W9-CCM-767

Measures of Personality and Social Psychological Attitudes

Contributors

Frank M. Andrews Institute for Social Research, Ann Arbor, Michigan 48106

Jim Blascovich Department of Psychology, State University of New York at Buffalo, Buffalo, New York 14260

Valerie A. Braithwaite Department of Psychology, Australian National University, Canberra ACT 2601, Australia

Kelly A. Brennan Department of Psychology, State University of New York at Buffalo, Buffalo, New York 14260

Richard Christie Department of Psychology, Columbia University, New York, New York 10027

Mark R. Leary Department of Psychology, Wake Forest University, Winston Salem, North Carolina 27109

Herbert M. Lefcourt Department of Psychology, University of Waterloo, Waterloo, Ontario, N2L 3G1 Canada

Ellen Lenney Department of Psychology, University of Maine, Orono, Maine 04473

Delroy L. Paulhus Department of Psychology, University of British Columbia, Vancouver, B.C., V6T 1W5 Canada

John P. Robinson Department of Sociology, University of Maryland, College Park, Maryland 20742

William A. Scott Department of Psychology, Australian National University, Canberra ACT 2601, Australia

Melvin Seeman Department of Sociology, University of California at Los Angeles, Los Angeles, California 99024

Phillip R. Shaver Department of Psychology, State University of New York at Buffalo, Buffalo, New York 14260

Joseph Tomaka Department of Psychology, State University of New York at Buffalo, Buffalo, New York 14260

Lawrence S. Wrightsman Department of Psychology, University of Kansas, Lawrence, Kansas 66045

Measures of Personality and Social Psychological Attitudes

Volume 1 of Measures of Social Psychological Attitudes

Edited by

John P. Robinson
Department of Sociology
University of Maryland
College Park, Maryland

Phillip R. Shaver
Department of Psychology
State University of New York at Buffalo
Buffalo, New York

Lawrence S. Wrightsman
Department of Psychology
University of Kansas
Lawrence, Kansas

ACADEMIC PRESS, INC.

Harcourt Brace Jovanovich, Publishers

San Diego   New York   Boston   London   Sydney   Tokyo   Toronto

Academic Press, Inc.
San Diego, California 92101

United Kingdom Edition published by
Academic Press Limited
24–28 Oval Road, London NW1 7DX

Library of Congress Cataloging-in-Publication Data

Measures of personality and social psychological attitudes / edited by
    John P. Robinson, Phillip R. Shaver, and Lawrence S. Wrightsman.
        p.   cm.
    Includes bibliographical references.
    ISBN   0-12-590241-7   (alk. paper). -- ISBN   0-12-590244-1   (pbk.:
alk. paper)
    1. Personality assessment. 2. Attitude (Psychology)--Testing.
3. Social interaction--Testing.   I. Robinson, John P. II. Shaver,
Phillip R. III. Wrightsman, Lawrence S.
    [DNLM: 1. Attitude. 2. Personality Assessment. 3. Psychology,
Social. 4. Psychometrics.   BF 39 M484]
BF698.4.M38   1990
155.2'8--dc20
DNLM/DLC
for Library of Congress   90-91
                                                                            CIP

Printed in the United States of America
90 91 92 93   9 8 7 6 5 4 3 2 1

Contents

v

CHAPTER 3

Measures of Subjective Well-Being   61

Frank M. Andrews and John P. Robinson

CHAPTER 4

Measures of Self-Esteem   115

Jim Blascovich and Joseph Tomaka

CHAPTER 5

Social Anxiety, Shyness, and Related Constructs   161

Mark R. Leary

CHAPTER 6

Measures of Depression and Loneliness   195

Phillip R. Shaver and Kelly A. Brennan

CHAPTER 7

Alienation and Anomie   291

Melvin Seeman

Interpersonal Trust and Attitudes toward Human Nature   373

Lawrence S. Wrightsman

CHAPTER 9

Locus of Control   413
Herbert M. Lefcourt

CHAPTER 10

Authoritarianism and Related Constructs   501
Richard Christie

CHAPTER 11

Sex Roles: The Measurement of Masculinity, Femininity, and Androgyny   573

Ellen Lenney

CHAPTER 12

Values   661

Valerie A. Braithwaite and William A. Scott

Preface

Our personality and attitude measurement series, originally published by the Institute for Social Research of the University of Michigan more than 20 years ago, has reached a wide international audience. Colleagues around the world tell us that these volumes are among the most frequently borrowed and stolen publications in their libraries. Buyers of this book should take heed: It has to be chained to its shelf! Evidently there is a worldwide hunger for measurement sourcebooks.

The original series has needed revising for some time, but we were daunted by the prospect of doing it alone. The number of measures has increased enormously since 1970. We kept looking toward a time when we could enlist the help of experts and specialists to produce an authoritative and timely collection of reviews. The wait was worth it. We are extremely pleased by the reviews and insights of the chapter authors who contributed to this volume.

Our series is intended as a basic reference work in the social sciences and is directed to three different audiences:

- Professionals actively involved in social science, especially those conducting personality and survey research in the fields of psychology, sociology, political science, communication, nursing, and social work
- Students taking courses in social research methods who are interested in becoming familiar with the measuring instruments of the social sciences and students wishing to conduct their own research projects
- Nonacademic professionals in fields related to the social sciences, such as practicing clinical psychologists, social commentators, journalists, political analysts, and market researchers

Our aim is to provide a comprehensive guide to the most promising and useful measures of important social science concepts. We hope to make the measures maximally accessible, so that readers can decide which one to use in a particular situation. Whenever possible—given copyright restrictions and authors' justifiable reservations—we have included actual scale items and scoring instructions. Nevertheless, these materials and our brief comments on them are no substitute for reading the original sources and subjecting the instruments to further item analyses and validation studies. This book is meant to be a starting point, an idea generator, a guide—not the last stop on the way to a perfect measure.

We are grateful to the Society for the Psychological Study of Social Issues (SPSSI), which helped make this new series possible. The warm encouragement and skillful diplomacy of Louise Kidder, former SPSSI Publications Chair, are especially appreciated.

Lynda Fuerstnau and her staff at the SPSSI central office contacted all the scale authors to seek reprint permission—an arduous task! Marie Hibbard helped compile the permission records. Marilyn Roundy was an excellent typist. Morris Rosenberg offered crucial substantive advice. Thank you all. John Robinson and Phillip Shaver are grateful to Lawrence Wrightsman, who joined them in editing the series and made their labor less difficult and more enjoyable.

Most important of all, we acknowledge the creative and dedicated scale authors whose work lies at the heart of this volume. Without their curiosity, imagination, and high technical standards, we would have nothing to pass along to you. Many scale authors not only granted permission to reproduce their work but also supplied supplementary references and information about recent research. It's a pleasure to showcase their work.

One final word: If all necessary information concerning a particular scale is included here, you are welcome to use the scale in your research. If more information is needed, please contact the scale's author or publisher. In many cases, we provide an address where permission or copies of commercial test forms can be obtained.

John P. Robinson
Phillip R. Shaver
Lawrence S. Wrightsman

CHAPTER 1

Criteria for Scale Selection and Evaluation

John P. Robinson, Phillip R. Shaver, and Lawrence S. Wrightsman

The original idea for this handbook of attitude and personality measures came from Robert Lane, a political scientist at Yale University. Like most social scientists, Lane found it difficult to keep up with the proliferation of social attitude measures. In the summer of 1958, he attempted to pull together a broad range of scales that would be of interest to researchers in the field of political behavior. Subsequently, this work was continued and expanded at the Survey Research Center of the University of Michigan under the general direction of Philip Converse, with support from a grant by the National Institute of Mental Health.

The result was a three-volume series, the most popular of which was the last, *Measures of Social Psychological Attitudes*. That is the focus of our first update of the original volumes.

Readers will note several differences between this work and its predecessors. Most important, we have given responsibility for each topic to experienced and well-known researchers in each field rather than choosing and evaluating items by ourselves. These experts were also limited to identifying the 10 or 20 most interesting or promising measures in their area, rather than covering all available instruments. This new structure has resulted in more knowledgeable review essays, but at the expense of less standardized evaluations of individual instruments.

There are many reasons for creating a volume such as this. Attitude and personality measures are likely to appear under thousands of book titles, in dozens of social science journals, in seldom circulated dissertations, and in the catalogues of commercial publishers, as well as in undisturbed piles of manuscripts in the offices of social scientists. This is a rather inefficient grapevine for the interested researcher. Too few scholars stay in the same area of study on a continuing basis for several years, so it is difficult to keep up with all of the empirical literature and instruments available. Often, the interdisciplinary investigator is interested in the relation of some new variable, which has come to attention casually, to a favorite area of interest. The job of combing the literature to pick a proper instrument consumes needless hours and often ends in a frustrating decision to forego measuring that characteristic, or worse, it results in a rapid and incomplete attempt to devise a new measure. Our search of the literature has revealed unfortunate replications of previous discoveries as well as lack of attention to better research done in a particular area.

The search procedure used by our authors included thorough reviews of *Psychological Abstracts* as well as the most likely periodical sources of psychological instruments (e.g., *Journal of Personality and Social Psychology, Journal of Personality Assessment, Journal of Social Psychology, Personality and Social Psychology Bulletin, Child Development,* and the *Journal of Applied Psychology*) and sociological and political measures (*Social Psychology Quarterly, American Sociological Review, Public Opinion Quarterly,* and *American Political Science Review*). Doctoral dissertations were searched by examining back issues of *Dissertation Abstracts.* Personal contact with the large variety of empirical research done by colleagues widened the search, as did conversations with researchers at annual meetings of the American Sociological Association and the American Psychological Association, among others. Papers presented at these meetings also served to bring a number of new instruments to our attention.

Our focus in this volume is on attitude and personality *scales* (i.e., series of items with homogeneous content), scales that are useful in survey or personality research settings as well as in laboratory situations. We have not attempted the larger and perhaps hopeless task of compiling single attitude items, except for ones that have been used in large-scale studies of satisfaction and happiness (see Chapter 3). While these often tap important variables in surveys and experiments, a complete compilation of them (even for happiness) is beyond our means.

Although we have attempted to be as thorough as possible in our search, we make no claim that this volume contains every important scale pertaining to our chapter headings. We do feel, however, that our chapter authors have identified most of the high quality instruments.

Contents of This Volume

A brief outline of the contents of our 12 chapters may prove useful. The remainder of this introductory chapter describes the background of our project and explains the major criteria for scale construction that we asked reviewers to use in evaluating the 150 scales covered in this volume. These evaluative criteria fall into three groups:

1. Item construction criteria (sampling of relevant content, wording of items, and item analysis);
2. Response set criteria (controlling the spurious effects of acquiescence and social desirability response sets); and
3. Psychometric criteria [representative sampling, presentation of normative data, reliability (both test–retest reliability and internal consistency), and validity (both convergent and discriminant)].

Of course, meeting these criteria does not in itself determine the value of a scale. For example, one can construct a scale with high internal consistency merely by including items that express the same idea in much the same way, and one can ensure significant discrimination of known groups merely by sampling two groups so divergent that they would be unlikely to respond the same way to any item. For this reason, we recommend that the choice of a scale from this volume be based as much as possible on decision theoretic criteria, such as those originally outlined by Cronbach and Gleser (1965).

The second chapter contains a review of measures of "response set," the main factor that confounds interpretation of items for researchers in all question domains. Delroy Paulhus describes three major kinds of response sets (social desirability, acquiescence, and extremity) and provides ways of collecting and analyzing attitude data that minimize the effects of these sets. He also reviews seven measures of the major response set, social desirability, and describes the advantages and disadvantages of each.

From this chapter we proceed to the 10 chapters dealing with specific social psychological measures. In Chapter 3, Frank Andrews and John Robinson review 10 scales dealing with the most general affective states: life satisfaction and happiness. Drawing upon Andrews' experience in conducting many national quality-of-life studies at the Survey Research Center of the University of Michigan, these authors identify background and attitudinal factors related to these affective states. They also describe several single-item measures of satisfaction and happiness as well as some promising new scales designed to measure related constructs.

Chapter 4 contains measures of self-esteem. Jim Blascovich and Joe Tomaka update Shaver's (1969) and Crandall's (1973) comprehensive reviews of these measures. They identify the most frequently cited measures in the literature and then review what they consider to be the 11 most worthwhile measures. Five of these are general measures for use with adolescents and adults, two are designed for use with younger children, and the remaining four cover specific aspects of self-esteem.

Chapter 5 reviews 10 measures of social anxiety, conceived as a major inhibitor of social interaction. Mark Leary notes the important distinction between subjective and behavioral manifestations of social anxiety and reviews four subjective measures and six that combine a subjective and a behavioral focus. One of the scales in the latter category has been used in hundreds of studies, although little use has been made of the two factors that are built into the scale. This supports Leary's general conclusion that the "link between subjective social anxiety and overt behavior is still poorly understood."

Chapter 6 is devoted to two related negative affective states, depression and loneliness. Phillip Shaver and Kelly Brennan explain similarities and differences between the two states, noting that measures of depression are inextricably tied to official clinical and psychiatric definitions. Both depression and loneliness have been measured in a variety of ways and in an extraordinary number of studies. Shaver and Brennan note that these emotional states have become central issues of our times.

Chapter 7 is concerned with alienation. The 24 scales Melvin Seeman reviews in this chapter cover a wide theoretical terrain and several decades of cumulative research. Seeman outlines separate dimensions of alienation, such as normlessness, powerlessness, and meaninglessness. His scale reviews are then organized in terms of seven of these dimensions and distinctions.

In contrast to these five areas, which directly concern positive and negative affective states, the remaining five chapters deal with beliefs, values, and traits. The first of them, attitudes toward people, is reviewed by Lawrence Wrightsman, who argues in Chapter 8 that these measures have generally been underused, given their strong predictive value in studies of occupational choice and racial attitude change. Work in this area has been hampered by ambiguities in operational definitions of trust. The most widely used and interesting of the eight scales in this chapter is Richard Christie's Machiavellianism Scale, which is based on astute observations of Italian political life recorded nearly four centuries ago in *The Prince*.

In Chapter 9 Herbert Lefcourt reviews 16 attitude scales related to locus of control, a term that refers to the presumed internal states that keep some people functioning in difficult periods, while others are overwhelmed with negative emotions. While research interest in this ability to feel that one can control one's own destiny has waned recently, Lefcourt finds locus of control to be "a stimulating and useful research tool" across a broad range of research. Recent variants of the scale have distinguished among three separate agents of control (internal, chance, and powerful others), different goal states, and different environments (e.g., personal, interpersonal, sociopolitical, work). Four of the scales Lefcourt reviews deal with general locus of control, three others are for use with children, four deal with specific goal areas, and five deal with health-related content.

Chapter 10 reviews 17 measures related to authoritarianism. In a broad-ranging historical essay, Richard Christie describes the origins of these scales and offers some fascinating insights into their development. He portrays authoritarianism as an under-utilized construct in social psychological research and notes the development of a superior measure in the area, one that transcends the severe methodological limitations of earlier measures. Although factor analytic studies have produced several divergent results, the importance of child-rearing themes in this area has been reinforced in several studies; submission to ingroup figures and institutional control are two further recurrent themes. Christie notes the need for more study with working-class samples and the need for behavioral measures.

In Chapter 11, Ellen Lenney describes eight measures of androgyny. She concludes that the creation of separate, largely orthogonal measures of masculinity and femininity provided an important breakthrough in this line of research. She notes several clear advantages of new measures based on the two-dimensional scheme, in contrast to earlier scales that treated masculinity–femininity as a single dimension.

In the final and most general chapter, Chapter 12, a variety of measures of values are presented. Included in this chapter are instruments based on the work of anthropologists and philosophers, as well as psychologists and sociologists. Valerie Braithwaite and William Scott devote most of their attention to the vast literature generated by Rokeach's value measures. They also review 14 other value scales, which tap such factors as concern for others, desire for status, individualism, and religiosity, among others. Of particular interest are four scales that measure non-Western orientations toward life. The lack of truly cross-cultural measures and of research relating values and behavior are two of the major shortcomings in this area.

A Broader Conceptual Framework

Stepping back from the specific contents of these 11 chapters, it can be argued that almost all of the measures bear some relation to the five basic emotional factors identified in recent multidimensional research (e.g., Epstein, 1984; Shaver, Schwartz, Kirson, & O'Connor, 1987). When research respondents in the Shaver *et al.* (1987) study were asked to sort the 135 most prototypical emotions into categories that were similar to one another, five major groupings emerged: love (liking), happiness, anger, sadness (depression), and fear (anxiety).

In the present volume, our chapter headings have been determined primarily by the degree to which various attitude constructs have been cited and reported in the social science literature. It can be seen that love or liking is assessed to some degree by the attitudes toward people scales in Chapter 8 and by the self-esteem (self-love) scales in Chapter 4. Happiness is obviously directly assessed with the measures in Chapter 3, and indirectly with the locus of control scales in Chapter 9. The struggle to maintain a positive affective state such as happiness or self-esteem is reflected in the measures in Chapter 2; social desirability bias can be considered a defensive or self-enhancing strategy. Both masculinity and femininity, discussed in Chapter 11, have been found to be related to measures of self-esteem and well-being.

Considering the hedonically negative emotional categories, anger (hostility, hatred) is related to measures of authoritarianism (Chapter 10) and to cynical or hostile attitudes

toward people (Chapter 8). Sadness is obviously related to depression, loneliness, alienation, (low) self-esteem, and low satisfaction with life, measures of which are reviewed in
Chapters 3, 4, 6, and 7. Sadness (depression) is also more common among people with an
external locus of control (Chapter 9). Fear and anxiety are directly assessed by the
measures of social anxiety in Chapter 5 and are present in people who are high in
dogmatism (Chapter 10). Finally, the superordinate categories of positive versus negative
emotions are reflected in certain measures of values (Chapter 12).

In this sense, then, the scale topics selected for review in this volume can be seen to
relate to basic emotional states. Given the growth of research on emotion in recent years
(e.g., Scherer & Ekman, 1984; Frijda, 1986; Izard, Kagan, & Zajonc, 1984; and the new
journal, *Cognition and Emotion*), it seems likely that these links between attitudes and
basic emotions will become more explicit. Some early evidence of the relation of many of
these measures to life satisfaction was reviewed by Robinson (1969).

Evaluative Criteria

We have tried to go beyond a simple listing of potential instruments and their psychometric properties. While most scale authors do provide useful statistical data in their scale
presentations, it is one thing to present statistical data and another to interpret them. The
casual reader or part-time researcher may find it difficult to assess such assets and liabilities when different authors use different statistical procedures. For example, few researchers seem to know that a Guttman reproducibility coefficient of .91 can be obtained
from a series of items with inter-item correlation coefficients around .30, or that a test–
retest reliability correlation of .50 may indicate a higher reliability than a split-half
reliability of .80.

Nor may scale authors be disposed to point out the limitations of their instruments
when they are writing articles for publication. Thus, many authors fail to alert readers to
their restricted samples, failure to deal with response sets, items that are too complicated
for respondents to understand, lack of item analyses, or failure to include certain behaviors and attitudes relevant to the construct at hand. We have tried, where possible, to make
such liabilities visible to the reader, although it was simply not feasible with the space and
resources available to note all such shortcomings. Originally we had hoped to order the
instruments in each chapter according to their probable research value, or to their ability to
meet certain desirable standards; that also was not possible. Within each topic area, the
instruments we had space to consider often differ so much in purpose or focus that they
cannot be arranged along a single quality dimension.

At present, when experienced researchers disagree with our reviewers' assessments,
they need to supplement them with their own. We hope that our reviewers have alerted
readers to a number of psychometric considerations, not only when deciding which
instrument to use, but also in evaluating their own new scales. We have tried to be fair,
honest, consistent, and not overly demanding in our evaluations, and we have tried to
highlight the merits as well as the limitations of each instrument.

The following brief description of our evaluative criteria proceeds in the general
chronological sequence in which attitude instruments are constructed.

Writing the Items

The first step for scale builders, and the first dimension on which their work can be
evaluated, is writing or locating items to include in a scale. It is usually assumed that the

scale builder knows enough about the field to construct an instrument that will cover an important theoretical construct well enough to be useful to other researchers. If it covers a construct for which instruments are already available, sound improvements over previous measures should be demonstrated.

Three minimal considerations in constructing a scale are:

1. *Proper Sampling of Content:* Proper sampling is not easy to achieve, nor can exact rules be specified for ensuring its achievement (as critics of Louis Guttman's concept of "universe of content" have noted). Nonetheless, one must be aware of the critical role of item sampling procedures in scale construction. Future research may better reveal the population of behaviors, objects, and feelings that ought to be covered in any area, but some examples may suggest ways in which the interested researcher can provide better coverage of a construct domain. Thus investigators of the "authoritarian personality" lifted key sentiments expressed in small group conversations, personal interviews, and written remarks and transformed them into scale items; some of the items consisted of direct verbatim quotations from such materials. In the job satisfaction area, Robinson, Athanasiou, and Head (1967) presented open-ended responses to such questions as "What things do you like best (or don't you like) about your job?" Responses to such questions offer invaluable guidelines to researchers, concerning both the universe of factors to be covered and the weight that should be given to each factor. Other instruments in the job satisfaction area (as elsewhere) were built either on the basis of previous factor analytic work or on responses to questions concerning critically satisfying or dissatisfying situations. Decisions remain to be made about the number of questions needed to cover each factor, but the important first step is to make sure that the main factors have been identified and covered.

2. *Simplicity of Item Wording:* One of the great advantages of obtaining verbatim comments from group discussions or open-ended questions, as people in advertising have discovered, is that such sentiments are usually couched in language easily comprehended and recognized by respondents. Comparing earlier and contemporary instruments, we see that more recently constructed scales contain question wording that is far less stuffy, complex, and esoteric. Even today, however, items developed from college student samples must be edited and adapted for use with more heterogeneous populations. Some helpful advice on these matters is contained in Sudman and Bradburn (1982), Robinson and Meadow (1982), and Converse and Presser (1986).

Many other undesirable item-wording practices seem to be going out of style as well: double-barreled items, which contain so many ideas that it is hard to tell why a person agrees or disagrees with them (e.g., "The government should provide low-cost medical care because too many people are in poor health and doctors charge so much money"); items that are so vague they mean all things to all people ("Everybody should receive adequate medical care"); or items that depend on familiarity with little-known facts ("The government should provide for no more medical care than that implied in the Constitution"). Advice about writing items in the negative versus the positive is offered in our discussion of response set.

3. *Item Analysis:* While item wording is something an investigator can manipulate to ensure coverage of intended content, there is no guarantee that respondents will reply to the items in the manner intended by the investigator. Item analysis is one of the most efficient methods for checking whether people are responding to the items in the manner intended. We have encountered several scales whose authors assumed that some a priori division of scale items corresponded to the way their respondents perceived them.

Many methods of item analysis are available, and, in fact, multidimensional analyses (described below under homogeneity, in our discussion of statistical procedures) can be considered the ultimate item analytic procedure. Researchers need not go so far as to factor-analyze their data to select items to be included or discarded, but an item intercorrelation matrix (on perhaps a small subsample or pretest sample) can be a simple and convenient surrogate for determining which items to include, particularly when using most of the statistical packages available for personal computers. If it is hypothesized that five items in a large battery of items (say those numbered 1, 2, 6, 12, and 17) constitute a scale of authoritarianism, then the majority of the 10 inter-item correlations between these five items should be substantial. At the minimum they should be significant at the .05 level. While this minimum may seem liberal, it is in keeping with the degree to which items in the most reputable scales intercorrelate for heterogeneous populations. If items 1, 2, and 17 intercorrelate substantially with each other but item 6 does not correlate well with any of them, then item 6 should be discarded or rewritten. Measuring the degree to which each of the five items correlates with external criteria or outside variables is a more direct device for the selection of items; this may even be preferable to high inter-item correlations. Such item validity approaches provide a built-in validational component for the scale. Wendt (1979), for example, used canonical correlation methods to find that a general alienation scale factored into two distinct scales with different demographic correlates. Exercises using LISREL programs may be similarly useful.

Robinson (1969) reported learning a valuable lesson about the myriad pitfalls in writing items from a simple item analysis of value questions in a national survey. Twelve items had been selected from a previous study that had uncovered four dimensions of value (authoritarianism, expression, individualism, and equalitarianism). One of the individualism items ("It is the man who starts off bravely on his own who excites our admiration") seemed in particular need of reframing for a cross-sectional survey. Accordingly, the item was reworded, "We should all admire a man who starts out bravely on his own." Item analysis revealed that this reformulated item was more closely associated with the three authoritarianism items than with the other two individualism items. Thus, this seemingly innocuous wording change completely altered the value concept tapped by the item.

For researchers who do not have the luxury of pretesting as a way to eliminate or revise unsatisfactory items, the item analysis phase of scale construction can be incorporated into the determination of the dimensionality or homogeneity of the test items. This will ensure that there is empirical as well as theoretical rationale for combining the information contained in various items into a scale.

Avoiding Response Set

A second large area of concern to scale builders is the avoidance of response set. Response set refers to a tendency on the part of individuals to respond to attitude statements for reasons other than the content of the statements. Thus, a person who might want to appear generally agreeable with any attitude statement is said to show an "agreement response set." One defense against response set is to make the scale as interesting and pleasant for the respondent as possible. The more that respondents find the instrument to be dull or unpleasant, the greater the chance that they will not answer carefully or will attempt to finish it as quickly as possible, agreeing indiscriminately or simply checking off the same answer column for each item.

As Delroy Paulhus details in Chapter 2, two major sources of response set need to be controlled:

1. *Acquiescence:* Most of us have observed people whose attitudes change in accord with the situation. Such people are said to "acquiesce" in anticipation of opposition from others. In the same way, some people are "yeasayers," willing to go along with anything

that sounds good, while others (perhaps optimists) are unwilling to look at the negative side of any issue. These dispositions are reflected in people's responses to attitude questions. Fortunately, it is often possible to separate their "real" attitudes from their tendency to agree or disagree.

There are various levels of attack, all of which involve abandoning a simple agree–disagree or yes–no format. One can first control simple order effects by at least an occasional switching of response alternatives between positive and negative. For simple "yes–no" alternatives, a few "no–yes" options should be inserted. Similarly, for the "strongly agree, agree, uncertain, disagree, strongly disagree" or Likert format, the five alternatives should occasionally be listed in the opposite order. This practice will offer some possibility of locating respondents who choose alternatives solely on the basis of the order in which they appear. It may also encourage overly casual respondents to think more about their answers, although at the cost of some confusion to respondents.

It is more difficult to shift the entire item wording from positive to negative, as those who have tried to reverse authoritarianism items (Chapter 10) have found. A logician may argue that the obverse of "Obedience is an important thing for children to learn" is not "Disobedience is an important thing for children to learn," and the investigator is on shaky ground in assuming that a respondent who agrees with both the first statement and the second is completely confused or vulnerable to agreement response set. Along the same line, the practice of inserting a single word in order to reverse an item can produce rather awkward sentences, while changing one word in an unusual context can produce items in which most respondents may not notice the change. In sum, writing item reversals requires considerable sensitivity and care. The interested researcher should check previous work on the subject (as referenced in Chapter 10).

A third and more difficult, yet probably more effective, approach involves the construction of forced-choice items. Here two (or more) replies to a question are listed and respondents are told to choose only one: "The most important thing for children to learn is (obedience) (independence)." Equating the popularity or social desirability of each of these alternatives provides even greater methodological purity but also entails more intensive effort on the part of both scale constructors and respondents. At the same time, the factor of social desirability is an important response set variable in its own right and needs to be controlled independently of acquiescence.

2. *Social Desirability:* In contrast to the theory that the acquiescent person reveals a certain desire for subservience in his willingness to go along with any statement, Edwards (1957) proposed more positively that such people are just trying to make a good impression. Decreasing social desirability responding usually involves the use of forced-choice items in which the alternatives have been equated on the basis of social desirability ratings. In more refined instruments, the items are pretested on social desirability, and alternative pairings (or item pairings) that do not prove to be equated are dropped or revised. DeMaio (1984) discusses approaches to the social desirability factor in the context of cross-section surveys.

We have mentioned the major sources of response set contamination, but there are others of which investigators should be aware. One of the more prevalent sources of contamination is the faking of responses according to some preconceived image that the respondent wants to convey. On a job satisfaction scale, for example, the respondent may try to avoid saying anything that might put his supervisor in a bad light or might involve a change in work procedures. College students may be aware of a professor's hypothesized relationship between two variables and try to answer in ways that confirm (or disconfirm) this prediction. Other undesirable variations of spurious response patterns that an investigator may wish to minimize can result from the respondents' wanting (a) to appear too consistent, (b) to use few or many categories in their replies, or (c) to choose extreme alternatives.

Statistical Criteria

The third area of instrument evaluation concerns the various statistical and psychometric procedures incorporated into its construction. These include respondent sampling, presentation of norms (usually means and standard deviations), reliability, and validity. While each of these statistical considerations is important, inadequate performance on any one of them does not render the scale worthless. Nevertheless, inadequate performance or lack of concern with many of them does indicate that the scale should be used with reservation. Recent scale authors have paid more heed to these considerations than their predecessors did, but few scales can be said to be ideal on all these factors.

The following eight statistical standards cover the basic requirements in the construction of a well-designed scale:

1. *Representative Sampling:* Too many researchers remain unaware of the fallacy of generalizing results from samples of college students to an older and much less well-educated general population (for an excellent review, see Sears, 1986). Indeed, some statisticians argue that a sample of a single classroom should be treated as a sample size of one, not the number of students in the classroom. Moreover, college students as a whole represent less than 5% of the population of the United States and diverge from the population on two characteristics that survey researchers usually find most distinctive in predicting attitude differences: age and education. Significant differences among college students are also likely to be found between freshmen and seniors, engineering and psychology students, and students at different colleges, so that one must be careful in expecting results from one classroom sample to hold for all college students. In the political attitude area, distinctions made by political elites may not be recognized by typical citizens, or even by politically sophisticated college students.

This is not meant to discourage researchers from improving the representativeness of whatever populations they do have available for study but rather to caution against generalizing from their findings to people not represented by their samples. Nor is it meant to imply that samples of college students are a useless group on which to construct scales. In areas like foreign affairs, one might well argue that college exposure is the best single criterion of whether a person can truly appreciate the intricacies of the issues involved.

However, an instrument constructed from replies of a random cross section of all students in a university has much more to offer than the same instrument developed on students in a single class in psychology (even if there are more students in the classroom than in the university sample). The prime consideration is the applicability of the scale and scale norms to respondents who are likely to use them in the future.

Problems arise with many samples of noncampus respondents as well. Poor sampling frames and low response rates are not uncommon, even for scales that are otherwise carefully designed and administered to community samples.

2. *Normative Information:* The adequacy of norms (mean scale scores, percentage agreements, etc.) is obviously dependent on the adequacy of the sample. The most basic piece of normative information is the difference between the researcher's sample and the sample on which the scale was developed in terms of mean scale score and standard deviation.

Additional topics of useful statistical information include: item means (or percentage agreements), standard deviations, and median scores (if the scale scores are skewed). Most helpful are means and standard deviations for certain well-defined groups (e.g., men and women, Catholics and Baptists) who have high or low scale scores. When such differences have been predicted the results bear on the *validity* of the scale, which is discussed below. Validity, reliability, and homogeneity are also important areas of basic normative information, of course, and they are covered below in more detail.

3. *Reliability (test–retest):* "Reliability" is one of the most ambiguous terms in psychometrics. There are at least three major referents: (1) the correlation between the same person's scores on the same items at two separate points in time; (2) the correlation between two different sets of items at the same time (called *parallel forms* if the items are presented in separate formats, and *split-half* if the items are all presented together); and (3) the correlation between the scale items for all who answer the items. The latter two indices refer to the internal structure or homogeneity of the scale items (the next criterion), while the former indicates stability of a respondent's item responses over time. It is unfortunate that test–retest measures, which require more effort and sophistication on the part of scale authors and may generate lower reliability figures for their efforts, are available for so few instruments. While the test–retest reliability level may be approximately estimated from indices of homogeneity, there is no substitute for the actual test–retest data. Some attempts to assess reliability and stability are discussed in Wheaton *et al.* (1977) and Bohrnstedt, Mohler, and Muller (1987).

4. *Internal Consistency:* In addition to split-half, parallel forms, and inter-item indices of the internal homogeneity of scale items, there exist other measures of reliability. Some of these item-test and internal consistency measures have known statistical relationships with one another, as Scott (1960) and others have shown. Even between such "radically" different procedures as the traditional psychometric approach and the Guttman cumulative approach, however, there likely exist reasonably stable relationships between indices based on inter-item, item–total, and total test homogeneity; as yet, however, these have not been charted. This includes the major reliability coefficient, Cronbach's α (1951).

Currently, the major difference between the indices seems to lie in a researcher's preference for large or small numbers. Inter-item correlations and homogeneity indices based on Loevinger's concepts seldom exceed .40. If one prefers larger numbers, a reproducibility coefficient or split-half reliability coefficient computed on the same data could easily exceed .90. While there is currently no way of relating the various indices, one minimal, but still imperfect, criterion is that of statistically significant correlations. Many researchers complain that this criterion depends too heavily on the sample sizes involved. To make the job even more difficult, statistical distributions of these various indices are not always available so that significance can be ascertained.

Of all the proposed indices, none combines simplicity with amount of information conveyed as well as the inter-item correlation matrix. Computing Pearson r correlation coefficients for more than five items is no longer a time-consuming operation for any researcher with access to a personal computer. Even the inter-item correlation matrix for a 20-item scale can now be generated in a matter of seconds. In the case of dichotomous (two-choice) items, the coefficient Yule's Y or Kendall's tau–B can easily be calculated to determine inter-item significance. Cronbach's α is now calculated on personal computer scaling programs. These, however, constitute only rule-of-thumb procedures for deciding whether a group of items should be added together to form a scale or index. Similarly, the criterion of statistical significance is proposed only because it is a standard that remains fairly constant across the myriad measures which are now, or have been, in vogue. Perhaps more satisfactory norms may be proposed in the future.

When the number of items goes beyond 10, however, the inter-item matrix becomes quite cumbersome to analyze by inspection. One is well advised to have the data analyzed by a multidimensional computer program. Program packages such as SPSS and SAS have the ability to factor-analyze 10–50 item intercorrelations in a few minutes, given a reasonably sized sample. These sorts of analyses will help one locate groups of items that go together much faster than could be done by inspecting the correlation matrix.[1] There are many kinds of factor analysis programs and options; under most circumstances, however, the differences between them usually do not result in radically different factor structures.

To say that factor analytic programs do not usually vary greatly in their output is not to imply that structures uncovered by factor analysis are without serious ambiguities. In particular, one common structure of attitudinal data seems to produce an indeterminant factor structure. This occurs when almost all the items are correlated in the range from about .15 to .45. Sometimes only a single factor will emerge from such a matrix and sometimes a solution will be generated that more clearly reflects item differentiation on a series of factors. We have encountered one instance in which an instrument that was carefully constructed to reflect a single dimension of inner- versus other-directedness (according to a forced-choice response format) was found to contain eight factors when presented in Likert format. Thus, one can offer no guarantee that building scales based on inter-item significance will invariably generate unidimensional scales. Nonetheless, only by these procedures can scale authors properly separate the apples, oranges, and coconuts in the fruit salad of items they have assembled.

One final word of caution: It is possible to devise a scale with very high internal consistency merely by writing the same item in a number of different ways. Obviously, such scales tap an extremely narrow construct. Sampling of item content, therefore, is crucial in assessing internal consistency. Internal consistency is a very desirable property, but it needs to be balanced by concept coverage, proper norms, and careful validity work.

5. *Known Groups Validity:* Validity is the more crucial indicator of the value of the scale. Nevertheless, group discrimination is not necessarily the most challenging hurdle to demonstrated validity. It is rather difficult to construct a liberalism–conservatism scale that will not show significant differences between members of The Heritage Foundation and members of the American Civil Liberties Union, or a religious attitude scale that will not separate Mormons from Jews or ministerial students from engineers. The more demanding criterion is whether the scale scores reliably distinguish happy from miserable people, liberals from conservatives, agnostics from believers within heterogeneous samples—or predict which of them will demonstrate behavior congruent with their attitudes.

6. *Convergent Validity (Predictions from Theory):* A second and more usual test of convergent validity involves obtaining results from the scale consistent with one's theory. For example, one might find that older people or better educated people or students with higher grades score higher on the scale, which would be consistent or convergent with some theoretical expectation or prediction. One might also expect that the scale scores would be higher among people who engaged in some type of behavior (such as joining a social group or contributing money) or expressed a particular attitude. The persuasiveness of this convergent or construct validation depends of course on the comprehensiveness and plausibility of the theory and the strength of the outside correlations. More formal attempts to establish construct validity have been attempted through causal modeling (e.g., Andrews, 1984).

---

[1]Researchers should not be deceived by what appear to be high factor loadings. Factor loadings need to be squared to reach levels that are equivalent to correlation coefficients.

Table 1

Some General Rating Criteria for Evaluating Attitude Measures

Criterion rating	4. Exemplary	3. Extensive	2. Moderate	1. Minimal	0. None
Theoretical development/structure	Reflects several important works in the field plus extensive face validity check	Either reviews several works or extensive face validity	Reviews more than one source	Reviews one (no sources)	Ad hoc
Pilot testing/item development	More than 250 items in the initial pool; several pilot studies	100–250 items in initial pool; more than two pilot studies	50–100 items in initial pool; two pilot studies	Some items eliminated; one small pilot study	All initial items included; no pilot study
Available norms	Means and SDs for several subsamples and total sample; extensive information for each item	Means and SDs for total and some groups; some item information	Means for some subgroups; information for some items	Means for total group only; information for 1–2 items	None; no item information
Samples of respondents	Random sample of nation/community with response rate over 60%	Cross-sectional sample of nation/community; random national sample of college students	Some representation of non-college groups; random sample of college students in same departments or colleges	Two or more college classes (some heterogeneity)	One classroom group only (no heterogeneity)

Inter-item correlations	Inter-item correlation average of .30 or better	Inter-item correlation average of .20–.29	Inter-item correlation average of .10–.19	Inter-item correlations below .10	No inter-item analysis reported
Coefficient α	.80 or better	.70–.79	.60–.69	<.60	Not reported
Factor analysis	Single factor from factor analysis	Single factor from factor analysis	Single factor from factor analysis	Some items on same factors	No factor structure
Test–retest	Scale scores correlate more than .50 across at least a 1-year period	Scale scores correlate more than .40 across a 3–12-month period	Scale scores correlate more than .30 across a 1–3-month period	Scale scores correlate more than .20 across a less than a 1-month period	No data reported
Known groups validity	Discriminate between known groups highly significantly; groups also diverse	Discriminate between known groups highly significantly	Discriminate between known groups significantly	Discriminate between known groups	No known groups data
Convergent validity	Highly significant correlations with more than two related measures	Significant correlations with more than two related measures	Significant correlations with two related measures	Significant correlation with one related measure	No significant correlations reported
Discriminant validity	Significantly different from four or more unrelated measures	Significantly different from two or three unrelated measures	Significantly different from one unrelated measure	Different from one correlated measure	No difference or no data
Freedom from response set	Three or more studies show independence	Two studies show independence	One study shows independence	Some show independence, others do not	No tests of independence

7. *Cross-Validation:* Cross-validation requires two different samples and measures of some criterion variable on each sample. The question to be answered by the test is whether the combination of items for sample A that best correlates with the criterion variable will also work for sample B, and conversely, whether the best set of sample B items works for sample A. Note that the crux of the procedure involves first identifying the items from sample A and then testing them independently on sample B.

8. *Discriminant Validation:* A more refined and powerful standard is the multitrait–multimethod matrix as proposed by Campbell and Fiske (1959). The method requires more than one index of each of the several constructs (say x, y, and z) one wants to measure with the instrument. It is best to include as many measures or indices of each construct as possible, as well as to measure for control purposes such variables as intelligence or response set that could also explain apparent relationships. In the resulting correlation matrix, the various items measuring each single construct (say x) should first correlate highly among themselves; second, the correlations among these items should be higher than their correlations with the items intended to measure constructs y or z, or any of the control variables. The latter is evidence of the scale's ability to discriminate from these other measures.

Needless to say, this is a gross oversimplification of the Campbell–Fiske criteria, and interested readers should peruse the authors' article thoroughly before attempting comparable analyses. At the time they were writing, Campbell and Fiske found only a few personality scales which met their conditions. One recent example of an attitude scale that meets them is Andrews and Crandall's (1976) life quality scale.

In certain chapters in our earlier volumes, in which a sufficient number of instruments to warrant comparison was present, we attempted to rate each scale on all such considerations. A current rating scheme is shown in Table 1.

Readers might consider using this scheme to evaluate the adequacy of measures they propose to use. Readers are also referred to the psychometric standards of the American Psychological Association (1985) and those in Heise and Bohrnstedt (1970), Bohrnstedt and Borgatta (1981), and Werts and Linn (1970), for "quick methods" of ascertaining reliability and validity.

Even this extensive list of proposed criteria is far from exhaustive. The actual choice of an instrument should be dictated by decision theoretic considerations. Thus the increasing of homogeneity by adding questionnaire items needs to be balanced against corresponding increases in administrative analysis and cost (as well as respondent fatigue and noncooperation) before one decides on how many attitude items to use. For assessing general levels of some attitude (e.g., separating believers from atheists), well-worded single items may do the job just as well as longer scales no matter how competently the scales are devised.

Future Volumes

As noted at the outset, this is the first of a planned series of updated measurement volumes. Subsequent volumes in this series will deal with (a) measures of role-related attitudes (e.g., toward work, marriage, parenthood) and (b) politically relevant scales (as in our *Measures of Political Attitudes*). Areas for further volumes are being considered, and further revisions of the present volume will appear as demand and changes in the field warrant.

Bibliography

American Psychological Association (1985). *Standards for educational and psychological tests.* Washington, DC: Author.

Andrews, F. (1984). Construct validity and error components of survey measures: A structural modeling approach. *Public Opinion Quarterly,* **48,** 409–422.

Andrews, F., & Crandall, R. (1976). The validity of measures of self-reported well-being. *Social Indicators Research,* **3,** 1–19.

Bohrnstedt, G., & Borgatta, E. (Eds.) (1981). *Social measurement: Issues.* Newbury Park, CA: Sage.

Bohrnstedt, G., Mohler, P., & Muller, W. (Eds.) (1987). *Empirical study of the reliability and stability of survey research items.* Newbury Park, CA: Sage.

Campbell, D., & Fiske, D. (1959). Convergent and discriminant validation by the multitrait multi-method matrix. *Psychological Bulletin,* **56,** 81–105.

Christie, R., Havel, J., & Seidenberg, B. (1958). Is the F scale irreversible? *Journal of Abnormal and Social Psychology,* **56,** 143–159.

Crandall, R. (1973). The measurement of self-esteem and related constructs. *In* J. Robinson and P. Shaver (Eds.), *Measures of Social Psychological Attitudes.* Ann Arbor, MI: Institute for Social Research.

Cronbach, L. (1951). Coefficient alpha and the internal structure of tests. *Psychometrika,* **31,** 93–96.

Cronbach, L., & Gleser, G. (1965). *Psychological tests and personnel decisions* (2nd ed.). Urbana: Univ. of Illinois Press.

Converse, J., and Presser, S. (1986). *Survey questions: Handcrafting the standardized questionnaire.* Newbury Park, CA: Sage.

DeMaio, T. (1984). The social desirability variable in survey research. In C. Turner & E. Martin (Eds.), *Surveying subjective phenomena* (Vol. 2). New York: Russell Sage Foundation.

Edwards, A. (1957). *The social desirability variable in personality assessment and research.* New York: Dryden Press.

Ekman, P., & Scherer, K. (Eds.) (1984). *Approaches to emotion.* Hillsdale, NJ: Erlbaum and Associates.

Epstein, S. (1984). Controversial issues in emotion theory. In P. Shaver (Ed.), *Review of personality and social psychology* (Vol. 5, pp. 64–88). Newbury Park, CA: Sage.

Frijda, N. H. (1986). *The emotions.* Cambridge, England: Cambridge Univ. Press.

Heise, D. R., & Bohrnstedt, G. W. (1970). Validity, invalidity, and reliability. In E. F. Borgatta & G. W. Bohrnstedt (Eds.), *Sociological methodology.* San Francisco: Jossey-Bass.

Izard, C. E., Kagan, J., & Zajonc, R. B. (Eds.) (1984). *Emotions, cognition, and behavior.* Cambridge, England: Cambridge Univ. Press.

Robinson, J. (1969). Life satisfaction and happiness. In J. Robinson and P. Shaver (Eds.), *Measures of Social Psychological Attitudes.* Ann Arbor, MI: Institute for Social Research (also see review of 1965 Withey scale, p. 533).

Robinson, J., Athanasiou, R., & Head, K. (1967). *Measures of occupational attitudes and characteristics.* Ann Arbor, MI: Institute for Social Research.

Robinson, J., & Meadow, R. (1982). *Polls apart.* Cabin John, MD: Seven Locks Press.

Scherer, K. S., & Ekman, P. (Eds.) (1984). *Approaches to emotion.* Hillsdale, NJ: Erlbaum.

Scott, W. A. (1960). Measures of test homogeneity. *Educational and Psychological Measurement,* **20,** 751–757.

Sears, D. (1986). College sophomores in the laboratory: Influences of a narrow data base on social psychology's view of human nature. *Journal of Personality and Social Psychology,* **51,** 515–530.

Shaver, P. (1969). Measurement of self-esteem and related constructs. In J. Robinson and P. Shaver (Eds.), *Measures of Social Psychological Attitudes.* Ann Arbor, MI: Institute for Social Research.

Shaver, P., Schwartz, J., Kirson, D., & O'Connor, C. (1987). Emotion knowledge: Further exploration of a prototype approach. *Journal of Personality and Social Psychology,* **52,** 1061–1086.

Sudman, S., & Bradburn, N. (1982). *Asking questions.* San Francisco: Jossey-Bass.

Wendt, J. (1979). Canonical correlation as an explanatory technique for attitude scale construction. *Public Opinion Quarterly,* **43,** 518–531.

Werts, C. E., & Linn, R. L. (1970). Cautions in applying various procedures for determining the reliability and validity of multiple item scales. *American Sociological Review,* **34,** 757–759.

Wheaton, B., *et al.* (1977). Assessing reliability and stability in panel models. In D. R. Heise (Ed.), *Sociological methodology.* San Francisco: Jossey-Bass.

CHAPTER 2

Measurement and Control of Response Bias

Delroy L. Paulhus

A *response bias* is a systematic tendency to respond to a range of questionnaire items on some basis other than the specific item content (i.e., what the items were designed to measure). For example, a respondent might choose the option that is most extreme or most socially desirable. A response bias might be a *response set,* that is, a temporary reaction to a situational demand, for example, time pressure or expected public disclosure. Alternatively, a bias may be induced by context effects such as the item format or the nature of previous items in the questionnaire (for a review, see Tourangeau & Rasinski, 1988). To the extent that an individual displays the bias consistently across time and situations, the bias is said to be a *response style* (Jackson & Messick, 1958; Wiggins, 1973).

Response biases continue to be a disturbing issue in psychological assessment, particularly with self-report measures such as those in the present volume. People's reports of their own traits, attitudes, and behavior may involve systematic biases that obscure measurement of content variables. For example, there is evidence that standard self-report methodologies distort the reporting of racist attitudes (Sigall & Page, 1971), nonnormative sexual attitudes (Knudson, Pope, & Irish, 1967), desirable behaviors (Phillips & Clancy, 1972), deviant behaviors (Clark & Tifft, 1966), and abortion (Wiseman, 1972). Another repercussion of response bias is that an assessment instrument may confound content with style. That is, the instrument may simultaneously assess the individual's response style as well as the content variable. If so, every observed correlation with this instrument will be open to (at least) two possible explanations.

Among the response biases cited in the literature are deviant responding (Berg, 1967), careless responding (Meehl & Hathaway, 1946), consistent responding (Dillehay & Jernigan, 1970), and omitting items (Cronbach, 1946). In this chapter, however, attention will be restricted to the three most prominent response biases: (1) socially desirable responding (including lying, faking bad, etc.), (2) acquiescence (tendency to agree), and (3) extremity bias (tendency to use extreme ratings).

Socially Desirable Responding

The most frequently studied response bias is socially desirable responding (SDR), the tendency to give answers that make the respondent look good. Over 50 years ago, psychometricians had already raised the issue of SDR effects on the validity of question-naires (e.g., Bernreuter, 1933; Vernon, 1934). Ten years later, Meehl and Hathaway (1946) were able to cite eight measures specifically developed to index SDR in self-reports.[1] Since the 1950s, SDR has been a prominent concern in measuring personality (e.g., Edwards, 1953), psychopathology (e.g., Gough, 1947; McKinley, Hathaway, & Meehl, 1948), attitudes (Lenski & Leggett, 1960), and self-reports of sensitive behavior (Goode & Hart, 1952).

The first section below reviews methods developed to control SDR in each of these realms. Where SDR cannot be controlled, it might still be measured: Accordingly, the second section below reviews the best available measures of SDR.

Controlling the Influence of SDR

Available methods for controlling SDR are varied and often complex [for reviews, see DeMaio (1984), Nederhof (1985), or Paulhus (1981)]. Only a brief summary can be rendered here. Four types of methods may be distinguished: rational, factor analytic, covariate, and demand reduction methods.

1. Rational techniques are control features that are built into the self-report instrument. Their purpose is to prevent the subject from responding in a socially desirable fashion. For example, one may use a forced-choice format in which the two statements are equated for social desirability. If single statements are used, they might be restricted to those that are roughly neutral with respect to social desirability. Alternatively, one could select statements with high content saturation, that is, statements in which the relative influence of content over desirability is high (see Jackson, 1967).

2. Factor analytic techniques may be applied during test construction if the procedure involves choosing the highest loading items in a factor analysis. If one principal component appears to represent SDR, it may be deleted before the factors are rotated (Paulhus, 1981). Even better, if a measure of SDR is administered along with the content items, then the first factor may be rotated to the SDR measure (e.g., Morf & Jackson, 1972; Norman, 1969). In both techniques the highest loading items on the remaining factors necessarily tap individual differences above and beyond the effects of SDR. Hence, these items may be used to construct SDR-free content measures.

3. In covariate techniques, no attempt is made to prevent respondents from answering in a desirable fashion. Instead, a measure of SDR, for example, one of the measures provided at the end of this chapter, is administered along with the content measures. SDR may then be partialed out of correlations between two content scales to control for spurious correlation.

Alternatively, to improve the validity of individual scores, the raw score may be adjusted by an amount commensurate with the contamination by SDR. This adjustment may be effected by regressing the content score on SDR: The residual then represents the content score corrected for SDR (e.g., Norman, 1967). This procedure is systematized in scoring the MMPI, in which certain clinical scale scores are adjusted using the K scale as a measure of SDR (McKinley et al., 1948). A similar procedure is now used in adjusting several scales of the 16PF (Karson & O'Dell, 1976).

4. A wide-ranging form of control, demand reduction, includes those methods that

---

[1]Precedence should be granted to Hartshorne and May (1928), who in the twenties had already developed a lie scale to directly assess dishonesty in school children.

reduce the situational press for desirable responding. Perhaps the most obvious strategy is to assure respondents of anonymity. In classroom administrations, perceived anonymity is increased by (1) physically separating respondents (especially acquaintances), (2) insisting that they put no identifying marks on the questionnaire (Becker, 1976), and (3) telling them beforehand that they will seal the completed questionnaire in an envelope and drop it in a box on the way out. Presumably because of perceived anonymity, mail surveys appear to be less susceptible to SDR (Wiseman, 1972). Computerized assessments show lower SDR than face-to-face interviews, but higher SDR than paper-and-pencil tests (Martin & Nagao, 1989; Davis & Cowles, 1989; Lautenschlager & Flaherty, in press).

If it is necessary to match responses across two administrations, respondents could be asked to give their birthdates, or to use a consistent pseudonym for all administrations. Despite all such precautions, at least some subjects may still suspect that their identity can be determined by the experimenters.

A more aggressive technique, the bogus pipeline (Jones & Sigall, 1971), is essentially a pseudo lie detector. Respondents are hooked up to electronic equipment that the operator claims can assess their attitudes directly through physiological measures. The equipment is said to be, in effect, "a pipeline to the soul." As a putative test of their own self-insight, subjects are asked to guess the machine's reading for each attitude question. The rationale is that subjects want to avoid being embarrassed by the machine: Hence, their guesses should be less contaminated with SDR than are ordinary self-reports.

The efficacy of the technique is documented by its ability to increase admissions of such undesirable behavior as (a) racist attitudes (Sigall & Page, 1971), (b) sexist attitudes (Faranda, Kaminski, & Giza, 1979), (c) inconsistent attitudes (Paulhus, 1982), (d) dislike for a handicapped confederate (Sigall & Page, 1972), and (e) having prior knowledge of test answers (Quigley-Fernandez & Tedeschi, 1978).

Some related techniques are milder versions of the bogus pipeline. For example, before respondents complete a questionnaire they are warned that the measure contains methods for detecting faking. In a complex variant of this technique, respondents are given an especially transparent lie scale, which is then scored, and they are advised whether their score indicates faking (Montag & Comrey, 1982).

A technique useful for face-to-face interviews is the Randomized Response Method (Greenberg, Abdula, Simmons, & Horvitz, 1969; Warner, 1965). The desirability-loaded question (e.g., Have you ever had an abortion?) is posed along with an innocuous question (Are your mother's eyes blue?). The respondent is instructed to flip a coin and (without telling the interviewer how the flip came out) answer question 1 if heads; question 2, if tails. Since the interviewer is not aware which question is being answered, the respondent is under less pressure to respond desirably. Nonetheless, the abortion rate in the sample can ultimately be estimated from three group statistics: the observed proportion of "yes" responses, the assumption that .50 of the respondents answered the abortion question, and the known rate of blue eyes in the population. The bulk of the evidence suggests that the randomized response technique does increase reports of sensitive behaviors, although not quite up to their true rates (Dawes & Smith, 1985).

Psychological assessment through biographical data is a unique approach that tends to reduce SDR demand (Shaffer, Saunders, & Owens, 1986). The rationale is that, when reporting on concrete, verifiable facts, subjects are less tempted to dissimulate.

Finally, some researchers have tried to reduce SDR by employing proxy subjects: Instead of the target person, a close acquaintance is questioned about the target's behavior. According to evidence collected by Sudman and Bradburn (1974), this technique is satisfactory for measuring publicly observable types of behavior, but not for attitudes. The evidence for its efficacy in measuring personality is mixed (Kane & Lawler, 1978; Mc-Crae, 1982).

5. The last category, stress minimization, refers to basic guidelines for reducing tension during the test administration. Among the factors known to increase desirable responding are: (a) speed instructions (Sutherland & Spilka, 1964), (b) emotional arousal (Paulhus & Levitt, 1987), and distraction (Paulhus, Graf, & Van Selst, 1989). Hence, these factors should all be minimized.

Measurement of SDR

There are a number of reasons why a researcher might want a direct measure of SDR such as those included in this chapter. The most common usage is for supporting the discriminant validity of a content instrument. To ensure that the content instrument is not confounded with SDR, the researcher would administer both measures to the same sample, hoping to see a low intercorrelation. An SDR measure would also be necessary to use the covariate and target rotation techniques described above.

In some cases, rather than correcting a biased score, one might prefer to discard an individual's data if an accompanying SDR measure detected a high degree of SDR. Optimal cutoff scores may be derived for detecting faking good and faking bad (e.g., Helmes & Holden, 1986; Karson & O'Dell, 1976; Lanning, 1989).

Such cutoff scores may then be useful in evaluating the fakeability of content instruments. A content scale is resistant to faking if, under fake-good instructions, the SDR scale exceeds the cutoff point but the content scale does not change. Note that demonstrating that one can fake good on an instrument does not prove that it is confounded with SDR under ordinary conditions (Furnham, 1986). Moreover, faking good can be idiosyncratic (Lautenschlager, 1986).

Situational demands can also be assessed with SDR measures. For example, organizational researchers have used such measures to determine the extent to which various work environments encourage SDR (see Zerbe & Paulhus, 1987, for a review). SDR measures may also assist in determining the best interviewer characteristics (Weiss, 1968) or test conditions (e.g., Martin & Nagao, 1989; Paulhus, 1984; Schriesheim, 1979) to promote disclosure. Computerized testing, for example, has been evaluated with several measures of SDR (Davis & Cowles, 1989; Lautenschlager & Flaherty, in press).

In practice, the primary use for SDR measures has been to assess consistent individual differences, that is, response styles. There is a longstanding concern that response styles interfere with accurate assessment of content variables (e.g., Edwards, 1953; Goode & Hart, 1952; Gough, 1947; McKinley et al., 1948). Such styles have also been claimed to reflect deeper psychological constructs of interest in their own right (Block, 1965; Damarin & Messick, 1965; Sweetland & Quay, 1953). The classic example is Crowne and Marlowe's work (1964) on the need for approval construct, which emerged from studies on their 1960 measure of SDR (Crowne & Marlowe, 1960). Other personality constructs postulated to underlie response styles include repression–sensitization (Byrne, 1964), censure avoidance (Allaman, Joyce & Crandall, 1972; Millham & Jacobson, 1978), and self-deception (Paulhus, 1984; Sackeim & Gur, 1978). Measures of several of these constructs are included at the end of this chapter.

The widespread concern about SDR in test responses is reflected in the fact that major personality batteries invariably include an SDR measure. The MMPI includes two such scales: the Lie scale to detect blatant dissimulation and the K scale to tap more subtle distortions (McKinley *et al.*, 1948). The Eysenck Personality Inventory (Eysenck & Eysenck, 1964) and the Eysenck Personality Questionnaire (Eysenck & Eysenck, 1975) both contain a rationally developed lie scale. Comrey (1980) includes the Response Bias scale in the Comrey Personality Scales. The Personality Research Form (Jackson, 1967) contains the Desirability scale assembled from diverse items of extreme desirability. The Differential Personality Questionnaire (Tellegen, 1982) contains the Unlikely Virtues scale as well as a Desirability Inconsistency scale. The California Psychological Inventory contains the Good Impression and Well-Being scales (Gough, 1987). Measures of both faking good and faking bad have been developed for the 16-PF (Winder, O'Dell, & Karson, 1975).

With the exception of the MMPI validity scales, little direct research has been conducted on these commercially published SDR measures. One reason is that these instruments are often tailored to be similar in format and content to the inventory as a whole and hence may have little application outside the inventory. Because of the limitations in empirical evidence, such measures are not presented in detail here; rather, the reader is referred to the manuals cited above for each of the inventories.

Varieties of SDR

A disturbing feature of SDR measures is the low intercorrelation among several of the more well-known instruments, for example, Edwards's SD scale, the Marlowe–Crowne scale and Wiggins's Sd scale. The frustration of nonspecialists is epitomized in the title of one article: "Will the real social desirability scale please stand up?" (Strosahl, Linehan, & Chiles, 1984). Factor analyses of SDR instruments have consistently revealed two primary factors (Borkenau & Ostendorf, 1989; Edwards & Walsh, 1964; Jackson & Messick, 1962; Paulhus, 1984; Wiggins, 1964). One cluster is associated with *Alpha,* the general anxiety factor of the MMPI (Block, 1965). The second cluster is associated with the another MMPI factor called *Gamma* (Wiggins, 1964), which is linked to agreeableness and traditionalism. Paulhus (1984, 1986) provided evidence that these two SDR factors represent (a) self-deceptive positivity (an honest but overly positive self-presentation) and (b) impression management (self-presentation tailored to an audience). This distinction was outlined many years before by Damarin and Messick (1965). As depicted in Fig. 1, the gamut of SDR measures may usefully be characterized in terms of their relative weighting of self-deception and impression management. The Desirability scale of the PRF and Edwards's SD scale load primarily on the self-deception factor; Wiggins's Sd scale and Eysenck's Lie scale load primarily on the impression management factor. The Marlowe–Crowne scale loads on both factors, although more so on impression management.

The term "impression management" was chosen to represent one traditional view of SDR: that some subjects are purposefully tailoring their answers to create the most positive social image. Of the many impressions that one may try to present, this factor represents only one: a socially conventional, dependable persona. The label "impression management" is preferable to "lying," which is an overly harsh and sweeping indictment. After all, such individuals may misrepresent themselves only to avoid social disapproval (Crowne, 1979). Whatever the label,[2] this tendency will vary according to situational

---

[2]This factor has also been given such diverse interpretations as moralistic hypocrisy (Cattell, Pierson, & Finkbeiner, 1976), interpersonal sensitivity (Holden & Fekken, 1989), defensiveness (Weinberger, Schwartz, & Davidson, 1979), extraverted adjustment (McCrae & Costa, 1983), and test-taking intelligence (P. Borkenau, personal communication).

SELF-DECEPTION
    FACTOR

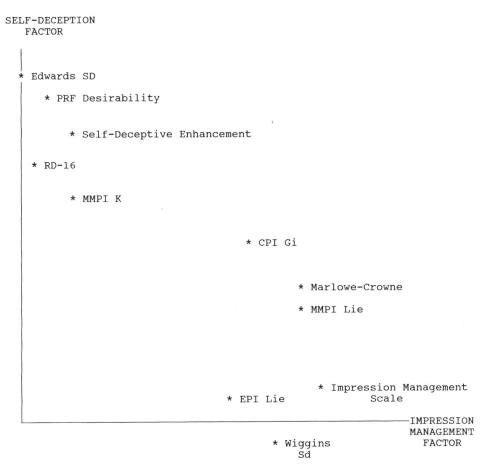

Fig. 1 Typical factor loadings of SDR measures.

demands and transient motives and that variation may obscure the validity of the respondent's self-reports.

The concept of self-deceptive positivity, on the other hand, appears to be intrinsically linked to such personality constructs as adjustment (Taylor & Brown, 1988), optimism (Scheier & Carver, 1985), self-esteem (M. Rosenberg, personal communication), and a sense of general capability (Holden & Fekken, 1989). These conceptual links are supported by significant correlations between measures of self-deception and measures of mental health (Linden, Paulhus, & Dobson, 1986; Sackeim & Gur, 1979), self-esteem (Paulhus & Reid, in press; Winters & Neale, 1985), and various cognitive biases (Paulhus, 1988; Paulhus & Reid, in press). The label "self-deceptive" was chosen in reference to the verifiable distortion by high scorers on certain forms of self-information (Paulhus, 1988).

This two-factor distinction helps resolve several issues in the SDR literature. Research typically shows a positive relation between SDR and adjustment, whereas traditional theories (as well as common sense) presume a negative relation. Self-deceptive SDR bears a strong positive relation with adjustment whereas impression management bears little relation. Thus the relation with adjustment depends on the type of SDR.

The second issue clarified by the self-deception versus impression management distinction is what should be done about the SDR that pervades such central personality variables as perceived control, social dominance, and adjustment. Norman (1967, 1990) argued that removing a general index of SDR from personality ratings clarifies the content dimensions. However, most relevant studies have shown that controlling SDR, if anything, actually *reduces* the predictive validity of content measures (Borkenau & Amelang, 1985; Kozma & Stones, 1988; McCrae, Costa, Dahlstrom, Barefoot, Siegler, & Williams, 1989; McCrae & Costa, 1983; Ruch & Ruch, 1967). Indeed, it now appears that controlling any SDR measure that taps self-deception (e.g., the Edwards scale, the Borkenau–Ostendorf SD scale, the K scale, and to a lesser degree, the Marlowe–Crowne scale) will lower the predictive validity of measures involving a self-deceptive positivity (e.g., anxiety, achievement motivation, dominance, well-being, perceived control, self-esteem). This form of SDR is inextricably linked to content variance and should not be controlled.

In contrast, impression management should be controlled under certain circumstances (Paulhus, 1986), namely, when impression management is conceptually independent of the trait being assessed but still contributes to the self-report scores of that trait. In personnel selection, for example, transient motives ("I'll say anything to get this job because my business just burned down") satisfy those criteria. Many of the techniques listed earlier were designed to control such conscious impression management.

The ideal procedure would involve establishing the distribution of impression management scores in the specific job-selection situation. In addition, the distribution of subjects asked to fake good would be established. If the scores of faking subjects sat several standard deviations above the mean of the no-fake group, then an efficient cutoff point would be easy to specify.

Finally, a set of measures with uncertain status must be mentioned—the so-called honesty or integrity scales. These are questionnaires administered in industrial–organizational settings to determine whether employees or job candidates can be trusted. They fall into two groups. One type contains direct questions about the respondent's integrity, of the form: "Are you now, or have you ever been, a crook?" The second type targets more general traits, such as conscientiousness and impulsiveness, that bear on employee trustworthiness (e.g., Hogan & Hogan, 1989).

Although widely used in business, the direct measures have had a poor reputation among psychologists (e.g., Sackett & Harris, 1984). This reputation may be due in part to the difficulty in obtaining the measures for research purposes. In addition, some honesty scales show positive correlations with lie scales. Thus the same individuals could be labeled honest or dishonest depending on whether honesty scales or lie scales are used. Nonetheless, the more recent evidence about the validity of certain honesty scales is more encouraging (Cunningham, 1989; Sackett, Burris, & Callahan, 1989).

Guidelines

The comments above suggest several practical implications for researchers. Caution must be exercised in interpreting reports of high correlations between self-report instruments and SDR: Such relations must not blithely be assumed to represent contamination and, therefore, deficits in the instruments. Indeed, the SDR component may be a legitimate aspect of the construct being measured.

If individual differences in SDR are evidenced in one's data, one must carefully consider why this has occurred. In a personnel selection situation, for example, a correlation between self-reported motivation and a measure of impression management has a number of plausible interpretations. A stylistic interpretation would suggest that chronic impression managers are faking high motivation. Alternatively, the nature of the position (e.g., public relations) may be such that chronic impression managers would continue to be motivated and are, therefore, ideal candidates. A third interpretation is that the observed relation is due, not to stylistic impression management, but to a temporary response set: By chance, some respondents are temporarily motivated and are, therefore, presenting a good impression that is unlikely to predict future behavior.

Measures Reviewed Here

In selecting an SDR measure from the eight provided below, the researcher must consider which form of SDR is relevant and select an appropriate measure. The eight measures are

1. Edwards (1957) Social Desirability Scale,
2. Marlowe–Crowne Social Desirability Scale (Crowne & Marlowe, 1960),
3. MMPI Lie Scale (Hathaway & McKinley, 1951),
4. MMPI K Scale (Meehl & Hathaway, 1946),
5. Balanced Inventory of Desirable Responding (Paulhus, 1984, 1988),
6. RD-16 (Schuessler, Hittle, & Cardascia, 1978), and
7. Children's Social Desirability Scale (Crandall, Crandall, & Katkovsky, 1965).

It is difficult to order the measures in terms of their value because they each have specialized applications. Instead, they will be presented in descending order of the amount of research published on the measure. No implication should be drawn that SDR measures not included here are deficient. There is simply less information available on other measures (except for the Eysenck Lie scale, which is reviewed by Furnham [1986]).[3]

The Edwards Social Desirability (SD) scale contains 39 items from the MMPI that have extremely high or low desirability ratings. The scale falls squarely on the first factor of SDR: hence it correlates highly with many standard measures of adjustment (e.g., anxiety, self-esteem, depression) and personality (e.g., perceived control, assertiveness). A high correlation with the SD does not invalidate an individual difference measure but suggests that the measure may involve some positivistic bias.

The Marlowe–Crowne (MC) scale contains 33 True–False items about behaviors that are desirable but rare or undesirable but common. The behaviors concern everyday events, not psychopathology. The scale loads on both factors of SDR but more highly on the impression management factor. The MC scale generally correlates less highly than the SD with measures of adjustment.

The MMPI Lie scale contains 15 statements about attitudes and practices that are socially undesirable, but common. Saying "false" to 8 or more is considered evidence that the respondent is faking good on the MMPI. The measure falls toward the second factor of SDR, highly correlated with other lie scales and the Marlowe–Crowne scale. The scale can detect faking good only in naive test-takers.

The MMPI K scale contains 30 items designed to identify abnormal persons whose MMPI scores appear normal. In contrast to the MMPI Lie scale, it is a more subtle

---

[3]Nor is there sufficient information concerning two new SDR measures: (1) the Borkenau–Ostendorf Social Desirability scale (Borkenau & Ostendorf, 1989), and (2) the Self-Presentation Scale (Roth, Harris, & Snyder, 1988). A promising technique that requires standardization is Phillips and Clancy's (1972) overclaiming index.

measure of SDR. Its status is rather complex, given that it is said to index psychological health in normal samples, but defensiveness in maladjusted samples.

The CPI Good Impression scale contains 40 items designed to measure faking good. The high scorer wants to present the impression of being dependable, cooperative, and moral. A good deal of validity data are available for this measure (Gough, 1987; Tellegen, 1982).

The Balanced Inventory of Desirable Responding (BIDR) contains separate measures of impression management (audience-driven self-presentation) and self-deceptive enhancement (an honest positivistic bias). The sum of the two measures correlates highly with the MC scale.

The RD-16 instrument was specifically designed to detect SDR in surveys of attitudes and opinions on the general population. An impressive set of norms is available from a national probability sample. The items were screened to preclude differences across such subgroups as race and education.

The Children's Social Desirability Scale was designed for children from grades 6–12. The item content largely follows that of the Marlowe–Crowne scale but is worded in children's language. Additional items involve child-specific content.

Edwards Social Desirability Scale (SD)

(Edwards, 1957)

Variable

Edwards (1957) described the SD as measuring "the tendency to give socially desirable responses in self-description" (p. 35), more specifically, an individual's characteristic level of self-presentation without special instructions or motivation to do so (p. 230).

Description

Edwards (1957) asked ten judges to rate whether "True" or "False" was the most desirable response to 79 items assembled from the K, F, and Lie scales of the MMPI. The 39 items on which the judges unanimously agreed formed the SD. Most of the items (30 of 39) are keyed negatively. As on the MMPI, respondents must answer "True" or "False," with one point added for each response that matches the key. Hence, possible scores range from 0 to 39, higher scores indicating more socially desirable responding. Given their source, it is not surprising that item content is heavily laden with references to psychological distress.

Samples

Edwards (1957) reported means of 28.6 (s.d. = 6.5) and 27.1 (s.d. = 6.5) for males and females in a sample of 192 college students. Edwards and Walsh (1964) found a mean of 28.8 in a sample of 130 paid students. More recently, Paulhus (1984) reported means of 28.4 (s.d. = 5.5) and 30.3 (s.d. = 4.9) for students in anonymous ($n = 60$) and public disclosure conditions ($n = 40$), respectively. In a sample of 503 students, Tanaka–Matsumi and Kameoka (1986) found means of 26.7 (s.d. = 6.3) and 20.9 (s.d. = 5.3) in normal and depressed samples, respectively.

Reliability

Internal Consistency

Alpha coefficients range from .83 to .87 in the samples reported above.

Test–Retest

Test–retest reliabilities of .66 (males) and .68 (females) after 2 weeks were reported by Rorer and Goldberg (1965).

Validity

Convergent

The ESD is robust in that it correlates highly with scales from a variety of content areas if they too were assembled from items with extreme desirability ratings (Edwards, 1970; Jackson & Messick, 1962). For example, the SD correlates .71 with the Desirability scale of Jackson's (1967) PRF, which comprises items of extreme desirability chosen from diverse personality domains (Holden & Fekken, 1989).

Discriminant

Early critics alleged that, because 22 of the 39 items overlapped with Taylor's (1953) anxiety scale, the SD was simply another anxiety measure. Similarly, Crowne and Marlowe (1960) complained that the scale was intrinsically confounded with psychopathology because many of the items referred to psychological distress. Edwards and Walsh (1964) responded by showing that the pattern of correlations with other measures was unchanged when the psychopathology items were replaced.

Edwards distinguished the construct measured by the SD from tendencies to lie deliberately as measured by impression management scales (Edwards, 1957, 1970). This conceptual distinction has been clearly sustained by the data (Edwards & Walsh, 1964; Paulhus, 1984; Wiggins, 1964).

A major controversy was stirred by reports of a very high correlation between SD and the first factor of the MMPI (e.g., Jackson & Messick, 1962). To some observers this correlation suggested that the MMPI assesses SDR instead of psychopathology. Block (1965), however, argued forcefully that the SD reflects a substantive trait, namely, ego resiliency. Although most commentators agree that the SD reflects a more general disposition, the precise nature of the disposition remains moot (Paulhus, 1986).

Location

Because the items are taken directly from the MMPI (a copyrighted instrument), only a few sample items can be provided. However, the 39 MMPI booklet numbers are listed so that the full scale may be assembled by the reader. The MMPI is available from University of Minnesota Press, Minneapolis, Minnesota 55455.

Comments

Despite his many reports on the SD, Edwards has said very little about the nature of the underlying construct. Even in his most recent comment (Edwards *et al.*, 1988), he has adhered closely to an operational definition: the tendency to respond desirably to the sort of item in his scale. Because the construct is not well defined, it is difficult to marshall evidence for it. As noted in the literature review, the SD falls clearly on the first factor of SDR, indicating an honest form of positivistic bias.

Edwards's original implication that a high correlation with SD invalidates a self-report measure is no longer tenable. In fact, controlling for SD may actually reduce the validity of adjustment-related measures (e.g., Kozma & Stones, 1988; McCrae, 1986).

Fortunately, Edwards's colleagues (L. K. Edwards & Clark, 1987) have finally published his alternative version (Edwards, 1963)—one comprising nonpsychopathology items. The scale appears to perform similarly to the original, thereby challenging certain critiques going back 30 years (Edwards, Edwards, & Clark, 1988). Nevertheless, the new version has yet to be subjected to scrutiny by other researchers.

Edwards Social Desirability Scale

Sample Items

True	False	1. I am happy most of the time. (T)
True	False	2. My hands and feet are usually warm enough. (T)
True	False	3. No one cares much what happens to you. (F)
True	False	4. I sometimes feel that I am about to go to pieces. (F)

Complete Scale

The MMPI booklet numbers for the 9 items keyed "True" are as follows: 7, 18, 54, 107, 163, 169, 257, 371, 528. The 30 items keyed "False" are 32, 40, 42, 43, 138, 148, 156, 158, 171, 186, 218, 241, 245, 247, 252, 263, 267, 269, 286, 301, 321, 335, 337, 352, 383, 424, 431, 439, 549, 555.

Marlowe–Crowne Social Desirability Scale (MCSD)

(Crowne and Marlowe, 1960)

Variable

Although Crowne and Marlowe (1960) originally constructed the MCSD to be a measure of SDR in self-reports, their subsequent research on the construct convinced them that the scale was tapping a more general motive: They dubbed it *need for approval* (Crowne & Marlowe, 1964).[4] In the most recent statement, Crowne (1979) refined the concept to be an avoidance of disapproval.

Description

Crowne and Marlowe (1960) set out to build an SDR measure that improved upon the Edwards scale. Noting that Edwards's items were largely pathological in content, they

---

[4]Although Crowne was the senior author on both reports, the scale itself was labeled the Marlowe–Crowne scale, presumably to balance the credit.

focused instead on ordinary personal and interpersonal behaviors. Fifty such items were assembled and reduced to 33 by item analyses and ratings of experienced judges. The correlations with MMPI scales were still sizable, but not as high as those shown by the Edwards scale (e.g., Katkin, 1964).

The 33 items describe either (a) desirable but uncommon behaviors (e.g., admitting mistakes) or (b) undesirable but common behaviors (e.g., gossiping). Respondents are asked to respond "True" or "False" to 18 items keyed in the true direction and 15 in the false direction. Hence, scores range from 0 to 33, with higher scores representing higher need for approval.

Samples

Crowne and Marlowe (1964) reported a mean of 15.5 (s.d. = 4.4) in a sample of 300 college students. In a more recent study of 100 students, Paulhus (1984) reported means of 13.3 (s.d. = 4.3) and 15.5 (s.d. = 4.6) in anonymous and public disclosure conditions, respectively. In a sample of 503 students, Tanaka-Matsumi and Kameoka (1986) reported means of 14.0 and 12.3 for normal and depressed respondents, respectively. In a sample of 650 Peace Corps volunteers (90% college graduates), Fisher (1967) found means of 16.1 (s.d. = 6.8) and 16.4 (s.d. = 6.5) for males and females, respectively.

Reliability

Internal Consistency

Alpha coefficients ranged from .73 to .88 in the samples reported above.

Test–Retest

Crowne and Marlowe (1964) reported a test–retest correlation of .88 over 1 month. Fisher (1967) reported a value of .84 over a 1-week interval.

Validity

Convergent

The scale, as published in 1960, was intended as a measure of SDR in self-reports. A series of studies, summarized in Crowne and Marlowe (1964), uncovered a broad range of correlates suggesting the existence of an underlying motivational construct, namely, need for approval. For example, evidence showed that, compared to low scorers, high scorers on the MCSD respond more to social reinforcement, inhibit aggression, and are more amenable to social influence. Their task performance is more influenced by the evaluations of others. They prefer low-risk behaviors and avoid the evaluations of others, even when there is as much possibility for positive as for negative evaluation (for reviews of the research, see Crowne, 1979; Millham & Jacobson, 1978; Strickland, 1977).

Discriminant

As noted in the introduction, the MCSD falls primarily on the second SDR factor, showing only low to moderate correlations with such measures as Edwards SD and Self-Deceptive Enhancement.

Location

Crowne, D. P., & Marlowe, D. (1960). A new scale of social desirability independent of psychopathology. *Journal of Consulting Psychology,* **24,** 349–354.

Comments

The MCSD continues to sustain a dual existence as an SDR scale and a measure of the approval-dependent personality. Both interpretations are consistent with analyses showing the scale taps predominantly the second factor of SDR, that is, impression management (Paulhus, 1984).

One review (Strickland, 1977) was generally supportive of the need for approval construct, but recommended the label "approval motivation." Millham and Jacobson (1978) seem to prefer "evaluative dependence." The original prefix "need" was fashionable when the scale was developed but now seems presumptuous.

In addition, the weight of evidence has gradually shifted the interpretation to avoiding disapproval, rather than seeking approval, as implied by the original label (Allaman *et al.,* 1972; Crowne, 1979; Millham & Jacobson, 1978). Finally, some work has suggested that the attribution and denial items may be tapping distinct constructs (Millham, 1974; Paulhus & Reid, in press; see also Roth, Snyder, & Pace, 1986).

Use of the MCSD scale as a measure of situational demand is well-supported: Several studies have demonstrated its sensitivity to various audience effects (Davis & Cowles, 1989; Paulhus, 1984). Such effects, however, do not prove that subjects *consciously* modified their self-presentations.

More controversial is the question of whether high MCSD scores predict a proneness to dissimulation. A classic supporting example is Kiecolt-Glaser and Murray (1980): After an assertiveness training program, high MCSD scorers rated themselves as more assertive than low scorers although the program trainers rated them as *less* assertive. Other evidence suggests that high scorers will actually lie for reasons related to social approval (Jacobson, Berger, & Millham, 1970), but there is no clear evidence that they will lie for other reasons.

A complicating factor in interpreting certain studies is that, according to their spouses, high MCSD scorers actually do possess such desirable qualities as good adjustment, friendliness, and openness to experience (McCrae & Costa, 1983). Nonetheless, correlations in that study suggest that high MCSD scorers may further exaggerate their claims to such good qualities. A further complication is that high MCSD scorers also possess an honest demeanor: That is, judges tend to believe them and trust them even when they are instructed to lie (Riggio, Salinas, & Tucker, 1988). Indeed there is some evidence for a self-deceptive component (Millham & Kellogg, 1980; Weinberger, in press).

Marlowe–Crowne Scale

Listed below are a number of statements concerning personal attitudes and traits. Read each item and decide whether the statement is true or false as it pertains to you.

T   F   1. Before voting I thoroughly investigate the qualifications of all the candidates.

T	F	2. I never hesitate to go out of my way to help someone in trouble.
T	F	*3. It is sometimes hard for me to go on with my work if I am not encouraged.
T	F	4. I have never intensely disliked anyone.
T	F	*5. On occasion I have had doubts about my ability to succeed in life.
T	F	*6. I sometimes feel resentful when I don't get my way.
T	F	7. I am always careful about my manner of dress.
T	F	8. My table manners at home are as good as when I eat out in a restaurant.
T	F	*9. If I could get into a movie without paying and be sure I was not seen, I would probably do it.
T	F	*10. On a few occasions, I have given up doing something because I thought too little of my ability.
T	F	*11. I like to gossip at times.
T	F	*12. There have been times when I felt like rebelling against people in authority even though I knew they were right.
T	F	13. No matter who I'm talking to, I'm always a good listener.
T	F	*14. I can remember "playing sick" to get out of something.
T	F	*15. There have been occasions when I took advantage of someone.
T	F	16. I'm always willing to admit it when I make a mistake.
T	F	17. I always try to practice what I preach.
T	F	18. I don't find it particularly difficult to get along with loud-mouthed, obnoxious people.
T	F	*19. I sometimes try to get even, rather than forgive and forget.
T	F	20. When I don't know something I don't at all mind admitting it.
T	F	21. I am always courteous, even to people who are disagreeable.
T	F	*22. At times I have really insisted on having things my own way.
T	F	*23. There have been occasions when I felt like smashing things.
T	F	24. I would never think of letting someone else be punished for my wrongdoings.
T	F	25. I never resent being asked to return a favor.
T	F	26. I have never been irked when people expressed ideas very different from my own.
T	F	27. I never make a long trip without checking the safety of my car.
T	F	*28. There have been times when I was quite jealous of the good fortune of others.
T	F	29. I have almost never felt the urge to tell someone off.
T	F	*30. I am sometimes irritated by people who ask favors of me.

T	F	31. I have never felt that I was punished without cause.
T	F	*32. I sometimes think when people have a misfortune they only got what they deserved.
T	F	33. I have never deliberately said something that hurt someone's feelings.

Note: Items marked with an asterisk are keyed negatively.

MMPI Lie (L) Scale
(Meehl & Hathaway, 1946)

Variable

The L scale was designed to identify respondents who are deliberately trying to appear socially desirable while completing the MMPI.

Description

The scale comprises 15 statements about attitudes and practices that are socially undesirable but common. Topic areas include minor dishonesties, aggression, bad thoughts, and weaknesses of character. As on the MMPI as a whole, the response format is True–False. For all items, "False" is the response scored as a lie. In current usage, scores of 8 or above are considered suggestive of purposeful self-presentation (Greene, 1980).

Samples

Hathaway and McKinley (1951) reported means of 4.2 (s.d. = 2.6) and 4.5 (s.d. = 2.6) for males and females, respectively. In a more recent sample of 765 college students, Goldberg (1972) reported means of 2.5 (s.d. = 1.9) and 2.7 (s.d. = 1.8) for males and females, respectively. In a massive sample of 50,000 medical outpatients, Swenson, Pearson, and Osbourne (1973) reported means of 4.2 (s.d. = 2.3) and 4.8 (s.d. = 2.3) for males and females, respectively.

Reliability

Internal Consistency

Gocka (1965) reported an alpha coefficient of .72 on a patient sample. Paulhus (1984) reported an alpha value of .60 on a student sample.

Test–Retest

Test–retest correlations for intervals of up to 1 week range from .70 to .85. For intervals of 1 year or more, correlations range from .35 to .60 (Greene, 1980; Rorer & Goldberg, 1965).

Validity

Convergent

Evidence for concurrent validity is available from studies showing high correlations with similar constructs, for example, Eysenck's Lie scale (Paulhus, 1986) and the Marlowe–Crowne scale (e.g., Edwards & Walsh, 1964). As noted in the introduction, the L scale loads on both factors of SDR but primarily on the second factor, impression management.

No claim has been made that high scores should predict lying outside of self-reports. In the only known laboratory study, high scorers performed better than lows in a stressful situation (Burish & Houston, 1976).

Discriminant

The measure shows low correlations with measures loading on the first factor of SDR. For example, correlations with the K scale, the alternative SDR measure from the MMPI, range from low to moderate (Dahlstrom, Welsh, & Dahlstrom, 1972).

Location

Hathaway, S. R., & McKinley, J. C. (1951). *MMPI manual.* New York: Psychological Corporation.
Dahlstrom, W. G., Welsh, G. S., & Dahlstrom, L. E. (1972). *An MMPI handbook* (Vol. 1). Minneapolis: University of Minnesota Press.

Comments

It was soon apparent to the constructors of the L scale that the desirability demand of the items was less than subtle: "The L score was a trap for the naive subject but easily avoided by more sophisticated subjects" (Meehl & Hathaway, 1946). It is obvious to a sophisticated test-taker that, even if one is trying to appear desirable, it is unrealistic to deny such ubiquitous attributes.

Given its negative correlation with intelligence, some have construed the L scale as a measure of psychological sophistication. College-educated persons and those of higher

---

MMPI Lie Scale

Sample Items

1. At times I feel like swearing. (F)

    TRUE   FALSE

2. I get angry sometimes. (F)

3. Sometimes when I am not feeling well I am cross. (F)

Complete Scale

The MMPI booklet numbers for the 15-item Lie scale are 15, 30, 45, 60, 75, 90, 105, 120, 135, 150, 165, 195, 225, 255, 285. All items are keyed negatively, that is, one point is assigned for each "False."

socioeconomic status rarely score above 4 (Dahlstrom *et al.*, 1972). When they do, it may suggest a gross lack of insight into their own behavior (Greene, 1980).

MMPI K Scale

(Meehl & Hathaway, 1946)

Variable

The K scale was designed as a subtle measure of SDR on the MMPI. It is used to identify persons with psychopathology whose MMPI protocols appear normal.

Description

The 30 items were selected empirically. First, MMPI responses from normals were compared to those of persons with known psychopathology who scored as normals on the clinical scales. This procedure yielded 22 discriminating items. Depressed and schizophrenic patients, however, scored low on these items. Therefore, eight items were added to differentiate these two groups from normals. In current usage, scores of 16 or above are said to suggest invalid MMPI protocols (Greene, 1980).

Samples

In the original MMPI sample of 610 normals (a cross section of Minnesota residents), McKinley *et al.* (1948) reported means of 12.8 (s.d. = 5.6) and 12.1 (s.d. = 5.1) for males and females, respectively. In their mixed sample of 968 psychiatric cases, the means were 14.6 (s.d. = 5.9) and 14.3 (s.d. = 5.2) for males and females, respectively. In their sample of 100 university students, the means were 16.1 (s.d. = 5.1) and 15.7 (s.d. = 5.0) for males and females, respectively.

In a more recent sample of college students, Goldberg (1972) reported means of 15.4 (s.d. = 4.7) and 15.5 (s.d. = 4.3) for males and females, respectively. In a massive sample of 50,000 medical outpatients, Swenson *et al.* (1973) reported means of 15.4 (s.d. = 4.9) and 15.5 (s.d. = 4.8) for males and females, respectively.

Reliability

Internal Consistency

Gocka (1965) reported an alpha coefficient of .82 on a patient sample.

Test–Retest

Correlations range from .78 to .92 for an interval up to 2 weeks and range from .52 to .67 for intervals from 8 months to 3 years (Greene, 1980; Rorer & Goldberg, 1965).

Validity

Convergent

According to the original test constructors, the scale "was not assumed to be measuring anything which in itself is of psychiatric interest" (Meehl & Hathaway, 1946, p. 544). The validation of the scale was considered to rest on its value as a correction factor. That is, controlling other measures for K should improve their predictive validity.

In this respect, the validational evidence is weak. A few studies have shown improved validity of the MMPI scales after correcting scores as recommended in the MMPI manual (e.g., Wooten, 1984). Most studies have shown, if anything, decreases in validity (e.g., Heilbrun, 1963; McCrae *et al.*, 1989; Yonge, 1966).

The validity of K as a measure of defensiveness is better supported but appears to vary according to the type of respondent. In maladjusted college students, there is evidence that K indexes defensiveness (e.g., Heilbrun, 1961; Reis, 1966). In normal college students, K appears to tap a healthy positive self-image (e.g., McCrae *et al.*, 1989; Yonge, 1966).

Location

Meehl, P. E., & Hathaway, S. R. (1946). The K factor as a suppressor variable in the Minnesota Multiphasic Personality Inventory. *Journal of Applied Psychology, 30,* 525–564.
Dahlstrom, W. G., Welsh, G. S., & Dahlstrom, L. E. (1972). *An MMPI handbook* (Vol. 1.) Minneapolis: University of Minnesota Press.

Comments

As noted in the introduction, the K scale falls on the first factor of SDR. This association is consistent with the original conception of the K scale as a subtle measure of desirable responding. At the same time, this association suggests that at least some high scores result from a positive bias in self-image.

MMPI K Scale

Sample Items

1. I like to let people know where I stand on things. (T)
    TRUE   FALSE
2. I have very few quarrels with members of my family. (T)
3. People often disappoint me. (F)

Complete Scale

The MMPI booklet numbers for the items keyed "False" are 30, 39, 71, 89, 124, 129, 134, 138, 142, 148, 160, 170, 171, 180, 183, 217, 234, 267, 272, 296, 316, 322, 374, 383, 397, 398, 406, 461, 502. The sole item keyed "True" is MMPI booklet number 96.

CPI Good Impression (Gi) Scale
(Gough, 1952)

Variable

The Gi scale was designed to measure what people say about themselves when trying to create an extremely favorable impression (Gough, 1987, p. 36).

Description

Following Ruch (1942), test development involved contrast groups. Subjects first took an experimental booklet of items under normal circumstances and then repeated the testing with "good impression" instructions: "Try to give just as favorable an impression of yourself as you would if you were actually applying for an important position, or were trying to create a very favorable impression. . ."

The items tested included some adopted from Ruch (1942) and others newly written to measure impression management. The 40 best-differentiating items were included on Gough's (1957) CPI and five were modified for the revised CPI (Gough, 1987). Scores can range from 0 to 40 with scores above 30 suggestive of faking good.

Samples

Gough (1987) reported means and standard deviations for a wide variety of samples including 4126 college students (18.5, s.d. = 5.9), 100 nurses (18.6, s.d. = 5.5), and 345 prison inmates (17.9, s.d. = 7.0).

Reliability

Internal Consistency

Gough (1987) reported alpha coefficients of .77 for both male and female college students.

Test–Retest

Gough (1987) reported test–retest correlations of .68 after 1 year for both male and female high school students.

Validity

Convergent

A total of 400 CPI respondents were rated by their spouses using Q-sorts. The four Q-sort items showing the largest positive correlations with respondents' Gi scores were: (1) A conscientious and serious-minded person, (2) Well-organized, capable, patient, and industrious; values achievement, (3) Gentle, considerate, and tactful in dealing with others, and (4) Gets along well with others; able to "fit in" easily in most situations. In addition, 793 respondents were rated on Q-sorts by trained assessors. The four highest correlating items were (1) Is fastidious, (2) Favors conservative values in a variety of areas, (3) Is a genuinely dependable and responsible person, (4) Tends toward overcontrol of needs and impulses; binds tensions excessively; delays gratification unnecessarily. These and other validity data suggest that the high scorer is a highly controlled individual who behaves in a socially conventional manner.

Location

Gough, H. G. (1987). *California Psychological Inventory administrator's guide.* Palo Alto, CA: Consulting Psychologists Press.

Comments

The substantial validity data on the Gi highlight the dualistic nature of SDR measures. According to people who should know (spouses, peers, interviewers), the high scorer actually is a socially desirable person in being dependable, industrious, and cooperative.

However, the raters also see the high scorer as overcontrolled, suggesting an unwillingness to acknowledge undesirable qualities. This defensiveness is borne out by the fact that to score high on the Gi the respondent had to claim desirable qualities well beyond those validated by the judges (e.g., cultured interests, social skills). Other evidence of the high scorer's tendency to put the best foot forward is that interviewers rated him/her as well groomed, well dressed, and polite.

This dualism in the target construct is handled by giving a substantive interpretation to scores up to the cutoff point of 30, after which respondents are assumed to be faking good (Lanning, 1989).

The qualities measured by a scale developed through role-playing instructions depend wholly on the instructions given to the experimental group. As the reader may see above, the instructions used to select Gi items mentioned the job interview, thereby targeting the conventional, dependable, industrious, and cooperative types. This persona is, of course, only one of many possible good impressions.

CPI Gi Scale

Sample Items

1. I always follow the rule: business before pleasure. (T)
   TRUE   FALSE
2. I have never deliberately told a lie. (F)
3. I enjoy hearing lectures on world affairs. (T)

Complete Scale

The CPI booklet numbers for the items keyed "True" are 14, 103, 127, 133, 140, 165, 195, 222, 254. The items keyed "False" are 10, 30, 34, 38, 42, 44, 48, 56, 66, 70, 78, 81, 91, 101, 102, 109, 120, 150, 153, 159, 170, 178, 203, 207, 231, 238, 248, 262, 268, 273, 289, 293.

Balanced Inventory of Desirable Responding (BIDR)

(Paulhus, 1984, 1988)

Variable

The BIDR measures two constructs: self-deceptive positivity (the tendency to give self-reports that are honest but positively biased) and impression management (deliberate self-presentation to an audience).

Description

The BIDR is a descendant of the Self- and Other-Deception Questionnaires developed by Sackeim and Gur (1978). The original self-deception items were rationally developed on the assumption that individuals with a propensity for self-deception tend to deny having psychologically threatening thoughts or feelings. The threats were based on psycho-analytic theory (e.g., hating one's parents, enjoying one's bowel movements, having sexual fantasies). In contrast, the more recent version of the scale (Paulhus, 1988) empha-sizes exaggerated claims of positive cognitive attributes (overconfidence in one's judg-ments and rationality). Thus the focus has shifted from ego defense to ego enhancement. Given that the newer measure of self-deception is presented here, the psychometric information reported below applies only to that version.

The impression management items were rationally developed on the assumption that some respondents systematically overreport their performance of a wide variety of desir-able behaviors and underreport undesirable behaviors. Because the claims involve overt behaviors (e.g., I always pick up my litter), any distortion is presumably a conscious lie.

The 40 BIDR items are stated as propositions. Respondents rate their agreement with each statement on a seven-point scale. The scoring key is balanced. After reversing the negatively keyed items, one point is added for each extreme response (6 or 7). Hence, total scores on SDE and IM can range from 0 to 20. This scoring ensures that high scores are attained only by subjects who give exaggeratedly desirable responses. All 40 items may be summed to yield an overall measure of SDR that correlates highly with the MCSD. (An extended version including 20 denial items is also available.)

Samples

Self-Deception

In a large sample of 884 religious adults, Quinn (1989) found means of 7.6 (s.d. = 3.1) and 7.3 (s.d. = 3.1) for males and females, respectively. In a sample of 433 college students, Paulhus (1988) reported corresponding means of 7.5 (s.d. = 3.2) and 6.8 (s.d. = 3.1).

Impression Management

Quinn (1989) reported male and female means of 7.3 (s.d. = 3.1) and 8.9 (s.d. = 3.2) in a sample of 884 religious adults. In a sample of 433 college students, Paulhus (1988) reported means of 4.3 (s.d. = 3.1) and 4.9 (s.d. = 3.2) for males and females, respec-tively. In a sample of 100 college students, Paulhus (1984) reported an overall mean of

11.9 (s.d. = 4.5) in a public disclosure condition. In a sample of 48 members of alcoholics anonymous, Mellor, Conroy, and Masteller (1986) reported a mean of 11.2 (s.d. = 4.9).

Reliability

Internal Consistency

In the studies reported above, values of coefficient alpha range from .68 to .80 for the SDE and from .75 to .86 for the IM scale. When all 40 items are summed as a measure of SDR, the alpha is .83 (Paulhus, 1988).

Test–Retest

Paulhus (1988) reported test–retest correlations over a 5-week period of .69 and .65 for the SDE and IM scale, respectively.

Validity

The sum of all 40 BIDR items shows concurrent validity as a measure of SDR in correlating .71 with the Marlowe–Crowne scale (Paulhus, 1988) and .80 with the Multidimensional Social Desirability Inventory of Jacobson, Kellogg, Cauce, and Slavin (1977).

Convergent: Self-Deception

In general, measures of self-deception show concurrent validity in correlating strongly with other first factor SDR measures (see introduction). Paulhus (1988) found that the SDE measure provided here correlates positively with the following traditional measures of defense and coping: (1) repressive style as measured by Byrne's R-S scale ($r = .51$), (2) reversal, as measured by Ihilevich and Gleser's (1986) Defense Mechanisms Inventory ($r = .34$), and (3) positive re-appraisal ($r = .44$), distancing ($r = .33$), and self-controlling ($r = .39$) as measured with the Ways of Coping scale (Folkman, Lazarus, Dunkel-Schetter, DeLongis, & Gruen, 1986).

Several experimental studies have supported the construct validity of the SDE. After a failure experience, high self-deception subjects were more likely than lows to show a self-serving bias (Paulhus, 1988). High self-deception subjects also showed more illusion of control, belief that they are safe drivers, and proneness to love (Paulhus & Reid, in press) and to intrinsic religiosity (Leak & Fish, 1989). High scorers also show excessive confidence in memory judgments and more hindsight bias; they also claim familiarity with non-existent products (Paulhus, 1988).

All these mechanisms may contribute to the positive adjustment reported by high SDE subjects including high self-esteem as well as low neuroticism, depression, empathic distress, and social anxiety (Paulhus & Reid, in press). Note that all these measures of adjustment have been validated in the past by clinical judgment, behavioral measures, and/or peer-ratings.

Convergent: IM Scale

As noted in the introduction, the IM scale correlates highly with a cluster of measures traditionally known as lie scales (e.g., Eysenck's Lie scale, MMPI Lie scale) and role-playing measures (e.g., Wiggins' Sd, Gough's Gi). Correlations with the MCSD and agreeableness and conscientiousness ratings (Paulhus, 1988) suggest that a social approval motive underlies anonymous responses.

The IM scale is particularly responsive to demands for impression management. For example, in a comparison of six SDR measures, the IM scale showed the largest increase from private to public conditions (Paulhus, 1984). Lautenschlager and Flaherty (in press) showed that IM, but not SDE, was sensitive to test administration conditions (paper and pencil vs. computer; public vs. private).

Discriminant

Measures of self-deception and impression management show discriminant validity in forming separate factors in factor analyses (Paulhus, 1984, 1988). Earlier versions of the self-deception measure showed positive correlations with impression management ranging from .35 to .65, depending on the situational demand for self-presentation. The version presented here, however, exhibits much lower correlations, ranging from .05 to .40. Note that males score higher than females on self-deception, but lower on impression management.

Location

Paulhus, D. L. (1988). *Assessing self deception and impression management in self-reports: the Balanced Inventory of Desirable Responding.* (Manual available from the author at the Department of Psychology, University of British Columbia, Vancouver, B.C., Canada V6T 1Y7.)

Comments

The predecessors of these measures, the Self-Deception and Other-Deception Questionnaires, were first described in Sackeim and Gur (1978), although the items have never been published. Subsequently, Paulhus (1984) refined the measures and integrated them into one inventory. The two major refinements were (a) writing reversals to balance the keys, and (b) replacing the psychopathology items. The latter refinement eliminated any spurious correlation with psychopathology measures. Five preliminary versions of the BIDR preceded the version presented here (Paulhus, 1988). A French language version is also available (Sabourin, Bourgeois, Gendreau, & Morval, 1989).

A major feature of the BIDR is the provision for separate measures of the two major SDR factors, self-deceptive enhancement and impression management. It is often critical to know which component is responsible for a correlation observed between SDR and some other variable. In addition, the dichotomous scoring procedure (assigning points only for *extremely* desirable responses) provides some assurance that style rather than content is being tapped. IM is more likely to tap style as anonymity decreases.

Note that substantial correlations are observed between SDE and measures of adjustment even though the content of the SDE measure is free of psychopathology. These findings suggest that self-deceptive positivity is intrinsically linked to the adjusted personality, consistent with current views of adjustment (Alloy & Abramson, 1979; Taylor & Brown, 1988). Research is required on the personality of extreme scorers: Peer-raters may not see them as well-adjusted as they see themselves. They may also snap under stress.

Validation of a measure of self-deception is constrained by the uncertain status of the construct (see Lockard & Paulhus, 1988). Conceptually similar labels for the construct are available, for example lack of insight, overconfidence, or dogmatism. Whatever the label, it is clear that the SDE scale is tapping a specific form of SDR, one that is less subject to purposeful manipulation than measures in the impression management category.

BIDR Version 6—Form 40

Using the scale below as a guide, write a number beside each statement to indicate how much you agree with it.

1 —————— 2 —————— 3 —————— 4 —————— 5 —————— 6 —————— 7
NOT TRUE   SOMEWHAT   VERY TRUE
                                      TRUE

_____ 1. My first impressions of people usually turn out to be right.

_____ *2. It would be hard for me to break any of my bad habits.

_____ 3. I don't care to know what other people really think of me.

_____ *4. I have not always been honest with myself.

_____ 5. I always know why I like things.

_____ *6. When my emotions are aroused, it biases my thinking.

_____ 7. Once I've made up my mind, other people can seldom change my opinion.

_____ *8. I am not a safe driver when I exceed the speed limit.

_____ 9. I am fully in control of my own fate.

_____ *10. It's hard for me to shut off a disturbing thought.

_____ 11. I never regret my decisions.

_____ *12. I sometimes lose out on things because I can't make up my mind soon enough.

_____ 13. The reason I vote is because my vote can make a difference.

_____ *14. My parents were not always fair when they punished me.

_____ 15. I am a completely rational person.

_____ *16. I rarely appreciate criticism.

_____ 17. I am very confident of my judgments.

_____ *18. I have sometimes doubted my ability as a lover.

_____ 19. It's all right with me if some people happen to dislike me.

_____ *20. I don't always know the reasons why I do the things I do.

_____ *21. I sometimes tell lies if I have to.

_____ 22. I never cover up my mistakes.

_____ *23. There have been occasions when I have taken advantage of someone.

_____ 24. I never swear.

_____ *25. I sometimes try to get even rather than forgive and forget.

_____ 26. I always obey laws, even if I'm unlikely to get caught.

_____ *27. I have said something bad about a friend behind his or her back.

_____ 28. When I hear people talking privately, I avoid listening.

_____ *29. I have received too much change from a salesperson without telling him or her.

_____ 30. I always declare everything at customs.

_____ *31. When I was young I sometimes stole things.

_____ 32. I have never dropped litter on the street.

_____ *33. I sometimes drive faster than the speed limit.

_____ 34. I never read sexy books or magazines.

_____ *35. I have done things that I don't tell other people about.

_____ 36. I never take things that don't belong to me.

_____ *37. I have taken sick-leave from work or school even though I wasn't really sick.

_____ 38. I have never damaged a library book or store merchandise without reporting it.

_____ *39. I have some pretty awful habits.

_____ 40. I don't gossip about other people's business.

Items 1–20 assess SDE; items 21–40 assess IM. Add one point for every "6" or "7" (minimum = 0; maximum = 20).
*, Items keyed in the "False" (negative) direction.

Responding Desirably on Attitudes and Opinions (RD-16)

(Schuessler, Hittle, & Cardascia, 1978)

Variable

This measure of SDR was specially designed to detect socially desirable responding in attitude and opinion surveys of the general population.

Description

The scale development involved several stages. A set of 270 items was taken from over 100 tests of attitudes, morale, and related concepts. These were rated for desirability and items showing neutral ratings, above average variance, or interactions between race and education were discarded. Sixteen items were selected rationally to cover the widest range of topics. The scale was normed in a national probability sample of 1522 adults.

The 16-item scale comprises eight pairs, one pair from tests of dejection, social estrangement, social opportunism, trust, social contentment, anomie, expediency, and self-determination. Each pair (and therefore, the entire set) is key-balanced. The subject is asked to agree or disagree with each item. Possible scores range from 0 to 16 with higher scores indicating more desirable responding.

Samples

In their national probability sample of 1522 adults, Schuessler *et al.* (1978) reported an overall mean of 12.7 (s.d. = 2.4). On a shortened 10-item version, Krebs and Schuessler

(1987) reported means of 7.9 (s.d. = 1.6) and 7.2 (s.d. = 1.6) on American and German samples, respectively.

Reliability

Internal Consistency

Schuessler *et al.* (1978) reported an overall alpha coefficient of .64 in the national probability sample.

Test–Retest

No test–retest reliabilities are available.

Validity

Convergent

Concurrent validity is supported by a correlation of .55 with a 10-item version of Jackson's (1967) Desirability scale.

Discriminant

According to Schuessler *et al.* (1978), discriminant validity is supported by low intercorrelations with the Marlowe–Crowne scale (r = .07 to .16). Low to moderate (−.18 to −.36) negative correlations were found with measures of acquiescence (Krebs & Schuessler, 1987; Schuessler *et al.*, 1978).

Location

Schuessler, K., Hittle, D., & Cardascia, J. (1978). Measuring responding desirably with attitude-opinion items. *Social Psychology*, **41**, 224–235.

Comments

Several attributes make the RD-16 appropriate for use in attitude and opinion surveys. First, the items were drawn from a wide pool of general attitude and opinion measures. Second, the items were selected from ratings done by a cross section of adults rather than the usual college sophomores. Third, the items were screened so that none would differ in desirability across race and education.

It is notable that, although the items were taken from attitude and opinion surveys, the statistical selection procedures yielded personality-oriented items like those on other SDR measures. The measure falls clearly on the first factor of SDR (see introductory material at the beginning of this chapter). A major feature is the national probability sample of norms broken down by social status categories. A German language version is also available (Krebs & Schuessler, 1987). Note that the items below should be randomized for presentation: They are listed below in all-desirable then all-undesirable order.

RD-16

Please circle "A" or "D" to indicate whether you agree or disagree with the following statements. Do not omit any items.

A   D   1. I find that I can help others in many ways.

A   D   2. I feel that I am better off than my parents were at my age.

A   D   3. In spite of many changes, there are still definite rules to live by.

A   D   4. One can always find friends if he [one] tries.

A   D   5. Anyone can raise his standard of living if he [one] is willing to work at it.

A   D   6. Most people really believe that honesty is the best policy.

A   D   7. In general, I am satisfied with my lot in life.

A   D   8. People will be honest with you as long as you are honest with them.

A   D   *9. It is difficult to think clearly about right and wrong these days.

A   D   *10. Many people are friendly only because they want something from you.

A   D   *11. If the odds are against you, it's impossible to come out on top.

A   D   *12. At times I feel that I am a stranger to myself.

A   D   *13. The future looks very bleak.

A   D   *14. I often feel that no one needs me.

A   D   *15. I am so fed up that I can't take it any more.

A   D   *16. To get along with people one must put on an act.

Note: *, Items keyed in "False" (negative) direction. Nonsexist wording is suggested in brackets.

Children's Social Desirability Scale (CSD)

(Crandall, Crandall, & Katkovsky, 1965)

Variable

Modeled after the Marlowe–Crowne scale, the CSD assesses SDR in children as motivated by a need for approval. Subsequently, the construct was reinterpreted as fear of disapproval (Crandall, 1966).

Description

The scale contains 48 statements in True–False format with 26 items keyed true. Much of the item content follows that of the Marlowe–Crowne items. Additional items involve child-specific content (e.g., "Sometimes I want to do things my parents think I am too young to do.") or items that are worded in children's language (e.g., "Sometimes I wish I could just mess around instead of having to go to school."). Possible scores range from 0 to 48 with high scores indicating a fear of disapproval.

Samples

In a total sample of 956 grade school and high school students, Crandall *et al.* (1965) reported means monotonically decreasing from 29.3 (s.d. = 10.4) in Grade 3 to 12.7 (s.d. = 7.6) in Grade 12.

Reliability

Internal Consistency

Crandall *et al.* (1965) reported corrected split-half reliabilities ranging from .82 to .95.

Test–Retest

Crandall *et al.* (1965) reported a test–retest correlation of .85 after a 1-month interval. Allaman *et al.* (1972) reported test–retest correlations of .90 after 1 month and of .43 and .19 over 3 years for males and females, respectively.

Validity

Convergent

Correlations of .78 and .51 were found between scores on the CSD and scores on the Marlowe–Crowne and Good Impression scales, respectively. High scorers were more religious (Crandall & Gozali, 1969) but had lower self-esteem (Crandall, 1966). In observational studies, high CSD scorers were less aggressive, participated less, avoided achievement activities (Crandall, 1966), and ate less candy in the presence of others (Staub & Sherk, 1970). Some evidence is less consistent with the construct (for a review, see Strickland, 1977).

Discriminant

No relevant information has been reported.

Location

Crandall, V., Crandall, V. J., & Katkovsky, W. A. (1965). A children's social desirability scale. *Journal of Consulting Psychology, **29**,* 27–36.
The actual items are presented in Strickland (1977).

Comments

Crandall *et al.* (1965) also developed a version for younger children (Grades 3–5). The items are posed in question format and are usually presented via a recording for standardization purposes. In a sample of 43 fifth graders, this measure correlated .85 with the written true–false version (Brannigan, 1974).

The developmental data are provocative in suggesting that SDR tendencies result from maternal tendencies such as hostility, criticism, restrictiveness, punitiveness, and lack of encouragement. In addition, noncompliance and dominance in infancy were related to adult SDR (Allaman *et al.*, 1972).

Developmental stability is a critical issue. Test–retest correlations are high after 1 month but low after 3 years. Crandall *et al.* (1965) interpret the latter as developmental instability. Interestingly, the correlation with the Marlowe–Crowne noted earlier (.78) was after an average delay of several years. Although the sample size was very small ($n = 12$), Allaman *et al.* (1972) suggest that SDR may stabilize by adolescence.

CSD

This questionnaire lists a number of experiences that most children have at one time or another. Read each of these carefully. After you have read one, decide whether it does or does not fit you. If it does, put a T (for true) in front of the statement; if it doesn't, put an F (for false) in front of the statement.

_____ 1. I always enjoy myself at a party.

_____ *2. I tell a little lie sometimes.

_____ 3. I never get angry if I have to stop in the middle of something I'm doing to eat dinner, or go to school.

_____ *4. Sometimes I don't like to share my things with my friends.

_____ 5. I am always respectful of older people.

_____ 6. I would never hit a boy or girl who was smaller than me.

_____ *7. Sometimes I do not feel like doing what my teachers want me to do.

_____ 8. I never act "fresh" or "talk back" to my mother or father.

_____ 9. When I make a mistake, I always admit I am wrong.

_____ *10. I feel my parents do not always show good judgment.

_____ 11. I have never felt like saying unkind things to a person.

_____ 12. I always finish all of my homework on time.

_____ *13. Sometimes I have felt like throwing or breaking things.

_____ 14. I never let someone else get blamed for what I did wrong.

_____ *15. Sometimes I say something just to impress my friends.

_____ 16. I am always careful about keeping my clothing neat, and my room picked up.

_____ 17. I never shout when I feel angry.

_____ *18. Sometimes I feel like staying home from school even if I am not sick.

_____ *19. Sometimes I wish that my parents didn't check up on me so closely.

_____ 20. I always help people who need help.

_____ *21. Sometimes I argue with my mother to do something she doesn't want me to do.

_____ 22. I never say anything that would make a person feel bad.

_____ 23. My teachers always know more about everything than I do.

_____ 24. I am always polite, even to people who are not very nice.

_____*25. Sometimes I do things I've been told not to do.

_____ 26. I never get angry.

_____*27. I sometimes want to own things just because my friends have them.

_____ 28. I always listen to my parents.

_____ 29. I never forget to say "please" and "thank you."

_____*30. Sometimes I wish I could just "mess around" instead of having to go to school.

_____ 31. I always wash my hands before every meal.

_____*32. Sometimes I dislike helping my parents even though I know they need my help around the house.

_____ 33. I never find it hard to make friends.

_____ 34. I have never been tempted to break a rule or a law.

_____*35. Sometimes I try to get even when someone does something to me I don't like.

_____*36. I sometimes feel angry when I don't get my way.

_____ 37. I always help an injured animal.

_____*38. Sometimes I want to do things my parents think I am too young to do.

_____*39. I sometimes feel like making fun of other people.

_____ 40. I have never borrowed anything without asking permission first.

_____*41. Sometimes I get annoyed when someone disturbs something I've been working on.

_____ 42. I am always glad to cooperate with others.

_____ 43. I never get annoyed when my best friend wants to do something I don't want to do.

_____*44. Sometimes I wish that the other kids would pay more attention to what I say.

_____ 45. I always do the right things.

_____*46. Sometimes I don't like to obey my parents.

_____*47. Sometimes I don't like it when another person asks me to do things for him.

_____*48. Sometimes I get mad when people don't do what I want.

Note: *, Items keyed in "False" (negative) direction.

Acquiescence

Acquiescence is the tendency to agree rather than disagree with propositions in general (e.g., Lentz, 1938). A few studies have examined the effects of test situation and item format (e.g., Schuman & Presser, 1981; Trott & Jackson, 1967), but the bulk of the research has addressed acquiescence as a response style. Some individuals, called *yeasayers,* tend to agree with statements or say "yes" to questions; other individuals, called *naysayers,* tend to disagree with statements or say "no" to questions. Rather than a mechanical response to any question, this tendency is assumed to emerge when the subject is uncertain (Peabody, 1966). Acquiescence has often been viewed as an individual difference variable in its own right, a personality trait with conceptual links to conformity and impulsiveness (e.g., Couch & Keniston, 1960; Gough & Heilbrun, 1980; Messick, 1967).

A problem arises when a self-report instrument measures acquiescence as well as the construct it was designed to measure. For example, on many anxiety scales subjects are asked to indicate with a "yes" or "no" which anxiety-related symptoms they have experienced. The respondent who says "yes" to all the symptoms may indeed be a very anxious person. Alternatively, the respondent may merely be a yeasayer.

Some researchers have claimed that acquiescence can be a serious confound in self-reports of attitudes (Carr, 1971; Ray, 1983; Schuman & Presser, 1981), ability and achievement (Cronbach, 1946), personality (Jackson & Helmes, 1979), and psychopathology (Jackson & Messick, 1958). Moreover, acquiescence has been found to interact with social status variables such as race and education (Bachman & O'Malley, 1984a; DeLamater & McKinney, 1982). In contrast, other researchers have concluded that acquiescence effects are insignificant (Gove & Geerken, 1977; Rorer, 1965; Rorer & Goldberg, 1965; Wright, 1975).

With a view to reconciling these conflicting data, Bentler, Jackson, and Messick (1971) distinguished two types of acquiescence: agreement acquiescence and acceptance acquiescence. *Agreement* acquiescence is the tendency to agree with (or give positive ratings) to all types of items, even an item and its own negation ("happy" and "not happy"). *Acceptance* acquiescence is the tendency to endorse all qualities (even apparently contrary ones) as true of one's self. This form is indicated by agreeing that one is both "happy" and "sad" and disagreeing that one is "not happy" and "not sad." Bentler *et al.* (1971) concluded that the effects of agreement acquiescence are insignificant, whereas acceptance acquiescence remains a problem. Block (1971) was skeptical.

There is little disagreement that acquiescence is more problematic in attitude and survey research than in personality assessment (Bentler *et al.,* 1971; Ray, 1983; Schuman & Presser, 1981). In survey research, the percentage agreement with an item (e.g., I favor capital punishment) is usually more critical than in personality items (e.g., I am friendly), in which relative agreement across items is the issue. Moreover, in many personality inventories, the items are simply trait adjectives, thereby simplifying the control of acquiescence. In sharp contrast, Schuman and Presser (1981) have shown that the complex statements required in much survey research are highly susceptible to acquiescence in agree–disagree, interrogative, or true–false format. Moreover, Ray's (1983) work suggests that acquiescence may be a generalized style across attitude scales.

Control

Despite continuing disagreement about the pervasiveness of acquiescence, most scale constructors now make an effort to balance the scoring key. Usually, half the items are keyed positively (a high rating indicates possession of the construct being assessed) and half the items are keyed negatively (a low rating indicates possession of the construct). In dichotomous formats (e.g., True–False), this procedure is equivalent to keying half the items true and half false.

This simple precaution controls the classical form of acquiescence (agreement acquiescence) because, to get an overall high score, the respondent must agree with many items and disagree with many others. In other words, one cannot get a high score simply by yea-saying or nay-saying (for a cautionary note, see Wiggins, 1968).

It is more difficult to correct an imbalanced scale post hoc. If the correlations are high between positively and negatively keyed subtotals and their correlations with other variables are comparable, then one may safely combine the two. One could then differentially weight the positively and negatively keyed subtotals to simulate a balanced key (Winkler, Kanouse, & Ware, 1982). Partial correlation techniques have also been applied to remove acquiescence statistically (Webster, 1958).

According to Bentler *et al.* (1971), however, it is acceptance acquiescence that specifically requires controlling. Simply adding a negation (not happy) for each item worded as an assertion (happy) will not suffice.[5] One must add conceptual opposites that are also worded as assertions. When collecting ratings on the personality trait "dominance," for example, one must also include the conceptually opposite trait, "submissive." In applications where the conceptual opposite is not clear (as in many survey items), preliminary studies may be necessary to find an appropriate assertion to match the original (for examples, see Schuman & Presser, 1981). Combining these matched options in a forced-choice format is even better. Only one known personality instrument has been designed to control both forms of acquiescence: the Multidimensional Social Desirability Inventory (Jacobson, Brown, & Ariza, 1983; Jacobson *et al.*, 1977).[6] Note, however, that the instrument targets only one domain, socially desirable responding.

Measurement

A small number of instruments have been designed to measure individual differences in the tendency to acquiesce in self-reports. The Couch–Keniston (1960) agreement response scale, for example, was included in the first edition of the present volume. On the basis of empirical work (e.g., Rorer, 1965), however, such measures have fallen into disrepute and none is widely used. Moreover, the original proponents of the importance of acquiescence, Messick and Jackson, shifted their focus to acceptance acquiescence, a form that seems to be domain-specific. In short, none of the instruments claiming to measure general acquiescence tendencies can be recommended to the researcher. Therefore, no such measures are presented in this chapter.

A number of larger assessment batteries permit computation of an acquiescence index across all the items in the battery. Gough and Heilbrun's (1965) Adjective Check List, for example, permits calculation of the "checking factor," that is, the total number of adjectives checked as true of the self. This score is often factored out of subsequent analyses (e.g., Wiggins, 1979). Note that this procedure may eliminate some content unless one has administered the ACL in true–false format to ensure some response to each item. The MMPI permits detection of "all true" or "all false" protocols through computation of the Carelessness scale (Greene, 1980).

Several statistical techniques have been designed to separate the contributions of item content from both forms of acquiescence (Bramble & Wiley, 1974; Morf & Jackson, 1972). If, however, acceptance acquiescence is domain-specific, one may require a separate measure for each personality dimension or narrow battery. Indeed, one may even require separate measures for the positively and negatively keyed items within a scale (Paulhus & Reid, in press).

---

[5]Another problem with negating items may be a loss in validity (Holden *et al.*, 1985).

[6]Sample items of each type are: "I always keep my promises," "I daydream about sexual acts," "I do not always vote," and "I never feel worthless."

Extremity Response Bias (ERB)

Extremity response bias (ERB) is the tendency to use the extreme choices on a rating scale (e.g., 1s and 7s on a seven-point scale). Situational factors such as ambiguity (Shulman, 1973), emotional arousal, and speededness (Paulhus, 1987) induce temporary increases in ERB. The individual exhibiting a consistent ERB across time and stimuli may be said to have an extremity response style; low scorers on this construct may be said to have a moderacy response bias, tending to use the midpoint as often as possible. Early reviews by Peabody (1962) and Hamilton (1968) concluded that ERB is a consistent individual difference, and more recent studies have sustained this conclusion. Bachman and O'Malley (1984a) found ERB in attitudes to be highly stable over time. A study of trait ratings found ERB to be the major source of individual differences across raters (Van der Kloot, Kroonenberg, & Bakker, 1985). Race differences in ERB have also been found (Bachman & O'Malley, 1984a). There is little support, however, for a link between ERB and any traditional personality dimensions (Bonarius, 1971; Schneider, 1973).

Not all extreme responding represents a response bias in test-taking. There is substantial evidence that extreme responses are valid indicators of extreme opinions. Most convincing is the evidence that extreme test responses predict extreme behavior (Schuman & Presser, 1981; cf. Peabody, 1962).

Not to be confused with ERB is the so-called deviant response style (Berg, 1967), the tendency to make ratings as different as possible from the norm. Berg hypothesized links between this style and a wide range of behaviors and collected some relevant data. Its failure to gain credibility is summarized by Wiggins's (1973) statement that "There is good reason to question both the evidence for and the explanatory value of the deviation hypothesis" (p. 419).

Problems

ERB precludes the direct comparability of one subject's scores to another's: One cannot ordinarily distinguish whether an extreme rating indicates a strong opinion or a tendency to use the extremities of rating scales. A second problem is that ERB induces spurious correlations among otherwise unrelated constructs. Another source of problems is the interaction between ERB and social status variables such as gender (Hamilton, 1968), race (Bachman & O'Malley, 1984a), and education (Shulman, 1973).

Control

In some situations, ERB can be controlled by putting questions in multiple-choice format. ERB cannot be corrected simply by balancing the key because extremity operates in both directions. Reducing the number of response options to two does eliminate the problem but simultaneously reduces the sensitivity of the measure. Standardizing the within-subjects variance equates subjects on extremity but subject variances may contain content because they are often inextricably confounded with subject means. In measuring self-esteem, for example, most responses are on the positive portion of the rating scale, thus confounding high self-esteem and ERB (Bachman & O'Malley, 1984b).

Measurement

There are no standard instruments for assessing ERB as a response style. In some applications, the variance of a subject's ratings across an inventory has been used as an index (e.g., Van der Kloot *et al.*, 1985). Of course, this is inappropriate if the key for each dimension is not balanced or if the means depart substantially from the scale midpoint. Note that if only one dimension is being assessed, it is difficult to distinguish any index of ERB from a measure of dimensional importance or salience for that topic.

Future Research Directions

Although the debates are less heated than in the 1960s, the issue of response bias in self-reports continues to be rather polarized through the 1990s. Some researchers, citing Block (1965) and Rorer (1965), believe that the fear of response biases is unwarranted. Others continue to balk at using instruments that have unbalanced keys or that correlate highly with some measure of SDR.

Consequently, the more recent disputes about SDR often give one a sense of déjà vu. In the well-being literature, for example, Carstensen and Cone (1983) alleged that the popular measures were invalid because of high correlations with Edwards's Social Desirability scale. McCrae (1986) responded that such correlations were due to the fact that social desirability scales measure substance, not style. A similar debate recently occurred over the high correlations found between SD and measures of depression (Linehan & Nielsen, 1981; Nevid, 1983). One possible resolution to such standoffs lies in the separation of SDR instruments of self-deception and impression management (e.g., Sabourin *et al.*, 1989). Advances on these issues will be possible only if researchers abandon the all-or-none positions taken in the past.

With regard to SDR, two critical issues need to be addressed by researchers in this area. One issue is the clarification of the link between adjustment and an exaggerated positivity. Do all well-adjusted persons exaggerate? Is it only the extreme scorers? Alternatively, is it only a subset of maladjusted individuals who defensively report being adjusted? (See Paulhus, Fridhandler, & Hayes, in press.)

The second pressing need is for increased specificity in the measurement of impression management (called for some time ago by Norman, 1963). Few would disagree that respondents bent on impression management tailor their self-reports to suit the audience. Yet the target audience on available scales is a vague notion of society at large (DeMaio, 1984). Among the most useful scales would be those targeted at such audiences as job interviewers, psychology experimenters, and college peers.[7] Moreover, separate measures may be required to index faking good, faking bad, and faking mad (Furnham & Henderson, 1982; Winder *et al.*, 1975). Finally, more research is needed to clarify what impression management scores mean when completed under anonymous conditions.

The current situation is more stable with respect to acquiescence. In personality, the pro forma compromise has been to balance the keying of new instruments without necessarily conceding that acquiescence makes a difference. In survey research, some difficult issues remain (Schuman & Presser, 1981).

Extremity response bias is typically ignored by contemporary test developers, although evidence confirms that it is pervasive (Van der Kloot *et al.*, 1985). A number of researchers are actively pursuing questions about which item contexts (e.g., Eiser & van der Pligt, 1984; Romer, 1983) and emotional states (Paulhus, 1987) are conducive to extreme responding.

---

[7]The scales in the Hogan Personality Inventory (1986) represent various images of self presentation. These images, however, are cross-situationally stable because they derive from motives and eventually become automatic.

Some researchers dismiss the importance of response bias contamination by pointing to significant validity coefficients for their content scales. They must be reminded that modest validity coefficients leave much unexplained variance in the predictor, some of which may be response bias. Moreover, the impression management demand of most *practical* assessment situations makes it likely that at least some respondents are faking.

While I fully intend to end on a negative note, there is at least one reason to be optimistic about a future break in the deadlocks over the nature of response styles. That reason is the growing interest in the *process* of questionnaire responding (e.g., Cliff, 1977; DeBoeck, 1981; Jackson, 1986; Novakowska, 1970; Rogers, 1971, 1974; Schwarz, Strack, Muller, & Chassein, 1988). Much of this research exploits the techniques of modern cognitive psychology, for example, computer-controlled presentation of stimuli and measurement of reaction times (Holden, Fekken, & Jackson, 1985; Hsu, Santelli, & Hsu, 1989; Knowles, 1988; Paulhus & Levitt, 1987). It may be some time, however, before any benefits trickle down to test consumers.

Acknowledgments

Work on this chapter was supported by a grant from the Social Sciences Research Council of Canada. Among those who assisted by commenting on the chapter were Lew Goldberg, Stanley Presser, Peter Schmolk, Howard Schuman, and Jerry Wiggins.

Bibliography

Allaman, J. D., Joyce, C. S., & Crandall, V. C. (1972). The antecedents of social desirability response tendencies of children and young adults. *Child Development, 43,* 1135–1160.

Alloy, L. B., & Abramson, L. Y. (1979). Judgment of contingency in depressed and nondepressed students: Sadder but wiser? *Journal of Experimental Psychology: General, 108,* 441–485.

Bachman, J. G., & O'Malley, P. M. (1984a). Yea-saying, nay-saying, and going to extremes: Black–white differences in response styles. *Public Opinion Quarterly, 48,* 491–509.

Bachman, J. G., & O'Malley, P. M. (1984b). Black–white differences in self-esteem: Are they affected by response styles? *American Journal of Sociology, 90,* 624–639.

Becker, W. M. (1976). Biasing effect of respondents' identification on responses to a social desirability scale: A warning to researchers. *Psychological Reports, 39,* 756–758.

Bentler, P. M., Jackson, D. N., & Messick, S. (1971). Identification of content and style: A two-dimensional interpretation of acquiescence. *Psychological Bulletin, 76,* 186–204.

Berg, I. A. (1967). The deviation hypothesis: A broad statement of its assumptions and postulates. In I. A. Berg (Ed.), *Response set in personality assessment* (pp. 146–190). Chicago: Aldine.

Bernreuter, R. G. (1933). Validity of the personality inventory. *Personality Journal, 11,* 383–386.

Block, J. (1965). *The challenge of response sets.* New York: Appleton-Century-Crofts.

Block, J. (1971). On further conjectures regarding acquiescence. *Psychological Bulletin, 76,* 205–210.

Bonarius, J. C. J. (1971). *Personal construct psychology and extreme response style.* Amsterdam: Swets and Zeitlinger.

Borkenau, P., & Amelang, M. (1985). The control of social desirability in personality inventories: A study using the principal-factor deletion technique. *Journal of Research in Personality, 19,* 44–53.

Borkenau, P., & Ostendorf, F. (1989). Descriptive consistency and social desirability in self- and peer reports. *European Journal of Personality, 3,* 31–45.

Bramble, W. J., & Wiley, D. E. (1974). Estimating content-acquiescence correlation by covariance structure analysis. *Multivariate Behavioral Research, 9,* 179–190.

Brannigan, G. G. (1974). Comparison of yes–no and true–false forms of the children's social desirability scale. *Psychological Reports,* **34,** 898.

Burish, T. G., & Houston, B. K. (1976). Construct validity of the Lie scale as a measure of defensiveness. *Journal of Clinical Psychology,* **32,** 310–314.

Byrne, D. (1964). Repression–sensitization as a dimension of personality. In B. A. Maher (Ed.), *Progress in experimental personality research* (Vol. 1, pp. 169–220). New York: Academic Press.

Carr, L. G. (1971). The Srole items and acquiescence. *American Sociological Review,* **36,** 287–293.

Carstensen, L. L., & Cone, J. D. (1983). Social desirability and measurement of psychological well-being in elderly persons., *Journal of Gerontology,* **38,** 713–715.

Cattell, R. B., Pierson, G., & Finkbeiner, C. (1976). Alignment of personality source trait factors from questionnaires and observer ratings: The theory of instrument-free patterns. *Multivariate Experimental Clinical Research,* **2,** 63–88.

Clark, J. P., & Tifft, L. L. (1966). Polygraph and interview validation of self-reported deviant behavior. *American Sociological Review,* **31,** 516–523.

Cliff, N. (1977). Further study of cognitive processing models for inventory response. *Applied Psychological Measurement,* **1,** 41–49.

Comrey, A. L. (1980). *Handbook of interpretations for the Comrey Personality scales.* San Diego: EdITS.

Couch, A., & Keniston, K. (1960). Yeasayers and naysayers: Agreeing response set as a personality variable. *Journal of Abnormal and Social Psychology,* **60,** 151–174.

Crandall, V. C. (1966). Personality characteristics and social and achievement behaviors associated with children's social desirability response tendencies. *Journal of Personality and Social Psychology,* **4,** 477–486.

Crandall, V. C., & Gozali, J. (1969). The social desirability responses of children of four religious–cultural groups. *Child Development,* **40,** 751–762.

Crandall, V. C., Crandall, V. J., & Katkovsky, W. (1965). A children's social desirability questionnaire. *Journal of Consulting Psychology,* **29,** 27–36.

Cronbach, L. J. (1946). Response sets and test validity. *Educational and Psychological Measurement,* **6,** 475–494.

Crowne, D. P. (1979). *The experimental study of personality.* Hillsdale, NJ: Erlbaum.

Crowne, D. P., & Marlowe, D. (1960). A new scale of social desirability independent of psychopathology. *Journal of Consulting Psychology,* **24,** 349–354.

Crowne, D. P., & Marlowe, D. (1964). *The approval motive.* New York: Wiley.

Cunningham, M. R. (1989). Test-taking motivations and outcomes on a standardized measure of on-the-job integrity. *Journal of Business and Psychology,* **3,** 120–125.

Dahlstrom, W. G., Welsh, G. S., & Dahlstrom, L. E. (Eds.) (1972). *An MMPI handbook* (Vol. 1). Minneapolis: Univ. of Minnesota Press.

Dahlstrom, W. G., Welsh, G. S., & Dahlstrom, L. E. (Eds.) (1975). *An MMPI handbook* (Vol. 2). Minneapolis: Univ. of Minnesota Press.

Damarin, F., & Messick, S. (1965). *Response styles as personality variables: A theoretical integration of multivariate research* (Res. Bull. No. 65-10). Princeton, NJ: Educational Testing Service.

Davis, C., & Cowles, M. (1989). Automated psychological testing: Method of administration, need for approval, and measures of anxiety. *Educational and Psychological Measurement,* **49,** 311–320.

Dawes, R. M., & Smith, T. L. (1985). Attitude and opinion measurement. In G. Lindzey & E. Aronson (Eds.), *Handbook of social psychology* (3rd ed., pp. 509–566). New York: Random House.

DeBoeck, P. (1981). Individual differences in the validity of a cognitive processing model for responses to personality inventories. *Applied Psychological Measurement,* **5,** 481–492.

DeLamater, J., & McKinney, K. (1982). Response-effects of question content. In W. Dijkstra & J. van der Zouwen (Eds.), *Response behaviour in the survey-interview.* New York: Academic Press.

DeMaio, T. J. (1984). Social desirability and survey measurement: A review. In C. F. Turner & E. Martin (Eds.), *Surveying subjective phenomena* (Vol. 2, pp. 257–282). New York: Russell Sage Foundation.

Dillehay, R. C., & Jernigan, L. R. (1970). The biased questionnaire as an instrument of opinion change. *Journal of Personality and Social Psychology, 15,* 144–150.

Edwards, A. L. (1953). The relationship between the judged desirability of a trait and the probability that the trait will be endorsed. *Journal of Applied Psychology, 37,* 90–93.

Edwards, A. L. (1957). *The social desirability variable in personality assessment and research.* New York: Dryden Press.

Edwards, A. L. (1963). A factor analysis of experimental social desirability and response set scales. *Journal of Applied Psychology, 47,* 308–316.

Edwards, A. L. (1970). *The measurement of personality traits by scales and inventories.* New York: Holt-Rinehart-Winston.

Edwards, A. L., & Walsh, J. A. (1964). Response sets in standard and experimental personality scales. *American Educational Research Journal, 1,* 52–61.

Edwards, L. K., & Clark, C. L. (1987). Social desirability values and dispersions for the items in two SD scales: The MMPI SD scale and an experimental SD scale. *Psychological Reports, 60,* 1083–1086.

Edwards, L. K., Edwards, A. L., & Clark, C. L. (1988). Social desirability and the frequency of social-reinforcement scale. *Journal of Personality and Social Psychology, 54,* 526–529.

Eiser, J. R., & van der Pligt, J. (1984). Accentuation theory, polarization, and the judgment of attitude statements. In J. R. Eiser (Ed.) *Attitudinal judgment* (pp. 43–63). New York: Springer-Verlag.

Eysenck, H. J., & Eysenck, S. B. G. (1964). *The manual of the Eysenck Personality Inventory.* London: Univ. of London Press.

Eysenck, H. J., & Eysenck, S. B. G. (1975). *The Eysenck Personality Questionnaire manual.* London: Hodder & Stoughton.

Faranda, J. A., Kaminski, J. A., & Giza, B. K. (1979). *An assessment of attitudes toward women with the bogus pipeline.* Paper presented at the meeting of the American Psychological Association, New York.

Fisher, G. (1967). Normative and reliability data for the standard and the cross-validated Marlowe–Crowne Social Desirability Scale. *Psychological Reports, 20,* 174.

Folkman, S., Lazarus, R. S., Dunkel-Schetter, C., DeLongis, A., & Gruen, R. J. (1986). Dynamics of a stressful encounter: Cognitive appraisal, coping, and encounter outcomes. *Journal of Personality and Social Psychology, 50,* 992–1003.

Furnham, A. (1986). Response bias, social desirability, and dissimulation. *Personality and Individual Differences, 7,* 385–400.

Furnham, A., & Henderson, M. (1982). The good, the bad, and the mad: Response bias in self-report measures. *Personality and Individual Differences, 3,* 311–320.

Gocka, E. (1965). American Lake norms for 200 MMPI scales. Unpublished data cited in Dahlstrom, Welsh, & Dahlstrom (1975).

Goldberg, L. R. (1972). Student personality characteristics and optimal college learning conditions: An extensive search for trait-by-treatment interaction effects. *Instructional Science, 1,* 153–210.

Goode, W. J., & Hart, P. K. (1952). *Methods in social science.* New York: McGraw-Hill.

Gough, H. G. (1947). Simulated patterns on the Minnesota Multiphasic Personality Inventory. *Journal of Abnormal and Social Psychology, 42,* 215–225.

Gough, H. G. (1952). On making a good impression. *Journal of Educational Research, 46,* 33–42.

Gough, H. G. (1957). *California Psychological Inventory manual.* Palo Alto, CA: Consulting Psychologists Press.

Gough, H. G. (1987). *California Psychological Inventory administrator's guide.* Palo Alto, CA: Consulting Psychologists Press.

Gough, H. G., & Heilbrun, A. B. (1965). *The adjective checklist manual.* Palo Alto, CA: Consulting Psychologists Press.

Gough, H. G., & Heilbrun, A. B. (1980). *The adjective checklist manual*. Palo Alto, CA: Consulting Psychologists Press.

Gove, W. R., & Geerken, M. (1977). Response bias in surveys of mental health: An empirical investigation. *American Journal of Sociology, 82,* 1289–1317.

Greenberg, B. C., Abdula, A. L., Simmons, W. L., & Horvitz, D. G. (1969). The unrelated question in randomized response model, theoretical framework. *Journal of the American Statistical Association, 64,* 520–539.

Greene, R. L. (1980). *The MMPI: An interpretive manual*. New York: Grune & Stratton.

Hamilton, D. L. (1968). Personality attributes associated with extreme response style. *Psychological Bulletin, 69,* 192–203.

Hartshorne, H., & May, M. A. (1928). *Studies in deceit*. New York: Macmillan.

Hathaway, S. R., & McKinley, J. C. (1951). *The MMPI manual*. New York: Psychological Corporation.

Heilbrun, A. B. (1961). The psychological significance of the MMPI K scale in a normal population. *Journal of Consulting Psychology, 25,* 486–491.

Heilbrun, A. B. (1963). Revision of the MMPI K correction for improved detection of maladjustment in a normal college population. *Journal of Consulting Psychology, 27,* 161–165.

Helmes, E., & Holden, R. R. (1986). Response styles and faking on the Basic Personality Inventory. *Journal of Consulting and Clinical Psychology, 54,* 853–859.

Hogan, R. (1986). *Hogan Personality Inventory*. Minneapolis, MN: National Computer Systems.

Hogan, J., & Hogan, R. (1989). How to measure employee reliability. *Journal of Applied Psychology, 74,* 273–279.

Holden, R. R., & Fekken, G. C. (1989). Three common social desirability scales: Friends, acquaintances, or strangers? *Journal of Research in Personality, 23,* 180–191.

Holden, R. R., Fekken, G. C., & Jackson, D. N. (1985). Structured personality test item characteristics and validity. *Journal of Research in Personality, 19,* 386–394.

Hsu, L. M., Santelli, J., & Hsu, J. R. (1989). Faking detection validity and incremental validity of response latencies to MMPI subtle and obvious items. *Journal of Personality Assessment, 53,* 278–295.

Ihilevich, D., & Gleser, G. C. (1986). *Defense mechanisms: Their classification, correlates, and measurement with the Defense Mechanisms Inventory*. Owosso, MI: DMI Associates.

Jackson, D. N. (1967). *Personality Research Form manual* (3rd ed.). Port Huron, MI: Research Psychologists Press.

Jackson, D. N. (1986). The process of responding in personality assessment. In A. Angleitner & J. S. Wiggins (Eds.) *Personality assessment via questionnaire: Current issues in theory and measurement* (pp. 123–142). New York: Springer-Verlag.

Jackson, D. N., & Helmes, E. (1979). Personality structure and the circumplex. *Journal of Personality and Social Psychology, 37,* 2278–2285.

Jackson, D. N., & Messick, S. (1958). Content and style in personality assessment. *Psychological Bulletin, 55,* 243–252.

Jackson, D. N., & Messick, S. (1962). Response styles and the assessment of psychopathology. In S. Messick & J. Ross (Eds.), *Measurement in personality and cognition* (pp. 129–155). New York: Wiley.

Jacobson, L. I., Berger, S. E., & Millham, J. (1970). Individual differences in cheating during a temptation period when confronting failure. *Journal of Personality and Social Psychology, 15,* 48–56.

Jacobson, L. I., Brown, R. F., & Ariza, M. J. (1983). A revised multidimensional social desirability inventory. *Bulletin of the Psychonomic Society, 21,* 391–392.

Jacobson, L. I., Kellogg, R. W., Cauce, A. M., & Slavin, R. S. (1977). A multidimensional social desirability inventory. *Bulletin of the Psychonomic Society, 9,* 109–110.

Jones, E. E., & Sigall, H. (1971). The bogus pipeline: A new paradigm for measuring affect and attitude. *Psychological Bulletin, 76,* 349–364.

Kane, J. S., & Lawler, E. E. (1978). Methods of peer assessment. *Psychological Bulletin, 85,* 555–586.

Karson, S., & O'Dell, J. W. (1976). *A guide to the clinical use of the 16PF*. Champaign, IL: Institute for Personality and Ability Testing.

Katkin, E. S. (1964). The Marlowe–Crowne Social Desirability Scale: Independent of psychopathology? *Psychological Reports*, **15**, 703–706.

Kiecolt-Glaser, J., & Murray, J. A. (1980). Social desirability bias in self-monitoring data. *Journal of Behavioral Assessment*, **2**, 239–247.

Knowles, E. S. (1988). Item context effects on personality scales: Measuring changes the measure. *Journal of Personality and Social Psychology*, **55**, 312–320.

Knudson, D. D., Pope, H., & Irish, D. P. (1967). Response differences to questions on sexual standards. *Public Opinion Quarterly*, **31**, 290–297.

Kozma, A., & Stones, M. J. (1988). Social desirability in measures of subjective well-being: Age comparisons. *Social Indicators Research*, **20**, 1–14.

Krebs, D., & Schuessler, K. (Eds.) (1987). *Soziale Empfindungen: Ein interkultureller Skalenvergleich bei Deutschen und Amerikanern*. New York/Frankfurt: Campus Verlag.

Lanning, K. (1989). Detection of invalid response patterns on the California Psychological Inventory. *Applied Psychological Measurement*, **13**, 45–56.

Lautenschlager, G. J. (1986). Within-subject measures for the assessment of individual differences in faking. *Educational and Psychological Measurement*, **46**, 309–316.

Lautenschlager, G. J., & Flaherty, V. L. (in press). Computer administration of questions: More desirable or more social desirability? *Journal of Applied Psychology*.

Leak, G. K., & Fish, S. (1989). Religious orientation, impression management, and self-deception. Toward a clarification of the link between religiosity and social desirability. *Journal for Scientific Study of Religion*, **28**, 355–359.

Lenski, G. E., & Leggett, J. C. (1960). Caste, class and deference in the research interview. *American Journal of Sociology*, **65**, 463–467.

Lentz, T. F. (1938). Acquiescence as a factor in the measurement of personality. *Psychological Bulletin*, **35**, 659.

Linden, W., Paulhus, D. L., & Dobson, K. S. (1986). Effects of response styles on the report of psychological and somatic distress. *Journal of Consulting and Clinical Psychology*, **54**, 309–313.

Linehan, M. M., & Nielsen, S. L. (1981). Assessment of suicide ideation and parasuicide: Hopelessness and social desirability. *Journal of Consulting and Clinical Psychology*, **49**, 773–775.

Lockard, J. S., & Paulhus, D. L. (Eds.) (1988). *Self-deception: An adaptive mechanism?* New York: Prentice-Hall.

Martin, C. L., & Nagao, D. H. (1989). Some effects of computerized interviewing on job applicant responses. *Journal of Applied Psychology*, **74**, 72–80.

McCrae, R. R. (1982). Consensual validation of personality traits: Evidence from self-reports and ratings. *Journal of Personality and Social Psychology*, **43**, 293–303.

McCrae, R. R. (1986). Well-being scales do not measure social desirability. *Journal of Gerontology*, **41**, 390–392.

McCrae, R. R., & Costa, P. T. (1983). Social desirability scales: More substance than style. *Journal of Consulting and Clinical Psychology*, **51**, 882–888.

McCrae, R. R., Costa, P. T., Dahlstrom, W. G., Barefoot, J. C., Siegler, I. C., & Williams, R. B. (1989). A caution on the use of the MMPI K-correction in research on psychosomatic medicine. *Psychosomatic Medicine*, **51**, 58–65.

McKinley, J. C., Hathaway, S. R., & Meehl, P. E. (1948). The Minnesota Multiphasic Personality Inventory. IV. The K scale. *Journal of Consulting Psychology*, **12**, 20–31.

Meehl, P. E., & Hathaway, S. R. (1946). The K factor as a suppressor variable in the Minnesota Multiphasic Personality Inventory. *Journal of Applied Psychology*, **30**, 525–564.

Mellor, S., Conroy, L., & Masteller, B. K. (1986). Comparative trait analysis of long-term recovering alcoholics. *Psychological Reports*, **58**, 411–418.

Messick, S. (1967). The psychology of acquiescence: An interpretation of research evidence. In I. A. Berg (Ed.), *Response set in personality assessment* (pp. 115–145). Chicago: Aldine.

Millham, J. (1974). Two components of need for approval score and their relationship to cheating following success and failure. *Journal of Research in Personality*, **8**, 378–392.

Millham, J., & Jacobson, L. I. (1978). The need for approval. In H. London & J. E. Exner (Eds.), *Dimensions of personality* (pp. 365–390). New York: Wiley.

Millham, J., & Kellogg, R. W. (1980). Need for social approval: Impression management or self-deception? *Journal of Research in Personality, 14,* 445–457.

Montag, I., & Comrey, A. L. (1982). Personality construct similarity in Israel and the United States. *Applied Psychological Measurement, 6,* 61–67.

Morf, M. E., & Jackson, D. N. (1972). An analysis of two response styles: True responding and item endorsement. *Educational and Psychological Measurement, 32,* 329–353.

Nederhof, A. J. (1985). Methods of coping with social desirability bias: A review. *European Journal of Social Psychology, 15,* 263–280.

Nevid, J. S. (1983). Hopelessness, social desirability and construct validity. *Journal of Consulting and Clinical Psychology, 51,* 139–140.

Norman, W. T. (1963). Personality measurement, faking, and detection: An assessment method for use in personnel selection. *Journal of Applied Psychology, 47,* 225–241.

Norman, W. T. (1967). On estimating psychological relationships: Social desirability and self-report. *Psychological Bulletin, 67,* 273–293.

Norman, W. T. (1969). "To see oursels as ithers see us!": Relations among self-perceptions, peer-perceptions, and expected peer-perceptions of personality attributes. *Multivariate Behavioral Research, 4,* 417–443.

Norman, W. T. (1990). On separating substantive, stylistic, and evaluative components in personality measurements: A cross-national comparison. *Journal of Personality and Social Psychology.*

Novakowska, M. (1970). A model of answering to a questionnaire item. *Acta Psychologica, 34,* 420–439.

Paulhus, D. L. (1981). Control of social desirability in personality inventories: Principal-factor deletion. *Journal of Research in Personality, 15,* 383–388.

Paulhus, D. L. (1982). Individual differences, self-presentation, and cognitive dissonance: Their concurrent operation in forced compliance. *Journal of Personality and Social Psychology, 43,* 838–852.

Paulhus, D. L. (1984). Two-component models of socially desirable responding. *Journal of Personality and Social Psychology, 46,* 598–609.

Paulhus, D. L. (1986). Self-deception and impression management in test responses. In A. Angleitner & J. S. Wiggins (Eds.), *Personality assessment via questionnaire* (pp. 143–165). New York: Springer-Verlag.

Paulhus, D. L. (1987). *Emotional arousal and evaluative extremity: A dynamic complexity analysis.* Manuscript submitted for publication.

Paulhus, D. L. (1988). *Assessing self-deception and impression management in self-reports: The Balanced Inventory of Desirable Responding.* Unpublished manual, University of British Columbia, Vancouver, Canada.

Paulhus, D. L., Fridhandler, B., & Hayes, S. (in press). Psychological defense. In S. R. Briggs, R. Hogan, & W. Jones (Eds.), *Handbook of personality psychology.* San Diego, CA: Academic Press.

Paulhus, D. L., & Levitt, K. (1987). Desirable responding triggered by affect: Automatic egotism? *Journal of Personality and Social Psychology, 52,* 245–259.

Paulhus, D. L., & Reid, D. B. (in press). Attribution and denial in socially desirable responding. *Journal of Personality and Social Psychology.*

Paulhus, D. L., Graf, P., & Van Selst, M. (1989). Attentional load increases the positivity of self-presentation. *Social Cognition, 7,* 389–400.

Peabody, D. (1962). Two components in bipolar scales: Direction and extremeness. *Psychological Review, 69,* 65–73.

Peabody, D. (1966). Authoritarianism scales and response bias. *Psychological Bulletin, 65,* 11–23.

Phillips, D. L., & Clancy, K. J. (1972). Some effects of social desirability in survey studies. *American Journal of Sociology, 77,* 921–940.

Quigley-Fernandez, B., & Tedeschi, J. T. (1978). The bogus pipeline as lie-detector: Two validity studies. *Journal of Personality and Social Psychology, 36,* 247–256.

Quinn, B. A. (1989). *Religiousness and psychological well-being: An empirical investigation.* Unpublished dissertation, Wayne State Univ., Detroit.

Ray, J. J. (1983). Reviving the problem of acquiescent response bias. *Journal of Social Psychology,* **121,** 81–96.

Reis, H. A. (1966). The MMPI K scale as a predictor of prognosis. *Journal of Clinical Psychology,* **22,** 212–213.

Riggio, R. E., Salinas, C., & Tucker, J. (1988). Personality and deception ability. *Personality and Individual Differences,* **9,** 189–191.

Rogers, T. B. (1971). The process of responding to personality items: Some issues, a theory and some research. *Multivariate Behavioral Research Monographs,* 6 Whole No. 2.

Rogers, T. B. (1974). An analysis of two central stages underlying responding to personality items: The self-referent decision and response selection. *Journal of Research in Personality,* **8,** 128–138.

Romer, D. (1983). Effects of own attitude on polarization of judgment. *Journal of Personality and Social Psychology,* **44,** 273–284.

Rorer, L. G. (1965). The great response style myth. *Psychological Bulletin,* **63,** 129–156.

Rorer, L. G., & Goldberg, L. R. (1965). Acquiescence and the vanishing variance component. *Journal of Applied Psychology,* **49,** 422–430.

Roth, D. L., Harris, R. N., & Snyder, C. R. (1988). An individual differences measure of attributive and repudiative tactics of favorable self-presentation. *Journal of Social and Clinical Psychology,* **6,** 159–170.

Roth, D. L., Snyder, C. R., & Pace, L. M. (1986). Dimensions of favorable self-presentation. *Journal of Personality and Social Psychology,* **51,** 867–874.

Ruch, F. L. (1942). A technique for detecting attempts to fake performance on the self-inventory type of personality test. In J. F. Dashiell (Ed.), *Studies in personality.* New York: McGraw-Hill.

Ruch, F. L., & Ruch, W. W. (1967). The K factor as a (validity) suppressor variable in predicting success in selling. *Journal of Applied Psychology,* **51,** 201–204.

Sabourin, S., Bourgeois, L., Gendreau, P., & Morval, M. (1989). Self-deception, impression management, and consumer satisfaction with mental health treatment. *Psychological Assessment: A Journal of Consulting and Clinical Psychology,* **1,** 126–129.

Sackeim, H. A., & Gur, R. C. (1978). Self-deception, self-confrontation and consciousness. In G. E. Schwartz & D. Shapiro (Eds.), *Consciousness and self-regulation: Advances in research* (Vol. 2, pp. 139–197). New York: Plenum.

Sackeim, H. A., & Gur, R. C. (1979). Self-deception, other-deception, and self-reported psychopathology. *Journal of Consulting and Clinical Psychology,* **47,** 213–215.

Sackett, P. R., & Harris, M. M. (1984). Honesty testing for personnel selection: A review and critique. *Personnel Psychology,* **37,** 221–245.

Sackett, P. R., Burris, L. R., & Callahan, C. (1989). *Integrity testing for personnel selection: An update.* Unpublished manuscript, University of Minnesota, Minneapolis.

Scheier, M. F., & Carver, C. S. (1985). Optimism, coping, and health: Assessment and implications of generalized outcome expectancies. *Health Psychology,* **4,** 219–247.

Schneider, D. J. (1973). Implicit personality theory: A review. *Psychological Bulletin,* **79,** 294–309.

Schriesheim, C. A. (1979). Social desirability and leader effectiveness. *Journal of Social Psychology,* **108,** 89–94.

Schuessler, K., Hittle, D., & Cardascia, J. (1978). Measuring responding desirably with attitude–opinion items. *Social Psychology,* **41,** 224–235.

Schuman, H., & Presser, S. (1981). *Questions and answers in attitude surveys.* New York: Academic Press.

Schwarz, N., Strack, F., Muller, G., & Chassein, B. (1988). The range of response alternatives may determine the meaning of the question: Further evidence on informative functions of response alternatives. *Social Cognition,* **6,** 107–117.

Shaffer, G. S., Saunders, V., & Owens, W. A. (1986). Additional evidence for the accuracy of biographical data: Long-term retest and observer ratings. *Personnel Psychology,* **39,** 791–809.

Shulman, A. (1973). A comparison of two scales on extremity response bias. *Public Opinion Quarterly, 37,* 407–412.

Sigall, H., & Page, R. (1971). Current stereotypes: A little fading, a little faking. *Journal of Personality and Social Psychology, 18,* 247–255.

Sigall, H., & Page, R. (1972). Reducing attenuation in the expression of interpersonal affect via the bogus pipeline. *Sociometry, 35,* 629–642.

Staub, E., & Sherk, L. (1970). Need for approval, children's sharing behavior and reciprocity in sharing. *Child Development, 41,* 243–252.

Strickland, B. R. (1977). Approval motivation. In T. Blass (Ed.), *Personality variables in social behavior* (pp. 315–356). Hillsdale, NJ: Erlbaum.

Strosahl, K. D., Linehan, M. M., & Chiles, J. A. (1984). Will the real social desirability scale please stand up?: Hopelessness, depression, social desirability, and the prediction of suicidal behavior. *Journal of Consulting and Clinical Psychology, 52,* 449–457.

Sudman, S., & Bradburn, N. M. (1974). *Response effects in surveys.* Chicago: Aldine.

Sutherland, B. V., & Spilka, B. (1964). Social desirability, item-response time, and item significance. *Journal of Consulting Psychology, 28,* 447–451.

Sweetland, A., & Quay, H. A. (1953). A note on the K scale of the MMPI. *Journal of Consulting Psychology, 17,* 314–316.

Swenson, W. M., Pearson, J. S., & Osbourne, D. (1973). *An MMPI sourcebook: Basic item, scale, and pattern data on 50,000 medical patients.* Minneapolis: Univ. of Minnesota Press.

Tanaka-Matsumi, J., & Kameoka, V. A. (1986). Reliabilities and concurrent validities of popular self-report measures of depression, anxiety, and social desirability. *Journal of Consulting and Clinical Psychology, 54,* 328–333.

Taylor, J. A. (1953). A personality scale of manifest anxiety. *Journal of Abnormal and Social Psychology, 48,* 285–290.

Taylor, S. E., & Brown, J. D. (1988). Illusion and well-being: A social–psychological perspective on mental health. *Psychological Bulletin, 103,* 193–210.

Tellegen, A. (1982). *Brief manual for the Differential Personality Inventory.* Unpublished manuscript, University of Minnesota, Minneapolis.

Tourangeau, R., & Rasinski, K. A. (1988). Cognitive processes underlying context effects in attitude measurement. *Psychological Bulletin, 103,* 299–314.

Trott, D. M., & Jackson, D. N. (1967). An experimental analysis of acquiescence. *Journal of Experimental Research in Personality, 2,* 278–288.

Van der Kloot, W. A., Kroonenberg, P. M., & Bakker, D. (1985). Implicit theories of personality: Further evidence of extreme response style. *Multivariate Behavioral Research, 20,* 369–387.

Vernon, P. E. (1934). The attitude of the subject in personality testing. *Journal of Applied Psychology, 18,* 165–177.

Warner, S. L. (1965). Randomized response: A survey technique for eliminating evasive answer bias. *Journal of the American Statistical Association, 60,* 63–69.

Webster, H. (1958). Correcting personality scales for response sets or suppression effects. *Psychological Bulletin, 55,* 62–64.

Weinberger, D. A. (in press). The construct validity of the repressive coping style. In J. L. Singer (Ed.), *Repression and dissociation: Defense mechanisms and personality styles.* Chicago: Univ. of Chicago Press.

Weinberger, D. A., Schwartz, G. E., & Davidson, R. J. (1979). Low-anxious, high-anxious, and repressive coping styles: Psychometric patterns and behavioral and physiological responses to stress. *Journal of Abnormal Psychology, 88,* 369–380.

Weiss, C. H. (1968). Validity of welfare mothers' interview responses. *Public Opinion Quarterly, 32,* 622–633.

Wiggins, J. S. (1964). Convergences among stylistic response measures from objective personality tests. *Educational and Psychological Measurement, 24,* 551–562.

Wiggins, J. S. (1968). Personality structure. *Annual Review of Psychology, 19,* 293–350.

Wiggins, J. S. (1973). *Personality and prediction: Principles of personality assessment.* Reading MA: Addison-Wesley.

Wiggins, J. S. (1979). A psychological taxonomy of trait-descriptive terms: The interpersonal domain. *Journal of Personality and Social Psychology, 37,* 395–412.

Winder, P., O'Dell, J. W., & Karson, S. (1975). New motivational distortion scales for the 16 PF. *Journal of Personality Assessment, 39,* 532–537.

Winkler, J. D., Kanouse, D. E., & Ware, J. E., Jr. (1982). Controlling for acquiescence response set in scale development. *Journal of Applied Psychology, 67,* 555–561.

Winters, K. C., & Neale, J. M. (1985). Mania and low self-esteem. *Journal of Abnormal Psychology, 94,* 282–290.

Wiseman, F. (1972). Methodological bias in public opinion surveys. *Public Opinion Quarterly, 36,* 105–108.

Wooten, A. J. (1984). Effectiveness of the K correction in the detection of psychopathology and its impact on profile height and configuration among young adult men. *Journal of Consulting and Clinical Psychology, 52,* 468–473.

Wright, J. D. (1975). Does acquiescence bias the "index of political efficacy"? *Public Opinion Quarterly, 39,* 219–226.

Yonge, G. D. (1966). Certain consequences of applying the K factor to MMPI scores. *Educational and Psychological Measurement, 26,* 887–893.

Zerbe, W. J., & Paulhus, D. L. (1987). Socially desirable responding in organizations: A reconception. *Academy of Management Review, 12,* 250–264.

CHAPTER 3

Measures of Subjective Well-Being

Frank M. Andrews and John P. Robinson

Introduction

The primary focus of this chapter is on people's subjective well-being. The main concern is with measuring "global" well-being, that is, happiness or satisfaction with life-as-a-whole or life in general. Subjective well-being may involve a focus on global well-being, but it may also refer to specific life concerns or domains, such as one's job, housing, family, or income. Most of what is said here about measuring global well-being is also applicable to measuring well-being with regard to specific life concerns. Most research has been done in the context of surveys or group-administered questions.

Subjective well-being is important as a psychological summing up of the quality of an individual's life in a society. Several social psychological concepts tap aspects of the quality of life indirectly, such as self-esteem, depression, locus of control, or alienation, but only life satisfaction and happiness have a "bottom-line" finality in terms of consequences for the individual. It is clear, however, that perceived happiness and satisfaction are closely related to these other concepts (Robinson, 1969).

Research on subjective well-being is extensive, broad-ranging, and conceptually diffuse. It has sailed under at least three flags: mental health, quality of life, and social gerontology. Investigators with allegiance to each of these fields have coined their own terms to refer to the topic of this chapter. These terms, which overlap to some extent but are not all synonymous, include satisfaction, happiness, morale, positive affect, negative affect, affect balance, cognitive evaluations, elation, subjective well-being, sense of well-being, psychological well-being, perceived well-being, subjective welfare, (subjective/sense of/psychological/perceived) ill-being, anxiety, depression, distress, tension, and perceived life quality. Undoubtedly there are other terms as well. Later in the chapter some of the conceptual distinctions between these terms are considered.

The research literature on subjective well-being is growing rapidly. The chapter titled "Life Satisfaction and Happiness" in the first edition of this volume (Robinson, 1969) discussed results from about a half-dozen surveys and made reference to about a dozen others. However, in the two decades since that chapter was written, several thousand new studies relevant to subjective well-being have been published. Diener (1984) reports "over 600" appeared between 1968 and about 1983, and Michalos (1986a), who used a computer search for titles including the words "satisfaction" or "happiness," found 2545 just during the period 1979–1982! Kammann, Farry, and Herbison (1984), after a brief review of the field, concluded "well-being is a robust, primary dimension of human experience, and . . . happiness research is alive and well. . ." (p. 91). Although not itself a comprehensive review of the large literature on life quality, this chapter does refer to some useful general reviews of this literature.

Organization of the Chapter

In addition to this Introduction, this chapter consists of three major sections plus a set of scale reviews. The first section briefly reviews some of the recent research on subjective well-being. Key concepts and the distinctions between them are described and some current ideas about how people come to feel as they do about their well-being are noted. The second section briefly describes some of the more prominent scales used to measure subjective well-being (more details appear in the individual scale reviews). The third section presents recommendations for choosing among scales of subjective well-being and some ideas about topics for future research. The individual scale reviews provide certain standard specific information about most of the multi-item scales discussed in the chapter, including the actual items that compose the scale and some information about the scale's reliability and validity.

Research on Subjective Well-Being

Theoretical Perspectives

Cognitive and Affective Components

Subjective well-being is an attitude, and it is widely accepted that attitudes include at least two basic components: cognition and affect (e.g., Ostrom, 1969). The cognitive component refers to the rational or intellectual aspects; the affective component involves emotional aspects. By distinguishing between the cognitive and affective components of subjective well-being, one has a perspective that is useful for understanding the numerous concepts and measures that fall within this arena.

Before elaborating on this, however, one further distinction needs to be noted: It has proven useful to subdivide the affective component into two portions—positive affect and negative affect. Bradburn's (1969) scales of positive and negative affect, which are described in the section Measuring Subjective Well-Being, have sometimes been used as relatively pure measures of these concepts.

Some measures of happiness have been shown to reflect relatively large amounts of affect, particularly positive affect, but relatively little cognition. In contrast, measures of satisfaction reflect relatively more cognition. Satisfaction measures, however, seem not to be pure indicators of the cognitive component but include some positive and negative affect as well. Questions that ask about worrying, anxiety, or depression reflect mainly negative affect. Elation, presumably, is mainly positive affect. The Delighted–Terrible Response Scale (Andrews & Withey, 1976) tends to produce a "balanced" measure reflecting approximately equal amounts of affect and cognition and, within affect, approximately equal amounts of positive and negative affect (Andrews & McKennell, 1980). McKennell, Atkinson, and Andrews (1980) have shown that these results are replicable crossnationally (America, England, and Canada), and Horley and Little (1985) have independently replicated the results on American respondents. Hox (1986) has identified separate factors of cognition and affect in data from Dutch respondents. After an extensive review of the literature on subjective well-being, Veenhoven (1984a) also concluded that the affect–cognition distinction is a useful one.

Distinguishing between cognitive and affective components of measures of subjective well-being helps to make sense of what otherwise would be puzzling data. For example, surveys of global subjective well-being often find that older adults show lower levels of happiness than do younger adults, but higher levels of satisfaction (e.g., Campbell, Converse, & Rodgers, 1976). Given the cognitive–affective conceptual framework, this suggests that cognitive evaluations of life-as-a-whole may rise with age, while positive affect may decline. Perhaps individuals become somewhat jaded emotionally as they age but increase their level of achievement and/or adjust their aspirations.

This conceptual framework also helps to make sense of the finding that life quality evaluations obtained using the Delighted–Terrible Scale show little change across the age range. As noted above, the Delighted–Terrible Scale tends to produce balanced measures, and presumably the gains across the age ranges in the cognitive component are offset by the declines in the positive affect component.

The Relationship Between Positive and Negative Affect   A specialized literature in the subjective well-being arena has addressed the question of the statistical relationship between positive and negative affect. One might expect the two would be highly, perhaps even perfectly, negatively correlated. Some studies have shown, however, that certain measures of these two concepts are virtually independent of each other. Bradburn (1969) was surprised when this finding emerged in his data, and it has been replicated on independent samples several times since (e.g., Andrews & Withey, 1976; Cherlin & Reeder, 1975; Hox, 1986).

Other work has debated the reasons for this result and suggested it may be due to the particular measures employed as indicators of the concepts and/or the time frame over which positive and negative affect are assessed (Diener & Emmons, 1985; Diener & Larsen, 1984; Kammann *et al.,* 1984; Stones & Kozma, 1985; Warr, Barter, & Brownbridge, 1983).

Although Headey and his colleagues have focused their work more broadly than on just the affective components of subjective well-being, they also have identified conceptually distinct but statistically related factors of well-being and ill-being (Headey, Holström, & Wearing 1984a, 1985).

There is some evidence in the literature for positive and negative affect as being the results of activation of different areas of the brain (e.g., Stein, 1964).

The Psychodynamics of Subjective Well-Being Ratings

A question that has received attention is, How do people come to have the feelings about subjective well-being that they do? One obvious answer is that it depends on people's external circumstances, that is, what happens to them. While true, this still leaves the psychodynamic question: Given whatever goes on "outside," what can be said about internal mental processes that lead to subjective well-being attitudes?

Two lines of investigation have been pursued, and neither has a widely accepted name. We designate them: (1) the gap or ratio approach, and (2) the social psychological influences approach.

The Gap/Ratio Approach to Understanding Subjective Well-Being   It is widely believed that attitudes about subjective well-being reflect some "gap" or perhaps a "ratio" involving what people aspire to and what they perceive themselves as having (Andrews,

1981; Mason & Faulkenberry, 1978; Michalos, 1980, 1983; Parducci, 1968). Whether the formulation should involve a gap or ratio depends partly on how aspirations and achievements are measured and will not be addressed here.

In the gap formulation, the gap is the difference between the aspired level and the achieved level. It is presumed that aspirations will usually be higher than perceived achievements, and that the smaller the difference, the higher will be subjective well-being. Negative differences (i.e., when perceived achievements exceed aspirations) are presumed to produce high levels of subjective well-being, but perhaps not higher than zero differences.

In the ratio formulation, the ratio is calculated as perceived achievements divided by aspirations, and the larger the ratio, the higher subjective well-being is presumed to be. The gap/ratio approach has much appeal because it helps to explain otherwise puzzling results in both cross-sectional and longitudinal data.

Cross-sectionally, it is sometimes observed that people who seem objectively better off than the average individual show below average levels of subjective well-being. For example, middle-aged adults with relatively large, well-equipped homes may be less satisfied with their housing than older adults living in more modest homes. One explanation is that although the well-housed individuals may be "better off," their aspirations may be much higher than those of people living in the modest homes. The greater gap (or smaller ratio) leads to lower subjective well-being.

The gap/ratio conceptualization also explains some longitudinal results. Why is it that, even if given a chance, many people would not want to return to the "good old days"? Presumably the "good old days" refer to a time when the gap between aspiration and achievement was smaller (or is remembered as being smaller) than the present gap is perceived to be, but the absolute levels of achievement may have been substantially lower. (A parallel argument can be made for ratios.) Those who would not go back in time presumably realize that to do so would require giving up real gains in actual achievements.

Given the presumed significance of gaps or ratios, a "complete" research design for measuring subjective well-being and monitoring it over time would require separate measures of three constructs: aspirations, perceived achievements, and subjective well-being. Little has been done in this regard. If one has data only on subjective well-being one may be able to observe a difference between groups (or a change over time), but one is left with a question about why the difference or change occurred: Are the actual conditions different, or are the aspirations different, or both? Given information on any two of the three concepts (subjective well-being, achievement, aspiration) one could make useful statements about the causes of subjective well-being differences between groups or times *if* one accepts the gap/ratio theory. For example, subjective well-being might have been higher at time A than B because perceived achievement levels rose slowly but aspirations rose faster. Only if one has data on all three constructs, however, can one test the appropriateness of the theory itself.

Multiple Discrepancies Theory   Some of the most elegant work testing the theory and identifying the sources of people's aspirations is currently being done within the framework of Multiple Discrepancies Theory (Michalos, 1985). This theory assumes that an individual's subjective well-being with regard to a particular aspect of life (e.g., life-as-a-whole, housing) is determined by that individual mentally combining information about several distinct gaps. These are the gaps between what one perceives oneself to have and a set of aspirations (i.e., what one wants) that are determined by (1) what relevant others have, (2) the best one has had in the past, (3) what one expected to have by now, (4) what one expects to have in the future, (5) what one deserves, and (6) what one believes one needs. In one study Michalos (1985) found that Multiple Discrepancies Theory could account for about 50% of the variance in ratings of global happiness and satisfaction. Michalos's work follows some early work on the same topic by Andrews and Withey (1976) and by Campbell *et al.* (1976) and is presently being extended in a number of studies by Michalos himself (1986b), Emmons and Diener (1985a), Wright (1985), and in a large multinational project that Michalos has organized and that involves data collected from students in 66 universities in 46 countries (data for 38 countries had been collected and analyzed as of June 1987) (Michalos, 1987).

The Social Psychological Influences Approach   An approach that is complementary to the gap/ratio approach for explaining people's levels of subjective well-being is what might be called the "social psychological influences" approach. The goal here has been to explore a number of social and psychological factors that might be expected to influence people's feelings of subjective well-being to see to what extent the expected linkages emerge.

Concepts that have received considerable research attention in the field of social psychology and that one might presume to be relevant to feelings of subjective well-being include the following: stress, social support, internal control (e.g., belief that one can control one's own fate), external control (which some theorists have subdivided into perceived control by other people and perceived control by chance), and role performance (i.e., how well a person performs home, work, and social roles).

In a longitudinal causal modeling analysis, Abbey and Andrews (1985) showed that measures of these social psychological concepts do link in expected ways to subjective well-being as assessed by measures of both depression and quality of life. In one analysis, they showed that 34% of the variance in people's feelings of depression could be explained by the levels of the social psychological factors measured 6 weeks earlier, and that depression plus the social psychological factors could explain 54% of the variance in feelings of life quality assessed 6–12 weeks later.

Descriptive Studies of Subjective Well-Being

National Studies: The United States
The literature on subjective well-being includes more than a dozen major studies that provide as at least part of their output important descriptive results on the subjective well-being of certain national populations. Some of these studies also contain extensive data on subgroups within the national population. Most of these studies include evaluations both of life-as-a-whole and of a wide range of more specific life concerns such as housing, family, job, income, oneself, local government, and many others.

These studies are the primary source of normative data for subjective well-being measures: From them one can determine what was (at the time the study was done) the typical level of subjective well-being expressed by many different demographically defined groups within a national population. Most studies also report distributions of the subjective well-being ratings.

Some of these studies, presented in chronological order, are briefly described in the following paragraphs.

The first major study of subjective well-being was conducted during the late 1950s in the United States by Gurin, Veroff, and Feld (1960). The study sailed under the banner of "mental health," rather than the "life quality" flag commonly used by subjective well-being studies in the 1970s and 1980s. Almost two decades later, in the mid-1970s, this study was replicated on another sample of American adults (Veroff, Douvan, & Kulka, 1981).

In the early- and mid-1960s Bradburn and Caplovitz collected data on "psychological well-being" from five samples in the United States (Bradburn, 1969). While four of these samples were small (ranging from 252 to 542), the fifth only of medium size ($n = 1277$), and none was intended to be a national sample, together they provide data from a wide range of heterogeneous American respondents. The Positive Affect, Negative Affect, and Affect Balance scales emerged from this work and have been widely used since.

During the early- and mid-1970s, a series of national studies conducted in the United States by Andrews and Withey (1974, 1976) and by Campbell *et al.* (1976; also Campbell, 1981) explored Americans' feelings about "life quality" and developed a number of response scales that have been used by other investigators. Andrews and Withey presented data on almost 200 different measures of life quality (68 measures of "global" well-being and 123 measures at the level of specific life concerns) that were assessed on between one and four nationally representative samples in 1972–1973 and/or on more restricted groups of respondents. Campbell *et al.* completed a national survey in 1971 and then replicated it in 1978. Their 1978 survey included a panel component in which many of the respondents interviewed in 1971 were reinterviewed 7 years later.

Although not a study focusing exclusively on subjective well-being, an important series of subjective well-being data are provided by the annual (sometimes biannual) General Social Survey (GSS) for most of the 1970s and continuing through the 1980s. The GSS has included a battery of items assessing global happiness and satisfaction with certain specific life concerns. In 1984 these concerns were: city/place, nonworking activities, family life, friendships, and health and physical condition. J. A. Davis (1984) presented a useful summary, noting that marital status and recent financial changes are among the most useful predictors of happiness. The GSS has been the major source for national-level data on subjective well-being in the United States during the 1980s.

National Studies: Other Countries

Cantril (1967) conducted the first large multinational study of subjective well-being. He developed the Self-Anchoring Ladder Scale (described more fully below) to assess the well-being of people in 13 countries: Brazil, Cuba, Dominican Republic, Egypt, India, Israel, Nigeria, Panama, Philippines, Poland, United States, West Germany, and Yugoslavia.[1] People were asked to indicate the level of their subjective well-being 5 years prior to the study, at the time of the study, and their expected level 5 years after the study. Cantril's surveys were conducted in the late 1950s and early 1960s.

In 1972 the Research Group for Comparative Sociology, based at the University of Helsinki (Finland), undertook the Scandinavian Welfare Study. This involved surveys of nationally representative samples in each of the four Scandinavian countries: Denmark, Finland, Norway, and Sweden. The study covered a broad range of topics, including global happiness and satisfaction with "position" (i.e., job) and income (Allart & Uusitalo, 1977).

A tantalizing set of results on subjective well-being is provided in a short journal article by Gallup (1976). He reports on a series of surveys carried out in the mid-1970s on samples in 60 countries said to represent "nearly two-thirds of the world's population" (p. 460) by the Gallup International Research Institutes. The surveys included items on personal happiness (at the present time, 5 years ago, and 5 years hence) and also assessed satisfaction with life concerns that included job, leisure and recreation, education, health,

---

[1]A little information from Japan is also presented.

family life, standard of living, and personal safety. Unfortunately, analyses going beyond simple means and proportions by country or geographical region were never completed and published because the data tapes were lost (G. H. Gallup, personal communication).

Another large multinational set of data on subjective well-being has been developed through the "Eurobarometer" surveys conducted annually beginning in 1973 in most of the countries of the European Economic Community. Elegant analyses of these data, showing the effects of nation, time period, generation (i.e., birth cohort), and various social psychological factors have been published by Inglehart and Rabier (1986). Using these data, Andrews and Inglehart (1979) showed substantial similarities in the structure of perceptions of well-being among the European countries and between them and the United States.

One of the most ambitious national-level studies involving subjective well-being was that begun in the latter 1970s by a research team at York University in Canada. The study was titled "Social Change in Canada." The design involved three surveys of nationally representative samples of Canadian adults with data collections in 1977, 1979, and 1981, as well as a three-wave panel study of representative samples of residents of Canada's two largest cities, Toronto and Montreal, with data collections timed to match the national surveys, and a nationally representative survey of decisionmakers ("elites") in major Canadian institutional sectors (government, politics, academia, business, labor, religion, etc.). The planned data collections were completed, and the data have been cleaned and placed into an archive, but as yet no book-length report on subjective well-being has been published. However, some results on subjective well-being are presented in Atkinson (1981) and Blishen and Atkinson (1980).

Another large national project involving subjective well-being is that conducted by Zapf, Glatzer, and their colleagues in West Germany. They carried out three nationally representative "welfare" surveys in 1978, 1980, and 1984. An English-language summary appears in Zapf and Glatzer (1987).

There have been relatively few national level studies of subjective well-being in Third World countries. However, the work of Shinn and his colleagues on samples of respondents in South Korea provides a fascinating exception. A 1980 survey included some of the same questions on subjective well-being and used the same seven-point satisfaction rating scale as has been used in several surveys on nationally representative samples in the United States. In general, levels of satisfaction and happiness were lower in Korea than in the United States, and the positive relationships between well-being and education or income were stronger (Lee, Kim, & Shinn, 1982; Shinn, 1986; Shinn, Ahn, Kim, & Lee, 1983).

Subnational Studies

The number and variety of subnational studies on subjective well-being is immense. Some are oriented toward particular geographic units: states or provinces (e.g., Oklahoma, Oregon, Alberta); regions of states (e.g., northern Michigan, southeastern Oklahoma, northern Wisconsin); counties (e.g., Oakland County, Michigan); and cities (e.g., Fairbanks, Alaska; Flint, Michigan; and many others). Others focus on particular social groups (old people, teenagers, blacks, Chicanos). And still others are oriented toward particular organizations (e.g., West Point Academy).

One of the most significant subnational studies from the standpoint of contribution to general knowledge about subjective well-being is a major undertaking in Australia by Headey, Wearing, and their colleagues (Headey, 1981; Headey, Glowacki, Holström, & Wearing, 1985; Headey, Holström, & Wearing, 1985). Beginning in 1981 they undertook to interview the same panel of respondents every 2 years until 1991. The panel is intended to be reasonably representative of the population in the state of Victoria.

Laboratory and Observational Studies

In general, researchers in the area have confined themselves to self-report measures, arguing that only the respondents themselves are fit to judge how happy or satisfied they are. At the same time, one would expect these self-assessments to relate to environmental circumstances (e.g., stress, poverty), and to a limited extent that has been found to be the case, at least for self-reported circumstances. Other than the studies by Neugarten, however, few studies have attempted to link happiness measures to objectively verified outside behavior. One exception is a study Caplan *et al.* (1985) of life quality evaluations as linked to use of a tranquilizer 6 weeks earlier. There was no marked relationship, either positive or negative, between use of Diazepam (the active ingredient in Valium) and subjective well-being 6 weeks later. Because it is hard to imagine laboratory conditions that would be both ethical and powerful enough to produce experimentally induced levels of happiness, this attitude area has attracted almost no interest among experimental social psychologists.

Relationships of Subjective Well-Being to Other Variables

The three subsections that follow sketch in brief fashion the general nature of results that have emerged when global measures of subjective well-being have been related to (1) demographic and social classification variables, (2) personality variables, and (3) evaluations of specific life concerns. More detailed summaries of these and other relationships can be found in works cited below.

Links to Demographic and Social Classification Variables

One of the surprises of research on subjective well-being has been the general weakness of relationships between global happiness, satisfaction, etc. and standard demographic variables such as age, sex, race, education, income, and marital status. Even taken together, such demographic variables rarely explain more than about 10% of the variance in people's general happiness or satisfaction with life-as-a-whole (e.g., Andrews & Withey, 1976; E. E. Davis, Fine-Davis, & Meehan, 1982; Michalos, 1985; Veenhoven, 1984a). This is not to say, however, that there are no relationships between global subjective well-being and demographic variables.

J. A. Davis (1984) summarized some of the links to demographic variables in an article titled "New Money, An Old Man/Lady, and 'Two's Company' . . .": He found subjective well-being higher among people who experienced increases in income, who were married, and who had social support—results that are replicated in many other studies. It is also common to find that subjective well-being tends to be a little higher in the United States for people with more wealth and/or more education. [If one examines mean levels of subjective well-being by country, one finds results parallel to those for individuals: Richer countries tend to show higher subjective well-being, though the relationship is only moderate and there are notable exceptions (Cantril, 1967; Gallup, 1976).]

Males rarely are much different from females. Trends across the age groups are weak and depend on the particular measure used to assess subjective well-being (Herzog & Rodgers, 1981, 1986).

Links to Personality Variables

An intriguing portion of the literature on subjective well-being, one with important implications for how one conceptualizes and measures the concept, examines relationships between subjective well-being and various personality variables. Several investigators have found that positive affect tends to relate positively to measures of extraversion, interest in other people, active social involvement, optimism, and self-esteem (i.e., liking of oneself) but is much less related to neuroticism; in contrast, negative affect tends to relate to neuroticism and to low levels on a "personal competence" trait, but not to extraversion (Costa & McCrae, 1980; Emmons & Diener, 1985b; Headey *et al.*, 1984a; Heady, Holström, & Wearing, 1985; Kammann *et al.*, 1984).

A particularly interesting finding by Costa and McCrae (1980) is that the personality traits of extraversion and neuroticism were significantly related to people's reported levels of happiness 10 years later. While no one is claiming that subjective well-being is a personality trait, this finding suggests that certain trait variables are either components of subjective well-being or causally related to it.

Links to Evaluations of Specific Life Concerns

Some of the most powerful statistical predictors of global well-being (e.g., general happiness, satisfaction with life-as-a-whole) have proven to be assessments of specific life concerns (sometimes called *domains*) such as evaluations of family, housing, job, or community. This line of investigation has been pursued by many investigators, including Andrews and Withey (1976), Campbell *et al.* (1976), E. E. Davis *et al.* (1982), Headey (1981), Kozma and Stones (1983), Michalos (1980, 1983), and Zapf *et al.* (1987).

A typical result is that a set of 5–15 heterogeneous life concern assessments can "explain" 40–60% of the variation in evaluations of global subjective well-being. Predictions of satisfaction with life-as-a-whole tend to be more successful (show higher multiple correlations) than predictions of happiness. Andrews and Withey (1976) showed that after allowing for correlated and random measurement errors virtually all of the potentially explainable variance in their global measure (Life 3) could be explained by several different sets of life concern assessments. The domains with the strongest links to global well-being tapped concerns that were close to self and home: assessments of one's own self-efficacy, family, financial resources, amount of fun, and housing. More remote concerns, such as assessments of community services, local government, and the national government, also made independent, but much smaller, contributions to explaining global well-being.

The implicit (and reasonable) causal assumption underlying all these analyses is that feelings about specific life concerns are somehow combined by people to form their assessments about life-as-a-whole. Many investigators have been surprised by the simplicity of the prediction models that work well here. Although complex interaction schemes that attempt to weigh life concerns according to their importance, and procedures that introduce curvilinear transformations have been tried, it has been difficult to improve upon the simplest linear additive prediction model. This suggests that once the life concern assessments are determined, a rather simple combination system may underlie individuals' feelings about global subjective well-being. If this is the case, one of the key scientific questions moves back a step, and one must consider how people come to feel as they do about specific life concerns.

Of course, one could argue that causality might also work in the opposite direction: Feelings about life-as-a-whole have some influence on feelings about specific life concerns. So far, no one has provided a compelling exploration of this possibility, and such an analysis would be difficult to implement.

Reviews of the Literature

Over the past 20 years there have been numerous reviews of the research literature on subjective well-being. These provide extensive summaries of relationships between subjective well-being and other variables and some discussion of how subjective well-being has been conceptualized and measured. A comprehensive review is a book by Veenhoven (1984a). A doctoral dissertation by Flett (1986) is also extensive. Article- or chapter-length reviews include those by Diener (1984), Kammann *et al.* (1984), and Michalos (1986a). Earlier reviews include those by Wilson (1967), Tatarkiewicz (1976), Larson (1978), and George (1981).

Diener and Griffin (1982) have assembled an annotated bibliography listing research on subjective well-being. Veenhoven (1984b) has published a "Databook" that presents more than 3500 statistical results from 150 empirical investigations of happiness conducted between 1911 and 1975.

Measuring Subjective Well-Being

Subjective well-being has been assessed in a great many different ways and by many different investigators. There is no single scale, or even small set of scales, that stands out as especially widely used or markedly better than others. Many "scales" are merely single items with particular response categories. From a formal psychometric scaling perspective, these measures based on single items are relatively crude, but they have proven useful, as noted below.

In the measurement of subjective well-being, the term "scale" is used in two distinct ways. One, the usual psychometric use, is as a measure or indicator of subjective well-being. The measure may be based on information either from a single question or from multiple questions that are combined to produce a single score.

In contrast, a scale is also a set of *response categories*. Examples of this second use include the Ladder Scale, Faces Scale, Delighted–Terrible Scale, Mountain Scale, etc., all of which have seen extensive use in studies of subjective well-being. Typically, one of these scales may be used to elicit and record people's answers to a large number of different subjective well-being items. These items may subsequently be combined to form a single measure of subjective well-being, or they may be kept separate as measures of distinct concepts of subjective well-being.

The discussion that follows illustrates both of the above uses of the term "scale." Of course, when a measure is based on information from a single question, the two uses of the term coalesce; however, when information from multiple items is combined to produce a measure, then it is important to distinguish the set of questions that are asked from the set of response categories that are offered for answering those questions.

Happiness Scales

Questions about happiness have been asked over a longer period of time than questions about any other subjective well-being concept. Smith (1979) reports data on happiness from almost 50 national surveys of Americans over the period 1946–1977.[2] Additional surveys since 1977 including the General Social Surveys and the survey reported by Campbell (1981) have also included questions on happiness.

In a fascinating analysis, Smith shows that apparently minor variations in the way a happiness question is phrased and/or in the response categories that are used has systematic effects on the distribution of answers, and hence on the average measured level of

[2]Veenhoven (1984b) presents data on "happiness" from 121 surveys in 32 countries between 1940 and 1975. Veenhoven's definition of "happiness," however, is more inclusive than that used in this paper and approximates what is here called "subjective well-being."

happiness. However, asking the same question at different times generates a time trend, and the trend generated by one measure of happiness tends to parallel the trends from other versions. (Happiness tended to be relatively high in the late 1950s and early 1960s, declined through the mid- and late 1960s, reached a low point in the early 1970s, then rose sharply and has remained relatively high through the late 1970s and into the 1980s.)

There are two "standard" happiness measures, both based on single questions. Unfortunately, even the standard versions have occasionally varied slightly from survey to survey, presumably due to oversights or errors when the questionnaire was designed.

The first standard happiness question (see Table 1) has been used by the University of Michigan's Survey Research Center (SRC) and the National Opinion Research Center (NORC) at the University of Chicago. The second standard happiness measure (also shown in Table 1) is that used by the Gallup Organization (American Institute for Public Opinion, AIPO). This "standard" also has varied a bit over the years. Smith (1979) presented the distributions obtained from the above happiness questions in each of 45 national surveys and an additional 24 local or special-population surveys. A consistent finding is that the SRC–NORC happiness measure shows substantially fewer people (typically 8–15%) reporting themselves as "very happy" than does the AIPO measure.

Happiness has been assessed in numerous other ways. None, however, has seemed markedly better than the measures presented above, and none has as long a history of observation in the United States (or anywhere else).

Single-Item Satisfaction Scales

For the purposes of this discussion, satisfaction scales will be defined as those scales that ask explicitly about satisfaction. Scales that measure subjective well-being without explicitly using the word satisfaction are presented in later sections.[3]

Typical satisfaction scales are single-item measures that ask a respondent "How satisfied are you with . . ." (e.g., as in Campbell et al., 1976) or "How much satisfaction do you get from . . ." (e.g., as in the General Social Survey). The question is completed with reference to a global concept, such as "your life-as-a-whole," or to a specific life concern such as "your family life" or "your job."

The response scales used vary from short to long and, for face-to-face interviews, are often printed on a card that is handed to the respondent. For example, the satisfaction scale used in the 1984 General Social Survey had seven on-scale categories and one off-scale category. This scale and several others are shown in Table 1.[4]

Other Response Scales for Assessing
Subjective Well-Being

In addition to the happiness and satisfaction scales described above, the literature on subjective well-being includes several other response scales that have received substantial use.

In each case, they were developed in an attempt to elicit an assessment of subjective well-being that would be more general than asking about either "happiness" or "satisfaction." As noted above, for some purposes "happiness" is too narrow a concept because it

---

[3]An exception is the Mountain Scale, discussed below with other graphic scales, whose instructions have sometimes explicitly referenced "satisfaction."

[4]The numbering shown in Table 1 for the categories of the satisfaction scale used by Campbell et al. (1976)—with higher numbers referring to higher levels of satisfaction—is reversed from that originally used by Campbell and his colleagues.

Table 1

Happiness and Satisfaction Items

Happiness items

1. The University of Michigan's Survey Research Center (SRC) and the National Opinion Research Center (NORC) at the University of Chicago: "Taken all together, how would you say things are these days—would you say that you are very happy, pretty happy, or not too happy?" (The most common variant reads "Taking all things together, how would you say things are these days—would you say that you're very happy, pretty happy, or not too happy these days?)

VERY HAPPY	PRETTY HAPPY	NOT TOO HAPPY
1	2	3

2. Gallup Organization (American Institute for Public Opinion, AIPO): "In general, how happy would you say you are—very happy, fairly happy, or not happy?" ("Not at all happy" is an additional codeable response that has sometimes been offered to the respondent.)

VERY HAPPY	FAIRLY HAPPY	NOT HAPPY
1	2	3

Satisfaction items

1. General Social Survey:
"For each area of life I am going to name, tell me the number that shows how much satisfaction you get from that area."

A VERY GREAT DEAL	A GREAT DEAL	QUITE A BIT	A FAIR AMOUNT	SOME	A LITTLE	NONE	DON'T KNOW
1	2	3	4	5	6	7	98

2. Campbell *et al.* (1976):
"How satisfied or dissatisfied are you with . . . ? Which number comes closest to how satisfied or dissatisfied you feel?"

COMPLETELY DISSATISFIED			NEUTRAL			COMPLETELY SATISFIED
1	2	3	4	5	6	7

3. Eurobarometer surveys (e.g., Inglehart & Rabier, 1986)
(4-point item) "On the whole are you very satisfied, fairly satisfied, not very satisfied, or not at all satisfied with the life you lead?"
(11-point item) "Now I would like you to indicate on this scale to what extent you are satisfied with . . . . Zero means you are completely dissatisfied and ten means you are very satisfied."

0	1	2	3	4	5	6	7	8	9	10

---

neglects the cognitive component of the attitude. Also, some investigators have felt that "satisfaction" also was too narrow because a respondent might be "completely satisfied" but still not very ecstatic, that is, satisfaction has the potential of neglecting the affective component.

Other motivations for developing some of the scales that follow were (1) to use a graphic device that would not depend on the words of a particular language, particularly attractive for multinational studies, and (2) to obtain a distribution that was less skewed than that produced by some happiness and satisfaction measures.

Ladder Scale

Cantril (1967) developed the Ladder Scale, which he called the Self-Anchoring Striving Scale, and used it extensively in his 13-nation study described previously. Other investigators have used this scale, or adaptations of it, since then.

As shown in Table 2, the scale is presented to the respondent as a picture of a ladder with 10 rungs and with 11 numbers (0–10) in the spaces above and below the rungs. The respondent is asked to define the meaning of the top and bottom of the ladder according to his/her own ideas regarding what constitutes good and bad, best and worse, etc.

Parallel questions were constructed to elicit assessments of specific life concerns and also for getting the respondent's evaluations of how well-off the nation was.

Mountain Scale, Faces Scale

Like the Ladder Scale, these two response scales are graphic scales intended to elicit subjective well-being assessments without the use of specific words.

The Mountain Scale was developed by Cantril for use in countries where ladders were not common and it would be difficult for respondents to understand the idea of using rungs on a ladder to indicate degrees of well-being. The Gallup International Research Institutes adopted the Mountain Scale as the primary measuring device for use in their multinational study of subjective well-being (described above). The Mountain Scale consists of a line drawing of a mountain with eleven ascending steps. Instructions for its use are shown in Table 2.

The Faces Scale, developed by Andrews and Withey (1976), is another means of eliciting assessments of subjective well-being without using verbal labels for the scale categories. Seven schematic faces whose expressions vary from very positive to very negative are printed on a card and shown to the respondent. The scale format and one of the questions used with it are shown in Table 2.

Delighted–Terrible Scale

The Delighted–Terrible Scale, as developed by Andrews and Withey (1976), is a seven-category response scale designed for assessing subjective well-being in such a way that affective and cognitive components would both be represented. Several additional off-scale categories allow respondents not to make an assessment for various reasons. The scale is printed on a card, which is handed to the respondent. The instructions used with it and a copy of the scale are shown in Table 2.

Headey (1981) modified the Delighted–Terrible Scale by inserting two additional categories, thereby providing nine on-scale categories. The two new categories were "very pleased" (between "delighted" and "pleased") and "very unhappy" (between "terrible" and "unhappy").

Measures Reviewed Here

Although single items used to assess satisfaction or happiness, either at the global level or at the level of specific life concerns, are the most widely used measures of subjective well-being, a substantial number of multi-item scales also exist. Multi-item scales of subjective well-being, as in any scaling operation, generally have higher validity and/or reliability because random measurement errors that may affect one item are likely to be at least

Table 2
Other Response Scales for Assessing Subjective Well-Being

Ladder Scale (Cantril, 1967):
  "Here is a picture of a ladder. Suppose we say that the top of the ladder represents the best possible life for you and the bottom represents the worst possible life for you. Where on the ladder do you personally stand at the present time?" ". . . where on the ladder would you say you stood five years ago?" ". . . where do you think you will be 5 years from now?"

10
9
8
7
6
5
4
3
2
1
0

Mountain Scale: a line drawing of a mountain with eleven ascending steps (Gallup, 1976):
  "Now I would like to ask you how satisfied you are with your . . . If you are extremely satisfied, you would point to the top of the mountain. If you are dissatisfied, you would point to the bottom. If you are satisfied with some parts of it and dissatisfied with others, you would point to some step between the top and bottom of the mountain. Just point to the step on the mountain that comes closest to how satisfied you are with . . . . Remember, the higher the step, the more satisfied you are; the lower, the more dissatisfied."

Faces Scale (Andrews & Withey, 1976):
  "Here are some faces expressing various feelings. Below each is a letter. Which face comes closest to expressing how you feel about [your life as a whole]?"

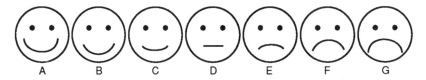

Delighted–Terrible Scale (Andrews & Withey, 1976):
  "In the next section of this interview we want to find out how you feel about parts of your life, and life in this country as you see it. Please tell me the feelings you have now—taking into account what has happened in this last year and what you expect in the near future. . . . just tell me what number on this card gives the best summary of how you feel, 'seven' for delighted, 'six' for pleased, and so forth on to 'one' for you feel terrible about it. If you have no feelings at all on the question, tell me letter 'A.' If you have never thought about something I ask you, and this probably will not happen, then tell me letter 'B.' And I may ask you a question that does not apply to you, if so tell me letter 'C'."

(Table continues)

Table 2 *(Continued)*

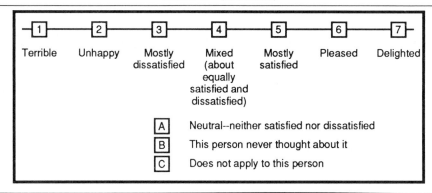

1	2	3	4	5	6	7
Terrible	Unhappy	Mostly dissatisfied	Mixed (about equally satisfied and dissatisfied)	Mostly satisfied	Pleased	Delighted

A Neutral--neither satisfied nor dissatisfied
B This person never thought about it
C Does not apply to this person

partially canceled by opposite errors in other items. Also, multi-item scales, because of their broader information base, may be able to reflect more of the different components of subjective well-being.

The multi-item scales discussed below all focus on *global* well-being. The scales are presented below in chronological order of publication.[5]

1. Life Satisfaction Scales (Neugarten, Havighurst, & Tobin, 1961)
2. Affect Scales (Bradburn, 1969)
3. PGC Morale Scale (Lawton, 1975)
4. Indices of General Affect and Well-Being (Campbell *et al.,* 1976)
5. Life 3 Scale (Andrews & Withey, 1976)
6. General Well-Being Schedule (Fazio, 1977)
7. MUNSH–Happiness Scale (Kozma & Stones, 1980)
8. Affectometer 2 (Kammann & Flett, 1983)
9. PSYCHAP Inventory (Fordyce, 1986)

Among the "classic" measures of subjective well-being are three Life Satisfaction scales proposed by Neugarten *et al.* (1961), and a revision of one of them proposed by Wood, Wylie, and Sheafor (1969). All four scales in this group come from social gerontology and are designed for use with elderly people. Each scale is a set of items that is intended to tap several different dimensions: zest versus apathy, resolution and fortitude, congruence between desired and achieved goals, positive self-concept, and mood tone. The three scales developed by Neugarten *et al.* are the Life Satisfaction Rating (LSR), the Life Satisfaction Index A (LSIA), and the Life Satisfaction Index B (LSIB). Wood *et al.* (1969) proposed a modification of the LSIA, which they called the Life Satisfaction Index Z (LSIZ). The multidimensional set of items that compose LSIA has recently been shown to include a second-order factor that can be designated Subjective Well-Being (Liang, 1984).

Three Affect scales (Positive Affect, Negative Affect, and Affect Balance) developed by Bradburn and Caplovitz (Bradburn, 1969) have received substantial attention in the literature on subjective well-being. Positive affect and negative affect are each measured by five-item scales; affect balance is simply the difference between positive affect and negative affect.

The Philadelphia Geriatric Center's (PGC) Morale Scale is a widely used measure of subjective well-being for older populations. It was developed and later revised by Lawton (1972, 1975) and consists of 17 (originally 22) items. The original conceptualization of

[5]Considerable additional information about each scale, including its actual items and notes about its reliability and validity, appears in the individual Scale Reviews.

subjective well-being assumed it was multidimensional, and the Morale Scale is believed to reflect at least three factors: dissatisfaction–loneliness, agitation, and attitudes toward one's own aging. A more recent second-order confirmatory factor analysis suggests these three factors can themselves be subsumed under a more general factor designated Global Life Satisfaction (Liang & Bollen, 1983), which was subsequently renamed Subjective Well-Being (Liang & Bollen, 1985).

The Campbell *et al.* (1976) Index of General Affect is based on eight items in which respondents describe the nature of their lives. The items were presented in semantic differential format (i.e., as the opposite poles of 7-point scales). The Index of Well-Being (Campbell *et al.*, 1976) combines the above Index of General Affect and a single item on satisfaction with life as a whole (answered on the seven-point satisfaction scale shown in Table 1). The combination weights the satisfaction item much more heavily than the others.

The Life 3 Scale developed by Andrews and Withey (1976) is a simple averaging of two questionnaire items, each of which asks respondents "How do you feel about your life as a whole?" using the categories of the Delighted–Terrible Response Scale described in Table 2. The two questions are typically separated by 10–15 minutes of other questions, which may ask for evaluations of more specific life concerns. (Despite the fact the second question repeats the first, respondents rarely express any objection.) This simple scale was found to have good psychometric properties in data on subjective well-being from several national surveys.

Dupuy developed what came to be called the General Well-Being Schedule for the National Center for Health Statistics in 1970. The schedule contains 33 items that can be combined to produce a score on general well-being and/or subscales measuring six aspects of well-being: health worry, energy level, satisfying and interesting life, depressed–cheerful mood, emotional–behavioral control, and relaxed versus tense–anxious. Fazio (1977) presented the schedule, a scoring key, and information on how GWB scores relate to a variety of indicators of mental health.

Kozma and Stones (1980) have developed a multi-item scale of subjective well-being named the Memorial University of Newfoundland Scale of Happiness (MUNSH). This scale represents an attempt to improve upon several prior scales: Bradburn's Affect Scales, the PGC Morale Scale, and the Life Satisfaction Index-Z Scale. Although the MUNSH has good psychometric properties when used with the kinds of people for whom it was developed (elderly individuals in Newfoundland), its applicability to other populations remains to be assessed.

Kammann and his colleagues at the University of Otago in New Zealand have developed a measure of subjective well-being that they have named the Affectometer: A Rapid Inventory of Subjective Well-Being (Flett, 1986; Kammann & Flett, 1983; Kammann, Christie, Irwin, & Dixon, 1979). The instrument was (as of 1988) in its second version (Affectometer 2) and consists of 20 self-descriptive statements and 20 adjectives. Together, the statements and adjectives aim to reflect 10 qualities of subjective well-being: confluence, optimism, self-esteem, self-efficacy, social support, social interest, freedom, energy, cheerfulness, and thought clarity.

The PSYCHAP Inventory (PHI) of Fordyce (1986) is a new measure that has been used with a variety of populations. The inventory includes 320 items spread across four 80-item forms. The items on each form can be used to produce a total score on happiness and four subscores intended to reflect attributes that are associated with happiness: achieved happiness, happy personality, happy attitudes and values, and happiness lifestyle. One interesting feature of the inventory is that it is linked to an outreach program to increase people's life satisfaction and happiness.

Life Satisfaction Scales

(Neugarten, Havighurst, & Tobin, 1961)

Variables

This study developed three separate measures of life satisfaction, one based on interviews and expert ratings (LSR) and two on self-report scales (LSIA and LSIB). These then became the basis for a later revision, the LSIZ.

Description

The scales were explicitly developed as measures "that would use the individual's own evaluations as the point of reference and that would be relatively independent of level of activity or social participation."

The LSR measure was based on inferences drawn from raters who reviewed extensive in-depth information obtained from respondents over four rounds of interviews spaced over a 30-month period. There were five rating scales using a 1–5 system, so that scores ran between 5 (lowest satisfaction) to 25 (highest possible satisfaction).

Because of the time and effort required to calculate LSR, the authors used this as a validity criterion to select items for the two self-response indices. The first (Life Satisfaction Index A) consisted of 20 agree–disagree items that correlated most highly with LSR and the second (Life Satisfaction Index B) consisted of the 12 open-end and checklist items that correlated highest with LSR. LSIA scores vary from 0 (lowest satisfaction) to 20 (highest satisfaction) and LSIB scores vary from 0 (lowest satisfaction) to 22 (highest satisfaction).

Sample

The total sample consisted of 177 adults aged 50 and older, about half of whom were part of a panel interviewed at several points in time and from whom most of the reliability and validity data were obtained. The larger sample consisted of 91 men and 86 women, with 50 rated as being upper middle-class, 55 as lower middle-class, and 72 as upper lower-class. Mean score on the LSR for the 177 respondents was 17.8 (SD = 4.6). Mean scores for the 92 panel respondents for the LSIA was 12.4 (SD = 4.4) and for the LSIB 15.5 (SD = 4.7).

Reliability

Internal Consistency

Two independent judges gave LSR ratings that correlated .78 with each other (after correction for attenuation).

Apparently because the item analysis to construct the scale was external rather than internal, data on the internal consistency of the items were not reported for LSIA and LSIB scales.

Test–Retest

No test–retest data were reported.

Validity

Convergent

The LSR scale correlated .64 with independent ratings made by clinical psychologists after lengthy personal interviews with 80 respondents, a figure that may have been lowered by the failure of several low satisfaction respondents to remain in the study.

The LSIA and LSIB scales correlated .55 and .58, respectively, with LSR and .39 and .47 with the ratings of the clinical psychologists, again possibly lowered because of sample attrition and the 14-month interval between measurement periods. The LSIA and LSIB scales correlated .73.

Discriminant

No data on discriminant validity were reported.

Location

Neugarten, B. L., Havighurst, R. J., & Tobin, S. (1961). The measurement of life satisfaction. *Journal of Gerontology,* **16,** 134–143.

Results and Comments

The authors concluded that the LSIA and LSIB scales correlate "only moderately" with LSR.

Relatively small differences were found between men and women and between younger and older people; however, the scale intercorrelations were much lower among younger respondents, congruent with earlier findings about the "greater consistency between measures for respondents of advanced age."

All life satisfaction measures correlated significantly with the respondent's social status ($r = .21-.41$).

Items 1,2,3,4,6,7,9,12,16,17,18,19, and 20 were found to provide a more useful scale (LSIZ) according to a 1969 article by Wood, Wylie, and Sheafor that appeared in the *Journal of Gerontology*. This LSIZ scale has been used rather often subsequently.

Although the LSIA was originally intended to reflect the five scales of the LSR, actual factor analyses of the LSIA have sometimes failed to produce all five factors. For example, Adams (1969) reported the following factor structure: I (Mood Tone): LSIA items 3, 4, 5, 6, 7, 18; II (Zest for Life) 1, 8, 9, 10, 15, 16; III (Congruence): 12, 13, 19; IV (Unnamed factor): 2, 17, 20; Remaining items: 11, 14.

Life Satisfaction Rating Scales

SCALE A. Zest versus Apathy

5. Speaks of several activities and relationships with enthusiasm. Feels that "now" is the best time of life. Loves to do things, even sitting at home. Takes up new activities; makes new friends readily, seeks self-improvement. Shows zest in several areas of life.

4. Shows zest, but it is limited to one or two special interests, or limited to

certain periods of time. May show disappointment or anger when things go wrong, if they keep him from active enjoyment of life. Plans ahead, even though in small time units.

3. Has a bland approach to life. Does not seem to get much pleasure out of the things he does. Seeks relaxation and a limited degree of involvement. May be quite detached (aloof) from many activities, things, or people.

2. Thinks life is monotonous for the most part. May complain of fatigue. Feels bored with many things. If active, finds little meaning or enjoyment in the activity.

1. Lives on the basis of routine. Doesn't think anything worth doing.

SCALE B. Resolution and Fortitude

5. Try and try again attitude. Bloody but unbowed. Fights back: withstanding, not giving up. Active personality: take the bad and the good and make the most of it. Wouldn't change the past.

4. Can take life as it comes. "I have no complaints on the way life has treated me." Assumes responsibility readily. "If you look for the good side of life, you'll find it." Does not mind talking about difficulties in life, but does not dwell on them either. "You have to give up some things."

3. Says, "I've had my ups and downs; sometimes on top, sometimes on the bottom." Shows a trace of extrapunitiveness or intropunitiveness concerning his difficulties in life.

2. Feels he hasn't done better because he hasn't gotten the breaks. Feels great difference in life now as compared to age 45; the change has been for the worse. "I've worked hard but never got anywhere."

1. Talks of hard knocks which he has not mastered (extrapunitive). Blames self a great deal (intropunitive). Overwhelmed by life.

SCALE C. Congruence between Desired and Achieved Goals

5. Feels he has accomplished what he wanted to do. He has achieved or is achieving his own personal goals.

4. Regrets somewhat the chances missed during life. "Maybe I should have made more of certain opportunities." Nevertheless, feels that he has been fairly successful in accomplishing what he wanted to do in life.

3. Has a fifty-fifty record of opportunities taken and opportunities missed. Would have done some things differently, if he had his life to live over. Might have gotten more education.

2. Has regrets about major opportunities missed but feels good about accomplishment in one area (may be in his avocation).

1. Feels he has missed most opportunities in life.

SCALE D. Self-Concept

5. Feels at his best. "I do better work now than ever before." There was never any better time. Thinks of self as wise, mellow, and attractive; feels important to others. Feels he has the right to indulge himself.

4. Feels more fortunate than the average. Is sure that he can meet the exigencies of life. "When I retire, I'll just substitute other activities." Compensates well for any difficulty of health. Feels worthy of being indulged. "Things I want to do, I can do, but I'll not overexert myself." Feels in control of self in relation to the situation.

3. Sees self as competent in at least one area, e.g., work; but has doubts about self in other areas. Acknowledges loss of youthful vigor, but accepts it in a realistic way. Feels relatively unimportant, but doesn't mind. Feels he takes, but also gives. Senses a general, but not extreme, loss of status as he grows older. Reports health better than average.

2. Feels that other people look down on him. Tends to speak despairingly of older people. Is defensive about what the years are doing to him.

1. Feels old. Feels in the way, or worthless. Makes self-disparaging remarks. "I'm endured by others."

SCALE E. Mood Tone

5. "This is the best time of my life." Is nearly always cheerful, optimistic. Cheerfulness may seem unrealistic to an observer but shows no sign of "putting up a bold front".

4. Gets pleasure out of life, knows it, and shows it. There is enough restraint to seem appropriate in a younger person. Usually feels positive affect. Optimistic.

3. Seems to move along on an even temperamental keel. Any depressions are neutralized by positive mood swings. Generally neutral-to-positive affect. May show some irritability.

2. Wants things quiet and peaceful. General neutral-to-negative affect. Some depression.

1. Pessimistic, complaining, bitter. Complains of being lonely. Feels "blue" a good deal of the time. May get angry when in contact with people.

Life Satisfaction Index A

Here are some statements about life in general that people feel differently about. Would you read each statement on this list, and if you agree with it, put a check mark in the space under AGREE. If you do not agree with a statement, put a check mark in the space under DISAGREE. If you are not sure one way or the other, put a check mark in the space under "?". PLEASE BE SURE TO ANSWER EVERY QUESTION ON THE LIST.

(Key: score 1 point for each response marked in parentheses.)

*1. As I grow older, things seem better than I thought they would be. (A)

AGREE   DISAGREE   ?

*2. I have gotten more of the breaks in life than most of the people I know. (A)

*3. This is the dreariest time of my life. (D)

*4. I am just as happy as when I was younger. (A)

5. My life could be happier than it is now. (D)

*6. These are the best years of my life. (A)

*7. Most of the things that I do are boring or monotonous. (D)

8. I expect some interesting and pleasant things to happen to me in the near future. (A)

*9. The things I do are as interesting to me now as they ever were. (A)

10. I feel old and somewhat tired. (D)

11. I feel my age, but it does not bother me. (A)

*12. As I look back on my life, I am fairly well satisfied. (A)

13. I would not change my past life even if I could. (A)

14. Compared to other people my age, I've made a lot of foolish decisions in my life. (D)

15. Compared to other people my age, I make a good appearance. (A)

*16. I have made plans for things I'll be doing a month or a year from now. (A)

*17. When I think back over my life, I didn't get most of the important things I wanted. (D)

*18. Compared to other people, I get down in the dumps too often. (D)

*19. I've gotten pretty much what I expected out of life. (A)

*20. In spite of what people say, the lot of the average man is getting worse, not better. (D)

Note: *, Items in Life Satisfaction Index Z of Wood et al. (1969).

Life Satisfaction Index B
(with scoring key)

Would you please comment freely in answer to the following questions?

1. What are the best things about being the age you are now?
   1.....a positive answer
   0.....nothing good about it

2. What do you think you will be doing five years from now? How do you expect things will be different from the way they are now, in your life?
   2.....better, or no change
   1.....contingent—"It depends."
   0.....worse

3. What is the most important thing in your life right now?
   2.....anything outside of self, or pleasant interpretation of future.
   1....."hanging on"; keeping health, or job
   0.....getting out of present difficulty, or "nothing now," or reference to the
         past

4. How happy would you say you are right now, compared with the earlier
   periods in your life?
   2.....this is the happiest time; all have been happy; or hard to make a
         choice
   1.....some decrease in recent years
   0....earlier periods were better, this is a bad time

5. Do you ever worry about your ability to do what people expect of you—
   to meet demands that people make on you?
   2.....no
   1.....qualified yes or no
   0.....yes

6. If you could do anything you pleased, in what part of (name of country)
   would you most like to live?
   2.....present location
   0.....any other location

7. How often do you find yourself feeling lonely?
   2.....never; hardly ever
   1.....sometimes
   0.....fairly often; very often

8. How often do you feel there is no point in living?
   2.....never; hardly ever
   1.....sometimes
   0.....fairly often; very often

9. Do you wish you could see more of your close friends than you do, or
   would you like more time to yourself?
   2.....O.K. as is
   1.....wish could see more of friends
   0.....wish more time to self

10. How much unhappiness would you say you find in your life today?
    2.....almost none
    1.....some
    0.....a great deal

11. As you get older, would you say things seem to be better or worse than
    you thought they would be?
    2.....better
    1.....about as expected
    0.....worse

12. How satisfied would you say you are with your life?
    2.....very satisfied
    1.....fairly satisfied
    0.....not very satisfied

Affect Scales: Positive Affect, Negative Affect, Affect Balance

(Bradburn, 1969)

Variables

These three scales were developed as measures of psychological well-being for the general population, with Positive Affect tapping positive emotions, Negative Affect tapping negative emotions, and Affect Balance reflecting the difference between positive and negative emotions.

Description

These scales were built on a "utility" or "pleasure–pain" model of well-being resulting from an individual's position on two independent dimensions, one positive and one negative. This model was developed from previous survey results in four small communities in which a variety of negative and positive experiences were investigated and found to be uncorrelated. The 10 items are asked as a series of yes–no questions about feelings during "the past few weeks." One point is given for each positive response to the Positive Affect items, and one point for each negative response to the Negative Affect items. (In order to have enough cases for analysis, the two categories at the low-frequency end of each scale, 0 and 1 for Positive Affect, and 4 and 5 for Negative Affect, were combined to produce scores ranging from 0 to 4 for each scale.) Affect Balance is computed as Positive Affect minus Negative Affect plus a constant of 5 (to avoid negative values) and thus ranges from +1 (lowest Affect Balance) to +9 (highest Affect Balance).

Sample

The scale was applied to 2735 adults, with 1256 respondents in Washington (D.C.) suburbs, 538 in Detroit suburbs, 430 in Detroit city, 247 in Chicago and 264 in ten metropolitan areas. National data were reported for a June, 1965, sample of 1469 respondents.

No overall mean score was reported for these samples, but extrapolation from the individual item percentages indicates an average score of 6.7 for the national sample. In the overall sample of 2726 respondents, some 369 reported ABS scores of +8 and +9 (top of the scale) and only 180 scores of +1 and +2 (bottom of the scale).

Reliability

Internal Consistency

Reported inter-item correlations (Q) varied between .19 and .75 for the Positive Affect Scale and between .38 and .72 for the Negative Affect Scale. Overall correlations between Negative and Positive Scale items were less than .10.

Test–Retest

Across a 3-day interval, a γ value of .76 was reported for the ABS scale, with .83 for the Positive Affect items and .81 for the Negative Affect items. Across longer periods, these correlations dropped to .47 and .46 for the positive and negative scales, respectively.

Validity

Convergent

The ABS scores correlated between .45 and .51 (γ values) with a general question about reported happiness, .47 and .40 with an item about getting what one wants out of life and −.33 and −.36 with wanting to change one's life. In addition, affect balance scores were found to change regularly with changes in these measures.

Discriminant

No data on discriminant validity were reported.

Location

Bradburn, N. (1969). *The structure of psychological well-being.* Chicago: Aldine.

Results and Comments

Affect balance was unrelated to gender and age but was higher among college graduates and higher income individuals. The combination of low income and heavy family responsibilities results in particularly low scores on well-being.

It should be noted that the correlation coefficient γ (and Q) usually give larger values (for the same data table) than Pearson's r, τ_b and other coefficients.

Affect Balance Scale

Now let's talk about something else. We are interested in the way people are feeling these days.

During the past few weeks, did you ever feel . . .

		% ANSWERED YES
P1	A. Particularly excited or interested in something?	54
	YES NO	
N	B. Did you ever feel so restless that you couldn't sit long in a chair?	53
P	C. Proud because someone complimented you on something you had done?	71
N	D. Very lonely or remote from other people?	26
P	E. Pleased about having accomplished something?	84
N	F. Bored?	34
P	G. On top of the world?	33
N	H. Depressed or very unhappy?	30
P	I. That things were going your way?	71
N	J. Upset because someone criticized you?	18

Note: *P, positive affect; N, negative affect.

PGC Morale Scale (Revised)
(Lawton, 1975)

Variable

Subjective well-being for older populations is measured.

Description

The original PGC Morale Scale consisted of 22 items, mainly in agree–disagree format, developed by Lawton (1972), who later revised it to 17 items (Lawton, 1975). It was originally developed and validated based on correlations with adjustment ratings of three groups from homes for the aged. Subjective well-being is assumed to be a multidimensional concept reflecting at least three factors: dissatisfaction–loneliness, agitation, and attitudes towards one's own aging.

Scores on the scale run from 0 (lowest morale) to 17 (highest morale).

Sample

The revised scale was developed on a sample of 1086 residents of several elderly housing projects in the East and Midwest (72% female, 32% married, 76% white, 43% Jewish, and mainly functionally independent). No average scores on the revised scale were reported.

Reliability

Cronbach α coefficients for 828 of these respondents for the three subscales were .85, .81, and .85. No data are reported for the entire scale.

Validity

Convergent

No data bearing on the convergent validity of the scale were reported by Lawton, but Lohmann (1977) reported an average .73 correlation with nine other well-being measures.

Discriminant

No data bearing directly on the discriminant validity of the PGC was reported by Lawton.

Location

Lawton, M. P. (1975). The Philadelphia Geriatric Center morale scale: A revision. *Journal of Gerontology*, **30**, 85–89.

Results

The author recommended that additional areas be included in future scales of morale, including health, social accessibility, attitudes toward aging, and positive affect. A second-order confirmatory factor analysis suggested these three factors can themselves be subsumed under a more general factor designated Global Life Satisfaction (Liang & Bollen, 1983); this was subsequently renamed Subjective Well-Being (Liang & Bollen, 1985).

PGC Morale Scale*

Factor 1—Agitation

1   Little things bother me more this year (No)
                YES   NO
2   I sometimes worry so much that I can't sleep (No)
3   I have a lot to be sad about (No)
4   I am afraid of a lot of things (No)
5   I get mad more than I used to (No)
6   Life is hard for me most of the time (No)
7   I take things hard (No)
8   I get upset easily (No)

Factor 2—Attitude Toward Own Aging

1   Things keep getting worse as I get older (No)
2   I have as much pep as I had last year (Yes)
3   Little things bother me more this year (No)
4   As you get older you are less useful (No)
5   As I get older, things are better/worse than I thought they would be (Better)
6   I sometimes feel that life isn't worth living (No)
7   I am as happy now as when I was younger (Yes)

Factor 3—Lonely Dissatisfaction

1   How much do you feel lonely? (Not much)
2   I see enough of my friends and relatives (Yes)
3   I sometimes feel that life isn't worth living (No)
4   Life is hard for me much of the time (No)
5   How satisfied are you with your life today? (Satisfied)
6   I have a lot to be sad about (No)
7   People had it better in the old days (No)
8   A person has to live for today and not worry about tomorrow (Yes)

Note: *, High morale response in parentheses.

Index of Well-Being, Index of General Affect

(Campbell et al., *1976)*

Variable

The Index of Well-Being is a two-part measure of self-reported well-being with life as currently experienced; it was developed with a national sample.

Description

The Index of Well-Being is the sum of (1) the average score on an Index of General Affect (a set of eight items on semantic differential scales) and (2) a single-item assessment of life satisfaction. The satisfaction item was weighted 1.1 and added to the average General Affect response to compute the final score.

Scores can thus range from 0.0 (lowest) to 14.7 (highest well-being).

Sample

The scale was applied to a national probability sample of 2160 American adults aged 18 and older in the summer of 1971; about one-sixth of the respondents were reinterviewed in the spring of 1972. Average scores on the index were 11.8 for the entire sample (s.d. = 2.2), with 31% of the sample scoring 13 or higher on the index. Persons over the age of 65 scored above average on the index, as did high-income individuals, married people without children and residents of rural areas. Particularly low scores were found among unemployed, low-income, divorced–separated, and never-married young adults. Women scored slightly higher than men on the index and whites higher than blacks after controlling for income.

Reliability

Internal Consistency

The eight items in the Index of General Affect had a Cronbach α of .89. This Index correlated .55 with the life satisfaction question.

Test–Retest

Test–retest correlations for 285 respondents about 8 months later were .43 for the Index of Well-Being and .56 for the Index of General Affect.

Validity

Convergent

The Well-Being Index correlated .20–.26 with measures of fears and worries. It correlated more highly (.35) with a measure of personal competence. The Index of Affect correlated .52 with a measure of happiness.

Discriminant

The Well-Being Index correlated .20 with the Crowne–Marlowe Social Desirability Scale, being higher for the Deny Bad subscale (.29) than with the Assert Good subscale (.12).

Location

Campbell, A., Converse, P. E., & Rodgers, W. L. (1976). *The quality of American life: Perceptions, evaluation and satisfaction.* New York: Russell Sage.

Results and Comments

The study found the major domains of life that correlated with the Well-Being Index were nonwork activities, family life, standard of living, work, and marriage. Some 54% of the variance in well-being scores was accounted for by 17 of these domain measures.

Several resource factors correlated positively with the Well-Being Index, including numbers of friends (.23), time (.21), family income (.14), intelligence (.13), health (.13), and religious faith (.11).

Index of Well-Being

1. Index of General Affect (weighted 1.0)

Mean
Rating

(5.5)	a) Interesting	1 2 3 4 5 6 7	Boring
(5.7)	b) Enjoyable	1 2 3 4 5 6 7	Miserable
(5.9)	c) Worthwhile	1 2 3 4 5 6 7	Useless
(5.9)	d) Friendly	1 2 3 4 5 6 7	Lonely
(5.8)	e) Full	1 2 3 4 5 6 7	Empty
(5.8)	f) Hopeful	1 2 3 4 5 6 7	Discouraging
(5.6)	g) Rewarding	1 2 3 4 5 6 7	Disappointing
(5.2)	h) Brings out the best in me	1 2 3 4 5 6 7	Doesn't give me much chance

2. Life Satisfaction (weighted 1.1)

How satisfied or dissatisfied are you with your life as a whole?
Which number comes closest to how satisfied or dissatisfied you feel?

COMPLETELY   1   2   3   4   5   6   7   COMPLETELY
DISSATISFIED   SATISFIED
             (1%) (2%) (4%) (11%) (21%) (39%) (22%)

Note: In the actual questionnaire, items a, c, f, and g (as listed above) were reversed to minimize position effects.

Life 3 Scale

(Andrews & Withey, 1976)

Variable

This measure is based on two questions that ask respondents to evaluate "their life as a whole" on a 1–7 (terrible–delighted) response scale.

Description

The response scale categories were developed as a "measuring device that would yield more valid and discriminating information about people's evaluation of different aspects of life" by providing explicit labels for each scale point and by including more affect than previous satisfaction scales. The Life 3 Scale consists of the same item asked twice of each respondent, separated by 15–20 minutes of other questions related to the quality of life using this and other scales. Scale scores run from 2 (lowest evaluation) to 14 (highest evaluation).

Sample

The scale was administered to several national samples totaling nearly 4000 respondents in 1972 and 1973.

In the April 1973 survey ($n = 1433$) a mean score of 10.8 was reported.

Reliability

Internal Consistency

The two items correlated .68 in the April national sample, from which a Cronbach $\alpha = .81$ can be derived.

Test–Retest

No test–retest data for the combined scale are reported.

Validity

Life 3 correlated .54 with Cantril's ladder ratings, .52 with the circles measure, and .57 with interviewers' ratings of the respondent's life satisfaction in the April survey. Using a complex LISREL analysis, a validity estimate of .77 was obtained, higher than for the ladder rating (.73), the circles measure (.72), and the interviewers' ratings (.66).

Location

Andrews, F. M., & Withey, S. B. (1976). *Social indicators of well-being.* New York: Plenum.

Results and Comments

One of the most attractive features of this scale is the extremely broad set of predictors and conditions that the authors related to it. For example, the Life 3 scale was found to relate most strongly in the November survey to scale ratings on the following factors: amount of fun, family life, money index, and yourself, with multivariate β values for the four running from .23 to .17. These studies examined more than 200 other life areas and circumstances in terms of their relation to Life 3.

The authors found that few respondents object to answering this same question twice and many may not notice it.

Life 3 Scale

In the next section of this interview we want to find out how you feel about parts of your life, and life in this country as you see it. Please tell me the feelings you have now, taking into account what has happened in the last year and what you expect in the near future. Just tell me what number on this card gives the best summary of how you feel, "seven" for delighted, "six" for pleased, and so forth on to "one" for you feel terrible about it. If you have no feelings at all on the question, tell me letter "A." If you have never thought about something I ask you, and this probably will not happen, then tell me letter "B." And I may ask you a question that does not apply to you; if so, tell me letter "C."

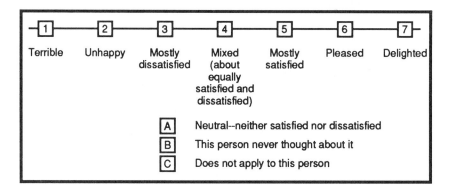

1. How do you feel about your life as a whole? _____(Number)

   (15–20 minutes of other questions using the above scale.)

2. How do you feel about your life as a whole? _____(Number)

General Well-Being Schedule

(Fazio, 1977)

Variable

The General Well-Being Schedule (GWB), developed for the National Center for Health Statistics, is a structured instrument for assessing self-representations of subjective well-being.

Description

The schedule contains 33 items, 14 with six response options, 4 with 0–10 rating bars, and 15 self-evaluation behavioral items. The items were developed based on a simple two-process model of effective psychotherapy from a problem-solving framework, one in which patients develop a positive rapport with a therapist through therapeutic exercises. A variety of techniques for assessing depression were computer-searched.

Scale scores run from 14 (lowest well-being) to 134 (highest well-being) for the first 18 items as described in Fazio (1977).

Sample

Scale norms are available from a sample of 79 male and 119 female students at the University of Wisconsin, Milwaukee, in a freshman psychology class (Fazio, 1977). Average scores for the first 18 items of the schedule were 75 for men and 71 for women (SD = 15 and 18) and are shown for individual items below. The scale was also administered to a national sample of 6931 adults aged 25–74 between 1971 and 1975, although no normative data were reported.

Reliability

Internal Consistency

Item–total scale correlations ranging from .48 to .78 were reported for the college student sample; subscale–total correlations ranged from .56 to .88. An internal consistency coefficient was .91 for men and .95 for women.

Test–Retest

A test–retest correlation for 41 of these students over a 3-month period was .85. Average group scale scores also remained similar; they were 75 at time 1 and 73 at time 2 (SD = 17 and 17).

Validity

Convergent

In the Wisconsin student survey, the total GWB score correlated .47 with an independent interviewer assessment of depression, with the six subscale correlations ranging from .27 (free from health worry) to .44 (cheerful–depressed mood). It correlated .69 with six other measures such as the PFI, PSS, and CHQ anxiety scales (.41, .40, and .10), and the HQ, Zung, and MMPI depression scales (.35, .28, and .21). The correlation with the PFI depression scale, however, was slightly higher (.50).

Location

The items and evidence for concurrent validity in the student study are presented in Fazio, A. F. (1977). *A concurrent validation study of the NCH1 general well-being schedule.* (Dept. of HEW Publ. No. HRA-78-1347). Hyattsville, MD: National Center for Health Statistics.

Results and Comments

The availability of representative national data for this schedule is an important advantage of the scale as is the evidence for its better performance than alternative measures of anxiety and depression. Its six subscale components ensure that a diversity of content is included in the total scores. In addition to producing a score on general well-being, the items can be grouped to yield scores on six aspects of well-being: health worry, energy level, satisfying and interesting life, depressed–cheerful mood, emotional–behavioral control, and relaxed versus tense–anxious.

General Well-Being Schedule

(2.9)   How have you been feeling in general? (DURING THE PAST MONTH)

	VERY GOOD SPIRITS	GOOD SPIRITS	UP AND DOWN SPIRITS	LOW SPIRITS	VERY LOW SPIRITS
EXCELLENT					
1	2	3	4	5	6

(3.7)   Have you been bothered by nervousness or your "nerves"? (DURING THE PAST MONTH)

VERY MUCH SO	QUITE A BIT	SOME	A LITTLE	NOT AT ALL
1	2	3	4	5

(3.7)   Have you been in firm control of your behavior, thoughts, emotions OR feelings? (DURING THE PAST MONTH)

	YES, FOR THE MOST PART	GEN-ERALLY SO	NOT TOO WELL	NO, SOME-WHAT DIS-TURBED	VERY DIS-TURBED
DEFINITELY SO					
1	2	3	4	5	6

(4.0)   Have you felt so sad, discouraged, hopeless, or had so many problems that you wondered if anything was worthwhile? (DURING THE PAST MONTH)

	VERY MUCH SO	QUITE A BIT	SOME	A LITTLE	NOT AT ALL
EXTREMELY					
1	2	3	4	5	6

(2.7)   Have you been under or felt you were under any strain, stress, or pressure? (DURING THE PAST MONTH)

YES, QUITE A BIT	YES, SOME MORE	YES, ABOUT SAME	YES, A LITTLE	NOT AT ALL
1	2	3	4	5

(2.7)   How happy, satisfied, or pleased have you been with your personal life? (DURING THE PAST MONTH)

VERY HAPPY	FAIRLY HAPPY	SATISFIED	SOMEWHAT DIS-SATISFIED	VERY DIS-SATISFIED
1	2	3	4	5

(4.3)   Have you had reason to wonder if you were losing your mind, or losing control over the way you act, talk, think, feel, or of your memory? (DURING THE PAST MONTH)

NOT AT ALL	ONLY A LITTLE	SOME, NOT CON-CERNED	SOME, CON-CERNED	SOME, QUITE CON-CERNED	YES, VERY CON-CERNED
1	2	3	4	5	6

(3.3) Have you been anxious, worried, or upset? (DURING THE PAST MONTH)

EXTREMELY	VERY MUCH SO	QUITE A BIT	SOME	A LITTLE	NOT AT ALL
1	2	3	4	5	6

(2.8) Have you been waking up fresh and rested? (DURING THE PAST MONTH)

EVERY DAY	MOST EVERY DAY	FAIRLY OFTEN	LESS OFTEN	RARELY	NONE OF THE TIME
1	2	3	4	5	6

(4.0) Have you been bothered by any illness, bodily disorder, pains, or fears about your health? (DURING THE PAST MONTH)

ALL THE TIME	MOST OF THE TIME	A GOOD BIT OF THE TIME	SOME OF THE TIME	A LITTLE OF THE TIME	NONE OF THE TIME
1	2	3	4	5	6

(3.2) Has your daily life been full of things that were interesting to you? (DURING THE PAST MONTH)

ALL THE TIME	MOST OF THE TIME	A GOOD BIT OF THE TIME	SOME OF THE TIME	A LITTLE OF THE TIME	NONE OF THE TIME
1	2	3	4	5	6

(3.5) Have you felt down-hearted and blue? (DURING THE PAST MONTH)

ALL THE TIME	MOST OF THE TIME	A GOOD BIT OF THE TIME	SOME OF THE TIME	A LITTLE OF THE TIME	NONE OF THE TIME
1	2	3	4	5	6

(3.5) Have you been feeling emotionally stable and sure of yourself? (DURING THE PAST MONTH)

ALL THE TIME	MOST OF THE TIME	A GOOD BIT OF THE TIME	SOME OF THE TIME	A LITTLE OF THE TIME	NONE OF THE TIME
1	2	3	4	5	6

(3.2)   Have you felt tired, worn out, used up, or exhausted? (DURING THE
        PAST MONTH)

ALL THE TIME	MOST OF THE TIME	A GOOD BIT OF THE TIME	SOME OF THE TIME	A LITTLE OF THE TIME	NONE OF THE TIME
1	2	3	4	5	6

(7.2)   How concerned or worried about your HEALTH have you been?
        (DURING THE PAST MONTH)

NOT   VERY
CONCERNED   0   1   2   3   4   5   6   7   8   9   10   CONCERNED

(5.4)   How RELAXED or TENSE have you been? (DURING THE PAST
        MONTH)

RELAXED   0   1   2   3   4   5   6   7   8   9   10   TENSE

(6.0)   How much ENERGY, PEP, VITALITY have you felt? (DURING THE
        PAST MONTH)

                                                                    VERY
LISTLESS   0   1   2   3   4   5   6   7   8   9   10   ENERGETIC

(6.2)   How DEPRESSED or CHEERFUL have you been? (DURING THE
        PAST MONTH)

VERY   VERY
DEPRESSED   0   1   2   3   4   5   6   7   8   9   10   CHEERFUL

(3.5)   Have you had severe enough personal, emotional, behavioral, or
        mental problems that you felt you needed help? (DURING THE PAST
        YEAR)

YES, SOUGHT HELP	YES, DID NOT SEEK HELP	SEVERE PROBLEMS, DID NOT SEEK HELP	FEW PERSONAL PROBLEMS	NO PERSONAL PROBLEMS
1	2	3	4	5

(2.6)   Have you ever felt that you were going to have, or were close to
        having, a nervous breakdown?

YES, DURING PAST YEAR	YES, MORE THAN YEAR AGO	NO
1	2	3

(2.9)   Have you ever had a nervous breakdown?

YES, DURING PAST YEAR	YES, MORE THAN YEAR AGO	NO
1	2	3

(2.9) Have you ever been a patient (or outpatient) at a mental hospital, a mental health ward of a hospital, or a mental health clinic, for any personal, emotional, behavior, or mental problems?

YES, DURING PAST YEAR	YES, MORE THAN YEAR AGO	NO
1	2	3

(2.9) Have you ever seen a psychiatrist, psychologist or psychoanalyst about any personal, emotional, behavior, or mental problem concerning yourself?

YES, DURING PAST YEAR	YES, MORE THAN YEAR AGO	NO
1	2	3

(4.7) Have you talked with or had any connection with any of the following about some personal, emotional, behavior, mental problem, worries, or "nerves" concerning yourself? (DURING THE PAST YEAR)

	YES	NO
a. Regular medical doctor (except for definite physical conditions or routine check-ups)	1	2
b. Brain or nerve specialist	1	2
c. Nurse (except for routine medical conditions)	1	2
d. Lawyer (except for routine legal services)	1	2
e. Police (except for simple traffic violations)	1	2
f. Clergyman, minister, priest, rabbi, etc.	1	2
g. Marriage Counselor	1	2
h. Social Worker	1	2

i. Other formal assistance   YES _____   What kind? ___
                                      NO _____

Do you discuss your problems with any members of your family or friends?

YES, HELPS A LOT	YES, HELPS SOME	YES, DOESN'T HELP AT ALL	NO, NO ONE TO TALK WITH	NO ONE WANTS TO TALK	NO, DON'T WANT TO TALK	NO PROB-LEMS
1	2	3	4	5	6	7

Memorial University of Newfoundland Scale of Happiness

(Kozma & Stones, 1980)

Variable

This scale was developed as a self-appraised measure of mental health among the elderly.

Description

Items in the MUNSH scale were chosen on the basis of their correlation with avowed happiness and were intended to overcome shortcomings in Bradburn's Affect Balance Scale. More than 70 items from the ABS and other scales were included in the initial pool of items, from which 24 items were selected after cross-validation. The final forms of MUNSH contained five positive affect (PA) items, five negative affect (NA) items, seven items of positive experience (PE), and seven of negative experience (NE).

Scores range potentially from 0 (lowest happiness) to 48 (highest happiness).

Sample

The item analysis phase of the study was conducted with a random sample of 301 adults aged 65–95 equally drawn from lists of elderly people living in urban, in rural, and in institutional settings in Newfoundland. The results were cross-validated with a similar sample of 297 Newfoundland residents.

No data on means or standard deviations for these groups were reported.

Reliability

Internal Consistency

Coefficient α values above .85 were reported for both samples for the overall MUNSH scale.

Test–Retest

A test–retest correlation of .70 was reported for 23 respondents interviewed 6–12 months after the initial interview.

Validity

Convergent

The scale's items were initially "validated" in terms of their higher correlation (at the .005 significance level) with avowed happiness. The overall MUNSH scale correlated .67 with avowed happiness, compared to .50, .55, and .49 for three alternative scales of well-being, and showed much internal consistency, indicating discriminant validity as well.

Location

Kozma, A., & Stones, M. J. (1980). The measurement of happiness: Development of the Memorial University of Newfoundland Scale of Happiness (MUNSH). *Journal of Gerontology,* **35,** 906–912.

Results and Comments

The authors were looking forward to extending their results to respondents in Toronto and London (Ontario) and Buffalo (New York) and to collecting further data on the scale's discriminant validity.

"Happiness" is part of the title of this scale because it was validated against self-ratings of happiness. It could be argued, however, that the scale is actually a more general measure of subjective well-being because it includes the following four subscales: Positive Affect, Negative Affect, General Positive Experience, and General Negative Experience.

The MUNSH Scale

We would like to ask you some questions about how things have been going. Please answer "Yes" if a statement is true for you and "No" if it does not apply to you. In the past months have you been feeling:

(1) On top of the world? (PA)

1	2	3
YES	NO	DON'T KNOW

(2) In high spirits? (PA)

(3) Particularly content with your life? (PA)

(4) Lucky? (PA)

(5) Bored? (NA)

(6) Very lonely or remote from other people? (NA)

(7) Depressed or very unhappy? (NA)

(8) Flustered because you didn't know what was expected of you? (NA)

(9) Bitter about the way your life has turned out? (NA)

(10) Generally satisfied with the way your life has turned out? (PA)

The next 14 questions have to do with more general life experiences:

(11) This is the dreariest time of my life. (NE)

(12) I am just as happy as when I was younger. (PE)

(13) Most of the things I do are boring or monotonous. (NE)

(14) The things I do are as interesting to me as they ever were. (PE)

(15) As I look back on my life, I am fairly well satisfied. (PE)

(16) Things are getting worse as I get older. (NE)

(17) How much do you feel lonely? (NE)

(18) Little things bother me more this year. (NE)

(19) If you could live where you wanted, where would you live? (PE)

(20) I sometimes feel that life isn't worth living. (NE)

(21) I am as happy now as I was when I was younger. (PE)

(22) Life is hard for me most of the time. (NE)

(23) How satisfied are you with your life today? (PE)

(24) My health is the same or better than most people my age. (PE)

Note: PA, Positive affect; NA, negative affect; PE, positive experience; NE, negative experience. Scoring: Yes = 2; Don't know = 1; No = 0. Item 19: Present location = 2; other locations = 0. Item 23: Satisfied = 2; not satisfied = 0. MUNSH Total = PA − NA + PE − NE.

Affectometer 2

(Kammann & Flett, 1983)

Variable

Affectometer 2 is a measure of general happiness based on the balance of positive and negative feelings in recent experience.

Description

This is a 40-item self-report scale patterned most closely on Bradburn's Affect Balance Scale, but using a frequency response scale rather than a "yes–no" format. Its items were empirically selected from an initial pool of 435 adjectives and sentences and are mainly a subset of the 96-item Affectometer 1. Four items were chosen from these measures to represent each of ten categories: confluence, optimism, self-esteem, self-efficacy, social support, social interest, freedom, energy, cheerfulness, and thought clarity.

Scale scores apparently run from −200 (low happiness) to +200 (high happiness), based on responses to the 20 statements and the 20 adjectives.

Sample

The scale was developed based on a random sample of 110 adults in Dunedin, New Zealand.

Data on mean scores were not reported.

Reliability

Internal Consistency

A coefficient α of .95 is reported, with a median item–total correlation of .57.

Test–Retest

Estimated test–retest reliability (based on Affectometer 1 studies) was .80 for a 2-week period; over an 8-month period it was estimated at .53.

Validity

Convergent

The Affectometer 2 correlated $-.84$ with the Beck Depression Inventory (BDI) and, as predicted, the negative items correlated more highly with the BDI than the positive items. The earlier Affectometer 1 correlated between .63 and .75 with several measures of happiness and neuroticism and loaded highest (.88) on the strong first factor emerging from factor analysis.

Discriminant

Although no data on discriminant validity were reported for the present inventory, Affectometer 1 scores were found to correlate between .22 and .37 with three measures of response set.

Location

Kammann, R., & Flett, R. (1983). Affectometer 2: A scale to measure current level of general happiness. *Australian Journal of Psychology, 35,* 259–265.

Results and Comments

The shorter Affectometer 2 scale has a "comparable" coefficient α to that of Affectometer 1. Unlike Bradburn's ABS, the Affectometer's negative and positive affect scales correlate $-.66$.

   More details on the earlier Affectometer research can be found in "The analysis and measurement of happiness as a sense of well-being," an unpublished paper by Kammann *et al.* available from the Department of Psychology at the University of Otago in New Zealand.

Affectometer 2

(CO)   1. My life is on the right track.

NOT AT ALL	OCCASIONALLY	SOME OF THE TIME	OFTEN	ALL OF THE TIME
1	2	3	4	5

(CO)   2. I wish I could change some part of my life.
(O+)   3. My future looks good.
(O−)   4. I feel as though the best years of my life are over.
(SE+)   5. I like myself.
(SE−)   6. I feel there must be something wrong with me.
(SF+)   7. I can handle any problems that come up.
(SF−)   8. I feel like a failure.
(SS+)   9. I feel loved and trusted.

(SS−)	10.	I seem to be left alone when I don't want to be.
(SI+)	11.	I feel close to people around me.
(SI−)	12.	I have lost interest in other people and don't care about them.
(F+)	13.	I feel I can do whatever I want to.
(F−)	14.	My life seems stuck in a rut.
(E+)	15.	I have energy to spare.
(E−)	16.	I can't be bothered doing anything.
(Ch+)	17.	I smile and laugh a lot.
(Ch−)	18.	Nothing seems very much fun any more.
(TC+)	19.	I think clearly and creatively.
(TC−)	20.	My thoughts go around in useless circles.

Adjective items

	Positive (+)		Negative (−)
(CO)	21. Satisfied		31. Discontented
(O)	22. Optimistic		32. Hopeless
(SE)	23. Useful		33. Insignificant
(SF)	24. Confident		34. Helpless
(SS)	25. Understood		35. Lonely
(SI)	26. Loving		36. Withdrawn
(F)	27. Free-and-easy		37. Tense
(E)	28. Enthusiastic		38. Depressed
(Ch)	29. Good-natured		39. Impatient
(TC)	30. Clear-headed		40. Confused

Note: The symbols + and − indicate positive and negative affect items. (CO), Confluence; (O), optimism; (SF), self-esteem; (SE), self-efficacy; (SS), social support; (SI), social interest; (F), freedom; (E), energy; (Ch), cheerfulness; (TC), thought clarity.

The PSYCHAP Inventory

(Fordyce, 1986)

Variable

This scale was designed to measure happiness in general populations by examining an individual's status on other facets of happiness.

Description

This inventory comes in two sets, each with two equivalent forms of 80 items each, with no repeat items. Each item consists of a forced-choice statement, with answers to distinguish happy from unhappy people. In addition to the total test score, subscales tap achieved happiness, happy personality, happy attitudes and values, and happiness lifestyle; all subscales were derived conceptually and not empirically.

Forms A and B are the original, most equivalent pair; forms C and D have been more recently developed to produce a greater range of responses and scores less skewed in the happiness direction. Items were developed from a larger pool of items asked of an adult community college sample and were chosen on the basis of their correlation with a previously validated two-item happiness measure and a depression measure.

Scores vary from 6 (low happiness) to 80 (high happiness) on each form.

Sample

Normative data were obtained from 437 adult community college students from forms A and B and from 527 students for forms C and D. Average age was about 26 years and 80% came originally from areas outside of Florida.

The mean score for forms A and B was 55 (SD about 12) and for forms C and D was 45 (SD about 13.5).

Reliability

Internal Consistency

Parallel-forms reliability averaged .92, ranging from .86 to .95 and with subscale reliabilities in the high .70s to low .90s. Moreover, very stable internal consistency properties are reported.

Test–Retest

Test–retest correlations averaged .86 over a 2–3-week interval and .74 over a 3-month period.

Validity

Convergent

The four forms show average correlations of .65 with Fordyce's Happiness Index, of −.73 with the depression scale of the MAACL, of −.51 with the depression scale of the Profile of Mood states, of −.67 with the Depression Adjective Check List, of .72 with the Affectometer, and of −.68 with the IPAT depression scale. The author also cites several additional studies in which the scale has produced predictions in expected directions with variables such as self-esteem, health, love relationships, and extroversion. He also cites several studies in which the scale showed clear "known-groups" validity.

Discriminant

No data on discriminant validity were reported, although in about half of the studies reported, the scale correlated significantly with measures of social desirability. The author suggested that this might be appropriate.

Location

Fordyce, M. (1986). The Psychap Inventory: A multi-item test to measure happiness and
its concomitants. *Social Indicators Research,* **18,** 1–33. (A "materials package" can be
ordered from the author at Edison Community College, Fort Myers, Florida 33907.)

Results and Comments

The scale was formerly known as the Self-Description Inventory (SDI). It is designed to
be related to training courses in happiness skills developed by the author.

The author notes that the four subscales also show great overlap with each other,
although they also predict differential relations with outside variables as one would
predict.

Only a few items from Form D are presented here. All forms are available from the
author at the above address. All forms are copyrighted.

The PSYCHAP Inventory

Form D

DIRECTIONS:

The Psychap Inventory is a questionnaire that gives you the chance to describe
yourself and compare your personality to that of others.

Each item consists of two statements, a statement marked "A" and a statement
marked "B." Read each of the statements and decide which of the two describes
you better, then mark your choice on the answer sheet you've been given. If
statement "A" is true or more true of you than statement "B," blacken the "A"
answer slot. If statement "B" seems more like you, blacken the "B" answer slot on
the answer sheet. (An example of correct marking is shown below.) DO NOT make
answers or marks in this question booklet.

Columns Correctly
Marked

      a   b

1.

      a   b

2.

In most cases, you will find it easy to choose between the two statements.
Sometimes, however, you may feel both statements are somewhat true of you (or
that neither are). Even still, try and pick between them the one that is more like you

more of the time, for it is important to answer every question to get accurate feedback.

Also, the questions are meant to be answered in a general manner, not just based on how you feel today.

If you understand these directions, put your name and other information on the answer sheet and begin describing yourself, starting with item 1.

Sample Items

1. A. I'm very industrious.
   B. I'm not overly industrious.
2. A. I am content.
   B. I am not content.
3. A. I place a very strong value on my happiness.
   B. I don't place too strong a value on my happiness.
4. A. I'm pretty certain about where I'm going in life.
   B. Right now, I'm not too certain about where I'm going in life.
5. A. I don't have much time to spend in activities I enjoy.
   B. I spend most of my time in activities I enjoy.

Copyright, Dr. Michael W. Fordyce. These booklets are available from Cypress Lake Media, Suite 4, Cypress Lake Professional Center, 1178 Cypress Lake Drive, Fort Myers, Florida 33907.

Other Scales for Assessing Subjective Well-Being

There are a large number of scales of subjective well-being that are not described above. Among them, two sets are briefly noted here: (1) some promising new scales that have received little attention up to now, and (2) some classics that are rarely thought of as primary measures of subjective well-being, though perhaps they should be.

Two promising new scales have been proposed by Larsen, Diener, and their colleagues. One is called the Affect Intensity Measure (Larsen, 1983). It consists of 40 items that seek to assess the intensity (rather than the duration or frequency) with which individuals experience positive and negative emotions. The other is the Satisfaction With Life Scale, a 5-item measure of global well-being that seeks to tap only the cognitive component of evaluation (Diener, Emmons, Larsen, & Griffin, 1985).

Another promising new scale is an Index of Happiness developed by Fordyce (1977). This index is based on two items. One asks "In general, how happy or unhappy do you usually feel?" and is answered on a fully labeled 11-category response scale; the other asks people to report "On the average, what percent of the time do you feel happy, what percent of the time do you feel unhappy, and what percent of the time do you feel neutral?"

Among the "classic scales" not usually thought of as primary measures of subjective well-being, one should note the existence of a rich and well-developed tradition of measurement in the fields of personality psychology and psychiatry. While personality measures per se do not meet our definition for a subjective well-being measure, some of the concepts assessed in these fields do. Examples are anxiety and depression. The Hopkins Symptom Checklist (Derogatis, Lipman, Rickels, Uhlenhuth, & Covi, 1974) is a battery of items that includes widely used measures of both anxiety and depression. The Langner Index (Langner, 1962) has also been used to measure psychological well-being.

Recommendations

Given the large number of different measures of subjective well-being in the literature and the thousands of published studies that report their development and/or relationships to other variables, one might hope to make clear recommendations about which are the "best" measures of subjective well-being. That, however, is not possible.

There are several reasons. First, what would be "best" (if that could be determined) for one theoretical purpose, or for one type of respondent, or within one set of resource constraints would not be optimal in other circumstances. Second, the nature of assessing subjective well-being makes it infeasible to try all the different measures of global well-being on the same set of respondents: People would object to being asked similar questions repeatedly. While a few different measures of the same concept can be used together, this provides only a slow accumulation of comparative information. Third, despite the large number of studies of subjective well-being, relatively few investigators have given high priority to investigating the measurement properties of the subjective well-being scales they used. Given that a measure works at least reasonably well, it has generally seemed more important to investigate substantive matters than methodological ones.

However, several general comments can be made about the quality of subjective well-being measures. These are followed by more detailed discussion of some of the criteria and by references to empirical analyses in which the psychometric properties of some scales of subjective well-being have been compared.

Some General Comments

Each of the scales described above should work reasonably well when administered by skilled interviewers to cooperative respondents of the type for which the scale was designed and when used to measure the aspects of subjective well-being that it does in fact reflect. Of course, the measures based on just a single item tend to include more measurement error than those based on multiple items, but this is to be expected; the researcher designing an instrument must make decisions between measurement precision and economy in data collection. As is discussed below, some studies need greater precision than others and/or can afford to achieve greater precision.

Several sophisticated comparative studies of the psychometric properties of certain subjective well-being scales are very useful for providing general ideas about the measurement quality one can expect. Quantitative statements about this are included in the subsections that follow. However, extensive tables showing various validity and reliability coefficients do not appear because, as yet, there is relatively little convergence with regard to which scale is best: Results of one study that show a given scale being a little better than others tend not to be replicated in other studies. Nevertheless, for those who care to look, references are given to some of the more significant psychometric studies.

The considerations that we believe should govern one's choice of a measure of subjective well-being are the following:

1. What is the specific concept of subjective well-being that is to be measured? This is a broad theoretical concern.
2. What is the availability of financial resources and interviewing time? How much can/should one burden the respondents? How much precision is really needed? To what extent does one need to compare one's new results with findings from the past and/or with relevant "norms"? These are all practical considerations that must be taken into account.

3. Given the general absence of replicable comparative advantages of one scale over another, what general psychometric results can one use to help in choosing a scale? The matters of skew and number of scale points are surely among them.

Each of these considerations receives more detailed discussion in the sections that follow.

Considerations for Choosing Scales

Theoretical Considerations

An obvious and crucial concern is to be clear with regard to the concept one intends the scale to reflect and to choose a scale designed to indicate that concept.

One theme of this chapter is that subjective well-being is a broad notion consisting of various components, some or all of which may be interrelated. As yet there is no consensus on how one should identify those components, but several schemes have been described in preceding sections of this chapter. The affect-and-cognition approach is one that has proved useful; so also is the well-being and ill-being approach. (Combining the two provides four possible sets including positive and negative affect and positive and negative cognition; only some of these have been investigated.) Other ways of conceptualizing the area are illustrated in the preceding discussions of the factors inherent in the PGC Morale Scale and in the Life Satisfaction Index A.

Given the sensitizing nature of the past 20 years of research, one should decide between general measures of subjective well-being, such as is provided by the Delighted–Terrible Scale or the Ladder Scale, and more focused assessments of affect (e.g., happiness or depression) or of assessments of cognition (e.g., satisfaction). Unfortunately, as noted above, satisfaction measures seem not to be pure indicators of cognition but reflect some affect as well. Pure measures of cognition are only now beginning to receive attention (Diener *et al.*, 1985).

While it seems important to be aware of distinctions among different measures of subjective well-being, one may ask how important are those distinctions. The answer here depends, at least in part, on one's reasons for measuring subjective well-being. If the study merely seeks a crude differentiation among people with regard to their subjective well-being, the precise composition of the measure one chooses may be unimportant. All of the subjective well-being measures described above (and numerous others as well) tend to show somewhat similar results across groups or across times. Stones and Kozma (1985), for example, have shown that many subjective well-being scales load substantially on a single general factor. However, if one is pursuing a more exact, fine-grained investigation, then choice of the theoretically relevant measure becomes important. For example, as noted previously, what one concludes about levels of subjective well-being across the age range apparently depends on the measure one uses. If one doesn't know which measure will theoretically be most relevant, an obvious though more expensive solution is to use several different measures.

A second conceptual consideration has to do with the global versus specific dimension of subjective well-being. One must decide whether one wants assessments of *global* subjective well-being (i.e., about life-as-a-whole) or about subjective well-being with regard to specific life concerns/domains (and if so, which concerns). These are not mutually exclusive choices, and many studies opt for both global and specific assessments.

A third conceptual matter is the importance (or lack of importance) in a particular study of understanding how respondents come to report whatever level of subjective well-being they do. The two "explanations" described above (the gap/ratio approach and the social psychological influences approach) provide one perspective. If a study is to compare the subjective well-being of different groups of respondents and/or monitor changes in subjective well-being over time, it may be important not only to measure subjective well-being itself but also to measure some of the relevant factors (aspirations, perceived achievements, various social psychological factors, etc.) that are presumed to affect subjective well-being.

Practical Considerations

In addition to the theoretical considerations discussed above, practical considerations do, and should, influence the design of empirical research, including one's choice of a measure of subjective well-being.

One of the reasons single-item measures of subjective well-being have been widely used is their economy: They take less time to administer than does a 10-, 20-, or 40-item scale. While it is widely acknowledged that a single-item measure usually provides a less precise indication of a given individual's subjective well-being than a multi-item measure, whether this is important depends on one's purposes. Individual-level precision is important if one is doing relational analysis or making predictions or recommendations for particular individuals; it is much less important if one's primary goal is simply to report an average level of subjective well-being for a large group, to compare groups, or to monitor changes in levels of subjective well-being over time for a group.

One also needs to consider the nature of the respondents. Some of the subjective well-being scales discussed above were developed for use on elderly individuals (the PGC Morale Scale, the LSIA, the LSIZ) and would not be appropriate, or would need to be adapted, for use with general populations.

Another practical consideration is the relative need for comparative data from prior studies. If one wants to compare one's new results with "norms" for general population samples from any of a substantial number of nations, or subgroups in certain nations, one should choose a subjective well-being measure that has been used on that particular group in the past. Preceding portions of this chapter should be helpful in guiding one to relevant studies.

After reviewing the literature on happiness, Veenhoven (1984a) proposed four "working rules" for enhancing the quality of data about happiness (presumably the rules would also apply to other aspects of subjective well-being): (1) Self-ratings are to be preferred over ratings by others, (2) anonymous questionnaires work better than personal interviews, (3) the context of the question should focus clearly on overall ratings of life-as-a-whole, and (4) questions should leave room for "no answer" or "don't know" responses. Our own experience in measuring subjective well-being is, in general, in accord with Veenhoven's rules, but we would add that the third rule (focusing on life-as-a-whole) applies only if one's interest is at the global level; good measures can also be obtained of more specific life concerns or domains.

Psychometric Considerations

Validity   The validity of a measure is the extent to which it reflects the concept it is intended to reflect. Substantial validity is a necessity for any measure. Estimating the validity of measures of attitudes, including measures of subjective well-being, however, poses severe challenges. The problem is that there is no independent "external" indicator of an attitude with which one's attitude measure can be compared. The title of one article puts this succinctly: "If you want to know how happy I am, you'll have to ask me" (Irwin, Kammann, & Dixon, 1979).

With respect to measures of subjective well-being, several general strategies have been pursued for estimating validity. One strategy, subsequently abandoned, was to attempt to show that subjective well-being had strong covariation with various "objective" indicators of well-being. But investigators found that the covariation was often rather weak: Satisfaction with housing did not vary strongly with house size or elegance; satisfaction with neighborhood safety was not highly correlated with crime rates; etc. It was concluded the low linkages often were due not to big measurement problems with the subjective well-being measures, but to their reflecting something different from what the "objective" measures indicated. [A detailed discussion appears in Andrews (1981); some of the reasons subjective well-being measures reflect different things have to do with aspirations, a topic discussed previously in this chapter.]

A second strategy has been to show that subjective well-being measures are well-behaved in the sense that they relate highly to one another and are reasonably stable over short periods of time. These are reliability criteria (and are discussed below) but do not directly address the validity question.

A third strategy has been to show that subjective well-being measures are responsive to certain changes in people's lives. Example: People who develop serious health problems "should" become less satisfied with their health, at least in the short term. Several elegant analyses (e.g., Atkinson, 1982; Headey, Holström, & Wearing, 1984b; Martinson, Wilkening, & Linn, 1985) show that the expected changes do tend to occur, thereby lending support to the validity of the subjective well-being measures. And as Robinson (1969) noted, the groups in society that report lowest satisfaction or happiness also tend to be those with the highest suicide rates or other "escape" behaviors (e.g., taking drugs).

A fourth strategy has been to perform a latent-variable causal modeling analysis using multimethod–multitrait data to estimate construct validity directly. The logic here is that the latent variables represent individuals' "true" levels of subjective well-being, or identifiable sources of random or correlated measurement error, and that the observed relationships among a set of measures can be explained by the relationships among the latent variables and the strength of their causal impacts on the observed measures. Andrews and Crandall (1976; also Andrews & Withey, 1976) applied this estimation technique to 35 measures of subjective well-being and found that the better measures had estimated construct validities in the .7–.8 range (i.e., that half to two-thirds of the total variance in a measure reflected the intended well-being concept). The "better" measures included those assessed using several of the scales discussed previously in this chapter: the seven-point Delighted–Terrible Scale, the Seven-point Satisfaction Scale used by Campbell *et al.* (1976), the Faces Scale, and the Ladder Scale. These validity results compare well with validity estimates for a broad range of other survey-based measures, for which median validities were about .7 (Andrews, 1984).

Reliability   Reliability is the extent to which two or more measures intended to tap the same concept agree with one another. Reliability is used as a quality indicator for measures because it is usually assumed that if two measures of the same concept are highly correlated with one another this is because both measures are reflecting the intended concept to a substantial degree. While this will usually be the case, it is also possible that the agreement between the measures arises from their both reflecting something other than the intended concept (i.e., from correlated error). In such a situation reliability might be high, but validity low.

There are two kinds of reliability that have been considered in evaluating measures of subjective well-being: homogeneity reliability and stability reliability.

Homogeneity reliability is the extent to which two or more measures taken at about the same time agree with one another. It is usually expressed either as the (average) correlation coefficient among the measures or as a "reliability coefficient." Among the reliability coefficients, coefficient α (Cronbach, 1951) is the most commonly used, but there are others. Reliability coefficients estimate how well the items, after being combined into a scale, would reflect the intended concept assuming there were no correlated error. This is expressed as a percentage of the scale score variance that represents true score variance. Of course, homogeneity reliability can be computed only for scales that are based on more than a single measure.

Coefficient α values for the multi-item scales described previously tend to fall in the range .7–.9; the longer scales tend to have the higher α values (as would be expected if all items were about equally related to one another, which tends to be the case).

Stability reliability is the extent to which two identical measures of the same concept taken at different points in time (on the same individuals) agree with one another. It is usually expressed as a simple correlation coefficient and is interpretable as an indicator of measurement quality only if it is reasonable to assume that the concept itself did not change between the two measurements. Stability reliability coefficients have been reported in several studies of subjective well-being, and the time intervals between measurements have usually ranged from 10–20 minutes up to about 8 months. Of course, as the time interval lengthens, the likelihood of real change having occurred increases (and hence correlations decrease). Stability reliability coefficients for subjective well-being measures tend to range from .5 to .7, with the lower values typically being obtained from the longer intervals.

Number of Scale Points The number of scale points (i.e., answer categories) in a measure has a direct effect on the extent to which the measure can reflect the actual variation that exists in a population. Short scales (two- or three-point scales) tend to capture less of the variation than do longer scales (five or more points). Scales with 7–11 points, however, reflect virtually all of the variation that exists, so little is to be gained by lengthening a scale still further.

The exact percentages of variation reflected by response scales of different lengths depend on the shape of the distribution in the population and how the scale categories match that distribution. However, given a reasonably "normal" distribution and an optimal match-up, the following figures result: two-point scales reflect roughly 67% of the underlying variation; three-point scales, roughly 80%, four-point scales, roughly 90%; five-point scales, roughly 95%; seven-point scales, roughly 97%; 11-point scales, roughly 99% (e.g., Cochran, 1968; Cox, 1980). In an empirical estimation of validities, Andrews (1984) showed that response scales having more categories tended to yield measures with higher validities.

The implications for choosing a measure of subjective well-being are clear but need to be considered in the light of competing criteria. Other things being equal, it is desirable to choose a measure based on a response scale that has at least five (better, seven) answer categories. This will be especially important for measures based on just one or two items. The "standard" three-point happiness measures clearly violate this recommendation, but many of the other scales described above, including the Delighted–Terrible, seven-point Satisfaction, Faces, Mountain, and Ladder scales, are in accord with it.

Competing criteria, however, also need consideration. Response scales with fewer than five–seven answer categories may be easier to administer, especially to older respondents and/or over the telephone. Ultimately, the study designer has to balance ease of administration against loss in precision. Pilot tests of various measures of subjective well-being on people similar to the intended respondents may provide useful guidance.

Distribution, Skew   The final psychometric consideration concerns the distribution and skew of scores obtained from the measure of subjective well-being. Most studies find respondents giving predominantly positive responses to questions on subjective well-being. Few respondents remain chronically unhappy or dissatisfied. Skew may be a problem because many statistical techniques assume that distributions are "normally" distributed. Although many techniques work well despite modest departures from normality (i.e., they work well on practically any unimodal and reasonably symmetrical distribution), severe skews and/or marked multimodality may cause significant problems. It follows that if the data are to receive extensive statistical analysis, using measures of subjective well-being that are well behaved distributionally will simplify the analysis and its interpretation.

A second argument in favor of choosing subjective well-being measures that yield distributions that are not heavily skewed has to do with discrimination power. If a large proportion of respondents all receive the same score on a measure, it is not possible to differentiate among them. This can be a problem if one wants to do an extensive analysis; it may not be a concern if the study's goal is simple description (e.g., to show that about 60% of people are "completely satisfied" with their marriage) (Campbell *et al.,* 1976).

Of course, the distribution produced by a given response scale depends partly on the definition of the scale categories, and partly on the aspect of subjective well-being being assessed. Assessments of marriage tend to produce highly skewed distributions on a satisfaction scale, but satisfaction with income tends to show a more nearly normal distribution.

The response categories of the Delighted–Terrible Scale were deliberately chosen in an attempt to reduce the substantial skews that tend to characterize satisfaction scales. Certain other scales (the Ladder, Faces, and Mountain scales) also tend to produce measures with more symmetrical distributions.

Reviews of Subjective Well-Being Scales

The literature on subjective well-being includes few comprehensive reviews of a large number of scales. Furthermore, most existing reviews consider only a few of the potentially relevant quality criteria. Nevertheless, as indicated above, these reviews do provide some basic quantitative assessments of the quality of subjective well-being measures and show that subjective well-being can be measured with substantial validity and reliability.

As also noted above, the fine-grained differences among subjective well-being measures in relative quality tend not to be well replicated from one psychometric assessment to another. This is at least partly attributable to reviewers using different combinations of subjective well-being measures, different types of respondents, and different assessment criteria. It is also probably attributable to the fact that the better scales, including those described above, do not differ radically in measurement quality: All are pretty good; none seem *markedly* better than the others.

Reviews that are relatively recent, at least somewhat sophisticated with respect to measurement criteria, and examine more than just a few subjective well-being measures include the following: Andrews and Crandall (1976); also reported in Andrews and Withey (1976), Carp and Carp (1983), Connidis (1984), Diener (1984), George and Bearon (1980), Kammann *et al.* (1984), Larsen, Diener, and Emmons (1985), Lohmann (1977), and Stones and Kozma (1985). Those who seek comparative information on factor structures, reliabilities, and/or validities will find such information in these reviews.

Future Research Directions

Over the past quarter-century much has been learned about specific concepts that fit within the general realm of subjective well-being, and substantial progress has been made with regard to developing measures of those concepts. These measures, in turn, have made possible numerous descriptive studies of the subjective well-being of a wide range of different populations and demographically defined groups. Key portions of the conceptual, measurement development, and descriptive work are summarized in preceding sections of this chapter. Among the problems that remain relatively unexplored, however, are issues concerning the causes (i.e., generation) of subjective well-being, including appropriate causal models, relevant social policies, and matters of time lags and change.

The causes of happiness may be one of the oldest of philosophical issues and is also one of the most central to humankind. Although it is unlikely that the issue will (or should) be fully resolved by social scientists, one would hope that modern social science might have new knowledge and insights to contribute. In the current parlance of empirical research, what is needed are causal models that can explain the interrelationships among measures of subjective well-being, and the interrelationships between well-being measures and the social and psychological factors that we suspect may influence well-being. Some of the research in this area was briefly summarized in the first major section of this chapter, but much remains to be accomplished at both the basic and applied levels.

At the macro–applied level of social policymaking, the usefulness of subjective well-being measures has yet to be compellingly demonstrated to policymakers. Although it is true that some social impact statements are partially based on measures of subjective well-being (and some social scientists see this use of well-being measures as a "growth industry"), it also is true that many governments and international organizations were doing less in the late 1980s with regard to any form of social indicators, including indicators of subjective well-being, than was the case 10 years previously. The role of subjective well-being measures in social policymaking needs to be further explored and developed.

Part of the task in doing this will be to sort out the issue of time lags. There are two perspectives that pervade theoretical discussions of subjective well-being. One focuses on change: If conditions get better, subjective well-being will increase; if things deteriorate, well-being will decline. The other perspective, however, emphasizes stability achieved through adaptation and comparison: People adapt to their circumstances (at least within broad limits); people accommodate themselves to what is available; people compare themselves to others, or to themselves at prior times, or to their ideals (which may themselves adapt). Interesting research has demonstrated both the change and the stability perspectives, and there is as yet no widely accepted unifying theory that incorporates both perspectives. The time lag over which one considers change or accommodation may hold part of the answer, but that remains to be examined.

It is unrealistic to expect that great issues such as these will be resolved in the short term, but now that a substantial set of reasonably good measures of subjective well-being exists, as documented in this chapter, it is not unreasonable to hope that progress can be made in relating those measures to a variety of socially important causes and consequences.

Bibliography

Abbey, A., & Andrews, F. M. (1985). Modeling the psychological determinants of life quality. *Social Indicators Research,* **16**(1), 1–34.

Adams, D. (1969). Analysis of a life satisfaction index. *Journal of Gerontology*, **24**, 470–474.

Allart, E., & Uusitalo, H. (1977). *Questionnaire and code book of the Scandinavian Welfare Survey in 1972* (Research Report No. 14 of the Research Group for Comparative Sociology.) Helsinki: University of Helsinki.

Andrews, F. M. (1981). Objective social indicators, subjective social indicators, and social account systems. In F. T. Juster & K. C. Land (Eds.), *Social accounting systems* (pp. 377–419). New York: Academic Press.

Andrews, F. M. (1984). Construct validity and error components of survey measures: A structural modeling approach. *Public Opinion Quarterly*, **48**, 409–442.

Andrews, F. M., & Crandall, R. (1976). The validity of measures of self-reported well-being. *Social Indicators Research*, **3**, 1–19.

Andrews, F. M., & Inglehart, R. F. (1979). The structure of subjective well-being in nine western societies. *Social Indicators Research*, **6**(1), 73–90.

Andrews, F. M., & McKennell, A. C. (1980). Measures of self-reported well-being: Their affective, cognitive, and other components. *Social Indicators Research*, **8**, 127–155.

Andrews, F. M., & Withey, S. B. (1974). Developing measures of perceived life quality: Results from several national surveys. *Social Indicators Research*, **1**(1), 1–26.

Andrews, F. M., & Withey, S. B. (1976). *Social indicators of well-being: American's perceptions of life quality*. New York: Plenum.

Atkinson, T. (1981). Public perceptions of the quality of life. *Perspective Canada III*. Ottawa: Statistics Canada.

Atkinson, T. (1982). The stability and validity of quality of life measures. *Social Indicators Research*, **10**(2), 113–132.

Blishen, B., & Atkinson, T. (1980). Anglophone and francophone differences in perceptions of the quality of life in Canada. In A. Szalai & F. M. Andrews (Eds.), *The quality of life: Comparative studies* (pp. 25–39). London: Sage.

Bradburn, N. M. (1969). *The structure of psychological well-being*. Chicago: Aldine.

Campbell, A. (1981). *The sense of well-being in America*. New York: McGraw-Hill.

Campbell, A., Converse, P. E., & Rodgers, W. L. (1976). *The quality of American life: Perceptions, evaluations, and satisfactions*. New York: Russell Sage Foundation.

Cantril, H. (1967). *The pattern of human concerns*. New Brunswick, NJ: Rutgers Univ. Press.

Caplan, R. D., Andrews, F. M., Conway, T. L., Abbey, A., Abramis, D. J., & French, J. R. P., Jr. (1985). Social effects of Diazepam use: A longitudinal field study. *Social Science and Medicine*, **21**, 887–898.

Carp, F. M., & Carp, A. (1983). Structural stability of well-being factors across age and gender, and development of scales of well-being unbiased for age and gender. *Journal of Gerontology*, **38**, 572–581.

Cherlin, A., & Reeder, L. G. (1975). The dimensions of psychological well-being. *Sociological Methods and Research*, **4**, 189–214.

Cochran, W. G. (1968). The effectiveness of adjustment by subclassification in removing bias in observational studies. *Biometrics*, **24**, 295–313.

Connidis, I. (1984). The construct validity of the Life Satisfaction Index A and Affect Balance Scales: A serendipitous analysis. *Social Indicators Research*, **15**, 117–130.

Costa, P. T., Jr., & McCrae, R. R. (1980). Influence of extraversion and neuroticism on subjective well-being: Happy and unhappy people. *Journal of Personality and Social Psychology*, **38**, 668–678.

Cronbach, L. J. (1951). Coefficient Alpha and the internal structure of tests. *Psychometrika*, **16**, 297–334.

Cox, E. P., III (1980). The optimal number of response alternatives for a scale: A review. *Journal of Marketing Research*, **17**, 407–422.

Davis, E. E., Fine-Davis, M., & Meehan, G. (1982). Demographic determinants of perceived well-being in eight European countries. *Social Indicators Research*, **10**(4), 341–35.

Davis, J. A. (1984). New money, an old man/lady, and "two's company": Subjective welfare in the NORC General Social Surveys, 1972–1982. *Social Indicators Research*, **15**(4), 319–350.

Derogatis, L. R., Lipman, R. S., Rickels, K., Uhlenhuth, E. H., & Covi, L. (1974). The Hopkins

Symptom Checklist (HSCL): A measure of primary symptom dimensions. In P. Pichot (Ed.), *Psychological measurements in modern psychopharmacology: Modern problems in pharmacopsychiatry* (Vol. 7) (pp. 79–110). Karger: Basel.

Diener, E. (1984). Subjective well-being. *Psychological Bulletin,* **95,** 542–575.

Diener, E., & Emmons, R. A. (1985). The independence of positive and negative affect. *Journal of Personality and Social Psychology,* **47**(5), 1105–1117.

Diener, E., & Griffin, S. (1982). *Subjective well-being: Happiness, life satisfaction, and morale—Comprehensive bibliography.* Champaign: University of Illinois, Department of Psychology.

Diener, E., & Larsen, R. J. (1984). Temporal stability and cross-situational consistency of positive and negative affect. *Journal of Personality and Social Psychology,* **47,** 871–883.

Diener, E., Emmons, A., Larsen, R. J., & Griffin, S. (1985). The satisfaction with life scale: A measure of life satisfaction. *Journal of Personality Assessment,* **49,** 71–75.

Emmons, R. A., & Diener, E. (1985a). Factors predicting satisfaction judgments: A comparative examination. *Social Indicators Research,* **16**(2), 157–168.

Emmons, R. A., & Diener, E. (1985b). Personality correlates of subjective well-being. *Personality and Social Psychology Bulletin,* **11,** 89–97.

Fazio, A. F. (1977). *A concurrent validational study of the NCHS General Well-Being Schedule* (Dept. of H.E.W. Publ. No. HRA-78-1347). Hyattsville, MD: National Center for Health Statistics.

Flett, R. (1986). *Subjective well-being: Its measurement and correlates.* Ph.D. dissertation, University of Otago, Dunedin, New Zealand.

Fordyce, M. W. (1977). *The happiness measures.* Unpublished paper available from the author at Edison Community College, Fort Myers, FL.

Fordyce, M. W. (1986). The PSYCHAP Inventory: A multi-item test to measure happiness and its concomitants. *Social Indicators Research,* **18,** 1–33.

Gallup, G. H. (1976). Human needs and satisfaction: A global survey. *Public Opinion Quarterly,* **40,** 459–467.

George, L. K. (1981). Subjective well-being: Conceptual and methodological issues. *Annual Review of Gerontology and Geriatrics,* **2,** 345–382.

George, L. K., & Bearon, L. B. (1980). *Quality of life in older persons: Meaning and measurement.* New York: Human Sciences Press.

Gurin, G., Veroff, J., & Feld, S. (1960). *Americans view their mental health.* New York: Basic.

Headey, B. (1981). The quality of life in Australia. *Social Indicators Research,* **9**(2), 155–182.

Headey, B., Glowacki, T., Holström, E., & Wearing, A. (1985). Modeling change in perceived quality of life. *Social Indicators Research,* **17**(3), 267–298.

Headey, B., Holström, E., & Wearing, A. (1984a). Well-being and ill-being: Different dimensions? *Social Indicators Research,* **14**(2), 115–140.

Headey, B., Holström, E., & Wearing, A. (1984b). The impact of life events and changes in domain satisfaction on well-being. *Social Indicators Research,* **15**(3), 203–228.

Headey, B., Holström, E., & Wearing, A. (1985). Models of well-being and ill-being. *Social Indicators Research,* **17**(3), 211–234.

Herzog, A. R., & Rodgers, W. (1981). Age and satisfaction. *Research on Aging,* **3,** 142–165.

Herzog, A. R., & Rodgers, W. (1986). Satisfaction among older adults. In F. M. Andrews (Ed.), *Research on the quality of life.* Ann Arbor: University of Michigan, Institute for Social Research.

Horley, J., & Little, B. R. (1985). Affective and cognitive components of global subjective well-being measures. *Social Indicators Research,* **17**(2), 189–198.

Hox, J. J. (1986). *Het gebruik van hulptheorieen by operationalisering [Using auxiliary theories for operationalization: A study of the construct 'subjective well-being'].* Ph.D. dissertation, University of Amsterdam, Department of Education.

Inglehart, R., & Rabier, J. R. (1986). Aspirations adapt to situations—but why are the Belgians so much happier than the French? In F. M. Andrews (Ed.), *Research on the quality of life.* Ann Arbor: University of Michigan, Institute for Social Research.

Irwin, R., Kammann, R., & Dixon, G. (1979). If you want to know how happy I am, you'll have to ask me. *New Zealand Psychologist,* **8,** 10–12.

Kammann, R., & Flett, R. (1983). Affectometer 2: A scale to measure current level of general happiness. *Australian Journal of Psychology*, **35**, 259–265.

Kammann, R., Christie, D., Irwin, R., & Dixon, G. (1979). Properties of an inventory to measure happiness (and psychological health). *New Zealand Psychologist*, **8**, 1–9.

Kammann, R., Farry, M., & Herbison, P. (1984). The analysis and measurement of happiness as a sense of well-being. *Social Indicators Research*, **15**(2), 91–116.

Kozma, A., & Stones, M. J. (1980). The measurement of happiness: Development of the Memorial University of Newfoundland Scale of Happiness (MUNSH). *Journal of Gerontology*, **35**, 906–912.

Kozma, A., & Stones, M. J. (1983). Predictors of happiness. *Journal of Gerontology*, **38**, 626–628.

Langner, T. S. (1962). A twenty-two item screening score of psychiatric symptoms indicating impairment. *Journal of Health and Human Behavior*, **3**, 269–276.

Larsen, R. J. (1983). *Manual for the affect intensity measure*. Unpublished manuscript, Department of Psychology, Purdue University, West Lafayette, IN.

Larsen, R. J., Diener, E., & Emmons, R. A. (1985). An evaluation of subjective well-being measures. *Social Indicators Research*, **17**(1), 1–18.

Larson, R. (1978). Thirty years of research on the subjective well-being of older Americans. *Journal of Gerontology*, **33**, 109–125.

Lawton, M. P. (1972). The dimensions of morale. In D. Kent, R. Kastenbaum, & S. Sherwood (Eds.), *Research, planning and action for the elderly* (pp. 145–165). New York: Behavioral Publications.

Lawton, M. P. (1975). The Philadelphia Center Morale Scale: A revision. *Journal of Gerontology*, **30**, 85–89

Lee, H., Kim, K. D., & Shinn, D. C. (1982). Perceptions of quality of life in an industrializing country: The case of the Republic of Korea. *Social Indicators Research*, **10**(3), 297–318.

Liang, J. (1984). Dimensions of the Life Satisfaction Index: A structural formulation. *Journal of Gerontology*, **39**, 613–622.

Liang, J., & Bollen, K. A. (1983). The structure of the Philadelphia Geriatric Center Morale Scale: A reinterpretation. *Journal of Gerontology*, **38**, 181–189.

Liang, J., & Bollen, K. A. (1985). Gender differences in the structure of the Philadelphia Geriatric Center Morale Scale. *Journal of Gerontology*, **40**, 468–477.

Lohmann, N. P. L. (1977). *Comparison on life satisfaction morale, and adjustment scales on an elderly population*. Ph.D. dissertation, Brandeis University, Waltham, MA.

Martinson, O. B., Wilkening, E. A., & Linn, J. G. (1985). Life change, health status and life satisfaction: A reconsideration. *Social Indicators Research*, **16**, 301–313.

Mason, R., & Faulkenberry, G. D. (1978). Aspirations, achievements, and life satisfactions. *Social Indicators Research*, **5**(2), 133–150.

McKennell, A. C., Atkinson, T., & Andrews, F. M. (1980). Structural constancies in surveys of perceived well-being. In A. Szalai & F. M. Andrews (Eds.), *The quality of life: Comparative studies* (pp. 111–128). London: Sage.

Michalos, A. (1980). Satisfaction and happiness. *Social Indicators Research*, **8**, 385–422.

Michalos, A. (1983). Satisfaction and happiness in a rural northern resource community. *Social Indicators Research*, **13**, 225–252.

Michalos, A. C. (1985). Multiple discrepancies theory (MDT). *Social Indicators Research*, **16**(4), 347–414.

Michalos, A. C. (1986a). Job satisfaction, marital satisfaction, and the quality of life: A review and a preview. In F. M. Andrews (Ed.), *Research on the quality of life* (pp. 57–83). Ann Arbor: University of Michigan Institute for Social Research.

Michalos, A. C. (1986b). An application of multiple discrepancies theory (MDT) to seniors. *Social Indicators Research*, **18**, 349–374.

Michalos, A. C. (1987). *Global report on student well-being: Applications of multiple discrepancies theory*. Unpublished final progress report, University of Guelph, Guelph, Ontario, Canada.

Neugarten, B. L., Havighurst, R. J., & Tobin, S. (1961). The measurement of life satisfaction. *Journal of Gerontology*, **16**, 134–143.

Ostrom, T. M. (1969). The relationship between affective, behavioral and cognitive components of attitude. *Journal of Experimental Psychology, 5,* 12–30.

Parducci, A. (1968). The relativism of absolute judgments. *Scientific American, 219*(6), 84–89.

Robinson, J. P. (1969). Life satisfaction and happiness. In J. P. Robinson & P. R. Shaver (Eds.), *Measures of social psychological attitudes* (pp. 11–41). Ann Arbor: University of Michigan, Institute for Social Research.

Shinn, D. C. (1986). Education and the quality of life in Korea and the United States: A cross-cultural perspective. *Public Opinion Quarterly, 50,* 360–369.

Shinn, D. C., Ahn, C., Kim, K., & Lee, H. (1983). Environmental effects on perceptions of life quality in Korea. *Social Indicators Research, 12,* 393–416.

Smith, T. W. (1979). Happiness: Time trends, seasonal variations, intersurvey differences and other mysteries. *Social Psychology Quarterly, 42,* 18–30.

Stein, L. (1964). Reciprocal action of reward and punishment mechanisms. In R. G. Heath (Ed.), *The role of pleasure in behavior.* New York: Harper & Row.

Stones, M. J., & Kozma, A. (1985). Structural relationships among happiness scales: A second order factorial study. *Social Indicators Research, 17*(1), 19–28.

Tatarkiewicz, W. (1976). *Analysis of happiness.* The Hague: Martinus Nijhoff.

Veenhoven, R. (1984a). *Conditions of happiness.* Dordrecht, Holland: Reidel.

Veenhoven, R. (1984b). *Databook of happiness.* Dordrecht, Holland: Reidel.

Veroff, J., Douvan, E., & Kulka, R. (1981). *The inner American: A self-portrait from 1957 to 1976.* New York: Basic.

Warr, P., Barter, J., & Brownbridge, G. (1983). On the independence of positive and negative affect. *Journal of Personality and Social Psychology, 44,* 644–651.

Wilson, W. (1967). Correlates of avowed happiness. *Psychological Bulletin, 67,* 294–306.

Wood, V., Wylie, M. L., & Sheafor, B. (1969). An analysis of a short self-report measure of life satisfaction: Correlation with rater judgment. *Journal of Gerontology, 24,* 465–469.

Wright, S. J. (1985). Health satisfaction: A detailed test of the Multiple Discrepancies Theory model. *Social Indicators Research, 17,* 299–313.

Zapf, W., & Glatzer, W. (1987). German social report: Living conditions and subjective well-being, 1978–1984. *Social Indicators Research, 19,* 1–171.

CHAPTER 4

Measures of Self-Esteem

Jim Blascovich and Joseph Tomaka

Self-esteem is a popular and important construct in the social sciences and in everyday life. The State of California has actually established a "Commission on Self-Esteem," presumably to devise and implement policies to increase feelings of self-worth among its citizens. Most Americans believe intuitively that "poor" or "low" self-esteem is undesirable, and indeed research links low self-esteem with loneliness (Peplau & Perlman, 1982), depression (Shaver & Brennan, this volume, Chap. 6), social anxiety (Leary, 1983), and alienation (Johnson, 1973).

The popular notion of self-esteem is straightforward. According to the dictionary definition, "To esteem a thing is to prize it, to set a high mental valuation upon it; when applied to persons, esteem carries also the warmer interest of approval, cordiality, and affection" (Williams, 1979, p. 309). In common parlance, then, self-esteem is the extent to which one prizes, values, approves, or likes oneself.

In the social sciences, self-esteem is a hypothetical construct that is quantified, for example, as the sum of evaluations across salient attributes of one's self or personality. It is the overall affective evaluation of one's own worth, value, or importance. This conception underlies the assumption that measuring attitudes toward, or evaluations of, one's self reflects a person's self-esteem. The concept of self-esteem goes by a variety of names (e.g., self-worth, self-regard, self-respect, self-acceptance) all of which are compatible with the dictionary definition of "esteem" ascribed to the self.

Regardless of the exact definition or label one chooses to employ, self-esteem is usually thought to be the evaluative component of a broader representation of self, the self-concept, the latter being a more inclusive construct than self-esteem, one that contains cognitive and behavioral components as well as affective ones. As a result, cognitions about the self (contained in the self-concept) may or may not influence self-esteem. For example, believing that one is a terrible singer may be a part of one's self-concept but may not bear any relation to one's feelings of self-worth. Feeling mildly or severely depressed because one cannot sing, however, is a matter of self-esteem, as is the behavioral consequence of jumping off the roof of an 18-story building to end one's humiliation over this deficiency.

According to current models of affect and attitudes (e.g., Frijda, 1986; Lazarus, 1984; Weiner, 1986), appraisals or judgments (e.g., "I'm attractive/unattractive," "intelligent/unintelligent," "hardworking/lazy") underlie positive or negative feelings about the self. To the extent that such evaluations cover a relatively broad spectrum of personal attributes, self-esteem is an appropriate label. Over time, consistency in such judgments results in a relatively stable affective appraisal that is readily accessible to the individual because of the salience of the self in everyday life. Narrower constructs such as self-confidence or body-esteem refer to narrower self-domains. Thus, self-esteem is more global than the evaluation of a specific attribute (e.g., height or academic ability) or a circumscribed set of related attributes (e.g., one's body or intelligence).

There is widespread acceptance of the psychological importance of self-esteem. Further, it is widely assumed that self-esteem is traitlike, thus self-esteem levels are consistent over time within individuals. Self-esteem is nearly as ubiquitous a construct as intelligence, but there is less agreement about how to measure it. Both self-esteem and intelligence are everyday trait concepts that psychologists attempt to quantify, and both are defined as much in terms of their measurement and correlates as in terms of well-developed theory. In fact "self-esteem has been related to almost every variable at one time or another" (Crandall, 1973, p. 45). This includes personality correlates such as happiness (Freedman, 1978) and shyness (Jones & Briggs, 1984); cognitive correlates such as self-serving attributional bias (Tennen & Herzberger, 1987); behavioral correlates such as task effort and persistence (Felson, 1984; McFarlin, Baumeister, & Blascovich, 1984); and clinical correlates such as depression (Tennen & Herzberger, 1987) and coping ability (S. E. Taylor, 1983).

Key Issues

Conceptual and methodological problems combine to make valid measurement of self-esteem difficult. Conceptual confusion is created by the fact that self-esteem, like other important concepts, is used in ordinary language and academic psychology concurrently (e.g., Blascovich & Ginsburg, 1978). Thus implicit, common-language notions of self-esteem are sometimes substituted for more precise, explicit, scientific definitions, creating the illusion of a universally accepted, well-defined, phenomenological entity (Wells & Marwell, 1976). The relatively recent call for a "standardized" measure of self-esteem (Greenwald, 1986), based on the assumption that a single measure would accommodate all needs, has only added to the confusion.

Although there is little dispute that global self-esteem involves self-evaluation, different hypothetical self-evaluation processes have been proposed (Wells & Marwell, 1976). Minimally, self-esteem is described simply as an attitude, the evaluative component of self-concept (Gergen, 1965; Rosenberg, 1965). More recent research (e.g., Fleming & Courtney, 1984; Shavelson, Hubner, & Stanton, 1976) has expanded this description to include "facets" of self-esteem, detailing in hierarchical fashion the more specific self-evaluational components and subcomponents that contribute to global self-esteem (e.g., math ability contributes to academic self-concept).

At a conceptually more complex level, self-esteem is thought to result from perceived discrepancies between actual and ideal self (Cohen, 1959). At an even more complex level, self-esteem is regarded as one's attitude toward the discrepancy between the actual and ideal self (Wells & Marwell, 1976).

Other writers concentrate less on the nature of the construct than on the adaptive and self-protective functions of self-esteem (Becker, 1973, 1975; Mossman & Ziller, 1968). For example, high self-esteem is hypothesized to protect the individual against environmental stressors (Ziller, Hagey, Smith, & Long, 1969) or even against the "terror" of facing mortality (Greenberg, Pyszczynski, & Solomon, 1986). Each of these approaches has important implications for strategies of self-esteem measurement.

Given the ultimately subjective nature of self-esteem, it has been measured almost exclusively by self-report. Indeed, it is difficult to conceive of a behavioral or physiological measure that would tap self-esteem directly. Considering the different theoretical approaches to the self-esteem construct as well as the vast number of studies in which self-esteem has been measured, it is not surprising that different measurement approaches have evolved. The relative merits of direct and indirect self-report measures have been debated (see Crandall, 1973). Some favor direct, face-valid questionnaires using items that are scored more or less additively (Levy, 1956; Wylie, 1961) while others favor more indirect measures using complexly scored questionnaires, using, for example, self–ideal discrepancy scores (Bills, Vance, & McLean, 1951; Miskimins & Braucht, 1971). Researchers apparently prefer the former. The use of simple self-report measures has increased dramatically while the use of more complex measures has declined. Self-esteem is typically measured in adults and adolescents by dichotomous or Likert-type responses to a number of questionnaire items, which are summed or scored to produce a self-esteem index. We are persuaded that the direct, self-report route is the most pragmatic.

Another issue concerns measurement specificity. For example, some (e.g., Rosenberg, 1965) argue that global self-evaluations hold the most predictive promise, while others (Marsh, Smith, & Barnes, 1983; Shavelson *et al.*, 1976) argue that more specific measures (i.e., based on facets of the self) are best. We do not take a stand regarding the specificity issue. Rather, we recommend that researchers choose a measure according to the level of specificity that seems theoretically justifiable and empirically sensitive. Thus five of the scales reviewed are general or global measures of self-esteem (e.g., the Rosenberg Scale and the Texas Social Behavior Inventory), while the remainder measure specific facets of self-esteem (e.g., the revised Janis and Field Feelings of Inadequacy Scale and the Tennessee Self-Concept Scale) or are specialized for children (Piers–Harris Children's Self-Concept Scale and the Self-Perception Profile for Children).

Self-esteem is best employed as a predictor or intervening (i.e., mediating or moderating) person variable, lending itself to correlational and other nonexperimental research designs. Like other person factors (e.g., intelligence, Type A behavior), self-esteem cannot be manipulated in a truly experimental manner, although participants in experiments can be chosen on the basis of self-esteem scores (e.g., Crocker, Thompson, McGraw, & Ingerman, 1987; Janis & Field, 1959; McFarlin & Blascovich, 1981). Since global self-esteem is a relatively stable characteristic, especially in adults, meaningful changes are difficult to detect when global self-esteem is employed as a dependent variable in an experiment. For example, experimentally manipulated success or failure experiences are unlikely to have any measurable impact when assessed against a lifetime of self-evaluative experiences. This inability to influence self-esteem in controlled settings creates a problem for researchers interested in testing variables hypothesized to influence levels of self-esteem or in evaluating interventions designed to raise self-esteem. Designing experiments to influence self-esteem in the laboratory, given that therapists and counselors have difficulty influencing the self-esteem of clients after years of rigorous interventions, presents a daunting challenge to researchers.

One approach to overcoming the problem of using self-esteem as a dependent variable is to focus on self-evaluations of very specific and/or novel attributes. For example, self-evaluations of one's ability to perform a certain arcane laboratory task might prove useful as a dependent measure in experiments because individual participants are unlikely to have a prior history of evaluating this specific ability. Of course, the rationale for such a procedure is based on theoretical associations between self-evaluations of specific attributes and overall self-esteem. Another strategy is to focus on threats to self-esteem. For example, differences in affective, cognitive, or even psychophysiological reactions to information that is consistent or inconsistent with subjects' established beliefs might prove useful to the extent that defending oneself against challenges to such beliefs is central to self-esteem.

Another methodological problem in assessment stems from the social desirability of high self-esteem. It is more socially desirable to present oneself as high rather than low in self-esteem and to respond to face-valid scale items accordingly, thereby inflating self-esteem scores. Demo (1985) has suggested decreasing the social desirability of self-esteem items by measuring "*presented* self-esteem" through the ratings of observers, which can then be used to complement an individual's self-ratings or "*experienced* self-esteem." In his study, Demo compared Rosenberg's (1965) and Coopersmith's (1967) traditional self-report measures of self-esteem with nontraditional "other-report" measures, either from ratings made by "peers" (acquaintances) or trained "observers." The peer measures were ratings completed by peers who had ongoing relationships with the individual in question, and the ratings by trained observers were completed following interactions with that individual. The convergence of these other-report measures with self-reports suggests considerable validity. Few researchers, however, have access to the specialized peer and observer populations that Demo did.

Presumably, verbal and nonverbal behaviors presented by individuals to peers and trained observers are less subject to social desirability effects than their responses to self-report scale items. However, these other-reports may be more susceptible than self-reports to another confounding factor in self-esteem assessment: the possible functional utility of attempting to exhibit high levels of self-esteem. Appearing high in self-esteem can be used defensively (consciously or unconsciously) against threats to the self such as failure or social rejection (Schneider & Turkat, 1975). Such defensive reactions may increase exhibited levels of self-esteem, thereby artifactually inflating other-report as well as self-report measures (Paulhus, 1986).

Locating and Selecting Measures

The initial set of self-esteem scales identified for review was based on the authors' knowledge, on inquiries to colleagues, and on the earlier chapter by Crandall (1973). These sources were supplemented and checked by an on-line query of title and abstract information in the psycINFO® computerized database. This database contains relevant information for all articles published since 1967 in over 1300 journals, as well as dissertations and monographs.

Query of the terms "self-esteem" and "self-concept" yielded over 30,000 separate references! This not only indicated the popularity of these constructs but ruled out even a cursory review of abstracts. The search was then limited to the following major journals: *American Psychologist, Developmental Psychology, Journal of Consulting and Clinical Psychology, Journal of Experimental Research in Personality, Journal of Experimental Social Psychology, Journal of Personality, Journal of Personality Assessment, Journal of Personality and Social Psychology, Journal of Research in Personality, Personality and Social Psychology Bulletin, Psychological Bulletin,* and *Psychological Review*. Still, over 15,000 references remained. The search was then limited to the following terms: "concurrent validity," "construct validity," "face validity," "test item analysis," "test item content," "test reliability," "factor analysis," and "multitrait–multimethod matrix." This reduced the search to 306 documents that were likely to include original articles using or describing newly developed scales. Careful reading of the resulting abstracts verified this assumption. The 40 scales listed and footnoted in Table 1 were identified using this procedure. The *Social Science Citation Index* was used to gauge the frequency with which each scale had been used (see Table 1). The resulting frequencies were then divided by the number of years since publication to arrive at the yearly frequency figures in Table 1.

There is neither a firm body of evidence nor a convincing definitional rationale to

Table 1

Various Self-Esteem and Self-Concept Scales Listed in Order of Number of Citations Per Year[a]

Scale	Frequency	Frequency/Year	%
*Self-Esteem (Rosenberg, 1965)	1285	61.2	25
*Self-Esteem Inventory (Coopersmith, 1967)	942	54.6	18
Tennessee Self-Concept (Roid & Fitts, 1988)	527	24.9	10
Piers–Harris Self-Concept (Piers, 1984)	365	20.3	7
*Barron Ego-Strength (Barron, 1953)	366	17.4	7
Janis and Field Feelings of Inadequacy (Janis & Field, 1959; Eagly, 1967; Fleming & Courtney, 1984)	253	12.0	5
Personal Orientation Inventory (Shoström, 1966)	252	12.0	5
Texas Social Behavior Inventory (Helmreich & Stapp, 1974)	137	10.5	3
Body-Cathexis (Secord & Jourard, 1953)	192	9.1	4
*Rosenberg–Simmons Self-Esteem (Rosenberg & Simmons, 1972)	103	6.9	2
Berger Self-Acceptance (Berger, 1952)	132	6.3	3
*McFarland and Ross Self-Esteem (McFarland & Ross, 1982)	30	6.0	1
*Ziller Social Self-Esteem (Ziller, Hagey, Smith, & Long, 1969)	103	5.7	2
SDQ III (Marsh, Smith, & Barnes, 1983)	27	5.4	1
Index of Adjustment and Values (Bills, Vance, & McLean, 1951)	111	5.3	2
Butler–Haigh Q-sort (Butler & Haigh, 1954)	108	5.1	2
*Self-Perception Inventories (Soares & Soares, 1970)	70	3.9	1
Self-Valuation Triads (Gergen, 1965)	59	2.8	1
Adjective Check List (Gough & Heilbrun, 1965)	55	2.6	1
Total	5117		100

[a]The Pictorial Scale of Self-Concept (Harter, 1985), Body-Esteem Scale (Franzoi & Shields, 1984), Self-Concept Stability (Brownfain, 1952), The 20-Statements (Kuhn & McPartland, 1954), Duncan Personality Integration (Duncan, 1966), Phillips Self-Acceptance (Phillips, 1951), Miskimins' Self-Goal-Other Discrepancy Scale (Miskimins & Braucht, 1971), Measure of Self-Consistency (Gergen & Morse, 1967), Sherwood Self-Concept Inventory (Sherwood, 1962), Inferred Self-Concept Scale (McDaniel, 1970), Unconscious Self-Esteem (Beloff & Beloff, 1959), Joseph Preschool Self-Concept (Joseph, 1979), Thomas-Zander Ego-Strength (Zander & Thomas, 1960), and Self-Report Inventory (Bown, 1961) all had percentage of total values of less than one and are thus not listed above. An asterisk indicates that an estimate may be inflated due to non-scale-related citations.

justify many of the "self-esteem" measures that exist. The subset of scales that we selected for review are based on the criteria of our limited outreach efforts, on popularity (i.e., frequency of use), judgments of promise, and need in the field. Certain less popular measures were included because of the needs they fill, while certain popular measures were included even when we were less enthusiastic about their value as measures of global self-esteem than as measures of related constructs.

Measures Reviewed Here

Our review of self-esteem scales is organized primarily by target population. Five scales that were developed for use with adolescents and adults are considered first, followed by two scales developed for use with children. Finally, a subset of five scales dealing with narrower or related constructs is considered.

Adolescent–Adult Scales

The first grouping includes the following five scales for adolescents and adults.

1. Rosenberg Self-Esteem Scale (1965)
2. Janis–Field Feelings of Inadequacy Scale (1959/1967/1980/1984)
3. Coopersmith Self-Esteem Inventory (1967)
4. Texas Social Behavior Inventory (1974)
5. Ziller Social Self-Esteem Scale (1969)

Few scale developers distinguish measures intended for adolescents from those intended for adults. This is not surprising given that most research subjects are college students in one of, or straddling, these two age categories.

As is evident from Table 1, Rosenberg's (1965) Self-esteem Scale (SES) is the most popular measure of global self-esteem. Indeed, it is the standard with which developers of other measures usually seek convergence. Rosenberg's definition of self-esteem as a favorable or unfavorable attitude toward oneself (Rosenberg, 1965, p. 15), while unidimensional, is strikingly face valid. The fact that the scale contains only 10 Likert-type items contributes to ease of administration, scoring, and interpretation. The measure's relatively high internal consistency and test–retest reliability undoubtedly contribute to its popularity. Possible susceptibility to social desirability effects has not dampened its use, probably because of similar problems with other scales. Although originally developed for use with adolescents, the SES is also used widely with adults. A subsequent adaptation of the scale for children by Rosenberg and Simmons (1972) does not enjoy similar popularity, probably because its administration requires an in-person interview.

The original Janis–Field Feelings of Inadequacy Scale (FIS) (1959) assessed self-esteem in a negative fashion. Its 23 items tapped the strength of such negative feelings as personal worthlessness, social anxiety, and self-consciousness. Eagly's major revision (1967) reduced the number of scale items to 20 and created a balance between negative and positive items, thereby eliminating possible acquiescence or response set problems inherent in the negatively framed original version. In an attempt to use the scale to measure self-esteem in a multidimensional fashion, Fleming and Watts (1980) and Fleming and Courtney (1984) have further revised the FIS, by adding five and eight items, respectively. These revisions are in line with the "hierarchical facet" approach to self-esteem (Shavelson et al., 1976), and produce measures of five primary factors hypothesized to be subordinate to self-esteem: social confidence, academic ability, emotionality, physical appearance, and ability.

The Coopersmith Self-Esteem Inventory (SEI) (1967), second to the Rosenberg SES in popularity, was developed originally for use with children and has been modified for use with adults (Ryden, 1978). Although Coopersmith (1975) reduced the original 50-item version to 25 items in an attempt to assess self-regard unidimensionally, various factor analyses of SEI data have revealed as many as 10 factors (e.g., Ahmed, Valliant, & Swindle, 1985; Gibbs & Norwich, 1985). While none of these factors were related directly to self-esteem, the overall scale has correlated as high as .55 with the Rosenberg

SES, .72 with the Janis–Field FIS, and .77 with the Tennessee Self-Concept Scale (Demo, 1985; Van Tuinen & Ramanaiah, 1979).

The Texas Social Behavior Inventory (TSBI) (Helmreich, Stapp, & Ervin, 1974) was developed to assess feelings of self-worth in terms of interpersonal interaction in the four domains of social confidence, dominance, social competence, and relations to authority figures. Although it is not as global a measure of self-esteem as others, it is likely that "social" self-esteem is usually an important determinant of overall self-esteem. One distinctive advantage of the TSBI is that it has two equivalent 16-item forms (Helmreich & Stapp, 1974), both of which correlate highly (.97) with the original 32-item form and with the other short form (.87). Thus two separate assessments can be made (e.g., test–retest, or pre- and post-test) with relatively little concern over the sensitization effects that affect other measures.

Ziller, Hagey, Smith, and Long's (1969) Social Self-Esteem (SSE) measure is also based on an assumption of the paramount importance of self-worth in interpersonal situations. The SSE uses a geometric format in which the location of paper and pencil representations of the self in relation to the location of representations of others is the ultimate quantifying criterion of self-esteem (as described in the scale section). To the extent that unconscious processes guide such representations, the assessment of self-esteem is not as subject as usual to social desirability or bias effects. While its psychometric record is not strong, it is included here for its novel and experimental approach to measuring self-esteem.

The Self-Esteem Scale

(Rosenberg, 1965)

Variable

This scale was originally designed to measure adolescents' global feelings of self-worth or self-acceptance.

Description

The 10 items that make up the Rosenberg Self-Esteem Scale (SES) were designed to optimize ease of administration, economy of time, unidimensionality, and face validity. Self-Esteem Scale items require the respondent to report feelings about the self directly. Although originally designed as a Guttman-type scale, the SES is typically scored using a four-point response format (strongly agree, agree, disagree, strongly disagree) resulting in a scale range of 10–40 with higher scores representing higher self-esteem. Some authors, however, have adopted more familiar Likert-style response formats employing 5- or 7-point scales resulting in broader ranges of SES scores.

Several studies have demonstrated that a unidimensional factor structure underlies the SES (e.g., Hensley, 1977; Simpson & Boyal, 1975), while others have identified two highly correlated factors, with the additional factor reflecting negatively worded questions (Dobson, Goudy, Keith, & Powers, 1979; Hensley & Roberts, 1976; Kaplan & Pokorny, 1969).

Sample

The original sample was a group of 5024 high school juniors and seniors from 10 randomly selected New York State high schools.

Reliability

Internal Consistency

Dobson *et al.* (1979) obtained a Cronbach α of .77 for their sample, while Fleming and Courtney (1984) reported a Cronbach α of .88.

Test–Retest

Silber and Tippett (1965) reported a test–retest correlation of .85 for 28 subjects after a 2-week interval. Fleming and Courtney (1984) reported a test–retest correlation of .82 for 259 male and female subjects with a 1-week interval.

Validity

Convergent

The SES is associated with many self-esteem-related constructs. For example, Lorr and Wunderlich (1986) reported a correlation of .65 between SES scores and confidence and .39 between SES scores and popularity. Reynolds (1988) found a correlation of .38 between SES scores and overall academic self-concept with correlations between SES scores and specific facets of academic self-concept ranging from .18 to .40. The Rosenberg measure correlated .72 with the Lerner Self-Esteem Scale, .24 with "beeper" self-reports of self-esteem (a series of self-esteem measurements requested at quasirandom times over an extended period of time), and .27 with peer ratings for an adolescent sample (Savin-Williams & Jaquish, 1981).

Fleming and Courtney (1984) demonstrated negative relationships between the SES and several concepts associated with low self-regard. For example, SES scores correlated −.64 with anxiety, −.54 with depression, and −.43 with anomie. In addition, these authors reported that SES scores correlated .78 with general self-regard, .51 with social confidence, .35 with school abilities, .42 with physical appearance, and .66 with scores on a revised Janis and Field scale. Finally, Demo (1985) found SES scores correlated .55 with scores on the Coopersmith SEI and .32 with peer ratings of self-esteem. Correlations with social desirability range from .10 (Reynolds, 1988) to .33 (Fleming & Courtney, 1984).

Discriminant

Considerable discriminant validity has also been demonstrated for the SES. Reynolds found no significant correlations between SES scores and grade point averages (.10), locus of control (−.04), Scholastic Aptitude Test verbal (−.06) and quantitative (.10) scores. Fleming and Courtney found no significant correlations between SES scores and gender (.10), age (.13), work experience (.07), marital status (.17), birth order (.02), grade point average (.01), or vocabulary (−.04).

Location

Rosenberg, M. (1965). *Society and the adolescent self-image*. Princeton, NJ: Princeton University Press.

Results and Comments

The Rosenberg SES has enjoyed widespread use and utility as a unidimensional measure of self-esteem. In fact, the SES is the standard against which new measures are evaluated. Its ease of administration, scoring, and brevity underlie our recommendation for the use of the SES as a straightforward estimate of positive or negative feelings about the self. Researchers interested in a more dimensionalized or faceted view of the self are advised to examine other scales reviewed in this chapter.

The Rosenberg, however, is not completely trouble-free. For example, the items may be susceptible to socially desirable responding. In addition, scale score distributions among college students tend to be negatively skewed so that even tripartite splits of the distribution produce "low" self-esteem groups that have relatively high self-esteem in an absolute sense. Alleviating this concern somewhat, however, is the argument that an individual who fails to endorse SES items at least moderately is probably clinically depressed.

In addition to the standard 10-item scale, a 6-item version (based on the original scale) is available for use with younger than high-school age populations (Rosenberg & Simmons, 1972). This scale is administered by interview and was designed to be applicable for both black and white children.

Self-Esteem Scale

1. I feel that I am a person of worth, at least on an equal basis with others.

  1. STRONGLY   2. AGREE   3. DISAGREE   4. STRONGLY
     AGREE   DISAGREE

  2. I feel that I have a number of good qualities.
 *3. All in all, I am inclined to feel that I am a failure.
  4. I am able to do things as well as most other people.
 *5. I feel I do not have much to be proud of.
  6. I take a positive attitude toward myself.
  7. On the whole, I am satisfied with myself.
 *8. I wish I could have more respect for myself.
 *9. I certainly feel useless at times.
 *10. At times I think I am no good at all.

  Note: Self-Esteem Scale (Rosenberg, 1965). Rights reserved by Princeton University Press. Reprinted here with permission. *, Reverse-scored item.

The Feelings of Inadequacy Scale
(Janis & Field, 1959)

Variable

This scale was originally developed to quantify a person's feelings of inadequacy, inferiority, self-consciousness, and social anxiety.

Description

The Janis and Field Feelings of Inadequacy Scale (FIS) was originally part of a larger instrument devised to assess individual differences in persuasibility (Janis & Field, 1959). The feelings of inadequacy subscale was intended to measure self-esteem, primarily by asking respondents to indicate how bad they feel about themselves. The original 23 FIS items appraise perceived social anxiety, self-consciousness, and feelings of personal worthlessness. Respondents indicate the extent of their agreement with each of the 23 statements, using five response alternatives: very, fairly, slightly, not very, and not at all. Item scores vary from 0 to 4 for a possible FIS range of 0 to 92, with low scores indicating high feelings of inadequacy (low self-esteem), and high scores reflecting high self-esteem.

The FIS has undergone several revisions. Eagly's (1967) was the first, balancing the scale for acquiescence response set (all items had been negatively worded) and discarding poor items, thereby reducing the scale to 20 items. Many of the new items pertained to success and social competence.

A second revision (Fleming & Watts, 1980) factored the scale in accordance with Shavelson *et al.*'s (1976) hierarchical facet model of self-esteem. Five items were added to the scale (four pertaining to school abilities and one to assertiveness) producing three subscales: social confidence, school abilities, and self-regard. In addition, response alternatives were changed to 7-point Likert format. The scale was revised once again to approximate the Shavelson *et al.* model (Fleming & Courtney, 1984) better. Eight items were added for a total of 33, producing two additional subscales: physical appearance and physical ability. In addition to the five subscales, factor analysis of the latest scale revision reveals a global self-esteem factor justifying an overall self-esteem score.

Sample

The original Janis and Field (1959) questionnaire was based on a sample of 184 male and female high school juniors. The Eagly (1967) version was based on samples of 33 and 160 male and female college students. The Fleming and Watts (1980) and Fleming and Courtney (1984) versions are both based on college student samples of 106 and 259 (males and females), respectively.

Reliability

Internal Consistency

Janis and Field (1959) reported a split-half reliability coefficient of .83 and a Spearman–Brown coefficient of .91 for their 23-item version. Eagly (1967) presented split-half reliabilities of .72 and .88 for her 20-item version. Cronbach α is .90 for the Fleming and Watts (1980) version and .92 for the Fleming and Courtney (1984) version with Cronbach α values ranging from .77 to .88 for the five subscales.

Test–Retest

No test–retest data were encountered.

Validity

Convergent

The Janis and Field version correlated .67 with the California Personality Inventory self-esteem measure and .60 with self-ratings of self-esteem (Hamilton, 1971). O'Brien (1985) found a correlation of .82 between the Eagly revision of the FIS and the Rosenberg Self-Esteem Scale. The Eagly version correlated .84 with the Berger Self-Acceptance Scale (Eagly, 1969). Fleming and Watts's version was related to locus of control ($-.30$), with high self-esteem individuals more internal (Fleming & Watts, 1980). The Fleming and Courtney version correlated $-.62$ with anxiety, $-.48$ with depression, and $-.38$ with anomie (Fleming & Courtney, 1984). This version is also moderately correlated with social desirability (.22).

Discriminant

Hamilton (1971) found low correlations between the FIS and self-ratings of dominance and open-mindedness. Fleming and Watts (1980) found no correlation between their total self-esteem score and verbal intelligence (.06), self-report of grade point average (.12), birth order (.12), number of siblings (.08), and empathic fantasy ($-.07$). In addition, this version was unrelated to social desirability, correlating .06 with the Marlowe–Crowne scale.

Location

Although the Fleming and Courtney (1984) FIS scale revision items are presented below, the original FIS and subsequent revisions are readily available.[1]

Original Janis and Field: Janis, I. L., & Field, P. B. (1959). Sex differences and factors related to persuasibility. In C. I. Hovland & I. L. Janis (Eds.), *Personality and persuasibility*. New Haven, CT: Yale University Press.

Eagly Revision: Eagly, A. H. (1967). Involvement as a determinant of response to favorable and unfavorable information. *Journal of Personality and Social Psychology Monographs, 7*(3, Pt. 2; Whole No. 643).

Fleming and Watts Revision: Fleming, J. S., & Watts, W. A. (1980). The dimensionality of self-esteem: Some results for a college sample. *Journal of Personality and Social Psychology, 39,* 921–929.

Fleming, J. S., & Courtney, B. E. (1984). The dimensionality of self-esteem II: Hierarchical facet model for revised measurement scales. *Journal of Personality and Social Psychology, 46,* 404–421.

Results and Comments

The extensive revisions of the FIS have produced a reliable and seemingly valid measure of both facet and global self-esteem. The Fleming and Courtney (1984) version is recommended. Factor structures and validity coefficients attest to the scale's appropriateness. Used for subscale scores or total scores, the questionnaire should produce an adequate estimation of an individual's level of self-esteem according to either a global or a facet conceptualization.

---

[1] J. S. Fleming reports that a new version of the instrument called the PASCI (Personal and Academic Self-Concept Inventory) is now available. The PASCI has six self-concept scales (Self-Regard, Social Acceptance, Verbal Ability, Math Ability, Physical Appearance, and Physical Ability), as well as a Social Anxiety scale. These scales are briefer than the previous version, with only five items each. Results of confirmatory factor analysis, reliability analysis, and correlations with some related scales for convergent and discriminant validity are available in "The Personal and Academic Self-Concept Inventory: Factor Structure and Gender Differences in High School and College Samples," by J. S. Fleming and D. J. Whalen, 1989 (available from the first author).

Feelings of Inadequacy Scale
(revised Janis and Field)

*1. How often do you feel inferior to most of the people you know?

I ————— I ————— I ————— I ————— I ————— I ————— I**
NEVER   ALWAYS

*2. Do you ever think that you are a worthless individual?

3. How confident do you feel that someday the people you know will look up to you and respect you?

*4. Do you ever feel so discouraged with yourself that you wonder whether you are a worthwhile person?

*5. How often do you dislike yourself?

6. In general, how confident do you feel about your abilities?

*7. How often do you have the feeling that there is nothing you can do well?

*8. How much do you worry about how well you get along with other people?

*9. How often do you worry about criticisms that might be made of your work by your teacher or employer?

*10. Do you ever feel afraid or anxious when you are going into a room by yourself where other people have already gathered and are talking?

*11. How often do you feel self-conscious?

*12. How much do you worry about whether other people will regard you as a success or failure in your job or in school?

*13. When in a group of people, do you have trouble thinking of the right things to talk about?

*14. When you make an embarrassing mistake or have done something that makes you look foolish, how long does it take you to get over it?

*15. Do you often feel uncomfortable meeting new people?

*16. How often do you worry about whether other people like to be with you?

*17. How often are you troubled with shyness?

*18. When you think that some of the people you meet might have an unfavorable opinion of you, how concerned or worried do you feel about it?

*19. How often do you feel worried or bothered about what other people think about you?

*20. When you have to read an essay and understand it for a class assignment, how worried or concerned do you feel about it?

*21. When you have to write an argument to convince your teacher, who may disagree with your ideas, how concerned or worried do you feel about it?

*22. How often do you have trouble expressing your ideas when you try to put them into writing as an assignment?

*23. How often do you have trouble understanding things you read for class assignments?

*24. How often do you imagine that you have less scholastic ability than your classmates?

25. In turning in a major assignment such as a term paper, how often do you feel you did an excellent job on it?

*26. Compared with classmates, how often do you feel you must study more than they do to get the same grades?

*27. Have you ever felt ashamed of your physique or figure?

*28. Do you often feel that most of your friends or peers are more physically attractive than yourself?

*29. Do you often wish or fantasize that you were better looking?

*30. Have you ever been concerned or worried about your ability to attract members of the opposite sex?

31. How confident are you that others see you as being physically appealing?

*32. Have you ever thought of yourself as physically uncoordinated?

*33. Have you ever felt inferior to most other people in athletic ability?

*34. When involved in sports requiring physical coordination, are you often concerned that you will not do well?

*35. Have you ever thought that you lacked the ability to be a good dancer or do well at recreational activities involving coordination?

*36. When trying to do well at a sport and you know other people are watching, how rattled or flustered do you get?

Note: *, Reverse-scored item. **, Labels of scale anchors vary as appropriate to specific items.

The Self-Esteem Inventory

(Coopersmith, 1967)

Variable

This scale measures evaluative attitudes across several domains pertaining to the self.

Description

The Self-Esteem Inventory (SEI) was originally designed for use with children. Items were drawn from work by Rogers and Dymond (1954) and from original research by Coopersmith. Five psychologists classified these items as reflecting high or low self-esteem. Of all possible items, 50 were selected on the basis of face validity. These items were designed to measure self-regard in four specific areas: peers, parents, school, and personal interests. Each item is a declarative, self-descriptive statement worded in the first person. Subjects are instructed to respond to each question by stating whether the statement is "like me" or "unlike me." One point is assigned for each item connoting high self-esteem that the respondent identifies as "like me" as well as for each item connoting low self-esteem that is identified as "unlike me." Thus SEI scores can range from 0 to 50.

In subsequent work, Coopersmith (1975) created Form B of the SEI by selecting the 25 items with the highest item–total correlations. This version was assumed to measure positive self-regard unidimensionally. In addition, others have modified the scale for use with adult samples (see Ryden, 1978). Authors continue to use both the 50- and 25-item versions. Factor analyses of both versions have proved troublesome. Kokenes (1978) found nine factors in the full 50-item version, while Gibbs and Norwich (1985) found 10 factors in their own 25-item version. Perhaps the most stable factors were obtained by Ahmed *et al.* (1985), who found Form B of the Coopersmith scale to have four interpretable factors: view of life, family relations, tolerance and confusion, and sociability. It should be noted that none of these analyses has produced factors that correspond to *a priori* theoretical constructs.

Sample

The original sample consisted of 87 fifth and sixth grade boys and girls; a second sample consisted of 1748 children attending public schools in Connecticut (Coopersmith, 1967).

Reliability

Internal Consistency

Using the 50-item version, J. B. Taylor and Reitz (1968) reported a split-half reliability of .90. Van Tuinen and Ramanaiah (1979) reported a Cronbach α of .83 for the 25-item version (Form B). Ahmed *et al.* (1985) obtained an α of .75 for the same version.

Test–Retest

Coopersmith reported test–retest correlations of .88 for a 5-week period and .70 over 3 years. Ryden (1978) reported test–retest correlations ranging from .78 to .80 for his shortened version over periods ranging from 6 to 58 weeks. Byrne (1983) obtained test–retest correlations on a general self subscale of .62 over a 1-week period.

Validity

Convergent

Demo (1985) found the 25-item version to correlate .44 with "beeper" self-reports of self-esteem, .55 with the Rosenberg Scale, .41 with peer ratings, .33 with observer Q-sorts of self-esteem, and .50 with a self-esteem interview. Correlations of .58 with social self-esteem, .75 with the Tennessee Self-Concept Scale, .72 with the Janis–Field Feelings of Inadequacy Scale, .58 with simple ratings of global self-esteem, and .47 with simple ratings of social self-esteem have been demonstrated (Van Tuinen & Ramanaiah, 1979). Finally, Byrne (1983) obtained correlations ranging from .58 to .60 with the Rosenberg Self-Esteem Scale. Correlations with social desirability have reached .44 (Ryden, 1978).

Discriminant

Discriminant validity has also been shown with the SEI. For example the SEI was unrelated to several measures of need for order or routine (Van Tuinen & Ramanaiah, 1979). Also, the scale was unrelated to the Eysenck Personality Inventory Lie Scale (Ahmed *et al.*, 1985). Finally, Gibbs and Norwich (1985) found no relationship between their version of the SEI and verbal IQ or reading age.

Location

Coopersmith, S. (1967). *The antecedents of self-esteem.* San Francisco: W. H. Freeman. Items for Form B are identified in Coopersmith, S. (1975). Self-concept, race, and education. In C. K. Verma & C. Bagley (Eds.), *Race and education across cultures.* London: Heinemann.

Results and Comments

There are several problems with the SEI. First, as is true of many global self-esteem instruments, the scale is negatively skewed; that is, most people score above the mean (Coopersmith, 1967). In addition, there is a high correlation with social desirability. These findings suggest that influences other than self-esteem contribute to SEI scores. The response format (like me, unlike me) is limiting and may contribute to socially desirable responding and range restriction. The most critical problem, however, has been the lack of a stable factor structure. The scale and subsequent revisions were originally intended to be unidimensional, but data have indicated multidimensionality. Solutions of 4, 9, and 10 factors have resulted in no stable interpretable pattern. This, in combination with the lack of face validity of many items, detracts from the value of the SEI.

Self-Esteem Inventory

Please mark each statement in the following way:

If the statement describes how you usually feel, put a check in the column "*Like Me.*"

If the statement does not describe how you usually feel, put a check in the column "*Unlike Me.*"

There are no right or wrong answers.

1. I spend a lot of time daydreaming.

Like Me   Unlike Me

_____   _____

2. I'm pretty sure of myself.
*3. I often wish I were someone else.
4. I'm easy to like.
5. My parents and I have a lot of fun together.
6. I never worry about anything.
*7. I find it very hard to talk in front of the class.

*8. I wish I were younger.

*9. There are lots of things about myself I'd change if I could.

10. I can make up my mind without too much trouble.

11. I'm a lot of fun to be with.

*12. I get upset easily at home.

13. I always do the right thing.

14. I'm proud of my school work.

*15. Someone always has to tell me what to do.

*16. It takes me a long time to get used to anything new.

*17. I'm often sorry for the things I do.

18. I'm popular with kids my own age.

19. My parents usually consider my feelings.

20. I'm never unhappy.

21. I'm doing the best work that I can.

*22. I give in very easily.

23. I can usually take care of myself.

24. I'm pretty happy.

25. I would rather play with children younger than me.

*26. My parents expect too much of me.

27. I like everyone I know.

28. I like to be called on in class.

29. I understand myself.

*30. It's pretty tough to be me.

*31. Things are all mixed up in my life.

32. Kids usually follow my ideas.

*33. No one pays much attention to me at home.

34. I never get scolded.

*35. I'm not doing as well in school as I'd like to.

36. I can make up my mind and stick to it.

*37. I really don't like being a boy/girl.

*38. I have a low opinion of myself.

*39. I don't like to be with other people.

*40. There are many times when I'd like to leave home.

41. I'm never shy.

*42. I often feel upset in school.

*43. I often feel ashamed of myself.

*44. I'm not as nice looking as most people.

45. If I have something to say, I usually say it.

*46. Kids pick on me very often.

47. My parents understand me.

48. I always tell the truth.
*49. My teacher makes me feel I'm not good enough.
*50. I don't care what happens to me.
*51. I'm a failure.
*52. I get upset easily when I'm scolded.
*53. Most people are better liked than I am.
*54. I usually feel as if my parents are pushing me.
55. I always know what to say to people.
*56. I often get discouraged in school.
57. Things usually don't bother me.
*58. I can't be depended on.

Note: *, Reverse-scored item.

Texas Social Behavior Inventory

(Helmreich, Stapp, & Ervin, 1974)

Variable

This scale is intended to be an objective measure of an individual's feelings of self-worth or social competence, constructs that are not distinguished conceptually or empirically.

Description

The original Texas Social Behavior Inventory (TSBI) consisted of 32 items selected from a larger pool on the basis of factor and item analyses. Shortly after the creation of the original scale, Helmreich and Stapp (1974) revised the scale to create two parallel 16-item forms. This split was based on the desire for rapid administration and for use in studies attempting to change self-esteem. The criteria for assignment to one of the forms were equivalence of part–whole correlations, equivalence of means between forms and between sexes, equivalence of score distributions, and parallel factor structures. Owing to their equivalence, the two scales correlate .97 with the full 32-item version and .87 with each other. Most researchers using the TSBI have employed one of the short forms.

Factor analyses of 32-item TSBI responses produce one large factor and four conceptually coherent correlated factors: confidence, dominance, social competence, and social withdrawal or relation to authority figures (Helmreich & Stapp, 1974). Items are straightforward, addressing degree of self-confidence in groups of people, fear of speaking to strangers, and security in social situations. Subjects are instructed to respond to statements using a five-point Likert-type format (not at all characteristic of me, not very, slightly, fairly, very much characteristic of me). Individual items are keyed from 0 to 4, and scores on the scale range from 0 to 64 with higher scores indicating higher self-esteem.

Sample

The original 32-item version was based on a sample of more than 1000 college students.

Reliability

Internal Consistency

Alternate-form reliability of the total 32-item scale is .89 (Helmreich & Stapp, 1974). McIntire and Levine (1984) reported a Cronbach α of .92 for the full 32-item version.

Test–Retest

No test–retest correlations were encountered.

Validity

Convergent

Sadowski, Woodward, Davis, and Elsbury (1983) found the TSBI to be significantly related to locus of control. For both males and females high self-esteem was positively associated with internality. Helmreich and Stapp (1974) reported that TSBI scores were correlated .81 with masculinity for males and .83 for females, and .42 with femininity for males and .44 for females. McIntire and Levine (1984) reported that the TSBI correlated .25 with the Ghiselli Self-Assurance Scale, .76 with performance self-esteem, .40 with academic self-esteem, .25 with athletic self-esteem, .39 with academic social self-esteem, and .23 with athletic social self-esteem. The TSBI correlated .26 (McIntire & Levine, 1984) and .32 (Helmreich & Stapp, 1974) with the Marlowe–Crowne Social Desirability Scale.

Discriminant

Helmreich and Stapp (1974) found no relationship between the TSBI and intelligence as measured by the Scholastic Aptitude Test, although it was predictive of academic and other honors.

Location

Helmreich R., & Stapp, J. (1974). Short forms of the Texas Social Behavior Inventory (TSBI), an objective measure of self-esteem. *Bulletin of the Psychonomic Society,* **4,** 473–475.

Results and Comments

The most troubling aspect of the TSBI is its focus: Does it measure self-esteem or social skill? While these two constructs are certainly related, they are still very distinct concepts in social psychological research. The scale authors treat the concepts as conceptually and empirically equivalent. Positive response bias is a potential problem, because only 5 of 16 questions on form A and 4 of 16 on form B are worded negatively. The remainder are positively worded.

We would expect this scale to correlate positively with measures tapping social skill and self-confidence. Given that high self-esteem is socially desirable, the modest correlations with social desirability are not unreasonable and are typical of self-esteem scales in general. In summary, the scale is a short, simple, and easy-to-use measure of self-esteem, particularly in social situations or environments. The TSBI is probably best used as a measure of social self-esteem.

Texas Social Behavior Inventory

Form A

*1. I am not likely to speak to people until they speak to me.

a	b	c	d	e
NOT AT ALL CHARACTERISTIC OF ME	NOT VERY	SLIGHTLY	FAIRLY	VERY MUCH CHARACTERISTIC OF ME

2. I would describe myself as self-confident.
3. I feel confident of my appearance.
4. I am a good mixer.
5. When in a group of people, I have trouble thinking of the right things to say.
*6. When in a group of people, I usually do what the others want rather than make suggestions.
7. When I am in disagreement with other people, my opinion usually prevails.
8. I would describe myself as one who attempts to master situations.
9. Other people look up to me.
10. I enjoy social gatherings just to be with people.
11. I make a point of looking other people in the eye.
*12. I cannot seem to get others to notice me.
*13. I would rather not have very much responsibility for other people.
14. I feel comfortable being approached by someone in a position of authority.
*15. I would describe myself as indecisive.
16. I have no doubts about my social competence.

Form B

*1. I would describe myself as socially unskilled.
*2. I frequently find it difficult to defend my point of view when confronted with the opinions of others.
3. I would be willing to describe myself as a pretty "strong" personality.
4. When I work on a committee I like to take charge of things.
5. I usually expect to succeed in the things I do.

6. I feel comfortable approaching someone in a position of authority over me.

7. I enjoy being around other people, and seek out social encounters frequently.

8. I feel confident of my social behavior.

9. I feel I can confidently approach and deal with anyone I meet.

10. I would describe myself as happy.

11. I enjoy being in front of large audiences.

*12. When I meet a stranger, I often think that he is better than I am.

*13. It is hard for me to start a conversation with strangers.

14. People seem naturally to turn to me when decisions have to be made.

15. I feel secure in social situations.

16. I like to exert my influence over other people.

Note: *, Reverse-scored item.

Social Self-Esteem

(Ziller, Hagey, Smith, & Long, 1969)

Variable

The Social Self-Esteem Scale (SSE) is based on the premise that self-esteem maintains the self under conditions of strain, such as the processing of new self-relevant information.

Description

The SSE was developed to assess self-esteem as it evolves from social interaction and exchange. High self-esteem is considered a self-protective mechanism and is said to insulate the individual from environmental strain (such as the processing of new information about the self) through selective consideration of relevant social elements. Self-esteem is viewed largely as a result of self-evaluation or social comparison processes stemming from social contexts.

The SSE is based on the assumption that individuals find it expedient to order and structure the surrounding environment. According to the SSE developers, empirical evidence demonstrates that individuals tend to order things from left to right. In addition, individuals assign more importance to things placed at the extreme left. For each "item" respondents are instructed to place representations of themselves and five significant others (e.g., "someone you know who is happy") arbitrarily in one of six circles arranged in a row. There are six different groups of significant others within which the self must be placed. A self-esteem score is derived by measuring the self's position relative to others. The farther left the self is placed, the greater the individual's inferred self-worth. The scale can also be scored as a function of how far left the self is placed relative to the most desirable other. If scored simply as a function of left-sided placement, the possible range of scores is 0–36, with higher scores indicating greater self-esteem.

Sample

Various samples were used by Ziller *et al.* (1969) ranging from college students to politicians and in size from 41 to 321.

Reliability

Internal Consistency

Split-half reliability estimates are reported by Ziller *et al.* (1969) ranging from .80 to .85.

Test–Retest

Test–retest correlation for 86 sixth and seventh grade students (unspecified time interval) was .54 (Ziller *et al.*, 1969) No test–retest data on adult subjects were encountered.

Validity

Convergent

The SSE has not correlated very highly with other measures of self-esteem. Ziller *et al.* (1969) reported nonsignificant correlations with the Coopersmith SEI, Bills Index of Adjustment and Values and Diggory's Self-Evaluations of .04, −.14, and .21, respectively. Zirkel and Gable (1977) obtained nonsignificant correlations of .03 with the SEI, .03 with the Primary Self-Concept Scale, −.03 with the Behavioral Rating Form, and −.11 with the Teacher Rating Form.

Some predictive validity has been shown for the SSE. Ziller *et al.* (1969) demonstrated that the scale differentiated winning from losing political candidates, sociometric stars from sociometric isolates in a grade school population, mental health status of one clinical population from another (e.g., acutely depressed from psychotic), psychiatric patients from normals, frequent and consistent contributors to psychiatric treatment group interaction from less frequent and consistent contributors, and subjects of higher versus lower socioeconomic status. The scale has also been used (in combination with a semantic differential measure of self-esteem) as a measure of "defensiveness," operationalized as a discrepancy between one's conscious and unconscious self-evaluations (Mann, 1981). Defensiveness was subsequently related to delinquent behavior of adolescents.

Discriminant

No studies of discriminant validity were encountered, although the low correlations with more conventional self-esteem measures might be interpreted as evidence for discrimination.

Location

Ziller, R. C., Hagey, J., Smith, M. D., & Long, B. (1969). Self-esteem: A self-social construct. *Journal of Consulting and Clinical Psychology*, **33**, 84–95.

Results and Comments

The format of the SSE is interesting but not immune to criticism. Problems suggested by Carlson (1970) include the failure of the scale to distinguish between the source and level of self-esteem; sex bias, making it questionable for females; and cultural bias. Additionally, the left-to-right tendency is not universally evident in subjects, and the order of significant others on the questionnaire can affect subjects' placement of them on the scale (Froehle & Zerface, 1971). Mann (1980) has investigated some of these problems and concluded that while the placement of significant others may bias responses, there are no effects of developmental stage or gender of respondent.

Because of the consistent lack of convergence with conventional measures, it is clear that this scale does not measure what has traditionally been thought of as self-esteem. Unconscious self-evaluation is certainly an interesting possibility. Thus, the instrument might be more useful as a tool for measuring true or actual self-esteem rather than defensive or presented self-esteem. More research along these lines is needed.

Social Self-Esteem

Sets of six circles are accompanied by lists of six "people."

The six sets of social objects included in the adult form of the instrument are:

a) doctor, father, a friend, a nurse, yourself, someone you know who is unsuccessful;

b) doctor, father, friend, politician, yourself, an employer;

c) someone you know who is a good athlete, someone you know who is popular, someone you know who is funny, someone who knows a great deal, yourself, someone you know who is unhappy;

d) an actor, your brother or someone who is most like a brother, your best friend, yourself, a salesman, a politically active person;

e) someone you know who is cruel, a judge, a housewife, a policeman, yourself, your sister or someone who is most like a sister.

Note: Social Self-Esteem (Ziller et al., 1969). Copyright 1969 by the American Psychological Association. Reprinted here with permission. Because the scale is now being distributed commercially, Dr. Ziller requests that researchers contact him (Dept. of Psychology, University of Florida, Gainesville, 32601) and the publisher (American Psychological Association) for permission to use the scale.

Children

Assessment of self-esteem in children, especially young children, presents some obvious measurement problems. Scale language must be relatively simple and scale responses must also be unsophisticated. Hence traditional Likert-type instruments are not used in the two scales reviewed here:

6. Piers–Harris Children's Self-Concept Scale (1984)
7. Harter Self-Perception Profile for Children (1985)

The Piers–Harris Children's Self-Concept Scale (CSCS) (Piers, 1984) was designed to assess self-attitudes based on an evaluation of one's behavior and attributes. The target population includes children and adolescents aged 8–18. A total or global self-esteem score is computed, as well as six subscale scores for behavior, abilities, intelligence, physical appearance, anxiety, and happiness. Response bias and inconsistency indexes are also available. Social desirability is thought not to be problematic for younger age populations because of the presumably unsocialized nature of children in this regard. However, this assumption may hold less well for adolescents.

Harter (1985) has developed the Self-Perception Profile for Children (SPPC), a promising scale designed for use with elementary school children. Overlapping versions are available for use with kindergarten-age children and children in first or second grade. The SPPC assesses global self-worth as well as five major domains: scholastic competence, social acceptance, athletic competence, physical appearance, and behavior conduct. The format of the SPPC appears well-chosen for young children. Pairs of pictures depicting skills and activities are presented to respondents. In each pair, one picture illustrates the skill or activity being performed well or optimally and the other picture suboptimally (i.e., negatively). The child chooses which one is most like him or her and how true a representation it is (i.e., "sort of true" or "really true").

Piers–Harris Children's Self-Concept Scale
(Piers, 1984)

Variable

This instrument is designed to measure children's and adolescent's self-concepts, defined by Piers as "a relatively stable set of self-attitudes reflecting both a description and an evaluation of one's own behavior and attributes" (1984, p. 1). Contrary to broader uses elsewhere, the term "self-concept" here is synonymous with self-esteem or self-regard.

Description

The Piers–Harris Children's Self-Concept Scale (CSCS) is an 80-statement self-report inventory. Statements are worded primarily in the first person and children are instructed to respond "yes" or "no" to indicate whether or not each statement is self-descriptive. Approximately half the items are high self-esteem statements and half are low. Total CSCS scores range from 0 to 80 with higher scores indicating greater self-esteem.

In addition to yielding a total score, the CSCS also produces six factor analytically derived clusters or subscales: behavior, intellectual and school status, physical appearance and attributes, anxiety, popularity, and happiness and satisfaction. The clusters demonstrate substantial overlap and many items contribute to more than one cluster.

The scale is designed for use with children and adolescents aged 8–18. It is self-administered, but the user may find it desirable to read the items aloud to younger children. Administration time is less than 30 minutes. A computerized version is also available that, in addition to yielding the scores listed above, also produces two validity indexes. A response bias index estimates the amount of response bias present in a score, and an inconsistency index examines the extent to which redundant questions were answered in opposing directions.

Sample

The original sample consisted of 1183 children aged 4–12 from a Pennsylvania school system. No consistent gender or age differences were found.

Reliability

Internal Consistency

Piers (1984) lists reliability coefficients (e.g., α, Spearman–Brown, and Kuder–Richardson 20) from nine samples ranging from .88 to .92.

Test–Retest

A summary of test–retest data was also presented by Piers (1984). Test–retest reliability was .72 for a 4-month period for the 95-item version. Three- to 4-week test–retest coefficients on the 80-item version ranged from .80 to .96 (Querry, 1970).

Validity

Convergent

Correlations as high as .54 with teacher ratings of self-concept have been demonstrated (Piers, 1984). Correlations with peer ratings have also been consistent, ranging from .26 to .49 (Piers, 1969). Correlations with other self-esteem measures have also been relatively consistent. The CSCS correlated .51 with the Tennessee Self-Concept Scale for males and .61 for females (Yonker, Blixt, & Dinero, 1974). Correlations with the Bills Index of Adjustment and Values were .40 for females and .42 for males (Yonker *et al.,* 1974). Correlations were .85 with the Coopersmith Inventory (Schauer, 1975) and .67 with the Personal Attribute Inventory for Children (Parish & Taylor, 1978). Correlations with social desirability have also been high, ranging from .25 to .45 (Millen, 1966).

The CSCS also has been related to several concepts believed to be negatively related to self-esteem. Cox (1966) reported correlations of $-.64$ between the CSCS and "big problems" and $-.48$ between the CSCS and "health problems." Correlations between the CSCS and the Children's Manifest Anxiety Scale ranged from $-.54$ to $-.69$ (Millen, 1966).

Discriminant

No discriminant validity data were encountered.

Location

The scale is copyrighted and available through Western Psychological Services, 12031 Wilshire Blvd., Los Angeles, California 90025.

Results and Comments

Because of potential problems with response bias and socially desirable responding, the CSCS is better suited to children than adolescents. When used with younger groups the scale appears to exhibit acceptable reliability and validity. Shorter versions, while not encountered in the literature we reviewed, may represent an improvement.

Piers–Harris Children's Self-Concept Scale

2. I am well behaved in school. (Behavior)

                        YES   NO

16. I have good ideas. (Intellectual and School Status)
54. I am good-looking. (Physical Appearance and Attributes)
*74. I am often afraid. (Anxiety)
51. I have many friends. (Popularity)
 2. I am a happy person. (Happiness and Satisfaction)

Note: Because of the commercial nature of this scale, only sample items can be reproduced here. *, Reverse-scored item.

Self-Perception Profile for Children

(Harter, 1985)

Variable

This scale measures several aspects of children's self-concept that are related primarily to competence and acceptance.

Description

Because of the rather dramatic change in skills that connote competence and acceptance at different ages (Harter & Pike, 1983), there are two versions of the 24-item Self-Perception Profile for Children (SPPC), one for kindergarteners, and one for first and second graders. The SPPC assesses five domains (scholastic competence, social acceptance, athletic competence, physical appearance, and behavioral conduct) as well as global self-worth. Harter advises that the global self-worth scores of children under 8 years of age be interpreted with caution, since younger children are less able to make abstract judgments. The two versions share 12 common core items, but each version has 12 unique items.

The SPPC utilizes a unique format consisting of pairs of pictures, one presen ing a positive behavioral depiction and the other a negative depiction. For example, one picture shows a child bouncing a ball, while the other shows the child dropping the ball. The pictorial format is appropriate for young children because it engages their interest and attention and makes it possible for them to portray their skills and activities concretely. For each pair of pictures, the child is asked to decide which is most like him or her. Next, the child is asked whether this is "sort of true" or "really true" for him or her. Thus the child is requested to make both an evaluative and an extent-of-agreement judgment.

Each of the six subscales is based on six items. Items are scored from one to four with the most positive answers receiving a four (positive picture, really true) and negative responses receiving a one (negative picture, really true). Domain scores can range from 6 to 24, while total scores range from 36 to 144. In both cases, higher scores indicate a more positive self-concept.

Sample

Four standardization samples were employed, encompassing a total of 1553 third through eighth grade boys and girls.

Reliability

Internal Consistency

Cronbach α values for each subscale are provided by Harter (1985). All are generally high, ranging from .71 to .85 across four samples.

Test–Retest

No test–retest correlations were encountered.

Validity

Convergent

Factor analyses have confirmed the a priori domains of self-concept (Harter, 1985). Some convergent evidence comes from unpublished data reported by S. Harter and R. G. Pike (personal communication, November 20, 1988) in which 96% of first and second grade children were readily able to give specific reasons why they felt competent or not and why they felt accepted or not. Also, a correlation of .42 was reportedly obtained between perceived competence and preferred level of difficulty in puzzle tasks.

Discriminant

No discriminant validity data were encountered.

Location

The scales are available from Dr. Susan Harter at the Psychology Department, University of Denver, Denver, Colorado 80208-0204.

Results and Comments

While most work using the SPPC has been performed by Harter and her colleagues, the scale is promising as a stable and useful instrument for assessing children's self-concept. The format is engaging for children and should hold their interest for the time necessary to complete the scale. Providing versions that are age-specific is an added advantage. One potential (and as yet untested) problem is susceptibility to socially desirable responding. Additional work is necessary to establish the validity of the instrument.

Harter and her colleagues are creating instruments with similar formats for older children, adolescents, and adults using words rather than pictures. The entire set of instruments may prove useful for developmental studies.

Self-Perception Profile for Children

This girl is pretty good at puzzles.
Are you:

Really good at puzzles   OR   Pretty good

This girl isn't very good at puzzles.
Are you:

Sort of good   OR   Not very good at puzzles

This boy isn't very good at numbers.
Are you:

Not too good at numbers   OR   Sort of good

This boy is pretty good at numbers.
Are you:

Pretty good   OR   Really good at numbers

Related Constructs

In many cases, researchers may be interested in constructs that, while related to self-esteem, are either defined more broadly or more narrowly. Here we consider two measures of the more general construct of self concept and two measures of more specific constructs.

8. Tennessee Self-Concept Scale (1965/1988)
9. Marsh Self-Description Questionnaire I, II, & III (1983/1984/1984)
10. Shrauger Personal Evaluation Inventory (1990)
11. Body-Esteem Scale (1984)

The Tennessee Self-Concept Scale (TSC), originally introduced by Fitts (1965) and recently revised by Roid and Fitts (1988), was developed to assess an individual's identity, behaviors, and satisfaction comprehensively across many domains. Indeed, 29 scores can be derived for each respondent. Presumably, satisfaction scores in these various domains can be construed as specific self-esteem measures. Although the TSC has been used as a research instrument, its major value may lie in clinical applications, allowing therapists to focus on specific attributes underlying pathologically low or high self-esteem.

The Self-Description Questionnaires (SDQ) were also developed in an attempt to measure self-concept multidimensionally. Marsh and his colleagues developed distinct versions for children (the SDQ-I) (Marsh, Smith, & Barnes, 1983), adolescents (the SDQ-II) (Marsh, Parker, & Barnes, 1984), and late adolescents or adults (the SDQ-III) (Marsh, & O'Neill, 1984). Each is based on the assessment of varying numbers of factors assumed to underlie self-concept in each age group.

Shrauger's Personal Evaluation Inventory (PEI) (1990) focuses on self-confidence, arguably an important evaluative component contributing to global self-esteem. The PEI is based on a multidimensional approach to self-confidence encompassing academic ability, athletics, physical appearance, romantic relationships, social interactions, and speaking with people. Clearly, this instrument is more appropriate for use with late adolescents and young adults than with other age groups.

The Body-Esteem Scale (BES) (Franzoi & Shields, 1984) is based on a revision of the widely used Body-Cathexis Scale of Secord and Jourard (1953). Unlike the earlier unidimensional scale, the BES is based on gender-specific multidimensional factor structures including physical attractiveness, concern about weight, and physical condition for males and attitudes toward sexual attractiveness, concern about weight, and physical condition for females. To the extent that physical appearance is an important underlying component of self-esteem, as argued by Berscheid and Walster (1978) and Hatfield and Sprecher (1985), measures like the BES tap an important component of self-esteem.

Tennessee Self-Concept Scale
(Roid & Fitts, 1988)

Variable

This scale is based on a multidimensional view of the self-concept derived primarily from a clinical perspective and emphasizes both general and specific factors.

Description

The Tennessee Self-Concept Scale (TSCS) was designed to be simple, widely applicable, and multidimensional. It is intended for use with individuals aged 12 and above. The scale consists of 100 self-descriptive, self-administered statements, the vast majority of which are phrased in the first person. Respondents are instructed to indicate the extent to which they agree or disagree with each statement. Response alternatives are completely false, mostly false, partly true and partly false, mostly true, completely true. Items are scored from one to five, and total scale scores can range from 100 to 500, with higher scores indicating a more positive self-concept.

Roid and Fitts (1988) reported that 29 major scores are calculable from the measure, but users have relied primarily on total score and five categorical scores: physical self, moral–ethical self, personal self, family self, and social self. Three additional measures can be computed for each of these categories: identity (how the individual describes his or her basic identity within each category), self-satisfaction (how satisfied the individual is with perceived self-image within each category), and behavior. The result is a 3 × 5 matrix of categories by item types. Other scales address self-criticism, true–false ratio, conflict, variability in response, defensive posture, general maladjustment, psychosis, personality disorder, neurosis, personality integration, deviant signs, and time score, in addition to others.

Sample

The original sample consisted of 626 participants from various parts of the United States. The group ranged in age from 12 to 68 and contained an approximate balance of females and males, blacks and whites, representatives of all social, economic, and intellectual levels, and educational levels from sixth grade to doctoral level. Normative scores on all subscales are available in Roid and Fitts (1988).

Reliability

Internal Consistency

Split-half reliability has been estimated to be .91 (Nunnelly, 1968). Roid and Fitts (1988) reported several α coefficients for total score that range from .89 to .94. Subscale coefficients were slightly lower.

Test–Retest

Fitts (1965) reported test–retest reliability coefficients based on 60 college students (2-week interval) ranging from .60 to .92 for total score. Roid and Fitts (1988) presented test–retest data on 472 respondents over a median interval of 6 weeks. Their test–retest coefficients ranged from .62 to .94 (total score).

Validity

Convergent

The TSCS has correlated .80 with the Piers–Harris Self-Concept Scale (Roid & Fitts, 1988). Fitts (1965) found total score to correlate .64 with a measure of positive feelings. The scale correlates .53 with the Eysenck Personality Questionnaire extraversion measure (Roid & Fitts, 1988). Van Tuinen and Ramanaiah (1979) provide the best evidence of convergence with other measures. They found that the TSCS total scale correlated .75 with the Coopersmith inventory, .45 with social self-esteem, and .65 with the Janis and Field questionnaire. In addition, correlations of .62 and .42 were found for simple self-ratings of global and social self-esteem, respectively. Finally, Fitts (1965) found the scale to be highly negatively correlated (−.70) with the Taylor Manifest Anxiety Scale.

Discriminant

Evidence of discriminant validity is provided by Fitts (1965), who found the scale to be uncorrelated with authoritarianism (California F-scale). Hall (1964) showed no relationship between the TSCS and agreement response set. Sundby (1962) found the scale unrelated to conformity. Roid and Fitts (1988) provide evidence for the discriminative power of the TSCS in terms of correlations with scales composing the Edwards Personal Preference Schedule. The TSCS failed to correlate with most measures including deference, order, exhibition, intraception, succorance, dominance, abasement, change, endurance, heterosexuality, and aggression.

Location

The TSCS is copyrighted and available through Western Psychological Services, 12031 Wilshire Blvd., Los Angeles, California 90025.

Results and Comments

A comprehensive analysis of the TSCS by Marsh and Richards (1988) demonstrated consistent validational support for only the family, social, and physical subscales. Although the scale purports to measure many aspects of self-concept, its popularity (see Table 1) is due to its use as a general measure of self-esteem.

Tennessee Self-Concept Scale

1. I have a healthy body. (Physical)

1	2	3	4	5
		PARTLY FALSE		
COMPLETELY	MOSTLY	AND	MOSTLY	COMPLETELY
FALSE	FALSE	PARTLY TRUE	TRUE	TRUE

25. I am satisfied with my moral behavior. (Moral)

38. I have a lot of self-control. (Personal)

57. I am a member of a happy family. (Family)

79. I am as sociable as I want to be. (Social)

Note: Because of the commercial nature of the scale, only sample items can be reproduced here.

Self-Description Questionnaire
(Marsh, Smith, & Barnes, 1983)

Variable

This instrument is designed to measure the self-concept and is derived from a hierarchical facet model of a dimensionalized self.

Description

The facet model incorporates a generalized sense of self, more specific facets or domain self-concepts, and even more specific skills and abilities. In short, specific skills and abilities contribute to facet selves, which in turn contribute to a generalized sense of self. The Self-Description Questionnaire (SDQ) was designed to measure the self-concept of children of less than adolescent age. Seven conceptual and factor analytically supported facets from two domains (academic and nonacademic) are measured. These domains are physical abilities, appearance, relationship with peers, relationship with parents, reading, mathematics, and (other) school subjects.

The scale consists of 66 items selected from an original pool of 100 items. The nonacademic subscales each contain eight positively worded and one negatively worded item. The academic scales each contain 10 parallel items, five of which are cognitive in content and five affective in content. Each contains four positively worded items and one negatively worded item. Most questions are worded in the first person, and subjects are instructed to respond to each item on a five-point response scale (true, mostly true, sometimes true, sometimes false, mostly false, and false). Items are scored in the direction of higher self-esteem, and total score can range from 66 to 330.

Sample

The scale is based on a sample of 654 male and female students attending one of six coeducational public schools in Sydney, Australia. The students were primarily in fifth or sixth grade and ranged in age from 9.5 to 13 years.

Reliability

Internal Consistency

Marsh, Smith, and Barnes (1983) report Cronbach α values for the seven subscales ranging from .80 to .92.

Test–Retest

Six-month subscale test–retest coefficients have ranged from .27 to .74 with most in the .50–.70 range (Marsh, Smith, & Barnes, 1983).

Validity

Convergent

Several factor analyses have confirmed the presence of seven factors within the scale (Marsh & Hocevar, 1983; Marsh, Barnes, & Hocevar, 1985; Marsh, Relich, & Smith, 1983) with all items loading on their expected factor. Evidence of convergence with related constructs is based on several data sets and includes correlations with physical abilities, .30–.53; appearance, .07–.31; relations with peers, .22–.58; mathematics .33–.74; all school subjects .22–.65.

Discriminant

No discriminant validity data were encountered.

Location

The scale is copyrighted and available through the Psychological Corporation, 555 Academic Court, San Antonio, Texas 78204-2498. Only paraphrased sample items can be reproduced here.

SDQ: Marsh, H. W., Smith, I. D., & Barnes, J. (1983). Multitrait–multimethod analyses of the Self-Description Questionnaire: Student–teacher agreement on multidimensional ratings of student self-concept. *American Education Research Journal, 20,* 333–357.

SDQ II: Marsh, H. W., Parker, J., & Barnes, J. (1984). Multidimensional adolescent self-concepts: Their relationship to age, sex, and academic measures. *American Education Research Journal, 22,* 422–444.

SDQ III: Marsh, H. W., & O'Neill, R. (1984). Self-description Questionnaire III: The construct validity of multidimensional self-concept ratings by late adolescents. *Journal of Educational Measurement, 21,* 153–174.

Results and Comments

The SDQ appears to be an adequate and comprehensive measure of the multidimensional aspects of self-concept. It is susceptible, however, to response bias and socially desirable responding. Its length and specificity limit its utility as a measure of overall self-evaluation (global self-esteem). In general we recommend this scale for researchers interested in specific aspects of self-concept, but not for those interested in global self-esteem.

Also available but not reviewed in this chapter are the Self-Description Questionnaire II (SDQ II) for use with adolescent samples and the Self-Description Questionnaire III (SDQ III) for use with late adolescent and adult samples. The SDQ II contains 122 items measuring 11 subscales including general self, mathematics, verbal, general school, physical abilities, physical appearance, relations with same-sex peers, relations with opposite-sex peers, relations with parents, honesty, and emotional stability. The SDQ III contains 13 scales, each represented by 10 or 12 items. The subscales are mathematics, verbal, general academic, problem solving and creativity, physical abilities, physical appearance, relations with same-sex peers, relations with opposite-sex peers, relations with parents, religion or spirituality, honesty or reliability, emotional stability or security, and general self-concept. Both the SDQ II and the SDQ III are balanced to avoid response set and have acceptable reliability and factor structures.

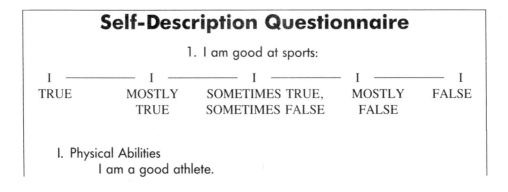

Self-Description Questionnaire

1. I am good at sports:

I ——————— I ——————— I ——————— I ——————— I
TRUE   MOSTLY   SOMETIMES TRUE,   MOSTLY   FALSE
              TRUE   SOMETIMES FALSE   FALSE

I. Physical Abilities
   I am a good athlete.

II. Appearance
   I am good looking.

III. Relationships with Peers
   I make friends easily.

IV. Relationship with Parents
   I get along well with my parents.

V. Reading
   I look forward to reading.

VI. Mathematics
   I am interested in maths.

VII. School Subjects
   I like all school subjects.

Note: Because of the commercial nature of this scale, only sample items can be reproduced here.

Personal Evaluation Inventory

(Shrauger, 1990)

Variable

This scale measures self-confidence, an aspect of self-evaluation defined as a person's sense of his or her own competence or skill and perceived capability to deal effectively with various situations.

Description

The Personal Evaluation Inventory (PEI) was designed to serve as a measure of self-evaluation that would not be as global as existing measures such as the Rosenberg Self-Esteem Scale. In development, an open-response format was employed to determine the most relevant self-confidence domains. The six most frequently mentioned dimensions were then chosen as subscales. These included academic performance, athletics, physical appearance, romantic relationships, social interactions, and speaking with people. In addition to these subscales, others were developed to assess general confidence level and mood state which might effect confidence judgments.

Item selection was based on four criteria: high item–subscale correlations; low correlations with other subscales; low correlations with the Marlowe–Crowne Social Desirability Scale; and balance between positively and negatively worded items within each subscale. All subscales contain seven items except for the athletics subscale, which contains five items. Thus, there are a total of 54 items, each scored from one to four with a possible range of total scores of 54–216, with higher scores indicating higher self-confidence.

Sample

The scale was developed on a sample of 211 college students.

Reliability

Internal Consistency

Cronbach α values for the subscales range from .74 to .89 for females and from .67 to .86 for males.

Test–Retest

Test–retest correlations of subscales after a 1-month interval ranged from .53 to .89 for women and from .25 to .90 for men. Total scale score correlations for the same interval were .80 for women and .93 for men.

Validity

Convergent

Evidence of convergence is displayed in a series of correlations reported by S. Shrauger (1990). The total PEI correlated .58 with the Rosenberg Self-Esteem Scale, .59 with the Janis–Field Feelings of Inadequacy Scale (Eagly, 1967 version), and .53 with optimism. In general, the subscales displayed patterns similar to total scale with the exception of the athletic subscale, which displayed no evidence of convergence (i.e., correlations reaching significance). Finally, Shrauger reports that scores on the PEI are related to peer ratings, task choice, and rejection of negative information about the self. Confidence scores were significantly related negatively to negative affect (−.43), to hopelessness (−.49), and to repressive tendencies (−.63).

Discriminant

Factor analytic results reported by Shrauger (1990) confirm the presence of six hypothesized factors accounting for 48% of the variance, with only two of 200 nontarget loadings greater than .3. The PEI appears to be free of socially desirable response set, does not correlate significantly with social desirability scales including the Marlowe–Crowne and the College Social Desirability Index (Shrauger & Sparrell, 1988). In addition, confidence scores were unrelated to socioeconomic level, religious affiliation, and degree of religious involvement.

Location

The scale is not yet published, but information can be obtained by writing Dr. Sidney Shrauger, Psychology Department, Park Hall, State University of New York at Buffalo, Buffalo, New York 14260.

Results and Comments

Although more validation studies are needed, the PEI is a promising measure of the self-confidence aspect of self-concept. The scale appears to be free of traditional scale limitations such as methodological artifact and response set, but there are still two problems. One is the scale's focus on domains within the college experience. Several subscales would be inappropriate for other settings such as work. A second problem is the utility of the athletic subscale. While it is clearly an independent factor, its applicability seems limited to domains such as sport psychology.

Personal Evaluation Inventory

Below are listed a number of statements that reflect common feelings, attitudes, and behaviors. Please read each statement carefully and think about whether you agree or disagree that it applies to you. Try to respond *honestly* and *accurately*, but it is not necessary to spend much time deliberating about each item. Think about how the item applies to you during the last two months unless some other time period is specified. Indicate your degree of agreement with each statement as follows:

1. I am a good mixer.

A	B	C	D
STRONGLY AGREE	MAINLY AGREE	MAINLY DISAGREE	STRONGLY DISAGREE

*2. Several times in the last few days I have gotten down on myself.

*3. It bothers me that I am not better looking.

4. I have no difficulty maintaining a satisfying romantic relationship.

5. I am happier right now than I have been in weeks.

6. I am pleased with my physical appearance.

*7. I sometimes avoid taking part in ball games and informal sports activities because I don't think I am good enough at them.

*8. Talking in front of a group makes me uncomfortable.

*9. I would like to know more people, but I am reluctant to go out and meet them.

10. Athletics is an area in which I excel.

11. Academic performance is an area in which I can show my competence and be recognized for my achievement.

12. I am better looking than the average person.

*13. I dread the thought of getting up and talking in public.

14. When I think about playing most sports I am enthusiastic and eager rather than apprehensive and anxious.

*15. I often feel unsure of myself even in situations I have successfully dealt with in the past.

*16. I frequently wonder whether I have the intellectual ability to achieve successfully my vocational and academic goals.

17. I am a better athlete than most people of my age and sex.

*18. I lack some important capabilities that may keep me from being successful.

19. When I have to talk before a group of people I usually feel assured that I can express myself effectively and clearly.

20. I am fortunate to be as good looking as I am.

*21. I have recognized that I am not as good a student as most of the people I am competing with.

*22. I have been more critical of myself in the last few days than I usually am.

*23. Being poor at sports is an important weakness of mine.

24. For me meeting new people is an enjoyable experience that I look forward to.

*25. Much of the time I don't feel as competent as many of the people around me.

26. I almost never feel uncomfortable at parties or other social gatherings.

27. I have fewer doubts about my abilities than most people.

*28. I have more trouble establishing a romantic relationship than most people do.

*29. I am more uncertain about my abilities today than I usually am.

*30. It bothers me that I don't measure up to others intellectually.

31. When things are going poorly, I am usually confident that I can successfully deal with them.

*32. I am more concerned than most people about my ability to speak in public.

33. I have more confidence in myself than most people I know.

*34. I feel apprehensive or unsure when I think about going on dates.

*35. Most people would probably consider me physically unattractive.

36. When I take a new course I am usually sure that I will end up in the top 25% of the class.

37. I am as capable as most people at speaking before a group.

*38. When I go to social gatherings I frequently feel awkward and ill at ease.

39. Usually I have a better love life than most people seem to.

*40. I have sometimes avoided taking classes or doing other things because they would require my making presentations before a group.

41. When I have to come through on important tests or other academic assignments I know that I can do it.

42. I am better at meeting new people than most people seem to be.

43. I feel more confident about myself today than I usually do.

*44. At times I have avoided someone with whom I might have a romantic relationship because I felt too apprehensive around them.

*45. I wish I could change my physical appearance.

46. I am less concerned than most people about speaking in public.

47. Right now I am feeling more optimistic and positive than usual.

48. Attracting a desirable boyfriend or girlfriend has never been a problem for me.

*49. If I were more confident about myself, my life would be better.

50. I seek out activities that are intellectually challenging because I know I can do them better than most people.

51. I can get plenty of dates without any difficulty.

*52. I don't feel as comfortable in groups as most people seem to.

*53. I am less sure of myself today than I usually am.

*54. I would be a lot more successful in dating if I were better looking.

Note: *, Reverse-scored item.

The Body-Esteem Scale

(Franzoi & Shields, 1984)

Variable

This scale is designed to measure a specific aspect of self-concept that is presumably importantly related to self-esteem: how one feels about his or her body and appearance.

Description

The Body-Esteem Scale (BES) (Franzoi & Shields, 1984) is a revision of Secord and Jourard's (1953) Body-Cathexis Scale. Body-cathexis is defined as "the degree of feeling of satisfaction or dissatisfaction with the various parts or processes of the body" (Secord & Jourard, 1953, p. 343). The Body-Cathexis Scale required respondents to rate 40 body parts and functions on a 5-point scale. Items were summed and divided by 40 to produce a total score ranging from one to five. Higher scores indicated greater body cathexis (i.e., greater satisfaction with one's body).

Based on their identification of three gender-specific factors in the Body-Cathexis Scale, Franzoi and Shields (1984) included three gender-specific subscales in the BES: physical attractiveness, upper body strength, and physical condition for men, and sexual attractiveness, weight concern, and physical condition for women. Carpentieri and Cheek (1985) confirmed this factor structure. The 32 BES items are scored on a five-point Likert scale ranging from 1 (have strong negative feelings) to 5 (have strong positive feelings). Likert scores are summed across all items to yield a total score, and across subsets of items to produce subscale scores. Total scores range from 32 to 160, with higher scores indicating greater esteem for one's body. Subscale score ranges are consistent with the number of subscale items.

Sample

The BES was developed using two samples, the first consisting of 366 females and 257 males, the second 301 females and 182 males. All were undergraduate students attending the University of California at Davis.

Reliability

Internal Consistency

The Body-Esteem Scale has shown adequate internal consistency with subscale α values ranging from .78 to .87 (Franzoi & Shields, 1984).

Test–Retest

No test–retest data were encountered for the BES. However, Balogun (1986) reported a 2-week test–retest correlation of .89 for the Body-Cathexis Scale from which the BES was derived.

Validity

Convergent

BES subscales are moderately correlated with overall self-esteem (Rosenberg SES, 1965), with rs ranging from .19 to .51 (Franzoi & Shields, 1984). Franzoi and Herzog (1986) reported BES subscale correlations of .21–.40 with the Rosenberg Self-Esteem Scale. In addition, they reported subscale correlations ranging from .08 to .27 with attractiveness, .24–.28 with body-consciousness, and .21–.63 with body-competence. In addition, the weight subscale was found to distinguish between people suffering from anorexia nervosa and a "normal" control group (Franzoi & Shields, 1984).

Discriminant

Although Franzoi and Shields (1984) and Franzoi and Herzog (1987) reported data supporting discriminant validity among the subscales, no data describing relationships between the BES scale and other variables were found.

Location

Franzoi, S. L., & Shields, S. A. (1984). The Body-Esteem Scale: Multidimensional structure and sex differences in a college population. *Journal of Personality Assessment*, **48**, 173–178.

Results and Comments

The extent of socially desirable response bias in the BES has not been determined. On the basis of scale content we expect social desirability to contribute moderately to scale scores. Much of our support for the BES is based on validity data for its predecessor, the Body-Cathexis Scale. We recommend the use of the Body-Esteem Scale instead of the earlier Body-Cathexis Scale because of its rationale and stable factor structure.

The Body-Esteem Scale

All items are scored on the following scale.

1 —————— 2 —————— 3 —————— 4 —————— 5

HAVE   HAVE
STRONG   STRONG
NEGATIVE   POSITIVE
FEELINGS   FEELINGS

Female
Sexual attractiveness: body scent, nose, lips, ears, chin, chest or breasts, appearance of eyes, cheeks/cheekbones, sex drive, sex organs, sex activities, body hair, face
Weight concern: appetite, waist, thighs, body build, buttocks, hips, legs, figure or physique, appearance of stomach, weight
Physical stamina: physical stamina, reflexes, muscular strength, energy level, biceps, physical coordination, agility, health, physical condition

Male
Physical attractiveness: nose, lips, ears, chin, buttocks, appearance of eyes, cheeks/cheekbones, hips, feet, sex organs, face
Upper body strength: muscular strength, biceps, body build, physical coordination, width of shoulders, arms, chest or breasts, figure or physique, sex drive
Physical condition: appetite, physical stamina, reflexes, waist, energy level, thighs, physical coordination, agility, figure or physique, appearance of stomach, health, physical condition, weight

---

Future Research Directions

During the review of self-esteem scales for possible inclusion in this chapter, several general problems became apparent. First, few if any measures are free from the conceptual and methodological criticisms raised by Wylie (1974) and Crandall (1973). Apparently, the perfect measure does not exist. The more serious of the methodological inadequacies contributed to our decision to review relatively few measures.

Second, since three very popular scales together account for 50% of the measurement-related citations in the literature during the last two decades (see Table 1), one might be tempted to conclude that self-esteem is only what the Rosenberg, Coopersmith, or Tennessee scales measure. However, as our review implies, these particular scales are not always appropriate measures of self-esteem. On the one hand, the Tennessee Self-Concept Scale is often much broader in scope and technically more complex than is necessary for self-esteem assessment. On the other hand, there is often a need for more specific self-evaluations than the global measures of self-esteem provided by the Rosenberg or Coopersmith scale.

Third, since self-esteem is a hypothetical construct, validation is mainly limited to convergence with other similar variables and constructs (and divergence from dissimilar ones) or to face validity. Thus, acceptance of a measure depends to a great extent on the acceptance of both the conceptual criteria or definition of self-esteem underlying the measure and the consonance of scale items with the definition.

Attempting to validate self-esteem measures against specified behaviors is problematic not only because a large set of representative behaviors is difficult to identify and measure, but also because such a procedure introduces circularity into the logic of the validation process. Is it the construct (i.e., self-esteem) or the behavior that is being validated? If one assumes the former, then the validity of the behavior must be established instead of the construct. Such validation would probably still rest on face or concept validity.

Finally, too little attention has been paid to possible group, subcultural, and cultural biases in self-esteem assessment. The typical scale has been developed primarily to assess self-esteem in white adolescents and young adults. Thus, the counterintuitive finding that blacks score much higher than whites on Rosenberg Self-Esteem Scale items (Johnston, Bachman, & O'Malley, 1986) may be reliable and consistent with certain theoretical explanations, such as high self-esteem serving a self-protective function for members of stigmatized groups (Crocker & Major, 1989), or may result from possible subcultural biases in the SES.

Certainly, even currently acceptable scales can be improved psychometrically, especially by periodic collection of validational, reliability, and normative data. However, development of new measures of global self-esteem or new measures of specific self-evaluations related to self-esteem is probably unnecessary unless advances in theory warrant them.

One promising example is the work of Luhtanen and Crocker (1990), who are currently validating a scale to measure the self-esteem or self-worth that individuals accrue from the groups to which they belong voluntarily (e.g., a work group) or involuntarily (e.g., a race or gender group). Unlike the "social" self-esteem scales described above, which assess self-esteem as a function of the individual's relative or comparative worth in interpersonal situations, Luhtanen and Crocker's Collective Self-Esteem Scale assesses self-esteem as a function of worth ascribed to and internalized by the individual via group membership. This scale assesses membership esteem (i.e., an individual's worthiness as a group member), private collective self-esteem (i.e., an individual's judgments of how his or her social group is perceived), public collective self-esteem (i.e., an individual's judgments of how outsiders perceive his or her social groups), and identity (i.e., the importance to the individual of membership in social groups).

Another area in which work remains to be done, but one without a promising solution in sight, concerns the defensive or health-maintaining nature of self-esteem (Cohen, 1954; Greenberg et al., 1986; Schneider & Turkat, 1975; Taylor & Brown, 1988). If there is such a thing as core self-esteem that is independent of defensive distortions, then it is necessary to develop self-esteem measures that are not subject to self-presentation and self-enhancement effects such as defensive agreement with socially desirable scale items. Alternatively, if one postulates that defensive or self-enhancing biases are critical to the nature and development of self, then self-presentation and self-enhancement biases are important components of the self-esteem construct and must be measured (see Chapter 2, this volume).

One way out of this apparent conflict might be a two-factor approach to self-esteem measurement in which both self-evaluation and self-protection tendencies or traits are assessed. Individuals could be assessed as high, moderate, or low on each dimension and the relative strength of the associations between either or both factors and criterion variables could be pursued. In this way, the relative contributions of "core" self-esteem and "functional" or "defensive" self-esteem could be determined. Although we are working on such a measurement approach, its development is still in its infancy.

Bibliography

Ahmed, S. M. S., Valliant, P. M., & Swindle, D. (1985). Psychometric properties of the Coopersmith Self-Esteem Inventory. *Perceptual and Motor Skills, **61**, 1235–1241.

Balogun, J. A. (1986). Reliability and construct validity of the Body-cathexis Scale. *Perceptual and Motor Skills, **62**, 927–935.

Barron, F. (1953). An ego-strength scale that predicts response to psychotherapy. *Journal of Consulting Psychology, **14**, 327–333.

Becker, E. (1973). *The denial of death.* New York: Free Press.

Becker, E. (1975). *Escape from evil.* New York: Free Press.

Beloff, H., & Beloff, J. (1959). Unconscious self-evaluation using a stereoscope. *Journal of Abnormal and Social Psychology, **59**, 275–278.

Berger, E. (1952). The relations between expressed acceptance of self and expressed acceptance of others. *Journal of Abnormal and Social Psychology, **47**, 778–882.

Berscheid, E., & Walster, E. (1978). *Interpersonal attraction* (2nd ed.). Reading, MA.: Addison-Wesley.

Bills, R., Vance, E., & McLean, O. (1951). An index of adjustment and values. *Journal of Consulting Psychology, **15**, 257–261.

Blascovich, J., & Ginsburg, G. P. (1978). Conceptual analysis of risk taking in "risky shift" research. *Journal for the Theory of Social Behaviour, **8**, 217–230.

Bown, O. (1961). The development of a self-report inventory and its function in a mental health assessment battery. *American Psychologist, **16**, 402.

Brownfain, J. (1952). Stability of the self-concept as a dimension of personality. *Journal of Abnormal and Social Psychology, **47**, 597–606.

Butler, J., & Haigh, G. (1954). Changes in the relation between self-concepts consequent upon client centered counseling. In C. R. Rogers & R. Dymond (Eds.), *Psychotherapy and personality change* (pp. 55–75). Chicago: Univ. of Chicago Press.

Byrne, B. M. (1983). Investigating measures of self-concept. *Measurement and Evaluation in Guidance, **16**, 115–126.

Carlson, R. (1970). On the structure of self-esteem: Comments on Ziller's formulation. *Journal of Consulting and Clinical Psychology, **34**, 264–268.

Carpentieri, A. M., & Cheek, J. M. (1985). *Shyness and the physical self: Body-esteem, sexuality, and anhedonia.* Unpublished honor's thesis. Wellesley College, Wellesley, MA.

Cohen, A. R. (1954). *The effects of individual self-esteem and situational structure on threat oriented reactions to power.* Unpublished doctoral dissertation, University of Michigan, Ann Arbor.

Cohen, A. R. (1959). Some implications of self-esteem for social influence. In C. Hovland & I. L. Janis (Eds.), *Personality and persuasibility* (pp. 102–120). New Haven, CT: Yale Univ. Press.

Coopersmith, S. (1967). *The antecedents of self-esteem.* San Francisco: Freeman.

Coopersmith, S. (1975). *Coopersmith Self-Esteem Inventory, technical manual.* Palo Alto, CA: Consulting Psychologists Press.

Cox, S. H. (1966). *Family background effects on personality development and social acceptance.* Unpublished doctoral dissertation, Texas Christian University, Fort Worth.

Crandall, R. (1973). The measurement of self-esteem and related constructs. In J. P. Robinson & P.

R. Shaver (Eds.), *Measures of social psychological attitudes* (pp. 45–167). Ann Arbor, MI: Institute for Social Research.

Crocker, J., & Major, B. (1989). Social stigma and self-esteem: The self-protective properties of stigma. *Psychological Review, 96,* 608–630.

Crocker, J., Thompson, L. L., McGraw, K. M., & Ingerman, C. (1987). Downward comparison, prejudice, and evaluation of others: Effects of self-esteem and threat. *Journal of Personality and Social Psychology, 52,* 907–916.

Demo, D. H. (1985). The measurement of self-esteem: Refining our methods. *Journal of Personality and Social Psychology, 48,* 1490–1502.

Dobson, C., Goudy, W. J., Keith, P. M., & Powers, E. (1979). Further analysis of Rosenberg's Self-esteem Scale. *Psychological Reports, 44,* 639–641.

Duncan, C. (1966). A reputation test of personality integration. *Journal of Personality and Social Psychology, 3,* 516–524

Eagly, A. H. (1967). Involvement as a determinant of response to favorable and unfavorable information. *Journal of Personality and Social Psychology Monographs, 7*(3, Whole No. 643).

Eagly, A. H. (1969). Sex differences in the relationship between self-esteem and susceptibility to social influence. *Journal of Personality, 37,* 581–591.

Felson, R. B. (1984). The effect of self-appraisals of ability on academic performance. *Journal of Personality and Social Psychology, 47,* 944–952.

Fitts, W. H. (1965). *Manual: Tennessee Self-Concept Scale.* Nashville, TN: Counselor Recordings & Tests.

Fleming, J. S., & Courtney, B. E. (1984). The dimensionality of self-esteem. II. Hierarchical facet model for revised measurement scales. *Journal of Personality and Social Psychology, 46,* 404–421.

Fleming, J. S., & Watts, W. A. (1980). The dimensionality of self-esteem: Some results for a college sample. *Journal of Personality and Social Psychology, 39,* 921–929.

Franzoi, S. L., & Herzog, M. E. (1986). The Body-Esteem Scale: A convergent and discriminant validity study. *Journal of Personality Assessment, 50,* 24–31.

Franzoi, S. L., & Herzog, M. E. (1987). Judging physical attractiveness: What body aspects do we use? *Personality and Social Psychology Bulletin, 13,* 19–33.

Franzoi, S. L., & Shields, S. A. (1984). The Body-Esteem Scale: Multidimensional structure and sex differences in a college population. *Journal of Personality Assessment, 48,* 173–178.

Freedman, J. (1978). *Happy people: What happiness is, who has it, and why.* New York: Harcourt, Brace, Jovanovich.

Frijda, N. H. (1986). *The emotions.* New York: Cambridge Univ. Press.

Froehle, T. C., & Zerface, J. P. (1971). Social self-esteem: A further look. *Journal of Consulting and Clinical Psychology, 37,* 73–75.

Gergen, K. (1965). The effects of interaction goals and personalistic feedback on the presentation of the self. *Journal of Personality and Social Psychology, 1,* 413–424.

Gergen, K. (1971). *The concept of self.* New York: Holt.

Gergen, K., & Morse, S. (1967). Self-consistency: Measurement and validation. *Proceedings of the 75th American Psychological Association Convention, 2,* 207–208.

Gibbs, J., & Norwich, B. (1985). The validity of a short form of the Coopersmith Self-Esteem Inventory. *British Journal of Educational Psychology, 55,* 76–80.

Gough, H., & Heilbrun, A. (1965). *The Adjective Check List manual.* Palo Alto, CA: Consulting Psychologists Press.

Greenberg, J., Pyszczynski, T., & Solomon, S. (1986). The causes and consequences of a need for self-esteem: A terror management theory. In R. F. Baumeister (Ed.), *Public self and private self* (pp. 189–212). New York: Springer-Verlag.

Greenwald, A. (1986). *The standardization of self-esteem measurement.* Symposium presented at the annual meeting of the Society of Experimental Social Psychology, Tempe, AZ.

Hall, J. D. (1964). *An investigation of acquiescence response set.* Unpublished doctoral dissertation, George Peabody College, Nashville, TN.

Hamilton, D. L. (1971). A comparative study of five methods of assessing self-esteem, dominance, and dogmatism. *Educational and Psychological Measurement, 31,* 441–452.

Harter, S. (1985). *Manual for the Self-Perception Profile for Children (revision of the Perceived Competence Scale for Children).* Denver, CO: University of Denver.

Harter, S., & Pike, R. G. (1983). *The Pictorial Scale of Perceived Competence and Acceptance for Young Children.* Denver, CO: University of Denver.

Hatfield, E., & Sprecher, S. (1985). *Measuring passionate love in intimate relationships.* Unpublished manuscript, University of Hawaii at Manoa.

Helmreich, R., & Stapp, J. (1974). Short forms of the Texas Social Behavior Inventory (TSBI): An objective measure of self-esteem. *Bulletin of the Psychonomic Society, 4,* 473–475.

Helmreich, R., Stapp, J., & Ervin, C. (1974). The Texas Social Behavior Inventory (TSBI): An objective measure of self-esteem or social competence. *JSAS Catalog of Selected Documents in Psychology, 4,* 79.

Hensley, W. E. (1977). Differences between males and females on Rosenberg scale of self-esteem. *Psychological Reports, 41,* 829–830.

Hensley, W. E., & Roberts, M. K. (1976). Dimensions of Rosenberg's scale of self-esteem. *Psychological Reports, 38,* 583–584.

Janis, I. S., & Field, P. B. (1959). A behavioral assessment of persuasibility: Consistency of individual differences. In C. I. Hovland & I. L. Janis (Eds.), *Personality and persuasibility,* (pp. 55–68). New Haven, CT: Yale Univ. Press.

Johnson, F. (1973). Alienation: Concept, term, and word. In F. Johnson (Ed.), *Alienation: Concept, term and meanings* (pp. 27–51). New York: Seminar Press.

Johnston, L., Bachman, J., & O'Malley, P. (1986). *Monitoring the future.* Ann Arbor: University of Michigan, Institute for Social Research.

Jones, W. H., & Briggs, S. R. (1984). The self–other discrepancy in social shyness. In R. Schwarzer (Ed.), *The self in anxiety, stress, and depression* (pp. 93–107). Amsterdam: North-Holland/Elsevier.

Joseph, J. (1979). *Pre-School and Primary Self-Concept Screening Test: Instruction manual.* Chicago: Stoelting Co.

Kaplan, J. B., & Pokorny, A. D. (1969). Self-derogation and psychosocial adjustment. *Journal of Nervous and Mental Disease, 149,* 421–434.

Kokenes, B. (1978). A factor analytic study of the Coopersmith Self-Esteem Inventory. *Adolescence, 13,* 149–155.

Kuhn, M., & McPartland, D. (1954). An empirical investigation of self-attitudes. *American Sociological Review, 19,* 58–76.

Lazarus, R. S. (1984). On the primacy of cognition. *American Psychologist, 39,* 124–129.

Leary, M. R. (1983). *Understanding social anxiety: Social, personality and clinical perspectives.* Beverly Hills, CA: Sage.

Levy, L. H. (1956). The meaning and generality of perceived and actual–ideal discrepancies. *Journal of Consulting Psychology, 20,* 396–398.

Lorr, M., & Wunderlich, R. A. (1986). Two objective measures of self-esteem. *Journal of Personality Assessment, 50,* 18–23.

Luhtanen, R., & Crocker, J. (1990). *A collective self-esteem scale: Self-evaluation of one's social identity.* Unpublished manuscript, SUNY at Buffalo.

Mann, D. W. (1980). Methodological, developmental, and sex biases in the Social Self-Esteem Test? Modest, no, and no. *Journal of Personality Assessment, 44,* 253–257.

Mann, D. W. (1981). Age and differential predictability of delinquent behavior. *Social Forces, 60,* 87–113.

Marsh, H. W., & Hocevar, D. (1983). Confirmatory factor analysis of multitrait–multimethod matrices. *Journal of Educational Measurement, 20,* 231–248.

Marsh, H. W., & O'Neill, R. (1984). Self-Description Questionnaire III: The construct validity of multidimensional self-concept ratings by late adolescents. *Journal of Educational Measurement, 24,* 153–174.

Marsh, H. W., & Richards, G. E. (1988). Tennessee Self-Concept Scale: Reliability, internal structure, and construct validity. *Journal of Personality and Social Psychology*, **55**, 612–624.

Marsh, H. W., Barnes, J., & Hocevar, D. (1985). Self–other agreement on multidimensional self-concept ratings: Factor analysis and multitrait–multimethod analysis. *Journal of Personality and Social Psychology*, **49**, 1360–1377.

Marsh, H. W., Relich, J. D., & Smith, I. D. (1983). Self-concept: The construct validity of interpretations based upon the SDQ. *Journal of Personality and Social Psychology*, **45**, 173–187.

Marsh, H. W., Smith, I. D., & Barnes, J. (1983). Multitrait–multimethod analyses of the Self-Description Questionnaire: Student–teacher agreement on multidimensional ratings of student self-concept. *American Education Research Journal*, **20**, 333–357.

Marsh, H. W., Parker, J., & Barnes, J. (1984). Multidimensional adolescent self-concepts: Their relationship to age, sex, and academic measures. *American Education Research Journal*, **22**, 422–444.

McDaniel, E. L. (1970). *A manual for the Inferred Self-Concept Scale*. Austin, TX: San Felipe Press.

McFarland, C., & Ross, M. (1982). Impact of causal attributions on affective reactions to success and failure. *Journal of Personality and Social Psychology*, **43**, 937–946.

McFarlin, D. G., & Blascovich, J. (1981). Effects of self-esteem and performance on future affective preferences and cognitive expectations. *Journal of Personality and Social Psychology*, **40**, 521–531.

McFarlin, D. G., Baumeister, R. F., & Blascovich, J. (1984). On knowing when to quit: Task failure, self-esteem, advice, and respondent persistence. *Journal of Personality*, **52**, 138–155.

McIntire, S. A., & Levine, E. L. (1984). An empirical investigation of self-esteem as a composite construct. *Journal of Vocational Behavior*, **25**, 290–303.

Millen, L. (1966). *The relationship between self-concept, social desirability and anxiety in children*. Unpublished master's thesis, Pennsylvania State University, College Park.

Miskimins, R. W., & Braucht, G. (1971). *Description of the self*. Fort Collins, CO: Rocky Mountain Behavioral Inst.

Mossman, B., & Ziller, R. (1968). Self-esteem and consistency of social behavior. *Journal of Abnormal Psychology*, **73**, 363–367.

Nunnelly, K. G. (1968). *The use of multiple therapy in group counseling and psychotherapy*. Unpublished doctoral dissertation. Michigan State University, East Lansing.

O'Brien, E. J. (1985). Global self-esteem scales: Unidimensional or multidimensional? *Psychological Reports*, **57**, 383–389.

Parish, T. S., & Taylor, J. C. (1978). The Personal Attribute Inventory for Children: A report on its validity and reliability as a self-concept scale. *Educational and Psychological Measurement*, **38**, 565–569.

Paulhus, D. L. (1986). Self-deception and impression management in test responses. In A. Angleutner & J. S. Wiggins (Eds.), *Personality assessment via questionnaire* (pp. 143–165). New York: Springer-Verlag.

Peplau, L. A., & Perlman, D. (1982). *Loneliness: A current source book of theory, research, and therapy*. New York: Wiley (Interscience).

Phillips, E. (1951). Attitudes toward self and others: A brief questionnaire report. *Journal of Consulting Psychology*, **15**, 79–81.

Piers, E. V. (1969). *Manual for the Piers–Harris Children's Self-Concept Scale*. Nashville, TN: Counselor Recordings and Tests.

Piers, E. V. (1984). *Piers–Harris Children's Self-Concept Scale: Revised Manual*. Los Angeles: Western Psychological Services.

Querry, P. H. (1970). *A study of the self-concept of children with functional articulation disorders and normal children*. Unpublished master's thesis, University of Pittsburgh, Pittsburgh, PA.

Reynolds, W. M. (1988). Measurement of academic self-concept in college students. *Journal of Personality Assessment*, **52**, 223–240.

Rogers, C. R., & Dymond, R. F. (Eds.) (1954). *Psychotherapy and personality change: Coordinated studies in the client-centered approach.* Chicago: Univ. of Chicago Press.

Roid, G. H., & Fitts, W. H. (1988). *Tennessee Self-Concept Scale* (revised manual). Los Angeles: Western Psychological Services.

Rosenberg, M. (1965). *Society and the adolescent self-image.* Princeton, NJ: Princeton Univ. Press.

Rosenberg, M., & Simmons, R. G. (1972). *Black and white self-esteem: The urban school child.* Washington, D.C.: American Sociological Association.

Ryden, M. B. (1978). An adult version of the Coopersmith Self-Esteem Inventory: Test–retest reliability and social desirability. *Psychological Reports, 43,* 1189–1190.

Sadowski, C. J., Woodward, H. R., Davis, S. F., & Elsbury, D. L. (1983). Sex differences in adjustment correlates of locus of control dimensions. *Journal of Personality Assessment, 47,* 627–631.

Savin-Williams, R. C., & Jaquish, G. A. (1981). The assessment of adolescent self-esteem: A comparison of methods. *Journal of Personality, 49,* 324–336.

Schauer, G. H. (1975). *An analysis of the self-report of fifth and sixth grade regular class children and gifted class children.* Unpublished doctoral dissertation, Kent State University, Kent, OH.

Schneider, D. J., & Turkat, D. (1975). Self-presentation following success or failure: Defensive self-esteem models. *Journal of Personality, 43,* 127–135.

Secord, P. F., & Jourard, S. M. (1953). The appraisal of body-cathexis: Body-cathexis and the self. *Journal of Consulting Psychology, 17,* 343–347.

Shavelson, R. J., Hubner, J. J., & Stanton, G. C. (1976). Self-concept: Validation of construct interpretations. *Review of Educational Research, 46,* 407–441.

Shaver, P. R., & Brennan, K. A. (1990). Measures of depression and loneliness. In J. P. Robinson, P. R. Shaver, & L. S. Wrightsman (Eds.), *Measures of Personality and Social Psychological Attitudes.* New York: Academic Press.

Sherwood, J. J. (1962). *Self-identity and self-actualization: A theory and research.* Unpublished doctoral dissertation, University of Michigan, East Lansing.

Shostrom, E. (1966). *EITS Manual for the Personal Orientation Inventory.* San Diego: Educational and Industrial Testing.

Shrauger, J. S., & Sparrell, J. (1988). *Development and validation of an empirically derived measure of social desirability in college students.* Unpublished data, State University of New York at Buffalo.

Shrauger, J. S. (1990). *Self-confidence: Its conceptualization, measurement, and behavioral implications.* Manuscript in preparation, SUNY at Buffalo.

Silber, E., & Tippett, J. (1965). Self-esteem: Clinical assessment and measurement validation. *Psychological Reports, 16,* 1017–1071.

Simpson, C. K., & Boyal, D. (1975). Esteem construct generality and academic performance. *Educational and Psychological Measurement, 35,* 897–907.

Soares, J. J., & Soares, L. (1970). Self-perceptions of culturally disadvantaged children. *American Educational Research Journal, 5,* 31–45.

Sundby, E. (1962). *A study of personality and social variables related to conformity behavior.* Unpublished doctoral dissertation, Vanderbilt University, Nashville, TN.

Taylor, J. B., & Reitz, W. E. (1968, April). *The three faces of self-esteem* (Res. Bull. No. 80). Department of Psychology, University of Western Ontario.

Taylor, S. E. (1983). Adjustment to threatening events: A theory of cognitive adaptation. *American Psychologist, 38,* 1161–1173.

Taylor, S. E., & Brown, J. D. (1988). Illusion and well-being: A social psychological perspective on mental health. *Psychological Bulletin, 103,* 193–210.

Tennen, H., & Herzberger, S. (1987). Depression, self-esteem, and the absence of self-protective attributional biases. *Journal of Personality and Social Psychology, 52,* 72–80.

Van Tuinen, M., & Rananaiah, N. V. (1979). A multimethod analysis of selected self-esteem measures. *Journal of Research in Personality, 13,* 16–24.

Weiner, B. (1986). *An attributional theory of motivation and emotion.* New York: Springer-Verlag.

Wells, L. E., & Marwell, G. (1976). *Self-esteem: Its conceptualization and measurement.* Beverly Hills, CA: Sage.

Williams, E. B. (1979). *The Scribner-Bantam English dictionary* (rev. ed.). New York: Bantam Books.

Wylie, R. C. (1961). *The self concept.* Lincoln: Univ. of Nebraska Press.

Wylie, R. C. (1974). *The self-concept* (Vol. 1. *A review of methodological considerations and measuring instruments*) (rev. ed.). Lincoln: Univ. of Nebraska Press.

Yonker, R. J., Blixt, S., & Dinero, T. (1974, April). *A methodological investigation of the development of a semantic differential to assess self-concept.* Paper presented at the annual meeting of the National Council on Measurement in Education, Chicago.

Zander, A., & Thomas, E. (1960). *The validity of a measure of ego strength.* Unpublished manuscript, University of Michigan, Institute for Social Research, Ann Arbor.

Ziller, R., Hagey, J., Smith, M. D., & Long, B. (1969). Self-esteem: A self-social construct. *Journal of Consulting and Clinical Psychology, 33,* 84–95.

Zirkel, P., & Gable, R. K. (1977). The reliability and validity of various measures of self-concept among ethnically different adolescents. *Measurement and Evaluation in Guidance, 10,* 48–55.

CHAPTER 5

Social Anxiety, Shyness, and Related Constructs

Mark R. Leary

Anxiety is a multifaceted response to threatening situations. It is characterized by cognitive apprehension, neurophysiological arousal, and a subjective experience of tension or nervousness. People may experience anxiety for a wide variety of reasons, but factor analyses of anxiety and fear inventories consistently obtain solutions that include at least one category of "social" or "interpersonal" anxieties (e.g., Bates, 1971; Endler, Hunt, & Rosenwein, 1962). Over the past 25 years, a great deal of behavioral research has been directed at the causes of socially based anxiety, as well as its behavioral concomitants and implications for the socially anxious individual (for reviews, see Jones, Cheek, & Briggs, 1986; Leary, 1983d; Schlenker & Leary, 1982; Zimbardo, 1977).

Empirical studies dealing with social anxiety can be split into three general categories. First, many researchers have been interested in social anxiety as an interpersonal phenomenon in its own right. Virtually everyone experiences social anxiety at least occasionally. When they do, people not only suffer subjective tension but behave in ways that often interfere with social interaction. When nervous, people may display overt indications of their inner arousal (e.g., trembling, fidgeting), avoidance of other people, and disruption of other ongoing behaviors (e.g., disfluent speech, difficult concentration). As a result, anxiety is a liability in social relations, because people who are nervous and inhibited may become less socially effective.

While most research has been directed toward understanding social anxiety and its impact on interpersonal behavior, other researchers have been interested in social anxiety in the process of studying other phenomena. For example, the construct of social anxiety has been used in studies of topics such as evaluation apprehension, impression management, self-consciousness, affect regulation, self-efficacy, alcohol abuse, conformity, and loneliness. This research has demonstrated that feelings of social inadequacy and concerns about others' evaluations play a central role in many psychological phenomena (see Jones, Cheek, & Briggs, 1986; Leary, 1983d).

A third focus of research involves understanding and treating extreme social anxiety in clinical and counseling settings. Although everyone may experience social anxiety occasionally, some individuals are plagued chronically by insecurity and anxiety in their dealings with others. Not surprisingly, clinical and counseling psychologists have been interested in developing the most effective ways of treating socially anxious clients. Researchers have examined the effectiveness of a variety of interventions, including systematic desensitization (Paul, 1966), social skills training (Curran, 1977), and cognitive therapy (Glass & Shea, 1986). Reviews of these literatures may be found in Leary (1983d, 1987a).

In the course of these three lines of research, several measures have been developed to identify individuals who are prone to being anxious and inhibited in social situations. The earliest measures of social anxiety and related constructs emerged during the development of early multifactorial personality inventories (e.g., Cattell, 1946; Comrey, 1965; Guilford & Guilford, 1936; see Crozier, 1979, for a review). However, these measures were seldom used to study social anxiety per se and did not stimulate much research on the topic.

Current interest in social anxiety among psychologists can be traced partly to the publication of the Social Avoidance and Distress Scale (Watson & Friend, 1969). Several other measures have appeared during the past 25 years that, in one way or another, assess people's discomfort in social situations. In this chapter, 10 scales related to social anxiety and similar constructs are examined.

Measures Reviewed Here

Although the cognitive, affective, and behavioral aspects of anxiety are interrelated, the correlations among them are not as strong as one might expect (Beatty, 1984). People may be quite anxious with few obvious indications of their inner distress or appear hesitant and avoidant even though they are not nervous. Social anxiety is sometimes related to observable behavior, but there is no necessary relationship between subjective anxiety and its behavioral concomitants (see Leary, 1983b, 1983c, 1983d, 1986a, 1987b, for discussions of the relationship between social anxiety and behavior). Put simply, it is taken as obvious that feeling anxious is conceptually distinguishable from behaving in an inhibited, avoidant, or "nervous" fashion.

This distinction is important because the scales discussed in this chapter differ in the degree to which they focus on subjective as distinct from behavioral manifestations of social anxiety. Some measure only subjective cognitive and/or affective aspects, whereas others tap both affective and behavioral components.

Thus, for heuristic purposes, the measures reviewed in this chapter can be grouped into two categories on the basis of their item content.

Subjective Focus:
1. Fear of Negative Evaluation Scale (Watson & Friend, 1969)
2. Interaction Anxiousness Scale (Leary, 1983c)
3. Personal Report of Communication Apprehension-24 (McCroskey, 1982)
4. Embarrassability Scale (Modigliani, 1968)

Subjective and Behavioral Focus:
5. Social Avoidance and Distress Scale (Watson & Friend, 1969)
6. Social Anxiety Scale (Fenigstein, Scheier, & Buss, 1975)
7. Shyness Scale (Cheek & Buss, 1981)
8. Social Reticence Scale (Jones & Briggs, 1986)
9. Social Anxiety Scale for Children (La Greca, Dandes, Wick, Shaw, & Stone, 1988)
10. Personal Report of Confidence as a Speaker (Paul, 1966)

Studies show that, despite differences in their item content, these scales correlate moderately to highly with one another (Jones, Briggs, & Smith, 1986; Leary, 1983d;

Leary & Kowalski, 1987). Thus, viewed from a purely empirical standpoint, it sometimes matters little which scale is used in certain research contexts. However, in terms of face validity, some measures are clearly more appropriate than others for particular purposes (as explained below). Further, data show that scores on these measures differentially predict other criteria. For example, the most behavioral measure, the Social Reticence Scale, correlates more highly with judges' ratings of people's behavior than the most affective measure, the Interaction Anxiousness Scale (Jones, Briggs, & Smith, 1986), supporting the contention that they measure somewhat different constructs. Researchers should select their measures carefully based on the focus of their particular study.

Overview of the Measures

The first four measures listed above focus on the tendency to experience subjective apprehension and anxiety in social contexts. However, they differ in important ways.

The Fear of Negative Evaluation (FNE) Scale assesses the degree to which people worry about how they are perceived and evaluated by others. Two versions of the FNE Scale exist, the original 28-item version (Watson & Friend, 1969) and a brief 12-item revision (Leary, 1983a). The two versions correlate .96 and both show strong evidence of construct and criterion validity. Unlike most of the other measures reviewed here, the FNE Scale focuses primarily on people's concerns with interpersonal evaluation rather than on the tendency to feel anxious per se. However, to the extent that social anxiety is closely related to people's concerns with how they are perceived and evaluated by others (Schlenker & Leary, 1982), fear of negative evaluation and social anxiety are closely related constructs.

Most early scales designed to measure social anxiety included items that assessed both subjective anxiety and overt behavior. Leary (1983b, 1983c) argued that using behavioral items to measure the tendency to experience social anxiety creates conceptual confusion and makes it difficult to study the relationship between subjective anxiety and particular behavioral reactions. When behavioral items are included on "social anxiety" scales, empirical associations between the scale and particular overt behaviors are often tautological. For this reason, Leary (1983c) constructed the 15-item Interaction Anxiousness Scale to measure the tendency to experience social anxiety independently of the tendency to behave in an inhibited, reticent, or awkward fashion.

Researchers in speech communication have long been interested in people's feelings of social anxiety when speaking before groups (sometimes called speech anxiety, audience anxiety, or stage fright). The 104-item Personal Report of Confidence as a Speaker (PRCS) developed by Gilkinson (1942) was used for many years, until it was supplanted by a shorter version of the scale developed by Paul (1966). Paul's PRCS has been widely used as a measure of speech anxiety in a number of contexts, particularly in studies that examined the effectiveness of various clinical interventions to reduce speech anxiety.

However, Paul's (1966) measure focused only on difficulties experienced when speaking before groups and included items assessing both affect (e.g., "I am terrified at the thought of speaking before a group of people") and behavior ("I always avoid speaking in public if possible"). As a result, McCroskey (1970, 1978) developed the Personal Report of Communication Apprehension (PRCA) to assess the tendency to become apprehensive across a variety of communication settings. He subsequently refined the PRCA twice. The most recent, 24-item version (PRCA-24) (McCroskey, 1982) contains subscales to assess communication apprehension in four distinct contexts: dyadic conversations, meetings, small groups, and public speaking. Both the PRCA and the

PRCA-24 are psychometrically strong, but they have been used nearly exclusively by researchers in speech communication and rarely by psychologists.

As its name indicates, the Embarrassability Scale (Modigliani, 1966, 1968) measures the tendency to become embarrassed. Embarrassment is a form of social anxiety that occurs when events damage the public identity an individual wishes to claim (Goffman, 1955; Miller, 1986; Schlenker, 1980). This scale presents 26 potentially embarrassing incidents (such as walking in on someone in the bathroom, falling down on a bus, or forgetting an appointment) and asks the respondent how embarrassed he or she would be in each. Unfortunately, this fascinating measure has been underutilized, partly because it appeared in an unpublished dissertation (see, however, Edelmann, 1985; Miller, 1986, 1987).

The next six scales assess both subjective and behavioral aspects of social anxiety and related constructs. Of all of the scales reviewed in this chapter, the Social Avoidance and Distress Scale (SAD) of Watson and Friend (1969) has received the most use among psychologists. It has been used in hundreds of studies to examine the effectiveness of clinical interventions for social anxiety, as well as in investigations of the personological and behavioral correlates of social anxiety. As its name implies, the SAD Scale includes items that assess both social avoidance and social distress (i.e., anxiety). Indeed, Watson and Friend discussed distinct avoidance and distress subscales, and a factor analysis by Patterson and Strauss (1972) revealed separate behavioral and anxiety factors. Despite this, most researchers have ignored the subscale structure and used the total scale score. However, one study showed that the avoidance and anxiety subscales differentially predict behavior in real interactions (Leary, Knight, & Johnson, 1987). Unfortunately, despite a wealth of data supporting the validity of the full scale as a combined measure of anxiety and avoidance, the validity of the individual subscales has not been studied.

In the process of factor analyzing items relevant to self-consciousness, Fenigstein *et al.* (1975) constructed a 6-item Social Anxiety Scale. Though it is the shortest of the scales reviewed in this chapter, it casts the biggest net. Items on the scale tap embarrassability, public speaking anxiety, reticence when talking to strangers, shyness, nervousness in large groups, and performance difficulties when under others' scrutiny. Thus, both affective and behavioral items are included, and the items span both conversational and public speaking situations. This measure, along with a revision for the general population (Scheier & Carver, 1985), may be useful when a brief, yet broad, index of affective and behavioral difficulties in a variety of situations is required.

The Cheek and Buss (1981) Shyness Scale assesses both social anxiety and the tendency to be inhibited in social situations. The original scale contained 9 items, but subsequent revisions have yielded 11- and 13-item versions (Cheek, 1983). The Shyness Scale has become the measure of choice when one desires a combined index of the anxiety and inhibition components of the shyness syndrome. It has good psychometric properties and has demonstrated its usefulness in a number of contexts. However, to repeat a theme carried throughout this chapter, the Shyness Scale should be used only when one desires a measure that combines affective and behavioral items. If one's research calls for a "pure" measure of either social anxiety or behavioral inhibition or avoidance, other measures should be used.

The Social Reticence Scale (SRS) reviewed here (Jones & Briggs, 1986) is a revision of an earlier scale by Jones and Russell (1982). Although the authors describe it as a measure of shyness (which they define as a type of social anxiety), the scale does not, in fact, contain any items that refer to anxiety. Rather, the item content reflects two domains: the degree of ease or difficulty one has in meeting people and making good impressions, and the degree to which one communicates easily and effectively with others. Thus, the scale is best viewed as a measure of the inhibition, hesitancy, and reticence that often accompany subjective social anxiety. Indeed, although scores on the SRS correlate highly with other measures of social anxiety, it seems to predict shy behavior better than some other scales (Jones, Briggs, & Smith, 1986). Thus, the SRS may be the scale of choice when one wishes to measure feelings of inhibition, isolation, and social ineffectiveness but is less preferable when a measure of subjective social anxiety per se is needed.

Aside from studies of wariness or stranger anxiety in infants, relatively little research has been conducted on social anxiety in children. However, La Greca et al. (1988) have developed the Social Anxiety Scale for Children (SASC), a 10-item scale that includes items assessing fear of negative evaluation, inhibition, and social anxiety. Although not yet widely used due to its novelty, the SASC shows promise as a self-report measure of social anxiety and inhibition for use with literate children.

All of the scales reviewed in this chapter have demonstrated reliability and validity as measures of social anxiety and related constructs. However, they are by no means interchangeable, and researchers should exercise care to select appropriate instruments for their particular research purposes.

Fear of Negative Evaluation Scale (FNE)
(Watson & Friend, 1969)

Variable

Watson and Friend (1969, p. 449) defined fear of negative evaluation (FNE) as "apprehension about other's evaluations, distress over their negative evaluations, and the expectation that others would evaluate oneself negatively."

Description

Item content is congruent with this conceptualization. The original FNE Scale (Watson & Friend, 1969) consists of 30 true–false items, approximately balanced between positively and negatively scored items. The revised, brief version of the scale (Leary, 1983a) contains 12 of the original items, which are answered on five-point scales (1, not at all characteristic of me; 5, extremely characteristic of me). Scale scores on the original FNE range from 0 (lowest FNE) to 30 (highest FNE); scores on the brief version range from 12 to 60. The opposite of high FNE is the lack of apprehension about others' evaluations, but not necessarily a desire or need to be evaluated positively.

Sample

The mean of the original sample of 205 university students was 15.5 (SD = 8.6), and the scores were rectangularly distributed. Responses from a second sample of 128 subjects obtained a mean of 13.6 (SD = 7.6). The sample used in the development of the 12-item scale (n = 150) had a mean of 35.7 and a standard deviation of 8.1.

Reliability

Internal Consistency

For the 30-item T–F scale, internal consistency (KR-20) is high (.92 and .94 in two samples). For the Brief FNE Scale, item–total correlations range from .43 to .75, and Cronbach's α coefficient is .90.

Test–Retest

One-month test–retest reliability for the 30-item T–F scale is .78; for the briefer scale a 4-week test–retest correlation is .75.

The original and brief versions of the scale correlate .96.

Validity

Convergent

FNE scores correlate moderately with other measures of apprehension in social situations, such as the SAD Scale ($r = .51$) and the Interaction Anxiousness Scale ($r = .32$). Compared to people who score low on the scale, high scorers are more uneasy about being evaluated, more likely to endorse "irrational beliefs" about the importance of being loved, and more concerned about making good impressions (Friend & Gilbert, 1973; Goldfried & Sobocinski, 1975; Leary, Barnes, & Griebel, 1986; Smith & Sarason, 1975). High FNE people also experience greater anxiety in evaluative settings and report being more bothered by the possibility of being negatively evaluated.

Discriminant

Scores on the original FNE correlate slightly ($r = -.25$) with the Marlowe–Crowne Social Desirability Scale.

Location

Original 30-item scale: Watson, D., & Friend, R. (1969). Measurement of social-evaluative anxiety. *Journal of Consulting and Clinical Psychology,* **33,** 448–457.

Revised 12-item scale: Leary, M. R. (1983). A brief version of the Fear of Negative Evaluation Scale. *Personality and Social Psychology Bulletin,* **9,** 371–375.

Results and Comments

As noted above, Watson and Friend (1969) conceptualized FNE as involving both apprehension over others' evaluations and the expectation that one will be evaluated negatively. However, the content of both versions of the scale leans heavily toward items that assess concerns regarding negative evaluations rather than the expectancy that one will be negatively evaluated. To the degree that data strongly support the utility of the FNE Scale as a measure of interpersonal evaluation apprehension, it may be regarded as an index of central cognitive aspects of social anxiety.

Fear of Negative Evaluation Scales
(Original and Revised)

1. I rarely worry about seeming foolish to others. (R)

1	2	3	4	5
NOT AT ALL CHARACTERISTIC OF ME				EXTREMELY CHARACTERISTIC OF ME

2. I worry about what people will think of me even when I know it doesn't make any difference. *

3. I become tense and jittery if I know someone is sizing me up.

4. I am unconcerned even if I know people are forming an unfavorable impression of me. (R)*

5. I feel very upset when I commit some social error.

6. The opinions that important people have of me cause me little concern. (R)

7. I am often afraid that I may look ridiculous or make a fool out of myself.

8. I react very little when other people disapprove of me. (R)

9. I am frequently afraid of other people noting my shortcomings. *

10. The disapproval of others would have little effect on me. (R)

11. If someone is evaluating me, I tend to expect the worst.

12. I rarely worry about what kind of impression I am making on someone. (R)*

13. I am afraid that others will not approve of me. *

14. I am afraid that people will find fault with me. *

15. Other people's opinions of me do not bother me. (R)*

16. I am not necessarily upset if I don't please someone. (R)

17. When I am talking to someone, I worry about what they may be thinking about me. *

18. I feel that you can't help making social errors, so why worry about it. (R)

19. I am usually worried about what kind of impression I make. *

20. I worry a lot about what my superiors think of me.

21. If I know someone is judging me, it has little effect on me. (R)*

22. I worry that others will think I am not worthwhile.

23. I worry very little about what others may think of me. (R)

24. Sometimes I think I am too concerned with what other people think of me. *

25. I often worry that I will say or do the wrong things. *

26. I am often indifferent to the opinions others have of me. (R)

27. I am usually confident that others will have a favorable impression of me. (R)

28. I often worry that people who are important to me won't think very much of me.

29. I brood about the opinions my friends have about me.

30. I become tense and jittery if I know I am being judged by my superiors.

Note: The 12 items of the Brief FNE Scale (Leary, 1983a) are marked with an asterisk (*). Reverse-score items marked "R" before summing. Source of the original, 30-item scale is Watson and Friend (1969). No standard instructions have been published.

Interaction Anxiousness Scale

(Leary, 1983c)

Variable

The Interaction Anxiousness Scale (IAS) was designed to provide a measure of the tendency to experience subjective social anxiety independently of accompanying behaviors.

Description

The Interaction Anxiousness Scale consists of 15 self-report items that are answered on a five-point scale (1, not at all characteristic of me; 5, extremely characteristic of me). Items were selected with regard to two criteria: (1) They referred to subjective anxiety (tension, nervousness) or its opposite (relaxation, calm), but not to specific overt behaviors; and (2) the items dealt with situations involving contingent social interactions, encounters in which an individual's responses follow from or are contingent upon the responses of other interactants (as opposed, for example, to public speaking situations). Item selection proceeded in four stages from an initial pool of 87 items to the 15 included in the scale. Scale scores range from 15 (low social anxiety) to 75 (high social anxiety).

Sample

Means and standard deviations on the IAS are quite stable across student samples from universities of varying sizes in different parts of the United States (see Leary & Kowalski, 1987). On a sample of 1140 respondents from three different universities (Denison University, University of Texas, Wake Forest University), the mean on the scale was 38.9 (SD = 9.7).

Reliability

Internal Consistency

All items correlate at least .45 with the sum of all other items in the scale, and Cronbach's α exceeds .87.

Test–Retest

Eight-week test–retest reliability is .80.

Validity

Convergent

IAS scores correlate highly (*r* values > .60) with other measures of social anxiousness and shyness (Jones, Briggs, & Smith, 1986; Leary & Kowalski, 1987).

Further, scores on the IAS correlate well with self-reported anxiety in real interactions. Compared to low scorers, high scorers report more anxiety and less confidence both before and during interpersonal encounters, are more concerned with what others think of them during interactions, feel more inhibited during conversations, and are judged by others as appearing more nervous and less confident (Leary, 1983c, 1986b). High scorers also tend to be more worried about how others evaluate their physical appearance (Hart, Leary, & Rejeski, 1989). Scores are also associated with increases in heart rate in face-to-face interactions (Leary, 1986b), and IAS scores correlate positively with social avoidance and inhibition (Leary, Atherton, Hill, & Hur, 1986). Finally, students who sought counseling for social problems at a university counseling center scored significantly higher on the scale than students who did not seek counseling (Leary, 1983c).

Discriminant

The correlation between the IAS and scores on the Marlowe–Crowne Social Desirability Scale is −.26, giving some evidence of discriminant validity.

Location

Leary, M. R. (1983). Social anxiousness: The construct and its measurement. *Journal of Personality Assessment, 47,* 66–75.

Results and Comments

As noted in the introduction, most measures of social anxiety assess both affective and behavioral aspects of people's social difficulties. However, for many purposes, the distinction between subjective feelings of anxiety and overt behaviors such as hesitancy, avoidance, and performance difficulties is critical (Leary, 1983b, 1983c, 1986a).

The IAS has demonstrated reliability and validity as a measure of the tendency to experience social anxiety in conversational settings. In the development of the scale, an explicit attempt was made to measure social anxiousness independently of behavior. Thus, when a measure of social anxiousness per se, uncontaminated by self-reported behavior, is needed, the IAS is preferred over measures that combine affective and behavioral elements.

Interaction Anxiousness Scale

Read each item carefully and decide the degree to which the statement is characteristic or true of you. Then place a number between "1" and "5" in the correct space according to the following scale.

1 = The statement is *not* at all characteristic of me.
2 = The statement is *slightly* characteristic of me.
3 = The statement is *moderately* characteristic of me.
4 = The statement is *very* characteristic of me.
5 = The statement is *extremely* characteristic of me.

_____ 1. I often feel nervous even in casual get-togethers.

_____ 2. I usually feel uncomfortable when I am in a group of people I don't know.

_____ 3. I am usually at ease when speaking to a member of the opposite sex. (R)

_____ 4. I get nervous when I must talk to a teacher or boss.

_____ 5. Parties often make me feel anxious and uncomfortable.

_____ 6. I am probably less shy in social interactions than most people. (R)

_____ 7. I sometimes feel tense when talking to people of my own sex if I don't know them very well.

_____ 8. I would be nervous if I was being interviewed for a job.

_____ 9. I wish I had more confidence in social situations.

_____ 10. I seldom feel anxious in social situations. (R)

_____ 11. In general, I am a shy person.

_____ 12. I often feel nervous when talking to an attractive member of the opposite sex.

_____ 13. I often feel nervous when calling someone I don't know very well on the telephone.

_____ 14. I get nervous when I speak to someone in a position of authority.

_____ 15. I usually feel relaxed around other people, even people who are quite different from myself. (R)

Note: Reverse-scored items marked (R) before summing. Source: Leary (1983c).

Personal Report of Communication Apprehension (PRCA-24)

(McCroskey, 1982)

Variable

Communication apprehension is "an individual's level of fear or anxiety associated with either real or imagined communication with another person or persons" (McCroskey, 1978, p. 78).

Description

Defined in this manner, the term is broader than "speech anxiety" and "audience anxiety," which refer to anxiety experienced when one must speak or perform before groups. However, it is narrower than "social anxiety," which does not connote concerns with communication per se. McCroskey (1970) originally developed three versions of the Personal Report of Communication Apprehension (PRCA), one for each of three age groups (college, 10th grade, 7th grade) as well as a version for preliterate children (McCroskey, 1976). He has subsequently revised the college (i.e., adult) version twice (McCroskey, 1978, 1982).

The original PRCA contained 20 items that were distilled from an initial pool of 76, 30 of which were taken directly from Paul's (1966) Personal Report of Confidence as a Speaker. Items covered anxiety experienced in interpersonal communication, small group discussion, and public speaking situations. The 1978 revision of the scale added five items.

However, items on the early versions of the PRCA were overrepresented by those that referred to anxiety experienced in public speaking contexts (Porter, 1979). In fact, 10 of

Table 1

Means and Standard Deviations for the PRCA-24[a]

Scale	Undergraduates (n = 12,418)		Pharmacy students (n = 10,223)	
	Mean	SD	Mean	SD
Total PRCA-24	65.6	14.1	65.2	16.3
Public speaking	19.9	5.1	18.7	5.2
Meetings	16.3	4.7	16.4	5.0
Groups	15.3	4.7	15.5	5.0
Dyadic interaction	14.1	3.9	14.5	4.4

[a]J. C. McCroskey (personal communication, 1987).

the 20 items on the original scale refer explicitly to public speaking, and several others are ambiguous regarding context. Thus, the original PRCA bordered on being a measure of speech anxiety rather than of generalized communication apprehension. To remedy this, McCroskey (1982) constructed a new version of the scale, the PRCA-24, to tap apprehension in four specific types of communication contexts.

The PRCA-24 contains four subscales of six items each. The subscales measure communication apprehension in group settings, dyadic interactions, meetings, and public speaking situations. Four subscale scores can be obtained, along with a total communication apprehension score. Items are answered on five-point Likert scales (1, strongly agree; 5, strongly disagree). Scores on each subscale range from 6 (low communication apprehension) to 30 (high communication apprehension). Total scores range from 24 to 120.

Sample

Norms for the PRCA-24 are available for several large samples, two of which are shown in Table 1. To classify people as low versus high in communication apprehension using the total PRCA-24 score, McCroskey used scores below 52 to indicate low apprehension and scores above 79 to indicate high apprehension.

Reliability

Internal Consistency

The subscale scores intercorrelate between .40 and .69. Alpha coefficients from several large samples consistently exceed .90 for the total PRCA-24 score, and .75 for all subscales.

Test–Retest

Test–retest correlations have not been published.

Validity

Convergent

Scores on the PRCA-24 correlate with state anxiety in communication contexts (Allen, Richmond, & McCroskey, 1984; McCroskey & Beatty, 1984) and with measures of assertiveness (McCroskey, Beatty, Kearney, & Plax, 1985). Further, the subscales that measure apprehension in dyadic and public speaking situations correlate moderately with general measures of shyness and social anxiousness (Jones, Briggs, & Smith, 1986). However, these correlations are lower than those among most other such measures, possibly due to the brevity of the subscales.

Discriminant

Although the total scale score has proven useful in a number of research contexts, the discriminant validity of the four subscales has not been adequately examined. In one study, the subscale scores did not differentially predict assertiveness. Further, the various subscales contribute little unique variance to total PRCA-24 scores, leading the authors to conclude that the items on the PRCA-24 are "tapping a generalized, trait-like response to communication" (McCroskey *et al.*, 1985). Thus, the subscale scores have not been shown to predict affective or behavioral criteria differentially.

Location

McCroskey, J. C. (1982). *An introduction to rhetorical communication* (4th ed.). Englewood Cliffs, NJ: Prentice-Hall.

Results and Comments

Early versions of the PRCA (McCroskey, 1970, 1978) have been used extensively in studies of communication apprehension and show strong evidence of reliability and validity. Although the PRCA-24 has not yet received the widespread use of its predecessors, every indication is that the PRCA-24 may become the instrument of choice for assessing generalized communication apprehension. The PRCA-24 appears to be both highly reliable and valid as a measure of apprehension regarding interpersonal communication. However, two qualifications regarding its use should be noted: The scale measures apprehension that is specific to communicating with others, and there is little evidence to support the differential validity of the four subscales. Until their discriminant validity is more extensively explored, use of the total scale score (based on all 24 items) is advised.

Personal Report of Communication Apprehension-24

Directions: This instrument is composed of 24 statements concerning your feelings about communication with other people. Please indicate in the space provided the degree to which each statement applies to you by marking whether you (1) Strongly Agree, (2) Agree, (3) Are Undecided, (4) Disagree, or (5) Strongly Disagree with each statement. There are no right or wrong answers. Many of the statements are similar to other statements. Do not be concerned about this. Work quickly, just record your first impression.

_____ 1. I dislike participating in group discussions.

_____ 2. Generally, I am comfortable while participating in group discussions.

_____ 3. I am tense and nervous while participating in group discussions.

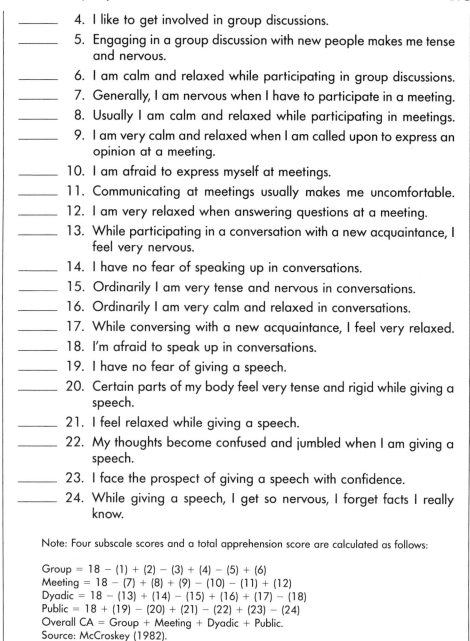

_____ 4. I like to get involved in group discussions.

_____ 5. Engaging in a group discussion with new people makes me tense and nervous.

_____ 6. I am calm and relaxed while participating in group discussions.

_____ 7. Generally, I am nervous when I have to participate in a meeting.

_____ 8. Usually I am calm and relaxed while participating in meetings.

_____ 9. I am very calm and relaxed when I am called upon to express an opinion at a meeting.

_____ 10. I am afraid to express myself at meetings.

_____ 11. Communicating at meetings usually makes me uncomfortable.

_____ 12. I am very relaxed when answering questions at a meeting.

_____ 13. While participating in a conversation with a new acquaintance, I feel very nervous.

_____ 14. I have no fear of speaking up in conversations.

_____ 15. Ordinarily I am very tense and nervous in conversations.

_____ 16. Ordinarily I am very calm and relaxed in conversations.

_____ 17. While conversing with a new acquaintance, I feel very relaxed.

_____ 18. I'm afraid to speak up in conversations.

_____ 19. I have no fear of giving a speech.

_____ 20. Certain parts of my body feel very tense and rigid while giving a speech.

_____ 21. I feel relaxed while giving a speech.

_____ 22. My thoughts become confused and jumbled when I am giving a speech.

_____ 23. I face the prospect of giving a speech with confidence.

_____ 24. While giving a speech, I get so nervous, I forget facts I really know.

Note: Four subscale scores and a total apprehension score are calculated as follows:

Group = 18 − (1) + (2) − (3) + (4) − (5) + (6)
Meeting = 18 − (7) + (8) + (9) − (10) − (11) + (12)
Dyadic = 18 − (13) + (14) − (15) + (16) + (17) − (18)
Public = 18 + (19) − (20) + (21) − (22) + (23) − (24)
Overall CA = Group + Meeting + Dyadic + Public.
Source: McCroskey (1982).

Embarrassability Scale

(Modigliani, 1966)

Variable

Embarrassment is a form of social anxiety that occurs when a person's public identity in a particular situation is threatened (Goffman, 1955; Miller, 1986; Modigliani, 1968); embarrassability refers to an individual's general susceptibility to becoming embarrassed.

Description

The Embarrassability Scale consists of brief descriptions of 26 social situations that may cause people to feel embarrassed, such as slipping on a patch of ice, walking in on someone in the bathroom, and falling victim to a coughing attack during a lecture. For each situation, respondents indicate how embarrassed they would feel. The original scale used a nine-point response format (1, not the least bit embarrassed; 9, acutely embarrassed), but some researchers have used five-point scales. The version of the scale presented at the end of this review is a slightly modified version of Modigliani's (1966) measure that has been reworded to make the items equally appropriate for male and female respondents (Miller, 1987). Also, this format employs a five-point response format; thus the possible range is from a high score of 130 to a low score of 26.

Sample

Because this scale has not been used extensively, normative data are scarce. Using the nine-point response scale, Edelmann (1985) reported a mean of 101.1 (SD = 33.0). Miller (1987) used a five-point scale and obtained a significant difference in the mean embarrassability scores for men (39.9) and women (45.8).

Reliability

Internal Consistency

Item–total correlations range from .64 to .85, with a mean of .78 (Modigliani, 1968). Cronbach's α was found to be .88 in two different samples using slightly different versions of the scale (Miller, 1987; Modigliani, 1968). Interestingly, different researchers have obtained somewhat different factor structures (Edelmann, 1985; Miller, 1987; Modigliani, 1966, 1968).

Validity

Convergent

Scores on the Embarrassability Scale correlate moderately ($r = .33$) with embarrassment in a real social situation (Modigliani, 1968). Further, scores correlate appropriately with measures of evaluation apprehension and concerns with one's social self, such as feelings of inadequacy ($r = .50$), test anxiety ($r = .33$), fear of negative evaluation ($r = .65$), public self-consciousness ($r = .36$), social anxiety ($r = .55$), and shyness ($r = .61$) (Edelmann, 1985; Miller, 1987; Modigliani, 1968).

Discriminant

Data relevant to discriminant validity have not been published.

Location

Modigliani, A. (1966). *Embarrassment and social influence*. Unpublished doctoral dissertation, University of Michigan, Ann Arbor.

Results and Comments

Not only do these data attest to the validity of the scale, they underscore the close relationships among interpersonal concerns, social anxiety, and embarrassment. Although the topic of embarrassment has received increasing attention (see Buss, 1980; Edelmann, 1981, 1985; Leary, 1983d; Miller, 1986), individual differences in embarrassability have attracted only passing interest. In part this may be due to the fact that the Embarrassability Scale has not been widely accessible. Although available data suggest that the scale is a reliable and valid measure of the tendency to experience embarrassment, additional research with this fascinating scale is badly needed.

Embarrassability Scale

These items ask you whether certain situations would cause you embarrassment. To be sure that we mean the same thing by "embarrassment," let's say a few words about it. Generally embarrassment involves feeling self-conscious, awkward, discomforted, or exposed because of the nature of the situation. Remember that you may feel embarrassed for yourself or for someone else. Remember also that mild embarrassment differs considerably from strong embarrassment while still being a form of embarrassment. Mild embarrassment generally involves a very slight self-consciousness, a mild sensation of awkwardness and uneasiness, and a slight feeling of uncertainty about what to do or say next. Strong embarrassment can be extremely unpleasant, involving blushing, fumbling, severe self-consciousness, strong sensations of awkwardness and discomfort, a panicky feeling of being unable to react appropriately to the situation that has been created, and a strong desire to escape the situation and the presence of others.

Try to imagine as vividly as possible that each of these events is happening to you. If they have occurred to you in the past, think back to how you felt at the time. Then, state how embarrassed you would feel if the event were actually happening to you by using the scale below to describe your own reaction.

1 = I would not feel the least embarrassed: not awkward or uncomfortable at all.
2 = I would feel slightly embarrassed.
3 = I would feel fairly embarrassed: somewhat self-conscious and rather awkward and uncomfortable.
4 = I would feel quite embarrassed.
5 = I would feel strongly embarrassed: extremely self-conscious, awkward, and uncomfortable.

1. Suppose you were just beginning a talk in front of the class.

1   2   3   4   5

2. Suppose you slipped and fell on a patch of ice in a public place, dropping a package of groceries.
3. Suppose you were a dinner guest, and the guest seated next to you spilled his plate on his lap while trying to cut the meat.
4. Suppose someone stopped you on the street by asking you something, and he turned out to be quite drunk and incoherent.
5. Suppose a group of friends were singing "Happy Birthday" to you.

6. Suppose you discovered you were the only person at a particular social occasion without a coat and tie (or dress).

7. Suppose you were watching an amateur show and one of the performers was trying to do a comedy act but was unable to make anyone laugh.

8. Suppose you were calling up a person you had just met for the first time in order to ask him/her for a date.

9. Suppose you were muttering aloud to yourself in an apparently empty room and discovered someone else was present.

10. Suppose you walked into a bathroom at someone else's house and discovered it was occupied by a member of the opposite sex.

11. Suppose you were watching a play from the audience when it suddenly became clear that one of the actors had forgotten his lines, causing the play to come to a standstill.

12. Suppose you were unable to stop coughing while listening to a lecture.

13. Suppose you were being lavishly complimented on your pleasant personality by your companion on your first date.

14. Suppose you were in a class and you noticed that the teacher had completely neglected to zip his fly.

15. Suppose you entered an apparently empty classroom, turned on the lights, and surprised a couple necking.

16. Suppose you were talking to a stranger who stuttered badly due to a speech impediment.

17. Suppose your mother had come to visit you and was accompanying you to all your classes.

18. Suppose you were a dinner guest and could not eat the main course because you were allergic to it.

19. Suppose you were alone in an elevator with a professor who had just given you a bad grade.

20. Suppose a shabbily dressed man accosted you on the street and asked you for a handout.

21. Suppose you were walking into a room full of people you did not know and were being introduced to the whole group.

22. Suppose you tripped and fell while entering a bus full of people.

23. Suppose you were opening some presents while the donors were around watching.

24. Suppose you asked someone on crutches if he had suffered from a skiing accident and he blushed and replied that, no, he was crippled by polio when a child.

25. Suppose you had forgotten an appointment with a professor, and remembered it as you met him in the hall the next day.

26. Suppose you were conversing in a small group which included a blind student, when someone next to him unthinkingly made a remark about everyone being "blind as a bat."

Note: This is a slightly modified version of Modigliani's (1966) Embarrassability Scale (Miller, 1987).

Social Avoidance and Distress Scale (SAD)

(Watson & Friend, 1969)

Variable

Social avoidance and distress refer to the tendency to avoid social interactions and to feel anxious while in them: Avoidance is a behavioral response and distress is an affective reaction.

Description

The Social Avoidance and Distress (SAD) Scale contains 28 items, 14 of which assess social avoidance and 14 of which measure social anxiety. The response format was originally true–false, but many researchers have used five-point scales. There are an equal number of positively and negatively worded items. Scale scores on the true–false scale range from 0 (lowest avoidance and distress) to 28 (highest avoidance and distress).

When constructing the scale, the authors paid careful attention to the conceptualization of social avoidance and distress. They distinguished between avoidance and the failure to approach, arguing that the opposite of avoidance is not social approach, but simply a lack of avoidance. Further, they deliberately included only items that assessed subjective distress and behavioral avoidance and excluded items that dealt with physiological indices of anxiety and impaired behavioral performance. Also, the initial pool of items was selected with consideration to social desirability and frequency of endorsement, and pilot testing was extensive.

Sample

When the true–false format is used, the mean for university students is 9.1, with a standard deviation of 8.0 (Watson & Friend, 1969). However, the distribution is quite skewed; indeed, the modal score is 0. This has led many researchers to use five-point scales in place of the T–F format. In the original sample males scored significantly higher than females.

Reliability

Internal Consistency

Internal consistency is very high. When the T–F format is used, the mean biserial item–total correlation is .77 and KR-20 is .94. When a five-point scale is used, Cronbach's α coefficient is close to .90.

A factor analytic study verified the subscale structure for avoidance and distress but suggested that the total scale score taps social avoidance more strongly than social anxiety (Patterson & Strauss, 1972). When subscale totals are obtained using the true–false version of the scale, the distress and avoidance subscales have reliability coefficients of .85 and .87, respectively; the two subscales correlate .54 for men and .71 for women (Leary *et al.*, 1987).

Test–Retest

Test–retest reliability for the T–F format was found to be .68 over 4 weeks (Watson & Friend, 1969).

Validity

Convergent

Scores on the SAD correlate highly (*r* values of .75 and above) with a variety of other measures of social anxiety and shyness (e.g., Jones, Briggs, & Smith, 1986). Correlations with measures of general anxiety (such as the Manifest Anxiety Scale) are positive but lower. High scorers on the SAD report greater anxiety in real interactions than low scorers and are less interested in participating in group discussions than lows (Watson & Friend, 1969). The SAD Scale has been used successfully in more than a hundred studies designed to test the effectiveness of various counseling interventions for chronic social anxiety.

Discriminant

Acquiescence response is controlled by the inclusion of an equal number of positively and negatively worded items. The SAD correlates −.25 (*n* = 205) with the Marlowe–Crowne Social Desirability Scale.

Location

Watson, D., & Friend, R. (1969). Measurement of social-evaluative anxiety. *Journal of Consulting and Clinical Psychology, 33,* 448–457.

Results and Comments

Although the scale has separate avoidance and distress subscales, most researchers have ignored the subscale structure and used the total of all scale items. Overall, the SAD scale is an unusually well-designed measure, and its usefulness as a measure of social anxiety and avoidance has been demonstrated in a number of contexts. One word of caution is in order, however. Because the items tap both subjective and behavioral aspects of social difficulties, the use of the full SAD Scale is appropriate only when a combined measure of anxiety and avoidance is desired. Although separate use of the two subscales may be appropriate in some contexts, the validity and reliability of the subscales have not been systematically explored.

Social Avoidance and Distress Scale

Directions: Circle the response that reflects your reaction.

1. I feel relaxed even in unfamiliar social situations. (R)

    TRUE   FALSE

2. I try to avoid situations that force me to be very sociable.
3. It is easy for me to relax when I am with strangers. (R)
4. I have no particular desire to avoid people. (R)
5. I often find social occasions upsetting.

6. I usually feel calm and comfortable at social occasions. (R)
7. I am usually at ease when talking to someone of the opposite sex. (R)
8. I try to avoid talking to people unless I know them well.
9. If the chance comes to meet new people, I often take it. (R)
10. I often feel nervous or tense in casual get-togethers in which both sexes are present.
11. I am usually nervous with people unless I know them well.
12. I usually feel relaxed when I am with a group of people. (R)
13. I often want to get away from people.
14. I usually feel uncomfortable when I am in a group of people I don't know.
15. I usually feel relaxed when I meet someone for the first time. (R)
16. Being introduced to people makes me tense and nervous.
17. Even though a room is full of strangers, I may enter it anyway. (R)
18. I would avoid walking up and joining a large group of people.
19. When my superiors want to talk with me, I talk willingly. (R)
20. I often feel on edge when I am with a group of people.
21. I tend to withdraw from people.
22. I don't mind talking to people at parties or social gatherings. (R)
23. I am seldom at ease in a large group of people.
24. I often think up excuses in order to avoid social engagements.
25. I sometimes take the responsibility for introducing people to each other. (R)
26. I try to avoid formal social occasions.
27. I usually go to whatever social engagements I have. (R)
28. I find it easy to relax with other people. (R)

Note: The avoidance subscale consists of items 2, 4, 8, 9, 13, 17, 18, 19, 21, 22, 24, 25, 26, and 27. The distress (anxiety) subscale consists of items 1, 3, 5, 6, 7, 10, 11, 12, 14, 15, 16, 20, 23, and 28. Reverse-score items marked (R) before summing. Source: Watson and Friend (1969); no standard instructions have been published.

Social Anxiety Subscale of the Self-Consciousness Scale

(Fenigstein, Scheier, & Buss, 1975)

Variable

Social anxiety is defined as discomfort in the presence of others.

Description

The Social Anxiety Scale consists of six items that are answered on a five-point scale (0, extremely uncharacteristic; 4, extremely characteristic). The six items tap not only subjective anxiety, but also reticence and performance difficulties. Thus, despite its name, the scale measures more than anxiety per se. The situations described in the items include new situations, being observed, embarrassing events, conversations with strangers, public speaking, and large groups.

The Social Anxiety Scale was developed empirically during construction of the Self-Consciousness Scale. Thirty-eight items were written to assess seven aspects of self-consciousness. Refinement of items and factor analyses resulted in three scales that tapped private self-consciousness, public self-consciousness, and social anxiety. The social anxiety subscale contains six items. Scale scores range from 0, indicating low anxiety, to 24, reflecting high anxiety.

Noting that nonstudent respondents often have difficulty understanding some of the original scale items, Scheier and Carver (1985) revised it to make the wording more appropriate for the general population. Although the content of the items on the social anxiety scale remained the same, the wording was modified slightly and the response format was changed to a four-point scale (0, not at all like me; 3, a lot like me). Scale scores range from 0 (low anxiety) to 18 (high anxiety). The revised scale correlates .86 with the original. Both the original and revised scales are included in this chapter.

Sample

Using the original scale (with a five-point response scale), the means for 179 male and 253 female university students were 12.5 (SD = 4.1) and 12.8 (SD = 4.5), respectively. On the revised scale (using a four-point response format), the means were 8.8 (SD = 4.3) and 8.6 (SD = 4.7) for 213 men and 85 women, respectively. A sample of 396 middle-age women scored slightly lower ($\bar{M}$ = 7.3, SD = 3.9).

Reliability

Internal Consistency

Cronbach's α for the original scale is about .70. For the Scheier and Carver revision, Cronbach's α is .79.

Test–Retest

Two-week test–retest reliability of the original scale is .73. The 4-week test–retest correlation for the Scheier and Carver version is .77.

Validity

Convergent

The original Social Anxiety Subscale of the Self-Consciousness Scale correlates significantly with the Interaction Anxiousness Scale (r = .78), test anxiety (r = .23), and self-esteem (r = −.35) (Turner, Scheier, Carver, & Ickes, 1978). Due to its novelty, the Scheier and Carver (1985) revision has not been validated, but there is little reason to expect it to be less valid than the original.

Discriminant

The original scale correlates slightly with scores on the Marlowe–Crowne Social Desirability Scale, $r = -.23$ ($p > .05$) (Turner *et al.*, 1978).

Location

Original scale: Fenigstein, A., Scheier, M. F., & Buss, A. H. (1975). Public and private self-consciousness: Assessment and theory. *Journal of Consulting and Clinical Psychology*, **43**, 522–527.
Revised scale for noncollege populations: Scheier, M. F., & Carver, C. S. (1985). The Self-Consciousness Scale: A revised version for use with general populations. *Journal of Applied Social Psychology*, **15**, 687–699.

Results and Comments

The Social Anxiety Subscale may be useful when a short, omnibus measure of social anxiety and related difficulties is needed. However, researchers interested in measuring social anxiety should bear two considerations in mind: (a) due to its length, the scale is less reliable than most of the other measures discussed in this chapter, and (b) the item content is quite broad, assessing a wide spectrum of affective and behavioral constructs including shyness, embarrassability, reticence, and speech anxiety.

Original and Revised Social Anxiety Subscale of the Self-Consciousness Scale

Original Scale

Instructions: Rate the degree to which each statement is characteristic or true of you:

$$0 = \text{extremely uncharacteristic}$$
$$1 = \text{somewhat uncharacteristic}$$
$$2 = \text{neither}$$
$$3 = \text{somewhat characteristic}$$
$$4 = \text{extremely characteristic}$$

1. It takes me time to overcome my shyness in new situations.

| 0 | 1 | 2 | 3 | 4 |

2. I have trouble working when someone is watching me.
3. I get embarrassed very easily.
4. I don't find it hard to talk to strangers.
5. I feel anxious when I speak in front of a group.
6. Large groups make me nervous.

Revised Scale

Instructions: Indicate the extent to which each of the following statements is like you, using the following format:

$$3 = \text{a lot like me}$$
$$2 = \text{somewhat like me}$$
$$1 = \text{a little like me}$$

1. It takes me time to get over my shyness in new situations.

    1   2   3

2. It's hard for me to work when someone is watching me.
3. I get embarrassed very easily.
4. It's easy for me to talk to strangers.
5. I feel nervous when I speak in front of a group.
6. Large groups make me nervous.

Shyness Scale

(Cheek & Buss, 1981)

Variable

Cheek and Buss (1981) define shyness as discomfort and inhibition in the presence of others. Thus, the Shyness Scale assesses both social anxiety and behavioral inhibition.

Description

The original Shyness Scale (Cheek & Buss, 1981) consisted of 9 items, but a 13-item revision (Cheek, 1983) has received increasing use. (An intermediate 11-item version was also used in a few studies.) Items on the Revised Cheek & Buss Shyness Scale are answered on a five-point scale (1, very uncharacteristic or untrue; 5, extremely characteristic or true). Scale scores are obtained by reverse-scoring four items and summing all responses. Scale scores on the 13-item scale run from 13 (lowest shyness) to 65 (highest shyness).

In an attempt to foster a discriminant relationship between shyness and sociability (the preference for being with others rather than alone), items were written to measure affective and behavioral aspects of shyness without reference to the desire to seek out or avoid social interactions. This attempt to discriminate between the two constructs was successful: shyness and sociability scores correlate only $-.30$, and shyness and sociability items load on separate factors in factor analyses.

Sample

Using the original nine-item scale (with responses scored from 0 to 4), the original sample (n = 912) had a mean of 14.6 (SD = 5.8) The 13-item scale (scored 1–5) has a mean of 33.3 for college men and 32.4 for college women.

Reliability

Internal Consistency

Cronbach's α for the 13-item scale is .90, the average inter-item correlation is .39. These reliability coefficients are slightly higher than those obtained on the original 9-item measure.

Test–Retest

The 45-day test–retest reliability is .88.

Validity

Convergent

Scores on the Shyness Scale correlate highly with other measures of shyness and social anxiety: Social Avoidance and Distress, .77; Interaction Anxiousness, .86; Social Reticence, .79 (Jones, Briggs, & Smith, 1986). Scores also correlate .68 with responses to the question, "How much of a problem is shyness for you?," .55 with scores on the EASI Fearfulness Scale, −.34 with Extraversion, and −.52 with self-esteem (Jones, Briggs, & Smith, 1986). Shyness scores on the 13-item scale also correlate well (r = .68), with aggregated ratings of individuals' shyness provided by three to five close friends and family members.

Behaviorally, high scorers talk less and engage in less eye contact in dyadic interactions and are rated by observers as more tense, unfriendly, and inhibited than low scorers. In addition, high scorers report greater subjective tension, inhibition, and awkwardness during actual conversations (Cheek & Buss, 1981).

Discriminant

Data relevant to the discriminant validity of the scale have not been published.

Location

Cheek, J. M., & Buss, A. H. (1981). Shyness and sociability. *Journal of Personality and Social Psychology,* **41,** 330–339.

Results and Comments

Whether the 9-item or 13-item measure is used, the Shyness Scale seems a reliable and valid index of individual differences in the tendency to be anxious and inhibited in social encounters. The high correlation between the two versions (r = .96) suggests that it may matter little which scale is used, although reliability estimates are slightly higher for the longer scale, as one would expect, and the content of the 13-item version is slightly broader.

To re-echo a theme of this chapter, the Shyness Scale explicitly assesses anxiety and inhibition and should be used only when both components of shyness are of interest (Leary, 1986a). In such contexts, it is probably the measure of choice.

Revised Shyness Scale

INSTRUCTIONS: Please read each item carefully and decide to what extent it is characteristic of your feelings and behavior. Fill in the blank next to each item by choosing a number from the scale printed below.

1 = very uncharacteristic or untrue, strongly disagree
2 = uncharacteristic
3 = neutral
4 = characteristic
5 = very characteristic or true, strongly agree

1. I feel tense when I'm with people I don't know well.
2. I am socially somewhat awkward.
3. I do *not* find it difficult to ask other people for information. (R)
4. I am often uncomfortable at parties and other social functions.
5. When in a group of people, I have trouble thinking of the right things to talk about.
6. It does *not* take me long to overcome my shyness in new situations. (R)
7. It is hard for me to act natural when I am meeting with new people.
8. I feel nervous when speaking to someone in authority.
9. I have *no* doubts about my social competence. (R)
10. I have trouble looking someone right in the eye.
11. I feel inhibited in social situations.
12. I do *not* find it hard to talk to strangers. (R)
13. I am more shy with members of the opposite sex.

Note: R, Reverse-scored item. Source: Cheek (1983).

Social Reticence Scale

(Jones & Briggs, 1986)

Variable

Jones and Briggs (1986) describe the Social Reticence Scale as a measure of social shyness: a "form of social anxiety in which self-focus and reticence prevent effective functioning in social situations" (p. 1).

Description

The Social Reticence Scale (SRS) described here is a revision of an earlier scale that was constructed by Jones and Russell (1982). The scale consists of 20 self-report items that span a broad range of social difficulties including problems meeting people and making friends, feelings of isolation, reticence, communication difficulties, and nonassertiveness. However, none of these items explicitly mentions subjective feelings of social anxiety. Items are answered on five-point scales (1, not at all characteristic; 5, extremely characteristic). Scale scores range from 20 (lowest) to 100 (highest degree of reticence). Sample items include: "I frequently feel isolated from other people" and "I make new friends easily."

Factor analyses show that the scale taps two major factors, one dealing with the difficulty or ease with which people report meeting others and making good impressions, and another involving the ease and effectiveness with which people communicate.

Sample

Available normative data are extensive, including data on college students, nonstudent adults, parents, and convicted felons (see Jones & Briggs, 1986). For college men (n = 877) the mean was 49.6 (SD = 12.2); for college women (n = 1373) the mean was 48.8 (SD = 13.0).

Reliability

Internal Consistency

The SRS has item–total correlations ranging from .38 to .76, with a mean of .55. Cronbach's α on a sample of over 1000 respondents was .92.

Test–Retest

The 8-week test–retest correlation on a sample of 101 respondents was .87.

Validity

Convergent

Jones and Briggs (1986) report that SRS correlates highly with other measures of social anxiety and shyness (Jones, Briggs, & Smith, 1986) and with relevant factors from the 16-PF. Scores correlate negatively with self-esteem ($-.60$) and assertiveness ($-.63$), and positively with loneliness (.68).

Jones and Carpenter (1986) found that high scorers on the SRS had fewer friends and a less extensive social support network than low scorers. SRS scores also correlate .50 with judges' ratings of shyness and .36 with judges' ratings of anxiety in laboratory interactions. Scores also correlate with friends' and family members' ratings of how talkative, outgoing, sociable, and extraverted respondents are.

Discriminant

The SRS correlates slightly with the Marlowe–Crowne Social Desirability Scale (r = $-.22$) but is uncorrelated with the Lie Scale of the Eysenck Personality Inventory.

Location

Jones, W. H., & Briggs, S. R. (1986). *Manual for the Social Reticence Scale*. Palo Alto, CA: Consulting Psychologists Press. Since the scale is published by a commercial press, its items are not duplicated here.

Results and Comments

The SRS casts a wider net than most of the other measures reviewed in this chapter, tapping a broad range of interpersonal difficulties that are associated with shyness. Thus, when a wide-ranging measure of such problems is desired, the SRS may be quite useful. Indeed, studies show strong relationships between SRS scores and a variety of social problems. However, even though SRS scores correlate highly with other trait measures of social anxiety, it does not appear to be as pure a measure of social anxiety per se as some other available measures.

Social Anxiety Scale for Children
(La Greca, Dandes, Wick, Shaw, & Stone, 1988)

Variable

The authors define social anxiety quite broadly to include not only subjective anxiety, but also social avoidance and fear of negative evaluation.

Description

Consistent with this conceptualization, items for the Social Anxiety Scale for Children (SASC) were selected to tap affective, cognitive, and behavioral concomitants of social anxiety. The ten items in the final version of the scale are shown at the end of this review. Items are answered on three-point scales (0, never true; 1, sometimes true; 2, always true). Scale scores run from 0, the lowest possible, to 20 the highest possible.

A principal components factor analysis revealed two large factors, one involving fear of negative evaluation (items 1, 2, 5, 6, 8, and 10) and the other involving social avoidance and distress (items 3, 4, 7, and 9). Scores on these two factors correlate modestly, but significantly ($r = -.27$). Psychometric data for the separate factors indicate that breaking the scale into subscales reduces reliability below acceptable limits.

Sample

Due to its newness, few normative data on the SASC are available. Subjects in the second and third grades ($\bar{M}$ values $= 10.4$ and 9.9) scored significantly higher on the scale than those in the fourth, fifth, and sixth grades ($\bar{M}$ values $= 8.9$, 7.7, and 8.4, respectively). Also, when the data were collapsed across grades, girls ($\bar{M} = 9.8$) scored significantly higher than boys ($\bar{M} = 8.3$).

Reliability

Internal Consistency

Cronbach's α for the total SASC score is .76.

Test–Retest

Two-week test–retest reliability (n = 102) was .67.

Validity

Convergent

Scores on the SASC correlate highly (r = .57) with scores on the Revised Children's Manifest Anxiety Scale (RCMAS), but not with the RCMAS Lie Scale. Also, popular children score significantly lower on the scale than less popular children (sociometrically "neglected" and "rejected" children). SASC scores correlated $-.18$ (p < .001) with overall liking by peers.

Discriminant

Data relevant to the discriminant validity of the scale have not been published.

Location

La Greca, A. M., Dandes, S. K., Wick, P., Shaw, K., & Stone, W. L. (1988). Development of the Social Anxiety Scale for Children: Reliability and concurrent validity. *Journal of Clinical Child Psychology, 17,* 84–91.

Results and Comments

Initial data support the validity of the SASC as a measure of children's social difficulties. However, it is difficult to tell from existing research whether the scale adequately discriminates social anxiety from other personal and interpersonal problems. Further, only 2 of the 10 items on the scale directly assess the tendency to experience social anxiety per se (items 3 and 7) as opposed to cognitive apprehension and social avoidance.

Even so, the SASC fills a void in the literature by providing a measure of social anxiety and related problems in children. Considerably more research regarding the validity of the SASC is needed, however, before a final verdict regarding its usefulness can be made.

Social Anxiety Scale for Children

Indicate how often each statement is true for you.

1. I worry about doing something new in front of other kids.

0	1	2
NEVER TRUE	SOMETIMES TRUE	ALWAYS TRUE

2. I worry about being teased.
3. I feel shy around kids I don't know.
4. I'm quiet when I'm with a group of kids.

5. I worry about what other kids think of me.
6. I feel that kids are making fun of me.
7. I get nervous when I talk to new kids.
8. I worry about what other children say about me.
9. I only talk to kids that I know really well.
10. I am afraid that other kids will not like me.

Note: Source: La Greca et al. (1988).

Personal Report of Confidence as a Speaker
(Paul, 1966)

Variable

Paul (1966) called the Personal Report of Confidence as a Speaker (PRCS) a measure of "interpersonal-performance anxiety," but it is more commonly referred to as a measure of "speech anxiety" or "audience anxiety."

Description

The original PRCS (Gilkinson, 1942) consisted of 104 items and was used widely during the 1940s, 1950s, and 1960s, particularly by researchers in speech communication (e.g., Dickens, Gibson, & Prall, 1952). Several shorter versions of the scale were developed for use when available administration time was limited; the most widely used revision was published by Paul (1966) in the context of research on the effectiveness of various clinical treatments for chronic speech anxiety. Paul's PRCS consists of 30 items that assess affective and behavioral reactions in public speaking situations. The items are answered in a true–false format; half are keyed "true" and half are keyed "false" to control for acquiescence response set. Scores range from a low of 0 to a high of 30; the higher the score, the greater the degree of anxiety.

Sample

The original sample of 523 students enrolled in a speech course had a mean of 11.6 and a standard deviation of 5.9 (Paul, 1966). Daly (1978) reported a mean of 14.8 (SD = 7.4).

Reliability

Internal Consistency

The scale is quite internally consistent; the α coefficient is .91.

Test–Retest

The test–retest correlation across an entire semester was .61.

Validity

The PRCS correlates well with related measures: the public speaking subscale from the S–R Inventory of Anxiousness ($r = .72$); Audience Anxiousness ($r = .84$); the IPAT Anxiety Questionnaire ($r = .32$); introversion-extraversion ($r = -.31$); and Interaction Anxiousness ($r = .63$) (see Daly, 1978; Leary, 1983c; Paul, 1966). The correlation with an early version of McCroskey's Personal Report of Communication Apprehension (PRCA) was .94, as high as the internal consistency of the measures. However, this version of the PRCA was weighted heavily by items referring to public speaking (Porter, 1979).

The correlation with the MMPI Lie Scale is small, but statistically significant ($r = -.13$, $n = 523$).

Location

Paul, G. L. (1966). *Insight vs desensitization in psychotherapy*. Stanford, CA: Stanford University Press.

Results and Comments

The PRCS has demonstrated reliability and validity as a measure of apprehension related to speaking in public. It has been used widely in treatment analog studies in counseling and clinical psychology, in which it has proven to be sensitive to experimental treatments designed to lower public speaking anxiety. Like many of the other measures reviewed in this chapter, it consists of a combination of subjective items (e.g., "I have no fear of facing an audience") and behavioral items (e.g., "I am fairly fluent"). When a measure of communication anxiety per se is desired, McCroskey's (1982) PRCA-24 is a better measure.

Personal Report of Confidence as a Speaker

This instrument is composed of 30 items regarding your feelings of confidence as a speaker. After each question there is a "true" and a "false."

Try to decide whether "true" or "false" *most* represents your feelings associated with your *most recent* speech, then put a *circle around* the "true" or "false." Remember that this information is completely confidential. *Work quickly* and don't spend much time on any question. We want your *first impression* on this questionnaire. Now go ahead, work quickly, and remember to answer every question

1. I look forward to an opportunity to speak in public. (F)

   TRUE   FALSE

2. My hands tremble when I try to handle objects on the platform. (T)
3. I am in constant fear of forgetting my speech. (T)
4. Audiences seem friendly when I address them. (F)
5. While preparing a speech I am in a constant state of anxiety. (T)
6. At the conclusion of a speech I feel that I have had a pleasant experience. (F)

7. I dislike to use my body and voice expressively. (T)

8. My thoughts become confused and jumbled when I speak before an audience. (T)

9. I have no fear of facing an audience. (F)

10. Although I am nervous just before getting up I soon forget my fears and enjoy the experience. (F)

11. I face the prospect of making a speech with complete confidence. (F)

12. I feel that I am in complete possession of myself while speaking. (F)

13. I prefer to have notes on the platform in case I forget my speech. (T)

14. I like to observe the reactions of my audience to my speech. (F)

15. Although I talk fluently with friends I am at a loss for words on the platform. (T)

16. I feel relaxed and comfortable while speaking. (F)

17. Although I do not enjoy speaking in public I do not particularly dread it. (F)

18. I always avoid speaking in public if possible. (T)

19. The faces of my audience are blurred when I look at them. (T)

20. I feel disgusted with myself after trying to address a group of people. (T)

21. I enjoy preparing a talk. (F)

22. My mind is clear when I face an audience. (F)

23. I am fairly fluent. (F)

24. I perspire and tremble just before getting up to speak. (T)

25. My posture feels strained and unnatural. (T)

26. I am fearful and tense all the while I am speaking before a group of people. (T)

27. I find the prospect of speaking mildly pleasant. (F)

28. It is difficult for me to search my mind calmly for the right words to express my thoughts. (T)

29. I am terrified at the thought of speaking before a group of people. (T)

30. I have a feeling of alertness in facing an audience. (F)

Note: Letter in parentheses indicates keyed response. Source: Paul (1966).

Future Research Directions

Research during the past 25 years has produced a wealth of data regarding the antecedents, concomitants, consequences, and remediation of social anxiety. Even so, several central questions have not been addressed adequately. In particular, four areas seem to have the most potential for advancing our understanding of social anxiety.

First, while episodes of social anxiety often are accompanied by hesitancy, reticence, and awkwardness, the nature of the link between subjective social anxiety and overt behavior is still poorly understood, "Shylike" behavior has been explained by various researchers as (a) a means of avoiding or reducing anxiety, (b) a form of learned helplessness, (c) the result of excessive self-preoccupation, (d) an interpersonal strategy designed to avoid negative evaluations, and (e) a primary cause of the anxiety state itself (see Leary, 1986a). Although these explanations are by no means mutually exclusive, there is scant evidence at present to support any of them. Given that the most troublesome aspect of social anxiety for many people is its impact on their interpersonal behavior, the anxiety–behavior link deserves concerted research attention.

Second, most research on the topic of social anxiety has been largely atheoretical, and this has been particularly true of studies that have focused on individual differences. Furthermore, only a few of the studies that have been rooted in a developed theory have attempted to test the relative utility of the various models that have been proposed. As a result, we have little basis for choosing among theoretical alternatives other than the ease with which they handle post hoc explanations of the data and the degree to which they offer an overriding conceptual structure. Promising theoretical directions include self-consciousness theory (Buss, 1980), self-presentation theory (Leary, 1987a; Schlenker & Leary, 1982), and self-efficacy theory (Bandura, 1977).

Third, the measures reviewed in this chapter ostensibly tap several different constructs (social anxiety, shyness, embarrassability, communication apprehension, and so on). However, despite discussions regarding the conceptualization of these various constructs (see Crozier, 1979; Jones, Briggs, & Smith, 1986; Leary, 1983b), little data exists regarding how they are related to one another. Are these different manifestations of the same general phenomenon or are some of them distinguishable from one another on the basis of cognitive, affective, behavioral, or physiological factors (e.g., Buss, 1980)?

A final question involves whether there is any utility in making finer distinctions in the conceptualization and measurement of these constructs. Are there identifiable subtypes of social anxiety that have theoretical or practical utility? Revisions of the PRCA, for example, identify four subtypes of communication apprehension (McCroskey, 1982), but these distinctions have not been supported by research. A related question is whether socially anxious people can be subdivided on the basis of the "cause" of their anxiety and whether it is worthwhile trying to measure the factors that predispose people to be socially anxious (e.g., Leary, 1987a). Finally, researchers have adopted everyday labels to refer to many of these constructs, and one wonders whether there are more useful ways to slice the conceptual pie than those suggested by everyday language. We need empirical verification of the conceptual distinctions that most researchers have taken for granted.

Acknowledgments

I would like to thank Rowland Miller, Jonathan Cheek, James McCroskey, and Annette La Greca for generously providing me with unpublished data and prepublication drafts for use in this review.

Bibliography

Allen, J., Richmond, V. P., & McCroskey, J. C. (1984). Communication and the chiropractic profession. Part I. *Journal of Chiropractic, 21,* 25–30.

Bandura, A. (1977). Self-efficacy: Toward a unifying theory of behavioral change. *Psychological Review, 84,* 191–215.

Bates, H. D. (1971). Factorial structure and MMPI correlates of a fear survey in a clinical population. *Behaviour Research and Therapy, 9,* 355–360.

Beatty, M. (1984). Physiological assessment. In J. A. Daly & J. C. McCroskey (Eds.), *Avoiding communication* (pp. 81–94). Beverly Hills, CA: Sage.

Buss, A. H. (1980). *Self-consciousness and social anxiety.* San Francisco: Freeman.

Cattell, R. B. (1946). *Description and measurement of personality.* New York: World Book.

Cheek, J. M. (1983). *The revised Cheek and Buss shyness scale.* Unpublished manuscript, Wellesley College, Wellesley, MA.

Cheek, J. M., & Buss, A. H. (1981). Shyness and sociability. *Journal of Personality and Social Psychology, 41,* 330–339.

Comrey, A. L. (1965). Scales for measuring compulsion, hostility, neuroticism, and shyness. *Psychological Reports, 16,* 697–700.

Crozier, W. R. (1979). Shyness as a dimension of personality. *British Journal of Social and Clinical Psychology, 18,* 121–128.

Curran, J. P. (1977). Skills training as an approach to the treatment of heterosexual-social anxiety. *Psychological Bulletin, 84,* 140–157.

Daly, J. A. (1978). The assessment of social-communication anxiety via self-reports: A comparison of measures. *Communication Monographs, 45,* 204–218.

Darwin, C. (1872/1955). *The expression of emotion in man and animals.* New York: Philosophical Library.

Dickens, M., Gibson, F., & Prall, C. (1952). An experimental study of the overt manifestations of stage fright. *Speech Monographs, 17,* 37–47.

Edelmann, R. J. (1981). Embarrassment: The state of research. *Current Psychological Reviews, 1,* 125–138.

Edelmann, R. J. (1985). Individual differences in embarrassment: Self-consciousness, self-monitoring, and embarrassability. *Personality and Individual Differences, 6,* 223–230.

Endler, N. S., Hunt, J., & Rosenwein, A. J. (1962). An S–R inventory of anxiousness. *Psychological Monographs, 79*(Whole No. 17), 1–33.

Fenigstein, A., Scheier, M., & Buss, A. H. (1975). Public and private self-consciousness: Assessment and theory. *Journal of Consulting and Clinical Psychology, 43,* 522–527.

Friend, R. M., & Gilbert, J. (1973). Threat and fear of negative evaluation as determinants of locus of social comparison. *Journal of Personality, 41,* 328–340.

Gilkinson, H. (1942). Social fears as reported by students in college speech classes. *Speech Monographs, 9,* 141–160.

Glass, C. R., & Shea, C. A. (1986). Cognitive therapy for shyness and social anxiety. In W. H. Jones, J. M. Cheek, & S. R. Briggs (Eds.), *Shyness: Perspectives on research and treatment* (pp. 315–327). New York: Plenum.

Goffman, E. (1955). On facework. *Psychiatry, 18,* 213–231.

Goldfried, M. R., & Sobocinski, D. (1975). Effect of irrational beliefs on emotional arousal. *Journal of Consulting and Clinical Psychology, 43,* 504–510.

Guilford, J. P., & Guilford, R. B. (1936). Personality factors S, E, and M and their measurement. *Journal of Psychology, 2,* 109–127.

Hart, E. A., Leary, M. R., & Rejeski, W. J. (1989). The measurement of social physique anxiety. *Journal of Sport and Exercise Psychology, 11,* 94–104.

Jones, W. H., & Briggs, S. R. (1986). *Manual for the Social Reticence Scale.* Palo Alto, CA: Consulting Psychologists Press.

Jones, W. H., & Carpenter, B. N. (1986). Shyness, social behavior, and relationships. In W. H. Jones, J. M. Cheek, & S. R. Briggs (Eds.), *Shyness: Perspectives on research and treatment* (pp. 227–238). New York: Plenum.

Jones, W. H., & Russell, D. (1982). The social reticence scale: An objective measure of shyness. *Journal of Personality Assessment, 46,* 629–631.

Jones, W. H., Briggs, S. R., & Smith, T. G. (1986). Shyness: Conceptualization and measurement. *Journal of Personality and Social Psychology, 51,* 629–639.

Jones, W. H., Cheek, J. M., & Briggs, S. R. (Eds.) (1986). *Shyness: Perspectives on research and treatment.* New York: Plenum.

La Greca, A. M., Dandes, S. K., Wick, P., Shaw, K., & Stone, W. L. (1988). Development of the Social Anxiety Scale for Children: Reliability and concurrent validity. *Journal of Clinical Child Psychology*, **17**, 84–91.

Leary, M. R. (1983a). A brief version of the Fear of Negative Evaluation Scale. *Personality and Social Psychology Bulletin*, **9**, 371–376.

Leary, M. R. (1983b). The conceptual distinctions are important: Another look at communication apprehension and related constructs. *Human Communication Research*, **10**, 305–312.

Leary, M. R. (1983c). Social anxiousness: The construct and its measurement. *Journal of Personality Assessment*, **47**, 66–75.

Leary, M. R. (1983d). *Understanding social anxiety: Social, personality, and clinical perspectives.* Beverly Hills, CA: Sage.

Leary, M. R. (1986a). Affective and behavioral components of shyness: Implications for theory, measurement, and research. In W. H. Jones, J. M. Cheek, & S. R. Briggs (Eds.), *Shyness: Perspectives on research and treatment* (pp. 27–38). New York: Plenum.

Leary, M. R. (1986b). The impact of interactional impediments on social anxiety and self-presentation. *Journal of Experimental Social Psychology*, **22**, 122–135.

Leary, M. R. (1987a). A self-presentational model for the treatment of social anxieties. In J. E. Maddux, C. D. Stoltenberg, & R. Rosenwein (Eds.), *Social processes in clinical and counseling psychology* (pp. 126–138). New York: Springer-Verlag.

Leary, M. R. (1987b). Socially-based anxiety: A review of measures. In C. Tardy (Ed.), *A handbook for the study of human communication: Methods and instruments for observing, measuring, and assessing communication processes.* Norwood, NJ: Ablex.

Leary, M. R., & Kowalski, R. M. (1987). Manual for the Interaction Anxiousness Scale. *Social and Behavioral Sciences Documents*, **16**(Ms. No. 2774), 2.

Leary, M. R., Atherton, S. C., Hill, S., & Hur, C. (1986). Attributional mediators of social inhibition and avoidance. *Journal of Personality*, **54**, 188–200.

Leary, M. R., Barnes, B. D., & Griebel, C. (1986). Cognitive, affective, and attributional effects of potential threats to self-esteem. *Journal of Social and Clinical Psychology*, **4**, 461–474.

Leary, M. R., Knight, P. D., & Johnson, K. A. (1987). Social anxiety and dyadic conversation: A verbal response analysis. *Journal of Social and Clinical Psychology*, **5**, 34–50.

McCroskey, J. C. (1970). Measures of communication-bound anxiety. *Speech Monographs*, **37**, 269–277.

McCroskey, J. C. (1976). *Alternative measures of communication apprehension.* Unpublished manuscript, West Virginia University, Morgantown.

McCroskey, J. C. (1978). Validity of the PRCA as an index of oral communication apprehension. *Communication Monographs*, **45**, 192–203.

McCroskey, J. C. (1982). *An introduction to rhetorical communication* (4th ed.). Englewood Cliffs, NJ: Prentice-Hall.

McCroskey, J. C., & Beatty, M. J. (1984). Communication apprehension and accumulated communication state anxiety experiences: A research note. *Communication Monographs*, **51**, 79–84.

McCroskey, J. C., Beatty, M. J., Kearney, P., & Plax, T. G. (1985). The content validity of the PRCA-24 as a measure of communication apprehension across communication contexts. *Communication Quarterly*, **33**, 165–173.

Miller, R. S. (1986). Embarrassment: Causes and consequences. In W. H. Jones, J. M. Cheek, & S. R. Briggs (Eds.), *Shyness: Perspectives on research and treatment* (pp. 295–311). New York: Plenum.

Miller, R. S. (1987). *The nature of embarrassability: Correlates and sex differences.* Unpublished manuscript, Sam Houston State University, Huntsville, TX.

Modigliani, A. (1966). *Embarrassment and social influence.* Unpublished doctoral dissertation, University of Michigan, Ann Arbor.

Modigliani, A. (1968). Embarrassment and embarrassability. *Sociometry*, **31**, 313–326.

Patterson, M. L., & Strauss, M. E. (1972). An examination of the discriminant validity of the social avoidance and distress scale. *Journal of Consulting and Clinical Psychology*, **39**, 1969.

Paul, G. L. (1966). *Insight vs desensitization in psychotherapy*. Stanford, CA: Stanford Univ. Press.

Porter, D. T. (1979). Communication apprehension: Communication's latest artifact? In D. Nimmo (Ed.), *Communication yearbook 3* (pp. 241–259). New Brunswick, NJ: Transaction Books.

Scheier, M. F., & Carver, C. S. (1985). The Self-Consciousness Scale: A revised version for use with general populations. *Journal of Applied Social Psychology*, **15**, 687–699.

Schlenker, B. R. (1980). *Impression management: The self-concept, social identity, and interpersonal relations*. Monterey, CA: Brooks/Cole.

Schlenker, B. R., & Leary, M. R. (1982). Social anxiety and self-presentation: A conceptualization and model. *Psychological Bulletin*, **92**, 641–669.

Smith, R. E., & Sarason, I. G. (1975). Social anxiety and evaluation of negative interpersonal feedback. *Journal of Consulting and Clinical Psychology*, **43**, 429.

Turner, R. G., Scheier, M. F., Carver, C. S., & Ickes, W. (1978). Correlates of self-consciousness. *Journal of Personality Assessment*, **42**, 285–289.

Watson, D., & Friend, R. (1969). Measurement of social-evaluative anxiety. *Journal of Consulting and Clinical Psychology*, **33**, 448–457.

Zimbardo, P. G. (1977). *Shyness*. New York: Jove.

CHAPTER 6

Measures of Depression
and Loneliness

Phillip R. Shaver and Kelly A. Brennan

The early post-World-War-II period was often called "the age of anxiety" (May, 1950). If eras can be characterized by salient emotions, ours must be the age of depression and loneliness. In everyday parlance, both of these emotions are forms of *sadness*. Recent research (Shaver, Schwartz, Kirson, & O'Connor, 1987) indicates that all of the common emotions (affection, pride, contempt, grief, horror, etc.) fit within five general, everyday language categories of feelings: love, happiness, anger, sadness, and fear. The age of anxiety was an age of fear; the present age is an age of sadness.

In addition to being parts of ordinary language, "depression" and "loneliness" are technical terms within psychiatry and clinical psychology. Depression, which often includes loneliness, has been medically defined and is frequently treated as a form of illness. In fact, depression is currently the most prevalent mental health problem in the United States (Dean, 1985). Loneliness, while not as extensively researched as depression, and not as carefully defined psychiatrically, is often treated in the process of treating depression (Young, 1982).

When ordinary concepts are used technically, definitional confusion may arise. Some measures of depression focus on a temporary feeling akin to sadness; others target the prolonged physical, psychological, and behavioral symptoms included in the medical definition. Because all forms of negative emotion, especially fear, loneliness, and sadness, are closely related (Shaver *et al.*, 1987), it is not surprising that measures of one are correlated with measures of the others. Moreover, these emotions are closely related to other states discussed in this book: alienation, low self-esteem, external locus of control (helplessness), and dissatisfaction with life. In ordinary language, this is as it should be; in professional social science it is problematic. Constructs with different names are supposed to be empirically distinct.

Another problem is that the terms "loneliness" and "depression" harbor implicit causal theories. As Seeman (1983) pointed out in "Alienation Motifs in Contemporary Theorizing: The Hidden Continuity of the Classic Themes" (see also Ch. 7, this volume), what was previously called alienation, a concept that emphasized social–structural determinants of human misery, tends today to be called loneliness or depression, terms that call attention to, if not place the blame on, individuals. When Durkheim (1897/1951) wrote about anomie and suicide, he emphasized societal forces that move a person toward meaningful integration into the activities of a community or toward meaningless isolation

Measures of Personality and Social Psychological Attitudes
Copyright © 1991 by Academic Press, Inc.

and hopeless self-destruction. When an American commits suicide, we are likely to think instead that he or she carried ill-fated genes (Mendlewicz, 1985), needed antidepressant medication (Noll, Davis, & DeLeon-Jones, 1985), held dysfunctional beliefs about success and failure (Sacco & Beck, 1985; Weiner, 1985), lacked the skills necessary to cope (Billings & Moos, 1985), or failed to build a supportive social network (Cohen & Syme, 1985). In other words, if we as Americans encounter pitfalls on the road to life, liberty, and the pursuit of happiness, the fault lies not in our societal and cultural stars but in ourselves.

As indicated above, the concept of depression raises a special problem not encountered in this volume's other chapters. Depression is an official diagnostic category in the American Psychiatric Association's *Diagnostic and Statistical Manual* (3rd ed.) (DSM-III) (1980). Scale designers may measure life satisfaction, authoritarianism, or social anxiety as they see fit, but designers of depression scales must keep an eye on DSM-III diagnostic criteria. When scales created for clinical diagnosis are used in broad survey studies of college students and nonstudent adults, one wonders whether the results should be interpreted in terms of mental illness or ordinary unhappiness and distress.

Fortunately, since our goal in this chapter is to make researchers aware of alternative measures, we need not take sides or adopt a single position regarding the ultimate nature and causes of depression and loneliness. We will present measures along with the conceptual frameworks favored by their authors. If the frameworks conflict across measures, we will identify resulting problems but not attempt to solve them. For us, then, depression and loneliness can be either normal feelings, such as forms of sadness brought on by perceived failures, setbacks, relationship problems, losses, and social isolation, or in some cases pathological states requiring medical intervention.

Just as researchers have found it somewhat difficult to disentangle depression from other forms of emotional distress, particularly anxiety, they have found it difficult to distinguish loneliness from depression and anxiety. Correlations between loneliness and depression scales are typically high, ranging between .30 and .80. (The correlation with self-esteem is usually around −.60.) Correlations between loneliness and anxiety are typically smaller but statistically significant.

Various attempts to separate these constructs have been made. One approach involves selecting items for loneliness scales that correlate least with measures of depression (e.g., Schmidt & Sermat, 1983). Another involves examining lay people's conceptions of loneliness and depression to see how they differ (e.g., Horowitz, French, & Anderson, 1982). This kind of study suggests, as mentioned earlier, that loneliness and depression are both forms of sadness or unhappiness, with depression being broader in scope. Essentially, individuals are thought to become unhappy ("depressed," in the ordinary language sense) when they fail at a task or when reality fails to meet their wishes and expectations. Loneliness is seen as due to a failure or deficiency in the interpersonal realm, whereas depression can be due either to interpersonal or to other kinds of problems (e.g., job failure). In other words, depression is roughly synonymous with sadness or unhappiness, and loneliness is a subtype of depression. Another approach to separating the two constructs is to use multivariate statistical modeling. Using this approach, Weeks, Michela, Peplau, and Bragg (1980) found that loneliness and depression are overlapping but distinct phenomena.

A final warning: Measures of loneliness and depression often contain overlapping item content, so it may be misleading to attempt to separate them empirically. Some depression measures assess respondents' loneliness and perceived distance from other people (not to mention loss of interest in sex and loss of interest in other people, which may be related to loneliness); and many measures of loneliness ask, in effect: Are you feeling sad (or depressed) because you are alone?

In preparing this chapter we searched social science abstracts, targeting the years 1970–1988 and seeking books and articles whose contents involved the intersection of the keywords "depression" and "measurement" or "loneliness" and "measurement." More than 500 titles were discovered. We evaluated each of these as likely or unlikely to be useful based on such considerations as publication in English, inclusion of measures written in English, and use of self-report rather than clinical-rating formats. Our goal was to locate all published, English language, self-report measures of loneliness and depression that have been used with reasonable frequency during the past 15 or so years. With over 30 measures in hand, we combed through the set to reduce the chapter to manageable length. Not all measures could be included, but our intent was to include the most widely used scales plus a range of alternatives varying in format, targeted population (e.g., children, the elderly), and theoretical foundation.

Measuring Depression

According to the DSM-III (American Psychiatric Association, 1980), depression is a syndrome—that is, a complex of symptoms. A "major depressive episode" is indicated, first, by "dysphoric mood or loss of interest or pleasure in all or almost all usual activities and pastimes. The dysphoric [person] is characterized by [adjectives] such as . . . depressed, sad, blue, hopeless, low, down in the dumps, irritable." Second, the mood disturbance must be "prominent and relatively persistent . . ." It is necessary that "at least four of the following symptoms have each been present nearly every day for a period of at least two weeks (in children under six, at least three of the first four)":

> (1) poor appetite or significant weight loss (when not dieting) or increased appetite or significant weight gain (in children under 6, consider failure to make expected weight gains); (2) insomnia or hypersomnia; (3) psychomotor agitation or retardation (but not merely subjective feelings of restlessness or being slowed down) (in children under 6, hypoactivity); (4) loss of interest or pleasure in usual activities, or decrease in sexual drive . . . (in children under 6, signs of apathy); (5) loss of energy; fatigue; (6) feelings of worthlessness, self-reproach, or excessive or inappropriate guilt . . . ; (7) complaints or evidence of diminished ability to think or concentrate, such as slowed thinking, or indecisiveness . . . ; (8) recurrent thoughts of death, suicidal ideation, wishes to be dead, or suicide attempt (pp. 120–121). (We have omitted various psychosis-related exclusionary criteria.)

Although some of the most widely used measures of depression were constructed before this definition was established, they too emerged from clinical work and are based on similar criteria.

Differences among depression measures arise naturally from the syndrome concept. Some emphasize behavior, some emphasize affect or mood, some emphasize cognitions, and some emphasize "vegetative" processes (appetite, sexual interest, sleep disturbances, etc.). Just as the DSM-III makes dysphoric mood primary, however, so do most measures of depression; despite the emphasis on visible or objective "symptoms," self-reports of distress are still central. Sadness, however, does not amount to depression, according to the DSM-III, unless it is accompanied for at least 2 weeks by four of eight symptoms (or, for children under 6, three of the first four, all physiological or behavioral). Hence, it is possible to criticize measures that inquire only about dysphoric feelings, even though they fare surprisingly well empirically, as we shall see. It is also possible to criticize "mood" or "state" measures, because they fail to make reference to the 2-week persistence criterion. Still, the precise boundary between trait and state is somewhat arbitrary.

Inherent in the disease framework is a criterion against which self-report measures of depression should be evaluated. In hundreds of studies, self-report measures stand or fall in relation to clinicians' observations and judgments. To the extent that clinical judgments vary, due to differences in clinical training or theoretical leanings, the criterion itself changes.

A problem with attempting to define "depression" is that it names what cognitive psychologists call a "fuzzy category" (Rosch, 1978). Depression shades naturally into normal unhappiness, so it is sometimes difficult to separate depression from serious disappointment (e.g., not getting into professional school), grief (hence the clinical concept, "inappropriate" grieving), aging (with its many necessary losses), and more or less normal periods of stagnation. There is an inevitable tension between the goals of clinical diagnosticians, who wish to separate sickness from health, and many social scientists, who wish to quantify a continuum of affect ranging from mild discontent to despair (sometimes even from euphoria to despair). Related to this difference in goals, as can be seen in our scale reviews, is a difference in the populations typically studied. Clinical researchers frequently compare small groups of depressed patients with small groups of patients bearing some other diagnostic label. Nonclinical researchers tend to study larger groups of college students and nonstudent adults.

Depression is also difficult to distinguish from forms of distress other than sadness: anxiety, boredom, and hostility, for example. The DSM-III's reference to irritability and "psychomotor agitation" indicates possible signs of anger and worry. This leads to at least moderate correlations between measures of depression and anxiety (and negative correlations with such opposites of depression as self-esteem, feelings of efficacy, and self-congratulatory attributions), which are commonly interpreted as threats to discriminant validity. These correlations are damning only if one believes that depression is a completely distinct entity.

The DSM-III definition of depression mentions explicitly that children should be diagnosed somewhat differently from adults. This has led to the development of specialized assessment devices for children. Not evident in the definition is an equally serious difficulty at the other end of the age spectrum. Elderly people can be misdiagnosed as depressed if somatic symptoms are over-emphasized; hence the creation of special depression scales for the elderly.

Defining depression as a syndrome (a set of concurrent, interrelated "symptoms") does circumvent one important danger: the confounding of cause and effect. As discussed below, researchers often embed assumptions about causes within their definitions of loneliness (e.g., "a reaction to insufficient communication with others," "a reaction to a lack of intimacy"). Because clinicians and depression researchers with different theoretical orientations have labored for decades to agree on an atheoretical definition, DSM-III criteria are silent concerning etiology. Nevertheless, researchers still argue about the causal role of certain "symptoms" included in the definition. Some, for example, believe that dysfunctional cognitions (or attributions) cause depression; others believe that physiological processes alter both mood and cognition.

Besides these conceptual differences, which can powerfully influence depression scales, reviewers of the literature on measures of depression encounter a diversity of methods. Respondents can be asked to describe symptom frequency or severity; agree or disagree with depression-related statements; make selections from a list of mood-related adjectives; interpret hypothetical scenarios (thereby revealing their characteristic cognitive processes). There are measures of depression that embody each of these approaches.

Readers wishing to gain rapid familiarity with the literature on depression and its measurement may consult the *Handbook of Depression* (Beckham & Leber, 1985) and *Assessment of Depression* (Sartorius & Ban, 1986). The former is extremely comprehensive; the latter contains brief reviews of more measures than we can cover here. It focuses on the assessment of depression in different countries (the book is sponsored by the World Health Organization). Finally, an interesting anthropologically oriented book about depression is *Culture and Depression* (Kleinman & Good, 1985).

Depression Measures Reviewed Here

We have chosen 11 depression scales for review. The first six are fairly general and assess depression either as a symptom complex or as a pervasive dysphoric mood. Among these scales are some of the most widely used clinical and research self-report measures of depression.

1. Beck Depression Inventory (BDI) (1967, 1972)
2. Zung Self-Rating Depression Scale (SDS) (Zung, 1965)
3. Carroll Rating Scale (CRS) (Carroll, Feinberg, Smouse, Rawson, & Greden, 1981)
4. Center For Epidemiologic Studies Depression Scale (CES-D) (Radloff, 1977)
5. Depression Adjective Checklist (DACL) (Lubin, 1965)
6. Depressive Experiences Questionnaire (DEQ) (Blatt, D'Afflitti, & Quinlan, 1976)

The Beck Depression Inventory (BDI) (Beck, 1967; Beck & Beck, 1972) is the most prominent and frequently cited self-report measure of depression. The BDI has become the standard by which the validity of other scales is evaluated, and for good reasons. First, the scale has excellent construct validity: The BDI contains 21 items (13 in the short version) encompassing four major components of depression: behavioral, affective, cognitive, and physiological. Second, the scale is brief, easy to administer, and widely available in various forms for different populations, cultures, and age groups. Third, the scale's creator, Aaron Beck, has made important, provocative contributions to the theory of depression (especially with respect to its cognitive components). Although the items were originally designed to measure intensity of depressive symptoms, the scale is primarily used today as a screening tool (i.e., for determining presence or absence of depression).

The Self-Rating Depression Scale (SDS) (Zung, 1965) and the Carroll Rating Scale for Depression (CRS) (Carroll, Feinberg, Smouse, Rawson, & Greden, 1981) are also widely used and relatively comprehensive self-report measures of depression. In some respects, both measures are similar to the BDI; both are short, easily administered self-report scales that include items to assess severity of depressive symptoms. In addition, both scales were designed to measure major symptom domains: physiological, psychomotor, and affective. Unlike the BDI, however, the SDS and the CRS stress behavioral and somatic symptoms of depression almost to the exclusion of cognitive and psychological indicators.

The BDI, SDS, and CRS are all suitable for clinical screening. However, researchers interested in using these scales to measure depression in the general population are faced with a potential difficulty. Depending on the population sampled, depression may differ not only in quantity or degree (as noted above), but also in quality. That is, nonclinically depressed individuals may not experience the somatic and psychomotor difficulties that accompany full-blown depressive episodes. For "normal" individuals, the experience of depression may be more a matter of extremely depressed mood, or extended periods of sad affect, without any of the behavioral or somatic correlates of a "major depressive disorder."

The Center for Epidemiologic Studies Depression Scale (CES-D) (Radloff, 1977) and the Depression Adjective Check Lists (DACL) (Lubin, 1965) are included here in part because they have performed well as measures of depression among nonclinical respondents. Depression in the general population, while perhaps less severe than in clinical populations, can still be extremely disturbing and debilitating for its victims. This, together with the prevalence of at least mild depression, indicates the need for reliable and valid survey measures of depression.

Finally, we included the Depressive Experiences Questionnaire (DEW) (Blatt, D'Afflitti, & Quinlan, 1976b) because of its unique theoretical foundation in contemporary psychodynamic theory. It promises to broaden the definition of depression to include dependency and overly stringent achievement standards.

The second set of three measures focuses on cognitive and psychological processes that accompany and/or cause depression. The possible influence of cognitive factors in depression has sparked a controversy related to the issue of causality. Whereas some theorists have long been proponents of the position that depressive, distorted, or dysfunctional cognitions cause depression, other more conservative theorists contend that negative cognitions are simply concomitants of depression. Although we cannot resolve the issue, we have selected three scales relevant to the controversy:

7. Attributional Style Questionnaire (ASQ) (Peterson et al., 1982)
8. Cognitive Bias Questionnaire (CBQ) (Hammen & Krantz, 1976; Krantz & Hammen, 1979)
9. Automatic Thoughts Questionnaire (ATQ) (Hollon & Kendall, 1980)

The Attributional Style Questionnaire (ASQ) (Peterson et al., 1982) is the most popular of the cognitive measures, judging from number of citations. The Cognitive Bias Questionnaire (Hammen & Krantz, 1976; Krantz & Hammen, 1979) was designed to assess the kinds of distortion that seem to accompany depression. The Automatic Thoughts Questionnaire (ATQ) (Hollon & Kendall, 1980) is also a measure of common depressive cognitions, based on statements elicited from depressed individuals. All three measures reflect the pervasive influence of Beck's cognitive approach to depression.

Another set of controversies in the assessment of depression concerns developmental issues. Such issues as whether children can become depressed, how to estimate the frequency and severity of depression among the various categories of elderly people ("old-old," "young-old," etc.), and how to coordinate the reading levels of target populations with the requirements of existing self-rated depression scales have led to the creation of depression measures for particular age groups. We have included two such scales:

10. Children's Depression Inventory (CDI) (Kovacs, 1980/1981; Kovacs & Beck, 1977)
11. Geriatric Depression Scale (GDS) (Brink et al., 1982)

The Children's Depression Inventory (Kovacs, 1981/1982; Kovacs & Beck, 1977) is the most widely used measure of childhood and adolescent depression. The CDI was derived from the Beck Depression Inventory for adults, with minor revisions in item content, number of items, and scoring, to accommodate differences in cognitive and linguistic ability. The Geriatric Depression Inventory (Brink et al., 1982) measures depression in the elderly. The somatic and behavioral items on standard adult depression inventories (the SDS, in particular) have sometimes led to false positive diagnoses of the elderly as depressed; the GDS, however, contains few somatic items, thereby reducing the problem of inaccurate diagnosis.

Beck Depression Inventory (Long Form and Short Form)

(Beck, 1967; Beck & Beck, 1972)

Variable

The Beck Depression Inventory (BDI) was designed to assess the intensity of depression in terms of 21 symptom–attitude categories.

Description

In his 1967 book, Beck defined depression by presenting a list of 21 "symptom–attitude categories." The BDI's items represent each of these categories: mood, pessimism, sense of failure, lack of satisfaction, guilt feelings, sense of punishment, self-dislike, self-accusation, suicidal wishes, crying, irritability, social withdrawal, indecisiveness, distortion of body image, work inhibition, sleep disturbance, fatigability, loss of appetite, weight loss, somatic preoccupation, and loss of libido.

In the 1967 version of the scale, each statement was ranked to reflect the range of severity of the symptom, from neutral to maximal severity. Numerical values from 0 to 3 were assigned to each statement to indicate degree of severity. "In many categories, two alternative statements [were] presented at a given level and [were] assigned the same weight; these equivalent statements [were] labeled *a* and *b* (e.g., 2a, 2b) to indicate that they are at the same level" (Beck, 1967, p. 189). For example, for the first category, sadness, the alternatives were presented and scored as follows:

0   I do not feel sad
1   I feel blue or sad
2a   I am blue or sad all the time and I can't snap out of it
2b   I am so sad or unhappy that it is quite painful
3   I am so sad or unhappy that I can't stand it

In more recent versions of the scale, including the one illustrated here, there is only one alternative at each level, so each of the 21 items has four alternatives ranging from 0 (low depression) to 3 (maximum depression). Total scores can therefore range from 0 to 63.

According to Steer, Beck, and Garrison (1986, p. 124), "although cutoff scores on the BDI should be based upon the purposes for which decisions about the intensity of depression are to be made," the following rough cutoffs can be used when reviewing the research literature: No depression or minimal depression, scores less than 4; mild (low), between 5 and 13; moderate (medium), between 14 and 20; and severe, 21 and above.

Beck and Beck (1972) created a short form of the scale by examining data from an earlier study of 598 psychiatric patients who had been rated by clinicians for depth of depression. Thirteen items were selected based on their high correlations with the total BDI score and their correlation with clinical ratings. The short form correlated .96 with the total BDI and .61 with clinical ratings. In their 1972 article, Beck and Beck suggested the following cutoffs: 0–4, none or minimal; 5–7, mild; 8–15, moderate; 16+, severe.

Sample

Beck (1967) reported data from two studies of inpatients and outpatients of urban psychiatric hospitals. The original sample ($n = 226$) was drawn over a 7-month period beginning in June 1959, and the second sample ($n = 183$), over a 5-month period beginning in February 1960. Demographically, the two samples were 39% male, 35% black, median age about 34, and 15% lower class. About two-thirds were outpatients, a third inpatients (Beck, 1967, p. 191). Of course, the scale has subsequently been administered to hundreds of other samples.

Reliability

Internal Consistency

In his 1967 book, Beck reported an odd–even split-half reliability coefficient of .86 (with Spearman-Brown correction, .93).

Test–Retest

According to Steel *et al.* (1986), stability coefficients are usually in the .70s over a period of weeks. These authors mention, however, that the psychological set which the respondent is asked to hold while taking the instrument is crucial. If the respondent is asked to describe himself or herself for just today, then the BDI is evaluating state depression, which would not be expected to display much stability. If the patient describes himself or herself for at least the past week, however, then the BDI is assumed to be measuring trait depression (in which case the stability coefficients would be higher).

Validity

Convergent

The BDI is consistently and significantly related to clinical ratings of depression. The magnitude of the correlations ranges from .60 to .90, with a variety of sample sizes. (See the reviews mentioned above.) BDI scores are also reasonably and significantly related to biological, electrophysiological, psychosocial, and cross-cultural manifestations and correlates of depression, and with observationally documented sleep disturbances (see Steer *et al.* for references).

The BDI is often used by other scale developers to validate new measures, so almost by definition it is highly related to many other measures (*r* values ranging from the .50s to the .80s) (see Mayer, 1977). Factor analyses of the BDI generally reveal three intercorrelated factors: negative attitudes or suicide, physiological, and performance difficulty. When second-order factors are extracted, a single "overall depression" factor emerges. The intercorrelation of the oblique first-order factors and the single second-order factor argue for the overall coherence of the scale.

Discriminant

In his 1967 book, Beck reported several pieces of evidence for the BDI's discriminant validity: for example, a higher correlation with clinical ratings of depression (.59) than with clinical ratings of anxiety (.14). Steer *et al.* (1986) mentioned that while some authors (e.g., Mayer, 1977; Meites, Lovallo, & Pishkin, 1980) have questioned the discriminant validity of the BDI (especially with respect to measures of anxiety), it distinguishes between different types of depression and different psychiatric diagnoses. Langevin and Stancer (1979) suggested that the BDI suffers from social desirability response set (the correlation between the BDI and the Edwards social desirability scale is around $-.80$). Steer *et al.* pointed out, however, that the Edwards scale may partially reflect self-esteem, in which case it should correlate negatively with the BDI. Other researchers (Reynolds & Gould, 1981) report correlations with the Marlowe–Crowne Social Desirability Scale (Crowne & Marlowe, 1960) that are negative but modest in size ($r = -.26$).

Location

Original 21-item scale: Beck, A. T. (1967). *Depression: Causes and treatment.* Philadelphia: University of Pennsylvania Press.

Revised 21-item scale: Beckham, E. E., & Leber, W. R. (Eds.) (1985). *Handbook of depression: Treatment, assessment, and research* (Appendix 3). Homewood, IL: Dorsey.

Short form (13 items): Beck, A. T., & Beck, R. W. (1972). Screening depressed patients in family practice: A rapid technic. *Postgraduate Medicine,* **52** (December), 81–85.

Results and Comments

The BDI is the most widely used self-report measure of depression in English, and it has been translated and used successfully in many other languages. It has been adapted for use with children and adolescents (Kovacs & Beck, 1977) and has been employed in studies of adults of all ages, including the elderly. Difficulties may be encountered when the BDI is used with the "old-old elderly" (those over 75 years of age), because of its emphasis on somatic symptoms which may occur in old age for reasons unrelated to depression.

In addition, slight variations of the BDI have been used in over 600 studies since 1967 with varying norms for different groups. These studies have been reviewed in a number of places; see, for example, Beck and Beamesderfer (1974), Mayer (1977), and Steer *et al.* (1986).

The BDI is available only from its publisher, Psychological Corporation (555 Academic Court, San Antonio, Texas 78204), so we have not included it here. We decided to review the scale anyway because, as mentioned above, it is so widely used. We have provided instructions and two sample items for (both long and short forms of the BDI) to aid potential scale users in deciding whether or not to purchase the measure.

Beck Depression Inventory (Standard Form)

On this questionnaire are groups of statements. Please read each group of statements carefully. Then pick out the one statement in each group which best describes the way you have been feeling during the PAST WEEK, INCLUDING TODAY! Circle the number beside the statement you picked. If several statements in the group seem to apply equally well, circle each one. **Be sure to read all the statements in each group before making your choice.**

(Sample items)
1.   0 I do not feel like a failure.
      1 I feel I have failed more than the average person.
      2 As I look back on my life, all I can see is a lot of failures.
      3 I feel I am a complete failure as a person.
2.   0 I don't feel disappointed in myself.
      1 I am disappointed in myself.
      2 I am disgusted with myself.
      3 I hate myself.

Beck Depression Inventory (Short Form)

Instructions: This is a questionnaire. On the questionnaire are groups of state-ments. Please read the entire group of statements in each category. Then pick out the one statement in that group which best describes the way you feel today, that is, **right now!** Circle the number beside the statement you have chosen. If several statements in the group seem to apply equally well, circle each one. **Be sure to read all the statements in each group before making your choice.**

(Sample items)
1.   3 I am so sad or unhappy that I can't stand it.
      2 I am blue or sad all the time and I can't snap out of it.
      1 I feel sad or blue.
      0 I do not feel sad.
2.   3 I get too tired to do anything.
      2 I get tired from doing anything.
      1 I get tired more easily than I used to.
      0 I don't get any more tired than usual.

Self-Rating Depression Scale

(Zung, 1965)

Variable

Zung developed the Self-Rating Depression Scale (SDS) in an effort to assess and dis-tinguish among the "psychic–affective," physiological, psychomotor, and psychological manifestations of depression.

Description

The SDS was intended to be an easily administered measure of the severity of state depression: It is short (20 items), self-rated, and quantitative (Zung, 1986). The 20 items on the SDS coincide with the specific symptoms that Zung associated with the four symptom categories mentioned above:

1. The psychic–affective component is represented by two questions, one measuring depressed mood and one referring to crying spells.
2. The physiological disturbance component is represented by questions about diurnal variation, sleep disturbance, decreased appetite, decreased libido, decreased weight, constipation, tachycardia, and increased fatigue.
3. Psychomotor disturbance is measured with two items referring to psychomotor retardation and psychomotor agitation.
4. The psychological disturbance index of depression focuses on confusion, hopelessness, irritability, indecisiveness, personal devaluation, emptiness, suicidal rumination, and dissatisfaction.

The items for each of the three symptom areas are presented together rather than being presented in random order, but Mikesell and Calhoun (1970) demonstrated that "there are no significant order effects on the SDS" (p. 22).

The SDS consists of 20 four-point items, in response to which respondents indicate how frequently each applies to them at the time of testing (Zung, 1965): "none or a little of the time," "some of the time," "a good part of the time," to "most or all of the time." To counter agreement response set, half of the items are worded positively ("Morning is when I feel the best"), and half are worded negatively ("I get tired for no reason"). Because the scale is constructed so that more depressed persons obtain higher scores, the positive items are reverse scored. An overall depression index for the SDS is derived by dividing the sum of the raw scores by the maximum possible score of 80 (most depressed); thus, the index is expressed as a proportion ranging from .25 to 1.00.

Sample

The original sample contained 156 people, 56 of whom were admitted over a 5-month period to a Veterans Administration Hospital with the primary diagnosis of depressive disorder. The other 100 members of the sample constituted the (nondepressed) control group, consisting of either professional staff, nonprofessional staff, or other patients hospitalized for nonpsychiatric illnesses. Of the 56 patients initially diagnosed as depressed, 31 were treated and discharged as cases of depressive disorders; the other 25 patients who had initially been diagnosed as depressive were later diagnosed and treated as cases of other psychiatric disorders (e.g., anxiety reactions, personality disturbances). The SDS has also been used in many subsequent studies.

Reliability

Internal Consistency

There seems to be surprisingly little information concerning the reliability of this scale. In an earlier review of the SDS (Shaw, Vallis, & McCabe, 1985), the relative lack of reliability information was also noted. Concerning internal consistency, Zung reported a statistically significant split-half correlation between even and odd SDS items of .73 (Zung, 1973). In a later study, he obtained an α of .92 (Zung, 1986). Knight, Waal-Manning, and Spears (1983) obtained an α coefficient of .79.

Test–Retest

No test–retest reliability information was encountered.

Validity

Convergent

In contrast to the sparse reliability data, there is a great deal of information concerning the validity of the SDS, particularly of the convergent variety. Studies of the relationship between the SDS and several other measures of depression, such as the Hamilton Rating Scale for Depression (HRSD), the Beck Depression Inventory (BDI), and the "D" scale of the Minnesota Multiphasic Personality Inventory (MMPI), reveal significant and moderate to high correlations (e.g., Biggs, Wylie, & Ziegler, 1978; Brown & Zung, 1972; Zung, 1967, 1969; Zung, Richards, & Short, 1965). In addition, Biggs *et al.* (1978) found that the SDS correlated well with physicians' global ratings of depression ($r = .69$, $p < .001$). In general, the SDS successfully discriminates between depressed and non-depressed individuals, but its usefulness in measuring severity of depression may be limited. The literature on this point is mixed. Carroll, Fielding, and Blashki (1973) found that the SDS did not discriminate well among individuals differing in severity of depression, but Biggs *et al.* (1978) found significant differences.

Discriminant

No information encountered.

Location

Zung, W. W. K. (1965). A self-rating depression scale. *Archives of General Psychiatry*, **12**, 63–70.

Results and Comments

The SDS, like the BDI, is one of the most widely used depression scales in both research and clinical settings. Since 1965, the SDS has been translated into at least 30 other languages and used as a measure of depression in over 300 studies (Zung, 1986). In contrast to the BDI, which asks for intensity ratings of depression, the SDS asks respondents to rate the frequency of depressive symptoms. This distinction may be important, depending on a researcher's goals.

According to Zung (1967), the SDS is not influenced by most demographic factors, such as age, sex, marital status, education, financial status, and intellectual level. We did not check the validity of these claims, but Kaszniak and Allender (1985), in their review of procedures for the assessment of depression in the elderly, note that the SDS may not be an acceptable screening test for use with "old-old" persons because of its emphasis on somatic complaints.

Finally, Zung (1972) has developed a parallel version of the measure, the Depression Status Inventory (DSI). The DSI provides clinicians with a quantitative depression-rating method, to be used in conjunction with clinical interviews.

The Self-Rating Depression Scale

1. I feel down-hearted, blue and sad.

1	2	3	4
NONE OR A LITTLE OF THE TIME	SOME OF THE TIME	GOOD PART OF THE TIME	MOST OR ALL OF THE TIME

2. Morning is when I feel the best. (R)
3. I have crying spells or feel like it.
4. I have trouble sleeping through the night.
5. I eat as much as I used to. (R)
6. I enjoy looking, talking to and being with attractive women/men. (R)
7. I notice that I am losing weight.
8. I have trouble with constipation.
9. My heart beats faster than usual.
10. I get tired for no reason.
11. My mind is as clear as it used to be. (R)
12. I find it easy to do the things I used to. (R)
13. I am restless and can't keep still.
14. I feel hopeful about the future. (R)
15. I am more irritable than usual.
16. I find it easy to make decisions. (R)
17. I feel that I am useful and needed. (R)
18. My life is pretty full. (R)
19. I feel that others would be better off if I were dead.
20. I still enjoy the things I used to do. (R)

Note: Response alternatives are scored from 1 to 4; "R" indicates reverse-scoring.
© Copyright, William Zung, 1965, 1966, 1974. All rights reserved. A complete copy of the SDS may be obtained by contacting DISTA Products, Eli Lilly Corporate Center, Indianapolis, Indiana 46285.

Carroll Rating Scale for Depression

(Carroll, Feinberg, Smouse, Rawson, & Greden, 1981)

Variable

The Carroll Rating Scale (CRS) was designed as a self-rated measure to parallel the widely used therapist-rated Hamilton Rating Scale for Depression (HRSD) (Hamilton, 1960).

Description

Carroll *et al.* developed the CRS to address the lack of congruence between clinician- and self-ratings of depression, as these were assessed at the time. The items on the CRS assess behavioral and somatic aspects of depression (Carroll *et al.*, 1981). The CRS, patterned after the HRSD, was designed as an index of severity of depressive symptomatology, not as a diagnostic measure. The 52 items on the CRS focus on symptoms related to motor retardation, agitation, sleep disturbances, weight loss and anorexic symptoms, fatigue, loss of libido, loss of concentration, loss of insight, psychological and general somatic anxiety, as well as suicidal ideation. In contrast to the HRSD, in which some statements were rated

0–4 and some 0–2 in severity, the same items in the CRS are represented by either four or two statements, which denote progressively more severe manifestations of the same symptom. The final form of the CRS comprises 52 items presented in random order.

All items on the CRS are worded in a forced-choice yes–no format. To partly counter response set, 40 of the items are worded so that a "yes" response is indicative of depression, and 12 are worded so that a "no" response indicates depression. After reversing the 12 negative items, the total score is calculated by assigning one point per item. Scores can range from 0 to 52. Carroll et al. (1981) suggest that if the CRS is to be used as a clinical screening test for depression, a score of 10 or above indicates depression.

Sample

Carroll et al. (1981) reported data from three separate samples. The first, a general population sample, consisted of 119 adults (age 18–64) employed at the University of Michigan Medical Center. The respondents were a "representative sample of the population [and] they covered a wide range of socioeconomic status" (p. 95).

The second study, conducted for comparison purposes, included CRS scores and psychiatrists' global ratings of severity obtained on 1191 occasions for over 200 patients who were suffering from endogenous depression rated on a scale of 0–3.

The third study was conducted to compare the CRS with the BDI and the HRSD, using sample of 278 inpatients with a range of psychiatric diagnoses (Carroll et al., 1981).

Reliability

Internal Consistency

Carroll et al. (1981) reported a split-half, odd–even correlation coefficient of .87, with item–total correlations ranging from .05 to .78 (median $r = .55$). The sum of each half-set of statements correlated very well with the total score (odd $r = .97$, even $r = .96$). In addition, the sum of the 12 "no" statements correlated .87 with the total score, and the sum of the 40 "yes" statements correlated .98 with the total score.

Test–Retest

No information.

Validity

Convergent

Because the CRS was designed to parallel clinician ratings on the HRSD, Carroll et al. (1981) and others (Feinberg, Carroll, Smouse, & Rawson, 1981; Nasr, Altman, Rodin, Jobe, & Burg, 1984) have reported extensive data pertaining to the convergent validity of the CRS in comparison with the HRSD. Carroll et al. (1981) published a correlation matrix of each of the CRS items with each of the HRSD items. The correlations between each CRS item and the corresponding HRSD item were moderate (r values ranging from −.06 to .73, median = .60), indicating that a direct translation of the HRSD into a self-report measure was only approximated. The correlation of the total CRS scale with the HRSD scale, however, was high ($r = .80$). In a separate study, Nasr et al. (1984) reported a similarly high relationship ($r = .84$). Feinberg *et al.* (1981) reported correlations ranging from .66 to .83, depending on the kind of depression exhibited by the sample (unipolar endogenous vs. bipolar endogenous vs. nonendogenous).

In addition to correlating highly with the HRSD, the CRS correlated well with clinicians' global ratings of severity of depressive symptoms (from the second sample of endogenous depressives, $r = .67$). In comparison with other self-rating measures, the CRS has been found to correlate well with the BDI: Carroll *et al.* (1981) reported an r of .86 (from the third sample of psychiatric inpatients). In addition, Feinberg *et al.* (1981) reported correlations with the Visual Analogue Scale (VAS) (a measure of positive mood) that ranged from $-.60$ to $-.87$ (again, depending on the sample's major form of depression).

Discriminant

The ability of the CRS to detect severity of depression in endogenous (unipolar and bipolar) depressives differed from its ability to detect severity in nonendogenous depressives (Feinberg *et al.*, 1981). That is, the correlation between clinicians' ratings (from the HRSD) and the self-rated CRS was attenuated for nonendogenous depressives. Feinberg *et al.* (1981) suggested that this attenuated correlation was due to the tendency for "nonendogenous [depressives to] report more symptoms than unipolar and bipolar depressed patients" (p. 27). Furthermore, for the global ratings, the correlation between the CRS and the HRSD diverged with increasing severity of symptoms; thus, as severity of depression increased, the congruence between the CRS and the HRSD diminished. This suggests that the CRS does not tap the same constructs as the HRSD in certain subject populations.

Location

Carroll, B. J., Feinberg, M., Smouse, P. E., Rawson, S. G. & Greden, J. F. (1981). The Carroll Rating Scale for depression: I. Development, reliability and validation. *British Journal of Psychiatry,* **138,** 205–209.

Results and Comments

The CRS is a generally valid and useful substitute or supplement for clinical ratings as assessed by both the HRSD and global ratings of severity of depressive symptomatology. However, the CRS should be used cautiously with severely depressed patients, due to the inflation of scores for such patients. For lower levels of depression, the CRS has been demonstrated to converge with clinical HRSD ratings.

Carroll Rating Scale for Depression

Complete **ALL** the following statements by **CIRCLING YES** or **NO**, based on how you have felt during the **past few days.**

Depression

1. I feel in good spirits. (no)
   YES   NO

2. I am miserable or often feel like crying. (yes)
3. I think my case is hopeless. (yes)
4. There is only misery in the future for me. (yes)

Guilt

5. I think I am as good a person as anybody else. (no)
6. I feel worthless and ashamed about myself. (yes)
7. Things which I regret about my life are bothering me. (yes)
8. I am being punished for something bad in my past. (yes)

Suicide

9. I feel that life is still worth living. (no)
10. I often wish I were dead. (yes)
11. I have been thinking about trying to kill myself. (yes)
12. Dying is the best solution for me. (yes)

Initial Insomnia

13. I take longer than usual to fall asleep at night. (yes)
14. Getting to sleep takes me more than half an hour. (yes)

Middle Insomnia

15. My sleep is restless and disturbed. (yes)
16. I wake up often in the middle of the night. (yes)

Delayed Insomnia

17. I wake up before my usual time in the morning. (yes)
18. I wake up much earlier than I need to in the morning. (yes)

Work and Interests

19. I get pleasure and satisfaction from what I do. (no)
20. I still like to go out and meet people. (no)
21. I have dropped many of my interests and activities. (yes)
22. I am still able to carry on doing the work I am supposed to do. (no)

Retardation

23. My mind is as fast and alert as always. (no)
24. My voice is dull and lifeless. (yes)
25. I get hardly anything done lately. (yes)
26. I am so slowed down that I need help with bathing and dressing. (yes)

Agitation

27. I think I appear calm on the outside. (no)
28. I am restless and fidgety. (yes)
29. It must be obvious that I am disturbed and agitated. (yes)
30. I have to keep pacing around most of the time. (yes)

Psychological Anxiety

31. I can concentrate easily when reading the papers. (no)
32. I feel irritable or jittery. (yes)
33. Much of the time I am afraid but don't know the reason. (yes)
34. I am terrified and near panic. (yes)

Somatic Anxiety

35. I am having trouble with indigestion. (yes)
36. My heart sometimes beats faster than usual. (yes)
37. I have a lot of trouble with dizzy and faint feelings. (yes)
38. My hands shake so much that people can easily notice. (yes)

Gastrointestinal

39. I still enjoy my meals as much as usual. (no)
40. I have to force myself to eat even a little. (yes)

General Somatic

41. I feel just as energetic as always. (no)
42. I am exhausted much of the time. (yes)

Libido

43. My sexual interest is the same as before I got sick. (no)
44. Since my illness began I have completely lost interest in sex. (yes)

Hypochondriasis

45. I worry a lot about my bodily symptoms. (yes)
46. I am especially concerned about how my body is functioning. (yes)
47. My trouble is the result of some serious internal disease. (yes)
48. My body is bad and rotten inside. (yes)

Loss of Insight

49. All I need is a good rest to be perfectly well again. (yes)
50. I got sick because of the bad weather we have been having. (yes)

Loss of Weight

51. I am losing weight. (yes)
52. I can tell that I have lost a lot of weight. (yes)

Center for Epidemiologic Studies
Depression Scale
(Radloff, 1977)

Variable

The CES-D was specifically constructed to assess current frequency of depressive symptoms, with emphasis on depressed affect or mood, and was intended for use with cross-sectional samples in survey research.

Description

In contrast to the BDI and the SDS, the CES-D was not designed as a "clinical intake [measure] and/or [for] evaluation of severity of [the] illness over the course of treatment" (Radloff, 1977, p. 385). The CES-D's 20 items represent the major components of symptomatology that Radloff identified in both the clinical literature and factor analytic studies of existing measures (Radloff, 1977, p. 386). A few items were selected to reflect each of the following six components: depressed mood, feelings of guilt and worthlessness, feelings of helplessness and hopelessness, psychomotor retardation, loss of appetite, and sleep disturbance.

   Respondents are asked to indicate how frequently they experienced the symptom within the past week. Responses include: "rarely or none of the time (less than 1 day)," "some or a little of the time (1–2 days)," "occasionally or a moderate amount of time (3–4 days)," "most or all of the time (5–7 days)." Each frequency level is assigned a numerical score ranging from 0 (rarely or none of the time) to 3 (most or all of the time). Four of the items are worded in a positive (nondepressed) direction, both to help avoid response set and to assess positive affect (or its absence). Scores range from 0 to 60, with higher scores indicating higher frequency of depressive symptomatology.

Sample

The CES-D was validated in household interview surveys, as well as in psychiatric settings. The household interview surveys were conducted in two different communities, at three different points in time, and contained over 300 structured items (in the first interview), in addition to the CES-D scale. Two studies were conducted in psychiatric settings for the purpose of clinical validation of the CES-D.

   The first household interview survey was conducted using probability samples representative of two communities: Kansas City, Missouri (from October 1971 to January 1973), and Washington County, Maryland (from December 1971 to July 1973). The response rate was about 75% (1173) in Kansas City and around 80% (1673) in Washington County. In her 1977 article, Radloff tells where the demographic characteristics of the samples can be found (p. 387).

The second survey was conducted in Washington County only, from March 1973 to July 1974; the response rate was 75% (1089). In this study, Radloff alternated the original version of the CES-D with a shorter version. In addition, respondents were asked to complete and mail back one retest of the CES-D at either 2, 4, 6, or 8 weeks following the original interview. The rate of mail-backs received was 56% ($n = 419$).

The third survey was a reinterview of a sample of the original respondents in the first or third surveys. This survey was conducted in Kansas City, from July 1973 through December 1973, with 343 respondents and a 78% response rate. The clinical validation studies were conducted in Washington County with 70 inpatients from a private psychiatric facility and in a private New Haven, Connecticut, psychiatric facility (Radloff, 1977, p. 388) with 35 people admitted for outpatient treatment of severe depression.

Radloff (1977) included comparison data across different groups defined by age, sex, race, and educational background for all participants except the New Haven sample.

Reliability

Internal Consistency

Split-half correlations were .85 for patient groups and .77 for normal groups. Coefficient α and Spearman-Brown coefficients were .90 or above for both normals and patients (Radloff, 1977).

Test–Retest

Radloff (1977) reported test–retest reliabilities ranging from .32 for 12 months to .67 for 4 weeks.

Validity

Convergent

For the patient sample, initial correlations of the CES-D with the nurse-clinicians' ratings and clinicians' ratings based on the Hamilton and Raskin scales (Raskin, Schulterbrandt, Reatig, & McKeon, 1969) indicate moderate convergent validity (r values of .44–.56). Radloff notes, however, that "after four weeks of treatment, the correlations were substantially higher (.69–.75)" (1977, p. 393). In the general population sample, the CES-D correlated moderately well with self-report measures of depression and depressed mood [e.g., Radloff included scales for depression (Lubin, 1966) and mood (Bradburn, 1969)]. Radloff also reported positive correlations between depression scores and number of negative life events (within the past year, 1977, p. 396). Other researchers (Weissman, Prussoff, & Newberry, 1975) have found that the CES-D correlates .81 with the BDI and .90 with the SDS, two depression measures reviewed earlier in this chapter.

Radloff stated that the CES-D scores "discriminated well between psychiatric inpatient and general population samples and discriminated moderately among levels of severity within patient groups" (1977, p. 393). Boyd, Weissman, Thompson, and Myers (1982), however, found that of respondents in Radloff's study who scored 16 or higher, only one-third were later diagnosed as having a major depressive disorder; in contrast, of those who scored 16 or below, 36% were later assessed as having a major depressive disorder. These figures suggest that alternative cutoffs for the CES-D may need to be established.

Discriminant

Radloff (1977) reported a low, negative correlation of the CES-D with the Marlowe–Crowne Social Desirability scale ($r = -.18$).

Location

Radloff, L. S. (1977). The CES-D scale: A self-report depression scale for research in the general population. *Applied Psychological Measurement,* **1,** 385–401.

Results and Comments

In addition to the adult scale, a version of the CES-D has been designed for research with children: the Center for Epidemiologic Studies Depression scale for Children (CES-DC) (Faulstich, Carey, Ruggiero, Enyart, & Gresham, 1986). The CES-D correlates highly with the BDI and the SDS but may be more useful for surveys of the general population because it assesses depressed mood, not the full range of depressogenic symptoms.

CES-D Scale

Instructions for Questions: Below is a list of the ways you might have felt or behaved recently. Please tell me how often you have felt this way during the past week. [Interviewer, hand respondent card showing answer alternatives below.]

During the past week:

1. I was bothered by things that usually don't bother me.

1	2	3	4
RARELY OR NONE OF THE TIME (LESS THAN 1 DAY)	SOME OR A LITTLE OF THE TIME (1–2 DAYS)	OCCASIONALLY OR A MODERATE AMOUNT OF TIME (3–4 DAYS)	MOST OR ALL OF THE TIME (5–7 DAYS)

2. I did not feel like eating; my appetite was poor.
3. I felt that I could not shake off the blues even with help from my family or friends.
4. I felt that I was just as good as other people. (R)
5. I had trouble keeping my mind on what I was doing.
6. I felt depressed.
7. I felt that everything I did was an effort.
8. I felt hopeful about the future.
9. I thought my life had been a failure.
10. I felt fearful.
11. My sleep was restless.
12. I was happy. (R)
13. I talked less than usual.

---

14. I felt lonely.

15. People were unfriendly.

16. I enjoyed life. (R)

17. I had crying spells.

18. I felt sad.

19. I felt that people dislike me.

20. I could not get "going."

Note: "R" indicates that an item is reverse-scored.

Depression Adjective Checklist

(Lubin, 1965)

Variable

Lubin developed the Depression Adjective Checklist (DACL) to measure "transient depressive mood, feeling, or emotion" (as opposed to chronic, enduring depression).

Description

Lubin wished to create an easily administered, brief, reliable, and valid measure of transient mood and affect. The DACL consists of seven lists, four containing 32 adjectives and three containing 34 adjectives. Respondents are asked to indicate whether each adjective "applies to me" or "does not apply to me." The four lists of 32 adjectives contain 22 "positive" adjectives (those more often checked by depressed subjects) and 10 "negative" adjectives (checked more often by normal subjects). The three lists of 34 items contain 22 positive and 12 negative adjectives.

Responses are scored so that high scores indicate higher levels of depression. The total score consists of the number of positive (depressive) items checked, plus the number of negative (normal) items *not* checked. Scores therefore range from 0 (no depression) to 32 (maximum depression) for set 1 (lists A, B, C, and D) and 0 to 34 for set 2 (lists E, F, and G). Each list takes approximately 2.5 min to complete (slightly longer for psychiatric samples; Lubin, 1981).

The DACL consists of two sets of lists which were developed from two separate sets of item analyses. The analyses were initially conducted on data from samples of depressed and nondepressed females, then later with samples of depressed and nondepressed males. There was no a priori reason for constructing separate lists for each gender, but initially Lubin had been studying pre- and postpartum depression; thus, the original lists (A–D) were derived from samples of females (B. Lubin, personal communication, 1988).

Sample

In the first set of item analyses, Lubin employed two samples, one of 48 female neuropsychiatric patients "who had been rated as 'marked' or 'severely' depressed" in a psychiatric interview and the other of 179 "normal" (i.e., nondepressed) females. Subjects were asked to rate 171 adjectives connoting varying degrees of depression. One hundred and twenty-eight adjectives differentiated sufficiently ($p < .001$) between the two samples and were included in the four lists (of 22 positive and 10 negative adjectives; set 1, lists A, B, C, and D).

The original 171 adjectives were then given to two separate samples in the second item analysis. The first sample consisted of 100 male normals. The second consisted of 47 clinically rated, depressed, male psychiatric patients. One hundred and eight items significantly discriminated between the two criterion groups ($p < .01$); 102 of the most discriminating items were included in the subsequent adjective lists (of 22 positive and 12 negative adjectives; set 2, lists E, F, and G).

The male and female normals (nondepressed subjects) were either college students or members of community service organizations. Depressed participants came from an "adult psychiatric clinic (65%), an acute intensive treatment hospital (25%), and the psychiatric ward of a general hospital (10%)" (Lubin, 1965, p. 57).

Reliability

Internal Consistency

Split-half correlations ranging from .82 to .93 are reported in Lubin's original (1965) article. He also reported high correlations between the seven lists (r values ranging from .80 to .93), indicating their equivalence. Recall that lists A, B, C, and D (set 1) all contain nonoverlapping items, as do lists E, F, and G (set 2); but both sets are based on the same original 171 adjectives, so they overlap with each other. This fact, however, does not seem important because correlations between the two sets are only slightly higher (average $r = .88$) than intercorrelations within each set (set 1, average $r = .87$; set 2, average $r = .87$) (Lubin, 1965; see also Lubin, 1981).

It may be worth noting that reliability coefficients are higher for the gender on which the lists were constructed. In other words, reliabilities for females are higher on set 1, and reliabilities for males are higher on set 2. Apparently these differences are negligible, however, because Lubin recommends the use of set 2 for both genders (lists E, F, and G; B. Lubin, personal communication, 1988; see also Lubin, Caplan, & Collins, 1980, for information pertaining to the comparability of the two sets of lists).

Test–Retest

According to Lubin (1981) test–retest reliability is not an appropriate indicator of reliability for a measure designed to assess depressed affect or mood because, by definition, moods are ephemeral. Lubin and Himelstein (1976) report predictably low 1-week test–retest reliabilities of .19, .24, and .22 for set 2 (E–G) ($n = 75$).

Validity

Convergent

The DACL has been found to correlate moderately with the MMPI-D (r values ranging from .25 to .53) (Lubin, 1965) and the BDI (r values ranging from .38 to .66) (Christenfeld, Lubin, & Satin, 1978; Lubin, 1965). Christenfeld *et al.* (1978) found that the DACL correlated moderately with clinicians' global ratings of depression (r for males $= .52$; r for females $= .23$; total $r = .35$) and with the SDS ($r = .41$). Marone and Lubin (1968) reported higher correlations, however, between the SDS and the second set of checklists (E, F, and G; r values ranging from .51 to .64).

Discriminant

Christenfeld *et al.* (1978) reported that the DACL correlated only −.08 with the Marlowe–Crowne Social Desirability Scale. Lubin (1981), however, reported mixed evidence on this issue. Some studies find no relationship, but others find negative correlations in the .20–.30 range.

Location

Lubin, B. (1965). Adjective checklists for measurement of depression. *Archives of General Psychiatry,* **12,** 57–62.
Lubin, B. (1981). *Manual for the Depression Adjective Check Lists.* San Diego, CA: Educational and Industrial Testing Service.

Results and Comments

The major advantage of these scales is their brevity and simple response format. Since they do not measure such standard symptoms of depression as sleep disturbance, weight loss, and loss of sexual interest, the scales presumably tap largely the dysphoric affect component of depression, which seems to be of most value in research on nonclinical populations.

For researchers interested in measuring primarily the mood component of depression, the DACL has several advantages. Normative data have been published for several different demographic and psychiatric groups (Levitt, Lubin, & Brooks, 1983; Lubin, 1981). Lubin and Levitt (1979; see also Levitt *et al.,* 1983) reported age, sex, and other norms (e.g., race, education) for the DACL, based on a national probability sample. Moreover, Lubin and Collins (1985; see also Lubin, Natalicio, & Seever, 1985, for detailed recommendations regarding use of the Spanish version in the Southwestern United States) published norms for Spanish, Hebrew, and Chinese as well as English versions of the DACL. In addition, even shorter versions of the lists are available (Lubin, 1966); the scale has been translated into a number of different languages (Lubin & Collins, 1985); and a children's version is available (B. A. Eddy & Lubin, 1988; Lubin, 1990; Sokoloff & Lubin, 1983). Finally, Lubin and his colleagues have developed a trait (dispositional dysphoria) version of the DACL and are currently writing a manual that includes norms, reliability and validity data, etc. for this new version.

For researchers interested in the checklist method, there is an alternative version with multiple subscales. The Multiple Affect Adjective Checklist (MAACL) (Zuckerman & Lubin, 1965) contains 132 items distributed across five subscales (anxiety, depression, hostility, positive affect, and sensation seeking). In addition, a brief version of the MAACL as well as an MAACL for lower reading levels are in preparation (B. Lubin, personal communication, 1988).

DACL FORM E

DIRECTIONS: Below you will find words which describe different kinds of moods and feelings. Check the words which describe *How You Feel Now—Today.* Some of the words may sound alike, but we want you to *check all the words that describe your feelings.* Work rapidly and check *all* of the words which describe how you feel today.

1. —— Unhappy
2. —— Active
3. —— Blue
4. —— Downcast
5. —— Dispirited
6. —— Composed
7. —— Distressed
8. —— Cheerless
9. —— Lonely
10. —— Free
11. —— Lost
12. —— Broken
13. —— Good
14. —— Burdened
15. —— Forlorn
16. —— Vigorous
17. —— Peaceful
18. —— Well
19. —— Apathetic
20. —— Chained
21. —— Strong
22. —— Dejected
23. —— Awful
24. —— Glum
25. —— Great
26. —— Finished
27. —— Hopeless
28. —— Lucky
29. —— Tortured
30. —— Listless
31. —— Safe
32. —— Wilted
33. —— Criticized
34. —— Fit

Words for DACL FORM F

1. Sorrowful
2. Lively
3. Uneasy
4. Tormented
5. Low-spirited
6. Clean
7. Discouraged
8. Suffering
9. Broken-hearted
10. Easy-going
11. Downhearted
12. Washed Out
13. Playful
14. Joyless
15. Despairing
16. Gay
17. Friendly
18. Successful
19. Rejected
20. Crestfallen
21. Jolly
22. Deserted
23. Grieved
24. Low
25. Steady
26. Wretched
27. Terrible
28. Inspired
29. Woeful
30. Unworthy
31. Joyous
32. Destroyed
33. Somber
34. Unconcerned

Words for DACL FORM G

1. Heartsick
2. Healthy
3. Sad
4. Afflicted
5. Lonesome
6. Fine
7. Alone
8. Gloomy
9. Depressed
10. Alive
18. Enthusiastic
19. Bleak
20. Griefstricken
21. Eager
22. Drained
23. Desolate
24. Miserable
25. Merry
26. Dull
27. Melancholy

11. Heavy-hearted	28. Interested
12. Failure	29. Unwanted
13. Glad	30. Gruesome
14. Despondent	31. Whole
15. Sunk	32. Oppressed
16. Optimistic	33. Lifeless
17. Jovial	34. Elated

Depressive Experiences Questionnaire

(Blatt, D'Afflitti, & Quinlan, 1976a)

Variable

Blatt, D'Afflitti, and Quinlan (1976a) developed the Depressive Experiences Question-naire (DEQ) to measure two major dimensions of depression proposed by Blatt (1974): (1) anaclitic depression (characterized by intense feelings of helplessness, neediness, fear of abandonment, and dependency on others); and (2) introjective depression (characterized by overly stringent standards for the self, feelings of guilt, worthlessness, and loss of self-esteem).

Description

Blatt (1974) characterized the propensity toward anaclitic or introjective depression as a stable personality trait rooted in early development. The DEQ was not intended to mea-sure symptoms of depression per se but to measure a "wide range of experiences that are frequently associated with depression" (Blatt *et al.*, 1976b, p. 383).

The original DEQ consists of 66 Likert-type items that ask respondents about their attitudes toward the self and interpersonal relations. Each statement is accompanied by a seven-point scale ranging from "strongly disagree" (1) to "strongly agree" (7), with a neutral point of 4. The following are typical items: "I enjoy sharp competition with others," "I worry a lot about offending or hurting someone who is close to me," and "I feel good about myself whether I succeed or fail."

To derive a scoring procedure for the two hypothesized dimensions, Blatt *et al.* (1976b) conducted a factor analysis from which three factors emerged. As predicted, Factor I corresponded to the anaclitic, interpersonally oriented personality style, and Factor II corresponded to the introjective or self-critical type described above. The third, rather different factor presented a positive picture of secure goal striving, pride, etc., perhaps indicating invulnerability to depression. Blatt *et al.* (1976b) named the three factors dependency (DEQ-A, for "anaclitic"), self-criticism (DEQ-I, for "introjective"), and efficacy (DEQ-E). The three factors were derived separately for males and females, so there are six different sets of scoring instructions.

To score the DEQ in its original form, the raw score for each item must be standard-ized according to the item means and standard deviations in Blatt *et al.*'s (1976b) standar-dization sample. The standard score is then multiplied by the appropriate factor weights from the original factor analysis, which can be different for males and females.

Welkowitz, Lish, and Bond (1985) recently proposed an alternative to this complicated scoring procedure:

> An item was assigned exclusively to one subscale if (a) its factor loading on that subscale for either gender was greater than .40, (b) it had the highest factor loading for that item, and (c) it had the highest factor loading for both genders even if for one gender the criterion of .40 was not met. (p. 90)

Using this rule, 21 items were assigned to the dependency (DEQ-A) subscale, 15 to the self-criticism (DEQ-I) subscale, and 8 to the efficacy (DEQ-E) subscale. The remaining 22 items were dropped. At the end of this review, all 66 items are reproduced along with the Welkowitz *et al.* scoring procedure.

Sample

In the original Blatt *et al.* (1976b) study, the sample was composed of 500 female and 160 male undergraduates enrolled in a local state college. In the Welkowitz *et al.* (1985) study, subjects were 55 male and 76 female psychology students at NYU. In a follow-up study comparing the original and revised DEQs, Klein (1989) tested 45 male and 118 female outpatients at a community mental health center and a university-based clinic; 49% of them met DSM-III criteria for current major depression. Klein also tested 73 adolescent and young adult offspring of patients with major affective disorders, 33 offspring of patients with chronic orthopedic and rheumatological conditions, and 38 offspring of parents with no personal or family history of psychopathology.

Reliability

Internal Consistency

As noted, Blatt *et al.* (1976b) extracted three factors from the DEQ: dependency, self-criticism, and efficacy. The factor structure provides indirect evidence for the internal consistency of the subscales. Welkowitz *et al.* (1985) reported the following α coefficients for subscales based on unit-weighted items: DEQ-A, .81; DEQ-I, .86; DEQ-E, .72. Klein Harding, Taylor, and Dickstein (1989) reported α coefficients of .79, .82, and .59 for clinic patients and .86, .83, and .72 for the normal offspring sample. Thus, across fairly different samples the α coefficients are comparable, and the A and I factors seem internally consistent.

Test–Retest

Zuroff, Moskowitz, Wielgus, Powers, and Franko (1983) computed separate test–retest correlations for the dependency and self-criticism scales at 5- and 13-week intervals for classes that did or did not receive a midterm examination. For the dependency scale the correlations ranged from .81 to .89; for the self-criticism scale, from .68 to .83. (The lowest value, .68, was obtained from the group that took an examination and received feedback on it shortly before the retest.) The clinic patients in the Klein study were followed up after 6 months; test–retest correlations were .64, .61, and .69, respectively, for the three DEQ scales. Both studies indicate considerable stability, suggesting that the scores reflect personality traits, as Blatt intended.

Validity

Convergent

Blatt *et al.* (1976b) correlated each of the three factor scores with the other measures administered in their study. Although DEQ-A (dependency) did not correlate with the Weissman–Ricks Mood Scale or with the semantic differential evaluation of the real self, it did correlate with ratings of the potency of the real self (in females) and with discrepancy between real and ideal self on the potency dimension. Blatt *et al.* (1976b) suggested that the dependency factor is consistent with "themes of the self as weak" (p. 386). DEQ-I (self-criticism) correlated with measures related to depression: the Weissman–Ricks Mood Scale and the discrepancy between real and ideal self as measured on the evaluation dimension of the semantic differential. Blatt *et al.* (1976b) noted that

> [because the] Self-Criticism Factor, with its themes of negative self-evaluation and guilt, correlated more highly [than the dependency factor] with measures that have been used in the literature as indexes of depression . . . these measures may be sensitive primarily to guilt and self-blame, a constellation traditionally viewed as a major aspect of depression. (p. 386)

In other studies the factor-based dependency and self-criticism scales have correlated in theoretically predictable ways with various measures of depressive symptomatology (Blatt, Quinlan, Chevron, McDonald, & Zuroff, 1982), self-concept, self-esteem, and interpersonal behavior (Blatt *et al.*, 1976a, 1982), oral responses on the Rorschach (Bornstein, Poynton, & Masling, 1985), sex-role orientation (Chevron, Quinlan, & Blatt, 1978), descriptions of parents (Blatt, Wein, Chevron, & Quinlan, 1979; McCranie & Bass, 1984), and differential vulnerability to interpersonal rejection and achievement failure (Zuroff & Mongrain, 1987).

Using the revised version of the DEQ, Welkowitz *et al.* (1985) correlated each of the three subscales with the Beck Depression Inventory (BDI) separately for males and females. The correlations for males and females were as follows for each DEQ scale: DEQ-A, .48, .39; DEQ-I, .62, .58; DEQ-E, −.18, −.14. Klein (1989) correlated scores based on the original DEQ scoring system with scores based on the Welkowitz *et al.* (1985) scoring system. Across sexes and samples, the correlations for the dependency scale ranged from .81 to .94; for the self-criticism scale, .85–.92; for the efficacy scale, .86–.93.

These correlations suggest that the original and revised scoring systems yield similar results. Both versions of the self-criticism and dependency scales correlated significantly with concurrent measures of depression; correlations were generally higher for self-criticism than for dependency and slightly higher for the revised scales than for the original scales (especially in the case of dependency). Correlations between original and revised efficacy scales and measures of depression were generally negative but small (as in the Welkowitz *et al.* study). All three scales were significantly (but modestly) correlated with depression-related outcome measures 6 months later.

One important difference between original and revised DEQ scoring systems is that, whereas dependency and criticism scales are essentially uncorrelated using the original system (based on orthogonal factors), they are substantially correlated when the revised system is used (*r* values ranging from .53 to .69 across sexes and samples in Klein's data). These findings are compatible with the discovery of Welkowitz *et al.* (1985) (using the revised measure) that dependency and self-criticism were correlated .60, and that dependency scores added nothing to the prediction of BDI scores in a multiple regression analysis if self-criticism scores were entered into the equation first.

Discriminant

DEQ scores do not seem to be simply redundant with other measures of depression. The dependency and self-criticism scales are clearly different from (and more relevant to depression) than the efficacy scale. The relatively high correlation between dependency and self-criticism scales, based on the revised scoring system, is a cause for concern. The revised version of the scales seem to correlate in similar ways with other variables (e.g., in Klein's study), but the self-criticism scale usually correlates higher. One has to wonder whether the correlations involving dependency are simply reflections of variance shared with self-criticism. This problem can be circumvented by using the original scoring system (based on factor weights), but one then has to wonder about the meaning of the orthogonalized scores. Further research into this matter is needed.

Table 1

DEQ Scoring System Devised by Welkowitz
et al. (1985); Item Numbers for the Three
Scales of the Revised DEQ

Anaclitic	Introjective	Efficacy	Dropped[a]
2	7	1	3
9[b]	11	14	4
10	13	15	5
18[b]	16	24	6
19	17	33	8
20	27	42	12
22	30	59	21
23	35	60	25
26[b]	36		29
28	37		31
32	43		39
34	53		40
38[b]	56		44
41	58		47
45	62[b]		48
46			49
50			51
52			54
55			57
65[b]			61
			63
			64
			66

[a]Items in the "dropped" column are not included
in the Welkowitz *et al.* scoring system.

[b]These items are scored in the reverse direction.

Location

Blatt, S. J., D'Afflitti, J. P., & Quinlan, D. M. (1976a). *Depressive Experiences Questionnaire.* New Haven, CT: Yale University Press.

Blatt, S. J., D'Afflitti, J. P., & Quinlan, D. M. (1976b). Experiences of depression in normal young adults. *Journal of Abnormal Psychology,* **85,** 383–389.

The scoring procedure is so complex we have elected not to reproduce it here. Instructions can be obtained from Dr. Sydney Blatt, Yale University School of Medicine, 25 Park Street, New Haven, CT 06519. A revised scoring system (Welkowitz *et al.,* 1985) is shown in Table 1.

Results and Comments

The DEQ is still controversial, but it is worth including here because of its unique content and its roots in psychodynamic theory. The measure has already generated many interesting findings, and its psychometric shortcomings do not seem intractable. Future research is needed to explore the unique correlates and meaning of the dependency and self-criticism scores, to examine the replicability of the factor weights in the standardization sample, and to resolve differences between alternative scoring systems.

Depressive Experiences Questionnaire

Listed below are a number of statements concerning personal characteristics and traits. Read each item and decide whether you agree or disagree and to what extent. If you *strongly agree,* circle 7; if you *strongly disagree,* circle 1; if you feel somewhere in between, circle any one of the numbers between 1 and 7. The midpoint, if you are neutral or undecided, is 4.

1. I set my personal goals and standards as high as possible.

1	2	3	4	5	6	7
STRONGLY DISAGREE						STRONGLY AGREE

2. Without support from others who are close to me, I would be helpless.
3. I tend to be satisfied with my current plans and goals, rather than striving for higher goals.
4. Sometimes I feel very big, and other times I feel very small.
5. When I am closely involved with someone, I never feel jealous.
6. I urgently need things that only other people can provide.
7. I often find that I don't live up to my own standards or ideals.
8. I feel I am always making full use of my potential abilities.
9. The lack of permanence in human relationships doesn't bother me.
10. If I fail to live up to expectations, I feel unworthy.
11. Many times I feel helpless.
12. I seldom worry about being criticized for things I have said or done.

13. There is a considerable difference between how I am now and how I would like to be.

14. I enjoy sharp competition with others.

15. I feel I have many responsibilities that I must meet.

16. There are times when I feel "empty" inside.

17. I tend not to be satisfied with what I have.

18. I don't care whether or not I live up to what other people expect of me.

19. I become frightened when I feel alone.

20. I would feel like I'd be losing an important part of myself if I lost a very close friend.

21. People will accept me no matter how many mistakes I have made.

22. I have difficulty breaking off a relationship that is making me unhappy.

23. I often think about the danger of losing someone who is close to me.

24. Other people have high expectations of me.

25. When I am with others, I tend to devalue or "undersell" myself.

26. I am not very concerned with how other people respond to me.

27. No matter how close a relationship between two people is, there is always a large amount of uncertainty and conflict.

28. I am very sensitive to others for signs of rejection.

29. It's important for my family that I succeed.

30. Often, I feel I have disappointed others.

31. If someone makes me angry, I let him (her) know how I feel.

32. I constantly try, and very often go out of my way, to please or help people I am close to.

33. I have many inner resources (abilities, strengths).

34. I find it very difficult to say "No" to the requests of friends.

35. I never really feel secure in a close relationship.

36. The way I feel about myself frequently varies: There are times when I feel extremely good about myself and other times when I see only the bad in me and feel like a total failure.

37. Often, I feel threatened by change.

38. Even if the person who is closest to me were to leave, I could still "go it alone."

39. One must continually work to gain love from another person: That is, love has to be earned.

40. I am very sensitive to the effects my words or actions have on the feelings of other people.

41. I often blame myself for things I have done or said to someone.

42. I am a very independent person.

43. I often feel guilty.

44. I think of myself as a very complex person, one who has "many sides."

45. I worry a lot about offending or hurting someone who is close to me.

46. Anger frightens me.
47. It is not "who you are" but "what you have accomplished" that counts.
48. I feel good about myself whether I succeed or fail.
49. I can easily put my own feelings and problems aside and devote my complete attention to the feelings and problems of someone else.
50. If someone I cared about became angry with me, I would feel threatened that he (she) might leave me.
51. I feel uncomfortable when I am given important responsibilities.
52. After a fight with a friend, I must make amends as soon as possible.
53. I have a difficult time accepting weaknesses in myself.
54. It is more important that I enjoy my work than it is for me to have my work approved.
55. After an argument, I feel very lonely.
56. In my relationships with others, I am very concerned about what they can give to me.
57. I rarely think about my family.
58. Very frequently, my feelings toward someone close to me vary: There are times when I feel completely angry and other times when I feel all-loving towards that person.
59. What I do and say has a very strong impact on those around me.
60. I sometimes feel that I am "special."
61. I grew up in an extremely close family.
62. I am very satisfied with myself and my accomplishments.
63. I want many things from someone I am close to.
64. I tend to be very critical of myself.
65. Being alone doesn't bother me at all.
66. I very frequently compare myself to standards or goals.

Attributional Style Questionnaire

(Peterson, Semmel, von Baeyer, Abramson, Metalsky, &
Seligman, 1982)

Variable

Peterson *et al.* (1982) developed the ASQ to measure a stable tendency to make particular kinds of causal inferences or attributions, which are hypothesized to play a causal role in depression.

Description

The role of attributions in eliciting emotions had been discussed by Weiner (1972; see Weiner, 1985, for a recent review), among others. Seligman and his co-workers incorporated this view into their "attributional reformulation of the learned helplessness model of depression" (e.g., Abramson, Garber, & Seligman, 1980; Peterson & Seligman, 1984). According to the attributional reformulation, people attribute positive and negative events in their lives to causes that vary along three dimensions: internal versus external, temporally stable versus unstable, and global versus specific.

The most damaging kinds of attributions for negative events (the kinds of attributions that predispose a person to depression) are internal, stable, and global; for example: "It's my fault; it's due to my stupidity (or unlovability), which isn't likely to change; and the effects are general, not just confined to this situation." The ASQ, which contains a number of hypothetical situations, was designed to be a reliable measure of an individual's propensity to make certain kinds of attributions for both positive and negative events.

The ASQ consists of 12 hypothetical situations, half with positive outcomes and half with negative outcomes. In addition, half of the situations are interpersonal, or affiliative, in nature, and half are achievement-oriented. Each situation is followed by a series of five questions, which are answered on seven-point scales. The first asks respondents to specu-late about what caused the outcome in the situation. Following this is a series of three questions asking whether the cause of the outcome is internal or external, stable or unstable, global or specific. Respondents are asked (1) whether the cause is due to characteristics of the person or of the situation (internal vs. external); (2) whether the cause will be present again in future situations or is only temporary (stable vs. unstable); and (3) whether the cause influences other areas of the person's life or influences only situations similar to the one described (global vs. specific). The final question asks respondents how personally important the situation would be if they were the main character. Scoring is achieved as follows:

> The three attributional dimension rating scales associated with each event description are scored in the directions of increasing internality, stability, and globality. Composite scores are created simply by summing the appropriate items in the composite.
> The construction of the scale allows for the derivation of 20 different subscales based on different composites of items. At the finest level of analysis, one can derive 12 subscales based on three items each (e.g., rated stability of the attributions for the three good-outcome achievement-related events). Collapsing across the achievement–affiliation distinction, one can obtain six subscales based on six items each (e.g., rated stability of the attributions for the six good-outcome events). Finally, one can combine the internality, stability, and globality scales into two composite attributional style scores, one for good and one for bad events, based on 18 items each. (Peterson *et al.*, 1982, p. 292)

Sample

The ASQ was originally given to a sample of 130 undergraduates enrolled in an abnormal psychology course at the State University of New York at Stony Brook (Peterson *et al.*, 1982). Five weeks later, 100 of these undergraduates completed the ASQ a second time.

Reliability

Internal Consistency

Cronbach's α was computed for the positive events (.75) and the negative events (.72). Reliabilities for each of the six subscales ranged from .44 to .69, with a mean of .54. The low reliabilities of the individual subscales indicate the indiscriminability of achievement from affiliation subscales; hence, in their 1982 article, Peterson *et al.* cautioned researchers "not to bother making a distinction between these items unless there is a specific interest in comparing correlations of achievement and affiliation subscales to external criteria that distinctly pertain to each of these goal areas" (p. 294).

Test–Retest

Peterson *et al.* (1982) computed test–retest reliabilities for all six subscales over a 5-week interval. The *r* values ranged from .57 to .69 (Peterson *et al.*, 1982). The composite *r* values for the positive and negative events were .70 and .64, respectively.

Validity

Convergent

In 1984, Peterson and Seligman published a narrative review of literature supporting the idea that a depressive attributional style, one that explains negative events in terms of internal, stable, and global causes, is a risk factor for subsequent depression. While individual studies could be criticized, the bulk of the evidence was supportive.

Sweeney, Anderson, and Bailey (1986) published a quantitative review of empirical studies on attributional style and depression. Their meta-analysis of over 104 studies on almost 15,000 subjects also indicated that attributions concerning negative events are related to depression. A correlation between attributional style and depression, however, does not necessarily indicate that attributions cause depression. Studies by Hammen and her colleagues (summarized in Hammen, 1988) suggest the reverse, that depression causes certain kinds of attributions (distorted cognitions). Even the longitudinal studies reviewed by Peterson and Seligman (1984) leave the causal direction ambiguous. Generally, these studies assessed cognitive style at Time 1 and depressed affect at Time 2, failing to address the possibility that self-blaming subjects were already depressed at Time 1. Overall, there is good evidence for a relationship between attributions and depression, which supports the ASQ's validity, but the question of causal direction remains open.

Discriminant

Although this issue is not usually addressed in the ASQ literature, much of the wider literature on attributions and emotions indicates that different attributional patterns are associated with different emotions (Weiner, 1985).

Location

Peterson, C., Semmel, A., von Baeyer, C., Abramson, L. Y., Metalsky, G. I., & Seligman, M. E. P. (1982). The Attributional Style Questionnaire. *Cognitive Therapy and Research*, **6**, 287–300.

Results and Comments

Hammen (1988) has criticized the ASQ indirectly by challenging the attributional approach to depression (Hammen & Krantz, 1985) and to the study of stressful life events (Hammen, 1988). Hammen noted, first, that with "the single exception" of Kayne, Alloy, Romer, and Crocker (1990): "Neither the research using the Attributional Style Questionnaire nor the very few studies of attributional style and actual stressors have tested the hypothesized [i.e., crucial] mediator between explanatory style and depression, that is, attributions for specific negative events" (p. 82).

Second, Hammen noted the lack of cross-situational and temporal stability for explanatory style (i.e., the tendency to make internal, stable, and global attributions for negative events). Third, Hammen noted a possible contradiction in the attributional model, which "implicitly assigns considerable significance to *events,* suggesting that features of stressful life events themselves may be important determinants of depression and cognition" (p. 83).

In Peterson and Seligman's (1984) review, they conceded that cognitions (explanatory style) and negative events, by themselves, may not predict depression; the interaction of the two, however, may serve to produce negative expectations, which in turn cause depression. Hammen acknowledged their claim, as well as their lack of specific data supporting it:

> These authors indicate that it is the expectation of uncontrollability over future outcomes that is the sufficient cause of depression, whereas explanatory style and its associated causal explanations for negative events are risk factors inasmuch as they affect the expectation. While knowledge of explanatory style usually helps predict expectations, there may not be an invariable relationship [between explanatory style and expectations]. (Hammen, in press, p. 83).

Still, the reviews by Peterson and Seligman (1984) and Sweeney *et al.* (1986) provide evidence for the utility of the ASQ. This, plus the enormous theoretical influence of Seligman's work, makes it likely that the ASQ or variants of it will continue to be used.

At the authors' request, the full scale has not been included in this chapter. We have included the scale instructions, along with one sample item. The scale may be obtained by writing to Dr. Martin E. P. Seligman (University of Pennsylvania, Department of Psychology, 3813-15 Walnut Street, Philadelphia, Pennsylvania 19104).

Attributional Style Questionnaire

Instructions: Please try to vividly imagine yourself in the situations that follow. If such a situation happened to you, what would you feel would have caused it? While events may have many causes, we want you to pick only one—the *major* cause if this event happened to *you.* Please write this cause in the blank provided after each event. Next we want you to answer some questions about the *cause* and a final question about the *situation.* To summarize, we want you to:

1. Read each situation and vividly imagine it happening to you.
2. Decide what you feel would be the *major* cause of the situation if it happened to you.
3. Write one cause in the blank provided.
4. Answer three questions about the *cause.*
5. Answer one question about the *situation.*
6. Go on to the next situation.

Sample Situation and Items:
You have been looking for a job unsuccessfully for some time.

1. Write down the one major cause _____ .

2. Is the cause of your unsuccessful job search due to something about you or to something about other people or circumstances? (circle one number)

TOTALLY DUE TO
OTHER PEOPLE
OR CIRCUMSTANCES   1   2   3   4   5   6   TOTALLY DUE
                                                  TO ME

3. In the future when looking for a job, will this cause again be present? (circle one number)

WILL NEVER AGAIN
BE PRESENT   1   2   3   4   5   6   WILL ALWAYS
                                                  BE PRESENT

4. Is the cause something that just influences looking for a job or does it also influence other areas of your life? (circle one number)

INFLUENCES JUST
THIS PARTICULAR   INFLUENCES
SITUATION   1   2   3   4   5   6   ALL SITUATIONS
                                                  IN MY LIFE

5. How important would this situation be if it happened to you? (circle one number)

NOT AT ALL   EXTREMELY
IMPORTANT   1   2   3   4   5   6   IMPORTANT

Note: Following each situation, item 2 measures internality, item 3 measures stability, and item 4 measures globality.

The Cognitive Bias Questionnaire

(Hammen & Krantz, 1976; Krantz & Hammen, 1979)

Variable

The CBQ was designed to measure negative thinking and cognitive biases hypothesized to be associated with depression, independent of dysphoric affect (Hammen & Krantz, 1985).

Description

The CBQ measures two dimensions, depression and cognitive distortion. "Depression," as represented by the CBQ, refers to depressed affect, or dysphoria, not to a depressive syndrome (with its full complement of symptoms) (Hammen & Krantz, 1985). Cognitive distortion is defined as the presence of inferences "that are unwarranted in light of the available information" (Hammen & Krantz, 1985). The CBQ was constructed to assess the specific cognitive distortions outlined by Beck (1967, 1970), such as overgeneralization, selective abstraction, arbitrary inference, minimization of positive assets or consequences, and maximization of negative assets or consequences.

The scale consists of six negative situations commonly encountered by college students (Hammen & Krantz, 1976) or psychiatric inpatients (Krantz & Hammen, 1979). Three of the situations are interpersonal in focus and three are achievement-oriented. Each situation is followed by a series of four questions (except one that is followed by only three questions). The four questions represent all possible combinations of the two dimensions of depression and distortion: depressed–nondistorted; depressed–distorted; nondepressed–nondistorted; nondepressed–distorted. Respondents are asked to circle the answer corresponding to the way they would feel if they were the person in that situation. Scores are summed for each of the four depression–distortion categories and can range from 0 to 23 on each scale.

Sample

Various samples have been studied, including (relatively) depressed and nondepressed college students, and depressed psychiatric in- and outpatients. The student sample consisted of two groups from introductory psychology courses: Group 1 contained 107 males and 105 females ($n = 212$; tested in 1976); Group 2 contained 117 males and 198 females ($n = 315$; tested in fall of 1977). The mean age was 18 (Krantz & Hammen, 1979).

The Hammen and Krantz (1976) sample contained 32 depressed and 33 nondepressed college women ($n = 65$), screened from introductory psychology classes on the basis of their BDI [and D30 (Dempsey, 1964)] scores. A cutoff score of 10 on the BDI was used to classify the two groups.

The clinically depressed intervention sample contained volunteers in a six-session depression intervention study (reported by Glass, 1978) who were defined as meeting the criteria for major depressive disorder. The final sample included 14 males and 15 females, with a mean age of 26.

The inpatient sample included 10 depressed and 10 nondepressed male psychiatric inpatients at a metropolitan Veterans Administration hospital (Krantz & Hammen, 1979) who either met all the criteria for a major or a minor depressive diagnosis or had a mixture of other psychiatric diagnoses (including schizophrenia, character disorder, and hypomania, a phase of bipolar affective disorder). The two groups did not differ with regard to age ($\bar{M} = 44$), length of hospitalization (4 weeks), or other relevant demographic characteristics.

Reliability

Internal Consistency

Krantz and Hammen (1979) computed KR-20 reliabilities of .62 and .69 for the large student sample ($n = 315$) and the second-largest sample ($n = 212$), respectively. Item–total correlations were computed for the first ($n = 315$) group ranging from .12 to .50 (with a mean of .34). Krantz and Hammen (1979) attribute these moderate reliabilities to the inherent heterogeneity of the construct of depressive distortion.

Test–Retest

Test–retest reliabilities ranged from .60 ($p < .001$) for the group of 315 undergraduates to .48 ($p < .001$) for two randomly selected groups from one of the large ($n = 212$) samples of undergraduates. The two groups were selected on the basis of their BDI scores, using a median split of 9 (n for the depressed group $= 19$; n for the nondepressed group $= 21$).

The time interval was 8 weeks for the group of 315 undergraduates, and 4–5 weeks for the two smaller samples.

Validity

Convergent

Overall, depressed persons select more depressed–distorted responses on the CBQ. In the 1976 study, Hammen and Krantz reported that depressed women selected more depressed–distorted responses than nondepressed women selected. In addition, the depressed women selected fewer nondepressed–nondistorted responses than the nondepressed women. There were no differences between the two groups on the other two categories (nondepressed–distorted and depressed–nondistorted).

Similarly, in the two large samples of undergraduates, depressed and nondepressed students (based on either a cutoff of 10 or a median split) differed in the predicted direction in amount of depressed–distorted responses selected. In the Hammen and Peters (1978) study, undergraduates role-playing depressed students gave a significantly higher proportion of depressive–distorted responses than did undergraduates asked to play the role of a nondepressed student.

In the clinically depressed psychiatric outpatient sample, correlations between depression (BDI) scores and depressed–distortion scores approached significance before treatment ($r = .33, p < .10$), and reached significance after treatment ($r = .46, p < .01$). Also, in the psychiatric inpatient sample, depressed and nondepressed persons differed significantly on number of depressed–distorted items endorsed, with depressed patients scoring higher than nondepressed patients. Inspection of the means shows, however, that even for the most highly depressed sample (from the entire series of studies), the mean was only 7 distortions out of a possible 23. The nondepressed inpatient group's mean was 1.5, considerably less than 7, but indicating a highly skewed distribution of scores.

Krantz and Hammen found that the CBQ correlated .31 ($p < .001$) with scores on Byrne's (1964) Repression–Sensitization (R-S) scale. The R-S scale measures a related construct, willingness to acknowledge negative experiences as well as pessimistic and self-critical thoughts.

Discriminant

In order to determine whether depressed–distorted responses are idiosyncratic to depressed persons or whether they are "characteristic of emotional upset in general" (Krantz & Hammen, 1979, p. 627), Krantz and Hammen (1979) correlated each depressed–distorted item with the depression, anxiety–tension, anger, confusion, fatigue, and vigor subscales of the Profile of Mood States questionnaire (McNair, Lorr, & Droppelman, 1971). The only significant correlations with the depressed–distorted scores, after controlling for the other mood states, were the depression and vigor subscales, suggesting good discriminant validity. Frost and MacInnis (1983) reported that anxiety was not related to depressed–distortion scores after controlling for depression; they did, however, report a correlation of depressed–distortion scores with hostility ($r = .29, p < .05$).

Location

Krantz, S., & Hammen, C. (1979). Assessment of cognitive bias in depression. *Journal of Abnormal Psychology*, **88**, 611–619.

Results and Comments

There are two potential problems with the scale. First, the content is geared toward specific samples. For example, the CBQ was derived on either a sample of college students (Hammen & Krantz, 1979) or a sample of psychiatric patients (Krantz & Hammen, 1979). As a result, the particular items are probably limited to two very specific contexts. Of course, this problem could be overcome by creating new versions for different samples, but then comparability would become an issue.

The second problem is more serious. Hammen and Krantz (1985) caution that "although the biased quality of the depressive–distortion score appears to correlate somewhat more highly with depression scores than do depressive–nondistortions, the dysphoric aspect of the depressive-distortion scale undoubtedly contributes to its association with depression inventories" (p. 412). Still, this measure represents a promising and carefully researched early step in the attempt to identify cognitive factors associated with depression.

Cognitive Bias Questionnaire

I. Peggy had joined a particular organization a couple of years ago because she was very committed to its goals and practices. She knew most of the members by now, and a few had even become fairly close friends. Peggy had never considered herself the "leader" type. Earlier in school she had been fairly active but had never really stood out. Several friends in her current group thought that her ideas were sound and they began to urge her to run for president of the organization in the upcoming election. Peggy was very reluctant at first, feeling she was unqualified, but finally she decided to run because she thought she did have energy and ideas to contribute. No woman had ever held the position before, but her friends thought she had a good chance to win. When elections were held, Peggy ran for the presidency but she lost.

Put yourself in Peggy's place, trying as vividly as you can to imagine what she probably thought and felt.

1. When you first heard you'd lost, you immediately:
   a. Feel bad and imagine I've lost by a landslide. (D-D)
   b. Shrug it off as unimportant. (ND-D)
   c. Feel sad and wonder what the total counts were. (D-ND)
   d. Shrug it off, feeling I've tried as hard as I could. (ND-ND)

2. After the election, you conclude:
   a. I feel really depressed about losing, but I'll continue to work for my goals once I get my enthusiasm back. (D-ND)
   b. It's okay that I lost, since it's a useful illustration of the inevitable prejudice against female leadership. (ND-D)
   c. I'm not a winner at anything. I never should have let myself be talked into running. (D-D)
   d. The campaign was a good experience even though I didn't win. (ND-ND)

3. When you compare the winner's "platform" to yours, you think:
   a. Mine was good for a first attempt and was vastly better than my opponent's. (ND-D)
   b. Despite what my friends said, mine wasn't good at all. (D-D)

   c. I feel bad that I didn't do a better job on it, but I'll know next time. (D-ND)

   d. Mine showed some inexperience but was pretty good for a first attempt. (ND-ND)

II. Lisa and Jason have been dating for the past few months. Lisa is neither pretty nor ugly and has a pleasant personality. Jason is usually fun to be with and often takes her to nice restaurants and theatres. Tonight she seemed to be somewhat unhappy despite his attempts to start light-hearted conversations. He asked her if anything was wrong. She replied that she was having some problems at work that she didn't want to talk about but was grateful for his concern. She seemed a little more cheerful after that.

Put yourself in Jason's place, trying to imagine as vividly as you can what he probably thought and felt.

1. You think about the future of this relationship and you imagine:
   a. It's a pretty good relationship, and we're getting to know each other better as time goes on. (ND-D)
   b. It's a pretty good relationship and I'm generally satisfied although I think the relationship has a few problems. (ND-ND)
   c. I would probably have a hard time finding someone else who would care about me, so I want to make this relationship work out. (D-D)
   d. It is not what I really want it to be and that makes me sad, so I will leave myself open to contacts with other women. (D-ND)

2. You wonder why Lisa hasn't called for several days.
   a. I decide I don't really know why and figure I should ask her. (ND-ND)
   b. All I can think of is that she must not care about me. (D-D)
   c. I imagine that she thinks so highly of me that she sometimes is afraid of risking rejection or pushing me too hard. (ND-D)
   d. I feel unhappy about it but figure that things sometimes do not happen exactly the way one would like. (D-ND)

3. Why do you think her mood changed after you asked her if there was a problem?
   a. I feel pleased and imagine I can be very therapeutic for her and most others. (ND-D)
   b. I don't know why since it may have been due to any number of things, but I am happy that her mood changed. (ND-ND)
   c. I just don't understand her moods, which worries and upsets me even though I know it's very hard to really understand another person. (D-ND)
   d. I wish I could believe that I had something to do with it, but I rarely have the ability to cheer anyone up. (D-D)

4. You wonder why she got in the bad mood, and imagine that:
   a. I feel bad that I don't understand her, but it's really difficult to understand everything about somebody else. (D-ND)
   b. Like most people, she has a few problems that bother her. (ND-ND)
   c. It's because she's extremely immature and moody; I, on the other hand, am calm and happy. (ND-D)
   d. It's because she's dating the most bleak, plain man in the city. (D-D)

III. Fred had started working in the main office last week. It felt like it had taken forever to find this job after he moved to L.A. He had grown up in a small town some distance away, and since he moved had met few people. The others who worked in the same office seemed friendly, although most of them were considerably older than he. One woman, Carolyn, was about his age, sort of pretty, but she worked down the hall and he saw her only occasionally. Taking his coffee break in the snack bar one afternoon, she came over and sat with him. They talked for awhile. He found her fun and pleasant, and they seemed to enjoy each other. The break ended and he had to get back to his office. He found himself thinking about her that afternoon, fantasizing about going out with her, wondering what she's like. He looked forward to seeing her the next day. At lunch the next afternoon, he sat alone in the snack bar and saw her come in. She saw him, smiled and waved, but she took her lunch to another empty table on the far side of the room.

Put yourself in Fred's place and try to imagine as vividly as you can what he might think and feel.

1. Your first reaction was to think:
   a. I might consider being a little assertive and pursue her. (ND-ND)
   b. I'm unhappy that she prefers to eat alone this afternoon. (D-ND)
   c. She dislikes me and wants me to get the message. (D-D)
   d. She's playing hard to get. (ND-D)

2. Seeing her makes you think of your romantic prospects in L.A.; you imagine:
   a. I get really discouraged about how hard it is to meet good people, but almost everyone has problems with it, too. (D-ND)
   b. I feel like I'll never meet anyone who is interested in me. (D-D)
   c. I can't expect the first woman to come along to be the Big Romance. (ND-ND)
   d. Women in L.A. are awfully conceited. (ND-D)

3. Thinking back on your conversation with Carolyn, your judgment is:
   a. I know she really was excited by me and I'm mystified about why she's avoiding me. (ND-D)
   b. I'm afraid it wasn't as interesting as I first thought. (D-ND)
   c. The conversation was pleasant; that probably had nothing to do with whether she's interested in me or not. (ND-ND)
   d. I must have failed at making a good impression. (D-D)

4. Reflecting on your life here in L.A., you think:
   a. I'll just have to wait and see what the future will bring; it's too soon to tell. (ND-ND)
   b. I have just about everything I want and I know I'll be a big hit in this town. (ND-D)
   c. Loneliness is a big problem for me, but then I suppose it's also a problem for all newcomers. (D-ND)
   d. No one in L.A. will ever really care about me, but at least I have a job. (D-D)

IV. Janice is a senior at a large university. She dislikes the lack of faculty–student contact, so she usually makes an effort to talk to her teachers outside the classroom. So after she received an average score on a midterm, she went to the professor, Dr. Smith, to talk over the test. Dr. Smith pointed out the correct answers and the reasons for them on the questions she missed. He also gave her some helpful tips on studying. After about 45 minutes, Dr. Smith said he was quite busy and hoped she would excuse him. He then walked her to the door and said it was nice talking to her.

Put yourself in Janice's place, trying to imagine as vividly as you can what she probably thought and felt.

1. Are you satisfied with your meeting with Dr. Smith?
   a. Yes, because he was quite pleased with my visit and will probably give me a good grade in the course. (ND-D)
   b. Although it's upsetting for me to realize it, I probably needed tips on studying. (D-ND)
   c. Yes, he answered all my questions and I made a good contact. (ND-ND)
   d. No, he probably thinks I'm dumb, which is why he gave me tips on study habits. (D-D)

2. Looking over the questions you missed, you decide:
   a. It's not my fault, the teacher should make a better test. (ND-D)
   b. Unfortunately, my performance on this test is indicative of my future ability. I'm a mediocre student. (D-D)
   c. I feel bad that I missed those questions. (D-ND)
   d. Now that you've talked to the teacher, you hope you'll do better on the final. (ND-ND)

3. You thought Dr. Smith was rather nice in walking you to the door. Your reaction to his gesture was:
   a. Embarrassment. He was trying to hurry me out. (D-D)
   b. Appreciation that he realized that it was worth his time to help me. (ND-D)
   c. Appreciation. He seemed interested and concerned. (ND-ND)
   d. Sort of sad and let down that the meeting had to end. (D-ND)

4. How did your meeting with the professor change your view of the large, impersonal, university?
   a. Dr. Smith helped to make the university seem less impersonal. (ND-ND)
   b. You realize that the faculty is always happy to talk with students. (ND-D)
   c. Although Dr. Smith was willing to talk to me, I still feel lost and a little lonely at the large, impersonal university. (D-ND)
   d. Even though the professor was polite, I still felt that he resented my taking up so much of his time, and that made me feel bad. (D-D)

V. Lou is a sophomore, living in one of the dorms. He's moderately good looking, friendly, a bit on the quiet side, an A student. He frequently admires men of his age who appear to be outgoing, although he's aware of the disadvantages of that personality as well. One of his concerns is making friends. In his freshman year he kept busy with school work and maintained relationships he'd had in high school. But this year he has become more aware that he wants to meet people and make friends on campus. He's uncertain quite how to go about it.

Tonight is Friday night, and Lou can't deny to himself that he feels lonely.

Most of the men on his floor are out for the evening or gone for the weekend. At the far end of the hall the men in two or three rooms are in tonight as well. While he's in the shower, he hears one of them mention plans for going out later for pizza to a place where they know some women are going to be.

Put yourself in Lou's place and try to imagine as vividly as you can how he might think and feel.

1. Your first reaction when you hear that they are going out is:
   a. Unhappiness. They probably would have asked me to come if they liked me more. (D-D)
   b. Unhappiness and increased loneliness. Sounds like I'll be practically alone on the floor. (D-ND)
   c. To wonder if they'd mind if I'd come along. (ND-ND)
   d. Relief. They seem unfriendly for not asking me, so I'm happy since I don't have to be with them. (ND-D)

2. Being alone on a Friday night:
   a. Doesn't bother me because I figure I'll have a date next weekend for sure. (ND-D)
   b. Upsets me and makes me feel lonely. (D-ND)
   c. Upsets me and makes me start to imagine endless days and nights by myself. (D-D)
   d. I can handle it because one Friday night alone isn't that important; probably everybody has spent one night alone. (ND-ND)

3. You sit at your desk trying to get some reading done. Your mind keeps flashing on:
   a. Pleasant memories of a recent date I've had. (ND-ND)
   b. An upcoming blind date which I expect will go very well. (ND-D)
   c. I'm lonely and down but everybody is lonely once in a while. (D-ND)
   d. The feeling that not having a date tonight is one of the most painful things I can imagine. (D-D)

4. People have always told you that you have a nice smile. You're thinking about your looks now and feel:
   a. It's unimportant what people think about my looks or anyone else's looks. (ND-D)
   b. Fairly satisfied about my looks. (ND-ND)
   c. Really ugly and undesirable. When someone compliments my looks I think they're just being polite. (D-D)
   d. Unhappy because even though I feel fairly good looking it didn't seem to be an asset in getting a date tonight. (D-ND)

VI. Ellen was a graduate student, and she aspired to be a good teacher. It was very important to her to communicate well with others, and she liked the idea of turning students on to particular viewpoints that they may never have considered before. Her father had been a professor in a small college and although their relationship was strained at times, she had always respected her father and thought that being a professor was a good life. Ellen was a sensitive person, perceptive and insightful, and she was aware that part of her motivation stemmed from the role of being an "expert" and having people be impressed by her knowledge.

An opportunity to test her teaching skills arrived in the form of a class presentation that all the students in one of her seminars were required to make. Ellen probably put in a bit more than average preparation on her topic. When the day came for her presentation, she seemed calm and poised (although rather nervous on the inside). During her talk, students commented and asked questions; no one yawned or dozed. One question had been rather hard to answer. No one said anything to her afterwards; since it was late in the day, everyone left immediately afterward.

Put yourself in Ellen's place and try to imagine as vividly as you can what she probably thought and felt.

1. You try to judge how well your talk went. You decide:
   a. I clearly did the best job of anyone. (ND-D)
   b. According to my own standards, I think it went okay. (ND-ND)
   c. I'm disappointed that no one complimented me. (D-ND)
   d. I hoped someone would tell me it went well, but since no one said anything, I'm afraid it wasn't very good. (D-D)

2. When you thought about it afterwards, the thing that mostly comes to mind is:
   a. I feel good; relieved that the whole thing is over. (ND-ND)
   b. I feel disappointed that I didn't get feedback about how I'd done. (D-ND)
   c. I feel bad about that one question I couldn't answer. I think it made me look ridiculous. (D-D)
   d. I feel good because now the teacher will see my genius. (ND-D)

3. You're wondering what grade you might be given for the presentation by the instructor.
   a. I feel that because of that one question that stumped me, he'll conclude that I didn't really prepare well enough to earn an A. (D-D)
   b. I saw him nod once or twice, so he was really impressed and I'll get an A. (ND-D)
   c. I'm quite worried about the grade but I don't know how he'll grade. (D-ND)
   d. I think I'll get an A because it's a graduate seminar and because I clearly did as much as anyone else and an A is usual under these circumstances. (ND-ND)

4. With respect to your future career as a college teacher, you conclude:
   a. I'm afraid I won't make it because I know the competition for jobs is stiff. (D-ND)
   b. I'm optimistic because I've always been lucky. (ND-D)
   c. Since my seminar presentation didn't go very well, I feel pretty pessimistic about my chances. (D-D)
   d. I'm optimistic since my grades are good. (ND-ND)

Note: D-D, depressed, distorted; ND-D, nondepressed, distorted; DN-D, depressed, nondistorted; ND-ND, nondepressed, nondistorted.

The Automatic Thoughts Questionnaire

(Hollon & Kendall, 1980)

Variable

The ATQ was designed to measure the frequency of automatic negative thoughts associated with depression and to "identify the covert self-statements reported by depressives as being representative of the kinds of cognitions [that depressed persons] experience" (Hollon & Kendall, 1980, p. 384).

Description

The ATQ deals with four facets of depression: (1) personal maladjustment and desire for change, (2) negative self-concept and negative expectations, (3) low self-esteem, and (4) helplessness. Respondents are asked to rate the frequency with which they recall experiencing 30 different thoughts during the previous week. Frequency ratings are made on a five-point scale: 1 = not at all, 2 = sometimes, 3 = moderately often, 4 = often, 5 = all the time. All of the items are scored "positively" for depression, so that high frequency ratings indicate depression; that is, all the thoughts listed on the questionnaire are negatively valenced (e.g., "I'm worthless," "My future is bleak," "I've let people down"). Scores range from 30 (little or no depression) to 150 (maximum depression). In their original article, Hollon and Kendall (1980) did not suggest screening cutoff scores for depression, but they did report a mean of 79.6 (SD = 22.3) for depressed subjects, and a mean of 48.6 (SD = 10.9) for nondepressed subjects.

The ATQ was constructed using two separate samples (see "Sample"), one to generate the items and the other one to select and cross-validate them. The first sample was asked to record their thoughts, without consideration of grammar or syntax. A total of 100 useful items were generated in this manner (redundant and incomprehensible items were deleted). These formed the initial scale (ATQ-100), which was administered to the second sample, along with the Beck Depression Inventory (BDI), the Minnesota Multiphasic Personality Inventory Depression Subscale (MMPI-D), and the State–Trait Anxiety Inventory (STAI). One subsample of the second sample was used for item selection and the other was used for cross-validation.

Independent *t*-tests were computed for each of the 100 ATQ items, comparing depressed and nondepressed subjects from the item-selection subsample (defined by both the BDI and the MMPI). The items that best discriminated between depressed and nondepressed undergraduates were retained in the final 30-item version of the scale, the ATQ-30. These 30 items also distinguished between depressed and nondepressed students in the cross-validation subsample.

Sample

The first sample consisted of 788 male and female undergraduates. The second sample consisted of 167 males and 145 females (with a mean age of 20), and was randomly divided into two subsamples of 156 each.

Reliability

Internal Consistency

The internal consistency of the ATQ is high; Hollon and Kendall (1980) reported both a split-half, odd–even correlation coefficient ($r = .97$) and an α coefficient ($r = .96$).

Harrell and Ryon (1983) reported a similar split-half coefficient (.96) and a coefficient α of .98. Harrell and Ryon (1983) also reported separate reliabilities for depressed and nondepressed groups: For depressed groups, r values ranged from .91 to .94; for non-depressed medical patients, r values ranged from .87 to .91; for the nondepressed psycho-pathology cases, r values ranged from .59 to .89. In addition, Harrell and Ryon (1983) reported item–total correlations ranging from .56 to .91.

Test–Retest

Test–retest information was not reported.

Validity

Convergent

Hollon and Kendall (1980) reported that correlations among the BDI, the MMPI-D, and the ATQ-30 were all statistically significant. Harrell and Ryon (1983) reported significant intercorrelations among the BDI, the MMPI-D, and the ATQ-30. Hollon and Kendall (1980) found that ATQ scores reliably discriminated between depressed and nondepressed subjects ($F(1, 27) = 43.48, p < .001$). Harrell and Ryon (1983) obtained similarly favorable results: significantly higher total scores on the ATQ-30 for depressed patients ($F (2, 58) = 78.20, p < .001$) than for both nondepressed medical patients and nondepressed psychopathology patients.

Discriminant

No information was encountered.

Location

Hollon, S. D., & Kendall, P. C. (1980). Cognitive self-statements in depression: Development of an Automatic Thoughts Questionnaire. *Cognitive Therapy and Research*, **4**, 383–395.

Results and Comments

The ATQ-30 and the ATQ-100 are both useful measures of negative thoughts associated with depression, but because the ATQ-30 is shorter and requires less time to administer, it is preferred over the ATQ-100. The ATQ-30 can be used as a screening device, both because of its high correlation with self-report measures of depression (especially the BDI) and because of its generalizability. The ATQ, unlike the Attributional Style Questionnaire (ASQ; Peterson *et al.*, 1982) and the Cognitive Bias Questionnaire (CBQ; Krantz & Hammen, 1979), is not limited to specific demographic groups or to specific contexts (Hammen & Krantz, 1985). One caveat should be mentioned, however. Although the ATQ asks respondents to recall their thoughts from the previous week, such estimates may not parallel more veridical, on-line assessments of cognition (Coyne & Gotlib, 1983, as discussed in Hammen & Krantz, 1985).

Automatic Thoughts Questionnaire

Instructions: Listed below are a variety of thoughts that pop into people's heads. Please read each thought and indicate how frequently, if at all, the thought occurred to you *over the last week*. Please read each item carefully and fill in the appropriate circle on the answer sheet in the following fashion: 1 = "not at all," 2 = "sometimes," 3 = "moderately often," 4 = "often," and 5 = "all the time."

1. I feel like I'm up against the world.

1	2	3	4	5
NOT AT ALL	SOMETIMES	MODERATELY OFTEN	OFTEN	ALL THE TIME

2. I'm no good.
3. Why can't I ever succeed?
4. No one understands me.
5. I've let people down.
6. I don't think I can go on.
7. I wish I were a better person.
8. I'm so weak.
9. My life's not going the way I want it to go.
10. I'm so disappointed in myself.
11. Nothing feels good anymore.
12. I can't stand this anymore.
13. I can't get started.
14. What's wrong with me?
15. I wish I were somewhere else.
16. I can't get things together.
17. I hate myself.
18. I'm worthless.
19. Wish I could just disappear.
20. What's the matter with me?
21. I'm a loser.
22. My life is a mess.
23. I'm a failure.
24. I'll never make it.
25. I feel so helpless.
26. Something has to change.
27. There must be something wrong with me.
28. My future is bleak.
29. It's just not worth it.
30. I can't finish anything.

Children's Depression Inventory

(Kovacs, 1980/1981; Kovacs & Beck, 1977)

Variable

The CDI was designed to parallel the Beck Depression Inventory (BDI) but was adapted to suit the developmental and reading-level needs of children.

Description

Like the BDI (for adults), the CDI assesses severity of several symptom–attitude categories: affective, cognitive, motivational, vegetative, and psychomotor (Kovacs & Beck, 1977; also, see the section in this chapter concerned with the BDI). The CDI is worded so as to be "clear to kids" (Kovacs & Beck, 1977); the number of items is changed and the coding scheme is slightly different. Otherwise, with the exception of one item, the CDI is comparable to the BDI. (The BDI item that gauges change in libido was transformed into a loneliness item for the children's version of the scale.) The CDI, like the BDI, consists of a series of statements focusing on a particular depressive symptom; each statement is ranked to reflect severity of the symptom, from minimum to maximum. Respondents are asked to circle the statement that best describes their condition during the past 2 weeks.

On the BDI, there are four statements per item and thus scores on each of the 21 items (or 13, depending on the version) range from 0–3, with total scores ranging from 0 (no depression) to 63 or 39 (maximum depression). The CDI contains only three statements per item; hence scores on each of the 27 items can range from 0–2, with total scores ranging from 0 to 54. For example, for the symptom "crying behavior," the response alternatives include the following: "I feel like crying every day," "I feel like crying many days," and "I feel like crying once in a while" (quoted by Saylor, Finch, Spirito, & Bennett, 1984). Kovacs (1980/1981) suggested interpreting scores of 19 and above as indicating depression. Sex and grade norms are available in Finch, Saylor, and Edwards (1985).

The CDI was constructed in two phases. In the first phase the adult BDI was administered to a group of adolescent schoolchildren. Items that reliably discriminated between depressed and nondepressed adolescents were retained for the children's inventory, the CDI. In the second phase, the CDI was validated on a second group of adolescents. Both samples are described below.

In addition to completing the BDI, the adolescents in the first sample were assessed with regard to six "adjustment items." Kovacs and Beck (1977) retained BDI items that were endorsed by a high percentage of the adolescents whose scores on the BDI fell into the "moderate to severely-depressed" range (according to the usual BDI criteria). These items were chosen as potential CDI items.

The items selected for the CDI were then rewritten according to the specifications of four children who were about to be discharged from the Philadelphia Child Guidance Clinic (Kovacs & Beck, 1977). Each of the four children, all 11–15 years old, was asked individually for feedback about how to rewrite the items to make them understandable to other children. The rewritten items were included on the preliminary CDI, which was then given to the second sample. Kovacs and Beck (1977) reported the individual scores for all seven children but did not actually validate the CDI until 1980–1981 (Kovacs).

Sample

The first sample ($n = 63$) consisted of seventh and eighth grade children attending a parochial school in suburban Philadelphia (Albert, 1973; Albert & Beck, 1975). There were 36 boys and 27 girls, with ages ranging from 11 to 15 years (Kovacs & Beck, 1977). The second sample consisted of seven children, ages 9–15.

Reliability

Internal Consistency

Saylor, Finch, Spirito, and Bennett (1984) reported both split-half (even–odd and first half–second half) and Kuder–Richardson reliabilities for both samples. For the psychiatric sample, the even–odd split-half $r = .74$; the first half–second half $r = .57$. For the normal sample, the even–odd split-half $r = .61$; the first half–second half $r = .73$. The Kuder–Richardson reliability coefficient was .80 for the psychiatric sample and .94 for the nonpsychiatric sample.

Test–Retest

The 1-week test–retest reliability for the two samples was .87 for the psychiatric sample and .38 for the nonpsychiatric sample (Saylor, Finch, Spirito, & Bennett, 1984). The same researchers reported a 6-week test–retest reliability for the psychiatric sample ($r = .59$) but no 6-week reliabilities were reported for the nonpsychiatric sample.

Validity

Convergent

In a 1983 chapter, Kovacs reported that an "early version" of the CDI correlated .55 with clinicians' ratings of depressive symptomatology based on the Interview Schedule for Children. Other evidence for convergent validity has been mixed, depending on whether research has been conducted using comparison groups or correlational analyses. Most of this validity information was obtained by Saylor, Finch, Spirito, and Bennett (1984), in an investigation of the psychometric properties of the CDI on both psychiatric and normal samples.

Saylor, Finch, Baskin *et al.* (1984) conducted validity studies on three sets of comparison groups: psychiatric inpatients versus normals; depressed psychiatric inpatients versus nondepressed psychiatric inpatients (as assessed by clinicians employing DSM-III criteria); depressed psychiatric inpatients versus nondepressed psychiatric inpatients (assessed from hospital charts, adhering to DSM-III criteria). In general, the CDI did not significantly differentiate depressed from nondepressed children but did differentiate distressed children (i.e., patients with nonspecific psychiatric diagnoses) from nondistressed (i.e., normal) children.

Saylor, Finch, Baskin *et al.* (1984) also correlated the CDI with clinicians' ratings on the Achenbach (1978) Child Behavior Checklist, $r = .30$ ($.05 < p < .10$). The CDI also correlated significantly with the Piers Harris Self-Concept scale, indicating that negative self-concept is correlated with depression in children.

The Peer Nomination Inventory of Depression (PNID) (Lefkowitz & Tesiny, 1980) was completed by children in the four psychiatric units of the Philadelphia hospital in which Saylor, Finch, Baskin *et al.* (1984) conducted their studies. No relationship was found between the CDI and the PNID in either the depressed or the nondepressed group.

In 1984, Strauss, Forehand, Frame, and Smith published more encouraging validity data from a sample of 641 schoolchildren (second–fifth grade) in two rural public schools. The children were divided into two groups based on their CDI scores (scores greater than 19 were considered high). Strauss *et al.* (1984) reported that high scorers had significantly more negative self-concepts (according to the Piers Harris scale; were more passive (according to the Children's Action Tendency Scale); were more anxious, fearful, and distressed (as assessed on the Revised Behavior Problem Checklist); received lower teacher ratings (were more withdrawn, had poorer academic performance, and received higher ratings of problem behavior); and received lower peer ratings (were viewed as more withdrawn and less popular, attractive, smart, and good at sports). Whereas none of these scales and rating devices were intended to measure depression, all of the subscales seem relevant to depression.

Discriminant

No information, except for the failure in one study to distinguish depression from other (unspecified) forms of distress.

Location

Kovacs, M. (1980/1981). Rating scales to assess depression in school-aged children. *Acta Paedopsychiatry*, **46**, 305–315.

Kovacs, M., & Beck, A. T. (1977). An empirical-clinical approach toward a definition of childhood depression. In J. G. Schulterbrandt & A. Raskin (Eds.), *Depression in childhood: Diagnosis, treatment, and conceptual models*. New York: Raven Press.

    The items are available at modest cost from Dr. Maria Kovacs (144 N. Dithridge St., Pittsburgh, PA 15213).

Results and Comments

Kovacs asked that we not publish the CDI here, primarily because publication might provide access to improperly trained users. We decided to review the scale anyway, because it seems to be the most widely used depression scale for children. We have provided instructions and two sample items to aid potential scale users in deciding whether or not to write for the measure.

    There are other child versions of the BDI (Short-CDI) (Carlson & Cantwell, 1979) [BDI-A (for adolescents)] (Chiles, Miller, & Cox, 1980) as well as child versions of other self-report depression scales, including the Zung (M-Zung) (Lefkowitz & Tesiny, 1980), the DACL (C-DACL) (B. A. Eddy & Lubin, 1988; Lubin, 1990; Sokoloff & Lubin, 1983), and the CES-D (CES-DC) (Weissman, Orvaschel, & Padian, 1980). The Children's Depression Scale (CDS) (Lang & Tisher, 1978) may prove useful because of its multidimensional structure.

    Many of these scales differ in ease of administration, complexity and number of items, duration and severity of depression measured, and range of age and cognitive development of intended respondents. (For a review of some of the issues involved in measuring childhood depression, see Kazdin and Petti, 1982). It is too early to tell which of the newly created child scales is the best in general or for particular purposes. The study of childhood depression is a relatively new, and still controversial, field.

Children's Depression Inventory

Instructions: Kids sometimes have different feelings and ideas. This form lists the feelings and ideas in groups. From each group, pick *one* sentence that describes you best for the past two weeks. After you pick a sentence from the first group, go on to the next group. There is no right answer or wrong answer. Just pick the sentence that best describes the way you have been recently. Put a mark like this, X, next to your answer. Put the mark in the box next to the sentence that you pick. Here is an example of how this form works. Try it. Put a mark next to the sentence that describes you *best*. Example:

    _____ I read books all the time
    _____ I read books once in a while
    _____ I never read books

Sample items:
1. _____ I am sad once in a while
   _____ I am sad many times
   _____ I am sad all the time
2. _____ I have trouble sleeping every night
   _____ I have trouble sleeping many nights
   _____ I sleep pretty well

The Geriatric Depression Scale
(Brink, Yesavage, Lum, Heersema, Adey, & Rose, 1982)

Variable

Brink *et al.* (1982) developed the Geriatric Depression Scale (GDS) as a geriatrically oriented alternative to other self-report screening tests for depression.

Description

Due to the higher prevalence of somatic concerns in aged populations, many persons with ordinary somatic complaints are misdiagnosed as depressed. The GDS was designed to be sensitive to the special somatic symptomatology of the elder depressive. In addition, its simple "yes–no" response format is easier to use than the graduated items of most self-report scales. The 30 items "represent the core of geriatric depression and include [the following symptoms:] lowered affect, inactivity, irritability, withdrawal, distressing thoughts, and negative judgments about past, present, and future" (Brink *et al.*, 1982, p. 40). Each item is worded as a question, and respondents are asked to reply in "yes" or "no" fashion. Ten of the 30 items are worded "negatively" (with disagreement indicating depression) and 20 items are worded "positively" (with agreement indicating depression). Each "yes" answer receives one point, except on reverse-scored items, where "no" receives one point.

Brink *et al.* suggest possible cutoff scores ranging from 9 to 14, depending on the researcher's goal (i.e., sensitivity or specificity). For most purposes, a score of 0–10 (out of a possible 30) can be considered the range for normal, nondepressed aged persons (Brink *et al.*, 1985); scores of 11–20 indicate mild depression; 21–30, moderate to major depression.

Sample

The GDS was validated in two separate studies, one of 47 elderly people residing in the San Francisco Bay Area who "had an ethnic, educational, and socioeconomic mix roughly proportionate to the Bay Area as a whole" (p. 40) and one of normal elders (*n* = 20) and elders receiving treatment for depression (*n* = 51). Brink *et al.* (1982) administered 100 yes–no questions to the sample in the first study; the items concerned seven "common manifestations of depression in later life: somatic concern, lowered affect, cognitive impairment, feelings of discrimination, impaired motivation, lack of future orientation, and lack of self esteem" (p. 40). Each of the 100 items was correlated with the total score to identify the 30 best items (i.e., those with the highest item–total correlations). In the second study, a 30-item version of the GDS was administered, along with the Hamilton

Rating Scale for Depression (HRSD), and the SDS (Zung, 1965). Brink *et al.* reported that the mean score for the normal sample was 5, and the mean score for the depressed sample was 19.2.

Reliability

Internal Consistency

Yesavage, Brink, Rose, and Adey (1983) reported four measures of internal consistency for the GDS: (1) the median correlation of each item with the total score (total score minus the score on the particular item involved); (2) the average inter-item correlation; (3) Cronbach's α coefficient; and (4) the split-half reliability coefficient. The median correlation with the total score was .56; the mean inter-item correlation was .36; α was .94; and the split-half reliability coefficient was .94.

Test–Retest

As reported in Yesavage, Brink, Rose, Lum *et al.* (1983), 20 subjects completed the questionnaire in sessions 1 week apart with a correlation of .85.

Validity

Convergent

Brink *et al.* (1982) reported correlations of the GDS with both the SDS and the HRSD of .82. In a subsequent validation study, Yesavage, Brink, Rose, Lum *et al.* (1983) published data comparing the GDS, the SDS, and the HRSD in three different samples of elderly respondents who varied in degree of depression. The participants were categorized as either normal ($n = 40$), mildly depressed ($n = 26$), or severely depressed ($n = 34$) on the basis of Research Diagnostic Criteria (RDC; a clinical rating procedure) for major affective disorder. Using an ANOVA procedure, Yesavage, Brink, Rose, Lum *et al.* (1983) found that depression scores on the GDS varied significantly, and in the predicted direction, across the three groups. Furthermore, to compare the GDS with the SDS and the HRSD, correlations with the RDC were computed; the GDS correlated .82, whereas the SDS and the HRSD correlated .69 and .83, respectively, with the RDC. The GDS seemed to be the better of the two self-report measures for this sample, using clinical ratings as a criterion. In addition, intercorrelations between the three rating scales were computed; the GDS correlated .84 and .83 with the SDS and the HRSD, respectively. In a different sample of elderly psychiatric inpatients, Hyer and Blount (1984) reported data comparing the GDS with the BDI. These researchers reported a correlation between the two of .73. The GDS outperformed the BDI in discriminating among nondepressed and moderately to severely depressed patients. Excluding the mildly depressed patients, the GDS had both lower false positive and lower false negative rates than the BDI, as compared to diagnoses by a "multidisciplinary psychiatric team" (Hyer & Blount, 1984, p. 612).

Discriminant

As already indicated, the GDS seems to converge better with systematic clinical ratings than the BDI and SDS, at least with elderly subjects, suggesting that the GDS is not quite the same as those measures when used with this age group.

Location

Brink, T. L., Yesavage, J. A., Lum, O., Heersema, P. H., Adey, M., & Rose, T. L. (1982). Screening tests for geriatric depression. *Clinical Gerontologist, 1,* 37–43.

Results and Comments

The GDS has the distinct advantage of being the only depression rating scale developed specifically for the elderly and standardized on elderly samples. The scale can therefore be recommended for use in screening for depression in the elderly. Selecting cutoff scores for the GDS may be problematic, however. It has been suggested that researchers use the following cutoffs unless some other level of specificity or sensitivity is desired: 0–10, normal; 11–20, mildly depressed; 21–30, moderately–severely depressed. In a critical review of six different depression scales that might be used with elderly individuals in general, and with the "old-old" population in particular, I. K. Weiss, Nagel, and Aronson (1986) concluded that, of the 13 most important symptoms idiosyncratic to elderly depression, the GDS measured six, which was more than any other scale. In addition to the GDS, I. K. Weiss *et al.* (1986) included the following scales: the HRSD, the Inventory of Psychic and Somatic Complaints of the Elderly, the SDS, the BDI, and the Center for Epidemiologic Studies Depression Scale (CES-D).

French, Spanish, Russian, Hebrew, and Yiddish translations of the short form of the GDS are available from T. L. Brink (1103 Church Street, Redlands, California 92374).

Geriatric Depression Scale

Instructions: Choose the best answer for how you felt over the past week.

1. Are you basically satisfied with your life? (N)
     YES   NO
2. Have you dropped many of your activities and interests? (Y)
3. Do you feel that your life is empty? (Y)
4. Do you often get bored? (Y)
5. Are you hopeful about the future? (N)
6. Are you bothered by thoughts you can't get out of your head? (Y)
7. Are you in good spirits most of the time? (N)
8. Are you afraid that something bad is going to happen to you? (Y)
9. Do you feel happy most of the time? (N)
10. Do you often feel helpless? (Y)
11. Do you often get restless and fidgety? (Y)
12. Do you prefer to stay at home, rather than going out and doing new things? (Y)
13. Do you frequently worry about the future? (Y)
14. Do you feel you have more problems with memory than most? (Y)
15. Do you think it is wonderful to be alive now? (N)

16. Do you often feel downhearted and blue? (Y)
17. Do you feel pretty worthless the way you are now? (Y)
18. Do you worry a lot about the past? (Y)
19. Do you find life very exciting? (N)
20. Is it hard for you to get started on new projects? (Y)
21. Do you feel full of energy? (N)
22. Do you feel that your situation is hopeless? (Y)
23. Do you think that most people are better off than you are? (Y)
24. Do you frequently get upset over little things? (Y)
25. Do you frequently feel like crying? (Y)
26. Do you have trouble concentrating? (Y)
27. Do you enjoy getting up in the morning? (N)
28. Do you prefer to avoid social gatherings? (Y)
29. Is it easy for you to make decisions? (N)
30. Is your mind as clear as it used to be? (N)

Administration: These items may be administered in oral or written format. If the latter is used, it is important that the answer sheet have printed YES/NO after each question, and the subject is instructed to circle the better response. If administered orally, the examiner may have to repeat the question in order to get a response that is more clearly a yes or no. The GDS loses validity as dementia increases. The GDS seems to work well with other age groups.

Scoring: Count 1 point for each depressive answer. 0–10 = normal; 11–20 = mild depression; 21–30 = moderate or severe depression.

Measuring Loneliness

Research on loneliness has flourished during the past 10 years, due to a number of social factors including the high divorce rate, the number of people living alone, the increased number of widowed elderly, and the distress associated with geographic mobility and urbanization. Also relevant are the pioneering efforts of a handful of investigators, including Robert S. Weiss, L. Anne Peplau, and Daniel Perlman. R. S. Weiss, whose work was heavily affected by contact with Bowlby's (1969) attachment theory, published an influential book entitled *Loneliness: The Experience of Emotional and Social Isolation* (1973). Peplau, then a graduate student, heard Weiss lecture about this work. In the latter half of the 1970s, she and her students began studying and writing about loneliness, in the process developing the widely used UCLA Loneliness Scale (Russell, Peplau, & Cutrona, 1980; Russell, Peplau, & Ferguson, 1978) and an attribution-theoretical approach to loneliness (e.g., Michela, Peplau, & Weeks, 1982; Peplau, Russell, & Heim, 1979). Together with Perlman, Peplau organized a conference on loneliness theory and research in 1979. This allowed several loneliness researchers to compare ideas and findings (see Peplau & Perlman, 1982a,b). The result was intellectual cross-fertilization, increased enthusiasm, and the subsequent creation of a literature containing hundreds of books and articles.

Because this literature is relatively new, the measurement issues it raises can be summarized briefly. One concerns the desirability of using the term "loneliness" in scale items. The UCLA scale does not; some measures do. In a 1985 article, Borys and Perlman argued that inclusion of "loneliness" causes males' scores to decline, probably because loneliness is not as socially acceptable for males as it is for females. On the other hand, leaving out the word provokes disagreements about what is measured by a particular scale, and (oddly, given the common decision to delete the word) most measures have been validated by showing that they correlate with direct self-reports of loneliness. There seems to be no way out of this bind, because loneliness is an emotion with no agreed-upon behavioral manifestations. Investigators have a hard time deciding that someone is lonely if he or she declines to say so.

A related issue concerns the indicators of loneliness that a particular scale designer chooses to highlight. Frijda (1986) and Shaver *et al.* (1987) have argued that emotions are complex systems that (1) begin with implicit or explicit values, desires, or concerns; (2) are triggered by perceptions of events as relevant to such concerns; and (3) include action tendencies (with physiological, psychological, and behavioral components) designed to respond functionally to the perceptions or appraisals. Given this complexity, researchers can focus on needs and concerns, appraised situations, affective experience, psychophysiological changes, or behavior. Some designers of loneliness measures emphasize appraisals, although not always calling them that (e.g., "I have no one to talk to," "The people around me seem distant."). Others emphasize affective experience: "I feel abandoned," "I feel lonely." Supporting the proposition that these are parts of a coherent emotional whole, measures targeting different aspects of loneliness usually correlate highly, but the reasons for asking about one aspect rather than another often go unmentioned. Weiss (1987) has expressed concern about the most popular measurement strategies, arguing that they confound definitions with theories:

> They define [loneliness] by the conditions that might theoretically give rise to it. I have in mind . . . such instances as ". . . the absence or perceived absence of satisfying social relationships . . ." and ". . . the unpleasant experience that occurs when a person's network of social relations is deficient in some important way, either quantitatively or qualitatively." Other definitions of loneliness . . . suggest a theoretical idea of what is at the heart of loneliness, such as ". . . an experience involving a total and often acute feeling that constitutes a distinct form of self-awareness signaling a break in the basic network of the relational reality of the self–world." . . . By wrapping together identification of the phenomenon ("*This* is loneliness") with an explanation for the phenomenon, they foreclose the critical research question. It is as though Galileo had defined gravity as the force that acts with equal effect on heavy objects and light objects. (p. 8)

A third issue concerns the structure of loneliness: Is it unidimensional or multidimensional? In Weiss's (1973) influential book, he distinguished between two kinds of loneliness: emotional isolation and social isolation. Some scale designers have attempted to capture that distinction. Others, focusing on the kinds of social deficits that might cause loneliness, have created scales with separate dimensions related, for example, to kinds of relationships (romantic, familial, organizational, etc.). Taking a more empirical approach, some investigators, implicitly viewing loneliness as a mixed or complex emotion, have attempted to discover its affective components (e.g., dejection, isolation, agitation).

A fourth issue concerns the temporal characteristics of loneliness: Is it a state, a trait, or both? To the extent that loneliness is a transient emotion, like anger or disappointment, it can be captured with state measures, measures that say, in effect, How are you feeling right now? To the extent that loneliness is a character trait for some people, like hostility or shyness, different kinds of questions are needed: Are you usually like this? Have you always been a lonely person? Some scale designers have attempted to distinguish between state and trait loneliness.

Loneliness Measures Reviewed Here

We have included eight kinds of loneliness measures. The order in which they appear is not quite random, but is not meant to indicate quality or rank on any other single dimension:

1. UCLA Loneliness Scale (Versions 2 & 3) (Russell & Cutrona, 1988; Russell *et al.*, 1980)
2. State versus Trait Loneliness Scales (Gerson & Perlman, 1979; Shaver, Fuhrman, & Buhrmester, 1985)
3. Loneliness Rating Scale (LRS) (Scalise, Ginter, & Gerstein, 1984)
4. Rasch-Type Loneliness Scale (and related subscales) (de Jong-Gierveld & van Tilburg, 1990)
5. Differential Loneliness Scale (DLS) (Schmidt & Sermat, 1983)
6. Emotional versus Social Loneliness Scales (Russell, Cutrona, Rose, & Yurko, 1984; Wittenberg, 1986)
7. Emotional/Social Loneliness Inventory (ESL) (Vincenzi & Grabosky, 1987)
8. Children's Loneliness Scale (CLS) (Asher, Hymel, & Renshaw, 1984)

The UCLA Loneliness Scale (Russell *et al.*, 1980) is reviewed first, because it is the most widely used loneliness measure and because of its role in the explosion of loneliness research. Although a few measures were proposed before the UCLA scale (e.g., Belcher, 1973; Bradley, 1969; Sisenwein, 1964), and some provided item pools and ideas for later scale developers, these early measures have essentially been lost in unpublished doctoral dissertations. The UCLA scale is a unidimensional Likert-type measure focusing on the quality of a respondent's relationships with others. None of its 20 items includes the term "lonely" or "loneliness."

Two state versus trait loneliness scales (Gerson & Perlman, 1979; Shaver *et al.*, 1985) are discussed next in a single review. Both are based on the UCLA scale and were constructed to distinguish short-term, situationally induced loneliness, the kind that any-one might experience when traveling alone or moving to a new city, from chronic, dispositionally based loneliness.

The Loneliness Rating Scale (Scalise *et al.*, 1984) is different from the UCLA scale in several ways: (1) It focuses on the emotional state of loneliness, not on its presumed social–relational causes; (2) It is multidimensional; (3) It is administered in an adjective checklist format.

The Rasch-Type Loneliness Scale and its related subscales (de Jong-Gierveld & van Tilburg, 1990) are unique in a number of ways. They are based on a three-dimensional conceptualization of loneliness, the dimensions being "type of deprivation" (nature and intensity of missing relationships), "time perspective" (temporary vs. unchangeable), and "emotional characteristics" (absence of positive feelings vs. presence of negative feel-ings). More recently, de Jong-Gierveld and Kamphuis have conducted psychometric stud-ies to test whether certain items on their scale meet the requirements of Rasch scaling (a kind of "fundamental measurement").

The Differential Loneliness Scale (Schmidt & Sermat, 1983) focuses on specific kinds of relationships that a person may experience as deficient: romantic–sexual relationships, friendships, family relationships, and relationships with groups or organizations. Like the UCLA scale and the de Jong-Gierveld scales, the DLS does not explicitly mention loneliness.

The fifth and sixth scale reviews deal with measures designed to distinguish between emotional and social loneliness, a distinction first discussed by Weiss (1973). According to Weiss, people can be lonely primarily because they long for an attachment relationship (which has been interpreted by later writers as a relationship involving intimacy and security, usually a romantic or marriagelike relationship) or because they long to be part of a network of friends or co-workers. The phenomenology and behavioral implications of these two kinds of loneliness are thought to be quite different, even though both may cause a person to score high on a general measure like the UCLA Scale or the LRS. The emotional–social distinction has been tackled in measures designed by Russell *et al.* (1984), Wittenberg (1986), and Vincenzi and Grabosky (1987). The first two measures are reviewed together, under the title Emotional versus Social Loneliness. The Russell *et al.* (1984) measure includes only two items, which ask respondents to indicate how well a description of each kind of loneliness applies to them. The Wittenberg measure uses 10 items in Likert format. The third measure, the Emotional–Social Loneliness Inventory (ESLI), contains 15 pairs of statements, 8 dealing with social isolation and loneliness, and 7 dealing with emotional isolation and loneliness. Vincenzi and Grabosky entertain the possibility that isolation and loneliness can be distinguished psychometrically, isolation being a social condition, loneliness being a feeling.

The Children's Loneliness Scale (CLS), developed by Asher *et al.* (1984), is one of the few scales available for use with children. It was designed in the context of studies of social skill training for isolated children and so focuses on children's perceptions of isolation and rejection.

Newcomers to the loneliness literature can obtain a quick overview of the field by consulting the anthologies edited by Peplau and Perlman (1982a) and Hojat and Crandall (1987). Both books, besides containing excellent articles and chapters concerning numerous research projects (and Russell's 1982 overview of measurement issues), also contain virtually exhaustive bibliographies.

UCLA Loneliness Scale (Versions 2 & 3)
(Russell, Peplau, & Cutrona, 1980; Russell & Cutrona, 1988)

Variable

These scales measure loneliness conceptualized as a unidimensional emotional response to a discrepancy between desired and achieved levels of social contact (Peplau & Perlman, 1982b).

Description

The original UCLA scale (Russell, Peplau, & Ferguson, 1978) contained 20 items from a 75-item pool developed in a dissertation by Sisenwein (1964). Many of the items were based on statements written by 20 psychologists who were asked to describe the experience of loneliness; some were based on an earlier scale by P. D. Eddy (1961). Each item was accompanied by a four-point frequency scale: 4, I often feel this way; 3, I sometimes feel this way; 2, I rarely feel this way; and 1, I never feel this way. All 20 items in the original UCLA scale were worded in the direction of greater loneliness.

Potential problems with the 1978 scale included vulnerability to response sets (because all 20 items were worded in the same direction) and lack of discriminant validity (failure to differ substantially from measures of depression, self-esteem, etc.). In a 1980 article, Russell *et al.* offered a revised version of the UCLA scale (that we refer to here as "Version 2"). Nineteen positively worded items (e.g., "I feel in tune with the people around me") were created and administered along with the 20 original items to 162 university students. Six additional questions (e.g., "During your lifetime, how often have you felt lonely?", "During the past two weeks, how lonely have you felt?") were used to construct an index of "explicit self-labels of loneliness," which had a coefficient α of .78. Ten positively worded and ten negatively worded items were chosen on the basis of their correlation with the index. These items, randomly presented, constitute Version 2 of UCLA Loneliness Scale, the most frequently used measure of loneliness.

Scores on the revised scale, as on the original, can range from 20 (lowest loneliness) to 80 (highest loneliness). Positively worded (i.e., nonlonely) items are reversed before total scores are computed.

As indicated in the first list of items presented at the end of this review, four- and eight-item versions of the scale have been extracted for use in survey studies. Even the four-item version has a respectable coefficient α (.75) (see Gutek, Nakamura, Gahart, Handschumacher, & Russell, 1980).

The second set of items listed at the end of the review was created by Russell and Cutrona (1988) for work with nonstudent adult populations. In conducting large surveys of the elderly, Russell encountered difficulties due to the fairly high reading level required by the UCLA items. The third version of the scale (Version 3) was designed to overcome this problem. It contains 11 items worded in the "lonely" direction and 9 in the "non-lonely" direction. (This slight imbalance is due to the difficulty of simplifying the language of one of the original reverse-scored items.)

Sample

Russell *et al.* (1980) reported two studies using Version 2 of the UCLA scale, one involving 162 university students and one involving 237 students. Norms were presented based on 102 males and 128 females in the second study. The mean for males was 37.1 (SD = 10.9); for females, the mean was 36.1 (SD = 10.1). The scale has been used in many subsequent studies, a few of which have been discussed in Russell (1982) and many of which have been listed in research bibliographies published by Peplau and Perlman (1982c) and Shapurian and Hojat (1987).

In a telephone survey study by Gutek *et al.* (1980), the four-item version of the scale was administered to 382 working adults in Los Angeles. With scores potentially ranging from 4–16, the mean was 8.3 for 18–30-year-olds and 7.3 for respondents over 60. The mild but significant negative correlation with age, which may seem counterintuitive given stereotypes of lonely old people, has been replicated in several other studies (see Harris & Associates, 1974, 1981, and Revenson & Johnson, 1984).

Version 3 of the UCLA scale has been administered to a variety of different populations, including 487 college students ($\bar{M}$ = 40.1, SD = 9.5), 305 nurses ($\bar{M}$ = 40.1, SD = 9.5), 311 teachers ($\bar{M}$ = 19.2 for a 10-item version of the scale, SD = 5.1), and 284 elderly ($\bar{M}$ = 31.5, SD = 6.9).

Reliability

Internal consistency

In the Russell *et al.* (1980) studies, coefficient α for the 20-item revised scale (Version 2) was .94. Similar figures have been obtained by other investigators. As mentioned above, α was .75 for the four-item survey version of the scale in a study of working adults (although Hays & DiMatteo, 1987, obtained a lower α, .63, for this brief version in their study of 199 college students). An eight-item short form developed by Hays and DiMatteo yielded an α coefficient of .84, and the short form correlated .91 with the 20-item version. Coefficient α's for Version 3 of the scale were: .92 for college students, .94 for nurses, .89 for teachers, and .89 for the elderly (Russell & Cutrona, 1988).

Test-Retest

Jones (cited in Russell *et al.,* 1978) obtained a two-month test–retest correlation of .73 using the original version of the scale. Cutrona (1982) obtained a correlation of .62 over a 7-month period in a longitudinal study of college freshmen. In the elderly sample of Russell, Kao, and Cutrona (1987), a one-year test–retest correlation of .73 was obtained using the third version of the scale.

Validity

Convergent

Like the original UCLA scale, the second version of the scale correlates significantly with measures of depression (*r* values of approximately .50) and anxiety (*r* values in the .30s). In the second study reported in Russell *et al.* (1980), positive correlations were found between loneliness and amount of time spent alone each day (*r* = .41), number of times the respondent had eaten dinner alone (.34), and number of times he or she had spent a weekend evening alone (.44); negative correlations were obtained with frequency of social activities with friends (−.28) and number of close friends (−.44). "Significant correlations were also found between loneliness scores and feeling abandoned, depressed, empty, hopeless, isolated, and self-enclosed, and with *not* feeling sociable or satisfied" (Russell, 1982, p. 93). Many subsequent studies have documented theoretically consistent relationships between loneliness, as measured by the UCLA scale, and variables as diverse as social behavior (e.g., Jones, Freemon, & Goswick, 1981; Solano, Batten, & Parrish, 1982), attribution patterns (e.g., Anderson, 1983; Anderson, Horowitz, & French, 1983; Solano, 1987) and immune functioning (Kielcolt-Glaser, Garner *et al.,* 1984; Kiecolt-Glaser, Ricker *et al.,* 1984). See Hays and DiMatteo (1987) and Russell and Cutrona (1988) for similar convergent validity data based on an eight-item scale and on the four-item scale.

Discriminant

The second study in the paper by Russell *et al.* (1980) was aimed at exploring the discriminant validity of Version 2 of UCLA scale. While a variety of personality and mood measures (combined via multiple regression) were able to account for a substantial portion of the variance in the UCLA scale, a "self-labelling index" of loneliness (Russell *et al.,* 1980) added significantly to the equation when entered last, indicating that it is not simply redundant with the other measures. Moreover, the relationships between UCLA scores and social variables (eating alone, etc.) were not eliminated when the personality and mood variables were partialled out. In a study using structural equation modeling techniques, Weeks *et al.* (1980) showed that loneliness and depression, while clearly related, were psychometrically distinct. Hays and DiMatteo (1987) found their eight-item version of the UCLA scale to be correlated with theoretically related variables, such as alienation and social anxiety, but not with several measures of health-related behaviors (exercise, meal regularity, alcohol use, hard drug use, smoking, hours of sleep).

In a study involving 489 college students, Russell, Kao, and Cutrona (1987) examined the discriminant validity of the new, simpler language (Version 3) of the UCLA scale in relation to measures of social support:

> Confirmatory factor analysis indicated that the measures of loneliness and social support defined distinct factors which, although intercorrelated, related differently to the other mood and personality measures included in the study. In general, the loneliness measures were found to be more strongly related to the mood and personality measures than were the social support measures. In a second investigation, Russell, Kao, and Cutrona (1987) examined the discriminant validity of measures of social support and loneliness in a sample of 301 elderly individuals. . . . The measures of loneliness and social support correlated significantly, but also appeared to be assessing different constructs. . . . Loneliness scores were found to be strongly related to the measures of mental health status, and were only weakly associated with physical health status. (pp. 8–9)

Location

Original scale: Russell, D., Peplau, L. A., & Ferguson, M. L. (1978). Developing a measure of loneliness. *Journal of Personality Assessment,* **42,** 290–294.

Version 2: Russell, D., Peplau, L. A., & Cutrona, C. E. (1980). The revised UCLA loneliness scale: Concurrent and discriminant validity evidence. *Journal of Personality and Social Psychology,* **39,** 472–480.

History, review, and scale: Russell, D. (1982). The measurement of loneliness. In L. A. Peplau & D. Perlman (Eds.), *Loneliness: A sourcebook of current theory, research, and therapy* (pp. 81–104). New York: Wiley (Interscience).

Version 3: Russell, D. W., & Cutrona, C. E. (1988). *Development and evolution of the UCLA Loneliness Scale.* Unpublished manuscript, Center for Health Services Research, College of Medicine, University of Iowa.

Results and Comments

The original and revised UCLA scales have been used in hundreds of studies of loneliness. The second version of the scale has well-established reliability and validity. The third version of the scale, although originally developed for nonstudent populations, works very well with students, too, and may superscede the already prominent second version (Russell, personal communication, 1990).

Three features of the scales deserve highlighting. First, the word "loneliness" does not appear in any of the items. Russell (1982) mentions that this may help reduce response bias, to the extent that loneliness is a socially undesirable, stigmatized state (Gordon, 1976). A review by Borys and Perlman (1985) offers support for this proposition: Sex differences in loneliness are rare when the UCLA scale is employed but more common when loneliness is explicitly mentioned, and a study of Borys and Perlman suggests that this is due to greater social disapproval of lonely males compared with lonely females.

A second important feature of the scales is their unidimensionality. Russell and colleagues conceptualized loneliness as a unidimensional affective state, and their scales were designed accordingly. Investigators pursuing a multidimensional conception of loneliness will obviously need a different or an additional measure. For those seeking a unidimensional, fairly general measure, the UCLA scale in one of its several incarnations (4-item, 8-item, 20-item, and 20-simplified-item forms) is a good choice.

Third, the UCLA scale does not specify a time frame for respondents, hence it is unclear whether the measure is primarily a trait or a state measure. The 2-month test–retest correlation of .73 and the 7-month correlation of .62 mentioned earlier suggest a substantial trait component in UCLA scale scores. Spielberger, Gorsuch, and Lushene (1970) report test–retest correlations in the .70–.80 range for their trait anxiety measure and .15–.55 for their state anxiety measure. If we use these findings as a benchmark, the UCLA scale seems to be primarily a trait measure. The distinction between trait and state loneliness motivated the development of the scales that are reviewed next.

At the authors' request, we have included only the instructions and a few sample items from Version 2. Version 3, however, is included in its entirety. A final note about Version 3 of the UCLA Loneliness Scale: Russell and Cutrona hold the copyright on this scale. Russell (personal communication, 1990) has asked us to urge those interested in reprinting the scale or any items from the scale to seek permission from him (write to Daniel Russell, Center for Health Services Research, The University of Iowa, Iowa City, Iowa 52242).

UCLA Loneliness Scale (Version 2, 1980)

Directions: Indicate how often you feel the way described in each of the following statements. *Circle* one number for each.

Sample Items:
1. There are people I feel close to. (R)

1	2	3	4
NEVER	RARELY	SOMETIMES	OFTEN

2. I lack companionship.
3. I feel part of a group of friends. (R)

Note: The total score on the scale is the sum of all items. "R" indicates reverse-scoring.

UCLA Loneliness Scale (Version 3, 1988)

Instructions: The following statements describe how people sometimes feel. For each statement, please indicate how often you feel the way described by writing a number in the space provided. Here is an example:

How often do you feel happy?
If you never felt happy, you would respond "never"; if you always feel happy, you would respond "always".

1	2	3	4
NEVER	RARELY	SOMETIMES	ALWAYS

*1. How often do you feel you are "in tune" with the people around you?

2. How often do you feel you lack companionship?

3. How often do you feel there is no one you can turn to?

4. How often do you feel alone?

*5. How often do you feel part of a group of friends?

*6. How often do you feel you have a lot in common with the people around you?

7. How often do you feel you are no longer close to anyone?

8. How often do you feel your interests and ideas are not shared by those around you?

*9. How often do you feel outgoing and friendly?

*10. How often do you feel close to people?

11. How often do you feel left out?

12. How often do you feel your relationships with others are not meaningful?

13. How often do you feel no one really knows you well?

14. How often do you feel isolated from others?

*15. How often do you feel you can find companionship when you want it?

*16. How often do you feel there are people who really understand you?

17. How often do you feel shy?

18. How often do you feel people are around you but not with you?

*19. How often do you feel there are people you can talk to?

*20. How often do you feel there are people you can turn to?

Scoring: Items that are asterisked should be reversed (i.e., 1 = 4, 2 = 3, 3 = 3, 4 = 1), and the scores for each item then summed together. Higher scores indicate greater degrees of loneliness.

State versus Trait Loneliness Scales

(Gerson & Perlman, 1979; Shaver, Furman, & Buhrmester, 1985)

Variable

The purpose of these scales is to distinguish short-term, possibly transient and situationally induced loneliness (called state loneliness) from chronic, dispositional loneliness (trait loneliness).

Description

Gerson and Perlman (1979) studied the communication skills of female undergraduates who were either chronically lonely, situationally lonely, or not lonely. In order to make these distinctions, the original, 1978 version of the UCLA Loneliness Scale (Russell *et al.*, 1978; also see the UCLA scale review in this chapter) was administered twice, once with instructions referring to "how you have felt during the past two weeks or so" and again referring to "how you have usually felt during your life." The nonlonely group ($n = 24$) had scores in the lower third of the distributions for both recent ($\bar{M} = 28$) and general ($\bar{M} = 29$) loneliness. The members of the situationally lonely group ($n = 19$) had scores in the top third of the distribution for recent loneliness ($\bar{M} = 52$), but in the lower third for general loneliness ($\bar{M} = 34$). Members of the chronically lonely group ($n = 23$) had scores in the top third for both recent ($\bar{M} = 55$) and general ($\bar{M} = 60$) loneliness.

Shaver *et al.* (1985) conducted a longitudinal study of college freshman, starting during the summer before the students entered college and continuing through the first three academic quarters (fall, winter, and spring). They created two parallel 11-item scales using 8 items from the revised UCLA scale (Russell *et al.*, 1980) and 3 from the NYU Loneliness Scale (Rubenstein & Shaver, 1982). The latter items were included because they specifically mention loneliness, which the UCLA items do not. Items borrowed from the UCLA scale were answered on a five-point Likert scale. Four of the UCLA scale items were worded in the lonely direction, four in the nonlonely direction. Each NYU item has its own five-point answer scale (see items at the end of this review). The instructions and items for the state scale refer to "the past few days." The trait scale is the same except that it substitutes "the past few years" for "the past few days." Scores on both scales can range from 11 (low loneliness) to 55 (high loneliness).

Sample

Gerson and Perlman screened 300 female undergraduate students at the University of Manitoba in order to find the 66 women included in their study. Shaver *et al.* studied 400 freshmen at the University of Denver but included in the state–trait analyses only the 166 who completed questionnaires at all four time periods.

Reliability

Internal Consistency

Gerson and Perlman did not report coefficient α for their scales, but since the UCLA scale itself is internally consistent ($\alpha > .90$), their adaptations of it probably are, too. The Shaver *et al.* scales were used at four different times across a 9-month period, always with coefficient α above .88.

Test–Retest

Gerson and Perlman did not assess test–retest reliability. Shaver *et al.* obtained different test–retest correlations for their two scales, as would be expected on theoretical grounds. (Trait loneliness should be more stable than state loneliness.) Approximately 2 months elapsed between administrations of the scales throughout the year. Test–retest correlations for trait loneliness varied between .77 and .83; for state loneliness, they varied between

.29 and .64. State loneliness was least stable in the period when the students were making the transition from home to college, as predicted.

Validity

Convergent

Gerson and Perlman predicted that state lonely subjects would be more expressive than trait lonely or nonlonely subjects, and this effect was obtained. Also, correlations between expressiveness and Beck Depression Inventory scores were computed for each of the three subject groups. The correlation was significantly negative for the trait lonely and non-lonely subjects (i.e., depressed subjects in these categories were less expressive) but near zero for the state lonely group. The results as a whole suggested that state lonely, but not trait lonely, subjects were making a greater effort to communicate or were more actively involved in communication.

As predicted, Shaver *et al.* found that trait loneliness was significantly related to poor social skills, poor coping strategies, and dysfunctional attributions for social failures (r values ranging from .31 to .49, all $p < .001$). State loneliness was correlated with social skills (r values ranging from $-.46$ to $-.64$), especially in the fall quarter when subjects were attempting to form new relationships.

Divergent

As indicated above, in two rather different studies state and trait loneliness exhibited theoretically predicted divergent patterns of relationships with other variables, even though they were substantially correlated with each other (.40 in the fall and .60 in the spring in the Shaver *et al.* study).

Location

Gerson, A. C., & Perlman, D. (1979). Loneliness and expressive communication. *Journal of Abnormal Psychology,* **88,** 258–261.

Shaver, P., Furman, W., & Buhrmester, D. (1985). Transition to college: Network changes, social skills, and loneliness. In S. Duck & D. Perlman (Eds.), *Understanding personal relationships: An interdisciplinary approach* (pp. 193–219). London: Sage Publications.

Results and Comments

Both scales need further testing and development. They are included here because the distinction between state and trait loneliness deserves further research. A number of studies have shown, for example, that "lonely" people have inadequate social skills (Jones, 1982; Jones, Hobbs, & Hackenbury, 1982), fail to follow normative patterns of self-disclosure (Solano *et al.,* 1982), and make self-defeating causal attributions (Peplau, Miceli, & Morasch, 1982). This makes it seem that loneliness in general involves serious social and psychological deficits. What if these deficits are due primarily to trait lonely people, who cannot be distinguished from state lonely people using most loneliness scales? On the other hand, Gerson and Perlman's study revealed extra communication effort on the part of people who were state lonely. The mapping of behavioral and psychological differences between lonely and nonlonely people might be more accurate and less misleading if the state–trait distinction were included in future studies.

The Gerson and Perlman trait and state scales (for which they preferred the terms "chronic" and "transient") are based directly on the UCLA scale presented at the end of the previous scale review, so they are not reproduced here. The Shaver *et al.* scales are presented in detail.

State versus Trait Loneliness

Instructions: Below is a list of statements concerning the way you have been feeling during the *past few days*. Please indicate the degree to which you agree or disagree with each statement by choosing one of the following answer alternatives: 1 = Agree Strongly, 2 = Agree, 3 = Uncertain or Mixed Agreement and Disagreement, 4 = Disagree, 5 = Disagree Strongly.

a. During the past few days, I have felt in tune with the people around me. (Circle one.)

1   2   3   4   5

b. During the past few days, I have lacked companionship. (R)

c. During the past few days, I have felt part of a group of friends.

d. During the past few days, my interests and ideas have not been shared by the people around me. (R)

e. During the past few days, there have been people I felt close to.

f. During the past few days, I have felt left out. (R)

g. During the past few days, no one has really known me well. (R)

h. During the past few days, there have been people I could turn to.

i. During the past few days, when I've been alone I have felt lonely. (R)

j. During the past few days, about how often have you felt lonely? (Circle one.) 1 = most of the time   2 = often   3 = about half the time 4 = occasionally   5 = never, or almost never (R)

k. During the past few days, when you felt lonely, how lonely did you usually feel? (Circle one.) 1 = very lonely   2 = pretty lonely 3 = moderately lonely   4 = slightly lonely   5 = I haven't felt lonely (R)

l. Compared to other people, how lonely do you think you've been during the past few days? (Circle one.) 1 = much lonelier than average   2 = somewhat lonelier than average   3 = about average   4 = somewhat less lonely than average   5 = much less lonely than average (R)

Instructions: In the next section, the items are repeated. Please answer them with respect to the way you have been feeling during the *past few years*. Please indicate the degree to which you agree or disagree with each statement by choosing one of the following answer alternatives: 1 = Agree Strongly, 2 = Agree, 3 = Uncertain or Mixed Agreement and Disagreement, 4 = Disagree, 5 = Disagree Strongly.

a.   During the past few years, I have felt in tune with the people around
     me. (Circle one.)

1   2   3   4   5

b.   During the past few years, I have lacked companionship. (R)
c.   During the past few years, I have felt part of a group of friends.
d.   During the past few years, my interests and ideas have not been
     shared by the people around me. (R)
e.   During the past few years, there have been people I felt close to.
f.   During the past few years, I have felt left out. (R)
g.   During the past few years, no one has really known me well. (R)
h.   During the past few years, there have been people I could turn to.
i.   During the past few years, when I've been alone I have felt lonely. (R)
j.   During the past few years, about how often have you felt lonely?
     (Circle one.) 1 = most of the time   2 = often   3 = about half the
     time   4 = occasionally   5 = never, or almost never (R)
k.   During the past few years, when you felt lonely, how lonely did you
     usually feel? (Circle one.) 1 = very lonely   2 = pretty lonely
     3 = moderately lonely   4 = slightly lonely   5 = I haven't felt lonely
     (R)
l.   Compared to other people, how lonely do you think you've been
     during the past few years? (Circle one.) 1 = much lonelier than
     average   2 = somewhat lonelier than average   3 = about
     average   4 = somewhat less lonely than average   5 = much less
     lonely than average (R)

Note: Items followed by a parenthesized "R" are reverse-scored.

Loneliness Rating Scale
(Scalise, Ginter, & Gerstein, 1984)

Variable

This multidimensional scale assesses the frequency and intensity of particular affects
reported by lonely people.

Description

The authors assembled 70 affect adjectives (e.g., empty, unloved, scared, sad) that
university students said describe their feelings when they are lonely. These were administered to a large group of students, each being placed within two sentence stems: (1) When
I experience loneliness, I feel _____ : never . . . always. (2) The feeling of being

_____ is: bothersome . . . overwhelming. The blanks were filled with each of the 70 single adjectives—e.g., empty or unloved or scared. The frequency and intensity statements were placed side by side for each adjective. The order of adjectives was randomly determined. Through factor analysis, the 70 adjectives were reduced to four 10-item subscales labeled Depletion, Isolation, Agitation, and Dejection. On the final measure, subscale scores can range from 0 to 30 for frequency and from 0 to 50 for intensity; an intensity score of 0 is assigned for each item when the frequency is "never."

Sample

The original 70 adjectives were solicited from an undisclosed "number of university students." They were then administered in the format described above to 763 people, mostly students, at a medium-sized university in Louisiana (277 males, 486 females). The mean scores and standard deviations for males and females, respectively, were as follows for the four subscales.

Subscale	Males		Females	
	Mean	(SD)	Mean	(SD)
Depletion frequency	8.2	(5.9)	9.8	(6.5)
Depletion intensity	11.3	(8.9)	13.7	(9.9)
Isolation frequency	7.5	(6.4)	8.6	(6.6)
Isolation intensity	10.8	(9.9)	12.6	(10.3)
Agitation frequency	7.6	(5.3)	8.3	(5.7)
Agitation intensity	11.3	(9.1)	12.2	(9.2)
Dejection frequency	13.3	(6.2)	16.2	(6.7)
Dejection intensity	18.8	(10.1)	22.4	(11.1)

All of the sex differences except those on the two Agitation scales were significant, females consistently obtaining higher scores.

Reliability

Internal Consistency

The four subscales were derived by factor analysis of the frequency ratings, using varimax rotation. All four factors had eigenvalues greater than 1.0, and together the four factors accounted for 42% of the total item variance. Coefficient α's for the four frequency scales were .86 for Depletion, .89 for Isolation, .82 for Agitation, and .87 for Dejection. No parallel analyses seem to have been done on the intensity data.

Test–Retest

This was not assessed.

Validity

Convergent

No evidence, except what has already been described, is available.

Divergent

This was not assessed.

Location

Scalise, J. J., Ginter, E. J., & Gerstein, L. H. (1984). A multidimensional loneliness measure: The Loneliness Rating Scale (LRS). *Journal of Personality Assessment*, **48**, 525–530.

Results and Comments

This measure needs further work, but the approach it represents is promising. The LRS focuses on the constellation of emotions experienced by lonely people, not on perceived deficiencies in their relationships, the focus of most other measures. Examination of the four subscales reveals why loneliness measures correlate fairly highly with depression and anxiety measures. The depletion and dejection factors are virtually synonymous with depressed affect; the agitation factor is related to anxiety (and hostility); the isolation factor may correlate with both depression and anxiety.

It would have been helpful if the authors had selected items more systematically, reported correlations among the four scales, and provided more evidence for the scale's validity. Still, their research marks a useful start on an interesting line of work.

Loneliness Rating Scale

Frequency Scale Format

1a) When I experience loneliness, I feel drained.

0	1	2	3
NEVER			ALWAYS

Intensity Scale Format

1b) The feeling of being drained is:

1	2	3	4	5
BOTHERSOME		OVERWHELMING		

The adjectives for the four subscales are listed below. Each gets inserted into the blanks in the item formats above.

Depletion	**Isolation**	**Agitation**	**Dejection**
Drained	Unloved	Angry	Low
Empty	Worthless	Nervous	Sad
Secluded	Hopeless	Humiliated	Depressed
Alienated	Disliked	Guilty	Blue
Broken	Abandoned	Tormented	Self-pitying
Withdrawn	Unacceptable	Aggressive	Hurt
Numb	Faceless	Hostile	Confused
Passive	Deserted	Sick	Discouraged
Detached	Excluded	Scared	Miserable
Hollow	Useless	Tense	Unhappy

A Rasch-Type Loneliness Scale

(de Jong-Gierveld & van Tilburg, 1990)

Variable

This scale is based on a multidimensional conceptualization of loneliness according to which "persons perceive, experience, and evaluate their isolation and lack of communication with others" (de Jong-Gierveld & Kamphuis, 1985, p. 289).

Description

Early in the authors' Dutch research program, three dimensions of loneliness were distinguished: intensity (concerning the nature and intensity of perceived social deprivation), time perspective (concerning the changeability vs. temporal stability of loneliness), and emotional characteristics (absence of positive feelings such as happiness and affection, and the presence of negative feelings such as fear, sadness, and uncertainty). Abbreviated versions of the original items (including both adjectives and statements with which respondents could agree or disagree) are shown in Table 2, organized first by dimension (emotions, type of deprivation, and time perspective) and second by subscales (positive, negative; intimate partner, emptiness, abandonment; etc.).

Based on these dimensions and subscales, four types of respondents were identified in a large survey study of Dutch adults: the nonlonely (59% of the sample); the "hopeless" (or dissatisfied) lonely, who are actively and intensely dissatisfied with their relationships (14% of the sample); the periodically and temporarily lonely (15%); and the resigned, hopelessly lonely (12%). Within the original multidimensional scale, de Jong-Gierveld and her colleagues found nine items that formed a "deprivation scale," which correlated .66 ($p < .001$) with a simple self-rating of loneliness. The nine items are the ones followed by asterisks in the table.

Because this nine-item loneliness (or "deprivation feelings") scale measured mainly "severe feelings of loneliness," de Jong-Gierveld and Kamphuis (1985) wished "to develop a loneliness scale that would (1) tap less intense loneliness feelings as well as severe feelings, (2) consist of negatively as well as positively formulated items, and (3) "represent a latent continuum" of deprivation. Specifically, their goal was to construct a scale of approximately 10 items, half worded in the socially deprived (or lonely) direction and half in the nondeprived (nonlonely) direction, that would conform to the criteria for a Rasch scale while spanning the various subcategories identified in earlier studies. [The Rasch model of scaling is designed for dichotomous items that are assumed to reflect a continuous latent variable (see Rasch, 1966; Wright & Stone, 1979)]. A secondary goal was to determine whether or not various subscales met Rasch criteria and could be said to measure continuous latent dimensions.

The 28 items of concern here were part of a follow-up questionnaire administered to a large representative sample of Dutch adults. Half of the questionnaires were selected for scale construction analyses and half were set aside for cross-validation. The items had been answered by respondents on a five-point scale: yes!, yes, more or less, no, no! These answers were recoded so that the first three alternatives received a 1 and the last two alternatives received a 0. A factor analysis was performed on the recoded data, and the first latent root was found to be much larger than the second or subsequent roots, suggesting unidimensionality. The full set of items did not meet Rasch criteria, however, so the authors undertook various kinds of item analyses to find a suitable subset. The 11 items marked by an asterisk in the list at the end of this review survived this testing. Cross-

Table 2

The Original 34 Items Used to Assess the Multidimensional
Construct of Loneliness[a]

Dimension	Items
1. Emotions	
Positive	Unique, beloved, useful, strong, happy, valued
Negative	Uncertain, frightened, sad, misunderstood, unsuccessful, failing, aimless, lacking feedback
2. Type of social deprivation	
E_1: Intimate partner	I miss a man/woman, especially mine*
	You actually have no one you'd want to share your joy or sorrow with*
	I miss having a really good friend*
	I regret not having a mate*
E_2: Emptiness	I experience emptiness around me*
	I miss having people around me*
	I miss good company around me*
E_3: Abandonment	I often feel deserted*
	You can no longer expect any interest, even from your closest kin*
	There's nobody who really cares for me
3. Time perspective	
E_6: Hopelessness	Ultimately, there is no hope for a lonely person in our society
	The worst of all is that this situation is so endless
	Once lonely, always lonely
	There's no cure for loneliness
	You can't resolve loneliness, not even in the long run
	Loneliness can't be cured, you've got to learn to live with it
E_7: Permanence	Speaking about loneliness, sooner or later you get yourself back on your feet
	Times of loneliness always go away
E_9: Blaming others	People are by nature unwilling to rescue you from your loneliness
	As a lonely person, one is left to one's own fate

[a]From deJong-Gierveld, J., & Raadschelders, J. (1982).

validation of the Rasch characteristics of these items in the half of the sample set aside for this purpose supported the scale's unidimensionality. Factor analyses of the 11 items suggested that they tap a single loneliness dimension but are affected by a second methodological factor on which the positively worded items load in one direction and the negatively worded items load in the other. This was judged to be an unavoidable and nonfatal consequence of including the two kinds of items.

The subscales labeled L1, L2, L3, and L5 in the list at the end of this review also met Rasch criteria and so were judged to measure coherent latent dimensions. (L4 was considered too short for such treatment.) The authors concluded that

> subscales L1, L2, L3, and L5 are good Rasch measures for feelings of severe loneliness, loneliness in problem situations, loneliness concerning missing companionship, and for the positive set, feelings of belongingness. Subscales L2 and L3 seem to be particularly suitable indicators for less severe loneliness. Subscale L1 seems to be a suitable indicator for severe loneliness. (de Jong-Gierveld & Kamphuis, 1985, pp. 296–297)

Sample

The items under consideration here were self-administered in 1982 and 1983 by a representative sample of 1230 Dutch men and women.

Reliability

Internal Consistency

As mentioned, the 11-item loneliness scale and the four retained subscales each meet Rasch criteria for unidimensionality. Factor analysis of the 11-item measure yielded a single content factor, as hoped, and a second methodological factor. Item–total correlations ranged from .50 to .59.

Test–Retest

Not mentioned.

Validity

Convergent

A measure similar, but not identical, to the Rasch measure was used as the final dependent variable in a LISREL analysis of predictors of loneliness (de Jong-Gierveld, 1987). It correlated significantly with theoretically reasonable variables such as being without a partner and being dissatisfied with current relationships. The 11-item Rasch scale itself was used in two studies of intimacy and loneliness (de Jong-Gierveld & van Tilburg, 1987). Based on dichotomous item-scoring (hence with total scores ranging potentially from 0 to 11), people without romantic partners ($n = 290$) had a mean score between 4.0 and 4.4 (in the two studies); those with a partner who was not also a confidant or intimate ($n = 432$) had scores between 2.9 and 3.3; and those whose partner was a confidant and intimate ($n = 398$) had scores between 1.9 and 2.1. The effect of partner support on Rasch-scale loneliness was highly significant in both studies. Something similar to the subscales (L1 etc.) were used in the de Jong-Gierveld and Raadschelders (1982) study to construct types of individuals. The resulting types related in meaningful ways to measures of depression and self-esteem.

Discriminant

Not mentioned.

Location

de Jong-Gierveld, J., & van Tilburg, T. (1990). *Manual of the loneliness scale.* Vrije Universiteit Amsterdam Koningslaan 22-24, 1075 AD Amsterdam, The Netherlands.

Results and Comments

The scale and the four subscales require further validation, and it would be useful to know how the subscales relate to each other. They are included here for several reasons:

1. The attempt to meet Rasch-scale criteria is unusual among social scientists, being more common in connection with ability testing.
2. The item pool has evolved through a series of thoughtful studies, beginning with qualitative phenomenological research and moving to recent studies involving Rasch scaling and structural equation modeling.
3. The items seem to be closer to the *experience* of loneliness than are the items on some of the better-known scales.
4. The scales have been developed on large representative samples of (Dutch) adults.

The de Jong-Gierveld Rasch-Type Scale and Subscales

Item	Percentage Agreeing (%)	Item–Total Correlation (r)
Severe Deprivation (L1)		
6. I wish I had a really close friend.*	27	.56
17. I experience a sense of emptiness around me.*	20	.60
28. There's no one really that I would like to share my ups and downs with.	31	.31
21. I don't really have any friends.	28	.37
22. There is no one who is particularly interested in you.	31	.28
12. Often, I feel rejected.*	20	.62
23. You can no longer expect any interest from even your own family.	32	.40
Deprivation Feelings Connected with Specific Problem Situations Such as Abandonment (L2)		
4. There are only a few people with whom you can really talk.	72	.41
15. There are only a few people who take the trouble to listen to you.	52	.48
14. When you feel good, you may be welcome, but when you're depressed it's quite a different matter.	43	.47

9. Recently, I feel misunderstood even by my closest family.	24	.43
24. I miss having people around me.*	18	.53
3. I have lost all my friends from previous years.	40	.45
20. I feel I'm a prisoner in my own home.	20	.51

Missing Companionship (L3)

8. It makes me sad that I have no company around me.*	21	.58
18. I feel ignored by people in my neighborhood.	14	.46
2. I wish I had contact with my neighbors.	23	.47
29. I feel my circle of friends and acquaintances is too limited.*	29	.59
11. The neighbors are very cold.	39	.45

A Feeling of Sociability (L4)

13. There are a few people that I have pleasant contact with.	14	.38
5. There are several people in the neighborhood that I can go to for a cozy chat.	40	.43
25. There is always someone around that I can talk to about my day to day problems.*	28	.53

A Feeling of Having Meaningful Relationships (L5)

26. There are plenty of people that I can depend on if I'm in trouble.*	37	.57
30. There are enough people that I feel close to.*	31	.57
10. I can rely on my friends whenever I need them.*	31	.54
1. I have a number of friends that I can rely on.	33	.47
19. There are many people that I can count on completely.*	53	.49
7. There are enough people who accept me for what I am.	18	.47

Note: Items 16 and 27 have been deleted because they did not appear in the de Jong-Gierveld and Kamphuis article. Items followed by asterisks are part of the 11-item Rasch scale, which measures intensity of loneliness. Subscales labeled L1, L2, L3, and L5 each meet Rasch criteria for unidimensionality. The answer alternatives used by the authors were yes!, yes, more or less, no, and no!, but more conventional true—false or Likert-type answer alternatives should work as well.

Differential Loneliness Scale

(Schmidt & Sermat, 1983)

Variable

The DLS asks respondents to evaluate the quality and quantity of their interactions in four kinds of relationships: romantic–sexual relationships, friendships, relationships with family, and relationships with larger groups or the community.

Description

The DLS is based on a definition of loneliness as "a felt discrepancy between the kinds of relationships the individual perceives himself as having and what he would like to have" (Schmidt & Sermat, 1983, p. 1039; Sermat, 1980). Within each of four kinds of relationships, dissatisfaction is assessed in terms of five interaction dimensions: presence versus absence, approach versus avoidance, cooperation, evaluation, and communication. Items were chosen in accordance with three objectives: (a) to lessen overlap with the constructs of depression, anxiety, and self-esteem; (b) to minimize social desirability response bias; and (c) to maximize homogeneity. Both positively and negatively worded items were included; no item includes the word "lonely" or "loneliness." Two versions were developed, a college student version and a nonstudent version, both of which had similar factor structures. The nonstudent version is described here.

Items were based on the psychiatric and psychological literature about loneliness, descriptions of loneliness experiences in popular literature, letters describing loneliness experiences written in response to a magazine article about Sermat's research, and 400 essays about loneliness (Sermat, 1980). A total of 320 items were created, 16 for each of the 20 relationships-by-dimensions categories. In each category, half of the items are scored in the satisfied direction and half in the dissatisfied direction. Each item is answered "true" or "false." The 320 items were reduced to 60 by selecting items that correlated more highly with the total 320-item score than with measures of social desirability, depression, anxiety, and self-esteem (see below). Items endorsed by less than 5% or more than 95% of the subjects were eliminated. Items meeting these criteria were rank-ordered according to their correlation with the total score. Since the top 60 items accounted for 96% of the variance in the top 120, the authors decided that a 60-item scale was sufficient. Among these 60 items, 22 concerned friendships, 18 concerned family relationships, 12 concerned romantic–sexual relationships, and 8 concerned relationships with groups. In other words, the final scale is not balanced with respect to types of relationships, because balancing would have reduced internal consistency. True or false answers indicating loneliness receive one point, so scores on the 60-item scale can range from 0 (not lonely) to 60 (extremely lonely).

Sample

The initial set of 320 items was administered to a student group and to a largely nonstudent adult group consisting of 264 visitors to the Ontario Science Centre, all over 25 years of age. After the 60-item version was created, it was administered to several additional groups: 255 men and 434 women who were visitors to the Ontario Science Centre, York University psychology and social science students, executives participating in management seminars, or members of various community groups. The majority (79%) were not married at the time they participated, and 73% had attended college at some time during their lives.

The original sample of 264 nonstudent adults had a mean score for the 60 items of 13.1 (SD = 11.6).

Reliability

Internal Consistency

The K-R 20 internal consistency coefficient for the initial nonstudent adult sample was .92. For the subsequent studies of nonstudent adults, K-R 20 was .89 for men and .92 for women. For this same group, the reliabilities of the subscales were as follows: Romantic–Sexual, .71; Family, .70; Friends, .72; Groups, .73.

Test–Retest

No data were mentioned.

Validity

Convergent

In the nonstudent groups studied with the 60-item scale a single-item loneliness question was asked: "How lonely would you say you are, generally?" Subjects replied on a 10-point scale ranging from "never" (1) to "all the time" (10). This variable was correlated with the DLS score, and the following results were obtained: for men (under 25 years), r = .45; for older men, .58; for younger women, .55; for older women, .45. (All r values were significant at $p < .001$.) This suggests that the scale items, which do not include the word "loneliness," do measure the kinds of relationship dissatisfaction associated with feeling lonely. The four subscales correlate .39 with each other, on the average, which is considerably below their reliabilities (averaging around .72). This suggests that the subscales do measure somewhat different content areas as designed. When the 60 items were factor-analyzed, the factors in both the student and nonstudent groups corresponded roughly to the four relationship-type categories (subscale dimensions).

Divergent

The items were selected to minimize correlations with the social desirability scale of Jackson's (1967) PRF, the depression scale of Jackson and Messick's (1971) DPI, and the anxiety and self-esteem scales of Jackson's (1976) JPI. Even so, the correlation with social desirability was −.59; with self-esteem, −.40; with anxiety, .42; and with depression, .62 (all highly significant). While these correlations are probably lower than they would be for other loneliness scales, they are still substantial, suggesting that this cluster of variables cannot be fully disentangled.

Location

Schmidt, N., & Sermat, V. (1983). Measuring loneliness in different relationships. *Journal of Personality and Social Psychology,* **44,** 1038–1047.

Results and Comments

The authors report that "married men and women received significantly lower DLS scores than did single, separated, widowed, or divorced men and women" (no figures provided).

Men obtained significantly higher DLS scores than women, and younger participants had higher scores than older participants.

The DLS is unusual in emphasizing loneliness in different kinds of relationships. Because of the way the scale was reduced from 320 to 60 items, however, it does not place equal weight on the four kinds of relationships; 40 of the 60 items concern friends and family, 20 concern romantic–sexual partners and relations with groups. Examination of the items suggests that the scale probably measures social provisions, social deficits, and social skills, not loneliness per se. The authors seem to agree with this assessment, as indicated in the following passage:

> Although the DLS attempts to assess the critical areas of relational deficit and provides a research tool for a greater in-depth study of the sources of loneliness feelings, it is not a direct measure of subjective feelings of loneliness. Different individuals have different quantitative and qualitative needs for relationships in various areas, different methods of coping with such deficits, and different ways of dealing with their feelings of loneliness. (p. 1046)

The DLS may be especially useful in studies in which investigators wish to distinguish loneliness optimally from anxiety, depression, and low self-esteem. For those studying college students, it might be worthwhile to obtain a copy of the student version of the scale from Dr. Vello Sermat, Department of Psychology, York University, Downsview, Ontario, Canada M3J 1P3. There is only 27% overlap between the items in the two versions, and comments by Schmidt and Sermat (1983) suggest that the emphasis placed on particular kinds of relationships may vary across versions.

Differential Loneliness Scale (Nonstudent Version)

Instructions. For each statement, decide whether it describes you or your situation or not. If it does seem to describe you or your situation, mark it TRUE. If not, mark FALSE. If an item is not applicable to you because you are currently not involved in the situation it depicts (e.g., a current romantic or marital relationship), then score it false.

1. I find it easy to express feelings of affection toward members of my family. (Fam.) (R)

      TRUE   FALSE

2. Most everyone around me is a stranger. (Gr.)
3. I usually wait for a friend to call me up and invite me out before making plans to go anywhere. (Fr.)
4. Most of my friends understand my motives and reasoning. (Fr.) (R)
5. At this time, I do not have a romantic relationship that means a great deal to me. (R.S.)
6. I don't get along very well with my family. (Fam.)
7. I have at least one good friend of the same sex. (Fr.) (R)
8. I can't depend on getting moral or financial support from any group or organization in a time of trouble.

9. I am now involved in a romantic or marital relationship where both of us make a genuine effort at cooperation. (R.S.) (R)

10. I often become shy and retiring in the company of relatives. (Fam.)

11. Some of my friends will stand by me in almost any difficulty. (Fr.) (R)

12. People in my community aren't really interested in what I think or feel. (Gr.)

13. My trying to have friends and to be liked seldom succeeds the way I would like it to. (Fr.)

14. I spend some time talking individually with each member of my family. (Fam.) (R)

15. I find it difficult to tell anyone that I love him or her. (R.S.)

16. I don't have many friends in the city where I live. (Fr.)

17. I work well with others in a group. (Gr.) (R)

18. I am an important part of the emotional and physical well-being of my lover or spouse. (R.S.) (R)

19. I don't feel that I can turn to my friends living around me for help when I need it. (Fr.)

20. I don't think that anyone in my family really understands me. (Fam.)

21. I have a lover or spouse who fulfills many of my emotional needs. (R.S.) (R)

22. My friends are generally interested in what I am doing, although not to the point of being nosy. (Fr.) (R)

23. Members of my family enjoy meeting my friends. (Fr.) (R)

24. I allow myself to become close to my friends. (Fr.) (R)

25. My relatives are generally too busy with their concerns to bother about my problems. (Fam.)

26. Few of my friends understand me the way I want to be understood. (Fr.)

27. No one in the community where I live cares much about me. (Gr.)

28. Right now, I don't have true compatibility in a romantic or marital relationship. (R.S.)

29. Members of my family give me the kind of support that I need. (Fam.) (R)

30. A lot of my friendships ultimately turn out to be pretty disappointing. (Fr.)

31. My romantic or marital partner gives me much support and encouragement. (R.S.) (R)

32. I am not very open with members of my family. (Fam.)

33. I often feel resentful about certain actions of my friends. (Fr.)

34. I am embarrassed about the way my family behaves. (Fam.)

35. People who say they are in love with me are usually only trying to rationalize using me for their own purposes. (R.S.)

36. I have a good relationship with most members of my immediate family. (Fam.) (R)

37. In my relationships, I am generally able to express both positive and negative feelings. (Fr.) (R)

38. I don't get much satisfaction from the groups I attend. (Gr.)

39. I get plenty of help and support from friends. (Fam.) (R)
40. I seem to have little to say to members of my family. (Fam.)
41. I don't have any one special love relationship in which I feel really understood. (R.S.)
42. I really feel that I belong to a family. (Fam.) (R)
43. I have few friends with whom I can talk openly. (Fr.)
44. My family is quite critical of me. (Fam.)
45. I have an active love life. (R.S.) (R)
46. I have few friends that I can depend on to fulfill their end of mutual commitments. (Fr.)
47. Generally I feel that members of my family acknowledge my strengths and positive qualities. (Fam.) (R)
48. I have at least one real friend. (Fr.) (R)
49. I don't have any neighbors who would help me out in a time of need. (Gr.)
50. Members of my family are relaxed and easy-going with each other. (Fam.) (R)
51. I have moved around so much that I find it difficult to maintain lasting friendships. (Fr.)
52. I tend to get along well with partners in romantic relationships. (R.S.) (R)
53. I find it difficult to invite a friend to do something with me. (Fr.)
54. I have little contact with members of my family. (Fam.)
55. My friends don't seem to stay interested in me for long. (Fr.)
56. There are people in my community who understand my views and beliefs. (Gr.) (R)
57. As much as possible, I avoid members of my family. (Fam.)
58. I seldom get the emotional security I need from a romantic or sexual relationship. (R.S.)
59. My family usually values my opinion when a family decision is to be made. (Fam.) (R)
60. Most of my friends are genuinely concerned about my welfare. (Fr.) (R)

Note: "True" receives one point except for items followed by an "R"; on those items "false" receives one point. R.S., romantic–sexual relationships; Fr., friendships; Fam., relationships with family; Gr., relationships with larger groups.

Emotional versus Social Loneliness Scales

(Russell, Cutrona, Rose, & Yurko, 1984; Wittenberg, 1986)

Variable

Based on R. S. Weiss (1973), these two measures were designed to distinguish emotional isolation (lack of a close, intimate attachment to another person) from social isolation (lack of a network of social relationships with friends who share common interests and activities).

Description

Two measures are included in this review because they are closely related conceptually and one (Wittenberg, 1986) is an unpublished extension of the other. Russell *et al.* (1984) designed two items, one to measure emotional loneliness and the other to measure social loneliness. Each item consists of a two-sentence description of a type of loneliness followed by a nine-point rating scale (anchored by the phrases "not at all" and "very much") indicating how intensely the respondent is experiencing that type at present. Hence, scores on each scale range from 1 to 9.

Wittenberg (1986) developed two five-item measures, one of social loneliness and the other of emotional loneliness. Each item is answered on a five-point scale, so scores range from 5 (lowest loneliness) to 25 (highest loneliness) on both scales.

Sample

Russell *et al.* studied 505 students at the University of Iowa, part of a randomly selected sample ($n = 1000$) spanning all four undergraduate levels and including graduate levels (55% were women, 45% were men).

Wittenberg studied 104 undergraduate psychology students at the University of Rochester (46 females and 58 males).

Reliability

Internal Consistency

Russell *et al.* used single items, so the internal consistency criterion is inapplicable. Wittenberg calculated coefficient α for her two five-item scales and obtained values of .78 and .76 for emotional and social loneliness, respectively.

Test–Retest

No information for either measure.

Validity

Convergent

The Russell *et al.* emotional loneliness item correlated .44 with the UCLA Loneliness scale, .40 with the item "There is no one I can turn to," and .44 with the item "I am no longer close to anyone." The social loneliness item correlated .47 with the UCLA scale, −.47 with the item "I feel part of a group of friends," and −.35 with the item "I have a lot in common with others." For each of these UCLA items, the correlation with the theoretically appropriate Russell *et al.* item was significantly higher than the correlation with the inappropriate Russell *et al.* item. The social and emotional loneliness items were correlated with measures of six provisions of relationships outlined by Weiss: attachment, social integration, opportunity for nurturance, reassurance of worth, reliable alliance, and guidance. Social loneliness was most related to needing reassurance of worth, while emotional loneliness was most related to needing attachment. Both social and emotional loneliness were significantly related to depression; only emotional loneliness was related to anxiety. In general, the results were compatible with Weiss's theorizing.

Wittenberg's social loneliness scale correlated .81 with the UCLA Loneliness scale; the correlation for the emotional loneliness scale was .59. The social scale related, as expected, to a variety of friendship network measures; the emotional scale related, also as expected, to a variety of romantic-relationship–dating measures. (Most of these correlations were in the .30–.70 range.)

Discriminant

Russell *et al.*'s social and emotional loneliness items correlated only .17 with each other and, as shown above, exhibited different patterns of correlations with other variables. (Not reported above, however, are many items and variables that correlated similarly with the two items.) Wittenberg's two social and emotional loneliness scales correlated .44 with each other, which is well below the scales' reliabilities, and exhibited different patterns of relationships with other variables. A troubling feature of Wittenberg's results is the high correlation between the social loneliness scale and the UCLA scale, although this may be partly due to an imbalance in the UCLA scale (i.e., it may place greater weight on friendship than on romantic involvement and attachment, although Russell *et al.*'s results did not corroborate this).

Location

Russell, D., Cutrona, C. E., Rose, J., & Yurko, K. (1984). Social and emotional loneliness: An examination of Weiss's typology of loneliness. *Journal of Personality and Social Psychology*, **46**, 1313–1321.
Wittenberg, M. T. (1986). *Emotional and social loneliness: An examination of social skills, attributions, sex role, and object relations perspectives*. Unpublished doctoral dissertation, University of Rochester.

Results and Comments

Both of these measures are very preliminary and are included here to encourage further work. R. S. Weiss (1973) distinguished between social and emotional loneliness when he discovered that members of a Parents Without Partners organization typically felt supported by their friends and fellow members but nevertheless yearned for a close attachment relationship with "one special person." At the same time, happily married couples who had just moved to a new city felt securely attached to each other but still missed spending time with their friends back home. As Russell *et al.* said in concluding their article:

> Social and emotional loneliness appear to be related to different forms of social deficits, with social loneliness resulting from the lack of satisfying friendship relationships and emotional loneliness resulting from the lack of satisfying romantic relationships. The subjective experiences of these two forms of loneliness appear to be qualitatively different, although both . . . are characterized by a substantial common core of experiences. It may be useful to view this common core as indicating the essence of the loneliness experience, with different forms of loneliness (such as social and emotional loneliness) adding certain qualities to that common experience. (p. 1320)

Emotional versus Social Loneliness

Instructions: Below are descriptions of two kinds of loneliness. Rate, on the nine-point scale beneath each description, how intensely you have been experiencing each kind of loneliness.

1. A possible type of loneliness involves not belonging to a group or social network. While this may be a set of friends who engage in social activities together, it can be any group that provides a feeling of belonging based on shared concerns, work or other activities.

NOT AT ALL   1   2   3   4   5   6   7   8   9   VERY MUCH

2. A possible type of loneliness is the lack of an intense, relatively enduring relationship with one other person. While this relationship is often romantic, it can be any one-to-one relationship that provides feelings of affection and security.

NOT AT ALL   1   2   3   4   5   6   7   8   9   VERY MUCH

Emotional and Social Loneliness Scale

Instructions: These questions refer to your feelings about the quality of your social relationships. Indicate how often you have felt the way described in each of the following statements during the past year.

1. Most everyone around me seems like a stranger. (Circle one.) (SL)

1	2	3	4	5
NEVER	RARELY	SOMETIMES	OFTEN	VERY OFTEN

2. I don't get much satisfaction from the groups I participate in. (SL)

*3. There are good people around me who understand my views and beliefs. (SL)

4. There is no one I have felt close to for a long time. (EL)

*5. I have a romantic partner who gives me support and encouragement. (EL)

*6. I belong to a network of friends. (SL)

*7. There are people I can count on for companionship. (SL)

8. I don't have one specific relationship in which I feel understood. (EL)

*9. I am an important part of the emotional well-being of another person. (EL)

10. I don't have a special love relationship. (EL)

Note: Emotional loneliness items are followed by EL, social loneliness items by SL, with items marked by an asterisk being reverse-scored.

Emotional–Social Loneliness Inventory

(Vincenzi & Grabosky, 1987)

Variable

The ESLI is a multidimensional measure designed to distinguish among four constructs related to R. S. Weiss's (1973) typology of loneliness: emotional and social isolation (conditions) and emotional and social loneliness (feelings).

Description

The ESLI contains 15 pairs of statements. The left-hand member of each pair concerns isolation ("what is true in my life at this time"); the right-hand member concerns loneliness ("what I feel in my life at this time"). For example, the first pair of items is "I don't have a close friend" and "I don't feel like I have a close friend." Each statement is answered on a four-point scale from 3 (usually true) to 0 (rarely true). Emotional isolation and loneliness are measured by the first eight pairs of items, social isolation and loneliness by the last seven items. Scores on emotional isolation and loneliness can range from 0 to 24, where 24 indicates extreme emotional isolation or emotional loneliness; scores on social isolation and loneliness can range from 0 to 21.

Scores below six indicate little or no isolation; scores of 6–8 indicate average isolation; scores of 9–12 indicate above average isolation; and a score of 13 or above indicates "severe isolation problems." A score below six on emotional loneliness indicates little or no loneliness; scores of 6–10 indicate average emotional loneliness; scores of 11–14 indicate above average emotional loneliness; a score of 15 or above indicates severe emotional loneliness problems. The parallel ranges for social loneliness are 0–4, 5–9, 10–13, and 14 or above.

The measure was created and validated in two steps. In the first step, a group of subjects containing high school students, college students, and group therapy patients were given 23 pairs of items. Factor analysis suggested reducing these to the 15 pairs of items currently constituting the measure. In a second step, a new and larger group of subjects from the same three categories took the 15-pair version of the measure.

Sample

The first sample included 95 people from a large city: 36 from an academically talented high school class, 33 from a masters-level class in psychology, and 26 from an adult psychotherapy program for clients believed to be having problems with loneliness or isolation. The second sample contained 229 people from the same city: 99 from average and below average classes, 65 from a college undergraduate population, and 99 from the adult psychotherapy program.

Reliability

Internal Consistency

Analyses began with the feeling (i.e., loneliness) items from the 23 pairs used in the first study. A factor analysis involving varimax rotation suggested emotional and social subscales involving eight and seven items, respectively. When only the 15 feeling items were refactored, two factors representing emotional and social isolation were extracted, accounting for 53% of the total variance. The corresponding 15 condition items were then factored, and two factors were obtained. All eight emotional items loaded on the first factor; five of the seven social items loaded on the second factor. Coefficient α for the four subscales were as follows: emotional isolation, .83 (8 items), social isolation, .80 (7 items), emotional loneliness, .86 (8 items), social loneliness, .82 (7 items). In the cross-validation sample, essentially the same factor structures were obtained, although one or two items cross-loaded, suggesting that the scales are not as distinct as they might be. When all 30 items were entered into a single factor analysis, two large factors emerged corresponding to the social–emotional distinction (not to the condition–feeling distinction). Nevertheless, correlations between condition and feeling within each pair of statements were generally around .50, indicating some discrimination. The authors said, regarding coefficient α values for the second study, that α "was .85 for emotional and social loneliness and .76 for emotional and social isolation" (p. 264). No reason was provided for aggregating the subscales in this way.

Test–Retest

The authors said: "Twenty subjects from the [first] clinical population were retested two weeks later. The test–retest reliability coefficient was .80 for the total score on the isolation and loneliness categories" (p. 262). The exact nature of these total scores, and the rationale for using them, are unclear.

Validity

Convergent

In both studies, the clinical group scored higher on all four subscales than the nonclinical groups.

Discriminant

No evidence was presented for discrimination between this measure and others, but evidence for subscale discrimination is provided. In the second study, the clinical group scored higher on the feeling items than on the condition items, especially for the emotional subscale. The nonclinical group did not exhibit this pattern, suggesting that for a given level of perceived isolation, the clinical group reacts with more intensely negative feelings.

Location

Vincenzi, H., & Grabosky, F. (1987). Measuring the emotional/social aspects of loneliness and isolation. *Journal of Social Behavior and Personality, 2,* (2, Part 2), 257–270.

Results and Comments

This is a new scale that needs further work. The factor structure seems to be only partially replicable, and the distinction between perceived conditions, on the one hand, and feelings, on the other, seems shaky. Nevertheless, like the measures discussed in the previous scale review, the ESLI supports R. S. Weiss's (1973) distinction between emotional and social loneliness and provides a useful basis for further psychometric analyses.

Emotional–Social Loneliness Inventory

The purpose of this questionnaire is to help you explore what is "TRUE" in your life versus how you "FEEL" at this time. For example, you may have a mate, but due to a poor relationship, you don't feel like you have a mate. Please use the last two weeks as a guideline to answer these questions.

Please respond to each question by circling the response that best describes you. Please respond to both categories for each question.

Rarely True = 0   Sometimes = 1   Often True = 2   Usually True = 3

What is true in my life at this time.	What I feel in my life at this time.
1. I don't have a close friend.	I don't feel like I have a close friend.
0 1 2 3	0 1 2 3
2. People take advantage of me when I'm involved with them.	I'm afraid to trust others.
3. I don't have a mate (or boyfriend/girlfriend).	I don't feel like I have a mate (or boyfriend/girlfriend).
4. I don't want to burden others with my problems.	Those close to me feel burdened by me when I share my problems.
5. There is nobody in my life who depends on me.	I don't feel needed or important to others.
6. I don't have any relationships that involve sharing personal thoughts.	I don't feel I can share personal thoughts with anyone.
7. There is no one in my life that tries to understand me.	I don't feel understood.
8. Nobody in my life really wants to be involved with me.	I don't feel safe to reach out to others.
9. I spend a lot of time alone.	I feel lonely.
10. I am not part of any social group or organization.	I don't feel part of any social group or organization.
11. I haven't spoken to anyone today.	I don't feel like I made contact with anyone today.
12. I don't have much in common to talk about with those around me.	I don't feel I have anything to say to people.
13. When I'm with others I don't disclose much about myself.	I don't feel I'm being myself with others.
14. I don't take social risks.	I fear embarrassing myself around others.
15. People don't see me as an interesting person.	I don't feel I am interesting.

Children's Loneliness Scale

(Asher, Hymel, & Renshaw, 1984)

Variable

The authors' goal was "to develop a reliable measure of children's feelings of loneliness and social dissatisfaction and to learn whether the children who are least accepted by their classmates are indeed more lonely" (Asher *et al.*, 1984, p. 1456).

Description

A 24-item questionnaire was developed to assess feelings of loneliness and social dissatisfaction among children in the third to sixth grade. Sixteen of the items, 10 worded in the lonely direction (e.g., "I am lonely," "I don't have any friends") and 6 in the nonlonely direction (e.g., "I have lots of friends," "I am well-liked by the kids in my class"), focus on feelings of loneliness, feelings of social adequacy versus inadequacy, and subjective estimates of peer status. Eight filler items focus on hobbies and preferred activities (e.g., "I like to paint and draw"). These are included to help children feel more open and relaxed about indicating their attitudes on the other questions.

Responses are recorded on a five-point scale ranging from "always true" to "not true at all." In the Asher *et al.* (1984) study, the 24 items were read to 506 children in their classrooms by an unfamiliar adult after the children had been trained to use the rating scale on statements such as "I like roller skating." Scores were computed on the 16 primary items so that high values (following appropriate reversal of certain items) indicated greater loneliness or social dissatisfaction. Scores could range from 16 (low loneliness) to 80 (high loneliness). The actual range was 16–79, with a mean of 32.5 (SD = 11.8).

The purpose of the scale, within the context of the study in which it first appeared, was to determine whether unpopular or sociometrically isolated children feel dissatisfied and lonely. In previous studies, unpopular children had been selected by external means (e.g., peer ratings) and placed, for example, in social skills training programs. The authors wanted to know whether subjective measures could also be used to identify children in need of such training. A substantial portion of the children admitted feeling lonely and left out; in response to the item "I'm lonely," 6% said "that's always true about me," and an additional 6% said "that's true about me most of the time."

Sample

Complete loneliness scale data were obtained from 506 children (243 females, 263 males) in 20 third through sixth grade classrooms in two schools in a "moderate-size midwestern city."

Reliability

Internal Consistency

The 16 primary and the 8 filler items were factor analyzed, and all 16 loneliness items loaded on a single factor. None of the filler items loaded significantly on this factor. Cronbach's α for the 16-item scale was .90. Uncorrected item–total correlations ranged from .50 (for "I'm good at working with other children") to .72 (for "I'm lonely").

Test–Retest

Although test–retest reliability was not directly assessed, there was a 2-week delay between assessment of loneliness and assessment of classroom sociometric status. The highly significant negative correlation between these two rather different variables over the 2-week period suggests considerable temporal stability in loneliness and social dissatisfaction.

Validity

Convergent

Loneliness correlated significantly with two measures of sociometric status. The 16-item summary score correlated approximately $-.30$ ($p < .001$) with peer ratings and peer nominations indicating popularity. (The correlation varied slightly as a function of children's age and sex.) The authors considered this correlation impressive, given that most of the loneliness items do not refer explicitly to the classrooms in which the sociometric ratings and nominations were collected. (Thus, a child could have had friends outside of class, outside of school, etc., who could counteract isolation in the particular classroom studied.)

The mean loneliness score of children not named as friends by anyone in the class was 36.3, while the mean for children named as friends by at least five peers was 27.8, a highly significant difference. (The overall mean of 32.5 falls approximately halfway between these two groups.)

Divergent

Loneliness was uncorrelated with the eight filler items. It was also virtually uncorrelated with two academic achievement tests, the Comprehensive Test of Basic Skills ($r = .02$) and the Stanford Diagnostic Reading Test ($r = .10$). The correlation between loneliness and sociometric status was not large enough to suggest that the two are indistinguishable.

Location

Asher, S. R., Hymel, S., & Renshaw, P. D. (1984). Loneliness in children. *Child Development,* **55,** 1456–1464.

Results and Comments

The Children's Loneliness Scale is similar in certain respects to the UCLA Loneliness Scale for adults. Both refer to a range of facts and feelings related to loneliness (perceived lack of social skills, lack of social confidence, feeling isolated). Most of the items seem to describe behavior and skills: e.g., "It's easy for me to make new friends at school." Only a few mention feelings ("I feel alone," "I feel left out of things," "I'm lonely"). Nevertheless, the scale coheres very well, and the conceptually crucial item, "I'm lonely," loads higher than any other item on the first principal component and correlates more highly than any other item with the total score. The authors seem justified in calling the scale a measure of childhood loneliness.

Personal communication with Dr. Hymel (1988) revealed that Asher is currently working to reduce ambiguity about the situations referred to in the items (e.g., to make them refer more directly to classes in which sociometric ratings are obtained), and Hymel and one of her co-workers are creating a longer, multidimensional scale for children that assesses emotional and social isolation in relationships with family members and peers. (Dr. Steven Asher is at the Bureau of Educational Research, University of Illinois. Dr. Hymel is at the Department of Psychology, University of Waterloo, Ontario.)

Children's Loneliness Scale

1. It's easy for me to make new friends at school.

1	2	3	4	5
ALWAYS TRUE				NOT AT ALL TRUE

2. I like to read. (Filler)
3. I have nobody to talk to. (R)
4. I'm good at working with other children.
5. I watch TV a lot. (Filler)
6. It's hard for me to make friends. (R)
7. I like school. (Filler)
8. I have lots of friends.
9. I feel alone. (R)
10. I can find a friend when I need one.
11. I play sports a lot. (Filler)
12. It's hard to get other kids to like me. (R)
13. I like science. (Filler)
14. I don't have anyone to play with. (R)
15. I like music. (Filler)
16. I get along with other kids.
17. I feel left out of things. (R)
18. There's nobody I can go to when I need help. (R)
19. I like to paint and draw. (Filler)
20. I don't get along with other children. (R)
21. I'm lonely. (R)
22. I am well-liked by the kids in my class.
23. I like playing board games a lot. (Filler)
24. I don't have any friends. (R)

Note: "R" indicates that an item is reverse-scored. "Filler" indicates that an item is not scored.

Future Research Directions

Several likely directions for future research on the measurement of depression and loneliness have been touched upon. In the study of depression, definitions and measures may change as more is learned about responses to specific treatments, including treatments as different as medication and cognitive therapy. Further clarification of the differences between clinical depression and normal unhappiness can be expected. The role of cognitive processes in causing and sustaining depression will receive continued attention, as will the role of genetic factors. Refinement of measures for particular developmental and cultural groups can be expected. Efforts will be made to establish a universal conception of depression that remains sensitive to differences in local meaning systems.

In the study of loneliness, which is less mature than the study of depression, researchers will continue to focus on the internal structure of loneliness (i.e., the multidimensionality of its causes and phenomenology) and on its differentiation from related concepts such as depression and perceived social support. Examination of the nature of loneliness in different age groups will continue.

Weiss's (1987) contention that definitions of loneliness seem to include implicit theories of loneliness should bring loneliness researchers closer to the recent literature on emotion. To the extent that loneliness is a subtype of sadness, as the data of Shaver *et al.* (1987) suggest, it may differ from other subtypes only in its antecedents. That is, loneliness may be a particular kind of sadness that is due to dissatisfaction with the level of social contact or intimacy in one's life, just as disappointment is a form of sadness that occurs when reality fails to live up to one's expectations. In other words, some emotions cannot be defined or understood without reference to their antecedents, contrary to Weiss's claims.

In general, the study of loneliness and depression should benefit from the increasing effort to understand human emotions. There are signs in the literature that a revolution in "emotion science" is about to follow the path blazed by the cognitive sciences. The emotion revolution is a logical outcome of the "age of depression and loneliness."

Acknowledgments

The authors are grateful to Cindy Hazan for help in the early phases of the literature search, to Dan Russell and Carolyn Cutrona for help with the discussion of loneliness measures, and to several other scale authors, who responded promptly and generously to our requests for further information.

Bibliography

Abramson, L. Y., Garber, J., & Seligman, M. E. P. (1980). Learned helplessness in humans: An attributional analysis. In J. Garber & M. E. P. Seligman (Eds.), *Human helplessness: Theory and applications* (pp. 3–34). New York: Academic Press.

Achenbach, T. M. (1978). The child behavior profile: I. Boys aged 6–11. *Journal of Consulting and Clinical Psychology*, **46**, 478–488.

Albert, N. (1973). *Evidence of depression in an early adolescent school population.* Unpublished manuscript, Villanova, Pennsylvania.

Albert, N., & Beck, A. T. (1975). Incidence of depression in early adolescence: A preliminary study. *Journal of Youth and Adolescence*, **4**, 301–307.

American Psychiatric Association (1980). *Diagnostic and statistical manual of mental disorders* (3rd ed.). Washington, DC: Author.

Anderson, C. A. (1983). Motivational and performance deficits in interpersonal settings: The effect of attributional style. *Journal of Personality and Social Psychology*, **45**, 1136–1147.

Anderson, C. A., Horowitz, L. M., & French, R. de S. (1983). Attributional style of lonely and depressed people. *Journal of Personality and Social Psychology*, **45**, 127–136.

Asher, S. R., Hymel, S., & Renshaw, P. D. (1984). Loneliness in children. *Child Development*, **55**, 1456–1464.

Beck, A. T. (1967). *Depression: Causes and treatment.* Philadelphia: Univ. of Pennsylvania Press.

Beck, A. T. (1970). Cognitive therapy: Nature and relation to behavior therapy. *Behavior Therapy,* **1,** 184–200.

Beck, A. T., & Beamesderfer, A. (1974). Assessment of depression: The depression inventory. In P. Pichot (Ed.), *Psychological measurements in psychopharmacology: Modern problems in pharmacopsychiatry* (Vol. 7, pp. 151–169). Basel, Switzerland: Karger.

Beck, A. T., & Beck, R. W. (1972). Screening depressed patients in a family practice: A rapid technic. *Postgraduate Medicine,* **52,** (Dec.), 81–85.

Beckham, E. E., & Leber, W. R. (Eds.) (1985). *Handbook of depression: Treatment, assessment, and research.* Homewood, IL: Dorsey.

Belcher, M. J. (1973). *The measurement of loneliness: A validation of the Belcher Extended Loneliness Scale (BELS).* Unpublished doctoral dissertation, Illinois Institute of Technology, Chicago.

Biggs, J. T., Wylie, L. T., & Ziegler, V. E. (1978). Validity of the Zung self-rating depression scale. *British Journal of Psychiatry,* **132,** 381–385.

Billings, A. G., & Moos, R. H. (1985). Psychosocial stressors, coping, and depression. In E. E. Beckham & W. R. Leber (Eds.), *Handbook of depression: Treatment, assessment, and research* (pp. 940–974). Homewood, IL: Dorsey Press.

Blatt, S. J. (1974). Levels of object representation in anaclitic and introjective depression. *Psychoanalytic Study of the Child,* **29,** 426–427.

Blatt, S. J., D'Afflitti, J. P., & Quinlan, D. M. (1976a). *Depressive experiences questionnaire.* New Haven, CT: Yale University.

Blatt, S. J., D'Afflitti, J. P., & Quinlan, D. M. (1976b). Experiences of depression in normal young adults. *Journal of Abnormal Psychology,* **85,** 383–389.

Blatt, S. J., Wein, S. T., Chevron, E., & Quinlan, D. M. (1979). Parental representations and depression in normal young adults. *Journal of Abnormal Psychology,* **88,** 388–397.

Blatt, S. J., Quinlan, D. M., Chevron, E. S., McDonald, C., & Zuroff, D. C. (1982). Dependency and self-criticism: Psychological dimensions of depression. *Journal of Consulting and Clinical Psychology,* **50,** 113–124.

Bornstein, B., Poynton, F. G., & Masling, J. M. (1985). Morality and depression: An empirical study. *Psychoanalytic Psychology,* **2,** 241–249.

Borys, S., & Perlman, D. (1985). Gender differences in loneliness. *Personality and Social Psychology Bulletin,* **11,** 63–74.

Bowlby, J. (1969). *Attachment and loss* (Vol. 1. *Attachment*). New York: Basic Books.

Boyd, J. H., Weissman, M. M., Thompson, W. D., & Myers, J. K. (1982). Screening for depression in a community sample: Understanding the discrepancies between depression symptom and diagnostic scales. *Archives of General Psychiatry,* **39,** 1195–1200.

Bradburn, N. M. (1969). *The structure of psychological well being.* Chicago: Aldine.

Bradley, R. (1969). *Measuring loneliness.* Unpublished doctoral dissertation, Washington State University, Pullman.

Brink, T. L., Yesavage, J. A., Lum, O., Heersema, P. H., Adey, M., & Rose, T. L. (1982). Screening tests for geriatric depression. *Clinical Gerontologist,* **1,** 37–43.

Brown, G. L., & Zung, W. W. K. (1972). Depression scales: Self-physician-rating? A validation of certain clinically observable phenomena. *Comprehensive Psychiatry,* **13,** 361–367.

Byrne, D. (1964). Repression-sensitization as a dimension of personality. In B. A. Maher (Ed.), *Progress in experimental personality research.* New York: Academic Press.

Carlson, G. A., & Cantwell, D. P. (1979). A survey of depressive symptoms in a child and adolescent psychiatric population. *Journal of American Academy of Child Psychiatry,* **18,** 587–599.

Carroll, B. J., Fielding, J. M., & Blashki, T. G. (1973). Depression ratings scales: A critical review. *Archives of General Psychiatry,* **28,** 361–366.

Carroll, B. J., Feinberg, M., Smouse, P. E., Rawson, S. G., & Greden, J. F. (1981). The Carroll Rating Scale for depression: I. Development, reliability and validation. *British Journal of Psychiatry,* **138,** 205–209.

Chevron, E. S., Quinlan, D. M., & Blatt, S. J. (1978). Sex roles and gender differences in the experience of depression. *Journal of Abnormal Psychology*, **87**, 680–683.

Chiles, J. A., Miller, M. L., & Cox, G. B. (1980). Depression in an adolescent delinquent population. *Archives of General Psychiatry*, **37**, 1179–1184.

Christenfeld, R., Lubin, B., & Satin, M. (1978). Concurrent validity of the Depression Adjective Check List in a normal population. *American Journal of Psychiatry*, **135**, 582–584.

Cohen, S., & Syme, S. L. (Eds.) (1985). *Social support and health*. Orlando, FL: Academic Press.

Coyne, J. C., & Gotlib, I. H. (1983). The role of cognition in depression: A critical appraisal. *Psychological Bulletin*, **94**, 472–505.

Crowne, D., & Marlowe, D. (1960). A new scale of social desirability independent of psychopathology. *Journal of Consulting Psychology*, **24**, 349–354.

Cutrona, C. E. (1982). Transition to college: Loneliness and the process of social adjustment. In L. A. Peplau & D. Perlman (Eds.), *Loneliness: A sourcebook of current theory, research, and therapy* (pp. 291–309). New York: Wiley (Interscience).

Dean, A. (1985). Introduction. In A. Dean (Ed.), *Depression in multidisciplinary perspective* (pp. xi–xix). New York: Brunner/Mazel.

de Jong-Gierveld, J. (1987). Developing and testing a model of loneliness. *Journal of Personality and Social Psychology*, **53**, 119–128.

de Jong-Gierveld, J., & Kamphuis, F. (1985). The development of a Rasch-type loneliness scale. *Applied Psychological Measurement*, **9**, 289–299.

de Jong-Gierveld, J., & Raadschelders, J. (1982). Types of loneliness. In L. A. Peplau & D. Perlman (Eds.), *Loneliness: A sourcebook of current theory, research, and therapy* (pp. 105–119). New York: Wiley (Interscience).

de Jong-Gierveld, J., & van Tilburg, T. (1987). The partner as source of social support in problem and non-problem situations. *Journal of Social Behavior and Personality*, **2**,(2, Part 2), 191–200.

de Jong-Gierveld, J., & van Tilburg, T. (1990). *Manual of the loneliness scale*. Vrije Universiteit Amsterdam Koningslaan 22–24, 1075 AD Amsterdam, The Netherlands.

Dempsey, P. A. (1964). A unidimensional depression scale for the MMPI. *Journal of Consulting Psychology*, **28**, 364–370.

Durkheim, E. (1897/1951). *Suicide*. New York: Free Press.

Eddy, B. A., & Lubin, B. (1988). The Children's Depression Adjective Checklist (C-DACL) with emotionally disturbed adolescent boys. *Journal of Abnormal Child Psychology*, **16**, 83–88.

Eddy, P. D. (1961). *Loneliness: A discrepancy within the phenomenological self*. Unpublished doctoral dissertation, Adelphi College, Garden City, New York.

Faulstich, M. E., Carey, M. P., Ruggiero, L., Enyart, P., & Gresham, F. (1986). Assessment of depression in childhood and adolescence: An evaluation of the Center for Epidemiological Studies depression scale for children (CES-DC). *American Journal of Psychiatry*, **143**, 1024–1027.

Feinberg, M., Carroll, B. J., Smouse, P. E., & Rawson, S. G. (1981). The Carroll Rating Scale for depression: III. Comparison with other rating instruments. *British Journal of Psychiatry*, **138**, 205–209.

Finch, A. J., Saylor, C. F., & Edwards, G. L. (1985). Children's Depression Inventory: Sex and grade norms for normal children. *Journal of Consulting and Clinical Psychology*, **53**, 424–425.

Frijda, N. (1986). *The emotions*. New York: Cambridge Univ. Press.

Frost, R. O., & MacInnis, D. J. (1983). The Cognitive Bias Questionnaire: Further evidence. *Journal of Personality Assessment*, **47**, 173–177.

Gerson, A. C., & Perlman, D. (1979). Loneliness and expressive communication. *Journal of Abnormal Psychology*, **88**, 258–261.

Glass, D. R. (1978). *An evaluation of a brief treatment for depression based on the learned helplessness model*. Unpublished doctoral dissertation, University of California, Los Angeles.

Gordon, S. (1976). *Lonely in America*. New York: Simon & Schuster.

Gutek, B., Nakamara, C., Gahart, M., Handschumacher, I., & Russell, D. (1980). Sexuality and the workplace. *Basic and Applied Social Psychology,* **1,** 255–265.

Hamilton, M. A. (1960). A rating scale for depression. *Journal of Neurology, Neurosurgery and Psychiatry,* **23,** 56–62.

Hammen, C. L. (1988). Depression and cognitions about personal stressful life events. In L. Alloy (Ed.), *Cognitive processes in depression.* New York: Guilford Press.

Hammen, C. L., & Krantz, S. E. (1976). Effects of success and failure on depressive cognitions. *Journal of Abnormal Psychology,* **85,** 577–586.

Hammen, C. L., & Krantz, S. E. (1985). Measures of psychological processes in depression. In E. E. Beckham & W. R. Leber (Eds.), *Handbook of depression* (pp. 408–444). Homewood, IL: Dorsey Press.

Hammen, C. L., & Peters, S. D. (1978). Interpersonal consequences of depression: Responses to men and women enacting a depressed role. *Journal of Abnormal Psychology,* **82,** 62–73.

Harrell, T. H., & Ryon, N. B. (1983). Cognitive–behavioral assessment of depression: Clinical validation of the Automatic Thoughts Questionnaire. *Journal of Consulting and Clinical Psychology,* **51,** 721–725.

Harris, L., & Associates (1974). *The myth and reality of aging in America.* Washington, DC: National Council on the Aging.

Harris, L., & Associates (1981). *Aging in the eighties: America in transition.* Washington, DC: National Council on the Aging.

Hays, R. D., & DiMatteo, M. R. (1987). A short-form measure of loneliness. *Journal of Personality Assessment,* **51,** 69–81.

Hojat, M., & Crandall, R. (Eds.) (1987). *Loneliness: Theory, research, and applications.* A special issue of the *Journal of Social Behavior and Personality,* **2,** (2, Part 2).

Hollon, S. D., & Kendall, P. C. (1980). Cognitive self-statements in depression: Development of an Automatic Thoughts Questionnaire. *Cognitive Therapy and Research,* **4,** 383–395.

Horowitz, L. M., French, R. de S., & Anderson, C. A. (1982). The prototype of a lonely person. In L. A. Peplau & D. Perlman (Eds.), *Loneliness: A sourcebook of current theory, research, and therapy* (pp. 183–205). New York: Wiley (Interscience).

Hyer, L., & Blount, J. (1984). Concurrent and discriminant validities of the Geriatric Depression Scale with older psychiatric inpatients. *Psychological Reports,* **54,** 611–616.

Jackson, D. N. (1967). *Personality Research Form manual.* Goshen, NY: Research Psychologists Press.

Jackson, D. N. (1976). *Jackson Personality Inventory manual.* Goshen, NY: Research Psychologists Press.

Jackson, D. N., & Messick, S. (1971). *Differential Personality Inventory.* London, Ontario, Canada: University of Western Ontario.

Jones, W. H. (1982). Loneliness and social behavior. In L. A. Peplau & D. Perlman (Eds.), *Loneliness: A sourcebook of current theory, research, and therapy* (pp. 81–104). New York: Wiley (Interscience).

Jones, W. H., Freemon, J. E., & Goswick, R. A. (1981). The persistence of loneliness: Self and other determinants. *Journal of Personality,* **49,** 27–48.

Kayne, N. T., Alloy, L. B., Romer, D., & Crocker, J. (1990). *Predicting depression and elation reactions in the classroom: A test of an attributional diathesis-stress theory of depression.* Manuscript submitted for publication.

Kaszniak, A. W., & Allender, J. (1985). Psychological assessment of depression in older adults. In G. M. Chaisson-Stewart (Ed.), *Depression in the elderly: An interdisciplinary approach* (pp. 107–160). New York: Wiley.

Kazdin, A. E., & Petti, T. A. (1982). Self-report and interview measures of childhood and adolescent depression. *Journal of Child Psychology and Psychiatry,* **23,** 437–457.

Kielcolt-Glaser, J. K., Garner, W., Speicher, C., Penn, G. M., Holliday, J., & Glaser, R. (1984). Psychological modifiers of immunocompetence in medical students. *Psychosomatic Medicine,* **46,** 7–14.

Kielcolt-Glaser, J. K., Ricker, D., George, J., Messick, G., Speicher, G. E., Garner, W., & Glaser,

W. (1984). Urinary cortisol levels, cellular immunocompetency, and loneliness in psychiatric inpatients. *Psychosomatic Medicine*, **46**, 15–23.

Klein, D. N. (1989). The Depressive Experiences Questionnaire: A further evaluation. *Journal of Personality Assessment*, **53**, 703–715.

Klein, D. N., Harding, K., Taylor, E. B., & Dickstein, S. (1989). Dependency and self-criticism and depression: Evaluation in the clinical population. *Journal of Abnormal Psychology*, **917**, 399–404.

Kleinman, A., & Good, B. (Eds.) (1985). *Culture and depression: Studies in the anthropology and cross-cultural psychiatry of affect and disorder*. Berkeley: Univ. of California Press.

Knight, R. G., Waal-Manning, H. J., & Spears, G. F. (1983). Some norms and reliability data for the State-Trait Anxiety Inventory and the Zung Self-Rating Depression Scale. *British Journal of Clinical Psychology*, **22**, 245–249.

Kovacs, M. (1980/1981). Rating scales to assess depression in school-aged children. *Acta Paedopsychiatry*, **46**, 305–315.

Kovacs, M. (1983). Definition and assessment of childhood depressions. In D. F. Ricks & B. S. Dohrenwend (Eds.), *Origins of psychopathology: Problems in research and public policy* (pp. 109–127). Cambridge, England: Cambridge Univ. Press.

Kovacs, M., & Beck, A. T. (1977). An empirical–clinical approach toward a definition of childhood depression. In J. G. Schulterbrandt & A. Raskin (Eds.), *Depression in childhood: Diagnosis, treatment, and conceptual models* (pp. 1–25). New York: Raven Press.

Krantz, S., & Hammen, C. (1979). Assessment of cognitive bias in depression. *Journal of Abnormal Psychology*, **88**, 611–619.

Lang, M., & Tisher, M. (1978). *Children's Depression Scale* (res. ed.). Hawthorn, Victoria: Australian Council for Educational Research.

Langevin, R., & Stancer, H. (1979). Evidence that depression rating scales primarily measure a social undesirability response set. *Acta Psychiatrica Scandinavica*, **59**, 70–79.

Lefkowitz, M. M., & Tesiny, E. P. (1980). Assessment of childhood depression. *Journal of Consulting and Clinical Psychology*, **48**, 43–50.

Levitt, E. E., Lubin, B., & Brooks, J. (1983). *Depression: Concepts, controversy and some new facts* (2nd ed.). Hillsdale, NJ: Erlbaum.

Lubin, B. (1965). Adjective checklists for measurement of depression. *Archives of General Psychiatry*, **12**, 57–62.

Lubin, B. (1966). Fourteen brief lists for the measurement of depression. *Archives of General Psychiatry*, **15**, 205–208.

Lubin, B. (1981). *Manual for the Depression Adjective Check Lists*. San Diego, CA: Educational and Industrial Testing Service.

Lubin, B. (1990). In preparation.

Lubin, B., & Collins, J. (1985). Depression Adjective Check Lists: Spanish, Hebrew, Chinese and English versions. *Journal of Clinical Psychology*, **41**, 213–217.

Lubin, B., & Himelstein, P. (1976). Reliability of the Depression Adjective Check Lists. *Perceptual and Motor Skills*, **3**, 1037–1038.

Lubin, B., & Levitt, E. E. (1979). Norms for the Depression Adjective Check Lists: Age group and sex. *Journal of Consulting and Clinical Psychology*, **47**, 192.

Lubin, B., Caplan, M. E., Collins, J. F. (1980). Additional evidence for comparability of set two (lists E, F, and G) of the Depression Adjective Check Lists. *Psychological Reports*, **46**, 849–850.

Lubin, B., Natalicio, L., & Seever, M. (1985). Performance of bilingual subjects on Spanish and English versions of the Depression Adjective Check Lists. *Journal of Clinical Psychology*, **41**, 218–219.

McCranie, E. W., & Bass, J. D. (1984). Childhood family antecedents of dependency and self-criticism: Implications for depression. *Journal of Abnormal Psychology*, **93**, 3–8.

McNair, D., Lorr, M., & Droppelman, L. (1971). *Profile of mood states*. San Diego: Educational and Industrial Testing Services.

Marone, J., & Lubin, B. (1968). Relationship between set 2 of the Depression Adjective Check

Lists (DACL) and Zung Self-Rating Depression Scale (SDS). *Psychological Reports*, **22**, 333–334.

May, R. (1950). *The meaning of anxiety*. New York: Ronald Press.

Mayer, J. M. (1977). Assessment of depression. In P. M. Reynolds (Ed.), *Advances in psychological assessment* (Vol. 4, pp. 358–425). San Francisco: Jossey–Bass.

Meites, K., Lovallo, W., & Pishkin, V. (1980). A comparison of four scales for anxiety, depression, and neuroticism. *Journal of Clinical Psychology*, **36**, 427–432.

Mendlewicz, J. (1985). Genetic research in depressive disorders. In E. E. Beckham & W. R. Leber (Eds.), *Handbook of depression: Treatment, assessment, and research* (pp. 795–815). Homewood, IL: Dorsey Press.

Michela, J. L., Peplau, L. A., & Weeks, D. G. (1982). Perceived dimensions of attributions for loneliness. *Journal of Personality and Social Psychology*, 43, 929–936.

Mikesell, R. H., & Calhoun, L. G. (1970). Response set on the Zung Self-Rating Depression Scale. *Perceptual and Motor Skills*, **3**, 22.

Nasr, S. J., Altman, E. G., Rodin, M. B., Jobe, T. H., & Burg, B. (1984). Correlation of the Hamilton and Carroll depression rating scales: A replication study among psychiatric outpatients. *Journal of Clinical Psychiatry*, **45**, 167–168.

Noll, K. M., Davis, J. M., & DeLeon-Jones, F. (1985). Medication and somatic therapies in the treatment of depression. In E. E. Beckham & W. R. Leber (Eds.), *Handbook of depression: Treatment, assessment, and research* (pp. 220–315). Homewood, IL: Dorsey Press.

Peplau, L. A., & Perlman, D. (Eds.) (1982a). *Loneliness: A sourcebook of current theory, research, and therapy*. New York: Wiley (Interscience).

Peplau, L. A., & Perlman, D. (1982b). Perspectives on loneliness. In L. A. Peplau & D. Perlman (Eds.), *Loneliness: A sourcebook of current theory, research, and therapy* (pp. 1–18). New York: Wiley (Interscience).

Peplau, L. A., & Perlman, D. (1982c). A bibliography on loneliness. In L. A. Peplau & D. Perlman (Eds.), *Loneliness: A sourcebook of current theory, research, and therapy* (pp. 407–417). New York: Wiley (Interscience).

Peplau, L. A., Miceli, M., & Morasch, B. (1982). Loneliness and self-evaluation. In L. A. Peplau & D. Perlman (Eds.), *Loneliness: A sourcebook of current theory, research, and therapy* (pp. 135–151). New York: Wiley (Interscience).

Peplau, L. A., Russell, D., & Heim, M. (1979). The experience of loneliness. In I. H. Frieze, D. Bar-Tal, & J. S. Carroll (Eds.), *New approaches to social problems: Applications of attribution theory* (pp. 53–78). San Francisco: Jossey–Bass.

Peterson, C., & Seligman, M. E. P. (1984). Causal explanations as a risk factor for depression: Theory and evidence. *Psychological Review*, **91**, 347–374.

Peterson, C., Semmel, A., von Baeyer, C., Abramson, L. Y., Metalsky, G. I., & Seligman, M. E. P. (1982). The Attributional Style Questionnaire. *Cognitive Therapy and Research*, **6**, 287–300.

Radloff, L. S. (1977). The CES-D scale: A self-report depression scale for research in the general population. *Applied Psychological Measurement*, **1**, 385–401.

Rasch, G. (1966). An item-analysis which takes individual differences into account. *British Journal of Mathematical and Statistical Psychology*, **19**, 49–57.

Revenson, T. A., & Johnson, J. L. (1984). Social and demographic correlates of loneliness in late life. *American Journal of Community Psychology*, **12**, 71–85.

Reynolds, W. M., & Gould, J. W. (1981). A psychometric investigation of the standard and short form Beck Depression Inventory. *Journal of Consulting and Clinical Psychology*, **49**, 306–307.

Rosch, E. (1978). Principles of categorization. In E. Rosch & B. B. Lloyd (Eds.), *Cognition and categorization* (pp. 27–48). Hilldale, NJ: Erlbaum.

Rubenstein, C., & Shaver, P. (1982). The experience of loneliness. In L. A. Peplau & D. Perlman (Eds.), *Loneliness: A sourcebook of current theory, research, and therapy* (pp. 206–223). New York: Wiley (Interscience).

Russell, D. (1982). The measurement of loneliness. In L. A. Peplau & D. Perlman (Eds.),

Loneliness: A sourcebook of current theory, research, and therapy (pp. 81–104). New York: Wiley (Interscience).

Russell, D., & Cutrona, C. E. (1988). *Development and evolution of the UCLA Loneliness Scale.* Unpublished manuscript, Center for Health Services Research, College of Medicine, University of Iowa, Iowa City.

Russell, D., Altmaier, E., & Van Velzen, D. (1987). Job-related stress, social support, and burnout among classroom teachers. *Journal of Applied Psychology,* **72,** 269–274.

Russell, D., Cutrona, C. E., Rose, J., & Yurko, K. (1984). Social and emotional loneliness: An examination of Weiss's typology of loneliness. *Journal of Personality and Social Psychology,* **46,** 1313–1321.

Russell, D., Kao, C., & Cutrona, C. E. (1987, June). *Loneliness and social support: Same or different constructs?* Paper presented at the Iowa Conference on Personal Relationships, Iowa City.

Russell, D., Peplau, L. A., & Cutrona, C. E. (1980). The revised UCLA loneliness scale: Concurrent and discriminant validity evidence. *Journal of Personality and Social Psychology,* **39,** 472–480.

Russell, D. Peplau, L. A., & Ferguson, M. L. (1978). Developing a measure of loneliness. *Journal of Personality Assessment,* **42,** 290–294.

Sacco, W. P., & Beck, A. T. (1985). Cognitive therapy of depression. In E. E. Beckham & W. R. Leber (Eds.), *Handbook of depression: Treatment, assessment, and research* (pp. 3–38). Homewood, IL: Dorsey Press.

Sartorius, N. & Ban, T. A. (Eds.) (1986). *Assessment of depression.* Berlin: Springer-Verlag.

Saylor, C. F., Finch, A. J., Baskin, C. H., Furey, W., & Kelly, M. M. (1984). Construct validity for measures of childhood depression: Application of multitrait–multimethod methodology. *Journal of Consulting and Clinical Psychology,* **52,** 977–985.

Saylor, C. F., Finch, A. J., Spirito, A., & Bennett, B. (1984). The Children's Depression Inventory: A systematic evaluation of psychometric properties. *Journal of Consulting and Clinical Psychology,* **52,** 955–967.

Scalise, J. J., Ginter, E. J., & Gerstein, L. H. (1984). A multidimensional loneliness measure: The Loneliness Rating Scale (LRS). *Journal of Personality Assessment,* **48,** 525–530.

Schmidt, N., & Sermat, V. (1983). Measuring loneliness in different relationships. *Journal of Personality and Social Psychology,* **44,** 1038–1047.

Seeman, M. (1983). Alienation motifs and contemporary theorizing: The hidden continuity of the classic themes. *Social Psychology Quarterly,* **46,** 171–184.

Sermat, V. (1980). Some situational and personality correlates of loneliness. In J. Hartog, J. R. Audy, & Y. A. Cohen (Eds.), *The anatomy of loneliness* (pp. 305–318). New York: International Universities Press.

Shapurian, R., & Hojat, M. (1987). Selected bibliography on loneliness. *Journal of Social Behavior and Personality,* **2,**(2, Pt. 2), 273–286.

Shaver, P., Furman, W., & Buhrmester, D. (1985). Transition to college: Network changes, social skills, and loneliness. In S. Duck & D. Perlman (Eds.), *Understanding personal relationships: An interdisciplinary approach* (pp. 193–219). London: Sage.

Shaver, P., Schwartz, J., Kirson, D., & O'Connor, C. (1987). Emotion knowledge: Further exploration of a prototype approach. *Journal of Personality and Social Psychology,* **52,** 1061–1086.

Shaw, B. F., Vallis, T. M., & McCabe, S. B. (1985). The assessment of the severity and symptom patterns in depression. In E. E. Beckham & W. R. Leber (Eds.), *Handbook of depression: Treatment, assessment, and research* (pp. 372–407). Homewood, IL: Dorsey Press.

Sisenwein, R. J. (1964). *Loneliness and the individual as viewed by himself and others.* Unpublished doctoral dissertation, Columbia University, New York.

Sokoloff, R. M., & Lubin, B. (1983). Depressive mood in adolescent, emotionally disturbed females: Reliability and validity of an adjective checklist (C-DACL). *Journal of Abnormal Child Psychology,* **11,** 531–536.

Solano, C. H. (1987). Loneliness and perceptions of control: General traits versus specific attributions. *Journal of Social Behavior and Personality,* **2**(2, Part 2), 201–214.

Solano, C. H., Batten, P. G., & Parrish, E. A. (1982). Loneliness and patterns of self-disclosure. *Journal of Personality and Social Psychology*, **43**, 524–531.

Spielberger, C. D., Gorsuch, R. L., & Lushene, R. E. (1970). *Manual for the State–Trait Anxiety Inventory*. Palo Alto, CA: Consulting Psychologists Press.

Steer, R. A., Beck, A. T., & Garrison, B. (1986). Applications of the Beck Depression Inventory. In N. Sartorius & T. A. Ban (Eds.), *Assessment of depression* (pp. 123–142). Berlin: Springer-Verlag.

Strauss, C. C., Forehand, R., Frame, C., & Smith, K. (1984). Characteristics of children with extreme scores on the children's depression inventory. *Journal of Clinical Child Psychology*, **13**, 227–231.

Sweeney, P. D., Anderson, K., & Bailey, S. (1986). Attributional style in depression: A meta-analytic review. *Journal of Personality and Social Psychology*, **50**, 974–991.

Vincenzi, H., & Grabosky, F. (1987). Measuring the emotional/social aspects of loneliness and isolation. *Journal of Social Behavior and Personality*, **2**(2, Pt. 2), 257–270.

Weeks, D. G., Michela, J. L., Peplau, L. A., & Bragg, M. E. (1980). The relation between loneliness and depression: A structural equation analysis. *Journal of Personality and Social Psychology*, **39**, 1238–1244.

Weiner, B. (1972). *Theories of motivation: From mechanism to cognition*. Chicago: Rand McNally.

Weiner, B. (1985). An attributional theory of achievement motivation and emotion. *Psychological Review*, **92**, 548–573.

Weiss, I. K., Nagel, C. L., & Aronson, M. K. (1986). Applicability of depression scales to the old old person. *Journal of the American Geriatrics Society*, **34**, 215–218.

Weiss, R. S. (1973). *Loneliness: The experience of emotional and social isolation*. Cambridge, MA: MIT Press.

Weiss, R. S. (1987). Reflections on the present state of loneliness research. *Journal of Social Behavior and Personality*, **2**,(2, Part 2), 1–16.

Weissman, M. M., Orvaschel, H., & Padian, N. (1980). Children's symptom and social functioning self-report scales: Comparison of mothers' and children's reports. *Journal of Nervous and Mental Disorders*, **168**, 736–740.

Weissman, M. M., Prusoff, B., & Newberry, P. B. (1975). *Comparison of CES-D, Zung, and Beck self-report depression scales* (Tech. Rep. ADM 42-47-83). Rockville, MD: Center for Epidemiologic Studies, National Institute of Mental Health.

Welkowitz, J., Lish, J. D., & Bond, R. N. (1985). The Depressive Experiences Questionnaire: Revision and validation. *Journal of Personality Assessment*, **49**, 89–94.

Wittenberg, M. T. (1986). *Emotional and social loneliness: An examination of social skills, attributions, sex role, and object relations perspectives*. Unpublished doctoral dissertation, University of Rochester, Rochester, NY.

Wright, B. D., & Stone, M. H. (1979). *Best test design: Rasch measurement*. Chicago: MESA Press.

Yesavage, J., Brink, T. L., Rose, T. L., & Adey, M. (1983). The Geriatric Depression Rating Scale: Comparison with other self-report and psychiatric rating scales. In T. Crook, S. Ferris, & R. Bartus (Eds.), *Assessment in geriatric psychopharmacology*. Madison, CT: Mark Powley & Associates.

Yesavage, J., Brink, T. L. Rose, T. L., Lum, O., Huang, V., Adey, M., & Leirer, V. O. (1983). Development and validation of a geriatric depression screening scale: A preliminary report. *Journal of Psychiatric Research*, **17**, 37–49.

Young, J. E. (1982). Loneliness, depression and cognitive therapy: Theory and application. In L. A. Peplau & D. Perlman (Eds.), *Loneliness: A sourcebook of current theory, research and therapy* (pp. 379–405). New York: Wiley (Interscience).

Zuckerman, M., & Lubin, B. (1965). *Manual for the Multiple Affect Adjective Checklist*. San Diego, CA: Educational and Industrial Testing Service.

Zung, W. W. K. (1965). A self-rating depression scale. *Archives of General Psychiatry*, **12**, 63–70.

Zung, W. W. K. (1967). Factors influencing the self-rating depression scale. *Archives of General Psychiatry*, **16**, 543–547.

Zung, W. W. K. (1969). A cross-cultural survey of symptoms of depression. *American Journal of Psychiatry, ***126,** 154–159.

Zung, W. W. K. (1972). The depression status inventory: An adjunct to the self-rating depression scale. *Journal of Clinical and Psychology, ***28,** 539–543.

Zung, W. W. K. (1986). Zung Self-Rating Depression Scale and Depression Status Inventory. In N. Sartorius & T. A. Ban (Eds.), *Assessment of depression* (pp. 221–231). Berlin: Springer-Verlag.

Zung, W. W. K., Richards, C. B., & Short, M. J. (1965). Self-rating depression scale in an outpatient clinic. *Archives of General Psychiatry, ***13,** 508–515.

Zuroff, D. C., & Mongrain, M. (1987). Dependency and self-criticism: Vulnerability factors for depressive affective states. *Journal of Abnormal Psychology, ***96,** 14–22.

Zuroff, D. C., Moskowitz, D. S., Wielgun, M. S., Powers, T. A., & Franko, D. L. (1983). Construct validation of the Dependency and Self-Criticism scales of the Depressive Experiences Questionnaire. *Journal of Research in Personality, ***17,** 226–241.

CHAPTER 7

Alienation and Anomie

Melvin Seeman

Alienation is a concept with a long and distinguished history. Its rediscovery in recent times has been part of a general reinvigoration of Marxist thought. For Karl Marx, especially the early Marx, whose philosophical manuscripts of 1844 were lost until the 1930s, the idea of alienation was a complex mixture of objective and subjective elements, concerning both social estrangement and depersonalization.

At the core of Marx's vision was a philosophy of human nature that emphasized creative self-realization in work, so the problem of alienated labor was crucial. It involved both the surrender of control over work and its products, and the worker's disengagement from both work and fellow workers. The emphasis in traditional Marxist thought has been on the worker's objectively defined exploitation and lack of control, but for the early Marx the subjective *sense* of powerlessness and self-estrangement were deeply implicated as well. These are the aspects of alienation tapped by most of the scales to be reviewed here.

With respect to "anomie," frequently defined in terms of normlessness, the derivation is from Emile Durkheim; and again there are a range of definitions pointing to mixtures of objective and subjective referents. In his customary antipsychological vein, Durkheim insisted that anomie is a state of society, not of persons, yet implications for a person's state of mind are surely present in his work, and they have been heavily exploited in the contemporary literature. Two rather different paths regarding anomie have been followed in the literature, both of them implicit in Durkheim's work. First, there is the idea of normlessness as a deviation from prescribed rules or customs (i.e., as social circumstances or a state of mind in which deviance and distrust are prevalent); second, there is the idea of normlessness as an absence or unclarity of prescriptions for behavior (i.e., as a state of meaninglessness).

The concept of alienation is always around in one form or another, but sometimes it goes by other names. It enjoyed a resurrection, using its straightforward name, during the turbulent 1960s and 1970s but appears to have gone underground in recent years. Still, the crucial concerns underlying the concepts of alienation and anomie have not been significantly bypassed or replaced. Indeed, the argument can be made (Seeman, 1983) that contemporary theorizing and research find the classical dimensions (if not the name) of alienation essential in a wide variety of fields (e.g., in studies of work, health, collective behavior, and political life). This is indicated, for example, by the current prominence of concepts and measures relating to a person's sense of (1) personal mastery (vs. powerlessness), (2) social isolation and loneliness (vs. community), (3) intrinsic engagement in work (vs. extrinsic, self-estranged activity), (4) consensual order (vs. norm-

Measures of Personality and Social Psychological Attitudes

lessness and distrust), (5) meaninglessness (ambiguity and unpredictability vs. coherence); and (6) shared values (vs. cultural estrangement).

These are, indeed, the major dimensions of alienation (Seeman, 1959, 1975), and
they provide a framework for reviewing the scales that seem most useful for measuring
alienation and anomie. As will be observed, considerably more effort has been devoted to
instrumentation in some alienation domains than in others. For example, powerlessness
and self-estrangement in work have been popular topics for study, while meaninglessness
and cultural estrangement have not. I have included a seventh category, "generalized
alienation," to accommodate indices of a more global nature.

A reader comparing the list of scales included in this chapter with the list included
earlier by Robinson and Shaver (1969, Chapter 5) will note that many of those 14 scales
have been omitted. The main reason is that considerable progress in scale development
has rendered the older measures dispensable. They have not been used with any consistency in the intervening years (e.g., Davids, 1955; Middleton, 1963), are too context-specific
and/or dated in content (e.g., Clark, 1959; Horton & Thompson, 1962; Hyman, Wright,
& Hopkins, 1962), or are generally pale versions of currently better-known variants (e.g.,
Gamson, 1961, on "helplessness" and Olsen, 1969, on political alienation). Streuning
and Richardson's (1965) early factor analysis of the alienation domain was very helpful,
but it too has been updated by the factor-based work included here (e.g., Kohn &
Schooler, 1983; Scheussler, 1982).

Before turning to details of the various scales, some general background comments
are in order to provide a clearer context for the measures selected to represent each of the
seven alienation domains.

Powerlessness Measures

The most extensive scale development has been done with respect to powerlessness (vs.
mastery), and six such scales will be reviewed here. Interest in a person's sense of control
over life events certainly predated the development of Rotter's I-E Scale (1966), but his
locus of control construct (see this volume, Chapter 9) served as an inspiration for several
of the scales reviewed in this chapter (e.g., Pearlin's mastery index, and even more
directly the Neal–Seeman powerlessness measure focusing on politicoeconomic events).
Useful measures bearing on the same basic theme of inefficacy, fatalism, powerlessness,
and lack of autonomy, can be found, in both early and recent versions, under various
names (i.e., without direct reference to the concepts of alienation, internal–external
control, or powerlessness).

Thus, although cross-cultural work on the powerlessness variant of alienation has
been limited (Guthrie & Tanco, 1980), the comparative work of Inkeles and Smith (1974)
examining modernization in developing countries involved creation of a "modernism"
scale. This scale incorporates an efficacy factor focusing, as does the I-E scale, on the role
of fate or luck and on the possibilities for management of one's destiny.[1] Another example
comes from studies of "achievement orientation," which, as a part of a long tradition in

---

[1]Two sample items reveal the similarity of this aspect of "modernism" with indices of powerlessness
versus mastery: (1) "Some say that accidents are due mainly to bad luck. Others say accidents can be prevented
by sufficient care. Do you think prevention depends: entirely on luck; mainly on luck; mainly on carefulness;
entirely on carefulness?" (2) "Which is most important for the future of the country: the hard work of the people;
good planning on the part of the government; God's help; good luck?" (The respondent is asked to make a first
and a second choice.)

sociological investigation, have regularly incorporated indices of the fatalistic compo-nents of that construct (see, for example, Kahl, 1965; Rosen, 1956; and the summary by Spenner & Featherman of the literature on "achievement ambitions," 1978). It is worth noting, too, that other components of alienation, in addition to powerlessness, are fre-quently included in measures of modernism or achievement orientation. For example, a trust dimension (which is treated below under the normlessness rubric) is included in Kahl's measurement scheme.

As these remarks highlight, scale-naming in the alienation–anomie domain presents a serious problem for researchers, because measures with similar content often go by different titles, and there is a tendency to adopt authors' labels uncritically. The result is intellectual disconnection where coordination would be more appropriate and/or spurious association between measures that carry different labels but embody similar content. An example of the first of these difficulties occurred in the literature on "learned help-lessness," in which disengagement between that literature and related research on locus of control and powerlessness was the rule for some time; however, the parallels have become more explicit (see the Attributional Style Questionnaire by Peterson et al., 1982, the discussion of depression and attributional style in Chapter 6 of the present volume; Burger & Arkin, 1980; Sergent & Lambert, 1979). An example of the second difficulty can be found in the work of Bacharach and Aiken (1979), who draw a distinction, as do many in the Marxist tradition (e.g., Israel, 1971), between the concept of "reification" and the concept of "alienation" (in their case, powerlessness) and then proceed to examine the relevance of each concept for supervisor and subordinate job satisfaction. The distinction is certainly feasible in principle, since reification refers to the worker's "lack of creative involvement in the work process; whereas, powerlessness refers to his inability to control this process" (p. 854). A difficulty arises, however, when these names for different constructs are operationalized through items that overlap considerably.[2]

That measures *can* be constructed which allow for discrimination among the various dimensions of alienation is clear from the range of evidence now available. The early factoring evidence on this point, supplied by Neal and Rettig (1963) and intended to establish independence among the various alienations, has been followed by a variety of similar findings using different measurement devices and more sophisticated analytic procedures. Thus, Kohn and Schooler (1983) developed a number of brief scales (in-cluded in this chapter) that distinguish powerlessness from normlessness, self-estrange-ment, and cultural estrangement. Similarly, Finifter (1970) distinguished between two components of political alienation using "political powerlessness" and "political norm-

---

[2]The measure of reification, for example, includes items (to be answered on a four-point true–false scale) which state: "In my bureau, there are well-defined procedures specifying the proper channel of communication in most matters" and "The same steps must be followed in processing every piece of work." The powerlessness measure carries the following similar items: "Going through channels is constantly stressed" and "Whenever I have a problem I can consult with whomever I want in my own service without my supervisor's permission."

This naming trouble, and consequent measurement overlap, occurs with surprising frequency and for many of the dimensions of alienation. With respect to work alienation (see the discussion of "self-estrangement" which follows), the problem surfaces regularly in discussions of job satisfaction vs. work alienation. Thus, Seybolt and Gruenfeld (1976) use a seven-item work alienation scale that has been employed in cross-cultural work (Seeman, 1972), along with an index of work satisfaction (Smith, Kendall, & Hulin, 1969), to demonstrate that these are simply different names for the same construct. They show, among other things, that the two measures are highly correlated (.68) and that controlling for job satisfaction radically reduces the variance accounted for by the alienation index. The result is hardly surprising in view of the overlap in the two measures, the "satisfaction" index in this case being heavily loaded with the worker's judgment about the intrinsically engaging qualities of the job (precisely what the work alienation index is intended to measure): creativity, challenge, accomplishment, and lack of routine.

lessness" scales. This distinction is echoed in Balch's (1974) and Jennings and Niemi's (1981) demonstration that the measure of "sense of political efficacy" used in many voting studies is not unitary; it reflects both the input (efficacy) and output (trust) aspects of the individual's relation to the political system, two features of alienation that can be measured separately and have distinctive consequences (Gamson, 1961). A factor analysis of political alienation items from the Michigan national election surveys (Mason, House, & Martin, 1985) makes a similar point. These items are not unidimensional; efficacy and trust dimensions are clearly distinguishable.

Discrimination with respect to powerlessness goes deeper than its separateness from the other alienations (i.e., from normlessness, self-estrangement, etc.). Not surprisingly, research following the development of Rotter's measure of generalized expectancies for control has shown that the original I-E Scale is not strictly unidimensional (e.g., Collins, 1974; Gurin, Gurin, & Morrison, 1978), and the same can be expected of other measures of control and powerlessness which have a clear affinity with I-E. The clearest distinction emerging from this work contrasts what might be called "personal control" with "social control" (i.e., the sense of personal competence or efficacy and the sense of effective sociopolitical control). Paulhus and Christie (1981) have developed 10-item scales reflecting this distinction, and they add a third discriminable sphere of control (the "interpersonal control" scale; sample item: "I'm not good at guiding the course of a conversation with others").

Recognition that the situation, domain, or sphere of alienation is important fits with recent emphasis, in both sociology and psychology, on person–situation interaction (Magnusson, 1981). Thus, a variety of powerlessness scales have been developed for use in delimited situations, one of the earliest being Clark's (1959) measurement of "alienation within a social system" (reviewed in Robinson & Shaver's 1969 volume), a measure of perceived powerlessness developed for use with members of an agricultural cooperative and referring to their sense of control within that organization. Since then, numerous efforts have been made to implement a context-specific approach to measurement including Epperson's (1963) work on "classroom alienation," which focuses on students' sense of task powerlessness and social powerlessness in the classroom; Holian's (1972) study of the connection between college students' alienation from "the immediate university situation" (their perception of college-based powerlessness, normlessness, etc.) and their feelings about the more distant spheres of politics and economics; and Martin, Bengston, and Acock's (1974) context-specific approach to the relation between age and alienation, which combines the several "modes" of alienation (powerlessness, etc.) with multiple social contexts (e.g., family, education, religion), yielding a 25-item scale based on the cross-classification of five modes of alienation with five institutional contexts.[3]

Finally, a word about the distinction between perceived mastery and desired mastery. The emphasis in measurement has been on the sense of powerlessness, conceived as an expectancy or a perception concerning the social world (whether that world is posed to the respondent in a generalized way or in a more context-specific way). The relation of such perceptions of powerlessness to the individual's values or preferences regarding control has been underplayed, however, perhaps because the desirability of control, being a value preference, has not been conceived as an integral part of the concept of alienation. Still,

---

[3]As implied, the same kind of contextual specification process (i.e., development of domain-specific and goal-specific measurement) has occurred in connection with the I-E Scale proper; see, for example, Lefcourt, von Baeyer, Ware, and Cox (1979). For a typical, brief (four-item) scale of the domain-specific type (in this case, a measure of "autonomy" in the family sphere), see Mortimer and Finch (1984). For health-specific scales, see Lau and Ware (1981), and Wallston and Wallston (1981).

there is an implicit "discrepancy" involved in the idea of alienation (the person is, after all, alienated—separated from something). Hence it is noteworthy that Burger and his colleagues (Burger & Cooper, 1979; Burger & Smith, 1985) have developed a 20-item "desirability of control" scale that exhibits discriminant validity and is relatively free of general social desirability influence.[4]

The following measures of the powerlessness component of alienation are described in the present chapter (for additional scales, see Campbell & Converse, 1976, and Shepard, 1971).

1. Powerlessness (Dean, 1961)
2. Powerlessness (Neal & Seeman, 1964)
3. Powerlessness (Neal & Groat, 1974)
4. Mastery Scale (Pearlin, Lieberman, Menaghan, & Mullan, 1981)
5. Doubt about Self-Determination (Scheussler, 1982)
6. Powerlessness (Kohn & Schooler, 1983)

These scales are covered in chronological order, since there is no basis for ordering them preferentially. They vary in abstractness and political vs. personal focus.

Dean's Powerlessness Scale is unusually heterogeneous in content, referring to "the future facing today's children," the feeling of being used, the sense of being a "cog in the machinery of life," and the feeling of being blocked from job promotion (unless one "gets a break"). Neal and Seeman's scale focuses on inability to influence world affairs; for example, "This world is run by the few people in power, and there is not much the little guy can do about it." Neal and Groat's scale is similar in content but different in format. Whereas Neal and Seeman used binary-choice items (similar to those on Rotter's, 1966 Locus of Control Scale), Neal and Groat used single statements with Likert-type answer alternatives.

The Pearlin et al. and Scheussler scales are more personal and abstract; they assess a feeling of powerlessness without referring to concrete life situations. The following is an example from Pearlin et al.: "I have little control over the things that happen to me." A typical item from Scheussler is, "The world is too complicated for me to understand." The Kohn and Schooler measure is the simplest and is meant for survey administration; a sample item is, "Do you feel that most of the things that happen to you are the result of your own decisions or of things over which you have no control?" Because the scales differ subtly in content and format, the reader should evaluate them in terms of the specific areas of powerlessness that he or she wishes to assess.

Powerlessness

(Dean, 1961)

Variable

Dean's powerlessness subscale is one part of a three-part general alienation measure in which the other components of alienation are normlessness and social isolation (reviewed below).

---

[4]The importance lies not so much in the development of the scale itself, but in reaffirming that researchers ought not to expect (as they often seem to do) that a measure of alienation in itself will explain very much, particularly when we note that these are often merely perceptual or cognitive measures having largely to do with a person's expectancies, but they typically do not account for other behaviorally relevant factors (e.g., the value placed on control, the available resources, the institutional context).

Description

Beginning with 139 items gleaned from the literature, seven judges (instructors and assistants in the Department of Sociology at Ohio State University) were requested to judge each item as to whether it specifically and exclusively referred to each of the three subscale concepts. It was necessary for at least five of the seven judges to agree in order to retain an item. The result was nine items in the final scale for powerlessness, six for normlessness, and nine for social isolation.

The alienation scale comprises 24 items presented in 5-point Likert format from 4 (strongly agree) to 0 (strongly disagree); five of the items are worded in the reverse direction. Scale scores can thus vary from 0 (lowest alienation) to 96 (highest alienation).

Sample

Data were collected in Columbus, Ohio, from four of the 19 wards of that city, selected by criteria related to voting incidence and socioeconomic variables, as part of Dean's study of political apathy. Precincts and individuals were selected by random sampling. The questionnaire was sent to 1108 individuals and 433 responded (38.8 percent). Of these, a final sample of 384 gave usable replies.

The following normative data were obtained in the original study:

Sample	Total	Powerlessness	Normlessness	Social isolation
Columbus men (n = 384)	36.6	13.7	7.6	11.8
Protestant college women (n = 75)	36.3	12.7	7.6	14.9
Catholic college women (n = 65)	30.2	10.9	3.6	15.2

No reason is given for the lack of correspondence between total scale scores and the sum of the three components. Scores form a normal distribution, with scores extending across almost the entire possible range.

Reliability

Internal Consistency

The reliabilities of the subscales, tested by the split-half method and corrected by the Spearman–Brown formula, were as follows: powerlessness, .78; normlessness, .73; social isolation, .84. The total alienation scale, with items rotated to minimize a possible halo effect, had a reliability of .78. Correlations among the various scores are shown below.

	Normlessness	Social isolation	Alienation
Powerlessness	.67	.54	.90
Normlessness		.41	.80
Social isolation			.75

Test–Retest

No data were reported.

Validity

Convergent

The total scale correlated about .30 with Srole's Anomia Scale and Nettler's (1957) Alienation Scale. It was hypothesized that (1) alienation and each of its components would correlate negatively with social status, (2) advancing age would be positively correlated with alienation, and (3) rural background would correlate negatively with alienation. While in most instances the hypotheses were sustained at significant levels, the correlation coefficients were generally low.

The component and total scores were correlated with the F scale (authoritarianism) in a sample of 73 college students. The r values were as follows: powerlessness and authoritarianism, .37, normlessness and authoritarianism, .33, social isolation and authoritarianism, .23, alienation and authoritarianism, .26.

Discriminant

No data were reported.

Location

Dean, D. (1961). Alienation: Its meaning and measurement. *Ame·ican Sociological Review,* **26,** 753–758.

Results and Comments

The scale has continued to be used. For example, Blocker and Riedesel (1978) drew a subsample from a 1976 sample of 407 Tulsa, Oklahoma, white, employed heads of households (n = 244). The study compared objective and subjective status inconsistency with respect to their possible consequences, one of which was powerlessness measured with Dean's subscale. Six items (each with five Likert-style responses) were used, two of them reversed to reduce acquiescence bias. (The split-half reliability of this powerlessness scale, corrected with the Spearman–Brown formula, was .84.) Results indicated that subjective status inconsistency (adjusted for education and occupational prestige) has a significant effect on powerlessness, whereas objective status inconsistency does not.

Benson, Severs, Tatgenhorst, and Loddengaard (1980) examined the relationship, in a sample of 113 college undergraduates, of nonspontaneous helping behavior to 21 intrapersonal factors. Seven personality and value measures were included in the analysis, one of which was the Dean alienation scale. It correlated significantly (although modestly) with nonspontaneous helping behavior: $r = -.24, p < .05$.

Burris (1983) used national survey data to assess the consequences of overeducation on a variety of worker attitudes, including political alienation. He found "no support for the hypothesis of a positive association between overeducation and political alienation. Consistent with the findings of previous research [(Dean, 1961), however,] we did find a negative correlation between political alienation and both education and occupational level" (p. 463).

In order to keep the scales in this chapter grouped according to conceptual domains—powerlessness, normlessness, and social isolation—the Dean subscales are presented in separate places, beginning here with powerlessness.

Powerlessness Items

Below are some statements regarding public issues with which some people agree and others disagree. Please give us your own opinion about these items, that is, whether you agree or disagree with the items as they stand. Please check in the appropriate blank, as follows:

_____ A (Strongly Agree)
_____ a (Agree)
_____ U (Uncertain)
_____ d (Disagree)
_____ D (Strongly Disagree)

2. I worry about the future facing today's children.

___ A   ___ a   ___ U   ___ d   ___ D

6. Sometimes I have the feeling that other people are using me.
9. It is frightening to be responsible for the development of a little child.
13. There is little or nothing I can do towards preventing a major "shooting" war.
15. There are so many decisions that have to be made today that sometimes I could just "blow up."
18. There is little chance for promotion on the job unless a man [person] gets a break.
20. We're so regimented today that there's not much room for choice even in personal matters.
21. We are just so many cogs in the machinery of life.
23. The future looks very dismal.

Note: Item numbers indicate placement in the general alienation questionnaire. See entries under normlessness and social isolation for the other numbered items. The word "person" in brackets is a suggested alternative to "man."

Powerlessness

(Neal & Seeman, 1964)

Variable

The authors define powerlessness as "low expectancies for control of events," with events being those of importance in mass societies (control over politics, the economy, etc.).

Description

The scale consists of seven forced-choice items, which were reduced from an original pool of 50 via pretesting (actually, 12 items were employed in the present study but only 7 were found to be scalable). The items were originally devised in collaboration with Liverant and Rotter at Ohio State University to measure an individual's internal or external locus of control (see scales reviewed in Chapter 9 of the present volume). One point is given for each response in the powerless (external) direction, resulting in scores ranging from 0 (high power) to 7 (low power, i.e., extreme powerlessness).

Sample

The sample consisted of 609 male respondents (out of 1094 contacted by mail) chosen at random from the Columbus city directory. Subsequent data collected from about a tenth of the 47% of the sample who did not return the mail questionnaire revealed that their powerlessness scores were similar to those in the original sample. The average score in the early 1960s for a random sample of males in Columbus, Ohio, was 2.7.

Reliability

Internal Consistency

The seven-item scale had a reproducibility coefficient of .87. Neal and Rettig (1963) reported for the same sample that 10 of the original 12 items had factor loadings over .30 and seven loadings over .50. Using many of the same items, Seeman and Evans (1962) obtained a split-half reliability of .70.

Test–Retest

No test–retest data were reported.

Validity

Convergent

As hypothesized by Neal and Seeman, members of work-related organizations felt less powerless (2.5) than those who were unorganized (2.9). The results held for manual workers and "mobility-oriented" nonmanual (white-collar) workers, but not for white-collar workers who were not mobility-oriented. In another study (Baer, Eitzen, Duprey, Thompson, & Cole, 1976), it was hypothesized that powerlessness would be related to measures of objective and subjective status inconsistency. The results were supportive, as shown below.

| | Consistent status | | | | Inconsistent status | | | |
| | Objective | | Subjective | | Objective | | Subjective | |
Powerlessness	(%)	(n)	(%)	(n)	(%)	(n)	(%)	(n)
Low	30	(55)	28	(52)	17	(9)	21	(12)
Middle	44	(80)	44	(81)	38	(20)	43	(24)
High	26	(48)	28	(52)	45	(24)	36	(20)

These findings are almost identical to those obtained with Rotter's (1966) internal–external locus of control scale "doubtless because, although different scales, they are tapping the same attitudinal dimension. The generalization seems clear that inconsistents tend to be externals and have feelings of powerlessness while consistents are evenly distributed in more of a bell-shaped curve" (Baer *et al.*, 1976, p. 392).

Discriminant

In the Neal and Seeman study, Srole's Anomia Scale (reviewed later in this chapter) did not produce as clear a pattern of findings as the Powerlessness Scale did. According to Neal and Rettig (1963), factor analysis revealed the Anomia Scale to be essentially independent of the Powerlessness Scale. In a subsequent article, Neal and Rettig (1967) concluded that alienation may be viewed as either unidimensional or multidimensional depending on one's level of analysis.

Location

Neal, A., & Seeman, M. (1964). Organizations and powerlessness: A test of the mediation hypothesis. *American Sociological Review*, **29**, 216–225.

Results and Comments

Besides the findings mentioned already, the Neal and Seeman data indicate that powerlessness and normlessness are jointly found among older, downwardly mobile, manual workers who reject mobility values. The least likelihood for both powerlessness and normlessness was found among the younger, stationary, non-manual workers who were mobility oriented. Seeman and Evans (1962) found powerlessness to predict tuberculosis patients' lack of knowledge concerning their illness but not dissatisfaction with medical care.

The Powerlessness Scale

This is a survey to find out what the public thinks about certain events that we face in our society. Each item consists of a pair of statements. Please select the one statement of each pair (and only one) that you more strongly believe to be true. Be sure to check the one you actually believe to be more nearly true, rather than the one you think you should check or the one you would like to be true. This is a measure of personal belief; obviously, there are no right or wrong answers. Again, be sure to make a choice between each pair of statements.

1. a. I think we have adequate means for preventing runaway inflation.
   b. There's very little we can do to keep prices from going higher.*
2. a. Persons like myself have little chance of protecting our personal interests when they conflict with those of strong pressure groups.*
   b. I feel that we have adequate ways of coping with pressure groups.
3. a. A lasting world peace can be achieved by those of us who work toward it.
   b. There's very little we can do to bring about a permanent world peace.*

4. a. There's very little persons like myself can do to improve world opinion of the United States.*
   b. I think each of us can do a great deal to improve world opinion of the United States.
5. a. This world is run by the few people in power, and there is not much the little guy can do about it.*
   b. The average citizen can have an influence on government decisions.
6. a. It is only wishful thinking to believe that one can really influence what happens in society at large.*
   b. People like me can change the course of world events if we make ourselves heard.
7. a. More and more, I feel helpless in the face of what's happening in the world today.*
   b. I sometimes feel personally to blame for the sad state of affairs in our government.

Note: Statements that indicate powerlessness are marked with asterisks.

Powerlessness

(Neal & Groat, 1974)

Variable

This conception of powerlessness focuses on low expectancy for control over the outcome of political and economic events.

Description

The 10-item scale taps only attitudes related to war and peace, power, government decisions, world opinion of the United States, and inflation. At its extreme, powerlessness implies fatalism and its absence, mastery. Responses range from "strongly agree" to "strongly disagree" on a four-point scale. The items originated in the Neal and Rettig (1963) powerlessness measure. Only eight were used in the data analyses described here. Scores range from 10 (low powerlessness) to 40 (high powerlessness) for the 10-item version and from 8 to 32 for the 8-item version.

Sample

The initial data were collected in 1963, by means of a mail questionnaire, from approximately 700 married women in the Toledo metropolitan area. Women in their child-bearing years were selected by random sampling procedures. The response rate was 68% and no significant differences in alienation were found between respondents and nonrespondents. In 1971, 408 of the original respondents were located and sent a second questionnaire. An 82% response rate yielded a sample of 334 respondents. Alienation scores and most demographic variables did not differ between respondents and nonrespondents, although the longitudinal sample underrepresented highly mobile subjects.

Reliability

Internal Consistency

A principal factor analysis with oblique rotation revealed the following factor loadings for each item (orthogonal varimax rotation yielded similar results):

	Factor loadings	
	1963	1971
Item 1	.71	.77
Item 2	.73	.74
Item 3	.65	.80
Item 4	.67	.69
Item 5	.51	.68
Item 6	.46	.65
Item 7	.51	.42
Item 8	.34	.41
Item 9*	.19	.50
Item 10*	.22	.27

*Factor loadings too low, item deleted from analysis.

The Ω reliability coefficient for 1963 was .83 and for 1971, .88.

Test–Retest

The factor scores on powerlessness obtained in the 1963 sample correlated with those of the 1971 sample with an r of .53. This high level of correspondence over 8 years suggests that the items tap "world views which have a high degree of consistency and stability through time" (p. 1201).

Validity

Convergent

The 1971 powerlessness scores were significantly related (in the hypothesized direction) to selected socioeconomic and demographic variables. Low levels of education, husband's occupational status, and family income were associated with higher levels of powerlessness.

Discriminant

No data were reported.

Location

Groat, H. T., & Neal, A. (1967). Social psychological correlates of urban fertility. *American Sociological Review, 32,* 945–959.

Neal, A., & Groat, H. T. (1974). Social class correlates of stability and change in levels of alienation. *Sociological Quarterly, 15,* 548–558.

Zeller, R., Neal, A., & Groat, H. T. (1980). On the reliability and stability of alienation measures. *Social Forces,* **58,** 1195–1204.

Results and Comments

The initial study focused on the relationship between various forms of alienation and fertility behaviors. It was found that powerlessness did not consistently discriminate fertility behavior: Powerlessness was positively associated with fertility among Catholics but not among Protestants. The longitudinal study revealed a relatively high level of consistency in powerlessness over a period of 8 years, as well as evidence of increasing levels of powerlessness. With regard to the various measures of alienation, Zeller, Neal, and Groat said:

> In conclusion, we believe that our longitudinal data have provided evidence to suggest that operationalizing dimensions of alienation is not only feasible, but may be accomplished with a high degree of confidence in the reliability of the measuring instruments. The obtained stability of alienation scores over a long period of time lends credence to the search for the causal, antecedent conditions. The key to the formation of alienative attitudes would appear to be deeply embedded in childhood and adolescent socialization, rather than within the adult responses to family events and to historical circumstances (1980, pp. 1202–1203).

Powerlessness

1 People like me can change the course of world events if we make ourselves heard.*

STRONGLY   AGREE   DISAGREE   STRONGLY
AGREE   DISAGREE

2 I think each of us can do a great deal to improve world opinion of the
United States.*

3 There's very little that persons like myself can do to improve world opinion
of the United States.

4 The average citizen can have an influence on government decisions.*

5 The world is run by the few people in power, and there is not much the
little guy can do about it.

6 It is only wishful thinking to believe that one can really influence what
happens in society at large.

7 A lasting world peace can be achieved by those of us who work toward
it.*

8 More and more, I feel helpless in the face of what's happening in the
world today.

9 There's very little we can do to keep prices from going higher.

10 Wars between countries seem inevitable despite the efforts of men to
prevent them.

Note: Items with asterisks are reverse-scored.

Mastery Scale

(Pearlin et al., 1981)

Variable

Mastery is defined as the "extent to which one regards one's life-chances as being under one's own control in contrast to being fatalistically ruled."

Description

The seven items in this scale are answered in a four-point agree–disagree format: strongly agree, agree, disagree, strongly disagree. In the studies described here the scale was administered as part of a face-to-face interview, but it seems amenable to self-administration. Scores can range from 7 (low mastery) to 28 (high mastery).

Sample

The authors' 1978 article was part of a larger investigation into the social origins of personal stress. Scheduled interviews were conducted in 1972–1973 with 2300 males and females (alternatively so as to obtain an equal number of each) in households selected by means of a cluster sample. The respondents were between the ages of 18 and 65 and lived in the Chicago urban area. The mean and SD for Time 1 Mastery scores were 3.8 and .7; for Time 2, 3.7 and .7.

The study published in 1981 utilized longitudinal data, which included the 1972–1973 interviews as a first wave. A second wave was administered to 1106 of the original respondents in 1976–1977. Attrition was somewhat disproportionate among young, non-white males of limited income.

Reliability

Unidimensionality of the seven-item scale was demonstrated via factor analysis. The correlation between Time 1 and Time 2 measures was .33. The longitudinal study utilized LISREL procedures, which allowed the authors to estimate the degree to which the scales were affected by correlated errors and the invariance of factor structure at the two points in time. The authors concluded that the relationship between constructs and indicators remained stable over time. Error over time was small and did not influence the stability of the estimates to a significant degree.

Validity

Convergent

The validity of the scale is indicated by its consistent relationships (in the hypothesized direction) with other scales and variables. Pairwise correlations for Mastery indices at Time 2 and Time 1 are as follows:

	Mastery-2	Mastery-1
Depression-2	−.43	−.20
Depression-1	−.16	−.30
Self-esteem-2	.54	.26
Self-esteem-1	.16	.48
Mastery-2	—	.33
Mastery-1	.33	—
Job description	−.17	−.13
Economic strain-2	−.33	−.22
Economic strain-1	−.15	−.33
Economic coping-2	.31	.18
Social supports	.19	.18
Income change	.09	−.05
Age	−.15	−.11
Marital status	−.08	−.13
Sex	.14	.14
Race	−.02	.01
Occupational rank	−.04	−.04
Education	.13	.21

Discriminant

The near-zero correlations above provide some evidence for discrimination.

Location

Pearlin, L., & Schooler, C. (1978). The structure of coping. *Journal of Health and Social Behavior, 19*, 2–21.
Pearlin, L., Lieberman, M., Menaghan, E., & Mullan, J. (1981). The stress process. *Journal of Health and Social Behavior, 22*, 337–356.

Results and Comments

Mastery was hypothesized to be one of three psychological resources that protect individuals from the stressful consequences of social strain. Results showed that mastery (as well as the other two psychological resources, low self-denigration and high self-esteem) can help blunt the emotional impact of persistent problems. A distinct order of relative importance among the psychological variables was discovered, and mastery was determined to be second in importance, following self-denigration. The importance of psychological resources was then assessed in comparison to the relevance of coping mechanisms (the specific responses to life strains). Findings indicate that "it is the psychological characteristics that are the more helpful in sustaining people facing strains arising out of conditions over which they may have little direct control—finances and job. But where one is dealing with problems residing in close interpersonal relations, it is the things one does that make the most difference" (Pearlin & Schooler, 1978, p. 13). The strains analyzed in the initial study are of the continuous and undramatic sort (those built into daily roles) and therefore are not inclusive of all types of strain.

The later study, which utilized longitudinal data, included the analysis of chronic life strains. In this analysis, mastery, along with self-esteem, seemed to be an important intermediary in the translation of life strains into actual stress. In particular, when life events and the role strains they generate resulted in a diminishment of self (reduced sense of mastery and lowered self-esteem), stress was more likely to occur.

A path analytic model reveals that disruptive job events are related to economic strains ($\beta = .18$), which are associated with the decline of self-esteem ($\beta = -.56$) and mastery ($\beta = -.70$), which in turn are both related to increased depression ($\beta = -.19$ and $-.11$, respectively). The authors show that self-esteem and mastery actually contribute to depression (rather than being symptomatic of it).

Mastery Scale

How strongly do you agree or disagree that:

1. I have little control over the things that happen to me.

| STRONGLY AGREE | AGREE | DISAGREE | STRONGLY DISAGREE |

2. There is really no way I can solve some of the problems I have.
3. There is little I can do to change many of the important things in my life.
4. I often feel helpless in dealing with the problems of life.
5. Sometimes I feel that I'm being pushed around in life.
6. What happens to me in the future mostly depends on me.*
7. I can do just about anything I really set my mind to do.*

Note: Items marked by asterisks are reverse-scored.

Doubt About Self-Determination

(Scheussler, 1982)

Variable

This scale measures whether a person feels shaped by social circumstances rather than capable of shaping them, with a high score reflecting the belief that the social world is unresponsive to planning and work.

Description

Respondents answer each of the 14 negatively worded items with either "agree" or "disagree." Scale scores range from 0 (low doubt) to 14 (high doubt) with a mean of 5.7 and a standard deviation of 3.6. The missing response rate was 3.6%. In the study summarized here, the scale was administered, with a simple agree–disagree choice for each item, by interviewers. It seems amenable to self-administration and to a more differentiated answer continuum, however.

Sample

A random sample of 1500 United States households was drawn in September 1974, and one adult was randomly selected from each. A relatively low response rate (61%) was explained by both the length of the questionnaire and its content. Completion rates differed by region (lower in the Pacific region), size of metropolitan area (higher in small areas), and type of area (higher in nonmetropolitan areas).

Reliability

Internal Consistency

The individual items had the following item–total correlations and factor loadings:

	Keyed response	% Keyed response	Item–total correlation	Factor loading
Item 1	Agree	51	.45	.51
Item 2	Agree	39	.47	.53
Item 3	Agree	34	.42	.47
Item 4	Agree	33	.43	.49
Item 5	Agree	35	.44	.49
Item 6	Agree	61	.46	.52
Item 7	Agree	41	.43	.47
Item 8	Agree	30	.41	.46
Item 9	Agree	48	.39	.44
Item 10	Agree	47	.33	.37
Item 11	Agree	35	.41	.46
Item 12	Agree	49	.49	.55
Item 13	Agree	35	.43	.48
Item 14	Agree	29	.32	.36

The scale has an α reliability of .80 and a Tucker–Lewis reliability of .94. Overall, the author considered the doubt about self-determination scale to be "good" in comparison to the other 11 scales constructed in the same study.

Validity

Convergent

Initially, this scale was taken to be a measure of social despair, but after reviewing the correlates with differently constructed tests and reevaluating its contents, it was determined to be a measure of doubt about self-determination. The scale is strongly correlated with Srole's Anomia Scale ($r = .78$, with three common items), yet it was decided that it is distinct because it refers to self-determination more than to self–other alienation. The self-determination scale is related (in the hypothesized direction) to several background characteristics. Higher scores on the scale were obtained for nonwhite, low income, low education, older, and divorced and separated respondents.

Discriminant

No data were reported.

Location

Scheussler, K. (1982). *Measuring social life feelings*. San Francisco: Jossey–Bass.

Results and Comments

The general goal of this research was to construct standard sociological scales. The author found a close correspondence between the 12 Social Life Feeling Scales and the more numerous scales found in the literature. He took this as an indication that only 12 social life feelings have been operationally distinguished, and therefore, the "twelve scales would suffice for maintaining those operational distinctions."

Social Life Feeling Scale 1: Doubt About Self-Determination

1. There are few people in this world you can trust, when you get right down to it.

          AGREE   DISAGREE

2. What happens in life is largely a matter of chance.
3. If the odds are against you, it's impossible to come out on top.
4. I have little influence over the things that happen to me.
5. I sometimes feel that I have little control over the direction my life is taking.
6. Nowadays a person has to live pretty much for today and let tomorrow take care of itself.
7. I've had more than my share of troubles.
8. For me, one day is no different from another.
9. The world is too complicated for me to understand.
10. I regret having missed so many chances in the past.
11. It's unfair to bring children into the world with the way things look for the future.
12. The future is too uncertain for a person to plan ahead.
13. I find it difficult to be optimistic about anything nowadays.
14. There are no right or wrong ways to make money, only easy and hard.

Powerlessness

(Kohn & Schooler, 1983)

Variable

Using Seeman's definition, Kohn and Schooler define powerlessness as "the expectancy or probability held by the individual that his own behavior cannot determine occurrence of the outcomes . . . he seeks" (p. 86).

Description

This scale focuses on the sense of being powerless (the lack of personal efficacy) rather than the fact of being powerless. In contrast to other indices in common use, this index has less abstract referents. Four items comprise a Guttman scale, these items being scored on an agree–disagree (or 0–1) basis. In the studies described here, the scale was administered as part of an interview conducted by the field staff of NORC, but it seems amenable to self-administration. Scores vary from 0 (low powerlessness) to 4 (high powerlessness).

Sample

The 1964 cross-sectional survey of 3101 United States men 16 years or older employed in civilian occupations was based on an area probability sample. Men not currently employed or employed in the military were excluded. Seventy-six percent of the selected men gave relatively complete interviews. The representativeness of the sample was tested by comparing respondent characteristics with population characteristics. For the cities where data were available, nonrespondents did not appear to differ from respondents in occupational level. In addition, there appeared to be no relationship between the occupational levels of nonrespondents and their reasons for refusing to be interviewed. Overall, the sample appears to be representative of the population, although larger cities were somewhat underrepresented.

A follow-up study was administered in 1974 with a subset of the men in the original sample who were less than 55 years old in 1964. Seventy-eight percent of those reselected were re-interviewed ($n = 687$). The generalizability of the 1974 sample was assessed by two independent tests, and the authors concluded that the longitudinal data could be generalized to the larger population of employed men in the United States.

Reliability

The powerlessness scale has a reproducibility in the .90s, scalability in the .70s, and essentially random patterns of error.

Validity

The powerlessness scale is one of five scales that comprise a larger measure of alienation. A second-order measurement model of alienation was developed by Roberts (1987) using Kohn and Schooler's data. The path of the second-order concept (alienation) to the first-order concept (powerlessness) is .83 in both 1964 and 1974. The measures of alienation at the two time periods correlated .52. The paths (first order concepts to indicators) are presented below for the two surveys:

	1964	1974
Item 1	−.23	−.27
Item 2	−.26	−.11
Item 3	n.a.	n.a.
Item 4	.68	.62

*n.a., Not applicable.

Location

Kohn, M., & Schooler, C. (1983). *Work and personality: An inquiry into the impact of social stratification.* Norwood, NJ: Ablex. See especially Chapter 4.

Slomczynski, K., Miller, J., & Kohn, M. (1981). Stratification, work, and values. *American Sociological Review,* **46,** 720–744.

Results and Comments

Kohn and Schooler examined the relationship between social structure (operationally defined as occupational structure) and the subjective experience of alienation. The point of origin was Marx's analysis of the occupational structure, which emphasized ownership of the means of production and the division of labor. Two hypotheses were tested: (1) loss of control over the products of labor is related to alienation (here, ownership and hierarchical position are crucial), and (2) loss of control over the process of work is conducive to alienation (here, occupational self-direction is important). Alienation was defined in terms of five subscales: powerlessness, self-estrangement, normlessness, cultural estrangement, and meaninglessness.

Ownership was found to be only weakly related to powerlessness ($r = -.04$), although position in the supervisory hierarchy was more strongly correlated ($r = -.13$). Bureaucratization (the index for division of labor) was slightly related ($r = -.09$), but in the reverse of the predicted direction. Occupational self-direction was more consistently related to powerlessness: close supervision (r = .16); routinized work (r = .08); and work of little substantive complexity ($r = -.19$) were all significantly related. The introduction of statistical controls reduced these correlations but left statistically significant relationships.

The authors concluded that "in this large-scale, capitalist system, control over the product of one's labor (ownership and hierarchical position) has only an indirect effect on alienation, whereas control over work process (closeness of supervision, routinization, and substantive complexity) has an appreciable direct effect on powerlessness" (p. 96). Moreover, there was evidence for a causal effect of "control over work" on powerlessness. The authors cautioned regarding the generalization of the findings beyond the United States or beyond the time the data were collected.

Powerlessness

1. Do you feel that most of the things that happen to you are the result of your own decisions or of things over which you have no control?

    0 OWN DECISIONS   1 NO CONTROL

2. I generally have confidence that when I make plans I will be able to carry them out.

0 AGREE   1 DISAGREE

3. There are things I can do that might influence national policy.

0 AGREE   1 DISAGREE

4. How often do you feel powerless to get what you want out of life?

0 RARELY   1 FREQUENTLY

Note: No answer alternatives were provided by Kohn and Schooler (1983) for item 4; see their Table 4.1, p. 86. We have inserted "rarely" and "frequently" on intuitive grounds.

Normlessness Measures

The idea of normlessness owes much to Durkheim's concept of "anomie," and sociologists are still quick to insist that this refers not to a state of mind but to a state of society (i.e., to a "breakdown" of the social order in which norms no longer regulate behavior). Unfortunately, little systematic work has been done to specify this structural version of normlessness empirically, and there are serious conceptual difficulties involved (Seeman, 1982). The six measures included here are all of the subjective variety (i.e., they deal with *perceived* normlessness). The core idea in this individual-centered viewpoint is that certain people at certain times may not respect the presumed norms, may not trust others to respect them, may not perceive that there is a consensus with respect to appropriate behavior, and may be prepared to act in deviant ways to achieve given goals (e.g., to get elected, to be occupationally successful, to have one's way).

Many of the points made in the previous section about powerlessness can also be made with respect to normlessness. Regarding the issue of scale names, for example, the well-known Machiavellianism scale (of Christie & Geis 1970) is heavily imbued with normlessness items (e.g., "Anyone who completely trusts anyone else is asking for trouble"; "It is hard to get ahead without cutting corners here and there"). Many of these are replicas of items in the Neal and Groat (1974) normlessness scale or the Rotter (1967, 1980) trust scale (see below and Chapter 8).

It is well to keep an eye on the distinctively different domains of trust, since (as with powerlessness) the evidence indicates that the various "spheres" of trust do not necessarily cohere. Jennings and Niemi (1981) and Lipset and Schneider (1983) have reported that indices of trust in government are distinct from indices of interpersonal trust; among both young adults and their parents there was only a modest decline in interpersonal trust between 1965 and 1973, a drop that "pales by comparison with [the one] found for political trust" (Jennings & Niemi, 1981, p. 185).[5]

Researchers need to be attuned to both (1) significant differences that lie behind the apparent similarity conveyed by scale names, and (2) dangers that inhere in too readily

[5]Jennings and Niemi also make a methodologically interesting comparison between answers obtained from respondents (over 1000 of them) in interviews and answers to mail questionnaires. They found, on the whole, that the personal interview produced more "socially desirable behavior" (e.g., presentations of self as less openly critical of school and government, and as more politically alert and efficacious), but that "the differences, fortunately, are not large" (1981, p. 399).

adopting a global and undifferentiated conception of "alienation." With respect to the first of these, for example, it matters whether the normlessness items represent (as they do in the well-known Srole Anomia Scale, presented below) generalized ideological statements characterizing the respondent's world view (e.g., "In spite of what some people say, the lot of the average man is getting worse, not better") or the respondent's personal tolerance or intolerance of specific deviant behaviors, as in the case of the scale of Jessor, Graves, Hanson, and Jessor (1968; see also Judd, Jessor & Donovan, 1986), which asks how wrong it is to engage in particular acts of deviance (e.g., taking something of value from a store without paying for it; lying about one's age when applying for a license or a job). Among other things, it is a distinction that is likely to produce quite different correlations with social class. The generalized anomia scale should (and does) yield relatively high correlations with socioeconomic status; but in the Jessor *et al.* community study, the *r* was a low .05 between SES and attitudes toward deviance.

With respect to the overly common global view of alienation, signs of respondent discrimination (between, for example, mistrust, despair, and sense of incompetence), rather than signs of undifferentiated alienation, are plentiful, depending in part on whether instrument effects are prevented from overriding potential distinctions among the various forms of alienation. Wright (1981), examining trends in political "disaffection" (mainly distrust and powerlessness), along with other forms of dissatisfaction or discontent (as in work), makes the case that

> political alienation must be seen as being conceptually and, it appears, empirically distinct from other forms of dissatisfaction or discontent . . . knowing that people are unhappy with the way the government is run tells us little or nothing about how they feel toward all other aspects of their lives. (p. 20)

In a similar vein, Jessor *et al.* (1968, p. 322) report a negligible correlation ($r = .02$) in their community survey between the tolerance of deviance scale described above and an index of internal versus external locus of control.

The normlessness scales selected for inclusion here fall mainly (though not exclusively) into two categories. They are either (1) Srole (or Srole-like) general scales about the state of society, made up of items that reflect generalized dyspepsia ("It's hardly fair to bring children into the world with the way things look for the future"); or (2) scales which, though still rather general in nature, are more directed at the issue of interpersonal trust (e.g., the Scheussler scale). The latter is specifically included because it derives from a nationally based effort to factor analyze "feeling state" items derived from a wide range of sources (beginning with some 1000 items).

A final remark about the normlessness scales brings us back to Durkheim. Clearly, they do not measure any structural version of anomie, although there are ways of approximating such a version through the use of these scales; this can be done either by aggregating individual responses in a given "community" of persons, thus estimating the state of the normative order faced by any individual (Johnson, 1960), or by deriving indices of consensus regarding these questions (Rossi & Berk, 1985). A further Durkheimian question concerns a debate about where the emphasis should lie in conceptions of anomie. A famous analysis by Merton (1957) made anomie a matter of instrumental failure. That is, anomie was a normative breakdown occasioned by disjunction between culturally prescribed values and limited available means for achieving them, hence the threat of "normlessness" in the sense proposed in this section: the threat of individual readiness to use nonnormative means, the widespread perception of such a threat, and the consequent social distrust. But Parsons (1968, pp. 316–317) claimed that the focus should be on "meaninglessness" rather than on instrumental "normlessness." Arguing that anomie has become "one of the small number of truly central concepts of contemporary social science," Parsons proceeded to specify that "anomie may be considered that state of a social system which makes a particular class of members consider exertion for success meaningless, not because they lack capacity or opportunity to achieve what is wanted, but because they lack a clear definition of what is desirable."

The following scales, presented in chronological order, are primarily measures of normlessness:

7. Anomia (Srole, 1956)
8. Normlessness (Dean, 1961)
9. Anomy (McClosky & Schaar, 1965)
10. Normlessness (Neal & Groat, 1974)
11. Doubt about Trustworthiness of People (Scheussler, 1982)
12. Normlessness (Kohn & Schooler, 1983)

The scales vary, in some cases only slightly, in emphasis.

Srole's Anomia Scale touches on several issues and feelings including pessimism ("The lot of the average person is getting worse"), meaninglessness and valuelessness ("You sometimes can't help wondering whether anything is worthwhile"), cynicism and lack of morality ("To make money, there are no right and wrong ways anymore, only easy and hard ways"). Dean's scale emphasizes normlessness due to cultural pluralism and rapid social change: "People's ideas change so much that I wonder if we will ever have anything to depend on," "Everything is relative, and there just aren't any definite rules to live by." McClosky and Schaar's items cover similar territory: "Everything changes so quickly these days that I often have trouble deciding which are the right rules to follow," "People were better off in the old days when everyone knew just how he was [they were] supposed to act." Neal and Groat emphasize the need to engage in immoral or undesirable behavior if one's goals are to be obtained: "Those running our government must hush up many things that go on behind the scenes if they wish to stay in office," "In getting a job promotion, some degree of 'apple polishing' is required." Scheussler's scale has to do with inability to trust others because of their selfishness: "Many people are friendly only because they want something from you." Finally, Kohn and Schooler's scale emphasizes cynicism and amorality: "If something works, it doesn't matter if it's right or wrong."

Anomia

(Srole, 1956)

Variable

Anomia was viewed by Srole as an individual's generalized, pervasive sense of social malintegration or "self–others alienation" (vs. self–others belongingness).

Description

This scale was operationalized in a way that emphasizes normlessness. The scale consists of five items, each measuring one aspect of anomia. They are presented as opinion statements, with possible answers of "agree," "disagree," and "can't decide." Only an unequivocal "agree" receives a score of 1. The possible range of scores, therefore, is 0 (low anomia) to 5 (high anomia). The scale can easily be administered by either respondents or interviewers.

Sample

The sample was drawn from Springfield, Massachusetts. Since the study measured attitudes toward minority groups, members of minority groups were excluded and the sample was limited to white, Christian, native-born residents who used mass transit. The sampling design combined random selection with age–sex quotas. There were 401 people between the ages of 16 and 69 (average age: 40.3).

The distribution of the original sample of 401 is given here in percentage terms (average score = 2.1) along with data on a random sample of 981 Los Angeles adults (average score = 1.7) in 1961 (Miller & Butler, 1966).

| | Anomia score | | Sample | |
			Springfield (%)	Los Angeles (%)
(Low)	0		16	29
	1		25	24
	2		20	17
	3		21	14
	4		13	9
(High)	5		5	7
		Total	100	100

Reliability

Internal Consistency

The unidimensionality of the anomia scale was originally assessed by latent structure analysis and was found to satisfy the criteria. In addition, in a study in New York City, it was determined that the anomia items satisfied the criteria of a Guttman scale. No quantitative estimates or test–retest data were reported originally, but subsequent studies (e.g., Abrahamson, 1980; Miller & Butler, 1966; Streuning & Richardson, 1965) have demonstrated the unidimensionality of these items using factor analytic procedures. Bell (1957) reported a coefficient of reproducibility of .90 and a coefficient of stability of .65. The average factor loading of the five anomia items on the first principal component in the Abrahamson study was .56. The average item intercorrelation in the Miller and Butler study was .30.

Test–Retest

No data were reported.

Validity

Convergent

Srole said originally that "a clue to [the scale's] validity is found in a datum from the current NYC study, involving a geographic probability sample of 1660 resident adults. A single indicator of latent suicide tendency was the agree–disagree item: 'You sometimes can't help wondering whether anything is worthwhile anymore.' The correlation between this item and the Anomia scale score is . . . .50." Bell (1957) found the Anomia Scale to relate significantly to social isolation. In Abrahamson's (1980) rather complex study, lottery winnings were correlated with anomia. There was a small direct path between size of winnings and anomia, indicating a weak (hypothesized) tendency for a rapid increase in affluence to create greater anomia. However,

> the larger indirect effects of the size of winnings tend to be anomia-reducing. By spurring a more permissive orientation toward gratifications and by depressing future attainment aspirations, larger winnings lead to lower anomia. . . . Thus, when anomia is interpreted as indicating anomie at an individual level, the strongest findings . . . seem to contradict the main thrust of Durkheim's anomie of affluence thesis. (p. 56)

Discriminant

Dworkin (1979) used the anomia scale in a study of feminist ideology formation. Using a sample of women from a small midwestern city, she tested the relative importance of (1) social structural conditions, (2) social psychological states (including anomia), and (3) peer variables as determinants of feminist attitudes. In general, social psychological variables (e.g., political orientation, status concern, experience of discrimination, and subjective status consistency) were related to feminism, but (despite its high reliability) the Srole Anomia Scale was not, suggesting some distinctness.

Location

Srole, L. (1956). Social integration and certain corollaries. *American Sociological Review*, **21**, 709–716.

Results and Comments

The early hypothesis that anomia would be related to negative attitudes toward minorities was confirmed in the Springfield sample ($r = .43$). When scores on authoritarianism were partialled out, the correlation was reduced from .43 to .35, indicating that the relationship between anomia (A) and minority attitudes (M) is somewhat independent of authoritarianism (F). Holding A constant, in contrast, reduces the correlation between F and M from .29 to .12. The correlation between F and M seems to be partially due to anomia.

Anomia was inversely related to SES. Consistent with this, Rose (1962) applied the items to 71 heads of organizations in Minnesota and found that only 3% of them agreed with any of the Srole items vs. 20% of a cross section of married people in Minneapolis–St. Paul. Angell (1962) also found a significant negative correlation between the anomia scale and occupational status ($r = -.25$), income ($-.19$), and education ($-.33$) in a cross-section of Detroit residents. Older people ($r = .16$) and blacks ($r = .25$) also scored higher on the scale.

Lenski and Leggett (1960) presented a strong case that the scale was highly susceptible to agreement response set. Richard Christie (personal communication) reports that the following five negatively scored items (four of which were devised by Srole but not included in the scale) may be useful in offsetting this response set:

1. Most people can still be depended upon to come through in a pinch.
2. If you try hard enough, you can usually get what you want.
3. Most people will go out of their way to help someone else.
4. The average man is probably better off today than he ever was.
5. Even today, the way that you make money is more important than how much you make.

Anomia

(Score 1 for agreement with each item)

	Agreement in the Miller & Butler study (%)
1. There's little use writing public officials because they often aren't really interested in the problems of the average man.	39
AGREE DISAGREE	
2. Nowadays a person has to live pretty much for today and let tomorrow take care of itself.	29
3. In spite of what some people say, the lot of the average person is getting worse, not better.	33
4. It's hardly fair to bring children into the world with the way things look for the future.	23
5. These days a person doesn't really know whom he [or she] can count on.	50

Four new items used in enlarging the scale are:

6. Most people really don't care what happens to the next fellow [to others].

7. Next to health, money is the most important thing in life.

8. You sometimes can't help wondering whether anything is worthwhile.

9. To make money there are no right and wrong ways anymore, only easy and hard ways.

Note: The first of the five original items is often changed to read: Most public officials (people in public offices) are not really interested in the problems of the average person. Nonsexist wordings are suggested in brackets for some of the other items.

Normlessness

(Dean, 1961)

Variable

Dean developed a three-part general alienation measure focusing on three important components of alienation, one of which was normlessness.

Description

Item selection was described in relation to Dean's powerlessness scale (reviewed earlier). There are six normlessness items on the final scale (from the 24-item alienation scale), each in five-point Likert format ranging from 4 (strongly agree) to 0 (strongly disagree); five of the items are reverse scored. Scale scores can vary from 0 (lowest normlessness) to 24 (highest normlessness).

Sample

The sample and normative data were described in the section on powerlessness.

Reliability

Internal Consistency

The reliabilities of the subscales, tested by the split-half method and corrected by the Spearman–Brown formula, were reported in the section on powerlessness. For normlessness, the reliability was .73. Normlessness correlated .67 with powerlessness, .54 with social isolation, and .80 with the total alienation score.

Test–Retest

No data were reported.

Validity

Convergent

The total scale correlated in the .30s with Srole's Anomia Scale and Nettler's (1957) Alienation Scale. It was hypothesized that (1) alienation and each of its components would correlate negatively with social status, (2) advancing age would be positively correlated with alienation, and (3) rural background would correlate negatively with alienation. While in most instances the hypotheses were sustained at significant levels, the correlation coefficients were generally low.

The component and total scores were correlated with the F scale (authoritarianism) in a sample of 73 college students. The result for normlessness was $r = .33$.

Location

Dean, D. (1961). Alienation: Its meaning and measurement. *American Sociological Review*, **26**, 753–758.

Results and Comments

The overall Dean alienation scale has continued to be used, but few studies seem to have focused specifically on the normlessness subscale.

Normlessness Items

Below are some statements regarding public issues, with which some people agree and others disagree. Please give us your own opinion about these items (i.e., whether you agree or disagree with the items as they stand).

Please check in the appropriate blank, as follows:

_____ A (Strongly Agree)
_____ a (Agree)
_____ U (Uncertain)
_____ d (Disagree)
_____ D (Strongly Disagree)

4. The end often justifies the means.

____ A   ____ a   ____ U   ____ d   ____ D

7. People's ideas change so much that I wonder if we'll ever have anything to depend on.
10. Everything is relative, and there just aren't any definite rules to live by.
12. I often wonder what the meaning of life really is.
16. The only thing one can be sure of today is that he can be sure of nothing.
19. With so many religions abroad, one doesn't really know which to believe.

Note: Item numbers indicate placement in the general alienation questionnaire. See entries under powerlessness and social isolation for the other numbered items.

Anomy

(McClosky & Schaar, 1965)

Variable

The authors define anomy as normlessness, revising the traditional sociological model (i.e., Durkheim's), which is based on the assumption that social conditions give rise to certain feelings (anomy) that in turn cause certain kinds of behavior (by giving equal weight to psychological variables that might cause anomy).

Description

The author's intention was to examine personality variables that might cause anomy. The nine-item anomy scale was one of several measures included in a large questionnaire. Answers to each item were either "agree" or "disagree," with one point given for each agree response. Scores ranged from 0 (low anomy) to 9 (high anomy). People scoring in the 6–9 range were considered anomic, the middle group scored in the 3–5 range, and the nonanomic respondents scored 0–2. The questionnaire was self-administered, but it could also be administered by an interviewer.

The original source of the items was not given. Through preliminary screening and pretesting, a large pool of items was reduced and given to a sample of 273 Minnesota adults. Their responses were examined for internal consistency, subjected to a Guttman reproducibility procedure, and finally reduced to nine items.

Sample

There were originally two samples. One was a cross-section of the population of Minnesota, designed by the Minnesota Poll in 1955, with an *n* of 1082. The other was a national sample drawn and administered by the Gallup polling organization in 1958 with an *n* of 1484.

The following distribution of scores was obtained in two early samples:

	National sample (%)	Minnesota sample (%)
Low (0–2)	26	38
Medium (3–5)	39	34
High (6–9)	35	28
Total	100	100

Reliability

Internal Consistency

The corrected split-half reliability coefficient was .76. The reproducibility coefficient for the national sample was .80; on another national sample of 3020 "political influentials" the reproducibility coefficient was .83. More recently, Taub, Surgeon, Lindholm, Betts, and Bridges (1977) reported a Cronbach α of .71 for a five-item version of the scale.

Validity

Convergent

The scale was judged by several groups of graduate students in political science and psychology, and by 40 Fellows at the Center for Advanced Study in the Behavioral Sciences (Stanford). For each item, the proportion of affirmative judgments (i.e., the proportion—not stated in the article—agreeing that the item embodies some aspect of anomy) was high enough to satisfy the authors. Some evidence for convergent (but not discriminant) validity is reproduced in the table below listing correlations between anomy and differently named constructs.

	National sample	Minnesota sample
Alienation	.60	.58
Bewilderment	NA	.62
Pessimism	.50	.43
Political Impotence	.54	.55
Political Cynicism	.59	.62
Life Satisfaction	− .41	− .39

Discriminant

None of the authors' results were significantly affected when measures of acquiescence, social status, and social frustration were introduced as controls.

Location

McClosky, H., & Schaar, J. H. (1965). Psychological dimensions of anomy. *American Sociological Review,* **30,** 14–40.

Results and Comments

The authors summarized their original studies as follows:

> In order to determine the efficacy of psychological, as opposed to sociological, factors in producing anomie three groups of measures were correlated with anomic feeling. It was found that individuals whose cognitive capacity was deficient (as indicated by high scores on Mysticism and Acquiescence; and low scores on Education, Intellectuality, and Awareness) tended to score high on anomie. It was also found that individuals predisposed to maladjustive emotional states (such as inflexibility, strong anxiety and aggression, and low ego strength) are high on anomie. Finally, those individuals who held extreme beliefs and had a rejective attitude towards people were also found to be high on anomie. All of these correlations were strong and in the predicted direction.

In the study by Taub *et al.* (1977) mentioned above, residents of a South Side Chicago neighborhood were studied using the anomy scale. It was found that organizational and social linkages of South Shore residents extended more frequently outside the community than within it, and that residents more often belonged to wide-area based organizations than to locally based ones. Nevertheless, this situation did not produce high anomie; there was "only a slight relationship between local visiting patterns, church attendance, membership in local voluntary associations, and anomie, once socioeconomic variables such as education and employment in large corporations or large organizations were controlled for" (p. 430).

Freudenburg (1984) compared adolescents and adults in a "booming" community to those in control communities with regard to support for energy development, satisfaction with locality, overall quality of life, and alienation (the latter being operationalized by the anomy scale). Adults generally had lower levels of anomy than adolescents. When length of residence was added as a control variable, the newcomer youths in the boomtown actually have a lower level of alienation than the newcomers in the three comparison communities, albeit by a nonsignificant margin, while the boomtown–other difference among long-time adolescent residents is even stronger than would have been expected on the basis of community-wide data (p. 700).

Anomy Scale

1. With everything so uncertain these days, it almost seems as though anything could happen.

AGREE   DISAGREE

2. What is lacking in the world today is the old kind of friendship that lasted for a lifetime.

3. With everything in such a state of disorder, it's hard for a person to know where he stands from one day to the next.

4. Everything changes so quickly these days that I often have trouble deciding which are the right rules to follow.

5. I often feel that many things our parents stood for are just going to ruin before our very eyes.

6. The trouble with the world today is that most people really don't believe in anything.

7. I often feel awkward and out of place.

8. People were better off in the old days when everyone knew just how he was expected to act.

9. It seems to me that other people find it easier to decide what is right than I do.

Normlessness

(Neal & Groat, 1974)

Variable

Following Seeman, Neal and Groat defined normlessness as "a high expectancy that socially unapproved behavior is necessary in goal attainment," thus emphasizing the "necessity of either coercion or deception in achieving socially desired political or economic goals."

Description

The scale is composed of eight items with response categories that range from "strongly agree" to "strongly disagree," responded to on a four-point continuum. Scores can range from a low of 8 (for respondents who disagree with all of the normlessness items) to 32 (high normlessness). In the study by Neal and Groat (1974), the items were self-administered as part of a mail questionnaire.

Sample

The reader should see the sample information provided earlier in connection with Neal and Groat's Powerlessness Scale.

Reliability

Internal Consistency

A principal factor analysis with oblique rotation revealed the following factor loadings for each item (orthogonal varimax rotation yielded similar results):

	Factor loadings	
	1963	1971
Item 1	.78	.50
Item 2	.52	.59
Item 3	.44	.63
Item 4	.56	.49
Item 5	.39	.45
Item 6	.33	.51
Item 7*	.56	.27
Item 8*	.11	.32

*Factor loadings too low, item deleted from analysis.

The Ω reliability coefficient for 1963 was .69; and for 1971, .69.

Test–Retest

The factor scores on normlessness obtained in the 1963 sample correlated .40 with those of the 1971 sample. This relatively high level of correspondence over 8 years suggests that the items tap "world views which have a high degree of consistency and stability through time" (Zeller *et al.*, 1980, p. 1201).

Validity

Convergent

Evidence of validity is displayed by the fact that the 1971 normlessness scores were significantly related (in the hypothesized direction) to selected socioeconomic and demographic variables. Low levels of education, husband's occupational status, and family income were associated with higher levels of normlessness.

Discriminant

No information was presented.

Location

Groat, H. T., & Neal, A. (1967). Social psychological correlates of urban fertility. *American Sociological Review, 32,* 945–959.
Neal, A., & Groat, H. T. (1974). Social class correlates of stability and change in levels of alienation. *Sociological Quarterly, 15,* 548–558.

Results and Comments

The initial study focused on the relationship between various forms of alienation and fertility behaviors. The hypothesis that high levels of normlessness would be related to high levels of fertility was supported. Those who scored high on normlessness had an average of 4.1 children while those who scored low had a mean of 3.6. This relationship is significant at the .02 level ($t = 2.1$) and is as prominent as the difference between Catholic and Protestant women. Normlessness operates differentially by religion: Catholics high in normlessness tend to be high in fertility, while among Protestants the differences are minimal.

The longitudinal study revealed the stability of relatively high levels of normlessness among working-class wives and the stability of relatively low levels of normlessness among middle-class wives. The socioeconomic variables did not account for the change in scores over time. These results were interpreted as support for a structural argument for the genesis of differential levels of alienation by socioeconomic status.

The study published in 1980 revealed a relatively high level of consistency in normlessness over a period of 8 years as well as evidence of increasing levels of normlessness. Of the four types of alienation studied (powerlessness, meaninglessness, social isolation, and normlessness), normlessness showed the greatest degree of increase.

Normlessness

1. In getting a good-paying job, it's necessary to exaggerate one's abilities (or personal merits).

| STRONGLY AGREE | AGREE | DISAGREE | STRONGLY DISAGREE |

2. In getting a job promotion, some degree of "apple polishing" is required.
3. In order to get elected to public office, a candidate must make promises he [or she] does not intend to keep.
4. Having "pull" is more important than ability in getting a government job.
5. Success in business can easily be achieved without taking advantage of gullible people.*
6. Those running our government must hush up many things that go on behind the scenes if they wish to stay in office.
7. In order to have a good income, salesmen must use high pressure salesmanship.
8. Those elected to public office have to serve special interests (e.g., big business or labor) as well as the public's interests.

Note: Item 5 is reverse-scored.

Doubt About Trustworthiness of People

(Scheussler, 1982)

Variable

This scale measures the extent to which people doubt that others are "generally fair, forthright, and honest" in their everyday lives.

Description

Eight items comprise the scale (five worded to affirm doubt, three to affirm trustworthiness). Respondents answer with either "agree" or "disagree" and scores range from 0 (low doubt) to 8 (high doubt) with a mean per item of .50. High scorers have doubts while low scorers feel that people are basically trustworthy. Scheussler based his study on interviews, but the scale could easily be adapted for self-administration.

Sample

A random sample of 1500 United States households was drawn in September 1974, and one adult was randomly selected from each. A relatively low response rate (61%) was explained by both the length of the questionnaire and its content. Completion rates differed by region (it was lower in the Pacific region), size of metropolitan area (higher in small areas), and type of area (higher in nonmetropolitan areas).

Reliability

Internal Consistency

The individual items had the following item–total correlations and factor loadings:

	Keyed response	% Keyed response	Item–total correlation	Factor loading
Item 1	Agree	63	.52	.58
Item 2	Agree	51	.57	.64
Item 3	Disagree	35	.56	.63
Item 4	Disagree	65	.39	.44
Item 5	Disagree	26	.49	.55
Item 6	Agree	48	.54	.62
Item 7	Agree	62	.56	.64
Item 8	Agree	47	.47	.53

The scale has an α reliability of .80 and a Tucker–Lewis reliability of .86. The missing response rate was 3.3%. Overall, the author considered the doubt about trustworthiness of people scale to be "good" in comparison to the other 11 scales constructed in the same study.

Validity

Convergent

Initially, this scale was intended to measure the feeling that people are untrustworthy (social distrust). The scale's correlations with different tests confirm this interpretation, but the author decided on the present more precise title for the scale. The trustworthiness scale correlates highly ($r = .77$, with one common item) with scores based on three items from Rosenberg's scale for measuring faith in people. The author concluded that the two scales measure closely similar feelings, if not exactly the same feeling.

Discriminant

No information reported, although the scale was derived from a large multidimensional item pool via factor analysis.

Location

Scheussler, K. (1982). *Measuring social life feelings*. San Francisco: Jossey–Bass.

Results and Comments

The general goal of this research was to construct standard sociological scales. The author found a close correspondence between the 12 Social Life Feeling scales and the more numerous scales found in the literature. This was taken as an indication that only 12 social life feelings have been operationally distinguished, and therefore, "twelve scales would suffice for maintaining those operational distinctions."

The following characteristics were associated with higher scores on the Doubt About Trustworthiness of People Scale: being young, divorced and separated, low in education, low in income, and nonwhite.

Social Life Feeling Scale 2: Doubt About the Trustworthiness of People

1. It is hard to figure out who you can really trust these days.

       AGREE   DISAGREE

2. There are few people in this world you can trust, when you get right down to it.
3. Most people can be trusted.*
4. Strangers can generally be trusted.*
5. Most people are fair in their dealings with others.*
6. Most people don't really care what happens to the next fellow.
7. Too many people in our society are just out for themselves.
8. Many people are friendly only because they want something from you.

   Note: Agree answers score 1 point; disagree answers score 0. Items followed by an asterisk are reverse-scored.

Normlessness

(Kohn & Schooler, 1983)

Variable

Kohn and Schooler base their index on Seeman's conceptualization, with an operationalization that includes a continuum ranging from the individual's belief that it is "acceptable to do whatever [one] can get away with" to "holding responsible moral standards" (1983, p. 87).

Description

Normlessness, a derivative of Durkheim's concept of anomie, is defined by Seeman as a situation in which "there is a high expectancy that socially unapproved behaviors are required to achieve given goals." Four items comprise a Guttman scale, these items being scored on an agree–disagree (or 0–1) basis. Scores range from 0 (low normlessness) to 4 (high normlessness).

Sample

See sample description provided earlier in this chapter in connection with the Kohn and Schooler Powerlessness Scale.

Reliability

Internal Consistency

The Normlessness Scale has a reproducibility in the .90s, scalability in the .70s, and essentially random patterns of error.

Test–Retest

No information was located.

Validity

Convergent

The Normlessness Scale is one of five scales that comprise a larger measure of alienation. A second-order measurement model of alienation was developed by Roberts (1987) using Kohn and Schooler's data. The path of the second-order concept (alienation) to the first-order concept (normlessness) was .30 in 1964 and .48 in 1974. The alienation measures for the two time periods correlated .52. The paths of the first-order concepts to indicators are given in Table 1.

Discriminant

No data were discussed.

Table 1

Paths: First-Order Concept (Normlessness)
to Indicators

	1964	1974
Item 1	.59	.65
Item 2	.58	.59
Item 3	.44	.30
Item 4	.32	.25

Source: Kohn and Schooler (1983).

Location

Kohn, M., & Schooler, C. (1983). *Work and personality: An inquiry into the impact of social stratification*. Norwood, NJ: Ablex. See especially Chapter 4.

Results and Comments

The scale was administered as part of an interview by the field staff of NORC, but the items could be adapted for self-administration. The reader should review the results reported for the Kohn and Schooler Powerlessness Scale (described earlier), since the normlessness index was used in the same investigation.

Ownership was found to be only weakly related to normlessness ($r = -.03$), although position in the supervisory hierarchy was somewhat more strongly correlated ($r = -.09$). Bureaucratization (the index for division of labor) was related ($r = -.11$), but in the direction opposite the hypothesis. Occupational self-direction was more consistently related to normlessness: Close supervision ($r = .23$); routinized work ($r = .13$); and work of little substantive complexity ($r = -.26$) were all significantly related. The introduction of statistical controls reduced these correlations, but left statistically significant, nontrivial relationships. The authors concluded that "in this large-scale, capitalist system, control over the product of one's labor (ownership and hierarchical position) has only an indirect effect on alienation, whereas control over work process (closeness of supervision, routinization, and substantive complexity) has an appreciable direct effect on . . . normlessness" (1983, p. 96). Moreover, there is evidence for a causal effect of control over work on normlessness. In effect, a learning generalization process is proposed, where the "lessons of the job are generalized to men's views of themselves and of the larger society" (Slomczynski, Miller, & Kohn, 1981, p. 721). The authors suggest caution regarding the generalization of the findings beyond the United States or beyond the time the data were collected.

Kohn and Schooler (1969) used a slightly different normlessness scale in their earlier study based on 1964 data. Here, five items (instead of four) made up the scale "criteria of morality." The items had the following factor loadings:

	Factor Loadings
Item 1	.66
Item 2	.54
Item 3	.57
Item 4	.51
Item 5*	.36

*Item 5 is not included in the Normlessness Scale presented below.

Kohn and Schooler (1973) analyzed the relationship between normlessness and work experience with the intention of determining the direction of causality. They used the "criteria of morality" scale, which was found to have a multiple–partial correlation with a set of 12 occupational conditions of .20 (which was reduced to .16 when controls were included in the analysis). When the direction of causality was assessed, the results were clear: The effect of "criteria of morality" on job complexity was not significant (standardized β-coefficient of .01), while that of job complexity on criteria of morality was significant (β of .14). Therefore, the authors concluded that the results supported a work generalization model.

Slomczynski *et al.* (1981) analyzed normlessness using the original 1964 United States sample and the 1974 follow-up sample (described above) and a 1978 Polish survey that was designed to be an "exact replication of the main parts of the U.S. study." The construction of a measurement model of "standards of morality" for the Polish data was somewhat problematic (there was no clear factor present in the orthogonal exploratory factor analysis) but a satisfactory model was developed. The correlates of social stratification position with standards of morality were very similar in the two countries: Holding a higher position was associated with having personally responsible standards of morality. Again, the generalizability of work experience is supported, here for both capitalist and socialist societies.

Normlessness

1. It's all right to do anything you want as long as you stay out of trouble.

   AGREE   DISAGREE

2. It's all right to get around the law as long as you don't actually break it.
3. If something works, it doesn't matter if it's right or wrong.
4. Do you believe that it's all right to do whatever the law allows, or are there some things that are wrong even if they are legal?

   WHATEVER LAW ALLOWS   SOME THINGS ARE WRONG EVEN
                                                       IF LEGAL

Meaninglessness Measures

Unfortunately, the kind of meaninglessness or lack of goal clarity emphasized by Parsons (1968) has not received much attention. Three rather different scales to tap the meaninglessness domain have been included here:

13. Meaninglessness (Neal & Groat, 1974),
14. Sense of Coherence (Antonovsky, 1987), and
15. Purpose in Life Test (Crumbaugh, 1968).

These scales begin to sketch the meaninglessness component of alienation, defined in terms of the absence of clear goals, cognitive clarity, and predictability; but it will be noted that their contents shade off in other directions as well.

Thus, although the Neal and Groat scale includes such items as "The international situation is so complex that it just confuses a person to think about it," it also includes less focused items which cause the scale to approximate a "generalized alienation" version of meaningless. That is, it becomes more or less a "life is meaningless" scale by including such items as "Most people lead lives of quiet desperation" and "One should live for today and let tomorrow take care of itself." There are a number of scales that go explicitly in this direction, measuring generalized life satisfaction, optimism versus hopelessness, and the like, and some have been included below (under the heading of generalized alienation). For the moment, however, the point is that "meaninglessness" here has a more delimited connotation than exhibited, for example, in the scaling work of Reker,

Peacock, and Wong (1987) on "meaninglessness." Obviously, the choice of scales depends on one's goals; and once again, it is essential to probe deeper than a scale's name.

In Antonovsky's work, the phrase "sense of coherence" carries the cognitive emphasis in "meaninglessness," as does the definition that he provides: ". . . the extent to which one perceives the stimuli that confront one, deriving from the internal and external environments, as making cognitive sense, as information that is ordered, consistent, structured and clear . . ." (pp. 16–17). The three subdimensions of the sense of coherence are (1) comprehensibility, (2) manageability, and (3) meaningfulness. So far as item content is concerned, the last of these domains sometimes brings the scale closer to a generalized sense of meaninglessness (e.g., "When you think about your life (do you) feel how good it is to be alive (or) ask yourself why you exist at all?"). The manageability component brings the content close to the powerlessness–competence issues discussed above. In these respects, the "sense of coherence" scale begins to resemble (as Antonovsky points out) the measurement of alienation and "hardiness" in the work of Kobasa (1981) and Maddi, Kobasa, and Hoover (1979), since it is a composite measure of the senses of control, commitment, and challenge in life (see "generalized alienation" below).

Finally, Crumbaugh's (1968) purpose-in-life test emphasizes another important aspect of meaninglessness: being without desirable and sensible goals. But it, too, brings in additional issues: control, freedom, and boredom, for example. In general, then, the three scales reviewed here go some way toward mapping the meaninglessness component of alienation, but more theoretical and empirical refinement is needed.

Meaninglessness

(Neal & Groat, 1974)

Variable

Meaninglessness is defined as an individual's perception that social and political events are "overwhelmingly complex, without purpose, and lacking in predictability."

Description

The scale is composed of nine items with response categories ranging over a four-point continuum: strongly agree, agree, disagree, strongly disagree. All items are keyed so that agreement equals high meaninglessness (lowest score, 9; highest score, 36).

Sample

The reader should see the Sample information provided in connection with the Neal and Groat Powerlessness Scale (discussed earlier in this chapter).

Reliability

Internal Consistency

A principal factor analysis with oblique rotation revealed the following factor loadings for each item (orthogonal varimax rotation yielded similar results):

| | Factor loadings | |
	1963	1971
Item 1	.40	.67
Item 2	.33	.68
Item 3	.52	.43
Item 4	.45	.30
Item 5*	.28	.47
Item 6*	.17	.40
Item 7*	.23	.25
Item 8*	.27	.14
Item 9*	.31	.05

*Factor loadings too low, item deleted from analysis.

The Ω reliability coefficient for 1963 was .64; and for 1971, .65.

Test–Retest

The factor scores on meaninglessness obtained in the 1963 sample correlated .52 with those of the 1971 sample. This high level of correspondence over 8 years suggests that the items tap "world views which have a high degree of consistency and stability through time" (Zeller, Neal, & Groat, 1980, p. 1201).

Validity

Convergent

The 1971 meaninglessness scores were significantly related (in the hypothesized direction) to selected socioeconomic and demographic variables. Low levels of education, husband's occupational status, and family income were associated with higher levels of meaninglessness.

Location

Neal, A., & Groat, H. T. (1974). Social class correlates of stability and change in levels of alienation. *Sociological Quarterly, 15,* 548–558.

Results and Comments

The initial study focused on the relationship between various forms of alienation and fertility behaviors. The hypothesis that high levels of meaninglessness would be related to high levels of fertility was supported. Those who scored highest on meaninglessness had an average of 4.38 children while those who scored low had a mean of 3.73. This relationship is significant at the .01 level ($t = 2.60$) and is greater than the difference between Catholic and Protestant women. In fact, "the obtained differentials by high and low meaninglessness within the Protestant ($d = .76$) and Catholic ($d = .58$) categories are greater than the overall differences between the religious groupings" (Groat & Neal, 1967, p. 951). Thus, meaninglessness is related to the number of children for Protestants, and less strikingly for Catholics.

The longitudinal study revealed a relatively high level of consistency in meaninglessness over a period of 8 years as well as evidence of increasing levels of meaninglessness.

Meaninglessness

1. It's hard to sleep nights when you think about recurrent crises in the world and what would happen if they exploded.

STRONGLY   AGREE   DISAGREE   STRONGLY
AGREE   DISAGREE

2. The tensions in the world today make one wonder whether he [or she] will be around in a few years or not.

3. The international situation is so complex that it just confuses a person to think about it.

4. The only thing one can be sure of today is that he [or she] can be sure of nothing.

5. Current political events have taken an unpredictable and destructive course.

6. In spite of what some people say, the lot of the average man [person] is getting worse not better.

7. Most people live lives of quiet desperation.

8. With so many religions around, one really doesn't know which one to believe.

9. One should live for today and let tomorrow take care of itself.

Note: Bracketed insertions suggest corrections of sexist wording.

Sense of Coherence

(Antonovsky, 1987)

Variable

Sense of coherence is a "global orientation that expresses the extent to which one has a pervasive, enduring though dynamic feeling of confidence" (p. 19).

Description

The sense of coherence has three core components: comprehensibility, or that the stimuli encountered in the course of living are structured, predictable, and explicable; manageability, or that the resources are available to one to meet the demands posed by these stimuli; and meaningfulness, or that these demands serve as challenges, worthy of investment and engagement (Antonovsky, 1987, p. 19). The three core components are not seen as equally important: The meaningfulness component is emphasized. The 29-item scale refers to a wide variety of stimuli and situations. These items were constructed using the "facet design" developed by Guttman to vary the content systematically along the dimensions of modality, source, demand (subject), time, and sense of coherence components. Each question has a seven-point response scale (ranging, for example, from "never have this feeling" to "always have this feeling"). Only the extremes of the continuum are labeled, the intermediate numerical positions being left unidentified (see scale description below). Scores vary from 29 (low sense of coherence) to 203 (high sense of coherence).

Sample

A pilot study was undertaken to aid in the process of concept operationalization. No concern for representativeness was involved at this stage. Fifty-one persons who had undergone severe trauma and were judged to be functioning "remarkably well" were interviewed in their homes in Israel. Respondents ranged in age from their teens to age 91 and included 51 who were male and 40 who were female. Twelve were born in Israel, 19 in Europe, and 20 in North Africa and the Middle East. A wide range of occupational and family statuses was represented, and the sample was relatively heterogenous, except for the fact that all respondents were Jewish.

Once completed, the scale was administered to several different samples (by both Antonovsky and his colleagues). The populations studied include an Israeli national sample, New York state production workers, United States undergraduate students (three separate samples), Israeli army officer trainees (three separate samples), and health workers (three separate samples). The total n in these samples was 1965. The scores obtained in some of the larger samples are given below.

Reliability

Internal Consistency

Cronbach α values for each of the above-mentioned samples are consistently high (range = .84–.93), reflecting a "respectable degree of internal consistency and the reliability of the instrument" (Antonovsky, 1987, p. 82).

Population	n	Range	Mean	SD	Coeff. of Var.	Cronbach's α
Israeli civilians	297	90–189	137	20	.15	.84
New York workers	111	62–189	133	27	.20	.93
United States undergrads	336	63–176	133	20	.15	.88
Israeli army officer trainees	338	90–199	160	17	.10	.88
Health workers in Edmonton	108	101–192	149	17	.12	.88

Validity

Convergent and Discriminant

Antonovsky and three colleagues read the in-depth interviews and classified respondents as strong, moderate, or weak on SOC in order to arrive at consensual validity. There was a "reasonable degree of agreement in classification" (p. 66). Before the scale was administered to respondents, four of Antonovsky's colleagues reviewed it for item appropriateness, in order to enhance face and content validity.

Criterion

Criterion validity is indicated by the evidence produced by independent researchers at the University of California, San Diego (Rumbaut, Anderson, & Kaplan, in press), who constructed a battery of 100 SOC items. Factor analysis produced a 22-item index, which proved to have internal consistency, convergent validity, and discriminant validity. Rumbaut administered his SOC scale and Antonovsky's SOC scale to a sample of 336 undergraduate students and found Cronbach α values of .90 and .88 respectively, and a correlation of .64 between the two scales. In addition, he found evidence of discriminant validity in the following correlations:

	Antonovsky's SOC	Rumbaut's SOC
Rotter's I-E Scale	.39	.43
Sarason Test Anxiety Scale	−.21	−.20

The rank order of means on SOC for the various populations studied (see table on page 332) conform to theoretical expectations, and thereby further supports the scale's validity.

Self-reports of health status in the Israeli national sample, which are related to SOC in the predicted direction, confirm the scale's predictive validity.

Location

Antonovsky, A. (1987). *Unraveling the mystery of health*. San Francisco: Jossey–Bass.

Results and Comments

"The central thesis of the salutogenic model is that a strong SOC is crucial to successful coping with the ubiquitous stressors of living and hence to health maintenance" (Antonovsky, 1987, p. 164). The results thus far have been consistent with the model. Dana (1985) reported SOC scores to be consistently and significantly related to positive health measures and negatively related to illness measures. Shortened versions of SOC were found to be related to drinking patterns (alcoholics was significantly lower on SOC) and to the Trait Scale of the Spielberger State-Trait Anxiety Inventory. Yet the author cautions that "judgement of the track record of the SOC scale must . . . be held in abeyance until published reports of the psychometric properties of the scale appear in refereed journals. There is, however, sufficient evidence to warrant the tentative conclusion that the scale is an adequate representation of the SOC construct" (p. 86), the evidence having been obtained through research in several societies.

Orientation to Life

*1. When you talk to people, do you have the feeling that they don't understand you?

| 1 | 2 | 3 | 4 | 5 | 6 | 7 |

NEVER HAVE   ALWAYS HAVE
THAT FEELING   THAT FEELING

2. In the past, when you had to do something which depends upon cooperation with others, did you have the feeling that it: surely wouldn't get done (surely would get done)?

3. Think of the people with whom you come into contact daily, aside from the ones to whom you feel closest. How well do you know most of them? you feel that they're strangers (you know them very well)

*4. Do you have the feeling that you don't really care about what goes on around you? very seldom or never (very often)

*5. Has it happened in the past that you were surprised by the behavior of people whom you thought you knew well? never happened (always happened)

*6. Has it happened that people whom you counted on disappointed you? [see item 5]

*7. Life is: full of interest (completely routine).

8. Until now your life has had: no clear goals or purpose at all (very clear goals and purpose).

9. Do you have the feeling that you're being treated unfairly? very often (very seldom or never)

10. In the past ten years your life has been: full of changes without your knowing what will happen next (completely consistent and clear).

*11. Most of the things you do in the future will probably be: completely fascinating (deadly boring).

12. Do you have the feeling that you are in an unfamiliar situation and don't know what to do? [see item 9]

*13. What best describes how you see life: one can always find a solution to painful things in life (there is no solution to painful things in life).

*14. When you think about your life, you very often: feel how good it is to be alive (ask yourself why you exist at all).

15. When you face a difficult problem, the choice of a solution is: always confusing and hard to find (always completely clear).

*16. Doing the things you do every day is: a source of deep pleasure and satisfaction (a source of pain and boredom).

17. Your life in the future will probably be: full of changes without your knowing what will happen next (completely consistent and clear).

18. When something unpleasant happened in the past your tendency was: "to eat yourself up" about it (to say "ok, that's that, I have to live with it," and go on).

19. Do you have very mixed-up feelings and ideas? [see item 9]

*20. When you do something that gives you a good feeling: it's certain that you'll go on feeling good (it's certain that something will happen to spoil the feeling).

21. Does it happen that you have feelings inside you would rather not feel? [see item 9]

22. You anticipate that your personal life in the future will be: totally without meaning or purpose (full of meaning and purpose).

*23. Do you think that there will always be people whom you'll be able to count on in the future? you're certain there will be (you doubt there will be)

24. Does it happen that you have the feeling that you don't know exactly what's about to happen? [see item 9]

*25. Many people—even those with a strong character—sometimes feel like sad sacks (losers) in certain situations. How often have you felt this way in the past? never (very often)

26. When something happened, have you generally found that: you over-estimated or underestimated its importance (you saw things in the right proportion).

*27. When you think of difficulties you are likely to face in important aspects of your life, do you have the feeling that: you will always succeed in overcoming the difficulties (you won't succeed in overcoming the difficulties).

28. How often do you have the feeling that there's little meaning in the things you do in your daily life? [see item 9]

29. How often do you have feelings that you're not sure you can keep under control? [see item 9]

Note: Responses in parentheses identify the seventh scale point for each item. Items preceded by asterisks are reverse-scored.

Purpose in Life Test

(Crumbaugh, 1968)

Variable

This scale is designed to measure the degree to which a person experiences a sense of meaning and purpose in life.

Description

The scale was devised to test Viktor Frankl's thesis that when meaning in life is absent, existential frustration results (or among mental patients, something that Frankl called noogenic neurosis). The Purpose in Life Test (PIL) comprises 20 items rated from 1 (low purpose) to 7 (high purpose). Total scores range from 20 (low purpose) to 140 (high purpose). Average scores tend to cluster at the purposeful end of the scale.

Sample

The following nonrepresentative samples were interviewed in Crumbaugh's original study.

Sample	n	Average Score	SD
Normal			
Successful businessmen and professionals	230	119	11
Active and leading Protestant parishioners	142	114	15
College undergraduates	417	109	14
Indigent hospital patients	16	106	15
Psychiatric			
Neurotics, outpatient	225	93	22
Neurotics, hospitalized	13	95	18
Alcoholics, hospitalized	38	85	19
Schizophrenics, hospitalized	41	97	16
Psychotics, hospitalized	18	81	18

All of the respondents were white and from the Columbus, Georgia, area.

Reliability

Internal Consistency

A split-half correlation of .85 was reported for 120 parishioners.

Test–Retest

No test–retest data were reported in the initial article, but in a more recent study (Morrison, 1977) the PIL yielded a Spearman ρ test–retest correlation, over a 3-week interval, of .88 ($n = 14$).

Validity

Convergent

The average scores reported above offer some support for the scale's validity. Within the two samples shown above, PIL scores correlated .47 with ministers' ratings (for the parishioner sample) and .38 with therapist ratings (for the outpatient sample).

Discriminant

In the 1977 study, Crumbaugh included both the PIL and a new scale that measures the "seeking of noetic goals" (SONG). He found, as hypothesized, that the two scales were negatively (but not highly) correlated. In a study of "career adaptivity" by Morrison (1977), self-esteem was positively related to adaptivity while PIL was not.

Location

Crumbaugh, J. (1968). Cross-validation of a purpose-in-life test based on Frankl's concepts. *Journal of Individual Psychology*, **24**, 74–81.

Results and Comments

In the original study the PIL correlated significantly with the Depression Scale of the MMPI ($r = -.65$) and Srole's Anomia Scale ($r = .40$). In his 1977 article, Crumbaugh concluded that the PIL and SONG scales "should be useful in group screening to determine the probability of successful therapeutic manipulations of types consistent with [Frankl's] logotherapy" (p. 907). (Frankl has estimated that about 20% of the case load in mental health clinics falls into his noogenic neurosis category.)

The Purpose in Life Test

For each of the following statements, circle the number that would be most nearly true for you. Note that the numbers always extend from one extreme feeling to its opposite kind of feeling. "Neutral" implies no judgment either way. Try to use this rating *as little* as possible.

1. I am usually:

1	2	3	4	5	6	7
completely bored			(neutral)			exuberant, enthusiastic

2. Life to me seems:

7	6	5	4	3	2	1
always exciting			(neutral)			completely routine

3. In life I have:

1	2	3	4	5	6	7
no goals or aims at all			(neutral)			very clear goals and aims

4. My personal existence is:

1	2	3	4	5	6	7
utterly meaningless, without purpose			(neutral)			very purposeful and meaningful

5. Every day is:

7	6	5	4	3	2	1
constantly new and different			(neutral)			exactly the same

6. If I could choose, I would:

1	2	3	4	5	6	7
prefer never to have been born			(neutral)			like nine more lives just like this one

7. After retiring, I would:

7	6	5	4	3	2	1
do some of the exciting things I have always wanted to			(neutral)			loaf completely the rest of my life

8. In achieving life goals I have:

1	2	3	4	5	6	7
made no progress whatever			(neutral)			progressed to complete fulfillment

9. My life is:

1	2	3	4	5	6	7
empty, filled only with despair			(neutral)			running over with exciting good things

10. If I should die today, I would feel that my life has been:

7	6	5	4	3	2	1
very worthwhile			(neutral)			completely worthless

11. In thinking of my life, I:

1	2	3	4	5	6	7
often wonder why I exist			(neutral)			always see a reason for my being here

12. As I view the world in relation to my life, the world:

1	2	3	4	5	6	7
completely confuses me			(neutral)			fits meaningfully with my life

13. I am a:

1	2	3	4	5	6	7
very irresponsible person			(neutral)			very responsible person

14. Concerning man's freedom to make his own choices, I believe man is:

7	6	5	4	3	2	1
absolutely free to make all life choices			(neutral)			completely bound by limitations of heredity and environment

15. With regard to death, I am:

7	6	5	4	3	2	1
prepared and unafraid			(neutral)			unprepared and frightened

16. With regard to suicide, I have:

1	2	3	4	5	6	7
thought of it seriously as a way out			(neutral)			never given it a second thought

17. I regard my ability to find a meaning, purpose, or mission in life as:

7	6	5	4	3	2	1
very great			(neutral)			practically none

18. My life is:

7	6	5	4	3	2	1
in my hands and I am in control of it			(neutral)			out of my hands and controlled by external factors

19. Facing my daily tasks is:

7	6	5	4	3	2	1
a source of pleasure and satisfaction			(neutral)			a painful and boring experience

20. I have discovered:

1	2	3	4	5	6	7
no mission or purpose in life			(neutral)			clear-cut goals and a satisfying life purpose

Note: Reprinted with permission of Crumbaugh, J. Purpose-in-Life Test in *Journal of Individual Psychology*, 24 (1968), pp. 74–81. Copyright 1968 by the American Society of Adlerian Psychology, Inc., c/o Heinz Ansbacher, University of Vermont, John Dewey Hall, Burlington, Vermont 05401.

Self-Estrangement Measures

This facet of alienation, in a sense the root meaning of alienation for Marx, is perhaps the most difficult to formulate both conceptually and operationally. Its scope and subtle resonance pose a formidable analytic challenge, but, as noted elsewhere (Seeman, 1983), a modicum of clarity is made possible by distinguishing three basic but distinctive conceptions of self-estrangement. The term refers to either (1) the despised self, (2) the disguised self, or (3) the detached self. The self-estrangement scales presented here concentrate on the last of these, but it is important to grasp the pertinence for alienation studies of the other two versions of self-estrangement.

The first of these, the despised self, refers essentially to low self-esteem (measures of which are presented in Chapter 4). This usage, which focuses on a negatively evaluated discrepancy between the individual's perceived actual self and some preferred ideal, is common in clinical psychology and in sociological social psychology, but historically it has not been associated very strongly with the idea of alienation. Still, the measurement of self-esteem frequently embodies some of the features of alienation discussed above. Thus, for example, the Texas Social Behavior Inventory (Helmreich & Stapp, 1974) is a measure of self-esteem in which, as Brown (1986, p. 357) remarks, "the majority of the items concern perceived confidence and competence in social situations" (i.e., mastery). Even more directly, Mortimer, Lorence, and Kumka (1986, pp. 49, 64–65) speak of "the competence dimension of the self concept" and present a factor-based four-item semantic differential measure of self-competence. Thus, measures of self-esteem and of the sense of competence share more than a passing connection, a point directly expressed in Franks and Marolla's (1976, p. 325) measurement of inner versus outer self-esteem, the former referring to "the individual's feelings of efficacy and competence" and the latter to externally based appraisals by significant others.

The disguised version of self-estrangement is, almost by definition, more complicated and more difficult to measure. It has a strong affinity with the Marxian idea of false consciousness, since the disguised self in one way or another involves a "deprivation of awareness" (Touraine, 1973, p. 201): for example, failure to realize one's true interests, truly human capacities, or true feelings (to be, as the saying has it, "out of touch" with oneself). There are numerous ways in which researchers have sought to approach this difficult topic, ranging from devising direct measures of "self-awareness" (Shrauger & Osberg, 1983) or "self-consciousness" (Fenigstein, Scheier, & Buss, 1975) to implementing research on "inauthenticity" (Seeman, 1966; Turner & Gordon, 1981; see also Turner & Schutte, 1981, on "the true self") and on clinical syndromes such as paranoia ("a profound form of social alienation," write Mirowsky & Ross, 1983).

Measures of the "detached" self have focused on detachment in the sphere of work, that is, on work that is not intrinsically rewarding, hence an activity in which the individual is not involved or engaged. Because such measures are so centrally tied to the workplace, the review of most of them (e.g., Featherman, 1971; Hackman & Oldham, 1975; Karasek, 1981; Shepard, 1971) will be reserved for a subsequent volume of this series. In various ways, these measures invoke the distinction between intrinsic and extrinsic rewards. They seek the respondent's perception of the occupational conditions involved in carrying out his or her job, presuming that activities described as creative, interesting, nonroutine, challenging, skill-invoking, and involving the worker's decision-making input are intrinsically rewarding, hence nonalienated in the self-estrangement sense.

Kohn and Schooler (1983, p. 15) comment "That the extrinsic–intrinsic distinction is a central line of cleavage is substantiated by a factor analysis that differentiates an extrinsic from an intrinsic dimension" in judgments about work. There is sharp disagreement, however, about the relative importance of objective versus subjective descriptions of such work dimensions. Kohn, for example, places primacy on the objective description of occupational conditions, that is, descriptions of "occupational self-direction," comprising chiefly the absence of close supervision, substantive complexity (requiring thought and independent judgment), and nonroutinized work. In an important sense, this view coordinates with the Marxian emphasis on the objective quality of alienated labor, though the precise basis for postulating the primacy of objective conditions over subjective worker perceptions is not well elaborated. Nor is the distinction as readily implemented as one might think. As Kohn and Schooler (1983, p. 26) remark, their indices of the complexity of work organization "are based on men's appraisals of what constitutes 'a complete job' in their occupation and of how repetitive their work is." One would expect, too, a substantial positive correlation between subjectively reported task perceptions and objective ratings such as those published in the *Dictionary of Occupational Titles;* there is considerable evidence for such a relationship (e.g., Kohn, 1981; Miller, Treiman, Cain, & Roos, 1980; Rousseau, 1982).[6]

Additional brief remarks about the scales in this section include:

1. The four-item Kohn and Schooler (1983, p. 87) measure of self-estrangement is a more general index than the others; it is not focused on work and shares the broad "meaninglessness" flavor discussed above ("it implies a sense of being detached from self, or being adrift—purposeless, bored with everything . . .").

2. There are measures of self-estrangement in work (not included here) that explicitly adopt a discrepancy scoring procedure, as in Wilensky's (1968) index of work alienation, which compares the respondent's actual experience at work with his "prized self-image" and finds a very low incidence of alienation by this measure (see also Shepard & Panko, 1974, on "power discrepancy" and Bonjean & Vance, 1968, on "self-actualization" in work).

3. There is some overlap between the idea of powerlessness discussed above and the items that make up many work alienation scales, since the latter regularly embody the idea of worker decision-making power, as in Karasek's (1981) concept of "decision latitude" (which, in his model, interacts with job demands to produce worker response). It would be wrong to assume, however, that this conceptual overlap necessarily produces high correlations between measures of generalized powerlessness and work alienation, or parallel correlations with other variables (Seeman, 1967, 1972).

The three scales included in this section are

16. Work Alienation (Seeman, 1967),
17. Job Involvement (Lorence & Mortimer, 1985), and
18. Self-Estrangement (Kohn & Schooler, 1983).

All three scales are recommended, given content relevance to the research task at hand.

Seeman's scale deals with alienated labor in the subjective Marxian sense: "Is your job too simple to bring out your best abilities, or not?" "On an ordinary workday, do you have the chance to make independent decisions in your work, or is it rather routine work?" (For a similar set of items, see Karasek, 1981.) Lorence and Mortimer's scale concerns absorption in and attachment to one's work: "How involved do you feel in your job . . . ?" "How often do you do some extra work for your job which isn't required of you?" The brief Kohn and Schooler scale is rather different; it measures self-estrangement and self-dissatisfaction: "How often do you feel that there isn't much purpose to being alive?"

Work Alienation

(Seeman, 1967)

Variable

Work alienation refers to work that is self-estranged in the sense that it provides little intrinsic satisfaction.

---

[6]Although item wording and the context of item presentation clearly make a difference, there is persuasive evidence regarding the validity of many questionnaire descriptions (e.g., on reported alcohol use, as in Armor, Polich, and Stambul, 1978).

Description

The scale consists of seven items that formed a clear cluster in a factor analysis of 15 work alienation questions, taken mostly from Blauner's (1964) study of work experience in various industries. The items offer dichotomous choices (except item 5, which is tri-chotomous) scored on a 0–1 basis (high scores equal high work alienation). Scores can range from 0 (low alienation) to 8 (high alienation). The scale was administered in an interview format in the cited studies but is amenable to self-administration.

Sample

The sample for the 1967 study consisted of 558 working males between the ages of 20 and 79 who were randomly selected from the population register of Sweden's third largest city, Malmo. The response rate was 83%, and the effective sample was 504.

The sample for a 1972 (Seeman, 1972) study included respondents from two distinct populations: (1) French (Parisian) workers (just before the 1968 uprisings) ($n = 488$), and (2) American (Los Angeleno) workers (interviewed at approximately the same time), chosen by means of block selection ($n = 400$).

Reliability

Internal Consistency

Factor analytic criteria were used to create a coherent scale: Seven items formed a clear cluster. The Kuder–Richardson reliability for the American sample was .51, .50 for the French sample.

Test–Retest

In a follow-up (re-interview) study in both countries (Seeman, 1984), significant stability of individual scores was exhibited: The correlation between work alienation scores in 1967 and in 1973 was .43 in the United States sample and .32 in France ($n = 86$ and 80, respectively).

Validity

Convergent

Evidence of the validity of the work alienation scale is provided, first, by its relationship (in the hypothesized direction) with workers' sense of job control: Among manual work-ers, with education controlled, work alienation was associated with low control ($r = -.21$; $n = 213$). Second, Blauner's original analysis of these items bears on the scale's validity. He found, as expected, that skill level and type of industry explained the greatest amount of variation in job conditions and workers' attitudes. In addition, he found work alienation among nonmanual workers to be correlated with income ($r = -.31$), and manual workers to be significantly higher in work alienation than nonmanual workers.

Discriminant

Seeman (1967) stressed the conceptual distinction between work alienation and job satis-faction: "The notion of work alienation employed here refers to intrinsic reward in work, an idea that is not equivalent to satisfaction with the job, even though the two may be correlated" (p. 280). Although the Swedish survey did not include an item on job satisfaction, an earlier American study did (Ransford, 1968). For his sample of 172 black male manual workers, the correlation was only −.02 between the work alienation scale and a job satisfaction item, and −.35 for white-collar blacks. For white workers in Los Angeles, the r values were −.38 and −.28 for manual workers and nonmanual workers, respectively, significant but low enough to indicate distinctness.

Location

Seeman, M. (1967). On the personal consequences of alienation in work. *American Sociological Review*, **32**, 273–285.

Results and Comments

Seeman's study of Swedish workers (1967) was aimed at assessing the consequences of work alienation for other areas of social life (i.e., the generalizability of work alienation). An examination of the correlates of work alienation shows that it is not consistently and significantly related to the frequently postulated outcomes, while powerlessness appears to be more significant in that respect. The correlations of work alienation and powerlessness with prejudice, anomia, and political knowledge were as follows:

	Ethnic prejudice		Anomia		Political Knowledge	
	Manual	Nonmanual	Manual	Nonmanual	Manual	Nonmanual
Powerlessness	.24	.29	.37	.39	−.21	−.17
Work alienation	.05	.02	.15	.06	.04	−.13

Overall, there was little evidence to support the generalization theme.

The comparative French–American study by Seeman (1972) analyzed the role of work alienation at a crucial point in French history (the eve of the 1968 uprisings) with the American sample serving as a comparison group. French workers were found to be significantly higher on work alienation, and differences were especially great regarding the sense of control over work. The percentage choosing alienated responses among French and American workers, by occupation, is presented below:

	% Manual		% Nonmanual	
	United States	France	United States	France
Item 1	25	48	22	42
Item 2	26	27	17	21
Item 3	26	31	11	13
Item 4	40	45	32	37
Item 5	18	27	6	15
Item 6	38	47	31	39
Item 7	30	37	11	24

Work Alienation

1. Would you say that your job makes you work too fast most of the time, or not?

    1 Too fast   0 Not

2. Is your job too simple to bring out your best abilities, or not?

    1 Too simple   0 Not

3. Does your work really give you a chance to try out your own ideas, or not?

    1 Try out ideas   0 Not

4. Can you do the work on the job and keep your mind on other things, or not?

    1 Other things   0 Not

5. Is your job interesting nearly all of the time, interesting most of the time but with some dull stretches, or pretty dull and monotonous most of the time?

    2 Monotonous   1 Dull stretches   0 Interesting

6. If you had the opportunity to retire right now, would you prefer to do that or would you prefer to go on working at your present job?

    1 Retire   0 Go on working

7. On an ordinary workday, do you have the chance to make independent decisions in your work, or is it rather routine work?

    1 Routine   0 Independent

Job Involvement

(Lorence & Mortimer, 1985)

Variable

The emphasis in this scale is on "psychological attachment to a particular job rather than on occupational and organizational commitment."

Description

Scale items were selected on the basis of their availability in the Quality of Employment Survey Panel data and differ for two time periods. The earlier (1973) survey yielded a three-item scale, which was originally developed to measure job morale (Patchen, 1965).

The 1977 scale included three questions similar to those in the first scale, as well as two items from the widely used Lodahl and Kejner (1965) job involvement index. Scores vary between 8 (low job involvement) and 33 (high job involvement).

Sample

A panel was drawn from the 1972–1973 and 1977 Quality of Employment Surveys. The 1973 survey drew a national (multistage area probability) sample of 1455 working adults. Seventy-six percent ($n = 1086$) were reinterviewed in 1977. The panel was composed of individuals who worked at least 20 hours per week in 1973 and 1977, and were younger than 65 in 1973. Eight hundred and eighty-two (81%) of the reinterviewed group fell into this category. Panel attrition was somewhat of a problem and may bias the results, since dropouts were found to be lower in job involvement; older; less educated; lower in income, occupational prestige, and work autonomy; and working fewer hours per week.

Reliability

Internal Consistency

The reliability of the scale is evidenced by factor analysis (using the entire panel). Factor loadings are listed below.

	1973 Job involvement	1977 Job involvement
Item 1	.34	
Item 2	.45	
Item 3	.53	
Item 4		.22
Item 5		.41
Item 6		.56
Item 7		.35
Item 8		.45

Test–Retest

No information was available.

Validity

Convergent

The authors argue that "the strong conceptual similarity among the five questions and those utilized in previous research on job involvement, coupled with these empirical findings, provide ample justification for use of these indicators" (p. 626). In addition, the 1973 job involvement index was found to be significantly related to education and work autonomy and to be stable over time. Job involvement in 1973 was found to be positively related to income in 1977. The 1977 job involvement scale was also significantly related to work autonomy.

Discriminant

No information was available.

Location

Lorence, J., & Mortimer, J. (1985). Job involvement through the life course. *American Sociological Review*, **50**, 618–638.

Results and Comments

The aim of this study was to examine the relationship between work experiences and job involvement while holding age constant. It was found that the youngest workers had the lowest stability of job involvement, and among this age group work autonomy had a particularly strong influence on job involvement. Job involvement reached its peak stability in the middle-age group and declined for older workers. The authors caution that "cohort effects may account, in full or in part, for the findings" and that "another problematic factor is the fact that the study ignores gender differences in labor-force experiences" (pp. 633–634).

In general, the authors conclude that

> while there are important limitations in the research, this study suggests the value of a life-span perspective in attempting to understand the interrelation of work orientations and occupational experiences. The findings demonstrate that the impact of work autonomy in job involvement varies with the particular phase of the work life. They suggest that the responsiveness of the person to differences in the work environment may decline with age. The influence of autonomy on job involvement, however, even among the oldest workers, attests to the continuing, though diminished importance of this facet of work experience for psychological change. (pp. 633–634)

Job Involvement (1973)

1. How often do you do some extra work for your job which isn't required of you? Would you say you do this:

    Often (4), Sometimes (3), Rarely (2), or Never (1)?

2. On most days of your job, how often does time seem to drag for you—

    Often (1), Sometimes (2), Rarely (3), or Never (4)?

3. Some people are completely involved in their job—they are absorbed by it night and day. For other people, their job is simply one of several interests. How involved do you feel in your job—

    Very little (1), Slightly (2), Moderately (3), or Strongly involved (4)?

Job Involvement (1977)

4. How much effort do you put into your job beyond what is required—

   A lot (4), Some (3), Only a little (2), or None (1)?

5. On most days on your job, how often does time seem to drag for you—

   Often (1), Sometimes (2), Rarely (3), Never (4)?

6. How often do you think about your job when you're doing something else—

   Often (4), Sometimes (3), Rarely (2), or Never (1)?

7. My main satisfaction in life comes from my work—

   Strongly disagree (1), Disagree (2), Agree (3), Strongly agree (4).

8. How much do you agree or disagree that the most important things that happen to you involve your job?

   Strongly disagree (1), Disagree (2), Neither agree nor disagree (3),
   Agree (4), Strongly agree (5).

Self-Estrangement

(Kohn & Schooler, 1983)

Variable

Departing from Seeman's conceptualization of self-estrangement as an individual's inability to find self-rewarding activities that engage him, Kohn and Schooler emphasize both a negative evaluation of self-worth and a sense of being detached from the self.

Description

Four items make up a Guttman scale. The items are answered on a frequency (dichotomized) or agree–disagree basis. Total scores range from 0 to 4. Whereas this scale was originally administered in an interview format, it could easily be adapted for self-administration.

Sample

See sample description earlier in this chapter for the Kohn and Schooler Powerlessness Scale.

Reliability

Internal Consistency

The self-estrangement scale has a reproducibility in the .90s, scalability in the .70s, and essentially random patterns of error.

Test–Retest

No information was available.

Validity

Convergent

The self-estrangement scale is one of five scales that comprise a larger measure of alienation. A second-order measurement model of alienation was developed by Roberts (1987) using Kohn and Schooler's data. The path of the second-order concept (alienation) to the first-order concept (self-estrangement) was .88 in 1964 and .90 in 1974. The alienation measures for the two time periods are correlated .52. The paths of the first-order concepts to indicators are given in Table 2.

Discriminant

No information was available.

Location

Kohn, M., & Schooler, C. (1983). *Work and personality: An inquiry into the impact of social stratification.* Norwood, NJ: Ablex. See especially Chapter 4.

Results and Comments

The reader should review the results reported for the Kohn and Schooler Powerlessness Scale (described earlier in this chapter), since the self-estrangement index was part of the same investigation.

Ownership was found to be only weakly related to self-estrangement ($r = -.02$), although position in the supervisory hierarchy was somewhat more strongly correlated ($r = -.09$). Bureaucratization (the index of division of labor) was related ($r = -.09$), but in the direction opposite the hypothesis. Occupational self-direction was more consistently related to self-estrangement: Close supervision ($r = .14$), routinized work ($r = .04$), and work of little substantive complexity ($r = -.17$) were all significantly related. The introduction of statistical controls reduced these correlations but left what the authors describe as statistically significant, nontrivial (although small) relationships.

Table 2
Paths: First-Order Concept (Self-Estrangement) to Indicators

	1964	1974
Item 1	.53	.46
Item 2	.50	.56
Item 3	.51	.48
Item 4	.20	.21

Source: Kohn and Schooler (1983).

Self-Estrangement

1. How often do you feel that there isn't much purpose to being alive?

(RARELY–FREQUENTLY)

*2. How often do you feel bored with everything?

(RARELY–FREQUENTLY)

3. At times, I think I am no good at all.

(AGREE–DISAGREE)

*4. Are you the sort of person who takes life as it comes or are you working toward some definite goal?

(AS IT COMES–WORKING TOWARD GOAL)

Note: Answer alternatives for items 1, 2, and 4 were not explicitly provided by Kohn and Schooler. The ones shown here represent our best guesses. Items preceded by an asterisk are presumably reverse-scored.

Social Isolation Measures

The days of high concern about the "loss of community" in mass society which coincided with the post-Depression days of rediscovery of the concept of alienation, have passed, and we have witnessed a replacement of the old concern about social isolation. The negative image of alienated isolation has been replaced by its obverse; namely the positive concept of "social supports" and thus by a burgeoning literature on friendship networks. The measures relating to social supports, which of course can also be read as indices of social isolation, are treated elsewhere in this series of volumes.

There has been a parallel resurgence of interest in the idea of "loneliness" (measures bearing on this development are reviewed in Chapter 6). Included here, however, is one of the established "social isolation" measures which derives from the alienation tradition:

19. Social Isolation (Dean, 1961).

The Dean scale has been relatively widely used, sometimes in modified form (Neal & Groat, 1974). Sample items include: "There are few dependable ties between people any more," "Sometimes I feel all alone in the world."

It should be mentioned in passing that (as with the domain of work) there is a strictly structural side to the current interest in social networks (i.e., investigations that focus on nonattitudinal features of networks: e.g., the influence of network centrality in the communication process, or the role of clique structures in economic affairs). Nevertheless, the network literature typically implicates the sense of social support, the obverse side of social isolation. (For a useful annotated bibliography, see Biegel, McCardle, & Mendelson, 1985. For an integration of the literatures on social support, social isolation, and loneliness, see Rook, 1984.)

Social Isolation

(Dean, 1961)

Variable

Dean developed a three-part general alienation measure, with one of the components being social isolation.

Description

Item selection was described earlier in relation to Dean's powerlessness scale. There were nine social isolation items on the final scale.

The items are presented in five-point Likert format, with answer alternatives ranging from 4 (strongly agree) to 0 (strongly disagree); five of the items are reverse-scored. Scale scores can vary from 0 (lowest social isolation) to 36 (highest social isolation). Normative data were presented in connection with Dean's powerlessness subscale.

Sample

The sample is described in the section on powerlessness.

Reliability

Internal Consistency

The reliability of the social isolation subscale, tested by the split-half method and corrected by the Spearman–Brown formula, was .84.

Test–Retest

No information was available.

Validity

Convergent

Social isolation correlated .54 with Dean's powerlessness scale, .41 with normlessness, and .75 with total alienation.

The component and total scores were correlated with the F scale (authoritarianism) in a sample of 73 college students. The result for social isolation was $r = .23$, significant but a bit lower than for powerlessness (.37) or normlessness (.33).

Discriminant

No information was available.

Location

Dean, D. (1961). Alienation: Its meaning and measurement. *American Sociological Review*, **26**, 753–758.

Results and Comments

The overall Dean Alienation Scale has continued to be used, but few studies have focused specifically on the social isolation subscale. The topic of social isolation and related topics such as social support and loneliness have continued to receive research attention, as explained in the introductory section of this chapter, but Dean's social isolation subscale per se does not seem to have been widely used. (See Rook, 1984, and Chapter 6 of the present volume.)

Social Isolation Items

Below are some statements regarding public issues with which some people agree and others disagree. Please give us your own opinion about these items (i.e., whether you agree or disagree with the items as they stand).

Please check in the appropriate blank, as follows:

———— A (Strongly Agree)
———— a (Agree)
———— U (Uncertain)
———— d (Disagree)
———— D (Strongly Disagree)

1. Sometimes I feel all alone in the world.

—— A   —— a   —— U   —— d   —— D

3. I don't get invited out by friends as often as I'd really like.
5. Most people today seldom feel lonely.*
8. Real friends are as easy as ever to find.*
11. One can always find friends if he shows himself friendly.*
14. The world in which we live is basically a friendly place.*
17. There are few dependable ties between people any more.
22. People are just naturally friendly and helpful.*
24. I don't get to visit friends as often as I'd really like.

Note: Items followed by asterisks are reverse-scored. Item numbers indicate placement in the general alienation questionnaire. See entries under powerlessness and social isolation for the other numbered items.

Cultural Estrangement Measures

Research interest in cultural estrangement (the individual's rejection of, or sense of removal from, dominant social values) has never been as strong as interest in the other varieties of alienation (e.g., powerlessness or self-estrangement). To some extent, that interest peaked when the communal and student movements became the inspiration and reflection of a counter/cultural period in the 1960s. As with social isolation, however, those concerns have passed, and with them any determined measurement of cultural estrangement.

Two indices that bear on this aspect of alienation include

20. Cultural Estrangement (Kohn & Schooler, 1983) and
21. Social Criticism Scale (Jessor & Jessor, 1977).

One of the earliest measures in this domain was the Nettler scale (1957), which focused on estrangement from American culture as reflected in attitudes toward mass culture, familism, religiosity, and politics (sample items: "Do you read *Reader's Digest?*; Do you think religion is mostly myth or mostly truth? Do you vote in national elections?"). Nettler's scale was revised in 1964 but would require further revision for contemporary use. The same focus on general "social criticism" is embodied in the scale developed by Jessor and his colleagues (1968; Jessor & Jessor, 1977). The measure of cultural estrangement developed by Kohn and Schooler (1983, p. 88) has a narrower focus, seeking to determine whether the respondent thinks that his (or her) ideas and opinions "differ from those of his friends, his relatives, other people of his religious background, and his compatriots generally."

Two messages are implied by including these scales. First, the level (or the social circle) in which any of these forms of alienation are experienced can be as small-scale or large-scale as one's research interests dictate. Thus, the alienation of self-estrangement can be experienced in a simple conversation (Goffman, 1957) or in a complex work institution, just as cultural estrangement can be experienced among a network of friends or in relation to American culture. Second, if one asks how normlessness and cultural estrangement differ, the simple answer is that the latter expresses a sense of difference rather than deviance, since the matter of sanctions is not at issue when one speaks of cultural estrangement.

Cultural Estrangement
(Kohn & Schooler, 1983)

Variable

This four-item scale assesses whether one believes that one's ideas and opinions about important matters differ from those of people in one's primary and secondary groups.

Description

This definition avoids focus on the rejection of dominant cultural themes (as in Seeman's and Nettler's work) in an attempt to overcome the problem of prejudging the dominant cultural themes or what the respondent assumes them to be. The scale does not distinguish between estrangement from primary and secondary groups. Kohn and Schooler note that they have found "unidimensionality in such estrangement, regardless of whether primary or secondary groups are involved" (1983, p. 88). Interviews were carried out by ʌe field staff of NORC in the Kohn and Schooler studies, but the scale could be self-administered.

The Cultural Estrangement Scale (or subscale) contains four items, each scored dichotomously. Scores range from 0 to 4, with high scores indicating greater estrangement.

Sample

See sample description for the Kohn and Schooler Powerlessness Scale (described earlier in this chapter).

Reliability

Internal Consistency

The cultural estrangement scale has a reproducibility in the .90s, scalability in the .70s, and essentially random patterns of error.

Test–Retest

No direct information was available, although the overall alienation measure showed a 4-year test–retest reliability of .52, and Cultural Estrangement contributed something to the overall score (see below).

Validity

Convergent

The cultural estrangement scale is one of five scales that comprise a larger measure of alienation. A second-order measurement model of alienation was developed by Roberts (1987) using Kohn and Schooler's data. The path of the second-order concept (alienation) to the first-order concept (cultural estrangement) was .20 in 1964 and .16 in 1974. The paths of the first order concepts to indicators are shown in Table 3.

Discriminant

No information was available.

Location

Kohn, M., & Schooler, C. (1983). *Work and personality: An inquiry into the impact of social stratification.* Norwood, NJ: Ablex. See especially Chapter 4.

Table 3
Paths: First-Order Concept (Cultural
Estrangement) to Indicators

	1964	1974
Item 1	.56	.51
Item 2	.77	.64
Item 3	.60	.58
Item 4	.57	.30

Source: Kohn and Schooler (1983).

Results and Comments

The reader should review the results reported for the Kohn and Schooler Powerlessness Scale (described earlier in this chapter), since the cultural estrangement index was part of the same investigation. The conditions that were positively related to the other forms of alienation were negatively related to cultural estrangement. This disparity has been noted in other studies and the authors (Kohn & Schooler, 1983) proposed as a likely explanation that

> powerlessness, self-estrangement, and normlessness, at least as we have indexed them, all represent a negative judgment of self—in the sense that the individual feels that he lacks personal efficacy, lacks basic worth, or lacks the ability to make his own moral decisions. Cultural estrangement, on the other hand, does not necessarily represent a negative judgment of self, but often means quite the opposite, that the individual is sufficiently secure in his judgment of self to be independent in his values. (p. 90)

In an earlier study (1969) using the 1964 data, Kohn and Schooler reported on an index called "idea-conformity," which is essentially the scale that was later labeled cultural estrangement. The items have the following factor loadings:

	Factor loadings
Item 1	.68
Item 2	.74
Item 3	.70
Item 4	.67

In 1981, Slomczynski *et al.* analyzed cultural estrangement (again, labeling it idea conformity) using the original 1964 United States sample and the 1974 follow-up sample (described above) and a 1978 Polish survey that was designed to be an "exact replication of the main parts of the U.S. study." The correlates of social stratification position with idea conformity are very similar for the two countries: "In both countries, the higher position is associated, to a modest but significant degree, with greater independence in one's ideas" (p. 279). Again, the generalizability of work experience is supported, here for both capitalist and socialist societies.

Cultural Estrangement

1. According to your general impression, how often do your ideas and opinions about important matters differ from those of your relatives?

   (RARELY–FREQUENTLY)

2. How often do your ideas and opinions differ from those of your friends?
3. How about from those of other people with your religious background?
4. Those of most people in the country?

   Note: No answer alternatives were provided in Kohn and Schooler's published version of the scale; "rarely–frequently" represents our best guess.

Social Criticism Scale

(Jessor & Jessor, 1977)

Variable

Jessor and Jessor define social criticism as the degree of acceptance or rejection of the values, norms, and practices of the society.

Description

The questions focus on areas such as social justice, economic opportunity, personal fulfillment, militarism, the environment, and education. The scale contained nine five-point items with a score range of 9–45 in a study of high school students, and thirteen items with a range of 13 (low social criticism) to 65 (high criticism) in a study of college students. The 13-item scale is presented below. The answer alternatives are strongly agree, agree, neither agree nor disagree, disagree, and strongly disagree. In Jessor and Jessor's studies, the items were self-administered as part of a large questionnaire battery.

Sample

The study examined two independent longitudinal samples of students in a small city in one of the Rocky Mountain states. The city had a population of 67,000 in 1970, with 93% white, 5% Chicano, and 1% black residents. The high school sample was selected in 1969 by randomly selecting (stratifying by sex and grade level) from every grade in three junior high schools and three senior high schools. Only students who were in junior high school at the time of the original study were eligible to be retested (three times) for the longitudinal study. Of the 1126 junior high school students originally selected in 1969, 52% participated in the initial study ($n = 589$). By the last year of testing, 483 students remained (82% retention of Year 1 participants), and 432 (188 males and 244 females) participated in all 4 years of testing. The latter comprise the longitudinal sample. The sample does not represent the socioeconomic and ethnic heterogeneity of American youth and cannot be generalized to the larger population.

The college sample consisted of male and female cohorts born in 1951, in their freshman year in 1970. The university from which they were selected was large (enrollment of 20,000) and was situated in the same community as the high school sample. A 10% random sample (which was stratified by sex) was drawn from the enrollment roster, and 60% of those available took part in the initial testing. Over the 3-year interval, 83% (226) remained in the sample, and 205 (92 males and 113 females) participated in all 4 years of testing. Participants differed from nonparticipants in the following ways: (1) Participants had a higher GPA, and (2) fewer of them were out-of-state students. Thus, generalization to the wider population is not possible. The students who completed all four questionnaires exhibited "essentially no differences" compared with those who completed only one or two (with the exception of "value on independence").

Reliability

Internal Consistency

Cronbach's α was .69 for the high school sample and .85 for the college sample.

Test–Retest

Stability reliability over a 1-year interval was excellent (greater than .6 in all cases) for both the high school and college samples.

Validity

Convergent

The authors attempted to reduce "inferential ambiguity" by means of the following strategies:

1. They employed a theoretical framework and theory-derived measures.
2. They relied on various kinds of replication (across time, sex, school, cohorts, and functionally related behaviors).
3. They examined time-extended relationships only when they demonstrated a cross-sectional relationship.
4. They utilized the longitudinal nature of the data to its fullest extent to avoid inferential ambiguity.

Thus, the measures in this study relied on "theory-derived, structured measures that had been psychometrically developed and, for the most part, construct validated in prior research" (Jessor & Jessor, 1977, pp. 234–235).

Discriminant

Low intercorrelations of this scale with others further reflects on its validity.

Location

Jessor, R., & Jessor, S. (1977). *Problem behavior and psychosocial development*. New York: Academic Press.

Results and Comments

The main hypothesis concerning the effects of personal belief structures is as follows: "Acceptance of social norms and practices . . . can serve as a powerful control over engaging in actions that . . . [are] included in the domain covered by the concept of problem behavior" (1977, p. 21). Social criticism was hypothesized as having a positive relationship with deviant behavior. The cross-sectional analysis (using data from Year 4) reveals the Pearson correlations shown in Table 4.

Overall, social criticism was found to be significantly related to problem behavior in the hypothesized direction. It was found that mean scores on the social criticism scale varied significantly by marijuana use and nonuse (the relationship held for males and females in high school and in college), but not for alcohol use.

Social criticism was also found to increase over time. In general, the study concludes that the personality system is important for the occurrence of problem behavior in youth, with the qualification that personality component structures have differential effectiveness: Personal controls are the most influential (the tolerance of deviance scale is the most prominent here), motivational instigations are next (with the independence achievement scale highest in prominence), and personal beliefs least influential (with the social crit-

Table 4
Pearson Correlations with Social Criticism Scale

	High school		College	
	Male	Female	Male	Female
Times drunk past year	−.10	−.01	.09	.15
Marijuana involvement	.33***	.35***	.40***	.38***
Deviant beh. past yr.	.19*	.18**	.15	.20*
Multiple-problem index	−.21**	.28***	.28**	.37***
Church att. past yr.	−.11	−.21**	−.14	−.14
GPA past year	.01	.07	−.28*	−.02

*$p < .05$; **$p < .01$; ***$p < .001$.

icism scale most prominent). There is a suggestion that "proneness to problem behavior rests upon a personality pattern that implicates unconventionality" (1977, p. 237). (For further information related to the Social Criticism Scale, see Jessor & Jessor, 1973, and Jessor, Jessor, & Finney, 1973.)

Social Criticism Scale

1. The experience with the war in Vietnam shows that our foreign policy is strongly controlled by the military and by large industry.

STRONGLY   AGREE   NEITHER AGREE   DISAGREE   STRONGLY
  AGREE   NOR DISAGREE   DISAGREE

2. Instead of providing students with a truly liberal education, American universities have increasingly become training centers for business firms and for the military.

*3. The government seems to be moving strongly on a program for cleaning up our air, our water, and our cities despite the cost and the opposition of vested interests.

4. All the talk about equality of opportunity for members of minority groups in the USA is just that—talk.

*5. Increasing American military strength and maintaining overseas bases are necessary ways of safeguarding world peace.

6. There is far too much emphasis on success and getting ahead in our society; people are becoming things or objects rather than human beings.

7. Government policy is getting to be so exclusively determined by powerful business and professional groups that the needs of the people as a whole are not being met.

*8. Women's position in our society is about as equal as could reasonably be expected.

9. The deterioration of our environment shows how bad things can become in a free enterprise system where profit comes before human needs.

*10. In the last couple of decades, the government has been highly effective in providing jobs and job training for the poor.

11. In a country like ours, with its wealth and technology, the fact there are millions of families living below the "poverty line" means that there is something terribly wrong with our economic system.

12. The fact that students have nothing to say about how a university is run is one reason why a college education has so little relevance to what's important today.

*13. If the people want change, they can make effective use of right to vote and to petition—that's the advantage of American democracy.

Note: Strongly agree = 5; items preceded by an asterisk are reverse-scored.

Generalized Alienation Measures

Since there is a common tendency to employ indices of alienation that are not readily classifiable under the above categories, two scales that tap appraisals of one's general life situation are included:

22. Alienation (Jessor & Jessor, 1977) and
23. Alienation Test (Maddi *et al.*, 1979).

Both capture feelings of pessimism, despair, helplessness, and isolation, the obverse of which would be generalized life satisfaction (see Chapter 3) and optimism (see Scheier & Carver, 1985). It is difficult to determine in some cases the most appropriate placement for a given scale, as in the case of the Srole "anomia" scale, discussed above, whose title carries a normlessness imprint but whose item content also includes aspects of powerlessness and generalized despair (e.g., "You can't help wondering whether anything is worthwhile").

Jessor and Jessor's scale is designed for adolescents. It is based on a definition of alienation that includes uncertainty about roles and daily activities, and the belief that one is isolated from others: "I sometimes feel uncertain about who I really am," "I generally feel I have a lot of interests in common with other students in this school" [reverse scored]. The unusually long (60-item) questionnaire of Maddi *et al.* is deliberately broad, examining four types of alienation (powerlessness, adventurousness, nihilism, and "vegetativeness") within five contexts (work, social institutions, family, other persons, and self).

One might anticipate that general scales of alienation, to the extent that they tap general distress, would not regularly correlate highly with the more specific indices that have been reviewed above; that expectation is borne out. For example, the Jessor group's tri-ethnic study (1968) reports a correlation of only .03 between their "alienation" index and the normlessness measure called "attitude toward deviance"; and Seeman (1967) reports a correlation among manual workers of only .07 between work alienation and Srole's anomia measure. The strength of such correlations varies, of course, as do researchers' judgments about how "strong" a given correlation is said to be. Campbell and Converse (1976, p. 363) report a correlation of .35 between feelings of personal competence (the reverse of powerlessness) and global well-being (the reverse of generalized alienation), and comment that these are, "not surprisingly, rather strongly associated."

But given that the explained variance (.12) is modest, one might be equally impressed by the degree of independence between these two measures of alienation.[7]

Finally, it should be noted that several of the subscales mentioned earlier in this chapter were designed by their authors as components of a comprehensive measure of alienation. In Dean's work, for example, alienation is the sum of powerlessness, normlessness, and social isolation scores. Neal and Groat similarly distinguish three domains: powerlessness, normlessness, and meaninglessness; scores for these domains can be summed. The same is true for all the other multipart measures.

Alienation

(Jessor & Jessor, 1977)

Variable

This scale measures generalized alienation in terms of uncertainty about the meaningfulness of daily roles and activities and a belief that one is isolated from others.

Description

The scale comprises 15 Likert-type items; scores can range from 15 (low alienation) to 60 (high alienation). The answer alternatives are strongly agree, agree, disagree, strongly disagree. In the Jessors' study the scale was self-administered as part of an extensive questionnaire battery.

Sample

The reader should review the Sample section for Jessor and Jessor's Social Criticism Scale, since the same samples are involved. There was one high-school and one college sample.

Reliability

Internal Consistency

Scott's Homogeneity Ratio for the social criticism scale in the fourth year was .23 for both the high school and the college samples. Cronbach's α was .81 for both samples.

Test–Retest

Stability reliability over a 1-year interval was good (the lowest correlation was for high school students in years 1 and 2, which is .49).

---

[7]A similar point could be made about the connection of alienation with the standard objective background factors (race, age, social class, etc.). The size of the association will depend on the kind of measure employed. On the whole (1) the more specific the measure, the less strong the association; and (2) the prevalent expectation for high correlations may be somewhat deceiving. Thus, Lipset and Schneider (1983) note that personal trust and general politically oriented trust are not strongly associated, and "the general sense of confidence does not appear to be strongly rooted in social groups" (p. 120). Inglehart (1978) makes a similar point about the association between objective social status and subjective life satisfaction.

Validity

Convergent

The authors' general approach to construct validation was described in the review of their Social Criticism Scale. The alienation scale correlates fairly highly with several other scales, as shown in Table 5. These are reasonable variables to be negatively correlated with a general measure of alienation.

Discriminant

Low correlations of the scale with other, conceptually unrelated variables in the study provide evidence for discriminant validity.

Location

Jessor, R., & Jessor, S. (1977). *Problem behavior and psychosocial development.* New York: Academic Press.

Results and Comments

The main hypothesis concerning the effects of personal belief structures is as follows: "Acceptance of social norms and practices . . . can serve as a powerful control over engaging in actions that . . . [are] included in the domain covered by the concept of problem behavior" (1977, p. 21). Alienation, since it implies a lack of social connectedness and purposiveness, was hypothesized to reduce regulatory influence and thereby increase the prevalence of problem behavior. Overall, the results of the cross-sectional analysis (using data from Year 4) showed no consistent relationship between alienation and problem behavior. The one exception to that pattern was a significant correlation ($r = .30$) between alienation and marijuana involvement in college females. College women who used marijuana at least once were significantly more alienated than nonusing college females.

When the initial year of the college sample was analyzed (Jessor et al., 1973), and marijuana use was more discretely defined, it was found that college male heavy users were significantly more alienated than were moderate and nonusers. High school males who moved from nonuser to user status during the first year of the study showed a significantly higher alienation score in the initial year.

The analysis of the Year 3 high school students (Jessor & Jessor, 1973) revealed higher levels of alienation among female problem drinkers.

Table 5
Correlation with Alienation Scale

	Females	Males
Expectation for affection	−.57	−.45
Self-esteem	−.60	−.52
Rotter's I-E	−.43	−.45
Friends' support	−.44	−.39
Parent–friend compatibility	−.37	−.38

Alienation Scale

1. I sometimes feel that the kids I know are not too friendly.

STRONGLY AGREE   AGREE   DISAGREE   STRONGLY DISAGREE

*2. Most of my academic work in school seems worthwhile and meaningful to me.

3. I sometimes feel uncertain about who I really am.

4. I feel that my family is not as close to me as I would like.

*5. When kids I know are having problems, it's my responsibility to try to help.

6. I often wonder whether I'm becoming the kind of person I want to be.

7. It's hard to know how to act most of the time since you can't tell what others expect.

8. I often feel left out of things that others are doing.

9. Nowadays you can't really count on other people when you have problems or need help.

10. Most people don't seem to accept me when I'm just being myself.

11. I often find it difficult to feel involved in the things I'm doing.

12. Hardly anyone I know is interested in how I really feel inside.

*13. I generally feel that I have a lot of interests in common with the other students in this school.

14. I often feel alone when I am with other people.

15. If I really had my choice I'd live my life in a very different way than I do.

Note: "Strongly agree" = 5; items preceded by asterisks are reverse-scored.

Alienation Test

(Maddi et al., 1979)

Variable

This measure was designed to be conceptually comprehensive of alienation and to assess a conscious subjective state.

Description

This scale was created to avoid the common problem with alienation scales of imprecision on the one hand and overly narrow focus on the other. Four types of alienation (powerlessness, adventurousness, nihilism, and vegetativeness) and five contexts of alienation (work, social institutions, family, other persons, and self) are measured. Each question is intended to tap one type and one context of alienation. The scale consists of 60 items (most of which are worded very strongly) with 15 items for each type of alienation and 12 items for each context of alienation. Respondents are asked to rate each item with a number from 0 (which indicates that the respondent feels the item is not true at all) to 100 (which indicates the respondent feels it is completely true). Scores vary between 0 (low alienation) and 6000 (high alienation) with higher scores reflecting greater alienation.

Sample

The 60 alienation items and other self-report measures were administered in group settings five times. Study 1 sampled college students (who were paid for their time) ($n = 89$), Study 4 sampled high school students (who were also paid for their time) ($n = 24$), Study 2 sampled adults who were engaged in religious activities ($n = 37$), Study 3 sampled middle and upper level management personnel at a large utilities corporation ($n = 316$), and Study 5 sampled clerical and sales personnel in an insurance company ($n = 38$).

Reliability

Internal Consistency

Internal consistency was found to be high. Following are the coefficient α values for studies 1 and 2:

Scale	Study 1	Study 2
Contexts		
Work	.83	.75
Social institutions	.80	.76
Interpersonal relations	.75	.72
Family	.77	.81
Forms of alienation		
Powerlessness	.90	.85
Vegetativeness	.88	.83
Nihilism	.82	.79
Adventurousness	.76	.74
Total alienation	.95	.93

The average intercorrelation of scales ranges from moderate to high, and correlations between individual scales and the total scale are all substantial (Table 6).

Table 6
Average Intercorrelation of Scales of the Alienation Test (Studies 1–5)

	1	2	3	4	5	6	7	8	9	Total
1 Work	—	.68	.63	.50	.62	.72	.76	.75	.65	.82
2 Social Inst.		—	.69	.50	.55	.73	.71	.74	.70	.82
3 Interp. Rel.			—	.60	.63	.79	.74	.83	.65	.85
4 Family				—	.66	.74	.72	.73	.66	.79
5 Self					—	.78	.82	.74	.59	.83
6 Powerlessness						—	.78	.80	.62	.91
7 Vegetativeness							—	.83	.59	.60
8 Nihilism								—	.61	.91
9 Adventurousness									—	.79

Test–Retest

Stability over a three-week period was described as moderate but adequate.

Validity

Convergent

Alienation scores tend to decrease with increasing age and socioeconomic level, and females are generally more alienated than males. Correlations of the alienation scores with other measures of relevance (in Study 2) revealed (S. R. Maddi, S. C. Kobasa, & M. Hoover, undated manual) that persons high in alienation tend to

> believe in an external locus of control, experience existential vacuum rather than a sense of purpose, do not fear death though they do experience considerable general anxiety, feel guilty over missed opportunities yet fearful of the future because of its uncertainty, and espouse conformist rather than individualistic values and views. (pp. 11–12)

Discriminant

Correlations of alienation scores with a general personality inventory (personal preference record) in Study 4 showed that alienated persons tend not to be oriented toward achievement, dominance, endurance, nurturance, or socially desirable responding. In addition, correlations with the Crowne and Marlowe index of social desirability were not significant in Study 5.

Location

Maddi, S. R., Kobasa, S. C., & Hoover, M. (1979). An alienation test. *Journal of Humanistic Psychology,* **19,** 73–76.

Maddi, S. R., Kobasa, S. C., & Hoover, M. The alienation test. Unpublished manual, University of Chicago.

Results and Comments

The authors suggest that further attention is needed to determine whether the various types and areas of alienation are really distinct enough to constitute different sources of information. The current results show adventurousness to be somewhat distinct from the other three types (although all four types show the expected positive relationship with the total alienation score).

In one study (Kobasa, 1979), it was found that hardy executives (those exposed to high levels of stress and yet resistant to illness) have the following characteristics: They (1) are committed rather than alienated from the self, (2) are vigorous rather than vegetative, (3) had a meaningfulness orientation rather than a nihilist orientation, and (4) exhibited internal rather than external locus of control.

The Alienation Test

Instructions. The items below consist of statements with which you may agree or disagree. Please indicate how you feel about each item by placing a number from 0 to 100 in the space provided. A zero indicates that you feel the item is not at all true; 100 indicates that you feel the item is completely true.

As you will see, *many of the items are worded very strongly.* This is so you will be able to decide the *degree* to which you agree or disagree.

Please read all the items very carefully. Be sure to answer all on the basis of the way you feel now.

These items have to do with your attitude toward WORK.

_____ 1. Those who work for a living are manipulated by the bosses. (P)

```
0    10    20    30    40    50    60    70    80    90    100
```

_____ 2. I wonder why I work at all. (V)

_____ 3. Most of life is wasted in meaningless activity. (N)

_____ 4. If you have to work, you might as well choose a career where you deal with matters of life and death. (A)

_____ 5. No matter how hard you work, you never really seem to reach your goals. (P)

_____ 6. I find it difficult to imagine enthusiasm concerning work. (V)

_____ 7. It doesn't matter if people work hard at their jobs; only a few bosses profit. (N)

_____ 8. Ordinary work is too boring to be worth doing. (A)

_____ 9. I feel no need to try my best at work for it makes no difference anyway. (P)

_____ 10. I don't like my job or enjoy my work; I just put in my time to get paid. (V)

_____ 11. I find it hard to believe people who actually feel that the work they perform is of value to society. (N)

_____ 12. If a job is dangerous, that makes it all the better. (A)

These items have do with your attitude toward SELF.

_____ 13. Thinking of yourself as a free person leads to great frustration and difficulty. (P)

_____ 14. The human's fabled ability to think is not really such an advantage. (V)

_____ 15. The attempt to know yourself is a waste of effort. (N)

_____ 16. I am really interested in the possibility of expanding my consciousness through drugs. (A)

_____ 17. No matter how hard I try, my efforts will accomplish nothing. (P)

_____ 18. Life is empty and has no meaning for me. (V)

_____ 19. The belief in individuality is only justifiable to impress others. (N)

_____ 20. I wish I could be carried away by a revelation, as apparently happened to some historically important persons. (A)

_____ 21. Often I do not really know my own mind. (P)

_____ 22. I long for a simple life in which body needs are the most important things and decisions don't have to be made. (V)

_____ 23. Unfortunately, people don't seem to know that they are only creatures after all. (N)

_____ 24. The most exciting thing for me is my own fantasies. (A)

These items have to do with your attitude toward SOCIAL INSTITUTIONS.

_____ 25. Politicians control our lives. (P)

_____ 26. Our laws are so unfair that I want nothing to do with them. (V)

_____ 27. The only reason to involve yourself in society is to gain power. (N)

_____ 28. I would drop almost anything in order to join some big cause. (A)

_____ 29. Most of my activities are determined by what society demands. (P)

_____ 30. In order to avoid being hassled by society, I feel I must go my own way and not get involved. (V)

_____ 31. No matter how sincerely you work for social change, society never really seems to improve. (N)

_____ 32. My most meaningful experiences have come through participation in social movements. (A)

_____ 33. There are only certain strict paths to follow if one is to be successful in our society. (P)

_____ 34. Our society holds no worthwhile values or goals. (V)

_____ 35. Why should I bother to vote; none of the candidates will be able to change things for the better. (N)

_____ 36. I admire those who participate in protest movements that are full of danger and drama. (A)

These items have to do with your attitude toward INTERPERSONAL RELATIONS.

_____ 37. Everyone is out to manipulate you toward his own ends. (P)

_____ 38. I am better off when I keep to myself. (V)

_____ 39. Most people are happy not to know that what they call love is really self-interest. (N)

_____ 40. Big parties are very exciting to me. (A)

_____ 41. Often when I interact with others, I feel insecure over the outcome. (P)

_____ 42. There is no point in socializing—it goes nowhere and is nothing. (V)

_____ 43. Why bother to try to love or care for people; they'll only hurt you in the end. (N)

_____ 44. What really turns me on about socializing is the challenge of a group of people disagreeing and arguing. (A)

_____ 45. I try to avoid close relationships with people so that I will not be obligated to them. (P)

_____ 46. Most social relationships are meaningless. (V)

_____ 47. People who believe that "Love makes the world go around" are fooling themselves. (N)

_____ 48. The best reason for getting involved with other people is participation in some action that can catch everybody up. (A)

These items have to do with your attitude toward FAMILY.

_____ 49. When you marry and have children you have lost your freedom of choice. (P)

_____ 50. I would just as soon avoid any contact with my children except an occasional letter. (V)

_____ 51. The idea of a family is a social invention to limit individual freedom of action. (N)

_____ 52. It would be really exciting to have another, secret life to supplement your family life. (A)

_____ 53. My parents imposed their wishes and standards on me too much. (P)

_____ 54. Parents work hard for their children only to be disappointed and rejected. (V)

_____ 55. The only reason to marry is for convenience and security. (N)

_____ 56. Strange though it may seem, it is at times of family crisis that I feel most alive. (A)

_____ 57. I am not sure I want to stay married because I don't want to feel tied down. (P)

_____ 58. For me, home and family have never had much positive meaning. (V)

_____ 59. Families do not provide security and warmth; they just restrict a person and give him many unnecessary responsibilities. (N)

_____ 60. What I really like about family life is the huge, action-filled reunions at holiday times. (A)

Note: Letters indicate the type of alienation to which each item is keyed. Space is provided before each item for the respondent to insert a number from 0 to 100.

Future Research Directions

We still have a long way to go in developing sophisticated and thoroughly tested measures of alienation. Too many of the present scales fail to balance positive and negative wordings (Reiser, Wallace, & Scheussler, 1986); the newer techniques of structural equation modeling need to be applied in the scale evaluation process (Judd *et al.*, 1986); and considerably more in the way of longitudinal and replicational work is needed.

These needs and infirmities, however, should be put in perspective. It is well to remember that the seemingly "classical" concept of alienation, in the sense at issue in these scales, did not appear in the first edition of the *Encyclopedia of the Social Sciences*. The idea was only rediscovered in the 1930s via Marx's Parisian manuscripts and became an object of modern empirical inquiry considerably later than that. The wedding of philosophy, social theory, and quantitative technique was never guaranteed to be easy, but that is the task that remains.

Bibliography

Abrahamson, M. (1980). Sudden wealth, gratification, and attainment. *American Sociological Review*, **45**, 49–57.

Angell, R. C. (1962). Preferences for moral norms in three problem areas. *American Journal of Sociology*, **67**, 650–660.

Antonovsky, A. (1987). *Unraveling the mystery of health: How people manage stress and stay well.* San Francisco: Jossey-Bass.

Armor, D. J., Polich, J. M., & Stambul, H. B. (1978). *Alcoholism and treatment.* New York: Wiley.

Bacharach, S. B., & Aiken, M. (1979). The impact of alienation, meaninglessness, and meritocracy on supervisor and subordinate satisfaction. *Social Forces,* **57,** 853–870.

Baer, L., Eitzen, D., Duprey, C., & Thompson, N. (1976). The consequences of objective and subjective status inconsistency. *Sociological Quarterly,* **17,** 389–400.

Balch, G. I. (1974). Multiple indicators in survey research: The concept "sense of political efficacy." *Political Methodology,* **1,** 1–43.

Bell, D. (1957). *Work and its discontents: The cult of efficiency in America.* Boston: Beacon Press.

Benson, P. L., Severs, D., Tatgenhorst, J., & Loddengaard, N. (1980). The social costs of obesity: A non-reactive field study. *Social Behavior and Personality,* **8,** 91–96.

Biegel, D. E., McCardle, E., & Mendelson, S. (1985). *Social networks and mental health: An annotated bibliography.* Beverly Hills, CA: Sage.

Blauner, R. (1964). *Alienation and freedom: The factory worker and his industry.* Chicago: Univ. of Chicago Press.

Blocker, T. J., & Riedesel, P. (1978). The nonconsequences of objective and subjective status inconsistency. *The Sociological Quarterly,* **19,** 332–339.

Bonjean, C. M., & Vance, G. G. (1968). A short-form measure of self-actualization. *Journal of Applied Behavioral Sciences,* **4,** 299–312.

Brown, J. D. (1986). Evaluations of self and others: Self-enhancement biases in social judgment. *Social Cognition,* **4,** 353–376.

Burger, J. M., & Arkin, R. M. (1980). Prediction, control, and learned helplessness. *Journal of Personality and Social Psychology,* **38,** 482–491.

Burger, J. M., & Cooper, H. M. (1979). The desirability of control. *Motivation and Emotion,* **3,** 381–393.

Burger, J. M., & Smith, N. G. (1985). Desire for control and gambling behavior among problem gamblers. *Personality and Social Psychology Bulletin,* **11,** 145–152.

Burris, B. H. (1983). The human effects of underemployment. *Social Problems,* **31,** 96–110.

Campbell, A., & Converse, P. E. (1976). *The quality of American life.* New York: Russell Sage Foundation.

Christie, R., & Geis, F. L. (1970). *Studies in Machiavellianism.* New York: Academic Press.

Clark, J. (1959). Measuring alienation within a social system. *American Sociological Review,* **24,** 849–852.

Collins, B. E. (1974). Four separate components of the Rotter I-E scale: Belief in a just world, a predictable world, a difficult world, and a politically responsive world. *Journal of Personality and Social Psychology,* **29,** 381–391.

Crumbaugh, J. (1968). Cross-validation of a purpose-in-life test based on Frankl's concepts. *Journal of Individual Psychology,* **24,** 74–81.

Crumbaugh, J. (1977). The Seeking of Noetic Goals Test (SONG): A complementary scale to the Purpose in Life Test (PIL). *Journal of Clinical Psychology,* **33,** 900–907.

Dana, R. H. (1985, April). *Sense of coherence: Examination of the construct.* Paper presented at the meeting of the Southwestern Psychological Association, Austin, TX.

Davids, A. (1955). Alienation, social apperception, and ego structure. *Journal of Consulting Psychology,* **19,** 21–27.

Dean, D. (1961). Alienation: Its meaning and measurement. *American Sociological Review,* **26,** 753–758.

Dworkin, A. (1979). Ideology formation: A linear structural model of the influences of feminist ideology. *Sociological Quarterly,* **20,** 345–358.

Epperson, S. C. (1963). Some interpersonal and performance correlates of classroom alienation. *School Review,* **71,** 360–376.

Featherman, D. L. (1971). The socioeconomic achievement of white, religio-ethnic sub-groups: social and psychological explanations. *American Sociological Review,* **36,** 207–222.

Fenigstein, A., Scheier, M. F., & Buss, A. H. (1975). Public and private self-consciousness: Assessment and theory. *Journal of Clinical and Consulting Psychology,* **43,** 522–527.

Finifter, A. (1970). Dimensions of political alienation. *American Political Science Review,* **64,** 389–410.

Franks, D. D., & Marolla, J. (1976). Efficacious action and social approval as interacting dimensions of self esteem: A tentative formulation through construct validation. *Sociometry,* **4,** 324–341.

Freudenburg, N. (1984). *Not in our backyards: community action for health and the environment.* New York: Monthly Review Press.

Gamson, W. (1961). The fluoridation dialogue: Is it an ideological conflict? *Public Opinion Quarterly,* **25,** 526–537.

Goffman, E. (1957). Alienation from interaction. *Human Relations,* **10,** 47–60.

Groat, H. T., & Neal, A. (1967). Social psychological correlates of urban fertility. *American Sociological Review,* **32,** 945–959.

Gurin, P., Gurin, G., & Morrison, B. M. (1978). Personal and ideological aspects of internal and external control. *Social Psychology,* **41,** 275–296.

Guthrie, G. M., & Tanco, P. P. (1980). Alienation. In H. M. Triandis & J. G. Draguns (Eds.), *Handbook of cross-cultural psychology* (Vol. 6, pp. 9–59). Boston: Allyn & Bacon.

Hackman, J. R., & Oldham, G. R. (1975). Development of the job diagnostic survey. *Journal of Applied Psychology,* **60,** 159–170.

Helmreich, R., & Stapp, J. (1974). Short forms of the Texas Social Behavior Inventory (TSBI), an objective measure of self-esteem. *Bulletin of the Psychonomic Society,* **4,** 473–475.

Holian, J. (1972). Alienation and social awareness among college students. *Sociological Quarterly,* **13,** 114–125.

Horton, J., & Thompson, W. (1962). Powerlessness and political negativism: A study of defeated local referendums. *American Journal of Sociology,* **67,** 485–493.

Hyman, H., Wright, C., & Hopkins, T. (1962). *Applications of methods of evaluation.* Berkeley: Univ. of California Press.

Inglehart, R. (1978). Value priorities, life satisfaction, and political dissatisfaction. In R. Tomasson (Ed.), *Comparative studies in sociology* (Vol. 1, pp. 173–202). New York: JAI Press.

Inkeles, A., & Smith, D. R. (1974). *Becoming modern: Industrial change in six developing countries.* Cambridge, MA: Harvard Univ. Press.

Israel, J. (1971). *Alienation: From Marx to modern society.* Boston: Allyn & Bacon.

Jennings, M. K., & Niemi, R. G. (1981). *Generations and politics.* Princeton, NJ: Princeton Univ. Press.

Jessor, R., & Jessor, S. (1973). Problem drinking in youth. In M. E. Chafetz (Ed.), *Psychological and social factors in drinking* (National Institute on Alcohol Abuse and Alcoholism). Washington, DC: U.S. Government Printing Office.

Jessor, R., & Jessor, S. L. (1977). *Problem behavior and psychosocial development.* New York: Academic Press.

Jessor, R., Graves, T., Hanson, R. C., & Jessor, S. L. (1968). *Society, personality, and deviant behavior.* New York: Holt, Rinehart & Winston.

Jessor, R., Jessor, S., & Finney, J. (1973). A social psychology of marijuana use. *Journal of Personality and Social Psychology,* **26,** 1–15.

Johnson, H. M. (1960). *Sociology: A systematic introduction.* New York: Harcourt, Brace.

Judd, C. M., Jessor, R., & Donovan, J. E. (1986). Structural equation models and personality research. *Journal of Personality,* **54,** 149–198.

Kahl, J. A. (1965). Some measures of achievement orientation. *American Journal of Sociology,* **70,** 669–681.

Karasek, R. A. (1981). Job socialization and job strain: The implications of two related psychosocial mechanisms for job design. In B. Gardell & G. Johnson (Eds.), *Working life* (pp. 75–94). New York: Wiley.

Kobasa, S. C. (1979). Stressful life events, personality, and health. *Journal of Personality and Social Psychology,* **37,** 1–11.

Kobasa, S. C. (1981). The hardy personality: Toward a social psychology of stress and health. In G. Suls (Ed.), *Social psychology of health and illness* (pp. 3–32). Hillsdale, NJ: Erlbaum.

Kohn, M. L. (1981). Personality, occupation, and social stratification. In D. J. Treiman & R. V. Robinson (Eds.), *Research in social stratification and mobility: A research annual* (Vol. 1, pp. 267–297). Greenwich, CT: JAI Press.

Kohn, M. L., & Schooler, C. (1969). Class, occupation, and orientation. *American Sociological Review,* **34,** 659–678.

Kohn, M. L., & Schooler, C. (1973). Occupation and psychological functioning. *American Sociological Review,* **38,** 97–118.

Kohn, M. L., & Schooler, C. (1983). *Work and personality: An inquiry into the impact of social stratification.* Norwood, NJ: Ablex.

Lau, R. R., & Ware, J. E. (1981). Refinements in the measurement of health-specific locus of control beliefs. *Medical Care,* **19,** 1147–1158.

Lefcourt, H. M., von Baeyer, C. L., Ware, E. E., & Cox, D. J. (1979). The multi-dimensional multi-attributional scale: The development of a goal specific locus of control scale. *Canadian Journal of Behavioural Science,* **11,** 286–303.

Lenski, G. E., & Leggett, J. C. (1960). Caste, class, and deference in the research interview. *American Journal of Sociology,* **65,** 463–467.

Lipset, S. M., & Schneider, W. (1983). *The confidence gap.* New York: Free Press.

Lodahl, T., & Kejner, M. (1965). The definition and measurement of job involvement. *Journal of Applied Psychology,* **49,** 24–33.

Lorence, J., & Mortimer, J. (1985). Job involvement through the life course. *American Sociological Review,* **50,** 618–638.

Maddi, S. R., Kobasa, S. C., & Hoover, M. (1979). An alienation test. *Journal of Humanistic Psychology,* **19,** 73–76.

Magnusson, D. (Ed.) (1981). *Towards a psychology of situations: An interactional perspective.* Hillsdale, NJ: Erlbaum.

Martin, W. C., Bengston, V. L., & Acock, A. C. (1974). Alienation and age: A context-specific approach. *Social Forces,* **53,** 266–274.

Mason, W. M., House, J. S., & Martin, S. S. (1985). On the dimensions of political alienation in America. In N. Tuma (Ed.), *Sociological methodology* (pp. 111–151). San Francisco: Jossey-Bass.

McClosky, H., & Schaar, J. H. (1965). Psychological dimensions of anomy. *American Sociological Review,* **30,** 14–40.

Merton, R. K. (1957). Social structure and anomie. In *Social theory and social structure.* Glencoe, IL: Free Press.

Middleton, R. (1963). Alienation, race, and education. *American Sociological Review,* **28,** 973–977.

Miller, C. R., & Butler, E. W. (1966). Anomia and eunomia: A methodological evaluation of Srole's anomia scale. *American Sociological Review,* **31,** 400–406.

Miller, A. R., Treiman, D. J., Cain, P. S., & Roos, P. A. (Eds.) (1980). *Work, jobs, and occupations.* Washington, DC: National Academy Press.

Mirowsky, J., & Ross, C. E. (1983). Paranoia and the structure of powerlessness. *American Sociological Review,* **48,** 228–239.

Morrison, R. (1977). Career adaptivity: The effective adaptation of managers to changing role demands, *Journal of Applied Psychology,* **62,** 549–558.

Mortimer, J. T., & Finch, M. D. (1984). *Autonomy as a source of self-esteem in adolescence.* Paper presented at the annual meeting of the American Sociological Association.

Mortimer, J. T., Lorence, J., & Kumka, D. (1986). *Work, family, and personality: Transition to adulthood.* Norwood, NJ: Ablex.

Neal, A. G., & Groat, H. T. (1974). Social class correlates of stability and change in levels of alienation. *Sociological Quarterly,* **15,** 548–558.

Neal, A. G., & Rettig, S. (1963). Dimensions of alienation among manual and non-manual workers. *American Sociological Review,* **28,** 599–608.

Neal, A. G., & Rettig, S. (1967). On the multidimensionality of alienation. *American Sociological Review,* **32,** 54–64.

Neal, A., & Seeman, M. (1964). Organizations and powerlessness: A test of the mediation hypothesis. *American Sociological Review, 29,* 216–226.

Nettler, G. (1957). A measure of alienation. *American Sociological Review, 22,* 670–677.

Nettler, G. (1964). *Scales of alienated attitude* (revised). Unpublished Manual, Department of Sociology, University of Alberta.

Olsen, M. (1969). Two categories of political alienation. *Social Forces, 47,* 288–299.

Parsons, T. (1968). Durkheim. In D. L. Sills (Ed.), *International encyclopedia of the social sciences* (pp. 311–320). New York: Macmillan and Free Press.

Patchen, M. (1965). *Participation, achievement, and involvement on the job.* Englewood Cliffs, NJ: Prentice-Hall.

Paulhus, D., & Christie, R. (1981). Spheres of control: An interactionist approach to assessment of perceived control. In H. Lefcourt (Ed.), *Research with the locus of control concept* (Vol. 1, pp. 161–186). New York: Academic Press.

Pearlin, L., & Schooler, C. (1978). The structure of coping. *Journal of Health and Social Behavior, 19,* 2–21.

Pearlin, L., Lieberman, M., Menaghan, E., & Mullan, J. (1981). The stress process. *Journal of Health and Social Behavior, 22,* 337–356.

Peterson, C., Semmel, A., von Baeyer, C., Abramson, L. Y., Metalsky, G. I., & Seligman, M. E. P. (1982). The attributional style questionnaire. *Cognitive Therapy and Research, 6,* 287–299.

Ransford, H. E. (1968). Isolation, powerlessness, and violence: A study of attitudes and participation in the Watts riot. *American Journal of Sociology, 73,* 581–591.

Reiser, M., Wallace, M., & Scheussler, K. (1986). Direction of wording effect in dichotomous social life feeling items. In N. Tuma (Ed.), *Sociological methodology* (pp. 1–25). San Francisco: Jossey-Bass.

Reker, G. T., Peacock, E. J., & Wong, P. T. P. (1987). Meaning and purpose in life and well-being: A life-span perspective. *Journal of Gerontology, 42,* 44–49.

Roberts, B. R., (1987). A confirmatory factor-analytic model of alienation. *Social Psychology Quarterly, 50,* 346–351.

Robinson, J. P., & Shaver, P. R. (1969). *Measures of social psychological attitudes.* Ann Arbor: University of Michigan, Institute for Social Research.

Rook, K. S. (1984). Research on social support, loneliness, and social isolation: Toward an integration. In P. Shaver (Ed.), *Review of personality and social psychology* (Vol. 5, pp. 239–264). Beverly Hills, CA: Sage.

Rose, A. M. (1962). *Human behavior and social process: An interactionist approach.* Boston: Houghton Mifflin.

Rosen, B. C. (1956). The achievement syndrome: A psychocultural dimension of social stratification. *American Sociological Review, 21,* 203–211.

Rossi, P. H., & Berk, R. A. (1985). Varieties of normative consensus. *American Sociological Review, 50,* 333–347.

Rotter, J. B. (1966). Generalized expectancies for internal versus external control of reinforcements. *Psychological Monographs, 80,* 1–28.

Rotter, J. B. (1967). A new scale for the measurement of interpersonal trust. *Journal of Personality, 35,* 651–665.

Rotter, J. B. (1980). Interpersonal trust, trustworthiness, and gullibility. *American Psychologist, 35,* 1–7.

Rousseau, D. M. (1982). Job perceptions when working with data, people, and things. *Journal of Occupational Psychology, 55,* 43–52.

Rumbaut, R. G., Anderson, J. P., & Kaplan, R. M. (in press). Stress, health, and the sense of coherence. In M. J. Magenheim (Ed.), *Geriatric medicine and the social sciences.* Philadelphia: Saunders.

Scheier, M. F., & Carver, C. (1985). Optimism, coping, and health: assessment and implications of generalized outcome expectancies. *Health Psychology, 4,* 219–247.

Scheussler, K. F. (1982). *Measuring social life feelings.* San Francisco: Jossey-Bass.

Seeman, M. (1959). On the meaning of alienation. *American Sociological Review, 24,* 783–791.

Seeman, M. (1966). Status and identity: The problem of inauthenticity. *Pacific Sociological Review*, **9**, 67–73.

Seeman, M. (1967). On the personal consequences of alienation in work. *American Sociological Review*, **32**, 273–285.

Seeman, M. (1972). The signals of '68: Alienation in pre-crisis France. *American Sociological Review*, **38**, 385–402.

Seeman, M. (1975). Alienation studies. *Annual Review of Sociology*, **1**, 91–123.

Seeman, M. (1982). A prolegomenon regarding empirical research on anomie. In S. G. Shoham & A. Grahame (Eds.), *Alienation and anomie revisited* (pp. 121–138). Tel Aviv, Israel: Ramot.

Seeman, M. (1983). Alienation motifs in contemporary theorizing: The hidden continuity of the classic themes. *Social Psychology Quarterly*, **46**, 171–184.

Seeman, M. (1984). A legacy of protest: The "events of May" in retrospect. *Political Psychology*, **5**, 437–464.

Seeman, M., & Evans, J. W. (1962). Alienation and learning in a hospital setting. *American Sociological Review*, **27**, 772–782.

Sergent, J., & Lambert, W. E. (1979). Learned helplessness or learned incompetence? *Canadian Journal of Behavioural Science*, **11**, 257–273.

Seybolt, J. W., & Gruenfeld, L. (1976). The discriminant validity of work alienation and work satisfaction measures. *Journal of Occupational Psychology*, **49**, 193–202.

Shepard, J. M. (1971). *Automation and alienation: A study of office and factory workers*. Cambridge, MA: MIT Press.

Shepard, J. M., & Panko, T. R. (1974). Alienation: A discrepancy approach. *Sociological Quarterly*, **15**, 253–263.

Shrauger, J. S., & Osberg, T. M. (1983). Self-awareness: The ability to predict one's future behavior. In G. Underwood (Ed.), *Aspects of consciousness* (Vol. 3, pp. 267–313). New York: Academic Press.

Slomczynski, K., Miller, J., & Kohn, M. (1981). Stratification, work, and values. *American Sociological Review*, **46**, 720–744.

Smith, P. C., Kendall, L. M., & Hulin, C. L. (1969). *The measurement of satisfaction in work and retirement*. Chicago: Rand McNally.

Spenner, K. I., & Featherman, D. L. (1978). Achievement ambitions. *Annual Review of Sociology*, **4**, 373–420.

Srole, L. (1956). Social integration and certain corollaries. *American Sociological Review*, **21**, 709–716.

Streuning, E. L., & Richardson, A. H. (1965). A factor analytic exploration of the alienation, anomie, and authoritarianism domain. *American Sociological Review*, **30**, 768–776.

Taub, R., Surgeon, G., Lindholm, S., Betts, P., & Bridges, A. (1977). Urban voluntary associations. *American Journal of Sociology*, **83**, 425–441.

Touraine, A. (1973). *Production de la société*. Paris: Editions de Seuil.

Turner, R. H., & Gordon, S. L. (1981). The boundaries of the self: The relationship of authenticity to inauthenticity in the self conception. In M. D. Lynch, A. A. Norem-Hebeisen, & K. J. Gergen (Eds.), *The self concept: Advances in theory and research* (pp. 39–57). Cambridge, MA: Ballinger.

Turner, R. H., & Schutte, J. (1981). The true self method for studying the self-conception. *Symbolic Interaction*, **4**, 1–12.

Wallston, K. A., & Wallston, B. S. (1981). Health locus of control scale. In H. M. Lefcourt (Ed.), *Research with the locus of control scale* (Vol. 1, pp. 189–243). New York: Academic Press.

Wilensky, H. (1968). Varieties of work experience. In H. Borow (Ed.), *Man in a world of work* (pp. 125–154). Boston: Houghton Mifflin.

Wright, J. D. (1981). Political disaffection. In S. Long (Ed.), *The handbook of political behavior* (Vol. 4, pp. 1–79). New York: Plenum.

Zeller, R., Neal, A., & Groat, H. T. (1980). On the reliability and stability of alienation measures. *Social Forces*, **58**, 1195–1204.

CHAPTER 8

Interpersonal Trust and Attitudes toward Human Nature

Lawrence S. Wrightsman

Human nature is a pervasive explanatory concept; most of us use it to justify our own behavior and that of others. Our beliefs about human nature may influence everything from how we bargain with a used-car salesperson to whether we accept or reject the latest proposal by the Soviet Union to reduce stockpiles of nuclear missiles.

We develop such attitudes because the behavior of other people is a great influence upon our success in life. Whatever goals we may have, obstacles to their achievement often result from the actions of other people as well as ourselves and the physical environment. Hence we seek to understand other people, to simplify them, and to make them appear to act in consistent ways. We also seek to develop substantive beliefs about people. Are they selfish? Can their word be trusted?

Not only do we form such general attitudes from our experiences but as previously noted, these attitudes, once formed, affect our dealings with other people. Each of us faces decisions about whether to permit a stranger to come in our house and use our telephone, whether to trust a friend with our innermost secrets, whether to loan money to a member of our family. Our attitudes toward human nature play a central part in our decisions about how to interact with others. Concepts such as Machiavellianism and "faith in people," detailed in this section, have as their foundation our conceptions of the nature of human nature.

Despite this breadth of influence, measures of general attitudes toward people show considerable underdevelopment and underutilization when we consider the number of phenomena that can be related to them. (This conclusion, from the 1969 edition of *Measures of Social Psychological Attitudes*, is even more relevant today.) Not only are these attitudes employed to interpret everyday experiences, but they also appear to be well-structured and concrete. In the course of a comprehensive, racial attitude change project, two of the scales reviewed in this section were virtually the only ones (out of 78 examined) that were predictive of change toward more favorable attitudes toward blacks (Wrightsman & Cook, 1965). As a further example, Rosenberg (1957) found significant correlations between the Faith in People scale and choice of an occupation.

More important, further development of constructs in this topic would assist social scientists in developing a taxonomy of basic attitudes similar to the recent "discovery" of the "big five" personality traits.

Measures Reviewed Here

Examination of the content of the scales to be described in this chapter reveals that trust is a central component to many of them. But the measurement of this concept has moved forward more rapidly than its conceptualization. In a thoughtful review of measures of trust, Stack (1978) observed that:

> A major problem in the study of trust has been that although all words carry multiple meanings to various listeners, abstract words such as *trust* have even more associative meanings than most. *Confidence, reliance,* and *faith* are often used interchangeably with the word *trust;* each of these words is also fraught with abstract associations. (p. 564, italics in original)

In subsequent sections of this chapter, this implicit conceptualization of trust (i.e., that it is reflective of several components, including reliability and faith) will be examined in more detail.

A total of eight scales receive review in this chapter. They are listed in an order that reflects two correlated aspects: their general usefulness and the amount of research they have generated. The eight scales are the following:

1. Machiavellianism Scale (Christie & Geis, 1970),
2. Philosophies of Human Nature Scale (Wrightsman, 1964, 1974),
3. Interpersonal Trust Scale (Rotter, 1967),
4. Specific Interpersonal Trust Scale (Johnson-George & Swap, 1982),
5. Trust Scale (Rempel & Holmes, 1986),
6. Faith in People Scale (Rosenberg, 1957),
7. Trust in People Scale (Survey Research Center, 1969), and
8. Acceptance of Others Scale (Fey, 1955).

Christie and Geis's (1970) Machiavellianism Scale (or Mach Scale) has the most demonstrable substantive rationale of the scales in this section. Christie based items for the scale on the writings of Niccolo Machiavelli in *The Prince.* In the two decades of its use, the scale has been employed in a wide variety of research settings and has repeatedly demonstrated its construct validity. It could be considered a showcase example of successful attitude scale construction.

The most central component of the scale taps a respondent's feelings about whether other people can be manipulated so as to achieve the respondent's goals. Thus, the person high in Machiavellianism reflects a rather perverse type of trust; that is, a confidence that others can be influenced or changed by a combination of techniques employed by the manipulator. The scale has relatively high internal consistency, and factor analyses reveal empirical factors in keeping with the content dimensions used to compose items for the scale. The scale is available in three different formats in order to control for response sets, although highly Machiavellian responses are still judged as quite socially undesirable and thus a respondent scoring high on the scale would seem to be relatively insensitive to social desirability concerns.

Although not all experiments using the scale have yielded positive results, most of the studies with negative results failed to optimize the conditions under which "high Machs" can operate. Geis and Christie (1970) reviewed 38 studies of this phenomenon that related Machiavellianism to interpersonal behavior in experimental situations. After a careful consideration of situations in which Machiavellianism did and did not make a difference, they concluded that the following three factors contributed to the emergence of a statistically significant relationship: (1) face-to-face interaction, (2) the degree of latitude for improvisation (that is, the opportunity to exaggerate, amplify, or innovate responses), and (3) the degree to which irrelevant emotion can be manifested. In situations in which these three qualities prevail, highly Machiavellian respondents are more successful in achieving their goals on the interpersonal task than are less Machiavellian subjects.

In general, Geis and Christie conclude that high Machs are most successful when given the opportunity to improvise in a face-to-face situation whereas in the same situation, low Machs are distracted by feelings that are responses to essentially irrelevant details. In such situations, high Machs "manipulate more, win more, are persuaded less, persuade others more, and otherwise differ significantly from Low Machs" (Geis & Christie, 1970, p. 312).

Wrightsman's Philosophies of Human Nature Scale is also rather elaborately conceived and has been applied in a variety of research settings. Although there are six subscales of attitudes toward human nature, the instrument was conceived of as two-dimensional in nature, the major dimension being favorability toward human nature. Factor analyses reveal that trust in other people is a central component of this general attitude toward people (Wrightsman, 1974). This instrument reflects quite satisfactory internal consistency and test–retest stability and has items scored in both positive and negative directions to control for agreement response set. The author also presents considerable evidence of the scale's essential validity.

Operating from social learning theory, Rotter (1954, 1967), in the Interpersonal Trust Scale, emphasized the expectancies the person has developed that a given behavior will lead to a specific positive or negative outcome. As Stack (1978) noted, "Each individual has different expectancies for reinforcement in interactions involving trust: He is not as likely to be reinforced for believing a stranger as for believing his best friend. . . . After many experiences with different agents in varying situations, an individual builds up generalized expectancies" (pp. 567–568). The purpose of the Interpersonal Trust Scale (IT) is to measure these expectancies.

Stack (1978), in reviewing the literature on trust, concluded that the IT questionnaire is remarkably similar to the Trustworthiness subscale on the Philosophies of Human Nature Scale. At least seven of the 25 IT items are quite similar to PHN items. But an attractive feature of the Interpersonal Trust Scale is that it permits distinction between different dimensions of trust, beyond its focusing on trust as defined by a belief in the credibility of others.

More recent measurements of trust have focused on more delimited aspects. The Specific Interpersonal Trust Scale, or SITS (Johnson-George & Swap, 1982), is designed to measure trust of another person under particular circumstances. Content of the items on the SITS generally falls into the following four categories: trusting another with material possessions, assuming that the other person is dependable, trusting the other with one's secrets and confidential information, and trusting another with one's physical safety.

The Trust Scale developed by Rempel and Holmes (1986) also concerns itself with trust in close relationships. In general the authors of this scale define trust as "the degree of confidence you feel when you think about a relationship" (Rempel & Holmes, 1986). Three fundamental aspects of trust are identified: predictability, dependability, and faith. The scale (18 items) is about the same length as the SITS.

Rosenberg's Faith in People Scale was one of the earliest scales to focus on this attitudinal area. The scale contains only five items and evidence for reliability is not impressive for the data that Rosenberg collected. However, validity of the scale was well reflected by predictable differences in respondents' occupational choice and a wide variety of related political attitudes. A limitation is that all of this research was conducted with college students.

The Survey Research Center (1969) at the University of Michigan has applied three of Rosenberg's items to a nationwide sample of adults. Here inter-item correlations are very impressive and hold up when controlled for educational level. The scale in national samples is associated as expected with optimistic and efficacious political attitudes, with feelings of personal efficacy, and with feelings of life satisfaction. Interesting differences in trust in people are also found by religious affiliation and for those with varying political views.

Fey's Acceptance of Others Scale (1955) is also mainly distinguished by the theoretically relevant results generated from its application: the findings that acceptance of others is associated with acceptance of self and estimated acceptance by others. This finding is in keeping with Erik Erikson's (1963) well-known stage theory of psychosocial development, in which resolution of the first crisis in infancy in the direction of trust rather than mistrust is considered necessary for mature development. The scale shows relatively high reliability but needs to be applied in a more comprehensive study than the one on which it was developed. Readers may find some interest in the short Estimated Acceptance by Others Scale that we have appended to this scale.

Machiavellianism

(Christie & Geis, 1970)

Variable

This measure is designed to tap a person's general strategy for dealing with people, especially the degree to which he or she feels other people are manipulable in interpersonal situations.

Description

In the construction of the original scale, 71 items were drawn from the writings of Machiavelli (*The Prince* and *The Discourses*). These were conceived as falling into three substantive areas: (1) the nature of interpersonal tactics (32 items), (2) views of human nature (28 items), and (3) abstract or generalized morality (11 items). An item analysis revealed that responses to about 60 of these were significantly correlated (at the .05 level or above) with a total "Mach" score based on the sum of all items (the items about human nature being most highly related, the ones about morality least highly related). The ten highest-related items of those worded in the Machiavellian direction were selected into the final scale (Mach IV) along with the ten highest-related items worded in the opposite direction.

An attempt was made to introduce as much content variety as possible. The balancing of items scored in both directions was designed to minimize the effects of indiscriminant agreement or disagreement.

Items are given in standard-category Likert format ("agree strongly" being scored 7, no answer 4, and "disagree strongly" 1). A constant score of 20 was added to make the lowest possible Machiavellianism score 40, the highest 160, and the neutral or midpoint score 100. A forced-choice version of this scale (Mach V) was developed to offset a significant negative correlation (*r* values around −.40) observed between Mach IV scores and Edwards's social desirability scale. Scores on Mach V also range between 40 and 160.

A "Kiddie Mach" scale (20 Likert-format items) was also developed for use with children or low education adults. Each of the three forms of the scale contains 20 items, and each has been normed so that the score 100 is the neutral point. The Kiddie Mach would seem to be the most rapidly administered, with Mach IV taking slightly more time to complete. Mach V would undoubtedly take the most time to complete. Additionally, Geis (1978, p. 307) notes about the forced-choice version, ". . . such a scale is frustrating to answer. The person is repeatedly faced with claiming one of two equally reprehensible attitudes, or with rejecting one of two equally attractive ones." Hence the authors added a third choice, removed from the other two in social desirability, to each forced-choice item.

The scales have been translated into a number of foreign languages (e.g., Chinese, Swedish).

Sample

During construction of the scales in the early 1960s, the items in the initial Mach scale were given to samples of 1196 college students in Iowa, North Carolina, and New York. A total of 1700 college students gave responses to the Mach scale, F scale, and anomie scale that formed the basis for the factor analysis reported below. The items have also been used to select students for many separate experiments to test hypotheses about Machiavellianism. Some items have also been applied to a national cross-section sample of Americans (Christie & Geis, 1970). The scale has also been applied in a number of other research settings.

Reliability

Internal Consistency

The average item–test correlation for the items in Mach IV was .38, with little difference in this value across the three content categories of items or positive versus negative item wording. Split-half reliabilities determined on subsequent samples averaged .79. (The values for comparable F scale items were .33 and .68, respectively.) Reliabilities for the forced-choice Mach V scale were somewhat lower (in the range .60–.70) but this might be expected to occur with most sets of items in which social desirability is as strictly controlled as it was in this scale.

Validity

Convergent

It is impossible to include all the evidence for the demonstrated convergent and discriminant validity of this scale. However, with respect to convergent validity, the Mach scale correlates to a very high degree (*r* values in the −.70–−.80) with the Trustworthiness subscale of the Philosophies of Human Nature Scale. The discriminant validity is reflected in the absence of significant correlations with measures of intelligence or social desirability. Suffice it to say that the scale is a model for careful construction and validation and to refer the reader to Christie and Geis (1970, Chapter 1) or Geis (1978) for details, since both of these provide extensive information about the reliability and validation of the scales. Some field study results bearing indirectly on validity are reported below (see Results and Comments).

Discriminant

With respect to divergent validity, a factor analysis of Mach items, F scale items, and anomie items resulted in four factors: one Mach factor, one F factor, one factor combining F and Mach, and one factor combining Mach and anomie. The items from Mach IV that loaded over .25 on each factor with Mach items were the following:

1. Duplicity: Items 7, 6, 9, 10, 15, 2, 3
2. Negativism: Items 8, 5, 12, 13, 1, 18, 20 (plus eight F scale items)
3. Distrust of People: Items 4, 14, 11, 16 (plus four anomie items)

Location

Christie, R., & Geis, F. L. (1970). *Studies in Machiavellianism.* New York: Academic Press.

Results and Comments

Despite the usual pejorative implications that surround the term "Machiavellian," none of Christie and Geis' evidence suggests that high Machs are more hostile, vicious, or vindictive than low Machs. Rather it appears that they have a "cool detachment" that makes them less emotionally involved with other people, with sensitive issues, or with saving face in embarrassing situations.

No differences have been found in Machiavellianism by intelligence, social status, or even social mobility. It is hypothesized that high Machs are less likely to arise from traditional societies because they operate most effectively in unstructured situations. Generational differences in Mach scores indicate that Americans are becoming more manipulative and impersonal in the Machiavellian sense (Wrightsman, 1974).

Field studies at medical schools have revealed the counterintuitive but plausible finding that psychiatrists score highest on the Mach scale and surgeons lowest (it is argued that the psychiatrist's role involves manipulation *per se* versus that of the surgeon, who has as little personal contact with patients as possible).

Mach IV (Version 1)

Listed below are a number of statements. Each represents a commonly held opinion and there are no right or wrong answers. You will probably disagree with some items and agree with others. We are interested in the extent to which you agree or disagree with such matters of opinion.

Read each statement carefully. Then indicate the extent to which you agree or disagree by circling the number in front of each statement. The numbers and their meaning are indicated below:

	Score	
	Original	Reversed
If you *agree strongly*, circle +3	7	1
If you *agree somewhat*, circle +2	6	2
If you *agree slightly*, circle +1	5	3
If you *disagree slightly*, circle −1	3	5
If you *disagree somewhat*, circle −2	2	6
If you *disagree strongly*, circle −3	1	7

First impressions are usually best in such matters. Read each statement, decide if you agree or disagree and the strength of your opinion, and then circle the appropriate number in front of the statement. *Give your opinion on every statement.*

If you find that the numbers to be used in answering do not adequately indicate your own opinion, use the one which is closest to the way you feel.

Item—test
Φ coeff.

1. Never tell anyone the real reason you did something unless it is useful to do so. .41

+3	+2	+1	−1	−2	−3
AGREE	AGREE	AGREE	DISAGREE	DISAGREE	DISAGREE
STRONGLY	SOMEWHAT	SLIGHTLY	SLIGHTLY	SOMEWHAT	STRONGLY

2. The best way to handle people is to tell them what they want to hear. .47

*3. One should take action only when sure it is morally right. .41

*4. Most people are basically good and kind. .35

5. It is safest to assume that all people have a vicious streak and it will come out when they are given a chance. .41

*6. Honesty is the best policy in all cases. .42

*7. There is no excuse for lying to someone else. .35

8. Generally speaking, men won't work hard unless they're forced to do so. .31

*9. All in all, it is better to be humble and honest than to be important and dishonest. .38

*10. When you ask someone to do something for you, it is best to give the real reasons for wanting it rather than giving reasons which carry more weight. .45

*11. Most people who get ahead in the world lead clean, moral lives. .33

12. Anyone who completely trusts anyone else is asking for trouble. .42

13. The biggest difference between most criminals and other people is that the criminals are stupid enough to get caught. .31

*14. Most men are brave. .29

15. It is wise to flatter important people.   .40

*16. It is possible to be good in all respects.   .37

*17. Barnum was wrong when he said that there's a sucker born
     every minute.   .37

18. It is hard to get ahead without cutting corners here and there.   .42

19. People suffering from incurable diseases should have the
    choice of being put painlessly to death.   .37

20. Most men forget more easily the death of their father than the
    loss of their property.   .35

Note: *, Reversed item.

Mach V Attitude Inventory (Version 2)

You will find 20 groups of statements listed below. Each group is composed of three statements. Each statement refers to a way of thinking about people or things in general. They reflect opinions and not matters of fact—there are no "right" or "wrong" answers and different people have been found to agree with different statements.

Please read each of the three statements in each group. Then decide *first* which of the statements is *most true* or comes *the closest* to describing your own beliefs. Circle a plus (+) in the space provided on the answer sheet.

Just decide which of the remaining two statements is *most false* or is the farthest from your own beliefs. Circle the minus (−) in the space provided on the answer sheet.

Here is an example:

	Most True	Most False
A. It is easy to persuade people but hard to keep them persuaded.	+	−
B. Theories that run counter to common sense are a waste of time.	⊕	−
C. It is only common sense to go along with what other people are doing and not be too different.	+	⊖

In this case, statement B would be the one you believe in most strongly and A and C would be ones that are not as characteristic of your opinion. Statement C would be the one you believe in least strongly and is least characteristic of your beliefs.

You will find some of the choices easy to make; others will be quite difficult. Do not fail to make a choice no matter how hard it may be. You will mark *two* statements in each group of three—the one that comes the closest to your own beliefs with a + and the one farthest from your beliefs with a −. The remaining statement should be left unmarked.

Do not omit any groups of statements.

1. A. It takes more imagination to be a successful criminal than a successful business man.
   B. The phrase "the road to hell is paved with good intentions" contains a lot of truth.
   C. Most men forget more easily the death of their father than the loss of their property.

2. A. Men are more concerned with the car they drive than with the clothes their wives wear.
   B. It is very important that imagination and creativity in children be cultivated.
   C. People suffering from incurable diseases should have the choice of being put painlessly to death.

3. A. Never tell anyone the real reason you did something unless it is useful to do so.
   B. The well-being of the individual is the goal that should be worked for before anything else.
   C. Once a truly intelligent person makes up his mind about the answer to a problem he rarely continues to think about it.

4. A. People are getting so lazy and self-indulgent that it is bad for our country.
   B. The best way to handle people is to tell them what they want to hear.
   C. It would be a good thing if people were kinder to others less fortunate than themselves.

5. A. Most people are basically good and kind.
   B. The best criterion for a wife or husband is compatibility—other characteristics are nice but not essential.
   C. Only after a man has gotten what he wants from life should he concern himself with the injustices in the world.

6. A. Most people who get ahead in the world lead clean, moral lives.
   B. Any man worth his salt shouldn't be blamed for putting his career above his family.
   C. People would be better off if they were concerned less with how to do things and more with what to do.

7. A. A good teacher is one who points out unanswered questions rather than gives explicit answers.
   B. When you ask someone to do something for you, it is best to give the real reasons for wanting it rather than giving reasons which might carry more weight.
   C. A person's job is the best single guide as to the sort of person he is.

8. A. The construction of such monumental works as the Egyptian pyramids was worth the enslavement of the workers who built them.
   B. Once a way of handling problems has been worked out it is best to stick to it.
   C. One should take action only when sure that it is morally right.

9. A. The world would be a much better place to live in if people would let the future take care of itself and concern themselves only with enjoying the present.

B. It is wise to flatter important people.

C. Once a decision has been made, it is best to keep changing it as new circumstances arise.

10. A. It is a good policy to act as if you are doing the things you do because you have no other choice.

B. The biggest difference between most criminals and other people is that criminals are stupid enough to get caught.

C. Even the most hardened and vicious criminal has a spark of decency somewhere within him.

11. A. All in all, it is better to be humble and honest than to be important and dishonest.

B. A man who is able and willing to work hard has a good chance of succeeding in whatever he wants to do.

C. If a thing does not help us in our daily lives, it isn't very important.

12. A. A person shouldn't be punished for breaking a law which he thinks is unreasonable.

B. Too many criminals are not punished for their crime.

C. There is no excuse for lying to someone else.

13. A. Generally speaking, men won't work hard unless they're forced to do so.

B. Every person is entitled to a second chance, even after he commits a serious mistake.

C. People who can't make up their minds aren't worth bothering about.

14. A. A man's first responsibility is to his wife, not his mother.

B. Most men are brave.

C. It's best to pick friends that are intellectually stimulating rather than ones it is comfortable to be around.

15. A. There are very few people in the world worth concerning oneself about.

B. It is hard to get ahead without cutting corners here and there.

C. A capable person motivated for his own gain is more useful to society than a well-meaning but ineffective one.

16. A. It is best to give others the impression that you can change your mind easily.

B. It is a good working policy to keep on good terms with everyone.

C. Honesty is the best policy in all cases.

17. A. It is possible to be good in all respects.

B. To help oneself is good; to help others even better.

C. War and threats of war are unchangeable facts of human life.

18. A. Barnum was probably right when he said that there's at least one sucker born every minute.

B. Life is pretty dull unless one deliberately stirs up some excitement.

C. Most people would be better off if they controlled their emotions.

19. A. Sensitivity to the feelings of others is worth more than poise in social situations.

B. The ideal society is one where everybody knows his place and accepts it.

C. It is safest to assume that all people have a vicious streak and it will come out when they are given a chance.

20. A. People who talk about abstract problems usually don't know what they are talking about.
    B. Anyone who completely trusts anyone else is asking for trouble.
    C. It is essential for the functioning of a democracy that everyone votes.

Scoring Key for Mach V (1968)
Points per Item by Response Patterns

Item number	1	3		5		7
1	A+	B+	A+	B+	C+	C+
	C−	C−	B−	A−	B−	A−
2	A+	B+	A+	B+	C+	C+
	C−	C−	B−	A−	B−	A−
3	C+	B+	C+	B+	A+	A+
	A−	A−	B−	C−	B−	C−
4	A+	C+	A+	C+	B+	B+
	B−	B−	C−	A−	C−	A−
5	A+	C+	A+	C+	B+	B+
	B−	B−	C−	A−	C−	A−
6	A+	B+	A+	B+	C+	C+
	C−	C−	B−	A−	B−	A−
7	B+	C+	B+	C+	A+	A+
	A−	A−	C−	B−	C−	B−
8	C+	A+	C+	A+	B+	B+
	B−	B−	A−	C−	A−	C−
9	C+	A+	C+	A+	B+	B+
	B−	B−	A−	C−	A−	C−
10	A+	C+	A+	C+	B+	B+
	B−	B−	C−	A−	C−	A−
11	A+	C+	A+	C+	B+	B+
	B−	B−	C−	A−	C−	A−
12	C+	A+	C+	A+	B+	B+
	B−	B−	A−	C−	A−	C−
13	C+	B+	C+	B+	A+	A+
	A−	A−	B−	C−	B−	C−
14	B+	A+	B+	A+	C+	C+
	C−	C−	A−	B−	A−	B−
15	C+	A+	C+	A+	B+	B+
	B−	B−	A−	C−	A−	C−
16	C+	A+	C+	A+	B+	B+
	B−	B−	A−	C−	A−	C−
17	A+	B+	A+	B+	C+	C+
	C−	C−	B−	A−	B−	A−
18	C+	B+	C+	B+	A+	A+
	A−	A−	B−	C−	B−	C−
19	B+	A+	B+	A+	C+	C+
	C−	C−	A−	B−	A−	B−
20	A+	C+	A+	C+	B+	B+
	B−	B−	C−	A−	C−	A−

Sum for all 20 items and add constant of 20. Range: 40–160.

Kiddie Mach (Version 3)

On the next two pages are some sentences. Each sentence says something about the world or about people. There are no right or wrong answers. You will probably agree with some of the sentences and disagree with others. We want to know *how much* you agree or disagree. You can show how much you agree or disagree with each sentence by circling one of the answers next to each sentence.

	Score	
	+ Item	− Item
If you *agree very much* with the sentence, put a circle around: Agree very much	5	1
If you *agree a little* with the sentence, put a circle around: Agree a little	4	2
If you *disagree a little* with the sentence, put a circle around: Disagree a little	2	4
If you *disagree very much* with the sentence, put a circle around: Disagree very much	1	5

Read each sentence, decide whether you agree or disagree and *how much*. Then you will put a circle around the answer that best tells how you feel about the sentence.

+ 1. Never tell anyone why you did something unless it will help you.

5	4	2	1
AGREE	AGREE	DISAGREE	DISAGREE
VERY MUCH	A LITTLE	A LITTLE	VERY MUCH

− 2. Most people are good and kind.

+ 3. The best way to get along with people is to tell them things that make them happy.

− 4. You should do something only when you are sure it is right.

+ 5. It is smartest to believe that all people will be mean if they have a chance.

− 6. You should always be honest, no matter what.

+ 7. Sometimes you have to hurt other people to get what you want.

+ 8. Most people won't work hard unless you make them do it.

− 9. It is better to be ordinary and honest than famous and dishonest.

−10. It's better to tell someone why you want him to help you than to make up a good story to get him to do it.

−11. Successful people are mostly honest and good.

+12. Anyone who completely trusts anyone else is asking for trouble.

+13. A criminal is just like other people except that he is stupid enough to get caught.

−14. Most people are brave.

+15. It is smart to be nice to important people even if you don't really like them.

−16. It is possible to be good in every way.

−17. Most people cannot be easily fooled.

+18. Sometimes you have to cheat a little to get what you want.

−19. It is never right to tell a lie.

+20. It hurts more to lose money than to lose a friend.

Philosophies of Human Nature

(Wrightsman, 1964, 1974)

Variable

The instrument is designed to assess philosophies of human nature, conceived of as the expectancies that people have about the ways in which other people generally behave.

Description

Unlike earlier investigations into how people perceive human nature, Wrightsman's conceptualization attempts to break the construct into six different components:

1. Trustworthiness: the extent to which people are seen as moral, honest, and reliable
2. Altruism: the extent of unselfishness, sincere sympathy, and concern for others
3. Independence: the extent to which a person can maintain his or her convictions in the face of society's pressures toward conformity
4. Strength of will and rationality: the extent to which people understand the motives behind their behavior and the extent to which they believe they have control over their outcomes
5. Complexity of human nature: the extent to which people are complex and hard to understand versus simple and easy to understand
6. Variability in human nature: the extent of individual differences in basic nature and the basic changeability in human nature

The first four dimensions are conceived of as essentially independent of the last two, a presupposition borne out empirically (see Reliability below). An overall favorability toward human nature score was therefore calculated from these first four subscales. A total of 120 items (20 for each of the six components with 10 scored positively, 10 negatively) were constructed and given to 177 undergraduate students. After an item analysis, the 24 least discriminating items were discarded. A further item analysis resulted in the discarding of an additional 12 items. The final form of the scale consists of six subscales of 14 items each, 7 scored positively and 7 negatively. Each item is presented in standard six-point Likert format from +3 (agree strongly) through −3 (disagree strongly). For each subscale, the possible range is from −42 (most negative) to +42, with a midpoint or neutral score of 0.

Samples

In addition to the samples used for item analyses and ascertaining reliability, the scale was administered in the early 1960s to 530 undergraduates (253 males and 277 females) at six colleges in the South, East, and Midwest. Means and standard deviations were as follows: Trustworthiness, M̄ = 1.4, SD = 13.0; Strength of Will and Rationality, M̄ = 7.4, SD = 10.2; Altruism, M̄ = −2.4, SD = 12.8; Independence, M̄ = −1.4, SD = 11.5; Complexity, M̄ = 11.4, SD = 11.3; and Variability, M̄ = 15.8, SD = 10.1. Data on self-concepts were obtained from 100 of these females.

Reliability

Internal Consistency

The following split-half reliabilities (corrected by the Spearman–Brown formula), test–retest reliabilities, and intersubscale correlations were obtained:

	Trust	Altruism	Independence	Strength	Complex	Variable
Split-half average	.74	.74	.68	.58	.58	.70
Test–retest (3 months)	.74	.83	.75	.75	.52	.84
Trustworthiness	—					
Altruism	.69	—				
Independence	.64	.61	—			
Strength	.35	.39	.30	—		
Complexity	−.20	−.21	−.16	−.26	—	
Variability	−.04	−.10	−.04	−.12	.40	—

Test–Retest

The test–retest correlation for the total favorability toward human nature scale (i.e., the 56 items from the first four subscales) was .90.

Validity

Convergent

Convergent validity was demonstrated by a number of predictions about hypothesized differences in favorableness in human nature that were confirmed.

1. Females had more favorable views toward human nature than men at each school tested (reflecting the evaluative aspect of this scale).
2. Students at a Fundamentalist college revealed themselves as feeling quite negative about human nature (reflecting the teachings of the basic sinfulness of humankind).
3. Students with positive scores on the PHN substantive subscales in two classroom studies rated their instructors more favorably than negatively oriented students. Similarly, those who had higher PHN variability scores made greater distinctions in their ratings of two instructors.
4. A strong correlation ($r = .65$) was found between negative views and dissatisfaction with one's self-concept.
5. Substantial correlations were found between favorableness toward human nature and other attitudes in the same conceptual area: Agger *et al.*'s political cynicism scale ($r = −.61$), Rosenberg's faith-in-people scale ($r = .77$), and Christie's Machiavellianism scale ($r = −.68$).

6. Behavioral correlates of responses to the PHN include choices to cooperate or to exploit another in a prisoner's dilemma game, a decision whether or not to return a questionnaire to the experimenter (Nottingham, 1972), and extent of grief in reaction to President Kennedy's assassination.

Location

Wrightsman, L. S. (1964). Measurement of philosophies of human nature. *Psychological Reports,* **14,** 743–751.

Wrightsman, L. S. (1974). *Assumptions about human nature: A social-psychological analysis.* Monterey, CA: Brooks/Cole.

Results and Comments

The intercorrelations reproduced above show that some of the theoretically based variables are in fact not empirically independent of each other. Further research (e.g., Walker & Mosher, 1970) affirms that people who are considered unreliable and dishonest are also perceived as selfish and uncooperative.

Two separate factor analyses of the PHN items (Wrightsman, 1974) produced empirically derived factors not always in keeping with the original theoretical structure of the scale. Two factors, a positive one labeled "Beliefs that People are Conventionally Good" (10 items) and a negative one labeled "Cynicism" (10 items), are composed mostly of Trustworthiness and Altruism subscale items. Interestingly, these two factors are correlated with each other only to a limited degree (−.27 and −.33 in two samples).

The above-mentioned factor analyses of PHN items generally produced factors that were narrower in operation than the original theoretical dimensions. Appendix C of Wrightsman (1974) reproduces these results; the author recommends an empirically based shorter scale of 20 items if one wishes to measure the central factors of trust and cynicism. These are reproduced here under the heading "Revised Philosophies of Human Nature Scale."

Philosophies of Human Nature
(Original 84-item scale)

Here is a series of attitude statements. Each represents a commonly held opinion and there are no right or wrong answers. You will probably disagree with some items and agree with others. We are interested in the extent to which you agree or disagree with such matters of opinion. Read each statement carefully. Then indicate the extent to which you agree or disagree by circling the number in front of each statement. The numbers and their meaning are indicated below:

If you agree strongly,	circle +3
If you agree somewhat,	circle +2
If you agree slightly,	circle +1
If you disagree slightly,	circle −1
If you disagree somewhat,	circle −2
If you disagree strongly,	circle −3

First impressions are usually best in such matters. Read each statement, decide if you agree or disagree and the strength of your opinion, and record your response, using the above scale.

If you find that the numbers to be used in answering do not adequately indicate your own opinion use the one that is closest to the way you feel.

Note: Items are not listed below as they appear to test takers; they have been categorized here by subscale.

Trustworthiness
(Positive Items)

2. Most students will tell the instructor when he or she had made a mistake in adding up their score, even if the instructor had given them *more* points than they deserved.

−3	−2	−1	+1	+2	+3
DISAGREE	DISAGREE	DISAGREE	AGREE	AGREE	AGREE
STRONGLY	SOMEWHAT	SLIGHTLY	SLIGHTLY	SOMEWHAT	STRONGLY

8. If you give the average person a job to do and leave him or her to do it, the person will finish it successfully.

14. People usually tell the truth, even when they know they would be better off lying.

20. Most students do not cheat when taking an exam.

26. Most people are basically honest.

62. If you act in good faith with people, almost all of them will reciprocate with fairness toward you.

86. Most people lead clean, decent lives.

Trustworthiness
(Negative Items)

32. People claim they have ethical standards regarding honesty and morality, but few people stick to them when the chips are down.

38. If you want people to do a job right, you should explain things to them in great detail and supervise them closely.

44. If most people could get into a movie without paying and be sure they were not seen, they would do it.

50. Most people are not really honest for a desirable reason; they're afraid of getting caught.

56. Most people would tell a lie if they could gain by it.

74. Most people would cheat on their income tax, if they had a chance.

92. Nowadays people commit a lot of crimes and sins that no one else ever hears about.

Altruism
(Positive Items)

4. Most people try to apply the Golden rule even in today's complex society.

10. Most people do not hesitate to go out of their way to help someone in trouble.

16. Most people will act as "Good Samaritans" if given the opportunity.

22. "Do unto others as you would have them do unto you" is a motto most people follow.

64. The typical person is sincerely concerned about the problems of others.

70. Most people with a fallout shelter would let their neighbors stay in it during a nuclear attack.

88. Most people would stop and help a person whose car is disabled.

Altruism
(Negative Items)

34. The average person is conceited.

40. It's only a rare person who would risk his own life and limb to help someone else.

46. It's pathetic to see an unselfish person in today's world because so many people take advantage of him.

52. People pretend to care more about one another than they really do.

58. Most people inwardly dislike putting themselves out to help other people.

76. Most people exaggerate their troubles in order to get sympathy.

94. People are usually out for their own good.

Independence
(Positive Items)

33. Most people have the courage of their convictions.

39. Most people can make their own decisions, uninfluenced by public opinion.

45. It is achievement, rather than popularity with others, that gets you ahead nowadays.

51. The average person will stick to his opinion if he thinks he's right, even if others disagree.

57. If a student does not believe in cheating, he will avoid it even if he sees many others doing it.

75. The person with novel ideas is respected in our society.

93. Most people will speak out for what they believe in.

Independence
(Negative Items)

3. Most people will change the opinion they express as a result of an

onslaught of criticism, even though they really don't change the way they feel.

9. Nowadays many people won't make a move until they find out what other people think.

15. The important thing in being successful nowadays is not how hard you work, but how well you fit in with the crowd.

27. The typical student will cheat on a test when everybody else does, even though he has a set of ethical standards.

63. It's a rare person who will go against the crowd.

69. Most people have to rely on someone else to make their important decisions for them.

87. The average person will rarely express his opinion in a group when he sees the others disagree with him.

Strength of Will and Rationality (Positive Items)

31. If a person tries hard enough, he will usually reach his goals in life.

37. The average person has an accurate understanding of the reasons for his behavior.

43. If people try hard enough, wars can be prevented in the future.

49. The average person is largely the master of his own fate.

55. In a local or national election, most people select a candidate rationally and logically.

73. Most persons have a lot of control over what happens to them in life.

79. Most people have a good idea of what their strengths and weaknesses are.

Strength of Will and Rationality (Negative Items)

1. Great successes in life, like great artists and inventors, are usually motivated by forces they are unaware of.

7. Our success in life is pretty much determined by forces outside our own control.

19. Attempts to understand ourselves are usually futile.

25. There's little one can do to alter his fate in life.

61. Most people have little influence over the things that happens to them.

67. Most people have an unrealistically favorable view of their own capabilities.

85. Most people vote for a political candidate on the basis of unimportant characteristics such as his appearance or name, rather than because of his stand on the issues.

Complexity of Human Nature
(Positive Items)

36. I find that my first impressions of people are frequently wrong.
42. Some people are too complicated for me to figure out.
48. I think you can never really understand the feelings of other people.
54. You can't accurately describe a person in just a few words.
60. You can't classify everyone as good or bad.
78. People are too complex to ever be understood fully.
90. People are so complex it is hard to know what "makes them tick."

Complexity of Human Nature
(Negative Items)

6. I find that my first impression of a person is usually correct.
12. People can be described accurately by one term, such as "introverted," or "moral," or "sociable."
18. It's not hard to understand what really is important to a person.
24. I think I get a good idea of a person's basic nature after a brief conversation with him.
30. If I could ask a person three questions about himself (and assuming he would answer them honestly), I would know a great deal about him.
72. When I meet a person, I look for one basic characteristic through which I try to understand him.
96. Give me a few facts about a person and I'll have a good idea of whether I'll like him or not.

Variability in Human Nature
(Positive Items)

11. A person's reaction to things differs from one situation to another.
17. Different people react to the same situation in different ways.
23. Each person's personality is different from the personality of every other person.
29. People are quite different in their basic interests.
65. People are pretty different from one another in what "makes them tick."
83. Often a person's basic personality is altered by such things as a religious conversion, psychotherapy, or a charm course.
89. People are unpredictable in how they'll act from one situation to another.

Variability in Human Nature
(Negative Items)

35. People are pretty much alike in their basic interests.

41. People are basically similar in their personalities.

47. If you have a good idea about how several people will react to a certain situation, you can expect most other people to react the same way.

53. Most people are consistent from situation to situation in the way they react to things.

59. A child who is popular will be popular as an adult, too.

77. If I can see how a person reacts to one situation, I have a good idea of how he will react to other situations.

95. When you get right down to it, people are quite alike in their emotional makeup.

Revised Philosophies of Human Nature Scale

This questionnaire is a series of attitude statements. Each represents a commonly held opinion, and there are no right or wrong answers. You will probably disagree with some items and agree with others. We are interested in the extent to which you agree or disagree with matters of opinion.

Read each statement carefully. Then indicate the extent to which you agree or disagree by circling a number for each statement. The numbers and their meanings are as follows:

If you agree strongly,	circle +3
If you agree somewhat,	circle +2
If you agree slightly,	circle +1
If you disagree slightly,	circle −1
If you disagree somewhat,	circle −2
If you disagree strongly,	circle −3

First impressions are usually best in such matters. Read each statement, decide if you agree or disagree and determine the strength of your opinion, and then circle the appropriate number on the answer sheet. Be sure to answer every statement.

If you find that the numbers to be used in answering do not adequately indicate your opinion, use the one closest to the way you feel.

1. If most people could get into a movie without paying and be sure that they would not be seen, they would do it.   (C)

−3	−2	−1	+1	+2	+3
STRONGLY	DISAGREE	DISAGREE	AGREE	AGREE	AGREE
DISAGREE	SOMEWHAT	SLIGHTLY	SLIGHTLY	SOMEWHAT	STRONGLY

2. Most people have the courage of their convictions.   (T)

3. The average person is conceited. (C)

4. Most people try to apply the Golden Rule, even in today's complex society. (T)

5. Most people would stop and help a person whose car was disabled. (T)

6. The typical student will cheat on a test when everybody else does, even though he has a set of ethical standards. (C)

7. Most people do not hesitate to go out of their way to help someone in trouble. (T)

8. Most people would tell a lie if they could gain by it. (C)

9. It's pathetic to see an unselfish person in today's world, because so many people take advantage of him. (C)

10. "Do unto others as you would have them do unto you" is a motto that most people follow. (T)

11. People claim that they have ethical standards regarding honesty and morality, but few people stick to them when the chips are down. (C)

12. Most people will speak out for what they believe in. (T)

13. People pretend to care more about one another than they really do. (C)

14. People usually tell the truth, even when they know they would be better off by lying. (T)

15. Most people inwardly dislike putting themselves out to help other people. (C)

16. Most people would cheat on their income tax if they had the chance. (C)

17. The average person will stick to his opinion if he thinks he's right, even if others disagree. (T)

18. Most people will act as "Good Samaritans" if given the opportunity. (T)

19. Most people are not really honest for a desirable reason; they're afraid of getting caught. (C)

20. The typical person is sincerely concerned about the problems of others. (T)

Note: Letters in parentheses indicate subscales. C, cynicism; T, trust.

Interpersonal Trust Scale

(Rotter, 1967, 1971)

Variable

This scale is designed to measure one's expectation that the behavior, promises, or (verbal or written) statements of other individuals can be relied upon.

Description

The Interpersonal Trust Scale is a Likert-type scale containing 25 trust items (and 15 filler items). Items included in the scale deal with the variable of interpersonal trust in a variety of situations, involving a number of different social agents including parents, salespeople, the judiciary, people in general, political figures, and the news media. Most items deal with the credibility of social agents, but some cover general optimism about the future of society. In the original testing, five Likert response categories were used, from (1) strongly agree to (5) strongly disagree. Scores thus can range from 25 (lowest trust) to 125 (highest trust), with a neutral score or midpoint of 75. Estimated administration time is 10–15 minutes, including 15 filler items to provide a greater mix of content.

Samples

The scale was standardized on groups of undergraduate students in the early 1960s. For example, the IT scale was administered to 4605 introductory psychology students at the University of Connecticut between 1964 and 1969 (Hochreich & Rotter, 1970).

Reliability

Internal Consistency

Reliabilities for the IT scale are as follows: Split-half reliability for the IT scale was .76, with .77 for males ($n = 248$) and .75 for females ($n = 299$).

Test–Retest

Test–retest reliability, across an average time interval of 7 months, was .56 ($p < .01$, $n = 24$). Across a 3-month interval, the test–retest figure was .68 ($n = 42$).

Validity

Convergent Validity

Several studies have provided evidence for the scale's *construct* validity (Boroto, 1970; Geller, 1966; Hamsher, Geller, & Rotter, 1968; Mulry, 1966; Roberts, 1967; Rotter, 1967), reflecting family background, social class, and religious differences (but, in contrast to the PHN, no sex difference), as well as relationships with behavioral measures of reactions to communications by partners and resistance to temptation.

Discriminant Validity

The discriminant validity of the scale is reflected in the selection of items for the final form of the scale. Rotter eliminated items that had high correlations with the Marlowe–Crowne Social Desirability Scale, thus reducing the impact of the need for social approval. Also with respect to discriminant validity, the IT scale does not correlate significantly with measures of scholastic aptitude in the college student populations sampled (Hochreich & Rotter, 1970).

Location

The IT trust items are included in this section. For research purposes, the complete scale, including the 15 filler items, may be obtained from Dr. J. B. Rotter, Department of Psychology, University of Connecticut, Storrs, Connecticut 06268.

Results and Comments

The Interpersonal Trust Scale is a useful advance in measurement, in that it specifies both the theoretical and operational definition of the term. However, even with this narrowing, a more specific factor structure emerges. Factor analysis suggests that there are two factors in the IT items. One of the factors on the IT is a trust of peers or other familiar social agents; this may be distinguished from a factor reflecting institutional or political trust (that is, trust in those with whom respondents have little direct contact) (see Stack, 1978).

Interpersonal Trust Scale

Directions: Indicate the degree to which you agree or disagree with each statement by using the following scale:

$$1 = \text{strongly agree}$$
$$2 = \text{mildly agree}$$
$$3 = \text{agree and disagree equally}$$
$$4 = \text{mildly disagree}$$
$$5 = \text{strongly disagree}$$

1. Hypocrisy is on the increase in our society.

| 1 | 2 | 3 | 4 | 5 |

2. In dealing with strangers one is better off to be cautious until they have provided evidence that they are trustworthy.
3. This country has a dark future unless we can attract better people into politics.
4. Fear and social disgrace or punishment rather than conscience prevents most people from breaking the law.
5. Using the honor system of *not* having a teacher present during exams would probably result in increased cheating.
6. Parents usually can be relied on to keep their promises.
7. The United Nations will never be an effective force in keeping world peace.
8. The judiciary is a place where we can all get unbiased treatment.
9. Most people would be horrified if they knew how much news that the public hears and sees is distorted.
10. It is safe to believe that in spite of what people say most people are primarily interested in their own welfare.

11. Even though we have reports in newspapers, radio, and T.V., it is hard to get objective accounts of public events.

12. The future seems very promising.

13. If we really knew what was going on in international politics, the public would have reason to be more frightened than they now seem to be.

14. Most elected officials are really sincere in their campaign promises.

15. Many major national sports contests are fixed in one way or another.

16. Most experts can be relied upon to tell the truth about the limits of their knowledge.

17. Most parents can be relied upon to carry out their threats of punishments.

18. Most people can be counted on to do what they say they will do.

19. In these competitive times one has to be alert or someone is likely to take advantage of you.

20. Most idealists are sincere and usually practice what they preach.

21. Most salesmen are honest in describing their products.

22. Most students in school would *not* cheat even if they were sure of getting away with it.

23. Most repairmen will not overcharge even if they think you are ignorant of their speciality.

24. A large share of accident claims filed against insurance companies are phony.

25. Most people answer public opinion polls honestly.

Scoring Key:
1. For the following items, use the recorded response as the score: Items 6, 8, 12, 14, 16, 17, 18, 20, 21, 22, 23, and 25.
2. For the remaining items, take the recorded response and convert it. If a 1, score it a 5; if a 2, score it a 4; if a 3, keep it at 3; if a 4, score it a 2; and if a 5, score it as a 1. Do this for the following items: Items 1, 2, 3, 4, 5, 7, 9, 10, 11, 13, 15, 19, and 24.
3. Add up the points for each item. This total is the score.
4. Higher scores indicate greater Interpersonal Trust.

Note: The filler items are not included on the above list.

Specific Interpersonal Trust Scale

(Johnson-George & Swap, 1982)

Variable

The SITS is oriented toward the measurement of the varieties of interpersonal trust held by one individual for a specific other person.

Description

This scale is based on a factor analysis of 43 items, approximately half of which are keyed in the negative direction. Emphasis was on the measurement of the kind of trust manifested in an intimate interpersonal relationship. Content of most of the items fell in one of the following four categories: trusting another with material possessions, a belief in the other's dependability or reliability, trusting another with personal confidences, and trusting another with personal safety (Johnson-George & Swap, 1982).

Items are in the standardized Likert format, but responses are generated on nine-point scales, anchored by "strongly agree" and "strongly disagree." Separate scales were created for males and for females. The SITS-M consists of 19 items, with a possible range from 19 to 171, with a neutral score of 95. The SITS-F scale consists of 13 items, with a possible range from 13 (lowest trust) to 117 (highest trust), with a neutral score of 65.

Samples

The scale was item-analyzed using 180 male and 255 female undergraduates at Tufts University. (In this internal analysis, 50 potential items for the SITS were administered, along with approximately 20 liking and loving items.)

Reliability

Internal Consistency

First, answers to the full 69-item questionnaire were factor analyzed to determine if trust, love, and liking were discriminable concepts. Second, a factor analysis of the 43 SITS items was conducted. For male subjects a general trust factor emerged (12 items), along with essentially separate liking and loving factors, plus two more trust item factors. Female subjects generated similar identifiable factors, although their first trust factor contained only items related to dependability. The 43 trust items with the highest interjudge agreement were subjected to a second factor analysis; data for males and females were analyzed separately. For males, four interpretable factors emerged:

Factor 1: General trust factor, with items covering a breadth of interpersonal situations and categories;

Factor 2: Emotional trust; the content of its items covers situations involving confiding, freedom from criticism and embarrassment, and other emotion-laden situations;

Factor 3: Called "Reliableness"; deals with keeping promises and commitments; and

Factor 4: Dependability, characterized by a confidence in the other's help or assistance when needed and in the other's sense of responsibility (Johnson-George & Swap, 1982, p. 1308).

For the female sample, three factors emerged and were replicated. Factor 1 is a mixture of the males' Factors 3 and 4 and was labeled Reliableness. Factor 2 closely resembled the Factor 2 of the males and was also called Emotional Trust, but the female's factor also included an element of the other's credibility or honesty. Factor 3, called Physical Trust, contained items dealing with one's physical safety and well-being.

On the basis of these factor analyses, factor-pure scales were generated separately for men and for women. The SITS-M consists of 19 items, including items that had substantial loadings on Factor 1, 2, or 3. The SITS-F includes 13 items from the Reliableness and Emotional Trust subscales. The authors observe that these five subscales have coefficient α values ranging from .71 to .83.

Test–Retest

No information was reported on test–retest reliability.

Validity

Convergent

Validity of the scales was demonstrated by placing subjects with a partner who behaved in either a reliable or unreliable manner toward them. Particularly in the case of males, scores on the resulting administration of the SITS were influenced by this manipulation, especially (as predicted) on the Reliableness subscale. A second validation study manipulated emotional trustworthiness and produced differences on that subscale. Sex differences on the SITS also add to convergent validity; females utilized more differentiated dimensions of interpersonal trust. The fact that females made more trusting ratings of partners is consistent with the previously reported sex differences on the PHN scale.

Location

The SITS items are included in this section. The reference for their construction and validation is Johnson-George, C., & Swap, W. C. (1982). Measurement of specific interpersonal trust: Construction and validation of a scale to assess trust in a specific other. *Journal of Personality and Social Psychology, 43,* 1306–1317.

Results and Comments

The SITS is a useful addition to the literature. It was meticulously constructed, and the experimental manipulations that tested its construct validity were thoughtful and generally successful. The scale's coverage is rather narrow and it is brief. Particularly given social scientists' renewed interest in the phenomenon of close relationships, the SITS will be useful in experimental and clinical research. Recent scholarly thinking on intimacy and close relationships has emphasized the importance of emotional trustworthiness and reliability, factors measured by this scale.

Specific Interpersonal Trust Scale (SITS)

Directions: Indicate how much you agree or disagree with each statement, using a scale ranging from 1 = strongly disagree to 9 = strongly agree. Whenever there is a blank in the item, use the name of the one person closest to you emotionally other than a member of your family.

Male Form

Response:
1. If _____ gave me a compliment I would question if _____ really meant what was said.

STRONGLY 1   2   3   4   5   6   7   8   9 STRONGLY
DISAGREE   AGREE

2. If we decided to meet somewhere for lunch, I would be certain _____ would be there.

3. I would go hiking with _____ in unfamiliar territory if _____ assured me he/she knew the area.

4. I wouldn't want to buy a piece of used furniture from _____ because I wouldn't believe his/her estimate of its worth.

5. I would expect _____ to play fair.

6. I could rely on _____ to mail an important letter for me if I couldn't get to the post office.

7. I would be able to confide in _____ and know that he/she would want to listen.

8. I could expect _____ to tell me the truth.

9. If I had to catch an airplane, I could not be sure _____ would get me to the airport on time.

10. If _____ unexpectedly laughed at something I did or said, I would wonder if he/she was being critical and unkind.

11. I could talk freely to _____ and know that _____ would want to listen.

12. _____ would never intentionally misrepresent my point of view to others.

13. If _____ knew what kinds of things hurt my feelings, I would never worry that he/she would use them against me, even if our relationship changed.

14. If _____ promised to do me a favor, he/she would follow through.

15. If _____ didn't think I handled a certain situation very well, he/she would not criticize me in front of other people.

16. If I told _____ what things I worry about, he/she would not think my concerns were silly.

17. If my alarm clock was broken and I asked _____ to call me at a certain time, I could count on receiving the call.

18. If _____ couldn't get together with me as planned, I would believe his/her excuse that something important had come up.

19. If _____ were going to give me a ride somewhere and didn't arrive on time, I would guess there was a good reason for the delay.

Scoring instructions for SITS-M:
1. For the following items, use the recorded number as the score: Items 2, 3, 5, 6, 7, 8, 11, 12, 13, 14, 15, 16, 17, 18, 19.

2. For the rest of the items, take the recorded response and convert it on the following scale: 9 becomes 1, 8 becomes 2, and so on.
   Do this for items numbers 1, 4, 9, and 10.

3. Add up the points for the total score.

4. A high score indicates greater interpersonal trust.

Female Form

1. If I were injured or hurt, I could depend on _____ to do what was best for

STRONGLY   1   2   3   4   5   6   7   8   9   STRONGLY
DISAGREE   AGREE

2. If _____ borrowed something of value and returned it broken, _____ would offer to pay for the repairs.

3. If my alarm clock was broken and I asked _____ to call me at a certain time, I could count on receiving the call.

4. If _____ agreed to feed my pet while I was away, I wouldn't worry about the kind of care it would receive.

5. If _____ promised to do me a favor, he/she would follow through.

6. If _____ were going to give me a ride somewhere and didn't arrive on time, I would guess there was a good reason for the delay.

7. I would be willing to lend _____ almost any amount of money, because he/she would pay me back as soon as he/she could.

8. If _____ couldn't get together with me as planned, I would believe his/her excuse that something important had come up.

9. I could talk freely to _____ and know that _____ would want to listen.

10. _____ would never intentionally misrepresent my point of view to others.

11. If _____ knew what kinds of things hurt my feelings, I would never worry that he/she would use them against me, even if our relationship changed.

12. I would be able to confide in _____ and know that he/she would not discuss my concerns with others.

13. I would expect _____ to tell me the truth.

Scoring instructions for SITS-F:
1. Add the recorded numbers to get the total score. No items on SITS-F are reverse-keyed.

Trust Scale

(Rempel & Holmes, 1986)

Variable

This is a measure of trust in close relationships, with trust being defined as "the degree of confidence you feel when you think about a relationship" (Rempel & Holmes, 1986, p. 28).

Description

The Trust Scale is an 18-item Likert-type scale. Three aspects of trust are covered: predictability, dependability, and faith. Predictability refers to "our ability to foretell our partner's specific behavior, including things we like and dislike" (p. 29). For the authors, a predictable person is someone whose behavior is consistent, even consistently bad. Volatile, unpredictable people, however, do not inspire confidence.

However, dependability, the second aspect, is ultimately more central to trust; the authors associate it with an emerging sense that the partner can be relied upon when it matters. The third and final element, faith, "enables people to go beyond the available evidence and feel secure that a partner will continue to be responsive and caring" (p. 31). Statements are responded to on a seven-point scale (1 = strongly disagree; 7 = strongly agree). The possible range is from 18 (lowest trust) to 126 (highest trust), with a midpoint score of 72.

Samples

Scale items were administered to both members of 47 couples. Because "our sample of 94 subjects was not large enough to guarantee stable results with certain analytic procedures, including factor analysis" (Rempel, Holmes, & Zanna, 1985, p. 103), the authors employed very conservative criteria in determining whether to retain an item.

Reliability

Internal Consistency

Of 26 items, 18 survived two analyses designed to detect and eliminate any items that clearly failed to measure trust adequately. Items with factor loadings less than .40 or correlations less than .30 with any of the three subscales (dependability, predictability, and faith) were eliminated.

Internal consistency of the scale as measured by Cronbach α is .81 for the total scale, .70 for predictability, .72 for dependability, and .80 for faith. The three subscales are moderately intercorrelated (range of .27–.46).

Test–Retest

No information is available on test–retest reliability.

Validity

Convergent

Rempel *et al.* (1985) describe a number of relationships with the Trust Scale, including attributions about the partner's motives and an intrinsic motivation for the relationship. Faith appeared to be a stronger determinant of such relationships than did the other components; it showed by far the highest correlations with measures of love and happiness, for example.

Location

Rempel, J. K., & Holmes, J. G. (1986, February). How do I trust thee? *Psychology*

Today, pp. 28–34. The authors are at the Department of Psychology, University of Waterloo, Waterloo, Ont., Canada N2L 3G1.

Rempel, J. K., Holmes, J. G., & Zanna, M. P. (1985). Trust in close relationships. *Journal of Personality and Social Psychology*, **49**, 95–112.

Results and Comments

This new Trust Scale and the previously described SITS have the same purpose and nearly the same number of items. Each includes a subscale that reflects dependability as a major aspect of trust. Yet their Gestalt differs. The Rempel and Holmes Trust Scale appears to tap into a more generalized trust of human nature; we would expect higher correlations between it and the Trustworthiness subscale of the PHN than we would between the SITS and the PHN. A strength of this scale is its firm grounding in theory, and its usefulness in understanding the determinants of close relationships.

Trust Scale

Directions: Read each of the following statements and decide whether it is true of your relationship with your partner. Indicate how strongly you agree or disagree by choosing the appropriate number from the scale below and placing it in the space provided in the left-hand margin.

1 = strongly disagree
2 = moderately disagree
3 = mildly disagree
4 = neutral
5 = mildly agree
6 = moderately agree
7 = strongly agree

1. I know how my partner is going to act. My partner can always be counted on to act as I expect. (P)

STRONGLY   1   2   3   4   5   6   7   STRONGLY
DISAGREE   AGREE

2. I have found that my partner is a thoroughly dependable person, especially when it comes to things that are important. (D)

*3. My partner's behavior tends to be quite variable. I can't always be sure what my partner will surprise me with next. (P)

4. Though times may change and the future is uncertain, I have faith that my partner will always be ready and willing to offer me strength, come what may. (F)

*5. Based on past experience, I cannot with complete confidence rely on my partner to keep promises made to me. (D)

*6. It is sometimes difficult for me to be absolutely certain that my partner will always continue to care for me; the future holds too many uncertainties and too many things can change in our relationship as time goes on. (F)

7. My partner is a very honest person and, even if my partner were to make unbelievable statements, people should feel confident that what they are hearing is the truth. (D)

*8. My partner is not very predictable. People can't always be certain how my partner is going to act from one day to another. (P)

9. My partner has proven to be a faithful person. No matter who my partner was married to, she or he would never be unfaithful, even if there was absolutely no chance of being caught. (D)

10. I am never concerned that unpredictable conflicts and serious tensions may damage our relationship because I know we can weather any storm. (F)

11. I am very familiar with the patterns of behavior my partner has established, and he or she will behave in certain ways. (P)

*12. If I have never faced a particular issue with my partner before, I occasionally worry that he or she won't take my feelings into account. (F)

*13. Even in familiar circumstances, I am not totally certain my partner will act in the same way twice. (P)

14. I feel completely secure in facing unknown new situations because I know my partner will never let me down. (F)

*15. My partner is not necessarily someone others always consider reliable. I can think of some times when my partner could not be counted on. (D)

*16. I occasionally find myself feeling uncomfortable with the emotional investment I have made in our relationship because I find it hard to set aside completely my doubts about what lies ahead. (F)

*17. My partner has not always proven to be trustworthy in the past, and there are times when I am hesitant to let my partner engage in activities that make me feel vulnerable. (D)

18. My partner behaves in a consistent manner. (P)

Scoring instructions for Rempel and Holmes' Trust Scale:

1. Use the recorded response as the score for items 1, 2, 4, 7, 9, 10, 11, 14, and 18. Add these together.

2. For the remaining items, convert the response because the item is reverse-scored. Change a recorded number of 1 to 7, 2 to 6, 3 to 5, 5 to 3, 6 to 2, and 7 to 1. Leave any response of 4 as 4. Add these converted scores for items 3, 5, 6, 8, 12, 13, 15, 16, and 17.

3. Add these two groups of scores to determine the total score.

4. The higher the score, the greater the trust.

5. Subscales are as follows:
    1. Predictability (P) subscale: Items, 1, 3, 8, 11, 13, and 18
    2. Dependability (D) subscale: Items 2, 5, 7, 9, 15, and 17
    3. Faith (F) subscale: Items 4, 6, 10, 12, 14, and 16.

Faith in People Scale

(Rosenberg, 1957)

Variable

This scale, alternatively called the "misanthropy scale," is designed to assess one's degree of confidence in the trustworthiness, honesty, goodness, generosity, and brotherliness of people in general.

Description

The instrument consists of a Guttman-type scale of two forced-choice and three agree–disagree statements, which was formed from nine related items culled by judges (five sociologists at Cornell) from an original group of 36 items. Positive responses are those indicating absence of faith in people. Range of scores is 1 (high faith on all 5 items) to 6 (low faith on all 5 items).

Rosenberg intended the dimension covered by this scale to be relevant to occupational choice, under the assumption that interpersonal attitudes could influence the individual's perception of his or her career. The following distribution along the scale was found for Cornell students:

Point on scale	%
High 1	15
2	28
3	24
4	17
5	11
Low 6	5
Total	100

Sample

The sample used was a nationwide sample of 4585 college students in 1952. The instrument was first administered to a sample of 2758 Cornell students in 1950, and to 1571 Cornell students in 1952.

Reliability

Internal Consistency

The coefficient of reproducibility for the five-item scale was .92. The author notes that while the fifth item did not meet the Guttman 80–20 positive–negative marginal standard, it was included because the other four items produced a coefficient of over .90.

Test–Retest

No information was available for test–retest reliability.

Validity

Convergent

Evidence of validity may be found in the fact that the group of respondents whose occupational choices were social work, personnel work, and teaching had the largest proportion of high scores on the scale, while the group choosing sales–promotion, business–finance, and advertising had the greatest proportion of low scores. This relationship remained even when sex differences were controlled. Consistent with these findings, students with a high faith in people were more likely to select people-oriented occupational values than were those with low faith in people.

Location

Rosenberg, M. (1957). *Occupations and values* (pp. 25–35). Glencoe, IL: Free Press.

Results and Comments

In correlating scores on the scale with single-question indices, Rosenberg found that high scorers were less willing to use unscrupulous means to get ahead, less likely to believe in the superior efficacy of "contacts" over ability, and less likely to believe it very important to get ahead in life.

In a separate analysis of data from the Cornell University students, Rosenberg (1956) found that students scoring low in faith in people were far more likely (than those showing high faith) to profess political attitudes that would be congruent with these general attitudes toward other people. These misanthropic students were more likely to agree that the general public was "not qualified to vote on today's complex issues" (68% of those scoring 6 on the scale vs. 32% of those scoring 1); "There's little use writing to public officials . . ." (45% vs. 12%); "political candidates are run by machines" (92% vs. 66%); "people who talk politics without knowing what they are talking about should be kept quiet" (40% vs. 21%); "unrestricted freedom of speech leads to mass hysteria" (32% vs. 16%); "people should be kept from spreading dangerous ideas because they might influence others to adopt them" (51% vs. 32%); "religions which preach unwholesome ideas should be suppressed" (32% vs. 16%); and "it's unwise to give people with dangerous social and economic viewpoints a chance to be elected" (46% vs. 25%). These results held after the researchers controlled for political party affiliation.

Faith in People Scale

(One point scored for each response noted with an *)

1. Some people say that most people can be trusted. Others say you can't be too careful in your dealings with people. How do you feel about it?

Most people can be trusted.   *You can't be too careful.   ?

2. Would you say that most people are more inclined to help others, or more inclined to look out for themselves?

To help others.   *To look out for themselves.   ?

3. If you don't watch yourself, people will take advantage of you.

Agree*   Disagree   ?

4. No one is going to care much what happens to you, when you get right down to it.

Agree*   Disagree   ?

5. Human nature is fundamentally cooperative.

Agree   Disagree*   ?

Trust in People

(Survey Research Center, 1969)

Variable

This scale consists of slight rephrasings of the first three items in Rosenberg's Faith in People Scale (see previous scale).

Description

The three items are presented in forced-choice format, a person being given a score of 1 for each trustworthy response. Scores therefore range from 0 (low trust) to 3 (high trust).
    The distributions along this scale for a cross section of Americans in 1964 and 1968 were:

		1964 (%)	1968 (%)
(Low)	0	27	21
	1	9	15
	2	23	20
(High)	3	41	44
	Total	100	100
Average score		1.78	1.87

Sample

The items were included in the 1964 postelection study of electoral behavior by the Survey Research Center. A national cross section of 1450 people answered these questions. The items were similarly applied to a cross section of 1330 postelection respondents in the 1968 election study.

Reliability

Internal Consistency

The following inter-item correlations were obtained in the two studies:

	1964			1968		
	PT	PH	TA	PT	PH	TA
People trusted	—			—		
People helpful	.48	—		.52	—	
Take advantage	.50	.54	—	.48	.54	—

These impressive inter-item correlations held at about the same magnitude for people with only a grade school education.

Test–Retest

No test–retest data are available.

Validity

Data collected in this study do not bear directly on validity. Validity is directly assessed in the previous scale description.

Location

Survey Research Center (1969). *1964 Election Study*. Ann Arbor, Michigan: Inter-University Consortium for Political Research, University of Michigan.

Results and Comments

When formed into a scale in the 1964 election study, the trust in people items correlated .24 with a short scale measuring trust in government, .23 with a scale tapping respondents' feelings that the government paid attention to the will of the people, and .25 with the SRC political efficacy scale. (These items and correlations appear in Robinson, Rusk, & Head, 1968.) Thus there seems to be a reasonable degree of carryover from trust of other people onto feelings toward government and the likelihood that one can influence the government.

The correlation of .28 between trust in people and the SRC measure of personal competence (see Chapter 3) indicates that feelings of self-worth are accompanied by an active trust of people. Trust in people correlated moderately with life satisfaction in the 1968 study.

Trust of people in 1964 was higher among the better-educated ($r = .28$), among whites (in 1968 the average score for black respondents was 1.12), and among residents of rural (vs. urban) areas. The relation with age was unusual in that highest trust was found in the 30–40 age group (average score = 1.97) and the lowest in the 20–29 age group (1.64). Differences in 1968, however, were in the same direction but much less dramatic (1.82 for those under 30 vs. 1.88 for those aged 30–59). Women were only slightly more trusting (about .10 points) than men in both studies.

Differences by religion were in the expected direction but were not as dramatic as one might anticipate in view of the general finding (see Wrightsman's scale results) that people belonging to Fundamentalist religions share a pessimistic credo about their fellow man.

Religion	Average score	
	1964	1968
Protestant	1.74	1.80
Reformation (e.g., Lutheran, Presbyterian)	1.98	2.25
Pietistic (e.g., Baptist, Methodist)	1.64	1.69
Neofundamentalist (e.g., Church of Christ)	1.46	1.38
Nontraditional (e.g., Quakers)	2.03	1.47
No denominational preference	2.08	1.75
Catholic	1.75	1.94
Jewish	2.34	2.14
No religious preference	1.44	1.60
Total Sample	1.78	1.87

There are, of course, further differences within the gross categories of Protestants in the above tabulation. For example, in 1968 Episcopalians (2.52) scored higher than Lutherans and Presbyterians within the category "Reformation" and Baptist (1.47 for both Southern and non-Southern) scored lowest in the Pietistic category. Whether any of the differences within Protestant religions cannot largely be attributed to differences in educational attainment (since members of religions whose members are better educated, such as Episcopalians, have highest faith in people) has not been thoroughly investigated in these data. However, the most interesting differences are between the high faith in people of Jewish respondents versus the low trust in people demonstrated by neo-Fundamentalists and respondents with no religious preference. The trust in people scale related in the following ways to various political orientations in the 1968 data:

1. People who voted for Alabama Governor George Wallace showed slightly less trust in people.
2. People who wanted to pull United States troops out of Vietnam (vs. those who wanted to stay there and those who wanted to invade North Vietnam) showed less trust in people.
3. People who thought the police used too much force with demonstrators in Chicago during the 1968 Democratic Party convention were no more trusting of people than people who thought the police used the right amount of force or not enough force.

Trust in People

1. Generally speaking, would you say that most people can be trusted or that you can't be too careful in dealing with people?

   *Most people can be trusted   Can't be too careful

2. Would you say that most of the time, people try to be helpful, or that they are mostly just looking out for themselves?

   *Try to be helpful   Look out for themselves

3. Do you think that most people would try to take advantage of you if they got the chance or would they try to be fair?

Take advantage   *Try to be fair

Note: * indicates trusting response.

Acceptance of Others
(Fey, 1955)

Variable

This scale was devised to test the relationship between three separate variables: feelings of self-acceptance, acceptance of others, and feelings of acceptability to others.

Description

The acceptance of others scale consists of 20 attitude statements, possible responses running from almost always (scored as 1) to very rarely (scored as 5). Scale scores thus run from 20 (low acceptance of others) to 100 (high acceptance). The mean score was 75.5 (SD = 8.4), with a range from 57 to 96. The items were apparently derived from an earlier scale by Phillips (1951).

Sample

The sample consisted of 58 third-year medical students.

Reliability

Internal Consistency

Split-half reliability for the acceptance of others scale was .90 (and for estimated acceptability to .89).

Test–Retest

No test–retest reliability data were presented.

Validity

No validity data were reported.

Location

Fey, W. F. (1955). Acceptance by others and its relation to acceptance of self and others: A revaluation. *Journal of Abnormal and Social Psychology,* **50,** 274–276.

Results and Comments

The author summarizes his results as follows:

> Analysis of the data indicated that individuals with high self-acceptance scores tend also to accept others, to feel accepted by others, but actually to be neither more nor less accepted by others than those with low self-acceptance scores. Individuals with high acceptance-of-others scores tend in turn to feel accepted by others, and tend toward being accepted by them. Persons who think relatively much better of themselves than they do of others tend to feel accepted by others, whereas actually they are significantly less well liked by them; this group significantly overestimates its acceptability to others. Estimated acceptability, in this study, is independent of actual acceptability. Comparison of most and least accepted groups shows only that the latter have a significantly larger gap between self acceptance and their acceptance of others. (p. 275)

The five items in the "estimated acceptance by others" scale are also reproduced below.

Acceptance of Others

1. People are too easily led.

ALMOST ALWAYS   1   2   3   4   5   VERY RARELY

*2. I like people I get to know.
3. People these days have pretty low moral standards.
4. Most people are pretty smug about themselves, never really facing their bad points.
*5. I can be comfortable with nearly all kinds of people.
6. All people can talk about these days, it seems, is movies, TV, and foolishness like that.
7. People get ahead by using "pull," and not because of what they know.
8. If you once start doing favors for people, they'll just walk all over you.
9. People are too self-centered.
10. People are always dissatisfied and hunting for something new.
11. With many people you don't know how you stand.
12. You've probably got to hurt someone if you're going to make something out of yourself.
13. People really need a strong, smart leader.
14. I enjoy myself most when I am alone, away from people.
15. I wish people would be more honest with you.
*16. I enjoy going with a crowd.
17. In my experience, people are pretty stubborn and unreasonable.

*18. I can enjoy being with people whose values are very different from mine.
*19. Everybody tries to be nice.
20. The average person is not very well satisfied with himself.

Note: *, Reversed item

Acceptability to Others

1. People are quite critical of me.
2. I feel "left out," as if people don't want me around.
*3. People seem to respect my opinion about things.
*4. People seem to like me.
*5. Most people seem to understand how I feel about things.

Note: *, Reversed item

Future Research Directions

In summary, the measurement of trust and general attitudes toward people has shown progress over the last two decades. But the most successful integration of theory development and ingenious research has been achieved with regard to a specific quantity, Machiavellianism. Although trust versus mistrust is a component of Machiavellianism, the general concept of trust deserves much more theoretical analysis. Measurement has advanced more rapidly than conceptual clarification, and research is needed on the relationships among the several recent measures of trust.

Acknowledgment

Marie Hibbard did the library research that served as a necessary and valuable basis for this chapter.

Bibliography

Boroto, D. R. (1970). *The Mosher forced choice inventory as a predictor of resistance to temptation.* Unpublished master's thesis, University of Connecticut, Storrs.

Christie, R., & Geis, F. L. (1970). *Studies in Machiavellianism.* New York: Academic Press.

Erikson, E. H. (1963). *Childhood and society* (2nd ed.). New York: Norton.

Fey, W. F. (1955). Acceptance by others and its relation to acceptance of self and others: A revaluation. *Journal of Abnormal and Social Psychology, 50,* 274–276.

Geis, F. L. (1978). Machiavellianism. In H. London & J. Exner (Eds.), *Dimensions of personality* (pp. 305–363). New York: Wiley.

Geis, F. L., & Christie, R. (1970). Overview of experimental research. In R. Christie & F. Geis (Eds.), *Studies in Machiavellianism* (pp. 285–313). New York: Academic Press.

Geller, J. D. (1966). *Some personal and situational determinants of interpersonal trust.* Unpublished doctoral dissertation, University of Connecticut, Storrs.

Hamsher, J. H., Geller, J. D., & Rotter, J. B. (1968). Interpersonal trust, internal–external control, and the Warren Commission Report. *Journal of Personality and Social Psychology, 9,* 210–215.

Hochreich, D. J., & Rotter, J. B. (1970). Have college students become less trusting? *Journal of Personality and Social Psychology, 15,* 211–214.

Johnson-George, C., & Swap, W. C. (1982). Measurement of specific interpersonal trust: Construction and validation of a scale to assess trust in a specific other. *Journal of Personality and Social Psychology, 43,* 1306–1317.

Mulry, R. C. (1966). *Personality and test-taking behavior.* Unpublished doctoral dissertation, University of Connecticut, Storrs.

Nottingham, J. A. (1972). The N and the out: Additional information on participants in psychological experiments. *Journal of Social Psychology, 88,* 299–300.

Phillips, E. L. (1951). Attitudes toward self and others: A brief questionnaire report. *Journal of Consulting Psychology, 15,* 78–82.

Rempel, J. K., & Holmes, J. G. (1986, February). How do I trust thee? *Psychology Today,* pp. 28–34.

Rempel, J. K., Holmes, J. G., & Zanna, M. P. (1985). Trust in close relationships. *Journal of Personality and Social Psychology, 49,* 95–112.

Roberts, M. D. (1967). *The persistence of interpersonal trust.* Unpublished master's thesis, University of Connecticut, Storrs.

Robinson, J., Rusk, G., & Head, K. (1968). *Measures of political attitudes.* Ann Arbor: Survey Research Center, University of Michigan.

Rosenberg, M. (1956). Misanthropy and political ideology. *American Sociological Review, 21,* 690–695.

Rosenberg, M. (1957). *Occupations and values.* Glencoe, IL: Free Press.

Rotter, J. B. (1954). *Social learning and clinical psychology.* Englewood Cliffs, NJ: Prentice-Hall.

Rotter, J. B. (1967). A new scale for the measurement of interpersonal trust. *Journal of Personality, 35,* 651–665.

Rotter, J. B. (1971). Generalized expectancies of interpersonal trust. *American Psychologist, 26,* 443–452.

Stack, L. C. (1978). Trust. In H. London & J. E. Exner, Jr. (Eds.), *Dimensions of personality* (pp. 561–599). New York: Wiley.

Survey Research Center (1969). *1964 Election Study.* Ann Arbor: Inter-University Consortium for Political Research, University of Michigan.

Walker, D. N., & Mosher, D. L. (1970). Altruism in college women. *Psychological Reports, 27,* 887–894.

Wrightsman, L. S. (1964). Measurement of philosophies of human nature. *Psychological Reports, 14,* 743–751.

Wrightsman, L. S. (1974). *Assumptions about human nature: A social-psychological analysis.* Monterey, CA: Brooks/Cole.

Wrightsman, L. S., & Cook, S. W. (1965). Factor analysis and attitude change. *Peabody Papers in Human Development, 3,* No. 2.

CHAPTER 9

Locus of Control

Herbert M. Lefcourt

Locus of control refers to assumed internal states that explain why certain people actively, resiliently, and willingly try to deal with difficult circumstances, while others succumb to a range of negative emotions. This failure to act in one's own behalf in trying to remedy an unpleasant situation, in the face of potential stress, or in trying to bring about rewarding outcomes is a shared focus of researchers in this area. Whether one focuses upon self-evaluated competence or upon beliefs about causal connections between efforts and outcomes, the interest is in why people act or fail to respond in the face of challenge.

In the first edition of *Measures of Social Psychological Attitudes,* MacDonald noted that the attention given to the locus of control construct was of "phenomenal proportions." It would not have seemed inappropriate at that time to predict that some 15 years later the interest in the locus of control construct would have diminished notably if not entirely. Yet there has been a continuous and stimulating amount of research published in journals as well as books. Three single-authored books (Lefcourt, 1976a, 1982; Phares, 1976) and three edited volumes (Lefcourt, 1981b, 1983a, 1984) present compilations of research conducted with the locus of control construct.

During this same period, much research has been reported with constructs that are cognates of locus of control. Perception of Control (Langer, 1983), Personal Causation (de Charms, 1976), Efficacy (Bandura, 1977), Personal Competence (Harter & Connell, 1984) Helplessness (Seligman, 1975), and Causal Attributions (Weiner, Heckhausen, Meyer, & Cook, 1972) have each been examined in extensive research programs. While the authors of these various cognate constructs insist upon the uniqueness of their contributions and draw detailed definitions to disentangle theirs from the terminologies of others, it is evident that there is much overlap in the meanings that are dealt with under these diverse rubrics. Although the foci of certain constructs emphasize the situational determinants of causal beliefs and others are cast more in motivational than in expectancy terminology, there is enough commonality among these constructs to have allowed researchers to become stimulated by the convergent findings obtained with their widely divergent methodologies.

Theoretical Background

The term *locus of control* refers to a construct that originated from within Rotter's social learning theory (Rotter, Chance, & Phares, 1972). In social learning terminology, locus of control is a generalized expectancy pertaining to the connection between personal characteristics and/or actions and experienced outcomes. It develops as an abstraction from accumulated specific encounters in which persons perceive the causal sequences occurring in their lives.

For some individuals, many outcomes are experienced as being dependent upon the effort expended in their pursuit. Such persons may come to believe that outcomes are generally contingent upon the work put into them, so that they are more apt to exert themselves when engaged in important tasks. On the other hand, individuals living in less responsive milieus may fail to perceive the connections between efforts and outcomes. In societies where nepotism, graft, and other inequitable practices may dominate the economic scene, for example, success is probably perceived as being more a function of luck or of being related to the right people than it is of effort or ability. Consequently, more time may be expended in prayer, gambling, or a search for succour than at instrumental acts that could help to create the desired ends.

When environments are extreme in terms of opportunity, we are less likely to ascribe such perceptions of response–outcome relationships to "personality." Rather, we are apt to discuss social constraints and opportunities with the assumption that behavior would change with alterations of environmental conditions. However, when the milieu is such that constraints are not all pervasive and obvious, then it becomes easier to speak of causal perceptions as personality characteristics or as relatively stable individual differences.

Locus of control, like helplessness, concerns the beliefs that individuals hold regarding the relationships between actions and outcomes. Whereas Seligman (1975) describes helplessness in terms of response–outcome independence, a generalized expectation of external control is defined as a pervasive belief that outcomes are not determinable by one's personal efforts. The converse, an internal locus of control, is the belief that outcomes are contingent upon actions. Within social learning theory it is possible to describe individuals as holding expectations that are more "internal" or "external" with regard to causation and thus to control.

The locus of control construct differs from some other constructs in that it is used primarily as a personality characteristic, an individual difference that is assumed to have some stability and generalization. Much of the earlier work with the locus of control construct helped to explicate the nomological network of variables and actions that the term helped to tie together. An internal locus of control was associated with a more active pursuit of valued goals, as would be manifested in social action (Levenson, 1974; Strickland, 1965), information seeking (Lefcourt & Wine, 1969; Seeman, 1963), alertness (Lefcourt, Gronnerud, & McDonald, 1973; Wolk & DuCette, 1974), autonomous decision making (Crowne & Liverant, 1963; Sherman, 1973), and a sense of well-being (Lefcourt, 1982). Those who were assumed to have a more external locus of control were more often found to be depressed (Abramowitz, 1969; Naditch, Gargan, & Michael, 1975), anxious (Feather, 1967; Watson, 1967), and less able to cope with stressful life experiences (Kobasa, 1979; Lefcourt, 1983b; Sandler & Lakey, 1982).

Despite the plenitude of research attesting to the value of the locus of control construct as a conceptual tool, the variance accounted for by many of the extant measures of locus of control has often left much to be desired, and it is in the realization of this fact that much of the recent work with the construct has developed. In this chapter we will attempt to present and review the wide range of new scale development that has characterized locus of control research. Investigators seem to have taken to heart the recommendations of Rotter (1975), Phares (1976), and Lefcourt (1976a, 1982) that maximal predictions are best obtained if the researcher tailors his or her measures to particular populations and their concerns rather than relying upon more global and less targeted measures, which may be irrelevant to the cares of the particular people being assessed for their locus of control beliefs.

Development of Measures

The first locus of control scales were constructed shortly after it had been demonstrated that people differ in the ways they respond to failure and success experiences if the outcomes of the tasks on which they perform are said to be due to skill or chance. This scale construction was a predictable development, for if people respond differentially to task instructions that emphasize different determinants of outcomes, it is also reasonable to assume that relatively stable attitudes regarding the causes of outcomes would also determine such responses.

The first locus of control scale evolved out of two dissertations completed at Ohio State University. Phares (1955) developed a brief scale that James (1957) expanded and refined into a 60-item Likert scale, 30 items of which were "fillers" used to disguise the purpose of the scale. This measure, referred to as the James–Phares Locus of Control Scale, provided the source from which the better-known Rotter Internal–External Control Scale was subsequently developed.

Contrary to common belief, these original scales were not designed to assess some highly general conceptions of locus of control. The more elaborate measure constructed by Julian Rotter, the late Shepherd Liverant, Melvin Seeman, Douglas Crowne, and the many Ohio State University graduate students who became involved in this project originally consisted of a large pool of items devised to assess control expectancies with regard to a number of different goal areas: for example, achievement, social recognition, love, and affection.

In their early attempt at creating a locus of control scale that focused on different goal areas, these investigators provided a model for subsequent researchers that is only now coming to fruition; and it is reflected in many of the contributions described in this chapter. This early scale, consisting of a number of theoretically discriminable subscales, would have allowed for a profile of control expectancies for a number of different goals, as well as a general, overall locus of control score. Unfortunately, this early attempt at creating a complex scale succumbed to the rigors of factor analysis, which reflected only one large factor and a number of smaller factors, each of them containing too few items to be of use. Consequently, after various refinements, the scale eventually developed into the well-known 23-item Rotter I-E Scale, a detailed description of which is included in this chapter.

Although it is regrettable that attempts to create a more complex measure failed, misgivings must be tempered by the success that has been achieved with this brief scale. For all the criticisms of its brevity and psychometric properties, it has proven to be a stimulating and useful research tool, a fact that is reflected in the great number of investigations that have been conducted with it.

One unfortunate consequence of the use of this presumably unifactor scale has been the developing tendency to view locus of control as a trait, or worse, a typology. As types, internals have been said to be potent, assertive, and effective persons whereas externals are held to be helpless, retiring, and incompetent. Although correlations between various scales designed to assess such characteristics might reveal weak if significant relationships in support of such supposed types, it should be self-evident that one 23-item questionnaire cannot sort people into types and that much error and confusion will result from attempts to interpret scalar differences in this way.

Not long after Rotter's I-E Scale was first published, a second locus of control scale was introduced. It contained several refinements that continue to have impact upon locus of control researchers. This was the Intellectual Achievement Responsibility (IAR) Questionnaire (Crandall, Katkovsky, & Crandall, 1965), which will also be presented in some detail in this chapter. This scale was targeted exclusively on childrens' achievement behavior. In addition to its goal specificity, the IAR scale contained two major subsets of items, one concerning success experiences and the other failure experiences. Another feature of the IAR Scale that differed from Rotter's I-E Scale was the selection of external causes of outcomes. In general the IAR Scale implied that external causes were "other persons." This external agent was thought to be more appropriate for the school-age child than fate, chance, social systems, or other causes that composed the external alternatives on Rotter's I-E Scale.

The IAR Scale, therefore, served to highlight three possible complexities to be considered in the conduct of locus of control research: goal specificity, the types of outcomes or experiences to be explained, and the specific agents that could exert an (external) influence of one's reinforcements. As will be noted, each of these issues has received some attention in the construction of a number of newer locus of control scales.

At the same time that researchers were becoming aware of the potential utility of the specific elements available in the IAR Scale, a number of investigators who had factor-analyzed Rotter's I-E Scale were reporting that this measure was not as unidimensional as it had been presumed to be. Mirels (1970), MacDonald and Tseng (1971), and several others have consistently obtained at least two factors in their factor analyses of Rotter's I-E Scale, which seemed accurately defined as personal and social system control. However, it was not until Reid and Ware (1974) lengthened each of the subscales representing these factors that it became possible to begin an examination of their utility. In addition, these investigators devised a subscale concerned with beliefs about self-regulation, or the control of inner urgings and impulses. With these three subscales, Reid and Ware became among the first to explore various realms of reinforcement control; in this case, the realms ranged from inner space (self-control) to immediate psychological interaction space (personal control) to person–system transactions (social system control).

Almost concurrent with the Reid and Ware studies, Levenson (1973a, 1973b) presented her own three-subscale version of Rotter's I-E Scale. Her scales (Internal, Chance, and Powerful Others) brought focus to the varied agents of control that could affect outcomes. Similar to the Reid and Ware scales, Levenson's measurement devices allowed for the possibility of examining profiles. It is entirely conceivable, for example, that someone could believe in the potency of luck at the same time that he or she espoused a belief in the efficacy of effort, a point too easily obscured by the format of Rotter's I-E Scale. Moreover, the behavior of such an individual could be rather different from that of a person who shares the beliefs about luck but does not believe that effort can alter his or her particular outcomes. That these attributions can be independent of one another has been demonstrated in the work of Collins and his colleagues (Collins, 1974; Collins, Martin, Ashmore, & Ross, 1973).

Several other scales were constructed to assess either general measures of locus of control for specific age samples or specific elements of locus of control similar to those explored with the IAR, the Reid–Ware three-factor scale, or Levenson's Internal, Chance, and Powerful Others subscales. These latter three scales, however, may be viewed as the prototypes for many of the newer assessment devices described in this chapter.

Following the example of the IAR Scale, which predicts to a rather specific reinforcement area, several goal-specific measures of locus of control have been reported in the literature. Following Kirscht (1972), the Wallstons (Wallston, Wallston, Kaplan, & Maides, 1976; Wallston & Wallston, 1978, 1981; Wallston, Wallston, & De Vellis, 1978), for example, constructed a health-focused locus of control device in which subjects were queried about their roles in maintaining their own health. This scale has been used with some success and may have helped to spawn a number of related measures pertaining to specific aspects of health, such as obesity (Saltzer, 1978, 1981, 1982), heart disease (O'Connell & Price, 1985), labor in childbirth (Schroeder, 1985), children's recovery from illness (DeVellis *et al.*, 1985), sexual functioning (Catania, McDermott, & Wood, 1984), and mental health (A. Calhoun, Pierce, & Dawes, 1973; Calhoun, Johnson, & Boardman, 1975; Hill & Bale, 1980, 1981; Wood & Letak, 1982). To help in the study of health among the elderly, Reid and Ziegler (1981a) have constructed a scale that measures elderly persons' beliefs about their ability to control reinforcements that they acknowledge as being important to them. This scale derives from a survey conducted among the elderly and focuses on reinforcements such as privacy, having company when desired, and keeping personal possessions. While not directly assessing beliefs about the control of health, this measure, as will be noted in the detailed description of it, is predictive of health outcomes. In addition to the above there are other health-focused locus of control measures, the Lau–Ware Health Locus of Control Scale (Lau, 1982; Lau & Ware, 1981) as well as a Children's Health Locus of Control Scale (Parcel & Meyer, 1978).

My colleagues and I (Lefcourt, von Baeyer, Ware, & Cox, 1979; Miller, Lefcourt, Holmes, Ware, & Saleh, 1986; Miller, Lefcourt, & Ware, 1983) have constructed three locus of control scales for different goals. It is our ambition eventually to create several goal-specific scales that will have salience at different ages and statuses. Thus far, we have constructed locus of control measures for predicting affiliative and achievement behaviors and for marital satisfaction. In addition, Wong (Wong & Sproule, 1984; Wong, Watters, & Sproule, 1978) and his colleagues have created the Trent Attribution Profile, which assesses locus of control for achievement, and Powers and Douglas (1985) have created a scale concerned only with achievement in mathematics. In a similar fashion to Lefcourt *et al.* (1979), Connell (1985) has constructed a multidimensional measure of locus of control for children that assesses causal beliefs in the cognitive, social, and physical competence areas.

Paulhus (1983) and Christie (Paulhus & Christie, 1981) have been exploring what they refer to as realms of control, with a focus on personal efficacy, interpersonal control, and sociopolitical control. The first of these realms refers to beliefs about the mastery of one's nonsocial environment and concerns personal achievements. Interpersonal control, in contrast, deals with the management of face-to-face interactions and relationships. Sociopolitical control is more like social system control, the matching of individuals against larger systems. For each of these scales there are some research results that attest to the scale's value. Another scale particularly designed to assess control beliefs in the political sphere is the Political Locus of Control Scale (Davis, 1983).

In addition to Paulhus and Christie's research pertaining to the nonsocial environment, there has been some research with locus of control for work-related reinforcements (Lewandowski, 1979; Pettersen, 1985) and for achievement in sports (Tenenbaum, Furst, & Weingarten, 1984), and there is a scale referred to as the Economic Locus of Control Scale (Furnham, 1986) that assesses causal beliefs about economic status. A specific measure concerned with teachers' beliefs about control of student behaviors has also been created that may have some use for understanding the burnout phenomenon that is so prominent among teachers (Rose & Medway, 1981). With regard to the interpersonal sphere, there are the aforementioned Affiliation Locus of Control (Lefcourt, 1981a; Lefcourt, Martin, Fick, & Saleh, 1985) and the Marital Locus of Control scales (Miller *et al.*, 1983, 1986), which assess perceived control in close and intimate relationships, and

Dahlquist and Ottinger (1983) have constructed a locus of control scale for children's perceptions of social interactions. In addition, there have been at least two attempts to develop measures of locus of control for parenting that are in the pioneering stage at the moment (Campis, Lyman, & Prentice-Dunn, 1986; Pancer, Cathro, & Favaro, 1983).

Though this compendium of locus of control measures seems quite extensive, it is by no means exhaustive. Specialty scales abound such that there is even a measure of locus of control constructed to assess causal beliefs among the deaf (Dowaliby, McKee, & Maher, 1983). Needless to say it would be impossible to present, discuss, and review every conceivable scale that has been constructed to assess locus of control. However, readers should be encouraged by these examples to entertain creating their own measures if their populations or problem foci should differ sufficiently from those for which extant scales were constructed.

Adult Measures Reviewed Here

Most of the scales to be described in detail are relatively tried and true in that there are sufficient reliability and validity data to justify their consideration for use in future research. Some scales are included, however, that are not of equivalent stature but that seem to have some real promise of addressing the vital problems that abound. This is not an exhaustive compilation of scales. However, it does represent what may be the most useful of the wide range of scales available. Many of the very focused measures are not included because of their great specificity, which naturally limits interest to a narrow group of specialists. This is not at all meant to reflect criticism of such measures and it will be the ultimate advice from this reviewer that specialists should try to construct measures that are germane to their problem areas. Even a four-item scale specifically designed to assess a particular area of concern may prove more useful and stimulating than would a longer, more established, but area-irrelevant locus of control measure.

The first four scales tap the internal–external control concept in general:

1. Internal–External Locus of Control Scale (Rotter, 1966)
2. Internality, Powerful Others, and Chance Scales (Levenson, 1981)
3. Spheres of Control Scale (Paulhus & Christie, 1981)
4. Adult Nowicki–Strickland Internal–External Control Scale (Nowicki & Duke, 1974a, 1983)

Rotter's (1966) Internal–External (I-E) Locus of Control Scale has been the most widely used and cited measure in the locus of control literature. It has been criticized extensively with regard to its presumed unidimensionality, its inherent social desirability response bias, and the difficulties and complications created by its forced-choice format. Since Collins (1974) first reported that the forced-choice internal and external alternatives did not correlate highly with each other when they were presented as separate scales, there has been growing skepticism about the use of this format. Much of the factor analytic research with Rotter's scale has been described in papers by Ashkanasy (1985) and Marsh and Richards (1987). These analyses offer equivocal evidence for the presumed unidimensionality of the scale, though given the brevity of the original scale, the plethora of subfactors seem to be of little utility.

Despite the extensive criticisms of the scale it has proven useful in exploratory research in which locus of control is suspected of being a contributing factor. High magnitude correlations, however, are not to be anticipated given the diversity of the items in the scale, though this very diversity may help to account for its suitability in exploratory investigations.

The Levenson (1981) Internality, Powerful Others, and Chance (IPC) Scales derive from a reconceptualization of the locus of control construct whereby it is assumed that one can believe in his or her own efficacy while believing at the same time that other powerful persons are also imbued with control, or that one can believe in the power of luck or chance happenings and yet also believe in one's own ability to control events. Evidently, these are not considered mutually exclusive. Control is within degrees, so that there is room for multicausation. As Levenson describes them, her scales are presented as Likert scales so that their three dimensions are more statistically independent of one another than are the two dimensions in Rotter's scale. Levenson's scales make a distinction between personal and ideological statements by having all items phrased in the first person as opposed to describing people in general. In addition, Levenson's items contain no wording that might imply modifiability of the specific issues presented. Finally, Levenson reports that there is no social desirability bias in her scales.

As will be noted, Levenson's scales have been used extensively, though few have developed the kinds of validity studies that equal those that Levenson had reported in the mid-1970s. Despite the relative paucity of investigations that have made good use of Levenson's scales, they have had some far-reaching influence in encouraging the development of multidimensional locus of control scales. The Multidimensional Health Locus of Control Scales, for example, owe their origins to the Levenson three-factor scale. Where many factor analytic studies have offered findings that argue the advisability of regarding locus of control as a multidimensional construct, rarely have the factors revealed been of sufficient length to have had any utility or discernible meaning. Levenson's conceptually constructed measure was among the earliest to create usable factors that offer profiles of control.

Paulhus' (1983) Spheres of Control Scale (SCS) differs considerably from Levenson's three-factor measure while sharing in the process of disaggregating the more general, unidimensional locus of control scales. Where Levenson focuses upon the sources of control (self, powerful others, and chance), Paulhus and Christie (1981) delineate realms or spheres of interest in which individuals could have varying degrees of control. The three spheres they assess include the nonsocial, in which feelings of competence or efficacy derive from actions directed at objects; the social, in which perceived control of social interactions is evaluated; and the political–social, in which perceived competence at effecting macro-social systems is assessed.

These scales bear some similarity to those that were created by Reid and Ware (1974) from a factor analysis of Rotter's scale, to which they added enough items to create usable subscales measuring personal control and social system control. A major difference inheres in the disaggregation of personal control into the nonsocial and social spheres, for which Paulhus and Christie have demonstrated divergent validity.

The Nowicki–Strickland Adult Internal–External Control Scale (ANSIE) (Nowicki & Duke, 1974a) takes aim at another problem inherent in other research than that immediately concerned with locus of control. This is the construction of measures that are appropriate to the subject pool being assessed. The concerns dealt with in items, the reading levels required, and the ease of subjects' understanding the task required of them comprise the motivating force for the construction of a battery of scales by these authors. The Adult Nowicki–Strickland Internal–External Control Scale (ANSIE) is designed to assess locus of control beliefs among noncollege adults. Thus, the reading level is less demanding and the simple true–false format makes it a more easily understood questionnaire to complete. The scale itself was simply an upgrading of the Nowicki–Strickland

Internal–External Control Scale for Children (CNSIE), the scale these authors constructed for assessing locus of control beliefs among children, which is also presented in this chapter.

The ANSIE is one measure of several that these authors have referred to as life-span locus of control scales (Nowicki & Duke, 1983). Though the authors have reported a number of studies demonstrating the utility of their age-focused scales, there has been controversy as to the intelligibility of the child-focused measure, and some question as to the "purity" of the scales that contain statements of contingency, competence, effectance, etc. However, the CNSIE and its variants were not constructed with closely defined attributes, causal agents, and kinds of outcomes in mind. Thus, the scales comprise varying numbers of items dealing with these different aspects of control, which, it may be argued, is appropriate for the more general measures of locus of control.

Internal–External Locus of Control Scale
(Rotter, 1966)

Variable

Locus of control refers to a generalized expectancy about the causation of reinforcements or outcomes, with one end of the unidimensional continuum labelled internal, and its opposite, external.

Description

An internal locus of control indicates that an individual believes that he or she is responsible for the reinforcements experienced; in effect, that the person's actions, characteristics, qualities, etc. are prominent determinants of the experiences being queried. An external locus of control, however, indicates that the person views his or her outcomes as being primarily determined by external forces, whether they be luck, social context, other persons, or whatever. The focus of the construct, then, is on the perceived contingency between actions, characteristics and events. As others have noted, contingency rather than competence or effectiveness is at the core of Rotter's unidimensional construct.

The history of the development of the test is detailed in Rotter's (1966) monograph, and more extensive descriptions and reviews may be found in Lefcourt (1976a, 1982) and Phares (1976). In its present form, it consists of 23 question pairs, using a forced-choice format, plus 6 filler questions.

Internal statements are paired with external statements. One point is given for each external statement selected. Scores can range from 0 (most internal) to 23 (most external).

The items are presented below along with their correlation to the total test score minus that item. The correlations were reported by Rotter (1966) for a sample of 400 subjects, 200 of each sex.

The scale is self-administered and can be completed in about 15 minutes. The scale has been most frequently used with college students, but has also been used with adolescent and older subjects. No upper or lower age limits have been established.

Rotter (1966) reported that two factor analyses had been completed; one by himself and the other by Franklin (1963). The results were much the same. Each revealed one general factor that accounted for much of the total scale variance (53% in Franklin's analysis) and several additional factors which involved only a few items and accounted for very little variance. Other factor analyses (Mirels, 1970) have shown the Rotter scale to be more multidimensional than the analyses of Rotter and Franklin indicated. (Still, there is generally one factor that accounts for most of the variance, and often this factor has to do with belief in one's own control: with items worded in the first person; a second factor that often emerges has to do with one's belief that people have control generally: items worded in the third person.) More recent factor analyses have most often found two-factor solutions to Rotter's I-E scale (Cherlin & Bourque, 1974; Gurin, Gurin, & Morrison, 1978; Parkes, 1985; Reid & Ware, 1973; Viney, 1974; J. M. Watson, 1981), the factors being characterized as Personal and Social–Political control. Another problem for this scale inheres in the fact that the internal and external items are not highly correlated with one another (Collins, 1974). This means that it is possible to endorse both alternatives, which were thought to be contrasting.

Sample

The Rotter I-E Scale has been administered to numerous samples. For details, see Lefcourt (1982) and Phares (1976).

Normative data are reported by Rotter (1966). Using the means reported for a variety of samples, and those from samples not reported by Rotter (for a total n of 4433), Owens computed the overall means for all groups combined: males, $\bar{M} = 8.2$ (SE $= 4.0$); females, $\bar{M} = 8.5$ (SE $= 3.9$); combined, $\bar{M} = 8.3$ (SE $= 3.9$). More recent norms have been substantially higher than those reported by Rotter and early users of the I-E scale. For example Strickland and Haley (1980) found I-E $\bar{M} = 11.3$ (SD $= 4.4$) for 113 males and $\bar{M} = 12.2$ (SD $= 4.2$) for 146 females. Similarly Parkes (1985) found $\bar{M} = 11.6$ (SD $= 3.3$) for 146 males and 12.6 (SD $= 3.7$) for 260 females.

Reliability

Internal Consistency

An internal consistency coefficient (Kuder–Richardson) of .70 was obtained from a sample of 400 college students (Rotter, 1966).

Test–Retest

For two subgroups of Rotter's (1966) sample test–retest reliability coefficients were computed, with a value of .72 for 60 college students after one month (for males, $r = .60$; for females, $r = .83$). After two months, an r of .55 was obtained for 117 college students (for males, $r = .49$; for females, $r = .61$). Rotter suggested that part of the decrease after the 2-month period was due to differences in administration (group vs. individual).

Validity

Convergent

Over 50% of the internal–external locus of control investigations have employed the Rotter scale. It is not possible to list all of the findings here. Detailed literature reviews are available (Lefcourt, 1981b, 1982, 1983a, 1984; Phares, 1976). The literature does indicate that there are individual differences in perception about one's control over one's destiny and that the Rotter scale is sensitive to these differences.

Discriminant

Rotter reports that correlations with the Marlowe-Crowne Social Desirability Scale range from −.07 to −.35. More recent studies have uncovered higher coefficients (Altrocchi, Palmer, Hellmann, & Davis, 1968; Feather, 1967; Hjelle, 1971) ranging from −.20 to −.42. Additionally, correlations with Edwards' Social Desirability Scales have been found to range between −.23 and −.70 (Berzins, Ross, & Cohen, 1970; Cone, 1971).

Correlations with measures of intelligence have ranged from .03 to −.22 (Rotter, 1966).

Location

Rotter, J. B. (1966). Generalized expectancies for internal versus external control of reinforcement. *Psychological Monographs*, **80** (1, Whole No. 609).

Comments

The scale has been used in a number of interesting and important studies. The group of studies that found significant correlations with measures of social desirability response bias, along with those that have found the scale tapping more than one factor, have called the validity of the scale into question. However, when one considers that (a) the correlations with measures of social desirability response bias are typically low, and (b) results of factor analyses are varied and sometimes difficult to compare, one must conclude that methodological questions have been more effectively raised than answered.

As mentioned above, factor analyses have uncovered one factor (named "personal control") on which the items with the highest loadings are phrased in the first person. This group of items would appear to be reflecting and measuring the construct as it has been defined by Rotter (see the definition under Variable above).

Although the first factor accounts for much of the scale variance, a second factor, social system control, has been found with some regularity. This factor pertains to causal beliefs relevant to influencing macrosystems, government, and other large social units.

Though there are methodological problems inherent in Rotter's I-E Scale, it has proven useful as a probing device. That is, if one wants to insert a general measure to ascertain the likelihood that perceived control plays some role in the prediction of some kinds of behavior, Rotter's I-E may still prove useful. However, psychometric problems such as those noted by Collins (1974) and the availability of more focused and psychometrically refined measures should lessen reliance on this more general and psychometrically "impure" measure.

Internal versus External Control

(Correlations are those of each item with total score, excluding that item.)

r

Filler   1.   a.   Children get into trouble because their parents punish them too much.

		b.	The trouble with most children nowadays is that their parents are too easy with them.
.26	2.	a.	Many of the unhappy things in people's lives are partly due to bad luck.
		b.	People's misfortunes result from the mistakes they make.
.18	3.	a.	One of the major reasons why we have wars is because people don't take enough interest in politics.
		b.	There will always be wars, no matter how hard people try to prevent them.
.29	4.	a.	In the long run people get the respect they deserve in this world.
		b.	Unfortunately, an individual's worth often passes unrecognized no matter how hard he tries.
.18	5.	a.	The idea that teachers are unfair to students is nonsense.
		b.	Most students don't realize the extent to which their grades are influenced by accidental happenings.
.32	6.	a.	Without the right breaks one cannot be an effective leader.
		b.	Capable people who fail to become leaders have not taken advantage of their opportunities.
.23	7.	a.	No matter how hard you try some people just don't like you.
		b.	People who can't get others to like them don't understand how to get along with others.
Filler	8.	a.	Heredity plays the major role in determining one's personality.
		b.	It is one's experiences in life which determine what one is like.
.16	9.	a.	I have often found that what is going to happen will happen.
		b.	Trusting to fate has never turned out as well for me as making a decision to take a definite course of action.
.24	10.	a.	In the case of the well-prepared student there is rarely if ever such a thing as an unfair test.
		b.	Many times exam questions tend to be so unrelated to course work that studying is really useless.
.30	11.	a.	Becoming a success is a matter of hard work, luck has little or nothing to do with it.
		b.	Getting a good job depends mainly on being in the right place at the right time.
.27	12.	a.	The average citizen can have an influence in government decisions.
		b.	This world is run by the few people in power, and there is not much the little guy can do about it.
.27	13.	a.	When I make plans, I am almost certain that I can make them work.

		b.	It is not always wise to plan too far ahead because many things turn out to be a matter of good or bad fortune anyhow.
Filler	14.	a.	There are certain people who are just no good.
		b.	There is some good in everybody.
.29	15.	a.	In my case getting what I want has little or nothing to do with luck.
		b.	Many times we might just as well decide what to do by flipping a coin.
.31	16.	a.	Who gets to be the boss often depends on who was lucky enough to be in the right place first.
		b.	Getting people to do the right thing depends upon ability, luck has little or nothing to do with it.
.36	17.	a.	As far as world affairs are concerned, most of us are the victims of forces we can neither understand nor control.
		b.	By taking an active part in political and social affairs, the people can control world events.
.31	18.	a.	Most people don't realize the extent to which their lives are controlled by accidental happenings.
		b.	There really is no such thing as "luck."
Filler	19.	a.	One should always be willing to admit mistakes.
		b.	It is usually best to cover up one's mistakes.
.27	20.	a.	It is hard to know whether or not a person really likes you.
		b.	How many friends you have depends on how nice a person you are.
.15	21.	a.	In the long run the bad things that happen to us are balanced by the good ones.
		b.	Most misfortunes are the result of lack of ability, ignorance, laziness, or all three.
.23	22.	a.	With enough effort we can wipe out political corruption.
		b.	It is difficult for people to have much control over the things politicians do in office.
.26	23.	a.	Sometimes I can't understand how teachers arrive at the grades they give.
		b.	There is a direct connection between how hard I study and the grades I get.
Filler	24.	a.	A good leader expects people to decide for themselves what they should do.
		b.	A good leader makes it clear to everybody what their jobs are.
.48	25.	a.	Many times I feel that I have little influence over the things that happen to me.
		b.	It is impossible for me to believe that chance or luck plays an important role in my life.

.20	26.	a.	People are lonely because they don't try to be friendly.
		<u>b.</u>	There's not much use in trying too hard to please people, if they like you, they like you.
Filler	27.	a.	There is too much emphasis on athletics in high school.
		b.	Team sports are an excellent way to build character.
.24	28.	a.	What happens to me is my own doing.
		<u>b.</u>	Sometimes I feel that I don't have enough control over the direction my life is taking.
.11	29.	<u>a.</u>	Most of the time I can't understand why politicians behave the way they do.
		b.	In the long run the people are responsible for bad government on a national as well as on a local level.

Note: Score is the total number of underlined choices (i.e., external items endorsed.)

Internality, Powerful Others, and Chance Scales

(Levenson, 1981)

Variable

These scales represent three separate components of the control construct, each viewed as independent and therefore to be used in a profile of causal beliefs.

Description

Internality (I) measures the extent to which people believe that they have control over their own lives. The Powerful Others (P) Scale concerns the belief that other persons control the events in one's life. The Chance (C) Scale measures the degree to which a person believes that chance affects his or her experiences and outcomes.

The I, P, and C subscales comprise items derived from Rotter's I-E Scale and some written specifically to assess these three components or attributions for control. The three subscales each comprise eight items with a seven-point Likert format that are presented as a unified scale of 24 items. This final scale was derived from a larger measure of 36 items that was reduced following item analyses and correlations with the Crowne–Marlowe Social Desirability Scale. All statements are worded in the first person. The Likert scale ranges from -3 (strongly disagree) to $+3$ (strongly agree) so that with a constant of 24 added to the total to eliminate negative scores, the range of scores per subscale is from 0 to 48.

Samples

The I, P, and C scales have been used with a wide variety of samples including psychiatric patients, reformatory prisoners, students, adults in different walks of life, and members of some non-American cultures (Japan). An extensive description of samples and norms can be found in Levenson (1981).

Levenson has presented extensive norms for the scale based on the results of more than a dozen studies. For the Internality subscale means range from the low 30s to the low 40s, with 35 being the modal mean, SD values approximating 7. The Powerful Others subscale has produced means ranging from 18 through 26, with 20 being characteristic of normal college student subjects (SD = 8.5). The Chance subscale produces means between 17 and 25, with 18 being a common mean among undergraduates (SD = 8).

Reliability

Internal Consistency

For a student sample of 152, the Kuder–Richardson reliabilities were .64 for I, .77 for P, and .78 for C. Similar estimates have been found among 115 adults (.51, .72, and .73). Split-half reliabilities (Spearman–Brown) were .62, .66, and .64 for the three scales.

Test–Retest

Test–retest reliabilities with a 1-week interval range between .60 and .79, while a 7-week interval produced values between .66 and .73. Factor analysis supports the independence of the three subscales (Levenson, 1974).

Validity

Convergent

The P and C subscales have been found to correlate with each other from .41 to .60, whereas the P and C scales correlated with I between −.25 and .19. With Rotter's I-E Scale, the P and C subscales produce values of .25 and .56, respectively, while the I scale is correlated negatively ($r = -.41$). Similar correlations (.24, .44, −.15; .22, .43, −.32) have been found among other samples. Extensive validity research has been conducted with the I, P, and C subscales related to achievement, occupational behavior, social–political involvement, interpersonal perception and behavior; much of it is reviewed in Levenson (1981).

Discriminant

The I, P, and C scales have been evaluated opposite the Crowne–Marlowe Social Desirability scale, and correlations for the subscales have been negligible (.09, .04, and −.10 in one study and .04, .11, .08 in a second study).

Location

Levenson, H. (1981). Differentiating among internality, powerful others, and chance. In H. M. Lefcourt (Ed.), *Research with the locus of control construct* (Vol. 1, pp. 15–63). New York: Academic Press.

Results and Comments

This measure was one of the first (along with the Crandalls' IAR) to disaggregate the components of locus of control and to create a multidimensional scale. As such, it has had considerable influence upon the development of other scales. At the same time, however, the very richness afforded by the profiles, wherein one can regard oneself as internal and yet also believe in the power of luck, results in some problems because conceptualization has not kept pace with empirical results. Although there has been much theoretical development for the unidimensional locus of control concept, little has been made of the meaning to be attributed to control profiles. This awaits future research, for which this scale seems well adapted. Whatever research is done will require foresight from theoretical considerations. In other words, this scale is not recommended if the researcher is not prepared to do the conceptual work necessary. Otherwise, he or she will be left with too many data, which will afford more confusion than knowledge.

I, P, and C Scales

Subscale

I   1. Whether or not I get to be a leader depends mostly on my ability.

−3	−2	−1	+1	+2	+3
STRONGLY DISAGREE	DISAGREE	SLIGHTLY DISAGREE	SLIGHTLY AGREE	AGREE	STRONGLY AGREE

C   2. To a great extent my life is controlled by accidental happenings.

P   3. I feel like what happens in my life is mostly determined by powerful people.

I   4. Whether or not I get into a car accident depends mostly on how good a driver I am.

I   5. When I make plans, I am almost certain to make them work.

C   6. Often there is no chance of protecting my personal interests from bad luck happenings.

C   7. When I get what I want, it's usually because I'm lucky.

P   8. Although I might have good ability, I will not be given leadership responsibility without appealing to those in positions of power.

I   9. How many friends I have depends on how nice a person I am.

C   10. I have often found that what is going to happen will happen.

P   11. My life is chiefly controlled by powerful others.

C   12. Whether or not I get into a car accident is mostly a matter of luck.

P   13. People like myself have very little chance of protecting our personal interests when they conflict with those of strong pressure groups.

C   14. It's not always wise for me to plan too far ahead because many things turn out to be a matter of good or bad fortune.

P   15. Getting what I want requires pleasing those people above me.

C   16. Whether or not I get to be a leader depends on whether I'm lucky enough to be in the right place at the right time.

P   17. If important people were to decide they didn't like me, I probably wouldn't make many friends.

I	18.	I can pretty much determine what will happen in my life.
I	19.	I am usually able to protect my personal interests.
P	20.	Whether or not I get into a car accident depends mostly on the other driver.
I	21.	When I get what I want, it's usually because I worked hard for it.
P	22.	In order to have my plans work, I make sure that they fit in with the desires of people who have power over me.
I	23.	My life is determined by my own actions.
C	24.	It's chiefly a matter of fate whether or not I have a few friends or many friends.

Note: I, Internality; C, Chance; P, Powerful others.

Spheres of Control

(Paulhus, 1983)

Variable

The SOC is a three-dimensional battery of measures pertaining to the domains of personal efficacy, interpersonal control, and sociopolitical control.

Description

The SOC comprises three 10-item scales, the Personal Efficacy Scale, Interpersonal Control Scale, and Sociopolitical Control Scale. These scales were refined by a succession of factor analytic studies. The original measure contained 90 items. Three studies with good-sized samples (334, 193, and 110) finally resulted in the three-factor measure described here. Items are rated on a seven-point Likert scale ranging from disagree to agree. Half of the items in each scale are keyed in opposite directions, and these are intermixed in the inventory. SOC scales are all keyed for scoring in the internal direction. Social desirability was dealt with during scale construction by the component-deletion method during the factor analyses (Paulhus, 1984). Since this measure is aimed toward university students, it is easily self-administered.

Samples

The samples used in the construction of the SOC have largely been drawn from university student populations. Validity research has subsequently been conducted among athletes and further university student samples. Though many data have been presented regarding the relationships between SOC and other scales, extensive norms have not been presented.

Reliability

Internal Consistency

Alpha reliabilities of the three 10-item scales were .75, .77, and .81 for the Personal, Interpersonal, and Sociopolitical scales.

Test–Retest

Test–retest correlations at 4-week intervals are above .90 and at a 6-month interval are above .70 for all three subscales. Factor structure confirms the three independent facets that Paulhus has advanced.

Validity

Convergent

Each SOC subscale correlates negatively with Rotter's I-E scale ($-.37$ with Efficacy, $-.28$ with Interpersonal Control, $-.50$ with Sociopolitical Control). The multiple R with the three SOC scales is .75. Validity studies have demonstrated the specificity of each realm such that Machiavellianism, while not related to personal efficacy, is decidedly related to Interpersonal and Sociopolitical Control. Likewise, voting behavior was predicted by Sociopolitical control but not by the other two control measures.

Discriminant

The Crowne–Marlowe Social Desirability Scale was not strongly related to the SOC scales (r values $= .19, .11, -.03$, respectively) in a sample of 110 students. Correlations between SOC subscales and a verbal comprehension measure from the Guilford–Zimmerman tests were .01, .16, and .15 for the three subscales.

Location

Paulhus, D. (1983). Sphere-specific measures of perceived control. *Journal of Personality and Social Psychology, 44,* 1253–1265.

Paulhus, D., & Christie, R. (1981). Spheres of control: An interactionist approach to assessment of perceived control. In H. M. Lefcourt (Ed.), *Research with the locus of control construct* (Vol. 1, pp. 161–185). New York: Academic Press.

Results and Comments

The SOC seems like a good refinement of Rotter's I-E Scale in presenting a well-developed expansion of the Personal and Social System Control factors of Rotter's scale. In addition, the interpersonal control scale provides a second measure associated with social behavior (like the affiliation control measure in Lefcourt's MMCS). Paulhus has argued that his measure assesses expectancies of outcomes in specific situations and without regard to goals, which he senses as being central to the MMCS. However, perusal of items suggests some overlap in direction. While this scale seems advantageous in its brevity and reliability, there is a dearth of normative data, and while validity studies were suggestive there have not been many subsequent to the publication of the original studies. Thus, the value of these measures has not yet been extensively assessed.

Spheres of Control Battery Items

Subscale 1: Personal Efficacy Scale

1. When I get what I want it's usually because I worked hard for it. (+)

7	6	5	4	3	2	1
AGREE						DISAGREE

2. When I make plans I am almost certain to make them work. (+)
3. I prefer games involving some luck over games requiring pure skill.
4. I can learn almost anything if I set my mind to it. (+)
5. My major accomplishments are entirely due to hard work and intelligence. (+)
6. I usually don't make plans because I have a hard time following through on them.
7. Competition encourages excellence. (+)
8. The extent of personal achievement is often determined by chance.
9. On any sort of exam or competition I like to know how well I do relative to everyone else. (+)
10. Despite my best efforts I have few worthwhile accomplishments.

Subscale 2: Interpersonal Control Scale

1. Even when I'm feeling self-confident about most things, I still seem to lack the ability to control interpersonal situations.
2. I have no trouble making and keeping friends. (+)
3. I'm not good at guiding the course of a conversation with several others.
4. I can usually establish a close personal relationship with someone I find sexually attractive. (+)
5. When being interviewed I can usually steer the interviewer toward the topics I want to talk about and away from those I wish to avoid. (+)
6. If I need help in carrying out a plan of mine, it's usually difficult to get others to help.
7. If there's someone I want to meet I can usually arrange it. (+)
8. I often find it hard to get my point of view across to others.
9. In attempting to smooth over a disagreement I usually make it worse.
10. I find it easy to play an important part in most group situations. (+)

Subscale 3: Sociopolitical Control Scale

1. By taking an active part in political and social affairs we, the people, can control world events. (+)

2. The average citizen can have an influence on government decisions. (+)

3. It is difficult for people to have much control over the things politicians do in office.

4. This world is run by the few people in power and there is not much the little guy can do about it.

5. With enough effort we can wipe out political corruption. (+)

6. One of the major reasons we have wars is because people don't take enough interest in politics. (+)

7. There is very little we, as consumers, can do to keep the cost of living from going higher.

8. When I look at it carefully I realize it is impossible to have any really important influence over what politicians do.

9. I prefer to concentrate my energy on other things rather than on solving the world's problems.

10. In the long run we, the voters, are responsible for bad government on a national as well as a local level. (+)

Note: Items marked with a (+) sign are positively keyed; all other items are negatively keyed.

Adult Nowicki–Strickland Internal–External Control Scale

(Nowicki & Duke, 1974a)

Variable

The ANSIE assesses the locus of control as a generalized expectancy of control with the poles of the dimension being internal versus external and thus has identical definitions and aims as Rotter's I-E.

Description

The ANSIE is a self-administered 40-item scale requiring yes or no answers. The questions were derived from the Children's Nowicki–Strickland I-E Scale (CNSIE) and were modified for adults by changing the tenses of some statements and substituting the word "people" for the word "children" in others. The language and format are viewed as being less difficult than in Rotter's I-E scale. Ostensibly the ANSIE allows for better assessment of locus of control among non-university student adults and given its similarity to the CNSIE allows for study of developmental trends.

Sample

Most available data have been collected from university students, as noted in Nowicki and Duke (1983). The original sample used for evaluating the psychometric properties of the scale comprised 156 students, though further statistics derived from 766 subjects in 12 separate studies.

Scores range from 0 (internal) to 40 (external). Among college students $\bar{M} = 9.1$, (SD = 3.9); among noncollege adults $\bar{M} = 11.0$ (SD = 5.6) out of a possible score of 40. The latter sample comprised only 33 adults, however, whereas the student sample numbered 156 in this originally presented normative data. Perusal of studies using the ANSIE indicate that most subsequent use has been with students.

Reliability

Internal Consistency

Split-half reliability indexes have varied mostly between .74 and .86. Factor analyses have often reported a large general factor, accounting for approximately 30% of the variance, that has been characterized as "helplessness."

Test–Retest

Test–retest reliability figures have varied from .65 with a 7-week interval to .83 with a 6-week interval and .56 with a 1-year interval.

Validity

Convergent

The ANSIE is related to Rotter's I-E scale with correlations ranging between .44 and .68; with Levenson's scale ANSIE was found to be related to the Internal factor ($r = -.24$, $p < .01$; Powerful Others ($r = .24$, $p < .01$) and Chance ($r = .40$, $p < .01$) with a large sample ($n = 1195$) (Mink, cited in Nowicki & Duke, 1983). In addition, the ANSIE is correlated with anxiety, achievement, and pathology in expected directions. In addition, blacks have been found to be more external than whites, and lower class subjects more external than middle class subjects (Duke & Nowicki, 1972), as is the case with Rotter's I-E scale.

Discriminant

ANSIE scores have been found to be relatively free of a social desirability bias and unrelated to intelligence test scores or gender (Nowicki & Duke, 1974a, 1983). Correlations with the Crowne–Marlowe scale have been of low magnitude ($r = .10$, .06) and insignificant, as have relationships with S.A.T. ($r = .11$).

Location

Nowicki, S., & Duke, M. P. (1983). The Nowicki–Strickland life span locus of control scales: Construct validation. In H. M. Lefcourt (Ed.), *Research with the locus of control construct* (Vol. 2, pp. 9–43). New York: Academic Press.

Results and Comments

The ANSIE would seem to have certain advantages over the Rotter I-E Scale, especially in its greater simplicity and its continuity with the other NOSIE measures which allows for better comparisons in groups differing in age and status. On the other hand, the ANSIE suffers from the same kind of problems inherent in the I-E Scale because the item contents have not been selected in any kind of a systematic or balanced way. Therefore, it is impossible to extricate subfactors that might help in interpreting whatever findings are obtained. If one examines the items it is apparent that there is a wide range of content, each area of which is not sufficiently sampled to allow for useful factor development. Thus, the ANSIE may be described as another "generalized expectancy" measure that can be profitably used as an investigative tool where specific predictions to particular criteria are not strong concerns.

Adult Nowicki–Strickland Internal–External Control Scale Items

1. Do you believe that most problems will solve themselves if you just don't fool with them? (Y)

   (YES)   (NO)

2. Do you believe that you can stop yourself from catching a cold? (N)
3. Are some people just born lucky? (Y)
4. Most of the time, do you feel that getting good grades meant a great deal to you? (N)
5. Are you often blamed for things that just aren't your fault? (Y)
6. Do you believe that if somebody studies hard enough, he or she can pass any subject? (N)
7. Do you feel that most of the time it doesn't pay to try hard because things never turn out right anyway? (Y)
8. Do you feel that if things start out well in the morning, it's going to be a good day no matter what you do? (Y)
9. Do you feel that most of the time parents listen to what their children have to say? (N)
10. Do you believe that wishing can make good things happen? (Y)
11. When you get punished, does it usually seem it's for no good reason at all? (Y)
12. Most of the time, do you find it hard to change a friend's opinion (mind)? (Y)
13. Do you think that cheering more than luck helps a team to win? (N)
14. Did you feel that it was nearly impossible to change your parents' minds about anything? (Y)
15. Do you believe that parents should allow children to make most of their own decisions? (N)

16. Do you feel that when you do something wrong, there's very little you can do to make it right? (Y)

17. Do you believe that most people are just born good at sports? (Y)

18. Are most of the other people your age stronger than you are? (Y)

19. Do you feel that one of the best ways to handle most problems is just not to think about them? (Y)

20. Do you feel that you have a lot of choice in deciding who your friends are? (N)

21. If you find a four-leaf clover, do you believe that it might bring you good luck? (Y)

22. Did you often feel that whether or not you did your homework had much to do with the kind of grades you got? (N)

23. Do you feel that when a person your age is angry at you, there's little you can do to stop him or her? (Y)

24. Have you ever had a good-luck charm? (Y)

25. Do you believe that whether or not people like you depends on how you act? (N)

26. Did your parents usually help you if you asked them to? (N)

27. Have you felt that when people were angry with you it was usually for no reason at all? (Y)

28. Most of the time, do you feel that you can change what might happen tomorrow by what you do today? (N)

29. Do you believe that when bad things are going to happen, they just are going to happen no matter what you try to do to stop them? (Y)

30. Do you think that people can get their own way if they just keep trying? (N)

31. Most of the time do you find it useless to try to get your own way at home? (Y)

32. Do you feel that when good things happen they happen because of hard work? (N)

33. Do you feel that when somebody your age wants to be your enemy there's little you can do to change matters? (Y)

34. Do you feel that it's easy to get friends to do what you want them to do? (N)

35. Do you usually feel that you have little to say about what you get to eat at home? (Y)

36. Do you feel that when someone doesn't like you there's little you can do about it? (Y)

37. Did you usually feel that it was almost useless to try in school because most other children were just plain smarter than you? (Y)

38. Are you the kind of person who believes that planning ahead makes things turn out better? (N)

39. Most of the time, do you feel that you have little to say about what your family decides to do? (Y)

40. Do you think it's better to be smart than to be lucky? (N)

Note: Answers keyed in external direction. If subject answers "yes" or "no" as indicated, one point is added to score.

Children's Measures Reviewed Here

The next three scales are general scales designed especially for children:

5. Crandall's Intellectual Achievement Responsibility Scale (V. C. Crandall & Crandall, 1983; V. J. Crandall et al., 1965)
6. The Nowicki–Strickland Internal–External Control Scale for Children (Nowicki & Duke, 1983; Nowicki & Strickland, 1973)
7. The Multidimensional Measure of Children's Perceptions of Control (Connell, 1985)

The V. J. Crandall et al. (1965) Intellectual Achievement Responsibility Scale (IAR), unlike Rotter's locus of control measure, was developed to predict a more specified set of criteria. As part of a larger program involved with the prediction of achievement behavior, the Crandalls made some innovative approaches in the construction of the IAR that were subsequently adopted by other investigators. Most obviously, this was the first scale to be specifically addressed to a focal area of concern and therefore to be not a "general" measure. Second, the scale was aimed at the assessment of control among children, thus becoming the first variant from the general scales aimed at the control beliefs of young adults. Given this focus upon children's beliefs, the Crandalls became more selective with regard to the attributes of cause, limiting external causes to "powerful others" rather than to such factors as chance or situational determinants, which adults can more easily comprehend. Thus, in the Crandalls' IAR, there was the first consideration of which causal agents are appropriate for given populations. Finally, the Crandalls also differentiated among causal beliefs that pertain to success from those that involve failure. As such, they opened up an area of interest that still is found to be highly significant, the different patterns of attribution between positive and negative experiences. These patterns have been found to be of significance in the literature concerned with sex differences in achievement (Dweck & Bush, 1976), with differential responses to rewards and punishments (Gregory, 1978), and with conceptualizations of depression (Seligman, Abramson, Semmel, & von Baeyer, 1979).

Though other scales directed towards children have been constructed, the IAR remains a standard measure used in studies where achievement behavior is the criterion of interest. Virginia Crandall has attempted to extend the IAR model to an assessment of adult achievement behavior as well, having constructed an Adult Achievement Responsibility Questionnaire (V. C. Crandall & Crandall, 1983), though the utility of this measure is yet to be proven as has the IAR.

The Nowicki–Strickland (1973) Children's Internal–External Control Scale (CNSIE) is an extensively used, general measure of locus of control. Its format, consisting of 40 true–false items that range in focus from efficacy in school work to winning games, feeling healthy, and being able to influence parents and friends, may be easier to complete than the forced-choice items in the IAR. However, Gorsuch, Henighan, and Barnard (1972) found some evidence to the effect that verbal facility was confounded with scores obtained on the CNSIE, though Halpin and Ottinger (1983) obtained data that refuted this claim.

Despite the wide variety of items present in the CNSIE, the internal consistency of the scale has been found to be quite adequate, indicating that about one-third of the variance in the scale can be accounted for by a general factor characterized as general helplessness. This scale has been translated into several languages and has been used in a number of cross-cultural studies. Like the IAR, this measure enjoys some status as a standard against which other scales are assessed to develop estimates of convergent validity. In order to assess locus of control beliefs among children younger than 9 years of age Nowicki (1981) has also constructed a brief 13-item measure entitled the Preschool and Primary Nowicki–Strickland Internal–External Control Scale (PPNSIE). In addition, this group of researchers at Emory University has created a measure for the aged, the Geriatric Nowicki–Strickland Internal–External Scale (GNSIE) (Duke, Shaheen & Nowicki, 1974), for young blacks (Black Preschool and Primary Internal–External Control Scale (BPPNSIE) (Duke & Lewis, 1979), and for learning disabled children (LDCNSIE) (Parrell-Burnstein, 1975). These latter scales have not yet attained anywhere near the familiarity or degree of use that the CNSIE or ANSIE measures have, but they do exemplify the approach of these investigators who readily create measures pertaining to the characteristics of particular subject populations.

The Connell (1985) Multidimensional Measure of Children's Perceptions of Control (MMCPC) grew out of a collaborative effort between the scale's author and Susan Harter, whose multidimensional perspective with regard to competence helped lead to the development of this newer measure of perceived control. In addition to the attractive elegance of this scale, which was constructed in a balanced and rational fashion, the measure allows for the assessment of control beliefs in a series of areas that are of concern to children. Thus the beliefs regarding one's competence in academic achievement (cognitive), friendship making (social), sports agility (physical), and general control are each assessed with attributions of internal, powerful others, and unknown control (in lieu of chance control, which children didn't seem to comprehend) for success and failure outcomes. One complication arising from the balanced multidimensionality of this scale is the very richness to be derived from a plethora of potential subscores. If users do not have a specific criterion in mind, they may be overwhelmed by the number of scores, judicious interpretation of which may prove difficult. However, if one does have singular criteria such as friendship or affiliation as target behaviors or approaches investigation with a strong conceptual basis, then this scale may afford valuable predictions, especially as one can contrast the utility of the relevant control belief with that of one that seems irrelevant. In essence, discriminant and convergent validity may be obtainable with the use of a single measure.

Since this measure is fairly new there is not enough evidence accrued to allow us to be overly sanguine about its value. However, given the extensive article by Connell (1985) and the sheer elegance of the scale construction, this scale would seem to have considerable promise.

Intellectual Achievement Responsibility Questionnaire

(Crandall, Katkovsky, & Crandall, 1965)

Variable

The IAR assesses children's beliefs about their control and responsibility for success and failure experiences in the intellectual achievement area.

Description

The IAR is composed of 34 forced-choice items. Each item stem describes a positive or negative achievement experience that routinely occurs in children's lives. Each stem is followed by one alternative stating that the event was caused by the child and another stating that the event occurred because of the behavior of someone else (parent, teacher, peer) in the child's environment. One half of the items measure the child's acceptance of responsibility for positive events, the other half deals with negative events. Thus, in addition to a total I (internal or self-responsibility) score, separate subscores can be obtained for beliefs in internal responsibility for successes (I+ score) and for failures (I− scores). The scale has been orally administered to children below the sixth grade and is self-administered for those above the sixth grade. Scores range from 0 (external) to 34 (internal).

In an NIMH Progress Report V. C. Crandall (1968) had reported upon the development of two 20-item short forms—one for third–fifth graders and one for sixth–twelfth graders. Each scale yields a total I score and I+ and I− 10-item subscale scores. Correlations between long- and short-form subscales are quite high: I+ = .90 and .89, I− = .91 and .88, for younger and older children respectively. In addition, an Adult Achievement Responsibility Scale has been constructed (V. C. Crandall & Crandall, 1983).

Sample

A variety of samples, ranging mostly from third–twelfth graders, has been studied. For convenience, two of these samples will be hereafter referred to by letter designations A and B.

Sample A consisted of 923 elementary and high school students drawn from five different schools. Included were students from a consolidated country school, a village school, a small-city school, a medium-city school, and a college laboratory school; there were 102 third graders, 103 fourth graders, 99 fifth graders, 166 sixth graders, 161 eighth graders, 183 tenth graders, and 109 twelfth graders (V. J. Crandall et al., 1965; McGhee & Crandall, 1968).

Sample B consisted of 134 students drawn from schools in a small central Ohio town; there were 35 seventh graders, 54 seventh graders, and 45 tenth graders (McGhee & Crandall, 1968).

The following are the norms and relationships between the two IARQ subscale scores (V. J. Crandall et al., 1965).

Grade	n	$\bar{M}$	SD	Correlation of I+ with I−
3	102	23.2	3.9	.14
4	103	24.8	3.4	.11
5	99	24.2	3.8	.11
6	166	25.8	4.1	.38
8	161	26.0	3.7	.40
10	183	25.9	4.3	.40
12	109	25.9	3.3	.17

Reliability

Internal Consistency

For 130 children split-half reliabilities were .54 for I+ and .57 for I− after correction with the Spearman–Brown Prophesy formula. For older children the correlations were .60 for I+ and I− (V. J. Crandall et al., 1965). The average item to total I+ scale correlation was .36; the equivalent for I− was .38 (Crandall, 1968).

Test–Retest

Test–retest reliabilities (2-month interval) were established on subsamples from Sample A: grades three through five, $r = .69$ for total I (.66 for I+, and .74 for I−) and for ninth graders, $r = .65$ for total I (.47 for I+ and .69 for I−).

Validity

Convergent

IAR scores were significantly related to report card grades (in all academic courses averaged over two marking periods) for the Sample A children with all grades combined. Those with higher IAR scores had higher report card averages, as shown by factorial analysis of variance. There was no significant sex difference or sex by IAR interactions.

The same analysis was used for achievement test scores as dependent variables: the Iowa Test of Basic Skills for grades 3–5, and the California Achievement Test for grades 6, 8, and 12. The tests provided separate subscores for reading, math, and language, in addition to total scores. High internal subjects of both sexes had significantly higher achievement test scores than low internal subjects on all subtest achievement scores and total achievement scores. Though IAR subscores were consistent for females, only the I− subscore showed significant differences for males.

The relation between IAR scores and report-card averages was again tested in Sample B. Unlike the results of the first study, no significant differences were obtained for females, although the differences were consistently in the same direction. For the males, high total I and I− subjects had significantly higher grade averages.

Other findings: internality was associated with the amount of time boys chose to spend in intellectual activities during free play ($r = .70$) and the intensity with which they were striving in these activities ($r = .66$); these relations were not significant for girls (V. J. Crandall, Katkovsky, & Preston, 1962).

Discriminant

Correlations with intelligence test scores (Sample A) were found to be only moderate but reached significance due to the large samples employed. The California Test of Mental Maturity was the intelligence test used for grades 6, 8, 10, and 12. The Lorge–Thorndike was used for grades 3, 4, and 5. Correlations were .26 for the total I scale (.22 for I+ and .14 for I−) for 233 children from grades 3–5; and .16 for the total I scale (.14 for I+ and I−) for 503 children from grades 6, 8, 10, and 12.

Correlations with social desirability have been found to be rather low. Of the six correlations between IAR scores and scores on the Children's Social Desirability Scale (V. C. Crandall, Crandall, & Katkovsky, 1965) (i.e., CSD with I+, I−, and total I for the younger children, and the same tests of association for the older children) only two were significant. Among the younger children in the A Sample, I− scores related negatively to CSD scores ($r = -.26$) and among the older children I+ scores were positively associated with CSD responses ($r = .15$).

Location

Crandall, V. C., Katkovsky, W., & Crandall, V. J. (1965). Children's beliefs in their own control of reinforcements in intellectual–academic achievement situations. *Child Development, 36,* 91–109.

Results and Comments

The IAR is a carefully developed scale that shows acceptable reliability and evidence of divergent and convergent validity. Studies in which it has been used are too numerous to summarize here. Reports of results and an Intellectual Achievement Responsibility Bibliography can be obtained from Virginia C. Crandall, Department of Psychology, The Fels Research Institute, Yellow Springs, Ohio, 45387. A fairly recent presentation of IAR data is to be found in V. C. Crandall and Crandall (1983).

In view of the multidimensional nature of this locus of control scale, factor analytic information would seem desirable though none is evident in the literature.

Little information is currently available regarding the Short Forms, but it appears they may be used with confidence (e.g., Crandall suggests they are less affected by social desirability response bias than the longer forms).

Intellectual Achievement Responsibility Questionnaire

This questionnaire describes a number of common experiences most of you have in your daily lives. These statements are presented one at a time, and following each are two possible answers. Read the description of the experience carefully, and then look at the two answers. Choose the one that most often describes what happens to you. Put a circle around the "A" or "B" in front of that answer. Be sure to answer each question according to how you really feel.

If, at any time, you are uncertain about the meaning of a question, raise your hand and one of the persons who passed out the questionnaires will come and explain it to you.

1. If a teacher passes you to the next grade, would it probably be
   A. because she or he liked you, or
   +B. because of the work you did?

2.ab When you do well on a test at school, is it more likely to be
   +A. because you studied for it, or
   B. because the test was especially easy?

3.ab When you have trouble understanding something in school, is it usually
   A. because the teacher didn't explain it clearly, or
   −B. because you didn't listen carefully?

4.a   When you read a story and can't remember much of it, is it usually
      A. because the story wasn't well written, or
    −B. because you weren't interested in the story?

5.ab   Suppose your parents say you are doing well in school. Is this likely to happen
    +A. because your school work is good, or
      B. because they are in a good mood?

6.ab   Suppose you did better than usual in a subject in school. Would it probably happen
    +A. because you tried harder, or
      B. because someone helped you?

7.   When you lose at a game of cards or checkers, does it usually happen
      A. because the other player is good at the game, or
    −B. because you don't play well?

8.   Suppose a person doesn't think you are very bright or clever.
    −A. can you make him change his mind if you try to, or
      B. are there some people who will think you're not very bright no matter what you do?

9.ab   If you solve a puzzle quickly, is it
      A. because it wasn't a very hard puzzle, or
    +B. because you worked on it carefully?

10.   If a boy or girl tells you that you are dumb, is it more likely that they say that
      A. because they are mad at you, or
    −B. because what you did really wasn't very bright?

11.ab Suppose you study to become a teacher, scientist, or doctor and you fail. Do you think this would happen
    −A. because you didn't work hard enough, or
      B. because you needed some help, and other people didn't give it to you?

12.ab When you learn something quickly in school, is it usually
    +A. because you paid close attention, or
      B. because the teacher explained it clearly?

13.   If a teacher says to you, "Your work is fine," is it
      A. something teachers usually say to encourage pupils, or
    +B. because you did a good job?

14.ab When you find it hard to work arithmetic or math problems at school, is it
    −A. because you didn't study well enough before you tried them, or
      B. because the teacher gave problems that were too hard?

15.ab When you forget something you had in class, is it
      A. because the teacher didn't explain it very well, or
    −B. because you didn't try very hard to remember?

16.   Suppose you weren't sure about the answer to a question your

teacher asked you, but your answer turned out to be right. Is it likely to happen

    A. because she wasn't as particular as usual, or

  +B. because you gave the best answer you could think of?

17.a   When you read a story and remember most of it, is it usually

  +A. because you were interested in the story, or

    B. because the story was well written?

18.a   If your parents tell you you're acting silly and not thinking clearly, is it more likely to be

  −A. because of something you did, or

    B. because they happen to feel cranky?

19.ab   When you don't do well on a test at school, is it

    A. because the test was especially hard, or

  −B. because you didn't study for it?

20.b   When you win at a game of cards or checkers, does it happen

  +A. because you play real well, or

    B. because the other person doesn't play well?

21.ab   If people think you're bright or clever, is it

    A. because they happen to like you, or

  +B. because you usually act that way?

22.   If a teacher didn't pass you to the next grade, would it probably be

    A. because she or he "had it in for you," or

  −B. because your school work wasn't good enough?

23.ab   Suppose you don't do as well as usual in a subject at school. Would this probably happen

  −A. because you weren't as careful as usual, or

    B. because somebody bothered you and kept you from working?

24.a   If a boy or girl tells you that you are bright, is it usually

  +A. because you thought up a good idea, or

    B. because they like you?

25.   Suppose you became a famous teacher, scientist, or doctor. Do you think this would happen

    A. because other people helped you when you needed it, or

  +B. because you worked very hard?

26.ab   Suppose your parents say you aren't doing well in your school work. Is this likely to happen more

  −A. because your work isn't very good, or

    B. because they are feeling cranky?

27.b   Suppose you are showing a friend how to play a game and he has trouble with it. Would that happen

    A. because he wasn't able to understand how to play, or

  −B. because you couldn't explain it well?

28.ab   When you find it easy to work arithmetic or math problems at school, is it usually

    A. because the teacher gave you especially easy problems, or

  +B. because you studied your book well before you tried them?

29.ab   When you remember something you heard in class, is it usually
         +A. because you tried hard to remember, or
          B. because the teacher explained it well?

30.b   If you can't work a puzzle, is it more likely to happen
         −A. because you are not especially good at working puzzles, or
          B. because the instructions weren't written clearly enough?

31.b   If your parents tell you that you are bright or clever, is it more likely
          A. because they are feeling good, or
         +B. because of something you did?

32.   Suppose you are explaining how to play a game to a friend and he
         learns quickly. Would that happen more often
         +A. because you explained it well, or
          B. because he was able to understand it?

33.b   Suppose you're not sure about the answer to a question your teacher
         asks you and the answer you give turns out to be wrong. Is it likely to
         happen
          A. because she was more particular than usual, or
         −B. because you answered too quickly?

34.a   If a teacher says to you, "Try to do better," would it be
          A. because this is something she might say to get pupils to try
             harder, or
         −B. because your work wasn't as good as usual?

Note: Item numbers preceded by + are those items that compose the I+ subscale. Those preceded by − compose the I− subscale. a, Recommended Short Form for younger (grades 3–5) subjects. b, Recommended Short Form for older (grades 6–12) subjects.

Nowicki–Strickland Internal–External Control Scale for Children

(Nowicki & Strickland, 1973)

Variable

The Nowicki–Strickland instrument was designed as a measure of generalized expectancies for internal versus external control of reinforcement among children, as defined by Rotter.

Description

The CNSIE Scale is a 40-item paper–pencil test having a Yes–No response format. The test was developed from a pool of 102 items. The 102 items were given to a group of nine clinical psychology staff members, who were asked to answer the items in an external direction. Items were dropped for which there was not complete agreement among the judges, leaving 59 items. Item analysis reduced the test further to the present 40 items (n = 152 children ranging from the third–ninth grades.)

The authors suggest two short forms, one for grades 3–6 and another for grades 7–12. These short forms are derived from a subset of items in the complete scale.

The test has been administered orally, with each item read twice, to a sample of 1017 children. It has also been self-administered. The authors make no recommendations about method of administration. Scores range from 0 (internal) to 40 (external).

An adult form of the Nowicki–Strickland Scale is also available (Nowicki & Duke, 1974a), and was presented earlier in this chapter with other adult scales.

Sample

A variety of samples, ranging from third grade through college, has been used. The main sample consisted of 1017 children (mostly Caucasian) ranging from third through twelfth graders in four different communities. See Validity for normative data.

Reliability

Internal Consistency

There have been a large number of studies reporting reliability data for the CNSIE that are included in Nowicki and Duke (1983).

Estimates of internal consistency via the split-half method corrected by the Spearman-Brown Prophesy Formula, are: $r = .63$ (grades 3–5); $r = .68$ (grades 6–8); $r = .74$ (grades 9–11); and $r = .81$ (grade 12). Approximate sample sizes for the first three groups are 300, and 87 for the grade 12 group.

Among 944 fourth and fifth grade children a Cronbach α of .64 was obtained (Tesiny, Lefkowitz, & Gordon, 1980) while α values ranging from .65 to .91 have been found among South African children, the magnitudes varying with verbal IQ levels.

Test–Retest

Test–retest reliabilities vary from .63 over a 9-month interval for 202 grades 3–6 children (Nowicki & Duke, 1983) to .76 over a 5-week interval for 81 grade 12 children (Nowicki & Rountree, 1971) and .52 over a year's interval for 499 children in grades 3 through 12 (Prawat, Grissom, & Parish, 1979). Generally, internal consistency measures are above the .60 level, though lower estimates are found in younger and less intelligent children. Factor analyses of the CNSIE generally report that the large first factor accounts for at least one-third of the common variance.

Validity

Convergent

Correlations with the Intellectual Achievement Responsibility Questionnaire (V. C. Crandall *et al.*, 1965) were computed for 182 third grade and 171 seventh grade blacks. Correlations with I− were not significant (Nowicki & Strickland, 1973). Correlations with I+ were significant for both groups: $r = .31$ and $r = .51$, respectively.

A correlation of .41 with the Bialer–Cromwell Scale (Bialer, 1961) was found in a sample of 29 children 9–11 years of age (Nowicki, 1981).

Internality was found to increase with age:

Grade	Males			Females		
	(n)	Mean	Standard deviation	(n)	Mean	Standard deviation
3	(44)	18.0	4.7	(55)	17.4	3.1
4	(59)	18.4	3.6	(55)	18.8	3.6
5	(40)	18.3	4.4	(41)	17.0	4.0
6	(45)	13.7	5.2	(43)	13.3	4.6
7	(65)	13.2	4.9	(52)	13.9	4.2
8	(75)	14.7	4.4	(34)	12.3	3.6
9	(43)	13.8	4.1	(44)	12.3	3.8
10	(68)	13.1	5.3	(57)	13.0	5.3
11	(37)	12.5	4.8	(53)	12.0	5.2
12	(39)	11.4	4.7	(48)	12.4	5.1

The CNSIE has been found to be associated with achievement scores on a host of achievement-related tasks including the SAT, CTEB, CAT, and grade point average with externals generally found to achieve less than internals. Extensive reporting of these data can be found in Nowicki and Duke (1983).

Discriminant

The CNSIE seems to be unrelated to IQ scores derived from the WISC (Nowicki & Duke, 1983). As well, nonsignificant correlations (not reported) with an abbreviated form (odd-numbered items only) of the Children's Social Desirability Scale (V. C. Crandall *et al.*, 1965) were found within each grade level.

Nowicki and Strickland (1973) report nonsignificant relationships between their scale and intelligence in one sample of twelfth graders and another sample of college students (statistics not reported).

Location

Nowicki, S., Jr., & Strickland, B. R. (1973). A locus of control scale for children. *Journal of Consulting and Clinical Psychology*, **40**, 148–154.

Comments

This test has been developed carefully by researchers of solid reputation. It has been used in many studies. Available results indicate the scale to have adequate internal consistency and temporal consistency. Data relevant to divergent and convergent validity are encouraging. In short, it appears to be one of the better measures of locus of control as a generalized expectancy presently available for children, though the difficulty level of items and their comprehensibility have been contested (Gorsuch *et al.*, 1972; Halpin & Ottinger, 1983).

Factor analyses of the scale generally support a unidimensional interpretation. The primary factor can most easily be construed as a "general feeling of helplessness."

Finally, inspection of the item correlations to the total score indicate that (as is generally true of IE scales) the "better" items are phrased externally. The bias is even more pronounced in the short forms, in which about 80% of the items are so phrased.

The Nowicki-Strickland Internal–External Control Scale for Children

+1. Do you believe that most problems will solve themselves if you just don't fool with them?

     (YES)   (NO)

 2. Do you believe that you can stop yourself from catching a cold? (N)

*3. Are some kids just born lucky? (Y)

 4. Most of the time do you feel that getting good grades means a great deal to you? (N)

+5. Are you often blamed for things that just aren't your fault? (Y)

 6. Do you believe that if somebody studies hard enough he or she can pass any subject? (N)

*+7. Do you feel that most of the time it doesn't pay to try hard because things never turn out right anyway? (Y)

 8. Do you feel that if things start out well in the morning that it's going to be a good day no matter what you do? (Y)

*+9. Do you feel that most of the time parents listen to what their children have to say? (N)

*10. Do you believe that wishing can make good things happen? (Y)

+11. When you get punished does it usually seem it's for no good reason at all? (Y)

+12. Most of the time do you find it hard to change a friend's (mind) opinion? (Y)

 13. Do you think that cheering more than luck helps a team to win? (N)

*+14. Do you feel that it's nearly impossible to change your parent's mind about anything? (Y)

 15. Do you believe that your parents should allow you to make most of your own decisions? (N)

*+16. Do you feel that when you do something wrong there's very little you can do to make it right? (Y)

*+17. Do you believe that most kids are just born good at sports? (Y)

*18. Are most of the other kids your age stronger than you are? (Y)

*+19. Do you feel that one of the best ways to handle most problems is just not to think about them? (Y)

 20. Do you feel that you have a lot of choice in deciding who your friends are? (N)

 21. If you find a four leaf clover do you believe that it might bring you good luck? (Y)

22. Do you often feel that whether you do your homework has much to do with what kind of grades you get? (N)

*+23. Do you feel that when a kid your age decides to hit you, there's little you can do to stop him or her? (Y)

24. Have you ever had a good luck charm? (Y)

25. Do you believe that whether or not people like you depends on how you act? (N)

26. Will your parents usually help you if you ask them to? (N)

*+27. Have you felt that when people were mean to you it was usually for no reason at all? (Y)

+28. Most of the time, do you feel that you can change what might happen tomorrow by what you do today? (N)

*+29. Do you believe that when bad things are going to happen they just are going to happen no matter what you try to do to stop them? (Y)

30. Do you think that kids can get their own way if they just keep trying? (N)

*+31. Most of the time do you find it useless to try to get your own way at home? (Y)

32. Do you feel that when good things happen they happen because of hard work? (N)

*+33. Do you feel that when somebody your age wants to be your enemy there's little you can do to change matters? (Y)

34. Do you feel that it's easy to get friends to do what you want them to? (N)

*+35. Do you usually feel that you have little to say about what you get to eat at home? (Y)

*+36. Do you feel that when someone doesn't like you there's little you can do about it? (Y)

*+37. Do you usually feel that it's almost useless to try in school because most other children are just plain smarter than you are? (Y)

*+38. Are you the kind of person who believes that planning ahead makes things turn out better? (N)

*+39. Most of the time, do you feel that you have little to say about what your family decides to do? (Y)

40. Do you think it's better to be smart than to be lucky? (N)

Note: *, Items selected for abbreviated scale for grades 3–6. +, Items selected for abbreviated scale for grades 7–12. External response shown in parentheses.

Multidimensional Measure of Children's Perceptions of Control

(Connell, 1985)

Variable

The MMCPC, like the MMCS, is designed to assess the different causal attributions that can be used to interpret both successful and unsuccessful experiences, seen not as unidimensional but as a profile of specific causal attributions.

Description

The MMCPC is a 48-item questionnaire that evolved from a larger scale that had been pilot tested with a sample of 277 children. The format is that of a four-point Likert scale, ranging from 1 to 4: 4 is "very true" and 1 is "not true at all." The scale comprises three sources of control, internal, powerful others, and unknown, within each of four domains: cognitive (school achievement), social (peer relations), physical (sports activity), and general. The outcomes queried are half success and half failure experiences. Each control source is represented by two items that are never presented consecutively, and the domains and types of outcome are randomly ordered throughout the scale.

The scale originally piloted had included a "chance" factor that did not demonstrate adequate internal consistency. Furthermore, interviews indicated that children of this age rarely used chance as an explanation for outcomes. Rather, "not knowing" seemed a more prevalent answer, which led to the construction of the "unknown" scale.

Sample

The samples for developing norms were more extensive than most of the other locus of control scales in the literature. Nearly 1300 children in third through ninth grades (8–14 years of age) from three states in the United States were used in the construction, standardization, and validation of the instrument.

Normative data collected from a sample of 355 third–sixth grade students revealed that Powerful Others and Unknown control item means clustered around 2.0 with a range of 1.5–3.2. Internal control item means cluster around 3.0 with a range of 2.5–3.8.

In contrast to the means, item standard deviations were relatively consistent across subscales, SD values fluctuating around .85. With a larger sample of 667 third through ninth grade children the norms shown in Table 1 were obtained.

Reliability

Internal Consistency

Cronbach α values for 9 of the 12 four-item subscales were greater than .6, with the range being .43–.70 in the elementary school samples. In the junior high school samples, the α values were lower with reliability estimates for 8 of the 12 four-item subscales being greater than .55 and having a range of .39–.67. Separate factor analyses were conducted on the 12 items within each domain. It was predicted that the strongest coherence would be between items sharing the same control source and the same outcome but that source of control would be the stronger organizing factor. The factor analytic results (pattern from

Table 1

Means and Standard Deviations of Subscales by Grade for a Combined California Elementary and Junior High School Sample ($n = 667$)[a]

	Grade													
	3		4		5		6		7		8		9	
	M̄	SD	M̄	SD	M̄	SD	M̄	SD	M̄	SD	M̄	SD	M̄	SD
Cognitive domain:														
Unknown	2.4	.8	2.3	.7	2.0	.7	2.0	.7	2.0	.5	1.9	.6	1.8	.5
Powerful others	2.5	.7	2.1	.7	2.1	.7	2.1	.6	2.1	.6	2.1	.5	2.1	.6
Internal	3.5	.4	3.6	.4	3.7	.4	3.6	.4	3.6	.4	3.6	.5	3.6	.4
Social domain:														
Unknown	2.9	.6	2.7	.7	2.6	.7	2.3	.5	2.4	.6	2.4	.5	2.4	.5
Powerful others	2.3	.9	2.2	.7	2.0	.7	2.1	.6	1.9	.5	1.9	.5	1.8	.6
Internal	3.1	.5	3.2	.6	3.0	.5	3.2	.5	2.9	.4	2.9	.4	3.0	.4
Physical domain:														
Unknown	2.4	.8	2.3	.7	2.1	.7	2.0	.6	2.1	.5	2.1	.6	1.8	.5
Powerful others	3.0	.6	2.8	.7	2.6	.6	2.6	.6	2.6	.6	2.5	.6	2.4	.5
Internal	3.4	.5	3.3	.5	3.1	.6	3.3	.5	3.1	.5	2.9	.6	2.8	.6
General domain:														
Unknown	2.8	.6	2.7	.6	2.7	.7	2.5	.6	2.5	.5	2.5	.5	2.4	.6
Powerful others	3.1	.6	3.0	.6	3.0	.6	2.8	.6	2.8	.5	2.7	.5	2.6	.6
Internal	2.8	.6	2.8	.6	2.8	.6	2.8	.5	2.7	.5	2.7	.6	2.7	.5

Source: Connell (1985).

[a]Numbers of subjects at each grade level were as follows: $n = 81$, 85, 120, 99, 98, 95, and 88 for grades 3–9 respectively.

an oblique Promax rotation) generally supported these hypotheses. Only in the social domain among junior high school students were these predictions not supported.

Test–Retest

Test–retest correlations for 129 pupils with a 9-month interval ranged between .30 and .48 with a mean $r = .34$, $p < .0001$ for the different subscales; a second group of 188 pupils with an interval of 17 months had test–retest correlations ranging between .25 and .50 with a mean $r = .32$, $p < .0001$.

Validity

Convergent

Extensive validity data were presented for criteria relevant to each domain. Standardized achievement tests were most consistently related to unknown control, internal control, and relative internality for success (internality less powerful others) in the cognitive domain, each variable showing four out of six possible correlations being significant at the .05 level. Relationships with teachers' ratings and scores on perceived competence revealed further validity for this domain's scale, though the details are complex due to all of the subscales being compared. Summarizing these data, each of the three attributions were systematically and predictably related to childrens' intrinsic versus extrinsic orientations in the classroom; unknown control appeared to be the most central control dimension related to self-cognitions, affects, and achievement in the academic domain.

In the social domain five perceived control variables (three sources of control and two components) were related to perceived peer acceptance. Self-ratings and teacher's ratings of acceptance were most highly related to the powerful others factor at low to moderate magnitudes, five out of six correlations being significant at the .01 level among three elementary school samples. In the physical domain self-ratings of physical competence were most consistently and strongly related to relative internality for success. Children who see their own effort determining whether they succeed at physical activities and who play down the role of the opponent's skills also tend to perceive themselves as more competent and are seen by their teachers as more competent in sports activities.

Discriminant

No significant relationships were found between the five control variables in the cognitive domain and the Otis–Lennon group-administered IQ test at each grade level. No other evidence of discriminant validity is offered, though the MMCPC offers opportunity to compare the control variables in predicting relevant criteria in one realm with the less relevant items in another realm.

Location

Connell, J. P. (1985). A new multidimensional measure of children's perceptions of control. *Child Development,* **56,** 1018–1041.

Results and Comments

The MMCPC is a promising device that was designed with conceptually derived elements that become integrated into larger units. However, since the components are known, they can be disaggregated and explored separately. Factor analyses and measures of internal consistency support the assumed structure of the MMCPC, which is impressive given the complexity of the scale. The contribution unique to this scale is the advancing of the "unknown control" variable. Findings by Ryan and Grolnick (1986), Harter and Connell (1984), and Matthews, Barabas, and Ferrari (1982) have attested to the value of this variable in the MMCPC. Though this scale does look promising and likely to stimulate interesting questions there is a dearth of discriminant validity work cited, questions of social desirability have not been addressed, and the paucity of items in each factor limit the utility of the measures for making high-magnitude predictions. The factor pattern also varies with different age groups, indicating that the conceptual distinctions between items may be more salient to some children in one domain than another and at one age than another. Nevertheless, even with these potential sources of error, this scale may prove to be one of the best for assessing a variety of control beliefs among children because of the meaningful components contained within it.

The Multidimensional Measure of Children's Perceptions of Control

Cognitive Domain

Unknown control

4	3	2	1
VERY TRUE	MOSTLY TRUE	A LITTLE TRUE	NOT TRUE AT ALL

7. When I do well in school, I usually can't figure out why.

46. When I don't do well in school, I usually can't figure out why.

22. If I get a bad grade in school, I usually don't understand why I got it.

Powerful others control

27. When I do well in school, it's because the teacher likes me.

3. The best way for me to get good grades is to get the teacher to like me.

18. If I have a bad teacher, I won't do well in school.

42. If I don't have a good teacher, I won't do well in school.

Internal control

11. If I want to do well in school, it's up to me to do it.

35. If I want to get good grades in school, it's up to me to do it.

38. If I get bad grades, it's my own fault.

14. If I don't do well in school, it's my own fault.

Social Domain

Unknown control

43. A lot of times there doesn't seem to be any reason why somebody likes me.

19. A lot of times I don't know why people like me.

28. When another kid doesn't like me, I usually don't know why.

4. If somebody doesn't like me, I usually can't figure out why.

Powerful others control

39. If I want my classmates to think that I am an important person, I have to be friends with the really popular kids.

15. If I want to be an important member of my class, I have to get the popular kids to like me.

36. If the teacher doesn't like me, I probably won't have many friends in that class.

12. If my teacher doesn't like me, I probably won't be very popular with my classmates.

Internal control

47. If somebody is my friend, it is usually because of the way that I treat him/her.

23. If somebody likes me, it is usually because of the way I treat them.

8. If somebody doesn't like me, it's usually because of something I did.

32. If someone is mean to me, it's usually because of something I did.

Physical domain

Unknown control

1. When I win at a sport, a lot of times I can't figure out why I won.

25. When I win at an outdoor game, a lot of times I don't know why I won.

40. When I don't win at an outdoor game, most of the time I can't figure out why.

16. Most of the time when I lose a game in athletics, I can't figure out why I lost.

Powerful others control

33. When I play an outdoor game against another kid, and I win, it's probably because the other kid didn't play well.

9. When I win at a sport, it's usually because the person I was playing against played badly.

24. When I lose at an outdoor game, it is usually because the kid I played against was much better at that game to begin with.

48. When I don't win at an outdoor game, the person I was playing against was probably a lot better than I was.

Internal control

5. I can be good at any sport if I try hard enough.

29. I can be good at any sport if I work on it hard enough.

20. If I try to catch a ball and I don't, it's usually because I didn't try hard enough.

44. If I try to catch a ball and I miss it, it's usually because I didn't try hard enough.

General Domain

Unknown control

37. When good things happen to me, many times there doesn't seem to be any reason why.

13. Many times I can't figure out why good things happen to me.

34. A lot of times I don't know why something goes wrong for me.

10. When something goes wrong for me, I usually can't figure out why it happened.

Powerful others control

45. To get what I want, I have to please the people in charge.

21. If there is something that I want to get, I usually have to please the people in charge to get it.

6. If an adult doesn't want me to do something I want to do, I probably won't be able to do it.

30. I don't have much chance of doing what I want if adults don't want me to do it.

Internal control

17. I can pretty much control what will happen in my life.

41. I can pretty much decide what will happen in my life.

2. When I am unsuccessful, it is usually my own fault.

26. When I don't do well at something, it is usually my own fault.

Measures for Specific Goal Areas Reviewed Here

The next four scales tap the internal–external control construct for specific goal areas. These include

    8. Multidimensional–Multiattributional Causality Scale (Lefcourt, 1981c; Lefcourt *et al.*, 1979),

    9. The Marital Locus of Control Scale (Miller *et al.*, 1983, 1986),

  10. The Desired Control Scale (Reid & Ziegler, 1981b), and

  11. The Parenting Locus of Control Scale (Campis *et al.*, 1986).

The Lefcourt *et al.* (1979) Multidimensional–Multiattributional Causality Scale (MMCS), like the preceding multidimensional scales, was created to take account of earlier work that had suggested specificity with regard to areas or realms of control, differential responses to success and failure experiences, and the findings from the attributional literature, which suggested that different attributions have different ramifications for goal-directed activity—even if those attributions shared similar directionality (internal versus external). Since the target population of these investigators was university students, the two goal areas selected for assessment were achievement and affiliation. Given that students are highly concerned with the demonstration of academic competence and the development and maintenance of friendships during their university careers, these areas were deemed to be of high reinforcement value for this age group. The MMCS therefore comprises two scales, one for achievement and one for affiliation. Outcomes are half successes and half failures. The attributions are derived from the attributional analyses of success and failure whereby ability and effort are the internal, and task difficulty and luck are the external, explanations for outcomes (Weiner et al., 1972).

When research has been conducted with the appropriate groups and the appropriate criteria, these scales have afforded some useful predictions, especially of social behaviors. However, when used as a general measure with inappropriate samples (random adult populations), the scale proves much less useful (Lewinsohn, Steinmetz, Larson, & Franklin, 1981). The scale has been translated into several languages and has been subjected to psychometric analyses by the authors and others (Powers, Douglas & Choroszy, 1983; Powers & Rossman, 1983). As with the Connell measure it is possible to obtain convergent and discriminant validity data by using both scales and contrasting the predictive power of the respective scales for specified criteria. The scales have been found to predict the manner in which university students respond to stressful experiences, expanding the nomological network surrounding the locus of control construct.

The Miller et al. (1983) Marital Locus of Control Scale (MLOC), similar to the MMCS, was constructed from items pertaining to marital satisfaction that were divided into success or good outcomes and failure or poor outcomes. Likewise, there were initially an equal number of items for each of four attributions: ability, effort, context, and luck. Through psychometric analyses, the appealing symmetry was sacrificed with differing numbers of attributional statements in the final form. The scale has been used with some degree of success in predicting both marital satisfaction per se, and in the prediction of actual problem-solving behavior by couples observed in laboratory situations that correspond to clinically relevant altercations. The scale has been employed in a number of investigations concerned with marital intimacy and problems and seems to offer considerable promise for clinical as well as research uses.

The Reid and Ziegler (1980, 1981a) Desired Control Scale (DCS) was designed to assess the values and control expectancies of an elderly population. What is most admirable about the scale construction is that the content of the items derives from an extensive survey conducted among the elderly that inquired into the kinds of experiences that contributed to their sense of well-being. Thus, the items deal explicitly with concerns that are paramount to that population. The scale itself is composed of two sections, one that asks how much the subject cares about the experience in question, and another that asks about the subject's beliefs about being able to affect the occurrence of that experience. These authors then have used the product of the two measures as a quasi-interaction term, along with the scores of each scale, to predict various behaviors and outcomes among the elderly. Impressive correlations with health and happiness indicators taken a year after assessments indicate the potential value of these scales for studying well-being among older persons. Reliability statistics likewise augur well for this measure.

The Campis et al. (1986) Parenting Locus of Control Scale (PLC) is clearly not at the stage of development of the preceding measures but is included largely because of the interest that has always been shown in this area by persons concerned with family difficulties. For many years I have received inquiries about the availability of a measure relevant to childrearing control beliefs and I have been aware of some other attempts to construct such a measure. This scale, however, is the first to my knowledge to have been published. It is admittedly narrow in scope, concerned only with control beliefs concerning parenting of elementary school age children. While its psychometric characteristics have only been briefly explored and developed and validity studies await execution, this scale may stimulate research and subsequent refinements. It is at least a beginning in an area that has been awaiting scale development, and it may prove to be a useful vehicle for establishing a new area of locus of control research.

The Multidimensional—Multiattributional Causality Scale

(Lefcourt, von Baeyer, Ware, & Cox, 1979)

Variable

The MMCS is composed of two parts, each dealing with causal beliefs about their respective areas: achievement and affiliation.

Description

As opposed to unidimensional I-E scales, this measure maps out four possible causal attributions to explain outcomes in these areas, which were originally described by Weiner *et al.* (1971).

The MMCS comprises 48 items, 24 dealing with achievement, 24 with affiliation. The present scale is the fifth revision that resulted from item analyses and elimination of items that reduced the Cronbach α values in each cluster. Successive versions had continually improved reliability figures. Half of each set concern successes and half failures. Within each 12-item set, there are four attributions composed of three items each. These consist of ability and effort as the internal attributions, and luck and context as the external attributions. Thus there are three items concerning ability as an explanation for success and three items pertaining to ability as an explanation for failure in achievement, likewise for effort, luck, and context.

There are a multitude of scores that can be derived from such a multidimensional scale. Most often the scale has produced overall scores for each reinforcement area by subtracting internal attribution scores (ability and effort) from the equivalent external scores. Since each item is scored in a five-point Likert format the potential range of scores for each area is 0–96 with high scores reflecting externality.

It is, however, possible to be concerned only with attributions for failure, for example, which would mean that 12 items with a range of 0–48 would yield the scores of interest. Likewise, scores for internal and external items may be treated separately, again meaning that 12-item (0–48) scales would be used. Though some have used the smaller six-item subscales, caution is needed as reliability decreases with lesser numbers of items.

This scale is self-administered and requires between 15 and 20 minutes.

Samples

The MMCS has been used with many samples and there are extensive norms for Japanese, Polish, and Korean students. The limitation is that the scales are most appropriate for university age students for whom the areas are pertinent and the reading level is appropriate.

Table 2

Normative Data for the MMCS Affiliation
and Achievement Scales

	Male (N = 102)		Female (N = 98)	
	M̄	SD	M̄	SD
Achievement				
Ability[a]	14.4	3.4	15.0	3.5
Effort	18.3	3.0	18.1	3.8
Context	13.4	4.0	12.6	3.7
Luck	12.0	4.3	11.6	4.6
Internality[b]	32.7	5.0	33.1	5.3
Externality	25.3	6.5	24.2	7.1
Success[b,d]	18.2	4.8	17.6	5.2
Failure	22.5	5.7	21.5	6.1
Total achievement[c,d]	40.7	8.0	39.1	9.1
Affiliation				
Ability[a]	13.4	4.4	13.2	3.7
Effort	13.1	4.5	13.6	4.3
Context	13.9	3.6	14.5	3.7
Luck	8.7	4.1	7.2	4.0
Internality[b]	26.4	7.7	26.7	6.7
Externality	22.6	6.4	21.7	6.3
Success[b,d]	21.1	5.0	19.7	4.8
Failure	23.1	6.3	23.3	5.2
Total affiliation[c,d]	44.2	8.9	43.0	8.3

Source: Lefcourt, von Baeyer, Ware, & Cox (1979).

[a]Six-item scales (0–24); higher scores indicate higher endorsement of attribution.

[b]Twelve-item scales (0–48).

[c]Twenty-four-item scales (0–96).

[d]The higher the score, the more external.

Norms for the various subscales and their composites are shown in Table 2. Intercorrelations of the attribution subscales are shown in Table 3.

Reliability

Internal Consistency

Measures of internal consistency were obtained from several samples. Cronbach α values have been found to range between .58 and .80 for the achievement locus of control scale (Externality–Internality) while α values for achievement internality have ranged from .50 to .77 and externality from .66 to .88. The equivalent values for affiliation range from .70 to .84 for internality and .62 to .81 for externality. Corrected Spearman–Brown split-half correlations range from .67 to .76 for achievement and .61 to .65 for affiliation.

Table 3

Intercorrelations among Subscale Scores within Each Goal Area[a]

Attributes	Achievement				Affiliation			
	Effort	Ability	Situation	Luck	Effort	Ability	Situation	Luck
Effort		.06	−.06	−.24*	.63***	.08	.18
Ability			.04	.30**			.18	.19
Situation				.48***				.53***
Luck								

Source: Lefcourt, von Baeyer, Ware, & Cox (1979).

   [a]$n = 68$; *$p < .05$; **$p < .02$; ***$p < .001$.

The correlations between achievement and affiliation locus of control range between .20 and .29, indicating significant but weak relationships. The average correlation of achievement items and the achievement locus of control score is .31, the equivalent for affiliation being .31. Relationships between achievement items with scores in the other area (affiliation) were .10, the equivalent for affiliation items being .09. Factor analyses (Powers *et al.*, 1983; Powers & Rossman, 1983) of the achievement locus of control scale have revealed evidence supporting the assumed factorial structure of that scale.

Test–Retest

Temporal stability has been assessed with intervals ranging from 1 week to 4 months with the achievement locus of control test–retest correlations ranging from .51 to .62, and the affiliation equivalent ranging from .50 to .70.

Validity

Convergent

The MMCS has been assessed along with Rotter's I-E scale, and the correlations have ranged between .23–.62 for achievement and .37–.55 for the affiliation locus of control scale. Validity data have been reported for achievement and affiliation-related criteria. Many of these data are reported in Lefcourt (1981c). Listening behavior, social interaction skills, etc. have been found as correlates of the affiliation locus of control scale (Lefcourt *et al.*, 1985) while behavior and affective responses in achievement tasks have been found to be related to the achievement locus of control scale (Lefcourt, 1981c; Lefcourt, Martin, & Ware, 1984).

Discriminant

Among 66 university students, social desirability, assessed by the Crowne–Marlowe Social Desirability Scale, was found to be related to the achievement ($r = −.33, p < .01$) but not the affiliation locus of control scale ($r = .01$). The significant relationship derived largely from correlations between the achievement–externality subscale and social desirability ($r = −.30, p < .02$) while achievement internality was not so related ($r = .11$, ns). Though social desirability is a "contaminant," the magnitude and specificity of the relationship with social desirability are such as to make one cautious but not dismissive in interpreting achievement locus of control findings.

Location

Lefcourt, H. M. (1981). The construction and development of the Multidimensional–Multiattributional Causality Scales. In H. M. Lefcourt (Ed.), *Research with the locus of control construct* (Vol. 1, pp. 245–277). New York: Academic Press.

Lefcourt, H. M., Van Baeyer, C. L., Ware, E. E., & Cox, D. J. (1979). The Multidimensional–Multiattributional Causality Scale. *Canadian Journal of Behavioural Science*, **11**, 286–304.

Results and Comments

The MMCS was carefully developed, undergoing four previous revisions that were refined by a succession of item analyses and examinations of internal consistency. There is some limited social desirability contamination, similar to Rotter's I-E Scale, which also concerns achievement. It is not very acceptable to attribute achievement outcomes to external causes while in an academic milieu.

The behavioral data collected as validity for the scales is extensive, ranging from time perspective (Wolf & Savickas, 1985) to social competence (Lefcourt *et al.*, 1985). If these scales in the MMCS are used with the samples intended, university students, the scales should have high utility. If, however, they should be used with inappropriate samples for whom these areas are of less interest, strong results should not be expected, as has been the case in some studies (Lewinsohn *et al.*, 1981).

MMCS Items Grouped According to Goal-Specific Subscales

Achievement

Ability

11. The most important ingredient in getting good grades is my academic ability.

0	1	2	3	4
DISAGREE				AGREE

27. I feel that my good grades reflect directly on my academic ability.

43. When I get good grades, it is because of my academic competence.

3. If I were to receive low marks it would cause me to question my academic ability.

19. If I were to fail a course it would probably be because I lacked skill in that area.

35. If I were to get poor grades I would assume that I lacked ability to succeed in those courses.

Effort

9. In my case, the good grades I receive are always the direct result of my efforts.

25. Whenever I receive good grades, it is always because I have studied hard for that course.

41. I can overcome all obstacles in the path of academic success if I work hard enough.

1. When I receive a poor grade, I usually feel that the main reason is that I haven't studied enough for that course.

17. When I fail to do as well as expected in school, it is often due to a lack of effort on my part.

33. Poor grades inform me that I haven't worked hard enough.

Context

6. Some of the times that I have gotten a good grade in a course, it was due to the teacher's easy grading scheme.

22. Some of my good grades may simply reflect that these were easier courses than most.

38. Sometimes I get good grades only because the course material was easy to learn.

14. In my experience, once a professor gets the idea you're a poor student, your work is much more likely to receive poor grades than if someone else handed it in.

30. Often my poorer grades are obtained in courses that the professor has failed to make interesting.

46. Some low grades I've received seem to me to reflect the fact that some teachers are just stingy with marks.

Luck

8. Sometimes my success on exams depends on some luck.

24. I feel that some of my good grades depend to a considerable extent on chance factors such as having the right questions show up on an exam.

40. Sometimes I feel that I have to consider myself lucky for the good grades I get.

16. Some of my lower grades have seemed to be partially due to bad breaks.

32. My academic low points sometimes make me think I was just unlucky.

48. Some of my bad grades may have been a function of bad luck, being in the wrong course at the wrong time.

Affiliation

Ability

15. It seems to me that getting along with people is a skill.

31. Having good friends is simply a matter of one's social skill.

47. It is impossible for me to maintain close relations with people without my tact and patience.

7. It seems to me that failure to have people like me would show my ignorance in interpersonal relationships.

23. I feel that people who are often lonely are lacking in social competence.

39. In my experience, there is a direct connection between the absence of friendship and being socially inept.

Effort

13. Maintaining friendships requires real effort to make them work.

29. In my case, success at making friends depends on how hard I work at it.

45. If my marriage were to succeed, it would have to be because I worked at it.

5. If I did not get along with others, it would tell me that I hadn't put much effort into the pursuit of social goals.

21. When I hear of a divorce, I suspect that the couple probably did not try enough to make their marriage work.

37. In my experience, loneliness comes from not trying to be friendly.

Context

2. My enjoyment of a social occasion is almost entirely dependent on the personalities of the other people who are there.

18. Some people can make me have a good time even when I don't feel sociable.

34. To enjoy myself at a party I have to be surrounded by others who know how to have a good time.

10. No matter what I do, some people just don't like me.

26. Some people just seem predisposed to dislike me.

42. It is almost impossible to figure out how I have displeased some people.

Luck

4. Making friends is a funny business; sometimes I have to chalk up my successes to luck.

20. In my experience, making friends is largely a matter of having the right breaks.

36. If my marriage were a long, happy one, I'd say that I must just be very lucky.

12. Often chance events can play a large part in causing rifts between friends.

28. I find that the absence of friendships is often a matter of not being lucky enough to meet the right people.

44. Difficulties with my friends often start with chance remarks.

Note: All items scored 0 = disagree, 4 = agree. First three items of each set of six refer to success, last three items refer to failure experiences. Numbering refers to order in which items appear in the questionnaire.

The Marital Locus of Control Scale

(Miller, Lefcourt, & Ware, 1983)

Variable

The MLOC assesses the locus of control orientation for the achievement of marital satisfaction.

Description

Though constructed like the MMCS (Lefcourt *et al.*, 1979) from a set of causal attribution statements derived from Weiner's attributional model (Weiner *et al.*, 1972) this scale has been interpreted as a singular dimension ranging from external to internal control beliefs for marital satisfaction.

The MLOC is a 44-item, self-administered scale with a six-point Likert scale format that was refined from a large pool of over 100 items and a preliminary form comprising 78 items by an iterative process using item and reliability analyses based on responses from 72 married students. Items that were negatively related to subscale totals or that had an item–total correlation less than .1 were deleted. Any item reducing the Cronbach α was eliminated, as were items with low variance in response.

The items were constructed to represent each of four attributional subsets reflecting ability, effort, chance or luck, and uncontrollable contextual characteristics as explanations for positive and negative marital experiences. The ability and effort subscales combine to form an internality index while chance and context combine to form an index of externality.

Six major concerns of marriage composed the content evaluated in the scale. These were (1) sexual functioning and affective behavior, (2) communication, (3) marital satisfaction, (4) compatibility, (5) pleasant and unpleasant experiences in marriage, and (6) children and child-rearing. Though these areas could be examined independently they have not yet been used in this fashion. Since a principal component factor analysis with varimax rotation produced only a two-factor solution, the factors characterized as internal and external, the subscales and attributions have not been evaluated separately as they have in the MMCS. Given the six-point format, scores could range from 44 to 264.

Since internal items were reverse-scored in the external direction, the total scale scores reflect externality: The higher the scores the higher the externality for marital satisfaction.

Sample

The normative samples were married university students, and couples drawn from a number of community organizations. Thus far, samples have comprised primarily well-functioning couples, or at least not ostensibly disturbed couples.

The first set of norms gathered from 230 university student couples (Miller *et al.*, 1983) were $\bar{M} = 133.4$ (SD = 20) for males and $\bar{M} = 131.4$ (SD = 20) for females. In a subsequent study with 87 older couples $\bar{M} = 111.9$, (SD = 17) for males and $\bar{M} = 113.0$, (SD = 13) for females.

Reliability

Internal Consistency

In the large normative sample ($n = 230$), Cronbach α for the MLOC was .83, the males and females being close to each other. The internal attributes (ability and effort) were strongly related ($r = .64, p < .001$) as were the external attributes (context and luck, $r = .62, p < .001$). Of the four correlations between each of the internal and external attributes, however, only one attained significance ($r = .26, p < .01$) that being between ability and luck. A principal component factor analysis with varimax rotation indicated a two-factor solution to the scale, with each factor being constituted by internal and external items respectively. In the second study of 88 couples (Miller *et al.*, 1986), the Cronbach α = .82.

Test–Retest

No measures of temporal stability have been reported.

Validity

Convergent

MLOC scores have been found correlated with MMCS scores for affiliation ($r = .48, p < .001$) and achievement ($r = .31, p < .02$), and with measures of intimacy ($r = -.37, p < .001$) and marital satisfaction ($r = -.29, p < .001$). The more external with regard to marital satisfaction the less intimate and the less satisfied with marriage was the respondent. In a study focusing upon actual interactions between spouses MLOC was related to marital problem solving. Internals were more active and more effective in solving common marital difficulties. Rotter's I-E Scale was used for contrast in this latter study. While related to MLOC ($r = .43, p < .001$), the I-E Scale was not related to any of the behavioral criteria.

Discriminant

Like other locus of control scales, MLOC was related to social desirability to some degree ($r = -.29, p < .05$) among a group of students asked to imagine their beliefs if they were married (they were all unmarried). When social desirability was partialled out, the achievement scale of the MMCS diminished in its relationship with MLOC ($r = .25, p < .05$) which was significantly less than the relationship with the more conceptually related affiliation scale ($r = .52, p < .001$). Thus MLOC shows stronger relationships with those constructs that have greater relevance to it.

Location

Miller, P. C., Lefcourt, H. M., & Ware, E. E. (1983). The construction and development of the Miller Marital Locus of Control Scale. *Canadian Journal of Behavioural Science*, **15**, 266–279.

Results and Comments

The MLOC enjoys higher internal consistency than would be expected given that it was constructed from attributional components. This very consistency makes analyses with components a less potentially fruitful enterprise. That behavioral data correlated with MLOC scores augurs well for the validity of the measure. Currently the scale is being used in research with troubled marriages. Two areas needing attention are temporal stability statistics and the control of social desirability effects. As noted above, partialling out social desirability scores may be a useful practice when using the MLOC.

Marital Locus of Control Scale Items

Ability

8. When things begin to go rough in my marriage I can see that I had a part to play in it. (.33)

1	2	3	4	5	6
STRONGLY AGREE					STRONGLY DISAGREE

11. I can always bring about a reconciliation when my spouse and I have an argument. (.29)

16. When we have unpleasant experiences in our marriage I can always see how I have helped to bring them about. (.25)

19. If parents discipline their children conscientiously they are sure to be well behaved. (.18)

20. If my spouse and I were to experience sexual difficulties we would certainly be able to overcome them. (.29)

25. It seems to me that maintaining a smooth functioning marriage is simply a skill; things like luck don't come into it. (.45)

26. Good communication between spouses is simply a matter of learning and applying the skills; nothing can really interfere with good communication. (.37)

33. A little planning can prevent most of the conflicts that occur between spouses over child-rearing. (.24)

34. Problems in our marriage never seem to sort themselves out over time; we usually end up having to do something about them. (.14)

36. My spouse and I get along well because we have the interpersonal skills; not because of things like luck or temperament. (.50)

38. There are always things I can do that will help to end an argument with my spouse that leave us feeling better. (.31)

43. Happy times in our marriage don't just happen by chance; planning is usually required. (.15)

Effort

3. Putting effort into the relationship will practically guarantee a successful marriage. (.29)

5. If my marriage were to end in divorce, I would suspect that I had not tried enough to make it work. (.19)

7. Circumstances play a very limited role in causing marital satisfaction; it is largely effort and concern that matter. (.30)

9. Raising children effectively is really just a matter of trying one's best; chance has absolutely nothing to do with it. (.32)

14. Some effort on my part is all that is required in order to bring about pleasant experiences in our marriage. (.07)

18. My spouse and I can get along happily in spite of the most trying circumstances if we decide to. (.35)

23. Even with the most loving couples a mutually satisfying emotional relationship doesn't just happen, it is the result of the couple working at it. (.33)

29. If my sexual relationship with my spouse was not entirely satisfactory, I would say that I wasn't putting enough effort into the relationship. (.18)

31. Good clear communication between spouses doesn't depend on things like compatibility or personality but on constant practice. (.08)

40. Couples who have a satisfying emotional relationship are constantly trying to improve their relationship; a good relationship doesn't just develop spontaneously. (.33)

Context

1. I am often at a loss as to what to say or do when I'm in disagreement with my spouse. (.33)

2. Sexual compatibility is something of a mystery to me; it is something that just happens. (.35)

6. The unhappy times in our marriage just seem to happen regardless of what I am doing. (.46)

10. I find that external circumstances like day-to-day events can have considerable influence on how my spouse and I get along. (.37)

12. When I want my spouse to do something she/he hadn't planned on, it's often difficult to bring her/him to my way of thinking. (.33)

13. Misunderstandings between my spouse and myself are generally purely circumstantial. (−.02)

17. Circumstances of one sort or another play a major role in determining whether my marriage functions smoothly. (.23)

24. At times, there doesn't seem to be any way out of a disagreement with my spouse. (.36)

27. It's more often up to my spouse to make an argument end peaceably. (−.05)

28. How well your kids grow up depends very much on external factors like what kind of neighborhood you live in. (.36)

35. I seem to have relatively little influence over when the intimate moments in our marriage will occur; they seem to happen of their own accord. (.25)

37. My spouse's moods are often mysterious to me in that I have little idea as to what may have set them off. (.40)

39. Some kids are unmanageable in spite of their parents' best efforts at discipline. (.41)

41. When my spouse and I are communicating effectively we aren't doing anything in particular to make it happen. (.22)

42. How well I get along with my spouse depends very much on how he/she is feeling that day. (.47)

Luck

4. Difficulties with my spouse often start with chance remarks. (.27)
15. Having a satisfactory sexual relationship with one's spouse is partly a matter of luck. (.42)
21. Successful child-rearing is a result of some good fortune along the way. (.40)
22. If my marriage were a long, happy one I'd say that I must just be very lucky. (.38)
30. When I look over the course of my marriage I can't help but wonder if it wasn't destined that way. (.21)
32. Couples who don't run into any marital conflict at some point in their marriage have simply been very lucky. (.31)
44. Something more than a couple's intentions and abilities is needed to bring about a mutually satisfying emotional relationship; it's really a kind of special magic that is there or isn't. (.28)

Note: Items are grouped according to goal-specific subscales. Item-total correlations in parentheses; total scores do not include the item score with which it was correlated.

The Desired Control Scale

(Reid & Ziegler, 1981a)

Variable

The DCS assesses the degree to which an elderly person feels in control of desirable events in everyday life.

Description

The original scale is composed of two parts, the desire of outcomes and the control expectancy of outcomes, each of which contain 35 items in a five-point Likert scale format. The range is from strongly disagree (1) to strongly agree (5). High scores indicate internality.

Since the long form has often required an hour or more to complete, a shortened form has been derived from the long form, the shortened version being a 16-item scale. The items selected for the short form had high item–total correlations within the long form and are representative of the variety of reinforcers found in the original measure.

The content of the scale was derived from the results of an interview survey with 143 elderly persons. These data were content-analyzed and from these analyses specific reinforcers and/or outcomes were identified and included in the questionnaire. The process of scale development is presented in an article by Reid and Ziegler (1977).

Scores from the scales are tabulated in two ways. Separate Desire and Expectancy scores are obtained and used in multiple regression predictions to given criteria, or scores of each Desire item are multiplied with the parallel Expectancy item, with the sum of the cross-products representing the total Desired Control score. Despite the possibility that some item pairs may contribute disproportionately to the total score variance (those that are both high or both low) both methods of calculating total scores have been found to produce similar correlations with criteria. The range of possible scores for both the Desire and Expectancy measures is 35–175.

The DCS has been collected most often as part of an interview so that it is commonly administered orally. No information is provided suggesting whether it differs if self-administered.

Sample

The samples ($n = 363$) used by Reid and Ziegler (1981a) come from five studies of the elderly, some of whom were institutionalized, some living in their own homes. Others were new residents of a recently built high-rise complex, or were from extended care units of a hospital, and others were drawn from a range of sittings. The mean Desire was 149 (SD = 14) and the Expectancy mean was 126 (SD = 18) for a sample of 363 elderly persons. For Desired Control, $\bar{M} = 543$ (SD = 107).

Reliability

Internal Consistency

Though the content of the scale is based on a series of categories of reinforcers that were reliably differentiated in a content analysis, the total Desired Control measure was found to have Cronbach α coefficients in the high .80s and low .90s throughout each of five studies. Separately, the Desire and Expectancy subscale α values were also high and generally in the .80s. Likewise item–total correlations for items were positive. A factor analysis with 469 cases produced three rotated factors that accounted for 76.6% of the variance. No meaningful interpretation of the three factors could be made. Consequently, the measure is treated as if it were unidimensional.

The short form of the DCS has produced Cronbach α values of .69 for Expectancy, .74 for Desire, and .73 for Desired Control with a sample of 135 persons. Factor analysis of the short form shows one dominant rotated factor accounting for 67.7% of the variance with a sample of 469 cases. Thus, the short form can easily be described as unidimensional.

Test–Retest

Test–retest reliability has ranged from .36 with a 6-month interval to .63 for a 1-year interval for the Desired Control index.

Validity

Convergent

The DCS has been studied along with a number of "adjustment" and "well-being" measures. Whether the measures are self-reports or ratings by others, the consistent finding is that the greater the Desired Control, the more positive is the psychological adjustment. In addition, the greater the Desired Control the more active were the subjects and the better was their functional health and the knowledge they had of available services, the more quickly they performed on a motor task, and the less stressed they were in their lives.

Most impressive are a set of cross-lagged correlations in which life satisfaction, health, and other variables were predicted a year after the DCS measures had been obtained. Life satisfaction was correlated positively with DCS (r values ranging between .23 and .44, $p < .001$) in four studies, and negatively with ill health in three of the four studies (r values ranging from $-.16$ to $-.49$). Similar results have been obtained for a 5-year interval as well (Reid & Ziegler, 1981a).

Discriminant

The Crowne–Marlowe Social Desirability measure was included in one study with 63 subjects. The r with Desired Control was .18. Partialling social desirability out from the correlations between Desired Control and the adjustment variables used in that study (life satisfaction, subjective senescence, and self concept) had negligible effects upon those relationships.

Location

Reid, D. W., & Ziegler, M. (1981). The Desired Control Measure and adjustment among the elderly. In H. M. Lefcourt (Ed.), *Research with the locus of control construct* (Vol. 1, pp. 127–157). New York: Academic Press.

Results and Comments

The DCS is exemplary in being derived from interviews designed to elicit what matters to the elderly in general. As such the items in the expectancy measure are pertinent to their intended subjects. However, the Desire measure seems superfluous in that the items tap issues that the larger samples have already claimed to be important. As it is, the Desire measure is highly skewed in a positive direction, a point the authors take as indicating that they were successful in eliciting the desires of the elderly.

For brevity then, the Expectancy variable could be used alone, which in its shortened version might be less onerous for the elderly to complete.

The longitudinal data that the authors have collected are impressive. The DCS should have clinical ramifications given its ability to predict health outcomes a year after assessment. Omissions are in the lack of presented norms for the shortened scale and in the absence of comparisons with other I-E scales.

Desired Control Measure

The purpose of this questionnaire is to determine your attitudes and beliefs on a variety of matters pertaining to everyday living. There are two parts to this study. The first part asks you to rate how desirable different events are to you. The second part asks you to rate the degree to which you agree or disagree with various statements.

Part I: Desire of Outcomes

There are many activities or events that happen to us in everyday living. Some of these events are more important or desirable to you than are others. Listed below are statements mentioning some of these activities or events. Working with the interviewer, would you please rate the extent to which each event described is important or not important to you. We emphasize that we are concerned here with the event's importance to you, not to others.

1. How desirable is it to you that your friends come and visit with you regularly?

5	4	3	2	1
VERY DESIRABLE	DESIRABLE	UNDECIDED	UNDESIRABLE	VERY UNDESIRABLE

*2. How desirable is it to you that people ask you for advice and suggestions?

*3. How important is it to you that you maintain your health?

4. Is getting involved in various activities important to you?

*5. Is being able to get along with people you meet important to you?

6. How desirable is it to you to be able to do the things you would like to do?

*7. Is being able to arrange outings important to you?

*8. Is being able to contact your family whenever you wish desirable to you?

*9. How important is being able to spend your time doing whatever you want?

*10. How important is it that you do the chores yourself without any help?

11. How much do you enjoy getting involved in interesting activities?

12. See #3. [repeated item]

*13. Is having your friends and family visit when you invite them important to you?

14. See #7. [repeated item]

15. How important is it that you have a say about where you are going to live?

16. Is making people happy important to you?

17. How important is it to you to be able to go to religious services?

18. Is being able to visit your friends important to you?

19. How important to you is being able to contact your family whenever you wish?

20. How important is it that you are given a chance to take on responsibility?

*21. How desirable is it to you that you can be active whenever you wish?

*22. How important is it that you find people who are interested in hearing what you have to say?

23. How desirable is it for you to see your family whenever you want?

*24. How desirable is it to you to get away from the house (or home)?

*25. How desirable to you is having your family visit you?

26. How important is it that you are able to return favors?

*27. How desirable is it to you to be able to help others?

28. Is being productive desirable to you?

*29. How important is it to you that you can have your friends over whenever you want?

30. See #13. [repeated item]

*31. Is keeping in contact with interesting ideas desirable to you?

32. See #21. [repeated item]

33. How desirable is it to you that your family writes or phones you?

*34. Is being able to find privacy important to you?

35. How important is it to you to be able to watch the T.V. programs you like?

Note: *, Sixteen items in Desired Control, short form.

Part II: Beliefs and Attitudes

The following are statements that may describe either yourself or the beliefs you have. Would you please respond to each statement by designating on the scale given with each item the degree to which you agree or disagree with the item. Once again, we emphasize that we are interested in your own opinion, not your judgment of what others think. From time to time you may find that some items seem to be repeated. Don't worry about this, for each item is purposefully different in terms of its specific wording. Would you please go ahead and rate your degree of agreement or disagreement to each statement.

1. I find that I am able to arrange for friends to come and visit me regularly.

5	4	3	2	1
STRONGLY AGREE	AGREE	UNDECIDED	DISAGREE	STRONGLY DISAGREE

*2. People tend to ignore my advice and suggestions.

*3. Maintaining my level of health strongly depends on my own efforts.

4. The circumstances in which I live make it very difficult (if not impossible) for me to be involved in numerous activities.

*5. It is difficult for me to get to know people.

6. I can rarely get out to do things I want.

*7. I can usually arrange to go on outings that I'm interested in.

*8. The situation in which I live prevents me from contacting my family as much as I wish.

*9. I spend my time usually doing what I want to do.

*10. Although it is sometimes strenuous, I try to do the chores by myself.

11. It is not possible for me to involve myself in interesting activities.

12. The future state of my health depends on fate.

*13. I find that if I ask my family (or friends) to visit me, they come.

14. It depends more on others and less on myself whether I get to go out for a good time (e.g., visiting, shopping, touring).

15. I would be very upset if I didn't have much say about where I was to live.

16. Making people happy is something that I don't get much opportunity to do.

17. It is not possible for me to go to religious services.

18. Going and visiting with friends is easy for me to do.

19. I often cannot get a hold of (e.g., by phone) members of my family when I want.

20. People don't give me a chance to take on a position of responsibility.

*21. I have quite a bit of influence on the degree to which I can be involved in activities.

*22. I can rarely find people who will listen closely to me.

23. Despite my circumstances, I can see my family when I want.

*24. My getting away from the house (or home) generally depends on someone else making the decisions.

*25. Visits from my family (or friends) seem to be due to their own decisions and not to my influence.

26. I find that I am able to return favors.

*27. People generally do not allow me to help them.

28. Circumstances prevent me from being more productive.

*29. I can entertain friends when I want.

30. Despite my efforts, my children (or other members of my family) will not (or cannot) come and visit me as often as I would like.

*31. Keeping in contact with interesting ideas is easy for me to do.

32. My living conditions prevent me from taking part in the activities I enjoy.

33. It is exceedingly difficult for me to get my family to either write or phone me.

*34. I am able to find privacy when I want it.

35. People keep me from watching the TV programs I want to see.

Note: *, Sixteen items in Desired Control, short form.

Parenting Locus of Control Scale

(Campis, Lyman, & Prentice-Dunn, 1986)

Variable

The PLOC assesses locus of control beliefs regarding the parent's perspective of child rearing successes and failures, assessed with regard to feelings of responsibility, efficacy, and a sense of control.

Description

The PLOC is a 47-item five-point Likert-type scale in which answers range from strongly disagree (1) to strongly agree (5). The items were derived from a series of procedures that began with item creation and rewording of items from older scales until there were 200 items, half internal and half external in orientation. Judges (faculty and graduate students) were then enlisted to rate each item on a nine-point scale from extremely internal (1) to extremely external (9). The disparities in ratings were then used for elimination of ambiguous items.

The resulting 109 items were then assembled on the five-point Likert scale format and distributed to 250 parents of elementary school age children. The test was self-administered by parents in their own homes in the normative sample. One hundred and forty-seven parents responded, and completed questionnaires were subjected to a principal-axis factor analysis that yielded a varimax rotation of five factors containing 68 of the original 109 items. Further reduction of items with lowest loadings and item–factor correlations left 47 items. The five factors are Parental Efficacy, Parental Responsibility, Child Control, Fate or Chance, and Parental Control.

Sample

The initial sample for scale refinement comprised 147 parents: 115 mothers and 32 fathers. A second group of 105 parents were used for validity work, 45 of whom had requested help for parenting problems. See Validity section for norms.

Reliability

Internal Consistency

The overall Cronbach α was .92 while for each subscale α values ranged from .65 for Parental Control to .77 for Parental Responsibility. In the second validity study, α values ranged from .62 for Parental Efficacy (after deleting one item) to .79 for Parental Responsibility.

Test–Retest

No measures of test–retest stability were reported.

Validity

Convergent

The overall PLOC was positively correlated with Rotter's I-E scale ($r = .33, p < .01, n = 105$). The factors of parental responsibility ($r = .26, p < .01$), child control ($r = .24, p < .01$) and fate–chance ($r = .27, p < .01$) were each related to I-E while efficacy and parental control were not ($r = .08$ and $.17$, respectively). In addition, parents seeking help for parenting problems scored in a more external direction on efficacy (means of 19.3 vs. 17.6 for control), child control (means of 16.3 vs. 14.4) and parental control (means of 31.4 vs. 26.6), each difference exceeding a probability of .02. Since the fate–chance dimension failed to discriminate parents with difficulties from those without, the authors recommend elimination of the fate–chance subscale. Furthermore, a correlation matrix with related parenting variables indicated utility for subscales, particularly Parental Control, which also differed most significantly between parents with and without parenting problems ($p < .0002$).

Discriminant

The Crowne–Marlowe Social Desirability Scale was included in the second validity study and it correlated significantly with two factors in the scale, Child Control ($r = -.21, p < .05$) and Parental Control ($r = -.38, p < .01$). With the entire scale the $r = -.27, p < .01$. The means for the larger sample of parents without parenting difficulties were 17.6 for Efficacy, 30.4 for Parental Responsibility, 14.4 for Child Control, 21.6 for Fate–Chance, and 26.6 for Parental Control.

Location

Campis, L. K., Lyman, R. D., & Prentice-Dunn, S. (1986). The parental locus of control scale: Development and validation. *Journal of Clinical Child Psychology,* **15,** 260–267.

Results and Comments

There is much missing in the presentation of this scale: clear norms for large samples, data pertaining to temporal stability, and sampling of parents of children of different ages and stages of development. Nevertheless, the scale has been developed with care and refined through a series of procedures that make it likely to become a useful measure. The robustness of the factor structure needs substantiation and the problem of social desirability needs to be dealt with but the promise for an area that has been of continuous interest should be high.

The exact procedures for the validity sample were not described. The items do seem easily read and pertinent to parental problems.

The Parenting Locus of Control Scale

Factor 1: Parenting Efficacy

1. What I do has little effect on my child's behavior. (.61)

1	2	3	4	5
STRONGLY DISAGREE	DISAGREE	NEITHER AGREE NOR DISAGREE	AGREE	STRONGLY AGREE

2. When something goes wrong between me and my child, there is little I can do to correct it. (.53)

3. Parents should address problems with their children because ignoring them won't make them go away. (R) (−.53)

4. If your child has tantrums no matter what you try, you might as well give up. (.51)

5. My child usually ends up getting his/her way, so why try. (.49)

6. No matter how hard a parent tries, some children will never learn to mind. (.44)

7. I am often able to predict my child's behavior in situations. (R) (−.44)

8. It is not always wise to expect too much from my child because many things turn out to be a matter of good or bad luck anyway. (.41)

9. When my child gets angry, I can usually deal with him/her if I stay calm. (R) (−.36)

10. When I set expectations for my child, I am almost certain that I can help him/her meet them. (R) (−.35)

Factor 2: Parental Responsibility

11. There is no such thing as good or bad children—just good or bad parents. (R) (.68)

12. When my child is well-behaved, it is because he/she is responding to my efforts. (R) (.59)

13. Parents who can't get their children to listen to them don't understand how to get along with their children. (R) (.54)

14. My child's behavior problems are no one's fault but my own. (R) (.53)

15. Capable people who fail to become good parents have not followed through on their opportunities. (R) (.52)

16. Children's behavior problems are often due to mistakes their parents made. (R) (.48)

17. Parents whose children make them feel helpless just aren't using the best parenting techniques. (R) (.47)

18. Most children's behavior problems would not have developed if their parents had had better parenting skills. (R) (.46)

19. I am responsible for my child's behavior. (R) (.40)

20. The misfortunes and successes I have had as a parent are the direct result of my own behavior. (R) (.35)

Factor 3: Child Control of Parents' Life

21. My life is chiefly controlled by my child. (.68)

22. My child does not control my life. (R) (−.65)

23. My child influences the number of friends I have. (.49)

24. I feel like what happens in my life is mostly determined by my child. (.48)

25. It is easy for me to avoid and function independently of my child's attempts to have control over me. (R) (−.44)

26. When I make a mistake with my child I am usually able to correct it. (R) (−.43)

27. Even if your child frequently has tantrums, a parent should not give up. (R) (−.39)

Factor 4: Parental Belief in Fate/Chance

28. Being a good parent often depends on being lucky enough to have a good child. (−.71)
29. I'm just one of those lucky parents who happened to have a good child. (−.61)
30. I have often found that when it comes to my children, what is going to happen will happen. (−.55)
31. Fate was kind to me; if I had had a bad child I don't know what I would have done. (−.51)
32. Success in dealing with children seems to be more a matter of the child's moods and feelings at the time rather than one's own actions. (−.47)
33. Neither my child nor myself is responsible for his/her behavior. (−.45)
34. In order to have my plans work, I make sure they fit in with the desire of my child. (−.44)
35. Most parents don't realize the extent to which how their children turn out is influenced by accidental happenings. (−.41)
36. Heredity plays the major role in determining a child's personality. (−.40)
37. Without the right breaks one cannot be an effective parent. (−.35)

Factor 5: Parental Control of Child's Behavior

38. I always feel in control when it comes to my child. (R) (.60)
39. My child's behavior is sometimes more than I can handle. (−.56)
40. Sometimes I feel that my child's behavior is hopeless. (.54)
41. It is often easier to let my child have his/her way than to put up with a tantrum. (.51)
42. I find that sometimes my child can get me to do things I really did not want to do. (.51)
43. My child often behaves in a manner very different from the way I would want him/her to behave. (.50)
44. Sometimes when I'm tired I let my children do things I normally wouldn't. (.48)
45. Sometimes I feel that I do not have enough control over the direction my child's life is taking. (.46)
46. I allow my child to get away with things. (.44)
47. It is not too difficult to change my child's mind about something. (R) (−.35)

Note: Factor loadings are given in parentheses after each item; (R) indicates items reversed for scoring.

Health-Related Measures Reviewed Here

The final five scales in this chapter deal with health-related variants of internal–external control. They are

12. The Multidimensional Health Locus of Control Scale (Wallston & Wallston, 1981; Wallston et al., 1978),
13. The Mental Health Locus of Control Scale (Hill & Bale, 1980, 1981),
14. The Drinking Internal–External Control Scale (originally constructed by Keyson & Janda, 1972, and subsequently published and revised by Donovan & O'Leary, 1983);
15. The Weight Locus of Control Scale (Saltzer, 1982); and
16. The Dyadic Sex Regulation Scale (Catania et al., 1984).

The Wallston et al. (1978) Multidimensional Health Locus of Control Scale (MHLC) is a well-known and frequently used device for the study of causal beliefs relevant to health. Initially, these authors had created a unidimensional scale with clear internal and external poles. However, this brief scale proved to be multidimensional via factor analyses and measures of internal consistency. This led the investigators to create a new measure modeled after that of Levenson. That is, a three-factor scale was created with factors of internality, powerful others, and chance, all pertaining to the maintenance of health. Social desirability is a factor only on the chance dimension. The Wallstons have collected a large body of data with their measures and it has been used far and wide by others. It would seem to have filled a need that was present in health studies. In addition, it has served as a stimulant to others who have designed health-related locus of control scales and has helped to spawn a literature concerned with activity versus passivity in the response to medical procedures and a concern for patient participation in the treatment process.

The Hill and Bale (1980, 1981) Mental Health Locus of Control (MHLC) and Mental Health Locus of Origin (MHLO) Scales should be of great interest to researchers studying persons suffering with mental illness. The items seem highly face valid as indicators of beliefs that should have portents for the development of psychopathology, the response to psychological treatment, and perhaps even the form of pathology that could be expected given such beliefs. However, it will be noted that there has been minimal psychometric clarification and refinement of these scales and the authors themselves have not added much to a literature that may yet evolve from these measures. The inclusion of this scale within this chapter is largely based on promise, for these scales offer exciting possibilities for clinical use.

The Keyson and Janda (1972), Donovan and O'Leary (1978, 1983) Drinking Internal–External Control Scale (DRIE) is modeled after Rotter's original unidimensional locus of control scale, containing a series of forced-choice items that have been factored into three aspects of control: inability to resist the impulse to drink, interpersonal pressures leading to drink, and a general control factor. The scale has been found to have adequate levels of internal consistency and reliability. The pertinence of locus of control to alcoholism and drinking behavior is self-evident given the belief that alcoholism is a disease that operates beyond the control of the sufferer. It is significant that the Alcoholics Anonymous prayer focuses upon accuracy of causal beliefs; that in early locus of control research alcoholics often presented paradoxical self-portraits in which they appeared to believe that they were more internal than nonalcoholic populations; and that one of the AA strategems is to have the alcoholic admit to his or her helplessness. This scale, then, has been in need of development. It should be noted that there is another alcohol-related scale, the Locus of Drinking Problems Scale (Stafford, 1980). The reliability of the several factors that compose this scale, however, has been questionable, with items of one assumed dimension being too highly related to items of another. Thus, although the trend is largely toward multidimensional scaling, at least in the area of concern with drinking and alcoholism, the unidimensional DRIE seems to be the best measure at this time.

The Saltzer (1982) Weight Locus of Control Scale (WLOC) is rather brief, comprising only four items, two internally and two externally oriented, presented with a Likert scale format. It seems to be relatively reliable and free of social desirability bias. Given the recent clinical concerns with eating disorders, obesity, and anorexia, the scale would seem to have considerable utility. Validity studies have shown that in interaction with measures revealing concern about appearance and health the WLOC affords some prediction of intentionality to control weight and persistence in weight control programs. This scale development grew from the same sources as the Wallstons' health-focused measures and would seem as promising for clinical uses. The author's own studies (Saltzer, 1978, 1981, 1982) are still the major reports demonstrating the scale's value.

The Catania et al. (1984) Dyadic Sexual Regulation Scale (DSR) is a brief 11-item Likert scale that picks up where the MLOC Scale leaves off. The MLOC assesses a range of matters related to intimacy, with the exception of sexual activity. The DSR contains a series of questions that were derived from open-ended interviews with heterosexual and homosexual couples. Not all of the questions ask directly about control beliefs but request answers from which control beliefs are inferred. The justifications offered for these inferences seem reasonable. The scale seems to have fair reliability and the few validity data offered are both positive and reasonable. While this scale is new and therefore much less substantiated than many of the above measures, it, like the WLOC, seems quite promising as a locus of control measure with clinical application. As with each of the preceding measures, when predictions to pertinent criteria are compared with predictions from more general locus of control measures, the specific targeted locus of control scale has proven to be a stronger predictor. In the present case sexual satisfaction in dyadic sexual relations is more strongly associated with the DSR than with the ANSIE.

Multidimensional Health Locus of Control Scale
(Wallston, Wallston, & DeVellis, 1978)

Variable

This measure assesses control beliefs relevant to health, building upon Levenson's dimensions of personal control or internality, the effectiveness of powerful others, and the role of chance in determining one's health status.

Description

The MHLC scales consist of three, six-item, self-administered subscales with two equivalent forms. Each form comprises 18 items. The three subscales are Internal Health Locus of Control (IHLC), Chance Health Locus of Control (CHLC), and Powerful Others Externality (PHLC). The scales are presented in a six-point Likert format ranging from strongly disagree (1) to strongly agree (6). The scale was developed initially with items from the original 11-item Health Locus of Control Scale (B. S. Wallston et al., 1976) and an additional 70 items constructed to represent these three subscales.

Separate item analyses were run on the items pertinent to each of the three subscales. Items were retained if the item mean was close to the midpoint (3.5), if there was suitable variance in response, if the item was significantly related to the whole scale (less that item), and if the item had a low correlation with social desirability. Scores for each subscale range from 6 to 36.

Samples

The MHLC has been given to dozens of samples so there is extensive information about groups with different health problems (diabetics, hypertensives, epileptics, patients undergoing hemodialysis and chemotherapy, etc.) as well as large unspecified groups (unspecified with regard to health) such as students, secretaries, wives of naval men, nurses, physicians, etc. The resulting 18-item scales (forms A and B) have been used extensively and the norms deriving from these studies are reported in detail (K. A. Wallston & Wallston, 1981). Generally, for IHLC, $\bar{M}$ = 26, (SD = 5); for CHLC, $\bar{M}$ = 15, (SD = 6); and for PHLC, $\bar{M}$ = 20 (SD = 5.5). The two forms seem to produce similar normative data.

Reliability

Internal Consistency

Several factor analyses reveal a replicable structure of three independent subscales. The subscales have Cronbach α values ranging between .61 and .80 (IHLC), .55–.83 (CHLC) and .56–.75 (PHLC). When forms A and B are added to each other α values increase with IHLC reaching .86, CHLC, .87 and PHLC, .83. Correlations between the two forms have ranged from .48 to .77 for IHLC, from .38 to .65 for CHLC, and from .46 to .53 for PHLC.

Test–Retest

With a time interval of 4–6 months test–retest correlations have been .66, .73, and .71 for IHLC, CHLC, and PHLC, respectively.

Validity

Convergent

The MHLC has been compared with Levenson's I, P, C scales in a reasonably sized sample of students (n = 115). IHLC is positively related to Levenson's Internality Scale (r = .57) while nonsignificantly related to the Powerful Others (r = −.12) or Chance scales (r = −.14). CHLC was negatively related to Levenson's Internality (r = −.30) and positively related to her P (r = .57) and C (r = .80) scales. The PHLC was most strongly related to the P Scale (r = .28), next with C Scale (r = .23), and least with I (r = −.07). The PHLC, then, seems least strongly related to Levenson's scale. Validity research with the MHLC is so extensive that no review can be offered that will do justice to it. Readers should consult K. A. Wallston and Wallston (1981). Groups with a range of medical problems that require their effective action have been assessed, as have patients with chronic disorders that breed helplessness.

Discriminant

Social desirability has been found related only to the CHLC measure and that was not a high-magnitude result ($r = -.24$). IHLC and PHLC showed little or no relationship with social desirability (r values $= .10$ and $.09$, respectively, $n = 115$). No differences have been found for sex, and weak relationships have been found between form A of PHLC and age ($r = .20, p < .05$) and educational level ($r = -.22, p < .05$) though not with form B or the other subscales.

Location

Wallston, K. A., & Wallston, B. S. (1981). Health Locus of Control Scales. In H. M. Lefcourt (Ed.), *Research with the locus of control construct* (Vol. 1, pp. 189–243). New York: Academic Press.

Wallston, K. A., Wallston, B. S., & DeVellis, R. (1978). Development of the Multidimensional Health Locus of Control Scales. *Health Education Monographs*, **6**, 161–170.

Results and Comments

Perhaps the Wallstons summed it up best when they stated that, despite its extensive use, their measure is not a panacea in explaining health-related behavior. As a dependent measure its validity appears greater than when it is used as an independent variable. Its reliability and internal structure seem sound, but it has been used too often without regard to other variables that are important as well. Actual control available, for example, may easily outweigh one's customary expectations of control and dictate behaviors in question.

Nevertheless, the Wallstons' scales seem a very useful device for studying health-related behavior. These authors have, as well, offered suggestions as to how the three scales may be used conjointly in predicting health-related behavior. Finally, the availability of alternate forms, a unique feature of this locus of control scale, makes it quite useful for assessment during treatment programs.

Multidimensional Health Locus of Control Scales

IHLC

Form A	Form B
1. If I get sick, it is my own behavior which determines how soon I get well again.	1. If I become sick, I have the power to make myself well again.

| 1 | 2 | 3 | 4 | 5 | 6 | | 1 | 2 | 3 | 4 | 5 | 6 |
STRONGLY DISAGREE   STRONGLY AGREE   STRONGLY DISAGREE   STRONGLY AGREE

6. I am in control of my health.   6. I am directly responsible for my health.

8. When I get sick I am to blame.

12. The main thing that affects my health is what I myself do.

13. If I take care of myself, I can avoid illness.

17. If I take the right actions, I can stay healthy.

8. Whatever goes wrong with my health is my own fault.

12. My physical wellbeing depends on how well I take care of myself.

13. When I feel ill, I know it is because I have not been taking care of myself properly.

17. I can pretty much stay healthy by taking good care of myself.

PHLC

Form A

3. Having regular contact with my physician is the best way for me to avoid illness.

5. Whenever I don't feel well, I should consult a medically trained professional.

7. My family has a lot to do with my becoming sick or staying healthy.

10. Health professionals control my health.

14. When I recover from an illness, it's usually because other people (for example, doctors, nurses, family, friends) have been taking good care of me.

18. Regarding my health, I can only do what my doctor tells me to do.

Form B

3. If I see an excellent doctor regularly, I am less likely to have health problems.

5. I can only maintain my health by consulting health professionals.

7. Other people play a big part in whether I stay healthy or become sick.

10. Health professionals keep me healthy.

14. The type of care I receive from other people is what is responsible for how well I recover from an illness.

18. Following doctor's orders to the letter is the best way for me to stay healthy.

CHLC

Form A

2. No matter what I do, if I am going to get sick, I will get sick.

4. Most things that affect my health happen to me by accident.

Form B

2. Often I feel that no matter what I do, if I am going to get sick, I will get sick.

4. It seems that my health is greatly influenced by accidental happenings.

9. Luck plays a big part in determining how soon I will recover from an illness.

9. When I am sick, I just have to let nature run its course.

11. My good health is largely a matter of good fortune.

11. When I stay healthy, I'm just plain lucky.

15. No matter what I do, I'm likely to get sick.

15. Even when I take care of myself, it's easy to get sick.

16. If it's meant to be, I will stay healthy.

16. When I become ill, it's a matter of fate.

Mental Health Locus of Control Scale

(Hill & Bale, 1980)

Variable

The MHLC is a bipolar measure of beliefs about control of therapeutic changes in which the internal pole reflects beliefs that the patient bears responsibility for changes and the external pole places the burden on the therapist.

Description

The self-administered 22-item MHLC scale derives from an initial pool of 61 items that were constructed to be face valid for the construct. The initial elongated scale (61 items) was administered to 226 university students along with other items representing different but related constructs. All items retained (14 external and 8 internal) had item–total correlations of at least .23, with the average $r = .40$. The mean scores for these items (from the six-point Likert format ranging from strongly agree to strongly disagree) were all within .87 of the midpoint (3.5), with the mean difference from the midpoint being .30.

Finally, all items were rated by 16 experts (psychology faculty and graduate students) for relevance to the construct. On a seven-point scale (7 being indicative of extreme relevance to external belief, 1 being indicative of extreme relevance to internal belief), all external items retained had a rating of at least 5.4. The internal items retained had mean ratings of 2.8 or less. The potential range for scale scores are from 22 (extreme internal) to 132 (extreme external).

Samples

Hill and Bale used one large university student sample of 226 subjects, 142 females, 84 males. All but 20 were white. The norms for the MHLC scale were $\bar{M} = 74, S.D. = 11, n = 226$.

Reliability

Internal Consistency

The coefficient α obtained from the above sample was .84.

Test–Retest

No retest data have been reported.

Validity

Convergent

The MHLC was not correlated with Rotter's I-E Scale ($r = .06$) but was related to beliefs about the origins of mental illness ($r = .40, p < .001$). Externality on MHLC was associated with beliefs that mental illness derives from uncontrollable endogenous forces, as opposed to more alterable social circumstances. Likewise, externality on the MHLC was negatively associated with information about psychopathology ($r = -.29, p < .001$). Socioeconomic status was negatively associated with Rotter's I-E ($r = -.16, p < .01$) and MHLC ($r = -.22, p < .001$). Information about psychopathology was also associated with SES but was unrelated to Rotter's I-E scale ($r = .00$). Finally, sex was related to MHLC ($r = -.21, p < .001$) with males being more external.

Location

Hill, D. J., & Bale, R. M. (1980). Development of the Mental Health Locus of Control and Mental Health Locus of Origin Scales. *Journal of Personality Assessment,* **44,** 148–156.

Hill, D. J., & Bale, R. M. (1981). Measuring beliefs about where psychological pain originates and who is responsible for its alleviation. In H. M. Lefcourt (Ed.), *Research with the locus of control construct,* (Vol. 1, pp. 281–320). New York: Academic Press.

Results and Comments

This scale offers promise, though the evidence is not in yet. The internal consistency and good scale refinement augur well for its potential. However, the complete absence of relationship with Rotter's scale leaves some doubt as to generalizability to other locus of control work. Much validity work is needed, especially, with persons undergoing therapeutic care. The authors know this and suggest it, but there has been no such work reported yet. The association with particular forms of psychopathology would seem an interesting target for research.

The MHLC Questionnaire

Instructions: This questionnaire consists of 28 statements about issues concerning mental health. Professionals in this field do not agree on many of these issues. The questionnaire is concerned with your own personal opinion about these statements.

Each statement is followed by a six-point scale on which you can express how much you agree or disagree with that statement. Please check one of the six spaces provided.

Filler   1. A person with an IQ of 160 would be considered abnormal in a statistical model of normality.

1	2	3	4	5	6
STRONGLY AGREE	AGREE	PROBABLY AGREE	PROBABLY DISAGREE	DISAGREE	STRONGLY DISAGREE

E   2. Psychotherapy is for people who can't make it alone and need someone stronger than themselves to lean on.

E   3. To recover from a serious mental problem you must first be willing temporarily to surrender all responsibility to an experienced professional.

Filler   4. According to psychoanalytic theory the stage of development in which the Oedipal conflict occurs is known as the penal stage.

I   5. People with psychological problems should play a large part in planning their own treatment.

E   6. Someone receiving psychiatric help should not make any important decisions without seeking advice.

Filler   7. In reactive schizophrenia the onset is slow and insidious.

E   8. When a psychiatric patient is trying out new behaviors a professional should decide which behaviors he/she should try first.

I   9. The decision as to when to end psychotherapy should be taken by the patient rather than the therapist.

E   10. The lives of people with psychological problems are so complicated that it is almost impossible for them to figure out what they should do to make things better.

E   11. If psychotherapy is like building a house, a good therapist should not only give you the tools but should design the house for you.

Filler   12. Thomas Szasz takes the view that mental illness is a myth.

E   13. Psychotherapists should tell their patients how to lead a healthy life instead of waiting to see if they find out for themselves.

E   14. Patients should try hard to accept their therapist's opinion as to what is right and wrong.

I   15. When an individual goes to a therapist for help, that individual should expect to take most of the responsibility for getting better.

Filler   16. The conscious and deliberate avoidance of thoughts that cause anxiety is known as rationalization.

I   17. In psychotherapy, what the therapist thinks is less important than what the client thinks.

E   18. Most patients leaving psychiatric hospitals should be strictly supervised for some period of time.

I   19. The goals of psychotherapy should be set by the client rather than the therapist.

E   20. In group therapy the individuals who benefit most are almost always those who pay most attention to the group leaders.

I   21. The mentally ill should not be encouraged to have others take care of their everyday needs.

I   22. If a psychiatric patient feels sure he/she is well enough to stop taking medication, that is what he/she should do.

E   23. The aim of anyone who gets into psychotherapy is to seek the advice of an expert and to act on it.

E   24. As a general rule psychiatrists should feel OK about making decisions on behalf of their patients.

Filler   25. The argument that normal and abnormal behaviors are acquired in a similar manner is a central part of the learning-theory approach to maladjustment.

I   26. A good psychotherapist expects clients to decide for themselves what they should do.

E   27. Going to a professional to discuss your problems is better than talking to friends because the advice of a professional is more valuable.

E   28. When experiencing psychological problems the person least likely to come up with solutions is oneself.

Mental Health Locus of Origin Scale

(Hill & Bale, 1980)

Variable

This scale measures locus-of-control beliefs about the etiology of psychopathology.

Description

At one end of the dimension ("endogenous") lie beliefs that emphasize unalterable sources of mental illness (genetic and physiological factors). The opposite pole consists of beliefs that focus on the more alterable social interaction sources of mental illness. This 20-item self-administered scale comprising 13 endogenous and 7 social interaction items was drawn from an original pool of 68 items. The same subject pool and raters as described for the MHLC scale were used.

Similar criteria were used to refine the MHLO scale as well: item–total scale correlations of $r = .17$ or greater, expert ratings (items with a mean rating of less than 5.3 were excluded for endogenous items, while only items rated 2.1 or less were selected for the interaction items), and proximation to the midpoint (no item more than 1.2 from the midpoint, 3.5, was included). The six-point Likert scale generates a potential range from 20 (internal–interactional extreme) to 120 (endogenous–unalterable extreme) with a midpoint of 70.

Sample

Hill and Bale used one large university student sample, 226 subjects, 142 females, 84 males. All but 20 were white. The norms for this scale are $\bar{M} = 61.60$ and $SD = 8.06$.

Reliability

Internal Consistency

Coefficient α is .76.

Test–Retest

No test–retest data were obtained.

Validity

Convergent

The MHLO scale is related to Rotter's I-E scale ($r = .18$, $p < .005$) and like the MHLC is negatively related to information about psychopathology. Thus, externals or those who believe in the unalterable sources of psychopathology tend to be more external on Rotter's scale and less informed. The relationship with the MHLC is likewise positive ($r = .40$, $p < .001$), with those who believe that the therapist is most responsible for outcomes also believing that pathology primarily results from organic, endogenous sources that are less alterable.

Discriminant

No information was specifically offered, but SES proved to be orthogonal with the MHLO ($r = -.08$). Likewise sex was unrelated to MHLO ($r = -.10$).

Location

Hill, D. J. & Bale, R. M. (1980). Development of the Mental Health Locus of Control and Mental Health Locus of Origin Scales. *Journal of Personality Assessment*, **44**, 148–156.

Hill, D. J. & Bale, R. M. (1981). Measuring beliefs about where psychological pain originates and who is responsible for its alleviation. In H. M. Lefcourt (Ed.), *Research with the locus of control construct* (Vol. 1, pp. 281–320). New York: Academic Press.

Results and Comments

Though on first glance the MHLO seems a different if related construct to locus of control, it shares in its use of attributions an assessment of orientations that bears commonality with locus of control. Endogenous sources, being unalterable, reflect a fatalistic view of psychopathology such that the individual's efforts are destined to be ineffectual. However, though interesting and a potentially valuable tool, the scale is relatively untested. The data offered by the authors barely scratch the surface. Hopefully, these scales will be used with clinic or hospital populations to examine the value for both diagnosis and prognosis.

The MHLO Questionnaire

Instructions: This questionnaire consists of 26 statements about issues concerning mental health. Professionals in this field do not agree on many of these issues. The questionnaire is concerned with your own personal opinion about these statements.

Each statement is followed by a six-point scale on which you can express how much you agree or disagree with that statement. Please check one of the six spaces provided.

It is very important that you respond to all the statements.

Filler   1. Senile dementia is an organic rather than a functional disorder.

1	2	3	4	5	6
STRONGLY AGREE	AGREE	PROBABLY AGREE	PROBABLY DISAGREE	DISAGREE	STRONGLY DISAGREE

E   2. Eventually medical science will discover a cure of psychosis.

E   3. The cause of most psychological problems is to be found in the brain.

Filler   4. In psychoanalysis childhood stresses and difficulties are thought to be the origins of patients' problems.

I   5. If the children of schizophrenics were raised by normal parents they would probably grow up to be mentally healthy.

E   6. Mental illness is usually caused by some disease of the nervous system.

E   7. Some people are born mentally unstable and are almost certain to spend some part of their lives in a mental hospital.

Filler   8. Thorazine is a drug commonly used in the treatment of schizophrenia.

E   9. Most people suffering from mental illness were born with some kind of psychological deficit.

Filler   10. Social learning theory considers higher level needs to be innate.

E   11. Some people are born depressed and stay that way.

E   12. Everybody's system has a breaking point and those of mental patients are probably weaker.

I   13. The mental illnesses of some people are caused by the separation or divorce of their parents during childhood.

E   14. Being hot-blooded is the cause of mental illness in some people.

Filler   15. Freud's view of socialization involves a progression of psychosocial stages that place great emphasis on social and cultural factors.

I   16. More money should be spent on discovering healthy methods

	of child-rearing than on determining the biological basis of mental illness.
E	17. Some people are born with the kind of nervous system that makes it easy for them to become emotionally disturbed.
I	18. Your choice of friends can have a lot to do with your becoming mentally ill.
Filler	19. An existentialist would state that anxiety arises as a result of repression.
I	20. Although they usually aren't aware of it, many people become mentally ill to avoid the difficult problems of everyday life.
E	21. Some people are born with a slightly greater tendency than others to commit suicide later in life.
I	22. Many normal people would become mentally ill if they had to live in very stressful situations.
E	23. Mental health professionals probably underestimate the extent to which brain damage is responsible for mental illness.
E	24. When a group of people is forced to live under extremely stressful conditions, the ones who crack under the strain are likely to be the ones who inherited a psychologically weak disposition.
I	25. The kind of nervous system you are born with has little to do with whether you become psychotic.
E	26. The cause of many psychological problems is bad nerves.

Drinking-Related Locus of Control Scale

(Keyson & Janda, 1972)

Variable

The DRIE is a measure of control expectancies dealing with a variety of drinking-related behaviors.

Description

The DRIE scale consists of 25 self-administered items in a forced-choice format pairing internal and external control alternatives. The external alternatives appear first in 10 items and in 15 as a second choice. The scale is scored in the external direction with higher scores indicating external control over drinking.

Sample

The sample of 120 men who were undergoing treatment for alcoholism at a VA hospital were on average 45 years of age (SD = 12) and had a mean educational level of 12 years (SD = 2); most were from a lower-middle-class background.

With a sample of 120 men the overall $\bar{M}$ = 6.3 (SD = 4.0) with scores ranging from 0 to 17. This mean is comparable with that reported by Oziel, Obitz, and Keyson (1972) which was 5.6 (SD = 4.8) for an n of 50. All subjects from both samples were alcoholics.

Reliability

Internal Consistency

Both the Cronbach α and Kuder Richardson coefficients of internal consistency were .77. The unequal length Spearman–Brown split–half reliability coefficient was .70, which was comparable to the previous study by Oziel *et al.* (1972) (r = .64). The mean inter-item and adjusted item total correlation coefficients were .10 (range, $-.19$–.48) and .28 (range, .08–.55), respectively. A factor analysis with factors rotated to orthogonal structure produced three factors with eigenvalues above 1.0 that accounted for 65.2% of the variance. The first factor, accounting for 39.6% of the variance, consisted of 7 items that concerned the inability to resist the temptation to drink and was referred to as the Intrapersonal Control factor. Factor 2 comprised seven items accounting for 15.3% of the variance. These items dealt with the inability to resist interpersonal pressures to drink and was therefore labeled the Interpersonal Control factor. Factor 3 consisted of three items, all with third person references and chance factors influencing abstinence. This factor was labeled the General Control factor and accounted for 10.3% of the variance. The latter was the least stable of the factors. Eight items failed to appear in any of the three factors.

Text–Retest

No test–retest data have been reported.

Validity

Convergent

With the same 120 subjects described above the DRIE was correlated significantly with Rotter's I-E scale (r = .28, $p < .01$) and with Levenson's Chance scale (r = .21, $p < .05$) but was not related to her measures of Internality (r = .15) or Powerful Others (r = .05). With 56 alcoholic subjects compared to 28 general medical patients and hospital employees, the DRIE differentiated the groups at the .001 level whereas Rotter's I-E scale did not. Likewise, out of 20 items on the Alcohol Use Inventory (Wanberg, Horn, & Foster, 1977), 10 were predicted significantly by the DRIE while none were predicted with Rotter's I-E scale.

Discriminant

The DRIE was assessed for its relationship with a variety of measures related to intellectual functioning. Neither educational level, intelligence, nor abstract thinking was associated with DRIE scores.

Location

Though Keyson and Janda created the DRIE, the bulk of the psychometric work and exploration with it have been conducted and written up by Donovan and O'Leary.

Donovan, D. M., & O'Leary, M. R. (1978). The Drinking-Related Locus of Control Scale. *Journal of Studies on Alcohol,* **39,** 759–784.

Donovan, D. M., & O'Leary, M. R. (1983). Control orientation, drinking behavior, and alcoholism. In H. M. Lefcourt (Ed.), *Research with the locus of control construct* (Vol. 2, pp. 107–154). New York: Academic Press.

Results and Comments

The DRIE seems to be a useful scale for helping to define the problems and sources of problems for alcoholics. It obviously predicts drinking-related problems better than generalized locus of control measures. One issue to note, however, is that Donovan and O'Leary report their factor analysis on only externally worded items. No reason is offered for the omission of internally worded items.

In addition, given Collins's work with Rotter's scale, which shows the internal and external items to be relatively unrelated, the DRIE may also be questioned as to the relationship of these assumed opposites. An examination of the items belonging to the respective factors leads one to question the labeling, as some of the "interpersonal" items seem much more relevant to the intrapersonal sphere. It would seem preferable to rely upon the total score at this time rather than the factors. Since the α values are moderately high this would seem to be the better strategy.

Though forced choice is often difficult, the specificity of the scale and its wording make it seem relatively easy to understand.

The Drinking-Related Locus of Control Scale

Factor

1. a. One of the major reasons why people drink is because they cannot handle their problems.
   b. People drink because circumstances force them to.

2. a. The idea that men or women are driven to drink by their spouses is nonsense.
   b. Most people do not realize that drinking problems are influenced by accidental happenings.

(2) 3. a. I feel so helpless in some situations that I need a drink.
   b. Abstinence is just a matter of deciding that I no longer want to drink.

4. a. I have the strength to withstand pressures at work.
(2) b. Trouble at work or home drives me to drink.

(3) 5. a. Without the right breaks one cannot stay sober.
   b. Alcoholics who are not successful in curbing their drinking often have not taken advantage of help that is available.

6. a. There is no such thing as an irresistible temptation to drink.
(2) b. Many times there are circumstances that force you to drink.

(2) 7. a. I get so upset over small arguments that they cause me to drink.
   b. I can usually handle arguments without taking a drink.

(3)
(1)

8. a. Successfully licking alcoholism is a matter of hard work, luck has little or nothing to do with it.
    b. Staying sober depends mainly on things going right for you.

9. a. When I see a bottle, I cannot resist taking a drink.
    b. It is no more difficult for me to resist drinking when I am near a bottle than when I am not.

10. a. The average person has an influence on whether he drinks or not.

11. a. When I am at a party where others are drinking, I can avoid taking a drink.
(1) b. It is impossible for me to resist drinking if I am at a party where others are drinking.

12. a. Those who are successful in quitting drinking are the ones who are just plain lucky.
    b. Quitting drinking depends upon lots of effort and hard work (luck has little or nothing to do with it).

(1) 13. a. I feel powerless to prevent myself from drinking when I am anxious or unhappy.
    b. If I really wanted to, I could stop drinking.

14. a. It is easy for me to have a good time when I am sober.
(1) b. I cannot feel good unless I am drinking.

15. a. As far as drinking is concerned, most of us are victims of forces we can neither understand nor control.
    b. By taking an active part in our treatment programs, we can control our drinking.

16. a. I have control over my drinking behavior.
(1) b. I feel completely helpless when it comes to resisting a drink.

17. a. If people want to badly enough, they can change their drinking behavior.
    b. It is impossible for some people to ever stop drinking.

18. a. With enough effort we can lick our drinking.
    b. It is difficult for alcoholics to have much control over their drinking.

19. a. If someone offers me a drink, I cannot refuse him.
    b. I have the strength to refuse a drink.

(3) 20. a. Sometimes I cannot understand how people can control their drinking.
    b. There is a direct connection between how hard people try and how successful they are in stopping their drinking.

21. a. I can overcome my urge to drink.
(1) b. Once I start to drink I can't stop.

22. a. Drink isn't necessary in order to solve my problems.
(2) b. I just cannot handle my problems unless I take a drink first.

(2) 23. a. Most of the time I can't understand why I continue drinking.
    b. In the long run I am responsible for my drinking problems.

24. a. If I make up my mind, I can stop drinking.
     b. I have no will power when it comes to drinking.
(1)   25. a. Drinking is my favorite form of entertainment.
     b. It wouldn't bother me if I could never have another drink.

Note: Factor 1, Intrapersonal control; Factor 2, interpersonal control; Factor 3, general control.

The Weight Locus of Control Scale
(Saltzer, 1982)

Variable

This measure assesses beliefs about how one's weight is determined, varying from internal to external sources of control.

Description

The WLOC is a four-item questionnaire composed of two internally and two externally worded items, presented in a six-point Likert scale format. The scoring is from 1 for strongly disagree to 6 for strongly agree. The WLOC is scored in the external direction and the Likert format is reverse-scored for the internally worded items. The possible range of scores is from 4 to 24 with 4 indicating extreme internality and 24 extreme externality.

Samples

Saltzer used three samples in developing norms for the WLOC scale. The first sample consisted of 115 (42 male, 73 female) college students, 110 of whom completed the scale twice. A second sample of 116 (55 male, 61 female) college students was, like the first sample, primarily middle class and white. The third sample comprised 115 women who chose to begin a weight reduction program.

Norms are as follows: A mean of 7.7 (SD of 3.2) for 115 college students in the first administration; a mean of 8.2 (SD of 3.0) for the same sample in a second administration. In other studies, a mean of 7.8 (SD of 3.5) was found for 116 college students and a mean of 7.0 (SD of 2.8) was found for 115 female weight control clinic patients.

This simple four-item scale can be self-administered in a minute or two. While there is no information about its readability, it seems a bit complex for someone without good verbal skills.

Reliability

Internal Consistency

Cronbach α values were .58 and .56 for the two administrations, respectively.

Test–Retest

Test–retest reliability with a 24-day interval was .67 ($p < .001, n = 110$).

Validity

Convergent

In the two descriptions of its use (Saltzer, 1981, 1982) the WLOC Scale is found to be correlated with Collins' revision of Rotter's I-E Scale (Collins, 1974), $r = .32, p < .001$, $n = 114$, and with a short form of the HLC (B. S. Wallston *et al.,* 1976), $r = .21, p < .02, n = 116$. In addition it is related to the internality ($r = -.30, p < .001, n = 112$) and the chance ($r = .35, p < .001, n = 113$) scales of the MHLOC scales (K. A. Wallston & Wallston, 1978). The powerful others scale from the MHLC was unrelated to the WLOC scale ($r = .11$, ns). Subjects who were internal on the WLOC scale and who highly valued health and/or physical appearance were influenced in their behavioral intentions for weight loss by their personal attitudes toward weight loss while those who were external on WLOC and had a high value for health and/or appearance were only influenced by perceived normative beliefs. That is, personal attitudes influenced intentions of internals while social pressures affected the intentions of externals. Neither Collins' version of Rotter's I-E Scale nor the HLC or MHLC scales generated the same interactions. Persistence in the program and weight loss itself were greatest among internals on the WLOC Scale who also had a high value for health and/or appearance.

Discriminant

WLOC and social desirability (short form of Crowne & Marlowe social desirability scale—Crowne & Marlowe, 1964) were unrelated ($r = -.03, n = 111$).

Location

Saltzer, E. B. (1981). Cognitive moderators of the relationship between behavioral intentions and behavior. *Journal of Personality and Social Psychology,* **41**, 260–271.
Saltzer, E. B. (1982). The Weight Locus of Control (WLOC) Scale: A specific measure for obesity research. *Journal of Personality Assessment,* **46**, 620–628.

Results and Comments

This scale has proven to be useful in predicting weight-related criteria that more general locus of control scales have failed to predict. As such it would seem to be the scale of choice for research concerned with weight control. The scale is, however, quite brief, an advantage in administration but a disadvantage with regard to reliability. Both the brevity of the scale and its having half external and half internal items limits potential reliability statistics.

Nevertheless, the internal consistency and temporal stability are adequate given the limiting features of the scale. The WLOC may need some refinement, and further research is necessary to assure its utility. However, the validity studies reported thus far are convincing as to its promise.

The Weight Locus of Control Scale

(I)   1. Whether I gain, lose, or maintain my weight is entirely up to me.

1	2	3	4	5	6
STRONGLY DISAGREE					STRONGLY AGREE

(E)   2. Being the right weight is largely a matter of good fortune.

(E)   3. No matter what I intend to do, if I gain or lose weight, or stay the same in the near future, it is just going to happen.

(I)   4. If I eat properly and get enough exercise and rest, I can control my weight in the way I desire.

Dyadic Sexual Regulation Scale

(Catania, McDermott, & Wood, 1984)

Variable

This scale assessed control beliefs relevant to sexual activity with partners (as opposed to masturbatory activity).

Description

The DSR is an 11-item, self-administered Likert-type scale with seven points (1, strongly disagree, 7, strongly agree). The scale items were derived from open-ended interviews about sexual attitudes with heterosexual and homosexual couples. Five items were reversed (items 2, 5, 6, 8, 10) for counter-balancing purposes. After reversing these items, total scores were computed so that higher scores indicate a greater degree of internal control.

No systematic refinement strategies were employed but the items are each well conceptualized with regard to their relevance to locus of control. Scale scores range from 11 (external) to 77 (internal).

Samples

Two samples were recruited from introductory psychology classes at a university. The samples were reduced to include only heterosexuals who had a current, regular sexual partner. Sample 1 consisted of 151 white students (59 males and 92 females) with a mean age of 27. Sample 2 consisted of 27 males and 43 females with similar demographic features as Sample 1. Normative data have not been presented.

Reliability

Internal Consistency

Cronbach α values were .74 in Sample 1 and .83 in Sample 2. A principal component analysis with varimax rotation was conducted on the DSR items for Sample 1. There were nonsignificant loadings beyond the first factor, which accounted for 95% of the variance.

Test–Retest

Test–retest reliability was .77 with a 2-week interval.

Validity

Convergent

The DSR and the ANSIE (Nowicki & Duke, 1974a) are significantly correlated ($r = .19$, $p < .05$, df = 149). The DSR was found to be related with each dyadic measure of sexual activity. Internality with regard to sexual activity is associated with higher frequencies of intercourse, oral sex from partner, orgasms with partner, sexual relations, affectionate behaviors, and sexual satisfaction, and with lesser anxiety in sexual situations. In contrast, the ANSIE was more weakly associated with each criterion.

Discriminant

Gender was unrelated to DSR in each sample.

Location

Catania, J. A., McDermott, L. V., & Wood, J. A. (1984). Assessment of locus of control: Situational specificity in the sexual context. *Journal of Sex Research*, **20**, 310–324.

Results and Comments

This scale is relatively straightforward; its reliability data are good, and the face validity fairly good. Only 5 of the 11 items are obvious control belief items, while the others each require some inference to obtain indications of control beliefs. Some of these items (#3 and #6) may be confounded with the satisfaction items, helping to account for certain validity findings. There is a need to check out social desirability factors in this scale, and the more inferred items may prove to be less valuable than the more obvious control-related items in fine-grained analyses in which items are matched singly against criteria. Nevertheless, the scale offers some promise for exploring this clinically relevant area.

Dyadic Sexual Regulation Scale

1. I often take the initiative in beginning sexual activity.

1	2	3	4	5	6	7
STRONGLY AGREE						STRONGLY DISAGREE

*2. If my sexual relations are not satisfying there is little I can do to improve the situation.

3. I have sexual relations with my partner as often as I would like.

4. My planning for sexual encounters leads to good sexual experiences with my partner.

*5. I feel that it is difficult to get my partner to do what makes me feel good during sex.

*6. I feel that my sexual encounters with my partner usually end before I want them to.

7. When I am not interested in sexual activity I feel free to reject sexual advances by my partner.

*8. I want my partner to be responsible for directing our sexual encounters.

9. I find it pleasurable at times to be the active member during sexual relations while my partner takes a passive role.

*10. I would feel uncomfortable bringing myself to orgasm if the stimulation my partner was providing was inadequate.

11. During some sexual encounters I find it pleasurable to be passive while my partner is the active person.

Note: *, Reverse-scored items.

Bibliography

Abramowitz, S. I. (1969). Locus of control and self-reported depression among college students. *Psychological Reports, 25,* 149–150.

Altrocchi, J., Palmer, J., Hellmann, R., & Davis, H. (1968). The Marlowe–Crowne, repressor–sensitizer, and internal–external scales and attribution of unconscious hostile intent. *Psychological Reports, 23,* 1229–1230.

Ashkanasy, N. M. (1985). Rotter's internal–external scale: Confirmatory factor analysis and correlation with social desirability for alternative scale formats. *Journal of Personality and Social Psychology, 48*(5), 1328–1341.

Bandura, A. (1977). Self-efficacy: Toward a unifying theory of behavioral change. *Psychological Review, 84*(2), 191–215.

Berzins, J. I., Ross, W. F., & Cohen, D. I. (1970). Skill versus chance activity preferences as alternative measures of locus of control: An attempted cross-validation. *Journal of Consulting and Clinical Psychology, 35,* 18–20.

Bialer, I. (1961). Conceptualization of success and failure in mentally retarded and normal children. *Journal of Personality, 29,* 303–320.

Calhoun, A., Pierce, J., & Dawes, A. (1973). Attribution theory concepts and outpatients' perceptions of the causal locus of their psychological problems. *Journal of Community Psychology, 1,* 52–58.

Calhoun, L., Johnson, R., & Boardman, W. (1975). Attribution of depression to internal–external and stable–unstable causes: Preliminary investigation. *Psychological Reports, 36,* 463–466.

Campis, L. K., Lyman, R. D., & Prentice-Dunn, S. (1986). The parental locus of control scale: Development and validation. *Journal of Clinical Child Psychology, 15*(3), 260–267.

Catania, J. A., McDermott, L. V., & Wood, J. A. (1984). Assessment of locus of control: Situational specificity in the sexual context. *Journal of Sex Research, 20,* 310–324.

Cherlin, A., & Bourque, L. B. (1974). Dimensionality and reliability of the Rotter I-E Scale. *Sociometry, 37*, 565–582.

Collins, B. E. (1974). Four components of the Rotter Internal–External Scale: Belief in a difficult world, a just world, a predictable world, and a politically reponsive world. *Journal of Personality and Social Psychology, 29*, 381–391.

Collins, B. E., Martin, J. C., Ashmore, R. D., & Ross, L. (1973). Some dimensions of the internal–external metaphor in theories of personality. *Journal of Personality, 41*, 471–492.

Cone, J. D. (1971). Locus of control and social desirability. *Journal of Consulting and Clinical Psychology, 36*, 449.

Connell, J. P. (1985). A new multidimensional measure of children's perceptions of control. *Child Development, 56*, 1018–1041.

Crandall, V. C. (1968). *Refinement of the IARQ Scale.* NIMH Progress Report, December 1968, Grant No. MH-02238, 60–67.

Crandall, V. C., & Crandall, B. W. (1983). Maternal and childhood behaviors as antecedents of internal–external control perceptions in young adulthood. In H. Lefcourt (Ed.), *Research with the locus of control construct* (Vol. 2). New York: Academic Press.

Crandall, V. C., Crandall, V. J., & Katkovsky, W. (1965). A children's social desirability questionnaire. *Journal of Consulting Psychology, 29*, 27–36.

Crandall, V. J., Katkovsky, W., & Crandall, V. C. (1965). Children's belief in their own control of reinforcement in intellectual–academic situations. *Child Development, 36*, 91–109.

Crandall, V. J., Katkovsky, W., & Preston, A. (1962). Motivational and ability determinants of young children's intellectual achievement behaviors. *Child Development, 33*, 643–661.

Crowne, D. P., & Liverant, S. (1963). Conformity under varying conditions of personal commitment. *Journal of Abnormal and Social Psychology 66*(6), 547–555.

Crowne, D. P., & Marlowe, D. (1964). *The approval motive.* New York: Wiley.

Dahlquist, L. M., & Ottinger, D. R. (1983). Locus of control and peer status: A scale for children's perceptions of social interactions. *Journal of Personality Assessment, 47*(3), 278–287.

Davis, J. (1983). Does authority generalize? Locus of control perceptions in Anglo-American and Mexican-American adolescents. *Political Psychology, 4*, 101–120.

de Charms, R. (1976). *Enhancing motivation: Change in the classroom.* New York: Irvington.

DeVelles, R. F., DeVellis, B. M., Revicki, D. A., Lurie, S. J., Runyan, D. K., & Briston, M. (1985). Development and validation of the child improvement locus of control (CILC) scales. *Journal of Social and Clinical Psychology, 3*(3), 307–324.

Donovan, D. M., & O'Leary, M. R. (1978). The Drinking-Related Locus of Control Scale. *Journal of Studies on Alcohol, 39*, 759–784.

Donovan, D. M., & O'Leary, M. R. (1983). Control orientation, drinking behavior, and alcoholism. In H. M. Lefcourt (Ed.), *Research with the locus of control construct* (Vol. 2, pp. 107–154). New York: Academic Press.

Dowaliby, F. J., McKee, B. G., & Maher, H. (1983). A locus of control inventory for postsecondary hearing-impaired students. *American Annals of the Deaf, 128*(7), 884–889.

Duke, M. P., & Lewis, G. (1979). The measurement of locus of control in Black preschool and primary school children. *Journal of Personality Assessment, 43*, 479–480.

Duke, M. P., & Nowicki, S. (1972). A new measure and social learning model for interpersonal distance. *Journal of Experimental Research in Personality, 6*, 119–132.

Duke, M. P., Shaheen, J., & Nowicki, S. (1974). The determination of locus of control in a geriatric population and a subsequent test of the social learning model for interpersonal distance. *Journal of Psychology, 86*, 277–285.

Dweck, C. S., & Bush, E. S. (1976). Sex differences in learned helplessness. I. Differential debilitation with peer and adult evaluators. *Developmental Psychology, 12*, 147–156.

Feather, N. T. (1967). Some personality correlates of external control. *Australian Journal of Psychology, 19*, 253–260.

Feather, N. T. (1968). Valence of outcome and expectation of success in relation to task difficulty and perceived locus of control. *Journal of Personality and Social Psychology, 7*(4), 372–386.

Franklin, R. D. (1963). Youth's expectancies about internal versus external control of reinforcement related to N variables. *Dissertation Abstracts*, **24**, 1684.

Furnham, A. (1986). Economic locus of control. *Human Relations*, **39**(1), 29–43.

Gorsuch, R. L., Henighan, R. P., & Barnard, C. (1972). Locus of control: An example of dangers in using children's scales with children. *Child Development*, **43**, 579–590.

Gregory, W. L. (1978). Locus of control for positive and negative outcomes. *Journal of Personality and Social Psychology*, **36**(8), 840–849.

Gurin, P., Gurin, G., & Morrison, B. M. (1978). Personal and ideological aspects of internal and external control. *Social Psychology Quarterly*, **41**, 275–296.

Halpin, B. M., & Ottinger, D. R. (1983). Children's locus of control scales: A reappraisal of reliability characteristics. *Child Development*, **54**(2), 484–487.

Harter, S., & Connell, J. P. (1984). A model of the relationships among children's academic achievement and their self-perceptions of competence, control, and motivational orientation. In J. Nicholls (Ed.), *The development of achievement motivation* (pp. 219–250). Greenwich, CT: JAI Press.

Hill, D. J., & Bale, R. M. (1980). Development of the Mental Health Locus of Control (MHLC) and Mental Health Locus of Origin (MHLO) Scales. *Journal of Personality Assessment*, **44**(2), 148–156.

Hill, D. J., & Bale, R. M. (1981). Measuring beliefs about where psychological pain originates and who is responsible for its alleviation: Two new scales for clinical researchers. In H. M. Lefcourt (Ed.), *Research with the locus of control construct* (Vol. 1). New York: Academic Press.

Hjelle, L. A. (1971). Social desirability as a variable in the locus of control scale. *Psychological Reports*, **31**, 311–327.

James, W. H. (1957). *Internal versus external control of reinforcement as a basic variable in learning theory*. Unpublished doctoral dissertation, Ohio State University, Columbus.

Keyson, M., & Janda, L. (1972). *The internal–external scale for alcoholism*. Unpublished manuscript, St. Luke's Hospital, Phoenix, AZ.

Kirscht, J. P. (1972). Perception of control and health beliefs. *Canadian Journal of Behavioural Science*, **4**, 225–237.

Kobasa, S. C. (1979). Stressful life events, personality, and health: An inquiry into hardiness. *Journal of Personality and Social Psychology*, **37**, 1–11.

Langer, E. J. (1983). *The psychology of control*. Beverly Hills, CA: Sage.

Lau, R. R. (1982). Origins of health locus of control beliefs. *Journal of Personality and Social Psychology*, **42**(2), 322–334.

Lau, R. R., & Ware, J. F. (1981). Refinements in the measurement of health-specific locus-of-control beliefs. *Medical Care*, **19**(11), 1147–1158.

Lefcourt, H. M. (1976a). *Locus of control: Current trends in theory and research*. Hillsdale, NJ: Erlbaum.

Lefcourt, H. M. (1976b). Locus of control and the response to aversive events. *Canadian Psychological Review*, **17**, 202–209.

Lefcourt, H. M. (1981a). *Locus of control: Current trends in theory and research* (2nd ed.). Hillsdale, NJ: Erlbaum.

Lefcourt, H. M. (Ed.) (1981b). *Research with the locus of control construct* (Vol. 1). New York: Academic Press.

Lefcourt, H. M. (1981c). The construction and development of the multidimensional–multiattributional causality scales. In H. M. Lefcourt (Ed.), *Research with the locus of control construct* (Vol. 1). New York: Academic Press.

Lefcourt, H. M. (1982). *Locus of control: Current trends in theory and research* (2nd ed.). Hillsdale, NJ: Erlbaum.

Lefcourt, H. M. (Ed.) (1983a). *Research with the locus of control construct* (Vol. 2). New York: Academic Press.

Lefcourt, H. M. (1983b). The locus of control as a moderator variable: Stress. In H. M. Lefcourt (Ed.), *Research with the locus of control construct* (Vol. 2, pp. 253–268). New York: Academic Press.

Lefcourt, H. M. (Ed.) (1984). *Research with the locus of control construct* (Vol. 3). New York: Academic Press.

Lefcourt, H. M., & Wine, J. (1969). Internal versus external control of reinforcement and the deployment of attention in experimental situations. *Canadian Journal of Behavioural Science,* **1,** 167–181.

Lefcourt, H. M., Gronnerud, P., & McDonald, P. (1973). Cognitive activity and hypothesis formation during a double entendre word association test as a function of locus of control and field dependence. *Canadian Journal of Behavioural Science,* **5,** 161–173.

Lefcourt, H. M., Martin, R. A., Fick, C., & Saleh, W. E. (1985). Locus of control for affiliation and behavior in social interactions. *Journal of Personality and Social Psychology,* **48,** 755–759.

Lefcourt, H. M., Martin, R. A., & Ware, E. E. (1984). Locus of control, causal attributions, and affects in achievement-related contexts. *Canadian Journal of Behavioural Science,* **16,** 57–64.

Lefcourt, H. M., von Baeyer, C. L., Ware, E. E., & Cox, D. V. (1979). The multidimensional-multiattributional causality scale: The development of a goal specific locus of control scale. *Canadian Journal of Behavioural Science,* **11,** 286–304.

Levenson, H. (1973a). Multidimensional locus of control in psychiatric patients. *Journal of Consulting and Clinical Psychology,* **41,** 397–404.

Levenson, H. (1973b). Perceived parental antecedents of internal, powerful others, and chance locus of control orientations. *Developmental Psychology,* **9**(2), 268–274.

Levenson, H. (1974). Activism and powerful others: Distinctions within the concept of internal-external control. *Journal of Personality Assessment,* **38,** 377–383.

Levenson, H. (1981). Differentiating among internality, powerful others, and chance. In H. M. Lefcourt (Ed.), *Research with the locus of control construct* (Vol. 1, pp. 15–63). New York: Academic Press.

Lewandowski, A. (1979). *An investigation of cognitive and attitudinal correlates of the coronary-prone behavior pattern.* Unpublished doctoral dissertation, University of Waterloo.

Lewinsohn, P., Steinmetz, J. L., Larson, D. W., & Franklin, J. (1981). Depression-related cognitions: Antecedent or consequence? *Journal of Abnormal Psychology,* **90,** 213–219.

MacDonald, A. P., Jr., & Tseng, M. S. (1971). *Dimensions of internal vs external control revisited.* Unpublished manuscript, West Virginia University, Morgantown.

Marsh, H. W., & Richards, G. E. (1987). *The Rotter locus of control scale: The comparison of alternative response formats and implications for reliability, validity and dimensionality.* Unpublished manuscript. University of Sydney, Australia.

Matthews, W. S., Barabas, G., & Ferrari, M. (1982). Emotional concomitants of childhood epilepsy. *Epilepsia,* **23,** 671–678.

McGhee, P. E., & Crandall, V. C. (1968). Beliefs in internal–external control of reinforcements and academic performances. *Child Development,* **39,** 91–102.

Miller, P. C. Lefcourt, H. M., Holmes, J. G., Ware, E. E., & Saleh, W. E. (1986). Marital locus of control and marital problem solving. *Journal of Personality and Social Psychology,* **51,** 161–169.

Miller, P. C., Lefcourt, H. M., & Ware, E. E. (1983). The construction and development of the Miller Marital Locus of Control Scale. *Canadian Journal of Behavioural Science,* **15,** 266–279.

Mirels, H. L. (1970). Dimensions of internal versus external control. *Journal of Consulting and Clinical Psychology,* **34,** 226–228.

Naditch, M. P., Gargan, M., & Michael, L. (1975). Denial, anxiety, locus of control, and the discrepancy between aspirations and achievements as components of depression. *Journal of Abnormal Psychology,* **84,** 1–9.

Nowicki, S., Jr. (1981). *A short form of the preschool and primary Nowicki–Strickland Internal-External Control Scale.* Unpublished manuscript, Emory University, Atlanta, GA.

Nowicki, S., Jr., & Duke, M. P. (1974a). The locus of control scale for college as well as noncollege adults. *Journal of Personality Assessment,* **38,** 36–137.

Nowicki, S., Jr., & Duke, M. P. (1974b). A preschool and primary locus of control scale. *Developmental Psychology,* **10,** 874–880.

Nowicki, S., Jr., & Duke, M. P. (1983). The Nowicki–Strickland life-span locus of control scales: Construct validation. In H. M. Lefcourt (Ed.), *Research with the locus of control construct* (Vol. 2, pp. 9–51). New York: Academic Press.

Nowicki, S., Jr., & Rountree, J. (1971). Correlates of locus of control in a secondary school population. *Developmental Psychology, 4*(3), 477–478.

Nowicki, S., Jr., & Strickland, B. R. (1973). A locus of control scale for children. *Journal of Consulting and Clinical Psychology, 40*, 148–154.

O'Connell, J. K., & Price, J. H. (1985). Development of a heart disease locus of control scale. *Psychological Reports, 56*, 159–164.

Owens, D. A. (1969). *Disability-minority and social learning.* Unpublished master's thesis, West Virginia University, Morgantown.

Oziel, L. V. Obitz, F. W., & Keyson, M. (1972). General and specific perceived locus of control in alcoholics. *Psychological Reports, 30*, 957–958.

Pancer, S. M., Cathro, S., & Favaro, P. (1983, June). *Parental locus of control: A measure for use in mental health programs for children and families.* Paper presented at the annual meeting of the Canadian Psychological Association, Winnipeg.

Parcel, G., & Meyer, M. (1978). Development of an instrument to measure children's health locus of control. *Health Education Monographs, 6*, 149–159.

Parkes, K. R. (1985). Dimensionality of Rotter's Locus of Control Scale: An application of the "Very Simple Structure" techniques. *Personality and Individual Differences, 6*, 115–119.

Parrell-Burnstein, M. (1975). *Locus of control orientation in children with and without learning problems.* Unpublished manuscript, Emory University, Atlanta, GA.

Paulhus, D. L. (1983). Sphere-specific measures of perceived control. *Journal of Personality and Social Psychology, 44*, 1253–1265.

Paulhus, D. L. (1984). Two-component models of socially desirable responding. *Journal of Personality and Social Psychology, 46*, 598–609.

Paulhus, D. L., & Christie, R. (1981). Spheres of control: An interactionist approach to assessment of perceived control. In H. M. Lefcourt (Ed.), *Research with the locus of control construct* (Vol. 1, pp. 161–188). New York: Academic Press.

Petterson, N. (1985). Specific vs. generalized locus of control scales related to job satisfaction. *Psychological Reports, 56*(1), 60–62.

Phares, E. J. (1955). *Changes in expectancy in skill and chance situations.* Unpublished doctoral dissertation, Ohio State University, Columbus.

Phares, E. J. (1976). *Locus of control in personality.* Morristown, NJ: General Learning Press.

Powers, S., & Douglas, P. (1985). Generalizability of the mathematics attribution scale norms to academically talented high school students. *Psychological Reports, 57*, 475–478.

Powers, S., & Rossman, M. H. (1983). The reliability and construct validity of the multidimensional–multiattributional causality scale. *Educational and Psychological Measurement, 43*, 1227–1231.

Powers, S., Douglas, P., & Choroszy, M. (1983). The factorial validity of the multidimensional–multiattributional causality scale. *Educational and Psychological Measurement, 43*, 611–615.

Prawat, R. S., Grissom, S., & Parish, T. (1979). Affective development in children, grades 3 through 12. *Journal of Genetic Psychology, 135*, 37–49.

Reid, D. E., & Ware, E. E. (1973). Multidimensionality of internal–external control: Implications for past and future research. *Canadian Journal of Behavioural Science, 5*, 264–271.

Reid, D. W., & Ware, E. E. (1974). Multidimensionality of internal versus external control: Addition of a third dimension and non-distinction of self versus others. *Canadian Journal of Behavioural Science, 6*, 131–142.

Reid, D. W., & Ziegler, M. (1977). A survey of the reinforcements and activities elderly citizens feel are important for their general happiness. *Essence, 2*, 5–24.

Reid, D. W., & Ziegler, M. (1980). Validity and stability of a new desired control measure pertaining to psychological adjustment of the elderly. *Journal of Gerontology, 35*(3), 395–402.

Reid, D. W., & Ziegler, M. (1981a). The desired control measure and adjustment among the elderly. In H. M. Lefcourt (Ed.), *Research with the locus of control construct* (Vol. 1, pp. 127–157). New York: Academic Press.

Reid, D. W., & Ziegler, M. (1981b). *Longitudinal studies of desired control and adjustment among the elderly*. Paper presented at joint meetings of the Gerontological Society of America and Canadian Association of Gerontology.

Rose, J. S., & Medway, F. J. (1981). Measurement of teachers' beliefs in their control over student outcome. *Journal of Educational Research,* **74**(3), 185–190.

Rotter, J. B. (1966). Generalized expectancies for internal versus external control of reinforcement. *Psychological Monographs,* **80**(1, Whole No. 609).

Rotter, J. B. (1975). Some problems and misconceptions related to the construct of internal versus external control of reinforcement. *Journal of Consulting and Clinical Psychology,* **43**, 56–67.

Rotter, J. B., Chance, J. E., & Phares, E. J. (1972). *Applications of a social learning theory of personality.* New York: Holt, Rinehart & Winston.

Ryan, R. M., & Grolnick, W. (1986). Origins and pawns in the classroom. *Journal of Personality and Social Psychology,* **50**, 550–558.

Saltzer, E. B. (1978). Locus of control and the intention to lose weight. *Health Education Monographs,* **6**, 118–128.

Saltzer, E. B. (1981). Cognitive moderators of the relationship between behavioral intentions and behavior. *Journal of Personality and Social Psychology,* **41**, 260–271.

Saltzer, E. B. (1982). The Weight Locus of Control (WLOC) Scale: A specific measure for obesity research. *Journal of Personality Assessment,* **46**, 620–628.

Sandler, I. N., & Lakey, B. (1982). Locus of control as a stress moderator: The role of control perceptions and social support. *American Journal of Community Psychology,* **10**(1), 65–80.

Schroeder, M. A. (1985). Development and testing of a scale to measure locus of control prior to and following childbirth. *Maternal-Child Nursing Journal,* **14**(2), 111–121.

Seeman, M. (1963). Alienation and social learning in a reformatory. *American Journal of Sociology,* **69**, 270–284.

Seligman, M. E. P. (1975). *Helplessness.* San Francisco: Freeman.

Seligman, M. E. P., Abramson, L. Y., Semmel, A., & von Baeyer, C. (1979). Depressive attributional style. *Journal of Abnormal Psychology,* **88**, 242–247.

Sherman, S. J. (1973). Internal–external control and its relationship to attitude change under different social influence techniques. *Journal of Personality and Social Psychology,* **26**(3), 23–29.

Stafford, R. A. (1980). Alcoholics' perception of the internal–external locus of their drinking problems. *Journal of Studies in Alcohol,* **41**, 300–309.

Strickland, B. R. (1965). The prediction of social action from a dimension of internal–external control. *Journal of Social Psychology,* **66**, 353–358.

Strickland, B. R., & Haley, W. E. (1980). Sex differences on the Rotter I-E Scale. *Journal of Personality and Social Psychology,* **39**, 930–939.

Tenenbaum, G., Furst, D., & Weingarten, G. (1984). Attribution of causality in sport events. Validation of the Wingate Sport Achievement Responsibility Scale. *Journal of Sport Psychology,* **6**(4), 430–439.

Tesiny, E. P., Lefkowitz, M. M., & Gordon, N. H. (1980). Childhood depression, locus of control, and school achievement. *Journal of Educational Psychology,* **72**, 506–510.

Viney, L. L. (1974). Multidimensionality of perceived locus of control: Two replications. *Journal of Consulting and Clinical Psychology,* **42**, 463–464.

Wallston, B. S., Wallston, K. A., Kaplan, G. D., & Maides, S. A. (1976). Development and validation of the Health Locus of Control (HLC) Scale. *Journal of Consulting and Clinical Psychology,* **44**, 580–585.

Wallston, K. A., & Wallston, B. S. (1981). Health Locus of Control Scales. In H. M. Lefcourt (Ed.), *Research with the locus of control construct* (Vol. 1, pp. 189–243). New York: Academic Press.

Wallston, K. A., Wallston, B. S., & DeVellis, R. (1978). Development of the multidimensional Health Locus of Control Scales. *Health Education Monographs,* **6**, 161–170.

Wanberg, K. W., Horn, V. L., & Foster, F. M. (1977). A differential assessment model for alcoholism: The scales of the Alcohol Use Inventory. *Journal of Studies on Alcohol,* **38**, 512–543.

Watson, J. M. (1981). A note on the dimensionality of the Rotter Locus of Control Scale. *Australian Journal of Psychology, 33,* 319–330.

Watson, J. S. (1967). Memory and "contingency analysis" in infant learning. *Merill-Palmer Quarterly of Behavior and Development, 13*(1), 55–76.

Weiner, B., Friese, I., Kukla, A., Reed, L., Rest, S., & Rosenbaum, R. M. (1971). *Perceiving the causes of success and failure.* New York: General Learning Press.

Weiner, B., Heckhausen, H., Meyer, V. W., & Cook, P. E. (1972). Causal ascriptions and achievement motivation: A conceptual analysis of effort and reanalysis of locus of control. *Journal of Personality and Social Psychology, 21,* 239–248.

Wolf, F. M., & Savickas, M. L. (1985). Time perspective and causal attributions for achievement. *Journal of Educational Psychology, 77,* 471–480.

Wolk, S., & DuCette, J. (1974). Intentional performance and incidental learning as a function of personality and task directions. *Journal of Personality and Social Psychology, 29,* 90–101.

Wong, P. T. P., & Sproule, C. F. (1984). An attribution analysis of the locus of control construct and the Trent Attribution Profile. In H. Lefcourt (Ed.), *Research with the locus of control construct* (Vol. 3). New York: Academic Press.

Wong, P. T. P., Watters, D. A., & Sproule, C. F. (1978). Initial validity and reliability of the Trent Attribution Profile (TAP) as a measure of attribution schema and locus of control. *Educational and Psychological Measurement, 38,* 1129–1133.

Wood, W. D., & Letak, J. K. (1982). A mental-health locus of control scale. *Personality and Individual Differences, 3,* 84–87.

CHAPTER 10

Authoritarianism and Related Constructs

Richard Christie

The American tradition of measurement is reflected in the initial empirical definition of right-wing authoritarianism as agreement with statements that were paraphrases of fascistic ideology developed by Stagner (1936). Less pragmatic and more speculative European theories broadened the construct into a *Weltanshauung* embracing themes about human nature and attitudes about society that were associated with a politically right-wing outlook. The topic then broadened to encompass such apparently nonideological individual difference variables as rigidity, anality, compulsivity, and similar variables.

These two approaches were linked in the pioneering synthesis in Adorno, Frenkel-Brunswik, Levinson, and Sanford's (1950) *The Authoritarian Personality* (referred to below as *TAP*). This monumental and controversial volume merged the then new techniques of attitude and personality measurement with speculative European psychoanalytic hypotheses about the nature of anti-Semitism. Beginning with a measure of anti-Semitism, the inquiry mushroomed into a landmark assessment of the personality of ethnocentric individuals. According to Deutsch, Platt, and Senghass (1971), the work on the authoritarian personality was one of the highly select group of 62 major advances in the social sciences between 1900 and 1965.

A major product of the research reported in *TAP* was the California F (for prefascist tendencies) scale, one of the most widely used scales of the past 40 years. This instrument and its modifications have been used in hundreds of studies, sometimes wisely but often without much appreciation of what the scale does and (more importantly) does not measure. Since it was correlated with such variables as ethnic prejudice, right-wing political beliefs, and similar topics, the scale immediately attracted the attention of social scientists. By relating these attitudes to presumed personality variables, the F scale provided a promising unifying concept. A major reason for continuing interest in the F scale has been the persistence of right-wing political activity and the relevance of the F scale and its myriad descendants in understanding this activity.

This selective review of F-scale type measures updates an earlier review (Christie, 1954), in which the situation recalled Augustine's intellectual agony in trying to clarify the concept of time. "For so it is, oh Lord my God, I measure it, but what it is that I measure I do not know." Three decades of research later, one can be more sanguine, although there is still no definition that would satisfy all its supporters and critics.

Historical Developments

This section reviews (1) the early empirical work on authoritarianism, (2) the psycho-analytic speculations on measures of authoritarianism and anti-Semitism, (3) the scales derived in *TAP,* and (4) some more provocative derivatives of that research. This roughly chronological account of how the concept originated and was modified will allow the pro and con arguments to be viewed in context. Following this review, selected instruments stemming from the original research are evaluated for three potential classes of users: personality researchers, survey researchers and political scientists, and social psychologists.

Early Empirical Studies

The pioneering attempts at measurement of attitudes in the United States (e.g., Likert, 1932; Thurstone, 1929, 1931), also came at a time of two major social upheavals, the Great Depression and the rise of Hitler in Europe. The double spur of burning social problems and new methodological techniques for their measurement led to the construction of a wide variety of attitude scales.

Stagner (1936) constructed the first known measure of authoritarianism and it was based on a content analysis of German and Italian fascist documents. Its 35 items were designed to tap seven different areas, with all items worded so that agreement was scored in the authoritarian direction. The statements were couched in terms of American domestic issues in the early 1930s and made no reference to Jews or members of other ethnic groups.

Newcomb (1943) noted how Stagner's items ". . . were precisely those which were then alive in the Bennington community . . . and made prominent by the New Deal administration" (p. 20). Newcomb was concerned about the role of response set and so wrote reversed items (worded so that acceptance was scored as anti-authoritarian) and also added content areas not covered by Stagner. His instrument, the P.E.P. (Political and Economic Progressivism) Scale, was the major variable used in his classic 1935–1939 study of changes in student values at Bennington College. His items included attitudes toward public relief, labor unions, and the public role of private and corporate wealth, with no explicit reference to members of minority groups.

Edwards' (1941) "Unlabeled Fascist Attitudes" scale was designed as a more subtle measure of fascist tendencies. Edwards believed that many Americans had fascistic beliefs but did not recognize them, so that references to militarism and nationalism were downplayed and items referring to birth control, education, the status of women, etc. were added; again, none referred to ethnic minority groups. The Likert format was used but only four items were reversed; of these one barely survived statistical analysis, presaging later difficulties in writing reversed items. In moving away from the direct reference to the political and economic issues in the Stagner and Newcomb scales, Edwards foreshadowed the content of the items in the California F scale.

Thus while there was some shift from sociopolitical and economic content to a more individual difference-oriented approach, a careful reading of these early scales shows they did not predict the content nor tenor of items in the F scale. Although aware of these studies, the authors of *TAP* were marching to another drummer, namely psychoanalytic theory.

Psychoanalysis, Marxism, and Authoritarianism:
The European Background

A clear statement of the relationship between Freudian theory and anti-Semitism appears in Brown's (1942) discussion of the origins of anti-Semitic attitudes: "This process makes use of three psychological mechanisms which are by now well understood by psychologists. These mechanisms are displacement, projection, and rationalization . . . viewed psychologically, anti-Semitism represents a displacement of aggression with a projection of guilt and a rationalization of motives."

Although Sigmund Freud had suffered from anti-Semitism, his published works apparently did not deal with the problem until his final book (1939), *Moses and Monotheism*. Freud cited three reasons for anti-Semitism: (1) the Jews' belief that they were the chosen people, (2) the practice of circumcision, which aroused Gentiles' castration fears, and (3) antireligious feelings held by nominal Christians, which could be more easily expressed by the projection of hostility toward Jews.

An additional prominent theme in European intellectual circles in the 1930s was Marxism, which was combined with psychoanalysis in Wilhelm Reich's (1946) *Massenpsychologie des Faschismus*. Samelson (1986, p. 195) notes how Reich

> found the deeper roots of the catastrophe [the Nazi takeover in Germany] in the character structure of lower middle-class and 'integrated' working-class Germans. In a patriarchal society, the family became the factory in which the state's structure and ideology were molded. It reproduced the authoritarian character structure by embedding sexual inhibition and fear in the child. (p. 195)

Reich specifically viewed 1930s anti-Semitism as part of the authoritarian character structure, and his unorthodox views achieved him the unique distinction of being ". . . unceremoniously drummed out of both the Communist Party and the psychoanalytic movement" (Jay, 1973, p. 86).

A more direct link to subsequent developments came from the Institut fur Socialforschung at Frankfurt, which while strongly influenced by both Marxism and Freudianism, was outside their inner circles of orthodoxy. Max Horkheimer, the Institut's director, sought psychoanalytic insights into the problem of false consciousness among workers. That is, why didn't workers realize they were being exploited and rebel against authority, rather than conform? Erich Fromm was hired to supervise interviews with German workers at a time when almost nothing was known about sampling theory or scale construction. The lengthy interviews covered many questions about the workers' life situation and their attitudes toward authority that were forerunners of those in *TAP*.

A qualitative analysis judged about 10% of the 700 respondents as authoritarian, roughly 75% as highly ambivalent, and 15% as anti-authoritarian. The conclusion that the German working class would be far less resistant to a right-wing seizure of power than its militant ideology would suggest (Jay, 1973, p. 117) was so provocative that the Institut deposited its endowment in a Dutch bank and its members were prepared to flee abroad when Hitler took power.

The Institut was partially reassembled at Columbia University in 1934. Horkheimer subsequently sought financial help from the American Jewish Committee essentially to repeat the German study with a focus on the personality correlates of anti-Semitism. This topic, which had not been examined in the earlier survey, involved the collaboration of American investigators familiar with new techniques of attitude and personality measurement. This led to Horkheimer's discovery of research being conducted at the University of California at Berkeley.

The Berkeley Studies in Authoritarianism

A $500 grant was given to the University of California in the early 1940s by a Jewish theater owner interested in anti-Semitism. It found its way to Nevitt Sanford, a young psychologist trained in personality research at Henry Murray's pioneering clinic at Harvard. Sanford recruited Daniel Levinson, then a graduate student in personality and social psychology, to assist him. They constructed a measure of anti-Semitism; a topic that a review of *Psychological Abstracts* of the time suggests had escaped the attention of eager measurers of almost everything else of political interest in the 1930s, despite Gerald Smith's widely circulated anti-Semitic publications and Father Coughlin's anti-Jewish sermons on radio (Lipset & Raab, 1970).

Levinson and Sanford's (1944) pioneering anti-Semitism (A-S) scale shared the psychoanalytic assumption that prejudice was at least partly based on the repression of one's own undesirable characteristics and their projection upon an external target (in this case Jews). The investigators subsequently found scales of attitudes toward Negroes, members of various minority groups, and superpatriotism were highly intercorrelated with one another, and thus concluded that they were tapping a common syndrome of ethnocentrism. It is important, however, to note that their measures of ethnocentrism were based on agreeing with negative statements about minority groups. There were no measures of identifying with the ingroup (which was implicitly white and non-Jewish since other respondents' protocols were excluded from the data analyses). After five revisions they suggested a 20-item Ethnocentrism (E) scale that contained six statements referring to Jews, six to blacks, and eight to members of minority groups and superpatriotism.

About the time the original A-S scale was constructed, Horkheimer discovered the Berkeley group, and funding from the American Jewish Committee broadened the study of prejudice in significant ways. Else Frenkel-Brunswik, who had been trained in psychology at the University of Vienna and had published on mechanisms of self-deception, then took primary responsibility for the clinical assessment of those high and low in prejudice. The fourth author, T. W. Adorno, was a member of the Institut who had not worked initially on the study of German workers but was psychoanalytically oriented. He was dually responsible for a study of authoritarianism among American workers and as a liaison between Horkheimer and the Berkeley group.

Frenkel-Brunswik and Sanford (1945) collaborated on a study of 20 women undergraduates (since there were few males in school during World War II) who had taken the A-S scale in psychology classes. In this pilot study eight extreme high scorers, eight extreme low scorers, and four middle scorers were given clinical interviews, selected cards from the Thematic Apperception Test, and the Rorschach ink blot technique.

The interviews from this pilot study not only illustrated the theoretical stance of subsequent research but also provided verbatim comments from the respondents that formed the basis of initial items for the F scale. It occurred to the research team that since high and low scorers on A-S appeared to have quite different sets of beliefs and attitudes on other topics, it might be possible to construct a disguised form of the A-S scale that never mentioned Jews at all. Items for the F scale were based partially on edited or paraphrased statements made by participants in the pilot study. These were augmented by other statements created by the authors or modified from ones taken from other sources. Criteria for item construction were not spelled out but were apparently based on the items' assumed congruence with the emerging but still implicit theory of the pre-Fascist personality.

There are four known versions of the resultant Berkeley F scale, each identified by the total number of items from the different scales included and successively identified as Forms 78, 60, 40–45, and 60A. Each revision of the F scale reflected sharpening and refinement of the items based upon analyses of data from earlier versions.

The argument that the E and F scales tapped personality differences was buttressed by the intensive clinical assessment of 45 individuals (20 males and 25 females) scoring high on the A-S and/or E scales and 35 low scorers (20 males and 15 females). Low and high scorers were selected and given clinical interviews, semiprojective questionnaires, and the Thematic Apperception Test.

Another scale (also described in Robinson, Rusk, & Head, 1973) developed during this period measured Political–Economic Conservatism (PEC). The Berkeley group treated overt left–right political ideology as separate from, although related to, the implicit ideology measured by the F scale. The PEC scale had overall a mean correlation of .52 with various forms of the F scale (Adorno *et al.*, 1950, p. 263).

The Authoritarian Personality had a major impact when published in 1950. The first paragraph of the concluding chapter noted,

> The most crucial result of the present study . . . is the close correspondence in the type of approach and outlook a subject is likely to have in a great variety of areas, ranging from the most immediate features of family and sex adjustment through relationships to other people in general, to religion and to social and political philosophy, ... conventionality, rigidity, repressive denial, and the ensuing breakthrough of one's weaknesses, fear, and dependency are but other aspects of the same fundamental personality pattern, and they can be observed in personal life as well as attitudes toward religion and social issues. (p. 971)

Authoritarianism after *The Authoritarian Personality*

The years immediately following World War II marked the high tide of interest in psychoanalytic theory in the social sciences. The authors of *TAP* had taken a subject that had been exposed to little systematic scrutiny, had wedded psychoanalysis with American empiricism in an original and creative way, and had generated an intuitively appealing theory. Since most social scientists viewed themselves as unprejudiced, the notion that prejudiced people projected their hostility onto outgroups and were personally rigid and generally permeated with anti-intellectualism was a cause for self-satisfaction if not smugness.

The F scale was viewed as an almost magical key for unlocking human personality and was used widely by scores of researchers, some of whom were carried away by the concept and used it uncritically. Abridgments or modifications of the scale and individual items from it, selected for sometimes idiosyncratic and unfathomable reasons, led to a vast literature, some of which is difficult to interpret. Although the authors of *TAP* acknowledged the influence of cultural and sociological variables in the prejudiced person, their focus on psychodynamics led some later investigators to an excessive preoccupation with individual differences in explaining prejudice.

The emergence in social psychology in the 1950s of a strong neo-Lewinian emphasis on situational determinants of behavior led to a research climate in which the manipulation of independent variables in laboratory situations was favored by funding agencies. Prestige in academic circles became tied to obtaining federal agency grants that supported laboratory-oriented research rather than personality-oriented inquiries. This trend was accelerated by political considerations related to the cold war and the lingering effects of

McCarthyism: Personality research on those to the right of the political spectrum was suspect.

Shils (1954) pointed out that the authors of *TAP* neglected authoritarianism of the political left. Throughout the text there was a focus on those who were prejudiced against Jews and other minority group members in the United States, and these individuals were, in the mid-1940s, to the right in political ideology. Since all the items were worded so that agreement was scored as authoritarian, one cannot tell from scale scores alone who among the low scorers are anarchists, civil libertarians, communists, liberals, socialists, or garden-variety curmudgeons who would disagree with any statement.

Psychoanalytic assumptions about prejudice as a projection of repressed characteristics were rooted in observations of bourgeois patients who grew up in central European patriarchal families, in which it was hypothesized that there was more repression of instinctual impulses than would be true in working-class families. As the authors of *TAP* (p. 229) phrased it, "it is a well-known hypothesis that susceptibility to fascism is most characteristically a middle-class phenomenon, that it is in the culture and, hence, that those who conform most to this culture will be most prejudiced." As Hyman and Sheatsley (1954) pointed out, many of the differences between high and low scorers on the E and F scales that showed up in the interviews reflected tastes in music, art, reading matter, etc. associated with social class that indicated greater social sophistication on the part of the low scorers, even within largely middle-class subjects. Christie (1954, p. 170) examined findings from a variety of noncollege student samples and found correlations from −.45 to −.54 between years of education and F-scale scores. These probably underestimated the true correlation between the two in a representative national sample.

Survey researchers have repeatedly found much stronger negative correlations between measures of social sophistication and authoritarianism than the more typical one of −.20 between F-scale scores and IQ among the mostly college-educated samples reported in the original research. It is one thing to replicate a relationship in descriptive research and another to understand, at least partially, why it should occur.

In Schooler's (1972) examination of demographic variables, interviews were conducted in 1964 with 3101 men "representative of all men throughout the United States employed in civilian occupations" (p. 301). Eleven slightly modified items from the original F scale correlated +.22 with respondents' age, −.24 with fathers' education, +.22 with rural residence in childhood, +.20 with being reared in the South, and +.20 with more fundamentalist religious beliefs. Multiple regression analyses that held the other background variables constant generated significant β weights of .19, .14, .10, .11, and .11.[1]

The generality of the relationship between authoritarianism and education was supported by Meloen and Middendorp (1988). They described national surveys in the Netherlands in 1970, 1975, 1980, and 1985 in which seven F-scale items correlated +.26 to +.28 with age, −.26 to −.32 with father's education, and −.40 with respondents' education. They also reported persistent mean F-scale scores for the same cohorts across time. Cohorts born from 1916 through 1953 showed a very slight decrease in F-scale scores as they aged. The older exiting cohorts (born from 1901 to 1915) had much higher F-scale scores whereas the younger entering cohorts had much lower scores. This led to a mean drop in F-scale item means for the total sample from 4.5 to 4.0 from 1970 to 1985

---

[1]Schooler (1976) reported on a fascinating further analysis of these data for 930 of these non-Jewish respondents who were either born in Europe or had a parent or grandparent born there. Areas of Europe were classified in seven categories based on the historical evidence of the abolishment of serfdom. When other variables were controlled, a β of .17 indicated a relationship between having ancestors from a feudal social system where serfdom had persisted longer and respondents' F Scale scores.

which was largely accounted for ". . . by the exit of the oldest and more authoritarian birth cohorts" (p. 24).

A score of 1.0 on the total scale (which is almost never found) means that a respondent strongly disagrees with every F-scale item; one of 7.0 (again, rarely found) that there is strong agreement with every item. A score of 4.0 therefore reflects the theoretical neutral point. Since various researchers have used differing numbers of total items, item mean scores permit easier comparisons of results from different studies. Since some investigators, particularly survey researchers, have used fewer than seven permitted response categories per item, Meloen's (1983) convention of converting scores to a seven-point scale will be followed in this chapter.

High F-scale scores in lower social classes that theoretically should be least subject to middle-class, 19th-century Viennese, repressive child-rearing practices thus raise questions about the generalizability of the theory.

The Great Response Set Controversy

A further question about the F scale attracted a great deal of attention in the mid 1950s. Since all of its items were worded in the authoritarian direction, one could not distinguish between respondents who agreed with the ideological content of the statements and respondents who would agree with almost any item.

Cronbach's (1946) much cited article alerted psychologists to the extent of the problem, arguing that response set was most likely to occur when an item was ambiguous. The relevance of this to the F scale is clear since many of its items were deliberately written to be semi-projective, e.g., "The wild sex life of the ancient Greeks and Romans was tame compared to some of the goings-on in this country, even in places where people might least expect it."

One control strategy for response set on F-scale items was to write item "reversals" and a handful of such attempts are of special interest. Bass (1955), among others, constructed logical reversals (e.g., "Familiarity breeds contempt" became "Familiarity does not breed contempt.") Eventually, he concluded that, ". . . three-fourths of the reliable variance of the F scale appears to be a function of acquiescence" (p. 622).

Similar findings by other investigators led Christie, Havel, and Seidenberg (1958) to criticize the wording of the reversals, which were frequently as unqualified and dogmatic as the original F-scale items. New reversals were written and couched in qualified language designed to be compatible with the ideology of a liberal low scorer. After item analyses, 10 reversed items were retained and combined with 10 original F-scale items. The counterbalanced scale was administered to eight new samples, with the highest correlation of +.58 between the two being found in a graduate student sample. Only those subsequent attempts at reversals that produced correlations of .50 are considered here (a positive correlation indicates ideological consistency between original and reversed items).

Lee and Warr (1969) used an expanded pool of 100 unpublished F-scale items developed by a Social Science Research Council committee and developed a 30-item counterbalanced F scale on 610 Princeton students that had a correlation of .51 between the positive and negative items.

Kohn (1972) developed an Authoritarianism–Rebellion scale that consisted of 15 original F-scale items and 15 reversals of the same items. In his original Canadian samples the correlations between the two subscales varied from .22 to .42. However, in a subsequent study (Kohn, 1974) on British undergraduates he modified some of the items and found greater ideological consistency, with the correlations ranging from .42 to .56.

The most successful early attempt at reversals was by Couch and Kenniston (1960), who focused narrowly on attitudes toward authority and constructed five reversals whose wording emphasized qualified statements and a lack of "exclamatory enthusiasm." They obtained a $+.70$ correlation between these items and five unspecified items from the original F scale, but with a select Harvard University sample.

A different approach to the problem of reversing items was taken by Ray (1971), who from a right-wing perspective asserted that the authoritarian as defined by Adorno *et al.* was ". . . an inflexible, paranoid deviant. . ." (p. 33). Although the inflexibility of the high scorer was a favorite theme in *TAP,* Ch. XXII of *TAP* found no significant relationships between measures of authoritarism and psychological ill-health using both psychiatric criteria and MMPI scores as criterion variables.

Ray redefined authoritarianism extremely narrowly explicitly to cover attitudes toward authority, so that most of his items appear to fall under the rubric submission to authority; the most discriminating ones refer to the acceptance of military authority. He reported a reliability of .80 and a .54 correlation between positively and negatively worded items on an Australian community sample.

Thus a major unresolved source of disillusionment with F scale was its contamination with response bias. The most successful attempts at reversals used relatively elite samples or a narrow definition of authoritarianism or both. No known report indicated a major success in eliminating acquiescent response set among more typical college samples.

Matters remained in limbo until Altemeyer's (1981) reformulation of the problem. First, he noted that items falling in the theoretical "superego" syndrome (R. N. Sanford, 1968) (i.e., authoritarian aggression, authoritarian submission, and conventionality) were the most discriminating items in the original research and that these held up best in subsequent revisions of the F scale. Items designed to measure anti-intraception, projectivity, etc. failed to be consistently discriminating. Altemeyer then scoured the literature for items falling in these three areas and began the extremely difficult task of writing reversals using strict psychometric criteria. After 10 successive revisions of his Right-Wing Authoritarianism (RWA) scale he succeeded in writing 12 reversals that met his criteria. These were balanced by 12 authoritarian items, only two of which were from the original F scale. The correlations between the positive and negative items consistently range from $+.65$ to $+.70$ and the α reliability on the counterbalanced scales was .88 (the highest since Newcomb's .90 for the P.E.P.).

Social Desirability

The Authoritarian Personality had been published and methodologically dissected before Edwards' (1957) book on the social desirability variable in personality research. Edwards argued that although some items might be answered truthfully, many reflected such negative aspects of the self that respondents would deny that they applied to themselves. Unpublished studies showed no correlation between either the Edwards' scale of Social Desirability or that of Crowne and Marlowe (1960) and various versions of the F scale. Given the ambiguous nature of F-scale items it should not be surprising that no significant correlations have been found.

The relevance of social desirability can arise, however, in studies in which the F scale has been correlated with other scales. If the other scale also has an element of ambiguity in its items and is also worded unilaterally, one would expect a spuriously high correlation (.35–.40) because yeasayers would be tending to agree with positively worded items in each scale whatever their content. If, however, the other scale was clearly affected by social desirability and not agreement response set, the independent contribution of the two biases would not necessarily affect the obtained correlation.

Thus the forced-choice versions of the F scale reproduced by Shaver (1973) are not included here because of their lower reliabilities and because the social desirability values of both the original F-scale items and the matched items have changed over time. Even with its erosion over time, Altemeyer's RWA Scale has higher reliability; moreover, agreement response set is balanced out and it takes less time to administer.

Measures Reviewed Here

The first three scales are general measures of authoritarianism that are outdated and primarily of historic interest.

1. Fascist Attitudes Scale (Stagner, 1936)
2. Political Economic Progressivism Scale (Newcomb, 1943)
3. Unlabeled Fascist Attitude Scale (Edwards, 1941)

The next set of scales was developed as part of *TAP* and highlight the development of instruments with items that may still be relevant.

4. Anti-Semitism (A-S) Scale (Levinson and Sanford, 1944)
5. Ethnocentrism Scale (Adorno *et al.* 1950)
6. The California F Scale (Form 78) (Adorno *et al.* 1950)
7. The California F Scale (Form 40–45 and Form 60A) (Adorno *et al.* 1950)

The A-S scale represents the beginning aspect of the Berkeley research and the suggested E scale was the final scale to measure prejudice. Similarly, the Form 78 version of the F scale represents their initial attempt and the Form 60A the final version; intermediate versions of the scales may be found in *TAP*. Most of the items on these scales are dated but may serve particularly as a source of items for updating or revision in studies on prejudice, particularly the 60A version, which represents their final distillation of items.

The following seven scales represent attempts at counterbalancing to minimize the persistent effects of acquiescent response bias.

8. G scale: Acquiescence Reversals (Bass, 1955)
9. Balanced F Scale (Christie *et al.,* 1958)
10. Balanced F Scale (Lee & Warr, 1969)
11. Authoritarianism–Rebellion Scale (Kohn, 1972)
12. Short Reversed Authoritarianism Scale (Couch & Keniston, 1960)
13. Attitude Toward Authority Scale (Ray, 1971)
14. Right-Wing Authoritarianism Scale (Altemeyer, 1981)

Three illustrative final scales are derivative.

15. Four-Item F Scale (Lane, 1955)
16. Traditional Family Ideology Scale (Levinson & Huffman, 1955)
17. Dogmatism Scale (Rokeach, 1956)

Lane's scale represents a thoughtful attempt to develop a short form of the F scale for survey purposes. Initially an eight-item simplified form of the scale was developed by Sanford and Older (1950); six of these items were included among 10 modified F-Scale items in the Survey Research Center's 1952 postelection survey.[2] Lane (1955) reanalyzed the data by selecting four items that met Guttman criteria for unidimensionality with amount of agreement on an item varying from 25 to 75% (which means that simple acquiescent response set was not a major factor in the endorsement of the least popular items).

Levinson and Huffman's (1955) Traditional Family Ideology Scale (TFI) contains 40 items dealing primarily with parent–child, husband–wife, and male–female relationships. Although many items are dated, it remains a comprehensive scale for this area.

The Dogmatism (D) scale was developed by Rokeach (1956) as an alternative measure of general rather than right-wing authoritarianism. The literature on this scale is almost as great as that as on the F Scale itself, as reviewed in Vacchiano, Strauss, and Hochman (1969). It is included here because it has been found to correlate from .54 to .77 with the F scale in various samples, mainly attributable to all of the items in both scales being worded in the agree direction. Kerlinger and Rokeach's (1966) factor analysis of the F and dogmatism items showed most of the items from the two scales fell on different factors. The first factor, however, (dubbed "virtuous self-denial") did have items from both scales although these did not meet Altemeyer's criteria for cluster membership. A study in which counterbalanced scales of F and D were used was that by Kline and Cooper (1984), who found no significant relationships between the two scales.

Fascist Attitudes Scale
(Stagner, 1936)

Variable

This initial measure of authoritarianism was based on a content analysis of German and Italian Fascist writings.

Description

Stagner's use of content analysis was not as systematized as later work with more carefully designed categories and reliability checks among coders. He paraphrased statements from original writings into an American context and sometimes added original statements that fit into the seven categories he detected.

The scale consists of 35 items with five items in each content category. Fifteen items dealing with the Great Depression were added as filler items and the scale was administered under the title, "Attitudes about the Depression." Scoring was on a simple agree–disagree basis with agreement scored as one and disagreement as 0 so the range of scores was from 0 (low fascism) to 35 (high fascism).

---

[2]In an administration of a short version of a counterbalanced F Scale in the 1958 SRC election study (Campbell, Converse, Miller, & Stokes, 1960, pp. 512–515), modifications of five of the Christie *et al.* reversals were administered together with five modified items from the original F Scale. Respondents with a grade school education were slightly less authoritarian (e.g., agreed more with the Christie *et al.* reversed items) than their college-educated counterparts. The usual strong inverse relationship between education and original F Scale items, in which those of low education agree more than those of high education, was found. These findings suggest that some of the relationship between the F Scale and education might be accounted for by response set.

Sample

Three groups of college undergraduates were used: (1) 91 students at a commuting college with mostly working and lower-middle-class backgrounds, (2) 71 students at Ohio State University, and (3) 62 students at "an expensive institution attended by well-to-do young people whose leanings are very conservative." The means and standard deviations were 16.9 (SD = 5.2), 16.7 (5.8), and 20.8 (3.9), respectively. The third group of students scored significantly higher than members of the first two groups.

Reliability

Internal Consistency

There was a correlation of .77 between items 1–22 and 22–50.

Test–Retest

No test–retest data were reported.

Validity

Only the difference between the first two and the third group was offered as evidence of validity.

Location

Stagner, R. (1936). Fascist attitudes: An exploratory study. *Journal of Social Psychology,* **6,** 309–319.

Results and Comments

In an effort to discover which items best discriminated between individuals who were in high agreement (the 46 highest scorers and the 46 with the lowest agreement), Stagner did an item by item comparison for the entire 50 items. Eighteen items had a discriminatory power (critical ratios, CRs) of 5.0 or more, 13 had between 3.0 and 4.9, and 19 ones of less than 3.0.

The items are all written and scored unilaterally, and the reliability and dimensionality are unclear. Since it has been superseded by more sophisticated scales it is of interest primarily as the first known attempt to quantify authoritarian ideology.

Fascist Attitudes Scale

High Critical Ratio

3. Recovery has been delayed by the large number of strikes.

    DISAGREE   AGREE

4. The U.S. should stop immigration to give American workers more jobs.

8. If we buy European made goods, we make the depression in this country last longer.

11. Building a bigger navy would give men jobs and protect our foreign markets, so that should be done.

12. Most labor trouble happens only because of radical agitators.

13. The unemployed should be given military training so our country could be protected in time of war.

16. The people who complain most about the depression wouldn't take a job if you gave it to them.

21. Any able-bodied man could get a job right now if he tried hard enough.

23. Most people on relief are living in reasonable comfort.

24. We must protect our trade in the Philippines against the Japanese.

27. The government must first balance the budget.

28. CCC camps where the boys learn military discipline and self-control would be a good idea.

30. The president was justified in protecting U.S. interests in Cuba.

34. Labor unions are all right, but we can't have strikes.

37. The U.S. should make European countries pay off their war debts.

42. While raising the standard of living we must safeguard property rights as guaranteed by the Constitution.

43. Unemployment insurance would saddle us with a nation of idlers.

46. These unemployed organizers are just a bunch of chronic complainers.

Moderate Critical Ratio

7. What we need is a strong president who will make people cooperate for recovery.

10. Recognition of Soviet Russia was a big mistake.

14. Capital and labor should get together for a fair wage and a fair profit.

15. The sales tax is an unfair way of raising relief money.

17. We must all sacrifice a little to build a strong American nation.

18. The president was all right until he became influenced by communistic ideals.

33. The formation of big trusts bankrupted many small businesses and so brought on the depression.

39. If the government didn't meddle so much with business everything would work out all right.

40. We should consider our duty to our country first in this time of crisis.

44. America has plenty of plans—what it needs is strong men who are willing to work for recovery.

45. If we have unemployment, we should deport the excess workers back to their home countries.

47. The NRA would have worked if so many strikes hadn't been organized.

48. People should not be allowed to vote unless they are educated and intelligent.

Lowest Critical Ratio

1. Conditions are likely to get better in 1935.

2. The farmers have been hit harder than the city workers.

5. The depression has caused an increase in crime.

6. This country should try to get more foreign markets so as to increase prosperity.

9. Many workers have been unemployed for 5 years through no fault of their own.

19. What we need is more international cooperation, not less.

20. Prosperity would come back if we could show businessmen that they could invest money at a profit.

22. Munitions makers probably don't have near as much to do with starting wars as the papers claim.

25. Italy has taken the wrong way out of the depression.

26. We will always have depressions.

29. The average person isn't intelligent enough to vote his way out of the depression.

31. Inflation would solve most of the problems of the depression.

32. There is no excuse for depressions.

35. The Wall Street bankers brought on the depression to clean up on the little fellows.

36. If we had stayed out of the World War, we would never have had this depression.

38. We'd get out of the depression quicker if we had a strong intelligent man with full power to run things.

41. The collapse in 1929 was due primarily to overproduction.

49. The U.S. ought to demand its fair share of trade with China.

50. What we need is more businesslike government.

Political–Economic Progressivism (P.E.P.) Scale

(Newcomb, 1943)

Variable

This is a measure of progressivism in terms of the main issues of the New Deal in the 1930s.

Description

In 1935 Newcomb launched a 4-year study of students at Bennington College. His key measure was a scale that would be administered repeatedly over the 4 years, which meant it could not be tied too closely to transitory events. However, he wanted a measure which tied into the key social issues of the day. Having discovered Stagner's as-yet-unpublished authoritarianism scale, which came close to what he desired, he used it as a basis for his P.E.P. scale.

The scale consists of 26 items, half of them worded in the liberal direction so that agreement is scored high on P.E.P. and half conservative so that agreement is scored in the opposite direction (i.e., low). A five-point Likert format was used with a score of three being assigned to the undecided option and each item was thus scored from one to five. Total scores can range from 26 (low progressivism) to 130 (high progressivism).

Samples

All available members of every Bennington class present in 1935 through 1938 were tested. There were very few refusals. In addition, material for comparisons was drawn from students at Skidmore and Williams Colleges.

Reliability

Internal Consistency

Split-half reliabilities were computed and are reported as ranging from .84 to .91 for freshmen and .91–.94 for juniors–seniors with medians of .89 and .92, respectively. The test-retest reliability was .86 over a 7-month period.

These are extremely high reliabilities for counterbalanced scales and would not be approached again until Altemeyer's RWA scale 30 years later. This success is probably due to (1) the careful construction of the scale, (2) the salience of the issues relating to the New Deal during the Depression, and (3) the highly selected student body, in which there was intensive interaction around these issues with the faculty.

Validity

Convergent

Concurrent validity was established by correlations with other scales measuring other controversial topics of the times such as attitudes toward Loyalist Spain, the fight between the AFL and CIO, and Roosevelt's attempt to add liberal members to the Supreme Court.

Discriminant

Discriminant validity was supported by analyses of participation in college community affairs and political activities.

Of unusual interest is the fact that Newcomb *et al.* (1967) did a follow-up study of the students 25 years later and found that the undergraduate P.E.P. scores predicted self reports of subsequent liberal political involvement.

Location

Newcomb, T. M. (1943). *Personality and social change*. New York: Dryden.

Results and Comments

This is a classic study in social psychology and its detailed appendices are worth careful study. Newcomb discovered, for example, that shifts in P.E.P. scores over the 4 years of college resulted largely from the decrease in endorsement of conservative statements with little change in endorsement of the liberal ones. He also computed reliabilities for tendency to agree scores (average of .68) and compared them over time on P.E.P. and found relatively low correlations. He also did a similar analysis of the tendency to make extreme responses (the sum of agree strongly and disagree strongly minus no opinion) and found similar results.

Unfortunately, so much of the item content refers to the late years of the Depression that the scale is no longer generally applicable. In fact, Newcomb, Koenig, Flacks, and Warwick (1967) did not use it in their follow-up study in 1964. It does, however, serve as a model of a skilled and insightful investigation.

P.E.P. Scale

Statements, agreement with which are considered conservative (i.e., scored low), are starred. Agreement with all other attitude statements is scored high.

1. The only true prosperity of the nation as a whole must be based upon the prosperity of the working class.

STRONGLY   DISAGREE   NEUTRAL   AGREE   STRONGLY
DISAGREE   AGREE

*2. Recovery has been delayed by the large number of strikes.

3. Some form of collective society, in which profits are replaced by reimbursements for useful mental or manual work, is preferable to our present system.

4. The depression occurred chiefly because the working classes did not receive enough in wages to purchase goods and services produced at a profit.

5. A "planned economy" is not enough unless it is planned for the welfare of workers rather than of business men.

*6. Most labor trouble happens only because of radical agitators.

*7. The people who complain most about the depression wouldn't take a job if you gave it to them.

8. The standard of living of the working class can be kept above the poverty line only as workers force it up by the use of strikes.

9. Labor organizations have as much right to bring in outside agitators as do businessmen to import outside technical experts.

*10. Any able-bodied man could get a job right now if he tried hard enough.

*11. Most people on relief are living in reasonable comfort.

*12. The budget should be balanced before the government spends any money on "social security."

 13. Our government has always been run primarily in the interests of big business, and so it is those interests which were chiefly responsible for the depression.

*14. Labor unions are justifiable only if they refrain from the use of strikes.

 15. Since it is impossible for working people to make any substantial savings, they have fully earned their right to old-age pensions.

*16. It is all right to try to raise the standard of living of the lower classes, provided that existing property rights are continually safeguarded.

 17. Most employers think only of profits and care little about their employees' welfare.

*18. Unemployment insurance would saddle us with a nation of idlers.

*19. Organizations of the unemployed are just a group of chronic complainers.

 20. We have no true democracy in this country, because only business and industrial concerns have economic opportunity.

*21. If the government didn't meddle so much in business everything would be all right.

*22. You can't expect democracy to work well as long as so many uneducated and unintelligent people have the vote.

*23. The vast majority of those in the lower economic classes are there because they are stupid or shiftless, or both.

*24. Those who have the ability and the foresight to accumulate wealth ought to be permitted to enjoy it themselves.

 25. The middle classes will never enjoy security or prosperity until they understand that their welfare is identified with that of the working class, and not with that of business and industrial groups.

 26. The real threat to prosperity in this country is the repressive activities of those who wish to keep wealth and economic power in the hands of those who now possess them.

Note: *, Reverse-scored item.

Unlabeled Fascist Attitudes

(Edwards, 1941)

Variable

This scale was developed as a more subtle measure of fascism than that of Stagner by broadening the concept by basing it on writings about the nature of fascism (which included items derogating women and academic freedom).

Description

A pool of items was constructed to meet the broadened meaning of fascism. These items were judged as pro- or antifascist by five judges and they agreed on 26 of them. These items were then given in a Likert format with five response categories to 91 students in general psychology at the University of Akron. The item scores of the top 16 and bottom 16 of the students were computed and four items were dropped because they had a critical ratio of less than 2.0. Only four of the original items had been worded in the antifascist direction and three of them failed to meet the criterion.

The possible range of scores therefore is from 1 to 5 on each item or 22 (low fascism) to 110 (high fascism) for the total scale.

Samples

The 22-item scale was given to two new groups of psychology students; 97 at the University of Akron and 146 at Ohio University. The range of obtained scores in the combined samples was 25–87.

Reliability

Internal Consistency

A split-half reliability of .84 is reported for the combined sample.

Test–Retest

No test-retest data are reported.

Validity

No external checks on validity are reported.

Location

Edwards, A. L. (1941). Unlabeled fascist attitudes. *Journal of Abnormal and Social Psychology,* **36,** 579–582.

Results and Comments

This scale is historically important since it introduced referents into measures of right-wing authoritarianism that dealt with civil liberties, sexism, academic freedom, etc. It thus makes a bridge between the earlier scales of Stagner and Newcomb to those embodied in the California F scales.

Unlabeled Fascist Attitudes

1. Children should be taught to be more obedient and to have more respect for authority by the public schools.

| STRONGLY DISAGREE | DISAGREE | NEUTRAL | AGREE | STRONGLY AGREE |

2. Whatever best serves the interests of government is generally right.

3. The public schools should place more emphasis upon physical training and loyalty and less upon the development of intellectual functions.

*4. Everyone should have the full liberty of propagandizing for what is not good for them.

5. The masses of people are capable of determining what is and what is not good for them.

6. America has reached a higher state of civilization than any other country in the world and as a consequence has a culture which is superior to any other.

*7. People should be given the opportunity to hear all sides of a question, regardless of how controversial it is.

8. Over 10% of the population is incapable of democratic participation in government by reason of their lack of inherited abilities.

9. Generally speaking, women are less intelligent and efficient than men.

10. The superior people in any culture are justified in dominating the national affairs by force if necessary, because of the very fact that they are superior.

*11. Many people who claim they believe in democracy have unconscious prejudices and attitudes which would make them sympathetic to a fascist movement.

12. Because many of the minor political parties merely confuse national issues, all political parties except the two major ones should be abolished.

13. The right to vote should be restricted to those individuals who have a specified amount of private property and therefore have a direct concern in the welfare of the country.

14. A large percentage of the taxes which citizens pay is wasted in an effort to educate individuals who are not capable or worthy of being educated.

15. The right of the working classes to call a general strike should be abolished because it is a potential threat to democracy and is not in the general interest of society.

16. Patriotism and loyalty to one's country are more important than one's intellectual convictions and should have precedence over them.

17. A standing army of 2,000,000 men or over is necessary for our national defense at all times.

18. Government should attempt to persuade people to have more children and if necessary restrict birth control information for the benefit of our national defense.

19. In the national interest, private schools should either be abolished or restricted in their teachings so that the control of education is largely in the hands of the federal government.

20. Regardless of who our next president is, he must be a strong intelligent man and be given full power to run things in the interest of the people.

21. Certain religious sects whose beliefs do not permit them to salute the flag should either be forced to conform or else be abolished.

22. There will always be superior and inferior races in the world and in the interests of all concerned it is best that the superior continue to dominate the inferior.

23. Our foreign markets are a vital necessity to our prosperity and must be protected at all costs.

24. Women have more ability and are more efficient at tasks around the home and as a result their rightful place is in the home and not in the business world.

25. Minor forms of military training such as drill, marching, and simple commands should be made part of the elementary school educational program.

26. Academic freedom is all right in principle, but instructors in high schools and colleges should not be allowed to express their convictions concerning their subject matter.

Note: *, Reversed items.

Anti-Semitism (A-S) Scale

(Levinson & Sanford, 1944)

Variable

This scale was designed to measure anti-Semitism in psychodynamic terms.

Description

Although Levinson and Sanford did not deny that social and historical factors were of importance they thought of anti-Semitism's manifestation in individual cases as more psychological. They viewed anti-Semitism as "an ideology, that is, as a relatively stable system of opinions, values, and attitudes concerning Jews and Jewish–Gentile relationships." The scale consisted of 52 items, each scored on a -3 (strong disagreement) to $+3$ (strong agreement) Likert format with no neutral option. A constant of $+4$ was added to the raw score of all items so they would have positive totals. All items were worded so that agreement was scored as anti-Semitic.

The scale was split into two 26-item forms for various comparative purposes. Scores thus range from 1 to 7 on each item, or from 26 (low anti-Semitism) to 182 (high anti-Semitism) for each form. Items were classified as falling into five categories.

1. Jews are personally offensive (PO)—12 items
2. Jews are socially threatening (ST)—12 items
3. Attitudes about what should be done to or against the Jews (A)—16 items
4. Jews as being too seclusive (S)—8 items
5. Jews as being too intrusive (I)—8 items

The classification appears to be primarily heuristic and four items were believed to belong to two categories.

Samples

Two groups of female undergraduates in psychology classes at the University of California Berkeley ($n = 77$ and 144) initially took the scale.

Reliability

Internal Consistency

A split-half reliability of .88 was obtained in the first sample. The average intercorrelation among the subscales was .79.

Test–Retest

The second sample took the first half one week and the second half a week later. The average intercorrelation among the subscales was again .79.

Validity

Convergent

As expected, Republican women had higher scores than their Democratic counterparts, Catholics and sectarian Protestants had higher scores than the nonreligious and nonsectarian Protestants, and members of sororities scored higher than nonmembers.

Discriminant

A small sample of 13 faculty and graduate students in the Department of Psychology at Berkeley scored significantly lower on the A-S scale (an item mean of 1.7) than the two samples of college women (3.0 and 2.7, respectively).

Location

Levinson, D. J., & Sanford, R. N. (1944). A scale for the measurement of anti-Semitism. *Journal of Psychology, 17,* 339–370.

Results and Comments

This scale is primarily of historical importance and was so long it was pared down. The investigators discovered (or more accurately, rediscovered) that items reflecting prejudice toward other minority groups correlated with A-S and the investigation, which started with anti-Semitism as the focus of attention, shifted to the more general phenomenon of ethnocentrism. The original scale has more A-S items than any other known scale, although many of the items are dated. Perhaps the greatest significance of the A-S scale was that the investigation by Frenkel-Brunswik and Sanford (1945) of personality characteristics of high and low scorers led to the development of the F scale.

The authors' belief in the irrationality of prejudice was bolstered by the finding that scores on the Intrusive and Seclusive subscales, which were viewed as logically opposite, actually correlated a strongly positive +.74, which ". . . reveals a deep contradiction in anti-Semitic ideology . . . these results suggest a deep-lying irrational hostility directed against a stereotyped image to which Jews correspond only partially if at all" (*TAP*, pp. 75–76).

Anti-Semitism Scale

Questionnaire A

1. Jews seem to prefer the most luxurious, extravagant, and sensual way of living. (PO)

DISAGREE   DISAGREE   DISAGREE   AGREE   AGREE   AGREE
STRONGLY SOMEWHAT SLIGHTLY SLIGHTLY SOMEWHAT STRONGLY

2. The Jews must be considered a bad influence on Christian culture and civilization. (ST)

3. In order to maintain a nice residential neighborhood it is best to prevent Jews from living in it. (A)

4. A major fault of the Jews is their conceit, overbearing pride, and their idea that they are a chosen race. (PO)

5. One trouble with Jewish businessmen is that they stick together and connive, so that a Gentile doesn't have a fair chance in competition. (ST & I)

6. Colleges should adopt a quota system by which they limit the number of Jews in fields which have too many Jews now. (A)

7. No matter how Americanized a Jew may seem to be, there is always something basically Jewish underneath, a loyalty to Jewry and a manner that is never totally changed. (PO)

8. Jewish power and control in money matters is far out of proportion to the number of Jews in the total population. (ST)

9. A step toward solving the Jewish problem would be to prevent Jews from getting into superior, profitable positions in society, for a while at least. (A)

10. Districts containing many Jews always seem to be smelly, dirty, shabby, and unattractive. (PO)

11. There are too many Jews in the various federal agencies and bureaus in Washington, and they have too much control over our national policies. (ST & I)

12. The Jewish problem is so general and deep that one often doubts that democratic methods can ever solve it. (A)

13. There are a few exceptions but in general Jews are pretty much alike. (PO)

14. Jews tend to lower the general standard of living by their willingness to do the most menial work and to live under standards that are far below average. (ST)

15. It is wrong for Jews and Gentiles to intermarry. (A)

16. The Jews should not pry so much into Christian activities and organizations nor seek so much recognition and prestige from Christians. (PO & I)

17. Much resentment against Jews stems from their tending to keep apart and to exclude Gentiles from Jewish social life. (S)

18. It is best that Jews should have their own fraternities and sororities, since they have their own particular interests and activities which they can best engage in together, just as Christians get along best in all-Christian fraternities. (A)

19. One thing that has hindered the Jews from establishing their own nation is the fact that they really have no culture of their own; instead they tend to copy the things that are important to the native citizen of whatever country they are in. (I)

20. The Jews should give up their un-Christian religion with all its strange customs (kosher diet, special holidays, etc.) and participate actively and sincerely in the Christian religion. (S)

21. It is sometimes all right to ban Jews from certain apartment houses. (A)

22. One big trouble with Jews is that they are never contented, but always try for the best jobs and the most money. (N)

23. Jews tend to remain a foreign element in American society, to preserve their old social standards, and to resist the American way of life. (S)

24. Anyone who employs many people should be careful not to hire a large percentage of Jews. (A)

25. Jews go too far in hiding their Jewishness, especially such extremes as changing their names, straightening noses, and imitating Christian manners and customs. (I)

26. There is little doubt that Jewish pressure is largely responsible for the U.S. getting into the war with Germany. (N)

Questionnaire S

1. The Jews should make sincere efforts to rid themselves of their conspicuous and irritating faults, if they really want to stop being persecuted. (PO)

2. Wars show up the fact that the Jews are not patriotic or willing to make sacrifices for their country. (ST)

3. It would hurt the business of a large concern if it had too many Jewish employees. (A & I)

4. There is something different and strange about Jews; one never knows what they are thinking or planning, nor what makes them tick. (PO)

5. Jews may have moral standards which they apply in their dealings with others, but with Christians they are unscrupulous, ruthless, and undependable. (ST)

6. The best way to eliminate the Communist menace in this country is to control the Jewish element which guides it. (A)

7. The trouble with letting Jews into a nice neighborhood is that they gradually give it a typically Jewish atmosphere. (PO & I)

8. The Jew's first loyalty is to Jewry rather than to his country. (ST)

9. In order to handle the Jewish problem, the Gentiles must meet fire with fire and use the same ruthless tactics with the Jews that the Jews use with the Gentiles. (A)

10. I can hardly imagine myself marrying a Jew. (PO)

11. Jews seem to have an aversion to plain hard work; they tend to be a parasitic element in society by finding easy, nonproductive jobs. (ST)

12. It is not wise for a Christian to be seen too much with Jews, as he might be taken for a Jew, or be looked down upon by his Christian friends. (A)

13. One general fault of Jews is their overaggressiveness, a strong tendency always to display their Jewish looks, manners, and breeding. (PO & S)

14. There seems to be some revolutionary streak in the Jewish makeup as shown by the fact that there are so many Jewish Communists and agitators. (ST)

15. One of the first steps to be taken in cleaning up the movies and generally improving the situation in Hollywood is to put an end to Jewish domination there. (A)

16. Jews should be more concerned with their personal appearance and not be so dirty, smelly, and unkempt. (PO)

17. The Jewish districts in most cities are results of the clannishness and stick-togetherness of Jews. (S)

18. Most hotels should deny admittance to Jews, as a general rule. (A)

19. The true Christian can never forgive the Jews for their crucifixion of Christ. (I)

20. Jewish millionaires may do a certain amount to help their own people, but little of their money goes into worthwhile American causes. (S)

21. Jewish leaders should encourage Jews to be more inconspicuous, to keep out of professions and activities already overcrowded with Jews, and to keep out of the public notice. (A)

22. There is little hope of correcting the racial defects of the Jews, since these defects are simply in their blood. (N)

23. The Jews keep too much to themselves, instead of taking the proper interest in community problems and good government. (S)

24. It would be to the best interests of all if the Jews would form their own nation and keep more to themselves. (A)

25. When Jews create large funds for educational or scientific research (Rosewald, Heller, etc.) it is mainly due to a desire for fame and public notice rather than a really sincere scientific interest. (I)

26. On the whole, the Jews have probably contributed less to American life than any other group. (N)

Note: Initials in parentheses at end of statement indicate subscales. The code is A, attitudes; I, intrusive; PO, personally offensive; S, seclusive; ST, socially threatening; N, not in subscales.

Ethnocentrism (E) Scale

(Adorno, Frenkel-Brunswik, Levinson, & Sanford, 1950)

Variable

This scale measures ethnocentrism, an ideological distinction "made between ingroups (those groups with which the individual identifies himself) and outgroups (with which he does not have a sense of belonging and which are regarded as antithetical to the ingroups)" (Adorno *et al.*, 1950, p. 104).

Description

One of the key steps in the Authoritarian Personality study was the gradual shift from the 52-item scale measuring anti-Semitism to a 20-item one measuring ethnocentric, hostile attitudes toward outgroups. "Outgroups are the objects of negative opinions and hostile attitudes; ingroups are the objects of positive opinions and uncritically supportive attitudes; and it is considered that outgroups should be socially subordinate to ingroups" (Adorno *et al.*, 1950, p. 104).

In the final version of the E scale, negative opinions and hostile attitudes toward outgroups were tapped by statements reflecting anti-Semitism (six items), anti-Negro attitudes (six items), and negative attitudes toward minority groups generally (eight items). Scores thus range from 1 to 7 per item or from 20 (low E) to 140 (high E).

Identification with ingroups was not tapped by statements eliciting feelings of membership but by excluding questionnaire protocols of minority group members from analysis. There were five versions of the Ethnocentrism scale.

1. The first exploratory version consisted of 12 items measuring attitudes toward minority groups in general and 10 referring to patriotism and was administered to a sample of 144 undergraduate women.

2. A second 14-item version of the E scale (excluding A-S) was included on TAP Form 78, which also included a 38-item version of the F scale, and a separate 10-item A-S scale (form numbers refer to the total number of items administered). The A-S scale correlated .68 with the E scale.

3. The third version of the E scale appeared in Form 60 and, for the first time, four A-S items were included in the E scale together with three items referring to Negroes (N) and five to minority groups generally and to patriotism (M).

4. The fourth version was included in Form 40–45. Form 40 had only 5 E items (none referring to Jews) and Form 45 contained 10 items, of which 4 referred to Jews.

5. A fifth and final 20-item version of the E Scale (presented here) appeared in Form 60A in research conducted after the data reported in *TAP*. Items that did not discriminate well were dropped from version to version and others were revised from version to version to increase their discriminatory power.

Samples

Form 78 was administered to three groups of college students and one group of professional women for a total of 295 respondents. Form 60 was given to three student samples and two composed of men in service clubs for a total of 286 respondents. Form 40 was taken by one sample of university women and seven groups of nonstudent samples for a total of 779 respondents. Form 45 was administered to one student sample and four nonstudent samples for a total of 440. Two additional samples of nonstudents ($n = 474$) were tested. Roughly half of each sample received Form 40 and the remainder Form 45. Both Form 40 and Form 45 had the same 30 F-scale items [Adorno *et al.*, 1950; Table 10 (VII) p. 263]. Form 60A was administered to 114 psychology students at the University of Tulsa and 386 at the University of California (Berkeley). It contained 30 F-Scale items, 20 final E-scale items, and 10 PEC-scale items (Christie & Garcia, 1951).

Reliability

Internal Consistency

The reliability of the initial 34-item version of the E scale is reported as .91. This dropped on the shorter version used in Form 78 to a range from .74 to .88 with an average of .80. It improved to .86 on the even shorter 12-item scale in Form 60 with a range from .82 to .88. No reliability was reported for the short Form 40 E scale but the range for the seven groups taking the 10-item Form 45 version varied from .65 to .91 with an average of .79. No reliability is reported on the 20-item suggested version but the patterns of intercorrelations of the A-S, M, and N subscales obtained by Christie and Garcia compare favorably with those reported in *TAP*, suggesting the reliability would be in the .80s.

Test–Retest

No test–retest data could be located.

Validity

Convergent

A scale that was a valid measure of prejudice among samples in the mid-1940s has lost most of its potency because of the stigma attached to overt expression of prejudice among most educated respondents in the United States, at least. Although no such demonstration is known, it would be a reasonable conjecture that endorsement of E-scale items would be judged socially undesirable by most educated respondents in the United States in the 1990s.

Location

Adorno, T. W., Levinson, D. J., Frenkel-Brunswik, E., & Sanford, R. N. (1950). *The authoritarian personality*. New York: Harper & Row.

Results and Comments

Many of the items on the suggested scale are outdated. The "secret" of the atomic bomb has long since been lost, most people today have no idea what a "zootsuiter" might be, etc. A more basic question is raised by changes since these scales were constructed in 1944–1946. The overt expression of prejudice toward minority groups was not as widely interpreted as a display of bad taste as it is today. Ironically, part of this change may be due to widely publicized interpretations of *TAP* which implied that there was something psychologically "bad" about being prejudiced.

Cronbach (1946) argued that acquiescent response tendencies were most prevalent when items were ambiguous. There is little ambiguity for most respondents on the items referring to Jews and Negroes in the suggested Ethnocentrism scale (Form 60A). Therefore the A-S and E scales should not have been much affected by agreement response set since they had specific references to members of minority groups.

Ethnocentrism Scale: Suggested Final Form

A. Jews (A-S)

1. One trouble with Jewish businessmen is that they stick together and prevent other people from having a fair chance in competition.

DISAGREE   DISAGREE   DISAGREE   AGREE   AGREE   AGREE
STRONGLY SOMEWHAT SLIGHTLY SLIGHTLY SOMEWHAT STRONGLY

2. I can hardly imagine myself marrying a Jew.
3. There may be a few exceptions, but in general Jews are pretty much alike.
4. The trouble with letting Jews into a nice neighborhood is that gradually they give it a typical Jewish atmosphere.
5. To end prejudice against Jews, the first step is for the Jews to try sincerely to get rid of their harmful and irritating faults.
6. There is something different and strange about Jews; it's hard to tell what they are thinking and planning, and what makes them tick.

B. Negroes (N)

1. Negroes have their rights, but it is best to keep them in their own districts and schools and to prevent too much contact with whites.
2. It would be a mistake ever to have Negroes for foremen and leaders over whites.
3. Negro musicians may sometimes be as good as white musicians, but it is a mistake to have mixed Negro—white bands.
4. Manual labor and unskilled jobs seem to fit the Negro mentality and ability better than more skilled or responsible work.
5. The people who raise all the talk about putting Negroes on the same level as whites are mostly radical agitators trying to stir up conflicts.
6. Most Negroes would become overbearing and disagreeable if not kept in their place.

C. Other Minorities and Patriotism (M)

1. Zootsuiters prove that when people of their type have too much money and freedom, they just take advantage and cause trouble.
2. The worst danger to real Americanism during the last 50 years has come from foreign ideas and agitators.

3. Now that a new world organization is set up, America must be sure that she loses none of her independence and complete power as a sovereign nation.

4. Certain religious sects who refuse to salute the flag should be forced to conform to such a patriotic action, or else be abolished.

5. Filipinos are all right in their place, but they carry it too far when they dress lavishly and go around with white girls.

6. America may not be perfect, but the American Way has brought us about as close as human beings can get to a perfect society.

7. It is only natural and right for each person to think that his family is better than any other.

8. The best guarantee of our national security is for America to have the biggest army and navy in the world and the secret of the atom bomb.

California F Scales

(Adorno et al., 1950)

Variable

The F scale was designed to measure ethnic prejudice and "prefascist tendencies" simultaneously, without mentioning members of minority groups or having specific reference to explicit fascist ideology.

Description

Although the scale was never called an "Authoritarianism" scale in *TAP*, it has since been commonly referred to as such. Four forms of the F scale constructed by the Berkeley group are known to exist. They were, respectively, Forms 78, 60, 40–45, and 60A, depending on the total number of items. Form 78 contained 38 F-Scale items and 40 relating to ethnocentrism, political–economic conservatism. Form 60 contained 30 revised F-scale items and 30 measuring ethnocentrism and PEC. Form 40–45 contained 30 further revised F-scale items and, depending on the form, 10 or 15 other items. Form 60A was a revision not mentioned in *TAP* but which was used in research at Berkeley from 1947 on.

The content of the items was based partly upon earlier scales of fascist attitudes, partly upon the grounds of psychoanalytic theory, partly on comments made in intensive interviews with high-scoring subjects, and partly on how well they fit into the authors' emerging conception of the authoritarian person. They isolated nine theoretical components as a guide to their thinking: authoritarian aggression, authoritarian submission, conventionalism, anti-intraception, superstition and stereotypy, power and "toughness," destructiveness and cynicism, projectivity, and overconcern with sex. Some items fell under more than one category but each of them was believed to be related to prejudice.

Each item was scored on a seven-point scale with strong disagreement being given a value of 1.0, strong agreement 7.0, and omissions being given the mid-point value of 4.0.

Samples

Form 78 was administered to four small samples of students and one of professional women for a total *n* of 295; Form 60 to three student samples and two men's service groups for a total *n* of 286; and Form 40–45 to 13 groups including more students but also reaching out to include psychiatric clinic patients, prisoners, and working-class respondents. Here the total *n* was 2150.

Reliability

Internal Consistency

The reliability (split half) of the Form 78 F Scale ranged from .56 to .88 in the five groups with a mean of .74; those of Form 60 from .81 to .91 with a mean of .87; and for Form 40–45 the reliabilities ranged from .81 to .97 with a mean of .90. There are no known published data on the reliability of Form 60A but it should have a reliability as high as Form 40–45. All of these reliabilities are enhanced to an unknown extent since with the exception of three of the 38 items on Form 78 they are all worded and scored positively.

Test–Retest

No test–retest data could be located.

Validity

Convergent

The Form 78 F scale correlated +.53 with the A-S scale and +.65 with the E scale. The Form 60 correlation with E was +.69 and that on Form 40 was .77 with E. The only known published report for Form 60A was by Christie and Garcia (1951), who reported correlations of +.56 and +.63 on two student samples in Oklahoma and California. In the clinically oriented studies reported in *TAP*, it is impossible to tell which measures of interview responses are valid because of lack of independence in the judgments. A single judge scored a complete individual protocol in the clinical interviews, for example, and overall the judges were able to identify five out of six protocols correctly as to whether the respondent was a high or low scorer. However, an analysis by Christie (1954) of the process indicated that the judges made a global evaluation of the interviewee and this affected their scoring of individual variables.

Discriminant

After *TAP* was published, Christie and Garcia (1951) found that the item mean score (4.1) of Oklahoma students was significantly higher than the mean for California students (3.3) and interpreted this as the result of being reared and living in a politically conservative subculture. Pettigrew (1959) challenged this interpretation with data collected on four towns in the South and four in New England and obtained item mean scores of 4.7 and 4.7, but these are higher scores than reported on representative national samples in the

1950s: an item mean of 3.7 in a 1950 NORC survey (Janowitz & Marvick, 1953); of 4.0 in a 1952 NORC survey (Lipetz, 1964); of 3.6 in the 1952 Survey Research Center postelection survey (Shaver, 1973); and of 3.8 in a 1953 NORC survey (Williams, 1966).[4]

Williams broke his national survey data into four regional categories and found the following item means: West 3.1; Northeast, 3.7, North-Central, 3.9; and South, 4.5. The higher score in the South is in accord with that found by Schooler noted in the introductory section. The present argument is that the South in the 1950s was much more politically conservative, more fundamentalist in religion, more prone to extol militarism, and more racially conservative than the rest of the country, consistent with the higher F-scale scores found there.

In the United States two-party system there is relatively little F-scale differentiation since both parties have broad based and demographically overlapping constituencies, although people who identify themselves as Republican tend to have slightly higher scores. Sharper differentiations are found in prenational convention studies with a greater spectrum of ideological choice [e.g., Milton's (1952) presidential preferences and item means among Tennessee students: Stevenson, 3.1; Eisenhower, 3.7; Kefauver, 3.7; Russell, 3.9; McArthur, 4.2, and Taft, known as "Mr. Conservative", 4.2].

In countries with a wider spectrum of political choice, Rokeach (1960) sampled English students and found the following ordering: Communist, 2.8; Labour-Liberal, 3.3; Labour, 3.4, and Conservative, 3.9. In India, Bushan (1969) found the following item mean scores: Communists, 4.4; Socialists, 5.1; Congress (the majority party), 5.4; and the right-wing Jana Sangh, 5.6. In the Netherlands, Meloen and Middendorp (1988) examined 5372 respondents according to their vote in elections: Radical Left (Communists, Pacifists, and Radical Christians), 3.4; Liberal Democrats 3.8; Social Democrats, 4.2; Conservative Liberals, 4.3; Christian Democrats, 4.4; and Fundamentalist Right, 4.5.

Although the preceding studies are in the direction one would predict from *TAP* they fall short of affixing the label "fascist" on the "pre-fascist" F scale. However, Hoogvelt (1969) obtained F-scale scores of 5.2 for pro-Powell (a British Fascist) supporters and 3.1 for anti-Powell respondents. In Steiner and Fahrenberg's (1970) samples of German veterans of World War II, members of the regular German Army scored 4.5 while former members of the elite Waffen-SS, the Nazi storm troopers, scored 5.3.

Moving to the anti-authoritarian pole of the F scale, Handlon and Squier (1955) reported on a sample of graduate student teaching assistants at the University of California at Berkeley who were required to sign a loyalty oath to retain their jobs in 1949–1950. The 24 who signed had an item mean of 2.73 on the F scale; those who refused to sign one of 1.88, which is the lowest group mean score known.

---

[4]Among the possible reasons for Pettigrew's higher item mean scores in contrast to those generally found in contemporaneous survey samples are (1) Seven of the 10 items he selected from the pool of items from the Form 40–45 (see his footnote 4, p. 28 and *TAP*, Table 9(V11), p. 160) have higher mean values than others on that form. This would add an estimated .3 to his item means; (2) His sample was composed of residents in towns varying from 4000 to 15,000 in population, similar to those found to score relatively high on the F Scale compared to representative samples including more urbanized localities; (3) His sampling was not a probability one but was based on the use of local directories, which overrepresent older and less transient populations, who again are more conservative. The failure to find North–South differences may be due to the fact that religion was not controlled. It appears (Table 8, p. 32) that about 40% of his northern sample was Catholic. Item mean scores on religious affiliation for which data were reported were approximately 5.0 for northern Catholics, 4.7 for southern Protestants, and 4.4 for northern Protestants. There were almost no southern Catholics in his samples.

Location

Adorno, T. W., Levinson, D. J., Frenkel-Brunswik, E., & Sanford, R. N. (1950). *The authoritarian personality*. New York: Harper.

Results and Comments

The F scale is still one of the most intriguing scales ever devised. Despite methodological criticisms of the research reported in *TAP* and criticisms of its theoretical orientation, it is still widely used because of the unique way it measures an extremely important variable, the proclivity to accept right-wing authoritarianism. One can use it whether or not one agrees with the authors' theories about personality.

California F Scale

Form 78

2. Although many people may scoff, it may yet be shown that astrology can explain a lot of things.

DISAGREE DISAGREE DISAGREE AGREE AGREE AGREE
STRONGLY SOMEWHAT SLIGHTLY SLIGHTLY SOMEWHAT STRONGLY

3. America is getting so far from the true American way of life that force may be necessary to restore it.

6. It is only natural and right that women be restricted in certain ways in which men have more freedom.

9. Too many people today are living in an unnatural, soft way; we should return to the fundamentals, to a more red-blooded, active way of life.

10. It is more than a remarkable coincidence that Japan had an earthquake on Pearl Harbor Day, December 7, 1944.

*12. The modern church, with its many rules and hypocrisies, does not appeal to the deeply religious person; it appeals mainly to the childish, the insecure, and the uncritical.

14. After we finish off the Germans and Japs, we ought to concentrate on other enemies of the human race such as rats, snakes, and germs.

17. Familiarity breeds contempt.

19. One should avoid doing things in public that appear wrong to others, even though one knows that these things are right.

*20. One of the main values of progressive education is that it gives the child great freedom in expressing those natural impulses and desires so often frowned upon by conventional middle class society.

23. He is indeed contemptible who does not feel an undying love, gratitude, and respect for his parents.

24. Today everything is unstable; we should be prepared for a period of constant change, conflict, and upheaval.

*28. Novels or stories that tell about what people think and feel are more interesting than those which contain mainly action, romance, and adventure.

30. Reports of atrocities in Europe have been greatly exaggerated for propaganda purposes.

31. Homosexuality is a particularly rotten form of delinquency and ought to be severely punished.

32. It is essential for learning or effective work that our teachers or bosses outline in detail what is to be done and exactly how to go about it.

35. There are some activities so flagrantly un-American that, when responsible officials won't take steps, the wide-awake citizen should take the law into his own hands.

38. There is too much emphasis in college on intellectual and theoretical topics, not enough emphasis on practical matters and on the homely virtues of living.

39. Every person should have a deep faith in some supernatural force higher than himself to which he gives total allegiance and whose decisions he does not question.

42. No matter how they act on the surface, men are interested in women for only one reason.

43. Sciences like chemistry, physics, and medicine have carried men very far, but there are many important things that can never be understood by the human mind.

46. The sexual orgies of the old Greeks and Romans are nursery school stuff compared to some of the goings-on in this country today, even in circles where people might least expect it.

47. No insult to our honor should ever go unpunished.

50. Obedience and respect for authority are the most important virtues children should learn.

53. There are some things too intimate or personal to talk about even with one's closest friends.

55. Although leisure is a fine thing, it is good hard work that makes life interesting and worthwhile.

56. After the war, we may expect a crime wave; the control of gangsters and ruffians will become a major social problem.

58. What a man does is not so important so long as he does it well.

59. Human nature being what it is, there will always be war and conflict.

60. Which of the following are the most important for a person to have or to be? Mark (X) the three most important.
   _____ Artistic and sensuous
   _____ Popular, good personality +
   _____ Drive, determination, will power +
   _____ Broad, humanitarian outlook
   _____ Neatness and good manners +
   _____ Sensitivity and understanding
   _____ Intellectual and serious

_____ Emotional expressiveness, warmth, intimacy
_____ Kindness and charity

65. It is entirely possible that this series of wars and conflicts will be ended once and for all by a world-destroying earthquake, flood or other catastrophe.

66. Books and movies ought not to deal so much with the sordid and seamy side of life: they ought to concentrate on themes that are entertaining or uplifting.

67. When you come right down to it, it's human nature never to do anything without an eye to one's own profit.

70. To a greater extent than most people realize, our lives are governed by plots hatched in secret by politicians.

73. Nowadays when so many different kinds of people move around so much and mix together so freely, a person has to be especially careful to protect himself against infection and disease.

74. What this country needs is fewer laws and agencies, and more courageous, tireless, devoted leaders whom the people can put their faith in.

75. Sex crimes, such as rape and attacks on children, deserve more than mere imprisonment; such criminals ought to be publicly whipped.

77. No sane, normal, decent person could ever think of hurting a close friend or relative.

Note: *, Reverse-scored items. +, The scoring key for this item is not reported, although, since the item is supposed to tap conventionalism, the "popular," "drive," "efficiency," and "neatness" replies would presumably be scored in the authoritarian direction.

Form 40–45

1. Obedience and respect for authority are the most important virtues children should learn.

DISAGREE   DISAGREE   DISAGREE   AGREE   AGREE   AGREE
STRONGLY SOMEWHAT SLIGHTLY SLIGHTLY SOMEWHAT STRONGLY

2. No weakness or difficulty can hold us back if we have enough will power.

3. Science has its place but there are many important things that can never be understood by the human mind.

4. Human nature being what it is, there will always be war and conflict.

5. Every person should have complete faith in some supernatural power whose decisions he obeys without question.

6. When a person has a problem or worry, it is best for him not to think about it, but to keep busy with more cheerful things.

7. A person who has bad manners, habits, and breeding can hardly expect to get along with decent people.

8. What the youth needs most is strict discipline, rugged determination, and the will to work and fight for your family and country.

9. Some people are born with an urge to jump from high places.

10. Nowadays when so many different kinds of people move around and mix together so much, a person has to protect himself especially carefully against catching an infection or disease from them.

11. An insult to our honor should always be punished.

12. Young people sometimes get rebellious ideas but as they grow up they ought to get over them.

[13. It is best to use some prewar authorities in Germany to keep order and to prevent chaos.]

14. What this country needs most, more than laws and political programs, is a few courageous, tireless leaders in whom the people can put their faith.

15. Sex crimes, such as rape and attacks on children, deserve more than mere imprisonment: such criminals ought to be publicly whipped, or worse.

16. People can be divided into two distinct classes: the weak and the strong.

17. There is hardly anything lower than a person who does not feel a great love, gratitude, and respect for his parents.

18. Some day it will probably be shown that astrology can explain a lot of things.

*[19. America is getting so far from the true American way of life that force may be necessary to restore it.]

20. Nowadays more and more people are prying into matters that should remain personal and private.

21. Wars and social troubles may someday be ended by an earthquake or flood that will destroy the whole world.

22. Most of our social problems could be solved if we could somehow get rid of the immoral, crooked, and feebleminded people.

23. The wild sex life of the old Greeks and Romans was tame compared to some of the goings-on in this country, even in places where people might least expect it.

24. If people would talk less and work more, everybody would be better off.

25. Most people don't realize how much our lives are controlled by plots hatched in secret places.

26. Homosexuals are hardly better than criminals and ought to be severely punished.

[27. The businessman and the manufacturer are much more important to society than the artist and the professor.]

28. No sane, normal, decent person could ever think of hurting a close friend or relative.

29. Familiarity breeds contempt.

[30. Nobody ever learned anything really important except through suffering.]

Note: *, This item was in the 30-item Form 40–45. [TAP, Table 9 (VII), item 30/28, p. 260]. It was inadvertently omitted in Table (VII), pp. 255–257, in which the items are assigned to clusters. This has led many people to conclude the scale had 29 instead of 30 items.

Form 60A

Form 60A of the F scale was the one used routinely in 1947–1949. Form 60A is actually a better measure of F than 40–45 because the bracketed items above were dropped (No. 13 was outdated, and the others had low discriminatory power) and the following four items, which had discriminated well in the earlier scales, were substituted.

The item numbers below are those in Form 60A, where they were evidently tacked onto the remaining 26 (see Christie & Garcia, 1951, Table 3, p. 464).

53. It is essential for learning or effective work that our teachers or bosses outline in detail what is to be done and exactly how to do it.
55. Some leisure is necessary but it is good hard work that makes life interesting and worthwhile.
58. Books and movies ought not to deal so much with the unpleasant and seamy side of life; they ought to concentrate on themes that are entertaining or uplifting.
59. When you come right down to it, it's human nature never to do anything without an eye to one's profit.

G Scale (Reversed F Scale)

(Bass, 1955)

Variable

Bass's (1955) reversals were among the first systematic attempts to construct reversed F-scale items to test the effect of agreement response set.

Description

Reversals were written for 29 F-scale items in Form 40–45 of the F scale. These were paired with the original items and undergraduates were asked to rate them on a five point scale in terms of similarity versus opposition in meaning. The items were divided into four subgroups in terms of judged level of opposition. Two forms were prepared with half the reversed items being included with 14 original F-scale items whose reversals were in the alternate form. Item mean scores vary from 0 to 6.

Sample

The original ratings of reversals were made by 63 undergraduates in a sociology class and 84 undergraduates in psychology classes took the F and G scales.

Reliabilities

Internal Consistency

Reliabilities of .83 and .50 were reported for the F and G scales, respectively.

Test–Retest

No test–retest data were given.

Validity

No validity data were reported.

Location

Bass, B. M. (1955). Authoritarianism or acquiescence? *Journal of Abnormal and Social Psychology,* **51,** 616–623.

Results and Comments

This was primarily a methodological exercise to determine the role of agreement response set in the F scale. As the statements became less opposed in meaning (more ambiguous) it was found that acquiescence increased. The correlation between the F and G scales was −.20. A factor analysis indicated that 59% of the variance was accounted for by an acquiescence factor and only 22% by authoritarianism as measured by the F scale.

G Scale (Bass Reversals)

1. Astrology will never explain anything.

DISAGREE   DISAGREE   DISAGREE   AGREE   AGREE   AGREE
STRONGLY SOMEWHAT SLIGHTLY SLIGHTLY SOMEWHAT STRONGLY

2. Sex criminals such as those who rape and attack children should be treated as sick people, not publicly whipped or worse.
3. A sane, normal, decent person might have to hurt a close friend or relative.
4. Young people sometimes get rebellious ideas. As they grow up they ought to try to carry them out and not be content to get over them and settle down.
5. Weaknesses and difficulties can hold us back; will power is not enough.
6. Our lives are not at all controlled by plots hatched in secret places.
7. Decent people can get along with a person who has bad manners, habits, and breeding.
8. Human nature being what it is, universal peace will come about eventually.
9. Familiarity does not breed contempt.
10. If people would discuss matters more before acting, everybody would be better off.
11. What a youth needs most is to be free to make up his own mind, to be flexible and to work and fight for what he considers right personally even though it might not be best for his family and country.

12. Nowadays, not enough investigating of personal and private matters is done.

13. The artist and the professor are much more important to society than the businessman and the manufacturer.

14. Because of science, it will be possible for the human mind to understand most important things.

15. Self-reliance, respect for democracy, and lack of need to submit to authority are the most important virtues children should learn.

16. Many fine people honestly could never bring themselves around to feeling a great love, gratitude, and respect for their parents.

17. Some of the goings-on in this country, even in places where people might least expect it, are tame compared to the wild sex life of the Greeks and Romans.

18. A person does not have to worry about catching an infection or disease just because many different kinds of people move around and mix together a great deal nowadays.

19. Homosexuals are not criminals and should not be punished.

20. People cannot be divided into two distinct classes, the weak and the strong.

21. When a person has a problem or worry, it is best for him to think about doing something about it, not be distracted by more cheerful things.

22. What this country needs most, more than a few courageous, tireless devoted leaders in whom the people can put their faith, is better laws and political programs.

23. An insult to our honor should be studied, not punished.

24. No people are born with an urge to jump from high places.

25. No person should have complete faith in some supernatural power whose decisions he obeys without question.

26. It is worst to use some prewar authorities in Germany to keep order and prevent chaos.

27. Nobody ever learned anything really important through suffering.

28. Wars and social troubles may someday be ended by wisdom and education, not by an earthquake or flood that will destroy the whole world.

29. Most of our social problems would be solved if we could somehow cure or help the immoral, crooked, and feeble-minded people.

Twenty-Item Counterbalanced F Scale

(Christie, Havel, & Seidenberg, 1958)

Variable

This was designed as a counterbalanced F scale with reversed items that were worded in probabilistic language intended to appeal to relatively sophisticated and liberal respondents.

Description

Reversals were written to meet criteria of logical opposition to the original item, avoidance of extremity of wording, and psychological opposition to the original item. The 10 most discriminating of these items as determined by item analysis were retained together with the 10 most discriminating of the other 20 original F-scale items. Scores range from 1 to 7, with high scores indicating authoritarianism.

Sample

The original item analysis was conducted on two geographically separate samples of psychology students ($n = 150$ and 79). Eight other samples varied from 57 to 152. A subsequent sample included 1507 students from a broad selection of 13 colleges (Christie & Geis, 1970).

Reliability

Internal Consistency

Internal consistency varied considerably with correlations between the two 10-item subscales varying from only $+.10$ in a sample of students in a nonelite college to $+.55$ in a lobbyist sample and $+.58$ in a sample of graduate students in the social sciences (reliabilities were reported only on the subscales and not on the combined scale). A reliability of .69 was found in a large heterogeneous college sample.

Test–Retest

No test–retest data are reported.

Validity

Convergent

Most of the correlations with social sophistication, preference for conservative presidential candidates (Goldwater over Johnson in 1964), etc. showed the same patterns as the original F scale. Scores on the scale were progressively higher for medical students intending to go into the following major specialties: psychiatry, pediatrics, internal medicine, obstetrics and gynecology, and surgery.

Location

Christie, R., Havel, J., & Seidenberg, B. (1958). Is the F scale irreversible? *Journal of Abnormal and Social Psychology,* **56,** 143–159.

Results and Discussion

Although the positive correlations between the subscales run counter to Bass's argument that the majority of the variance in the F scale is due to acquiescent response set, high amounts of response set were found, particularly among less sophisticated respondents. Christie *et al.* used a probability matrix and came to the conclusion that 23% of the nonelite undergraduate sample showed significant acquiescent response set. The amount of response set was linearly related to item mean scores on the total scale, which varied from 2.7 among graduate students to 4.1 in the undergraduate sample.

Some confusion is apparent in the earlier literature on the F scale because of the linguistic confusion between agreement response set, which is here interpreted as a result of confusion or ignorance about the interpretation of an item, and the hypothesized variable of submission to authority. Schulberg (1961) selected three groups of subjects: Consistent Highs, who agreed with original F-scale items and disagreed with reversals; Consistent Lows, who disagreed with the originals and agreed with the reversals; and High Agreement respondents, who agreed with both sets of items. Scodel and Freedman's (1956) experimental paradigm was followed in which subjects individually interacted with others from each category in a 15-minute discussion of movies, television, or radio. At the end they were asked to take the counterbalanced scale and fill it out as they thought their former colleague had. The acquiescent highs thought their targets also agreed with both sets of statements, the consistent highs judged others as agreeing with them on the original items but as being significantly less authoritarian on the reversed items. The consistent lows showed an opposite pattern to the consistent highs in thinking the others agreed with them on the reversed items but saw their partner as significantly toward the neutral point on the original items. None of the groups were more accurate in their judgments; they simply had different stereotypes of the other students whatever their actual scores.

In an attitude change experiment Marquis (1973) ran an experiment within an experiment using the same classification system. High F, Low F, and High Agreement "experimenters" gave a persuasive communication to "subjects" from the three groups in individual sessions. In this instance High Fs were unsuccessful as instigators of attitude change and the High Agree and Low F "experimenters" were significantly more successful in inducing attitude change. The High Agreement "subjects" did *not* display submission to authority when recipients of the communication; in fact they were less inclined to show compliance although not significantly so.

These two experiments raise questions about using only original F Scale items as a criterion of authoritarianism in experimental studies since in Schulberg's experiment the High Agrees performed more like consistent Highs and in Marquis' study more like consistent Lows. If only the original items had been used, a different conclusion would have been drawn about accuracy of perception in Schulberg's study, and Marquis study would probably not have found a significant difference between highs and lows as defined by scores on a positively worded F scale.

Twenty-Item Counterbalanced F Scale

1. Nowadays more and more people are prying into matters that should remain personal and private.

DISAGREE   DISAGREE   DISAGREE   AGREE   AGREE   AGREE
STRONGLY SOMEWHAT SLIGHTLY SLIGHTLY SOMEWHAT STRONGLY

*2. If it weren't for the rebellious ideas of youth there would be less progress in the world.

3. No weakness or difficulty can hold us back if we have enough will power.

4. Every person should have complete faith in some supernatural power whose decisions he obeys without question.

*5. It is highly unlikely that astrology will ever be able to explain anything.

6. What youth needs most is strict discipline, rugged determination, and the will to work and fight for family and country.

7. Most of our social problems would be solved if we could somehow get rid of the immoral, crooked, and feeble-minded people.

*8. An urge to jump from high places is probably the result of unhappy personal experiences rather than something inborn.

*9. The findings of science may some day show that many of our most cherished beliefs are wrong.

*10. People ought to pay attention to new ideas even if they seem to go against the American way of life.

*11. One of the most important things children should learn is when to disobey authorities.

12. In order for us to do good work, it is necessary that our bosses outline carefully what is to be done and exactly how to go about it.

13. Sex crimes, such as rape and attacks on children, deserve more than mere imprisonment; such criminals should be publicly whipped, or worse.

14. Most people don't realize how much our lives are governed by plots hatched in secret by politicians.

15. No sane, normal, decent person could ever think of hurting a close friend or relative.

*16. The artist and professor are probably more important to society than the businessman and manufacturer.

*17. Most honest people admit to themselves that they have sometimes hated their parents.

18. Human nature being what it is, there will always be war and conflict.

*19. In spite of what you read about the wild sex life of people in important places, the real story is about the same in any group of people.

*20. Books and movies ought to give a more realistic picture of life even if they show that evil sometimes triumphs over good.

Note: *, These are items in the reverse direction.

Counterbalanced F Scale

(Lee & Warr, 1969)

Variable

This was constructed as a counterbalanced authoritarianism scale in which the reversed items were worded so the semantic structure of each item was positive (and not simply a negation of an original F-scale item).

Description

The authors began with a pool of 100 items that had been constructed by a Social Science Research Council committee of social scientists experienced in using and modifying the original F scale. The 100-item pool was broader in content than the original F scale and had an equal number of positively and negatively worded items.

Lee and Warr did item analyses that eliminated the least discriminating items. The protocols were rescored and the process repeated until the pool of items was reduced to 15 positively and 15 negatively scored items. Scores range from 1 to 7.

Sample

The initial sample was composed of 54 Peace Corps trainees at Princeton and the final scale was given to 421 undergraduate and 135 graduate students at Princeton University.

Reliability

Internal Consistency

A split-half reliability of .84 was found for the total sample and the correlation between positive and negative items was .51.

Test–Retest

No test–retest data were reported.

Validity

Convergent

Negative relationships were found with measures of SAT verbal scores of $-.29$, which is greater than that usually reported, particularly among carefully recruited samples. The scale correlated $+.51$ with Tompkins' Conservatism (1964) scale and $+.39$ with the Gough–Sanford Rigidity scale as reported in Rokeach, 1960, Appendix III. The Rokeach 1956 Dogmatism Scale (all items worded positively) correlated $+.41$ with the positively worded Lee and Warr items, but only $+.01$ with those negatively worded, indicating that response set was playing a role even among these sophisticated respondents. In another study a correlation of $+.43$ was found with a Thurstone-type attitude scale with Negroes as a referent.

Discriminant

In studies involving known groups, humanities students scored lowest, engineering students highest. Perhaps most relevant to *TAP* were the mean scores of samples of political groups: Students at Princeton and the University of Pennsylvania who were members of Young Americans for Freedom had an item mean score of 3.9, politically unaffiliated students a score of 3.6, and members of the leftist Americans for Democratic Action and Students for a Democratic Society a score of 2.2.

Location

Lee, R. E., & Warr, P. B. (1969). The development and standardization of balanced F scale. *Journal of General Psychology*, **81**, 109–129.

Results and Comments

The item content of this scale is broader than that of any previously described authoritarianism scale. Despite the counterbalanced nature of the scale the interitem correlation is +.13, which is the same as that for the original F scale. The authors believe the correlation of only +.51 between the positive and negative items is in part due to the broad item coverage; they found 10 identifiable factors in a maximum likelihood factor analysis. The first factor concerns the family and parental discipline, which accords with the emphasis in *TAP*.

Counterbalanced F Scale

1. The minds of today's youth are being hopelessly corrupted by the wrong kind of literature.

DISAGREE   DISAGREE   DISAGREE   AGREE   AGREE   AGREE
STRONGLY   SOMEWHAT   SLIGHTLY   SLIGHTLY   SOMEWHAT   STRONGLY

*2. The church has outgrown its usefulness and should be radically reformed or done away with.

3. An insult to our honor should always be punished.

4. It is only natural and right for each person to think that his family is better than any other.

*5. What a youth needs most is the flexibility to work and fight for what he considers right personally even though it might not be best for his family and country.

*6. Most censorship of books or movies is a violation of free speech and should be abolished.

7. The facts on crime and sex immorality suggest that we will have to crack down harder on some people if we are going to save our moral standards.

*8. It is the duty of a citizen to criticize or censure his country whenever he considers it to be wrong.

*9. The resistance of medical pressure groups may have to be broken by strong governmental action in order for all of the people to get the full medical care to which they are entitled.

10. No person who could ever think of hurting his parents should be permitted in the society of normal decent people.

*11. A world government with effective military strength is one way in which world peace might be achieved.

12. Few weaknesses or difficulties can hold us back if we have enough will power.

13. Unless something drastic is done, the world is going to be destroyed one of these days by nuclear explosion or fallout.

14. The poor will always be with us.

---

15. The worst danger to the United States during the last 50 years has come from fringe ideas and agitators.

*16. Science declines when it confines itself to the solution of immediate practical problems.

17. We should be grateful for leaders who tell us exactly what to do and how to do it.

*18. One of the troubles with our present economy is that full employment depends on a substantial military budget.

*19. As young people grow up, they ought to try to carry out some of their rebellious ideas and not be content to get over them and settle down.

20. In the final analysis parents generally turn out to be right about things.

21. Divorce or annulment is practically never justified.

*22. Disobedience to the government is sometimes justified.

*23. Honesty, hard work, and trust in God do not guarantee material rewards.

24. There is a divine purpose in the operations of the universe.

25. Army life is a good influence on most men.

*26. One way to reduce the expression of prejudice is through more forceful legislation.

*27. One of the greatest threats to the American way of life is for us to resort to the use of force.

28. It usually helps the child in later years if he is forced to conform to his parents' ideas.

29. Sex crimes, such as rape and attacks on children, deserve more than mere imprisonment: Such criminals ought to be publicly whipped, or worse.

*30. Members of religious sects who refuse to salute the flag or bear arms should be treated with tolerance and understanding.

Note: *, Reverse-scored items.

Authoritarianism—Rebellion Scale (A-R)

(Kohn, 1972)

Variable

The A-R scale is a 30-item counterbalanced scale in which half the items are original or modified F-scale items with more extreme wording and half are reversals that are relatively extreme left-wing.

Discussion

One interesting aspect of the item criteria was that each reversal was worded so that "it would be clearly unreasonable for each person to agree with both it and the corresponding original. (However it should not be unreasonable to disagree with both statements . . .)." In the pilot study only 3% of the respondents showed double agreement and 24% showed double disagreement. After the original item analysis the scale was refined on a new sample and each statement from the contrasting 15 pairs was randomly interspersed in the questionnaire. The scoring was on a 1–6 basis with the theoretical neutral point being 3.5.

Sample

The pilot study was conducted on 107 undergraduates at York University. Two new student samples of 58 and 69 were used for the final scale as well as another sample of 66 students in political groups.

Reliability

Internal Consistency

A split-half reliability of +.84 was found for the two combined student samples. However, the original–reversal correlation was only +.42 for this group. P. M. Kohn (1974) followed up this study with one in England, using a scale administered to undergraduates at Oxford ($n = 51$) and two samples at the University of Reading ($n = 62$ and 62). Correlations between the two halves of the scale improved to +.43, +.51, and +.56 and the reliabilities were +.81, +.86, and +.93, with the Oxford sample showing the highest internal consistency.

Test–Retest

No test–retest data were reported.

Validity

Convergent

The usual positive correlations with age, religious fundamentalism, and frequency of church attendance were found. The latter two results were primarily due to the low scores made by atheists, agnostics, and " . . . persons of unconventional religious preference . . ." Upperclassmen obtained lower scores than younger students.

The same significant findings as in Canada emerged in England for religious preference, religious attendance, and political preference.

One of the Reading samples was given a variety of other scales. Correlations with A-R were: Conservatism (Wilson & Patterson, 1968), +.81; Ethnocentrism (Warr & Faust, 1967), +.56; Intolerance of Ambiguity (Budner, 1962), +.67; and Dogmatism (Trodahl & Powell, 1965), +.48.

Rokeach's (1956) Opinionation Scale was found to correlate +.60 with A-R.

Discriminant

More interestingly, the differences among the following political groups were highly significant in the Canadian sample: Trotskyists, 2.3; New Democrats 2.5; Liberals, 3.3; Conservatives, 3.5; and members of the ultra-right-wing Edmund Burke Society, 5.1.

Means for the student political groups at Reading were the Socialist Society, 2.0; Labour, 3.1; Liberal, 3.1; and Conservative, 4.6.

Conservatives in the Reading sample scored significantly higher than Socialists and Liberals on Intolerance of Ambiguity and the Liberals and Labour did not differ significantly among themselves. No significant relationships were found with Dogmatism.

In another study of 197 undergraduates using the A-R scale, P. M. Kohn and Mercer (1971) found low scorers were significantly more likely to have used a variety of drugs and to have more permissive attitudes toward their use.

Location

Kohn, P. M. (1972). The Authoritarianism–Rebellion scale: A balanced F Scale with left-wing reversals. *Sociometry,* **35,** 176–189.

Results and Comments

The A-R was designed to be a more ideologically explicit scale than the F scale. A factor analysis, which is not reported in detail, found that all 15 of the reversed items had a strong loading on the first factor and 11 of the 15 positively worded items had "appreciable" loading on the second factor. It is impossible to determine from available data to what extent this reflects response set as against item content.

The modest correlations between the positive and negatively worded subscales suggest a lack of unidimensionality. As P. M. Kohn (1972, p. 187) notes, "These findings suggest that such left–right ideological concepts as an authoritarianism–rebellion dimension do not apply meaningfully to North American college students in general; however, they apparently do apply to active members of political groups."

The Authoritarian–Rebellion Scale

1. Obedience and respect for authority are the most important virtues children should learn.

DISAGREE   DISAGREE   DISAGREE   AGREE   AGREE   AGREE
STRONGLY   SOMEWHAT   SLIGHTLY   SLIGHTLY   SOMEWHAT   STRONGLY

*2. What we need least is an authority to tell us what to do or how to do it.

3. Every person should have complete faith in some supernatural power whose decisions he obeys without question.

4. People can be divided into two distinct classes: the weak and the strong.

*5. To be a decent human being follow your conscience regardless of the law.

*6. No principle is more immoral than that of obedience.

7. Familiarity breeds contempt.

*8. Astrology will never explain anything because it is a fraud.

*9. The Canadian way of life is so resistant to progress that revolution is necessary to end its injustices and oppressions.

10. Nowadays, when so many different kinds of people move around and mix together so much, a person has to protect himself against catching an infection or disease from them.

---

*11. Children don't owe their parents a thing.

*12. Canada can't exert moral leadership among nations until it abandons its corrupt material values.

*13. Sex crimes like rape and child molesting reflect a sick society and we must change society rather than punishing individual offenders.

14. Obedience is the mother of success.

15. Strong discipline builds moral character.

16. Canada is spiritually predestined to lead the world.

17. Some day it will probably be shown that astrology can explain a lot of things.

*18. Peoples of different nationalities, social classes and races should mix together more. Everybody would benefit from it.

*19. To know people well is to love them.

20. The true Canadian way of life is disappearing so fast that force may be necessary to preserve it.

21. Sex crimes, such as rape and attacks on children, deserve more than mere imprisonment: such criminals ought to be publicly whipped, or worse.

*22. Obedience is the mother of enslavement.

*23. True morality only develops in a fully permissive environment.

24. There is hardly anything lower than a person who does not feel a great deal of love, gratitude, and respect for his parents.

25. No principle is more noble or holy than that of true obedience.

*26. The strong and the weak are not inherently different. They are merely the advantaged and disadvantaged members of an unfair society.

*27. Obedience and respect for authority aren't virtues and shouldn't be taught to children.

28. To be a decent person always stay within the law.

29. Our chief want in life is somebody to make us do what we should.

*30. Faith in the supernatural is a harmful self-delusion, and submission to religious authority is dangerous.

Note: *, Reverse-scored items.

Naysaying Low F Scale

(Couch & Keniston, 1960)

Variable

This five-item reversed F scale was designed to counterbalance positively worded items to provide a "true" measure of authoritarianism, as part of a larger study of personality correlates of response set.

Description

This 5-item "naysaying" scale correlated +.70 with items from a 10-item positive F scale that emerged from an earlier factor analysis of a value profile that included items from *TAP* (Bales & Couch, 1969). Response choices range from 1 (strongly disagree) to 7 (strongly agree). The range is from 5 (High F) to 35 (Low F).

Sample

Results were obtained on a sample of 54 students in an upper-level psychology course at Harvard.

Reliability

Internal Consistency

No data are given but it must be high given the correlation cited above.

Test–Retest

No test–retest data were reported.

Validity

No data were reported.

Location

Couch, A., & Keniston, K. (1960). Yeasayers and naysayers: Agreeing response set as a personality variable. *Journal of Abnormal and Social Psychology, 60,* 151–174.

Results and Comments

This scale is important because it demonstrates for the first time that it is possible to reverse F-scale items with a high degree of success. It should be noted, however, that these items were administered to a sophisticated sample and the basic content falls in the central core of the authoritarian syndrome, primarily tapping submission to authority.

The items in general are simpler than those in *TAP* and probably would be more easily interpreted by the general population.

Naysaying Low F Scale

1. People tend to place too much emphasis on respect for authority.

   1   2   3   4   5   6   7

2. It may well be that children who talk back to their parents respect them in the long run.

3. I seldom have any enthusiasm or respect and obedience for authority.

4. It would be preferable if there was less emphasis about strict discipline, rugged determination, and the will to work and fight for family and country.

5. I would not myself consider patriotism and loyalty to be the first requirements of a good citizen.

Attitude Toward Authority Scales
(Ray, 1971)

Variable

This is a unique measure of authoritarianism in that none of the items are taken or modified from ones in the California F scale.

Discussion

Ray defined authoritarianism narrowly as (1) viewing the leader as a guide or director rather than an "executive of democratic decisions," (2) approving authoritarian institutions and practices (notably Army), (3) preferences for regulation versus libertarianism. He developed three subscales designed to measure these concepts with 8, 11, and 9 items, respectively, and with half the 28 items being worded in the reverse direction. The correlation between the original and reversed items is reported as $+.54$ on the first of four samples, but similar correlations for three subsequent samples are not reported. Scores run from 1 (most negative to authority) to 5 (most positive to authority).

Sample

Four samples included: 96 Australian army conscripts, 95 day and evening social psychology students at Macquarie University, 95 boys in the fifth and sixth form class of high school, and 203 community residents (Ray attempted to find males of "as low a social class as possible" between the ages of 40 and 55). The item means and standard deviations for the four groups were 3.7 (SD = .6), 2.7 (.4), 2.9 (.5), and 3.2 (.5). On the 1–5 scoring system all of these groups score on the authoritarian side of the theoretical neutral point of 2.5.

Reliability

Internal Consistency

The reliabilities of the total scale in the four samples are reported as being .83, .81, .78, and .80, respectively.

Test–Retest

No test–retest data are reported.

Validity

Convergent

Basic demographic data are not systematically reported. In order to test the alleged "basic hypothesis" of Adorno *et al.* that the pro-authority person is "an inflexible, paranoid deviant," a counterbalanced group of items designed to measure "social adaptability" was reported to correlate +.22 with the Attitude to Authority scale for the conscript sample only.

Discriminant

Ray's data are in accord with the higher scores of presumably less well-educated conscripts in contrast to college students. Political party preferences were ranked along a left–right dimension from Communist to Democratic Labour (no number was given) and a correlation of +.47 was found with the Attitudes toward Authority Scale among the college students and one of +.21 among the high school students. A counterbalanced Political Conservatism Scale devised by Ray correlated +.61 with the Attitude toward Authority Scale.

Location

Ray, J. J. (1971). An "attitude toward authority" scale. *Australian Psychologist*, **6**, 31–50.

Results and Comments

Militarism was one of the seven key components in Stagner's (1936) pioneering analysis of fascism, and Edwards (1941) argued convincingly that the relationship was so obvious that scales of authoritarianism should focus on more psychologically relevant and less obvious aspects of the construct of authoritarianism. Since Ray does not allude to these studies it is unclear whether he rejected or was unaware of Edwards's argument. In any event, it is impossible to tell from his partial presentation of data whether everyone else is out of step with him or vice versa.

The scale is of dubious value to other researchers. The major conclusion to be drawn from the study is that it is possible to select a pool of items that is part of a more general conservative–authoritarian syndrome and find some moderately successful reversals.

A cluster analysis was done on the protocols of a conscript sample. One cluster was composed of nine items, and six of them were from the second "Army" Subscale, which led Ray (p. 36) to suggest, ". . . this subscale could well be used as a short form of the scale." It was subsequently found in a high school sample that six items showing part–whole correlations of less than .10 came from the first subscale. These items and two others were deleted from a 29-item scale given to the community sample.

Upon the basis of available information it is difficult to understand the basis of Ray's conclusion, ". . . the pro-authority person is well-adjusted. Thus, even the *most exact operationalization* (italics added) of the California hypothesis concerning authoritarian psychopathology leads to a decisive rejection of that hypothesis." A correlation of +.22 between a measure primarily of favorable attitudes toward the army and military discipline with one measuring the extent to which 96 conscripts say they are adapting well while in a military situation does not appear to be a "decisive rejection" of an hypothesis based on

Attitude to Authority Scales

Subset 1: (View of leader: executive vs. decision maker)

*1. If there is disagreement about a policy, a leader should be willing to give it up.

1   2   3   4   5

*2. A leader should always change his actions to ensure agreement and harmony in the community.

3. It is important for a leader to get things done even if he must displease people by doing them.

*4. A national leader should follow the wishes of the community, even if he thinks the citizens are mistaken.

5. If a leader is himself sure of what is the best thing to do, he must try to do this, even though he has to use some pressure on the people.

6. It is all right for a leader to do something unauthorized, if he is sure it will be for the good of the people in the long run.

*7. It is most important to have the participation of everybody in making decisions, regardless of their knowledge of the issues involved.

*8. It's always better to try to talk people into doing things, rather than give them straight out orders.

Subset 2: (Evaluation of authoritarian institutions and other examples of the exercise of authority)

9. There's generally a good reason for every rule and regulation in public service departments.

*10. In the Army, soldiers should not obey an order if it is obviously morally wrong.

*11. If the Army allowed more room for individuality it might be a better institution.

*12. There is something wrong with anybody who likes to wear a military uniform.

13. When the dictator Mussolini made Italy's trains run on time, that at least was an important thing to achieve.

14. Two years in the Army would do everyone a world of good.

15. The Army is very good for straightening men out and smartening them up.

16. Civilians could learn a lot from the Army.

*17. I disagree with what the Army stands for.

18. You can be sure that Army procedures will be good, because they have been tried and tested.

19. School children should have plenty of discipline.

Subset 3: (Freedom vs. regulation)

*20. People should be guided more by their feelings and less by the rules.

21. People should be made to be punctual.

*22. Efficiency and speed are not as important as letting everyone have their say in making decisions.

*23. There is far too much regimentation of people nowadays.

24. You know where you're going when you have an order to obey.

*25. People should not be expected to conform as much as they are today.

*26. People who say we don't have enough freedom here in Australia don't know what they're talking about.

27. I don't mind if other people decide what I am to do, or advise me how to do it.

28. It would be much better if we could do without politics altogether.

Note: *, Reverse-scored item.

an misinterpretation of *The Authoritarian Personality*. It could equally well be argued that "social adaptation" of high authoritarians in a military setting is exactly what Adorno *et al.* would have predicted. At the least, the relevance of the finding to Ray's ideosyncratically hypothesized "inflexible, paranoid deviant" appears to be a complete non sequitor.

Right-Wing Authoritarianism (RWA)
(Altemeyer, 1981)

Variable

This is a painstakingly constructed counterbalanced scale that combines variations of items used in studies following from *TAP* and items developed by Altemeyer.

Description

Altemeyer's (1981) initial reasons for revising measures of authoritarianism were based partially on his rejection of the psychoanalytic hypotheses underlying the construction of the F scale, partially on the perceived methodological inadequacies of much of the published research, and a strong belief that most counterbalanced versions of the F scale were flawed because they were not concerned sufficiently with the issue of reliability. His interpretation of the literature indicated that both the original item analyses in *TAP* and further revisions of the F scale pointed to the central importance of items dealing with the original authors' categories of authoritarian aggression, authoritarian submission, and conventionality.

Altemeyer's solution to the problem of reversals was ingenious in its simplicity. Items whose content was relevant to the three categories were required to meet three methodological criteria:

1. A reversed item ("contrait" in his terminology) should have a correlation of $+.40$ or better with a scale composed of positively worded ("pro-trait") items.
2. With reversed scoring for the contrait items the mean on a seven-point scale should be within plus or minus .40 of the protrait item being reversed.
3. The variance of responses to a contrait item should be plus or minus .20 that of the protrait item being reversed.

The last two criteria were based primarily upon test–retest findings over a 1-week period.

What Altemeyer proposed, in essence, was to construct contrait items that were mirror images psychometrically of protrait items. For example, if an original item had an item mean of 4.60 with a standard deviation of .80, the reversed item should have an item mean .60 below the theoretical neutral point of 4.00 and vary between 3.00 and 3.80, and a standard deviation within the .60–1.00 range. Meeting three criteria simultaneously was difficult: it took 10 attempts before he emerged with a 24-item counterbalanced scale which met them. Item mean scores could vary from 1 to 7 with a high score representing high authoritarianism.

Sample(s)

The development of the scale involved thousands of students recruited from the subject pool at the University of Manitoba, some samples being as large as 956.

Reliability

Internal Consistency

This varies from sample to sample. Altemeyer (1981) reported a reliability of .88 in the sample of 956 Manitoba students in 1973. Zwillenberg (1983) found reliabilities varying from .77 to .95 in small samples from a wide range of colleges, and the reliability for the combined total samples of .90 was even higher than Altemeyer's. There appear to be at least two explanations for the difference in reliabilities in various samples. One is obvious: the greater the heterogenity of a sample as indicated by the variance on RWA scores, the more likely a high reliability. Another reason is suggested by the fact that one of Zwillenberg's samples showing low reliability was composed in the main of humanities students at Columbia College, who had an item mean score of 2.83; this is more than a standard deviation below the mean of 3.81 found by Altemeyer at Manitoba. Another low reliability was found in a sample of students in a criminal justice class in a nonselective school; the mean was 4.63, far above Altemeyer's Manitoba mean. A possibility is that investigators should compare their own sample's means with those obtained by Altemeyer and expect that major discrepancies from his items fine-tuned on Manitoba samples will lead to lower reliabilities. There is evidence that the reliabilities found by Altemeyer may be suffering attrition over time, although the interitem correlations are still higher than those on the original F scale (Altemeyer, 1988, pp. 26–29). He reports on a newer, lengthier, and revised RWA scale to keep reliability satisfactorily high. In fact, he has been involved in a constant revision and updating of the items for the past 18 years.

Validity

Convergent

Highly reliable scales do not necessarily (and often do not) have predictive validity because they narrowly measure a construct. The RWA scale was deliberately designed to tap the essence of the most internally consistent items in the F scale. The question as to how it compared with the F scale (the 29-item version of Form 40–45) and other measures was the objective of a "pitting" study in which these scales were among those given to Altemeyer's largest reported sample ($n = 956$) of respondents. Among the other scales given were the 40-item version of Rokeach's D scale, the Lee and Warr counterbalanced F scale, Kohn's A-R scale, and the Wilson & Patterson (1968) conservatism scale. (The reliabilities of these were lower than of the RWA scale in this sample).

Altemeyer used a variety of paper and pencil tests designed to measure: (1) orientation toward acceptance of established authority and law, (2) acceptance of law as the basis of morality, and (3) punitiveness toward "sanctioned targets" (e.g., minority groups, social deviants, and "common criminals"). The RWA Scale had the highest correlation with the criterion variables in each case.

More impressive to those who have some skepticism of correlations of a variable (such as RWA) measured by a questionnaire and a dependent variable that involves a description of a hypothetical situation is Altemeyer's report on a subsample of males who were placed in a situation in which they were interacting with another person. A modification of the Milgram (1974) obedience paradigm was used in which a subject is faced with disobeying orders. The RWA Scale had the highest correlation ($+.44$) of the measures of conservatism or authoritarism with the persistence of "shocking" the other.

Overall, the Lee and Warr revision of the F Scale came out second best in the comparisons. Since this scale has a broader range of referrents than the RWA Scale, it may be inferred that the latter is not so narrowly devised that it lessens its validity. This is true at least for the types of studies conducted by Altemeyer, which are clearly related to social psychological dependent variables.

Location

Altemeyer, B. (1981). *Right-wing authoritarianism*. Winnipeg: University of Manitoba Press.

Results and Comments

The RWA scale is the best current measure of the essence of what the authors of *TAP* were attempting to measure. The interpretation of high scorers on the F scale was clear: Respondents who agreed with statements that were authoritarian in both overt and covert wording were potentially supportive of fascistic movements. Individuals who rejected the F-scale items were viewed as democratic. Altemeyer's reversals have an interesting and, at first glance, surprising aspect. They are almost all worded absolutely, e.g., Homosexuals *are just as good and virtuous* as anybody else and *there is nothing wrong* with being one (italics added).

Many Columbia College students who had low RWA scores objected to the wording of many of the reversals as being too dogmatic. Altemeyer's Manitoba students contained very few low scorers in absolute terms. However, he was using psychometric criteria and to get items worded to meet them he obviously had to sharpen them progressively to get the required discrimination. The reversals had to be stated so clearly negatively that the content caught a normally acquiescent respondent's attention. This raises the interesting question of how an absolute low scorer on the RWA scale (item mean of 2.0 or less) would be classified politically since he or she is clearly rejecting "hard" authoritarian items and endorsing "hard" anti-authoritarian items. The person would appear to be closer to the Frankfort Institut's idealized anti-authoritarian revolutionary than *TAP*'s idealized democratic liberal.

Those contemplating using the RWA Scale would be advised to compare their sample's mean RWA scores with those of Altemeyer's Manitoba sample in interpreting their results. The closer to his mean, the more evenly yea- and naysaying tendencies will be balanced, as strikingly lower scores increase the proportion of naysayers as well as legitimate low scorers, while markedly higher scores indicate the presence of more yeasayers as well as genuine authoritarians.

One point raised in Altemeyer's (1988) latest book is relevant in using and interpreting the RWA scale. In the process of revising his items from 1973 through 1987 there were some items which remained constant: "the continuing twelve." Item means on these increased from 4.04 to 4.75 during this period, which reflected the near disappearance of low scorers over the years with a proportionate increase in middle scorers and those above the theoretical neutral point. However, there was no marked increase in extreme high scorers. Just as Newcomb found that students exposed to a liberal school climate in the 1930s did not increase in endorsement of liberal items but rather learned to reject conservative ones, it would appear that new cohorts of Manitoba students exposed to an increasingly more conservative social climate are not increasing in strong endorsement of the RWA protrait items but are decreasing in endorsement of the contrait anti-authoritarian items.

The sensitivity of F-scale scores to changing political climates has been noted by Meloen (1983) for the period 1950–1980. Lederer (1983) documented a drop in teenagers' authoritarianism scores in the United States from 1945 to 1978 and an even sharper drop in West Germany from 1945 to 1978. That this trend is not irreversible is suggested by Meloen and Middendorp (1988, Table 18, p. 24) who found the trend for lower F Scale scores for their entering cohorts in their surveys in the Netherlands to be leveling out in 1985. This means that the interpretation of F and RWA scores needs to take account of not only the variables of age, education, religion, etc. but also the time at which the data are collected.

Only the earlier form of the RWA scale will be presented for illustrative purposes. Since Altemeyer is continuously revising the scale those wishing to use it would be well-advised to obtain a copy of the latest version before deciding which form to use.

The advent of perestroika and glasnost in the USSR has permitted a study which has produced some dramatic findings regarding Russian authoritarianism (McFarland, Agayev, and Abalakina, 1990). They used a Russian translation of Altemeyer's (1988) 30-item RWA scale on two quota samples ($n = 346$) in Moscow and Talinn (Estonia) and found demographic correlates of authoritarianism very similar to those found in the West.

They also predicted and found a high degree of polarization as indicated by an unusually high alpha reliability of .92. Counterbalanced scales of prejudice toward capitalists, Jews, women, dissidents, youth, advocates of free press, advocates of greater democracy, and the non-Russian minorities in the USSR were constructed and found to correlate significantly with one another and individually with the RWA scale. A summed prejudice scale correlated .83 with the RWA scale which is the highest known to be reported on any authoritarian–prejudice comparison.

Contrary to their expectations, however, was the mean score of their sample, 3.34

using Meloen's conversion, which is lower than that reported on Western cross-sectional samples. Lacking parallel data on strictly comparable Western samples, the interpretation of this provocative finding awaits further research.

One conclusion is clear. The RWA scale appears relevant to those interested in doing research across cultures.

The Right-Wing Authoritarianism Scale

1. Laws have to be strictly enforced if we are going to preserve our way of life.

DISAGREE   DISAGREE   DISAGREE   AGREE   AGREE   AGREE
STRONGLY   SOMEWHAT   SLIGHTLY   SLIGHTLY   SOMEWHAT   STRONGLY

*2. People should pay less attention to the Bible and the other old traditional forms of religious guidance, and instead develop their own personal standards of what is moral and immoral.

3. Women should always remember the promise they make in the marriage ceremony to obey their husbands.

4. Our customs and national heritage are the things that have made us great, and certain people should be made to show greater respect for them.

*5. Capital punishment should be completely abolished.

*6. National anthems, flags, and glorification of one's country should all be de-emphasized to promote the brotherhood of all men.

7. The facts on crime, sexual immorality, and the recent public disorders all show we have to crack down harder on deviant groups and troublemakers if we are going to save our moral standards and preserve law and order.

*8. A lot of our society's rules regarding modesty and sexual behavior are just customs which are not necessarily any better or holier than those which other peoples follow.

*9. Our prisons are a shocking disgrace. Criminals are unfortunate people who deserve much better care, instead of so much punishment.

10. Obedience and respect for authority are the most important virtues children should learn.

*11. Organizations like the army and the priesthood have a pretty unhealthy effect upon men because they require strict obedience of commands from supervisors.

12. One good way to teach certain people right from wrong is to give them a good stiff punishment when they get out of line.

*13. Youngsters should be taught to refuse to fight in a war unless they themselves agree the war is just and necessary.

14. It may be considered old-fashioned by some, but having a decent, respectable appearance is still the mark of a gentleman and, especially, a lady.

15. In these troubled times laws have to be enforced without mercy, es-

pecially when dealing with the agitators and revolutionaries who are stirring things.

*16. Atheists and others who have rebelled against the established religions are no doubt every bit as good and virtuous as those who attend church regularly.

17. Young people sometimes get rebellious ideas, but as they grow up they ought to get over them and settle down.

*18. Rules about being "well-mannered" and respectable are chains from the past that we should question very thoroughly before accepting.

*19. The courts are right in being easy on drug offenders. Punishment would not do any good in cases like these.

20. If a child starts becoming a little too unconventional, his parents should see to it he returns to the normal ways expected by society.

21. Being kind to loafers or criminals will only encourage them to take advantage of your weakness, so it's best to use a firm, tough hand when dealing with them.

*22. A "woman's place" should be wherever she wants to be. The days when women are submissive to their husbands and social conventions belong strictly in the past.

*23. Homosexuals are just as good and virtuous as anybody else, and there is nothing wrong with being one.

24. It's one thing to question and doubt someone during an election campaign, but once a man becomes the leader of our country we owe him our greatest support and loyalty.

Note: *, Reversed (contrait) items.

Four-Item F Scale

(Lane, 1955)

Variable

This is a very short F scale designed for use in survey research with cross-sectional samples.

Description

This scale was derived by a Guttman analysis of ten modified F-scale items included by the Survey Research Center in its 1952 postelection survey. Some of the items were based on ones modified from the original F scale for F. H. Sanford and Older's (1950) survey in Philadelphia. Interested in unidimensionality, Lane analyzed the 10 items and found 4 that met Guttman scale criteria.

Sample

The 565 respondents in this national survey were a subsample that had been randomly selected from a stratified sample of American adults. (The cutting point on classification as authoritarian is not specified but the authoritarians outnumbered the "equalitarians" by a ratio of roughly two to one).

Reliability

Internal Consistency

The four-item Guttman scale yielded a coefficient of reproducibility of 90.4, which meets the minimal criteria for unidimensionality.

Test–Retest

No test–retest data are reported.

Validity

Convergent

Lane found the high authoritarians to be less tolerant of ambiguity, more ethnocentric, more projective (at the lower educational levels), more moralistic, and more tough in their attitude on foreign affairs than are the equalitarian types.

Discriminant

At three educational levels (grade school, high school and college), Democratic voters were slightly less authoritarian than the Republican voters.

Location

Lane, R. E. (1955). Political personality and electoral choice. *American Political Science Review,* **49,** 173–190.

Results and Comments

Although all of the items are worded positively, the spread of agreement on individual items indicates that simple agreement response set cannot account for as much variance as is true on most versions of the F scale when administered to a cross-sectional sample. Although the items are almost 40 years old their content does not appear to be dated.

This would appear to be the best short form of the F scale currently available for use in large cross-sectional studies of the population.

Four-Item F Scale

1. What young people need most of all is strict discipline by their parents. (agree: 76%)

   DISAGREE   AGREE

2. Most people who don't get ahead just don't have enough will power. (agree: 64%)

3. A few strong leaders could make this country better than all the laws and talk. (agree: 51%)

4. People sometimes say that an insult to your honor should not be forgotten. Do you agree or disagree with that? (agree: 25%)

Note: Percentage agree response from a national sample in 1952.

Traditional Family Ideology (TFI)
(Levinson & Huffman, 1955)

Variable

This scale was designed to assess differences in family ideology along an authoritarian–democratic dimension as a direct extension of the *TAP* to more general areas.

Description

The scale is composed of 40 items scored along the usual 1–7 scale, with six of the items worded in the antitraditional direction and reverse scored. The items were divided into four a priori content areas; parent–child relationships, husband–wife relationships, general male–female relationships, and general values and goals. They were designed to tap the personality characteristics of extreme conventionalism, authoritarian submission, exaggerated masculinity and femininity, extreme emphasis on discipline, and a moralistic rejection of impulse life. Scores vary from 1 (low traditional ideology) to 7 (high traditional ideology).

Sample

The sample consisted of 109 full- and part-time students in adult evening Cleveland college psychology classes, with an average age in the middle 20s.

Reliability

Internal Consistency

The split-half reliability was .84.

Test–Retest

No test–retest data are reported.

Validity

Convergent

The TFI correlated .73 with an abbreviated form of the F scale. Although there was the expected relationship between judged authoritarianism of religious denominations, there was so much variability among members of individual groups in the sample that the overall difference was not significant. However, regular church attenders had a significantly higher TFI score than those who never went to church, and those who shifted away from their parents' religion had significantly lower scores than those who retained their parents' religion.

Location

Levinson, D. J., & Huffman, P. E. (1955). Traditional family ideology and its relation to personality. *Journal of Personality, 23,* 251–275.

Results and Comments

This scale is particularly relevant because the items relating to child rearing were among the most consistently discriminating items in *TAP* and this scale represents an elaboration by one of the original co-authors. With the dramatic changes in patterns of sex roles and attitudes over the years, many of the items in the TFI need updating.

This scale is mainly an historical source for items and needs to be reworked for contemporary populations.

Traditional Family Ideology Scale

A. Parent–Child Relationships: Child-Rearing Techniques

*39. A child should not be allowed to talk back to his parents, or else he will lose respect for them. (II, IV)

STRONGLY SOMEWHAT SLIGHTLY SLIGHTLY SOMEWHAT STRONGLY
DISAGREE DISAGREE DISAGREE AGREE   AGREE   AGREE

40. There is a lot of evidence such as the Kinsey Report that shows we have to crack down harder on young people to save our moral standards. (IV, V)

58. There is hardly anything lower than a person who does not feel a great love, gratitude, and respect for his parents. (II)

33. A well-raised child is one who doesn't have to be told twice to do something. (II, IV)

56. A woman whose children are messy or rowdy has failed in her duties as a mother. (II, V)

15. It isn't healthy for a child to like to be alone, and he should be discouraged from playing by himself. (I, V)

22. If children are told much about sex, they are likely to go too far in experimenting with it. (I, V)

57. A child who is unusual in any way should be encouraged to be more like other children. (I, V)

45. The saying "Mother knows best" still has more than a grain of truth. (I, II)

9. Whatever some educators may say, "Spare the rod and spoil the child" still holds, even in these modern times. (IV)

21. It helps the child in the long run if he is made to conform to his parents' ideas. (II, IV)

*3. A teen-ager should be allowed to decide most things for himself. (II, IV)

*27. In making family decisions, parents ought to take the opinions of children into account. (II, IV)

51. It is important to teach the child as early as possible the manners and morals of his society. (I)

52. A lot of the sex problems of married couples arise because their parents have been too strict with them about sex. (IV, V)

B. Husband and Wife Roles and Relationships

31. Women who want to remove the word obey from the marriage service don't understand what it means to be a wife. (II, III)

20. Some equality in marriage is a good thing, but by and large the husband ought to have the main say-so in family matters. (III)

28. One of the worst problems in our society today is "free love" because it mars the true value of sex relations. (I, V)

34. It is only natural and right for each person to think that his family is better than any other. (I, II)

4. A marriage should not be made unless the couple plans to have children. (I, V)

38. A man who doesn't provide well for his family ought to consider himself pretty much a failure as husband and father. (I, III)

14. Faithlessness is the worse fault a husband could have. (I, III)

44. In choosing a husband, a woman will do well to put ambition at the top of her list of desirable qualities. (III)

7. A wife does better to vote the way her husband does, because he probably knows more about such things. (II)

8. It is reflection on a husband's manhood if his wife works. (III, V)

*43. Women should take an active interest in politics and community problems as well as in their families. (I, III)

C. General Male–Female Relationships: Concepts of Masculinity and Femininity

46. A man can scarcely maintain respect for his fiancee if they have sexual relations before they are married. (III)

50. It goes against nature to place women in positions of authority over men. (II, III)

37. It is a woman's job more than a man's to uphold our moral code, especially in sexual matters. (III)

49. The unmarried mother is morally a greater failure than the unmarried father. (III)

26. The most important qualities of a real man are strength of will and determined ambition. (III)

25. Women can be too bright for their own good. (II, III)

*10. Women have as much right as men to sow wild oats. (III, V)

16. Petting is something a nice girl wouldn't want to do. (III, V)

13. Women think less clearly than men and are more emotional. (III)

1. Almost any woman is better off in the home than in a job or profession. (I, III)

32. It doesn't seem quite right for a man to be visionary; dreaming should be left to women. (III, V)

*19. Even today women live under unfair restrictions that ought to be done away with. (II, III)

2. It's a pretty feeble sort of man who can't get ahead in the world. (III)

D. General Values and Aims

55. The family is a sacred institution, divinely ordained. (I, II)

Note: *, Reverse scored. The numbers in parentheses at the end of each item refer to the following personality variables they are thought to tap: I, conventionalism; II, authoritarian submission; III, exaggerated masculinity and femininity: IV, extreme emphasis on discipline; V, moralistic rejection of impulse life.

Dogmatism (D) Scale

(Rokeach, 1956)

Variable

This scale was designed to measure individual differences in open versus closed belief systems, designed to encompass both right and *left* authoritarianism.

Description

The original scale consisted of 78 items designed to tap a variety of functional aspects of belief systems. All items were worded so that agreement was scored high on dogmatism and scored on a seven-point scale. After a number of item analyses Rokeach came to rely on a 40-item version, Form E. Scores can vary from 1 (low dogmatism) to 7 (high dogmatism).

Sample

The samples were composed of 202, 186, and 153 Michigan State University students, 207 college students in New York City, 137 students at the University of London, 80 students at Birkbeck College (England), and 60 English workers.

Reliability

Internal Consistency

The reliabilities (split-half) on Form E given to the Birkbeck students and English workers were reported as being .81 and .78 respectively. Altemeyer found a reliability of .82 for

Manitoba students, so the reliability seems stable although lower than most 40-item scales that are unilaterally worded.

Validity

Convergent

One finding that would support Rokeach's argument would be that members of politically extreme right and left groups have higher scores on the Dogmatism scale than members of the political center. Among his sample of 135 English college students, Communists and Conservatives were only slightly more dogmatic than Liberals or Laborites, whereas the F-scale differences displayed the usual significant linear pattern with Conservatives scoring highest and Communists lowest (Rokeach, 1956, Table 13, p. 34). In Kohn's (1974) English study, a weak and nonsignificant linear trend was found on the Dogmatism scale with Conservatives highest and "Socialists" (a mixture of Communists, Trotskyists, Maoists, and New Leftists) lowest. The most compelling evidence comes from a study of 134 members of the Italian House of Deputies. Di Renzo (1967) gave them the D scale and found highly significant (but not completely linear) differences among members of the major political parties. Those belonging to the two most right-wing political parties had significantly higher D-scale scores than those of the two most left-wing parties.

In a study involving extreme behavior rather than group membership, Barker (1963) compared 29 "organized leftists" (i.e., protestors against restriction of free speech at the university), 561 controls, and 26 "organized rightists" (i.e., supporters of the university administration) at Ohio State University. The F scale discriminated appropriately and linearly among the three groups at better than the .001 level; however, contrary to Rokeach's theory, the leftists did not differ significantly from the neutral group on dogmatism. The rightists were most dogmatic although not as sharply as on the F scale (.02 level of significance) when compared with the neutral group.

Granberg and Corrigan (1972) administered both the F and D Scales to University of Missouri students in regard to the Vietnam War and found " . . . F scale–VNW (a composite of attitudes and protest activity) relationships significantly stronger, more stable, and persistent than D (scale) and VNW relationship" (p. 475). In Altemeyer's "pitting" experiments, the D scale explained consistently lower variance (5%) than the RWA scale (27%) in reaction to governmental injustices. The D scales also were less predictive than any of the other scales in studies involving a modification of Kohlberg's moral dilemmas and a modification of the Milgram obedience paradigm.

Discriminant

Kline and Cooper's (1984) correlation of + .23 between a counterbalanced A-R Scale and a counterbalanced version of dogmatism with unclear psychometric properties suggests the two scales are relatively independent of one another. P. M. Kohn (1974) found a correlation of + .48 between the A-R Scale and a short unilaterally worded version of the Dogmatism Scale (which had a surprisingly low reliability of .48). However, Lee and Warr (1969) found an average correlation of only + .23 between their balanced F Scale and the D Scale in four American samples.

The pattern of markedly lower correlations when F is counterbalanced leads to the conclusion that the major part of the common variance of the F and D scales is due to agreement response set. The finding that there is some slight overlap between the factors in the two scales (Kerlinger & Rokeach, 1966) is believed to account for a smaller amount of the correlation, leaving practically no construct overlap between the two scales.

Location

Rokeach, M. (1956). Political and religious dogmatism: An alternative to the authoritarian personality. *Psychological Monographs*, **70** (Whole No. 425).

Results and Comments

Rokeach's intention in constructing the dogmatism scale was to design a scale that would be a better measure of general authoritarianism than the F Scale. Evaluation of this is complicated by the fact that the items in both scales are dogmatic in style and are all scored in the same direction. To what extent are the correlations between D and F of $+.62$ and $+.77$ in the two English samples enhanced by response set and how much are they tapping the same or similar constructs?

Similar magnitudes of correlations in other studies have led some investigators to assume the two scales are measuring essentially the same thing. The D Scale is clearly not measuring the right-wing authoritarianism tapped by the F Scale. It does not appear to be measuring "general" authoritarianism in the political sphere if the term implies that members of both right and left groups or those displaying radical or conservative behavior score higher than their more complacent peers. Use of the D Scale as an alternative to the F or RWA Scale, then, is not recommended, but dogmatism is an intriguing construct in its own right requiring separate investigation.

The Dogmatism Scale

1. The United States and Russia have just about nothing in common.

1	2	3	4	5	6	7
STRONGLY DISAGREE						STRONGLY AGREE

2. The highest form of government is a democracy and the highest form of democracy is a government run by those who are most intelligent.
3. It is only natural that a person would have much better acquaintance with ideas he believes in than with ideas he opposes.
4. Man on his own is a helpless and miserable creature.
5. It is only natural for a person to be rather fearful of the future.
6. It is better to be a dead hero than to be a live coward.
7. While I don't like to admit this even to myself, my secret ambition is to become a great man, like Einstein, or Beethoven, or Shakespeare.
8. Most of the ideas which get printed nowadays aren't worth the paper they are printed on.
9. In the history of mankind there have probably been just a handful of really great thinkers.
10. A man who does not believe in some great cause has not really lived.
11. When it comes to differences of opinion in religion we must be careful not to compromise with those who believe differently from the way we do.
12. A group which tolerates too much difference of opinion among its members cannot exist for long.

13. There are two kinds of people in this world: those who are for the truth and those who are against the truth.

14. In this complicated world of ours the only way we can know what's going on is to rely on leaders or experts who can be trusted.

15. The present is all too often full of unhappiness. It is only the future that counts.

16. If a man is to accomplish his mission in life it is sometimes necessary to gamble "all or nothing at all."

17. Even though freedom of speech for all groups is a worthwhile goal, it is unfortunately necessary to restrict the freedom of certain political groups.

18. Fundamentally, the world we live in is a pretty lonesome place.

19. There is so much to be done and so little time to do it in.

20. The main thing in life is for a person to want to do something important.

21. There are a number of people I have come to hate because of the things they stand for.

22. It is only when a person devotes himself to an ideal or cause that life becomes meaningful.

23. In times like these, a person must be pretty selfish if he considers primarily his own happiness.

24. The worst crime a person could commit is to attack publicly the people who believe in the same thing he does.

25. My blood boils whenever a person stubbornly refuses to admit he's wrong.

26. It is often desirable to reserve judgment about what's going on until one has had a chance to hear the opinions of those one respects.

27. In the long run the best way to live is to pick friends and associates whose tastes and beliefs are the same as one's own.

28. Unfortunately, a good many people with whom I have discussed important social and moral problems don't really understand what's going on.

29. Most people just don't give a "damn" for others.

30. Once I get wound up in a heated discussion I just can't stop.

31. If given the chance I would do something of great benefit to the world.

32. Of all the different philosophies which exist in this world there is probably only one which is correct.

33. In times like these it is often necessary to be more on guard against ideas put out by people or groups in one's camp than by those in the opposing camp.

34. A person who thinks primarily of his own happiness is beneath contempt.

35. Most people just don't know what's good for them.

36. I'd like it if I could find someone who would tell me how to solve my personal problems.

37. In a discussion I often find it necessary to repeat myself several times to make sure I am being understood.

38. A person who gets enthusiastic about too many causes is likely to be a pretty "wishy-washy" sort of person.

39. In a heated discussion I generally become so absorbed in what I am going to say that I forget to listen to what others are saying.

40. To compromise with our political opponents is dangerous because it usually leads to the betrayal of our own side.

Some Basic Comments on Authoritarianism

Research on authoritarianism over the past half century makes it possible to describe the key conceptual elements of a multifaceted syndrome. There have been at least a dozen factor analyses of the F scale on different samples that have indicated that *TAP*'s hypothesized variables of conventionality, authoritarian aggression, authoritarian submission, anti-intraception, superstition and stereotypy, power and "toughness," destructiveness and cynicism, projectivity, and concern with sex have not hung together empirically in any known sample. Furthermore, there is agreement neither about the number of factors nor which items falls empirically on which factor in these various studies.

It would be unrealistic to expect complete congruence since one would expect differences resulting from the use of samples varying in demographic background, the frequent use of small samples with a lack of stability of responses, and the assignment of items to categories reflecting the theories of the authors of *TAP* (rather than the many factors leading respondents to interpret semiprojective items from different frames of reference). At the same time, items referring to strictness in child rearing emerge on a main factor in almost every factor analytic study.

In his systematic revision of authoritarianism items, Altemeyer retained the following two from the original F scale: "Obedience and respect for authority are the most important virtues children should learn" (*TAP*, Conventionalism and Submission to Authority); and "Young people sometimes get rebellious ideas, but as they grow up they ought to get over them and settle down" (*TAP*, Authoritarian Submission). These 2 items also appear among the 10 on the first factor, acceptance of authority, found by Bales and Couch (1969) in their Value Profile, which began with a pool of 252 items. Two additional original F scale items appeared on this factor: "There is hardly anything lower than a person who does not feel a great love, gratitude, and respect for his parents" (*TAP*, Authoritarian Aggression); and "What youth needs most is strict discipline and rugged determination, and the will to work and fight for family and country" (*TAP*, Authoritarian Aggression and Power and "Toughness").

Schooler had used 11 modified F-scale items in his study of the antecedents of authoritarianism. Even in a popularized wording the item with the highest loading in a factor analysis was "The most important thing to teach children is absolute obedience to their parents" (Kohn & Schooler, 1969, Table 4, p. 668).

An additional twist was provided by Steiner and Fahrenberg (1970), who translated 21 items from various forms of the F scale and administered them to German veterans some 20 years after the end of World War II. Item-by-item scores of 229 veterans of the notorious Waffen-SS (the highly selected and indoctrinated storm troopers) and 202 veterans of the regular German army (the Wehrmacht) showed highly significant differences. The most discriminating item found the SS with an item mean of 6.2 compared with 4.3

for the Wehrmacht veterans (on a seven-point scale). The item was *"Was Die Jugend am meisten braucht, ist strenge Disziplin, feste Entschlossenheit und den Willen zur Arbeit und zum Kampf fur Familie und Vaterland."*

Steiner and Fahrenberg did not use the "obedience and respect for authority" item. (The closest item in meaning is the one above which Bales and Couch found loaded on their first factor.) This item also showed very high discriminatory value in the original work on the Form 60 F scale [Adorno *et al.,* 1950 item 19, Table G, VII, p. 253 and item 13 on the Form 40–45 (Table 9, [VII], p. 260)].

It would thus appear that the largest common element in the authoritarian syndrome emphasizes discipline and conventionality in child rearing. Submission to ingroup figures and to institutions are closely related and suspicion of and hostility toward outgroup figures are involved less centrally. This fits the theoretical scheme advanced in *TAP,* with individuals endorsing strict and conventional child-rearing practices being more likely to score highly authoritarian in broader social contexts. At the same time, there is no known scientifically convincing evidence that such beliefs are tightly tied to actual parental behavior, or, more crucially, that exposure on the part of the child to such rearing leads to authoritarianism. In the 1970 Dutch study, a correlation of $+.15$ was reported between respondents' reports of severity of parental punishment and scores on a short version of the F scale (Meloen & Middendorp, 1988, p. 13). Such retrospective evaluations, of course, are notoriously unreliable; yet the simultaneous correlation between parents and college students' F-scale scores is usually about $+.35$. As with the myriad demographic variables significantly related to F-scale scores, whether it is practices in the immediate family or extra-familial influences such as peers, schools, media, church, and the broader web of social interactions, it is unclear what the cause and effect relationships actually are.

Nonideological Personality Measures Related to Authoritarianism

All the original F-scale items were worded in the third person and captured an implicit *Weltanshauung* with right-wing authoritarian overtones. Inferences about personality characteristics such as rigidity, intolerance of ambiguity, or projectivity were based upon comparison of high and low scorers on the E and F scales on such instruments as projective sentences, Thematic Apperception tests, or the Rorschach. The only standardized personality questionnaire used was the MMPI, used on clinic patients.

Early efforts to relate the F scale to standardized personality instruments uncovered few significant relationships between authoritarianism and measures of psychopathology (Masling, 1954). The focus then changed to finding items of personality attributes that differentiated between high and low authoritarians. Among these are the New F scale (Webster, Sanford, & Freedman, 1955), the Pensacola Z scale (Jones, 1957), the Rigidity scale (Rehfisch, 1958), and the Intolerance of Ambiguity scale (Budner, 1962).

Not surprisingly, items from a variety of personality self-description scales tend to be associated with high scores on the California F scale. Without computers, it was unfeasible for these early studies to examine the interrelationships of large pools of items. It is therefore difficult to be precise about the underlying personality dimensions involved in the F syndrome except as some of the authors did by grouping the items in terms of apparent face content.

In a study that addressed this problem directly, Kline and Cooper (1984, p. 171) noted that although factor analysts have " . . . claimed to have sampled the whole field of personality variables . . ." that " . . . little evidence for the authoritarian personality could be found." Their examination of the matter led them to use two factorially based tests of personality variables in conjunction with five measures they believed relevant to authoritarianism.

Kline and Cooper used Cattell, Eber, and Tatsuoka's (1970) 16-PF global measure of personality and Eysenck and Eysenck's (1974) EPQ as examples of widely used tests measuring global personality variables. The Cattell *et al.* test was standardized on presumably normal samples; the Eysenck and Eysenck test was designed to be used with psychiatric patients.

They specified four criteria for measures believed relevant to the measurement of authoritarianism: (1) Common items that contributed to inflated correlations were excluded; (2) balanced scales that mitigated the effect of agreement response set were used; (3) other syndromes believed relevant to authoritarianism were covered; and (4) the effects of right-wing content were controlled.

Five scales that were believed to meet these criteria were used: (1) P. M. Kohn's (1972) A-R scale as a measure of authoritarianism; (2) Kline's (1971) Ai3Q test of anal or obsessive traits; (3) Ray's (1970) balanced Dogmatism scale; (4) Wilson and Patterson's (1968) Conservatism scale; and (5) Christie's (Christie & Geis, 1970) Machiavellianism scale.

The sample was composed of 94 carefully selected volunteer students from the University of Exeter who took the above tests in one 3-hour session that was part of a larger project. They were predominantly of high socioeconomic status and from a wide range of fields of study.

A very clear five-factor solution emerged in the analyses of data with correlations ranging from $-.14$ to $+.14$ among the factors (Kline & Cooper, 1984, Table 1, p. 174). The first factor clearly tapped authoritarianism with its highest loading (.84) on the Kohn A-R scale, followed by one of .67 on Cattell *et al.*'s 16-PF Conscientious Subscale, one of .60 on Kline's Ai3Q Obsessiveness scale, and one of .55 on Cattell *et al.*'s Q3 self-sentiment (high willpower) subscale. The interpretation of this factor was, " . . . our picture of the authoritarian personality—rigid, conscientious, and obsessive" (p. 175). As they noted (p. 174), "Now in the light of the original description of the authoritarian by Adorno and his colleagues, the findings are striking confirmation. . ."

In light of the earlier discussion it is interesting to note that this first factor did not correlate with the second factor measuring neuroticism. It also did not correlate with the third factor of Machiavellianism, which accords with the findings of Christie and Geis (1970). The fourth and fifth factors, which also did not correlate with the authoritarian factor, appear to tap primarily extroversion as measured by Eysenck and Eysenck and dominance as measured by Cattell. Since these two variables have not, as far as known, been postulated as being related to authoritarianism, this is not too surprising.

Authoritarianism and Social Psychological Research

Much early laboratory research was done by enthusiasts who were most interested in demonstrating that the construct measured by the F scale also manifested itself in other basic psychological ways. This literature is difficult to evaluate since it is very unevenly reported and many of the studies appear amateurish by contemporary standards.

The lack of standardization in laboratory research on authoritarianism contrasts with that using personality variables in which the instruments have known properties and in which cumulative knowledge has been obtained. Survey research, in which data collection is usually conducted by established organizations with systematized data collection procedures, is more similar to standardized personality research. Laboratory and/or field studies to date have involved much more idiosyncratic data collection procedures and there has been inadequate replication to permit solid conclusions. Altemeyer's (1981, 1988) programmatic research is a notable exception to one-shot studies.

Many of these studies were conducted before the importance of the interaction of persons in different situations became well understood. Many early investigators thus did not address the question of the conditions necessary for the elicitation of authoritarian behavior. In what situations do authoritarians display aggressive rather than submissive behavior? [See Altemeyer (1988) for provocative experimental evidence on this point.]

There are indications that authoritarianism measures can predict relevant behavior if that behavior is a response to conditions that would elicit authoritarian submission, authoritarian aggression, or conventionality. Crutchfield (1955) reported a correlation of +.39 between F-scale scores and yielding to group pressure in a variation of the Asch (1956) conformity paradigm. Altemeyer (1981, p. 201) reported a correlation of +.44 between the RWA scale and a replication of the Milgram (1974) obedience paradigm among a subsample of his Manitoba students. Zwillenberg (1983) found an overall correlation of +.38 between the RWA and severity of punishment for a variety of crimes in a factorial study which was based on a combination of variables used in previous research. Measures of authoritarianism (particularly the RWA) are robust enough, then, to predict behavior in relevant situations.

Future Research Directions

The construct of authoritarianism has been robust enough to weather over 40 years of methodological criticism varying from inept to ingenious, of political attack from right and left, and theoretical disputes as varied as the academic fields that touch upon the problems relating to individuals' relationship to authority. This review has highlighted a limited selection of material relevant to the best current ways of assessing authoritarian proclivities and some of the social variables that affect their measurement.

Despite myriad arguments and difficulties, there has been enough consistency in the basic research findings to justify further systematic research. Such research needs to build upon this base and attempt to specify conditions under which individuals with authoritarian proclivities are more or less likely to behave in an authoritarian manner.

One could also continue Kline and Cooper's (1984) line of analysis, which was conducted at the level of scales and subscales and did not indicate which items on the general scales were significantly related to the first factor of authoritarianism. One possibility for clarifying the relationship between ideological measures of authoritarianism and nonideological self-descriptive measures of personality would be to use as measures of authoritarianism Altemeyer's RWA scale, which focuses on the essence of authoritarianism, in conjunction with the Form 60A of the F scale, which has a broader range of referents. A combination of these two scales could be used as a baseline against which items in other nonideological personality scales, such as those used by Kline and Cooper and ones mentioned earlier, could be examined. One possibility would be to identify five groupings: consistent high, middle, and low scorers as well as those not responding primarily to content (e.g., yeasayers and naysayers).

Such a project would require a massive data collection attempt but the capacity of modern computers makes it a feasible one. A factor analysis of items would indicate which nonideological individual difference items fit together and how they are related to the best measures of the authoritarian syndrome.

An open question remains as to the generalizability of results to non-middle class samples. Very little is known about the nature or amount of variance accounted for by individual difference measures in these populations as compared with the major impact of demographic variables.

Survey and Political Science Research

One of the consistent findings in representative national samples is the high negative correlations between positively worded F-scale items and measures of socioeconomic status. Campbell *et al.* (1960) found the Christie *et al.* "soft" reversals were agreed to even more strongly by samples with low education than those with high school or college education. Altemeyer's "hard" RWA reversals show no difference in mean scores when compared with the original items among samples of college students who varied along a social sophistication dimension. In short, respondents who were older, in less selective colleges, were religiously fundamental, and in applied fields disagreed as strongly with the reversed items as they agreed with the originals (Zwillenberg, 1983).

Would this hold in representative national samples? Altemeyer (1981, p. 211) reports a correlation of $-.36$ between RWA and education among a nonrepresentative sample of Winnipeg 20–60-year-old males. He also reported (p. 242) a range of correlations of from $-.24$ to $-.30$ among respondents who are, of course, of higher social status and more homogeneous educationally than a representative sample.

Administering Altemeyer's items to a representative sample would reveal whether the negative correlation between authoritarianism and education found on unilaterally worded versions of the F scale is due to response set or to ideologically consistent authoritarianism. Would Altemeyer's items show greater ideological consistency among at least some working-class members than that reported using the Christie *et al.* "soft" reversals?[3]

Acknowledgments

The assistance of James Ortiz, who assiduously searched other libraries for journals and books purloined, lost, or otherwise not in the Columbia University Library system was invaluable. I am also indebted to James H. Johnson and Robert Dushay for statistical analyses of unpublished data, which strongly affected some of the evaluations made herein. A final word of thanks goes to Jos D. Meloen for providing information on European research on authoritarianism.

Bibliography

Adorno, T. W., Frenkel-Brunswik, E., Levinson, D. J., & Sanford, R. N. (1950). *The authoritarian personality*. New York: Harper.
Altemeyer, B. (1981). *Right-wing authoritarianism*. Winnipeg: University of Manitoba Press.
Altemeyer, B. (1988). *Enemies of freedom*. San Francisco: Jossey-Bass.
Asch, S. E. (1956). Studies of independence and conformity: a minority of one against a unanimous majority. *Psychological Monographs*, **70**, No. 9 (Whole Number 416).

[3]Since response set measures are orthogonal (i.e., psychometrically independent) to measures of content (authoritarianism), it would be worthwhile to conduct secondary analyses of RWA scale scores using a discrepancy score (the sum of scores on positive items minus the scores on reversed items). The expectation, based on research with the Christie *et al.* scale and Couch and Kenniston's work, would be that those with extreme discrepancy scores, the yeasayers and naysayers, would have different psychological and demographic background characteristics than the ideologically consistent high and low scorers on the RWA scale.

Bales, R., & Couch, A. (1969). The value profile: A factor analytic study of value statements. *Sociological Inquiry*, **39**, 3–17.

Barker, E. N. (1963). Authoritarianism of the political right, center, and left. *Journal of Social Issues*, **19**, 287–297.

Bass, B. M. (1955). Authoritarianism or acquiescence? *Journal of Abnormal and Social Psychology*, **51**, 616–623.

Brown, J. F. (1942). The origin of the anti-Semitic attitude. In I. Graeber & S. H. Britt (Eds.), *Jews in a gentile world*. New York: Macmillan.

Budner, S. (1962). Intolerance of ambiguity as a personality variable. *Journal of Personality*, **30**, 29–50.

Bushan, L. I. (1969). A comparison of four Indian political groups on a measure of authoritarianism. *Journal of Social Psychology*, **79**, 141–142.

Campbell, A., Converse, P. E., Miller, W., & Stokes, D. E. (1960). *The American voter*. New York: Wiley.

Cattell, R. B., Eber, H. W., & Tatsuoka, H. M. (1970). *Handbook to the 16 personality factor questionnaire*. Champaign, IL: Institute for Personality and Ability Testing.

Christie, R. (1954). Authoritarianism re-examined. In R. Christie & M. Jahoda (Eds.), *Studies in the scope and method of "The Authoritarian Personality."* Glencoe, IL: Free Press.

Christie, R., & Garcia, J. (1951). Subcultural variation in authoritarian personality. *Journal of Abnormal and Social Psychology*, **46**, 457–459.

Christie, R., & Geis, F. L. (1970). *Studies in Machiavellianism*. New York: Academic Press.

Christie, R., Havel, J., & Seidenberg, B. (1958). Is the F scale irreversible? *Journal of Abnormal and Social Psychology*, **56**, 143–159.

Couch, A., & Keniston, K. (1960). Yeasayers and naysayers: Agreeing response set as a personality variable. *Journal of Abnormal and Social Psychology*, **60**, 151–174.

Cronbach, L. J. (1946). Response sets and test validity. *Educational and Psychological Measurement*, **6**, 475–494.

Crowne, D. P., & Marlowe, D. (1960). A new scale of social desirability independent of psychopathology. *Journal of Consulting Psychology*, **24**, 349–354.

Crutchfield, R. (1955). Conformity and character. *American Psychologist*, **10**, 191–198.

Deutsch, K. W., Platt, J., & Senghass, D. (1971). Conditions favoring major advances in the social sciences. *Science*, **171** 450–479.

Di Renzo, G. J. (1967). *Personality, power, and politics*. Notre Dame, IN: Univ. of Notre Dame Press.

Edwards, A. L. (1941). Unlabeled fascist attitudes. *Journal of Abnormal and Social Psychology*, **36**, 579–582.

Edwards, A. L. (1957). *The social desirability variable in personality assessment and research*. New York: Dryden Press.

Eysenck, H. J., & Eysenck, S. B. G. (1964). *Manual of the Eysenck Personality Inventory*. London: London Univ. Press.

Frenkel-Brunswik, E., & Sanford, R. N. (1945). Some personality factors in anti-Semitism. *Journal of Psychology*, **20**, 271–291.

Freud, S. (1939). *Moses and monotheism*. New York: Knopf.

Granberg, D., & Corrigan, G. (1972). Authoritarianism, dogmatism, and orientations toward the Vietnam War. *Sociometry*, **35**, 468–476.

Handlon, B. J., & Squier, L. H. (1955). Attitudes toward special loyalty oaths at the University of California. *American Psychologist*, **10**, 121–127.

Hoogvelt, A. M. M. (1969). Ethnocentrism, authoritarianism, and Powellism. *Race*, **11**, 1–12.

Hyman, H. H., & Sheatsley, P. B. (1954). "The Authoritarian Personality.": A methodological critique. In R. Christie & M. Jahoda (Eds.), *Studies in the scope and method of "The Authoritarian Personality."* Glencoe, IL: Free Press.

Janowitz, M., & Marvick, D. (1953). Authoritarianism and political behavior. *Public Opinion Quarterly*, **17**, 185–201.

Jay, M. (1973). *The dialectical imagination*. Boston: Little, Brown.

Jones, M. B. (1957). The Pensacola-Z survey: A study of authoritarian tendency. *Psychological Monographs*, **71**, (Whole No. 452).

Kerlinger, F., & Rokeach, M. (1966). The factorial nature of the F and D scales. *Journal of Personality and Social Psychology*, **4**, 391–399.

Kline, P. (1971). *Ai3Q Test*. Windsor, Berks: National Foundation for Educational Research.

Kline, P., & Cooper, C. (1984). A factorial analysis of the authoritarian personality. *British Journal of Psychology*, **75**, 171–176.

Kohn, M. L., & Schooler, C. (1969). Class, occupation, and orientation. *American Sociological Review*, **34**, 659–678.

Kohn, P. M. (1972). The Authoritarianism–Rebellion scale: A balanced F scale with left-wing reversals. *Sociometry*, **35**, 176–189.

Kohn, P. M. (1974). Authoritarianism, rebelliousness, and their correlates among British undergraduates. *British Journal of Social and Clinical Psychology*, **13**, 245–255.

Kohn, P. M., & Mercer, G. W. (1971). Drug use, drug use attitudes, and the authoritarianism–rebellion dimension. *Journal of Health and Social Behavior*, **12**, 125–131.

Lane, R. E. (1955). Political personality and electoral choice. *American Political Science Review*, **49**, 173–190.

Lederer, G. (1983). *Jugend und authoritat*. Opladen: Westdeutscher Verlag.

Lee, R. E., & Warr, P. B. (1969). The development and standardization of balanced F scale. *Journal of General Psychology*, **81**, 109–129.

Levinson, D. J., & Huffman, P. E. (1955). Traditional family ideology and its relation to personality. *Journal of Personality*, **23**, 251–275.

Levinson, D. J., & Sanford, R. N. (1944). A scale for the measurement of anti-Semitism. *Journal of Psychology*, **17**, 339–370.

Likert, R. (1932). A technique for the measurement of attitudes. *Archives of Psychology*, No. 140.

Lipetz, M. E. (1964). Authoritarianism and the use of information for the assessment of attitudes. *Journal of Social Psychology*, **46**, 315–319.

Lipset, S. M., & Raab, S. M. (1970). *The politics of unreason*. New York: Harper & Row.

Marquis, P. C. (1973). Experimenter–subject interaction as a function of authoritarianism and response set. *Journal of Personality and Social Psychology*, **25**, 279–286.

Masling, J. M. (1954). How neurotic is the authoritarian? *Journal of Abnormal and Social Psychology*, **54**, 316–318.

McFarland, S., Agayev, V., & Abalakina, M. (1990). Russian authoritarianism. In W. F. Stone, & G. Lederer (Eds.). *Strength and weakness: The authoritarian personality today*. New York: Springer-Verlag.

Meloen, J. D. (1983). *De Autoritaire Reaktie in Tijden van Welvaart en Krisis*. Unpublished doctoral dissertation, University of Amsterdam.

Meloen, J. D., & Middendorp, C. P. (1988). *Authoritarianism in the Netherlands: Ideology, personality or subculture*. Paper presented at the 11th annual meeting of the International Meetings of the Society of Political Psychology.

Milgram, S. (1974). *Obedience to authority*. New York: Harper & Row.

Milton, O., (1952). Presidential choice and performance on a scale of authoritarianism. *American Psychologist*, **7**, 597–598.

Newcomb, T. M. (1943). *Personality and social change*. New York: Dryden Press.

Newcomb, T. M., Koenig, K. E., Flacks, R., & Warwick, D. F. (1967). *Persistence and change: Bennington College and its students after 25 years*. New York: Wiley.

O'Connor, P. (1952). Ethnocentrism, intolerance of ambiguity, and abstract reasoning. *Journal of Abnormal and Social Psychology*, **47**, 526–530.

Pettigrew, T. F. (1959). Regional differences in anti-Negro prejudice. *Journal of Abnormal and Social Psychology*, **59**, 28–36.

Ray, J. J. (1970). The development and validation of a balanced dogmatism scale. *Australian Journal of Psychology*, **22**, 253–260.

Ray, J. J. (1971). An "attitude to authority" scale. *Australian Psychologist*, **6**, 31–50.

Rehfisch, J. M. (1958). A scale of personality rigidity. *Journal of Consulting Psychology*, **22**, 10–15.

Reich, W. (1946). *The mass psychology of fascism*. (T. P. Wolfe, Trans.). New York: Orgone Press.

Robinson, J. P., Rusk, J. G., & Head, K. B. (Eds.) (1973). *Measures of Political Attitudes*. Ann Arbor: Survey Research Center, University of Michigan.

Robinson, J. R., & Shaver, P. R. (Eds.) (1973). *Measures of social psychological attitudes*. Ann Arbor: Institute for Social Research, University of Michigan.

Rokeach, M. (1956). Political and religious dogmatism: An alternative to the authoritarian personality. *Psychological Monographs*, **70** (Whole No. 425).

Rokeach, M. (1960). *The open and closed mind*. New York: Basic Books.

Samelson, F. (1986). Authoritarianism from Berlin to Berkeley: On social psychology and history. *Journal of Social Issues*, **42**, 191–208.

Sanford, F. H., & Older, H. J. (1950). *Authoritarianism and leadership*. Philadelphia: Stephenson Brothers.

Sanford, R. N. (1968). The theory of the authoritarian personality. In L. S. Wrightsman, Jr. (Ed.), *Contemporary issues in social psychology*. Belmont, CA: Brooks/Cole.

Schooler, C. (1972). Social antecedents of adult psychological functioning. *American Journal of Sociology*, **78**, 299–322.

Schooler, C. (1976). Serfdom's legacy. *American Journal of Sociology*, **81**, 1265–1286.

Schulberg, H. C. (1961). Authoritarianism, tendency to agree, and interpersonal perception. *Journal of Abnormal and Social Psychology*, **63**, 481–488.

Scodel, A., & Freedman, M. L. (1956). Additional observations on the social perceptiveness of authoritarians and nonauthoritarians. *Journal of Abnormal and Social Psychology*, **52**, 92–95.

Shaver, P. (1973). Authoritarianism, dogmatism, and related measures. In J. P. Robinson & P. Shaver (Eds.), *Measures of social psychological attitudes*. Ann Arbor: Survey Research Center, University of Michigan.

Shils, E. A. (1954). Authoritarianism: Right and left. In R. Christie & M. Jahoda (Eds.), *Studies in the scope and method of "The Authoritarian Personality."* Glencoe, IL: Free Press.

Stagner, R. (1936). Fascist attitudes: An exploratory study. *Journal of Social Psychology*, **6**, 309–319.

Steiner, J. M., & Fahrenberg, J. (1970). Die auspragung autoritarer Einstellung bei ehamaligen Angehorigen der SS und der Werhmacht. *Kolner Zeitschrift fur Soziolozie und Sozial Psychologie*, **22**, 551–566.

Thurstone, L. L. (1929). Theory of attitude measurement. *Psychological Bulletin*, **36**, 222–241.

Thurstone, L. L. (1931). The measurement of social attitudes. *Journal of Abnormal and Social Psychology*, **26**, 249–269.

Tompkins, S. (1964). *Polarity test*. NY: Springer.

Trodahl, V. C., & Powell, F. A. (1965). A short form of the dogmatism scale for use in field situations. *Social Forces*, **49**, 211–214.

Vacchiano, R. B., Strauss, P. S., & Hochman, L. (1969). The open and closed mind: A review of dogmatism. *Psychological Bulletin*, **71**, 261–273.

Warr, P. B., & Faust, J. (1967). A British Ethnocentrism scale. *British Journal of Social and Clinical Psychology*, **61**, 267–272.

Webster, H., Sanford, N., & Freedman, M. (1955). A new instrument for measuring authoritarianism in personality. *Journal of Personality*, **40**, 73–85.

Williams, J. A. (1966). Regional differences in authoritarianism. *Social Forces*, **45**, 273–277.

Wilson, G. D., & Patterson, J. R. (1968). A new measure of conservatism. *British Journal of Social and Clinical Psychology*, **7**, 264–269.

Zwillenberg, D. F. (1983). *Predicting biases in the punishment of criminals as a function of authoritarianism: The effects of severity of crime, degree of mitigating circumstances, and the status of the offender*. Unpublished doctoral dissertation, Columbia University, New York.

CHAPTER 11

Sex Roles:
The Measurement of
Masculinity, Femininity, and
Androgyny

Ellen Lenney

Throughout recorded history, a person's gender has been, and remains, a central determinant of that person's identity and relationships with others. Social psychologists have studied sex differences and, more recently, sex roles or gender roles extensively. The topics remain among the most important ones in the fields of psychology and sociology.

Ever since Terman and Miles published the first masculinity–femininity test in 1936, the number of citations appearing in *Psychological Abstracts* under the key words "sex role," "masculinity," "femininity," and (since 1981) "androgyny" has grown impressively: from 62 citations during the years 1927–1960, to 215 in 1961–1971, to 447 in '972–1980, and to 760 in 1981–1986.

Problems of Definition

In general we refer to sex role characteristics as those characteristics that actually differentiate the sexes, are stereotypically believed to differentiate the sexes, or are considered to be differentially desirable in the two sexes. Despite their enormous popularity, however, even the most basic constructs, masculine and feminine sex roles, have consistently eluded clear definition on both conceptual and operational levels.

Conceptual Definitions

In Constantinople's (1973) landmark review of the field and search for theoretical definitions, it was concluded that masculinity and femininity

> seem to be among the muddiest concepts in the psychologist's vocabulary. . . . The most generalized definitions of the terms as they are used by those developing tests of M-F would seem to be that they are relatively enduring traits which are more or less rooted in anatomy, physiology, and early experience, and which generally serve to distinguish males from females in appearance, attitudes, and behavior (p. 390).

Not only is such a definition unmanageably broad, but all researchers do not agree that sexual distinctions belong in the definition. For example, as Spence (1985) notes, some theoretical approaches define sex roles as "the characteristics, attitudes, values, and behaviors that society specifies as appropriate" for males and females (p. 68). Still other approaches emphasize social structure in their definitions. Consider, for example, Gilbert's (1985) statement that "sex roles refer to normative expectations about the division of labor between the sexes and to gender-related rules about social interactions that exist within a particular culture or historical context" (p. 163; see also Angrist, 1969).

Given the muddiness of the broad term "sex role," many authors have proposed the use of other terms referring to various narrower aspects of sex roles. The resultant proliferation of terms has, however, frequently generated more confusion. First, not all authors define the same term in the same way. Consider, for example, the different definitions of "sex role orientation" of Biller (1968, p. 92): "an underlying, and not necessarily conscious, perception of the maleness or femaleness of the self" and of Nash (1979, p. 272): "Measures of sex role orientation attempt to distinguish between traditional and nontraditional ('liberated') sex-related roles, activities, careers, and life styles." Second, some terms seem to appear interchangeably in the literature. For example, what is the difference between "sex role orientation" as Biller defined it (above) and "gender identity" as Cramer and Carter (1978, p. 63) define it ("a basic underlying sense of one's maleness or femaleness, which is at least partly unconscious")?

Thus, basic concepts remain at least as unclear as they were when Constantinople reviewed the field more than 15 years ago. Interested readers are referred to the excellent discussions by Morawski (1985, 1987), Myers and Gonda (1982b), Nash (1979), and Spence (1985).

Operational Definitions of Sex Role Phenomena

Not only have different measurement devices been designed to tap each of the various concepts in this field, but sex role tests differ in numerous other ways, each of which has basic implications for the construct being assessed. The failure to recognize these implications explicitly and consistently is, unfortunately, a prevalent theme in sex role research. Five major, nonoverlapping kinds of differences can be distinguished:

1. The assumption that masculinity and femininity anchor opposite ends of a single continuum versus their existence as separate entities, which vary independently.

2. A variety of item selection strategies, including differences in endorsement rate by the two sexes; endorsement rates by other theoretically relevant groups (e.g., "father-identified" males versus "mother-identified" females) (Gough, 1952); cultural beliefs about the ideal or socially desirable attributes of the two sexes; and/or cultural beliefs about the typical attributes of the two sexes.

3. How many, and what, domains are tapped. For example, tests may measure personality traits, activity and/or vocational preferences, overt behaviors, and/or attitudes of various sorts.

4. The extent to which scale authors intended their measures to be internally homogeneous. At one extreme are authors who are concerned that their tests be factorially "pure"; at the other extreme are those who feel that, since society defines sex roles as heterogeneous conglomerates, it is appropriate that their tests reflect this heterogeneity.

5. Whether tests are self-report devices, behavioral observation techniques, projective methods, or observer trait-rating devices.

Relationships between Operational Definitions and Conceptual Phenomena

An additional source of confusion lies in the loose connections many authors draw between constructs and measurement devices. Each test does, in fact, employ a different definition of sex roles (masculinity and femininity), which can be described by the above five dimensions. Too many authors proceed cavalierly to compare results across studies using radically different instruments as if these tests were actually measuring exactly the same construct. Simply because two tests are labeled sex role measures, the results of research employing each test are assumed to illuminate a single hypothetical entity.

Some authors, noting such problems, advocate an abandonment of global sex-role terms. Spence (1984), for example, argues that "Such imperialistic constructs as masculinity, femininity, androgyny, and sex role identification, as they have typically been conceived, are overly simplistic and of limited scientific utility" (p. 3). Although these broad terms will undoubtedly continue in use, the field will not progress until authors are consistently scrupulous in keeping their particular operational definitions at the forefront.

Selected Issues in Sex Role Research: An Historical Overview

A few themes have broad relevance to sex role measurement and/or to what some authors consider important for sex role tests' construct validity. As is not the case in better integrated fields, authors of the most influential scales vary in their theoretical approach to sex role phenomena, and research using the various scales differs in important respects.

Prior to the early 1970s, tests were built upon the assumption that masculinity and femininity were polar opposites having a necessarily inverse relationship within the individual. Such unidimensional devices, often called M-F tests, scored respondents who fell at one of the two extremes as either masculine or feminine and those who fell between the two extremes as having a given amount of the single entity M-F.

Although the prevailing bipolar view did not logically dictate that persons falling at different points along the M-F continuum would differ in the extent to which they possessed desirable attributes, such an idea seems to have been an inextricable part of most researchers' sex role conceptions. Appropriate sex-typing was seen as important for good adjustment and mental health, broadly construed. Thus, the masculine male and the feminine female were believed to be psychologically advantaged relative to their less sex-typed counterparts. (Bem, 1972, provides some examples of this viewpoint.)

Influences from three disparate sources produced the 1970s revolution in sex role research. First, a few authors had already hypothesized that masculinity and femininity could vary independently and that existing tests might be artifactually forcing them into a negative relationship. (See Constantinople's 1973 review for examples.) Second, scattered in the literature were empirical data that should have challenged the idea that appropriate sex-typing was uniformly conducive to mental health (see Bem, 1972, for examples). Third, with the growth of the women's movement, increasing numbers of lay authors eloquently argued that traditional sex roles, both masculine and feminine, were restrictive and harmful to individual development (e.g., Friedan, 1963; Greer, 1971).

These conceptual, empirical, and social influences swept the field within a remarkably short period, along with three landmark events that produced an altered Zeitgeist. First was Constantinople's (1973) review of existing M-F tests, which gathered together persuasive evidence that these tests had artificially constrained the relationship between masculinity and femininity.

Second was Bem's (1974) publication of the first sex role test specifically designed to provide independent measures of the individual's masculinity and femininity. Using the Bem Sex Role Inventory (BSRI), Bem found that, while some persons were more or less exclusively masculine or feminine, others, called androgynous, have balanced levels of traits from both domains. Bem also expressed a clear position on a more political, value-laden question, that androgynous persons may actually be more psychologically healthy than sex-typed persons.

Third was the publication of an inventory by Spence, Helmreich, and Stapp (1974, 1975), measuring masculinity and femininity separately (the Personal Attributes Questionnaire or PAQ). The PAQ was developed simultaneously with, but independently from, Bem's instrument.

A rash of new two-dimensional sex role tests quickly appeared, which demonstrated that (a) masculinity and femininity scores often do vary independently; (b) an appreciable percentage of both men and women have high or low scores on both M and F scales; and (c) the older M-F tests and the model they embodied are therefore empirically inadequate in many respects.

Bem's contention that androgynous persons are psychologically advantaged relative to other sex role groups has been a popular position and has, in fact, been carried to extremes she never envisioned. It should be noted, however, that the now well-confirmed view that M and F scores do not always vary in lockstep is different from the idea of what personal or social consequences attend various relationships between M and F.

Controversies in Modern Sex Role Research

While space limitations preclude full consideration, many issues are still under debate by sex role researchers. A partial list follows:

1. For discussions and criticisms of one-dimensional, two-dimensional, and multidimensional views of sex roles and/or of the androgyny-as-ideal position, see Baumrind (1982), Bernard, (1981, 1984), Furby (1983), Heilbrun and Bailey (1986), Lenney (1979a, 1979b), Locksley and Colten (1979), Lott (1981), Marsh and Myers (1986), Morawski (1985, 1987), Sampson (1977), and Spence (1984, 1985).
2. Some of these sources also consider whether current sex-role tests adequately capture the concepts underlying "masculinity" and "femininity." For further discussion, see Jackson (1985), Myers and Gonda (1982b), and Pedhazur and Tetenbaum (1979).
3. Studies have assessed the relationship of sex roles to self-esteem and psychological well-being; reviews of this research include Bassoff and Glass (1982), Taylor and Hall (1982), and Whitley (1983, 1985). All conclude that masculinity is more closely related to well-being than are either femininity or androgyny.

The Selection of Measures for Review

Since the eight scales given detailed consideration in this chapter represent only about 5% of the more than 150 available, it is important to describe the decision rules for selection, and to mention some of the more important scales which the chapter does not review.

Thus, among the excluded measures were those developed to assess:

1. Respondent's stereotypic perceptions of each sex: A variety of such measures exist; perhaps the most frequently cited is the Sex Role Stereotype Questionnaire, developed by Rosenkrantz, Vogel, Bee, Broverman, and Broverman (1968). This instrument provided the basis from which the PAQ (Spence *et al.,* 1975) was developed. Another example is the De Cecco–Shively Social Sex Role Inventory (Shively, Rudolf, & De Cecco, 1978; Smith, 1983).

2. Respondent's sex-role attitudes: There are dozens of these, including the Attitudes toward Women Scale (AWS; Spence & Helmreich, 1972), which has extensive reliability and validity evidence. Another widely used scale is the Inventory of Feminine Values (Fand, 1955; Steinmann & Fox, 1974). See also the Attitudes toward the Males' Sex Role Scale (Doyle & Moore, 1978).

3. Developmental aspects of cognitions concerning sex roles: Tests have been devised to assess children's attainment of gender identity (here, referring to knowledge of own and others' gender), of gender stability (knowledge that gender remains invariant over time), and/or of gender constancy (knowledge that gender remains invariant across situations). The technique of Slaby and Frey (1975) assesses all three constructs listed above (see also Beere, 1979; Bussey & Bandura, 1984; Fagot, 1985). Measures of children's gender schematic processing were also excluded (see Martin & Halverson, 1983a, 1983b; Serbin & Sprafkin, 1986).

Among the measures that tap children's knowledge of adult sex roles or of adult stereotypes of sex roles is the Sex Stereotype Measure (Williams, Bennett, & Best, 1975).

4. Certain specific aspects of sex roles: The best examples of such relatively narrow measures are the various vocational preference tests that have M, F, and/or M-F scoring systems such as the Strong–Campbell Interest Inventory (Campbell, 1966; Campbell, Crichton, Hansen, & Webber, 1974) (see also Constantinople, 1973, and Lunneborg, 1975, for commentary on the use of this and other versions of the Strong Vocational Interest Blank).

5. "Disturbed" sex roles: Interesting examples here include Freund's two tests of "cross-gender identity": the Feminine Gender Identity Scale for Males (Freund, Nagler, Langevin, Zajac, & Steiner, 1974) and the Masculine Gender Identity Scale for Females (Blanchard & Freund, 1983).

6. Exaggerated sex roles: Two interesting examples are the Masculine Role Inventory (Snell, 1986) and the Hypermasculinity Inventory (Mosher & Sirkin, 1984).

7. Measures of sex role strain or conflict: A very interesting example, which assesses such conflict in men, is the Gender Role Conflict Scale (O'Neil, Helms, Gable, David, & Wrightsman, 1986).

To select next from among the dozens of remaining tests required the application of several other criteria. Only those instruments which have the sole or overwhelmingly predominant purpose of sex role measurement were included. This excluded tests that have been frequently used to assess sex roles but include many other subscales as well. For instance, there are large literatures referring to the M-F scales of the Minnesota Multiphasic Personality Inventory (MMPI) (e.g., Hathaway, 1956; see also Constantinople's 1973 review), of the Omnibus Personality Inventory (OPI) (e.g., Heist & Younge, 1968), and of the California Psychological Inventory (CPI) (e.g., Gough, 1957). The interested reader is referred to the *Mental Measurements Yearbook* (Mitchell, 1985), which gives comprehensive reviews of these tests.

In the selection of adult measures, only direct self-report devices were included. This led to the exclusion of projective devices, such as the Franck Drawing Completion Test

(Franck & Rosen, 1949), which has a large literature (e.g., see Berg, 1985; Harkey, 1982). Also, in selecting adult measures, I included only those that contain separate M and F scales. This dramatically narrowed the field.

Two final criteria required more subjective judgment, namely, only those measures were included that have enjoyed relatively frequent use in the last 10–15 years and/or show promise of frequent use in the coming decade and that have some degree of theoretical basis or rationale. The second criterion excluded measures by researchers who appeared fortuitously to stumble upon a technique (for example, for finding a sex-differentiating pattern when collecting data for another purpose.) The criterion of frequent use excluded Baldwin, Critelli, Stevens, and Russell's (1986) promising Sex Rep Test, which assesses sex role by means of idiographically elicited sex role constructs and which permits separate assessments of masculinity and femininity.

Adult Sex Role Measures: Practical Considerations and Recommendations

Choosing a Sex Role Test

It is recommended that researchers selecting one of the six adult measures reviewed in this chapter do so by considering these six questions.

1. Do the particular research purposes suggest that scale items should have been selected by certain kinds of criteria? The scales variously contain items selected for both their perceived typicality and perceived desirability in the two sexes (PAQ and SRBS), for only their sex-typed social desirability (BSRI and PRF ANDRO), for their ability to discriminate between persons identified with their same-sex, sex-typed parent (ACL scales), or for their ability to discriminate between the sexes (Baucom's measure).

2. Do the particular research purposes suggest that certain content domain(s) should be sampled by scale items? The BSRI, PAQ, and ACL scales contain trait descriptors that sample a more or less broad range of personality characteristics (see next two points also). The SRBS contains subscales assessing interests and self-reported behaviors in the areas of recreational activities, vocational interests, social and dating behaviors, and marital behaviors. The PRF ANDRO and Baucom's scales each contain items drawn from a wide variety of domains, ranging from personality characteristics, to activity preferences and self-reports of past and/or typical behaviors.

3. Do the particular research purposes suggest that some of the items should be relatively negative in social desirability? The BSRI, PAQ, SRBS, and PRF ANDRO all contain only items that have a relatively high level of social desirability. Baucom's measure and the ACL scales contain a mixture of socially desirable and undesirable items. The Extended Personal Attributes Questionnaire (EPAQ) (Spence, Helmreich, & Holahan, 1979; see PAQ review) contains subscales designed specifically to tap certain negative characteristics.

4. Do the particular research purposes suggest the need for homogeneous, factorially pure scales? If so, the best selection is the PAQ, which provides M and F scales that are each unidimensional. Indeed, they are so factorially pure that Spence frequently (e.g., 1985) refers to them as instrumental and expressive scales, respectively. For Spence (see PAQ section) this unidimensionality is a major general advantage of her scales over those that are more heterogeneous. However, factorial impurity is not necessarily damning to a scale's validity. Bem, for example, is unconcerned over the common finding that her scales contain several factors. To state her position simply: Bem (e.g., 1979) holds that

sex roles are inherently heterogeneous conglomerates of attributes clustered loosely to- gether by the culture, and it is therefore appropriate that her measurement device reflect this heterogeneity. Detailed consideration of the multidimensionality of sex roles can be found in Bernard's (1981, 1984) writings.

5. Does the literature on the particular dependent variable(s) of interest contain studies that mostly use one or another of the sex role tests? If so, is it more desirable to link up with this literature by using the same test, or to extend it by using a different one? Most of these scales have been used in a broad variety of ways. However, some topics (e.g., research on learned helplessness in women using Baucom's scales) seem to refer more frequently to one scale.

6. There is a basic question that underlies all of the above: What scale best captures the researcher's own theoretical conception of sex roles? Most investigators seem to use whichever scale is handiest, without much thought as to that scale's specific appropri- ateness to the research topic. More judicious scale selection procedures would ultimately result in much greater conceptual and operational clarity than currently characterize the field.

Choosing a Method of Scoring and/or Subject Classification

Each of the methods described below may, in theory, be used with any sex-role test that has separate M and F scales. In practice, however, the various methods have been used with different frequency across tests. What follows is a brief overview of the more common methods, and of the practical decisions each entails, as these might apply across scales.

Each method represents a different position on what *combination* of masculinity and femininity best characterizes androgyny. Some researchers design their methods around a particular theoretical position concerning androgyny; more rarely, others first examine their specific research data and then design the most appropriate method to capture what these data reveal (see Lenney, 1979b; Spence & Helmreich, 1979c; Spence, 1984, for discussions of these two kinds of approaches).

The major positions are that androgyny is best expressed as: (a) relatively high absolute M and F scores; (b) relatively balanced M and F scores; or (c) both high and balanced M and F scores. (Discussion of a fourth position, that androgynous persons are those whose self-concepts are not organized into masculine and feminine categories, appears in the BSRI description; see also Bem, 1981b, 1981c, 1985.)

Scoring by Absolute Amount of M and F

This means that the researcher uses these two scores separately, not combining them into a single score. Therefore, on one level, this approach is simple. Complexities arise in the decision concerning how high M and F scores must be for a person to be categorized as androgynous, and in the attendant selection of cutoff points for subject classification.

By far the most common technique across tests is the median split method, which divides subjects into sex role groups by whether their scores fall above or below the median M and F scores. This method defines subjects as masculine if their M score is above the M median, and their F score is below the F median; as feminine if their F score is above the F median, and their M score is below the M median; as androgynous if both of their scores are above the respective scale medians; and as undifferentiated (or indeter- minate) if both of their scores are below the respective scale medians. The median split approach was originally proposed by Spence et al. (1975) when the PAQ was first published. It is the earliest and most successful rival to Bem's (1974) balance score method, discussed below. In 1977, Bem concurred with Spence and her colleagues that the median split method may be most appropriate in many cases. (See, especially, the BSRI and PAQ sections.)

There has been much controversy over how best to determine the particular medians to be used in a given application of the median split method. The two nonoverlapping questions here are whether medians should be derived (a) from the particular research sample or from a normative sample; and (b) separately from each sex's score distributions or from a combined-sex score distribution. In their own research, Spence and Bem most frequently use medians derived from the particular combined-sex sample under study. Others (e.g., Baucom, see appropriate scale description) most frequently use within-sex medians, often based on normative groups but sometimes based on the particular research sample.

Much research (e.g., Handal & Salit, 1985; Kaplan & Sedney, 1980) has convincingly shown the obvious point that subject classification depends, often critically, upon the choice of medians. Spence (e.g., Spence & Helmreich, 1979c; 1984) and others (e.g., Mendelsohn, Weiss, & Feimer, 1982; Tellegen & Lubinski, 1983) argue that this is not an appropriate matter for concern: The categories so derived merely represent convenient groupings of persons who can be simply described as to their M and F levels, and not an absolute typology.

With regard to debates over the validity of various median split approaches it becomes critically important for researchers to recognize explicitly that, whatever medians they choose, they are categorizing subjects *relative to* particular others. With this as a guide, the issues raised become appropriately empirical. Researchers should also recognize that median split techniques do represent the conception of androgyny as high M and high F, but they do not necessarily embody a larger theoretical model. Spence (e.g., Spence & Helmreich, 1979c; 1984), frequently uses the median split approach in part because it makes the fewest a priori assumptions regarding the nature of the contributions made by M and F to various criterion variables.

Other cutoff points on M and F score distributions may also be used in subject classification. For example, Baucom often adopts an extreme groups approach, defining "high" as in the upper third of the M and F distribution and "low" as in the lower third. In contrast, Spence (e.g., Spence & Helmreich, 1979c; 1984) notes that, especially in cases where M and/or F have nonlinear relationships with other variables, classification by three- or four-way splits on M and F may be preferred.

In general, use of these subject classification approaches is very inconsistent in the literature. Therefore, one should be extremely careful when drawing comparisons: It is ironic that despite the attention given to the above debates, researchers infrequently note how choices of cutoff points may have produced dissimilarities of research results across specific studies.

Scoring by a Balance Approach

This means that the researcher first combines M and F scores to reflect a conception of androgyny as roughly equal amounts of masculinity and femininity. The resultant "androgyny index" may then be used as a continuous variable in correlational analyses and/or may be used to divide subjects into sex role groups according to their level of androgyny. The best-known index of this type is that originally used by Bem (1974) in scoring the BSRI: She derived a *t*-ratio for each subject that represents the difference between his or her mean M and F scores normalized with respect to the standard deviations of the subject's own M and F scores. If the resultant Androgyny Score is significant, subjects are classified as masculine or feminine depending upon which score is higher; if it is less than or equal to one, subjects are classified as androgynous. Remaining subjects are called near-masculine or near-feminine (see BSRI review). While Bem now most often uses the median split approach, she still expresses the idea that her original *t*-score method may capture an important aspect of androgyny and sex-typing; namely, that sex-typed persons cluster and differentiate between masculine and feminine attributes while androgynous persons do not (see, especially, her writings on gender schema theory, which give prominence to this aspect of persons' information processing; Bem, 1981c, 1985).

Scoring by a Combination of Both Absolute Amount and Balance of M and F

This technique also has several advocates. For example, Orlofsky and his colleagues (e.g., Orlofsky, Aslin, & Ginsburg, 1977) have used a difference-median split approach that combines aspects of the separate approaches described above; Heilbrun (e.g., Heilbrun & Pitman, 1979) (see ACL section) often uses an Androgyny Index that takes account of both the sum and the absolute difference between M and F scores. (See also Downing, 1979, and Kalin, 1979, for two other balance approaches.)

General Considerations and Recommendations

Since the median split method is most frequently used, it has the advantage that researchers who use it can link their results to a large literature (bearing in mind the need to emphasize differences in particular medians across studies). Also, the median split method can be used to discover or elucidate a fairly broad variety of relationships among M, F, and criterion variables (e.g., Spence, 1984; Spence & Helmreich, 1979c). In contrast, any method that combines M and F scores into a single index presupposes a particular conception of how M and F relate together to given criterion variables and loses information on the separate contributions of M versus F. Nonetheless, such methods seem appropriate when a researcher is testing a specific model of androgyny and/or has discovered through initial correlational analyses that M and F indeed bear a particular joint relationship to variables of interest.

Choosing a Data Analysis Approach

Just as selections of particular scoring and subject classification techniques often emerge from researchers' models of androgyny, so too do choices of data analytic methods. The two basic approaches and their implications are as follows:

The relationship between any criterion variable and M and/or F may be analyzed through correlational techniques (multiple regression) and/or analysis of variance approaches (which classify subjects by sex role group). Correlational approaches, of course, can preserve all information on individual variability in M and F scores, while analysis of variance techniques cannot. Currently, the most common of the latter techniques, used in conjunction with median split subject categorization, is a two-way [2 (high versus low M) × 2 (high versus low F)] analysis (with sex as a third factor, if appropriate) on the particular dependent variable. Since this two-way approach permits identification of separate M and F main effects as well as of their interaction, it is preferable to the sometimes used one-way analysis, which simply looks at differences across the four sex-role groups. (When androgyny indices or cutoff points other than medians are used in subject categorization, of course, the specific form of an analysis of variance will be different.)

Both Bem (since her 1977 article) and Spence (1984; compare with her position in Spence & Helmreich, 1979c) now routinely advocate the use of both correlational and analysis of variance approaches in order to characterize research data fully. As Spence (1984) wisely advises:

> Assuming that the participants in an investigation have not been preselected [if they have, analyses of group means are the only choice], the relationship between each [M and F] scale and any given criterion should first be determined by means of a correlational analysis to reveal the degree and shape . . . of any association that is present. The next statistical step is to determine whether the joint effects of M and F yield relationships that could not be reconstructed from the information found in the separate M and F correlations. The final step is to specify the joint effects (combination rule) of M and F. [Analysis of variance techniques are useful in both of the last steps.] (p. 56)

The literature contains numerous discussions and/or empirical comparisons of scoring, subject classification, and data analytic techniques and of the different models of androgyny implied or tested by various combinations of these techniques (e.g., Anderson, 1986; Briere, Ward, & Hartsough, 1983; Hall & Taylor, 1985; Taylor & Hall, 1982).

Adult Measures Reviewed Here

The six adult measures reviewed are presented in an order that roughly approximates their date of publication and their frequency of use:

1. The Bem Sex Role Inventory (BSRI) (Bem, 1974),
2. The Personal Attributes Questionnaire (PAQ) (Spence *et al.,* 1975),
3. The Personality Research Form ANDRO Scales (PRF ANDRO) (Berzins, Welling, & Wetter, 1978),
4. The Adjective Check List (ACL) M and F scales (Heilbrun, 1976),
5. The M and F scales developed from the CPI (Baucom, 1976), and
6. The Sex Role Behavior Scale (SRBS) (Orlofsky, 1981).

The Bem Sex Role Inventory (BSRI) (Bem, 1974) assesses masculinity and femininity in terms of the respondent's self-perceived possession of positive personality characteristics having sex-typed social desirability. It can also be used as a measure of gender schematicity in that it assesses the extent to which respondents spontaneously sort self-relevant information into distinct masculine and feminine categories. In taking the BSRI, the respondent indicates the degree to which each of 60 items is self-descriptive; time to complete is about 15 minutes. The 20 Masculinity and 20 Femininity scale items cover a fairly broad range of personality characteristics. These two scales are empirically independent and are not factorially pure, in accordance with Bem's position that sex roles are inherently heterogeneous. The BSRI has excellent reliability. It has been employed in research on an enormous variety of topics and has been used with respondents from a broad range of ages, populations, countries, and cultures. Results show that the BSRI's validity is quite good, especially when it is used along lines appropriate to the theoretical rationale that guided its development. Indeed, one of its advantages is its grounding in a complete theoretical position. Controversy exists over certain of the BSRI's psychometric properties as well as over the number and exact nature of behaviors that scores should be expected to predict. Nonetheless, the BSRI is the most frequently used measure in sex-role research, and is most often used as a standard to which other instruments are compared.

Second in frequency of use is the Personal Attributes Questionnaire (PAQ) (Spence *et al.,* 1974, 1975), which assesses masculinity and femininity in terms of the respondent's self-perceived possession of personality traits stereotypically believed to differentiate the sexes but considered socially desirable in both sexes. In taking the most popular form of the PAQ, the respondent indicates the degree to which each of 24 characteristics, presented in bipolar format, is self-descriptive; time to complete is about 15 minutes. The Masculinity and Femininity scales each have eight items. The remaining eight items, forming a Masculinity–Femininity Scale with characteristics considered more socially desirable in one sex than in the other, is rarely used in research. The 24-item PAQ has excellent reliability. Its empirically independent Masculinity and Femininity scales are each factorially pure, in accordance with Spence's intention to tap only the instrumental and expressive characteristics of sex roles, respectively. Although Spence holds the PAQ scores should therefore be expected to relate well only to phenomena directly influenced by these particular characteristics, the PAQ has been employed in research on an enormous variety of topics. It has been used with respondents from early through middle adulthood, from a wide range of populations, and from differing countries and cultures. The PAQ has highly satisfactory validity when used in ways suggested by its underlying rationale. Indeed, the PAQ shares with the BSRI the advantage of grounding in a well-developed theoretical position, although the latter differs importantly between the two measures. A number of interesting PAQ variants are available, including an extended version having negatively valued traits, and a version shown to be psychometrically adequate for use in middle childhood.

The Personality Research Form ANDRO (PRF ANDRO) (Berzins et al., 1978) assesses masculinity and femininity in terms of the respondent's agreement or disagreement with self-descriptive statements pertaining to positive characteristics that have sex-typed social desirability. Items were selected from the Personality Research Form (PRF) (D. N. Jackson, 1967) to be consistent with Berzins et al.'s (1978) evaluation of the BSRI scales' content themes: social–intellectual ascendancy, autonomy, and orientation toward risk (Masculinity); and nurturance, affiliative–expressive concerns, and self-subordination (Femininity). PRF ANDRO items sample a wide variety of domains, from personality characteristics to activity preferences and self-reports of past and/or typical behaviors. There are 29 Masculine and 27 Feminine scale items. This 56-item measure has been administered by itself, as part of the 400-item PRF, or as part of an 85-item inventory developed by Berzins et al. (1978). The two component scales of the PRF ANDRO are empirically independent and are not factorially pure, usually showing a factor structure similar to that of the BSRI. The PRF ANDRO has good reliability. It has been used in research on a fairly wide variety of topics, mostly although not entirely with college student subjects. Evidence on the PRF ANDRO's validity is generally satisfactory. However, while its scales were intended to converge with the corresponding BSRI scales, correlations between the two measures are only moderate.

Heilbrun's (1976) Adjective Check List (ACL) scales ask respondents to indicate which of 54 trait adjectives are self-descriptive. Items tap both positive and negative traits from a fairly broad range of personality domains. The 28 Masculinity and 26 Femininity scale items all appear on the parent ACL's (Gough & Heilbrun, 1965) bipolar Masculinity–Femininity Scale, for which items were selected that discriminated between college males identified with masculine fathers and college females identified with feminine mothers. Heilbrun's (1976) scales differ from the older ACL scale only in scoring procedure: Usually, separate Masculinity and Femininity raw scores are transformed using sex-specific norm tables. Decisions needed to score this measure can be complicated. This measure may be administered by itself, or as part of the 300-item ACL. Given the largely empirical nature of the parent ACL, it is not surprising that Heilbrun's (1976) scales are only moderately independent and that each appears to have a fairly complex factorial structure. The scales have moderate to good reliability. Heilbrun appears to consider a broad variety of variables to be relevant to his measure's validity and implies that his instrument should operate in research much as the BSRI would. While most validating evidence is good, Heilbrun's scales do not show high correlations with those of the BSRI. This measure has generated a considerable amount of research on a fairly wide variety of topics, predominantly with college student subjects.

Baucom's (1976) scales assess sex role in terms of the respondent's agreement or disagreement with self-descriptive statements. Items from the full California Psychological Inventory (CPI) (Gough, 1957) that produced a sex difference in endorsement rates among college students were assigned to the separate 54-item Masculinity and 42-item Femininity scales. The chosen items appear to vary in their social desirability and cover an extremely broad range of content areas, including vocational and activity preferences, self-reports of past behavior, and diverse aspects of self-perception. This 96-item measure may be administered by itself or as part of the 480-item CPI. In a departure from other scale authors' usual strategies, Baucom typically uses an extreme groups approach, often employing standard cutoff scores, to assign subjects to sex role categories. The Masculinity and Femininity scales are empirically independent. No internal consistency or factor analytic data were encountered. Test–retest reliability appears quite satisfactory over short intervals. Baucom seems to expect his scales to operate in research much as the BSRI scales would, although correlations with the BSRI are not high. Nonetheless, most of the available validating evidence is good. Most studies have employed college student samples, and the vast majority of published references are those of Baucom and his colleagues.

The Sex Role Behavior Scale (SRBS-1) (Orlofsky, 1981) is a promising instrument, designed specifically to assess sex role interests and behaviors, as distinct from sex role traits or attitudes. Orlofsky modeled his scale development procedures on those used with the PAQ. Accordingly, his 51-item Male-Valued and 32-item Female-Valued scales each contain behaviors stereotypically believed to differentiate the sexes but considered socially desirable in both sexes. Like the PAQ, there is also a bipolar Masculinity–Femininity or Sex-Specific scale, having 77 items considered more socially desirable in one sex than in the other. In taking the SRBS-1, the respondent indicates the degree to which each of 160 behaviors is self-descriptive. Each scale contains four subscales tapping recreational activities, vocational interests, social and dating behaviors, and marital behaviors. Internal consistency is satisfactory for each of the three scales; no test–retest data were encountered. In accordance with his reasoning, Orlofsky has found moderate positive correlations between the Male- and Female-Valued scales, and fairly low relationships between these scales and the PAQ and Attitudes Toward Women Scale (AWS) (Spence, Helmreich, & Stapp, 1973). Because it is so new, the SRBS-1 does not have an extensive literature, and that which exists is entirely the work of Orlofsky and his colleagues and uses only college student samples. Nonetheless, existing validating evidence is good. The 240-item SRBS-2 (Orlofsky, Ramsden, & Cohen, 1982) has quite adequate subscale reliabilities and is suggested if individual behavior area subscores are desired.

There are a number of considerations relevant to these individual scale reports:

For example, the reader will find that the contents of the Validity and the Results and Comments sections vary across scales. This is because the distinction between what is and is not validating evidence is sometimes extremely hard to determine even within the same scale (see also Taylor & Hall, 1982). Certainly, there is no uniform rule for making this distinction across scales, since researchers offer different conceptual definitions of masculinity, femininity, and androgyny.

In an attempt to provide systematic scale evaluations, evidence was sorted into the various subsections, and/or particular emphasis was placed on that evidence, based on the specific scale authors' apparent intentions. These decisions may be legitimate matters for debate, as the subsections make clear. A few of the more salient points of dispute are summarized in the following paragraphs.

Spence (1984) expects PAQ M and F scales, as well as those of similar tests such as the BSRI, to relate well only to variables that are instrumental or expressive, respectively, in nature. Others (e.g., Bem, 1985) consider their M and F scales to be relevant to broader categories of variables. Thus, treatment of some of the more commonly measured variables in the current sex role literature (e.g., psychological adjustment and mental health; behavioral flexibility) appears in different subsections for different tests.

Also, authors vary in the extent to which they consider it important that M and F scales be homogeneous, discriminate between the sexes, etc. Finally, authors also vary in the extent to which they consider it important that their M and F scales converge with those of other instruments. For Bem, this appears to be largely irrelevant; for Spence, substantial correlations would be expected only with other primarily instrumental–expressive tests. Readers should interpret the convergent and discriminant validity implications of such correlational data with caution, bearing the scale authors' perspective in mind.

Tables 1–6 present a summary of some of the correlations between the corresponding M and F scales of tests reviewed in this chapter. Two cautions deserve emphasis here. First, while scales are often labeled "masculinity" and "femininity," they do *not* measure exactly the same constructs. This extremely important point continues to be ignored in the literature or given only brief mention. (See, for example, Taylor & Hall's otherwise excellent review, 1982.)

Table 1

Correlations between Corresponding BSRI and PAQ Scales

Source[a]	Subject sample[b]	Instruments[c]	Males[d] (n) M	F	Females[d] (n) M	F	Sexes combined[d] (n) M	F
1	1	A1	.83 (104)	.64	.84 (133)	.70		
2	2	A3	.70 (55)	.89				
3	1	A2	(n not given)		(n not given)		.56 (160)	.59
4	3	A2	(n not given)		(n not given)		.79 (132)	.71
5	1	A1	(65)		(65)		.85 (130)	.73
6	4	B2	(70)		(49)		.78 (119)	.86
7	1	B3	(87)		(85)		.72 (172)	.75
8	1	A1	.62 (92)	.70	.84 (131)	.67		
9	5	A2	(39)		(40)		.66 (79)	.75
10	6	A2	(98)		(183)		.76 (281)	.69

[a] 1, Cunningham & Antill, 1980; 2, Evans & Dinning, 1982; 3, Gaa & Liberman, 1981 (Study 1); 4, Gaa & Liberman, 1981 (Study 2); 5, Kelly, Furman, & Young, 1978; 6, Lamke, 1982; 7, Lubinski, Tellegen, & Butcher, 1983; 8, O'Grady, Freda, & Mikulka, 1979; 9, Smith, 1983; 10, Wilson & Cook, 1984.

[b] 1, undergraduate students; 2, psychiatric inpatients; 3, graduate students; 4, junior high school students; 5, mixed sample of homosexuals and heterosexuals, "mainly college students"; 6, graduate and undergraduate students.

[c] A, full BSRI M & F scales; B, Short BSRI M & F scales; 1, M & F scales of 55-item PAQ; 2, M & F scales of 24-item PAQ; 3, M + and F + scales of EPAQ.

[d] For all r values in this table, $p < .001$.

Table 2
Correlations between Corresponding BSRI and PRF ANDRO Scales[a,b]

Source[c]	Males[d] (n)		Females[d] (n)		Sexes combined[d] (n)	
	M	F	M	F	M	F
1	.60 (457)	.52	.65 (703)	.50		
2	.54 (104)	.44	.64 (133)	.50		
3	.65 (59)	.57	.62 (99)	.55		
4	(65)		(65)		.70 (130)	.62
5	(150)		(89)		.42 (239)	.45
6	(98)		(183)		.68 (281)	.52

[a]All subject samples are undergraduate students, except for Wilson and Cook (1984), whose sample included graduate and undergraduate students.

[b]All studies used the full BSRI M & F Scales.

[c]1, Berzins, Welling, & Wetter, 1978; 2, Cunningham & Antill, 1980; 3, Gayton, Havu, Ozmon, & Tavormina, 1977; 4, Kelly, Furman, & Young, 1978; 5, Ramanaiah & Martin, 1984; 6, Wilson & Cook, 1984.

[d]For all r values in this table, $p < .001$.

Table 3
Correlations between Corresponding BSRI and ACL Scales[a,b]

Source[c]	Males[d] (n)		Females[d] (n)		Sexes combined[d] (n)	
	M	F	M	F	M	F
1	(65)		(65)		.75 (130)	.68
2	.64 (92)	.21 $p < .05$	.64 (131)	r not given		
3	(150)		(89)		.58 (239)	.58
4	.59 (42)	.38 $p < .004$	.10 (96) $p > .05$	.19 $p > .05$		
5	(98)		(183)		.71 (281)	.57

[a]All subject samples are undergraduate students, except for Wilson & Cook (1984), whose sample included graduate and undergraduate students.

[b]All studies used the full BSRI M & F Scales.

[c]1, Kelly, Furman, & Young, 1978; 2, O'Grady, Freda, & Mikulka, 1979; 3, Ramanaiah & Martin, 1984; 4, Small, Erdwins, & Gross, 1979; 5, Wilson & Cook, 1984.

[d]Unless otherwise noted, all p levels $< .001$.

Table 4
Correlations between Corresponding PAQ and PRF ANDRO Scales

Source[a]	PAQ form[b]	Subject sample[c]	Males[d] (n)		Females[d] (n)		Sexes combined[d] (n)	
			M	F	M	F	M	F
1	1	1	.54 (104)	.49	.77 (133)	.48		
2	1	1	(65)		(65)		.66 (130)	.59
3	2	2	(98)		(183)		.57 (281)	.43

[a]1, Cunningham & Antill, 1980; 2, Kelly, Furman, & Young, 1978; 3, Wilson & Cook, 1984.

[b]1, M & F scales from 55-item PAQ; 2, M & F scales from 24-item PAQ.

[c]1, Undergraduate students; 2, graduate and undergraduate students.

[d]For all r values in this table, $p < .001$.

Table 5

Correlations between Corresponding PAQ and ACL Scales

Source[a]	PAQ form[b]	Subject sample[c]	Males[d] (n)		Females[d] (n)		Sexes combined[d] (n)	
			M	F	M	F	M	F
1	1	1	(65)		(65)		.70 (130)	.51
2	1	1	.48 (92)	.37	.57 (131)	.37		
3	2	2	(98)		(183)		.60 (281)	.45

[a]1, Kelly, Furman, & Young, 1978; 2, O'Grady, Freda, & Mikulka, 1979; 3, Wilson & Cook, 1984.
[b]1, M & F scales from 55-item PAQ; 2, M & F scales from 24-item PAQ.
[c]1, Undergraduate students; 2, graduate and undergraduate students.
[d]For all r values in this table, $p < .001$.

Table 6

Correlations between Corresponding ACL
and PRF ANDRO Scales

Source[a]	Subject sample[b]	Sexes combined[c] (n)	
		M	F
1	1	.61 (65 males, 65 females)	.57
2	1	.37 (150 males, 89 females)	.36
3	2	.62 (98 males, 183 females)	.54

[a]1, Kelly, Furman, & Young, 1978; 2, Ramaniah & Martin, 1984; 3, Wilson & Cook, 1984.
[b]1, Undergraduate students; 2, graduate and undergraduate students.
[c]For all r values in this table, $p < .001$.

Second, categorization into sex role groups by a given method generally depends upon the scale used. Many studies have shown only limited agreement in subject classification across scales. Given ambiguities in the categorization methods discussed above, percentages of categorization agreement across relevant studies are not shown. The following provide information for the interested reader: Cunningham and Antill, 1980 (comparison of subject classifications using the BSRI, PRF ANDRO, and PAQ); Gaa and Liberman, 1981 (BSRI and PAQ); Gayton, Havu, Ozmon, and Tavormina, 1977 (BSRI and PRF ANDRO); Kelly, Furman, and Young, 1978 (BSRI, PAQ, PRF ANDRO, and ACL); Small, Erdwins, and Gross, 1979 (BSRI and ACL); Wilson and Cook, 1984 (BSRI, PAQ, ACL, and PRF ANDRO).

Bem Sex Role Inventory
(Bem, 1974)

Variable

The BSRI provides independent assessments of masculinity and femininity in terms of the respondent's self-reported possession of socially desirable, stereotypically masculine and feminine personality characteristics. Under Bem's gender schema theory (Bem, 1981c, 1985), the BSRI can also be seen as a measure of the extent to which respondents spontaneously sort self-relevant information into distinct masculine and feminine categories.

Description and Original Subject Samples

The BSRI is a self-administered 60-item questionnaire, containing a Masculinity scale and a Femininity scale. The remaining 20 items are treated as neutral fillers. Each item is a personality characteristic. Respondents indicate how well each item describes themselves on a scale from 1 ("Never or almost never true") to 7 ("Always or almost always true"). The respondent's Masculinity score is the average of his or her ratings on the 20 Masculinity items, and the respondent's Femininity score is the average of his or her ratings on the Femininity items. Thus, both scores can range from 1 to 7. A Social Desirability score can be computed in similar fashion, using the 20 filler items.

The scale can be completed in about 15 minutes. Bem (1974) intended the BSRI to contain positive traits widely believed to be part of the culture's definitions of masculinity and femininity. Accordingly, she and her students compiled a list of 200 personality characteristics that seemed positively valued and stereotypically masculine or feminine, and 200 other characteristics that seemed neither masculine nor feminine. Of these latter traits half seemed positively valued and half seemed negatively valued.

These 400 items were presented to two samples of Stanford University undergraduates (20 males and 20 females in 1972, and 30 males and 30 females in 1973). In each sample, half of the subjects of each sex rated each trait in terms of its sex-typed social desirability for a man (e.g., "In American society, how desirable is it for a man to be assertive?") and the other half of the subjects rated each trait in terms of its desirability for a woman (e.g., "In American society, how desirable is it for a woman to be assertive?"). No subject rated any trait for both a man and a woman. The rating scale ranged from 1 ("Not at all desirable") to 7 ("Extremely desirable").

Traits that were judged by both males and females in both samples as significantly more desirable for a man than for a woman, or for a woman than for a man, qualified for inclusion in the Masculinity and Femininity scales, respectively. Of the eligible items, 20 were selected for each scale, with the mean social desirability rating of the Masculinity scale items when judged "for a man" being nearly identical to that of the Femininity scale items when judged "for a woman."

Traits that were judged by both males and females in both of Bem's (1974) samples as no more desirable for one sex than for the other qualified for inclusion in the Social Desirability scale. Of the eligible items, 10 positive and 10 negative characteristics were selected.

With regard to scoring the BSRI, there are several possible procedures: Currently, the most popular method of assigning subjects to sex role groups is a median split procedure (see above). Usually, it is advisable that the medians so used be determined for the particular research sample. However, researchers may choose to use medians derived from one of Bem's original large normative samples (Bem, 1977, 1981a). Bem (1977) reported median Masculinity and Femininity scores of 4.89 and 4.76, respectively, for a 1975 sample of 375 males and 290 females at Stanford University. The median split procedure resulted in classification of the following percentages of subjects as feminine, undifferentiated, androgynous, and masculine, respectively: males, 16, 27, 21, and 37%; females, 34, 20, 29, and 16%.

Bem's original definition of androgyny (1974), which she still considers to have theoretical merit (e.g., 1985), was not that androgynous persons possess high levels of both masculinity and femininity (as operationalized by the median split method), but rather that such persons possess relatively equal (balanced) levels of masculinity and femininity. She operationalized this balance definition in a t-ratio between the respondent's Masculinity and Femininity scores and classified persons as androgynous if their t-ratios were small, indicating approximately equal Masculinity and Femininity scores (see above and Bem, 1974).

The major distinction between the median split and t-ratio methods is that the former distinguishes between high–high (androgynous) and low–low (undifferentiated) scorers, while the latter method would consider both to be androgynous to the extent that their t-score is small. In 1975, Spence et al. argued for the median split procedure based in part upon results using their own Personal Attributes Questionnaire (PAQ), which showed high–high scorers to be higher on a measure of self-esteem than low–low scorers. In 1977, Bem responded to this challenge by comparing BSRI high–high versus low–low scorers on a variety of behavioral and self-report measures. Since she found differences on several measures, she concurred with Spence et al. (1975) that the median split classification should be used in most cases. However, Bem has consistently noted that high–high and low–low scorers are similar in that neither partitions self-concept into masculine and feminine categories (e.g., Bem, 1977), a fact that has conceptual relevance, particularly for gender schema theory (e.g., Bem, 1985). Nonetheless, pending further research, investigators should generally opt for the median split approach.

Discussions of the two scoring methods for the BSRI, as well as data comparing them in a variety of respects, may be found in Briere et al. (1983), Downing (1979), Handal and Salit (1985), and Jones, Chernovitz, and Hansson (1978).

Several other classification procedures have been suggested for use with the BSRI. Most commonly, these procedures involve some combination of balance and median split approaches. See, for example, Downing's (1979) "hybrid" scoring system and the "intersect" or "difference/median split" method proposed by Orlofsky et al. (1977; Briere et al., 1983).

Reliability

Internal Consistency

Bem (1974) computed coefficient α values on two samples. All three scores were highly reliable, both in the Stanford sample of 444 males and 279 females (Masculinity $\alpha = .86$; Femininity $\alpha = .80$; Social Desirability $\alpha = .75$) and in the junior college sample of 117 males and 77 females (α values of .86, .82, and .70, respectively). Androgyny difference scores showed reliabilities of .85 for the Stanford sample and .86 for the junior college sample. Bem (1981a) reports comparable coefficient α values for a Stanford sample of 476 males and 340 females.

Wilson and Cook (1984) report coefficient α values for their sample of 183 female and 98 male graduate and undergraduate students of .88 for Masculinity and .78 for Femininity.

Test–Retest

Bem (1974) found high reliability over a 4-week interval among 28 male and 28 female Stanford undergraduates for Masculinity ($r = .90$), Femininity ($r = .90$), Androgyny t-ratio ($r = .93$) and Social Desirability ($r = .89$) scores. Rowland (1977) administered the BSRI to Australian university students and found reliability over the 8-week interval for Masculinity (117 males, $r = .93$; 109 females, $r = .88$), Femininity (males, $r = .80$; females, $r = .82$), and Androgyny t-ratio (males, $r = .86$; females, $r = .91$) scores. Yanico (1985) administered the BSRI to 77 female university students twice. She found significant, moderately high reliability over a 4-year time period for both Masculinity ($r = .56$) and Femininity ($r = .68$).

Validity

Other chapters in this volume have organized this section into two standard subsections labeled "convergent validity" and "divergent validity." Unfortunately, however, such an organization would be potentially misleading for the field of sex role research. First, scale authors often have enormously disparate conceptual definitions of masculinity, femininity, and androgyny. They therefore necessarily also differ in important respects as to what data they consider relevant to their measures' convergent and divergent validity. Second, a number of issues whose theoretical importance crosses the field of sex role measurement cannot be sorted into convergent or divergent validity subsections across scales, since they are handled very differently (and sometimes unclearly) by the various scale authors. Thus, to avoid the potential confusion that might be generated by any implication that there are agreed-upon sorting rules in this area, validity sections in this chapter separate the relevant data by conceptual issues and are based largely upon the particular scale authors' apparent intentions. Previous sections discuss this and related points in detail.

Correlation between Masculinity and Femininity Scores

Bem's contention that masculinity and femininity are logically independent was supported by results from her (1974) normative samples; the correlations were .11 for 444 Stanford males, $-.14$ for 279 Stanford females, $-.02$ for 117 junior college males, and $-.07$ for 77 junior college females. While the two correlations for Stanford students were statistically significant ($p < .05$), they were quite low; the two correlations for the junior college sample are not significant. The empirical independence of BSRI Masculinity and Femininity scales is further supported by results of numerous factor analytic studies, which rarely find any items from the two scales loading on the same factors. In contrast, a few studies have found somewhat larger correlations between the two scales (e.g., Liberman & Gaa, 1986: 128 graduate students, breakdown by sex not given, $r = -.21$, $p < .05$).

Freedom from Response Set

Since Masculine and Feminine items were all selected to be positive and relatively desirable even for the "inappropriate" sex, it is important for the BSRI's validity that subjects classified as androgynous not be simply showing a social desirability response set. Using her Stanford and junior college normative samples, Bem (1974) reported correlations between the BSRI Social Desirability Scale and the Masculinity, Femininity, and Androgyny t-ratio scores. As expected, Masculinity and Femininity were somewhat related to Social Desirability (correlations ranged from .15 to .42), but Androgyny t-scores were not (correlations ranged from $-.07$ to .12; only the latter, for Stanford males, was significant, $p < .05$).

Berzins *et al.* (1978) administered the BSRI to 457 male and 703 female college students, who also completed the Personality Research Form (PRF) (D. N. Jackson, 1967) Desirability Scale and the Marlowe–Crowne Social Desirability Scale (Crowne & Marlowe, 1964). Correlations between Masculinity and BSRI Social Desirability, PRF Desirability, and Marlowe–Crowne Desirability, respectively, were .32, .25, and .02 for males and .21, .27, and .11 for females; between Femininity and these scales, correlations were .29, .19, and .15 for males and .22, .17, and .23 for females. While in this large sample correlations above .05 were significant at or beyond the .05 level, all are low.

Not surprisingly, given the underlying relationships among variables, there may be a small social desirability effect when subjects are assigned to sex role categories by the median split method. Liberman and Gaa (1986) administered the BSRI to 128 graduate students (breakdown by sex not given). They report that BSRI Social Desirability scores were significantly different across sex role categories ($p < .0001$); and that a post hoc test showed social desirability scores of androgynous subjects were significantly higher than those of subjects in all other categories. Nonetheless, the largest mean difference between any two sex role groups was only approximately one-half of a scale point on the seven-point Social Desirability rating scale. While Liberman and Gaa (1986) express concern over their findings, I disagree: The weight of the evidence demonstrates that BSRI scales have adequate freedom from socially desirable responding.

Millimet and Votta (1979) found that BSRI median split sex role categorizations (of 70 male and 72 female undergraduates) were independent from acquiescence response set, when the latter was assessed by the Couch–Keniston Agreement Response Scale (Couch & Keniston, 1960).

Validity of Bem's Item Selection Procedures

Several researchers have questioned whether Bem's decision to use sex-typed social desirability as the criterion for item selection, and her operationalization of this criterion (see Development section above), adequately capture even Bem's own "conception of the sex-typed person as someone who has internalized society's sex-typed standards of desirable behavior for men and women" (Bem, 1974, p. 155). Such criticisms most often hold that there was an ambiguity or other inadequacy in Bem's instructions to those subjects who rated the desirability of the items in her initial pool and suggest that alternative trait selection procedures should have been used that more clearly specified: (a) the meaning of the term "desirable" in its normative and/or prescriptive senses (e.g., Myers & Gonda, 1982a; Pedhazur & Tetenbaum, 1979); or (b) the specific target subjects had in mind when making their desirability ratings (e.g., Locksley & Colten, 1979). Bem's reply to these criticisms is that her item selection procedures were designed to assess widely shared cultural definitions of desirable masculine and feminine personalities, that these definitions inherently include both normative and prescriptive aspects, and that the consistency of desirability ratings she found across independent samples of judges indicates that the BSRI adequately taps these widely known cultural definitions (e.g., Bem, 1979).

Several investigators have attempted to cross-validate BSRI items according to various item selection criteria. Results of these studies are somewhat complex, since investigators have sometimes intentionally or unintentionally used instructions and rating scales that differed in important respects from those given to Bem's subjects during her item selection procedures (e.g., A. L. Edwards & Ashworth, 1977; Puglisi, 1980; Walkup & Abbott, 1978). However, when Bem's procedures are replicated exactly, it appears that almost all BSRI Masculinity and Femininity items continue to be acceptable by Bem's criteria (Heerboth & Ramanaiah, 1985; Ramanaiah & Hoffman, 1984; Walkup & Abbott, 1978).

Discrimination of Known Groups

Given the theory behind the BSRI, sex differences on the Masculinity and Femininity scales are not considered indicators of validity. That is, while the items in these scales do differ in sex-typed desirability, they were not selected by the extent to which they actually or stereotypically differentiate between the sexes, nor is there any necessary link between these items and biological sex.

Nonetheless, the sexes do typically differ in their scale scores. In Bem's (1974) normative samples, males scored significantly higher (444 Stanford males $\bar{M} = 4.97$; 117 junior college males $\bar{M} = 4.96$) than females (279 Stanford females $\bar{M} = 4.57$; 77 junior college females $\bar{M} = 4.55$) on the Masculinity Scale. Conversely, females scored significantly higher (279 Stanford females $\bar{M} = 5.01$; 77 junior college females $\bar{M} = 5.08$) than males (444 Stanford males $\bar{M} = 4.44$; 117 junior college males $\bar{M} = 4.62$) on the Femininity Scale. All probability levels are less than .001.

Concurrent and Predictive Validity within Bem's Theoretical Perspective

Behavioral Restriction and Flexibility Bem's original formulation of androgyny theory held that sex-typed persons should be behaviorally restricted, showing only behaviors consistent with their sex-typed self-image, while androgynous persons should show behavioral flexibility, behaving in both stereotypically masculine and feminine ways depending upon situational demands. With only minor deviations, the pattern of results in her own early studies categorizing college student subjects by the BSRI (in some cases, using median splits, in others, using the *t*-ratio method) strongly supported this idea. For example, in both sexes, masculine and androgynous subjects have been found to be significantly more likely than feminine subjects to demonstrate independence in a conformity paradigm (Bem & Lewis, 1975), and feminine and androgynous subjects have been found to be significantly more likely than masculine subjects to respond in a nurturant fashion toward both an infant and a lonely peer (Bem, Martyna, & Watson, 1976). Further, Bem and Lenney (1976) found that in both sexes sex-typed subjects were significantly more likely than androgynous subjects to avoid cross-sex behavior and to experience discomfort when performing such behavior. (See Helmreich, Spence, & Holahan, 1979, for a not entirely successful attempt to replicate this latter study, using the PAQ and several other methodological changes.)

The general concept underlying Bem's ideas of behavioral restriction and flexibility (i.e., that masculine persons restrict themselves to masculine behaviors, feminine persons restrict themselves to feminine behaviors, and androgynous persons do not show such restrictions) is addressed less directly by numerous other authors who have examined the BSRI scales' relationships to various "masculine" and "feminine" variables. M. C.

Taylor and Hall (1982) presented a meta-analysis of a large number of studies, divided into those that used "female-typed" or "male-typed" dependent measures. (Many of these studies used the BSRI. Although Taylor and Hall do not provide data separating studies using the BSRI from those using other modern sex-role tests, readers may do so themselves by using Taylor and Hall's reference list.) Results showed that masculinity related positively to male-typed measures in 93% of the cases, but femininity showed an almost even number of positive (56%) and negative (44%) relationships to such measures. Correspondingly, femininity related positively to female-typed measures in 80% of the cases, but masculinity showed an almost even number of positive (47%) and negative (53%) relationships to such measures. Orlofsky and Windle (1978), Ramanaiah and Martin (1984), D. Taylor (1984), and Wiggins and Holzmuller (1978, 1981), also presented evidence relevant to the convergent and discriminant validity of BSRI Masculinity and Femininity in relation to selected masculine and feminine dependent measures. Evidence across these sources is generally quite positive. In an interesting study, Anderson (1986) categorized college students by BSRI median split: She did not find androgynous subjects highest in self-perceived flexibility among the sex role groups.

Gender Schematicity In terms of Bem's gender schema theory (e.g., Bem, 1981c, 1985), BSRI scores indicate the degree of gender schematicity in subjects' self-concepts. That is, median split categorization as masculine or feminine reflects the respondent's spontaneous clustering of the test's traits into masculine and feminine groups (with only one cluster endorsed as self-descriptive); categorization of androgynous or undifferentiated, in contrast, reflects no such clustering. Bem predicts that sex-typed persons, who are gender-schematic, will organize and process information along gender lines more than do androgynous persons, who are gender-aschematic. Bem and others have found considerable evidence supporting this prediction, both in the processing of information related to the self (e.g., Bem, 1981c) and information unrelated to the self (Andersen & Bem, 1981; Bem, 1981c; Frable & Bem, 1985; Lippa, 1983). Bem (1985) provided a good review of this evidence, and Larsen and Seidman (1986) provided some data indicating that the BSRI is psychometrically adequate for use in gender schema theory research. In contrast, there have been failures to replicate certain of Bem's findings (e.g., Deaux, Kite, & Lewis, 1985; Mills & Tyrrell, 1983).

Bem's gender schema research is not without its critics. Most notably, Spence and her colleagues (e.g., Spence, 1984; Spence & Helmreich, 1981) have argued that measures such as the BSRI and PAQ should not be used to assess gender schematicity since (a) there is a logical contradiction in using these two-dimensional measures to assess a construct that is unidimensional, such as degree of gender schematicity (or, for that matter, degree of sex-typing); and (b) the BSRI and PAQ tap predominantly instrumental and expressive traits and as such have too limited a domain to assess adequately so broad a concept as gender schematicity. (For Bem's replies to these criticisms see Bem, 1981b.) V. J. Edwards and Spence (1987) and Payne, Conner, and Colletti (1987), using the PAQ, provided some evidence contrary to Bem's gender schema theory predictions. Alternatives to her theory include Markus, Crane, Bernstein, and Siladi's (1982) self-schema theory (see also Crane & Markus, 1982, and Bem's 1982 reply) and Spence's own gender identity theory (Spence, 1984, 1985).

Relationship of the BSRI to Other Sex Role Measures

The Adult Measures section of this chapter presents data on the BSRI's relationships to the various PAQ forms (Table 1), the PRF ANDRO (Table 2), and the ACL scales (Table 3).

A few studies have assessed the BSRI's relationships to older, bipolar tests. Bem

(1974) reported that, among 28 male and 28 female Stanford students, scores on the Masculinity–Femininity Scale of the Guilford–Zimmerman Temperament Survey (Guilford & Zimmerman, 1949) were not at all correlated with BSRI Masculinity, Femininity, or Androgyny t-ratio scores, while those on the Fe Scale of the California Psychological Inventory (Gough, 1957) were moderately correlated with all three BSRI scores (within-sex correlations ranged from $-.42$ to $.27$; only the correlation for males between BSRI Masculinity and CPI Fe was significant, $r = -.42$, $p < .05$). She interpreted these data as indicating that the BSRI measures an aspect of sex roles not tapped by either of these earlier scales. Similarly, low to moderate correlations between BSRI and CPI Fe scores have been reported by Bohannon and Mills (1979), and similar correlations between BSRI and MMPI M-F scores have been reported by Evans and Dinning (1982) and Volentine (1981, Study 1).

Bernard (1981) reports a factor analysis that included BSRI Masculinity and Femininity items along with items from the M-F scales of the MMPI, CPI, Guilford–Zimmerman Temperament Survey, and Strong Vocational Interest Blank. He found BSRI scores' loadings on all factors underlying these older scales to be low to moderate. (See also Wakefield, Sasek, Friedman, & Bowden, 1976, for similar factor analytic results involving items from the BSRI, MMPI, and CPI.)

Betz and Bander (1980) and Volentine (1981) found that MMPI M-F scores were significantly related to subjects' sex role classifications using the BSRI, but Adams and Sherer (1982) did not find such a relationship.

Location

Bem, S. L. (1974). The measurement of psychological androgyny. *Journal of Consulting and Clinical Psychology*, **42**, 155–162.

Bem, S. L. (1981). *Bem Sex Role Inventory professional manual*. Palo Alto, CA: Consulting Psychologists Press. (Long and Short BSRI.)

Results and Comments

Many factor analyses of the BSRI (e.g., Antill & Russell, 1982; Feather, 1978; Gaudreau, 1977; Moreland, Gulanick, Montague, & Harren, 1978; Pedhazur & Tetenbaum, 1979; Whetton & Swindells, 1977) have shown that the two BSRI scales are not factorially pure. Bem (e.g., 1979) has argued that this is fully consistent with the theory and purposes underlying the BSRI's development: The culture defines masculinity and femininity as two arbitrary clusters of different components, and the BSRI is designed precisely to assess the degree to which individuals endorse these heterogeneous cultural clusters as self-descriptive.

Factor analytic results differ to some extent by subject sample and other variables. However, they typically show two masculinity factors, which can be called "Dominance–Aggression" and "Self-Reliance–Personal Control," a femininity factor often called "Interpersonal Sensitivity and Warmth," and a fourth factor correlated with sex that contains the BSRI items "Masculine," "Feminine," and "Athletic" (Lippa, 1985).

Bem (1979, 1981a) developed a short BSRI partially in response to issues raised by these factor analyses. The short BSRI has half of the original items from each subscale. It eliminates the items "masculine," "feminine," and "athletic" as well as other items having relatively poor item–total correlations with Masculinity and Femininity scales. Bem (1981a) reported that the short BSRI scales correlate around $r = .90$ with the original BSRI scales.

It is important to note that, since the short BSRI deletes several femininity items that were relatively socially undesirable (e.g., "gullible," "flatterable"), Femininity scores on the short BSRI may be higher than those on the long BSRI. Therefore, the two forms are not comparable in absolute scores or medians.

There have been signs that the short form has problems connected with a feminine bias (e.g., McPherson & Spetrino, 1983), a loss of discriminatory power in classifying persons by sex role (Gruber & Powers, 1982), and failures to produce the same kinds of result patterns found when the long BSRI is used (e.g., Frable & Bem, 1985; L. A. Jackson, 1983). Bem no longer uses the short form in her own research (Frable & Bem, 1985).

Spence and her colleagues (e.g., Spence & Helmreich, 1979b, 1983) have argued that it is misleading to use the broad terms "masculinity" and "femininity" as labels for the BSRI scales. Instead, they contend that these scales assess the much more limited traits of instrumentality (socially desirable, self-assertive qualities) and expressiveness (socially desirable, interpersonally oriented qualities). According to these authors, sex roles are very complex and include many components not assessed by the BSRI and PAQ, such as attitudes toward the two sexes and sex-related behaviors. Since these components of sex roles are often unrelated within individuals, these authors argue that the BSRI should be expected to make adequate predictions only of attributes and behaviors closely related to instrumentality and expressiveness. Spence (1984) has provided an excellent discussion of this position and reviewed evidence supporting her contention that sex roles are multidimensional, with the BSRI and PAQ showing frequently weak and/or inconsistent relationships to gender-related dependent variables that go beyond instrumentality and expressiveness.

Bem (1985) has agreed that researchers using her scale are often too enthusiastic in their attempts to relate BSRI scores to nearly every aspect of the individual's gender psychology. However, she argues that research does show the relevance of the aspects of sex roles tapped by the BSRI to behaviors beyond instrumentality and expressiveness, when these behaviors are selected, as are those in her own research, with the theoretical rationale underlying the BSRI in mind.

Researchers have attempted to relate BSRI scores to a tremendous variety of other variables. Perhaps the most popular issue has concerned the extent to which masculinity, femininity, and androgyny predict various mental health indices. Among the better reviews of the more than 100 studies in this area are Whitley's (1983) meta-analysis of self-esteem studies and Bassoff and Glass's (1982), M. C. Taylor and Hall's (1982), and Whitley's (1985) meta-analyses of psychological adjustment and mental health studies. (Taylor and Hall did not provide separation of studies by sex role scale used; the other sources provided data relevant to such separation.) These and other sources indicate that mental health indices tend to show large and fairly consistent relationships with masculinity and small or no relationships with femininity. This evidence does suggest that androgyny is not the best predictor of mental health, broadly construed; however, much of the expectation that it would be the best predictor may have come from researchers' overinterpretation of Bem's original contention that those who are both masculine and feminine are best adjusted. As Bem (1985) noted, ". . . there is no real theoretical reason for expecting androgynous individuals to score higher on . . . [measures of mental health] . . . than sex-typed individuals in the context of a sex-typed society" (p. 190). She further notes her agreement with Nicholls, Licht, and Pearl (1982) that, because of item overlap and other issues, the correlation between masculinity and self-esteem may be "more artifactual than substantive" (Bem, 1985, pp. 190–191).

The list of other variables to which researchers have tried to relate BSRI scores includes parental behaviors (e.g., Baumrind, 1982; L. A. Jackson, Ialongo, & Stollak, 1986); life satisfaction (e.g., Windle, 1986); helping behavior (e.g., Senneker & Hendrick, 1983; Tice & Baumeister, 1985); various achievement behaviors (e.g., Cano, Solomon, & Holmes, 1984; Lippa & Beauvais, 1983; Wong, Kettlewell, & Sproule, 1985); person perception (e.g., Harackiewicz & DePaulo, 1982); marital intimacy, satisfaction, and division of household labor (e.g., Denmark, Shaw, & Ciali, 1985; White, Speisman, Jackson, Bartis, & Costos, 1986); feminism (e.g., Baucom & Sanders, 1978); values (e.g., Feather, 1984); and nonverbal behaviors (e.g., Lippa, Valdez, & Jolly, 1983).

The BSRI was developed with American college students, but it has also been used with other age groups, from high school age through elderly populations. Most such research does not discuss any salient problems in applying it to age groups differing from Bem's original samples. Windle (1986) and Windle and Sinnott (1985) discussed problems in using the BSRI with elderly adults. When used with high school children, the BSRI has sometimes been modified for clarity (e.g., Richmond, 1984). (Hyde and Phillis, 1979, presented a discussion of age differences in androgyny as measured by the BSRI.) Thomas and Robinson (1981) developed an adaptation of the BSRI for use with young adolescents.

The BSRI has also been used in other countries and cultures, sometimes with adaptations and/or translations as deemed appropriate. For example, there is an Indian BSRI (see Rao, Gupta, & Murthy, 1982); an Australian BSRI (see Ho & Zemaitis, 1980); a German BSRI (see Schneider & Schneider-Duker, 1984); and an Arabic BSRI (see Al-Qataee, 1984). Segall (1986) has discussed some issues in the cross-cultural use of the BSRI.

The BSRI has also been used to assess perceptions of the ideal man, woman or person (e.g., Scher, 1984; Silvern & Ryan, 1983) and of the typical man and woman (e.g., Heerboth & Ramanaiah, 1985). The psychometric adequacy of the BSRI as a tool to assess anything other than self-perceptions remains, of course, an open question.

Overall Assessment

The BSRI is currently the most frequently used sex role instrument; in fact, it is among the five most frequently used psychological tests reviewed in the widely referenced *Mental Measurements Yearbook* (Mitchell, 1985). Despite the tremendous amount of controversy it has engendered (see Spence, 1984, for an excellent summary), the BSRI has good reliability and its validity seems quite adequate when it is used in ways suggested by the theoretical rationale underlying its development.

Items on the BSRI

1	2	3	4	5	6	7
NEVER OR ALMOST NEVER TRUE						ALWAYS OR ALMOST ALWAYS TRUE

Masculine Items	**Feminine Items**	**Neutral Items**
(49) Acts as a leader	(11) Affectionate	(51) Adaptable
(46) Aggressive	(5) Cheerful	(36) Conceited
(58) Ambitious	(50) Childlike	(9) Conscientious
(22) Analytical	(32) Compassionate	(60) Conventional

(13) Assertive	(53) Does not use harsh language	(45) Friendly
(10) Athletic		(15) Happy
(55) Competitive	(35) Eager to soothe hurt feelings	(13) Helpful
(4) Defends own beliefs		(48) Inefficient
(37) Dominant	(20) Feminine	(24) Jealous
(19) Forceful	(14) Flatterable	(39) Likable
(25) Has leadership abilities	(59) Gentle	(6) Moody
	(47) Gullible	(21) Reliable
(7) Independent	(56) Loves children	(30) Secretive
(52) Individualistic	(17) Loyal	(33) Sincere
(31) Makes decisions easily	(26) Sensitive to the needs of others	(42) Solemn
		(57) Tactful
(40) Masculine	(8) Shy	(12) Theatrical
(1) Self-reliant	(38) Soft-spoken	(27) Truthful
(34) Self-sufficient	(23) Sympathetic	(18) Unpredictable
(16) Strong personality	(44) Tender	(54) Unsystematic
(43) Willing to take a stand	(29) Understanding	
	(41) Warm	
(28) Willing to take risks	(2) Yielding	

Note: This list contains all items on the 60-item BSRI. However, the reader wishing to administer the BSRI must obtain specific directions to the test-taker, actual scaled response alternatives, and detailed scoring instructions from Consulting Psychologists Press (see Location section, above). A general characterization of these procedures is provided in the Description section above.

Numbers in parentheses reflect the position of each adjective as it actually appears on the inventory. From Bem (1974).

Personal Attributes Questionnaire
(Spence, Helmreich, & Stapp, 1974, 1975)

Variable

The PAQ provides independent assessments of masculinity and femininity in terms of the respondent's self-perceived possession of personality traits stereotypically believed to differentiate the sexes but considered socially desirable in both sexes. It also provides an assessment of masculinity–femininity in terms of the respondent's self-perceived possession of personality traits stereotypically believed to differentiate the sexes but considered more socially desirable for one sex than for the other.

Description and Original Subject Samples

Because Spence intended the PAQ to tap only certain aspects of sex roles, Spence and her colleagues (e.g., Spence, 1984; Spence & Helmreich, 1979b) have stated that the PAQ measures not global masculinity, but self-assertive–instrumental traits; and not global femininity, but interpersonal–expressive traits. Typically, Spence and others still use the terms "masculinity" and "femininity" as labels for the trait clusters measured by the PAQ, although Spence stated that these labels "can be used only as descriptive, atheoretical terms that call attention to the fact that males and females differ stereotypically and in self-report" (Spence, 1984, p. 7).

In its original form (Spence *et al.*, 1974, 1975), the PAQ was a self-administered, 55-item questionnaire, containing a 23-item Male-Valued (Masculinity or M) Scale, an 18-item Female-Valued (Femininity or F) Scale, and a 13-item Sex-Specific (Masculinity–Femininity or M-F) Scale. (One of the 55 items is not classified by scale.) The authors quickly shortened the original PAQ to a 24-item questionnaire that contains 8 items from each of the original PAQ's M, F, and M-F scales (Spence & Helmreich, 1978). The 24-item PAQ has been used in the vast majority of research studies and Spence herself has abandoned use of the original version.

Each item on the PAQ is a personality characteristic, presented in a five-point bipolar format. Respondents are asked to select the letter or number that best describes where they fall along each continuum (e.g., A or 0 = not at all aggressive, to E or 4 = very aggressive).

Scores on the three scales are determined by adding the ratings for the relevant items. Each item is scored from 0 to 4, with higher scores on M and M-F scale items representing extreme masculine responses and higher scores on F scale items representing extreme feminine responses. Thus, for the 24-item PAQ, scores can range from 0 to 32 for each of the three scales. The PAQ 24-item version can be completed in about 15 minutes.

Spence *et al.* (1975) selected items for the 55-item PAQ from a pool of 138 bipolar items largely used in developing the Sex Role Stereotype Questionnaire (Rosenkrantz *et al.*, 1968). Rosenkrantz *et al.* (1968) compiled their list from college students' nominations of traits they believed to differentiate between adult men and women.

Spence *et al.* (1975) gave the pool of 138 items to large samples of male and female college students (numbers not reported in the 1975 publication) with instructions to rate on each item: (a) the typical adult male and typical adult female; (b) the typical male college student and typical female college student; or (c) the ideal male and ideal female. Finally, all subjects rated themselves on each item.

The authors chose for the PAQ 55 items which showed significant (test and significance level not given in the 1975 publication) stereotypes for both male and female subjects in both typical adult and typical student conditions. These items were then divided into three subscales based on ratings in the "ideal" condition. The Female-Valued (F) Scale had 18 items for which mean ratings of both ideal male and ideal female were toward the feminine end (defined by stereotype ratings) of the bipolar scale; the Male-Valued (M) Scale had 23 items for which mean ratings of both ideal male and ideal female were toward the masculine pole. The Sex-Specific (M-F) Scale had 13 items for which ratings of the ideal female were toward the feminine pole and ratings of the ideal male were toward the masculine pole. Thus, F scale items are "considered to be socially desirable in both sexes, but . . . females are believed to possess [them] to a greater degree than males"; M scale items are "considered to be socially desirable in both sexes but . . . males are believed to possess [them] in greater abundance than females"; M-F scale items are "characteristics whose social desirability appears to vary in the two sexes" (Spence & Helmreich, 1978, p. 19).

Spence and Helmreich (1978) state that the 24-item PAQ was derived by selecting 8 items from each of the original three scales, primarily based on the part–whole correlation between the item and its scale. Spence (1983) further asserts that "by design the M scale is confined to self-assertive traits . . . and the F scale is confined to emotive, interpersonally oriented traits" (p. 441). M-F items refer to instrumental–self-assertive or expressive–interpersonal characteristics, or to a combination of both (Spence & Helmreich, 1978). Spence and Helmreich (1978) report correlations for a sample of college students (number unspecified) between the 55-item and 24-item PAQ Scale scores of .93, .93, and .91 for M, F, and M-F, respectively.

Generally, only the M and F scales are used for subject classification. Indeed, the M-F scale is seldom included in empirical studies, since, "Perhaps because of its bipolar properties, investigators have had difficulty assimilating this scale into their conceptual models" (Spence, 1984, p. 5).

With regard to subject classification there are several possible procedures. Spence and her colleagues were the earliest advocates of the median split method of sex role categorization (Spence & Helmreich, 1978; Spence et al., 1975). The PAQ is rarely subjected to any other categorization scheme. Spence and Helmreich (1978) argued that it is usually advisable to derive median values for the particular research sample. However, some researchers may wish to use medians based upon one of Spence's large normative samples. Spence and Helmreich (1978) reported medians (for combined-sex distributions) on the 24-item PAQ of 20 on the M Scale, 23 on the F Scale, and 15 on the M-F Scale for a sample of 756 male and 1013 female high school students; and of 21, 23, and 15, respectively, for a sample of 715 college students (breakdown by sex not given).

When the high school and college samples described immediately above were divided into sex role groups by median splits on their own M and F score distributions, the following percentages of subjects were categorized as androgynous, masculine, feminine, and undifferentiated, respectively: male high school students, 32, 34, 8, and 25%; female high school students, 27, 14, 32, and 28%; male college students, 25, 44, 8, and 23%; female college students, 35, 14, 32, and 18%.

[For a median-split method which also takes into account respondents' M-F scores, see Spence and Helmreich (1978, pp. 52–53).]

In contrast to Bem's use of the four sex role grouping terms, but in line with her own argument that PAQ M and F scales do not measure global masculinity or global femininity, Spence (e.g., 1984) emphasizes that she uses the terms masculine, feminine, androgynous, and undifferentiated merely as nominal designations: "they are not intended to have explanatory significance or to represent theoretical constructs" (p. 7).

Spence and Helmreich (1978) stated that, depending upon the research question of interest, investigators may wish to use a more refined categorization scheme (e.g., by dividing scores on the M and F scales into quartiles rather than halves).

Spence and Helmreich (1979c) reported a variety of analyses using M and F scores from the 24-item PAQ obtained by 756 male and 1010 female high school students. They divided subjects into sex role groups by Bem's (1974) difference score procedure (see BSRI description), by the median split procedure, and by the hybrid difference–median method (Orlofsky et al., 1977). Spence and Helmreich (1979c) reported agreement rates in categorization among the various methods, as well as the differences among sex role groups (as defined by the various methods) in Attitudes toward Women scores (AWS) (Spence & Helmreich, 1972, 1978), self-esteem, and competitiveness. Their conclusion was that the median split method is superior because it does not presuppose any underlying relationship between M and F and any given dependent measure.

Reliability

Internal Consistency

Spence *et al.* (1974; reported in Beere, 1979) gave the 55-item PAQ to 248 college men and 282 college women. They found item–total correlations for women of .24–.70 for M items, .27–.55 for F items, and .19–.64 for M-F items. Item–total correlations for men were .23–.64, .22–.56, and .23–.61, respectively.

Spence and Helmreich (1978) reported Cronbach α values for the 24-item PAQ (male and female college students; numbers unspecified) of .85, .82, and .78 for M, F, and M-F, respectively.

Helmreich, Spence, and Wilhelm (1981) reported Cronbach α values for three subject samples given the 24-item PAQ. Alpha values for M, F, and M-F scales respectively were (a) among 674 female high school students, .71, .73, .62; among 509 male high school students, .67, .72, .53; (b) among 1585 female college students, .73, .73, .65; among 1251 male college students, .76, .76, .61; and (c) among 1028 mothers of college and elementary school students, .77, .79, .61; among 926 fathers of college and elementary school students, .78, .80, .56.

Wilson and Cook (1984) reported coefficient α values in their sample of 183 female and 98 male graduate students given the 24-item PAQ of .80 for both M and F scales.

Test–Retest

Spence *et al.* (1974, reported in Beere, 1979) gave the 55-item PAQ to 31 college students (breakdown by sex not reported in Beere) twice at a 13-week interval. Reliabilities for the three subscales ranged from .65 to .91.

Validity

Dimensionality of Masculinity and Femininity

In contrast to Bem, Spence (e.g., 1984) intended PAQ M and F scales each to be unidimensional. Helmreich *et al.* (1981) reported factor analyses of the 16 M and F items on the 24-item PAQ separately for their three large samples (described under Internal Consistency, above). Their summary of the results of the six factor analyses is that the best solution in each case identified only two factors, which reproduced the 24-item PAQ M and F scales. (Wilson and Cook, 1984, reported highly similar results.) Helmreich *et al.* (1981) repeated the same six factor analyses for the complete 24-item PAQ and found that M-F items mostly loaded on both factors identified above. This, argue these authors, supports both the bipolar nature of these items and the retention of the theoretically distinct M-F scale.

Antill and Cunningham (1982a) factor-analyzed the 54 items from the three subscales of the 55-item PAQ and found six factors. The first two factors concerned "femininity," on which 13 of the 18 F items loaded; and "masculinity," on which 17 of the 23 M items loaded. Gross, Batlis, Small, and Erdwins (1979) factor-analyzed responses to the items from the M and F scales of the 55-item PAQ, and reported a four-factor solution.

These results, taken together, indicate that the 55-item PAQ is not as factorially pure as the 24-item form.

Discrimination of Known Groups

For Spence, it is important that males and females achieve different scores on the three PAQ subscales, since this sex difference is part of her theoretical conception of masculinity and femininity.

In a sample of 248 male and 282 female college students, Spence *et al.* (1975) found highly significant sex differences in the expected directions on the M (male $\bar{M}$ = 60.61, female $\bar{M}$ = 57.73), F (male $\bar{M}$ = 48.73, female $\bar{M}$ = 53.16), and M-F (male $\bar{M}$ = 27.21, female $\bar{M}$ = 22.34) scales of the 55-item PAQ (all *p* levels ≤ .003). Similarly, in a sample of 715 college students (numbers within sex not given), Spence and Helmreich (1978) found significant sex differences on all three subscales of the 24-item PAQ (Masculinity $\bar{M}$ values: Males = 21.69, Females = 19.54; Femininity $\bar{M}$ values: Males = 22.43, Females = 24.37; Masculinity–Femininity $\bar{M}$ values: Males = 16.69, Females = 12.52; all *p* levels < .01).

Helmreich *et al.* (1981) conducted discriminant analyses by sex of respondent using the 24-item PAQ and found Wilks' λ values of .58, .68, and .58 in their large high school student, college student, and parent samples, respectively. They further reported correct gender classification in these samples of 80, 77, and 81% (all χ-square values significant beyond the .0001 level).

Spence and Helmreich (1978) reported analyses comparing the 24-item PAQ scores of 56 male and 54 female self-designated homosexuals to scores obtained by their own unselected college samples (Spence *et al.*, 1975). They found that male homosexuals scored lower than unselected males on M and M-F and higher on F and that lesbians scored higher than unselected females on M and M-F and lower on F. Spence and Helmreich (1978) reported further analyses supporting the 24-item PAQ's ability to discriminate unselected subjects from female varsity athletes, female Ph.D. scientists, and male Ph.D. scientists.

Freedom from Response Set

Spence *et al.* (1975) gave the 55-item PAQ and the Marlowe–Crowne Social Desirability Scale (Crowne & Marlowe, 1964) to 45 male and 97 female college students. They found correlations between social desirability and M, F, and M-F scores of .23, .35, and .16, respectively, for males; and .10, .36, and .08, respectively, for females (correlations of .23 and above were significant at the .05 level). These correlations are not impressive in size.

In developing the EPAQ (see Results and Comments below), Spence *et al.* (1979) found that the correlations for their college student sample (220 males and 363 females) between the 24-item PAQ M and F scales and the corresponding EPAQ negative Masculinity and negative Femininity scales were negative but quite low. This further indicates that a systematic social desirability set does not appear to contaminate responses to the 24-item PAQ M and F scales.

Concurrent and Predictive Validity within
Spence's Theoretical Perspective

Spence (e.g., 1983, 1984) has repeatedly asserted that the PAQ is a measure only of what its manifest content indicates. That is, she holds that sex roles are multidimensional and that therefore PAQ scores can be expected to relate well only to phenomena that are directly influenced by instrumental and expressive traits. Therefore, Spence's view requires convergent validity data only for the latter phenomena. Spence states that she would expect low and/or inconsistent relationships between PAQ scores and the majority of noninstrumental and nonexpressive gender-related attitudes, behaviors, characteristics, and preferences.

Most of the research to which Spence refers in discussing the PAQ's convergent and discriminant validity was originally reported in Spence and Helmreich (1978) and came from numerous studies using the 24-item PAQ. The results reported include, for example, correlations involving empathy (measured by Mehrabian and Epstein's Empathy Scale, 1972), which are significant and positive with PAQ F and negative and lower with PAQ M, and correlations involving the Work, Mastery, and Competitiveness subscales of the authors' own Work and Family Orientation Questionnaire (WOFO) (Spence & Helmreich, 1978), which are significantly positive with PAQ M and much lower with F. Spence (1984) also cited various validity data, including the results obtained by Lubinski *et al.* (1983) that the 24-item PAQ's F scale is moderately highly correlated with a measure of social closeness, while the M scale is much less highly correlated with this measure and that negative correlations, higher than those found with M, occurred between F and measures of alienation and aggression.

Also, M. C. Taylor and Hall (1982) provided a meta-analysis of studies using various sex role measures and measures of "male-typed" and/or "female-typed" characteristics, some of which are fairly clearly instrumental or expressive in nature. (Although these authors did not provide data separating studies using the PAQ from those using other modern sex role tests, readers may make this separation themselves by using M. C. Taylor and Hall's reference list.)

Evidence cited by Spence that PAQ scores show low and/or inconsistent relationships with noninstrumental and nonexpressive gender-related traits, attitudes, and behaviors abounds (see, e.g., Spence, 1984, 1985; Spence & Helmreich, 1978, 1980). For instance, relationships are small between the 24-item PAQ M and F scales and Spence and Helmreich's (1972) Attitudes toward Women Scale, anticipated comfort in performing cross-sex activities (Spence *et al.*, 1979), and Orlofsky's (1981) Sex-Role Behavior Scale. In addition, Spence and her colleagues have found low relationships between 24-item PAQ scales and gender schematicity as defined by Bem. For instance, V. J. Edwards and Spence (1987) found no relationship between PAQ M and F scores and subjects' recall of masculine and feminine words.

See also Bugen and Humenick (1983), Feather (1984), Lubinski *et al.* (1983), and McHale and Huston (1984) for additional convergent and discriminant validity data.

Relationship of the PAQ to Other Sex Role Measures

The Adult Measures section of this chapter presented the relationships found by various investigators between the M and F scales of the different PAQ versions and those of the full and short BSRI (Table 1), the PRF ANDRO (Table 4), and the ACL (Table 5).

Spence and Helmreich (1978) reported that J. Stapp and A. Kanner (unpublished; date and title not given) administered the CPI Fe Scale (Gough, 1966) and the 24-item PAQ to 31 male and 44 female college students and found correlations between CPI Fe and PAQ M of .04 for males and .13 for females (both nonsignificant); and between CPI Fe and PAQ F of $-.49$ for males and $-.42$ for females (both p values were $< .05$).

Betz and Bander (1980) reported that, in both sexes of college students, MMPI M-F scores differentiated 55-item PAQ-classified (median split) masculine from feminine and androgynous subjects; and that CPI Fe scores differentiated feminine from masculine subjects. In contrast, in Volentine's (1981; Study 2) mixed-sex college student sample MMPI M-F scores did not differ across the sex role groups defined by 24-item PAQ median split (see also Evans & Dinning, 1982).

Location

Spence, J. T., & Helmreich, R. L. (1978). *Masculinity and femininity: Their psychological dimensions, correlates, and antecedents.* Austin: University of Texas Press. (24-item PAQ)

Spence, J. T., Helmreich, R. L., & Holahan, C. K. (1979). Negative and positive components of psychological masculinity and femininity and their relationships to self-reports of neurotic and acting out behaviors. *Journal of Personality and Social Psychology*, **37**, 1673–1682. (EPAQ)

Spence, J. T., Helmreich, R. L., & Stapp, J. (1974). The Personal Attributes Questionnaire: A measure of sex role stereotypes and masculinity-femininity. *Journal Supplement Abstract Service Catalog of Selected Documents in Psychology*, **4**, 43–44. (55-item PAQ)

Results and Comments

Correlations between Subscale Scores

At least as the PAQ was originally presented (Spence *et al.*, 1975), data concerning M and F scale correlations are not relevant to assessing the PAQ's validity, since Spence took an atheoretical or empirical position on the question of relationships between masculinity and femininity. More recently Spence (e.g., 1984) seems to propose that the independence of these two trait spheres is of theoretical relevance.

Spence *et al.* (1975) gave the 55-item PAQ to 248 male and 282 female college students. They found correlations between the M and F scales of .47 for males and .14 for females (both p values $< .05$); between the M and M-F scales of .52 for males and .63 for females (both p values $< .05$); and between the F and M-F scales of .00 for males and $-.22$ for females (the latter $p < .05$). They interpret these findings to indicate that "masculinity and femininity are, if not orthogonal, actually positively related" (p. 34).

Spence and Helmreich (1978) gave the 24-item PAQ to various samples of subjects, including 715 college students (breakdown by sex not given). They found, in the latter sample, correlations between M and F scales of .22 for males and .09 for females; between M and M-F scales of .55 for males and .56 for females; and between F and M-F scales of $-.17$ for males and $-.24$ for females (all p values $< .05$). They report similar correlations for a large high school student sample. Spence *et al.* (1979) and Helmreich *et al.* (1981) report correlations between the 24-item PAQ M and F scales that range between .08 and .16 in samples of high school students, college students, and adults. It thus appears that, for the 24-item PAQ, Masculinity and Femininity are essentially uncorrelated, a position Spence now explicitly asserts (Spence, 1984).

The Extended Personal Attributes Questionnaire (EPAQ)

Spence *et al.* (1979) developed a 40-item EPAQ that contains the 24-item PAQ and three scales comprising negatively valued masculine and feminine traits. These new scales were added in the recognition that both stereotypically and in self-report the sexes differ in socially undesirable instrumental and expressive traits, as well as in the socially desirable traits tapped by the majority of sex role instruments developed recently.

The EPAQ contains one negative Masculinity (M −) scale consisting of items that were identified in pilot testing with college students as (a) socially undesirable in both sexes and (b) attributed to males more frequently than to females. Of the items meeting these criteria, eight were selected as instrumental in content (i.e., arrogant, boastful, egotistical, greedy, dictatorial, cynical, hostile, and looks out only for self). Corresponding pilot procedures were used to develop the two four-item negative Femininity scales. The F_C- scale contains items whose content refers to Bakan's (1966) concept of "unmitigated communion" (i.e., spineless, servile, gullible, and subordinates self to others). The $F_{VA}-$ scale contains items whose content refers to verbal passive aggressiveness (i.e., whiny, complaining, fussy, and nagging). All items appear on the EPAQ in the same five-point rating format as used in the PAQ, with extremes indicating a high or low degree of the trait. The M− scale is scored in a masculine direction, and both negative femininity scales are scored in a feminine direction.

Spence et al. (1979) reported a variety of psychometric properties of the EPAQ, as administered to 220 male and 363 female college students: For example, the sexes differed significantly in the expected directions on all six scales; the two F− scales had a positive, low correlation; and parallel positive and negative scales had small, negative correlations with each other. The authors also reported correlations between the new negative scales and measures of self-esteem, neuroticism, and acting-out behaviors. Patterns of correlations, which differed across these three measures, were taken to support the new scales' validity.

Helmreich et al. (1981) gave the EPAQ to 1465 female and 854 male college students. They reported coefficient α values for males and females, respectively, of .46 and .41 for F_C-; .60 and .63 for $F_{VA}-$; and .69 and .70 for M−. (Coefficient α values in both sexes were .74 for M+ and .75 for F+. See also Lubinski et al., 1983.) Factor analyses of the negative scales (Helmreich et al., 1981) showed a two-factor solution for males, but a three-factor solution, which reproduced the three scales, for females.

The EPAQ has been used in research with clinical populations. For example, Holahan and Spence (1980) found that M− and F− scores were higher among male and female college students seeking counseling than among unselected students. Evans and Dinning (1982) found that M− and F− were related negatively to self-reports of psychopathology in a male psychiatric sample. Hawkins, Turell, and Jackson (1983) and Butler, Giordano, and Neren (1985) have also discussed relations between the EPAQ and various behavior problems among college students.

Lubinski et al. (1983) gave 87 male and 85 female college students the EPAQ and A. Tellegen's (unpublished) Differential Personality Questionnaire (DPQ), a measure of 11 broad self-view dimensions. Of interest here is that, since their analyses showed little relationship between the EPAQ negative scales and relevant DPQ scales, the authors conclude that M− and F_C- do not "measure the mitigation of positively valued masculinity and femininity" (p. 437). In her reply, Spence (1983) asserted that Lubinski et al. made predictions that went beyond the manifest content of EPAQ scales and therefore their null results are unsurprising.

Researchers have attempted to relate PAQ scores to a large number of diverse measures. Results have been mixed. Spence (e.g., 1984), of course, expects a mixed pattern across gender-related phenomena, since these phenomena have varying degrees of relationship with the PAQ's instrumental and expressive content.

As with the BSRI, perhaps the most popular issue has been the degree to which masculinity, femininity, and androgyny relate to measures of psychological well-being. Typically, the PAQ M and F scales relate to such measures as do the corresponding BSRI scales: Masculinity shows a large and fairly consistent relationship to most measures of self-esteem and psychological adjustment, while Femininity shows a small or no relationship with such indices (see, e.g., Bassoff & Glass, 1982; M. C. Taylor & Hall, 1982; Whitley, 1983, 1984). M. C. Taylor and Hall did not provide data permitting the separation of studies by sex role test used; the other sources provided such data to varying degrees.)

Spence and her colleagues (Spence, 1984; Spence & Helmreich, 1978; Spence et al., 1975) reported that when the Texas Social Behavior Inventory (TSBI) (Helmreich & Stapp, 1974) is used as a measure of self-esteem and social competence, both PAQ M and F are significantly positively related to this socially oriented index of well-being, although M shows a stronger relationship than F. Nicholls et al. (1982) argued that the relationship between PAQ M and self-esteem measures may be largely due to item overlap and therefore may be more artifactual than real. In her reply, Spence (1984; Spence & Helmreich, 1983) has contended that this is not the case, since PAQ M and TSBI scores have dissimilar, but theoretically predictable, relationships to other variables.

To Spence, the relationship to be expected between PAQ scores and measures of well-being is exactly that predicted for other measures: Only to the extent that well-being is assessed in terms of possession of positive self-assertive and/or interpersonal qualities is a correlation with PAQ M and/or F to be anticipated.

The list of other variables to which researchers have tried to relate PAQ scores far exceeds the limits of this review. Just a few examples are helping behaviors (e.g., Siem & Spence, 1986); parenting behaviors (e.g., McHale & Huston, 1984; Spence, 1982); marital behaviors (e.g., Atkinson & Huston, 1984; Belsky, Lang, & Huston, 1986); loneliness (e.g., Wheeler, Reis, & Nezlek, 1983; Wittenberg & Reis, 1986); and moral judgments (e.g., Pratt, Golding, & Hunter, 1984).

The PAQ was developed with American college students and much research using it has been conducted on this population. The 24-item PAQ has, however, been used with other age groups, from high school age through middle adulthood. It is usually used without modification or discussion of problems with these age groups. Age effects are described in Spence and Helmreich (1979a).

The PAQ has been revised into a Children's PAQ (CPAQ). (See Hall & Halberstadt, 1980, for a full discussion of the CPAQ's psychometrics and construct validity; original reference is Simms et al., 1978.) The CPAQ is appropriate for children as young as third graders through sixth graders. The CPAQ has both long and short forms based closely on the 55- and 24-item PAQs. See also Silvern and Katz (1986) for an excellent study using the CPAQ with fourth–sixth graders. The CPAQ appears to be a very promising, psychometrically adequate instrument for use in middle childhood and it is hoped that future researchers will further substantiate its convergent and discriminant validity.

The PAQ has also been used in other countries and cultures, sometimes with adaptations and/or translations as deemed appropriate. For just two examples, there is a Mexican (Spanish) PAQ (e.g., Diaz-Loving, Diaz-Guerrero, Helmreich, & Spence, 1981) and an Italian PAQ (e.g., del Miglio & Nenci, 1983). The PAQ has been used with British adolescents (e.g., Keyes & Coleman, 1983), and students in Fiji (Basow, 1984) and Yugoslavia (Ajdukovic & Kljaic, 1984). Spence and Helmreich (1978) discuss additional cross-cultural studies.

The PAQ has frequently been used in ways other than as a self-descriptive instrument. Given scale development procedures, it seems acceptable to use the PAQ as a measure of stereotypical perceptions of males and females (see, e.g., Spence et al.,

1975). The PAQ has also been used to assess perceptions of homosexuals (e.g., A. Taylor, 1983) and of desirable characteristics in men and women (e.g., Ruble, 1983).

Overall Assessment

The PAQ is second only to the BSRI in its current frequency of use in sex role research. One possible reason it is less frequently used lies in Spence's oft-repeated admonition that the domain of its predictive power is limited only to certain aspects of sex roles.

   The 24-item PAQ demonstrates highly satisfactory reliability and validity when used in the ways suggested by its underlying rationale and development.

Abbreviated Unipolar Description of the Personal Attributes Questionnaire

Male-Valued Items

*Independent	Adventurous	*Self-confident
Not easily influenced	Outspoken	*Feels superior
Good at sports	Interested in sex	Takes a stand
Not excitable, minor crisis	*Makes decisions easily	Ambitious
*Active	Outgoing	*Stands up under pressure
*Competitive	Acts as leader	Not timid
Skilled at business	Forward	
Knows ways of world	Intellectual	
	*Not give up easily	

Female-Valued Items

*Emotional	Strong conscience	Creative
Not hide emotions	*Gentle	*Understanding
Considerate	*Helpful to others	*Warm to others
Grateful	*Kind	Likes children
*Devotes self to others	*Aware, other feelings	Enjoys art and music
Tactful	Neat	Expresses tender feelings

Sex-Specific Items

*Aggressive (M)	Mechanical aptitude (M)	Religious (F)
*Dominant (M)	*Needs approval (F)	Sees self running show (M)
Likes math and science (M)	*Feelings hurt (F)	*Needs for security (F)
	*Cries easily (F)	

*Excitable; major crisis   Loud (M)
   (F)
*Home-oriented (F)

> Note: The reader wishing to administer the 55-item PAQ must obtain specific directions to the test-taker, actual scaled response alternatives, and detailed scoring instructions from JSAS (see Location section, above). A general characterization of these procedures is provided in the Description Section, above. From Spence *et al.* (1975). Sex of ideal individual (male, M; female, F) corresponding to the listed pole is given in parentheses. Items with an asterisk are also found on the more widely used 24-item PAQ (Spence & Helmreich, 1978), see next scale.

The 24-Item PAQ

The items below inquire about what kind of a person you think you are. Each item consists of a *pair* of characteristics, with the letters A–E in between. For example:

Not at all artistic   A.....B......C.....D.....E   Very artistic

Each pair describes contradictory characteristics—that is, you cannot be both at the same time, such as very artistic and not at all artistic.

The letters form a scale between the two extremes. You are to choose a letter which describes where *you* fall on the scale. For example, if you think you have no artistic ability, you would choose A, if you think you are pretty good, you might choose D. If you are only medium, you might choose C, and so forth.

M-F	1. Not at all aggressive	A....B....C....D....E	Very aggressive
M	2. Not at all independent	A....B....C....D....E	Very independent
F	3. Not at all emotional	A....B....C....D....E	Very emotional
M-F	4. Very submissive	A....B....C....D....E	Very dominant
M-F	5. Not at all excitable in a MAJOR crisis	A....B....C....D....E	Very excitable in a MAJOR crisis
M	6. Very passive	A....B....C....D....E	Very active
F	7. Not at all able to devote self completely to others	A....B....C....D....E	Able to devote self completely to others
F	8. Very rough	A....B....C....D....E	Very gentle
F	9. Not at all helpful to others	A....B....C....D....E	Very helpful to others
M	10. Not at all competitive	A....B....C....D....E	Very competitive

M-F	11. Very home oriented	A. . . .B. . . .C. . . .D. . . .E	Very worldly
F	12. Not at all kind	A. . . .B. . . .C. . . .D. . . .E	Very kind
M-F	13. Indifferent to others' approval	A. . . .B. . . .C. . . .D. . . .E	Highly needful of others' approval
M-F	14. Feelings not easily hurt	A. . . .B. . . .C. . . .D. . . .E	Feelings easily hurt
F	15. Not at all aware of others' feelings	A. . . .B. . . .C. . . .D. . . .E	Very aware of others' feelings
M	16. Can make decisions easily	A. . . .B. . . .C. . . .D. . . .E	Has difficulty making decisions
M	17. Gives up very easily	A. . . .B. . . .C. . . .D. . . .E	Never gives up easily
M-F	18. Never cries	A. . . .B. . . .C. . . .D. . . .E	Cries very easily
M	19. Not at all self-confident	A. . . .B. . . .C. . . .D. . . .E	Very self-confident
M	20. Feels very inferior	A. . . .B. . . .C. . . .D. . . .E	Feels very superior
F	21. Not at all understanding of others	A. . . .B. . . .C. . . .D. . . .E	Very understanding of others
F	22. Very cold in relations with others	A. . . .B. . . .C. . . .D. . . .E	Very warm in relations with others
M-F	23. Very little need for security	A. . . .B. . . .C. . . .D. . . .E	Very strong need for security
M	24. Goes to pieces under pressure	A. . . .B. . . .C. . . .D. . . .E	Stands up well under pressure

Note: M, Masculinity Scale; F, Femininity Scale; M-F, Masculinity—Femininity Scale. Underlined poles are the extreme masculine response for the M and M-F scales, and the extreme feminine response for the F scale. Extreme responses are scored 4, next most extreme scored 3, etc. From Spence & Helmreich (1978).

PRF ANDRO

(Berzins, Welling, & Wetter, 1978)

Variable

The PRF ANDRO provides independent assessments of masculinity and femininity, in terms of the respondents' agreement or disagreement with self-descriptive statements pertaining to socially desirable, stereotypically masculine and feminine behaviors and characteristics.

Description and Original Subject Samples

The PRF ANDRO is a self-administered 56-item questionnaire. Each item is a statement to which respondents indicate "true" or "false" as it applies to themselves. Of the 29

Masculine (M) Scale items, 19 are keyed true and 10 are keyed false; of the 27 Feminine (F) Scale items, 17 are keyed true and 10 are keyed false. Respondents' M score is the sum of their keyed responses to M items and can vary from 0 to 29, with higher scores indicating greater masculinity; their F score is the sum of their keyed responses to F items and can vary from 0 to 27, with higher scores indicating greater femininity.

M scale items are described as relating to "a dominant-instrumental dimension comprised of themes of social–intellectual ascendancy, autonomy, and orientation toward risk"; F scale items are described as relating to "a nurturant–expressive dimension, containing themes of nurturance, affiliative–expressive concerns, and self-subordination" (Berzins et al., 1978, p. 128).

The PRF ANDRO can be administered in a variety of ways. Some researchers (e.g., Wilson & Cook, 1984) administer only the 56-item PRF ANDRO. Others (e.g., Berzins et al., 1978) administer the entire 400-item Personality Research Form (PRF) (D. N. Jackson, 1967), which comprises 20 content scales and includes the 56 items selected for the PRF ANDRO scale. Still others (e.g., Berzins et al., 1978; Douglas & Nutter, 1986) administer an 85-item Interpersonal Disposition Inventory (IDI) containing the 56 PRF ANDRO items; the 20-item PRF Desirability scale, which assesses socially desirable responding; 5 items from the PRF Infrequency scale, which detect careless responding; and 4 filler items. Berzins et al. (1978) note that PRF ANDRO items have a different order of appearance and "context" in the PRF and IDI.

Explicitly following the rationale used by Bem (1974) in developing the BSRI, Berzins et al. (1978) chose items from the PRF which appeared to (a) have sex-typed social desirability (e.g., in American society, a feminine characteristic should be perceived as more desirable for a woman than for a man), (b) have generally positive content, and (c) be consistent "with rationally derived abstract definitions of the main content themes of Bem's Masculinity and Femininity scales" (Berzins et al., 1978, p. 128). BSRI Masculinity themes were seen as autonomy, orientation toward risk, and social–intellectual ascendancy; BSRI Femininity themes were seen as self-subordination, nurturance, and affiliative–expressive concerns. Application of these criteria resulted in selection of 32 masculine and 32 feminine PRF items. Subsequent item analyses (sample and statistics not given) (Berzins et al., 1978) resulted in the shortening of the provisional scales to 29 M and 27 F items.

To evaluate these items' sex-typed social desirability, 177 college students rated each item. Thirty men and 57 women judged the items for a man; 31 men and 59 women judged them for a woman; no subject judged both sexes. Each item was followed by the question, "In American society how desirable is it for a MAN (or WOMAN) to mark this item TRUE?" Judges made ratings on a seven-point scale, ranging from "not at all desirable" to "extremely desirable." Analyses of variance on mean desirability ratings for the two scales showed no sex of judge effects or interactions, but highly significant (p values < .0001) sex of target effects for both scales in the predicted directions. Individual item analyses showed that all 56 target sex differences were in the expected direction, 53 being significant beyond the .05 level, and 50 beyond the .001 level.

Berzins et al. (1978) reported data from two college student samples: Sample 1 contained 457 men and 703 women, who completed the IDI and other measures to be discussed below; Sample 2 contained 434 men and 552 women, who completed the full PRF (Form AA).

By far the most popular method of assigning subjects to sex role groups is by a median split procedure. Usually, it is advisable that the medians so used be derived for the particular research sample. However, researchers may choose to use medians derived from normative samples described by Berzins et al. (1978). These authors combined both sexes and both samples and designated M scores of 15 or greater and 14 or less as high and low, respectively; and F scores of 17 or greater and 16 or less as high and low, respectively. Berzins *et al.* (1978) reported the following percentages of subjects, pooling Samples 1 and 2, classified as androgynous, masculine, feminine, and indeterminate (undifferentiated), respectively: Males, 19, 49, 10, and 22%; Females, 20, 14, 48, and 18%.

Penick, Powell, Read, and Mahoney (1980) reported data comparing medians derived from their own sample of 772 male and female college students (numbers within sex not specified; high M cut-off point was 16 or greater; high F cut-off point was 17 or greater) and for samples of male Veterans of Foreign Wars and alcoholics. Their evidence confirms that medians differ by samples and that therefore subject categorization depends critically on the sample from which medians are derived.

Cunningham and Antill (1980) provided data comparing the sex role categorization of 104 male and 133 female college students by the median split versus Bem's *t*-ratio (see BSRI section in this chapter) methods across the BSRI, PAQ, and PRF ANDRO.

Reliability

Internal Consistency

In the combined-sex original samples (Berzins *et al.*, 1978) (see Sample section above), M α coefficients were .76 for Sample 1 and .79 for Sample 2; F α coefficients were .67 and .70, respectively.

Wilson and Cook (1984) gave 183 female and 98 male graduate and undergraduate students the PRF ANDRO and obtained α coefficients of .73 for M and .62 for F. They consider these data to indicate modest internal reliability.

Test–Retest

Berzins *et al.* (1978) estimated test–retest reliability "using an interval of approximately 3 weeks" (pp. 129–130) among a separate sample of 55 male college students and 82 female college students. About half of the students completed the entire PRF in class and the IDI later at home; the other half followed the opposite sequence. Retest coefficients for both M and F scales were .81.

Validity

Correlation between M and F Scores

The authors adopted Bem's (1974) contention that the independence of masculinity and femininity is important for the validity of sex role instruments. Berzins *et al.* (1978) found low negative correlations (no significance level given) between PRF ANDRO scales in both sexes and both normative samples (Sample 1: men's $r = -.05$, women's $r = -.16$; Sample 2: men's $r = -.11$; women's $r = -.24$).

Freedom from Response Set

Subjects in Sample 1 (Berzins *et al.*, 1978) completed the BSRI, the Marlowe–Crowne Social Desirability Scale (Crowne & Marlowe, 1964), and the PRF Desirability Scale (the latter as part of the IDI). Correlations between PRF ANDRO M and BSRI Social Desirability, Marlowe–Crowne Social Desirability, and PRF Desirability, respectively, were

.09, −.00, and .22 for males and .09, .14, and .14 for females. Correlations between PRF ANDRO F and the three desirability scales were .15, .29, and .19 for males and .05, .18, and .15 for females. While in this large sample correlations above .05 were significant at or beyond the .05 level, all are low and demonstrate that the PRF scales have adequate freedom from socially desirable responding.

The IDI contains the five-item PRF Infrequency Scale, which can be used to identify subjects who are responding carelessly.

PRF ANDRO items are keyed to control for acquiescent response distortion, although there are slightly more items keyed true than keyed false on both M and F scales.

Discrimination of Known Groups

Since the PRF ANDRO authors based their scale development rationale and procedures on those used in developing the BSRI, sex differences on PRF ANDRO scales are not considered necessary to the scales' validity.

Nonetheless, the sexes do typically differ on both PRF ANDRO scales. In the earliest samples (Berzins et al., 1978), males scored significantly higher (Sample 1 $\bar{M}$ = 16.70, Sample 2 $\bar{M}$ = 16.18) than females (Sample 1 $\bar{M}$ = 12.86, Sample 2 $\bar{M}$ = 11.86) on the M Scale. Conversely, females scored significantly higher (Sample 1 $\bar{M}$ = 17.90, Sample 2 $\bar{M}$ = 18.37) than males (Sample 1 $\bar{M}$ = 14.29, Sample 2 $\bar{M}$ = 14.31) on the F Scale. All probability levels are less than .0001.

Convergent and Discriminant Validity

Relationship with the BSRI Berzins et al. (1978) intended the PRF ANDRO scales to converge with the corresponding BSRI scales. For Sample 1, convergent validity coefficients for the two M scales were .60 for men and .65 for women (.68, sexes combined); and for the F scales were .52 and .50, respectively (.61, sexes combined). All probability levels were less than .001. The authors took these data to indicate "substantial similarities between the constructs underlying the total scores on these instruments" (p. 132). Individual item analyses showed that all PRF ANDRO M items correlated significantly with overall BSRI Masculinity scores; and all PRF ANDRO F items correlated significantly with overall BSRI Femininity scores (all *p* values < .001).

Table 2 in the section on Adult Measures provides further data on correlations between corresponding BSRI and PRF ANDRO scales. Inspection of this table reveals that such correlations, though significant, are often only moderate in magnitude: Several authors (e.g., Cunningham & Antill, 1980; Ramanaiah & Martin, 1984) have taken their data to indicate that the two sex-role instruments are far from equivalent.

Using data from Sample 1, Berzins et al. (1978) conducted separate factor analyses on BSRI and PRF ANDRO responses. They expected, and found, similar factor structures for the two instruments: For the BSRI, four factors were defined exclusively by Masculinity items and were termed Social Ascendancy, Autonomy, Intellectual Ascendancy, and Physical Boldness; for the PRF ANDRO, four factors were also defined exclusively by M items and were termed Social–Intellectual Ascendancy, Autonomy, Orientation toward Risk, and Individualism. For the BSRI, three factors were defined exclusively by Femininity items and were termed Nurturant Affiliation, Self-Subordination, and Introversion; for the PRF ANDRO, two factors were defined exclusively by F items and were termed Nurturance and Affiliative–Self Subordination Concerns.

Correlations with Other Modern Masculinity and Femininity Scales Tables 4 and 6 in the Adult Measures section of this chapter display correlations between PRF ANDRO scales and those of the PAQ and ACL, respectively. Relevant correlations with these two instruments are, like those with the BSRI, moderate in size.

Discriminant Validity   Subjects in Sample 1 (Berzins *et al.*, 1978) completed a 33-item self-esteem scale designed especially for that study. Correlations between self-esteem and PRF ANDRO M scores were moderately high (.36 for men and .38 for women; sexes combined $r = .38$, $p < .001$). Correlations between self-esteem and PRF ANDRO F scores were negligible (sexes combined $r = -.06$, ns). Although Berzins *et al.* (1978) seemed to take this as evidence for less than ideal discriminant validity for the M scale, it probably should not be considered such in the light of evidence showing that self-esteem is more related to masculinity than to femininity across the newer sex role measures (e.g., Whitley, 1983).

Berzins *et al.* (1978) found uniformly very small correlations in Sample 1 between both PRF ANDRO scales and Rotter's (Rotter, 1966) Internal–External Locus of Control Scale (sexes combined: M $r = -.08$; F $r = .01$; both ns).

Berzins *et al.* (1978) gave 682 college students from Sample 2 the PRF ANDRO and the Masculinity–Femininity (M-F) Scale of the Omnibus Personality Inventory (OPI) (Heist & Younge, 1968). Correlations between OPI M-F and PRF ANDRO F scores were $-.22$ for men and $-.16$ for women; and between OPI and PRF ANDRO M scores were .04 and .08, respectively. Berzins *et al.* (1978) gave 206 male alcoholics the PRF ANDRO and the MMPI (Hathaway, 1956) M-F scale. Correlations with the PRF M and F scales were $-.06$ and .00, respectively. Thus, the PRF ANDRO taps aspects of sex roles not assessed by these earlier instruments.

Miscellaneous Evidence   Using a sample of college students (150 males and 89 females), Ramanaiah and Martin (1984) conducted a multitrait–multimethod analysis to investigate the convergent and discriminant validity of the PAQ, ACL, and PRF ANDRO scales, relative to a variety of self-report questionnaire measures of dominance and nurturance. They report that the PRF ANDRO showed lower validity than the other two sex role measures. M. C. Taylor and Hall (1982) presented a meta-analysis of studies that used "male-typed" and/or "female-typed" dependent measures. Some of the studies included used the PRF ANDRO, although these are not separated from studies using other sex role measures. Readers may identify the relevant studies by using M. C. Taylor and Hall's reference list.

Location

Berzins, J. I., Welling, M. A., & Wetter, R. E. (1977). *The PRF ANDRO Scale user's manual* (revised). Unpublished material, University of Kentucky. (Available from J. I. Berzins, Department of Psychology, University of Kentucky, Lexington, Kentucky, 40506.)

Results and Comments

Since the PRF ANDRO was constructed along the same lines as the BSRI, it is not surprising that factor analytic studies reveal that it too is multidimensional. As noted above (see Validity) Berzins *et al.* (1978) found comparable factor structures in the two instruments.

Wilson and Cook (1984), using a sample of 98 male and 183 female undergraduate and graduate students, found that when the PRF ANDRO M and F scales are analyzed separately 10 and 11 factors were extracted, respectively.

Antill and Cunningham (1982b) gave the PRF ANDRO to 104 male and 133 female college students. While they found a similar structure to that found by Berzins *et al.*

(1978), they argued that this structure reflects the PRF scales from which items were drawn and that there is little value in combining conglomerates of items from different PRF scales as was done in developing the two PRF ANDRO scales. Rather, they argued, the PRF Dominance and Nurturance scales might make more factorially pure measures of "masculinity" and "femininity," as these are defined by such unidimensional scales as those of the PAQ.

Researchers have attempted to relate PRF ANDRO scores to a variety of other variables. The list exceeds the limits of this review and includes self-esteem (e.g., Antill & Cunningham, 1979); personality factors as measured by PRF scales (Berzins *et al.*, 1978); mental health (see Bassoff & Glass's 1982 and Whitley's 1985 meta-analyses, both of which provide data allowing some degree of separation of studies by sex role measure used; see also M. C. Taylor & Hall's, 1982, meta-analysis, which does not provide data separately by sex role measure); perceived child-rearing practices (e.g., Kelly & Worell, 1976); alcoholism (e.g., Penick, Powell, & Read, 1984); defense preference and symptom distress (e.g., Frank, McLaughlin, & Crusco, 1984); and responses to dissatisfaction in close relationships (e.g., Rusbult, Zembrodt, & Iwaniszek, 1986).

Since the PRF ANDRO scales were developed based on Bem's scale rationale, it would seem that their theoretical domain of relevance should be the same as that of the BSRI scales. This is rarely made explicit in the PRF ANDRO literature.

While most research with the PRF ANDRO has employed college student subjects, other populations have also been tested. Berzins *et al.* (1978) reported score patterns in 18 different samples varying in age, occupation, education, and clinical status.

Overall Assessment

The PRF ANDRO scales have good test–retest reliability and adequate internal reliability given their intentionally heterogeneous item content. Further, they demonstrate adequate freedom from response set and, especially when given as part of the IDI, control for both acquiescent and careless responding. Evidence on the PRF ANDRO's validity is generally satisfactory, although to some extent the interpretation of this evidence depends upon whether one considers its exact comparability to the BSRI to be an indicator of validity. The PRF ANDRO and BSRI share certain aspects of their underlying rationale and do share variance in correlational studies, but they should not be considered equivalent measures.

Sample PRF ANDRO Items

Masculinity Scale

1. I seek out positions of authority.

   TRUE   FALSE

2. If I have a problem, I like to work it out alone.
3. I avoid some sports and hobbies because of their dangerous nature (keyed false).
4. I don't care if my clothes are unstylish, as long as I like them.
5. When I see a new invention, I attempt to find out how it works.

Femininity Scale

1. When I see a baby, I often ask to hold him.
2. I like to be with people who assume a protective attitude toward me.
3. I am usually the first to offer a helping hand when it is needed.

Note: The items appearing here are only those cited as illustrative in Berzins *et al.* (1978). The reader wishing to administer the 56-item PRF ANDRO must obtain specific directions to the test-taker, presentation of response alternatives, etc., from J. I. Berzins (see Location section above).

Masculinity and Femininity Scales from the Adjective Check List

(Heilbrun, 1976)

Variable

Heilbrun's (1976) instrument provides separate assessments of masculinity and femininity, in terms of respondents' indications of which of a series of adjectives they consider characteristic of their own behavior.

Description and Original Subject Samples

Heilbrun's (1976) measure is a self-administered 54-item questionnaire, containing a 28-item Masculinity Scale and a 26-item Femininity Scale. (Elsewhere, the Femininity Scale is described as having 25 items; e.g., Heilbrun, 1981, 1984, 1986.) Heilbrun (1976) describes each item as a "behavioral adjective," but items are equally well described as personality trait terms. The respondent is asked to check those items which are self-descriptive.

The respondent's raw Masculinity score is the total number of Masculine items checked; raw Femininity score is the total number of Feminine items checked. Thus, raw scores can range from 0 to 28 for Masculinity and from 0 to 26 for Femininity. Heilbrun (1976) recommends that both raw scores be transformed into *t*-scores with means of 50 and standard deviations of 10, using norm tables available from Heilbrun on request (see Location, below). These 16 norm tables were developed independently for each sex from the scores of 186 college males and 320 college females by a procedure designed to reduce correlations between each scale score and the total number of adjectives checked.

Heilbrun's instrument has also been used to derive a continuous androgyny score that varies with the magnitude and balance of the two separate scale scores.

All of the items appear on the parent 300-item Adjective Check List (ACL) (Gough & Heilbrun, 1965; see also Cosentino & Heilbrun, 1964). Accordingly, respondents may complete the entire ACL, with only the relevant items being used to compute their Masculinity and Femininity scores. This appears to be Heilbrun's own usual and recommended administration strategy.

Occasionally, researchers have administered only the items comprising the separate Masculinity and Femininity scales (e.g., Kelly *et al.*, 1978; Ramanaiah & Martin, 1984; Wilson & Cook, 1984).

Heilbrun (1976) developed his scales simply by separating the two components of the Masculinity–Femininity Scale, scored from the ACL (Gough & Heilbrun, 1965). The

ACL Masculinity–Femininity Scale contains 54 adjectives (28 keyed in a masculine direction and 26 in a feminine direction) that were selected because they discriminated between college males identified with masculine fathers and college females identified with feminine mothers (Cosentino & Heilbrun, 1964; Gough & Heilbrun, 1965). "This approach to scale development sought to compile items that distinguished between two extreme criterion groups differing not only in terms of biological maleness/femaleness but also in terms of psychological masculinity/femininity" (Heilbrun, 1976, p. 184). Masculinity–Femininity scores were derived by subtracting the number of feminine items checked from the number of masculine items checked and by then transforming these raw difference scores into t-scores based on independent college norms for men and women.

In developing his separate scales, Heilbrun stated that the bipolarity of the original Masculinity–Femininity Scale "is readily corrected by the simple expedient of developing separate norms for male and female college students and maintaining the masculine and feminine subscale items as independent scales" (Heilbrun, 1976, p. 185). Thus, the newer separate scales basically differ from the older bipolar scale only in scoring procedures.

To clarify the "meaning" of his separate Masculinity and Femininity scales, Heilbrun (1976) has referred to data from Parker (1969), who identified ACL items showing differential endorsement rates by male and female college students and to data from Williams and Bennett (1975), who identified ACL items showing differences between college students' (both males' and females') sex role stereotypes of "men and women." The percentage of Heilbrun (1976) Masculine items in Parker's masculine pool was 71, and of Heilbrun Feminine items in Parker's feminine pool was 96. The percentage of Heilbrun Masculine items in Williams and Bennett's masculine pool was 82, and of Heilbrun Feminine items in Williams and Bennett's feminine pool was also 82. Further, Heilbrun (1981, p. 1109) reported that all ACL Masculine and Feminine items "correspond to the appropriate sex role stereotypes according to norms published by Williams and Best (1977)."

In sum, Heilbrun holds that his Masculinity and Femininity scales adequately capture the underlying concepts as they can be defined by identification with the appropriate (same-sex) sex-typed parent, by self-report sex differences, and by differential stereotypes of the two sexes.

With regard to scoring this measure there are several possible procedures: Heilbrun (1976) did not report any medians used for a median-split approach. However, he apparently derived medians from a combined-sex sample of 90 male and 104 female undergraduates. Use of these medians classified the following percentages of these subjects as androgynous, masculine, feminine, and undifferentiated, respectively: Males, 28, 22, 34, and 16%; Females, 28, 22, 36, and 14%. (Heilbrun did not comment on the surprisingly high percentage of feminine males.)

Heilbrun (1986) reported raw score cutoff points apparently derived from medians for a combined sample of 56 male and 55 female college students (high Masculinity > 8, high Femininity > 13). Medians appear to vary dramatically across samples. For example, from their combined sample of 183 female and 98 male graduate and undergraduate students, Wilson and Cook (1984) reported raw score medians of 14.4 for Masculinity and 18.7 for Femininity.

Given Heilbrun's t-score transformations, mean scores on both scales automatically become 50, and standard deviations are 10. This information is sometimes used to classify subjects into more or less extreme groups whose Masculinity and Femininity scores fall the desired number of standard deviations away from their respective means (e.g., Heilbrun, 1976).

There are two cautionary notes of which researchers should be explicitly aware when using Heilbrun's *t*-score tables (see below) in scoring and/or subject classification: (a) Use of these tables will mean that scores in a particular subject sample are automatically being compared to those in Heilbrun's normative sample. (b) Heilbrun transformed raw scores "independently by sex" (Heilbrun, 1976, p. 185); accordingly, use of combined-sex medians within a particular sample (a common procedure in the sex role literature) may, if done incautiously, actually represent a complex combination of the within- and between-sex distributions. Heilbrun himself often preferred (e.g., 1981) to use medians derived within sex. The various issues raised by this paragraph have not been explicitly addressed in the literature.

With these considerations in mind, researchers may sometimes prefer to use raw scores or to develop *t*-score distributions by using their own subject sample in the appropriate manner suggested by the particular research purposes. This approach also appears in the literature (e.g., Heilbrun, 1986; Kelly *et al.*, 1978).

Heilbrun and Pitman (1979) developed a continuous, unidimensional androgyny score. This score can be used as a continuous variable in (a) correlational analyses (e.g., Heilbrun & Pitman, 1979) and (b) analyses of variance as a dependent variable (e.g., Heilbrun, 1981). It has also been used to divide subjects into high and low androgynous groups by median split on androgyny scores (e.g., Heilbrun, 1984; Heilbrun & Han, 1984).

The continuous androgyny score uses *t*-score transformed raw Masculinity and Femininity scores in the following formula: Androgyny $= [(M + F) - (M - F)]$. This formula is designed to reflect what Heilbrun considers "the two necessary properties of androgyny: (1) the common strength of M and F dispositions, and (2) the balance between these dispositions" (Heilbrun, 1983, p. 398). If a respondent has both of these properties, the sum of scores will be high, while their absolute difference will be low, resulting in a high androgyny score. Using a median split procedure in a college sample of 279 males and 251 females, Heilbrun (1984, Study 2) found that androgyny scores of 88 or higher defined high androgyny. He has reported the same cut-off point in other investigations (e.g., Heilbrun, 1984, Studies 1 and 3; Heilbrun & Han, 1984) also using college student samples.

Elackman (1982) criticized Heilbrun and Pitman's (1979) androgyny score, primarily on the grounds that it groups together as low androgynous subjects who would be categorized as masculine, feminine, or undifferentiated by a four-way (i.e., median split) typology and that, since it is a unidimensional score, it loses considerable information. Heilbrun's (1983) reply is that the androgyny score is valuable if the researcher's interest is in androgyny as a unique sex role outcome and that researchers may avoid loss of information by analyzing the same data using not only the androgyny score, but also Masculinity and Femininity scores separately.

Reliability

Internal Consistency

Wiggins and Holzmuller (1978) report Cronbach's α coefficients of .77 for Femininity and .83 for Masculinity, in a sample of 117 female and 70 male college students. While Heilbrun has frequently cited these data as substantiating his scales' internal consistency (e.g., Heilbrun, 1984, 1986; Heilbrun & Pitman, 1979), he fails to note that Wiggins and Holzmuller excluded two Masculine and one Feminine item and had subjects respond on a nine-point scale rather than in the usual checklist format.

Ramanaiah and Martin (1984) found α coefficients of .82 for Femininity and .85 for

Masculinity in a sample of 89 female and 150 male college students. Wilson and Cook (1984) reported α coefficients of .82 for Masculinity and a modest .69 for Femininity in a sample of 183 female and 98 male undergraduate and graduate students. O'Grady *et al.* (1979) also reported fairly modest α coefficients of .65 for Masculinity and .74 for Femininity, in their sample of 92 male and 131 female college students.

Test–Retest

Heilbrun (1976) gave the ACL twice to 29 male and 22 female college students. He reported significant reliability coefficients (*p* values < .001) over the 10-week interval for the two sexes combined: Masculinity $r = .67$ and Femininity $r = .62$. He notes that an attenuation of reliability may have occurred because the parent Masculinity–Femininity Scale ($r = .91$ for this sample) was broken into the shorter Masculinity and Femininity scales.

Validity

Heilbrun (e.g., 1976, 1981; Heilbrun & Pitman, 1979) sometimes has seemed to cite validating data obtained with the parent ACL bipolar Masculinity–Femininity Scale as if they pertained to the validity of the separate Masculinity and Femininity scales as well. For instance, Heilbrun (1976) reported that Masculinity–Femininity scores have been shown to have the predicted relationships with aggression anxiety in both sexes (Cosentino & Heilbrun, 1964), homosexual–heterosexual orientation in both sexes (Thompson, Schwartz, McCandless, & Edwards, 1973), and peer-rated differences in female instrumental orientation (Heilbrun, 1968).

However, results obtained with the older bipolar measure do not have a straightforward implication for the newer separate scales' validity: Even though there is complete item overlap between these measures, masculinity–femininity is a difference score and as such necessarily obscures the absolute level of its masculinity and femininity components.

Correlation between Masculinity and Femininity

Heilbrun (1976) did not explicitly design his measurements of masculinity and femininity to be statistically independent. Nonetheless, he seems to treat their relationship as relevant to his scales' validity (e.g., Heilbrun & Pitman, 1979). Heilbrun (1976) reported a correlation of − .42 for 186 college males; and of − .24 for 320 college females (both *p* values < .001). Correlations between the two scales reported by other investigators using combined-sex college student samples range from − .22 (Wiggins & Holzmuller, 1978) to + .16 (Ramanaiah & Martin, 1984; see also Wilson & Cook, 1984). To some extent, differences in correlations probably depend on whether the researchers used *t*-scores normed within sexes as Heilbrun (1976) did, or raw scores, as Wilson and Cook (1984) apparently did. Wiggins and Holzmuller (1978) and Ramanaiah and Martin (1984) did not report which of these two scoring strategies they used.

Given these considerations, and given the fact that it is usually the within-sex independence of masculinity and femininity that is considered in assessing the validity of current sex role measures (e.g., Bem, 1974), Heilbrun's (1976) correlations seem most relevant. These demonstrate that his two scales are only moderately independent. This conclusion is supported by O'Grady *et al.*'s (1979) finding of a − .34 (*p* < .001) correlation between the scales (scored by Heilbrun's norms), among 131 female college students.

Freedom from Response Set

Use of Heilbrun's norm tables (see below) controls for confounding of scores with the total number of adjectives checked and as such would seem to free scores fairly well from acquiescent responding. The full ACL has four indices that measure response sets: Number of Adjectives Checked (No Ckd), Defensiveness (Df), Number of Favorable Adjectives Checked (Fav), and Number of Unfavorable Adjectives Checked (Unfav) (see Gough and Heilbrun's (1965) ACL manual below).

Discrimination of Known Groups

Heilbrun (1976) reported no data on sex differences in scores per se but noted that 71% of his Masculine scale items and 96% of his Feminine scale items were found by Parker (1969) to have different endorsement rates among male and female students who completed the entire ACL. Thus, differential endorsement rates characterize the vast majority of the relevant items.

Heilbrun (1976) reported a reanalysis of ACL data obtained from 211 homosexuals (127 males and 84 females) and 217 heterosexuals (123 males and 94 females) by Thompson *et al.* (1973; the method of sampling was not described by Heilbrun). Heilbrun (1976) found that male homosexuals had a lower mean Masculinity (48.24) score than did heterosexual males (51.05) and that female homosexuals scored both more Masculine (58.55) and less Feminine (42.90) than did heterosexual females (51.02 and 47.71, respectively). All probability levels are less than .05.

Concurrent and Predictive Validity, General Considerations

A survey of Heilbrun's writings suggests that he considers a rather broad variety of variables to be relevant to his scales' validity. A sampling of findings on such variables follows.

Adjustment   Heilbrun (1976) expected androgynous persons to display better adjustment than masculine, feminine, or undifferentiated individuals. He categorized 90 male and 104 female college students into sex role groups by the median split method, and gave subjects a measure of ego identity. Analysis of variance (on ego identity) showed significant ($p < .05$) main effects for levels of both Masculinity and Femininity; comparisons showed that androgynous subjects were better adjusted than the other three sex role groups and that undifferentiated subjects were less well adjusted than the other three groups (p values $< .001$). Sex of subject did not interact with sex role.

Heilbrun (1976) also presented data comparing the incidence of the four sex role outcomes among a 3-year sample of 227 male and 171 female college students requesting service at a campus psychological center, to that among 90 male and 104 female unselected college students. The χ-square analysis for males was not significant, but that for females was ($p < .05$), with a higher percentage of "adjusted" than of "maladjusted" females being androgynous.

Heilbrun and his colleagues have reported further evidence that androgyny confers greater advantages among women than among men, in terms of self-esteem and attributed competence (Heilbrun, 1981), in terms of cognitive attributes contributing to effective social behavior (Heilbrun, 1981, 1984), and in terms of academic achievement (Heilbrun & Han, 1984). (See also Heilbrun, 1986, for a further discussion.)

Bassoff and Glass (1982) and Whitley (1985) provided meta-analyses of large numbers of studies employing various mental health or adjustment indices; some of the studies reviewed used the ACL scales, and these two reports provide data enabling some separation of studies by sex role measure used. M. C. Taylor and Hall's (1982) meta-analysis of studies on psychological well-being does not provide such data, although the reader may identify those using the ACL scales by referring to Taylor and Hall's reference list.

Flexibility in Sex Role Behavior   Heilbrun and Pitman (1979) gave the ACL to 22 male and 22 female college students and derived each subject's androgyny score. Subjects also completed a self-report measure of sex role behaviors across eight interpersonal situations. Subjects' actual behaviors were observed when they participated in a "contest" in same-sex pairs; a variety of "masculine" (e.g., competitive, self-enhancing) and "feminine" (e.g., noncompetitive, other-enhancing) behaviors were recorded. Higher androgyny scores were related to greater self-reported flexibility for males ($p < .01$) but not for females; however, higher androgyny scores were related to greater behavioral flexibility for females ($p < .05$), but not for males. The authors offer a complex interpretation of this pattern.

The general concept of behavioral flexibility and restriction (i.e., that masculine persons restrict themselves to masculine behaviors and feminine persons restrict themselves to feminine behaviors, but androgynous persons are not behaviorally restricted) was addressed less directly by M. C. Taylor and Hall's (1982) meta-analysis of studies, divided into those using "female-typed" and/or "male-typed" dependent measures. Some of the studies included used Heilbrun's scales, although Taylor and Hall did not provide data permitting their separation from studies using other sex role measures.

Self-Descriptions on Other Personality Dimensions   Wiggins and Holzmuller (1978) analyzed data from 117 female and 70 male college students who rated the self-applicability of 1710 trait-descriptive adjectives. Included were all but two Masculine adjectives and all but two Feminine adjectives appearing on Heilbrun's (1976) scales. Factor analyses resulted in an "Interpersonal Circumplex" (IC) consisting of eight 16-item scales from the initial item pool.

Correlations of ACL Masculinity and Femininity "scale set" scores with the eight IC scales were virtually identical to those of BSRI Masculinity and Femininity "scale set" scores with the same IC scales. In both cases, Masculinity scores had their highest positive correlations with "dominant–ambitious" and their highest negative correlations with "lazy–submissive"; the Femininity scales had their highest positive correlations with "warm–agreeable" and their highest negative correlations with "cold–quarrelsome." The authors regard this pattern of results as good evidence for the construct validity of Heilbrun's scales.

Ramanaiah and Martin (1984) had 150 male and 89 female college students complete the ACL, as well as selected measures of dominance and nurturance. The authors' interpretation of their findings is that Heilbrun's scales showed high convergent and discriminant validity when evaluated in a multitrait-multimethod analysis.

Relationship of Heilbrun's Scales to Other Sex Role Measures

The Adult Measures section of this chapter presents correlations between Heilbrun's scales and the corresponding scales of the full BSRI (Table 3), of the 55- and 24-item PAQ (Table 5), and of the PRF ANDRO (Table 6).

Wiggins and Holzmuller (1978) constructed five-item "Man" and "Woman" scales that "are, in effect, caricatures of 'traditional' masculinity–femininity scales based on items that empirically discriminate men from women" (p. 43). In their college student sample (117 females and 70 males), the correlation between Woman and ACL Femininity scales was .63; that between Man and ACL Masculinity scales was .42. These authors conclude that, although ACL scales "are conceptually distinct from the traditional masculinity–femininity measures, they share a considerable amount of variance in common" (p. 48).

Location

Gough, H. G., & Heilbrun, A. L. (1965). *The Adjective Check List manual.* Palo Alto, CA: Consulting Psychologists Press. (Full ACL)

Heilbrun, A. B. (1976). Measurement of masculine and feminine sex role identities as independent dimensions. *Journal of Consulting and Clinical Psychology, **44**,* 183–190.

Heilbrun, A. B., Jr., Department of Psychology, Emory University, Atlanta, Georgia 30322. (Norm tables)

Results and Comments

Heilbrun's scales are not factorially pure. Wilson and Cook (1984) factor-analyzed ACL responses of 183 female and 98 male college students and found that the Masculinity and Femininity scales yielded nine and seven factors, respectively. When they factor-analyzed pooled items from the ACL, PAQ, BSRI, and PRF ANDRO, they found Heilbrun's scales to have greater factorial complexity than those of the other three instruments. O'Grady *et al.* (1979) gave 92 male and 131 female college students the ACL, BSRI, and PAQ; their interpretation of their factor analyses is that the ACL Femininity scale shared only a modest amount of variance with the corresponding BSRI and PAQ scales.

Researchers have attempted to relate ACL Masculinity and Femininity scores to a variety of other variables, including (in addition to those listed in the Validity section above) intelligence (Humphreys, 1978); intraception, social insight, and personal defensiveness (Heilbrun, 1981); tolerance for ambiguity and decoding of facial expressions (Heilbrun, 1984); a measure of "blending" in sex-role behavior (Heilbrun, 1986); and a "gender schema task" (Heilbrun, 1986).

Overall Assessment

Heilbrun's ACL scales have generated a considerable amount of research. The scales have moderate test–retest reliability and inconsistent, though usually moderate or better, internal reliability. The Masculinity and Femininity scales show inconsistent relationships to each other across studies and appear to be only moderately independent (see also Kelly & Worell's, 1977, comments). This latter finding, of course, has different implications, depending upon the particular researcher's theoretical orientation.

The decision as to how to score Heilbrun's scales can be complicated. Further, comparability of results across studies is rendered difficult by researchers' inconsistent use of Heilbrun's norms, raw versus *t*-transformed scores, and between- versus within-sex medians. The implications of this inconsistency have not yet been systematically examined.

ACL Masculinity and Femininity scales' content reflect the largely empirical nature of the parent ACL. The scales include both desirable and undesirable traits (see also Kelly & Worell, 1977, on this point) and item selection criteria differ in important respects from those used in constructing other sex role scales. Heilbrun nowhere specifically comments on the implications these issues should have for theory-driven research using his scales; instead, he seems to have adopted the idea that his instrument should theoretically operate in research much as the BSRI would. While some researchers seem to agree with this idea (e.g., Ramanaiah & Martin, 1984; Wiggins & Holzmuller, 1978), others point to fairly low correlations between the relevant BSRI and Heilbrun scales and urge caution in assuming that these measures have equivalent domains of relevance (e.g., O'Grady *et al.*, 1979; Small *et al.*, 1979). The present author shares the latter point of view.

ACL Masculinity and Femininity Scale Items

Masculine Items	Feminine Items
Aggressive	Appreciative
Arrogant	Considerate
Assertive	Contented
Autocratic	Cooperative
Conceited	Dependent
Confident	Emotional
Cynical	Excitable
Deliberate	Fearful
Dominant	Feminine
Enterprising	Fickle
Forceful	Forgiving
Foresighted	Friendly
Frank	Frivolous
Handsome	Helpful
Hard-headed	Jolly
Industrious	Modest
Ingenious	Praising
Inventive	Sensitive
Masculine	Sentimental
Opportunistic	Sincere
Outspoken	Submissive
Self-confident	Sympathetic
Sharp-witted	Talkative
Shrewd	Timid
Stern	Warm
Strong	Worrying
Tough	
Vindictive	

Note: This list contains all 54 items on Heilbrun's (1976) ACL measure. However, the reader wishing to administer this measure must obtain specific directions to the test-taker, presentation format for items, and scoring details from A. B. Heilbrun and permission from Consulting Psychologists Press (see Location section, above).

Independent Masculinity and Femininity Scales from the California Psychological Inventory

(Baucom, 1976)

Variable

Baucom's (1976) scales provide independent assessments of masculinity and femininity in terms of the respondent's agreement or disagreement with self-descriptive statements of heterogeneous content that have been shown to produce sex differences in endorsement rates.

Description and Original Subject Samples

Baucom has frequently (e.g., Baucom, 1983; Baucom, Besch, & Callahan, 1985) called his instrument a measure of "sex role identity." Further, he stated that the masculine and feminine "types [as identified by his scales] are viewed as the cultural stereotypes of masculinity and femininity, respectively" (Baucom, 1976, p. 876). The cautious researcher will bear in mind that the scales actually assess the extent to which individuals respond as most men or most women do. (Issues pertaining to the exact variables measured by the scales are made somewhat more complex by Baucom's various subject classification schemes; see below.)

According to Baucom and Aiken (1984), several investigations (Baucom, 1976, 1980, 1983; Baucom & Danker-Brown, 1979, 1983, 1984; Baucom & Sanders, 1978; Baucom *et al.*, 1985) "indicate that masculinity, as measured by MSC, involves an active, assertive, goal-oriented set of attitudes and behaviors . . . [and that] Femininity, as measured by FMN, incorporates a sense of responsibility and commitment to society's mores . . ." (p. 439).

Baucom's scales are self-administered and contain a total of 96 statements, to each of which respondents indicate "true" or "false", as it applies to themselves. Of the 54 Masculine (MSC) Scale items, 11 are keyed true and 43 are keyed false; of the 42 Femininity (FMN) Scale items, 9 are keyed true and 33 are keyed false. Respondents' MSC score is the sum of their keyed responses to MSC items and can vary from 0 to 54; their FMN score is the sum of their keyed responses to FMN items and can vary from 0 to 42.

Baucom's 96 items are usually administered alone (e.g., Baucom, 1983; Baucom & Danker-Brown, 1979; Baucom & Sanders, 1978; Baucom *et al.*, 1985; House, 1986). Item order is not explicitly given in the literature; Baucom sometimes (e.g., Baucom & Danker-Brown, 1983) stated that he administers the items as two unlabeled scales. House (1986) administered MSC and FMN items in an "intermingled" order (p. 250).

Alternatively, respondents may (e.g., Baucom, 1976, 1980; Baucom & Weiss, 1986) complete the full 480-item CPI (Gough, 1957), which is composed of 18 content scales and includes the 54 MSC and 42 FMN items. One advantage of the latter approach is that the CPI's Gi (Good Impression) Scale may be used as a check on social desirability response set. Completion of the full CPI requires 45–60 min.

While Baucom (1976) selected all MSC and FMN items from the CPI, he stressed that his scales are in no way an update of the CPI Femininity (Fe) (Gough, 1966) scale. The latter is bipolar and was designed "for different purposes; to differentiate males from females and sexual deviates from normals; . . . and to operate cross-culturally" (Baucom, 1976, p. 876).

Baucom (1976) gave the full CPI to 159 male and 128 female college students and used sex differences in endorsement rates to select MSC and FMN items. Specifically, Baucom divided his subjects, separately by sex, into "a two-thirds and a one-third sample" (p. 876). Items were selected by a two-step process. First, if an item met the following criteria for both male and female samples it was included on MSC: At least 70% of the males responded to it in a given direction, and the females endorsed it at least 10% less than the males. Analogous procedures were used to select FMN items. (Baucom does not report the number of items meeting these criteria.) Second, items that correlated significantly ($p < .05$) with MSC in all four samples and that did not correlate with FMN in any sample were added to MSC. Analogous procedures were used to add FMN items. These procedures resulted in the final 54-item MSC and 42-item FMN scales.

Studies using MSC and FMN scores (see above) for subject classification into sex role groups have typically employed one of two very different approaches.

Extreme Groups Approach

In his original article, Baucom (1976) reported raw score cutoff points that he used to construct "A four-fold typology of sex roles (high MSC–high FMN, low MSC–low FMN, high MSC–low FMN, low MSC–high FMN) similar to that of Spence *et al.* (1975)" (p. 876). This statement is actually misleading, since Baucom's (1976) cutoffs were apparently not the scale medians (he did not report these), and apparently exclude some subjects from classification. Although the 1976 article did not explicitly state how cut-offs were derived, Baucom and Sanders (1978) strongly implied that the 1976 cutoffs represented an extreme groups approach; and Baucom explicitly used such an approach in his 1980 study to be described below. In his 1976 article, Baucom gave the following cutoffs: Males, high MSC $\geq$ 46, high FMN $\geq$ 28, low MSC $\leq$ 38, low FMN $\leq$ 23; Females, high MSC $\geq$ 33; high FMN $\geq$ 35, low MSC $\leq$ 29, low FMN $\leq$ 31. He does not report the percentages of subjects in this sample who fell into the four sex role groups. Baucom (1976) did report mean scores in his normative sample (Males: MSC = 40.4; FMN = 25.5; Females: MSC = 31.5, FMN = 33.0).

In 1980, Baucom reported a study in which he gave his scales to 172 female and 202 male college students (his 1976 sample, plus an additional 44 females and 43 males). He explicitly stated that "high" scores were those in the upper one-third of the same-sex distribution and "low" scores were those in the bottom one-third of the same-sex distribution. He reported exactly the same cutoffs for his expanded 1980 sample as for the normative sample. It is possible to calculate, from data given in Baucom's (1980) article, the percentages of subjects falling into the four sex role groups composed by use of these cutoffs: Of the males, 101 were classified; of these, 25% were high MSC–high FMN (androgynous), 23% were high MSC–low FMN (masculine), 30% were low MSC–high FMN (feminine), and 23% were low MSC–low FMN (undifferentiated). Of the females, 103 were classified; of these 33% were androgynous, 21% were masculine, 20% were feminine, and 25% were undifferentiated. (Baucom did not discuss the unusual fact that his system classified somewhat greater percentages of subjects as cross-sex-typed than as sex-typed.)

In several additional studies, Baucom and his colleagues have used either his exact 1976 cutoffs (e.g., Baucom & Danker-Brown, 1979, 1983, 1984; Baucom & Sanders, 1978; Baucom & Weiss, 1986) or have slightly modified them if scores in the particular sample are lower or higher than those in the normative sample (e.g., Baucom, 1983).

There are two important cautions to be noted concerning this classification system: (1) Since cutoffs were derived within sex, a particular comparison is implied by subjects' sex role assignments. As Baucom (1980) put it ". . . to refer to a female as masculine, for example . . . [means that] . . . the female is behaving more like a male than females typically behave" (p. 263). (2) Since Baucom's (1976, 1980) approach defines sex-role types as extreme groups, results obtained with this approach are not directly comparable to those obtained with a median split approach. This lack of comparability is readily obscured by Baucom's use of the same terms (i.e., androgynous, undifferentiated, masculine, and feminine) to refer to his sex role groups as are used by authors who routinely define these concepts (e.g., Spence, Bem) by median split procedures. (See Baucom & Sanders, 1978, for a rare instance in which differences between median split and extreme group classifications are explicitly noted.)

Median Split Approach

Baucom and others have also, although more rarely, classified subjects by a straightforward median split procedure, deriving medians (when specified) within each sex separately in the particular sample (e.g., Baucom & Aiken, 1984; Baucom *et al.,* 1985; House, 1986).

Treatment of MSC and FMN raw scores as continuous variables in correlational analyses also appears in the literature (Baucom, 1980; Baucom & Aiken, 1984; House, 1986).

Reliability

Internal Consistency

Baucom (1976) reported no data on this, and a search of the literature produced no relevant information.

Test–Retest

Baucom (1976) reported 3-week test–retest reliabilities obtained on data from 31 college students (breakdown by sex unspecified) of .93 for MSC and .80 for FMN. Baucom and Aiken (1984) gave Baucom's scales twice to husbands and wives in 18 "wait list" distressed couples seeking marital therapy. They reported no significant changes in either MSC or FMN during the 10-week period.

Validity

Correlation between MSC and FMN

Baucom (1976) intended to design scales that were statistically independent; therefore, the relationship between MSC and FMN scores is important validating evidence. Baucom's (1976) only comment on this was "In none of the four [normative] samples was MSC correlated with FMN at $p < .05$" (p. 876). A search of the literature produced no more specific data published on this question (although they are presumably available from Baucom; see Location, below). Baucom's (1976) smallest normative sample contained 43 females: For a correlation to reach a two-tailed p level of .05 in this sample, it would have to be around .30 or more. Therefore, it is safe to assume that the correlations between MSC and FMN was less than .30 in all normative samples and that Baucom's assertion that his scales are independent is indeed justified.

Freedom from Response Set

Since some MSC and FMN items are keyed true and some false, there is a degree of built-in protection against acquiescent response bias. This is somewhat attenuated by the fact that 80% of the MSC items and 79% of the FMN items are keyed false. This issue is not addressed in the literature.

If respondents complete the entire CPI, socially desirable responding may be assessed by scores on the Gi (Good Impression) Scale. Other CPI indices may be used to assess different response sets. (Gough, 1957, see Location, below.)

Discrimination of Known Groups

In Baucom's perspective, sex differences on MSC and FMN are important validity data. He reported that, in his 1976 (combined) sample, one-tailed *t*-tests showed significant ($p < .001$) sex differences in the expected direction for both scales (MSC: Males' $\bar{M} = 40.4$, Females' $\bar{M} = 31.5$; FMN: Males' $\bar{M} = 25.5$, Females' $\bar{M} = 33.0$). Data relevant to sex differences in scores may also be found in House (1986).

Concurrent and Predictive Validity within Baucom's
Theoretical Perspective

Baucom (1976) said that his "view resembles Bem's [1974] notion of androgyny," except that he holds that "In addition to balance, the absolute amounts of masculinity and femininity are important" (p. 876). This statement helps explain his obvious preference for using cutoffs or medians to classify subjects. Further, in line with his interpretation of Bem's (1974) ideas, Baucom (1976) expressed the expectations that high MSC–high FMN subjects will be "the most psychologically healthy of the four types . . . low-masculine/low-feminine [will be] . . . the most inadequate of the types," and the other two types will represent "the cultural stereotypes of masculinity and femininity" (p. 876). The evidence reviewed below was selected for this section by its degree of apparent relevance to these expectations.

Psychological Health and Other Variables Related to the Positivity–Negativity
of Masculinity and Femininity

1. Self-descriptions. Baucom (1980) gave 202 male and 172 female undergraduates the full CPI and ACL (Gough & Heilbrun, 1965). Correlations between MSC, FMN, and the 18 basic CPI scales were similar for both sexes. Baucom stated that results showed both masculinity and femininity to be positive concepts. According to his summary of the overall correlation patterns: "masculine persons are comfortable as leaders, understand other people, are accepting and nonjudgmental toward others, and have good intellectual skills . . . feminine individuals are dependable and conscientious, have emotional sensitivity, have good self-regulation, and are achievers" (p. 269). Baucom (1980) also categorized subjects by his 1976 cutoffs and provided descriptions of each sex role type based on their CPI and ACL responses. He noted that "androgynous and masculine sex-typed [persons] . . . described themselves in more positive terms than feminine sex-typed and undifferentiated persons" (p. 271).

2. Peer ratings. Baucom and Danker-Brown (1983) categorized 20 male and 20 female undergraduates into each of the four sex role groups, using the 1976 cutoffs. Each subject named a close same-sex friend who they felt could accurately describe them on the

ACL. Analysis of these peers' ratings showed that androgynous persons were perceived most positively overall and undifferentiated persons were perceived least positively. Interestingly, this effect seemed mostly due to positive perceptions of those high in FMN compared to those low in FMN.

3. Marital satisfaction. Baucom and Aiken (1984) studied 72 maritally distressed couples and 126 nondistressed couples. All husbands and wives completed the MSC and FMN scales and a measure of marital satisfaction. Data were analyzed correlationally using continuous scores and by analyses of variance using sex role categories derived by within-sex median splits on this sample's scores. Baucom and Aiken's results were complex, but the relevant points to note here are that (a) there were significantly more androgynous persons in the nondistressed than in the distressed sample and that (b) "both MSC and FMN were positively correlated with marital satisfaction, with some indications that femininity is the more important factor" (p. 442). House (1986) also reports a study of marital satisfaction.

4. Depression and learned helplessness. Baucom and his colleagues have conducted four separate investigations (Baucom, 1983; Baucom & Danker-Brown, 1979, 1984; Baucom & Weiss, 1986) that used different procedures to investigate depression and especially learned helplessness phenomena with particular reference to females. All subjects were college students. Baucom and Weiss's (1986) summary of findings across the four studies includes the following passage especially relevant here: "Androgynous women seek control, are granted more control on all but methodical tasks . . . and respond to a loss of control with minimal helplessness . . . feminine sex-typed women do not seek control as much as other women, are not granted much control by their peers on certain valued types of tasks, and respond to a loss of control with helplessness symptoms" (p. 1079).

5. M. C. Taylor and Hall's (1982) and Whitley's (1985) meta-analyses of psychological well-being studies include some that used Baucom's scales. While Taylor and Hall did not provide data permitting the separation of studies by sex role scale used, Whitley provides full separation by scales.

Evidence Relevant to MSC and FMN as Assessing "Cultural Stereotypes of Masculinity and Femininity," Respectively   Baucom (1980) found that, among 202 male and 172 female college students categorized into sex role groups by the 1976 cutoffs, CPI profiles were significantly different within each sex across the four sex role groups. In his summary, Baucom said that, in both sexes, "The self-description of high MSC/low FMN and low MSC/high FMN groups corresponded to stereotypic views of masculinity and femininity, respectively." (p. 262). (See Baucom & Danker-Brown, 1983, Table 1 for a similar kind of evidence concerning peer-rated adjectives characterizing the four sex role groups.)

M. C. Taylor and Hall (1982) meta-analyzed many studies, divided into those that used "female-typed" or "male-typed" dependent measures. While some of these studies used Baucom's scales, data permitting their separation from those using other sex role measures are not provided.

Relationship of MSC and FMN to Other Sex Role Measures

BSRI Scales

1. Correlations. Since Baucom (1976) explicitly referred to Bem's views and test, his scales' relationships to the BSRI scales deserve brief mention here. In a group of 109

female undergraduates, Baucom and Sanders (1978) found correlations of .56 and .23 (both *p* values < .01) between the two instruments' masculinity and femininity scales, respectively. These authors considered the masculinity correlation to be high; they offered two possibilities as explanations for the low femininity correlation: (a) restricted score ranges on the two scales; and (b) the fact that Baucom's scale contains items that actually differentiate the sexes, whereas Bem's contains items that have differential sex-typed social desirability.

2. Similarity in result patterns. Separate analyses of variance on Attitudes toward Women (AWS) (Spence *et al.*, 1973) scores, which categorized Baucom and Sanders' (1978) 109 female undergraduates by median splits on the BSRI, and by Baucom's (1976) cutoffs on MSC and FMN, showed that, for both sex role instruments: (a) High masculine scorers were more profeminist than low masculine scorers, and (b) high and low feminine scorers did not differ in level of feminism.

Baucom *et al.* (1985) gave 84 female college students both the BSRI and Baucom's scales. They did not report correlations between the relevant scores. However, they did find a similar result pattern in two analyses that categorized subjects by median splits separately on the BSRI scales, and on MSC and FMN: In both analyses, feminine women had the lowest concentrations of salivary testosterone; and females high in masculinity had somewhat higher concentrations of salivary testosterone than did feminine women.

CPI Fe   Baucom (1976) reported correlations for his normative sample with CPI Fe scores: Males, *r* with MSC = −.32, *r* with FMN = .60; females *r* with MSC = −.34, *r* with FMN = .20 (all *p* values < .01, in the expected directions). He (1980) reported exactly these same correlations when his original sample was expanded by adding 44 female and 43 male college students. Baucom (1976) notes that there is item overlap: 12 MSC items (22%) and 12 FMN items (29%) are on CPI Fe.

Location

Baucom, D. H. (1976). Independent Masculinity and Femininity scales on the California Psychological Inventory. *Journal of Consulting and Clinical Psychology*, **44**, 876. (Lists CPI item numbers appearing on MSC and FMN scales.)

Donald H. Baucom, Psychology Department, Davie Hall 013A, University of North Carolina, Chapel Hill, North Carolina 27514. (Extended report of above study.)

Gough, H. G. (1956). *California Psychological Inventory*. Palo Alto, CA: Consulting Psychologists Press. (CPI items)

Results and Comments

Extensive efforts failed to discover any factor analyses of MSC and FMN items. These scales are extremely heterogeneous in content. However, this is apparently not an issue for Baucom, since he never explicitly refers to item heterogeneity and since his sole item selection criterion (of sex differences in endorsement rates for CPI items) guaranteed heterogeneity.

Despite its irrelevance to Baucom's perspective, researchers should be aware that MSC and FMN cover a very broad range of content areas, from vocational preferences (e.g., MSC, CPI #28: "I think I would like the work of a dress designer;" FMN, CPI #82: "I think I would like the work of a garage mechanic") to activity preferences (e.g., FMN, CPI #122: "I like poetry;" MSC CPI #269: "I like science") to self-reports of past behavior (e.g., MSC, CPI #72: "I used to keep a diary;" FMN, CPI #420: "I used to steal sometimes when I was a youngster") to a host of other different aspects of self-description (see also sample items in list following this review). Since Baucom's published articles never give item examples, internal consistency information, or factor analytic data, this diversity of content is easily overlooked.

According to Baucom's (1976) list of item numbers, CPI item #87 ("I like adventure stories better than romantic stories") appears on both MSC and FMN, scored in opposite directions.

(Actual CPI item content provided in both points above were taken from Gough, 1956. See Location, above.)

MSC and FMN both include some seemingly undesirable characteristics. Baucom explicitly mentioned this only once, in passing (Baucom, 1980, p. 269).

Given all of the above points, future research should more fully characterize MSC and FMN's content. Such information would make possible more discriminating comparisons with other scales than are now feasible. Such data would also permit more intelligent assessment of whether Baucom and Aiken's (1984) description of MSC and FMN (see Variable, above) is fully warranted: This description makes Baucom's scales seem to share the largely instrumental–expressive content of the BSRI and PAQ to a greater extent than they actually may. It will be recalled that the corresponding BSRI and Baucom scales do not correlate highly.

Overall Assessment

Some characteristics of Baucom's scales are quite satisfactory: For example, test–retest reliability is good; MSC and FMN are independent; response set problems may be addressed when subjects complete the full CPI; and MSC and FMN scores differentiate the sexes, as is necessary given Baucom's intention. Further, Baucom's own research, reviewed under Validity above, lends substantial credence to the construct validity of MSC and FMN.

However, the heterogeneity of the scales is not addressed, and the issues raised by the use of various cutoffs for subject categorization (see above) may pose some problems for researchers using Baucom's scales. (For example, one wonders to what extent the construct validity "success" of MSC and FMN depends upon the extreme groups approach.)

Most, though not all (e.g., Baucom & Sanders, 1978; House, 1986) research has employed college student samples, and the vast majority of published references are those of Baucom and his colleagues.

Masculinity and Femininity Scales from the California Psychological Inventory (CPI)

MSC Items

Keyed TRUE: 53, 87, 100, 108, 126, 202, 259, 269, 320, 359, 399

Sample items: I think I would enjoy having authority over other
                 people. (53)
                 I prefer a shower to a bathtub. (100)

Keyed FALSE: 7, 13, 27, 28, 31, 35, 38, 40, 58, 68, 70, 72, 76, 85, 91, 111, 124, 144, 145, 147, 177, 186, 187, 227, 232, 238, 240, 252, 258, 272, 284, 286, 301, 309, 334, 369, 383, 391, 418, 422, 429, 452, 480.

Sample items: When in a group of people I usually do what the others want rather than make suggestions. (7)
I become quite irritated when I see someone spit on the sidewalk. (35)

FMN Items

Keyed TRUE: 110, 122, 146, 150, 212, 230, 328, 348, 443

Sample items: The thought of being in an automobile accident is very frightening to me. (110)
I would like to wear expensive clothes. (146)

Keyed FALSE: 19, 26, 29, 33, 36, 39, 49, 82, 87, 114, 117, 129, 143, 171, 196, 210, 211, 214, 239, 249, 263, 268, 291, 393, 420, 428, 431, 456, 468, 469, 470, 474, 479

Sample items: I think I would like the work of a building contractor. (19)
When I was going to school I played hookey quite often. (36)
At times I feel like picking a fist fight with someone. (114)

Note: This list contains all CPI item numbers for Baucom's (1976) 96-item measure, and a few illustrative examples for each kind of item. The reader wishing to administer this measure must obtain specific directions to the test-taker, presentation format for items, and scoring details from D. H. Baucom, as well as permission from Consulting Psychologists Press (see Location section above). Sources for this list: Item numbers and keying, Baucom, D. H. (1976); Sample items, Gough, H. G. (1956).

Sex Role Behavior Scale

(Orlofsky, 1981)

Variable

The SRBS assesses "the interest/role behavior level of sex roles," which Orlofsky (1981) considered to be distinct from sex role personality traits and sex role attitudes.

Description and Original Subject Samples

Orlofsky (1981) stated that he modeled his scale development procedures on the rationale used in constructing the PAQ (Spence *et al.*, 1975) and that in doing so he intended to identify aspects of masculine and feminine behavior that are independent or even positively related to each other, as well as aspects that are negatively related and follow a bipolar pattern.

Analogous to the PAQ's assessment of personality traits, the SRBS provides separate assessments of masculine and feminine interests and behaviors, in terms of the respondent's endorsement (as self-descriptive) of behaviors stereotypically believed to differentiate the sexes but considered socially desirable in both sexes. It also provides an assessment of the respondent's endorsement (as self-descriptive) of behaviors stereotypically believed to differentiate the sexes but considered more socially desirable for one sex than the other.

The SRBS-1 (Orlofsky, 1981) is a self-administered 160-item questionnaire that has Male-Valued, Female-Valued, and Sex-Specific subscales in each of the four behavior areas of recreational activities, vocational interests, social and dating behaviors, and marital behaviors. Subjects rate themselves on each item, from 1 or "not at all characteristic of me" to 5 or "extremely characteristic of me." (See list at the end of this section for sample items from each category.)

Orlofsky (1981) states that he garnered items from existing sex-role inventories and from anecdotal sources relevant to the four behavioral areas listed above.

Orlofsky (1981) had 528 college students rate each of the 239 items that resulted under one of three instructional sets: Approximately one-third of the subjects (83 males and 85 females) directly compared the typical young adult man and woman on a five-point scale whose midpoint was labeled "no difference, equally characteristic;" one-third (104 males, 85 females) rated the desirability of the items for a young man, and separately, for a young woman (order of ratings counterbalanced) on a four-point scale ranging from "very undesirable or inappropriate" to "very desirable and appropriate;" and the remaining subjects rated themselves on a five-point scale ranging from "not at all" to "extremely characteristic of me." SRBS-1 items were selected by using the desirability and typicality ratings. Those that both males and females rated as significantly more typical of one sex than the other (individual item t-tests for differences from the scale midpoint with an α level of .001) but as desirable for both sexes (above the midpoint of the desirability scale) were assigned to the 51-item Male-Valued and 32-item Female-Valued scales. Items rated by both sexes as significantly more typical of one sex than the other, and as significantly more desirable for that sex than the other (again, individual t-tests, α level .001) were assigned to the Sex-Specific Scale, which consists of 46 masculine sex-specific and 31 feminine sex-specific items.

In discussing the nature of the items that satisfied these criteria for inclusion in the SRBS-1, Orlofsky (1981) notes parallels with PAQ trait scales and with general conceptions of masculinity and femininity: Specifically, he states that Male- and Female-Valued items generally seem to reflect instrumental and expressive behaviors, respectively; while Sex-Specific items reflect "role behaviors involving physical strength, dominance, and aggressiveness versus those involving accommodation and domesticity" (p. 938).

Persons completing the SRBS-1 receive three scores for their self-ratings: The Male-Valued score is the sum of the Male-Valued item ratings, and can range from 255 (most masculine) to 51; the Female-Valued score is the sum of the Female-Valued item ratings, and can range from 160 (most feminine) to 32; the Sex-Specific score is the sum of the masculine Sex-Specific item ratings (with the most masculine choice for each item coded as 5) and the feminine Sex-Specific item ratings (with the most feminine choice for each item coded as 1). The Sex-Specific score is thus bipolar and can range from 385 (most masculine and least feminine) to 77 (most feminine and least masculine).

These three scores may not only be obtained for the overall SRBS-1, as described above, but a corresponding set of three scores may also be derived by following the same procedures within each of the four behavior areas. However, if individual behavior area subscores are desired, it is recommended that the Revised SRBS or SRBS-2 (Orlofsky *et al.*, 1982) be used, since some of the area subscales of the SRBS-1 demonstrated poor internal consistency. The SRBS-2 is described below.

While most research with the SRBS-1 and SRBS-2 has treated subjects' scores as continuous variables, it is possible to use the same kind of median split procedures employed with other sex role tests reviewed in this chapter to categorize subjects into sex role groups. Orlofsky himself (Orlofsky & O'Heron, 1987) reported only one study in which he used a median split procedure on SRBS-2 scores (see below).

For consideration of the scale's psychometric properties, the relevant sample is the 95 male and 77 female college students who rated themselves on the items in Orlofsky's (1981) initial item pool.

Reliability

Internal Consistency

Orlofsky (1981) reported α coefficients of .81 for men and .82 for women on the overall Male-Valued scale, .78 for men and .59 for women on the overall Female-Valued scale, and .88 for men and .87 for women on the overall Sex-Specific scale.

Alpha coefficients for the Sex-Specific behavior area subscales and for three of the Male-Valued behavior area subscales were satisfactory (ranging from .56 to .88) but were less so for the Female-Valued behavior area subscales (ranging from .40 to .74) and for the Male-Valued social and dating behavior subscale (.06 for males and .40 for females). The SRBS-2 (Orlofsky *et al.*, 1982; see below) was developed to improve behavior area subscales' reliability and should be used by researchers who wish to employ area subscale scores.

Test–Retest

Orlofsky (1981) did not assess this.

Validity

Relationships among Male-Valued, Female-Valued, and Sex-Specific Scales

In accordance with his reasoning in developing the SRBS-1, Orlofsky (1981) found significant (p values $< .001$) correlations between the overall Male-Valued and Female-Valued scales for both men ($r = .50$) and women ($r = .38$), suggesting that these stereotypical behaviors are not only not bipolar but are actually moderately positively related. Also in accordance with his reasoning and scale development procedure, Orlofsky (1981) found a substantial negative correlation (r for both sexes combined $= -.69$, $p < .0001$) between scores on the masculine Sex-Specific and feminine Sex-Specific items included in the overall Sex-Specific scale. Finally, scores on the overall Sex-Specific Scale showed, as expected, small positive correlations with overall Male-Valued scale scores ($r = .29$, $p < .01$, for men; $r = .16$, ns, for women) and negative correlations with overall Female-Valued scale scores ($r = -.20$, $p < .05$, for men; $r = -.46$, $p < .001$, for women).

Discrimination of Known Groups

Males and females in Orlofsky's (1981) self-rating sample differed significantly (p values $< .001$) on the overall Male-Valued (male $\bar{M} = 156.77$; female $\bar{M} = 140.77$) and Female-Valued (means of 88.65 and 111.79, respectively) scales. Significant (p values $< .001$)

sex differences were also found in the expected directions on all of the area subscales except Male-Valued vocational interests.

Miscellaneous

Orlofsky (1981) reasoned that sex role interests and behaviors would exhibit minimal relationships with sex role traits and attitudes. His findings support this reasoning. Subjects in the SRBS-1 self-rating group of Orlofsky's (1981) initial sample also completed the Personal Attributes Questionnaire (Spence *et al.*, 1975) and the Attitudes toward Women Scale (25-item version, Spence *et al.*, 1973). Correlations between the corresponding PAQ and SRBS overall Male-Valued, Female-Valued, and Sex-Specific scales computed for males and females separately showed that all relationships were small (ranging from $-.22$ to $.38$), with only some of those involving the Female-Valued scales significant. Further, a Sex $\times$ PAQ Sex Role Category (median split) analysis of variance on SRBS scores showed few sex role group differences, indicating that there is minimal relationship between traditionality–nontraditionality of sex role traits and masculine and feminine interests or behaviors.

Correlations between AWS and SRBS scores were significant, though small, only for the SRBS Sex-Specific scale (males, $r = -.27$; females, $r = .29$; both p values $< .01$), indicating that individuals with more egalitarian attitudes are somewhat less sex-typed in behavior than those with more traditional attitudes.

Location

Jacob L. Orlofsky, Department of Psychology, University of Missouri, St. Louis, MO 63121. (SRBS-1 and SRBS-2)

Results and Comments

Other Uses for the SRBS

While the SRBS is intended primarily as a self-report test, Orlofsky (1981) notes that it may also be used to assess subjects' "attitudes or beliefs concerning appropriate or desirable behavior for the sexes and differences between them (using ideal ratings and ideal female–ideal male difference ratings)" (p. 931). Orlofsky (1981) reports some data relevant to such uses of the SRBS.

Development of the SRBS-2

Orlofsky himself (Orlofsky, 1981; Orlofsky *et al.*, 1982) noted two shortcomings of the SRBS-1: Some behavior area subscales contained disproportionately few items, and internal consistency for some area subscales was poor. In 1982, Orlofsky *et al.* generated additional items garnered from existing sex role tests and anecdotal sources, to supplement the SRBS-1 vocational preferences, social interaction, and marital behavior subscales. Two hundred and sixteen items not on the SRBS-1 were given to 260 male and 260 female college students. Approximately one-third of the males and one-third of the females rated each of these items under each of the same three instructional sets used by Orlofsky in 1981. Subjects in the self-rating condition also described themselves on the 160 SRBS-1 items. Those new items that met the same selection criteria used in 1981 (see above) and that resulted in acceptable scale and area subscale reliabilities in the self-rating condition were assigned to the Male-Valued, Female-Valued, and Sex-Specific scales. The resultant SRBS-2 has 240 items, divided into Recreational and Leisure Activities (40 items), Vocational Preferences (48 items), Social Interaction (46 items), and Marital Behavior (106 items) area subscales.

The pattern of sex differences on the SRBS-2 is the same as that on the SRBS-1 (see above). Internal consistency analyses on the SRBS-2 show that this revision is indeed an improvement: "Alpha coefficients for the overall SRBS-2 scales and area subscales were all equal to or greater than .70 for the combined sexes, though these were somewhat lower for some area subscales when the sexes were considered separately" (p. 636; Orlofsky *et al.*, 1982, did not report more specific internal consistency data.)

Intercorrelations among SRBS-2 area subscales, examined for men and women separately, were all positive, though of small to moderate magnitude. Orlofsky *et al.* (1982) stated that this pattern shows that persons are partially consistent in sex-typing across behavior areas but that sex role behaviors are not unidimensional. Thus, they suggest that SRBS-2 area subscales "should be used separately as well as collectively" (p. 637).

Subject Classification Using the SRBS-2

As noted earlier, most research using the SRBS-1 and SRBS-2 has used continuous scores rather than any subject classification scheme. However, Orlofsky and O'Heron (1987) used SRBS-2 scores to classify 200 male and 211 female undergraduates, using a median split procedure. In doing so, they first averaged each subject's responses across items separately within overall SRBS-2 Male-Valued and Female-Valued scales: They reported medians on these scales of 3.06 and 3.02, respectively. Percentages of subjects classified as androgynous, masculine, feminine, and undifferentiated, respectively, were for males, 18, 53, 3, and 27% and females, 30, 2, 54, and 14%. The authors note that SRBS-2 cross-sex-typed subjects (masculine females and feminine males) made up only 2% of the combined-sex sample; whereas 24-item PAQ cross-sex-typed subjects made up 10% of this sample.

Additional Research Using the SRBS-2

Orlofsky, Cohen, and Ramsden (1985) gave 100 male and 100 female college students the SRBS-2, the 24-item PAQ (Spence & Helmreich, 1978), and the 25-item AWS (Spence *et al.*, 1973). Their goal was to examine the intercorrelations among these measures to test two competing perspectives:

> The social-learning point-of-view of Janet Spence and her colleagues [which] asserts a general independence of sex role personality traits, attitudes, and behaviors . . . [and the] . . . cognitive-developmental theory of Sandra Bem [which] asserts that sex role phenomena are fairly closely interrelated, at least for sex-typed individuals whose gender schemas cause them to adhere closely to traditional sex role norms in their self-concepts and behavior. (p. 377)

In contrast to Orlofsky's own (1981) findings with the SRBS-1, results of this study showed moderate relationships for each sex between both overall and behavior subarea SRBS-2 Male-Valued, Female-Valued and Sex-Specific scales and the corresponding PAQ scales and between AWS scores and certain SRBS-2 overall scales. The authors concluded that their findings lend partial support for both Bem's and Spence's positions.

Orlofsky and O'Heron (1987) gave 200 male and 211 female college students the

SRBS-2, the 24-item PAQ, and the 25-item AWS. Subjects also completed self-report questionnaires measuring self-esteem and social adjustment. The authors' goal was to test whether traditional sex-typing (sex role congruence), androgyny, or masculinity is best associated with psychological health. Results showed that sex role traits (PAQ) and behaviors (SRBS-2) both covaried with individual adjustment, but sex role attitudes (AWS) did not. Masculine traits and behaviors were positively associated with all self-esteem and adjustment indices in both sexes; feminine traits and behaviors related less strongly and less consistently to these indices but did play an important role in communal self-esteem components. Thus, adjustment advantages were found for both masculinity and androgyny.

Blackman (1986) gave the Recreational and Leisure Activities, Vocational Preferences, and Social Interaction items from the SRBS-2 to two groups of college women: 75 in a "math group" (enrolled in mathematics courses at the level of introductory calculus and beyond) and 104 in a "non-math group." Subjects also completed the BSRI and AWS. Multiple discriminant analysis showed that the math group had less feminine vocational interests (as shown by lower scores on the relevant Female-Valued SRBS-2 subscale) than the nonmath group. Stepwise multiple regression designed to determine predictors of group membership showed that the Female-Valued SRBS-2 Vocational Interests subscale was the only significant predictor ($p < .001$) among the AWS, BSRI, and SRBS-2 subscales. This result is also relevant to the construct validity of the SRBS-2.

Overall Assessment

The SRBS, especially the SRBS-2, is a very promising instrument. It is the only recent and reasonably psychometrically adequate measure that assesses masculine and feminine behaviors independently. Orlofsky and his colleagues' contention that sex-role behaviors are at least relatively independent from sex-role traits and attitudes seems supported and is certainly in keeping with other arguments that sex roles are multidimensional and should be assessed as such (e.g., Huston, 1983; Spence, 1984).

The major drawbacks of the SRBS and research using it to date are

1. Because it has been developed so recently, it does not have an extensive background literature. That which exists is nearly all the work of Orlofsky and his colleagues. This shortcoming is expected to be remedied as the SRBS is more widely used.

2. The SRBS-2 is a lengthy (240-item) instrument.

3. The assertion that this measure assesses *behavior* should be carefully tempered by the awareness that it operationally defines behavior in terms of individuals' self-reports of the degree to which activities and interests are characteristic of themselves. This is an important distinction in that the SRBS may share some method variance with other self-report scales. It is hoped that future researchers will assess relationships between SRBS scores and those on more overt behavioral measures.

4. As Orlofsky *et al.* (1982) themselves noted, items were assigned to specific behavior subareas on a rational basis, and factor analyses of the entire SRBS will be needed to determine whether these area divisions are the most empirically appropriate.

5. All existing research with the SRBS has been done with college student samples. The usefulness of the SRBS with other populations remains an empirical question. Problems associated with the use of college students in scale development may be particularly acute with respect to the Marital Behavior Subscale, in which subjects not currently married or living with a partner are apparently asked to respond in terms of their expectations of what such a relationship will be like for them (Orlofsky *et al.*, 1985).

Sex Role Behavior Scale Sample Items

Category of items	Male-Valued	Female-Valued	Sex-Specific
Recreational activities	Sailing Hiking Playing chess Reading science fiction	Volleyball Disco dancing Gardening Playing bridge	Football (M) Wrestling (M) Knitting (F) Reading romantic novels (F)
Vocational interests	Accountant Physician Business executive Optician	Social worker Flight attendant Elementary school teacher Bank teller	Nurse (F) Telephone operator (F) Minister (M) Plumber (M)
Social and dating behavior	Taking the first step to start a relationship with a person of the opposite sex Deciding where to go on a date Preferring to remain single through one's 20s	Preferring to avoid a sexual relationship unless one is in love with the other person Taking special care with one's appearance Using cologne or scent	Ordering in restaurant for both people (M) Helping opposite-sex persons on with their coat (M) Primping in front of the mirror (F)
Marital behavior	Being the one to initiate sexual interactions Preparing income tax returns Painting inside of the house; putting up wallpaper Disciplining male children	Being sexually faithful to one's spouse Buying groceries Decorating the house or apartment Regulating what the children eat	Yard work (M) Doing the driving when going out with one's spouse (M) Doing laundry (F) Buying clothing for children (F)

Note: The items appearing in this list are only those cited as illustrative in Orlofsky (1981). The reader wishing to administer the SRBS must obtain specific directions for giving the test, presentation format for items and for scaled response alternatives, and scoring details from J. L. Orlofsky (see Location section above). M, masculine sex-specific behavior; F, feminine sex-specific behavior.

Children's Sex Role Measures: General Considerations

As in the adult literature, researchers employ a tremendous number of construct labels (e.g., sex role preference, orientation, adoption, identity, knowledge; gender identity, constancy, and stability) and frequently differ in their conceptual and/or operational definitions of these constructs. The reader interested in pursuing issues raised by definitional complexity in the child literature is referred to the excellent discussions by Brenes, Eisenberg, and Helmstadter (1985), Eisenberg (1983), Huston (1983), and Nash (1979).

Diversity of Tests and General Problems

This chapter describes only two child measures in detail and discusses one recommended observational technique (see below). The decision to be highly selective was based upon three factors: the questionable validity and/or reliability of most children's measures; the fact that children's sex roles are clearly multidimensional (a point that, interestingly, has been emphasized more consistently and for a longer period in the child than in the adult literature), and that most measures are low in construct validity. Eisenberg (1983), Huston (1983), Katz and Boswell (1986), and Nash (1979) provide thorough discussions of each of these issues and their implications. Also, Beere (1979) and Johnson (1976) provide reviews of numerous tests.

Paucity of Androgyny Measures

A striking aspect of the child literature is the lack of measures permitting masculinity and femininity to vary independently. As Katz and Boswell (1986) point out, the vast majority of studies "use a single, unidimensional measure of sex role behavior, typically one that is bipolar in nature" (pp. 110–111). As for adults, early empirical evidence (largely ignored until the last few years) showed an independence in children of masculinity and femininity indicators (e.g., Huston, 1983). Nash (1979) expresses the situation nicely: "Most of the measures of sex role used in the developmental studies do not treat masculinity and femininity as independent variables and thus their validity and predictive value are questionable" (p. 290).

Given these considerations, researchers again need to obtain separate assessments of masculinity and femininity. [Older bipolar tests may sometimes be modified to do this through the inclusion of neutral items or by other modifications. See the IT Scale for Children Results and Comments section and Hargreaves, Stoll, Farnworth, and Morgan (1981) for examples.]

For children 8 years of age and older the Children's Personal Attributes Questionnaire (CPAQ) (see PAQ section) seems a good choice. There is also a BSRI adaptation for use with 10- to 14-year-olds (Thomas & Robinson, 1981).

For younger children, techniques for deriving androgyny scores, especially from naturally occurring behaviors (rather than from extant scales), seem highly promising. The reader is advised to consult Brenes *et al.* (1985) and Cameron, Eisenberg, and Tryon (1985), who studied preschool children, and Katz and Boswell (1986), who studied kindergarten and third grade children. (See below.) It is appropriate to note that one possible reason for the scarcity of "androgyny measures" among quite young children may be that such children tend to be rather overwhelmingly sex-typed. Cameron *et al.* (1985) discuss this problem well.

An alternative recommended methodology for assessing preschool children's sex roles is based upon naturalistic observation of their toy preferences during free play periods in their normal environments. Descriptions and critiques of this technique appear in Cameron *et al.* (1985), Connor and Serbin (1977), and Eisenberg (1983). Basically, this procedure involves using established norms to categorize toys as masculine, feminine, or neutral and then assessing the amount of time a child plays with toys in each of the categories. This technique has relatively high stability (Connor & Serbin, 1977); it avoids the kinds of demand characteristics of structured tests (Eisenberg, 1983); and it allows independent assessments of masculinity and femininity. (See O'Brien and Huston, 1985, for a related technique, and see Serbin & Sprafkin, 1982, for a comparison of laboratory and naturalistic observation procedures.)

Children's Measures Reviewed Here

The two children's measures given detailed reviews in this chapter are the following:

7. The IT Scale for Children (ITSC) (Brown, 1956a)
8. The Sex Role Learning Index (SERLI) (Edelbrock & Sugawara, 1978)

They are reviewed in that order because the IT Scale is the most frequently cited children's measure. Both measures are appropriate for children from preschool age through about 8 years old.

The ITSC was proposed as a measure of sex role preference, but there are disagreements in the literature concerning what aspect(s) of sex role it actually assesses. The ITSC has a projective format in which the child makes choices among drawings for "IT," a stick-figure drawing of a child intended to be ambiguous as to sex. Children are tested individually. There are three sections, in which the child selects one toy in each of 16 pairs of stereotypically masculine and stereotypically feminine toys, one alternative in each of eight pairs of stereotypically masculine and stereotypically feminine objects or people, and the one of four figures (girl, "girlish boy," "boyish girl," and boy) which IT would rather be. Bipolar scoring ranges from "exclusively feminine" to "exclusively masculine." The ITSC has fair reliability. It has been employed in research on an enormous variety of topics and with respondents from a variety of populations and cultures. Its validity is questionable, since studies yield inconsistent results and since the conceptual interpretation to be placed upon ITSC scores is unclear. Its use with girls may be especially problematic. There are numerous modifications of the ITSC that attempt to minimize its flaws and/or to alter its projective assumptions. The major advantage of the ITSC is its extensive prior research base; despite its problems, researchers developing new sex role measures for children usually compare their measures to the ITSC.

The SERLI was proposed as a measure of early sex role acquisition. In the Child and Adult Figures sections, children rank order from arrays of 10 pictures (5 masculine stereotyped and 5 feminine stereotyped) those portraying the activities and roles they would like to do, or be, when they grow up. In the Objects section, children sort 10 pictures of stereotypically masculine and 10 pictures of stereotypically feminine items into groups they consider appropriate for boys, girls, or both sexes. Individual testing sessions take about 10 minutes. Scoring procedures permit the separate assessment of (1) sex role discrimination (SRD), or the child's awareness of sex role stereotypes; (2) sex role preference (SRP), or the child's desire to adhere to cultural stereotypes of masculine and feminine behavior; and (3) sex role confirmation (SRC), or the child's desire to adhere to his or her own conception of what is sex appropriate. This measure has numerous advantages over most other child tests, including the facts that it does not rely solely upon adult standards, it does permit children to define items as appropriate for both sexes, and it is well grounded in a good theoretical rationale. The SERLI has satisfactory reliability over brief periods if certain aspects of the testing session are held constant; no data on internal consistency were encountered. The SERLI does not yet have an extensive background literature, and researchers often administer only portions of this instrument. However, existing validating evidence indicates that this is a very promising measure.

IT Scale for Children
(Brown, 1956b)

Variable

Brown (1956b) proposed his scale as a measure of sex role preference or "the preferential responses of children to sex-typed objects and activities" (p. 4), appropriate for children aged 3–8 years (Beere, 1979).

Description and Original Subject Sample

Brown's (1956b) stated intention was to provide a measure of sex role preference uncontaminated by conformity to social pressures or expectations. To achieve this, an indirect or projective format was devised in which the child makes choices among drawings for "IT," a stick-figure drawing of a child intended to be ambiguous or unstructured as to sex. (See Results and Comments below regarding the probable masculine cue value of the IT figure.) As will be noted below (see Validity and Results and Comments sections) there are disagreements in the literature concerning exactly what aspect of sex role the ITSC actually assesses.

In an individual testing session, the child is first shown a picture card containing the IT figure, which remains visible throughout administration of each of the three ITSC sections. Each section uses 3- × 4-inch cards containing black-and-white drawings. In the toy pictures section, 16 drawings are displayed simultaneously and the child is asked "Which toy would IT like the best?" This procedure is repeated until eight toy choices have been made. Eight of the drawings depict stereotypically masculine toys (pocket knife, soldiers, earthmover, racer, rifle, train engine, dump truck, and tractor); and eight depict stereotypically feminine toys (necklace, doll, purse, high chair, cradle, dishes, doll buggy, and baby bath). One point is given for each masculine choice, and scores can range from 0 (all feminine choices) to 8 (all masculine choices). In the eight paired pictures section, pairs of drawings of objects or people are shown, one pair at a time, and the child is asked which item IT would rather be (or have, or play with, depending on the paired items involved). Each pair contains a stereotypically masculine and a stereotypically feminine alternative (Indian princess–chief, trousers–dress, sewing materials–airplane parts, cosmetic–shaving articles, tools–household objects, men's–women's shoes, girls–boys playing, building–baking articles). Eight points are given for each masculine choice, and scores can range from 0 (all feminine choices) to 64 (all masculine choices). In the four child-figures section, the child is simultaneously shown pictures of a girl, a girlish boy (boy dressed as a girl), a boyish girl (girl dressed as a boy), and a boy. The child is asked which IT would rather be. Choice of the boy is given 12 points, of the girlish boy 8 points, of the boyish girl 4 points, and of the girl zero points.

Order of presenting the sections and items within sections, as well as the spatial arrangement of items, is randomly determined with the restriction that male and female items are alternated.

No explanation is provided for the differential weighting of items across sections. Total scores can range from the "exclusively feminine" score of zero to the "exclusively masculine" score of 84.

Brown (1956b) stated that, in devising the ITSC, he relied upon stereotyping data gathered by earlier research (e.g., Benjamin, 1932; Rabban, 1950) to select objects, activities, and people "commonly associated with masculine or feminine roles" (p. 4) in American culture. No more specific information on item selection is provided.

Brown (1956b) said that preliminary testing (sample not specified) using a direct, nonprojective approach indicated that children responded more in terms of conformity to social expectations than in terms of their own preferences. Use of the "IT" figure was designed to overcome this problem.

Brown's (1956b) sample was 78 male and 68 female middle-class kindergarten children aged 5 years 4 months to 6 years 4 months.

Reliability

Internal Consistency

Feinman and Ross (1975) administered the ITSC to 38 boys and 39 girls in nursery school through second grade. They report α coefficients of .64 for boys and .88 for girls. See Beere (1979) for studies estimating the ITSC's split-half reliability: Estimates cluster closely around .86.

Test–Retest

Brown (1956b) reports rank-difference coefficients of .69 for boys and .82 for girls between scores at two testings approximately 1 month apart. See also Beere (1979) for other studies estimating test–retest reliability: Coefficients range from .64 to .91 over intervals up to 1 month, and the ITSC seems not to be consistently more reliable for one sex than for the other.

Validity

Discrimination of Known Groups

Brown (1956b) assumed that young boys as a group would "identify with" items socially defined as masculine, while girls would "identify with" items socially defined as feminine. This implies that a sex difference in ITSC scores is basic to the scale's validity. In his sample (above) Brown (1956b) indeed found a significant difference ($p < .01$) between boys' mean score of 66.36 and girls' mean score of 38.40. Numerous other studies have also found that the ITSC discriminates between males and females (e.g., Brown, 1957; see Beere, 1979, and Eisenberg, 1983, for reviews).

The ITSC has also been found to discriminate between young boys (aged 4–10 years) described by parents as masculine (*n* = 25) and those described by parents as feminine (*n* = 30) (Green, Fuller, & Rutley, 1972).

Convergent and Discriminant Validity

It is extremely difficult to determine what pattern of correlations between the ITSC and other sex-role measures would best support or refute the scale's validity. This difficulty is in part due to differences among authors in their interpretations of what specific aspects of sex roles the ITSC actually taps. For just one example, while Brown (1956b) proposed the ITSC as a fairly straightforward, albeit indirect, measure of the child's own sex-role preference, Biller (1968) considers it a measure of sex-role orientation (the "underlying, and not necessarily conscious, perception of the maleness or femaleness of the self") (p. 92). Thus, for some authors the ITSC should show low correlations with measures of latent or "underlying sex role identity," while for others, these correlations should be high. Accordingly, even if a consistent pattern of correlations involving the ITSC were found, its implications for the scale's validity would be unclear. In fact, correlations supporting each of the two positions outlined above (Biller, 1968; Brown, 1956b) have been found: For example, Lansky and McKay (1969) found a negative correlation ($r = -.41, p < .10$) for 20 kindergarten boys and a zero correlation for 16 kindergarten girls between scores on the ITSC, which they assumed measured "manifest M-F," and the Franck Drawing Completion Test (Franck & Rosen, 1949), which they assumed measured "latent M-F." In contrast, Biller (1968) found a positive correlation ($r = .58, p < .0005$) among 186 kindergarten boys between the ITSC and the Draw-a-Person Test (e.g., Farylo & Paludi, 1985), both of which he considered measures of sex-role orientation.

Inconsistency seems to be the rule in correlations between the ITSC and various measures of sex-role preference, knowledge, and adoption (e.g., Biller, 1968, 1969; Sears, Rau, & Alpert, 1965; see Eisenberg, 1983, for a partial review). Further, Eisenberg (1983) reviews a number of studies that report observations of the actual play behavior of children who had taken the ITSC. She concludes that ITSC scores are generally not related to children's actual toy choices.

Finally, consideration of the scale's convergent and discriminant validity is made even more complex in that methodological inadequacies in the original ITSC have led to the proliferation of modified IT Scales (see below). Thus, there is no coherent body of literature relating a particular IT Scale version to a consistent set of other sex role measures.

Location

Brown, D. G. (1956a). *The IT Scale for Children*. Missoula, MT: Psychological Test Specialists.

Brown D. G. (1956b). Sex role preference in young children. *Psychological Mono-graphs, 70* (Whole No. 421).

Results and Comments

Modifications of the ITSC

One recurrent issue concerning the ITSC's validity is that, while girls typically score less masculine than boys, girls very frequently score in the masculine range of 42–84 (Brinn,

Kraemer, Warm, & Paludi, 1984; Paludi, 1981; see also Beere, 1979, and Eisenberg, 1983, for reviews.)

Brown (1956b, 1957) took this finding to indicate that girls in fact do not have the same degree of preference for the feminine role as boys do for the masculine role. Others (e.g., Fling & Manosevitz, 1972; Sher & Lansky, 1968) reported data indicating that this finding may be due to "masculine cues" in the IT figure (i.e., IT may look more like a boy than like a girl; see also Beere, 1979).

Modifications of the ITSC designed wholly or in part to address this issue include keeping the IT figure concealed in an envelope throughout test administration (developed by Lansky & McKay, 1963); replacing the IT figure with only "the androgynous face of a child" (Eisenberg, 1983, p. 49; developed by Biller, 1968; see also Burge, 1982); using a blank card and asking the child to imagine that a child named "IT" is drawn on the card (e.g., Dickstein & Seymour, 1977). Beere (1979) and Eisenberg (1983) both review studies using these and other variations. Results appear to be highly inconsistent.

A variety of other modified ITSC versions or administration strategies have been used. For example, Thompson and McCandless (1970) gave the scale to 36 kindergarten boys and 36 kindergarten girls, using "projective" (IT concealed in an envelope), "semi-projective" (usual ITSC procedure), or "objective" ("It-is-you") (see also Hartup & Zook, 1960) instructions. ITSC scores across instruction conditions varied in complex interaction with children's sex and race (white or black).

In one of the more interesting variations, Dickstein and Seymour (1977) included sex-role-neutral items in the ITSC, and administered it to 28 male and 29 female kindergarteners. They report that this "demasculinized" the scores of males by providing "reasonable alternatives" to stereotyped masculine items, but made no difference in females' scores. They interpret this pattern in terms of the more narrow sex role standards typically applied to boys' behavior. The addition of neutral items has the appeal of allowing a greater freedom in children's responses. It also seems to be the beginning of an approximation toward the recognition in current adult measures that masculinity and femininity are separate and may vary independently (see Children's Sex Role Measurement section above).

Hundreds of studies have used the ITSC or its numerous modifications, and researchers have attempted to relate ITSC scores to many different variables. The list of such variables far exceeds the limits of this review and includes parental dominance and power (e.g., Biller, 1969), as well as many other parental variables; dependence and independence (e.g., Lansky & McKay, 1969); and race and socioeconomic class (e.g., Doll, Fagot, & Himbert, 1973). Beere (1979) provides an extensive bibliography of such studies.

The ITSC has been adapted to fit other cultures, including India (Dixit, 1971), Australia (Perry & Perry, 1975), and Yugoslavia (Smiljanic-Colanovic, 1972). Brown (1958) commented on age and cross-cultural factors relevant to the ITSC.

Overall Assessment

The ITSC appears to have fair reliability. However, its validity is questionable, both because studies yield inconsistent results and because the conceptual interpretation placed upon ITSC scores is unclear and therefore varies across authors (see Validity above). Eisenberg (1983) provided and supported an excellent overview of the various complexities in interpretation of ITSC scores. Further, she stated that researchers have often assumed that the ITSC reflects children's basic underlying masculinity or femininity. However . . . As Brown originally suggested, the ITSC could be a measure of . . . sex role preferences. Furthermore, as it is not clear whether children really project themselves or their own preference onto the IT, it is quite possible that the IT functions as a test of sex-role knowledge . . . [children] may make choices based on the sex they attribute to IT, not on the basis of their own preferences (p. 48)

She notes that the ITSC may also assess different things, depending upon "how attuned the child is to pressures to give sex-appropriate responses, . . . and how strong, in reality, these pressures are" (p. 55).

The major advantage to using the ITSC is that its extensive prior research base allows comparison with previous findings. It is therefore perhaps not surprising that comparisons with the ITSC, despite its flaws, are still made when researchers describe the characteristics of new sex role measures for children (e.g., the SERLI, see description in this chapter) (Edelbrock & Sugawara, 1978).

Given considerations discussed above, researchers using the ITSC with girls need to be cautious in their conclusions.

Beere (1979) notes two other criticisms deserving mention here: (1) Five of the eight masculine toys are vehicles, and five of the eight feminine toys are dolls and doll accessories. Therefore, there is a sense in which each group really includes only four toy types. (2) Brown apparently did not attempt to control for these toys' attractiveness and manipulative potential.

Sex-Role Learning Index

(Edelbrock & Sugawara, 1978)

Variable

Edelbrock and Sugawara (1978) proposed the SERLI as a measure of "early sex role acquisition" (p. 615) in preschool age children. It has been used with children through age 9.

Description and Original Subject Samples

The SERLI assesses three concepts: (1) Sex role discrimination (SRD), or the child's awareness of sex role stereotypes, operationally defined by the degree of agreement between a child's classification of items and the sex role stereotypes of those items; (2) sex role preference (SRP), or the child's desire to adhere to cultural stereotypes of masculine and feminine behavior, operationally defined in terms of the order in which a child chooses items that the culture defines as appropriate for his or her sex; and (3) sex-role confirmation (SRC), or the child's desire to adhere to his or her own conception of what is sex appropriate, operationally defined in terms of the order in which a child chooses items that the child has defined as sex-appropriate, including items he or she has defined as appropriate for both sexes.

The authors intended their measure to overcome certain method and conceptual problems in previous instruments. In particular, by comparing children's choices of items not only to cultural stereotypes but to children's own conceptions of what is sex-appropriate, the authors intended to avoid the sole reliance on adult standards implicit in most measures. Further, the SERLI is different from pre-existing measures in (1) permitting children to define items as appropriate for *both* sexes, (2) permitting a comparison between children's views of adult and child activities and roles, and (3) using a probabilistic scoring system sensitive to the order of children's choices of sex appropriate items.

The SERLI contains black-and-white line drawings, organized into a Child Figures Section (in which drawings are of a child engaged in various activities), an Adult Figures Section (in which drawings are of an adult occupying various roles or engaged in various activities), and an Objects Section. The first two sections contain 10 items each, 5 masculine stereotyped and 5 feminine stereotyped. The Objects Section contains 20 items representing the activities and roles in the first two sections. (See list of SERLI contents.)

There are separate SERLI forms for boys and girls, with the only difference being that figures in the Child and Adult Figures sections are of the same sex as the child being tested. The use of same-sex figures is intended to overcome social desirability influences.

Item selection procedures are not described in detail, but Edelbrock and Sugawara (1978) do state that item choice was based both on content analyses of existing children's sex role measures and on pilot studies with a pool of 200 items. Items were chosen that represented common themes in children's play and stories and that children considered desirable.

The SERLI is administered individually. The entire procedure takes about 10 minutes. In the Objects Section, each item is presented to the child on a separate card. In each of the other two sections, all items are presented simultaneously in an array having three items in a top row, four items in a middle row, and three items in a bottom row. (Items and arrays are available from Edelbrock; see Location, below.)

For the Objects Section, the child is first shown three boxes, labeled "for boys," "for girls," and "for both boys and girls;" then, free-choice classifications are obtained: The child is shown each item, one at a time, and is asked, "Here is a picture of a/an (object name). Who would use a/an (object name) to (activity name): boys? girls? or both boys and girls?" (Order of these alternatives is alternated across items.) The child responds verbally, and then is given the drawing to place in the appropriate box. Next, to obtain a forced-choice classification of items which the child sorted into the "both boys and girls" box, the child is again shown these items, and is asked, "Who would use a/an (object name) more: boys? or girls?"

For the Child Figures Section, the child is shown the appropriate array, and the examiner names each item and asks the child, "If you could do any one of these things, which one would you like to do best?" The chosen item is removed and the procedure is repeated until all items are removed. Administration of the Adult Figures Section follows the same procedure, with the child being asked, "Which one of these things would you like to do or be when you grow up?"

The three sections may be given in any order and are scored as follows:

Objects Section

The child's SRD scores are the percentages of agreement between his or her forced-choice classification of objects and the objects' sex role stereotypes. "Own SRD" score is obtained for objects stereotyped as appropriate for the child's sex, while "Opposite SRD" score is obtained for objects stereotyped as appropriate for the other sex. So, if a girl classifies 7 out of 10 feminine objects "for girls" and 5 out of 10 masculine objects "for boys," her Own SRD score is 70 and her Opposite SRD score is 50, indicating greater awareness of her own sex role than of the masculine role.

Child and Adult Figures Sections

Definition of the sex-appropriate items in these sections is by sex role stereotypes for SRP and by the child's own sorting of objects (corresponding to the activities and roles) for

SRC. (In scoring SRC, items which the child sorted for "both boys and girls" are considered sex-appropriate.) For each section, scoring of SRP and SRC is based upon the order of choosing sex-appropriate items and the probabilities of these choices. Probabilities initially depend, of course, on the number of items defined as sex-appropriate. Further, probabilities change following each choice and depend upon the number of sex-appropriate items that remain after the child has made each selection.

Edelbrock and Sugawara (see Location, below) have developed simplified scoring tables that take into account the order of the child's choices and, for SRC, the number of sex-appropriate items as initially defined by the child. For example, for SRC, nine probability distributions have been normalized and standardized with means of 50 and standard deviations of 10. A score of 50 represents random choosing with respect to sex roles. Scores increase with increasing sex appropriate preference, and range from 20 to 80. Most important to these authors, the probabilistic scoring system is quite sensitive to individual differences in order of selecting sex-appropriate items, which is considered a ranking of their desirability to the child.

Edelbrock and Sugawara (1978) reported five studies, using a total sample of 63 boys and 56 girls enrolled in preschool and day-care centers. Subjects averaged 51.4 months of age, and were of average or above average intelligence, predominantly white, and from upper and upper-middle socioeconomic groups.

Reliability

Internal Consistency

Edelbrock and Sugawara (1978) reported no data on internal consistency. It is clear that they would not expect a perfect relationship among the various subscales, since these are intended to measure different aspects of sex role.

Test–Retest

Eighteen boys and 18 girls from Edelbrock and Sugawara's (1978) original sample were retested 3 weeks after the initial test. The same experimenter conducted both test sessions; a male experimenter tested half of the children and a female tested the other half. Product-moment correlations were higher for subjects tested by a same-sex experimenter (all correlations $p < .05$; highest $r = .90$ for Child Figures SRP, lowest $r = .51$ for Adult Figures SRC), than for subjects tested by an opposite-sex experimenter. In the latter case, correlations were significant for Own and Opposite SRD (r values $= .61$ and $.63$, respectively, both p values $< .01$) and for Adult Figures SRP ($r = .57$, $p < .05$); the correlation was .43 (ns) for Child Figures SRP, and correlations were very low for Child and Adult Figures SRC ($r = .09$, ns, and $-.17$, ns, respectively).

Validity

Discrimination of Known Groups

While Edelbrock and Sugawara (1978) did not explicitly state that they would expect a sex difference, with boys being masculine and girls being feminine, their discussion of sex-typing processes does suggest such an expectation. The most relevant comparisons, of course, would be between the sexes' scores on SRP and SRC. However, as noted above, these SERLI indices range, not from "masculine" to "feminine," but from "sex-inappropriate" to "sex-appropriate," with higher scores representing more appropriate (masculine for boys, feminine for girls) sex-typing. Thus, it is not possible to extract the most relevant comparisons from Edelbrock and Sugawara's (1978) data. It should be noted, however, that the relevant means presented in this article were all above 50, indicating appropriate sex-typing in both sexes.

Edelbrock and Sugawara (1978) noted three group differences in their data that match patterns found in previous research:

1. Boys scored higher than girls on SRP ($p < .01$) in the Child Figures Section, which accords with previous findings that boys adhere more to the masculine role than girls do to the feminine role.

2. Older children (52–65 months) scored higher than younger children (35–51 months) on SRD (across Own and Opposite SRD scores, $p < .001$), which accords with previous findings that children's awareness of sex role stereotypes increases with age.

3. Girls scored higher than boys on Opposite SRD ($p < .001$), but not on Own SRD, which accords with previous findings that girls are more aware of the masculine role than boys are aware of the feminine role.

Convergent and Discriminant Validity

Edelbrock and Sugawara (1978) noted a variety of problems with the IT scale for Children (see ITSC section in this chapter) and discussed a number of important differences between the ITSC and the SERLI. Thus, it is not fully clear what, if any, pattern of relationships between ITSC scores and SERLI scores would best validate the SERLI. Nonetheless, Edelbrock and Sugawara (1978) presented product-moment correlations between scores on the two measures, as well as partial correlations between scores, controlling for both CA (chronological age) and MA (mental age). Subjects were 39 boys and 39 girls from the original sample who were assessed with the two instruments in a "randomly determined" order. ITSC scores were transposed so that higher scores would indicate greater preference for the child's own sex role, in both sexes. For 29 of these boys and 23 of these girls, MA was assessed with the Peabody Picture Vocabulary Test (PPVT) (Dunn, 1965).

For boys, all SERLI scales except SRC in the Adult Figures Section were significantly (r values ranged from .35 to .56, p values $< .05$) related to the ITSC, and remained so even after MA and (except for Opposite SRD) CA were partialled out. For girls, only SRP ($r = .49$) and SRC ($r = .45$) in the Child Figures Section were significantly (p values $< .05$) related to the ITSC, but partialling out MA reduced these correlations to nonsignificant levels, indicating that the original correlations were due to shared developmental rather than trait variance.

Location

Edelbrock, C., and Sugawara, I. (1978). Acquisition of Sex-typed preferences. *Developmental Psychology*, **14**, 614–623.

Material available from Craig Edelbrock, Laboratory of Developmental Psychology, Building 15K, National Institute of Mental Health, Bethesda, Maryland 20014.

Results and Comments

Edelbrock and Sugawara (1978) report a number of findings that differ from or expand on previous research and that raise interesting issues concerning sex role socialization. For example:

1. Girls scored higher in the Adult Figures than in the Child Figures Section, while boys showed the reverse pattern. This suggested that girls have a clear notion of adult feminine behavior and conform to this notion but show a range of preferences for their own current play behaviors; boys are more influenced by the masculine role in their play behaviors than in their notions of, or conformity to, adult behaviors.

2. In the Child Figures Section, older girls adhered more to their own conceptions of what is sex-appropriate than to sex role stereotypes, while boys (both younger and older) were as influenced by stereotypes as they were by their own definition of what is masculine.

3. In addition, results suggested that both boys and girls prefer sex-appropriate choices more when tested by an opposite-sex than when tested by a same-sex experimenter.

Other investigators have employed various parts of the SERLI. For example, Martin and Halverson (1983a) assessed SRP in a sample of 5- to 6-year-old children. SRP for child and adult activities were summed for each subject and summed scores were split at the median for the sample to designate low-stereotyped versus high-stereotyped children. All children were shown stimuli depicting males and females performing sex-consistent (e.g., boy playing with trains) and sex-inconsistent (e.g., girl sawing wood) activities. It was predicted that, when children's memory for these stimuli was tested 1 week later, high-stereotyped children would make more distortion errors (e.g., misremembering the sex of the actor in the picture) on sex-inconsistent activities than would low-stereotyped children. However, results showed no effect of level of stereotyping on distortion; instead, some distortion of sex-inconsistent stimuli occurred regardless of level of stereotyping. The authors note that this lack of effect may reflect the narrow range of stereotyping in their sample, with most children being moderately to highly stereotyped.

List, Collins, and Westby (1983) used only the Adult Figures Section SRP subtest of the SERLI. Third grade males and females were split into high-stereotype, low-stereotype (scores above or below own-sex mean by .5 standard deviation or more, respectively) or medium-stereotype (within .5 standard deviation from the mean) groups. Children viewed both a traditional television program, in which the main female character was a wife and mother, and a nontraditional program, in which the main female character was an army officer and doctor. After viewing, children completed a recognition measure that included questions concerning information about the main character's role (role-relevant) and concerning information not pertaining to this role (role-irrelevant). The only stereotype result was that children higher in sex-role stereotypy remembered less role-irrelevant information than did low-stereotype children, across both programs. There were no differences between stereotype groups in recognition of role-relevant information from the two programs. The authors conclude that stereotypes do affect processing of program content but do not generally distort memory for contrasting sex role portrayals.

Serbin and Sprafkin (1986) studied children 3–7 years old. To assess sex-typing, they administered the SRP measures from the Child and Adult Figures Sections. To assess sex role flexibility, they administered the Objects Section in the free-choice fashion, computing a "flexibility score" from the number of "both boys and girls" responses. Sex role knowledge was assessed by the usual forced-choice method in the Objects Section. Children also completed measures assessing their use of gender as a basis for (1) classifying photographs of adults engaged in various activities, and (2) expressing affiliation preferences with same or opposite sex adults. As predicted, over the age span tested, gender-based classification declined as sex role knowledge increased, and sex role flexibility increased after gender-based classification declined. Sex-typing, in contrast, did not relate to gender-based classification but was positively related to gender-based affiliation choices.

Stoneman, Brody, and MacKinnon (1986) administered the SRD subtest to the younger siblings (4.5–6.5 years old) in 40 sibling dyads. Girls with older brothers had lower Own SRD scores than did the younger siblings in any other gender combination; and boys with older sisters had lower Opposite SRD scores than did the younger siblings in the other gender composition groups. Bradbard, Martin, Endsley, and Halverson (1986) reported a study in which SRD scores were used to confirm level of sex role knowledge among 4- to 9-year-olds.

Overall Assessment

The SERLI is a promising instrument that has the advantage of separately assessing a number of different aspects of sex role. It appears to have satisfactory reliability over brief time periods if certain aspects of the testing situation (e.g., experimenter sex) are held constant. It is grounded in a good theoretical rationale and avoids some of the most salient methodological problems of other measures. In part because of its relatively recent publication, the SERLI has not been as widely used as other measures. Further, researchers often use only part(s) of the SERLI. Accordingly, until there is a larger and more consistent literature on the SERLI it will be difficult to provide a clear overall summary of this instrument's value in various areas of sex role research.

Sex Role Learning Index

Section Contents

Masculine Stereotype		Feminine Stereotype	
activity	**object**	**activity**	**object**

Child Figures

Hammering	Hammer–nails	Ironing	Iron
Digging	Shovel	Sewing	Needle–Thread
Baseball	Ball–bat	Cooking	Stove
Car play	Car	Dishwashing	Dishes
Boxing	Boxing gloves	Sweeping	Broom

Adult Figures

Sawing	Saw	Feeding baby	Baby bottle
Policeman	Badge	Teacher	Desk–Books
Soldier	Rifle	Serving juice	Pitcher–Glasses
Fire fighter	Fire hat	Combing hair	Hairbrush–
Doctor	Stethoscope	Making pie	Mirror
			Apples–Knife–
			Bowl

Note: This list contains verbal descriptions for the activities and objects pictures used in the SERLI. The reader wishing to administer the SERLI must obtain the test materials, exact administration protocol, and scoring details from C. Edelbrock (see Location section). From Edelbrock, C., & Sugawara, A. I. (1978).

Future Research Directions

Both lay people and psychologists have always been fascinated by sex differences and sex roles. With the infusion of new ideas and enthusiasm provided by the recent "androgyny revolution," there is every reason to expect that this field of research will remain enormously vigorous and popular. Foretelling the future seems especially hazardous in an area characterized by so much ferment and dissension. Nonetheless, we may expect continued controversy and problems over certain major issues, we may hope for a general improvement in several areas, and we may predict increasing emphasis on a number of research foci.

For some time to come, there will certainly continue to be controversies and confusion posed by the persistent lack of a clear consensus over conceptual definitions for even basic sex-role terms. Inextricably intertwined with these theoretical problems, of course, are the numerous and still hotly debated issues of operational measurement. Thus, one can expect a continued plethora of approaches; to some extent at least, sex-role research is likely to remain an area plagued by confusion.

However, the modern (postandrogyny revolution) era is still quite young, which may mean that such conceptual and technical controversies will not rage indefinitely. As suggested earlier, improvements are to be hoped for in (a) the clarity with which authors keep their particular operational definitions, and the theoretical implications thereof, at the forefront in any discussions of research findings; and (b) the degree to which choices among the potentially bewildering variety of measurement options (scales, scoring methods, etc.) are theory-driven rather than largely fortuitous. If such improvements do occur, then a few of the definitional problems plaguing this area may ultimately be settled by consensus over the best solution, and more may be settled by a clear specification of the range of convenience for particular measures, methods, and concepts.

It is also to be hoped that improvement will occur in the relationship between the literatures on children's and adults' sex roles. Both literatures could fruitfully borrow ideas and approaches from each other to a much greater extent than they do currently. For example, there are already some promising signs that children's sex role measurement is about to be swept by its own, undoubtedly overdue, androgyny revolution. If so, one hopes that this revolution will profit from some of the mistakes made in the early years of androgyny measurement in adults.

In general, two trends, currently in their infancy, will probably grow as research foci. First, acknowledgment of sex roles' multidimensionality is becoming more explicit, and one may expect that future measures will be developed to tap more precisely specified aspects of sex roles. Thus, rather than seeing the complexity of sex roles as a nuisance factor, future researchers may devote more attention to analyzing sex roles' components and to determining the potentially quite different correlates of such aspects as personality traits, interests, activities, affects, and so on. Both the SRBS and the SERLI, reviewed in this chapter, seem to represent healthy moves in this direction. Second, the growth of interest in the cognitive aspects of sex roles is likely to accelerate, especially as cognitive emphases in the broader realms of social and personality psychology continue. In both the adult and child sex role literatures there are already several theories concerning schematic processing of gender-relevant information (e.g., Bem's gender schema theory, 1981c; Martin & Halverson's theory, 1983a). These and other approaches should generate considerable future research.

Bibliography

Adams, C. H., & Sherer, M. (1982). Sex-role orientation and psychological adjustment: Comparison of MMPI profiles among college women and housewives. *Journal of Personality Assessment, 46,* 607–613.

Ajdukovic, D., & Kljaic, S. (1984). Personal attributes, self-esteem, and attitude towards women: Some cross-cultural comparisons. *Studia Psychologica, 26,* 193–198.

Al-Qataee, A. (1984). The effect of exposure to Western cultures on the sex-role identity of Saudi Arabians. *Contemporary Educational Psychology, 9,* 303–312.

Andersen, S. M., & Bem, S. L. (1981). Sex-typing and androgyny in dyadic interaction: Individual differences in responsiveness to physical attractiveness. *Journal of Personality and Social Psychology, 41,* 74–86.

Anderson, K. L. (1986). Androgyny, flexibility, and individualism. *Journal of Personality Assessment, 50,* 265–278.

Angrist, S. S. (1969). The study of sex roles. *Journal of Social Issues, 25,* 215–232.

Antill, J. K., & Cunningham, J. D. (1979). Self-esteem as a function of masculinity in both sexes. *Journal of Consulting and Clinical Psychology, 47,* 783–785.

Antill, J. K., & Cunningham, J. D. (1982a). Comparative factor analyses of the Personal Attributes Questionnaire and the Bem Sex-Role Inventory. *Social Behavior and Personality, 10,* 163–172.

Antill, J. K., & Cunningham, J. D. (1982b). A critical appraisal of the PRF ANDRO Scale. *Current Psychological Research, 2,* 223–230.

Antill, J. K., & Russell, G. (1982). The factor structure of the Bem Sex-Role Inventory: Method and sample comparisons. *Australian Journal of Psychology, 34,* 183–193.

Atkinson, J., & Huston, T. L. (1984). Sex role orientation and division of labor early in marriage. *Journal of Personality and Social Psychology, 46,* 330–345.

Bakan, D. (1966). *The duality of human existence.* Chicago: Rand McNally.

Baldwin, A. C., Critelli, J. W., Stevens, L. C., & Russell, S. (1986). Androgyny and sex role measurement: A personal construct approach. *Journal of Personality and Social Psychology, 51,* 1081–1088.

Basow, S. A. (1984). Cultural variations in sex-typing. *Sex Roles, 10,* 577–585.

Bassoff, E. S., & Glass, G. V. (1982). The relationship between sex roles and mental health: A meta-analysis of twenty-six studies. *Counseling Psychologist, 10,* 105–112.

Baucom, D. H. (1976). Independent masculinity and femininity scales on the California Psychological Inventory. *Journal of Consulting and Clinical Psychology, 44,* 876.

Baucom, D. H. (1980). Independent CPI masculinity and femininity scales: Psychological correlates and a sex-role typology. *Journal of Personality Assessment, 44,* 262–271.

Baucom, D. H. (1983). Sex role identity and the decision to regain control among women: A learned helplessness investigation. *Journal of Personality and Social Psychology, 44,* 334–343.

Baucom, D. H., & Aiken, P. A. (1984). Sex role identity, marital satisfaction, and response to behavioral marital therapy. *Journal of Consulting and Clinical Psychology, 52,* 438–444.

Baucom, D. H., & Danker-Brown, P. (1979). Influence of sex roles on the development of learned helplessness. *Journal of Consulting and Clinical Psychology, 47,* 928–936.

Baucom, D. H., & Danker-Brown, P. (1983). Peer ratings of males and females possessing different sex role identities. *Journal of Personality Assessment, 47,* 494–506.

Baucom, D. H., & Danker-Brown, P. (1984). Sex role identity and sex-stereotyped tasks in the development of learned helplessness. *Journal of Personality and Social Psychology, 46,* 422–430.

Baucom, D. H., & Sanders, B. S. (1978). Masculinity and femininity as factors in feminism. *Journal of Personality Assessment, 42,* 378–384.

Baucom, D. H., & Weiss, B. (1986). Peers' granting of control to women with different sex role identities: Implications for depression. *Journal of Personality and Social Psychology*, **51**, 1075–1080.

Baucom, D. H., Besch, P. K., & Callahan, S. (1985). Relation between testosterone concentration, sex role identity, and personality among females. *Journal of Personality and Social Psychology*, **48**, 1218–1226.

Baumrind, D. (1982). Are androgynous individuals more effective persons and parents? *Child Development*, **53**, 44–75.

Beere, C. A. (1979). *Women and women's issues*. San Francisco: Jossey-Bass.

Belsky, J., Lang, M., & Huston, T. L. (1986). Sex typing and division of labor as determinants of marital change across the transition to parenthood. *Journal of Personality and Social Psychology*, **50**, 517–522.

Bem, S. L. (1972, May). *Psychology looks at sex roles: Where have all the androgynous people gone?* Paper presented at the University of California Symposium on Women, Los Angeles.

Bem, S. L. (1974). The measurement of psychological androgyny. *Journal of Consulting and Clinical Psychology*, **42**, 155–162.

Bem, S. L. (1977). On the utility of alternative procedures for assessing psychological androgyny. *Journal of Consulting and Clinical Psychology*, **45**, 196–205.

Bem, S. L. (1979). Theory and measurement of androgyny: A reply to the Pedhazur–Tetenbaum and Locksley–Colten critiques. *Journal of Personality and Social Psychology*, **37**, 1047–1054.

Bem, S. L. (1981a). *Bem Sex-Role Inventory professional manual*. Palo Alto, CA: Consulting Psychologists Press.

Bem, S. L. (1981b). The BSRI and gender schema theory: A reply to Spence and Helmreich. *Psychological Review*, **88**, 369–371.

Bem, S. L. (1981c). Gender schema theory: A cognitive account of sex typing. *Psychological Review*, **88**, 354–364.

Bem, S. L. (1982). Gender schema theory and self-schema theory compared: A comment on Markus, Crane, Bernstein, and Siladi's "Self-schemas and gender." *Journal of Personality and Social Psychology*, **43**, 1192–1194.

Bem, S. L. (1985). Androgyny and gender schema theory: A conceptual and empirical integration. In T. B. Sonderegger (Ed.), *Nebraska Symposium on Motivation, 1984* (Vol. 32, pp. 179–266). Lincoln: Univ. of Nebraska Press.

Bem, S. L., & Lenney, E. (1976). Sex typing and the avoidance of cross-sex behavior. *Journal of Personality and Social Psychology*, **33**, 48–54.

Bem, S. L., & Lewis, S. A. (1975). Sex role adaptibility: One consequence of psychological androgyny. *Journal of Personality and Social Psychology*, **31**, 634–643.

Bem, S. L., Martyna, W., & Watson, C. (1976). Sex typing and androgyny: Further explorations of the expressive domain. *Journal of Personality and Social Psychology*, **34**, 1016–1023.

Benjamin, H. (1932). Age and sex difference in the toy preferences of young children. *Journal of Genetic Psychology*, **41**, 417–429.

Berg, R. (1985). The Franck Test for gender identity: Correlation with occupation and long-term stability of scores in normal men. *Social Behavior and Personality*, **13**, 83–89.

Bernard, L. C. (1981). The multidimensional aspects of masculinity–femininity. *Journal of Personality and Social Psychology*, **41**, 797–802.

Bernard, L. C. (1984). The multiple factors of sex role identification: Rapprochement of unidimensional and bidimensional assessment. *Journal of Clinical Psychology*, **40**, 986–991.

Berzins, J. I., Welling, M. A., & Wetter, R. E. (1977). *The PRF ANDRO Scale user's manual (revised)*. Unpublished material, University of Kentucky, Lexington.

Berzins, J. I., Welling, M. A., & Wetter, R. E. (1978). A new measure of psychological androgyny based on the Personality Research Form. *Journal of Consulting and Clinical Psychology*, **46**, 126–138.

Betz, N. E., & Bander, R. S. (1980). Relationships of MMPI Mf and CPI Fe scales of fourfold sex role classifications. *Journal of Personality and Social Psychology*, **39**, 1245–1248.

Biller, H. B. (1968). A multi-aspect investigation of masculine development in kindergarten age boys. *Genetic Psychology Monographs, 78,* 89–138.

Biller, H. B. (1969). Father dominance and sex role development in kindergarten age boys. *Developmental Psychology, 1,* 87–94.

Blackman, S. (1982). Comments on three methods of scoring androgyny as a continuous variable. *Psychological Reports, 51,* 1100–1102.

Blackman, S. (1986). The masculinity–femininity of women who study college mathematics. *Sex Roles, 15,* 33–41.

Blanchard, R., & Freund, K. (1983). Measuring masculine gender identity in females. *Journal of Consulting and Clinical Psychology, 51,* 205–214.

Bohannon, W. E., & Mills, C. J. (1979). Psychometric properties and underlying assumptions of two measures of masculinity/femininity. *Psychological Reports, 44,* 431–450.

Bradbard, M. R., Martin, C. L., Endsley, R. C., & Halverson, C. F. (1986). Influence of sex stereotypes on children's exploration and memory: A competence versus performance distinction. *Developmental Psychology, 22,* 481–486.

Brenes, M. E., Eisenberg, N., & Helmstadter, G. C. (1985). Sex role development of preschoolers from two-parent and one-parent families. *Merrill-Palmer Quarterly, 31,* 33–46.

Briere, J., Ward, R., & Hartsough, W. R. (1983). Sex-typing and cross-sex-typing in "androgynous" subjects. *Journal of Personality Assessment, 47,* 300–302.

Brinn, J., Kraemer, K., Warm, J. S., & Paludi, M. A. (1984). Sex-role preferences in four age levels. *Sex Roles, 11,* 901–910.

Brown, D. G. (1956a). *The IT Scale for Children.* Missoula, MT: Psychological Test Specialists.

Brown, D. G. (1956b). Sex-role preference in young children. *Psychological Monographs, 70* (Whole No. 421).

Brown, D. G. (1957). Masculinity–femininity development in children. *Journal of Consulting Psychology, 21,* 197–202.

Brown, D. G. (1958). Sex-role development in a changing culture. *Psychological Bulletin, 55,* 232–242.

Bugen, L. A., & Humenick, S. S. (1983). Instrumentality, expressiveness, and gender effects upon parent–infant interaction. *Basic and Applied Social Psychology, 4,* 239–251.

Burge, P. L. (1982). The relationship between sex-role identity and self-concept of preschool children. *Child Study Journal, 12,* 249–257.

Bussey, K., & Bandura, A. (1984). Influence of gender constancy and social power on sex-linked modeling. *Journal of Personality and Social Psychology, 47,* 1292–1302.

Butler, T., Giordano, S., & Neren, S. (1985). Gender and sex-role attributes as predictors of utilization of natural support systems during personal stress events. *Sex Roles, 13,* 515–524.

Cameron, E., Eisenberg, N., & Tryon, K. (1985). The relations between sex-typed play and preschoolers' social behavior. *Sex Roles, 12,* 601–615.

Campbell, D. P. (1966). *Revised manual for Strong Vocational Interest Blanks.* Stanford, CA: Stanford University Press.

Campbell, D. P., Crichton, L., Hansen, J. I., & Webber, P. (1974). A new edition of the SVIB: The Strong–Campbell Interest Inventory. *Measurement and Evaluation in Guidance, 7,* 92–95.

Cano, L., Solomon, S., & Holmes, D. S. (1984). Fear of success: The influence of sex, sex-role identity, and components of masculinity. *Sex Roles, 10,* 341–346.

Connor, J. M., & Serbin, L. A. (1977). Behaviorally based masculine- and feminine-activity-preference scales for preschoolers: Correlates with other classroom behaviors and cognitive tests. *Child Development, 48,* 1411–1416.

Constantinople, A. (1973). Masculinity–femininity: An exception to a famous dictum? *Psychological Bulletin, 80,* 389–407.

Cosentino, F., & Heilbrun, A. B. (1964). Anxiety correlates of sex-role identity in college students. *Psychological Reports, 14,* 729–730.

Couch, A., & Keniston, K. (1960). Yeasayers and naysayers: Agreeing response set as a personality variable. *Journal of Abnormal and Social Psychology, 60,* 151–174.

Cramer, P., & Carter, T. (1978). The relationship between sexual identification and the use of defense mechanisms. *Journal of Personality Assessment, 42*, 63–73.

Crane, M., & Markus, H. (1982). Gender identity: The benefits of a self-schema approach. *Journal of Personality and Social Psychology, 43*, 1195–1197.

Crowne, D. P., & Marlowe, D. (1964). *The approval motive.* New York: Wiley.

Cunningham, J. D., & Antill, J. K. (1980). A comparison among five masculinity–femininity–androgyny instruments and two methods of scoring androgyny. *Australian Psychologist, 15*, 437–448.

Deaux, K., Kite, M. E., & Lewis, L. L. (1985). Clustering and gender schemata: An uncertain link. *Personality and Social Psychology Bulletin, 11*, 387–397.

del Miglio, C., & Nenci, A. M. (1983). Problematica dell'identita femminile: Evoluzione del ruolo e/o cambiamento. [Female identity: Change and evolution of its role.] *Archivio di Psicologia, Neurologia e Psichiatria, 44*, 93–106.

Denmark, F. L., Shaw, J. S., & Ciali, S. D. (1985). The relationship among sex roles, living arrangements, and the division of household responsibilities. *Sex Roles, 12*, 617–625.

Diaz-Loving, R., Diaz-Guerrero, R., Helmreich, R. L., & Spence, J. T. (1981). Comparacion transcultural y analisis psicometrico de una medida de rasgos masculinos (instrumentales) y femininos (expresivos). [Cross-cultural comparison and psychometric analysis of masculine (instrumental) and feminine (expressive) traits.] *Revista de la Asociacion Latinoamericana de Psicologia Social, 1*, 3–37.

Dickstein, E. B., & Seymour, M. W. (1977). Effect of the addition of neutral items on It Scale Scores. *Developmental Psychology, 13*, 79–80.

Dixit, R. C. (1971). Sex-role preference in children as a function of birth space. *Psychologia: An International Journal of Psychology in the Orient, 14*, 175–178.

Doll, P. A., Fagot, H. J., & Himbert, J. D. (1973). Examiner effect on sex role preference among black and white lower-class female children. *Psychological Reports, 32*, 427–434.

Douglas, J. J., & Nutter, C. P. (1986). Treatment-related change in sex roles of addicted men and women. *Journal of Studies on Alcohol, 47*, 201–206.

Downing, N. E. (1979). Theoretical and operational conceptualizations of psychological androgyny: Implications for measurement. *Psychology of Women Quarterly, 3*, 284–292.

Doyle, J. J., & Moore, R. J. (1978). Attitudes toward the male's role scale (AMR): An objective instrument to measure attitudes toward the male's sex role in contemporary society. *JSAS Catalog of Selected Documents in Psychology, 8*, 35.

Dunn, L. (1965). *The Peabody Picture Vocabulary Test: Expanded manual.* Minneapolis, MN: American Guidance Service.

Edelbrock, C., & Sugawara, A. I. (1978). Acquisition of sex-typed preferences. *Developmental Psychology, 14*, 614–623.

Edwards, A. L., & Ashworth, C. D. (1977). A replication study of item selection for the Bem Sex Role Inventory. *Applied Psychological Measurement, 1*, 501–507.

Edwards, V. J., & Spence, J. T. (1987). Gender-related traits, stereotypes and schemata. *Journal of Personality and Social Psychology, 53*, 146–154.

Eisenberg, N. (1983). Sex-typed toy choices: What do they signify? In M. B. Liss (Ed.), *Social and cognitive skills: Sex roles and children's play* (pp. 45–70). New York: Academic Press.

Evans, R. G., & Dinning, W. D. (1982). MMPI correlates of the Bem Sex Role Inventory and Extended Personal Attributes Questionnaire in a male psychiatric sample. *Journal of Clinical Psychology, 38*, 811–815.

Fagot, B. I. (1985). Changes in thinking about early sex role development. *Developmental Review, 5*, 83–98.

Fand, A. B. (1955). *Sex role and self-concept: A study of the feminine sex role as perceived by eighty-five college women for themselves, their ideal woman, the average woman, and men's ideal woman.* Unpublished doctoral dissertation, Cornell University, Ithaca, NY. (*Dissertation Abstracts International*, 1955, *15*, 1135–1136.)

Farylo, B., & Paludi, M. A. (1985). Research with the Draw-A-Person Test: Conceptual and methodological issues. *Journal of Psychology, 116*, 575–580.

Feather, N. T. (1978). Factor structure of the BEM Sex-Role Inventory: Implications for the study of masculinity, femininity, and androgyny. *Australian Journal of Psychology*, **30**, 241–254.

Feather, N. T. (1984). Masculinity, femininity, psychological androgyny, and the structure of values. *Journal of Personality and Social Psychology*, **47**, 604–620.

Feinman, S., & Ross, S. L. (1975). Homogeneity reliability of the It Scale for Children. *Psychological Reports*, **36**, 415–420.

Fling, S., & Manosevitz, M. (1972). Sex typing in nursery school children's play interests. *Developmental Psychology*, **7**, 146–152.

Frable, D. E., & Bem, S. L. (1985). If you are gender schematic, all members of the opposite sex look alike. *Journal of Personality and Social Psychology*, **49**, 459–468.

Franck, K., & Rosen, E. (1949). A projective test of masculinity–femininity. *Journal of Consulting Psychology*, **13**, 247–256.

Frank, S. J., McLaughlin, A. M., & Crusco, A. (1984). Sex role attributes, symptom distress, and defensive style among college men and women. *Journal of Personality and Social Psychology*, **47**, 182–192.

Freund, K., Nagler, E., Langevin, R., Zajac, A., & Steiner, B. (1974). Measuring feminine gender identity in homosexual males. *Archives of Sexual Behavior*, **3**, 249–260.

Friedan, B. (1963). *The feminine mystique*. New York: Norton.

Furby, L. (1983). "Consistency" and "contradiction" in the development of gender role characteristics. *New Ideas in Psychology*, **1**, 285–297.

Gaa, J. P., & Liberman, D. (1981). Categorization agreement of the Personality [sic] Attributes Questionnaire and the Bem Sex Role Inventory. *Journal of Clinical Psychology*, **37**, 593–601.

Gaudreau, P. (1977). Factor analysis of the Bem Sex-Role Inventory. *Journal of Consulting and Clinical Psychology*, **45**, 299–302.

Gayton, W. F., Havu, G. F., Ozmon, K. L., & Tavormina, J. (1977). A comparison of the Bem Sex Role Inventory and the PRF ANDRO Scale. *Journal of Personality Assessment*, **41**, 619–621.

Gilbert, L. A. (1985). Measures of psychological masculinity and femininity: A comment on Gaddy, Glass, and Arnkoff. *Journal of Counseling Psychology*, **32**, 163–166.

Gough, H. G. (1952). Identifying psychological femininity. *Educational and Psychological Measurement*, **12**, 427–439.

Gough, H. G. (1956). *California Psychological Inventory*. Palo Alto, CA: Consulting Psychologists Press.

Gough, H. G. (1957). *California Psychological Inventory: Manual*. Palo Alto, CA: Consulting Psychologists Press.

Gough, H. G. (1966). A cross-cultural analysis of the CPI Femininity scale. *Journal of Consulting Psychology*, **30**, 136–141.

Gough, H. G., & Heilbrun, A. L. (1965). *The Adjective Check List manual*. Palo Alto, CA: Consulting Psychologists Press.

Green, R., Fuller, M., & Rutley, B. (1972). It-Scale for Children and Draw-A-Person Test: 30 feminine vs. 25 masculine boys. *Journal of Personality Assessment*, **36**, 349–352.

Greer, G. (1971). *The female eunuch*. New York: McGraw-Hill.

Gross, R., Batlis, N., Small, A., & Erdwins, C. (1979). Factor structure of the Bem Sex Role Inventory and the Personal Attributes Questionnaire. *Journal of Consulting and Clinical Psychology*, **47**, 1122–1124.

Gruber, K. J., & Powers, W. A. (1982). Factor and discriminant analysis of the Bem Sex-Role Inventory. *Journal of Personality Assessment*, **46**, 284–291.

Guilford, J. P., & Zimmerman, W. S. (1949). *The Guilford–Zimmerman Temperament Survey: Manual of instructions and interpretations*. Beverly Hills, CA: Sheridan Supply.

Hall, J. A., & Halberstadt, A. G. (1980). Masculinity and femininity in children: Development of the Children's Personal Attributes Questionnaire. *Developmental Psychology*, **16**, 270–280.

Hall, J. A., & Taylor, M. C. (1985). Psychological androgyny and the Masculinity × Femininity interaction. *Journal of Personality and Social Psychology*, **49**, 429–435.

Handal, P. J., & Salit, E. D. (1985). Gender-role classification and demographic relationships: A function of type of scoring procedures. *Sex Roles*, **12**, 411–419.

Harackiewicz, J. M., & DePaulo, B. M. (1982). Accuracy of person perception: A component analysis according to Cronbach. *Personality and Social Psychology Bulletin,* **8,** 247–256.

Hargreaves, D., Stoll, L., Farnworth, S., & Morgan, S. (1981). Psychological androgyny and ideational fluency. *British Journal of Social Psychology,* **20,** 53–55.

Harkey, N. J. (1982). The Franck Drawing Completion Test: A tool for research in sex-role identification. *Journal of Personality Assessment,* **46,** 32–43.

Hartup, W. W., & Zook, E. A. (1960). Sex-role preferences in three- and four-year-old children. *Journal of Consulting Psychology,* **24,** 420–426.

Hathaway, S. R. (1956). Scales 5 (Masculinity-Femininity), 6 (Paranoia), and 8 (Schizophrenia). In G. S. Welsh & W. G. Dahlström (Eds.), *Basic readings on the MMPI in psychiatry and medicine* (pp. 104–112). Minneapolis: Univ. of Minnesota Press.

Hawkins, R. C., Turell, S., & Jackson, L. J. (1983). Desirable and undesirable masculine and feminine traits in relation to students' dieting tendencies and body image dissatisfaction. *Sex Roles,* **9,** 705–718.

Heerboth, J. R., & Ramanaiah, N. V. (1985). Evaluation of the BSRI masculine and feminine items using desirability and stereotype ratings. *Journal of Personality Assessment,* **49,** 264–270.

Heilbrun, A. B. (1968). Sex role, instrumental-expressive behavior, and psychopathology in females. *Journal of Abnormal Psychology,* **73,** 131–136.

Heilbrun, A. B. (1976). Measurement of masculine and feminine sex role identities as independent dimensions. *Journal of Consulting and Clinical Psychology,* **44,** 183–190.

Heilbrun, A. B. (1981). Gender differences in the functional linkage between androgyny, social cognition, and competence. *Journal of Personality and Social Psychology,* **41,** 1106–1118.

Heilbrun, A. B. (1983). Scoring androgyny as a continuous variable: A reply to Blackman. *Psychological Reports,* **53,** 398.

Heilbrun, A. B. (1984). Sex-based models of androgyny: A further cognitive elaboration of competence differences. *Journal of Personality and Social Psychology,* **46,** 216–229.

Heilbrun, A. B. (1986). Androgyny as type and androgyny as behavior: Implications for gender schema in males and females. *Sex Roles,* **14,** 123–139.

Heilbrun, A. B., & Bailey, B. A. (1986). Independence of masculine and feminine traits: Empirical exploration of a prevailing assumption. *Sex Roles,* **14,** 105–122.

Heilbrun, A. B., & Han, Y. L. (1984). Cost-effectiveness of college achievement by androgynous men and women. *Psychological Reports,* **55,** 977–978.

Heilbrun, A. B., & Pitman, D. (1979). Testing some basic assumptions about psychological androgyny. *Journal of Genetic Psychology,* **135,** 175–188.

Heist, P., & Younge, G. (1968). *The Omnibus Personality Inventory: Form F.* New York: Psychological Corporation.

Helmreich, R., & Stapp, J. (1974). Short forms of the Texas Social Behavior Inventory, an objective measure of self-esteem. *Bulletin of the Psychonomic Society,* **4,** 473–475.

Helmreich, R. L., Spence, J. T., & Holahan, C. K. (1979). Psychological androgyny and sex role flexibility: A test of two hypotheses. *Journal of Personality and Social Psychology,* **37,** 1631–1644.

Helmreich, R. L., Spence, J. T., & Wilhelm, J. A. (1981). A psychometric analysis of the Personal Attributes Questionnaire. *Sex Roles,* **7,** 1097–1108.

Ho, R., & Zemaitis, R. (1980). Behavioral correlates of an Australian version of the Bem Sex Role Inventory. *Australian Psychologist,* **15,** 459–466.

Holahan, C. K., & Spence, J. T. (1980). Desirable and undesirable masculine and feminine traits in counseling clients and unselected students. *Journal of Consulting and Clinical Psychology,* **48,** 300–302.

House, E. A. (1986). Sex role orientation and marital satisfaction in dual- and one-provider couples. *Sex Roles,* **14,** 245–259.

Humphreys, L. G. (1978). Research on individual differences requires correlational analyses, not ANOVA. *Intelligence,* **2,** 1–5.

Huston, A. C. (1983). Sex-typing. In P. H. Mussen (Ed.), *Handbook of child psychology* (4th ed., Vol. 4, pp. 387–467). New York: Wiley.

Hyde, J. S., & Phillis, D. E. (1979). Androgyny across the lifespan. *Developmental Psychology,* **15,** 334–336.

Jackson, D. N. (1967). *Personality Research Form manual.* Goshen, NY: Research Psychologists Press.

Jackson, L. A. (1983). The perception of androgyny and physical attractiveness: Two is better than one. *Personality and Social Psychology Bulletin,* **9,** 405–413.

Jackson, L. A. (1985). Self-conceptions and gender role: The correspondence between gender-role categorization and open-ended self-descriptions. *Sex Roles,* **13,** 549–566.

Jackson, L. A., Ialongo, N., & Stollak, G. E. (1986). Parental correlates of gender role: The relations between parents' masculinity, femininity, and child-rearing behaviors and their children's gender roles. *Journal of Social and Clinical Psychology,* **4,** 204–224.

Johnson, O. G. (1976). *Tests and measurements in child development handbook II* (Vol. 1 and 2). San Francisco: Jossey Bass.

Jones, W. H., Chernovitz, M. D., & Hansson, R. O. (1978). The enigma of androgyny: Differential implications for males and females? *Journal of Consulting and Clinical Psychology,* **46,** 298–313.

Kalin, R. (1979). Method for scoring androgyny as a continuous variable. *Psychological Reports,* **44,** 1205–1206.

Kaplan, A. G., & Sedney, M. A. (1980). *Psychology and sex roles.* Boston: Little, Brown.

Katz, P. A., & Boswell, S. (1986). Flexibility and traditionality in children's gender roles. *Genetic, Social, and General Psychology Monographs,* **112,** 105–147.

Kelly, J. A., & Worell, L. (1976). Parent behaviors related to masculine, feminine, and androgynous sex role orientations. *Journal of Consulting and Clinical Psychology,* **44,** 843–851.

Kelly, J. A., & Worell, J. (1977). New formulations of sex roles and androgyny: A critical review. *Journal of Consulting and Clinical Psychology,* **45,** 1101–1115.

Kelly, J. A., Furman, W., & Young, V. (1978). Problems associated with the typological measurement of sex roles and androgyny. *Journal of Consulting and Clinical Psychology,* **46,** 1574–1576.

Keyes, S., & Coleman, J. (1983). Sex-role conflicts and personal adjustment: A study of British adolescents. *Journal of Youth and Adolescence,* **12,** 443–459.

Lamke, L. K. (1982). The impact of sex-role orientation on self-esteem in early adolescence. *Child Development,* **53,** 1530–1535.

Lansky, L. M., & McKay, G. (1963). Sex role preferences of kindergarten boys and girls. Some contradictory results. *Psychological Reports,* **13,** 415–421.

Lansky, L. M., & McKay, G. (1969). Independence, dependence, manifest, and latent masculinity–femininity: Some complex relationships among four complex variables. *Psychological Reports,* **24,** 263–268.

Larsen, R. J., & Seidman, E. (1986). Gender schema theory and sex role inventories: Some conceptual and psychometric considerations. *Journal of Personality and Social Psychology,* **50,** 205–211.

Lenney, E. (1979a). Androgyny: Some audacious assertions toward its coming of age. *Sex Roles,* **5,** 703–719.

Lenney, E. (1979b). Concluding comments on androgyny: Some intimations of its mature development. *Sex Roles,* **5,** 829–840.

Liberman, D., & Gaa, J. P. (1986). The effect of response style on the validity of the BSRI. *Journal of Clinical Psychology,* **42,** 905–908.

Lippa, R. (1983). Sex typing and the perception of body outlines. *Journal of Personality,* **51,** 667–682.

Lippa, R. (1985). Review of the Bem Sex-Role Inventory. In J. V. Mitchell, Jr. (Ed.), *The 9th mental measurements yearbook* (pp. 176–178). Lincoln, NE: The Buros Institute of Mental Measurement.

Lippa, R., & Beauvais, C. (1983). Gender jeopardy: The effects of gender, assessed femininity and masculinity, and false success/failure feedback on performance in an experimental quiz game. *Journal of Personality and Social Psychology,* **44,** 344–353.

Lippa, R., Valdez, E., & Jolly, A. (1983). The effects of self-monitoring on the expressive display of masculinity–femininity. *Journal of Research in Personality,* **17,** 324–338.

List, J. A., Collins, W. A., & Westby, S. D. (1983). Comprehension and inferences from traditional and non-traditional sex-role portrayals on television. *Child Development,* **54,** 1579–1587.

Locksley, A., & Colten, M. E. (1979). Psychological androgyny: A case of mistaken identity? *Journal of Personality and Social Psychology,* **37,** 1017–1031.

Lott, B. (1981). A feminist critique of androgyny: Toward the elimination of gender attributions for learned behavior. In C. Mayo & N. M. Henley (Eds.), *Gender and nonverbal behavior* (pp. 171–180). New York: Springer-Verlag.

Lubinski, D., Tellegen, A., & Butcher, J. N. (1983). Masculinity, femininity, and androgyny viewed and assessed as distinct concepts. *Journal of Personality and Social Psychology,* **44,** 428–439.

Lunneborg, P. W. (1975). Interpreting other-sex scores on the Strong–Campbell Interest Inventory. *Journal of Counseling Psychology,* **22,** 494–499.

Markus, H., Crane, M., Bernstein, S., & Siladi, M. (1982). Self-schemas and gender. *Journal of Personality and Social Psychology,* **42,** 38–50.

Marsh, H. W., & Myers, M. (1986). Masculinity, femininity, and androgyny: A methodological and theoretical critique. *Sex Roles,* **14,** 397–431.

Martin, C. L., & Halverson, C. F. (1983a). The effects of sex-typing schemas on young children's memories. *Child Development,* **54,** 563–574.

Martin, C. L., & Halverson, C. F. (1983b). Gender constancy: A methodological and theoretical analysis. *Sex Roles,* **9,** 775–790.

McHale, S. M., & Huston, T. L. (1984). Men and women as parents: Sex role orientations, employment, and parental roles with infants. *Child Development,* **55,** 1349–1361.

McPherson, K. S., & Spetrino, S. K. (1983). Androgyny and sex-typing: Differences in beliefs regarding gender polarity in ratings of ideal men and women. *Sex Roles,* **9,** 441–451.

Mehrabian, A., & Epstein, N. A. (1972). A measure of emotional empathy. *Journal of Personality,* **40,** 525–543.

Mendelsohn, G. A., Weiss, D. S., & Feimer, N. R. (1982). Conceptual and empirical analysis of the typological implications of patterns of socialization and femininity. *Journal of Personality and Social Psychology,* **42,** 1157–1170.

Millimet, C. R., & Votta, R. P. (1979). Acquiescence and the Bem Sex-Role Inventory. *Journal of Personality Assessment,* **43,** 164–165.

Mills, C. J., & Tyrrell, D. J. (1983). Sex-stereotypic encoding and release from proactive interference. *Journal of Personality and Social Psychology,* **45,** 772–781.

Mitchell, J. V., Jr. (Ed.) (1985). *The 9th mental measurements yearbook.* Lincoln, NE: The Buros Institute of Mental Measurement.

Morawski, J. G. (1985). The measurement of masculinity and femininity: Engendering categorical realities. *Journal of Personality,* **53,** 196–223.

Morawski, J. G. (1987). The troubled quest for masculinity, femininity, and androgyny. In P. Shaver & C. Hendrick (Eds.), *Review of personality and social psychology* (Vol. 7, pp. 44–69). Newbury Park, CA: Sage.

Moreland, J. R., Gulanick, N., Montague, E. K., & Harren, V. A. (1978). Some psychometric properties of the Bem Sex Role Inventory. *Applied Psychological Measurement,* **2,** 249–256.

Mosher, D. L., & Sirkin, M. (1984). Measuring a macho personality constellation. *Journal of Research in Personality,* **18,** 150–163.

Myers, A. M., & Gonda, G. (1982a). Empirical validation of the Bem Sex-Role Inventory. *Journal of Personality and Social Psychology,* **43,** 304–318.

Myers, A. M., & Gonda, G. (1982b). Utility of the masculinity–femininity construct: Comparison of traditional and androgyny approaches. *Journal of Personality and Social Psychology,* **43,** 514–523.

Nash, S. C. (1979). Sex role as a mediator of intellectual functioning. In M. A. Wittig & A. C. Peterson (Eds.), *Sex related differences in cognitive functioning* (pp. 263–302). New York: Academic Press.

Nicholls, J. G., Licht, B. G., & Pearl, R. A. (1982). Some dangers of using personality question-naires to study personality. *Psychological Bulletin*, **92**, 572–580.

O'Brien, M., & Huston, A. C. (1985). Development of sex-typed play behavior in toddlers. *Developmental Psychology*, **21**, 866–871.

O'Grady, K. E., Freda, J. S., & Mikulka, P. J. (1979). A comparison of the Adjective Check List, Bem Sex Role Inventory, and Personal Attributes Questionnaire Masculinity and Femininity subscales. *Multivariate Behavioral Research*, **14**, 215–225.

O'Neil, J. M., Helms, B. J., Gable, R. K., David, L., & Wrightsman, L. S. (1986). Gender-Role Conflict Scale: College men's fear of femininity. *Sex Roles*, **14**, 335–350.

Orlofsky, J. L. (1981). Relationship between sex role attitudes and personality traits and the Sex Role Behavior Scale-1: A new measure of masculine and feminine role behaviors and interests. *Journal of Personality and Social Psychology*, **40**, 927–940.

Orlofsky, J. L., & O'Heron, C. A. (1987). Stereotypic and nonstereotypic sex role trait and behavior orientations: Implications for personality adjustment. *Journal of Personality and Social Psychology*, **52**, 1034–1042.

Orlofsky, J. L., & Windle, M. T. (1978). Sex-role orientation, behavioral adaptability and personal adjustment. *Sex Roles*, **4**, 801–811.

Orlofsky, J. L., Aslin, A. L., & Ginsburg, S. D. (1977). Differential effectiveness of two classifica-tion procedures on the Bem Sex Role Inventory. *Journal of Personality Assessment*, **41**, 414–416.

Orlofsky, J. L., Cohen, R. S., & Ramsden, M. W. (1985). Relationship between sex-role attitudes and personality traits and the Revised Sex-Role Behavior Scale. *Sex Roles*, **12**, 377–391.

Orlofsky, J. L., Ramsden, M. W., & Cohen, R. S. (1982). Development of the Revised Sex-Role Behavior Scale. *Journal of Personality Assessment*, **46**, 632–638.

Paludi, M. A. (1981). Sex role discrimination among girls: Effect on It Scale for Children scores. *Developmental Psychology*, **17**, 851–852.

Parker, G. V. (1969). Sex differences in self-description on the Adjective Check List. *Educational and Psychological Measurement*, **29**, 99–113.

Payne, T. J., Connor, J. M., & Colletti, G. (1987). Gender-based schematic processing: An em-pirical investigation and re-evaluation. *Journal of Personality and Social Psychology*, **52**, 937–945.

Pedhazur, E. J., & Tetenbaum, T. J. (1979). Bem Sex Role Inventory: A theoretical and meth-odological critique. *Journal of Personality and Social Psychology*, **37**, 996–1016.

Penick, E. C., Powell, B. J., & Read, M. R. (1984). Sex-role affiliation among male alcoholics. *Journal of Clinical Psychology*, **40**, 359–363.

Penick, E. C., Powell, B. J., Read, M. R., & Mahoney, D. (1980). Sex-role typing: A meth-odological note. *Psychological Reports*, **47**, 143–146.

Perry, D. G., & Perry, L. C. (1975). Observational learning in children: Effects of sex of model and subject's sex role behavior. *Journal of Personality and Social Psychology*, **31**, 1083–1088.

Pratt, M. W., Golding, G., & Hunter, W. J. (1984). Does morality have a gender? Sex, sex role, and moral judgment relationships across the adult lifespan. *Merrill-Palmer Quarterly*, **30**, 321–340.

Puglisi, J. T. (1980). Equating the social desirability of Bem Sex-Role Inventory masculinity and femininity subscales. *Journal of Personality Assessment*, **44**, 272–276.

Rabban, M. (1950). Sex role identification in young children in two diverse social groups. *Genetic Psychology Monographs*, **42**, 81–158.

Ramanaiah, N. V., & Hoffman, S. C. (1984). Effects of instructions and rating scales on item selection for the BSRI Scales. *Journal of Personality Assessment*, **48**, 145–152.

Ramanaiah, N. V., & Martin, H. J. (1984). Convergent and discriminant validity of selected masculinity and femininity scales. *Sex Roles*, **10**, 493–504.

Rao, S., Gupta, G. R., & Murthy, V. N. (1982). B.S.R.I. (A): An Indian adaptation of the Bem Sex Role Inventory. *Personality Study and Group Behavior*, **2**, 1–10.

Richmond, P. G. (1984). An aspect of sex-role identification with a sample of twelve-year-olds and sixteen-year-olds. *Sex Roles*, **11**, 1021–1032.

Rosenkrantz, P., Vogel, S., Bee, H., Broverman, I., & Broverman, D. M. (1968). Sex-role stereotypes and self-concepts in college students. *Journal of Consulting and Clinical Psychology*, **32**, 287–295.

Rotter, J. B. (1966). Generalized expectancies for internal versus external control of reinforcement. *Psychological Monographs*, **80**(1, Whole No. 609).

Rowland, R. (1977). The Bem Sex Role Inventory. *Australian Psychologist*, **12**, 83–88.

Ruble, T. L. (1983). Sex stereotypes: Issues of change in the 1970's. *Sex Roles*, **9**, 397–402.

Rusbult, C. E., Zembrodt, I. M., & Iwaniszek, J. (1986). The impact of gender and sex-role orientation on responses to dissatisfaction in close relationships. *Sex Roles*, **15**, 1–20.

Sampson, E. E. (1977). Psychology and the American ideal. *Journal of Personality and Social Psychology*, **35**, 767–782.

Scher, D. (1984). Sex-role contradictions: Self-perceptions and ideal perceptions. *Sex Roles*, **10**, 651–656.

Schneider, J., & Schneider-Duker, M. (1984). Sex roles and nonverbal sensitivity. *Journal of Social Psychology*, **122**, 281–282.

Sears, R. R., Rau, L., & Alpert, R. (1965). *Identification and child rearing*. Stanford, CA: Stanford Univ. Press.

Segall, M. H. (1986). Culture and behavior: Psychology in global perspective. *Annual Review of Psychology*, **37**, 523–564.

Senneker, P., & Hendrick, C. (1983). Androgyny and helping behavior. *Journal of Personality and Social Psychology*, **45**, 916–925.

Serbin, L. A., & Sprafkin, C. (1982). Measurement of sex-typed play: A comparison between laboratory and naturalistic observation procedures. *Behavioral Assessment*, **4**, 225–235.

Serbin, L. A., & Sprafkin, C. (1986). The salience of gender and the process of sex-typing in three- to seven-year-old children. *Child Development*, **57**, 1188–1199.

Sher, M. A., & Lansky, L. M. (1968). The It Scale for Children: Effects of variations in the sex-specificity of the It figure. *Merrill-Palmer Quarterly*, **14**, 322–330.

Shively, M. G., Rudolf, J. R., & De Cecco, J. P. (1978). The identification of the social sex-role stereotypes. *Journal of Homosexuality*, **3**, 225–234.

Siem, F. M., & Spence, J. T. (1986). Gender-related traits and helping behaviors. *Journal of Personality and Social Psychology*, **51**, 615–621.

Silvern, L. E., & Katz, P. A. (1986). Gender roles and adjustment in elementary-school children: A multidimensional approach. *Sex Roles*, **14**, 181–202.

Silvern, L. E., & Ryan, V. L. (1983). A re-examination of masculine and feminine sex-role ideals and conflicts among ideals for the man, woman, and person. *Sex Roles*, **9**, 1223–1248.

Simms, R. E., Davis, M. H., Foushee, H. C., Holahan, C. K., Spence, J. T., & Helmreich, R. L. (1978). *Psychological masculinity and femininity in children and their relationships to trait stereotypes and toy preferences*. Paper presented at the meeting of the Southwestern Psychological Association, New Orleans.

Slaby, R. G., & Frey, K. S. (1975). Development of gender constancy and selective attention to same-sex models. *Child Development*, **46**, 849–856.

Small, A. C., Erdwins, C., & Gross, R. B. (1979). A comparison of the Bem Sex-Role Inventory and the Heilbrun Masculinity and Femininity Scales. *Journal of Personality Assessment*, **43**, 393–395.

Smiljanic-Colanovic, V. (1972). [Development of sex-roles]. (Srcr) In *Psiholoske razprave: IV. Kongres psihologov SERJ*. Ljubljana, Yugoslavia: Ljubljana Press.

Smith, S. G. (1983). A comparison among three measures of social sex role. *Journal of Homosexuality*, **9**, 99–107.

Snell, W. E. (1986). The Masculine Role Inventory: Components and correlates. *Sex Roles*, **15**, 443–445.

Spence, J. T. (1982). Comments on Baumrind's "Are androgynous individuals more effective persons and parents?" *Child Development*, **53**, 76–80.

Spence, J. T. (1983). Comment on Lubinski, Tellegen, and Butcher's "Masculinity, femininity, and androgyny viewed and assessed as distinct concepts." *Journal of Personality and Social Psychology, 44,* 440–446.

Spence, J. T. (1984). Masculinity, femininity, and gender-related traits: A conceptual analysis and critique of current research. In B. A. Maher & W. B. Maher (Eds.), *Progress in experimental personality research* (Vol. 13, pp. 1–97). Orlando, FL: Academic Press.

Spence, J. T. (1985). Gender identity and its implications for the concepts of masculinity and femininity. In T. B. Sonderegger (Ed.), *Nebraska Symposium on Motivation* (Vol. 32, pp. 59–95). Lincoln: Univ. of Nebraska Press.

Spence, J. T., & Helmreich, R. L. (1972). The Attitudes toward Women Scale: An objective instrument to measure attitudes toward the rights and roles of women in contemporary society. *JSAS Catalog of Selected Documents in Psychology, 2,* 66–67.

Spence, J. T., & Helmreich, R. L. (1978). *Masculinity and femininity: Their psychological dimensions, correlates, and antecedents.* Austin: Univ. of Texas Press.

Spence, J. T., & Helmreich, R. L. (1979a). Comparison of masculine and feminine personality attributes and sex-role attitudes across age groups. *Developmental Psychology, 15,* 583–584.

Spence, J. T., & Helmreich, R. L. (1979b). The many faces of androgyny: A reply to Locksley and Colten. *Journal of Personality and Social Psychology, 37,* 1032–1046.

Spence, J. T., & Helmreich, R. L. (1979c). On assessing "androgyny." *Sex Roles, 5,* 721–738.

Spence, J. T., & Helmreich, R. L. (1980). Masculine instrumentality and feminine expressiveness: Their relationships with sex role attitudes and behaviors. *Psychology of Women Quarterly, 5,* 147–163.

Spence, J. T., & Helmreich, R. L. (1981). Androgyny versus gender schema: A comment on Bem's gender schema theory. *Psychological Review, 88,* 365–368.

Spence, J. T., & Helmreich, R. L. (1983). Beyond face validity: A comment on Nicholls, Licht, and Pearl. *Psychological Bulletin, 94,* 181–184.

Spence, J. T., Helmreich, R. L., & Holahan, C. K. (1979). Negative and positive components of psychological masculinity and femininity and their relationships to self-reports of neurotic and acting out behaviors. *Journal of Personality and Social Psychology, 37,* 1673–1682.

Spence, J. T., Helmreich, R., & Stapp, J. (1973). A short version of the Attitudes toward Women Scale (AWS). *Bulletin of the Psychonomic Society, 2,* 219–220.

Spence, J. T., Helmreich, R., & Stapp, J. (1974). The Personal Attributes Questionnaire: A measure of sex role stereotypes and masculinity–femininity. *JSAS Catalog of Selected Documents in Psychology, 4,* 43–44.

Spence, J. T., Helmreich, R., & Stapp, J. (1975). Ratings of self and peers on sex role attributes and their relation to self-esteem and conceptions of masculinity and femininity. *Journal of Personality and Social Psychology, 32,* 29–39.

Steinmann, A. G., & Fox, D. J. (1974). *The male dilemma.* New York: Jason Aronson.

Stoneman, Z., Brody, G. H., & MacKinnon, C. E. (1986). Same-sex and cross-sex siblings: Activity choices, roles, behavior, and gender stereotypes. *Sex Roles, 15,* 495–511.

Taylor, A. (1983). Conceptions of masculinity and femininity as a basis for stereotypes of male and female homosexuals. *Journal of Homosexuality, 9,* 37–53.

Taylor, D. (1984). Concurrent validity of the Bem Sex Role Inventory: A person–environment approach. *Sex Roles, 10,* 713–723.

Taylor, M. C., & Hall, J. A. (1982). Psychological androgyny: Theories, methods, and conclusions. *Psychological Bulletin, 92,* 347–366.

Tellegen, A., & Lubinski, D. (1983). Some methodological comments on labels, traits, interactions, and types in the study of "femininity" and "masculinity": Reply to Spence. *Journal of Personality and Social Psychology, 44,* 447–455.

Terman, L. M., & Miles, C. C. (1936). *Sex and personality.* New York: McGraw-Hill.

Thomas, S., & Robinson, M. (1981). Development of a measure of androgyny for young adolescents. *Journal of Early Adolescence, 1,* 195–209.

Thompson, N. L., Jr., & McCandless, B. R. (1970). It score variations by instructional style. *Child Development, 41,* 425–436.

Thompson, N. J., Jr., Schwartz, D. M., McCandless, B. R., & Edwards, D. A. (1973). Parent–child relationships and sexual identity in male and female homosexuals and heterosexuals. *Journal of Consulting and Clinical Psychology, 41*, 120–127.

Tice, D. M., & Baumeister, R. F. (1985). Masculinity inhibits helping in emergencies: Personality does predict the bystander effect. *Journal of Personality and Social Psychology, 49*, 420–428.

Volentine, S. Z. (1981). The assessment of masculinity and femininity: Scale 5 of the MMPI Compared with the BSRI and the PAQ. *Journal of Clinical Psychology, 37*, 367–374.

Wakefield, J. A., Sasek, J., Friedman, A. F., & Bowden, J. P. (1976). Androgyny and other measures of masculinity–femininity. *Journal of Consulting and Clinical Psychology, 44*, 766–770.

Walkup, H., & Abbott, R. D. (1978). Cross-validation of item selection on the Bem Sex Role Inventory. *Applied Psychological Measurement, 2*, 63–71.

Wheeler, L., Reis, H., & Nezlek, J. (1983). Loneliness, social interaction, and sex roles. *Journal of Personality and Social Psychology, 45*, 943–953.

Whetton, C., & Swindells, T. (1977). A factor analysis of the Bem Sex-Role Inventory. *Journal of Clinical Psychology, 33*, 150–153.

White, K. M., Speisman, J. C., Jackson, D., Bartis, S., & Costos, D. (1986). Intimacy maturity and its correlates in young married couples. *Journal of Personality and Social Psychology, 50*, 152–162.

Whitley, B. E. (1983). Sex role orientation and self-esteem: A critical meta-analytic review. *Journal of Personality and Social Psychology, 44*, 765–778.

Whitley, B. E. (1985). Sex-role orientation and psychological well-being: Two meta-analyses. *Sex Roles, 12*, 207–225.

Wiggins, J. S., & Holzmuller, A. (1978). Psychological androgyny and interpersonal behavior. *Journal of Consulting and Clinical Psychology, 46*, 40–52.

Wiggins, J. S., & Holzmuller, A. (1981). Further evidence on androgyny and interpersonal flexibility. *Journal of Research in Personality, 15*, 67–80.

Williams, J. E., & Bennett, S. M. (1975). *The definition of sex stereotypes via the Adjective Check List.* Unpublished manuscript, Wake Forest University, Winston-Salem, NC.

Williams, J. E., & Best, D. L. (1977). Sex stereotypes and trait favorability on the Adjective Check List. *Educational and Psychological Measurement, 37*, 101–110.

Williams, J. E., Bennett, S. M., & Best, D. L. (1975). Awareness and expression of sex stereotypes in young children. *Developmental Psychology, 11*, 635–642.

Wilson, F. R., & Cook, E. P. (1984). Concurrent validity of four androgyny instruments. *Sex Roles, 11*, 813–837.

Windle, M. (1986). Sex role orientation, cognitive flexibility, and life satisfaction among older adults. *Psychology of Women Quarterly, 10*, 263–273.

Windle, M., & Sinnott, J. D. (1985). A psychometric study of the Bem Sex Role Inventory with an older adult sample. *Journal of Gerontology, 40*, 336–343.

Wittenberg, M. T., & Reis, H. T. (1986). Loneliness, social skills, and social perception. *Personality and Social Psychology Bulletin, 12*, 121–130.

Wong, P. T., Kettlewell, G. E., & Sproule, C. F. (1985). On the importance of being masculine: Sex role, attribution, and women's career achievement. *Sex Roles, 12*, 757–769.

Yanico, B. J. (1985). BSRI scores: Stability over four years for college women. *Psychology of Women Quarterly, 9*, 277–283.

CHAPTER 12

Values

Valerie A. Braithwaite and William A. Scott

The study of values is central to and involves the intersection of interests of philosophers, anthropologists, sociologists, and psychologists. Values are presumed to encapsulate the aspirations of individuals and societies: They pertain to what is desirable, to deeply engrained standards that determine future directions and justify past actions. Values have been postulated as key constructs in the socialization process, and have found their way into cultural, religious, political, educational, occupational, and family research. Other intellectual traditions see values as also having an individual function shaped by the biological and psychological needs of each person. This perspective has fostered research linking values to the attitudes and personality of individuals and to the maintenance and enhancement of self-esteem.

In spite of widespread acceptance of the relevance of values to human activity at both the individual and social levels of analysis, developments in the field have been hampered by problems of definition and doubts about the empirical viability of the construct. Concern about theoretical fragmentation and conceptual diversity was a major theme in Levitin's (1968) review. Smith (1969) concurred that the empirical study of values had "started from different preconceptions and . . . altogether failed to link together and yield a domain of cumulative knowledge" (p. 98). Much has happened in the past two decades to improve this situation, most of it attributable to the innovative contribution of the late Milton Rokeach (1968, 1973). Convergence of views at the conceptual level, however, is still not reflected in the scales that are available to measure values. They are testaments to the diverse ways in which the value construct was conceptualized some thirty years ago.

Although the notion of value as an absolute attribute of an object had been firmly rejected by the 1950s, social scientists differed on the appropriate referent for value (Adler, 1956). Was value an attribute of the person "doing the valuing" or the object "receiving the valuing"?

A second widely discussed topic was the distinction between value as the desirable and value as the desired, the difference between what one "ought" to do and what one "wants" to do. Out of such deliberations in the 1950s and 1960s a unifying consensus emerged that values were "person-centered" and pertained to "the desirable," a consensus captured in the definition proposed by Clyde Kluckhohn (1951):

> A value is a conception, explicit or implicit, distinctive of an individual or characteristic of a group, of the desirable which influences the selection from available modes, means, and ends of action. (p. 395)

In spite of a unifying theme at the conceptual level, convergence in empirical values research did not follow. The first drawback was that the most established measures of personal and cultural values at that time were not consistent with the notion of "conceptions of the desirable." The Allport, Vernon, and Lindzey *Study of Values* (1960) assessed personal interests and preferences. Florence Kluckhohn and Strodtbeck's (1961) measure of cultural values was concerned with existential and general beliefs about human beings, and their relationships with each other and with their world.

A second factor blocking progress in values research was that although Clyde Kluckhohn's (1951) definition specified the desirable, the elements that constituted that domain could relate to anything from the way a person interacted with another through individual lifestyles or philosophies of life to the way a person thought the world should be. Adequate operationalization was made difficult by an inability to specify the elements of the value domain to ensure systematic item sampling. The result has been the adoption of piecemeal approaches in which a few dimensions have been measured with little justification for why they were the most important.

A third operational difficulty concerned the appropriate level of abstraction for item sampling. Values were widely accepted as general rather than specific: as "generalized ends" (Fallding, 1965, p. 227), as "nearly independent of specific situations" (Williams, 1968, p. 284), as "abstractions concerning general classes of objects" (Katz & Stotland, 1959, p. 432) or as generalized attitudes (Bem, 1970; Dukes, 1955; Newcomb, Turner, & Converse, 1965; Smith, 1963). It has never been clear, however, whether values were to be inferred from responses to specific attitude statements or more directly from general orienting responses. Furthermore, at what point on the specific–general continuum did attitudes become values?

Thus, while some conceptual agreement was being reached in the late 1960s about the nature of value, there was no emerging consensus on the operationalization of the construct. Handy (1970) was led to conclude that "the official definitions given sometimes do not conform to what was studied, and there often appears to be little effective control over what putatively was measured" (p. 207). This was the state of the art when Rokeach's (1968, 1973) work first appeared, providing the conceptual and operational synergy that had been eluding value research for so long.

Rokeach's Contribution to Empirical Values Research

Rokeach set about measuring values by asking respondents first to rank-order 18 instrumental values (modes of conduct) and second, 18 terminal values (end-states of existence) in terms of their importance as guiding principles in their lives. A *value* was defined as "an enduring belief that a specific mode of conduct or end-state of existence is personally or socially preferable to an opposite or converse mode of conduct or end-state of existence". Sets of values formed *value systems,* defined as "enduring organization[s] of beliefs concerning preferable modes of conduct or end-states of existence along a continuum of importance" (1973, p. 5).

These value systems were regarded as part of a functionally integrated cognitive system in which the basic units of analysis are beliefs. Clusters of beliefs form attitudes that are functionally and cognitively connected to the value systems. Rokeach further postulated classes of beliefs concerned with self-cognitions representing "the innermost core of the total belief system, and all remaining beliefs, attitudes and values can be conceived of as functionally organized around this innermost core" (1973, p. 216). Like other beliefs, then, values serve to maintain and enhance the self-concept.

Rokeach capitalized on the emerging consensus of the 1960s by accepting values as general beliefs, as having a motivational function, as not merely evaluative but prescriptive and proscriptive, as guiding actions and attitudes, and as individual as well as social phenomena. (See Allport, 1961, Smith, 1963, and Kluckhohn, 1951, for a discussion of these issues.) As well as consolidating these themes, Rokeach integrated a number of other strands of thought and research from the values literature. A significant body of work has focused on the attitude–value relationship (Carlson, 1956; Constantinople, 1967; Nelson, 1968; Ostrom & Brock, 1969; Peak, 1955; Rosenberg, 1956, 1960; Smith, 1949; Woodruff & Di Vesta, 1948). According to this view, values were more central concepts than attitude, were determinants of attitude, and were more resistant to change, with favorable attitudes emerging toward objects instrumental in the attainment of important values.

Rokeach also incorporated the views of those claiming strong ties between an individual's self-esteem and values (Katz & Stotland, 1959; Kluckhohn, 1951; Smith, 1963). Kluckhohn noted how some values acted "as components of super-ego or ego-ideal; . . . if violated, there is guilt, shame, ego-deflation, intropunitive reaction" (cited in Kluckhohn, 1951, p. 398). Guilt arising from value violation was an important part of Scott's (1965) conceptualization. Smith (1963) extended this idea to include protection of self-esteem as well: "In the long pull of maintaining 'face' before others and self-esteem within, we all become thoroughly practiced in evoking values to justify ourselves." (p. 345).

A third feature of earlier work that Rokeach integrated into his model was the notion that values are hierarchically organized (Katz & Stotland, 1959; Kluckhohn, 1951; Mukerjee, 1965; Tanaka, 1972; Williams, 1970; Woodruff & Di Vesta, 1948). Although the exact form of the hierarchy (e.g., linear or otherwise) remained unresolved, the notion of "prioritizing" values had proven popular to explain and resolve value conflict according to some systematic, learned organization of rules.

Fourth, Rokeach's operationalization of the value construct identified values as both modes of conduct and end-states. These concepts are similar to Kluckhohn's (1951) modes, means and ends of action, although Kluckhohn saw them not as values but as behaviors selected *through* values. Scott (1965) had identified values, in part, through the fact that they are ultimate (final sufficient ends) and Fallding (1965) through their being associated with "satisfactions that are self-sufficient" (p. 223). Modes of conduct gained prominence through the work of Lovejoy (1950), who distinguished adjectival values (i.e., modes of conduct) and terminal values (i.e., end states of existence). By defining values as either modes of conduct or end-states, Rokeach was able to build on and move beyond the content covered by the existing value instruments.

Rethinking Beliefs

While integrating much of contemporary thinking on values, Rokeach departed from the mainstream in three ways. First, his definition of belief served to differentiate more clearly the hitherto interrelated concepts of attitude and value. Traditionally, beliefs have been linked with information about an object, attitudes to evaluation of that object (Fishbein & Ajzen, 1975; Kluckhohn, 1951). Beliefs are not just cognitions in Rokeach's conceptual schema, but predispositions to action capable of arousing affect around the object of the belief. Attitudes and values have been defined and differentiated by Rokeach in terms of the types of beliefs composing them. Value refers to a single proscriptive or prescriptive belief that transcends specific objects or situations, while attitude refers to an organization of several beliefs focused on a specific object or situation. Together they constitute the value–attitude system, embedded in the wider belief system.

Rokeach's second departure from mainstream thought was in separating "instrumental" and "terminal" value systems. Apart from subsuming much of the empirical work that had already been conducted under the umbrella of values, identifying values as modes of conduct or end-states of existence clearly delimited the boundaries of the value domain. Rokeach's extension of this model, however, and proposal that modes of conduct are instrumental to the achievement of desirable ends cannot be readily justified. Many have argued convincingly against such thinking. Kluckhohn (1951) adopted the position that modes of conduct, the personal qualities or traits which individuals like to think of themselves as having, may serve as either means or ends. Lovejoy (1950) also strongly opposed linking modes with means in a means–end model. According to Lovejoy, the choice of a particular course of action may be influenced either by how one wishes to be perceived (adjectival values), or by the end-states one wishes to attain (terminal values), or by both. Although adjectival and terminal values are likely to affect and interact with each other, one is not in the service of the other.

Rokeach's third innovation was the notion that values can be conceptualized as two simple linear hierarchies. Criticisms of this proposition (Gorsuch, 1970; Kitwood & Smithers, 1975; Ng, 1982) have pointed to the likelihood that people have values that are *equally* important and that, in real life, some values are not likely to be compared with others. Thus, rank-ordering two sets of values is seen as a highly artificial task. Increasingly, however, research is supporting the feasibility of the rank-ordering approach, demonstrating that similar results emerge when fewer restrictions are placed on the respondent (Alwin & Krosnick, 1985; Feather, 1973; Moore, 1975; Munson & McIntyre, 1979; Rankin & Grube, 1980; Reynolds & Jolly, 1980).

Overall, Rokeach's (1968, 1973) departure from the mainstream at the conceptual level has offered clarity and order. At a methodological level, however, criticisms have been made of Rokeach's work that have far-reaching implications for the field of value measurement. In particular, item sampling and single-item measurement have been problematic issues for Rokeach, as they have been for others. Few measures in this chapter either provide justification for focusing on particular facets of the value domain or involve systematic sampling of items to represent these facets. With regard to single-item measurement, the practice continues to be a popular option for researchers who seek economy in their value measures (Christenson, Hougland, Gage, & Hoa, 1984; Hill & Stull, 1981; Kohn, 1969). These problems are endemic to as broad a field as values.

Item Sampling

Rokeach's identification of the 36 most important terminal and instrumental values has been criticized as arbitrary and subjective (R. A. Jones, Sensenig, & Ashmore, 1978; Keats & Keats, 1974; Kitwood & Smithers, 1975; Lynn, 1974). Rokeach (1973) himself acknowledged the overall procedure to be "an intuitive one" (p. 30). In this case, however, the subsequent literature has uncovered few omissions. Braithwaite and Law (1985), using 115 semistructured interviews to obtain a more comprehensive coverage of the universe of content, concluded that Rokeach's item sampling was basically sound. The interviews identified 54 goals in life and 71 ways of behaving, which factor analysis reduced to 19 basic dimensions corresponding quite well with the Value Survey items. Of the four major omissions identified in this study, only physical well-being and individual rights have been mentioned by other researchers. The omission of individual rights, more specifically justice, has been a cause of concern in cross-cultural contexts (Feather & Hutton, 1973; Ng, 1982). In examining the value correlates of preventive health behavior, Kristiansen (1985) noted the absence of "health" as a terminal value, an item which Rokeach added in a recent revision of his instrument.

The Value Survey has been examined closely for the adequacy of its item sampling and in the final analysis has fared well. Other instruments, however, have not been similarly scrutinized and there is often little in the development of these measures to reassure users of their adequacy on this criterion.

Single-Item Measures

Concerns about single-item measurement arise with the Value Survey because each value is assessed only by one- or two-word items in a heading (e.g., FREEDOM) and then one or two phrases in brackets underneath (e.g., independence, free choice) (Braithwaite & Law, 1985; Gorsuch & McFarland, 1972; Mueller, 1974).

According to psychometric theory, no single item is a pure measure of the construct of interest, since each reflects error, some attributable to other irrelevant constructs and some to random fluctuations. Constructs are best measured, therefore, by a number of different items that converge on the theoretical meaning of the construct while diverging on the irrelevant aspects that are being unavoidably assessed. Such a strategy is the conventional approach to arriving at a reliable and valid measure of a construct. Rokeach (1967) departed from this tradition with abstract concepts that are highly ambiguous and open to a variety of interpretations. As Gorsuch and McFarland (1972) have suggested, Rokeach opted for single-item measures because of economy. The Value Survey offers a wide coverage of items using a simple rank-ordering procedure that facilitates its use in a variety of research contexts. For example, respondents have been asked to complete the Value Survey twice: to represent their own values in the first instance, and their perceptions of the values of others or of institutions in the second (Feather, 1979a, 1980; Rokeach, 1979). Multiple-items would lengthen and complicate the measurement procedure enormously and the flexibility of the instrument would be lost.

Overriding the issue of cost, however, is the more fundamental criterion of validity (Gorsuch & McFarland, 1972). Are single items as valid as multi-item scales? Gorsuch and McFarland's work suggests that there is no simple answer; it depends on the items and the research questions being asked. Findings based on the Value Survey's measures of "salvation" and "equality," for instance, are highly consistent (Billig & Cochrane, 1979; Bishop, Barclay, & Rokeach, 1972; Cochrane, Billig, & Hogg, 1979; Feather, 1970b, 1975b; Joe, Jones, & Miller, 1981; Rawls, Harrison, Rawls, Hayes, & Johnson, 1973; Rokeach, 1969a, 1973; Tate & Miller, 1971; Thomas, 1986). In contrast, studies relying on the measures of "helpful" and "freedom" have produced discrepant results (Braithwaite, 1982; Cochrane et al., 1979; Feather, 1977, 1984a; Homant & Rokeach, 1970; Joe et al., 1981; Penner, Summers, Brookmire, & Dertke, 1976; Shotland & Berger, 1970; Staub, 1974).

The seriousness of the problem for users of the Value Survey is demonstrated by Feather's (1971, 1975a) inconsistent findings across data collected in the same place but at different times. In examining the values of science and humanities students across 2 consecutive years, Feather (1971) reported 13 significant differences in his 1970 data and 7 in his 1969 data. Only four were common to both analyses. In a second paper relating income level to values, Feather (1975a) reported 10 significant differences in 1972 and 11 in 1973, with four findings being replicated. In a third paper on the value correlates of dogmatism, Feather (1970a) was unable to replicate any from one year to the next.

Reliance on single-item measures becomes particularly problematic in cross-cultural comparisons of value systems, an area in which the Value Survey has attracted considerable attention (Feather, 1986; Furnham, 1984; Mahoney, 1977; Moore, 1976; Penner & Anh, 1977; Rokeach, 1973). The difficulties of transporting value constructs across cultures and of obtaining equivalent measures are legendary (Feather, 1986; Hofstede, 1980; Hui & Triandis, 1985; Triandis, Kilty, Shanmugam, Tanaka, & Vassiliou, 1972; Zavalloni, 1980). Translations are generally possible, but comparable interpretation is less easily assured.

As great as the problems of cross-cultural value inquiry are, the use of single-item measures is likely to magnify them further. Detracting from their advantage of efficiency is the danger of incorrectly inferring cultural similarity or dissimilarity because the data base was a single response to a highly abstract concept. In contrast, multi-item measurement provides a stronger basis for inferring group differences. Five items that tap different aspects of equality, for example, provide researchers with a clearer basis for interpretation than one item. Respondents have more than one chance to communicate their views and researchers have several sources of data on which to rely when interpreting the results.

Measures Reviewed Here

This review has given priority to the work of Rokeach, a bias that reflects the sheer dominance of his contribution to integrating and clarifying the value concept. In view of the measurement shortcomings of the Value Survey, however, other multi-item scales offer useful alternatives. The instruments reviewed in this chapter are:

1. The Study of Values (Allport, *et al.,* 1960)
2. The Value Survey (Rokeach, 1967)
3. The Goal and Mode Values Inventories (Braithwaite & Law, 1985)
4. Ways to Live (Morris, 1956b)
5. Revised Ways to Live (Dempsey & Dukes, 1966)
6. Value Profile (Bales & Couch, 1969)
7. Life Role Inventory—Value Scales (Fitzsimmons, Macnab, & Casserly, 1985)
8. Conceptions of the Desirable (Lorr, Suziedelis, & Tonesk, 1973)
9. Empirically Derived Value Constructions (Gorlow & Noll, 1967)
10. The East–West Questionnaire (Gilgen & Cho, 1979a)
11. Value Orientations (Kluckhohn & Strodtbeck, 1961)
12. Personal Value Scales (Scott, 1965)
13. Survey of Interpersonal Values (Gordon, 1960)
14. The Moral Behavior Scale (Crissman, 1942; Rettig & Pasamanick, 1959)
15. The Morally Debatable Behaviors Scales (Harding & Phillips, 1986)

These scales demonstrate that values have been measured by using abstract philosophical issues that transcend cultural boundaries (Nos. 4, 5, 10, and 11), by drawing upon a broad range of goals, ways of behaving, and states of affairs that are valued in Western societies (Nos. 1, 2, 3, 6, 7, 8, and 9), and by focusing more narrowly on personal, interpersonal or moral behavior held in high regard in Western cultures (Nos. 12, 13, 14, and 15).

There is considerable diversity as well in the dimensions used for item evaluation.

Judgments are made in terms of preference (1, 4), agreement (6, 10), importance (7, 13), goodness (14), justifiability (15), importance as guiding principles (2, 3), and consistent admiration (12). The semantic distinctiveness of these dimensions has been well documented (see Levitin, 1968), but less is understood about their empirical distinctiveness. Some work has addressed this issue showing equivalence of some (Bolt, 1978) and nonequivalence of others (Morris, 1956b).

In the midst of this variability, one can also detect some common threads. While few value researchers have empirically examined cross-instrument relationships, some recurring themes emerge in the dimensions identified through factor analytic studies of these instruments. Related scales falling under each category are as follows:

1. Concern for the welfare of others: Benevolence (13), Kindness (12), Social Orientation (1, 7), Equalitarianism (6), Humanistic Orientation (8), A Positive Orientation to Others (3), and Receptivity and Concern (4);

2. Status Desired or Respected: Recognition and Leadership (13), Status (12), Personal Achievement and Development (7), Philistine Orientation [identified in (1) by Duffy & Crissy, 1940, and Lurie, 1937], Acceptance of Authority (6), Status–Security Values (9), an Authoritarian Orientation (8), and Social Standing (3);

3. Self-control: Self-control (12) and Social Restraint and Self-control (4);

4. Unrestrained Pleasure: Self-Indulgence (4), Need-Determined Expression versus Value-Determined Restraint (6), and a Hedonistic Orientation (8);

5. Individualism: Independence (13, 12, 7), Withdrawal and Self-Sufficiency (4), Individualism (6), the Rugged Individualist (9), and the Work Ethic (8);

6. Social Adeptness: Social Skills (12) and Conformity (13); and

7. Religiosity: Religious Orientation (1), Traditional Religiosity (3), and Religiousness (12).

Selection from among the 15 scales reviewed must ultimately depend on the research question and the context in which values are to be assessed. The scales can be differentiated on the following decision-making criteria:

1. Conceptual breadth. Instruments 1–11 are based on a broad conceptualization of the value domain, while 12 and 13 are restricted in scope to interpersonal values and 14 and 15 more narrowly to moral values.

2. Representative sampling of items from the domain of inquiry. This issue has generally not been given much attention, although the relevance and comprehensiveness of items has been addressed with Instruments 2, 3, 6, and 12.

3. Representation of Western values rather than cross-culturally relevant values. Most value scales are biased toward Western values, but Instruments 4, 5, 10, and 11 are oriented to measuring values that transcend Western cultural boundaries.

4. Reliance on multi-item rather than single-item measurement. The scales reviewed in this chapter are strong on this criterion, but Instruments 2, 4, and 5 adopt a single-item approach.

5. Use in nonstudent populations. Most value scales have been developed and used with American college students, but there are some notable exceptions. Instruments 1, 2, 7, 13, and 15 have been used extensively in nonstudent populations, 2 and 15 with large probability samples from the general population.

6. Availability of basic data on instrument reliability and validity. Instruments 6, 8, 9, 10, 11, 14, and 15 are weak on this criterion.

7. Compatibility with the dominant conceptualization of value. Instruments 1, 4, 5, 6, 10, 11, and 13 do not measure conceptions of the desirable.

8. Relevance of items. Instruments 6 and 14 are older measures in which the language and content of some items have become dated.

Omissions

At this point the limits imposed on the scales reviewed should be specified. Excluded are measures of specific values such as altruism (e.g., Rushton, Chrisjohn, & Fekken, 1981), equality (e.g., Bell & Robinson, 1978), and materialist–postmaterialist goals (Inglehart, 1971, 1977), measures of moral judgment ability (e.g., Rest, 1972), measures of broader concepts such as modernity (e.g., Kahl, 1968), measures that focus on values in work, family, or other specific contexts (e.g., England, 1967; Harding & Phillips, 1986; Hofstede, 1980; Kohn, 1969), children's measures (e.g., Lortie-Lussier, Fellers, & Kleinplatz, 1986; Smart & Smart, 1975), and projective measures (e.g., Kilmann, 1975; Rorer & Ziller, 1982). Four instruments from the previous edition of *Measures of Social-Psychological Attitudes* have also been excluded because of less frequent usage in the past decade: Ewell's (1954) Inventory of Values, Perloe's (1967) Social Values Questionnaire, Shorr's (1953) Test of Value Activities, and Withey's (1965) Dimensions of Values. Reference to the latter, however, is included under Bales and Couch's (1969) Value Profile.

While the above limitations restrict the scales that can be reviewed in detail, there are other interesting contributions to value measurement that warrant attention. Five have been singled out as illustrative of approaches to meeting the most pressing problems facing value researchers at this time: inadequate methodologies for cross-cultural comparisons (Zavalloni, 1980) and a dearth of theory to guide values research (Spates, 1983).

The first stems from the work of Schwartz and Bilsky (1987). Schwartz and co-workers are developing and testing a broadly based values instrument which seeks to provide multi-item and cross-culturally valid scales. Their work extends Rokeach's definition of values both conceptually and methodologically. Values are defined as trans-situational goals that serve as guiding principles in a person's life. The values are differentiated in terms of three criteria. First, they may be instrumental or terminal goals. Second, their focus may be individualistic, collectivist, or both. Third, they relate to 12 motivational domains. The domains are assumed to be present in every culture since they arise from three universal human requirements: the biological needs of individuals, the requisites of coordinated social interaction, and the survival and welfare needs of groups.

The second noteworthy contribution is the antecedent–consequent method of Triandis *et al.* (1972) for comparing values across cultures. These authors selected 20 abstract concepts that were expected to highlight cultural differences in values (e.g., anger, freedom, punishment, death, love). Respondents indicated what each of these concepts meant to them by selecting from a list of five words one that identified the cause of the concept. Respondents were presented with six such lists, allowing them to choose six antecedents for each concept. After selecting antecedents, the same procedure was followed to identify consequences or the results of the concept. The frequencies with which 30 antecedents and 30 consequents were endorsed by members of different cultures were then tabulated and compared (see Triandis *et al.*, 1972). Triandis *et al.* have argued that "common themes found among such As [antecedents] and Cs [consequents] reveal underlying values, that is, cultural patterns of preferences for certain outcomes" (p. 258). On the negative side, however, these value preferences constitute only a small part of the cognitions measured through Triandis's procedure, and the "themes" involve a considerable amount of inferential work.

An alternative cross-cultural methodology for values has been proposed by Triandis and his co-workers (1986) in relation to the specific value orientation of individualism–collectivism. A large item pool was generated by cooperating researchers in nine countries and only those items that half or more of the researchers found relevant and none found irrelevant were used. The resulting 21 items were then subjected to an item and factor analysis within each culture. The analyses ensured relevance to the collectivism construct within each culture and comparable interrelationships among items across cultures. On this basis, the assumption could be made that items were being given similar meanings by the different cultural groups. Finally, Triandis *et al.* (1986) factor-analyzed the 21 items across all respondents from the nine cultures. From this pancultural factor analysis, Triandis *et al.* were able to identify four etic factors for cross-cultural comparisons.

A fourth approach offering both conceptual and methodological insights for value researchers is that of Hofstede (1980) on work values. Four value dimensions were identified as "basic problems of humanity with which every society has to cope" (p. 313): Power Distance (social inequality and the authority of one person over another), Uncertainty Avoidance (the way societies deal with the uncertainty of the future), Individualism versus Collectivism (the individual's dependence on the group), and Masculinity versus Femininity [the endorsement of masculine (e.g., assertive) goals as opposed to feminine (e.g., nurturant) goals within the group]. These dimensions are not too dissimilar from the value orientations outlined by Kluckhohn and Strodtbeck (1961) and Bales and Couch (1969) and may be modified for use outside the work context. Methodologically, Hofstede (1980) has emphasized the importance of analyzing data at the ecological level as distinct from the individual level. Hofstede derived his value measures through analyzing the scores of 40 countries rather than the scores of individuals.

The final contribution deserving mention is Inglehart's (1971, 1977) work on social values. Inglehart has focused on one major dimension representing desirable national goals. At one end are the materialist values that arise in response to needs for economic and physical security. The other pole is defined by postmaterialist values, that is, by values concerned with social and self-actualizing needs. Inglehart (1977) has measured the materialist–postmaterialist value dimension through the ranking of 12 national policy objectives, half of which represent materialist values (e.g., fighting rising prices), the remainder nonmaterialist values (e.g., giving people more say in important government decisions).

Inglehart's conceptualization is based on Maslow's (1962) need hierarchy. The materialist values representing sustenance and safety needs must be satisfied before the postmaterialist values tapping belongingness, esteem, intellectual and aesthetic needs are given priority. Inglehart argues that postmaterialist values are characteristic of younger generations, who have been the beneficiaries of an era of peace and economic prosperity.

Inglehart's (1977) work warrants special consideration because of its theoretical base in Maslow's (1962) theory of human needs. In contrast, so much of values research has not been guided by theory. The contrast in approaches can be well illustrated by a comparison of Inglehart's notion of materialism–postmaterialism and Rokeach's (1973) two-value model of political ideology. Conceptually they have much in common, although Inglehart's model is unidimensional and Rokeach's is two-dimensional. In terms of guiding future research, however, Inglehart's work has the advantage of being articulated with grand development themes, both in terms of human history and individual functioning. Rokeach's model, however, merely provides a means for differentiating political behavior. Values research could benefit considerably from theoretical developments of the kind offered by Inglehart.

To appraise values research and identify strengths and weaknesses is to make assumptions about how values should be studied. Before concluding this review, our assumptions will be delineated and alternative approaches acknowledged.

First, the assumption is made that the nature of values in a society can be understood by aggregating the values espoused by individuals. It is, of course, possible to adopt a methodologically holistic approach to the measurement of a society's values. Such an approach might involve an analysis of the language of a cultural group or a content analysis of the most widely consumed mass media or of seminal legislative enactments arising out of the political process. We have put all of these methods outside the scope of this review, but they nevertheless represent important alternative approaches.

At the opposite extreme we have neglected the ideographic approach, which seeks to redirect attention away from the group entirely and toward the individual. The practice of analyzing group data by aggregating scores across unique individuals is firmly rejected within the ideographic tradition (Caird, 1987; Lamiell, 1981). Clearly, the present review is at odds with this viewpoint. Our bias is toward nomothetic procedures. While ideographic techniques may well provide new insights into the nature of values, this review rests on the assumption that the more researchers refine, consolidate, and bridge available nomothetic measures, the sooner we will have a strong empirical base for understanding human values.

Study of Values
(Allport, Vernon & Lindzey, 1960)

Variable

The instrument measures "the relative prominence of six basic interests or motives in personality: the *theoretical, economic, aesthetic, social, political,* and *religious*" (Allport *et al.,* 1960, p. 3).

Description

The six-way classification is based on Spranger's (1928) ideal *Types of Men.* The theoretical person has intellectual interests, his/her major pursuit being the discovery of truth. The economic person has a practical nature and is interested in that which is useful. The aesthetic person looks for form and harmony in the world, each experience being judged according to grace, symmetry, or fitness. The social person values others and is altruistic and philanthropic. The political person is one who seeks power, influence, and renown. The religious person values unity above all else and is mystical, seeking communion with the cosmos.

The 1931 edition of the Study of Values was revised in 1951 and again in 1960. The test content, however, has not changed since 1951. The 1960 version consists of two parts. Part I comprises 30 questions, each of which presents respondents with two alternative answers. Respondents are required to indicate the strength of their preference by distributing three points between the two alternatives (3 to one and 0 to the other or 2 to one and 1 to the other). In Part II, respondents are asked 15 questions and are required to rank the four alternative answers to each question from the most preferred (4) to the least preferred (1).

Respondents are given 20 opportunities to endorse each of the six value orientations, 10 in Part I and 10 in Part II. Scores for each value are obtained by summing item scores and adding or subtracting correction figures provided on the last page of the test booklet. The corrections are made in order to equalize the popularity of the six values, giving each a mean of 40.

The test is self-administered, most respondents requiring about 20 minutes for completion. The test can also be self-scored, using instructions for both scoring and interpretation on the last page of the test booklet.

Sample

This instrument has been developed for use with college students or with adults who have had some college education (or its equivalent). In the 1960 manual, norms are provided for 8369 male and female American college students. Norms are also provided for men and women representing 13 occupational groups.

Reliability

Internal Consistency

Allport et al. (1960) report that split-half reliability coefficients ranged from .84 for theoretical values to .95 for religious values and that item–total correlations for each scale were all significant at the .01 level.

Test–Retest

With a 1-month interval, Allport et al. (1960) report coefficients ranging from .77 for social values to .92 for economic values ($n = 34$). After a 2-month interval, test–retest reliabilities ranged from .84 for economic values to .93 for religious values ($n = 53$). Test–retest reliabilities obtained by Hilton and Korn (1964) over seven occasions at 1-month intervals with a sample of 30 students ranged from .74 for political values to .89 for religious values, the mean being .82.

Validity

Convergent

The Study of Values has successfully differentiated students in different fields of study, as well as individuals in different occupations and with different vocational interests. Reviews by Allport et al. (1960), Cantril and Allport (1933), Duffy (1940), Dukes (1955), and Hogan (1972) provide details of this early validation work.

The instrument has performed impressively in documenting value changes among college graduates over a span of 38 years (Hoge & Bender, 1974), including both social changes due to historical events and individual changes accompanying experiences of frustration and personal inadequacy. The Study of Values Scale has also contributed to identifying gender differences (Duffy, 1940), findings that have been largely confirmed in a study of male and female business students by Palmer (1982). Other work has shown the instrument to differentiate women who are homemakers from career women (Pirnot & Dustin, 1986; Wagman, 1966), and in a somewhat less "Middle American" context, to differentiate heavy marijuana users from nonusers (Weckowicz & Janssen, 1973; Weckowicz, Collier, & Spreng, 1977).

Discriminant

The factorial structure of the scale has been examined in a variety of ways (Brogden, 1952; Duffy & Crissy, 1940; Gordon, 1972a; Lurie, 1937; Sciortino, 1970) and produces partial support for Spranger's (1928) conceptualization. Support was found in five studies for the social value orientation, in four for both the theoretical and religious orientations, and in two for the aesthetic orientation. The most consistent departure from Spranger's conceptualization is for the political and economic scales to correlate so highly as to be indistinguishable, forming a "philistine" orientation in the studies of Duffy and Crissy (1940), Gordon (1972a), and Lurie (1937).

Location

Allport, G. W., Vernon, P. E., & Lindzey, G. (1960). *Study of Values. Manual and test booklet* (3rd ed.). Boston: Houghton Mifflin.

Results and Comments

The Study of Values stands with the Value Survey as the most popular measures of human values, with much encouraging data available on its usefulness in a variety of contexts. Four notes of caution are appropriate for those considering its use:

1. The data produced by the instrument are ipsative, so that the researcher learns only of the relative and not absolute strength of each value. Ipsative data are also awkward to analyze statistically, with the zero-sum interdependence of the different scales creating problems for data analysis.

2. The Study of Values has been mainly used with college students or with those who are reasonably well educated.

3. This instrument measures preference, interest, beliefs, choice and behavioral intentions, with fewer than 20% of items tapping conceptions of the desirable.

4. The Study of Values is dated with sexist language appearing in several questions (e.g., "Assuming that you are a man with the necessary ability, . . . would you prefer to be a (a) mathematician, (b) sales manager, (c) clergyman, (d) politician").

Study of Values

Sample Items

Part I (30 questions—choose one answer and note strength of preference)

1. The main object of scientific research should be the discovery of truth rather than its practical application.
   (a) Yes
   (b) No

4. Assuming that you have sufficient ability, would you prefer to be:
   (a) a banker?
   (b) a politician?

15. At an exposition, do you chiefly like to go to the buildings where you can see:
   (a) new manufacturing products?
   (b) scientific (e.g., chemical) apparatus?

Part II (15 questions—rank order highest preference with a 4, next highest with a 3, next with a 2, and least preferred with a 1)

3. If you could influence the educational policies of the public schools of some city, would you undertake
   _____ a. to promote the study and participation in music and fine arts?
   _____ b. to stimulate the study of social problems?
   _____ c. to provide additional laboratory facilities?
   _____ d. to increase the practical value of courses?

12. Should one guide one's conduct according to, or develop one's chief loyalties toward
   _____ a. one's religious faith?
   _____ b. ideals of beauty?
   _____ c. one's occupational organization and associates?
   _____ d. ideals of charity?

The Value Survey

(Rokeach, 1967)

Variable

The instrument assesses goals in life (terminal values) and modes of conduct (instrumental values) in terms of their relative importance as guiding principles in life; the goals and modes are restricted to those transcending specific objects and situations.

Description

Rokeach's values were selected largely on an intuitive basis after reviewing the American literature on values and personality traits and interviewing individuals in Lansing, Michigan.

Several forms of this instrument are available. The most popular are Forms D (gummed labels) and E (rank orders are written alongside values). In Form D, respondents are presented with 18 alphabetically listed terminal values, each printed on a removable gummed label. Respondents rearrange these gummed labels to form a single rank order of values with the most important at the top and the least important at the bottom. On the following page, the procedure is repeated for 18 alphabetically listed instrumental values. In Form E of the Value Survey, gummed labels are not provided; instead, the values are ranked by placing 1 next to the value considered to be most important, 2 next to the value that is second most important, etc. All 18 values must be assigned a rank. A new version of the Value Survey has become available, Form G (gummed labels). Form G replaces the terminal value "happiness" with "health" and the instrumental value "cheerful" with "loyal."

A number of options exist for analyzing data from the Value Survey: median ranks for individual items within a group, conversion of ranks to Z scores, similarity of value systems at the individual level (Spearman's ρ), and similarity of value systems at the group level (Spearman's ρ). Feather (1975b) has provided a detailed discussion of these procedures (pp. 23–27).

The Value Survey is self-administered with estimates of completion time ranging from 10 to 20 min for Form D and from 15 to 30 min for Form E.

Sample

The Value Survey was developed and tested extensively on adult samples drawn from students and the general population in the United States. The instrument has also been tested extensively by Feather (1975b) in student and general population samples in Australia. It is of note that the Value Survey is one of the few value instruments that has been administered to random samples. In the United States, the National Opinion Research Center administered it to a national area probability sample of Americans over 21 in 1968 ($n = 1409$) and 1971 ($n = 1430$). Median rankings based on these samples have been reported by Rokeach (1974).

Reliability

Internal Consistency

This is not relevant for single-item measures.

Test–Retest

The test–retest reliability for the terminal or instrumental value system is given by the median for the distribution of rank correlations calculated over 18 items for each respondent in the sample. The medians reported by Rokeach (1973) using Form D with adults for varying time intervals of 3–7 weeks range from .76 to .80 for the terminal value system and .65 to .72 for the instrumental value system. For longer time intervals of 14–16 months, the median test–retest reliability for the terminal value system was .69 and for the instrumental value system .61. Rokeach's data show that comparable statistics for Form E tend to be somewhat lower than Form D. For time intervals of 3–12 weeks with Form E, Rokeach reported median test–retest reliabilities of .74 for the terminal value system and .65–.70 for the instrumental value system. Feather (1975b) reported median test–retest reliabilities for Form E for a 5-week interval of .74 (terminal value system) and .70 (instrumental value system). For a 2.5-year interval, the median reliabilities were .60 and .51, respectively.

Rokeach (1973) reported individual item test–retest reliabilities for a 3–7-week interval using Form D of the Value Survey. For terminal values, the reliabilities ranged from .51 to .88 (median .65), for instrumental values from .45 to .70 (median .61). Feather (1975b) reported item reliabilities for a 5-week interval for Form E. For terminal values, reliabilities ranged from .40 to .87 (median .63) and for instrumental values from .37 to .76 (median .56).

Reliability data have been obtained primarily from student samples. Rokeach included a sample from the general population and obtained reliability data from children.

Reliabilities for children were lower than those for adults and have not been included in the above summary (see Rokeach, 1973, p. 32).

Validity

Convergent

The Value Survey has been used successfully to differentiate religious (Brown & Lawson, 1980; Rokeach, 1969a), political (Billig & Cochrane, 1979; Bishop et al., 1972; C. H. Jones, 1982; Rawls et al., 1973; Rokeach, 1973), occupational (Mahoney & Pechura, 1980; Pedro, 1984; Rokeach, Miller, & Snyder, 1971; Vecchiotti & Korn, 1980), educational (Feather, 1970a, 1971), and cultural (Clare & Cooper, 1983; Feather & Hutton, 1973) groups. Deviants have also been distinguished from nondeviants in terms of their responses to the Value Survey (Cochrane, 1971; Feather & Cross, 1975; Toler, 1975). The construct validity of the Value Survey has been supported by studies that have linked values to conservatism (Feather, 1979b; Joe et al., 1981), the Protestant ethic (Feather, 1984a), social compassion (Rokeach, 1969b), androgyny (Feather, 1984b), attributions (Feather, 1982, 1985), interpersonal perception and behavior (Feather, 1980; Walker & Campbell, 1982), and adjustment (Feather, 1975b). Predicted behavioral correlates of the Value Survey are also widely documented, including cheating (Homant & Rokeach, 1970), returning lost or borrowed property (Penner et al., 1976; Shotland & Berger, 1970), volunteering (Raymond & King, 1973), social activism (Rokeach, 1973; Thomas, 1986), and preventive health (Kristiansen, 1985). In addition, the Value Survey has been shown to provide a relatively comprehensive coverage of the domain it aims to represent (V. A. Braithwaite & Law, 1985) and alternative assessment procedures have tended to converge on similar findings (Alwin & Krosnick, 1985; Bolt, 1978; Feather, 1973; Rankin & Grube, 1980; B. Thompson, Levitov, & Miederhoff, 1982).

Discriminant

Studies of order effects (Greenstein & Bennett, 1974) and social desirability (Kelly, Silverman, & Cochrane, 1972) have supported the validity of the instrument.

Location

Rokeach, M. (1967). *Value survey*. Sunnyvale, CA: Halgren Tests (873 Persimmon Ave., 94087).
Rokeach, M. (1973). *The nature of human values*. New York: Free Press.

Results and Comments

The factorial structure of the Value Survey has been examined on several occasions (Alker, Rao, & Hughes, 1972; Feather & Peay, 1975; Kilmann, 1975; Mahoney & Katz, 1976; Munson & Posner, 1980; Rokeach, 1973). Overall, the degree of overlap in the findings of these researchers is not impressive. All regard their solutions as interpretable, but salient item loadings on factors tend to be either too low or too few to give one confidence in the interpretations. A lack of enthusiasm about the meaningfulness of the solutions is apparent in the conclusions reached by Rokeach (1973): "the 36 terminal and instrumental values are not readily reducible" (p. 48) and Feather and Peay (1975): "the possibility of reducing the set of values to a smaller number did not seem apparent" (p. 161).

Feather (1975b) and Rokeach (1973) regard Form D gummed labels as the preferred research tool. The advantages of the new version, Form G, over Form D have yet to be established empirically, although the changes are in accord with inadequacies which have been identified in the Value Survey.

While there is much to be commended in the Value Survey, three notes of caution are warranted. First, because the data are ipsative, information is provided only on the relative and not the absolute importance of values, and statistical analysis can prove awkward. Second, users should look critically at inferences drawn from responses to single-item measures, since some are less psychometrically sound than others. Third, although the Value Survey has been used with children (Beech & Schoeppe, 1974; Brown & Lawson, 1980; Feather, 1975b), relatively little is known about the validity of the instrument with younger age groups.

Value Survey

Instructions

On the next page are 18 values listed in alphabetical order. Your task is to arrange them in order of their importance to YOU, as guiding principles in YOUR life. Each value is printed on a gummed label which can be easily peeled off and pasted in the boxes on the left-hand side of the page.

Study the list carefully and pick out the one value which is the most important for you. Peel it off and paste it in Box 1 on the left.

Then pick out the value which is second most important for you. Peel it off and paste it in Box 2. Then do the same for each of the remaining values. The value that is least important goes in Box 18.

Work slowly and think carefully. If you change your mind, feel free to change your answers. The labels peel off easily and can be moved from place to place. The end result should truly show how you really feel.

1		A COMFORTABLE LIFE (a prosperous life)
2		AN EXCITING LIFE (a stimulating, active life)
3		A SENSE OF ACCOMPLISHMENT (lasting contribution)
4		A WORLD AT PEACE (free of war and conflict)
5		A WORLD OF BEAUTY (beauty of nature and the arts)
6		EQUALITY (brotherhood, equal opportunity for all)
7		FAMILY SECURITY (taking care of loved ones)
8		FREEDOM (independence, free choice)

9		HAPPINESS (contentedness)
10		INNER HARMONY (freedom from inner conflict)
11		MATURE LOVE (sexual and spiritual intimacy)
12		NATIONAL SECURITY (protection from attack)
13		PLEASURE (an enjoyable, leisurely life)
14		SALVATION (saved, eternal life)
15		SELF-RESPECT (self-esteem)
16		SOCIAL RECOGNITION (respect, admiration)
17		TRUE FRIENDSHIP (close companionship)
18		WISDOM (a mature understanding of life)

WHEN YOU HAVE FINISHED, GO TO THE NEXT PAGE.

Below is another list of 18 values. Arrange them in order of importance, the same as before.

1		AMBITIOUS (hard-working, aspiring)
2		BROADMINDED (open-minded)
3		CAPABLE (competent, effective)
4		CHEERFUL (lighthearted, joyful)
5		CLEAN (neat, tidy)
6		COURAGEOUS (standing up for your beliefs)
7		FORGIVING (willing to pardon others)
8		HELPFUL (working for the welfare of others)

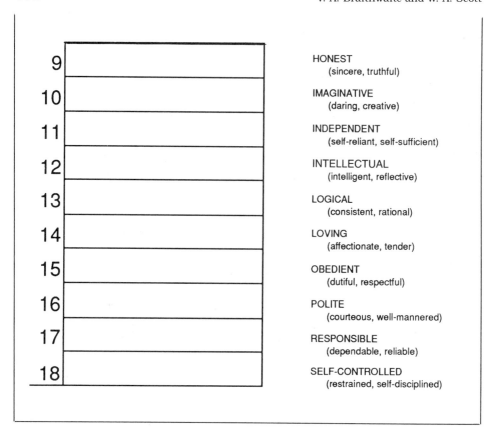

9		HONEST (sincere, truthful)
10		IMAGINATIVE (daring, creative)
11		INDEPENDENT (self-reliant, self-sufficient)
12		INTELLECTUAL (intelligent, reflective)
13		LOGICAL (consistent, rational)
14		LOVING (affectionate, tender)
15		OBEDIENT (dutiful, respectful)
16		POLITE (courteous, well-mannered)
17		RESPONSIBLE (dependable, reliable)
18		SELF-CONTROLLED (restrained, self-disciplined)

The Goal and Mode Values Inventories

(Braithwaite & Law, 1985)

Variable

Based on Rokeach's (1973) conceptualization of values, this instrument comprises an expanded set of goals and modes of conduct, measures absolute rather than relative importance, and separates social goals from personal goals.

Description

Interviews with a community sample, selected randomly within a demographically hetero-geneous geographical area in Brisbane, Australia, resulted in the representation of 36 personal goals, 18 social goals, and 71 modes of conduct in a values questionnaire. Rokeach's Value Survey had been used as a starting point to define the universe of content for respondents. Factor analyses of the data collected with this instrument led to the development of 14 multi-item scales. Of the original 125 items, 79 items clearly and consistently contributed to defining one of these factors and were included in the final inventories.

The instrument is self-administered in three parts: personal goals, followed by modes of conduct and finally social goals. Social goals are differentiated from personal goals through being directed toward the nature of society rather than the behavior of the individual. For personal goals and modes of conduct, respondents are asked to indicate how strongly they accept or reject each one "as a principle for you to live by." Ratings are made using an asymmetrical seven-point scale ranging from "I reject this" (1) through to "I accept this as of the greatest importance" (7). Because social goals are not part of everyday life, their instructions were modified to "principles that guide your judgments and actions." To avoid overuse of the positive end of the scale, respondents are encouraged to read quickly through the lists of values to get a feel for how they should use the response categories.

The Goal Value Scales are (1) International Harmony and Equality (10 items), (2) National Strength and Order (4 items), (3) Traditional Religiosity (4 items), (4) Personal Growth and Inner Harmony (6 items), (5) Physical Well-being (3 items), (6) Secure and Satisfying Interpersonal Relationships (5 items), (7) Social Standing (3 items), and (8) Social Stimulation (2 items). The Mode Value Scales are (1) A Positive Orientation to Others (13 items), (2) Competence and Effectiveness (13 items), (3) Propriety in Dress and Manners (7 items), (4) Religious Commitment (4 items), (5) Assertiveness (3 items), and (6) Getting Ahead (2 items). Scales are scored by summing across the relevant items with different maximum and minimum totals for each scale. All items are positively worded with two exceptions.

Sample

The inventories were developed and tested using two community samples in Brisbane, Australia ($n = 73, 483$) and two student samples from the University of Queensland, Australia ($n = 208, 480$).

Reliability

Internal Consistency

From the student and community samples, the α reliability coefficients for the two-item scales (Social Stimulation and Getting Ahead) were barely adequate, .53 and .66, respectively. For the remaining scales, α reliability coefficients ranged from .66 for Religious Commitment to .89 for A Positive Orientation to Others and for Competence and Effectiveness (median .74).

Test–Retest

Based on a sample of 208 students, reliability coefficients over a 4-week period ranged from .43 to .92 (median .62) for individual items. For the scales, the range was .58 for Social Stimulation to .93 for Traditional Religiosity (median .75).

Validity

Convergent

All scales were successfully related to expected counterparts in the Value Survey with the exception of Physical Well-being, for which there was no counterpart at that time. Further evidence of validity was obtained through correlating the scales with Scott's (1960) Measures of Foreign Policy Goals, Scott's (1965) Personal Value scales, and Wilson and Patterson's (1968) Conservatism Scale. Expected correlations varied in strength from a low .21 to a high .79, but all were significant and in the expected direction. In addition, the religiosity scales were found to correlate with church attendance and involvement in church organizations. The Personal Growth and Inner Harmony Scale was related to a preference among students for university courses that emphasized the development of self-awareness and for a liberal education in philosophy, history, and contemporary society.

Discriminant

To ensure the factorial distinctiveness of the scales, items were included in a scale only if they clearly and consistently defined one factor and no other. Factors were accepted only if they were stable across analytical procedures and across samples of respondents.

Location

Braithwaite, V. A., & Law, H. G. (1985). Structure of human values: Testing the adequacy of the Rokeach Value Survey. *Journal of Personality and Social Psychology, 49,* 250–263.

Results and Comments

The usefulness of these instruments has yet to be established, but the scales are expected to provide multi-item measures of the constructs represented by single items in Rokeach's Value Survey.

The major weakness of these scales is that the distributions of scores are likely to be skewed, in spite of the precautions taken to avoid overuse of the extreme positive categories. This result is not surprising since all the scales represent socially accepted value orientations. Skewed distributions, however, can place restrictions on choice of statistical analyses.

In developing these instruments, considerable emphasis was placed on representatively sampling items from the value domain. It is of note, therefore, that 12 items that represent important facets of the domain do not appear in the final scales because they were not highly correlated with other items (i.e., freedom, privacy, the protection of human life, a leisurely life, carefree enjoyment, comfort but not luxury, happiness, a sense of accomplishment, being thrifty, acting on impulse, being independent, being honest).

Goal and Mode Values Inventories

Part One

Instructions: Listed below are 23 goals* that various people have used as guiding principles in their lives. By goal we mean any state of affairs that a person might strive for as well as any state of affairs that a person may wish to preserve or keep as is.

Please indicate the extent to which you accept or reject each of these goals *as a principle for you to live by*. Do this by circling one of the following numbers which you will find listed below each question.

1	2	3	4	5	6	7
I reject this	I am inclined to reject this	I neither reject nor accept this	I am inclined to accept this	I accept this as important	I accept this as very important	I accept this as of the greatest importance

You are to circle the one that is closest to your own feelings about that particular goal as a guiding principle in your life. Before you start, quickly read through the entire list of goals in Part 1 to get a feel for how to score your answers. Remember there are no right or wrong answers. When you have completed Part 1 go on to Part 2 and then Part 3.

TRADITIONAL RELIGIOSITY

Salvation (being saved from your sins and at peace with God)

1   2   3   4   5   6   7

Religious or Mystical Experience (being at one with God or the universe)

Upholding Traditional Sexual Moral Standards (opposing sexual permissiveness and pornography)

* * Sexual Intimacy (having a satisfying sexual relationship)

PERSONAL GROWTH AND INNER HARMONY

Self-Knowledge or Self-Insight (being more aware of what sort of person you are)

The Pursuit of Knowledge (always trying to find out new things about the world we live in)

Inner Harmony (feeling free of conflict within yourself)

Self-Improvement (striving to be a better person)

Wisdom (having a mature understanding of life)

Self-Respect (believing in your own worth)

PHYSICAL WELL-BEING

Physical Development (being physically fit)

Good Health (physical well-being)

Physical Exercise (taking part in energetic activity)

SECURE AND SATISFYING INTERPERSONAL RELATIONSHIPS

Mature Love (having a relationship of deep and lasting affection)

True Friendship (having genuine and close friends)

Personal Support (knowing that there is someone to take care of you)

Security for Loved Ones (taking care of loved ones)

Acceptance by Others (feeling that you belong)

SOCIAL STANDING

Recognition by the Community (having high standing in the community)

Economic Prosperity (being financially well off)

Authority (having power to influence others and control decisions)

SOCIAL STIMULATION

An Active Social Life (mixing with other people)

An Exciting Life (a life full of new experiences or adventures)

> *Only the items that belong to the scales are reproduced here.
> **Reverse-scored.

Part Two

Instructions: Below are listed 42 ways of behaving. Please indicate the extent to which you accept or reject each way of behaving *as a guiding principle in your life*, in the same way as you did in Part 1. Again quickly read through the entire list before you start. Remember there are no right or wrong answers.

1	2	3	4	5	6	7
I reject this	I am inclined to reject this	I neither reject nor accept this	I am inclined to accept this	I accept this as important	I accept this as very important	I accept this as of the greatest importance

A POSITIVE ORIENTATION TO OTHERS

Tolerant (accepting others even though they may be different from you)

1	2	3	4	5	6	7

Helpful (always ready to assist others)

Forgiving (willing to pardon others)

Giving Others a Fair Go (giving others a chance)

Tactful (being able to deal with touchy situations without offending others)

Considerate (being thoughtful of other people's feelings)

Cooperative (being able to work in harmony with others)

Loving (showing genuine affection)

Trusting (having faith in others)

Grateful (being appreciative)

Understanding (able to share another's feelings)

Friendly (being neighborly)

Generous (sharing what you have with others)

COMPETENCE AND EFFECTIVENESS

Bright (being quick thinking)

Adaptable (adjusting to change easily)

Competent (being capable)

Resourceful (being clever at finding ways to achieve a goal)

Self-Disciplined (being self-controlled)

Efficient (always using the best method to get the best results)

Realistic (seeing each situation as it really is)

Knowledgeable (being well informed)

Persevering (not giving up in spite of difficulties)

Progressive (being prepared to accept and support new things)

Conscientious (being hardworking)

Logical (being rational)

Showing Foresight (thinking and seeing ahead)

PROPRIETY IN DRESS AND MANNERS

Polite (being well-mannered)

Patriotic (being loyal to your country)

Prompt (being on time)

Refined (never being coarse or vulgar)

Clean (not having dirty habits)

Neat (being tidy)

Reliable (being dependable)

RELIGIOUS COMMITMENT

Committed (being dedicated to a cause)

Devout (following your religious faith conscientiously)

Self-Sacrificing (putting the interest of others before your own)

Idealistic (living according to how things should be rather than how things are)

ASSERTIVENESS

Standing up for Your Beliefs (defending your beliefs no matter who opposes them)

Having Your Say (confidently stating your opinions)

Determined (standing by your decisions firmly)

GETTING AHEAD

Ambitious (being eager to do well)

Competitive (always trying to do better than others)

Part Three

Instructions: Below are 14 goals that refer to our society, our nation, and to people in general. Although most of us do not directly affect the course of national affairs, we all have principles or standards we prize highly in our society. We use these standards to make judgments about national policies and about world and community events, and at times, we may even use them to guide our actions (e.g., when we join certain organizations or when we vote in elections).

Please indicate the extent to which you reject or accept each of the following *as principles that guide your judgments and actions,* in the same way as you did previously. Again, quickly read through the entire list before you start. Remember there are no right or wrong answers.

1	2	3	4	5	6	7
I reject this	I am inclined to reject this	I neither reject nor accept this	I am inclined to accept this	I accept this as important	I accept this as very important	I accept this as of the greatest importance

INTERNATIONAL HARMONY AND EQUALITY

A Good Life for Others (improving the welfare of all people in need)

1	2	3	4	5	6	7

Rule by the People (involvement by all citizens in making decisions that affect their community)

International Cooperation (having all nations working together to help each other)

Social Progress and Social Reform (readiness to change our way of life for the better)

A World at Peace (being free from war and conflict)

A World of Beauty (having the beauty of nature and the arts: music, literature, art, etc.)

Human Dignity (allowing each individual to be treated as someone of worth)

Equal Opportunity for All (giving everyone an equal chance in life)

Greater Economic Equality (lessening the gap between the rich and the poor)

Preserving the Natural Environment (preventing the destruction of nature's beauty and resources)

NATIONAL STRENGTH AND ORDER

National Greatness (being a united, strong, independent, and powerful nation)

National Economic Development (having greater economic progress and prosperity for the nation)

The Rule of Law (punishing the guilty and protecting the innocent)

National Security (protection of your nation from enemies)

Ways to Live
(Morris, 1956b)

Variable

Descriptions of 13 philosophies of life are evaluated by respondents in terms of the kind of life they personally would like to live. Morris' (1956b) operational definition of conceptions of the preferable (conceived values) was "conceptions of the good life" (p. 13).

Description

The Ways to Live items were originally derived from combining three basic components of personality (Dionysian: tendency to release and indulge existing desires; Promethean: tendency to change and remake the world; and Buddhistic: tendency to regulate self by holding desires in check) that expressed themselves in major religious, ethical, and philosophical systems in the world (Morris, 1956a). Because a substantial number of college students did not find the original seven Ways to their liking, a further six were added over time, resulting in 13 Ways to Live for evaluation.

Each way is presented to respondents as a paragraph (between 100 and 150 words). The paragraphs are simply labeled as Way 1–Way 13.

After reading each paragraph, the respondent rates the way on a seven-point scale from 7 (liking it very much) through 1 (disliking it very much). After rating each of the 13 Ways to Live, respondents are asked to rank them according to how much they like them.

The test is self-administered and completion time is estimated to be 30 minutes–1 hour. Variation can be expected in view of the need for some to reread the complex paragraphs several times.

Sample

Large samples of students have been involved in Morris' work. Data from 2015 male and 831 female students in the United States are reported in *Varieties of Human Values* (Morris, 1956b). In a replication study, Morris and Small (1971) collected data from 703 male and 514 female college students. In a more recent replication, K. S. Thompson (1981) administered the Ways to Live to 468 male and 538 female students in the United States. The instrument has also been used cross-culturally with Indian, Chinese, Japanese, Canadian, and Norwegian students, although American college students have made the major contribution to its development.

Reliability

Internal Consistency

Because this is a single-item measure, internal consistency is not relevant.

Test–Retest

Morris (1956b) reported a test-retest correlation of .85 between two sets of ratings provided by 20 students 3 weeks apart. With a longer interval of 14 weeks, the average correlation was slightly lower, .78 ($n = 30$), although Morris noted that during this time the Ways to Live instrument was discussed with the students and changes in their views may have been a consequence. Morris also has provided some information on the test–retest reliabilities of each of the Ways. Their mean reliability based on 21 students tested over a 3-week interval was .67, with Ways 3, 8, and 13 showing the lowest reliabilities.

Validity

Convergent

Morris (1956b) has presented a mass of data relating the Ways to Live to population and economic indicators, religious practice, and personality and biological characteristics with varying degrees of success. He has used his instrument extensively to compare cultural groups and to map value changes over time (Morris, 1956b; Morris & Small, 1971). Bhatt and Fairchild (1984) found the Ways to Live useful in showing that the length of time Indian students spent in America was related to endorsement of typically American values. Hofstede (1980) also has made use of the Ways to Live instrument to validate his own value measures.

Discriminant

The factorial structure of the Ways to Live has been examined by Morris and his co-workers (Morris, 1956b; Morris & Jones, 1955), by K. S. Thompson (1981), and by Hofstede (1980). Morris has reported a five-factor solution based on ratings from United States male students: (1) Social restraint and self-control, (2) Enjoyment and progress in action, (3) Withdrawal and self-sufficiency, (4) Receptivity and sympathetic concern, and (5) Self-indulgence. A similar solution was reported for Indian college students. Thompson, however, reported a two-factor solution, not only for his own data but for a reanalysis of L. Jones and Morris' (1956) data. Thompson attributed the difference to the factoring techniques used, but details of his factor solutions are not provided. Hofstede's (1980) reanalysis of Morris' Ways to Live data from six countries also pointed to a two-factor solution. He identified the first factor as "enjoyment" (Ways 4, 7, 8, and 12) versus "duty" (Ways 2, 3, 6, and 10). The second factor was labelled "engagement" (Ways 5 and 13) versus "withdrawal" (Ways 1, 9, and 11). Although Thompson and Hofstede both identified two bipolar factors, the solutions themselves differ considerably. Until these problems are resolved, the Ways to Live are probably best conceived as 13 separate, though clearly not independent, variables. L. Jones and Morris' (1956) intercorrelations of ratings among the Ways for 250 male students show variation from −.27 to +.28. The Ways do not appear to be highly interrelated.

Location

Morris, C. W. (1956b). *Varieties of human value*. Chicago: University of Chicago Press.

Results and Comments

The Ways to Live has earned praise through its pioneering contribution to studying values across cultures. It covers a broad range of value concepts and has been designed to incorporate non-Western philosophies of life. Like many instruments of its era, the text of the Ways to Live needs minor revision to avoid sexist language (male personal pronouns and "man" appear throughout).

Other more fundamental criticisms have been made on psychometric grounds. First, the paragraphs or ways have been regarded as overly complex; not only are too many ideas presented to the respondent, but they are expressed in a verbose style. Second, reliance is placed on a single response to indicate a value preference. In this regard, Triandis (1972) sees the paragraphs as a strength; at least the cross-cultural researcher is relying on the translations of several sentences rather than one. Nevertheless, the fact remains that it is impossible to know how respondents have weighted the various ideas to arrive at one number to indicate preference. Indeed, the work of Dempsey and Dukes (1966) and Gorlow and Barocas (1965) suggest that the ideas within each way do not form a coherent whole. Dempsey and Dukes have prepared a revised and shortened form of the Ways to Live that may overcome some of its problems. This instrument is reviewed next in this chapter.

A third warning for potential users is that the Ways to Live has more to do with the desired than the desirable. Morris (1956b) has reported some interesting data on the dimension of evaluation (liking for the way of life). Morris asked respondents to rate the ways in terms of "goodness" or "badness" and in terms of how they ought to live. On average, liking correlated .64 with goodness–badness and .68 with how one ought to live. For a detailed appraisal of the Ways to Live, the reader is referred to Winthrop (1959).

Ways to Live

Instructions: Below are described thirteen ways to live which various persons at various times have advocated and followed.

Indicate by numbers, which you are to write in the margin, how much you yourself like or dislike each of them. Do them in order. Do not read ahead.

Remember that it is not a question of what kind of life you now lead, or the kind of life you think it prudent to live in our society, or the kind of life you think good for other persons, *but simply the kind of life you personally would like to live.*

Use the following scale of numbers, placing one of them in the margin alongside each of the ways to live:

> 7 I like it very much
> 6 I like it quite a lot
> 5 I like it slightly
> 4 I am indifferent to it
> 3 I dislike it slightly
> 2 I dislike it quite a lot
> 1 I dislike it very much

WAY 1: In this "design for living" the individual actively participates in the social life of his community, not to change it primarily, but to understand, appreciate, and preserve the best that man has attained. Excessive desires should be avoided and moderation sought. One wants the good things of life but in an orderly way. Life is to have clarity, balance, refinement, control. Vulgarity, great enthusiasm, irrational behavior, impatience, indulgence are to be avoided. Friendship is to be esteemed but not easy intimacy with many people. Life is to have discipline, intelligibility, good manners, predictability. Social changes are to be made slowly and carefully, so that what has been achieved in human culture is not lost. The individual should be active physically and socially, but not in a hectic or radical way. Restraint and intelligence should give order to an active life.

WAY 2: The individual should for the most part "go it alone," assuring himself of privacy in living quarters, having much time to himself, attempting to control his own life. One should stress self-sufficiency, reflection and meditation, knowledge of himself. The direction of interest should be away from intimate associations with social groups, and away from the physical manipulation of objects or attempts at control of the physical environment. One should aim to simplify one's external life, to moderate those desires whose satisfaction is dependent upon physical and social forces outside of oneself, and to concentrate attention upon the refinement, clarification, and self-direction of oneself. Not much can be done or is to be gained by "living outwardly." One must avoid dependence upon persons or things; the center of life should be found within oneself.

WAY 3: This way of life makes central the sympathetic concern for other persons. Affection should be the main thing in life, affection that is free from all traces of the imposition of oneself upon others or of using others for one's own purposes. Greed in possessions, emphasis on sexual passion, the search for power over persons and things, excessive emphasis upon intellect, and undue concern for oneself are to be avoided, for these things hinder the sympathetic love among persons that alone gives significance to life. If we are aggressive we block our receptivity to the personal forces upon which we are dependent for genuine personal growth. One should accordingly purify oneself, restrain one's self-assertiveness, and become receptive, appreciative, and helpful with respect to other persons.

WAY 4: Life is something to be enjoyed—sensuously enjoyed, enjoyed with relish and abandonment. The aim in life should not be to control the course of the world or society or the lives of others, but to be open and receptive to things and persons, and to delight in them. Life is more a festival than a workshop or a school for moral discipline. To let oneself go, to let things and persons affect oneself, is more important than to do—or to do good. Such enjoyment, however, requires that one be self-centered enough to be keenly aware of what is happening and free for new happenings. So one should avoid entanglements, should not be too dependent on particular people or things, should not be self-sacrificing; one should be alone a lot, should have time for meditation and awareness of oneself. Solitude and sociality together are both necessary in the good life.

WAY 5: A person should not hold on to himself, withdraw from people, keep aloof and self-centered. Rather merge oneself with a social group, enjoy cooperation and companionship, join with others in resolute activity for the realization of common goals. Persons are social and persons are active; life should merge energetic group activity and cooperative group enjoyment. Meditation, restraint, concern for one's self-sufficiency, abstract intellectuality, solitude, stress on one's possessions all cut the roots that bind persons together. One should live outwardly with gusto, enjoying the good things of life, working with others to secure the things that make possible a pleasant and energetic social life. Those who oppose this ideal are not to be dealt with too tenderly. Life can't be too fastidious.

WAY 6: Life continuously tends to stagnate, to become "comfortable," to become sickled o'er with the pale cast of thought. Against these tendencies, a person must stress the need of constant activity—physical action, adventure, the realistic solution of specific problems as they appear, the improvement of techniques for controlling the world and society. Man's future depends primarily on what he does, not on what he feels or on his speculations. New problems constantly arise and always will arise. Improvements must always be made if man is to progress. We can't just follow the past or dream of what the future might be. We have to work resolutely and continually if control is to be gained over the forces which threaten us. Man should rely on technical advances made possible by scientific knowledge. He should find his goal in the solution of his problems. The good is the enemy of the better.

WAY 7: We should at various times and in various ways accept something from all other paths of life, but give no one our exclusive allegiance. At one moment one of them is the more appropriate; at another moment another is the most appropriate. Life should contain enjoyment and action and contemplation in about equal amounts. When either is carried to extremes we lose something important for our life. So we must cultivate flexibility, admit diversity in ourselves, accept the tension which this diversity produces, find a place for detachment in the midst of enjoyment and activity. The goal of life is found in the dynamic integration of enjoyment, action, and contemplation, and so in the dynamic interaction of the various paths of life. One should use all of them in building a life, and no one alone.

WAY 8: Enjoyment should be the keynote of life. Not the hectic search for intense and exciting pleasures, but the enjoyment of the simple and easily obtainable pleasures: the pleasures of just existing, of savory food, of comfortable surroundings, of talking with friends, of rest and relaxation. A home that is warm and comfortable, chairs and a bed that are soft, a kitchen well stocked with food, a door open to the entrance of friends—this is the place to live. Body at ease, relaxed, calm in its movements, not hurried, breath slow, willing to nod and rest, grateful to the world that is its food—so should the body be. Driving ambition and the fanaticism of ascetic ideals are the signs of discontented people who have lost the capacity to float in the stream of simple, carefree, wholesome enjoyment.

WAY 9: Receptivity should be the keynote of life. The good things come of their own accord, and come unsought. They cannot be found by resolute action. They cannot be found in the indulgence of the sensuous desires of the body. They cannot be gathered by participation in the turmoil of social life. They cannot be given to others by attempts to be helpful. They cannot be garnered by hard thinking. Rather do they come unsought when the bars of the self are down. When the self has ceased to make demands and waits in quiet receptivity, it becomes open to the powers which nourish it and work through it; and sustained by these powers it knows joy and peace. To sit alone under the trees and the sky, open to nature's voices, calm and receptive, then can the wisdom from without come within.

WAY 10: Self-control should be the keynote of life. Not the easy self-control that retreats from the world, but the vigilant, stern, manly control of a self that lives in the world, and knows the strength of the world and the limits of human power. The good life is rationally directed and holds firm to high ideals. It is not bent by the seductive voices of comfort and desire. It does not expect social utopias. It is distrustful of final victories. Too much cannot be expected. Yet one can with vigilance hold firm the reins to his self, control his unruly impulses, understand his place in the world, guide his actions by reason, maintain his self-reliant independence. And in this way, though he finally perish, man can keep his human dignity and respect and die with cosmic good manners.

WAY 11: The contemplative life is the good life. The external world is no fit habitat for man. It is too big, too cold, too pressing. Rather it is the life turned inward that is rewarding. The rich internal world of ideals, of sensitive feelings, of reverie, of self-knowledge is man's true home. By the cultivation of the self within, man alone becomes human. Only then does there arise deep sympathy with all that lives, an understanding of the suffering inherent in life, a realization of the futility of aggressive action, the attainment of contemplative joy. Conceit then falls away and austerity is dissolved. In giving up the world one finds the larger and finer sea of the inner self.

WAY 12: The use of the body's energy is the secret of a rewarding life. The hands need material to make into something: lumber and stone for building, food to harvest, clay to mold. The muscles are alive to joy only in action, in climbing, running, skiing, and the like. Life finds its zest in overcoming, dominating, conquering some obstacle. It is the active deed that is satisfying, the deed adequate to the present, the daring and adventuresome deed. Not in cautious foresight, not in relaxed ease does life attain completion. Outward energetic action, the excitement of power in the tangible present—this is the way to live.

WAY 13: A person should let himself be used. Used by other persons in their growth, used by the great objective purposes in the universe that silently and irresistibly achieve their goal. For persons and the world's purposes are dependable at heart, and can be trusted. One should be humble, constant, faithful, uninsistent. Grateful for the affection and protection that one needs, but undemanding. Close to persons and to nature, and secure because close. Nourishing the good by devotion and sustained by the good because of devotion. One should be a serene, confident, quiet vessel and instrument of the great dependable powers that move to their fulfillment.

Instructions for ranking your preferences: Rank the thirteen ways to live in the order you prefer them, putting first the number of the way to live you like the best, then the number of the way you like next best, and so on down to the number of the way you like the least.

Final Word: If you can formulate a way to live you would like better than any of the thirteen alternatives, please do so.

A Short Form Ways to Live

(Dempsey & Dukes, 1966)

Variable

This instrument is a shortened form of Morris' (1956b) Ways to Live, retaining those elements within each way that were most highly intercorrelated.

Description

The instrument follows that of Morris closely except that the 13 Ways to Live have been cut back to less than 50 words each in almost all cases. The 13 Ways to Live were transformed into 110 statements or items. Through item analyses, discordant or poorly interrelated elements within each paragraph were eliminated. The result is an instrument that is much easier to read and considerably shorter. Like the Ways to Live instrument, it is self-administered.

Sample

The shortened version was developed using 230 students in an undergraduate psychology class.

Reliability

Internal Consistency

Data on internal consistency are not relevant for this single-item measure.

Test–Retest

The mean test–retest coefficient for a sample of 32 students was .80 with a time interval of 10 days.

Validity

Convergent

The authors focused their attention on comparing the shortened form with another revised form and the original. The shortened and revised forms were developed from analyses of the same 110 items. Dempsey and Dukes (1966) reported the average intercorrelations for sets of items representing each Way in the original, the revised form, and the shortened form. They also reported the correlations between the average ratings of the items and the rating given to the original paragraph describing that way to live. The short form proved to be superior on both criteria, the exceptions being Way 7 and Way 9, which retained considerable heterogeneity. Dempsey and Dukes interpreted the findings as indicating that the short form expressed "the core conception of Morris' document more adequately than the original paragraphs themselves" (p. 879).

Discriminant

The average correlation of the shortened form with the original over a 10-day interval was .57 ($n = 35$). The authors concluded that "while there is a substantial relationship between the original and short forms, there are also important differences between them" (p. 881). On comparing the content of the short form with the original Ways to Live, Dempsey and Dukes define their ways in the following manner (italics indicate Dempsey and Dukes' additions).

> Way 1: *Appreciate and* preserve the best man has attained.
> Way 2: Cultivate independence *and self-knowledge*.

Way 3: Show sympathetic concern for others.
Way 4: Experience festivity *and sensuous enjoyment.*
Way 5: Act and enjoy life through group participation.
Way 6: Master *threatening* forces by constant *practical work.*
Way 7: *Admit diversity and accept something from all ways of life.*
Way 8: *Enjoy the simple, easily obtainable pleasures.*
Way 9: Wait in quiet receptivity *for joy and peace.*
Way 10: Control the self *and hold firm to high ideals.*
Way 11: Meditate on the inner life.
Way 12: *Use the body's energy* in daring and adventurous deeds.
Way 13: *Let oneself be used by* the great cosmic purposes.

Location

Dempsey, P., & Dukes, W. F. (1966). Judging complex value stimuli: An examination and revision of Morris's *"Paths of Life." Educational and Psychological Measurement,* **26,** 871–882.

Results and Comments

The instrument looks as if it could be a promising substitute for the highly complex Ways to Live. It has not been used widely, however, although other shortened forms with no accompanying data to support reliability and validity have appeared in the literature (e.g., see Feifel & Nagy, 1981, and Sommers & Scioli, 1986). Increased usage would provide much needed validating data on the short form Ways to Live. As is the case for its parent instrument, minor adjustments to avoid male referents may be necessary.

Short Form Ways to Live

Instructions: On the following page are described 13 ways to live, which various persons at various times have advocated and followed. In the left margin rank these ways in the order you prefer them, so that the number 1 is by the path you like best, the number 2 by that you like next best, and so on, with number 13 by the path you like least.

It is not a question of what kind of life you now lead, or the kind of life you think it prudent to live in our society, or the kind of life you think good for other persons, but simply the kind of life you personally would like to live.

WAY 1: An individual should actively participate in the social life of his community, not to change it primarily, but to understand, appreciate, and preserve the best that man has attained. Life should have clarity, balance, refinement, control.

WAY 2: The individual should for the most part "go it alone," having much time to himself, stressing self-sufficiency, reflection and meditation, knowledge of himself. The center of life should be found within the self.

WAY 3: This way of life makes central the sympathetic concern for other persons. Whatever hinders sympathetic love among persons should be avoided, for such love alone gives significance to life. One should become receptive, appreciative, and helpful with respect to others.

WAY 4: Life should be more a festival than a workshop, or a school for moral discipline; it should be enjoyed, sensuously enjoyed, enjoyed with relish and abandonment. To let oneself go, to let things and persons affect oneself, is more important than to do—or to do good.

WAY 5: A person should merge himself with a social group, enjoy cooperation and companionship, join with others in resolute activity for the realization of common goals. Life should merge energetic group activity and cooperative group enjoyment.

WAY 6: We should stress the realistic solution of specific problems as they appear and the improvement of techniques for controlling the world and society. We have to work resolutely and continually if control is to be gained over the forces that threaten us.

WAY 7: We should at various times and in various ways accept something from all other paths of life, but give no one our exclusive allegiance. We must cultivate flexibility, admit diversity in ourselves, accepting the tension which this diversity produces.

WAY 8: The enjoyment of simple, easily obtainable pleasures should be the keynote of life: the pleasures of just existing, of savory food, of comfortable surroundings, of talking with friends, of rest, relaxation.

WAY 9: The good things in life cannot be found by resolute action, or by participation in the turmoil of social life. One should cease to make demands, waiting in quiet receptivity, open to the powers that nourish the self and work through it. Sustained by these powers, one knows joy and peace.

WAY 10: Self-control should be the keynote of life, not the easy self-control that retreats from the world, but the vigilant, stern, manly control of a self that lives in the world. One should hold firm to high ideals and not be bent by the seductive voices of comfort and desire.

WAY 11: The contemplative life is the good life, the life that is rewarding. The rich internal world of ideals, of sensitive feelings, of reverie, of self-knowledge is man's true home.

WAY 12: The use of the body's energy is the secret of a rewarding life. Not in cautious foresight, not in relaxed ease does life attain fulfillment, for it is the active deed that is satisfying, the deed adequate to the present, the daring and adventurous deed.

WAY 13: One should let himself be used by other persons in their growth, and by the great objective purposes in the universe. One should be a serene, confident, quiet vessel, guided by the great dependable powers that silently and irresistibly achieve their goal.

The Value Profile

(Bales & Couch, 1969)

Variable

Bales and Couch developed the Value Profile to measure agreement with a set of value statements considered relevant to interaction with others in laboratory group studies (see

Bales, 1970). They defined a value statement in the concrete interaction context as "a statement of an existing norm, or a proposal for a new norm" (p. 4).

Description

An initial pool of 872 items was generated to represent as large and as varied a coverage of the domain as possible. Sources included listening to group discussions, other value instruments, personality scales, and the experiences of their co-workers. These items were then reduced to 252 by the researchers and were presented to respondents for rating on an agree–disagree continuum. Item analyses to exclude value statements that were not discriminating well led to a final set of 144 items to be rated on the agree–disagree dimension. These items were factor-analyzed and 40 items were selected to represent four value dimensions.

The four scales in the Value Profile assess (1) Acceptance of Authority, (2) Need-Determined Expression (vs. Value-Determined Restraint), (3) Equalitarianism, and (4) Individualism. Each is represented by 10 items, which respondents evaluate on a six-point rating scale from strongly disagree (1) through to strongly agree (6). A score of 4 is reserved for cases in which no response is made. The instrument is self-administered.

Sample

The 144-item questionnaire was completed by 552 respondents, predominantly undergraduate college students but including some graduate students, faculty members, and officer candidates in the Air Force.

Reliability

No reliability data were encountered.

Validity

No validity data were encountered.

Location

Bales, R., & Couch, A. (1969). The value profile: A factor analytic study of value statements. *Sociological Inquiry, 39,* 3–17.

Results and Comments

The agree–disagree response continuum is not consistent with values as conceptions of the desirable, but it is of note that the notion of "oughtness" is incorporated into some of the value statements. Other items, however, can probably be more accurately described as related beliefs or attitudes than as values. A second weakness is that the language used in the scales has dated somewhat (e.g., the repeated reference to "man" in the Individualism Scale). As well as modernized scales, reliability and validity data are required before these measures can be used with confidence. In spite of these criticisms, the instrument has considerable strengths. Enormous effort was directed toward obtaining a broad coverage of the value domain. The item sampling procedure was an exhaustive one, and the dimensions identified from this firm basis should be given serious attention by value researchers.

A shortened 12-item version of the Value Profile was developed by Withey (1965), who adapted the three highest-loading items on each of Bales and Couch's four factors for use in a nationwide study of public civil defense practices. Respondents judged the statements on a five-point rating scale from strongly agree to strongly disagree. Many of the items used by Withey were reworded slightly, but their counterparts in the Value Profile are indicated by a W in the right hand margin. The reader is referred to Withey (1965) for further details or to the previous edition of *Measures of social psychological attitudes*.

Value Profile

Directions: This questionnaire is designed to measure the extent to which you hold each of several general attitudes or values common in our society. On the following pages you will find a series of general statements expressing opinions of the kind you may have heard from other persons around you. After each statement there is a set of possible responses as follows:

1	2	3	4	5	6
Strongly Disagree	Disagree	Slightly Disagree	Slightly Agree	Agree	Strongly Agree

You are asked to read each of the statements and then to *circle* the response which best *represents* your immediate reaction to the opinion expressed. Respond to each opinion as a whole. If you have reservations about some part of a statement, circle the response that most clearly approximates your *general feeling*.

Acceptance of Authority

1. Obedience and respect for authority are the most important virtues children should learn. (W)

1	2	3	4	5	6

2. There is hardly anything lower than a person who does not feel a great love, gratitude, and respect for his parents.

3. What youth needs most is strict discipline, rugged determination, and the will to work and fight for family and country.

4. You have to respect authority and when you stop respecting authority, your situation isn't worth much. (W)

5. Patriotism and loyalty are the first and the most important requirements of a good citizen.

6. Young people sometimes get rebellious ideas, but as they grow up they ought to get over them and settle down. (W)

7. A child should not be allowed to talk back to his parents, or else he will lose respect for them.

8. The facts on crime and sexual immorality show that we will have to crack down harder on young people if we are going to save our moral standards.

9. Disobeying an order is one thing you can't excuse—if one can get away with disobedience, why can't everybody?

10. A well-raised child is one who doesn't have to be told twice to do something.

Need-Determined Expression
(vs. Value-Determined Restraint)

1. Since there are no values that can be eternal, the only real values are those that meet the needs of the given moment.   (W)

2. Nothing is static, nothing is everlasting, at any moment one must be ready to meet the change in environment by a necessary change in one's moral views.

3. Let us eat, drink, and be merry, for tomorrow we die.   (W)

4. The solution to almost any human problem should be based on the situation at the time, not on some general moral rule.   (W)

5. Life is something to be enjoyed to the full, sensuously enjoyed with relish and enthusiasm.

6. Life is more a festival than a workshop or a school for moral discipline.

7. The past is no more, the future may never be, the present is all that we can be certain of.

*8. Not to attain happiness, but to be worthy of it, is the purpose of our existence.

*9. No time is better spent than that devoted to thinking about the ultimate purposes of life.

*10. Tenderness is more important than passion in love.

Equalitarianism

1. Everyone should have an equal chance and an equal say.   (W)

2. There should be equality for everyone—because we are all human beings.

3. A group of equals will work a lot better than a group with a rigid hierarchy.   (W)

4. Each one should get what he needs—the things we have belong to all of us.   (W)

5. No matter what the circumstances, one should never arbitrarily tell people what they have to do.

6. It is the duty of every good citizen to correct antiminority remarks made in his presence.

7. Poverty could be almost entirely done away with if we made certain basic changes in our social and economic system.

8. There has been too much talk and not enough real action in doing away with racial discrimination.

9. In any group it is more important to keep a friendly atmosphere than to be efficient.

10. In a small group there should be no real leaders—everyone should have an equal say.

Individualism

1. To be superior a man must stand alone.

2. In life an individual should for the most part "go it alone," assuring himself of privacy, having much time to himself, attempting to control his own life. (W)

3. It is the man who stands alone who excites our admiration. (W)

4. The rich internal world of ideals, of sensitive feelings, of reverie, of self knowledge, is man's true home.

5. One must avoid dependence upon persons or things; the center of life should be found within oneself. (W)

6. The most rewarding object of study any man can find is his own inner life.

7. Whoever would be a man, must be a nonconformist.

8. Contemplation is the highest form of human activity.

9. The individualist is the man who is most likely to discover the best road to a new future.

10. A man can learn better by striking out boldly on his own than he can by following the advice of others.

* Reverse-scored.

Life Roles Inventory—Value Scales

(Fitzsimmons, Macnab, & Casserly, 1985)

Variable

The instrument measures the importance of 20 kinds of values considered relevant to assessing the relative importance of the work role in relation to other major life roles in different cultures.

Description

Initially 22 values were derived from the literature: Ability Utilization, Achievement, Advancement, Aesthetics, Associates and Social Interaction, Authority, Autonomy, Creativity, Cultural Identity, Economic Rewards, Economic Security, Environment, Intellectual Stimulation, Life Style, Participation in Organizational Decision Making, Prestige, Physical Activity, Responsibility, Risk-Taking and Safety, Spiritual Values, Supervisory Relations, and Variety. Items were written to represent each of these facets of the value domain in English and in French, and as a consequence of a series of psychometric analyses, 20 multi-item scales were developed.

The 20 scales making up the LRI-VS are (1) Ability Utilization, (2) Achievement, (3) Advancement, (4) Aesthetics, (5) Altruism, (6) Authority, (7) Autonomy, (8) Creativity,

(9) Economics, (10) Life Style, (11) Personal Development, (12) Physical Activity, (13) Prestige, (14) Risk, (15) Social Interaction, (16) Social Relations, (17) Variety, (18) Working Conditions, (19) Cultural Identity, and (20) Physical Prowess. Each scale comprises five items, three of which are common to all countries (Australia, Canada, Portugal, Spain, United States) and two of which are unique to each national project. The items are preceded by the stem "It is now or will be important for me to . . ." and respondents are required to rate each item on a four-point scale: Little or no importance (1), Of some importance (2), Important (3), and Very important (4). Originally, the authors developed a general values instrument and a work-related values instrument. In the final version, both general and work-related items are brought together in one single instrument.

Sample

The scales were developed with English- and French-speaking samples of Canadian adult workers ($n = 6382$) and high school students ($n = 3115$), and an English-speaking sample of postsecondary education students ($n = 623$). Although the samples are not random, the authors did attempt to obtain a broad cross section. Norms are provided for males and females in each group and for the French and English forms where appropriate, and breakdowns are provided for adults by type of work.

Reliability

Internal Consistency

Alpha reliability coefficients have been reported for each scale in each of the three major samples. For the English form, reliabilities ranged from .67 (Achievement) to .88 (Altruism) (median .80) for adults, .68 (Achievement) to .91 (Altruism) (median .83) for postsecondary students, and .65 (Cultural Identity) to .90 (Altruism) (median .78) for the high school students. Reliabilities for the French form are comparable to the English in the adult samples but somewhat lower in the high school sample.

Test–Retest

Reliability coefficients over a 4–6-week interval with the high school student sample ranged from .63 (Ability Utilization) to .82 (Physical Prowess, Physical Activity) (median .69) in the English version. For the French form, coefficients ranged from .53 (Cultural Identity) to .83 (Physical Prowess) (median .65). Again, using high school students, the authors examined the correlation between the French and English forms with a short time interval. The correlation coefficients ranged from .62 (Achievement) to .88 (Physical Prowess) (median .74).

Validity

Convergent

The scales have been used to differentiate students enrolled in business, education and rehabilitation medicine and have been successfully related to measures from the Minnesota Importance Questionnaire (Gay, Weiss, Hendel, Dawis, & Lofquist, 1971), the

Work Aspect Preference Scale (Pryor, 1979), and the Work Values Inventory (Super, 1970). Eight value scales were postulated as having counterparts in these instruments: Authority, Social Relations, Creativity, Autonomy, Economics, Altruism, Work Conditions, and Prestige. The patterns of intercorrelations and confirmatory factor analysis supported not only the convergent but the discriminant validity of these scales (Macnab & Fitzsimmons, 1987).

Discriminant

In examining the relationship between the LRI-VS and the Vocational Preference Inventory (Fitzsimmons *et al.*, 1985), only 49 of the possible 120 correlations were significant, leading the authors to conclude that their value domain cannot be subsumed under that of interests.

Location

Fitzsimmons, G. W., Macnab, D., & Casserly, C. (1985). *Technical Manual for the Life Roles Inventory Values Scale and the Salience Inventory*. Edmonton, Alberta, Canada: PsiCan Consulting Limited.

Results and Comments

The factorial structure of the instrument has been examined for each of the norm samples (Fitzsimmons *et al.*, 1985), suggesting higher-order factors underlying the scales. Principal components analyses and varimax rotations on intercorrelations between the 20 scales consistently have revealed five factors emerging across samples: (1) Personal Achievement and Development, (2) Social Orientation, (3) Independence, (4) Economic Conditions, and (5) Physical Activity and Risk.

The LRI-VS is relatively new but it is currently being used internationally and further examples of its use should appear soon in the literature. Data provided on reliability and validity are impressive and its applicability to the work role as well as to other roles gives it special status. Previous instruments have focused primarily on work values or general values, rarely on both.

The major criticism that can be made of the LRI-VS at this point is its lack of consistency with the dominant definition of values. Respondents are asked to indicate what is important to them without any reference to desirability. Although the value scales have been empirically differentiated from interests, they have not been differentiated from needs. Importance is an appropriate dimension on which to assess needs and is relevant to values only when the instructions make it clear that respondents are considering the desirable, that is, guiding principles in life.

Life Roles Inventory—Value Scales

Instructions: Once you have completed the personal information on the answer sheet please start answering the questions below. Please answer every question. Work rapidly. If you are not sure, guess; your first thought is most likely to be the right answer for you.

For each of the following statements, indicate how important it is to you. Use the following scale:

1 Means of little or no importance
2 Means of some importance
3 Means important
4 Means very important

Use a pencil to fill in the circle of the number on the answer sheet that shows how important the statement is to you. For example:

Enjoy myself while working   1   2   ●   4

Now please respond to all the questions, using the answer sheet.

Sample items:

It is now or will be important for me to . . .

1. use all my skills and knowledge   1   2   3   4
2. do things that involve some risk
3. have a good income

Conceptions of the Desirable

(Lorr, Suziedelis, & Tonesk, 1973)

Variable

Values are conceptualized as personal goals, social goals, and modes of conduct deemed personally or socially preferable, and assessed in terms of their importance in the respondent's life.

Description

The initial pool of items (235) represented 10 bipolar constructs derived from the work of Morris (1956b), F. R. Kluckhohn and Strodtbeck (1961), Scott (1965), and Bales and Couch (1969). The constructs for item selection were (1) authoritarian versus rule-free, (2) equalitarian versus elitist, (3) achieving versus hedonistic, (4) altruistic versus self-interested, (5) controlled versus spontaneous, (6) adventurous versus cautious, (7) religious versus secular, (8) stoic versus comfort-seeking, (9) intellectual versus pragmatic, and (10) principled versus opportunistic.

The final form of the inventory is self-administered and comprises 139 items that respondents must rate on a five-point scale according to how desirable they think the goal is or how they think they ought to behave. The rating scale is defined by labels reflecting five levels of importance from Not at all (1) through to Extremely (5). On the basis of first-order and second-order factor analyses, the authors claim that four ethical orientations can be measured through 12 value scales: Acceptance of authority by the (1) Authoritarian, (2) Religious, and (3) Elitist scales, the work ethic by the (4) Self-reliant, (5) Stoic, (6) Achieving, and (7) Adventurous scales, the humanitarian orientation by the (8) Socially Concerned, (9) Intellectual, and (10) Conscientious scales, and the hedonistic orientation by the (11) Hedonistic and (12) Self-Interested scales. Unfortunately, details are not available to relate particular items to each of the scales.

Sample

The instrument was developed using two samples of adult men and women ($n = 365, 300$) who varied widely in educational level and social class.

Reliability

Neither internal consistency nor test–retest coefficients are provided.

Validity

Convergent

Limited information is provided on the religious and authoritarian subscales with both correlating with an attitudinal measure of liberalism–conservatism.

Discriminant

No data are provided.

Location

Lorr, M., Suziedelis, A., & Tonesk, X. (1973). The structure of values. *Journal of Research in Personality*, **7**, 139–147.

Results and Comments

The inventory has not received widespread use; there is neither sufficient information for scoring nor adequate data on reliability and validity. Further psychometric work is clearly needed to make this a useful instrument and language needs to be modernized. The inventory has two major strengths, however. First, a broad range of values is represented (personal and social goals and modes of conduct are included). Second, the authors have operationalized values in a manner that is consistent with the dominant conceptualization of values as conceptions of the desirable.

Conceptions of the Desirable

Directions: The purpose of this inventory is to find out what goals you regard as *desirable* and ways you believe you *ought* to behave. Please read each value statement and indicate how *important* it is in your life.

Indicate the degree of importance of each value to you by recording the number of the appropriate answer on the line. If the value is not at all important record a *1*. If the value is quite important record a *4*, and so on, using numbers as follows:

1. Not at all
2. Somewhat
3. Moderately
4. Quite
5. Extremely

Be sure to select an answer for each statement.

1. Do something for others without expecting any reward

1	2	3	4	5
NOT AT ALL	SOMEWHAT	MODERATELY	QUITE	EXTREMELY

2. Recognize that some people are born superior
3. Make the best use of time
4. Respect and obey the laws of the land
5. Trust in the providence of God
6. Try out new ideas
7. Bear my burdens without complaining
8. Avoid the stereotyped and the traditional
9. Look out for myself first
10. Promise nothing I can't fulfill
11. Make allowances for the peculiarities of gifted people
12. Challenge authority when I disagree with it
13. Give help to the hungry and poor
14. Be practical and efficient in whatever I do
15. Show respect for my parents
16. Strengthen and toughen myself for any hardships
17. Follow the rule "every man for himself"
18. Be guided by my conscience
19. Understand the reasons for things
20. Have a plan for whatever I do and stick to it
21. Solve my problems by myself
22. Recognize that some people deserve special privileges
23. Be an innovator
24. Honor my commitments
25. Be free from any religious constraints
26. Always be active and busy
27. Have fun and a good time
28. Appreciate great men and great minds
29. Face risks boldly
30. Keep my word no matter what
31. See that all men are guaranteed the same rights and privileges
32. Not be bound by any religious beliefs
33. Take advantage of opportunities even though it violates a few rules
34. Avoid obedience to authority
35. Use my intellectual powers to the fullest
36. Act responsibly when I take on a commitment
37. Strive to get ahead in some line of work

38. Seek the adventure of the unexpected
39. Take care of myself before helping others
40. Get as much pleasure out of living as I can
41. Never lie to anyone
42. Recognize that others have the same rights as I do
43. Strike down laws that don't make sense anymore
44. Enjoy the beauty of nature
45. Promote cooperation among peoples of different countries
46. Avoid sticking my neck out for anyone
47. Be self-sufficient
48. Obey lawful authority
49. Be loyal to my friends
50. Bring back religious values to our society
51. Understand the meaning and purpose of things
52. Show love for my country
53. Take time to enjoy myself without care
54. Make decisions on my own
55. Be honest and truthful
56. Acknowledge that rulers of countries are different from common people
57. Be always ready to meet my Creator
58. Show sympathy for others
59. Feel free to break any law I consider wrong
60. Enjoy music and the arts
61. Just take it easy; not push myself too hard
62. Stand apart from the crowd
63. Worship God
64. Not be governed by society's rules
65. Live in a world where nations are at peace with one another
66. Enjoy the here and now instead of worrying about tomorrow
67. Show respect for those in authority
68. Recognize that some people deserve a higher standing in society than others
69. Keep my promises
70. Never obey any law blindly
71. Maintain law and public order
72. Plan things ahead of time and carry them out
73. Do the will of God
74. Be able to appreciate the best in art, music, and literature
75. Enjoy the present and let the future take care of itself
76. Leave the problems of the world in the hands of the specially gifted

77. Eliminate traditions that are kept for tradition's sake
78. Keep cool and collected in the face of panic or disaster
79. Set clear goals to work for
80. Treat fellow human beings as equals
81. Trust God to save mankind
82. Respect the traditions of our society
83. Enjoy life to the fullest
84. Seek explanations for the way things are
85. Give leadership to the most intelligent people
86. Avoid doing favors for anybody
87. Take pride in my work
88. Reduce the number of useless rules in our society
89. Let no one influence me against my better judgment
90. Make God the final purpose of life
91. Endure problems and difficulties with courage
92. Satisfy my immediate needs and impulses
93. Defend my national heritage
94. Enjoy giving to others
95. Always do my best
96. Get all the pleasures of life
97. Maintain emotional control over myself at all times
98. Follow my belief, even if contrary to law
99. Be free from sin
100. Work for mutual acceptance and understanding between nations
101. Finish jobs that I start
102. Study the workings of the universe
103. Follow the social customs of my country
104. Keep my head no matter what is happening around me
105. Be my own man
106. Seek new roads to travel
107. Show respect for my elders
108. Give to those who are in need of help
109. Be able to take pressures and stress
110. When things get rough, go it alone
111. Seek out life's little comforts
112. Complete what I set out to do
113. Make sure to get my fair share of rewards and benefits
114. Seek out new experiences
115. Enjoy great cultural achievements
116. Keep myself physically fit

117. Be able to determine my own future
118. Recognize the common brotherhood of man
119. Know ahead of time what I will do
120. Protect our country's way of life
121. Accept the fact that some people are born leaders
122. Enjoy the challenge of danger
123. Avoid relying on others
124. Enjoy all of life's pleasures
125. Take the hard knocks of life without complaining
126. Follow a definite schedule
127. Do exciting things even if they involve some risk or danger
128. Accept the fact that some people are more important than others to our society
129. Indulge myself
130. Preserve our system of government
131. Help others less fortunate than myself
132. Strive to get ahead
133. Endure pain without flinching
134. Not be dependent on anyone
135. Get what is coming to me
136. Try daring things
137. See that all men are treated equally
138. Leave as little to chance as possible
139. Follow the conventions of our society

Empirically Derived Value Constructions

(Gorlow & Noll, 1967)

Variable

A set of empirically derived values representing sources of meaning in life, sources of pleasure in life, and goals in life are sorted in terms of their value to respondents.

Description

The first stage in the development of the instrument was the generation of 1500 statements by a group of respondents. Another group of respondents reduced this list to 75 non-overlapping clearly stated values. The final 75 value statements are expressed in infinitive form (e.g., to accept others, to excel generally) and are administered to respondents as a 13-pile Q-sort task. The first pile represents statements "of lowest value to you" while the 13th pile represents statements "of highest value to you."

Gorlow and Noll used the Q-sorts to generate a correlation matrix among persons that was subjected to a principal components factor analysis with a varimax rotation. Eight factors accounting for 64% of the variance were extracted and interpreted. The clusters of individuals identified were (1) the affiliative–romantic, (2) the status–security valuer, (3) the intellectual humanist, (4) the family valuer, (5) the rugged individualist, (6) the undemanding–passive group, (7) the Boy Scout, and (8) the Don Juan. Correlations were computed between loadings on the factors that emerged and the Q-sort placements of the value statements in order to identify which statements were related to each of the factors. No procedures were explored for scoring statements, however. The basic unit of analysis was the individual's factor score on each dimension.

Sample

The statements were generated by 75 introductory psychology students but the Q-sort data were obtained from 105 persons of varying backgrounds in the university community (approximately half were undergraduates, the others were graduate students, faculty members, and persons in the surrounding community).

Reliability

No information on reliability was encountered.

Validity

Convergent

The loadings for individuals on each factor were correlated with demographic and social variables. Affiliative–romantics were more likely to be women, status–security valuers were less likely to be actively religious, intellectual humanists tended to be politically active, family valuers tended to be women and married, rugged individualists tended not to have strong political feelings, and the Don Juans were more likely to be single and young.

Discriminant

No data were presented.

Location

Gorlow, L., & Noll, G. A. (1967). A study of empirically derived values. *Journal of Social Psychology*, **73**, 261–269.

Results and Comments

This instrument provides a set of empirically derived statements that overlap considerably with the dominant definition of value. They are not as broad and abstract as the concepts of Rokeach (1973), but at the same time they are not as specific as attitude statements. They represent behaviors that transcend specific objects and situations.

Unlike other scales reviewed in this chapter, the item set has been used to identify types of individuals. Developing scales of value statements (or types of items) is quite a different task. All Gorlow and Noll have provided are correlations between each of their statements and the factors representing types of people. Most statements correlate significantly with more than one type. It is not at all clear how these items might group if the factor analysis had been performed on items averaging across respondents.

The major drawback of this questionnaire is that it is not one that can be used "off the shelf." Gorlow and Noll (1967) emphasize that they are proposing a methodology rather than reporting generalizable findings, concluding with the point that "different constructions of values might be expected to emerge when groups different from college sophomore populations are studied" (p. 269). Thus different factor structures should emerge in other groups and need to be identified in each new study. Modifications to the item set may also be required.

Empirically Derived Value Constructions

Items: (To be sorted into 13 piles from 1—of lowest value to you—through 13—of highest value to you.)

1. To be respected
2. To be wealthy
3. To be politically wise
4. To have formal higher education
5. To be financially secure
6. To like yourself
7. To be on affectionate terms with family
8. To have sexual prowess
9. To love all mankind
10. To know that you are the best at something
11. To excel generally
12. To solve difficult problems
13. To succeed in your work
14. To be strong physically
15. To be physically attractive
16. To be well-known
17. To have close friendships
18. To be remembered after death
19. To be married
20. To have sexual relations
21. To have children
22. To make others happy
23. To have self-control
24. To be artistically creative
25. To be religious
26. To seek truth

27. To be accepted by others
28. To accept others
29. To relax and feel content
30. To feel you own what you want
31. To be an individual
32. To confide in others
33. To have help when you want it
34. To be unafraid
35. To go to Heaven
36. To have recreations
37. To work hard
38. To prevail in intellectual give and take
39. To be alone
40. To own things
41. To direct others
42. To be useful
43. To be in love
44. To be active
45. To pray
46. To appreciate nature
47. To remember your past
48. To have status
49. To be loyal to friends
50. To be loyal to your country
51. To stand by your beliefs
52. To be optimistic
53. To share what you have
54. To be a part of social groups
55. To affiliate with humanitarian efforts
56. To be involved in politics
57. To have a tradition
58. To make decisions
59. To be in charge
60. To respect your parents
61. To provide for relatives
62. To be unselfish
63. To teach
64. To live up to others' expectations for you
65. To be your own boss
66. To be part of a productive organization

67. To be loved
68. To not be in physical pain
69. To be free of wrongdoing
70. To appreciate beauty
71. To have high moral and ethical standards
72. To be sober and clearheaded
73. To be sensitive to others' feelings
74. To be able to respond emotionally
75. To contribute to society

East—West Questionnaire

(Gilgen & Cho, 1979a)

Variable

The instrument is designed to measure Eastern versus Western orientations in belief systems. The Eastern perspective is conceptualized as a monistic (nondualistic) view of existence expressed in the four major Eastern religious traditions of Hinduism, Buddhism, Confucianism, and Taoism. Nondualistic beliefs emphasize wholeness: "Man should recognize his basic oneness with nature, the spiritual, and the mental rather than attempt to analyze, label, categorize, manipulate, control, or consume the things of the world" (p. 836).

The Western perspective, with Judeo-Christian and Greek foundations, is dualistic such that reality is divided into two parts with one part being set off against the other. From this perspective, "man has characteristics which set him apart from nature and the spiritual," "man is divided into a body, a spirit, and a mind," "there is a personal God who is over man," and "man must control and manipulate nature to ensure his survival" (p. 836).

Description

The questionnaire is self-administered and comprises 68 items, half representing the Eastern world view while the other half represent the corresponding Western world view. Each item is rated on a five-point scale from "agree strongly" (1) through to "disagree strongly" (5). The authors recommend using the questionnaire to derive an Eastern Thought Score. This score is obtained by assigning a weight of 2 to "strongly agree" responses and a weight of 1 to "agree, but with some reservations" responses. All other responses are ignored. The agreement scores are summed first across the Eastern world view items and second across all items. The Eastern agreement score is then divided by the total agreement score and multiplied by 100. Eastern Thought scores range maximally from 0 to 100. Cho and Gilgen (1980) also report five subscales within the questionnaire: Spiritual, Nature, Society, Man, and Rational Thought.

Sample

The questionnaire has been used with United States college students ($n = 210$ in the largest study), transpersonal psychologists ($n = 69$), and business people ($n = 46$), and in Korea with medical and nursing students ($n = 87$).

Reliability

Internal Consistency

Compton (1983) reported an α reliability coefficient for the instrument of .70, although this coefficient may be more a function of the large number of items in the scale than the cohesiveness of the items. No reliability data were encountered for the subscales.

Test–Retest

Over a 2-week period, Gilgen and Cho (1979a) report a test–retest reliability for the scale of .76.

Validity

Convergent

Gilgen and Cho (1979a) contrasted the Eastern Thought Scores of business majors and executives, students majoring in art, philosophy, and religion, transpersonal psychologists, and Buddhists in a preliminary investigation of the validity of the instrument. Cho and Gilgen (1980) subsequently showed Korean students to be more Eastern in their orientation than American students, and Compton (1983) has used the scale to differentiate practitioners of Zen meditation from nonpractitioners. Gilgen and Cho (1979b) examined the construct validity of the instrument by relating it to scores on Rokeach's Value Survey (1967) and Morris' Ways to Live (1956b). The results generally are in the direction expected, but they are not consistent across males and females.

Location

Gilgen, A. R., & Cho. J. H. (1979a). Questionnaire to measure eastern and western thought. *Psychological Reports,* **44,** 835–841.

Results and Comments

The instrument has the attraction of being specifically designed to compare Eastern and Western world views. Further research is needed, however, to examine issues of reliability and validity, particularly in relation to the five subscales. In addition, the degree of internal consistency of the scale as a whole needs clarification. Users may also wish to alter the wording of some items (e.g., Man should strive to free himself. . .) to ensure acceptability for both male and female respondents.

The East–West Questionnaire

Instructions: We are interested in finding out how much you *agree* or *disagree* with each of the statements which follow. Please read each statement carefully and then decide whether you:

> 1—AGREE strongly
> 2—AGREE, but with some reservations
> 3—Have no opinion
> 4—DISAGREE, but only moderately
> 5—DISAGREE strongly

When you have made your decision, note the number that corresponds to it and blacken in the proper space on your answer sheet using the pencil provided.

At the bottom of each page you will find a KEY that presents the five response alternatives. Refer to this KEY in order to avoid errors.

Man and the Spiritual

Eastern World View	**Western World View**

I do not believe in a personal god.

1   2   3   4   5

I believe in a personal god to whom I must account after death.

1   2   3   4   5

If there is a soul, I believe that after I die it will lose its individuality and become one with the overall spirituality of the universe.

I believe in a personal soul which will continue to exist after death.

Man and Nature

Eastern World View	**Western World View**

Man should try to harmonize with nature rather than manipulate and control it.

Man's progress has resulted primarily from his ability, through science and technology, to control and modify the natural world.

Man should strive to return to nature.

Man should strive to free himself from the uncompromising forces of nature.

I feel a real sense of kinship with most plants and animals.

While plants and animals are essential to human existence, I have no personal bond with most of them.

I hate to kill anything, even insects.

I cannot honestly say that it bothers me very much to step on an ant or bee deliberately.

I love to sit quietly just watching the clouds or a wild flower.

Inaction makes me very nervous and uncomfortable.

I like to travel alone sometimes to new places.

I feel ill at ease by myself in strange places.

I enjoy being by myself in the dark.

I am usually afraid when I find myself alone in a dark place.

We should only consume what we actually need.

A high level of consumption, even if it means some waste, is essential to a strong economy and a high standard of living.

Man and Society

Eastern World View	Western World View
The world keeps passing through cycles, over and over again, never really changing.	Man is moving by some grand plan toward an historical goal.
The ideal society is one in which each person subordinates his or her own desires and works consciously for the good of the community.	The ideal society is one in which each person by working individually for his own goals benefits everyone.
People should accept the role in life they are given by their parents' status in society.	People should have the opportunity to work themselves out of the situation in life they are born into.
A meaningful life depends more on learning to cooperate than learning to compete.	One of the most important things you can teach your children is how to compete successfully in the world.
Money tends to enslave people.	Money frees us from drudgery and meaningless work.
I get very little pleasure from material possessions.	Material possessions are for me a deep source of satisfaction.
I find most strangers interesting and easy to get to know.	I feel awkward and self-conscious with most strangers.
I enjoy eating by myself in a restaurant.	I cannot stand eating by myself.

Man and Himself

Eastern World View	Western World View
Meditation properly practiced can be a rich source of personal enlightenment; even when practiced by amateurs it may offer a way to relax.	Meditation is at best a form of relaxation and at worst a dangerous escape from reality and our responsibilities.
It is within his deep inner self that man will find true enlightenment.	The deep inner realm of man is basically primitive and evil.
True learning is directed toward self-understanding.	The main purpose of learning is to be able to get a good job.
I feel that my dreams are an integral part of me.	My dreams seem like an alien part of me.
Knowing that we shall die gives meaning to life.	Death really doesn't make much sense to me.
Suicide is sometimes a noble and natural choice.	Suicide is just plain wrong.

| Suffering, while painful and unpleasant, is basically a positive experience. | Suffering should be avoided at all cost because it destroys the meaning of life. |
| Anxiety usually results in personal growth. | Anxiety usually leads to unproductive and even self-destructive behavior. |

The Rationality of Man

Eastern World View	**Western World View**
Thoughts tend to isolate us from our feelings.	It is primarily through thinking and classifying that our experiences take on meaning.
Complex problems cannot be understood by breaking them into smaller components and then analyzing each component.	The best way to understand something is to subdivide it into smaller components and analyze each component carefully.
Language tends to interfere with our ability to experience things naturally and fully.	Language gives form and meaning to our experiences.
A new idea should be treasured whether it is useful or not.	Only ideas that help us do something better have much value.
Science and technology have provided man with an illusion of progress, an illusion he will later pay for dearly.	The only real progress man has achieved has been through science and technology.
Science is a destructive force in the long run.	Science is our main hope for the future.
The use of artificial kidneys and plastic hearts is going too far; it is unnatural.	Heart and kidney transplants are natural and wonderful medical advances.
Administering questionnaires is not a very effective way to find out about people.	Probably some useful information about people can be acquired through questionnaires.

Value Orientations

(Kluckhohn & Strodtbeck, 1961)

Variable

The instrument measures the orientations of respondents toward four dilemmas, representing "common human problems for which all peoples at all times must find some solution" (p. 10).

Description

The statements are considered to be "value orientations," conceived as

> principles, resulting from the transactional interplay of three analytically distinguishable elements of the evaluative process—the cognitive, the affective, and the directive elements—which give order and direction to the ever-flowing stream of human acts and thoughts as these relate to the solution of "common human" problems. (p. 4)

For each dilemma, two or three alternative orientations are postulated: the relation to other humans may be faced in individual, lineal (rank-defined), or collateral (group-related) terms; the relation to nature may be seen as one of submission, subjugation, or harmonious adaptation; the time perspective may be focused predominantly on the past, present, or future; and self-expression may appear predominantly as either activity or passive "being."

Kluckhohn and Strodtbeck assessed these orientations through an individual interview in which 22 questions were asked, posing 23 choices for the interviewees. Preferred solutions were indicated by rank-ordering the alternative responses for each of the postulated dilemmas. The "relational orientation" (to other humans) is represented by seven questions, and the "man–nature orientation," the "time orientation" and the "activity" orientation each by five questions.

Thus, within each question, items pertaining to a single "orientation" are ipsatively administered, yielding total scores on choices within each orientation that are ipsative. (It is impossible, for instance, to score high simultaneously on individual, lineal, and collateral orientations.) This scoring procedure follows from theoretical postulates, rather than from empirical evidence concerning mutual exclusiveness of the alternatives. Between orientations, item responses and their sums within a type are independent, and can be compared via standardized scores (e.g., an individual relational orientation against a subjugative orientation to nature).

Sample

The instrument was developed in the 1950s for use with 23 Spanish-Americans, 20 Texans, 20 Mormons, 22 off-reservation Navajo, and 21 Zuni in a comparative ethnology of five neighboring communities in the southwest United States.

Reliability

No conventional reliability coefficients have been encountered. Some inferences regarding reliability can be made, however, through cross-community comparisons of items and scale totals (i.e., summed scores over responses reflecting a particular solution to the type of dilemma posed). The intercultural differences observed with the scales of collateral relations, past and future time orientations, and harmonious orientation to nature tend to be clearer than those obtained with their constituent items, suggesting positive reliabilities for these scales at least.

Validity

Convergent

A group-differences analysis provided the sole basis for ascertaining scale validity; no independent measures from the communities were reported to substantiate the investigators' predicted rank-ordering of the five samples. Interpretation of the results as demonstrating validity of the measures depends, therefore, on two assumptions: uncontaminated criteria and intercommunity differences that reflect only the postulated underlying orientations, rather than extraneous characteristics. Although the effects of extraneous determinants might be considered random over large, representative samples of cultures, irrelevant variables cannot be effectively controlled when the number of cultures is small. Despite this limitation (which applies to virtually all cross-cultural studies), the statistical analyses (by A. K. Romney) provide a useful model of intercultural validation.

Each orientation (mean of similarly classified replies to a given dilemma) was subject to an analysis of variance over the five samples; in addition, clusters of items (two or three responses to each question) were similarly analyzed to ascertain the consistency of intercultural differences that emerged within sets representing a common orientation. (Both procedures were complicated by the ipsative scoring.) Consistent intercultural differences were noted (e.g., Texans tended to score higher than others on four of the seven "individual" and on three of the five "subjugation" items; Spanish-Americans on three of the five "past" and three of the six "being" items).

It is such interitem consistencies that lend confidence to the interpretation of intercultural differences in total scale scores, because they imply that cultural differences do not depend on a particular way of measuring the variable. Although results from this study do not speak to the general question of scale validity, they do pertain to the validity of the scales for the authors' purpose (i.e., distinguishing among the five cultures studied) under the assumption that their judgment provides a sufficiently valid criterion.

Location

Kluckhohn, F. R., & Strodtbeck, F. L. (1961). *Variations in value orientations*. Evanston, IL: Row, Peterson.

Results and Comments

Given the cultural specificity of the measure, its continued use in the original form is unlikely. However, the theory underlying it may be regarded by some as sufficiently universal to generate other specific measures of the same attributes. For example, derived instruments in written questionnaire form have been used by Platt (1985) and by Triandis, Leung, Villareal, and Clark (1985).

Value Orientations

1. Job Choice (Activity: Items A1 and A2)

A man needed a job and had a chance to work for two men. The two bosses were different. Listen to what they were like and say which you think would be the best one to work for.

A (Doing)	One boss was a fair enough man, and he gave somewhat higher pay than most men, but he was the kind of boss who insisted that men work hard, stick on the job. He did not like it at all when a worker sometimes just knocked off work for a while to go on a trip or to have a day or so of fun, and he thought it was right not to take such a worker back on the job.

B
(Being)

The other paid just average wages but he was not so firm. He understood that a worker would sometimes just not turn up—would be off on a trip or having a little fun for a day or two. When his men did this he would take them back without saying too much.

(Part One)

Which of these men do you believe that it would be better to work for in most cases?

Which of these men would most other _____ think it better to work for?

(Part Two)

Which kind of boss do you believe that it is better to be in most cases?

Which kind of boss would most other _____ think it better to be?

2. Well Arrangements (Relational: Item R1)

When a community has to make arrangements for water, such as drill a well, there are three different ways they can decide to arrange things like location and who is going to do the work.

A
(Lin)

There are some communities where it is mainly the older or recognized leaders of the important families who decide the plans. Everyone usually accepts what they say without much discussion since they are the ones who are used to deciding such things and are the ones who have had the most experience.

B
(Coll)

There are some communities where most people in the group have a part in making the plans. Lots of different people talk, but nothing is done until almost everyone comes to agree as to what is best to be done.

C
(Ind)

There are some communities where everyone holds to his own opinion, and they decide the matter by vote. They do what the largest number want even though there are still a very great many people who disagree and object to the action.

Which way do you think is usually best in such cases?

Which of the other two ways do you think is better?

Which way of all three ways do you think most other persons in _____ would usually think is best?

3. Child Training (Time: Item T1)

Some people were talking about the way children should be brought up. Here are three different ideas.

A
(Past)

Some people say that children should be taught well the traditions of the past (the ways of the old people). They believe the old ways are best, and that it is when children do not follow them too much that things go wrong.

B (Pres)	Some people say that children should be taught some of the old traditions (ways of the old people), but it is wrong to insist that they stick to these ways. These people believe that it is necessary for children always to learn about and take on whatever of the new ways will best help them get along in the world of today.
C (Fut)	Some people do not believe children should be taught much about past traditions (the ways of the old people) at all except as an interesting story of what has gone before. These people believe that the world goes along best when children are taught the things that will make them want to find out for themselves new ways of doing things to replace the old.

Which of these people had the best idea about how children should be taught?

Which of the other two people had the better idea?

Considering again all three ideas, which would most other persons in _____ say had the better idea?

4. Livestock Dying (Man–Nature: Item MN1)

One time a man had a lot of livestock. Most of them died off in different ways. People talked about this and said different things.

A (Subj)	Some people said you just can't blame a man when things like this happen. There are so many things that can and do happen, and a man can do almost nothing to prevent such losses when they come. We all have to learn to take the bad with the good.
B (Over)	Some people said that it was probably the man's own fault that he lost so many. He probably didn't use his head to prevent the losses. They said that it is usually the case that men who keep up on new ways of doing things, and really set themselves to it, almost always find a way to keep out of such trouble.
C (With)	Some people said that it was probably because the man had not lived his life right—had not done things in the right way to keep harmony between himself and the forces of nature (i.e., the ways of nature like the rain, winds, snow, etc.).

Which of these reasons do you think is most usually true?

Which of the other two reasons do you think is more true?

Which of all three reasons would most other persons in _____ think is usually true?

5. Expectations about Change (Time: Item T2)

(20–40 Age Group)

Three young people were talking about what they thought their families would have one day as compared with their fathers and mothers. They each said different things.

C
(Fut)

The first said: I expect my family to be better off in the future than the family of my father and mother or relatives if we work hard and plan right. Things in this country usually get better for people who really try.

B
(Pres)

The second one said: I don't know whether my family will be better off, the same, or worse off than the family of my father and mother or relatives. Things always go up and down even if people do work hard. So one can never really tell how things will be.

A
(Past)

The third one said: I expect my family to be about the same as the family of my father and mother or relatives. The best way is to work hard and plan ways to keep up things as they have been in the past.

Which of these people do you think had the best idea?

Which of the other two persons had the better idea?

Which of these three people would most other _____ your age think had the best idea?

(40–Up Age Group)

Three older people were talking about what they thought their children would have when they were grown. Here is what each one said.

C
(Fut)

One said: I really expect my children to have more than I have had if they work hard and plan right. There are always good chances for people who try.

B
(Pres)

The second one said: I don't know whether my children will be better off, worse off, or just the same. Things always go up and down even if one works hard, so we can't really tell.

A
(Past)

The third one said: I expect my children to have just about the same as I have had or bring things back as they once were. It is their job to work hard and find ways to keep things going as they have been in the past.

Which of these people do you think had the best idea?

Which of the other two persons had the better idea?

Which of these three people would most other _____ your age think had the best idea?

6. Facing Conditions (Man–Nature: Item MN2)

There are different ways of thinking about how God (the gods) is (are) related to man and to weather and all other natural conditions which make the crops and animals live or die. Here are three possible ways.

C
(With)

God (the gods) and people all work together all the time; whether the conditions that make the crops and animals grow are good or bad depends upon whether people themselves do all the proper things to keep themselves in harmony with their God (gods) and with the forces of nature.

B (Over)	God (the gods) does (do) not directly use his (their) power to control all the conditions which affect the growth of crops or animals. It is up to the people themselves to figure out the ways conditions change and to try hard to find the ways of controlling them.
A (Subj)	Just how God (the gods) will use his (their) power over all the conditions which affect the growth of crops and animals cannot be known by man. But it is useless for people to think they can change conditions very much for very long. The best way is to take conditions as they come and do as well as one can.

Which of these ways of looking at things do you think is best?

Which of the other two ways do you think is better?

Which of the three ways of looking at things would most other people in _____ think is best?

7. Help in Misfortune (Relational: Item R2)

A man had a crop failure, or, let us say, had lost most of his sheep or cattle. He and his family had to have help from someone if they were going to get through the winter. There are different ways of getting help. Which of these three ways would be best?

B (Coll)	Would it be best if he depended mostly on his brothers and sisters or other relatives all to help him out as much as each one could?
C (Ind)	Would it be best for him to try to raise the money on his own outside the community (his own people) from people who are neither relatives nor employers?
A (Lin)	Would it be best for him to go to a boss or to an older important relative who is used to managing things in his group, and ask him to help out until things get better?

Which way of getting the help do you think would usually be best?

Which way of getting the help do you think is next best?

Which way do you think you yourself would really follow?

Which way do you think most other people in _____ would think best?

8. Family Work Relations (Relational: Item R3)

I'm going to tell you about three different ways families can arrange work. These families are related and they live close together.

C (Ind)	In some groups (or communities) it is usually expected that each of the separate families (by which we mean just husband, wife, and children) will look after its own business separate from all others and not be responsible for the others.
B (Coll)	In some groups (or communities) it is usually expected that the close relatives in the families will work together and talk over among themselves the way to take care of whatever problems come up.

When a boss is needed they usually choose (get) one person, not necessarily the oldest able person, to manage things.

A
(Lin)
In some groups (or communities) it is usually expected that the families which are closely related to each other will work together and have the oldest able person (*hermano mayor* or father) be responsible for and take charge of most important things.

Which of these ways do you think is usually best in most cases?

Which of the other two ways do you think is better?

Which of all the ways do you think most other persons in _____ would think is usually best?

9. Choice of Delegate (Relational: Item R4)

A group like yours (community like yours) is to send a delegate—a representative—to a meeting away from here (this can be any sort of meeting). How will this delegate be chosen?

B
(Coll)
Is it best that a meeting be called and everyone discuss things until almost everyone agrees so that when a vote is taken almost all people would be agreed on the same person?

A
(Lin)
Is it best that the older, important, leaders take the main responsibility for deciding who should represent the people since they are the ones who have had the long experience in such matters?

C
(Ind)
Is it best that a meeting be called, names be put up, a vote be taken, then send the man who gets the majority of votes even if there are many people who are still against this man?

Which of these ways of choosing is usually best in cases like this?

Which of the other two ways is usually better?

Which would most other persons in _____ say is usually best?

10. Use of Fields (Man–Nature: Item MN3)

There were three men who had fields with crops (were farmers). The three men had quite different ways of planting and taking care of crops.

C
(With)
One man put in his crops, worked hard, and also set himself to living in right and proper ways. He felt that it is the way a man works and tries to keep himself in harmony with the forces of nature that has the most effect on conditions and the way crops turn out.

A
(Subj)
One man put in his crops. Afterwards he worked on them sufficiently but did not do more than was necessary to keep them going along. He felt that it mainly depended on weather conditions how they would turn out, and that nothing extra that people do could change things much.

B
One man put in his crops and then worked on them a lot of time

(Over)	and made use of all the new scientific ideas he could find out about. He felt that by doing this he would in most years prevent many of the effects of bad conditions.

Which of these ways do you believe is usually best?

Which of the other two ways do you believe is better?

Which of the three ways would most other persons in _____ think is best?

11. Philosophy of Life (Time: Item T3)

People often have very different ideas about what has gone before and what we can expect in life. Here are three ways of thinking about these things.

B (Pres)	Some people believe it best to give most attention to what is happening now in the present. They say that the past has gone and the future is much too uncertain to count on. Things do change, but it is sometimes for the better and sometimes for the worse, so in the long run it is about the same. These people believe the best way to live is to keep those of the old ways that one can—or that one likes—but to be ready to accept the new ways that will help to make life easier and better as we live from year to year.
A (Past)	Some people think that the ways of the past (ways of the old people or traditional ways) were the most right and the best, and as changes come things get worse. These people think the best way to live is to work hard to keep up the old ways and try to bring them back when they are lost.
C (Fut)	Some people believe that it is almost always the ways of the future—the ways that are still to come—that will be best, and they say that even though there are sometimes small setbacks, change brings improvements in the long run. These people think the best way to live is to look a long time ahead, work hard, and give up many things now so that the future will be better.

Which of these ways of looking at life do you think is best?

Which of the other two ways do you think is better?

Which of the three ways of looking at life do you think most other persons in _____ would think is best?

12. Wage Work (Relational: Item R5)

There are three ways in which men who do not themselves hire others may work.

C (Ind)	One way is working on one's own as an individual. In this case a man is pretty much his own boss. He decides most things himself, and how he gets along is his own business. He only has to take care of himself and he doesn't expect others to look out for him.

B
(Coll)

One way is working in a group of men where all the men work together without there being one main boss. Every man has something to say in the decisions that are made, and all the men can count on each other.

A
(Lin)

One way is working for an owner, a big boss, or a man who has been running things for a long time (a *patrón*). In this case, the men do not take part in deciding how the business will be run, but they know they can depend on the boss to help them out in many ways.

Which of these ways is usually best for a man who does not hire others?

Which of the other two ways is better for a man who does not hire others?

Which of the three ways do you think most other persons in _____ would think is best?

13. Belief in Control (Man–Nature: Item MN4)

Three men from different areas were talking about the things that control the weather and other conditions. Here is what they each said.

A
(Subj)

One man said: My people have never controlled the rain, wind, and other natural conditions and probably never will. There have always been good years and bad years. That is the way it is, and if you are wise you will take it as it comes and do the best you can.

B
(Over)

The second man said: My people believe that it is man's job to find ways to overcome weather and other conditions just as they have overcome so many things. They believe they will one day succeed in doing this and may even overcome drought and floods.

C
(With)

The third man said: My people help conditions and keep things going by working to keep in close touch with all the forces which make the rain, the snow, and other conditions. It is when we do the right things—live in the proper way—and keep all that we have— the land, the stock, and the water—in good condition, that all goes along well.

Which of these men do you think had the best idea?

Which of the other two men do you think had the better idea?

Which of the three men do you think most other persons in _____ would think had the best idea?

14. Ceremonial Innovation (Time: Item T4)

Some people in a community like your own saw that the religious ceremonies (the church services) were changing from what they used to be.

C
(Fut)

Some people were really pleased because of the changes in religious ceremonies. They felt that new ways are usually better than old ones, and they like to keep everything—even ceremonies— moving ahead.

A (Past)	Some people were unhappy because of the change. They felt that religious ceremonies should be kept exactly—in every way—as they had been in the past.
B (Pres)	Some people felt that the old ways for religious ceremonies were best but you just can't hang on to them. It makes life easier just to accept some changes as they come along.

Which of these three said most nearly what you would believe is right?

Which of the other two ways do you think is more right?

Which of the three would most other _____ say was most right?

15. Ways of Living (Activity: Item A3)

There were two people talking about how they liked to live. They had different ideas.

A (Doing)	One said: What I care about most is accomplishing things—getting things done just as well or better than other people do them. I like to see results and think they are worth working for.
B (Being)	The other said: What I care most about is to be left alone to think and act in the ways that best suit the way I really am. If I don't always get much done but can enjoy life as I go along, that is the best way.

Which of these two persons do you think has the better way of thinking?

Which of the two do you think you are more like?

Which do you think most other _____ would say had the better way of living?

16. Livestock Inheritance (Relational: Item R6)

Some sons and daughters have been left some livestock (sheep or cattle) by a father or mother who has died. All these sons and daughters are grown up, and they live near each other. There are three different ways they can run the livestock.

A (Lin)	In some groups of people it is usually expected that the oldest able person (son or daughter, *hermano mayor*) will take charge of, or manage, all the stock held by himself and the other sons and daughters.
C (Ind)	In some groups of people it is usually expected that each of the sons and daughters will prefer to take his or her own share of the stock and run his or her own business completely separate from all the others.
B (Coll)	In some groups of people it is usually expected that all the sons and daughters will keep all their cattle and sheep together and work together and decide among themselves who is best able to take charge of things, not necessarily the oldest, when a boss is needed.

Which way do you think is usually best in most cases?

Which of the other two ways do you think is better?

Which of all three ways do you think most other persons in _____ would think is usually best?

17. Land Inheritance (Relational: Item R7)

Now I want to ask a similar question concerning farm and grazing land instead of livestock.

Some sons and daughters have been left some farm and grazing land by a father or mother who has died. All these sons and daughters are grown and live near each other. There are three ways they can handle the property.

A (Lin)	In some groups of people it is usually expected that the oldest able person (*hermano mayor*) will take charge of or manage the land for himself and all the other sons and daughters, even if they all share it.
C (Ind)	In some groups of people it is usually expected that each son and daughter will take his own share of the land and do with it what he wants—separate from all the others.
B (Coll)	In some groups of people it is usually expected that all the sons and daughters will make use of the land together. When a boss is needed, they all get together and agree to choose someone of the group, not necessarily the oldest, to take charge of things.

Which of these ways do you think is usually best in most cases?

Which of the other two ways do you think is better?

Which of all three ways do you think most other persons in _____ would think is usually best?

18. Care of Fields (Activity: Item A4)

There were two men, both farmers (men with fields). They lived differently.

B (Being)	One man kept the crops growing all right but didn't work on them more than he had to. He wanted to have extra time to visit with friends, go on trips, and enjoy life. This was the way he liked best.
A (Doing)	One man liked to work with his fields and was always putting in extra time keeping them clean of weeds and in fine condition. Because he did this extra work, he did not have much time left to be with friends, to go on trips, or to enjoy himself in other ways. But this was the way he really liked best.

Which kind of man do you believe it is better to be?

(*For men only*): Which kind of man are you really most like?

Which kind of man would most other _____ think it better to be?

19. Length of Life (Man–Nature: Item MN5)

Three men were talking about whether people themselves can do anything to make the lives of men and women longer. Here is what each said.

B (Over)	One said: It is already true that people like doctors and others are finding the way to add many years to the lives of most men by discovering (finding) new medicines, by studying foods, and doing other such things as vaccinations. If people will pay attention to all these new things they will almost always live longer.
A (Subj)	The second one said: I really do not believe that there is much human beings themselves can do to make the lives of men and women longer. It is my belief that every person has a set time to live, and when that time comes it just comes.
C (With)	The third one said: I believe that there is a plan to life which works to keep all living things moving together, and if a man will learn to live his whole life in accord with that plan, he will live longer than other men.

Which of these three said most nearly what you would think is right?

Which of the other two ways is more right?

Which of the three would most other persons in _____ say was most right?

20. Water Allocation (Time: Item T5)

The government is going to help a community like yours to get more water by redrilling and cleaning out a community well. The government officials suggest that the community should have a plan for dividing the extra water, but don't say what kind of plan. Since the amount of extra water that may come in is not known, people feel differently about planning.

A (Past)	Some say that whatever water comes in should be divided just about like water in the past was always divided.
C (Fut)	Others want to work out a really good plan ahead of time for dividing whatever water comes in.
B (Pres)	Still others want to just wait until the water comes in before deciding on how it will be divided.

Which of these ways do you think is usually best in cases like this?

Which of the other two ways do you think is better?

Which of the three ways do you think most other persons in _____ would think best?

21. Housework (Activity: Item A5)

There were two women talking about the way they liked to live.

B (Being)	One said that she was willing to work as hard as the average, but that she didn't like to spend a lot of time doing the kind of extra

things in her house or taking up extra things outside like _____ .
Instead she liked to have time free to enjoy visiting with people—
to go on trips—or to just talk with whoever was around.

A   The other woman said she liked best of all to find extra things to
(Doing)   work on which would interest her—for example, _____ . She said
            she was happiest when kept busy and was getting lots done.

Which of these ways do you think it is usually better for women to live?

(*For women only*): Which woman are you really more like?

Which way of life would most other _____ think is best?

22. Nonworking Time (Activity: Item A6)

Two men spend their time in different ways when they have no work to do.
(This means when they are not actually on the job.)

A   One man spends most of this time learning or trying out things that
(Doing)   will help him in his work.

B   One man spends most of this time talking, telling stories, singing,
(Being)   and so on with his friends.

Which of these men has the better way of living?

Which of these men do you think you are more like?

Which of these men would most other _____ think had the better way of living?

Personal Value Scales

(Scott, 1965)

Variable

A value is defined as a moral ideal, an "individual's concept of an ideal relationship (or
state of affairs) . . . [used] to assess the "goodness" or "badness," the "rightness" or
"wrongness," of actual relationships . . . [which are observed or contemplated]" (p. 3).

Description

"A person may be said to entertain a value to the extent that he [or she] conceives a
particular state of affairs as an ultimate end, an absolute good under all circumstances, and
a universal 'ought' toward which all people should strive" (p. 15).

Values were identified through an open-question survey of college students and a
consideration of the values relevant to Greek student organizations.

On this basis, a self-administered instrument was developed comprising 12 scales: (1)
Intellectualism, (2) Kindness, (3) Social Skills, (4) Loyalty, (5) Academic Achievement,
(6) Physical Development, (7) Status, (8) Honesty, (9) Religiousness, (10) Self-Control,
(11) Creativity, and (12) Independence. Each scale is represented by a set of items that are

rated on a three-point scale: "always dislike," "depends on situation," and "always admire." "Always" captures the absolute nature of values, while "admire" was initially regarded by Scott as a more socially acceptable way of assessing goodness or badness, rightness or wrongness. Subsequent analyses suggested that "admired," "right," and "good" were equivalent dimensions for evaluation.

Short and long versions of the scales are available, the short version having 4–6 items per scale, the long version 20 items per scale. The items in the short version are positively worded with three exceptions. The long version is balanced with positively and negatively worded items. For scoring purposes, responses are collapsed so that "depends on situation" is scored as nonacceptance of the value. This means that for positively worded items "always dislike" and "depends on situation" will be scored 0 and "always admire" 1. For negatively worded items, "always admire" and "depends on situation" will be scored 0 and "always dislike" 1. Scale scores are obtained by summating across items.

Sample

The scales were developed and used with samples of college students, selected from fraternities and sororities, the undergraduate population, and psychology classes. For the reliability and validity studies, sample sizes tended to be around 200, although they were smaller in cases in which known groups validation procedures were used.

Reliability

Internal Consistency

The α reliability coefficients for the short form ranged from .55 for Independence to .78 for Religiousness, leading Scott to conclude that the scales, while adequate for distinguishing between large groups, were not sufficiently reliable to permit accurate measurement of individual subjects. Thus, the long form was developed. Alpha reliability coefficients for the long forms ranged from .80 (Honesty) to .89 (Physical Development). Among a sample of Australian university students, V. A. Braithwaite (1979) reported comparable α reliability coefficients, ranging from .78 for Independence and Status to .92 for Religiousness.

Test–Retest

Reliabilities over a 2-week interval using the short form ranged from .58 for Loyalty to .77 for Religiousness.

Validity

Convergent

Correlations between the short and long forms of each value are reasonably high, ranging from .66 for Intellectualism to .81 for Physical Development and Religiousness. The construct validity of the scales was further investigated by examining the correlations among traits which people "personally admire," consider "the right thing to do," and prescribe as traits that "other people should admire." Correlations between admiration and rightness ranged from .52 for Academic Achievement to .78 for Religiousness (median .69). Correlations between admiring the value oneself and prescribing the value for others were a little lower, ranging from .44 for Intellectualism to .63 for Physical Development (median .54). These lower correlations are consistent with the finding of a sizeable minority of "moral relativists" in the sample: people who indicated acceptance of divergent values in others. Another test of construct validity involved correlating value strength with expected guilt over hypothetical transgressions. Significant correlations (median $r = .26$) were obtained with 9 of the 12 scales. The exceptions were Loyalty, Status, and Creativity.

Known groups validation hypotheses were tested and supported in the case of seven scales: Religiousness (Jesuit seminarians vs. male college students), Independence (college club of nonconformists vs. college students), Physical Development (women's physical education club vs. female college students), Creativity (art majors vs. college students), Academic Achievement (college students with high grades vs. college students with low grades), and Loyalty and Social Skills (students belonging to Greek organizations vs. independent students). Scott also developed 12 behavioral indices representing activities that were relevant to each of the 12 values measured. Eleven of the 12 correlations were significant (median $r = .20$), the exception being Independence.

Discriminant

Intercorrelations among the short form scales ranged from $-.27$ to .51, but Scott noted that in all cases these correlations were less than the internal consistency reliability coefficients of the scales concerned. The scales appeared to be measuring distinct, though correlated, values.

Location

Scott, W. A. (1965). *Values and organizations: A study of fraternities and sororities.* Chicago: Rand McNally.

Results and Comments

The Personal Value Scales have been relatively well validated for use with American college students. Using the scales, Scott (1965) confirmed several hypotheses concerning the importance of value similarity in seeking membership in organizations, in recruitment of potential members, in satisfaction with the group, in popularity within a group, and in friendship patterns. Scott (1960) has also demonstrated that the kinds of international relations that students advocate bear some correspondence to the kinds of interpersonal relations which they admire. The scales have been used more recently with American military cadets (Priest, Fullerton, & Bridge, 1982) to look at changes in values over time, changes interpreted as reflecting the growth of moral relativism (i.e., a pragmatic situation-dependent mode of judgment).

The long form of the Personal Value Scales is clearly the more sophisticated measure. Not only are these scales more reliable, but they are balanced to control for an acquiescence response bias. Assessing values through ratings on 240 items, however, is not economical and is likely to be impossible in many research contexts. Under such circumstances, a choice may have to be made between the 12 short-form scales or a subset of the long-form scales that hold special interest. Further analyses that seek to reduce the 12 scales to a smaller subset may provide a solution to the current dilemma facing researchers interested in their use.

Personal Value Scales

Instructions: Please read over the following statements, and for each one indicate (by a check in the appropriate space) whether it is something you *always admire* in other people, or something you *always dislike*, or something that *depends on the situation* whether you admire it or not.

Examples:

	Always Admire	Depends on Situation	Always Dislike	
1.	_____	_____	_____	Having a strong intellectual curiosity.
2.	_____	_____	_____	Creating beautiful things for the enjoyment of other people.

Intellectualism

Having a keen interest in international, national, and local affairs.　(SL)

Having a strong intellectual curiosity.　(SL)

Developing an appreciation of the fine arts—music, drama, literature, and ballet.　(SL)

Having an active interest in all things scholarly.　(SL)

Having cultural interests.

Striving to gain new knowledge about the world.

Enjoying books, music, art, philosophy, and sciences.

Keeping abreast of current events.

Knowing what's going on in the world of politics.

Keeping up with world news through regular reading or by watching informative programs.

Being an intellectual.　(S)

*Having restricted and narrow interests.

*Having no knowledge of current events.

*Being interested only in one's work.

*Having no opinions about the world situation.

*Knowing only one's specialty.

*Having little interest in arts, theater, music, and other cultural activities.

*Being uninterested in national and world affairs.

*Showing little interest in the finer things of life.

*Ignoring what goes on in the world around one.

*Reading only things that don't pose any intellectual challenge.

Kindness

Being kind to people, even if they do things contrary to one's beliefs. (SL)

Helping another person feel more secure, even if one doesn't like him. (SL)

Helping another achieve his own goals, even if it might interfere with your
own.   (SL)

Turning the other cheek, and forgiving others when they harm you.   (SL)

Being considerate of others' feelings.

Finding ways to help others less fortunate than oneself.

Being utterly selfless in all one's actions.

Having a deep love of all people, whoever they are.

Going out of one's way to help someone new feel at home.

Being concerned about the happiness of other people.

*Looking out for one's own interests first.

*Ridiculing other people.

*Being selfish.

*Ignoring the needs of other people.

*Revenging wrongs that other people have done to one.

*Being unable to empathize with other people.

*Hurting other people's feelings.

*Making jokes at the expense of other people.

*Letting each person go it alone, without offering help.

*Refusing any aid to people who don't deserve it.

Social Skills

Being well mannered and behaving properly in social situations.   (SL)

Dressing and acting in a way that is appropriate to the occasion.   (SL)

Being able to get people to cooperate with one.   (SL)

Being poised, gracious, and charming under all circumstances.   (SL)

Always doing the right thing at the right time.

Being informed in proper etiquette.

Being able to plan social functions smoothly.

Being popular with everyone.

Always behaving properly in public.

Being concerned about what kind of impression one makes on others.

Being able to get along with all kinds of people, whether or not they are
worthwhile.   (S)

Being the person in the group who is the most popular with the opposite sex.
                                                                       (S)

*Being a social isolate.

*Dressing sloppily.

*Displaying unpleasant personal habits in public.

* Interrupting others while they are talking.

* Constantly making social blunders.

* Talking constantly and attracting attention to oneself.

* Having bad manners.

* Being discourteous.

* Being unable to act in a way that will please others.

* Being ignorant of the rules of proper behavior.

Loyalty

Defending the honor of one's group whenever it is unfairly criticized.   (SL)

Working hard to improve the prestige and status of one's groups.   (SL)

Helping organize group activities.   (SL)

Attending all meetings of one's groups.

Upholding the honor of one's group.

Supporting all activities of one's organizations.

Doing more than one's share of the group task.

Performing unpleasant tasks, if these are required by one's group.

Remembering one's group loyalties at all times.

Taking an active part in all group affairs.

Treating an attack on one's group like an attack on oneself.   (S)

Concealing from outsiders most of one's dislikes and disagreements with fellow members of the group.   (S)

Doing all one can to build up the prestige of the group.   (S)

* Betraying one's group to outsiders.

* Letting other people do all the work for the group, and not getting involved oneself.

* Letting people get away with unfair criticism of one's group.

* Being unconcerned with what other people think about one's group.

* Being uncooperative.

* Failing to support group functions.

* Paying little attention to what the members of one's group think.

* Criticizing one's own group in public.

* Getting by with as little involvement in organizations as possible.

* Not taking one's group memberships seriously.

Academic Achievement (Grades)

Studying hard to get good grades in school.   (SL)

Working hard to achieve academic honors.   (SL)

Trying hard to understand difficult lectures and textbooks.

Striving to get the top grade-point average in the group.   (SL)

Studying constantly in order to become a well-educated person.   (SL)

Being studious.

Getting the top grade on a test.

Treating one's studies as the most important thing in college life.

Doing well in school.

Priding oneself on good grades.

*Being content with a "gentlemanly C" grade.

*Making fun of academic grinds.

*Being satisfied with poor grades.

*Priding oneself on being able to get by in school with little work.

*Not doing well in one's coursework.

*Not letting studies interfere with one's college life.

*Doing one's best to avoid working hard in a course.

*Being proud of poor grades.

*Paying no attention to lectures and textbooks that are difficult.

*Taking snap courses that don't require any work.

Physical Development

Being graceful and well coordinated in physical movements.   (SL)

Taking good care of one's physical self, so that one is always healthy.   (SL)

Being good in some form of sport.   (SL)

Developing physical strength and agility.   (SL)

Developing an attractive body that others will admire.   (SL)

Having a good figure or physique.

Having good muscular coordination.

Being a well-developed, outdoors type who enjoys physical activity.

Keeping in good physical shape.

Exercising regularly.

*Being physically weak and puny.

*Being an indoor type, and avoiding outdoor activities.

*Being poorly proportioned physically.

*Being uninterested in sports.

*Being listless and uninterested in strenuous activity.

*Being awkward in bearing and walk.

*Being unable to do anything that requires physical effort.

*Being unskilled in any form of athletics.

*Ignoring one's own physical condition.

*Avoiding any form of exercise.

Status

Being respected by people who are themselves worthwhile.   (SL)

Gaining recognition for one's achievements.   (SL)

Being in a position to direct and mold others' lives. (SL)

Making sure that one is respected.

Doing what one is told.

Being in a position to command respect from others.

Having all the respect that one is entitled to.

Being dignified in bearing and manner.

Being looked up to by others.

Enjoying great prestige in the community.

Having the ability to lead others. (S)

Showing great leadership qualities. (S)

* Acting beneath one's dignity.

* Not being able to do anything better than other people.

* Not being recognized for one's true worth.

* Being in a subordinate position.

* Having little effect on other people's actions.

* Being unable to exert any influence on things around one.

* Failing to develop contacts that could improve one's position.

* Being content with an inferior position all one's life.

* Associating with worthless people.

* Not taking pride in one's achievements.

Honesty

Never cheating or having anything to do with cheating situations, even for a friend. (SL)

Always telling the truth, even though it may hurt oneself or others. (SL)

Never telling a lie, even though to do so would make the situation more comfortable. (SL)

Sticking up for the truth under all circumstances.

Always representing one's own true thoughts and feelings honestly.

Speaking one's mind truthfully, without regard for the consequences.

Testifying against friends, if need be, in order that the truth be known.

Presenting oneself completely and honestly, even if it is unnecessary to do so.

Going out of one's way to bring dishonest people to justice.

Volunteering information concerning wrongdoing, even if friends are involved.

* Helping a close friend get by a tight situation, even though one may have to stretch the truth a bit to do it. (SL)

* Taking things that don't belong to one.

* Telling white lies.

* Deceiving others.

*Using others' property without asking permission.
*Telling falsehoods in order to help other people.
*Helping a friend through an examination.
*Using a false ID card to get into restricted places.
*Stealing when necessary.
*Being dishonest in harmless ways.

Religiousness

Being devout in one's religious faith.   (SL)
Always living one's religion in his daily life.   (SL)
Always attending religious services regularly and faithfully.   (SL)
Avoiding the physical pleasures that are prohibited in the Bible.   (SL)
Encouraging others to attend services and lead religious lives.   (SL)
Saying one's prayers regularly.
Seeking comfort in the Bible in time of need.
Adhering to the doctrines of one's religion.
Having an inner communication with the Supreme Being.
Having faith in a Being greater than man.
*Being an atheist.
*Denying the existence of God.
*Paying little attention to religious matters.
*Treating man, rather than God, as the measure of all things.
*Abstaining from trivial religious rituals.
*Not falling for religious mythology.
*Taking a skeptical attitude toward religious teachings.
*Seeking scientific explanations of religious miracles.
*Treating the Bible only as an historical or literary work.
*Regarding religions as crutches for the primitive peoples of the world.

Self-Control

Practicing self-control.   (SL)
Replying to anger with gentleness.   (SL)
Never losing one's temper, no matter what the reason.   (SL)
Not expressing anger, even when one has a reason for doing so.   (SL)
Suppressing hostility.
Keeping one's feelings hidden from others.
Suppressing the urge to speak hastily in anger.
Hiding one's feelings of frustration from other people.
Keeping one's hostile feelings to himself.
Not getting upset when things go wrong.

Always being patient with people.   (S)

*Losing one's temper easily.

*Showing one's feelings readily.

*Telling people off when they offend one.

*Expressing one's anger openly and directly when provoked.

*Getting upset when things don't go well.

*Letting others see how one really feels.

*Letting off steam when one is frustrated.

*Swearing when one is angry.

*Becoming so angry that other people know about it.

*Letting people know when one is annoyed with them.

Creativity (Originality)

Being able to create beautiful and artistic objects.   (SL)

Developing new and different ways of doing things.   (SL)

Constantly developing new ways of approaching life.   (SL)

Inventing gadgets for the fun of it.   (SL)

Trying out new ideas.

Being original in one's thoughts and ways of looking at things.

Always looking for new roads to travel.

Doing unusual things.

Creating unusual works of art.

Being an innovator.

Creating beautiful things for the enjoyment of other people.   (S)

Devoting one's entire energy to the development of new theories.   (S)

*Doing routine things all the time.

*Not having any new ideas.

*Always doing things in the same way.

*Enjoying a routine, patterned life.

*Doing things the same way that other people do them.

*Abiding by traditional ways of doing things.

*Repeating the ideas of others, without any innovation.

*Working according to a set schedule that doesn't vary from day to day.

*Painting or composing or writing in a traditional style.

*Keeping one's life from changing very much.

Independence

Being a freethinking person, who doesn't care what others think of his opinions.

Being outspoken and frank in expressing one's likes and dislikes.   (SL)

Being independent.

Standing up for what one thinks right, regardless of what others think.

Going one's own way as he pleases.

Being a nonconformist.

Being different from other people.

Encouraging other people to act as they please.

Thinking and acting freely, without social restraints.   (SL)

Living one's own life, independent of others.

Being independent, original, nonconformist, different from other people. (S)

*Conforming to the requirements of any situation and doing what is expected
of one.   (SL)

*Going along with the crowd.

*Acting in such a way as to gain the approval of others.

*Keeping one's opinions to himself when they differ from the group's.

*Being careful not to express an idea that might be contrary to what other
people believe.

*Always basing one's behavior on the recognition that he is dependent on
other people.

*Acting so as to fit in with other people's way of doing things.

*Always checking on whether or not one's intended actions would be accept-
able to other people.

*Never acting so as to violate social conventions.

*Suppressing one's desire to be unique and different.

*Working and living in harmony with other people.   (S)

*, Reverse-scored. Note: Items with SL in the right margin were included in both short and
long versions of the instrument. Items with S were included in the short but not the long version. All
other items appeared only in the long version.

Survey of Interpersonal Values (SIV)

(Gordon, 1960)

Variable

This instrument measures the relative importance of six values (support, conformity, recognition, independence, benevolence, and leadership) associated with the way in which people relate to one another.

Description

A factor analysis of 210 items representing 10 constructs selected from the needs, interests, and values literature led to the identification of seven interpersonal values. One of these constructs, aggression, was eliminated in the development of the final instrument because of the relative unpopularity of its items.

The SIV is made up of 30 sets of three statements, with each statement representing a different value dimension. The respondent's task is to select the statements that are most important and least important to him/herself within each triad. For each scale, a response of most important is given a score of 2, no response a score of 1, and least important a score of 0. Scale scores are obtained by summation over the 15 statements representing that value and range maximally from 0 to 30. The instrument is self-administered and should take approximately 15 minutes for completion.

Sample

The instrument has been used with large samples (n of 2667–3941) of American high school students and college students and with somewhat smaller samples from the military, the Peace Corps, a wide range of occupational groups, clinical groups, and foreign students. Norms are provided by the authors in the test manual and are based on ninth grade, high school, junior college and college student samples and a general population sample. Descriptive statistics are provided for other groups within the population as well.

Reliability

Internal Consistency

Coefficients based on a high school student sample and a college student sample ranged from .71 (Recognition) to .86 (Conformity, Independence, and Benevolence) (median = .82).

Test–Retest

Scale reliability coefficients are reported for five different samples with varying time intervals. For a 10-day interval, the reliability coefficients ranged from .78 for Recognition to .89 for Independence (median = .84). For longer test–retest intervals of 12 weeks–1 year, the coefficients ranged from .55 (Recognition and Leadership) to .82 (Independence) (median = .70).

Validity

Convergent

A Q-sort with the 90 value statements produced results that were very similar to those obtained with the SIV. Correlations ranged from .84 for Support to .92 for Leadership (median = .88). Gordon (1960) also claimed validity for the SIV on the basis of its interpretable correlations with the Allport–Vernon–Lindzey Study of Values and with scales that measure personality, needs, and work orientations. The scales have been linked with self-judgments about values, with peer ratings, and with expert ratings of group behavior. Other validity data have come from the differentiation of occupational groups and of supervisors and subordinates in various work roles. The reader is referred to the SIV manual for further details of convergent validity.

Discriminant

The scales intercorrelate negatively with each other as expected, given the forced-choice format, the exception being Recognition and Support. Across three samples, these measures were consistently positively correlated. Interscale correlations, however, were notably lower than the internal consistency coefficients, suggesting that the scales were measuring distinct constructs. Gordon also correlated the SIV with a battery of ability measures and reported little overlap in these domains. Four of the six scales, however, were found to have low but significant correlations with the Marlowe–Crowne Social Desirability Scale.

Location

Gordon, L. V. (1960). *Survey of interpersonal values*. Chicago: Science Research Associates (155 North Wacker Drive, 60606-1780).

Results and Comments

The SIV has been used by the author as well as other researchers in a wide variety of contexts: in the workplace (e.g., Matsui, 1978; Morrison, 1977), with prisoners (e.g., Bassett, Schellman, Kohaut, & Gayton, 1977), in non-Western cultures (e.g., Finlay, Simon, & Wilson, 1974; Matsui, 1978), in the educational domain (e.g., Knight, White, & Taff, 1972; McAvin & Gordon, 1981; Rootman, 1972), and in the analysis of social attitudes and political behavior (e.g., Finlay *et al.*, 1974; Gordon, 1972b, 1972c). Furthermore, data provided on the reliability and validity of the instrument is extensive (see SIV Manual).

Nevertheless, the instrument is not without weaknesses. Apart from the ipsative nature of the data, the SIV suffers from ambiguity in what is being measured. It is not clear that the SIV measures conceptions of the desirable. Strong correlations of the value scales with measures of needs suggest that Gordon may not be differentiating these two concepts adequately. Values should refer to what one ought to do and not to what one needs or wants to do.

Gordon (1967) has developed another instrument called the Survey of Personal Values. Once again six values are measured, using the same procedure as in the SIV. The values are (1) practical mindedness, (2) achievement, (3) variety, (4) decisiveness, (5) orderliness, and (6) goal orientation. These scales have not been reviewed in this chapter, however, because they bear a stronger resemblance to personality traits than to values.

Survey of Interpersonal Values

Instructions: In this booklet are statements representing things that people consider to be important to their way of life. These statements are grouped into sets of three. This is what you are asked to do: Examine each set. Within each set, find the ONE STATEMENT of the three which represents what you consider to be *most important* to you. Blacken the space beside that statement in the column headed M (for *most*). Next, examine the remaining two statements in the set. Decide which *one* of these statements represents what you consider to be *least important* to you. Blacken the space beside that statement in the column headed L (for *least*).

For every set you will mark *one statement* as representing what is *most important* to you, one statement as representing what is *least important* to you, and you will leave *one statement unmarked*.

Sample Items	M	L
1. a. To be in a position of not having to follow orders	[ ]	[ ]
b. To follow rules and regulations closely	[ ]	[ ]
c. To have people notice what I do	[ ]	[ ]
2. a. To be able to do pretty much as I please	[ ]	[ ]
b. To be in charge of some important project	[ ]	[ ]
c. To work for the good of other people	[ ]	[ ]

Moral Behavior Scale

(Crissman, 1942; Rettig & Pasamanick, 1959)

Variable

A list of ethically disputable or "morally prohibited" activities are rated by respondents in terms of their rightness or wrongness.

Description

Fifty behaviors are presented in a self-administered questionnaire, the vast majority of items being expressed in a proscriptive form (i.e., ought not to). Each statement is rated in terms of its rightness or wrongness from 1 ("least wrong" or "not wrong at all") to 10 ("most wrong" or "wrongest possible"). "In-between numbers" are used for "in-between degrees of wrongness."

    The scale has been scored in a variety of ways. Individual items have been used for the purposes of data analysis, as has the mean over all 50 items and the means for a number of subscales. The subscales vary across populations (cf. Gorsuch & Smith, 1972; Rettig, 1966; Rettig & Pasamanick, 1959, 1960, 1961, 1962, 1963).

Sample

The scale has been used with large samples of male and female college students, alumni, blue collar and white collar workers, three generations of the Kibbutz and the Moshava, Korean college students, and priests and teachers of moral theology.

Reliability

Internal Consistency

Kuder–Richardson reliability coefficients have been reported by Rettig and Pasamanick (1959) across a number of samples. The total scale produced a coefficient of .93 among college students, .95 among alumni, .96 among blue collar workers, and .93 among white collar workers. The modified Hebrew translation had somewhat lower reliabilities ranging from .84 to .89. Such coefficients, however, do not necessarily imply a notable degree of internal consistency. High reliabilities may result from the large number of items (50) in the scale.

Test–Retest

No reliability coefficients were encountered.

Validity

Convergent

Rettig (1966) cited validation for the religious items in the scale through a comparison of various groups (e.g., priests and teachers of moral theology at the Vatican, nonbelieving Korean students) but did not provide further details.

Discriminant

Most attention has been directed to the factorial structure of the scale across samples of students, alumni, different socioeconomic groups, and different cultural groups. Both similarities and differences are observed in these solutions. Questions about the scoring of the instrument have been raised by Gorsuch and Smith (1972), who identified a different factor structure by using new rotational procedures on the data collected by Rettig and Pasamanick (1959, 1960, 1961, 1962, 1963).

Location

Rettig, S., & Pasamanick, B. (1959). Changes in moral values among college students: A factorial study. *American Sociological Review, 24,* 856–863.

Results and Comments

The subscales proposed by Gorsuch and Smith (1972) have been examined for their convergent and discriminant validity in a sample of students and their parents ($n = 585$). Internal consistency reliabilities across three data sets were reported for five subscales that were not highly correlated with each other.

1. Misrepresentation (Coefficient $\alpha = .88-.90$)
   (Items 24, 27, 34, 41, 42, 43, 45)
2. Irreligious Hedonism (Coefficient $\alpha = .76-.80$)
   (Items 23, 25, 31, 39, 49)
3. Sexual Misbehavior (Coefficient $\alpha = .59-.65$)
   (Items 3, 16, 48)
4. Nonphilanthropic Behavior (Coefficient $\alpha = .62-.70$)
   (Items 20, 21, 35)
5. Nonconservative Marriage Pattern (Coefficient $\alpha = .69-.70$)
   (Items 32, 33)

Gorsuch and Smith also considered two single items to be worthy of consideration along with these scales: Item 40 and Item 46.

The scale has proven most popular among researchers who wish to document and analyze changes in moral values across time and across generations. For this purpose, stability in the item set is important. Nevertheless, sexist language and references to "bootleg liquor under prohibition law" and "girls smoking cigarettes" date the instrument and possibly reduce the seriousness with which respondents complete the task. In addition, Gorsuch and Smith (1972) note an important omission in the instrument: No items are included concerned with either drugs or prejudice.

Moral Behavior Scale

This questionnaire presents fifty acts or situations which you are to evaluate in terms of 'rightness' or 'wrongness' ranging from one to ten. Circle the one if the item seems least wrong or not wrong at all, and the ten if the item is judged most wrong or 'wrongest' possible. Use the in-between numbers for in-between degrees of wrongness; the higher the number, the more wrong it becomes.

1. Killing a person in defense of one's own life.

1	2	3	4	5	6	7	8	9	10
LEAST WRONG									MOST WRONG

2. Kidnapping and holding a child for ransom.
3. Having sex relations while unmarried.
4. Forging a check.
5. Habitually failing to keep promises.
6. Girls smoking cigarettes.
7. An industry maintaining working conditions for its workers known to be detrimental to their health.
8. A doctor allowing a badly deformed baby to die when he could save its life but not cure its deformity.
9. A legislator, for a financial consideration, using his influence to secure the passage of a law known to be contrary to public interest.
10. Testifying falsely in court when under oath.
11. Betting on horse races.
12. A nation dealing unjustly with a weaker nation over which it has power.
13. A jury freeing a father who has killed a man for rape against his young daughter.
14. Living beyond one's means in order to possess luxuries enjoyed by friends and associates.
15. Bootlegging under prohibition law.
16. Having illicit sex relations after marriage.
17. Driving an automobile while drunk but without accident.
18. A prosperous industry paying workers less than a living wage.
19. Holding up and robbing a person.
20. Not giving to charity when able.
21. Not taking the trouble to vote at primaries and elections.
22. A strong commercial concern selling below cost to crowd out a weaker competitor.
23. Falsifying about a child's age to secure reduced fare.
24. A student who is allowed to grade his own paper reporting a higher grade than the one earned.

25. Not giving to support religion when able.
26. Keeping over-change given by a clerk in mistake.
27. Copying from another's paper in a school examination.
28. Speeding away after one's car knocks down a pedestrian.
29. Charging interest above a fair rate when lending money.
30. Falsifying a federal income tax return.
31. Buying bootleg liquor under prohibition law.
32. Married persons using birth-control devices.
33. Seeking divorce because of incompatibility when both parties agree to separate (assuming no children).
34. Depositing more than one ballot in an election in order to aid a favorite candidate.
35. Living on inherited wealth without attempting to render service to others.
36. Taking one's own life (assuming no near relatives or dependents).
37. Using profane or blasphemous speech.
38. Being habitually cross or disagreeable to members of one's own family.
39. Seeking amusement on Sunday instead of going to church.
40. Refusing to bear arms in a war one believes to be unjust.
41. Advertising a medicine to cure a disease known to be incurable by such a remedy.
42. Misrepresenting the value of an investment in order to induce credulous persons to invest.
43. Taking money for one's vote in an election.
44. Newspapers treating crime news so as to make hoodlums and gangsters appear heroic.
45. A man having a vacant building he cannot rent sets it on fire to collect insurance.
46. Nations at war using poison gas on the homes and cities of its enemy behind the lines.
47. Slipping out secretly and going among people when one's home is under quarantine for a contagious disease.
48. A man deserting a girl whom he has got into trouble without himself taking responsibility.
49. Disbelieving in God.
50. A man not marrying a girl he loves because she is markedly his inferior socially and in education.

The Morally Debatable Behaviors Scales

(Harding & Phillips, 1986)

Variable

This instrument assesses the justifiability of behaviors reflecting contemporary moral issues which adults confront in their lives or have an opinion about.

Description

Twenty-two morally debatable behaviors make up this inventory, but the authors do not provide details of how they sampled either behaviors or issues from the domain of enquiry. Each item is rated on a 10-point scale ranging from 1, meaning the behavior is "never justified," to 10, meaning the behavior is "always justified." Harding and Phillips included the questions as part of a lengthy interview, and the morally debatable behaviors were reverse-ordered for alternate interviewers to overcome order effects.

The inventory measures three aspects of moral behavior: (1) personal–sexual morality (nine items) focusing on matters of life and death as well as sexual relations, (2) self-interest morality (eight items), which brings together items concerned with personal integrity and honesty, and (3) legal–illegal morality (eight items), which is defined by behaviors which are formally proscribed by law. Three items are common to self-interest and legal–illegal morality. The authors also calculate an average score over all 22 items for each respondent.

Sample

The instrument has been administered to very large random and quota samples in 10 European countries. Norms are available for item and scale scores in Denmark, Holland, Eire, Northern Ireland, Great Britain, Belgium, West Germany, France, Italy, and Spain.

Reliability

Neither test–retest nor internal consistency coefficients were encountered.

Validity

Convergent

Harding and Phillips examined the relationship of the scales to other value measures that they constructed and to the social demographic characteristics of the population under investigation. Those who showed greatest tolerance in moral outlook were the young, the more highly educated, those who were more left-wing politically, and those who described themselves as either nonreligious or atheist. While these were not direct tests of the validity of the scales, the findings are consistent and interpretable, and in this sense supportive of the validity of the measure.

Discriminant

The three morality scales emerged repeatedly in factor analyses of data sets from different countries. Furthermore, the scales showed different patterns of relationships with the social demographic variables. Higher levels of education and income were associated with greater tolerance of issues represented in the personal–sexual dimension, but this pattern was not reflected so clearly with items making up the other two dimensions.

Location

Harding, B., & Phillips, D. (1986). *Contrasting values in Western Europe: Unity, diversity and change.* London: Macmillan.

Results and Comments

The instrument is relatively new and was developed specifically for use in the European Value Systems Study. Although sufficient time has not elapsed for it to be used in a variety of research contexts, the authors have collected a considerable amount of data on the scale in different countries and the normative data presented are superior to those provided for most other scales reviewed in this chapter.

Harding and Phillips tap moral issues that are relevant to the 1980s, providing a more updated list of value-related behaviors than Crissman (1942). Users should be sensitive, however, to possible omissions depending on the social context in which the scales are to be administered. Further research providing information on reliability and validity should enhance the attractiveness of this instrument.

Of note in relation to the issue of scale validity is the work of Truhon, McKinney, and Hotch (1980), who suggest that moral behaviors are structured differently for women and men, with greater differentiation in the former than the latter. Obtaining comparable measures of moral values for men and women may be more difficult than has been assumed previously.

Morally Debatable Behaviors Scale

Please tell me for each of the following statements whether you think it can always be justified, never be justified, or something in between. (Show respondent card with justification scale on it. Read out statements, reversing order for alternate respondents. Mark an answer for each statement.)

1. Claiming state benefits that you are not entitled to

1	2	3	4	5	6	7	8	9	10
NEVER									ALWAYS

2. Avoiding a fare on public transport
3. Cheating on tax if you have the chance
4. Buying something you knew was stolen
5. Taking and driving away a car belonging to someone else (Joyriding)
6. Taking the drug marijuana or hashish
7. Keeping money that you have found
8. Lying in your own interest
9. Married men or women having an affair
10. Sex under the legal age of consent
11. Someone accepting a bribe in the course of their duties
12. Homosexuality
13. Prostitution
14. Abortion
15. Divorce
16. Fighting with the police

17. Euthanasia (terminating the life of the incurably sick)
18. Suicide
19. Failing to report damage you've done accidentally to a parked vehicle
20. Threatening workers who refuse to join a strike
21. Killing in self-defence
22. Political assassination

Future Research Directions

Rokeach's conceptualization of values has done much to bridge the gap between studies that in the past have appeared to have little in common. Progress in conceptual clarity, however, has not always been accompanied by methodological sophistication. The assumption that single items are adequate measures when the concepts being assessed are as abstract as values is likely to create serious problems both for the population being studied and the researcher interpreting the results. The findings emerging from single-item measures could be regarded with greater confidence if they were buttressed by multi-item scales.

Diverse specific multi-item measures are available to be used in conjunction with broad based single-item indices. Less satisfactory is the diversity of criteria incorporated into the instructions given to those responding to value scales. The value construct has too frequently been operationalized in a way that is not consistent with conceptions of the desirable. Response criteria that have been used include agreement, importance and liking. In practice, responses on these dimensions may correlate so highly with conceptions of the desirable that they can be considered synonymous. This is an empirical question, however, to which we do not have a satisfactory answer.

A third theme that runs through this review is that instruments cannot be translated and assumed appropriate in other cultures. None of the reviewed measures of values can be regarded truly as cross-cultural instruments. This problem stems not from ignorance of the ideal, but rather from difficulty in achieving or even approximating the ideal. The recent emergence of multinational research teams, each striving to develop measures that are both appropriate within their own culture and comparable across cultures, offers the greatest hope for the future.

Finally, values have always been regarded as important because they are assumed to play a major role in explaining behavior. While the literature provides some support for this assumption (see Rokeach and Feather's work in particular), behavioral prediction from values has often proved disappointing (Braithwaite & Braithwaite, 1981; Hughes, Rao, & Alker, 1976; Pitts & Woodside, 1983). Behavioral prediction may be hindered by reliance on abstract single-item measures. Highly abstract measures run the risk of being too far removed from behavior while single-item measures may lack reliability and validity.

Alternatively, closer scrutiny of our theoretical formulations may be warranted. Little attention has been directed either to the situations in which values are most likely to influence behavior or to the individuals for whom value–behavior consistency is most likely to occur. Like traits, values may at best explain what some of the people do some of the time. Our knowledge of the contexts in which principles conflict with needs, desires, and environmental demands is limited, as is our appreciation of how different individuals resolve such conflicts. Therefore, it may be timely for value researchers to change tack, take stock of research findings, and propose a set of parameters to define the circumstances in which values are useful in explaining human behavior.

Bibliography

Adler, F. (1956). The value concept in sociology. *American Journal of Sociology, 62,* 272–279.

Alker, H. A., Rao, V. R., & Hughes, G. D. (1972). Value consistent and expedient decision making. *Proceedings of the 80th Annual Convention,* American Psychological Association, pp. 149–150.

Allport, G. W. (1961). *Pattern and growth in personality.* New York: Holt, Rinehart & Winston.

Allport, G. W., Vernon, P. E., & Lindzey, G. (1960). *Study of values. Manual and test booklet* (3rd ed.). Boston: Houghton Mifflin.

Alwin, D. F., & Krosnick, J. A. (1985). The measurement of values in surveys: A comparison of ratings and rankings. *Public Opinion Quarterly, 49,* 535–552.

Bales, R. F. (1970). *Personality and interpersonal behavior.* New York: Holt, Rinehart & Winston.

Bales, R., & Couch, A. (1969). The value profile: A factor analytic study of value statements. *Sociological Inquiry, 39,* 3–17.

Bassett, J. E., Schellman, G. C., Kohaut, S. M., & Gayton, W. F. (1977). Norms for prisoners and reliability of two value surveys. *Psychological Reports, 41,* 383–386.

Beech, R. P., & Schoeppe, A. (1974). Development of value systems in adolescents. *Developmental Psychology, 10,* 644–656.

Bell, W., & Robinson, R. V. (1978). An index of evaluated equality: Measuring conceptions of social justice in England and the United States. In R. F. Tomason (Ed.), *Comparative studies in sociology: An annual compilation of research* (Vol. 1, pp. 235–270). Greenwich, CT: JAI Press.

Bem, D. J. (1970). *Beliefs, attitudes and human affairs.* Belmont, CA: Brooks/Cole.

Bhatt, A. K., & Fairchild, H. H. (1984). Values of convergence of Indian students in the United States. *Psychological Reports, 55,* 446.

Billig, M., & Cochrane, R. (1979). Values of British political extremists and potential extremists: A discriminant analysis. *European Journal of Social Psychology, 9,* 205–222.

Bishop, G. F., Barclay, A. M., & Rokeach, M. (1972). Presidential preferences and freedom—equality value patterns in the 1968 American campaign. *Journal of Social Psychology, 88,* 207–212.

Bolt, M. (1978). The Rokeach Value Survey: Preferred or preferable. *Perceptual and Motor Skills, 47,* 322.

Braithwaite, J. B., & Braithwaite, V. A. (1981). Delinquency and the question of values. *International Journal of Offender Therapy and Comparative Criminology, 23,* 129–134.

Braithwaite, V. A. (1979). *Exploring value structure: An empirical investigation.* Unpublished doctoral dissertation, University of Queensland.

Braithwaite, V. A. (1982). The structure of social values: Validation of Rokeach's two value model. *British Journal of Social Psychology, 21,* 203–211.

Braithwaite, V. A., & Law, H. G. (1985). Structure of human values: Testing the adequacy of the Rokeach Value Survey. *Journal of Personality and Social Psychology, 49,* 250–263.

Brogden, H. E. (1952). The primary personal values measured by the Allport–Vernon test, A Study of Values. *Psychological Monographs, 66,* No. 348.

Brown, N. W., & Lawson, R. (1980). Values in parochial and public schools: Alike or different? *Psychological Reports, 47,* 279–282.

Caird, H. D. (1987). *Measuring personal values: An approach to the study of individuals.* Unpublished doctoral dissertation, University of Queensland.

Cantril, H., & Allport, G. W. (1933). Recent applications of the Study of Values. *Journal of Abnormal and Social Psychology, 28,* 259–273.

Carlson, E. R. (1956). Attitude change through modification of attitude structure. *Journal of Abnormal and Social Psychology,* **52,** 256–261.

Cho, J. H., & Gilgen, A. R. (1980). Performance of Korean medical and nursing students on the East–West Questionnaire. *Psychological Reports,* **47,** 1093–1094.

Christenson, J. A., Hougland, J. G., Gage, B. A., & Hoa, L. V. (1984). Value orientations of organized religious groups. *Sociology and Social Research,* **68,** 194–207.

Clare, D. A., & Cooper, D. R. (1983). Ethnicity and personal values among Nigerian business students. *Journal of Social Psychology,* **119,** 137–138.

Cochrane, R. (1971). Research and methodology: The structure of value systems in male and female prisoners. *British Journal of Criminology,* **11,** 73–79.

Cochrane, R., Billig, M., & Hogg, M. (1979). Politics and values in Britain: A test of Rokeach's two-value model. *British Journal of Social and Clinical Psychology,* **18,** 159–167.

Compton, W. C. (1983). On the validity of the East–West Questionnaire. *Psychological Reports,* **52,** 117–118.

Constantinople, A. (1967). Perceived instrumentality of the college as a measure of attitudes toward college. *Journal of Personality and Social Psychology,* **5,** 196–201.

Crissman, P. (1942). Temporal changes and sexual difference in moral judgments. *Journal of Social Psychology,* **16,** 29–38.

Dempsey, P., & Dukes, W. (1966). Judging complex value stimuli: An examination and revision of Morris's "Paths of Life." *Educational and Psychological Measurement,* **26,** 871–882.

Duffy, E. (1940). A critical review of investigations employing the Allport–Vernon Study of Values and other tests of evaluative attitudes. *Psychological Bulletin,* **37,** 597–612.

Duffy, E., & Crissy, W. J. E. (1940). Evaluative attitudes as related to vocational interests and academic achievement. *Journal of Abnormal and Social Psychology,* **35,** 226–245.

Dukes, W. F. (1955). Psychological studies of values. *Psychological Bulletin,* **52,** 24–50.

England, G. W. (1967). Personal value systems of American managers. *Academy of Management Journal,* **10,** 53–68.

Ewell, A. H., Jr. (1954). *The relationship between the rigidity of moral values and the severity of functional psychological illness: A study with war veterans of one religious group.* Unpublished doctoral dissertation, New York University.

Fallding, H. (1965). A proposal for the empirical study of values. *American Sociological Review,* **30,** 223–233.

Feather, N. T. (1970a). Educational choice and student attitudes in relation to terminal and instrumental values. *Australian Journal of Psychology,* **22,** 127–144.

Feather, N. T. (1970b). Value systems in state and church schools. *Australian Journal of Psychology,* **22,** 299–313.

Feather, N. T. (1971). Similarity of value systems as a determinant of educational choice at university level. *Australian Journal of Psychology,* **23,** 201–211.

Feather, N. T. (1973). The measurement of values: Effects of different assessment procedures. *Australian Journal of Psychology,* **25,** 221–231.

Feather, N. T. (1975a). Values and income level. *Australian Journal of Psychology,* **27,** 23–29.

Feather, N. T. (1975b). *Values in education and society.* New York: Free Press.

Feather, N. T. (1977). Value importance, conservatism and age. *European Journal of Social Psychology,* **7,** 241–245.

Feather, N. T. (1979a). Human values and the work situation: Two studies. *Australian Psychologist,* **14,** 131–141.

Feather, N. T. (1979b). Value correlates of conservatism. *Journal of Personality and Social Psychology,* **37,** 1617–1630.

Feather, N. T. (1980). Value systems and social interaction: A field study in a newly independent nation. *Journal of Applied Social Psychology,* **10,** 1–19.

Feather, N. T. (1982). Reasons for entering medical school in relation to value priorities and sex of student. *Journal of Occupational Psychology,* **55,** 119–128.

Feather, N. T. (1984a). Protestant ethic, conservatism, and values. *Journal of Personality and Social Psychology,* **46,** 1132–1141.

Feather, N. T. (1984b). Masculinity, femininity, psychological androgyny, and the structure of values. *Journal of Personality and Social Psychology*, **47**, 604–620.

Feather, N. T. (1985). Attitudes, values, and attributions: Explanations of unemployment. *Journal of Personality and Social Psychology*, **48**, 876–889.

Feather, N. T. (1986). Cross-cultural studies with the Rokeach Value Survey: The Flinders program of research on values. *Australian Journal of Psychology*, **38**, 269–283.

Feather, N. T., & Cross, D. G. (1975). Value systems and delinquency: Parental and generational discrepancies in value systems for delinquent and non-delinquent boys. *British Journal of Social and Clinical Psychology*, **14**, 117–129.

Feather, N. T., & Hutton, M. A. (1973). Value systems of students in Papua New Guinea and Australia. *International Journal of Psychology*, **9**, 91–104.

Feather, N. T., & Peay, E. R. (1975). The structure of terminal and instrumental values: Dimensions and clusters. *Australian Journal of Psychology*, **27**, 151–164.

Feifel, H., & Nagy, V. T. (1981). Another look at fear of death. *Journal of Consulting and Clinical Psychology*, **49**, 278–286.

Finlay, D. J., Simon, D. W., & Wilson, L. A., II (1974). The concept of left and right in cross-national research. *Comparative Political Studies*, **7**, 209–221.

Fishbein, M., & Ajzen, I. (1975). *Belief, attitude, intention and behavior: An introduction to theory and research*. Reading, MA: Addison-Wesley.

Fitzsimmons, G. W., Macnab, D., & Casserly, C. (1985). *Technical Manual for the Life Roles Inventory Values Scale and the Salience Inventory*. Edmonton, Alberta, Canada: PsiCan Consulting Limited.

Furnham, A. F. (1984). Value systems and anomie in three cultures. *International Journal of Psychology*, **19**, 565–579.

Gay, E. G., Weiss, D. J., Hendel, D. D., Dawis, R. V., & Lofquist, L. H. (1971). *Manual for the Minnesota Importance Questionnaire*. Minnesota Studies in Vocational Rehabilitation, 28.

Gilgen, A. R., & Cho, J. H. (1979a). Questionnaire to measure eastern and western thought. *Psychological Reports*, **44**, 835–841.

Gilgen, A. R., & Cho, J. H. (1979b). Performance of Eastern- and Western-oriented college students on the Value Survey and Ways of Life Scale. *Psychological Reports*, **45**, 263–268.

Gordon, L. V. (1960). *Survey of interpersonal values*. Chicago: Science Research Associates.

Gordon, L. V. (1967) *Survey of personal values*. Chicago: Science Research Associates.

Gordon, L. V. (1972a). A typological assessment of "A Study of Values" by Q-methodology. *Journal of Social Psychology*, **86**, 55–67.

Gordon, L. V. (1972b). Value correlates of student attitudes on social issues: A multinational study. *Journal of Applied Psychology*, **56**, 305–311.

Gordon, L. V. (1972c). The image of political candidates: Values and voter preferences. *Journal of Applied Psychology*, **56**, 382–387.

Gorlow, L., & Barocas, R. (1965). Value preferences and interpersonal behavior. *Journal of Social Psychology*, **66**, 271–80.

Gorlow, L., & Noll, G. A. (1967). A study of empirically derived values. *Journal of Social Psychology*, **73**, 261–269.

Gorsuch, R. L. (1970). Rokeach's approach to value systems and social compassion. *Review of Religious Research*, **11**, 139–143.

Gorsuch, R. L., & McFarland, S. G. (1972). Single vs. multiple-item scales for measuring religious values. *Journal for the Scientific Study of Religion*, **11**, 53–64.

Gorsuch, R. L., & Smith, R. A. (1972). Changes in college students' evaluations of moral behavior: 1969 versus 1939, 1949, and 1958. *Journal of Personality and Social Psychology*, **24**, 381–391.

Greenstein, T., & Bennett, R. R. (1974). Order effects in Rokeach's Value Survey. *Journal of Research in Personality*, **8**, 393–396.

Handy, R. (1970). *The measurement of values*. St. Louis, MO: Warren H. Green.

Harding, S., & Phillips, D. (1986). *Contrasting values in Western Europe: Unity, diversity and change*. London: Macmillan.

Hill, C. T., & Stull, D. E. (1981). Sex-differences in effects of social and value similarity in same-sex friendship. *Journal of Personality and Social Psychology, 41,* 488–502.

Hilton, T., & Korn, J. (1964). Measured change in personal values. *Educational and Psychological Measurement, 24,* 609–622.

Hofstede, G. (1980). *Culture's consequences: International differences in work-related values.* Beverly Hills, CA: Sage.

Hogan, R. (1972). Characterological and personality nonprojectives. In O. K. Buros (Ed.), *The seventh mental measurement yearbook* (Vol. 1, pp. 68–389). Highland Park, NJ: Gryphon Press.

Hoge, D. R., & Bender, I. E. (1974). Factors influencing value change among college graduates in adult life. *Journal of Personality and Social Psychology, 29,* 572–585.

Homant, R., & Rokeach, M. (1970). Value for honesty and cheating behavior. *Personality, 1,* 153–162.

Hughes, G. D., Rao, V. R., & Alker, H. A. (1976). The influence of values, information, and decision orders on a public policy decision. *Journal of Applied Social Psychology, 6,* 145–158.

Hui, C. H., & Triandis, H. C. (1985). Measurement in cross-cultural psychology. *Journal of Cross-Cultural Psychology, 16,* 131–152.

Inglehart, R. (1971). The silent revolution in Europe: Intergenerational change in post-industrial societies. *American Political Science Review, 65,* 991–1017.

Inglehart, R. (1977). *The silent revolution.* Princeton, NJ: Princeton Univ. Press.

Joe, V. C., Jones, R. N., & Miller, P. M. (1981). Value pattern of a conservative. *Personality and Individual Differences, 2,* 25–29.

Jones, C. H. (1982). College students' values and presidential preference in the 1980 election. *Psychological Reports, 50,* 886.

Jones, L., & Morris, C. (1956). Relations of temperament to the choice of values. *Journal of Abnormal and Social Psychology, 53,* 346–349.

Jones, R. A., Sensenig, J., & Ashmore, R. D. (1978). Systems of values and their multidimensional representations. *Multivariate Behavioral Research, 13,* 255–270.

Kahl, J. A. (1968). *The measurement of modernism: A study of values in Brazil and Mexico.* Austin: Univ. of Texas Press.

Katz, D., & Stotland, E. (1959). A preliminary statement to a theory of attitude structure and change. In S. Koch (Ed.), *Psychology: A study of a science* (pp. 423–475). New York: McGraw-Hill.

Keats, D. M., & Keats, J. A. (1974). Review of "The nature of human values" by M. Rokeach. *Australian Journal of Psychology, 26,* 164–165.

Kelly, K., Silverman, B. I., & Cochrane, R. (1972). Social desirability and the Rokeach Value Survey. *Journal of Experimental Research in Personality, 6,* 84–87.

Kilmann, R. H. (1975). A scaled-projective measure of interpersonal values. *Journal of Personality Assessment, 39,* 34–40.

Kitwood, T. M., & Smithers, A. G. (1975). Measurement of human values: An appraisal of the work of Milton Rokeach. *Educational Research, 17,* 175–179.

Kluckhohn, C. K. M. (1951). Values and value orientations in the theory of action. In T. Parsons & E. Shils (Eds.), *Toward a general theory of action* (pp. 388–433). Cambridge, MA: Harvard Univ. Press.

Kluckhohn, F. R., & Strodtbeck, F. (1961). *Variations in value orientations.* Evanston, IL: Row, Peterson.

Knight, J. H., White, K. P., & Taff, L. K. (1972). The effect of school desegregation, sex of student, and socioeconomic status on the interpersonal values of southern Negro students. *Journal of Negro Education, 41,* 4–11.

Kohn, M. (1969). *Class and conformity: A study in values.* Homewood, IL: Dorsey Press.

Kristiansen, C. M. (1985). Value correlates of preventative health behavior. *Journal of Personality and Social Psychology, 49,* 748–758.

Lamiell, J. T. (1981). Towards an idiothetic psychology of personality. *American Psychologist, 36,* 276–289.

Levitin, T. (1968). Values. In J. P. Robinson & P. R. Shaver (Eds.), *Measures of social psychological attitudes* (pp. 405–501). Ann Arbor: University of Michigan, Survey Research Center, Institute for Social Research.

Lorr, M., Suziedelis, A., & Tonesk, X. (1973). The structure of values: Conceptions of the desirable. *Journal of Research in Personality*, **7**, 137–147.

Lortie-Lussier, M., Fellers, G. L., & Kleinplatz, P. J. (1986). Value orientations of English, French, and Italian Canadian children: Continuity of the ethnic mosaic? *Journal of Cross-Cultural Psychology*, **17**, 283–299.

Lovejoy, A. O. (1950). Terminal and adjectival values. *Journal of Philosophy*, **47**, 593–608.

Lurie, W. A. (1937). A study of Spranger's value-types by the method of factor analysis. *Journal of Social Psychology*, **8**, 17–37.

Lynn, R. (1974). Review of "The nature of human values" by M. Rokeach. *British Journal of Psychology*, **65**, 453.

Macnab, D., & Fitzsimmons, G. W. (1987). A multitrait–multimethod study of work-related needs, values, and preferences. *Journal of Vocational Behaviour*, **30**, 1–15.

Mahoney, J. (1977). Values and neurosis: A comparison of American and Israeli college students. *Journal of Social Psychology*, **102**, 311–312.

Mahoney, J., & Katz, G. M. (1976). Value structures and orientations to social institutions. *Journal of Psychology*, **93**, 203–211.

Mahoney, J., & Pechura, C. M. (1980). Values and volunteers: Axiology of altruism in a crisis center. *Psychological Reports*, **47**, 1007–1012.

Maslow, A. H. (1962). *Toward a psychology of being*. Englewood Cliffs, NJ: Van Nostrand.

Matsui, T. (1978). Impacts of management styles on the relations between supervisor needs and leadership patterns. *Journal of Applied Psychology*, **63**, 658–661.

McAvin, M. W., & Gordon, L. V. (1981). Attributions of interpersonal values and teaching effectiveness. *Psychological Reports*, **49**, 539–542.

Moore, M. (1975). Rating versus ranking in the Rokeach Value Survey: An Israeli comparison. *European Journal of Social Psychology*, **5**, 405–408.

Moore, M. (1976). A cross-cultural comparison of value systems. *European Journal of Social Psychology*, **6**, 249–254.

Morris, C. W. (1956a). *Paths of life*. New York: Braziller.

Morris, C. W. (1956b). *Varieties of human value*. Chicago: Univ. of Chicago Press.

Morris, C. W., & Jones, L. (1955). Value scales and dimensions. *Journal of Abnormal and Social Psychology*, **51**, 523–535.

Morris, C. W., & Small, L. (1971). Changes in the conceptions of the good life by American college students from 1950 to 1970. *Journal of Personality and Social Psychology*, **20**, 254–260.

Morrison, R. F. (1977). Career adaptivity: The effective adaptation of managers to changing role demands. *Journal of Applied Psychology*, **62**, 549–558.

Mueller, D. J. (1974). A test of the validity of two scales on Rokeach's Value Survey. *Journal of Social Psychology*, **94**, 289–290.

Mukerjee, R. (1965). *The social structure of values*. New Delhi: Chand.

Munson, J. M., & McIntyre, S. H. (1979). Developing practical procedures for the measurement of personal values in cross-cultural marketing. *Journal of Marketing Research*, **16**, 48–52.

Munson, J. M., & Posner, B. Z. (1980). The factorial validity of a modified Rokeach Value Survey for four diverse samples. *Educational and Psychological Measurement*, **40**, 1073–1079.

Nelson, C. (1968). Anchoring to accepted values as a technique for immunizing beliefs against persuasion. *Journal of Personality and Social Psychology*, **9**, 329–334.

Newcomb, T. M., Turner, R. H., & Converse, P. E. (1965). *Social Psychology*. New York: Holt, Rinehart & Winston.

Ng, S. H. (1982). Choosing between the ranking and rating procedures for the comparison of values across cultures. *European Journal of Social Psychology*, **12**, 169–172.

Ostrom, T. M., & Brock, T. C. (1969). Cognitive bonding to central values and resistance to a communication advocating change in policy orientation. *Journal of Experimental Research in Personality*, **4**, 42–50.

Palmer, D. D. (1982). Personal values and priorities of organizational goals. *Psychological Reports,* **51,** 55–62.

Peak, H. (1955). Attitude and motivation. In M. R. Jones (Ed.), *Nebraska symposium on motivation.* Lincoln: Univ. of Nebraska Press.

Pedro, J. D. (1984). Induction into the workplace: The impact of internships. *Journal of Vocational Behavior,* **25,** 80–95.

Penner, L. A., & Anh, T. (1977). A comparison of American and Vietnamese value systems. *Journal of Social Psychology,* **101,** 187–204.

Penner, L. A., Summers, L. S., Brookmire, D. A., & Dertke, M. C. (1976). The lost dollar: Situational and personality determinants of a pro- and antisocial behavior. *Journal of Personality,* **44,** 274–293.

Perloe, S. I. (1967). *The factorial structure of the social values questionnaire.* Unpublished manuscript.

Pirnot, K., & Dustin, R. (1986). A new look at value priorities for homemakers and career women. *Journal of Counseling and Development,* **64,** 432–436.

Pitts, R. E., & Woodside, A. G. (1983). Personal value influences on consumer product class and brand preferences. *Journal of Social Psychology,* **119,** 37–53.

Platt, S. D. (1985). A subculture of parasuicide? *Human Relations,* **38,** 257–297.

Priest, R., Fullerton, T., & Bridge, S. C. (1982). Personality and value changes in West Point cadets. *Armed Forces and Society,* **8,** 629–642.

Pryor, R. G. L. (1979). In search of a concept: Work values. *Vocational Guidance Quarterly,* **27,** 250–258.

Rankin, W. L., & Grube, J. W. (1980). A comparison of ranking and rating procedures for value system measurement. *European Journal of Social Psychology,* **10,** 233–246.

Rawls, J., Harrison, C. W., Rawls, D. J., Hayes, R. L., & Johnson, A. W. (1973). Comparison of Wallace, Nixon and Humphrey supporters along certain demographic, attitudinal, and value-system dimensions. *Psychological Reports,* **32,** 35–39.

Raymond, B., & King, S. (1973). Value systems of volunteer and nonvolunteer subjects. *Psychological Reports,* **32,** 1303–1306.

Rest, J. R. (1972). *Defining Issues Test.* Minneapolis: Moral Research Projects. (Available from 330 Burton Hall, 178 Pillsbury Avenue, University of Minnesota, Minneapolis 55455)

Rettig, S. (1966). Relation of social systems to intergenerational changes in moral attitudes. *Journal of Personality and Social Psychology,* **4,** 409–414.

Rettig, S., & Pasamanick, B. (1959). Changes in moral values among college students: A factorial study. *American Sociological Review,* **24,** 856–863.

Rettig, S., & Pasamanick, B. (1960). Differences in the structure of moral values of students and alumni. *American Sociological Review,* **25,** 550–555.

Rettig, S., & Pasamanick, B. (1961). Moral value structure and social class. *Sociometry,* **24,** 21–35.

Rettig, S., & Pasamanick, B. (1962). Invariance in factor structure of moral value judgments from American and Korean college students. *Sociometry,* **25,** 73–84.

Rettig, S., & Pasamanick, B. (1963). Some observations on the moral ideology of first and second generation collective and non-collective settlers in Israel. *Social Problems,* **11,** 165–178.

Reynolds, T. J., & Jolly, J. P. (1980). Measuring personal values: An evaluation of alternative methods. *Journal of Marketing Research,* **17,** 531–536.

Rokeach, M. (1967). *Value survey.* Sunnyvale, CA: Halgren Tests (873 Persimmon Ave., 94087).

Rokeach, M. (1968). *Beliefs, attitudes and values.* San Francisco: Jossey-Bass.

Rokeach, M. (1969a). Value systems in religion. *Review of Religious Research,* **11,** 3–23.

Rokeach, M. (1969b). Religious values and social compassion. *Review of Religious Research,* **11,** 24–38.

Rokeach, M. (1973). *The nature of human values.* New York: Free Press.

Rokeach, M. (1974). Change and stability in American value systems, 1968–1971. *Public Opinion Quarterly,* **38,** 222–238.

Rokeach, M. (1979). From individual to institutional values: With special reference to the values of science. In M. Rokeach (Ed.), *Understanding human values: Individual and societal* (pp. 47–70). New York: Free Press.

Rokeach, M., Miller, M. G., & Snyder, J. A. (1971). The value gap between police and policed. *Journal of Social Issues,* **27,** 155–171.

Rootman, I. (1972). Voluntary withdrawal from a total adult socializing organization: A model. *Sociology of Education,* **45,** 258–270.

Rorer, B. A., & Ziller, R. C. (1982). Iconic communication of values among American and Polish students. *Journal of Cross-Cultural Psychology,* **13,** 352–361.

Rosenberg, M. J. (1956). Cognitive structure and attitudinal affect. *Journal of Abnormal and Social Psychology,* **53,** 367–372.

Rosenberg, M. J. (1960). An analysis of affective–cognitive consistency. In M. J. Rosenberg, C. I. Hovland, W. J. McGuire, R. P. Abelson, & J. W. Brehm (Eds.), *Attitude organization and change: An analysis of consistency among attitude components* (pp. 15–64). New Haven, CT: Yale Univ. Press.

Rushton, J. P., Chrisjohn, R. D., & Fekken, G. C. (1981). The altruistic personality and the Self-Report Altruism Scale. *Personality and Individual Differences,* **2,** 293–302.

Schwartz, S. H., & Bilsky, W. (1987). Toward a universal psychological structure of human values. *Journal of Personality and Social Psychology,* **53,** 550–562.

Sciortino, R. (1970). Allport–Vernon–Lindzey Study of Values: 1. Factor structure for a combined sample of male and female college students. *Psychological Reports,* **27,** 955–958.

Scott, W. A. (1960). International ideology and interpersonal ideology. *Public Opinion Quarterly,* **24,** 419–435.

Scott, W. A. (1965). *Values and organizations: A study of fraternities and sororities.* Chicago: Rand McNally.

Shorr, J. (1953). The development of a test to measure the intensity of values. *Journal of Educational Psychology,* **44,** 266–274.

Shotland, R. L., & Berger, W. G. (1970). Behavioral validation of several values from the Rokeach Value Scale as an index of honesty. *Journal of Applied Psychology,* **54,** 433–435.

Smart, R. C., & Smart, M. S. (1975). Group values shown in preadolescents' drawings in five English speaking countries. *Journal of Social Psychology,* **97,** 23–37.

Smith, M. B. (1949). Personal values as determinants of a political attitude. *Journal of Psychology,* **28,** 477–486.

Smith, M. B. (1963). Personal values in the study of lives. In R. W. White (Ed.), *The study of lives* (pp. 324–347). New York: Atherton Press.

Smith, M. B. (1969). *Social psychology and human values.* Chicago: Aldine.

Sommers, S., & Scioli, A. (1986). Emotional range and value orientation: Toward a cognitive view of emotionality. *Journal of Personality and Social Psychology,* **51,** 417–422.

Spates, J. L. (1983). The sociology of values. *Annual Review of Sociology,* **9,** 27–49.

Spranger, E. (1928). *Types of men.* New York: Stechert-Hafner.

Staub, E. (1974). Helping a distressed person: Social, personality and stimulus determinants. In L. Berkowitz (Ed.), *Advances in Experimental Social Psychology* (Vol. 7, pp. 293–341). New York: Academic Press.

Super, D. E. (1970). *Work Values Inventory.* Boston: Houghton Mifflin.

Tanaka, Y. (1972). Values in the subjective culture: A social psychological view. *Journal of Cross-Cultural Psychology,* **3,** 57–69.

Tate, E. D., & Miller, G. R. (1971). Differences in value systems of persons with varying religious orientations. *Journal for the Scientific Study of Religion,* **10,** 357–365.

Thomas, C. B. (1986). Values as predictors of social activist behavior. *Human Relations,* **39,** 179–193.

Thompson, B., Levitov, J. E., & Miederhoff, P. A. (1982). Validity of the Rokeach Value Survey. *Educational and Psychological Measurement,* **42,** 899–905.

Thompson, K. S. (1981). Changes in the values and life-style preferences of university students. *Journal of Higher Education,* **52,** 506–518.

Toler, C. (1975). The personal values of alcoholics and addicts. *Journal of Clinical Psychology,* **31,** 554–557.

Triandis, H. C. (1972). *The analysis of subjective culture.* New York: Wiley.

Triandis, H. C., Bontempo, R., Betancourt, H., Bond, M., Leung, K., Brenes, A., Georgas, J., Hui, C. H., Marin, G., Setiadi, B., Sinha, J. B. P., Verma, J., Spangenberg, J., Touzard, H., & de Montmollin, G. (1986). The measurement of the etic aspects of individualism and collectivism across cultures. *Australian Journal of Psychology,* **38,** 257–267.

Triandis, H. C., Kilty, K. M., Shanmugam, A. V., Tanaka, Y., & Vassiliou, V. (1972). Cognitive structures and the analysis of values. In H. C. Triandis (Ed.), *The analysis of subjective culture* (pp. 181–263). New York: Wiley.

Triandis, H. C., Leung, K., Villareal, M. J., & Clark, F. L. (1985). Allocentric versus idiocentric tendencies: Convergent and discriminant validation. *Journal of Research in Personality,* **19,** 395–415.

Truhon, S. A., McKinney, J. P., & Hotch, D. F. (1980). The structure of values among college students: An examination of sex differences. *Journal of Youth and Adolescence,* **9,** 289–297.

Vecchiotti, D. I., & Korn, J. H. (1980). Comparison of student and recruiter values. *Journal of Vocational Behavior,* **16,** 43–50.

Wagman, M. (1966). Interests and values of career and homemaking oriented women. *Personnel and Guidance Journal,* **44,** 794–801.

Walker, W. V., & Campbell, J. B. (1982). Similarity of values and interpersonal attraction of whites toward blacks. *Psychological Reports,* **50,** 1199–1205.

Weckowicz, T. E., & Janssen, D. V. (1973). Cognitive functions, personality traits, and social values in heavy marijuana smokers and nonsmoker controls. *Journal of Abnormal Psychology,* **81,** 264–269.

Weckowicz, T. E., Collier, G., & Spreng, L. (1977). Field dependence, cognitive functions, personality traits, and social values in heavy cannabis users and nonuser controls. *Psychological Reports,* **41,** 291–302.

Williams, R. M. (1968). Values. In E. Sills (Ed.), *International encyclopedia of the social sciences* (pp. 283–287). New York: Macmillan.

Williams, R. M. (1970). *American society: A sociological interpretation* (rev. ed.). New York: Knopf.

Wilson, G. D., & Patterson, J. R. (1968). A new measure of conservatism. *British Journal of Social and Clinical Psychology,* **7,** 264–269.

Winthrop, H. (1959). Psychology and value: A critique of Morris' approach to evaluation as behavior. *Journal of General Psychology,* **61,** 13–37.

Withey, S. (1965). The U.S. and the U.S.S.R.: A report of the public's perspective on United States–Russian relations in late 1961. In D. Bobrow (Ed.), *Components of defense policy* (pp. 164–174). Chicago: Rand McNally.

Woodruff, A. D., & Di Vesta, F. J. (1948). The relationship between values, concepts and attitudes. *Educational and Psychological Measurement,* **8,** 645–659.

Zavalloni, M. (1980). Values. In H. C. Triandis & R. W. Brislin (Eds.), *Handbook of cross-cultural psychology: Social psychology* (Vol. 5, pp. 73–120). Boston: Allyn & Bacon.